Political Violence, Crises, and Revolutions

Ekkart Zimmermann

Political Violence, Crises, and Revolutions:
Theories and Research

G.K. Hall & Co., Boston, Massachusetts 1983

Schenkman Publishing Co. Cambridge, Massachusetts

The author gratefully acknowledges the cooperation of the following publishers and authors in granting permission to quote from the sources listed:

Academic Press: Homans, George, C. 1976. "Commentary," in Leonard Berkowitz and Elaine Walster (eds.) *Equity theory: toward a general theory of social interaction*; Russell, D.E.H. 1974. *Rebellion, revolution, and armed force: a comparative study of fifteen countries with special emphasis on Cuba and South Africa*. Addison-Wesley Publishing Company: Huntington, Samuel, P., and Domínguez, Jorge I. 1975. "Political development," in Fred I. Greenstein and Nelson W. Polsby (eds.) *Handbook of political science*, vol. 3; Tilly, Charles. © 1978, Addison-Wesley Publishing Company, Inc. *From mobilization to revolution*; Tilly, Charles. 1975. "Revolutions and collective violence," in Fred I. Greeinstein and Nelson W. Polsby (eds.) *Handbook of political science*, vol. 3. Reprinted with permission. George Allen & Unwin: Seton-Watson, Hugh. 1972. "Revolution in Eastern Europe," in P.J. Vatikiotis (ed.) *Revolution in the Middle East and other case studies*. American Association for the Advancement of Science: Hauser, Robert M., and Featherman, David L. 1974. "Socioeconomic achievements of U.S. men: 1962-1972." *Science* 185 (July 26). American Historical Association: Kaplow, Jeffry. 1965. Review of Cobban (1964). *American Historical Review* 70, no. 4 (July); Nelson, William H. 1965. "The revolutionary character of the American Revolution." *American Historical Review* 70, no. 4 (July). American Political Science Association: Gurr, Ted. 1968. "A causal model of civil strife: a comparative analysis using new indices." *American Political Science Review* 62, no. 4 (Dec.); Jackman, Robert W. 1978. "The predictability of coups d'état: a model with African data." *American Political Science Review* 72, no. 4 (Dec.); Korpi, Walter. 1974. "Conflict, power and relative deprivation." *American Political Science Review* 68, no. 4 (Dec.); McKinlay, R.D., and Cohan, A.S. 1976. "Performance and instability in military and nonmilitary regime systems." *American Political Science Review* 70, no. 3 (Sept.); Muller, Edward N., and Jukam, T.O. 1977. "On the meaning of political support." *American Political Science Review* 71, no. 4 (Dec.); Taylor, Michael, and Herman, V.M. 1971. "Party systems and government stability." *American Political Science Review* 65, no. 1 (Mar.); Welfling, Mary B. 1975. "Models, measurement and sources of error: civil conflict in Black Africa." *American Political Science Review* 69, no. 3 (Sept.); Zolberg, Aristide. 1968. "The structure of political conflict in the new states of tropical Africa." *American Political Science Review* 62, no. 1 (Mar.). American Psychological Association: Feshback, Seymour. 1971. "Dynamics and morality of violence and aggression: some psychological considerations." *American Psychologist* 26, no. 3 (Mar.). American Sociological Association: Gurin,

Library of Congress Cataloging in Publication Data

Zimmermann, Ekkart, 1946–
   Political violence, crises, and revolutions.

   Bibliography.
   Includes index.
   1. Violence. 2. Revolutions. I. Title
JC328.6.Z54   303.6'2   81–6970
ISBN 0-8161-9027-5   AACR2
ISBN 0-87073-894-1 (pbk.)

Patricia; Gurin, Gerald; and Morrison, Betty M. 1978. "Personal and ideological aspects of internal and external control." *Social Psychology* 41, no. 4 (Dec.); Jenkins, J. Craig, and Perrow, Charles. 1977. "Insurgency of the powerless: farm workers movements (1946–1972)." *American Sociological Review* 42, no. 2 (Apr.); McPhail, Clark. 1971. "Civil disorder participation: a critical examination of recent research." *American Sociological Review* 36, no. 6 (Dec.); Shapiro, Gilbert. 1967. Review of Moore (1966). *American Sociological Review* 32; Spilerman, Seymour. 1970. "The causes of racial disturbances: a comparison of alternative explanations." *American Sociological Review* 35, no. 4 (Aug.); Spilerman, Seymour. 1976. "Structural characteristics of cities and the severity of racial disorders." *American Sociological Review* 41, no. 5 (Oct.); Stark, Margaret J. Abudu; Raine, Walter J.; Burbeck, Stephen L.; and Davison, Keith K. 1974. "Some empirical patterns in riot process." *American Sociological Review* 39, no. 6 (Dec.). Annual Reviews, Inc.: Oberschall, Anthony. © 1978, Annual Reviews Inc. "Theories of social conflict." *Annual Review of Sociology* 4. Beacon Press: Moore, Barrington, Jr. 1966. *Social origins of dictatorship and democracy. Lord and peasant in the making of the modern world.* Bobbs-Merrill Co., Inc.: Useem, Michael. © 1975, The Bobbs-Merrill Co., Inc. *Protest movements in America.* Brooks/Cole Publishing Company: Welch, Claude E., Jr., and Taintor, Mavis Bunker, eds. 1972. *Revolution and political change.* Carnegie-Mellon University Press: Pinkney, David H. 1972. "The revolutionary crowd in Paris in the 1830s. *Journal of Social History* 5, no. 4 (Summer). Collins Publishers: Rudé, George. 1970. *Paris and London in the 18th century: studies in popular protest.* Doubleday & Company, Inc.: Rejai, Mostafa. 1973. *The strategy of political revolution.* Elsevier Scientific Publishing Company: Aya, Rod. 1979. "Theories of revolution reconsidered: contrasting models of collective violence." *Theory and Society* 8, no. 1 (July); Disch, Arne. 1979. "Peasants and revolts: review of Paige." *Theory and Society* 7, nos. 1–2 (Jan.–Mar.); Tilly, Charles. 1976. "Major forms of collective action in Western Europe 1500–1975." *Theory and Society* 3, no. 3 (Fall); Zimmermann, Ekkart. 1979. "Crises and crises outcomes: towards a new synthetic approach." *European Journal of Political Research* 7, no. 1 (Mar.); Zimmermann, Ekkart. 1979. "Explaining military coups d'état: towards the development of a complex causal model." *Quality and Quantity* 13, no. 5 (Oct.). Encyclopaedia Britannica: Marx, G.T. 1970. "Riots." *Encyclopaedia Britannica*, vol. 19. Faber & Faber: Wolf, Eric R. 1969. *Peasant wars of the twentieth century.* Free Press: Paige, Jeffery M. 1975. *Agrarian revolution: social movements and export agriculture in the underdeveloped world.* Government and Opposition (London School of Economics): Castles, Francis D. 1973. "Barrington Moore's thesis and Swedish political development." *Government and Opposition* 8, no. 3 (Summer). Harper & Row: Hagopian, Mark N. 1974. *The phenomenon of revolution.* International Institute for Strategic Studies: Huntington, Samuel P. 1971. "Civil violence and the process of development." *Adelphi Papers* 83. Journal of Social Issues: Caplan, Nathan. 1970. "The new ghetto man: a review of recent empirical studies." *Journal of Social Issues* 26, no. 1. Little, Brown: Luard, Evan. 1968. *Conflict and peace in the modern international system.* Macmillan & Co., and International Institute for Labour Studies: Hobsbawm, Eric J. 1974. "Social banditry," in Henry A. Landsberger (ed.) *Rural protest: peasant movements and social change.* Penguin Books: Finer, S.E. 1976. *The man on horseback*; Finer, S.E. 1970. *Comparative government.* Geertz, Clifford. 1963. "The integrative revolution: primordial sentiments and civil politics in the new states," in Clifford Geertz (ed.) *Old societies and new states: the quest for modernity in Asia and Africa*; Gove, Walter R. 1976. "Deviant behavior, social intervention, and labeling theory," in Lewis A. Coser and Otto N. Larsen (eds.) *The uses of controversy in sociology*; Gurr, Ted Robert, and Duvall, Raymond D. 1976. "Introduction to a formal theory of political conflict," in Lewis A. Coser and Otto N. Larsen (eds.) *The uses of controversy in sociology*; Huntington, Samuel P. 1968. "Civil military relations," in *International Encyclopedia of the Social Sciences*, vol. 2; Lerner, Daniel. 1958. *The passing of traditional society: modernizing the Middle East*; Prentice-Hall, Inc.: Bandura, Albert. 1973. *Aggression: a social learning analysis*; Greene, Thomas H. 1974. *Comparative revolutionary movements*; Gurr, Ted Robert. 1972. *Politimetrics: an introduction to quantitative macropolitics*; Oberschall, Anthony. 1973. *Social conflict and social movements*; Pinard, Maurice. 1971. *The rise of a third party. A study in crisis politics*; Wolfinger, Raymond E., Shapiro, Martin, and Greenstein, Fred I. 1976. *Dynamics of American politics.* Russell Sage Foundation: Balbus, Isaac D. 1973. *Dialectics of legal repression: black rebels before the American criminal courts.* Sage Publications: Doran, Charles F. © 1976, Sage Publications. Domestic conflict in state relations: the American sphere of influence. *Sage Professional Paper, International Studies Series*, Series no. 02–037; Duvall, Raymond, and Welfling, Mary. © 1973, Sage Publications. "Social

Contents

List of Figures

List of Tables

Acknowledgments

The author's thanks go to the Leverhulme Foundation which awarded him a research fellowship at the University of Essex, Department of Government, from October 1973 to July 1974. The intellectually stimulating atmosphere there greatly contributed to the present undertaking. Generous support from the staff of the library and from the Institute of Applied Social Research of the University of Cologne is gratefully acknowledged. I should like to thank all those colleagues, particularly Ted Robert Gurr (Northwestern University) and Charles Tilly (University of Michigan), who were so kind as to send copies of unpublished papers at my request. I am also grateful to the participants in two European Consortium for Political Research Workshops (Mannheim, April 1973, and Louvain, 1976) and in two European Conferences of the Peace Science Society (International) in Zürich (August 1975) and Mannheim (August 1977) for their critique on several working papers dealing with topics also covered in this much more extended study. A small grant from the Deutsche Forschungsgemeinschaft (German Science Foundation) for clerical assistance is gratefully acknowledged. My special thanks go to Mrs. Klinkhammer for her capacity to bear with my scribbled notes and to translate them into a readable manuscript. I am obliged also to Michael Stohl (Purdue University) and Erich Weede (University of Cologne) for comments on various portions of this work. The study has been accepted as partial fulfillment of the *Habilitation* requirements of the Department of Social Science at the University of Wuppertal (West Germany). Financial support from the Society of Friends of the University of Wuppertal is gratefully acknowledged.

In addition, I am greatly indebted to the various scholars from whose works I have quoted at length in this study in order to present their arguments as clearly as possible. Any equivalent paraphrasing would have increased the size of this study even more. None of these colleagues is, of course, to be blamed for the errors of omission and commission unavoidable in such a venture. These remain solely my responsibility. I will thus be grateful for critical comments on the present study as I have expressed my criticisms of research my colleagues have done in the fields of political violence, crises, and revolutions. I wish to express my gratitude to Ann Lacy for her painstaking efforts in copyediting the manuscript. Final thanks go to my wife Gisela for having kept her promise *not* to read a single page of this study.

The manuscript was basically finished in February 1978 with revisions done in 1979. Materials that either appeared in 1980 or came to my attention in that year have largely been ignored (see my recent book in German, *Krisen, Staatsstreiche und Revolutionen: Theorien, Daten und neuere Forschungsansätze*, published in autumn 1981 by Westdeutscher Verlag, Opladen, West Germany). In some of the most important instances, however, brief references have been incorporated here as well.

Chapter 1

Introduction

"Some 68 million human beings, according to the most careful estimates, perished from all forms of deliberate human violence—murder, riot, revolution, and war—in the 150 years from 1820 to 1970" (PROSTERMAN 1976: 339). If the victims of state violence suffering from pogroms, brutal repression, and other forms of state coercion were added, the figure would probably be more than twice as high. Obviously, political violence, meaning (for the most part antigovernment or antisystem) violence occurring within a political system and having political consequences, is an issue that deserves the close attention of the social scientist. When carrying out analyses, he or she should bear in mind that, after all, "violence is an issue about which most people have strong opinions, perhaps even violent ones" (MOORE 1968:1).

While there have been several systematic analyses of political violence before 1960, the best known being the classic studies by WRIGHT (1942) and RICHARDSON (1960) on the determinants of war and, more in line with the topics of this study, by SOROKIN (1937) on internal (and external) disturbances, political violence as a distinct field of study developed only recently in the 1960s. The late but extremely rapid development of this branch of study may be attributed to a number of factors:

1. the development of computers of increasing capacity and the concomitant availability of computer-based programs for data analyses which are relatively easy to handle and produce an enormous output of statistical results;

2. the growing interest in cross-national analyses, leading to the development of a number of data banks described in such publications as *Cross Polity Time Series Data* (BANKS 1971), *Black Africa: A Comparative Handbook* (MORRISON et al. 1972), *The Wages of War* (SINGER/SMALL 1972), *World Handbook of Political and Social Indicators* (2d ed., TAYLOR/HUDSON 1972) as well as to numerous other data collections referred to later in the text; and, providing the final and perhaps strongest impetus,

3. the riots among American blacks during the second half of the 1960s. This led to an enormous research program, perhaps second only to the study of voting behavior and to the other dominant issue in social science analyses during the 1960s, student protests in the United States and elsewhere in the world.

In 1965 ECKSTEIN opened up a number of analytical perspectives in a now classic article on cross-national analyses of political violence, the perspective in which we are primarily interested. Other pioneering works are the factor analyses of various forms of conflicts by RUMMEL (from 1963 to the present), the first broad comparative analysis of political violence published (FEIERABEND/FEIERABEND 1966), and GURR's study of civil strife (GURR 1968a), a first high point in theoretical and methodological sophistication. The end of the 1960s and first half of the 1970s have witnessed an enormous and continuing outpouring of studies on political violence, both comparative (cross-national) analyses and case studies. Most of these cross-national analyses study phenomena of political violence taking place after the Second World War. This focus is considerably broadened in the analyses of revolutions which are dealt with in later chapters of this study. Most of those analyses are comparative only in a very limited sense. Our aim is to evaluate these studies and to provide some guidelines as to the possibilities of cross-national analyses of revolutions. In the chapters on military coups d'état, one of the dominant patterns of political violence in many parts of the world, and on crises and political violence, reference is again made to a number of studies generally covering periods after the Second World War, but occasionally, longer periods are treated, and in one instance a period of approximately one hundred fifty years is considered. As might be expected in cross-national analyses of this sort, variations in time and space are considerable, rendering the development of universally valid theoretical statements a herculean task. One purpose of the present study is to bring together various strands of research and to show or suggest where and how they might be fruitfully related to each other. In addition, our book is intended as a critique of existent research.

A few words are in order about what is excluded from this study. First of all, the focus here is on *sociostructural* and *political conditions* of political violence, crises, and revolutions and not on the variety of ideological factors (or the structure of idea systems) and their impact on the phenomena mentioned. This is not to deny the importance of ideas. In the present context, this is a necessary limitation in order to find a way through the many studies already published on these explanatory factors. In addition, together with most social scientists, we share the premise that the impact of sociostructural and political conditions is likely to be stronger than that of idea systems (at least in the short run). Secondly, case studies on particular topics are generally not treated here, although some references to their usefulness have been made. This is true as well for other monographic works, be they historical or biographical in nature. Thirdly, at least one topic of current public interest is not considered here in detail: the explanation of the various forms of international terrorism (as well as the possibilities of combatting these forms of international disorder, a topic beyond the scholar's primary role of analyzing the phenomena objectively). To our knowledge, at this time there is not sufficient data to allow for systematic causal analyses of international terrorism. (When writing this, MICKOLUS 1980 was not yet published). Variability in the forms of international terrorism is still too great. However, throughout this study there is a set of recurrent conditions that probably will prove to be of considerable importance for an understanding of terrorist phenomena including irredentist claims, claims for sociocultural autonomy, and separation of certain cultural, ethnic, racial, or other groups (cf. also chapter 8.4.4 for some preliminary considerations).

Concerning the organization of the present study, only a few guidelines will be given here, with additional ones found in each of the major chapters. Chapter 2 deals with conceptual problems in the analysis of political violence. A discussion of various definitional criteria of violence, of typologies of violence, and of the relationships between violence and other key concepts will be found in this chapter. The following two chapters deal with background theories. Especially in cross-national aggregate data analyses of political violence, references are often made to microexplanations of aggressive behavior and to theories of social comparison processes. Our aim is to be more explicit concerning these theories by giving a brief summary of the findings of experimental studies of aggressive behavior (chapter 3) and of theories of social comparison processes (chapter 4). The weaknesses of these theories are discussed, as well as their possible contributions to better studies of political violence and other forms of political protest behavior. After the more preliminary chapters, chapter 5 deals with cross-national approaches to the study of political violence, the stress being on rather broadly defined dependent variables often representing clusters of phenomena of political violence as they emerged from factor analyses. In the first part of this section (chapter 5.1.1) the pioneering approaches of GURR, the FEIERABEND group, and HIBBS (1973) are described, compared, and evaluated. In the second part (chapter 5.1.2) several key variables for explaining political violence are traced through numerous cross-national analyses. A summary discussion of several methodological aspects concludes the section dealing with cross-national analyses of political violence. A chapter on case studies of political violence follows, focusing mainly on the fascinating analyses of social banditry given by HOBSBAWM (cf. 1959, 1969). The richness in detail of this section is lacking in the statistics encountered in the earlier studies. Chapter 5, dealing with approaches to the study of political violence, ends with a presentation and evaluation of theories and empirical results on the causes of the riots of American blacks during the 1960s. These events have been studied in greater detail than any other phenomena in the field of political violence. However, many important questions remain unanswered. It is interesting to compare the theories for explaining political violence on a cross-national basis with those explaining a more homogeneous phenomenon of political violence. As might be expected, there is considerable overlapping in the theories proposed. In addition, numerous other explanations based on survey data have been developed and tested to account for the blacks' riots.

In cross-national analyses of political violence, quite often it is equated with political instability or crises phenomena, yet no justification for such an equation is given. Consequently, in chapter 6 the present study (1) defines crises phenomena and discusses several general approaches to the study of crises; (2) differentiates analytically between crises and political violence, showing possible interrelationships between the two; (3) lists and discusses those cross-national analyses bearing on crises phenomena and/or the relationship between crises and political violence; and (4) develops a causal model of crises and crises outcomes (with persistence of a polity as the final dependent variable) and proposes suggestions as to the development of a cross-national crises science.

The chapter on crises and political violence is also the first in a series of three bearing on the analysis of revolutions, the subject of chapter 8. Prior to the study of revolution, however, a chapter on cross-national analyses of military coups d'état has been included. Crises, military coups d'état, and revolutions are topics that, for analytical reasons, must be considered separately. Empirically, however, there is some evidence that they are intricately linked. The behavior of the military and the police forces is of crucial importance when crises situations escalate to revolutionary proportions. However, the behavior of the military and the police forces is only one of the major variables considered in causal modeling of revolutions.

Compared with other sections in this study, the treatment of theories and empirical results dealing with the causes of military coups is more homogeneous, thus facilitating comparisons of theories and results. In contrast with chapter 5.1 where, within the cross-national analyses of political violence, coups were sometimes incorporated into the particular dependent variables, in this chapter the interest is solely on military coups d'état and not on other phenomena of political violence (at least not as far as the *dependent* variable is concerned). Thus, in chapter 7 some of the theories referred to in chapter 5.1 will be considered, while at the same time theoretical notions and empirical results bearing on later parts of this study will also be treated. This interlocking of theories can perhaps best be demonstrated by the fact that HUNTINGTON's hypotheses (1968) pervade all of these chapters and are dealt with at various points in our discussion. At the end of chapter 7 a causal model of military coups d'état is developed summarizing theoretical and empirical evidence and to some extent going beyond it by suggesting new theoretical linkages to be considered in future cross-national analyses of military coups d'état.

The chapter on the cross-national study of revolutions attempts critical assessment. Of the myriad studies on revolutions, a sizable portion hardly deals with revolutions at all. This also holds true for some of the cross-national analyses of revolutions, as will be shown in chapter 8.4.6. Consequently, the present study attempts to develop a more precise definition of revolutions, to discuss various typologies found in the literature, and to deal with some of the numerous variables which are suggested to explain the occurrence of revolutions. Some of the more elaborate explanations of revolutions, such as HUNTINGTON's (1968) comparison of Western and Eastern models of revolution, MOORE's (1966) broad sociohistorical analyses of the social origins of dictatorship and democracy, and PAIGE's (1975) study of agrarian revolution, are taken up in greater detail. Having criticized the very few quantitative cross-national studies of revolutions, the chapter focuses on historical analyses of revolutionary protests. The quantitative analyses of collective violence in France, Italy, and Germany from 1830 to 1930 (cf., e.g., TILLY et al. 1975) and the largely qualitative analyses of revolutionary crowds by RUDÉ (1964, 1970) are good examples of the way a comparative study of revolutions might proceed (they do not arrive at a dead end as do several cross-national analyses of revolutions which are actually analyses of military coups, and not even recommendable at that). A causal model of revolutions is developed, bringing together the various strands that have been discussed throughout the rather lengthy chapter on revolutions. Finally, several analytical suggestions are made which might be helpful in setting up more successful designs in the study of revolutions.

In the final chapter the three causal models developed in earlier chapters, concerning (1) crises and the persistence of polities, (2) military coups d'état, and (3) revolutions, are briefly compared, providing a short analytical summary of this study. In the concluding paragraphs, reference is made to some other neglected aspects in the study of political violence, crises, and revolutions. The chapter concludes with some comments on other social phenomena that come into focus once the frame of reference is broadened beyond the subjects considered here. The aim of the present study is one of constructive criticism, criticism concerning much of what has been done in analyses of political violence, crises, and revolutions. Suggestions are proposed as to how some of the errors committed in the past might be avoided in more carefully designed future studies. At various points, this text attempts to build on the critical evaluations given here. The author hopes that other scholars will go on in these areas of study, progressing further than we have done in the present context.

Chapter 2

Conceptual Problems

2.1. Toward a Definition of Political Violence

Violence has been a subject for human reflection for hundreds of years. However, rather than presenting an anthology of the different views on violence as found, for example, in the Sermon on the Mount and the writings of MACHIAVELLI, HOBBES, SOREL, and many others, we wish to discuss the usefulness of various definitional criteria proposed by social scientists. *Webster's Third International Dictionary* defines violence as "exertion of any physical force so as to injure or abuse."[1] An important distinction is added in the *Oxford English Dictionary* which denotes violence as "the exercise of physical force so as to inflict injury on, cause damage to, persons or property." Differentiating between violence against human beings and violence against nonhuman objects is generally accepted among social scientists.

In the introduction to *The History of Violence in America* (National Commission on the Causes and Prevention of Violence) violence is defined "narrowly . . . as behavior designed to inflict physical injury to people or damage to property" (in GRAHAM/GURR 1969:xxxii; cf. the similar definitions of VAN DEN HAAG 1972:54, and SKOLNICK 1969:4). This definition, sometimes with slight variations, is also used in the various works of GURR (cf. GURR/McCLELLAND 1971:17/19; GURR 1973b:360: "deliberate uses of force to injure or destroy physically"). GURR also points to additional variables that will be dealt with in this study: "This definition is independent of agents, objects, or contexts of violence" (GURR 1973b:360).

Having specified that violence denotes certain *intentions* as well as the use of *specific means* (cf. also the discussion in COUZENS 1971), criteria to be discussed in detail below, the attribute "political" remains to be defined. Some general criteria for political violence can be given, but the distinction between violence and political violence nevertheless often remains arbitrary (see the references to the labeling approach below). The following criteria are offered in an effort to distinguish violence from political violence:

1. The number of persons involved. Other things being equal, the probability that acts of violence will be thought of as political in nature is greater, the more persons are involved in these acts. Yet, an increase in the number of people involved does not necessarily mean that political violence is taking place. A street gang committing crimes connotes, narrowly speaking, no more of a political phenomenon than an individual acting in a certain manner against the law. On the other hand, a violent activity carried out by just one person, e.g., the assassination of a public figure (cf. the results in KIRKHAM et al. 1969; HAVENS et al. 1970; CROTTY 1971; FEIERABEND et al. 1971; GROSS 1974:161-75), could be highly political in nature. These examples lead to another important criterion of political violence, the reaction of the respective community or public (see under [3]).

The broader terms *collective violence* and *civil violence* ("all collective, non-governmental attacks on persons or property, resulting in intentional damage to them, that occur within the boundaries of an autonomous . . . political unit," GURR 1968c:247; cf. also MASOTTI/BOWEN 1968:13), rather than political violence, cover some of the problems just mentioned. GURR, for example, views the *potential* for collective violence as "a function of the extent and intensity of shared discontents among members of a society" (GURR 1970a:8). The more these discontents are "blamed on the political system and its agents," the greater the *potential* for *political violence* (ibid.). "Political violence refers to all collective attacks within a political community against the political regime, its actors—including competing political groups as well as incumbents—or its policies" (GURR 1970a:3-4).

To give an example which demonstrates some of the difficulties even this definition of political violence is likely to create: Is a violent strike of workers against the factory owners or the management political in nature if it is not directed against the state or its institutions? Probably not, but conditions may change once clashes between strikers and coercive forces of the state have occurred. A local protest could turn into a highly significant political event. Thus, the distinction between collective or civil violence and political violence remains imprecise, unless one restricts the *defining element* of political violence to *deliberate* and *unambiguous* attacks against the state, its agents, or specific policies (or, more generally, against "socially inclusive authority patterns," GURR/DUVALL 1976:141).[2] In the literature, however, such a clear-cut distinction is seldom found. It might not even be a useful one, as will become apparent below. In any case, the foregoing discussion should make it clear that another important definitional criterion must be added in speaking of political violence, that is,

2. The intentions of the actors. However, intentions of the actors alone would be an insufficient and sometimes misleading criterion if one were to distinguish collective violence from political violence. Probably more important than this second criterion is the third,

3. The reactions of the particular community or public. Thus, violent acts, originally simply collective in nature, could become acts of political violence according to the reactions of the particular audience (e.g., segments of the population, institutions of the state, political parties, or the media). This analytical perspective is particularly important in the *labeling approach* where the basic question is whether there are any consequences and consequences of what sort and for whom once official institutions or the public have attached a certain label to a specific phenomenon.[3]

What is needed, then, is data on the criteria the public uses to define violent acts as political or nonpolitical in nature (cf. also the empirical studies of BLUMENTHAL et al. 1972[4] and chapter 9; MARSH 1974; OLSEN/ BADEN 1974; OLSEN 1968a; cf. also KAASE, 1976; BARNES/KAASE et al. 1979). A definition of political violence based on these three criteria would, however, omit significant categories of political violence, e.g., acts of official violence which should be taken into consideration, as will become clear in following chapters. Even if researchers do start from other working definitions of political violence, as we ourselves will do, the three criteria mentioned might prove helpful in roughly delineating phenomena of political violence from other violent acts.

However, rather than accepting GURR's definition of political violence, we would advocate that of NIEBURG as a *working definition*. NIEBURG views the intentions of the actors in a different light than does GURR. GURR has more than once been criticized (cf. NARDIN 1971) for viewing political violence mainly through the perspective of the state or its institutions. He himself notes his failure to take state violence into consideration in his analyses (GURR 1972a:98). NIEBURG defines political violence as *"acts of disruption, destruction, injury whose purpose, choice of targets or victims, surrounding circumstances, implementation, and/or effects have political significance, that is, tend to modify the behavior of others in a bargaining situation that has consequences for the social system"* (NIEBURG 1969:13).

This rather effect-oriented definition[5] may cause some difficulties if one is to specify the definitional components. Particularly the bargaining aspect stressed in this definition may lead to distortions of analysis. As used by NIEBURG, bargaining would cover a wide range of situations and acts. It might be more useful to speak of bargaining only in a *limited* sense, as there may be acts of political violence which are not to be thought of as acts in a bargaining process but rather as strict coercive measures of the state or as acts of terror on behalf of the protesters.[6] (On the other hand, even extreme statements such as MAO's famous formula that "political power grows out of the barrel of a gun" could be interpreted, though at serious risk, in terms of bargaining.)

A clear boundary between the *bargaining model*, the *coercion model*, and the *terror model* of political violence is often difficult to define. Furthermore, there are often changes over time. Terror elements may replace bargaining elements as the position of one of the acting groups weakens. Or terror may be used initially, giving way to bargaining elements later on. In any case, "violence may occur without terror, but not terror without violence" (WALTER 1964a:251). Subscribing to the bargaining model of political violence may be more useful if less intense forms of political violence are to be analyzed. Limited forms of political violence at times may be seen as a special kind of demonstration, in the words of ETZIONI (1970:18), as an "interim election tool." Conventional nonviolent means may be judged insufficient to call attention to grievances of the protesters. Therefore, they use stronger forms of protest behavior. In cases of revolutionary overthrows (cf. chapter 8) the bargaining aspect in this working definition would, of course, be of little help. In these cases the issue is not how to make limited use of protest resources to gain some concession or to reach a compromise, but rather how to carry out a life and death struggle.

In NIEBURG's definition two important aspects are taken into account: Political violence must be seen as a *process* that takes place between various groups or categories of actors within a political system. Furthermore, the term political violence should not be limited to acts performed by rebels against the state, but should also apply to violent activities carried out by state agents against its citizens (e.g., pogroms). As will be shown in this study, the latter aspect is gravely neglected in the analyses of political violence to be discussed here. The definition of NIEBURG contrasts with other definitions in the literature and with those mentioned above. There are some advantages in retaining such a definition, but it should be accepted only with the modifications suggested. By now it should be apparent that none of the available definitions of political violence is satisfying. As long as the concept of political violence has so many connotations[7] not yet studied in systematic cross-national comparisons, agreement as to the usefulness of a single definition of political violence cannot be reached. Consequently, we forgo developing our own definition and merely suggest using NIEBURG's as a kind of working definition. HUNTINGTON's definition does not show the weaknesses of NIEBURG's but lacks its advantages: "By *civil* [political] violence I mean violence which differs from *international* (or, more correctly, inter-state) violence in that at least one participant is not a government and which differs from *criminal* violence in that it is designed to affect the make-up or functioning of the political system" (HUNTINGTON 1971a:1).

2.2. A Note on Typologies of Violence

Typologies are often constructed as a first step to organize empirical evidence. In the literature there are numerous typologies of the various forms of violence. Rather than proposing a "perfect" typology here, we want to mention some of the analytical problems one is likely to encounter in characterizing the concept of violence.

1. Violence against persons vs. violence against nonhuman objects. This is a clear-cut differentiation also used in empirical studies on political violence (cf. chapter 5.3.2).

2. Direct vs. indirect violence. Violence is indirect if a connecting link, be it persons, objects, or specific conditions, comes between the actor and the victim (object). Operational problems naturally will be greater with the more indirect forms of violence, the question then being whether remote and unobservable phenomena may be called violence at all (cf. also [7]). (The dichotomy *manifest violence* vs. *latent violence* is also quite often used in the sense that manifest violence stands for direct violence whereas latent violence implies more indirect forms.) Moreover, the distinction between direct and indirect violence should not automatically be equated with the differentiation between violence and the *threat*[8] to use violence.

3. Physical vs. psychological violence. The boundaries between the two forms of violence are sometimes difficult to draw (e.g., in cases of ecological damages). A fourfold typology distinguishing between the presence and absence of these forms of violence would show the various possible relationships between the two aspects. In addition, one form of violence could cause (or merely precede) others. Even in cases of very subtle psychological aggression the victim may show bodily reactions as well as psychological responses. One would expect bodily as well as psychological reactions in cases of severe physical aggression.

4. Individual vs. collective violence (cf. the discussion in the preceding section).

5. Organized vs. spontaneous violence. This is one of the major differentiations, as will become apparent as we proceed.

6. Criminal vs. political violence. Though there may be activities that could be classified under both forms, normally one should distinguish between criminal and political violence, the former merely denoting specific acts of violence that are against the law, the latter denoting political intentions.[9]

7. Personal vs. structural violence. This dichotomy has been proposed by GALTUNG: "We shall refer to the type of violence where there is an actor that commits the violence as *personal* or *direct*, and to violence where there is no such actor as *structural* or *indirect*" (GALTUNG 1969:170—italics in original).[10] More generally GALTUNG defines violence "as the cause of the difference between the potential and the actual" (ibid., p. 168). Violence is said to occur "when human beings are being influenced so that their actual somatic and mental realizations are below their potential realizations" (ibid.). According to GALTUNG one may distinguish two forms of personal and structural violence: (1) when the difference between the potential and the actual is enlarged; (2) when a reduction of this difference is prevented. "Thus, if a person died from tuberculosis in the eighteenth century it would be hard to conceive of this as violence since it might have been quite unavoidable, but if he dies from it today, despite all the medical resources in the world, then violence is present" (ibid.). In a way, structural violence is said to occur objectively. According to GALTUNG it seems possible that an individual behaves subjectively in a peaceful manner; however, objectively his way of behavior may be classified as within the range of structural violence.

If this dichotomy is to be at all useful (we know of no investigation that provides for much more than definitions),[11] another object of comparison, such as another nation (cf. the efforts of KÖHLER/ALCOCK 1976 and HØIVIK 1977), must be present. Otherwise there would be no criterion of how to delineate structural violence. One may ask whether there will be any case not included under structural violence. Operational criteria to define and evaluate the discrepancy between the possible and the actual levels of development are lacking. If these specifications are not made, the notion of structural violence leads to an *inflation* of the concept of violence which should be reserved to certain human *actions* and not cover inactions as well. Occasionally, GALTUNG equates structural violence with social injustice; this seems to be a more adequate, yet still quite evaluating, concept. (As far as the dichotomy direct vs. indirect violence is concerned, see [2]).

8. Legal vs. illegal violence and legitimate vs. illegitimate violence. Max WEBER's analysis of legal violence still plays an important role today. "One can rather define the modern state in sociological terms only by a specific *means* that is characteristic of it as of any political association: that of physical violence.[12] 'Every state is founded on violence,' Trotzkij said in his days in Brest-Litowsk. That is truly correct" (WEBER 1964:1043; italics in original, my translation). Yet, violence is not the sole means of the state, but only "specific to it" (WEBER, ibid.). WEBER considers the state monopoly of violence to be the result of increasingly different demands which cannot be fulfilled any longer in the traditional manner and are thus raised against the community (cf. WEBER's general remarks 1964:659-60). WEBER goes on to say: "The state, as well as the political associations historically preceding it, is an *authority* relation of people over people founded on the means of legitimate (i.e.: regarded as legitimate) violence" (WEBER 1964:1043, my translation). The state may demand obedience from its citizens (WEBER 1964:1045), but at the same time one may have to consider the reverse: if the institutions of the state do not succeed in attaining their prescribed goals within the limits of certain accepted rules, a loss of legitimacy of these institutions may result. (The charismatic rule might be an exception here.) As we proceed, it will become evident that a loss of legitimacy of the state, of its institutions or actors, is one of the fundamental conditions conducive to severe forms of political violence, crises, and revolutions. Thus, WEBER's analysis of the state monopoly of legal violence must be expanded in this respect.)[13]

If one constructs a typology using the dichotomies legal vs. illegal violence and legitimate vs. illegitimate violence (as in Table 2.1), types 2, 3, and 4 are particularly noteworthy. (Type 1 would simply imply that the state monopoly of violence is accepted by the particular population.)

The violent behavior of some white policemen in the United States who provide black neighborhoods with services less adequate than those in white areas is an example of the second type. The use of violent means by the police may be legally justified. Yet, it is not considered legitimate ("desirable or justifiable," GRAHAM/GURR 1969:xxxiii) as far as large portions of the black population are concerned. The majority of white people may think differently about this issue.

Table 2.1. Four General Types of Violence

		Dimension of Legality	
		Legal violence	Illegal violence
Dimension of Legitimacy	Legitimate violence	1	3
	Illegitimate violence	2	4

Black riots in America during the 1960s also serve as an example of type 3: Even though the use of violent means by members of the black minority is defined as illegal, it is nevertheless regarded as legitimate behavior by large portions of the black population (for references see chapter 5.3.2.1). This constellation of illegal yet legitimate violence is a characteristic of *classic* cases of protest. Whenever the protesters believe in the legitimacy of their behavior, in their cause, opposition is likely to be more intensive.

The terrorism of small violent gangs is an example of type 4. Of course, these gangs consider their behavior to be legitimate, but at the same time they are not able to convince the public of their course. Instead, the public remains aloof (cf. the terrorism of the Baader-Meinhof group in West Germany, of Irish radicals in England, of the Symbionese Liberation Army in the United States, or of the Rengo Sekigun in Japan).

Many authors define violence "roughly as the illegal employment of methods of physical coercion for personal or group ends" (HOOK 1934:264); or, quoting DE GRAZIA, "Force is the legitimate use of physical coercion, and violence is the illegitimate use of physical coercion" (DE GRAZIA 1962:65). As IGLITZIN (1972:25–26) correctly remarks, in these definitions "force is seen as ethically neutral, and law-enforcement officers, whether soldiers or policemen, as simply agents of this unbiased force. Violence, on the other hand, has been viewed as something irrational and excessive, committed by irrational groups or individuals against the good of the whole society" (IGLITZIN 1972:25–26. For the implications of such a definition see the much debated McCone Report in chapter 5.3.2.1). We think that our typology is much more open to and adequate for empirical studies of political violence than the "black and white" stereotypes in these definitions which are drawing on the distinction between *potestas* and *violentia* found in earlier philosophy of state.[14]

Occasionally one is confronted with a distinction similar to that just discussed:

9. Institutionalized vs. non-institutionalized violence. This differentiation, however, is not necessarily identical with the foregoing. Institutionalized violence does not always mean legal violence. There is the possibility of institutionalized violence which is at the same time *illegal* but not illegitimate. The *violencia* in Columbia provides an example, as do the *barbagia* in Sardinia and perhaps even the *mafia* in Sicily.

There are various other typologies of violence in the literature (cf. NIE–BURG 1969:13; TILLY/RULE 1965:56ff.; LAWRENCE 1970; CHANDLER 1973; WALLACE/SINGER 1973; GALTUNG 1978). Unfortunately, neither these nor the differentiations proposed here are sufficiently precise. There will always be examples that cut across types (cf. also the typology in GURR/ BISHOP 1976, which will be considered later). At the same time we do not yet know enough about the clustering of certain attributes to construct more convincing empirical typologies of (political) violence or even to develop a general theory of political violence.

If one reduces the current typologies found in the literature, one arrives at the following seven basic differentiations: *goals, objects, means, participants, spreading, intensity,* and *forms of organization.* These have been the basic categories in numerous empirical studies on political violence.

2.3. Political Violence and Some Related Concepts: An Attempt at Clarification

One of the related or even alternative concepts to political violence is *protest behavior.* There are reasons for using this concept to denote forms of political violence (as we will do at various points), but, at the same time one thus limits the objects of explanation to attacks against the state or its institutions (as has been done in most of the research on political violence). Thus, in one way the term *protest behavior* would be too specific, while, on the other hand, it would be more general than the term *political violence* since it would include nonviolent protest behavior as well. The same would hold for *civil disobedience* (as to the latter, cf. also chapter 9).

Unconventional or unorthodox political behavior ("behavior that does not correspond to the legal and customary regime norms regulating political participation," KAASE 1972:1) is another concept not precise enough for our purposes. Though it may be possible to define unconventional political behavior without resorting to value judgements, simply by making quantitative comparisons between conventional and unconventional forms of political behavior, the term is nevertheless too broad for the aims of the present study.

Another related and more general concept is *aggression* (see chapter 3.1 for definitions). Acts of physical violence are the extreme form of aggressive behavior. Violence can be considered as one means of achieving aggression.

Social conflict ("struggle over values or claims to status, power, and scarce resources, in which the aims of the conflicting parties are not only to gain the desired values but also to neutralize, injure, or eliminate their rivals," COSER 1968:232) is a more general framework within which violence or aggression would occur. "Violence . . . refers to the choice of means for carrying out the conflict rather than the degree of involvement of the participants" (ibid., p. 234).

Although we will frequently use conflict terminology, the *general* literature on social conflicts (cf. COSER 1956, 1967; DAHRENDORF 1958, 1965a; for a recent overview see TURNER 1974:77-177 and FINK 1968; NELSON 1971 and SCHMIDT/KOCHAN 1972 for critical evaluations) remains somewhat imprecise as far as adequate explanations of phenomena of political violence are concerned. Of course, there are numerous propositions concerning conflict to be found in this body of literature; what is lacking, however, is *systematic* empirical evidence for these propositions.

Finally,[15] the concept of *internal war* as defined by ECKSTEIN ("any resort to violence within a political order to change its constitution, rulers, or policies," ECKSTEIN 1965:133) must be ruled out, as internal war should be reserved for *special* forms of political violence (cf. chapter 5.3.1) rather than used as a common denominator of "any resort to violence within a political order."

More difficult than the choice of a basic concept seems to be the differentiation among the following concepts: *violence, force, coercion, power, authority,* and *terror.* In discussing possible interrelationships between these concepts, theoretical issues are even more involved here than in the foregoing discussion.

Obviously, *force* is a more general concept than violence: "we define it here as the actual or threatened use of violence to compel others to do what they might not otherwise do" (GRAHAM/GURR 1969:xxxii; cf. also ROUCEK 1957:12). There is a means-ends relationship between violence and force (as between violence and aggression or between violence and social conflict), but there are other ways to obtain compliance as well (cf. the list in VAN DEN HAAG 1972:53f.).

Coercion is a term often used synonymously with force. Here we speak of coercion when the state applies force against its population (for further definition see chapter 5.1.2.5).

Power, in turn, can be thought of as a more general concept[16] than force. If one subscribes to WEBER's definition of power,[17] force may be considered a means to "carry out [one's] own will despite resistance" (WEBER).

Once again following WEBER,[18] *authority* may be understood as power that need not be tested.[19] (Some writers consider "domination" a more adequate translation of WEBER's *Herrschaft*; cf. the discussion in LUKES 1978.) This wording leads to reflections about the relationship between authority and violence. As will become clear in this study, it does not always pay for the powerholders to use violent means to make their citizens comply. Certain authors consider the relationship between authority and violence to be antithetical (but see the greater differentiations of WALTER 1964a). They view violence as *ultima ratio regis* (the last resort of the ruler), a slogan put on the canons of Louis XIV for the first time. Any unnecessary use of violence reduces the resources of legitimacy upon which the regime can rely. Similarly to CLAUSEWITZ's notion that war is the continuation of politics through different means, violence is considered as the continuation of efforts to influence through other means. If the severest means of control are used by the powerholders, this often leads to a "stabilization" of the authority; yet at the same time discontent among the population increases. The issue then becomes the relationship of the resources of both sides, the government and the protesting segments of the population, to each other. As confirmed in results from research on political violence, violent political protests do not reach their maximum during periods of strict coercion.[20] Yet, if coercion is reduced to an intermediate level and applied with some reluctance, violent political protests are much more likely to rise. A number of revolutions demonstrate the point: revolution occurs just at that point when the *ancien régime* is showing its willingness to reform itself and starts reducing the severity of its coercive measures.

Having discussed some of the conceptual[21] as well as analytical problems that one faces in research on political violence, we will study two groups of background theories often considered in studies on political violence: firstly, sociopsychological experiments on aggressive behavior and resulting theories, and, secondly, theories on social comparison processes or mechanisms. The first group of theories elaborates a set of conditions conducive to individual discontent, whereas the latter group focuses on determinants (group processes) accounting for collective discontent.

Chapter 3

Experimental Studies of Aggressive Behavior: A Brief Overview

One of the basic concepts in research on political violence is the frustration-aggression nexus. "The frustration-aggression mechanism is in this sense analogous to the law of gravity: men who are frustrated have an innate disposition to do violence to its source in proportion to the intensity of their frustration, just as objects are attracted to one another in direct proportion to their relative masses and inverse proportion to their distance" (GURR 1970a:37). GURR overstates the point somewhat, as will become clear. Besides frustrations there are other classes of variables which can lead to aggressive behavior. We shall enumerate certain variables which experimental research on human aggressive behavior has shown to be important. These variables should be integrated into research on political violence, although it may at times be difficult to find appropriate indicators for some of them. Of the various experimental approaches to the study of aggression, we will consider here only the *frustration-aggression approaches* and the *social learning approach*. *Ethological* research on aggression (e.g., LORENZ 1966; JOHNSON 1972; SCOTT 1975; for an excellent summary of the devastating criticism of LORENZ's theoretical position see NELSON 1974;[1] see also the essays in MONTAGU 1973 and BOICE 1976), *psychoanalytic* concepts (e.g., FREUD; for a critique see BERKOWITZ 1962:8-12; FROMM 1973),[2] *personality* studies (cf. BUSS 1961:160-82; SELG/MEES 1974 for a summary), *physiological* (cf. MOYER 1969, 1971a) as well as *genetic*[3] approaches (see OWEN 1972; CORNING 1973:131-37; HOOK 1973) will not be considered in any detail. Although they may be relevant to the study of political violence, we consider them far less important than the approaches discussed here. In any case, it may be helpful to remember that "the critical issue is not whether aggressive behavior is multiply determined, but [the] extent [to which] biological, psychological, and social influences contribute to variations in aggression between different people and in the same individual at different times and under different circumstances" (BANDURA 1973:31).

3.1. Aggression: Some Definitional Problems

Definitional problems are once again (as in chapter 2.1) considerable (cf. KAUFMANN 1965, 1970:1–12; SELG/MEES 1974; BARON 1977). Only a few comments will be made here. One of the definitions of aggression, namely aggression as "the delivery of painful or noxious stimuli to another organism" (BUSS 1969a:65) has been criticized (e.g., by BERKOWITZ 1965a:323ff.) for not taking the intentions of the actor into consideration. BERKOWITZ's own definition, and similarly the classic definition of DOLLARD et al. (1939:11), reads instead: "Aggression is defined . . . as behavior whose goal is the injury of some person or object" (BERKOWITZ 1965a: 302). Yet, this definition as well is open to criticism. Critics such as BUSS (1961:1f.) maintain that intentions are often difficult to measure and moreover are not useful in behavioral science which should avoid teleological statements. BANDURA objects that in this definition aggression is unnecessarily restricted to *one* goal, i.e., to damage another person or object intentionally. He maintains that individuals often have various goals in mind when acting aggressively. One of the commonest (cf. BUSS 1961:2ff.; FESHBACH 1964) differentiations in aggression theory has indeed been between *hostile aggression* (aggression with the sole purpose of injuring a person or damaging an object) and *instrumental aggression* (aggression as a means for obtaining other goals).[4] This dichotomy, however, is dubious because the "so-called hostile aggression is equally instrumental except that the actions are used to produce injurious outcomes rather than to gain status, power, resources, or some other types of results. Whatever its merits, the distinction reflects differences in desired outcomes, not in instrumentality. It would therefore be more accurate to differentiate aggressive actions in terms of their functional value rather than in terms of whether or not they are instrumental. Most aggressive acts serve ends other than solely to produce injury" (BANDURA 1973:3). (The necessary changes having been made, the last statement seems to hold true for some forms of political violence as well.)

BANDURA himself proposes a definition similar to that of BUSS but also more comprehensive since it includes property damage and self-aggression as well: "Aggression is defined as behavior that results in personal injury and destruction of property. The injury may be psychological (in the form of devaluation or degradation) as well as physical" (BANDURA 1973:5). This definition also has its shortcomings because the labeling of certain acts as aggressive or nonaggressive (e.g., performing a medical operation) is not taken into account. As BANDURA himself writes: "A full explanation of aggression must consider both *injurious behavior* and *social judgments* that determine which injurious acts are labeled as aggressive" (ibid., p. 5). Even if one wants to avoid an intentional definition of aggression, the inclusion of social judgments as a defining element would nevertheless lead to evaluating the *intentions of the actors* (cf. also BANDURA/WALTERS 1973:113).[5] Thus in this respect there are clear parallels with the definition of political violence as well as in respect to labeling certain forms of behavior.[6]

Some writers have tried to cope with the difficulties in defining aggression by proposing typologies of aggressive behavior (see FESHBACH 1964; SELG 1968:64; MOYER 1968; 1976; BUSS 1971:8), but none of these typologies is based on sufficient systematic empirical evidence. Furthermore, there are always many examples in reality cutting across the various types which, therefore, are not sufficiently distinctive.

3.2. Frustration and Aggression: Some Explanatory Variables

According to DOLLARD et al. a frustration is an "interference with the occurrence of an instigated *goal*-response at its proper time in the behavior sequence" (DOLLARD et al. 1939:7, our emphasis). As BERKOWITZ (1969:6) points out, one must distinguish between mere *deprivation* (deprivation in the absence of a goal-oriented and blocked activity) and *frustration* (in the sense given above). Frustration (rather than deprivation in this sense) is one of the important conditions of political violence. It should be kept in mind, however, that many researchers of political violence speak of forms of *deprivation* when they mean forms of *frustration*, in the sense delineated here. Contrary to the original hypothesis of DOLLARD et al. that frustration is a necessary and sufficient condition for aggression to occur, several *intervening* variables must be taken into account if this relationship is to hold at all (cf. also the discussion in BARON 1977:83–87). In addition there are several *other* variables bearing some relationship to the hypothesis under consideration here. Firstly, the self-criticism of MILLER, one of the authors of the Yale group (DOLLARD et al.), must be noted: "Frustration produces instigation to a number of different types of response, one of which is an instigation to some form of aggression" (MILLER 1941:340). Two aspects of this reformulation deserve special attention: (1) frustration now leads only to an instigation to aggression; (2) the probability that aggression is to occur is determined by the position of the aggressive reaction in a hierarchy of other possible reactions.

With the intervening variable *instigation* (or drive)[7] *to aggression* BERKOWITZ's intervening variable *anger* ("the emotional state presumably resulting from frustration, which, in the presence of a suitable cue, instigates aggressive responses," BERKOWITZ 1962:1) has been anticipated. However, both specifications (the intervening variable anger and the idea of a response hierarchy), are useful only if (1) it is specified in advance where in the response hierarchy an aggressive reaction is located, and (2) the strength of the instigation to react aggressively is measured *independently* of its occurrence. Otherwise, circular statements result. Moreover, physiological states as well as psychological states such as anger, stress, or fear are difficult to isolate (cf. LAZARUS 1966; MOYER 1971a; but see also AX 1953).

The YALE group has already named a number of other variables that should be considered when dealing with frustration-aggression relationships: e.g., norms concerning the appropriateness of aggressive behavior, the resources of the potential object of aggression to punish the aggressor or to retaliate against him, the degree of interference with the originally intended behavior, the degree of instigation to perform the intended act, habits of reacting aggressively, and the number of frustrations in the past. Instrumental considerations (cf., e.g., LANGE/VAN DE NES 1973; THOMPSON/ KOLSTOE 1974) may also be important determinants of the occurrence of aggressive behavior. On the basis of his experimental results, BUSS states the following proposition: "When aggression has no instrumental value, its intensity is unrelated to that of frustration; when aggression has instrumental value, its intensity covaries with the intensity of frustration" (BUSS 1969:73). The converse hypothesis may, however, be somewhat more plausible.

Whereas some of the variables mentioned seem to influence the frustration-aggression relationship as a *whole* (e.g., aggressive habits, norms regulating where aggressive behavior is an appropriate reaction) or seem to have a more direct effect on *frustration* (e.g., the degree of interference, the instigation to act as originally intended, the number of frustrations), there are others which seem to be important in the *evaluation process* whether the victim of a frustration acts aggressively or not. Among these more *intermediate variables* are anger, resources of the object of aggression to punish or to retaliate, and norms regulating where aggressive behavior is allowed and where not. In addition to those variables already mentioned, there are others which determine the intensity of frustrations. Among these is the *arbitrariness* of the interference (cf. PASTORE 1952). There seem to be less aggressive reactions if the frustrations are the result of *accidental* behavior or of unintended interferences (cf. BURNSTEIN/WORCHEL 1962 and the findings of the replication study by RULE et al. 1978; cf. also EPSTEIN/ TAYLOR 1967). Moreover, one might find it necessary to distinguish not only between arbitrary and nonarbitrary frustrations but also between *reasonable* and *nonreasonable* frustrations (KREGARMAN/WORCHEL 1961; cf. also MALLICK/McCANDLESS 1966, though their results do not sufficiently confirm this distinction). Furthermore, the probability that frustrations will lead to aggressive behavior seems to be greater the more the ego of the actor is threatened (cf. WORCHEL 1960).

Finally, BERKOWITZ's *cue* variable deserves attention: "The anger in itself or the previous learning creates only a readiness for aggression; appropriate cues must also be present in order to set the response sequence into operation" (BERKOWITZ 1965a:324; see the various experiments in BERKOWITZ 1964, 1965; BERKOWITZ/GEEN 1967; BERKOWITZ/BUCK 1967; GEEN/BERKOWITZ 1966; cf. also TURNER/BERKOWITZ 1972). BERKOWITZ even goes so far as to maintain that "the victim's stimulus properties draw aggression from the aggressor independently of internal arousal" (BERKOWITZ 1969b:117). Moreover, "an angry person can pull the trigger of his gun if he wants to commit violence; but the trigger can also pull the finger or otherwise elicit aggressive reactions from him, if he is ready to aggress and does not have strong inhibitions against such behavior" (BERKOWITZ 1973:132).[8] Mere situational cues such as weapons seem to be sufficient to elicit aggressive behavior of subjects previously angered by another person who later becomes the target of aggression (BERKOWITZ/

LePAGE 1967). However, the experimental settings of BERKOWITZ and his colleagues are rather artificial.[9] An overview of nine such experiments similar in basic design provides mixed results (SCHMIDT/SCHMIDT-MUMMENDEY 1974; cf. also BUSS et al. 1972; LEYENS/PARKE 1975). These authors discuss several of the variables that should be controlled in such experiments if one is to isolate cue effects. The evidence provided thus far is inconclusive, to say the least.

Nevertheless, easy access to weapons seems to be an important determinant of aggressive behavior, especially in the United States, as indicated in the following finding: "Since 1900, guns have killed over 800,000 Americans. The total casualties from civilian gunfire in the 20th century exceed the military casualties in all wars from the Revolutionary War through the Vietnamese War. . . . Following the Detroit riots of June, 1967, it was found that 90 percent of the guns confiscated were not registered as required under Michigan law" (JOHNSON 1972:167, 168 on the basis of various studies; cf. also GILLIN/OCHBERG 1970). According to NEWTON/ZIMRING (1970:xii) in the United States there are nearly three thousand victims of gun accidents per year. Thus far it has proved impossible to pass *strict* legal measures in favor of tight gun control because of the vigorous opposition of the National Rifle Association (cf. also ETZIONI 1976:718-21). It remains doubtful, especially in the latter case, whether results can be generalized to situations outside the laboratory. The *ecological validity* (BRUNSWIK 1949) of the experimental settings seems to be very limited.

   There are, of course, other determinants of aggression besides the many forms of frustration (see BUSS 1961:171ff; LAWSON 1965:41-47). *Attacks* (see GENTRY 1970) a well as *painful stimuli* (see ULRICH 1966; ULRICH et al. 1973) are two of the more important classes of determinants (cf. also AMSEL's theory of frustrative nonreward; AMSEL 1962; chapter 5.3.2.3). In addition, one must consider various forms of aggression (see the references to aggression typologies above) not reducible to a one-dimensional continuum. Finally, there are many other reactions (such as avoidance, apathy, regression, autism, constructive coping) to frustrations besides aggressive behavior. BERKOWITZ's modified frustration-aggression theory has come under attack from a number of directions, especially from researchers like BANDURA (1973) who have a social learning approach. One of the main arguments against experiments based on the frustration-aggression theory is that the experimental setting quite often leads to confounding aggressive behavior with the evaluation of performance. To disclose the real dependent variable, experimental subjects must deliver electric shocks to other subjects (said to be "real" subjects but actually coworkers of the experimenter) to "improve their learning behavior." Thus, the measure of aggressiveness might be confounded with evaluating the performance of the "subjects." Even if there are differences in the number or intensity of shocks given which may be due to different degrees of frustration or anger, the alternative explanation puts the validity of this kind of experiment into question. "The measure thus incorporates both performance evaluations and punitiveness" (BANDURA 1973:134).

3.3. The Social Learning Approach to the Study of Aggression

In the social learning theory of aggression developed by BANDURA (1973), several of the variables also used in BERKOWITZ's theory are retained. However, according to BANDURA there are various additional variables that must also be considered. While BERKOWITZ maintains that anger and/or cues, together or alone, if sufficiently strong, may lead to aggressive behavior, BANDURA does not consider either of them necessary for explaining aggression. In his theory *model effects* and *inhibitions* of aggressive behavior are considered stronger determinants of aggressive behavior than anger or cues. Inhibitions, one of the central variables in the social learning theory of aggression, may be weakened through a number of variables, such as habits to act aggressively, insufficient resources of the attacked person to retaliate accordingly, anonymous situations, and justifications (e.g., norms, blaming the subject) for acting aggressively (cf. the techniques mentioned in BANDURA 1973:211ff.; see also BANDURA et al. 1975). An aggressive reaction may also be observed in situations resembling those where a model aggressed successfully.[10] In the social learning theory of aggression, arousal and anger serve merely as facilitating conditions for aggression, not as necessary factors. The *anticipated consequences* of aggression (or other forms of behavior) form another class of important predictors of aggressive behavior.[11] If negative consequences, like retaliation of the attacked person,[12] are likely to be stronger than positive consequences, aggressive behavior does not occur.[13] Furthermore, the behavior of a model can have various effects: "The empirical evidence, taken together, reveals that models can serve as teachers,[14] as elicitors, as disinhibitors, as stimulus enhancers, and as emotion arousers. A complete account of how models affect observers must encompass the diverse functions of modeling influences" (BANDURA 1973:130).[15]

The differences between the two approaches become clearer in the following statement: "Unlike BERKOWITZ's theory, which assigns response-priming functions to anger provocation and modeling stimuli, and response-eliciting functions to other environmental stimuli, social learning theory regards all three sources of influence as having response-activating properties. Aversive stimulation, in the form of personal insult or physical assault, is in fact a much more potent elicitor of aggression than some environmental cue that has merely been previously associated with anger-arousing experiences. Thus, people often counteraggress when insulted or struck without requiring additional stimulus prompts; they aggress on slight provocation when they see that such actions are effective in gaining desired outcomes" (BANDURA 1973:135–36). However, one should not overlook the parallels existing between the two approaches, as expressed in the following statement which sums up some of the variables mediating between frustration and aggression:

> Whether a person becomes openly aggressive after being thwarted depends upon such things as his characteristic degree of optimism and trust, the extent to which he has learned to respond construc-

tively to the problem confronting him, his judgment as to how safe
it is to attack the available targets or how proper it is to show any
aggression in the given situation, his attitude toward the potential
targets, the motives he attributes to his frustrator, the degree to
which the people around him are also suffering from the frustration
inflicted upon him, and his interpretation of his own emotional reaction to the frustration. These and other factors . . . lessen the inevitability of aggressive reactions to thwarting.[16] But to acknowledge
this does not mean we must discard the frustration-aggression hypothesis altogether. Barriers to goal attainment do increase the probability of aggressive responses, even if this heightened likelihood is
only relatively small in many situations (BERKOWITZ 1973:102-3).

As pointed out in a summary of a number of studies already mentioned
(cf. also PETERSON 1971; BARON 1971, 1973, 1974a; MEYER 1972;
BERKOWITZ/ALIOTO 1973; GEEN/STONNER 1973, 1974):

Evidence indicates that the sight of violence can (1) lower restraints
against aggression and even (2) elicit aggressive tendencies within the
observer. These tendencies might then lead to open attacks upon
available targets if (a) the observed violence was not regarded as
improper or unjustified, (b) the individual does not anticipate being
punished for aggressing, (c) strong inhibitions against aggression have
not been evoked in him, and (d) the available target also has appropriate stimulus properties, for example through being associated
with other victims of aggression (BERKOWITZ 1973:132).

The controversy between BERKOWITZ and BANDURA is perhaps best
summarized in STONNER's recent review of the literature: "The exact nature
of the interaction between arousal and its effects on the perceived consequences of aggression is an area deserving more attention" (STONNER
1976:241).

The social learning theory of aggression considers aggression as having
multiple determinants as well as multiple functions and strongly emphasizes
the conditions for acquiring aggressive responses. Without going into detail
here (see BANDURA 1973), one must agree with BANDURA that the social
learning theory of aggression is more comprehensive than BERKOWITZ's
revised formulation of the frustration-aggression theory. Nevertheless, many
of the issues raised in the controversy between the two approaches have not
as yet been settled. In the social learning theory of aggression, there is a clear
need to specify the anticipated consequences in advance, for otherwise the
theory would prove correct in every instance and thus lead to tautological
statements. Moreover, while one must admire BANDURA's skill in interpreting a wide variety of experimental results from the point of view of social
learning theory, much less attention seems to be paid to the operational
aspects of suggested theoretical explanations. Thus, a series of carefully
designed crucial experiments is called for to determine the predictive power
of the numerous independent variables isolated thus far.

3.4 Summary and Evaluation of These Studies with Respect to Political Violence

The frustration-aggression theory and the social learning theory of aggression both emphasize important perspectives that must be taken into account if one wishes to explain aggressive behavior or, more specifically here, phenomena of political violence. In Figure 3.1 we attempt to locate some of the classes of variables that appear to be important in various experiments. Although there are many other predictive variables of aggressive behavior,[17] some of which have already been mentioned, those in Figure 3.1 seem to be the most significant. Reactions other than aggression are omitted in this model. The signs in the inhibitions or reinforcements box refer to either an increasing (+) or a decreasing (−) probability of an aggressive response.

In some respects this is the basic model used in many studies on political violence, even if many of those studies treat only the relationships between two variables of the model at a time rather than use the model as a whole. It will become apparent that such a model touches on a number of perspectives worth considering in cross-national research on political violence. The subtle experimental results as to the conditions and consequences of aggressive behavior should be carefully studied by researchers concerned with political violence and should prevent them from relying uncritically on frustration-aggression explanations. However, experimental studies on the conditions of aggressive behavior have not yet provided us with information as to causal "paths" among a set of independent or intermediate variables. Many of the results which have been found either varied from study to study or were obtained at a cost of neglecting other possibly important causal variables (which, in part, is a condition of a successful experimental design requiring orthogonalization of independent variables).

Finally, it must be stressed that many experimental studies on aggression lack ecological validity. The experimental subjects are largely children or college students; most of these studies examine only short-term influences. An aggression machine like the one BUSS developed is hardly an equivalent for aggressive behavior likely to occur outside the laboratory (cf. also BARON/EGGLESTON 1972). The same holds true for many other dependent variables used in these experiments (cf. the overview and the discussion in BARON 1977:39–75). Many experiments on aggression give results that can be interpreted ambiguously (see the evidence in BANDURA 1973). One must demand more ecologically valid experimental settings so that results will have meaning outside the laboratory (but cf. also the study designs and results in LEYENS et al. 1975; TURNER et al. 1975). Another factor to be examined is whether conditions isolated by researchers working in the field of political violence, such as the various deprivation conditions (see GROFMAN/MULLER 1973 and chapter 5.3.2.3), have their equivalent in the laboratory[18] (see also STONNER 1976 for some other prospects in aggression research).

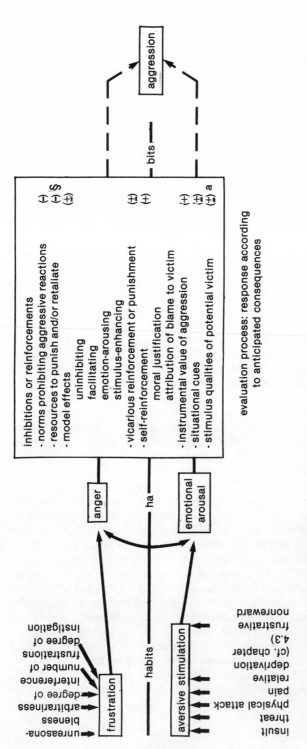

Figure 3.1.   A Simple Model for Explaining Aggression

Notes.   §: Curvilinear relationship (cf. chapter 5.1.2.5)
a: a rather ambiguous variable, as can be seen in the
outcome of an experiment by SWART/BERKOWITZ (1976).
Whereas one would be inclined to assume that normally
subjects would feel restrained to increase their aggressive
behavior against victims suffering pain, it has been
demonstrated that "because of its prior associations
with reinforced aggression" (BERKOWITZ 1974:174)
victim's pain could lead to an increase of aggression
by the experimental subject.

While most of the variables mentioned in this chapter are important for explaining aggressive behavior, evidence in research on political violence bearing on the theoretical variables suggested here is much more indirect in nature. Furthermore, many of the possibilities inherent in the approaches discussed here have not yet been considered by the majority of researchers doing cross-national research on political violence. The theoretical rationale discussed here for linking variables will be encountered again and again throughout this study. The problems start when we turn to the operationalizations used. Does a low score on a scale of political trust, as used in studies on the American black riots of the 1960s, adequately capture the notion of "anger"? Or are political trust and distrust indicators of alienation and retreat which might be more likely reactions to discontent than political violence? Is the police force in areas of discontent likely to be perceived as arbitrarily causing frustrations? Do economic and social indicators—moreover on an aggregated basis—adequately measure states of deprivation which might lead to political violence? Are habits of aggressive reaction adequately operationalized by measuring the "efficacy of past violence"? Are inhibitions sufficiently measured through the strength and loyalty of the coercive forces of the state and of the rebel forces? What are the cues in situations when political or even revolutionary violence will "precipitate"? What kind of cues are being emitted by the objects of political violence? What can be said about violent acts on behalf of protesters, subsequent official reactions and counterreactions of these or other groups? Which courses do processes of escalation of political violence take? Is it easier for groups to use political violence to influence the public in countries with a history of political violence than in other countries? Under what kind of conditions is it possible to contain political violence? These are some of the questions with which one must deal in research on political violence. There are answers, but they are hardly sufficient at this point. Obviously, *time series* data as well as *process data* are needed (cf. also chapters 5.1.3 and 9) to answer some of these questions. Before we consider theories of political violence in detail, a few remarks concerning other background theories, namely theories on social comparison processes, are in order.

Chapter 4

Theories of Social Comparison Processes

In the following section we discuss several theories of social comparison processes which should be more integrated into the study of political violence. Obviously, comparison processes between segments of the population are important if discontent and later a potential for protest behavior are to develop. The basic questions are then: comparisons with whom, in what respect, with what consequence, and at what time? More will be said about specific conditions for comparison processes that may lead to discontent and/or protest potential. Here it will be our aim to draw attention to several theories and mechanisms of social comparison processes which have been somewhat neglected in research on political violence (at least in those studies relying on macrolevel measures).

Rather than discussing general theories of social comparison processes such as FESTINGER's theory (FESTINGER 1954; SULS/MILLER 1977) or reference group theory (concerning the various types of reference groups that have been suggested, see CAIN 1968 and URRY 1973 for an overview), we will be more concerned with *mechanisms* of comparison used in such processes. Three mechanisms are the subject of our discussion:

4.1. HOMANS's Concept of Distributive Justice

"A man in an exchange relation with another will expect that the rewards of each man be proportional to his costs—the greater the rewards, the greater the costs—and that the net rewards, or profits, of each man be proportional to his investments—the greater the investments, the greater the profit" (HOMANS 1961:75). If these conditions hold, distributive justice is said to exist. Profits are defined simply as the difference between rewards (e.g., money, power, prestige, sympathy) and costs[1] (the rewards of *another* exchange relation a person is giving up). The definition of investments, however, creates problems: "Because some of a man's background characteristics[2] increase in value with the time and ability he has 'put in' various groups and jobs, we speak of them for the purposes of distributive justice as investments" (HOMANS 1961:236; italics omitted). According to HOMANS, investments can be sex, race, education, experience, or age. If formalized, HOMANS's rule of distributive justice reads:[3]

$$\frac{\text{A's rewards} - \text{A's costs}}{\text{A's investments}} = \frac{\text{B's rewards} - \text{B's costs}}{\text{B's investments}}$$

Without going into detail here (see EKEH 1974:127-65), problems arise if one tries to work with this concept:[4] HOMANS states that the judgements of each other's rewards, investments, and costs need not be based on the same criteria. Therefore, as measurements at the required interval level are not possible, problems of comparison obviously arise if one is to make *inter*-personal comparisons of states lacking in distributive justice. There is no obligatory interpersonal standard of comparison, no common currency (cf. M. DEUTSCH 1964:161) for evaluating particular situations. (Moreover, GOODE cites many examples which demonstrate that "with reference to most evaluated activities, people believe rewards should be commensurate with accomplishments or output, rather than costs and investments," GOODE 1978:343-44; for arguments in accord with HOMANS, however, see BLALOCK/WILKEN 1979:236ff.)

> Note that if all parties are to accept a distribution as just, they must agree on three different points. First, they must agree on the rule of distributive justice itself: that rewards ought to be proportional to contributions. Second, they must agree on what kinds of rewards and contributions are to be legitimately taken into account in applying the rule. Third, they must agree in their assessment of the amounts of these contributions each makes and the amounts of these rewards each receives. Experience seems to indicate that people are much more likely to reach agreement on the rule itself than on the other two issues. They agree on the rule but not on its concrete applications (HOMANS 1976:232).

For example, poor whites may feel relatively deprived when comparing themselves with blacks, whereas poor blacks at the same time could feel relatively deprived (and not relatively rewarded) when comparing themselves with whites. The problem is not only that different criteria—or in this case differentially evaluated criteria—are used for these intergroup comparisons. Applying a criterion like race also leads to different interpretations of other criteria, like income, schooling, or welfare benefits, that may be used by both sides in the evaluation process.

HOMANS was realistic enough to limit his statements concerning the principle of distributive justice strictly to *individual* comparisons. However, he introduces a concept like investments that (even if HOMANS himself does not define it this way) presupposes a certain amount of consensus about what are basic input criteria in groups or perhaps in societies. HOMANS's theory is clearly incomplete as concerns the social processes that may result from the fact that the same criteria are used in comparison processes but are differently evaluated. In short, HOMANS describes what is or may be there but does not give explanations as to why this is so. He should have gone on to develop a theory of persistence and change of values of a group, community, or society and to indicate criteria used in the process of *status evaluation*.[5]

There are two other basic arguments against HOMANS's notion of distributive justice. Firstly, the position of the principle of distributive justice within the context of HOMANS's exchange theory is debatable (see TURK/SIMPSON 1971 for a summary of further arguments and especially CHADWICK-JONES 1976 for a comprehensive evaluation and criticism of the approaches of HOMANS and ADAMS; as to the latter see the next chapter). Whereas the principle of distributive justice as the fifth proposition in HOMANS's theory is based on *fair* exchange, the first four propositions are built on *profitable* exchange, i.e., getting the highest profit from exchange relationships. However, one may have to reverse HOMANS's entire theoretical system as EKEH shows. "In two-person groups, whose members are engaged in restricted exchanges, *inter*personal comparisons and fair exchange prevail. In multi-person groups, with an emphasis on generalized exchange, *intra*personal comparisons and profitable exchange prevail" (EKEH 1974: 131; my italics).

Secondly, to take up a prior argument, if one were to work with subjective definitions of distributive justice, one would not be able to make general predictions or provide explanations as to behavior. If a situation "objectively" not fulfilling the conditions of distributive justice is differently evaluated by the particular actors, there would not be much sense in using such a concept in social science. If this concept is to be of any use in social science, one has to find out whether there are *inter*personally obligatory and accepted criteria for evaluating social situations. One must, of course, ask persons what they consider to be their investments, costs, and rewards, and how they would rate the alternatives open to them in specific situations (cf. also THIBAUT/KELLEY 1959). If the researcher finds out that there is a *consensus* within or between groups about basic criteria relevant for distributive justice,[7] the concept may be useful for explanatory purposes. It is maintained here that only if such interpersonally relevant criteria are established will a hypothesis like the following prove to be of any value in social science: "The more to a man's disadvantage the rule of distributive justice fails of realization, the more likely he is to display the emotional behavior we call anger" (HOMANS 1961:75). Before we take up the last hypothesis, however, a theoretical concept similar to that of HOMANS should be mentioned briefly.

4.2. ADAMS's Inequity Theory

"Inequity exists for Person whenever his perceived job inputs and/or outcomes stand psychologically in an obverse relation to what he perceives are the inputs and/or outcomes of Other" (ADAMS 1969:214; for formalized versions cf. ADAMS 1965 and the critiques and new developments in ANDERSON 1976; R. J. HARRIS 1976a; WALSTER et al. 1978: especially

pp. 262-66; JASSO 1978; ALESSIO 1980; see also the numerous extensions and specifications of equity theorizing in BLALOCK/WILKEN 1979:
222-87). Once again, "the relation necessary for inequity to exist is psychological in character, not logical" (ibid., p. 215). Thus the notion of inequity
is similar to HOMANS's rule of distributive justice. HOMANS, however, does
not limit his principle to job-related comparisons. ADAMS, on the other
hand, explicitly discusses strategies to reduce inequity. In general, the arguments raised against HOMANS apply to ADAMS as well. Furthermore, indicators for inputs could serve as indicators for outcomes as well (cf. TORNOW
1971) so that temporary solutions of inequity may lead to new forms of
inequity (WEICK 1966; cf. also COOK/PARCEL 1977:77; and the review
of findings in CAMPBELL/PRITCHARD 1976:104-10). "It is also possible
that particular inputs among themselves, outcomes among themselves and
inputs and outcomes in combination interact in peculiar ways" (ADAMS/
FREEDMAN 1976:54). Thus AUSTIN admonishes researchers "to uncover
how individuals *combine* outcome/input information into *one total* judgment of fairness" (AUSTIN 1977:283; latter italics added). In the same vein
VAN AVERMAET et al. (1978) point out that one should distinguish between equity as a goal and equity as a strategy.[8] Moreover, one must keep
in mind that in empirical studies bearing on equity theory[9] (these are for the
most part sociopsychological experiments) frequently situations have been
studied in which a third person rewards or punishes two parties for their
respective inputs (cf. the overview in LEVENTHAL 1976a). The basically
dyadic orientation in equity theorizing, however, has not been realized in
those experimental settings (cf. BURGESS/NIELSEN 1974 for an exception
and NEWPORT 1975 for a critique of their study). As HOMANS (1976:242)
correctly points out, facets of social power and its consequences rather than
equity theory in a narrower sense have been the subject of these experiments.
(It should also be noted that there is a strong undercurrent in equity theorizing favoring the position and the feelings of the underdog.)[10]

In general, we must be sceptical (cf. HOMANS 1976:240) of efforts at
extending equity theorizing to a general theory of social interaction (as to
these developments cf. of some of the approaches in BERKOWITZ/WALSTER
1976; more recently see WALSTER et al. 1978). It has been pointed out that
there are other concepts of justice besides equity, e.g., the concept of equality
(rewards distributed so that each individual gets the same share independently
of his inputs)[11] or the distribution of rewards according to needs (cf. also
DEUTSCH 1975, the typologies in LERNER 1975; DONNENWERTH/TÖRN-
BLOM 1975; TÖRNBLOM 1977; WALSTER et al. 1978; and the theoretical
considerations in LEVENTHAL 1976b:214 and passim as to combining
several of these concepts of justice on a numerical basis).[12] Theoretical justifications as well as empirical findings bearing on the relevance of these alternative conceptualizations of justice[13] are also found in the overviews in
BERKOWITZ/WALSTER (1976) and in the *Journal of Social Issues* 31,
no. 3 (1975). Whereas all of these concepts still focus on comparisons between two persons or two groups, a perspective originally stressed in equity
theory, there are some new efforts to extend equity theory beyond dyadic

relationships ("person-specific equity"). Thus, it has been discovered in experiments on "equity with the world" (i.e., equity relationships comprising *several* dyads, see AUSTIN/WALSTER 1975) that temporary violations of person-specific equity (which may not be attributed to the individual itself) will be compensated through rewards in other relationships (equity with the world). The individual obviously compensates for setbacks in one relationship with higher than proportional rewards in other dyadic relationships. Interestingly enough, such behavior apparently is approved of by other persons who are not the victims of inequity (see AUSTIN/WALSTER 1974; AUSTIN 1977:299–300). These new theoretical developments (cf. also WALSTER et al. 1978:205ff.) not only provide for an extension of the originally rather narrow equity conception (cf. also the developments in HARROD 1980), but also consider time as a variable more explicitly. In studies on political violence (cf. GROFMAN/MULLER 1973 and chapter 5.3.2.3) some empirical evidence has shown that individuals apply certain discount or surtax rates when evaluating their social positions over time; thus, very recent improvements of their positions do not lead to the decomposition of protest potentials, but rather serve to accentuate the degree of subjective relative deprivation. There may be some progress for the individual, yet in relation to his expectation or, more precisely, to that to which he feels legitimately entitled, these improvements still fall short and the result is still an increase in protest potential. (However, this empirical finding might in part be explained, as GROFMAN/MULLER 1973 themselves point out, in that these respondents want to protect their recent gains which they perceive as being threatened from the outside.) Similar variants of discount rate calculations might hold as to future positions to which individuals or groups will feel legitimately entitled. These are some of the most fascinating new developments in protest research. It should be made clear, however, that the work of GROFMAN/MULLER (1973) is the first and only one of its kind (but see also the recent studies of MILLER et al. 1977; MARSH 1977) and that their data base is too limited to allow for testing of the several substantial explanations of the relationships observed. These theoretical considerations have hardly been considered in the works on political violence to be discussed in chapter 5.1. However, there is no question that the *underlying* theoretical notions are prominent in that body of research as well. They will become even more important when the limits of cross-sectional analyses are overcome and new types of data have been collected (cf. also chapter 5.1.3 and chapter 9). To return to equity theorizing if one considers the antecedent conditions of political violence (not only of protest potential) one might expect that neither the conditions of person-specific equity nor of equity with the world will be met. However, one cannot infer the existence of protest potentials (all the less of political violence) from the presence of inequity relationships. As BURGESS/NIELSEN (1974:441), following THIBAUT/KELLEY (1959), point out, much depends on the alternatives available, a point to which we shall return several times in this study.

Whatever the merits of these theoretical notions, two things should be kept in mind: (1) The bulk of evidence stems either from experimental studies or from studies in economic settings (wage comparisons, etc.). (2) These concepts may be culture-specific in the sense that they hold only for highly competitive modernized societies (or for modernized segments of particular populations). In underdeveloped countries these notions may be largely irrelevant (cf. OBERSCHALL 1969 and chapter 5.1.1.2.1). As people in these countries often do not know what their inputs and possible outcomes are, such comparisons may be unimportant to them (cf. also COOK 1975: 387). They may, however, become important if people suffering from severe forms of injustice (e.g., from lack of distributive justice) are told about these relationships by the mass media or by political leaders. The theories of HOMANS and ADAMS seem to be more relevant for application in detailed nation-wide surveys in economically developed countries but of minor importance as far as economically underdeveloped countries are concerned.

4.3. The Theory of Relative Deprivation

What has been said in the two preceding sections applies as well to the theory of relative deprivation. Relative deprivation occurs when the equity relation (ADAMS) or the rule of distributive justice (HOMANS) is violated. The relatively deprived individual (group) judges the ratio of his (its) own job input to his (its) own outcome to be less than the ratio of another person (group). States of relative deprivation are most likely to occur when feelings of legitimately deserving certain benefits are violated. It is not that a person wants a certain object or benefit which is important, as RUNCIMAN (1968:70) erroneously maintains, but that he feels legitimately entitled to it or believes to have a right to share in it.

RUNCIMAN (1961) has, however, suggested a useful theoretical differentiation between *egoistic deprivation* (relative deprivation within one's own group) and *fraternalistic deprivation* (relative deprivation of one's own group in comparison to other groups in society).[14] One of the more promising yet almost completely neglected works on the theory of relative deprivation is an article by DAVIS (1959; in addition see the classic outline in MERTON/ROSSI in MERTON 1957:225–386, and recently WILLIAMS 1975). From his many hypotheses only one will be quoted here: "If a given social categorization is correlated with objective deprivation, relative deprivation will be more frequent among the deprived in the *more* favorite category" (DAVIS 1959:286).[15] This hypothesis will be of some use in explaining violent protest behavior, particularly among segments of the American black population during the 1960s (cf. chapter 5.3.2.3), among students, and among elites in general.

A noteworthy explanation and extension of the theory of relative deprivation or, more precisely, of egoistical relative deprivation, can be found in CROSBY (1976; cf. also COOK et al. 1977). She conceives relative deprivation to be based on the following twenty conditions:

Personality traits

    1.   Self-blame/fate-blame
    2.   Need for achievement

Personal past

    3.   Length of time Person possessed X
    4.   Recency of loss of X
    5.   Closeness of attaining goal X
    6.   Rate of acquisition of X
    7.   Visibility of lost X

Immediate environment

    8.   Proportion of others possessing X
    9.   Contact with others possessing X
    10.   Attractiveness of others possessing X
    11.   Power of others possessing X
    12.   Similarity between Person and Other possessing X
    13.   Length of time Other has possessed X

Societal dictates

    14a.   Message that Person is member of group A and
    14b.   Message that Group A correlates with X
    15.   Message that some people in society possess X
    16.   Message that X is good
    17.   Message that Person deserves X
    18.   Message that Person can obtain X
    19.   Social preoccupation with justice

Biological survival

    20.   Centrality of X to biological survival

Source: CROSBY (1976:93)

In opposition to CROSBY, we maintain that, in this list of conditions and determinants of relative deprivation, conditions 14 to 16 (and perhaps even 20), while relevant, are of less importance as far as the development of theoretical models linking these conditions with each other are concerned. CROSBY strongly emphasizes that the individual must "think it feasible to obtain X, and lack a sense of personal responsibility for not having X" (CROSBY 1976:90; as to the latter condition, cf. MULLER's approach in chapter 5.3.2.3). She then goes on to examine the rather diverse literature bearing on her conceptualization and finds out "that the overwhelming majority of data corroborate the present model" (CROSBY 1976:104).

The variety of conditions of relative deprivation touched upon in CROSBY's list (and some others as well) will be encountered throughout our entire study. Unfortunately, researchers have not always distinguished as clearly as CROSBY has done among these various forms of relative deprivation. Another advantage of her approach is that it allows for deriving a variety of new and possibly fruitful hypotheses.

The theory of relative deprivation has also been extended in another direction. In its traditional version the position of other groups is used as a frame of reference for evaluating the position of one's own group. GURR, following ABERLE (1962), proposes a conceptualization of relative deprivation, in which the position of one's *own* group (or one's own standing) in the past, present and/or future is used as a reference point. Whether changes in one's own standing over time or comparisons with the standing of other groups are more important determinants of relative deprivation is, of course, an empirical question. In any case, a fully developed theory of relative deprivation would have to cover over time comparisons of the positions of one's own group as well as of the standing of other groups used in comparison processes (cf. also GURR 1970a:105-9). Knowing more about the perceptions of other groups' positions (i.e., measuring the *scope* and *intensity* of feelings of relative deprivation) may also be useful for making predictions about possible allies in fighting against averse societal or economic conditions or against other groups perceived as causing their own deprivations. Thus, there are linkages between the theory of relative deprivation and coalition theory. Coalition formation for voicing political protest is a much neglected aspect[16] in research on political violence.

GURR distinguishes four forms of relative deprivation (for more details as to GURR's theoretical system, see chapter 5.1.1.1.1).

If one looks at the antecedent conditions of political violence, progressive deprivation is probably the most important among these four forms of deprivation (see chapter 5.3.2.3). Most of the evidence, however, is indirect in nature, as several measurement requirements have been violated (see chapter 5.1.1.1.3.2). There are various other forms of relative deprivation (or relative gratification, if the principle of distributive justice is violated in favor of one's own position) as individuals compare their positions over time. In chapter 5.3.2.3 some of these possibilities (see also FEIERABEND/FEIERABEND/NESVOLD 1969:637-44) will be discussed on the basis of empirical evidence (GROFMAN/MULLER 1973; cf. also PORTER/NAGEL 1976, in chapter 5.3.2.4).

When applying reference group notions to empirical research, scholars often ask their subjects to compare their various positions (or those of their own group) over time. For example, CANTRIL's (1965) self-anchoring striving scale is used to obtain answers on one's own positions (or those of one's own group) as far as housing, jobs, or general standing in society are concerned. Rarely is the question raised in sufficient detail[18] concerning which positions of which *other* groups are used as reference points. Thus, in general, theoretical possibilities inherent in the theory of relative deprivation, or more generally, in reference group theory,[19] are not yet adequately considered in empirical studies on political violence.

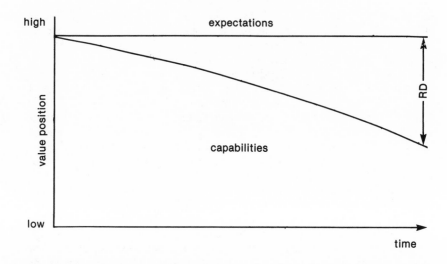

1.   *decremental deprivation* (expectations — constant, capabilities — declining)

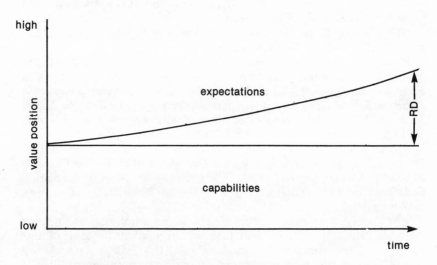

2.   *aspirational deprivation* (expectations — increasing, capabilities — constant)

Figure 4.1.   Four Forms of Relative Deprivation (RD)

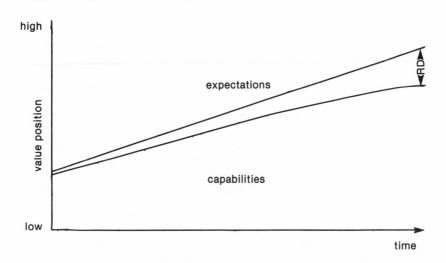

3. *progressive deprivation* (expectations — increasing,
    capabilities — increasing, but at a lower rate)

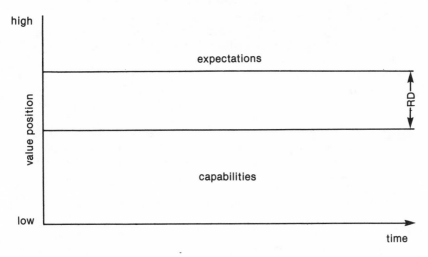

4. *persisting deprivation* (expectations — constant,
    capabilities — constantly lagging behind expectations)

Source: GURR (1969a:598-601, slightly modified; GURR
          actually speaks of collective value positions, cf.
          chapter 5.1.1.1.1).

To summarize, relative deprivation can and often does lead to anger. However, anger in itself is neither a sufficient nor a necessary condition for violent political protest. Anger must be felt collectively as well as mobilized to become politically relevant discontent.[20] "By collectivization of discontent, we mean that, in order for collective, violent behavior to occur, individuals must come to share a definition of a situation as irritating or intolerable, and they must feel social support for their violent behavior" (COOPER 1974:269). In contrast with our focus in chapter 3 where anger was the result of individual frustrations or individual averse conditions (Figure 2.1), we are here concerned with mobilized collective[21] discontent. The basic questions are now: what sort of comparisons, with whom and at what time, are likely to lead to discontent, and how is discontent mobilized and brought into the political arena? We have some indirect evidence as to the conditions making people politically angry. Our empirical knowledge of mobilization processes, however, is still relatively underdeveloped (cf. also chapter 9). In any case, as objective descriptions of social situations or positions in society may differ from subjective evaluations of these aspects, a theory of social comparison processes (here mainly the theory of relative deprivation) must be employed as an "interpretative concept" (MERTON/ ROSSI 1957:230). Restricting the analysis to aggregate data may be sufficient for explaining political violence in *statistical* terms but not in *theoretical* terms. The concepts outlined in this chapter must be integrated into theories of political violence and measured accordingly, i.e., on an individual level. Some researchers satisfied with the degree of prediction reached may consider this an unnecessary step. However, they tend to overlook the fact that their theories may have changed in the process of operationalization so that a test of the original theory becomes impossible. This has been the case more than once in cross-national research on political violence. As VROOM sums up: "A complete explanation of the role of social comparisons in determining individuals' attitudes toward their roles must specify how specific others are selected for comparison, how information about self and others is combined to yield judgments of the equity or fairness of any reward differential, and by what mechanisms inequity or unfairness will be reduced or eliminated" (VROOM 1969:206).

Finally, one must remember that, apart from the mechanisms in social comparison processes, there are other explanations of the occurrence of or participation in events of political violence (as to those explanations see chapter 5.1.1.1.3.1 and chapter 9): "People may resort to collective violence because they are frustrated, as GURR suggests, but they may also resort to violence because they sympathize with oppressed groups, because they see violence as the optimum strategy to obtain political power, because they enjoy the excitement of violent action, and so on" (DUFF/McCAMANT 1976:21).

Chapter 5

Approaches to the Study
of Political Violence

If there is one remarkable feature of recent research on political violence, it is its largely *cross-national* nature ("cross-national" denoting here *quantitative* cross-national studies). Accordingly, most of this rather lengthy chapter is devoted to these cross-national studies of political violence. Without exception these studies are based on aggregate data. Data on individuals and/or groups participating in acts of political violence are still to be collected on a cross-national basis (but cf. also the approach of the TILLY group in chapter 8.4.6.6.1). Although there are a number of noteworthy studies at the individual level, studies growing out of dealing with the causes of the American black riots in the 1960s (see chapter 5.3.2 and especially chapter 5.3.2.3), none of these is cross-national in perspective. One may have serious doubts as to whether constructs such as political distrust, political efficacy, internal control, etc. employed in studies on the black riots would also be meaningful explanations in other contexts.

Taking these aspects into consideration, we opted for two main divisions within this chapter. (Section 5.2 focuses on case studies and is rather brief.) In section 5.1 there is a discussion and comparison of three approaches to the cross-national study of political violence, those of GURR, the FEIERABENDs and their coworkers, and HIBBS, followed by an analysis of the relationships between various independent variables and political violence.[1] Due to the nature of some of the approaches discussed, various facets of political violence are taken as dependent variables. In section 5.3, on the other hand, *specific* topics are chosen for explanation, most of the chapter (5.3.2) containing a summary discussion of one of the best studied cases in the field of political violence: the riots of American blacks during the 1960s.

5.1. Cross-national Studies of Political Violence

5.1.1. A Comparison of the Approaches of GURR,
the FEIERABENDs and HIBBS

5.1.1.1. The Study of Civil Strife (GURR)

In our discussion of GURR's works we will be less concerned with his broad theoretical outline (GURR 1970a) than with the theoretical model used in various of his empirical studies. We will discuss GURR's works on a more or less chronological basis. It should be pointed out, however, that some of his later works (e.g., GURR/DUVALL 1973) contain important revisions of the original formulation dealt with here. In the subsequent critical evaluation some arguments highly specific in nature and others applying to many other writers' works as well will be discussed.

5.1.1.1.1. The Theoretical and Operational Model

Two theoretical approaches are basic for GURR's system: the frustration-aggression nexus as worked out by BERKOWITZ and the theory of relative deprivation ("the basic precondition for civil strife of any kind," GURR 1968a:1104).

> Relative deprivation is defined as actors' perceptions of discrepancy between their value expectations (the goods and conditions of the life to which they believe they are justifiably entitled) and their value capabilities (the amounts of those goods and conditions that they think they are able to get and keep). The underlying causal mechanism is derived from psychological theory and evidence to the effect that one innate [*sic*] response to perceived deprivation is discontent or anger, and that anger is a motivating state for which aggression is an inherently satisfying response (ibid.).

It is not the discrepancy between an ideal position and reality which is important for feelings of relative deprivation to occur, but rather the discrepancy between a position that one perceives as *possible* to achieve *and* to which one is *legitimately*[2] entitled, but still does not get. The stronger these positions are in the planning of individuals, the more they feel relatively deprived if they do not succeed in achieving their goals and can put the *blame on others* (or other instances; cf. also chapter 5.3.2.3).

Values are defined by GURR as "the desired events, objects, and conditions for which men strive" (GURR 1970a:25), whereas the *"value capabilities* of a collectivity are the average value positions its members perceive themselves capable of attaining or maintaining. Value capabilities also have both present and future connotations. In the present, value capabilities are represented by what men have actually been able to attain or have been provided by their environment: their *value position*. In the future, value capabilities are what men believe their skills, their fellows, and their rulers will, in the course of time, permit them to keep or attain: their *value potential"* (GURR 1970a:27).

GURR's theoretical scheme can best be summarized thus far by quoting a longer passage:

> The intensity of our anger at its onset is a function of four psycho-cultural variables. The greater the discrepancy we see between our expectations and capabilities, the greater is our discontent. The greater the importance we attach to the values affected, and the fewer the other satisfactions we have to fall back on, the greater is our discontent. If we have many alternative ways of trying to satisfy our expectations, we are likely to defer discontent over our failures; if we have few alternatives we are likely to feel the anger of despera-tion. A fifth determinant is time: if our anger is denied expression in the short run it intensifies before it subsides. The greater its inten-sity, the longer it persists; many men carry the burden of profound grievances throughout their lives and pass them on to their children (GURR 1970a:59).

GURR (1970a:92–154) presents a long list of the various facets of his com-prehensive relative deprivation variable. Later in this study these variables will be discussed in some detail.

The frustration-aggression nexus and the theory of relative deprivation are both employed in the analysis of protest potentials. The potential for political violence ("politicized discontent") is said to depend also on the following three conditions: "intensity of normative justifications for political violence," "intensity of utilitarian justification for political violence," and "scope of justifications for political violence." The relation between *potential* for political violence and *actual* political violence is *mediated* by a number of variables referring (1) to beliefs and traditions about the justifiability of conflict, and (2) to the balance between coercive and institutional resources of the rebels vs. the state. Depending upon the relationships among these intermediate variables, the protest potential may not be influenced at all or, more likely, be enlarged, reduced, stalemated, or diverted to another object. The balance of these intermediate variables thus determines the various possible outcomes with respect to political violence.

As to the *coercive potential*, a list of five hypotheses may suffice at this point. These hypotheses will be taken up later on.

1. "The magnitude of political violence varies strongly and directly with the ratio of dissident coercive control to regime coercive control to the point of equality, and inversely beyond it" (GURR 1970a:234).

2. "Regime coercive control varies curvilinearly with the severity of regime-administered negative sanctions, control being lowest when severity is at intermediate levels" (ibid., p. 240).

3. "Regime coercive control varies strongly with the loyalty of coercive forces to the regime" (ibid., p. 251).

4. "Regime control varies strongly with the consistency of regime-admin-istered negative sanctions" (ibid., p. 256).

5. "Dissident coercive control varies strongly with the extent to which dissidents are geographically concentrated in areas to which regime forces have limited access" (ibid., p. 265).

GURR's "second intervening variable is *institutionalization*, i.e., the extent to which societal structures beyond the primary level are broad in scope, command substantial resources or personnel, and are stable and persisting" (GURR 1968a:1105).[3] A third intervening variable is *facilitation*, i.e., "social and environmental conditions . . . that facilitate the outbreak and persistence of strife" (ibid., p. 1106). "Two aspects of facilitation are treated separately in this study: *past levels of civil strife* and *social and structural facilitation per se*" (ibid.). The final intervening variable, *legitimacy*, refers to the "degree of popular support for a regime" (ibid.). GURR's operational model is summarized in Figure 5.1.

GURR's theoretical justifications for selecting indicators cannot be discussed here in detail. Some critical remarks will be made later on, however. The dependent variable *civil strife* ("all collective, nongovernmental attacks on persons or property that occur within the boundaries of an autonomous or colonial political unit," GURR 1968a:1107) is divided into three aspects:

(1) *Turmoil*: relatively spontaneous, unstructured mass strife, including demonstrations, political strikes, riots, political clashes, and localized rebellions.

(2) *Conspiracy*: intensively organized, relatively small-scale civil strife, including political assassinations, small-scale terrorism, small-scale guerrilla wars, coups, mutinies, and plots and purges, the last two on grounds that they are evidence of planned strife.

(3) *Internal war*: large-scale, organized, focused civil strife, almost always accompanied by extensive violence, including large-scale terrorism and guerrilla wars, civil wars, private wars, and large-scale revolts (ibid.).[4]

(In later studies other operational definitions of the dependent variables are used, most often the distinction between protest and rebellion, the latter comprising conspiracy and internal war. This distinction also has dominated GURR's more recent work.)

GURR uses the following measures for his three dependent variables:

(1) *Pervasiveness*: the extent of participation by the affected population, operationally defined for this study as the sum of the estimated number of participants in all acts of strife as a proportion of the total population of each polity expressed in terms of participants per 100,000 population.

(2) *Duration*: the persistence of strife, indexed here by the sum of the spans of time of all strife events in each polity, whatever the relative scale of the events, expressed in days.

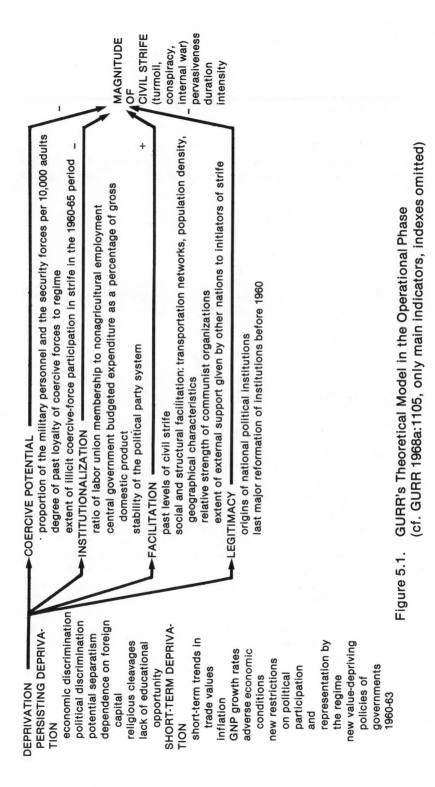

DEPRIVATION ──────────→ COERCIVE POTENTIAL ─────────
PERSISTING DEPRIVA-   · proportion of the military personnel and the security forces per 10,000 adults
TION   degree of past loyalty of coercive forces to regime
  economic discrimination   extent of illicit coercive-force participation in strife in the 1960-65 period   –
  political discrimination
  potential separatism   INSTITUTIONALIZATION
  dependence on foreign   ratio of labor union membership to nonagricultural employment
    capital   central government budgeted expenditure as a percentage of gross
  religious cleavages   domestic product
  lack of educational   stability of the political party system
    opportunity
SHORT-TERM DEPRIVA-   FACILITATION   +
TION   past levels of civil strife
  short-term trends in   social and structural facilitation: transportation networks, population density,
    trade values   geographical characteristics
  inflation   relative strength of communist organizations
  GNP growth rates   extent of external support given by other nations to initiators of strife
  adverse economic
    conditions   LEGITIMACY
  new restrictions   origins of national political institutions
    on political   last major reformation of institutions before 1960
    participation
    and
    representation by
    the regime
  new value-depriving
    policies of
    governments
    1960-63

MAGNITUDE
OF
CIVIL STRIFE
(turmoil,
conspiracy,
internal war)   –
pervasiveness
duration
intensity

Figure 5.1.   GURR's Theoretical Model in the Operational Phase
              (cf. GURR 1968a:1105, only main indicators, indexes omitted)

(3) *Intensity*: the human cost of strife, indexed here by the total estimated casualties, dead and injured, in all strife events in each polity as a proportion of the total population, expressed as casualties per 10,000,000 population (GURR 1968a :1107-8).[5]

All strife events in 114 polities (i.e., nations or colonies with more than one million inhabitants in 1962) during 1961-65 are counted. (For a discussion of problems arising during the data collection process see chapter 5.1.3).

5.1.1.1.2. Empirical Results

Sine GURR's three dependent variables are taken from factor analytic studies of internal conflicts by RUMMEL (1963) and TANTER (1965), a brief look[6] at some of the results of these studies may be in order.

5.1.1.1.2.1. Excursus: Conflicts within Nations— Some Factor Analytic Results

In Table 5.1 results of several factor analyses of conflicts within nations are listed.

In general, the factor dimensions seem to be relatively stable over *time*. "The results tend to support RUMMEL in the sense that three-factor solutions delineating 'turmoil,' 'revolutionary,' and 'subversive' dimensions are possible at varying points of time after World War I, but the precise structure of the latter two dimensions tends to vary through time, while TANTER's two-fold distinction between 'turmoil' and 'internal warfare' dimensions remains relatively invariate throughout the contemporary era" (BANKS 1972:50). Variability mainly consists in whether internal conflicts can be reduced to either two or three dimensions and not so much in which variables load on the internal war factor or on the other two factors (revolutionary and subversive). RUMMEL, the pioneer of this kind of factor analytic studies, comments on the available studies up to 1965 as follows: "The comparison of the conflict subspaces of the various studies indicates that *turmoil* is certainly a distinct and separate dimension of domestic conflict behavior. *Revolution* and *subversion* also appear as distinct dimensions, but not generally separate" (RUMMEL 1965:195). From his point of view the major difference between the first conflict dimension and the other two dimensions consists in the degree of organization that is characteristic of the particular forms of conflict. Whereas the *turmoil* dimension is described as "disorganized, spontaneous conflict behavior," the *revolutionary* dimension is said to represent "overt organized conflict behavior" and the *subversion* dimension "covert, organized conflict behavior" (RUMMEL 1963:12-13).

The differentiation between various forms of violent conflicts according to their degree of spontaneity and/or organization will be important later on, both in theoretical and empirical terms. It should be pointed out, however, that RUMMEL's terminology (and that of other authors like BWY 1968b; see the criticism in WEST 1973:73ff.) is to be criticized on several grounds: "It seems a distortion of the language of political theory to label a dimension measuring elite imprisonments and executions (purges) and mutinies, coups, and plots as revolution, and to label a dimension measuring civil war and organized guerrilla warfare as subversion. RUMMEL's revolution dimension seems more appropriately defined as an elite instability factor, and his sub-version dimension is a measure of communal and mass instability" (MORRISON/STEVENSON 1971:358; cf. also RUMMEL 1976:368). As holds true of other works (cf. chapter 5.1.1.2.4), the gap between the concepts used and the measures employed is much too wide.[7]

Besides variations over time in the dimensions of conflicts within nations, there may be *regional* variations as well. Actually, at least for African states (sample: 33 independent nations, period: 1963-65), strikingly different results emerge from a factor analysis: "Seventy-one percent of the total variation was accounted for by three factors in RUMMEL's analysis, whereas five factors in the African data were required to account for 69.4 percent of the total variance. The 64.4 percent of the total variance accounted for by TANTER's two-factor solution of the domestic data required four factors in the African data" (COLLINS 1973:264). In their study of internal conflicts in thirty-two black African nations (period: 1960-69) MORRISON/STEVENSON also come up with results that differ from those of RUMMEL and TANTER: "elite and communal instability are well defined independent dimensions of political instability in these nations, although mass instability is not. This last observation, however, is not surprising given the few isolated instances of revolt, and the absence of revolution . . . in the post-independence history of black African nations" (MORRISON/STEVENSON 1971: 367). If different methods of factor extraction are used (HAZLEWOOD 1973a), there seems to be some *technical stability* in these factor analytic results (except for the period 1962-64). Finally, controls of the *political systems* of the countries as well as of their level of *economic development* have been introduced into the analysis, leaving the factorial structure basically unchanged only in polyarchic systems and in four out of six groupings according to the level of economic development (HAZLEWOOD 1973a).

At first GURR did not carry out a factor analysis on his own, but took over the tripartition of the dependent variable from RUMMEL (1963). In a new study, however, GURR/BISHOP (1976) perform a factor analysis on thirty-one conflict variables, measuring internal as well as external conflicts in eighty-six nations during the 1950s and 1960s, and find support for the two dominant dimensions of internal conflicts: protest and internal war explaining 11.7% and 8.8% of the variance (64.8%)[8] JACKMAN/BOYD (1979) also generally confirm the two-factor solution.

Table 5.1. Summary of Some Factor Analytic Results of Conflicts Within Nations

Author	No. of Countries	Period	Conflict Variables	Factors	Proportion of Total Variance	
(1) Rummel (1963)	77	1955–57	assassinations; general strikes; guerrilla war; major government crises; purges; riots; revolutions; antigovernment demonstrations; domestic killed	I. turmoil II. revolutionary III. subversive	27.7 26.7 16.6	71.0
(2) Rummel (1966)	113	1946–59	internal warfare; turmoil; rioting; large-scale terrorism; small-scale terrorism; mutinies; coups; plots; administrative actions; quasi-private violence; total number of unequivocal acts of violence; same + equivocal acts of violence; extended violence	I. revolutionary II. subversive III. turmoil	26.8 13.7 23.8	64.3
(3) Tanter (1966)	83	1958–60	as (1)	I. turmoil II. internal war	32.7 31.7	64.4
(4) Tanter (1965)	75	1955–60	as (1)	I. turmoil II. internal war	35.4 32.0	67.4
(5) Bwy (1968b)	20	1958–60	as (1)	I. organized violence II. anomic violence	36.6 22.4	59.0

Study	N	Period	Variables	Factors	%	Total	%	Total
(6) Hoole (1964)[a]	68	1948–62	assassinations; strike; guerilla war; major government crises; purges; riots; revolutions, demonstrations	I. internal war	35.3			
				II. turmoil	25.3	60.6		
(7) Feierabend, Feierabend and Litell (1966)	84	1948–62	30 variables; among them: general strikes; macro demonstrations; macro riots; imprisonment of significant persons; terrorism and sabotage; civil war; coup d'état; revolts	9 factors, including				
				I. turmoil	23.3			
				II. revolt	11.1			
				III. purge	7.5	41.9		
(8) Banks (1972)	51	1922–36 and 1949–63	as (1)	I. turmoil	54.2	and	10.4	
				II. revolutionary	14.5		14.0	
				III. subversive	8.3	77.0	48.2	72.6
		1922–63	as well as 2-factor solution	I. turmoil	50.3			
				II. internal war	13.7	64.0		
(9) Hibbs (1973)	108	1948–57	riots; antigovernment demonstrations; political strikes; assassinations; armed attacks; deaths	I. collective protest	41.9			
				II. internal war	41.5	83.4		
		1958–67	same	I. collective protest	49.3			
				II. internal war	34.5	83.8[b]		

[a] According to the reanalysis of Tanter (1965). [b] Principal component analysis. Using principal factor method leads to the following results: 1st period: collective protest 38.4% and internal war 35.2% = 73.6% of the total variance; 2nd period: collective protest 38.1% and internal war 31.0% = 69.1% of the total variance.

Source: Zimmermann (1976:268–69)

5.1.1.1.2.2. Determinants of the Magnitude of Civil Strife

After performing various multiple regressions and other analyses, GURR finally presents the following causal model:

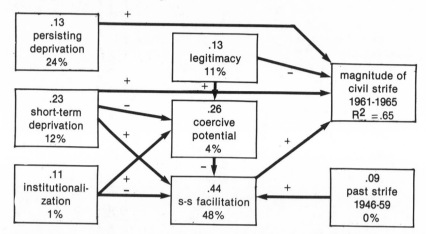

Figure 5.2.   GURR's Causal Model of the Magnitude of Civil Strife

Source: GURR (1968a:1121).

In each cell the values at the top are simple r's. The percentage values give the amount of the total explained variance that is explained by the particular variable when all other independent variables are controlled.

Whereas in a bivariate analysis all independent variables (with the exception of coercive force size—see below) correlate with the dependent variables in the predicted direction, in the multivariate case several important changes occur:

> None of the mediating variables appear to affect the relationship
> between *persisting deprivation* and strife, i.e., there is a certain
> inevitability about the association between such deprivation and
> strife. Persisting deprivation is moreover equally potent as a source
> of conspiracy, internal war, and turmoil. With the partial and weak
> exception of institutionalization, no patterns of societal arrange-
> ments nor coercive potential that are included in the model have any
> consistent effect on its impact (GURR 1968a:1120).

Some of the final results are summarized in the following longer quotation:

> The most proximate and potent variable is social and structural facil-
> itation, which accounts for nearly half the explained variance. The
> deprivation variables account directly for over one-third the magni-
> tude of strife; legitimacy and institutionalization for one-eighth. But

these proportions refer only to direct effects, and in the case of both coercive potential and facilitation part of that direct effect, i.e., the illicit participation of the military in strife and the provision of foreign support for initiators, can be determined only from the characteristics of strife itself. The more remote causes of strife, namely deprivation, institutionalization, legitimacy, and prior strife, are the more fundamental and persisting ones. Some additional regression analyses provide some comparisons. Four of the independent variables relate to inferred states of mind: the two short-term deprivation measures, persisting deprivation, and legitimacy. The R based on these variables is .65, compared with .81 when the remaining four variables are added. The R based on the three deprivation variables alone is .60. These analyses show that all 'states of mind' conditions contribute significantly[9] to magnitude of strife, but that long-term deprivation has a partial controlling effect on political deprivation. The inference is that short-term political deprivation, as indexed in this study, is most likely to lead to strife if it summates with conditions of persisting deprivation (GURR 1968a: 1121-22).

This statement is based on causal analyses using the so-called SIMON-BLALOCK technique and not on path analysis as the more potent technique for specifying relationships between independent variables. The causal ordering among some of the independent variables might be called into question, e.g., between short-term deprivation and coercive potential (cf. also the following chapter). Civil strife in general can be much better explained (R^2=.650) than its three components (conspiracy R^2=.397; internal war R^2=.420; turmoil R^2=.284) as it seems much less affected by skewed distributions.

5.1.1.1.2.3. Determinants of Turmoil

In another paper GURR (1968b) analyzes the causes of turmoil, one of the components of civil strife, again using the SIMON-BLALOCK technique rather than path analysis. Once more, persisting deprivation and legitimacy are direct determinants of the dependent variable (strife in the past is the third one) whereas the explanatory power of social and structural facilitation, the main determinant of civil strife in general, is almost negligible.[10] Little more than a quarter of the variance in turmoil is explained by the causal model GURR proposes:[11] "The most likely substantive interpretation of the relatively low predictability of turmoil ... is that much turmoil is a response to a variety of locally-incident deprivations and social conditions of a sort not represented in the indices used in this study" (GURR 1968a:1117).

Furthermore, turmoil may often be used as a means of introducing certain demands into the political process and thus be understood not only as a dependent variable but also as an independent variable. By using violent protest, dissidents may want to improve their bargaining position (and not just react to adverse social conditions). There may be tactical elements in the use of turmoil, as in other forms of political violence, not covered with the techniques used thus far. "Discussions of frustration and aggression, even if preceded by a consideration of social conditions conducive to these, tell us little about the sturggle for power and interaction among competing social groups which is so crucial to the occurrence, magnitude, and consequences of political violence" (MARX 1972:129).

Starting from GURR's work COOPER (1974) proposes a new model for explaining turmoil. Though he can explain larger portions of the variance than GURR, his study seems to be inconclusive for several reasons. He proposes a grouping of nations, as GURR himself has done (see chapter 5.1.1.1.2.6), according to their degree of modernity (using the FEIERA-BEND indicators, see chapter 5.1.1.2.2) as well as along geocultural lines (Western, Latin American, Middle Eastern, Asian, African, using the BANKS/TEXTOR 1963 classification). In general this homogenization of the objects under study increases the statistical explanation achieved.

The amount of unexplained variance is further reduced when two additional variables are introduced: interest articulation (using the measures of BANKS/TEXTOR 1963) and representation of interest articulation (using the same source for measures of the degree of polyarchy of the political system). Neither COOPER's theoretical rationale[12] nor his highly inferential measures are convincing. If turmoil is viewed as "situationally determined, unstructured, mass behavior" (COOPER 1974:268), then COOPER's very indirect indicators of organizational aspects of certain demands obviously do not make much sense in explaining the dependent variable, notwithstanding a high degree of statistical (but not substantial) explanation. Less tentative than some of his other results is COOPER's summary statement (cf. the following two chapters): "In general, we find that short-term deprivations become less and less a cause of turmoil as societies become more economically advanced and established. At the same time, we find that the means by which deprivations are mediated are more important in the societies that are economically less developed" (COOPER 1974:286).

5.1.1.1.2.4. Determinants of Protest and Rebellion in Western Nations

The sample is now limited to twenty-one Western societies, whereas the period remains the same (1961-65). The dependent variables differ somewhat from those in the former studies: "Magnitude of strife is indexed here using man-days of strife per 100,000 population, which combines duration and pervasiveness, and deaths from strife per 100 million population, which excludes injuries—reports of which are usually less precise and often missing. The distinctions made are between *violent* and *nonviolent* strife,[13] and between *turmoil* and *rebellion*" (GURR 1970b:131).[14] As in GURR's first study (1968a), only weak relationships between the dependent variables are found, thus refuting the idea that milder forms of protest may function as an alternative to more violent conflicts; instead of negative correlations, there are slight positive correlations between these various forms of protest.

The number of independent variables is reduced to three in this study, though many of the original indicators are retained. Thus, even more complex indexes (than in GURR 1968a) are formed here. If the three independent variables are used in a multiple regression analysis, the following results emerge: *relative deprivation* (measured as in GURR 1968a) is the variable with the *lowest* explanatory power. Only in the case of rebellion is it the most important determinant (partial r=.53). It is also of some importance as a cause of nonviolent strife, though third after the other two variables. There is other evidence in GURR's paper that short-term economic deprivation is unrelated to strife, but this is not true for *persisting* deprivation or *political* deprivation.[15] The second independent variable, *justifications*, differs slightly here from that of facilitation in previous analyses, being indexed through "governmental legitimacy; the relative extent of past strife, 1946-1959 . . .; and the historical success of strife" (GURR 1970b: 135). It is the most important determinant, except in the case of the dependent variable rebellion where its explanatory power is slight. Almost equally important (and even more significant in the case of rebellion) is the third determinant: *balance* (coercive and institutional balances being commanded by the regime or the dissidents, here comprising twenty-one different indicators). The greater the coercive potential of the regime, the less the amount of rebellion (r=-.47). On the other hand, the greater the coercive resources of the dissidents, the greater the probability of the various forms of violent strife. There are strong bivariate relationships between institutional support of dissidents and milder forms of protest (r=.70), but not in the case of rebellion (r=0.39). Thus, institutionalized channels for participation in the political process are not a means of inhibiting protest but may in fact act as a catalyst for milder forms of protest (see also chapter 5.1.1.1.2.5).[16]

The three independent variables explain over two-thirds of the variance of the dependent variables. Interestingly, GURR's fundamental causal variable, relative deprivation, does not do well in explaining turmoil in Western societies (but cf. also chapter 5.3.2.3). As a possible explanation GURR points to some deficiencies in research: "In real-world terms this does not mean that deprivation is unimportant as a cause of these forms of strife, but that the magnitude of its effect depends on how it is channeled by peoples' attitudes and social situations" (GURR 1970b:142). Turmoil in this sample of GURR's universe of 114 countries is much better explained than in the earlier study (GURR 1968b). Moreover, the structure of a causal model for explaining turmoil in Western societies would be different than the one proposed for 114 countries (GURR 1968b; see chapter 5.1.1.1.2.3; COOPER 1974).

5.1.1.1.2.5. Determinants of Civil Strife in Democracies

The sample comprises thirty-eight democracies. The dependent variables are similar to those in the previous study and show somewhat higher inter-correlations than have been found thus far. *Relative deprivation, justifications*, and *balance* are once again employed as independent variables, but this time GURR does not make use of his highly complex indices. Rather he uses some of the components of these main variables for predicting the scores on the dependent variables. The variance explained lies in general around 60%. The amount of *non-violent strife* is mainly determined by illegitimacy of the regime and institutional support of the dissidents, while historical justifications and regime institutional support lose their explanatory power in a multivariate analysis. A similar result is found in the case of *turmoil*. In addition, persisting deprivation and coercive potential of the dissidents lose their predictive power. Thus, channels of institutionalization for voicing discontent seem to have an impact on the amount of milder forms of protest that occurs in a political system. If *total strife* is to be explained, illegitimacy of the regime and institutional support for the dissidents are again the strongest predictors, followed by a group of variables including short-term deprivation, long-term deprivation, historical justifications, and institutional resources of the regime. Their influence is more than halved in the multivariate case. *Violent strife* is mainly determined by five equally strong predictors: the deprivation variables, illegitimacy, historical justifica-tions, and dissident institutional support. Finally, *rebellion* is determined by two of the last mentioned predictors: short-term deprivation and historical justification. The third independent variable of major importance is regime coercive control: the greater the coercive resources of the regime, the less likely are rebellions as forms of protest behavior. Long-term deprivation and illegitimacy lose their predictive power after the other independent variables have been taken into account.

Comparing the results of this study with those of the foregoing study, mediating variables, like justifications and balance, while occasionally show-ing irregularities, are more important determinants (besides illegitimacy, an aspect of justifications) of the forms of protest behavior than are the depriva-tion variables. In short, there does *not* seem to be a direct covariation be-tween deprivation (as indirectly measured) and protest behavior. If protest behavior is to be explained, at least in these two samples, it cannot be directly accounted for by referring to a protest potential presumably caused by deprivation and now finding its outlet. Rather it is the *structural transforma-tions* of protest potentials (cf. the emphasis on organizational aspects at various points in this study such as in chapter 8) which are of major impor-tance if certain forms of protest *behavior* are to occur. The statement—the greater the amount of discontent, the greater the likelihood of violent pro-tests—does not hold for *milder* forms of political violence, since turmoil (or nonviolent protest) often occurs in the absence of severe deprivation. Thus, one cannot infer the magnitude of protest potentials from the degree of deprivation nor, conversely, trace protest potentials or protest behavior back to deprivations.

"The greater the justifications for strife, the greater the magnitude of strife. This hypothesis is also supported, on the basis of indicators of governmental legitimacy and cultural traditions of violence. Legitimacy tends to inhibit the less violent forms of strife but not the more violent ones. Violent traditions cause an intensification of strife's more violent forms" (GURR 1972a:194; italics omitted). The greater the dissidents' control of coercive resources, the greater the likelihood of more violent protests. The coercive potential of the regime, however, seems to be more effective in preventing the more intense (but not the milder) forms of violent protests. Once again, institutional resources of potential dissidents do not lead to a reduction of the protest potential, but seem to be used rather as a means of voicing protest (cf. also COOPER 1974:287). Thus, if potential dissidents have access to institutional channels for expressing their protests, a better *overall* integration of the political system may result (this is not meant as a simple functionalistic statement). However, if these channels are nonexistent or blocked, in the long run the whole political system may be at stake, since the protest potential may accumulate over time. If one were to use HIRSCHMAN's terminology (1970; see also chapter 8.4.3.2), *exit* rather than *voice* may be the result.

Considering the impact of the variables, regime coercive control and regime institutional support (the latter showing weak positive relationships with the dependent variables in four out of five cases), a similar conclusion emerges: democratic societies obviously are strong enough to prevent intense and more violent forms of civil strife but show a tendency for weaker forms of protest behavior to occur *in spite of* their command of considerable coercive resources. If a regime is judged legitimate, its citizens do have clear expectations as to the regime's output. If it appears inadequate, milder forms of protest behavior may result paradoxically because of the higher overall legitimacy of these regimes (for more detailed arguments cf. chapter 6.3.4.1)[17] compared to more coercive regimes which seem able to prevent most kinds of protest but are more susceptible to rebellion (cf. also the findings for the entire 1960s in GURR/DUVALL, forthcoming).

Two warnings, however, should be kept in mind. Firstly, there may be sampling errors; for example, it remains questionable whether Libya could be counted as a democracy. Secondly, some of the interpretations given above are based on indirect measures and have generated highly inferential statements, e.g., the arguments concerning channels open to dissidents and alternative courses of action. The degree of institutional resources available to potential protest groups in a society is assessed on a general level, but we do not have sufficient information whether the assessment will also hold true on the level of *specific* groups of protesters. There may be great institutional resources available to various groups in society but not to the particular protesting groups who may thus feel excluded from the political process. Moreover, objectively there may be resources that could be used as institutional support for certain claims, but these resources may not be perceived as such by the protesters. In short, there are severe measurement problems[18] to be overcome before some of these apparently plausible statements can be tested on a more rigorous basis.

Some of GURR's results may be affected by characteristics of the samples used and/or by his measures of the independent variables as well as by variations in the dependent variables. In general, however, his theoretical model did well enough to explain large portions of the variances. Unfortunately, results of similar multivariate analyses using other samples, such as countries at a medium level of development, and perhaps other operationalizations have not been reported.

5.1.1.1.2.6. Forms and Determinants of Civil Strife: A Comparison of Nation Clusters

Grouping nations according to geocultural and other criteria[19] provides control of at least some of the variance in the data. There are, of course, many more variables which should be controlled in detailed multivariate analyses, provided that the number of cases does not become too small. Thus, even if some of the results selected for discussion in this chapter lead to interesting speculations, it should be remembered that the groupings of nations lack sufficiently strict controls and that further test variables are not included in these analyses. By grouping nations, one gets some information as to whether the proposed causal explanations are universally true or whether they hold only in specific contexts. GURR (1969a) once again starts from his universe of 114 nations.[20] They are grouped according to (1) the level of *economic development* (high, medium, low);[21] (2) the type of *political system* (using the Q-factor analytic results of BANKS/GREGG, 1965,[22] who propose the following classification: *polyarchic*, Western democracies and nations which "approximate Western democratic political structures and processes; *centrist*, Communist and other non-Latin American authoritarian regimes; *elitist*, recently independent, predominantly African states with relatively small, modernizing elites; *personalist*, predominantly Latin regimes characterized by unstable personalistic political leadership" [GURR 1969a:631] ; and *traditional* states, which are reclassified by GURR), and (3) the *geocultural region* (*Latin*, Latin American countries including Puerto Rico, Spain, and Portugal; *Islamic; African*, including non-Islamic states and colonies; *Asian; European*, with the subdivisions to Anglo-Nordic, Western European, and Eastern European).

Results are as follows: "Short-term deprivation is more important as a cause of turmoil [but cf. COOPER 1974 and preceding chapters for somewhat diverging results] than of conspiracy in the most developed nations, whereas it is more important as a cause of conspiracy in the less-developed nations. This difference also is apparent among the geocultural regions: short-term deprivation leads to conspiracy in the least-developed, Asian and

African nations; and to turmoil in the more-developed, European and Latin nations" (GURR 1969a:603).

The correlations between legitimacy and the dependent variables in general show the expected negative signs. There are, however, some interesting differences worth noting. Legitimacy seems to have a strong inhibiting effect on turmoil and conspiracy in moderately developed nations. In polyarchies there is a stronger influence on turmoil (r=-.46) and in personalist regimes on conspiracy as well (-.43; on turmoil: -.66). In Anglo-Nordic countries there is a strong negative relation with conspiracy (-.72), whereas an equally strong positive relationship emerges in Eastern European nations.

Traditions of civil strife (1946-59) mostly show a positive relation to political violence at a later point, a result which may (partly) be caused by autocorrelated residuals or by stable implicit variables, such as certain unmeasured political system variables (cf. the discussion in HEISE 1970:21ff.; HIBBS 1974, and WEEDE 1977c:40ff.). In the case of Eastern European nations, there is, however, a negative correlation between strife in the past and conspiracy (-.49) at some later date. One may speculate as to whether the causal link can be found in a strengthening of the coercive and internal security forces following past strife, thus inhibiting conspiracy later on. Of course, given the present data, this hypothesis cannot be tested. For African and Latin American countries there are moderately strong correlations; for Western European, polyarchic, and/or highly developed nations, however, stronger relations between past strife and present disorders emerge. Obviously, even in some of the economically more developed countries there is a culture of violence, stemming from long-term historical conflicts that often developed along religious, social, linguistic, and/or ethnic differences (see also chapter 5.1.2.4 and 5.1.2.8). Northern Ireland may serve as an example here (cf. JENKINS/MACRAE 1968; ELLIOT/HICKIE 1971; ROSE 1971 with survey data; ROSE 1976; BIRRELL 1972; BUDGE/O'LEARY 1973 with a comparison between Belfast and Glasgow;[23] BELL 1974, 1976; SCHMITT 1974; LIJPHART 1975; HULL 1976). Between 1969 and 1977, 1800 people have been killed in acts of political violence in Northern Ireland, including 275 British soldiers and 1,337 civilians (CLUTTERBUCK 1978).

While the relation between coercive force size and civil strife is inconclusive, the predicted negative influence can be determined if coercive force size is weighted by loyalty and then related to the dependent variable. Strength of institutions has the strongest impact on strife in Anglo-Nordic countries (-.75) as might be expected. However, the relation holds as well in African countries (-.45), in polyarchic nations (-.36), in elitist political systems (-.35), and in the total (-.32). Finally, the correlations between facilitation and civil strife are generally positive and reach modest to high coefficients, as could be expected.

Using the independent variables from GURR (1968a), more than half of the variance of the dependent variables in the different groups can be explained; more than two-thirds can be explained when total strife is the dependent variable. More interesting than these over-all results, however, would be the development of causal models accounting for the interrelationships between the independent variables. There are many plausible bivariate results within the particular nation groupings, yet without a multivariate analysis we do not know which of these are "spurious correlations"[24] or spurious noncorrelations.

COOPER (1974; cf. chapter 5.1.1.1.2.3) has gone one step further in performing a multivariate analysis of the conditions of turmoil after forming clusters of nations. In general, the amount of variance explained is somewhat greater than in GURR's analysis. This may be due in part to the different groupings of nations. Though there are some "deviating" results within each group of nations, several generalizations are worth noting: (1) legitimacy is consistently and strongly related (negative sign) to the dependent variable. (2) There is considerable evidence for GURR's culture-of-violence hypothesis (which may, however, be attributed to autocorrelated residuals or to stable implicit variables) in almost all of the clusters, with the exception of Latin American countries which show a strong reversal of the sign (negative impact of past strife). (3) Persisting deprivation and political deprivation in particular are positively related to turmoil, as predicted; however, Middle Eastern countries (persisting deprivation) and African countries (political deprivation) are deviating cases. (4) Surprisingly, coercive potential (size of coercive forces, weighted by loyalty) has a negative impact on turmoil only in the case of African nations, whereas in Latin American countries there is a partial $r=.41$. Perhaps loyalty of coercive forces in Latin America is no guarantee of low levels or the absence of turmoil. In general, the coercive potential does not seem to be among the more decisive factors in the explanation of turmoil, a less intensive form of political violence. (5) Facilitation behaves as predicted (positive sign). Turmoil in African and Asian countries, however, elicits different explanations. COOPER proposes a threshold explanation, namely that facilitative conditions are an asset to the dissidents only after a minimum level of organization has been achieved. "Moreover, these nations have extremely high inaccessibility scores. Inaccessibility, which may be almost a prerequisite for internal warfare, may have little effect on turmoil. In fact, turmoil usually requires concentrations of population and intensive communication" (COOPER 1974:284). (6) Finally, in Western countries institutionalization seems to lose its negative impact on turmoil. Thus, contrary to expectations that greater institutional means for dissidents would lower the amount of turmoil, in more advanced countries institutional means for voicing protest may serve as an amplifier of discontent.

Most of the above conclusions are tentative. Especially in the last case, one needs data on the institutional resources which dissidents *themselves* command rather than on the degree of openness of the whole system. All in all, these results seem to provide additional evidence for GURR's basic theory while concomitantly eliciting different explanations for specific clusters of nations. It should also be pointed out that some of these multivariate results (once again there is no causal model of the interrelationships among independent variables) may be seriously distorted through the two variables COOPER adds to the analysis (see the critique in chapter 5.1.1.1.2.3).

To return to GURR's study, some of the more descriptive results are also worth noting. If one compares the magnitude of strife in the United States (1963-68) with that in seventeen European democracies and in the total grouping, in the United States there are almost twice as many people participating in strife as in European countries or in the total (1,116 vs. approximately 680 per 100,000 inhabitants) and four times as many casualties (477 vs. 121 per 10,000,000 inhabitants) than in the European group of nations. The last two figures, however, are far below the score in the total (20,100 per 10,000,000).[25] Considering the score of total strife, the United States ranks at the top of comparable countries, followed by France and Belgium. When deaths are taken as the indicator of conflict intensity, the United States ranks first among eighteen Western democracies during the period 1961-70. When man-days of protest and man-days of rebellion are used as measures of the extent of civil conflict during the same period, the United States ranks fourth behind countries like France and Italy. "An estimated 350 people died and more than 12,000 were reported injured" during the 1960s in the United States (GURR 1979:53). Studying fewer countries over a longer period (1948-65),[26] FEIERABEND/FEIERABEND/ NESVOLD reach the conclusion that "the United States falls generally at the median position of world violence: half of the nations exceed our violence level: half do not attain it" (FEIERABEND/FEIERABEND/NES-VOLD 1969:673). There are, of course, historical background conditions for this extraordinary position[27] of the United States. Most commonly mentioned are the violent frontier tradition, explosive labor disputes, the Civil War, the use of violence in racial conflicts, and the easy access to weapons[28] (cf. GRAHAM/GURR 1969:793ff.; WALLACE 1970-71; and BROWN 1975; see ROSENBAUM/SEDERBERG 1976 as to the tradition of vigilantism, sometimes also called establishment violence).[29]

The following results have been confirmed in other studies as well (see chapter 5.1.2.1 ff.): turmoil is greatest in (in decreasing order) countries with medium economic development, personalist political systems, Africa, multiracial societies, Latin America. The United States, however, is far ahead of all these countries (at least for GURR's periods of observation 1961-65 vs. 1963-68 for the United States). One of the reasons may have been simply better reporting of events (cf. chapter 5.1.3). Conspiracy is greatest in personalist regimes as well as in Africa and in Latin countries. Internal war reaches its peak in elitist political systems, in Asia and Africa, in multiracial societies, and in countries with intermediate development. Strife in general is greatest in elitist political systems, followed by moderately developed countries, personalist systems, African and Asian polities, and multiracial countries.

A comparison of nation blocks leads to the general conclusion that countries on a medium level of development, elitist and personalist political systems, Asian and African nations, and multiracial societies are all to varying degrees susceptible to various forms of strife.[30] For industrial democracies a probability of minor forms of strife exists, but the probability that more intense forms of political violence will occur is much less (cf. the summary discussion of theories and empirical evidence on protest and turmoil in ZIMMERMANN 1980). In general, this is also the finding of the factor analysis of GURR/BISHOP (1976). If one standardizes (z-scores) two to four variables each (which load high on one of the eight factors which the authors report in their study) and calculates the means of these z-scores, a scale of nations according to their summary violence scores may be derived. Such a listing of nations is, however, of dubious value since the periods of observation are not the same. (The best example is the variable external wars covering the period from 1816 to 1965 in contrast with conflicts in the 1950s and 1960s; data on wars taken from SINGER/SMALL 1972.) Furthermore, phenomena of political violence are included with phenomena of structural violence (cf. the criticism of this concept in chapter 2.2) in order to develop a "summary violence score." GURR/BISHOP (1976) themselves are astonished that the Soviet Union and the United States have adjoining positions (twenty-third and twenty-fourth), whereas their individual profiles differ considerably. Without anticipating the criticism in chapter 5.1.1.1.3, we must point out that GURR and coworker reduce their data sets to a degree hardly justifiable on a theoretical or conceptual basis leading, in the end, to artifacts.

5.1.1.1.2.7. Actors, Objectives, and Human Costs of Political Violence

Due to lack of space, only very few of GURR's interesting results can be mentioned here. *Regime classes* (military, police, civil servants, political elite) participate in 70% of all conspiracy events in the total, but only in 23% of the cases in European countries (including English-speaking countries outside of Europe). If there are conspiracies in European countries, the participation of *workers* is much greater than in the total (62% vs. 25% in all events). Furthermore, participation of working class groups is greatest in case of internal war (100%), less in turmoil events (73%), and 25% in acts of conspiracy. On the other hand, *elites* participate in 70% of all conspiracies and 7% of the turmoil events. After working class groups, the *middle classes* are among the most frequent participants in internal wars. (One should not be too surprised at these results considering the way the dependent variables have been defined.)

Considering the *initiators* of strife, GURR distinguishes between communal groups ("members of territorial, religious, ethnic, or linguistic groups, whether or not formally organized," GURR 1969a:585), economic groups, political groups, governmental groups and clandestine groups. In reality some of these categories overlap. Moreover, political violence may be a reaction to preceding actions by other groups or by the government. Thus, the classification of strife events according to the initiators may be distorted by a systematic error of reporting directly in the original sources (see chapter 5.1.3). Nevertheless, some of these results deserve attention.

In most of the nation blocks (42%), strife is initiated by *political* groups, especially in the Latin (55%) and polyarchic (50%) countries. *Communal* groups are the initiators of strife in 20% of the cases, 34% in Europe and 32% in Africa. In European countries communal groups generally use political violence to protest against sociostructural deprivations, whereas in African nations resistance against national unification seems to be a much stronger instigation. *Governmental* groups turn to violence in conflict in 10% of the cases, a proportion higher in personalist systems (18%), in less developed nations (16%), and in Latin and elitist countries (13% each). European countries have the lowest score (1%). Finally, *clandestine* groups seem to be involved to a similar proportion in events of political violence (in general 15%).[31]

In addition to the question of who initiates strife, the *intentions* of these initiators must be considered. GURR here distinguishes between political objectives (e.g., retaliation, seizure of political power), economic objectives, and social objectives (e.g., to promote or oppose belief systems, to increase social goods). Once again, the categories overlap. Political goals dominate[32] in the vast majority of strife events (90%+), followed by social objectives, accounting for less than half as many events (for 71% of the turmoil cases and for 59% of the conspiracies in Europe). Of course, more limited political aims are pursued in instances of turmoil than in conspiracies. Seizure of political power is an objective more often found in African and Latin countries, as well as in less developed and in personalist countries (22% each). Strife for oppositional reasons is more often found in highly developed countries (56%), Latin (55%) and European countries (49%), and in polyarchic countries (49%) as opposed to 26% in the total. The predominance of political objectives comes as no surprise as the state takes over more and more functions, as popular expectations are more and more projected into the political arena, and, finally, as the state is often the sole agent to blame for the discontent experienced, at least from the point of view of the protesters.

The *human costs* of strife are generally lower in highly developed nations than elsewhere. The number of people dead in strife events varies from 1.7 per 1,000,000 inhabitants in economically developed countries, to 1,604 in elitist political systems and 841 in lowly developed countries. The average number of dead per turmoil or conspiracy event is about equal (approximately 18), whereas the number of dead per internal war is almost 14,000 (35,000 in Asian countries compared to 160 in highly developed nations). "An estimated 750,000 people lost their lives in civil violence between 1961 and 1965, the great majority of them victims of internal wars" (GURR 1969a:594).

The figures mentioned in this section are only approximations. Guess work is apparently unavoidable when coding so much information from such a large sample. The aim here was not to provide necessarily representative figures, but rather to show the variety of findings which might be gathered in this type of research. Replication studies (in which different methods are employed and/or different samples or periods are studied) are needed to find out whether these figures are typical or not. With the exception of the data sets collected by TILLY and his coworkers (see chapter 8.4.6.6.1), these are the first data of this kind in cross-national research on political violence. They go beyond the level of explanation (that of nations) dealt with in the context of chapter 5.1 and have been added mainly to demonstrate the variety of GURR's findings. (Findings comparable in part for the entire 1960s and for N=87 countries may be found in GURR 1979;[33] see also GURR/ DUVALL, forthcoming, and GURR et al., forthcoming.)

5.1.1.1.3. Some Critical Remarks Concerning GURR's Studies of Civil Strife

Throughout the foregoing discussion several critical points have been raised concerning the classification of nations into blocks or GURR's causal modelling. Here we shall list other arguments against GURR's analyses. Several of the following remarks, mainly the methodological ones, apply to other writers' works as well. Having discussed GURR's works in considerable detail, it may be convenient to use these studies as our paradigm when dealing with some of the more general methodological issues in this type of research. The theoretical issues mentioned here also have methodological implications and vice versa. Thus, occasionally we present our arguments in the context which seems to be most suitable for discussion.

5.1.1.1.3.1. Theoretical Issues

One of the basic issues also pertinent to many other studies on political violence is how the various independent variables are related to each other. In the beginning GURR (1968a, 1968b, 1972a) uses a linear-additive model for combining the various independent variables. On the more concrete level of indicators, there are, however, many examples of combining variables differently (e.g., linear-multiplicative combination, using square root figures, etc.). As the assumption of linear-additive relationships between independent variables is the easiest to work with, it was natural to start from this point. In recent works (GURR/DUVALL 1973; GURR et al., forthcoming) linear-multiplicative combinations of independent variables are employed, thus attaining a greater correspondence between theory and empirical model than before (see chapter 5.1.1.1.4). In any case, as research on political violence progresses, researchers should be prepared to test for other than linear-additive combinations of their independent variables.

The fundamental causal variables in GURR's theory, the deprivation variables, are not always of primary importance in explaining various forms of political violence. Rather, there are instances where the mediating variables, whose importance is clearly stressed in GURR's writings, hold the key to whether deprivational states are to end in forms of political violence and if so, in what forms. These results should help refute the claims sometimes raised against GURR's theory of civil strife, namely that the concept of relative deprivation is employed in a circular manner. GURR himself is aware of most of the arguments brought forward against his approach as can be seen in the following statement: "Conceptually, we neglected to include two important sets of variables in the coding: the kinds of events that precipitated violence, and the immediate social and political consequences of strife. We also failed to distinguish between casualties and damage caused by 'initiators' and casualties and damage caused by 'coercive forces.' This later made it impossible to distinguish adequately between the intensity of initiators' actions and the intensity of the regime's response to them, a distinction which is important to the theory" (GURR 1972a:98, italics omitted). One may add that GURR's theory is not as developed along these lines as are other portions of this theory. There is also reason to question the use of national average scores on the particular variables if variation within nations can be so large as to render such a summary score useless: "It seems, for instance, impossible, to find one scale-point of a variable (say legitimacy) that reflects its magnitude for the Sumatra separatist, the Djakarta student and the organizing peasant" (BLOM 1973:11). Obviously, *within*-nations variation (e.g., deprivation scores within segments of the population) should be considered as well as variance between nations.

These two issues lead to one of the fundamental problems of this kind of cross-national research: the issue of indicator equivalence. In GURR's theory a stable party system is said to be an inhibiting condition for political violence. According to experts on particular countries, however, occasionally it seems to work the other way around (see ANDERSON et al. 1967 on Columbia, quoted in BIENEN 1968:89; cf. also the references in chapter 5.2).

When constructing his inaccessibility index for measuring aspects of facilitation, GURR starts from the assumption that inaccessible territory (e.g., "limited transportation networks and large portions of rugged terrain," GURR 1968a:1114; but cf. also GURR et al., forthcoming, p. 85ff. for more discriminatory considerations) may be an advantage for dissidents. In case of urban guerrilla attacks in Latin America, however, the rationale could have been just the reverse. Yet, the alleged territorial advantages as proclaimed by leading theorists or ideologists of urban guerrilla warfare such as MARIGH-ELLA and GUILLÉN (see HODGES 1973) never prevailed (cf. ALLEMANN 1974 for a sensible evaluation; cf. also LAQUEUR 1975 and the references in chapter 8.4.4).

The operationalization of legitimacy provides another example of the lack of equivalence among indicators. Obviously, legitimacy of a political system is a sociopsychological concept (see chapter 6.3.4.1). Thus, data as to how individuals think about their government should be gathered. In measurements of the origins of national political institutions as well as the last major reformation of institutions, as in GURR, countries like Ethiopia, Switzerland, and Sweden have an equal (in fact, the highest) score of legitimacy. The rationale for this (that autochthonous and stable political institutions are more legitimate) may, however, be fulfilled only in the case of nations economically and politically highly developed, but not in the case of a former traditional autocracy like Ethiopia. Interestingly enough, judging from recent developments (cf. OTTAWAY 1976), the legitimacy of the Ethiopian political system seemed to be much lower than one would have expected according to GURR's method. Even if cases like this do not prove the point in general, one should nevertheless be critical of highly inferential measures of political legitimacy.

The general issue behind these questions is that of *system interference*, which "occurs when the inferences from the same direct measurement statements to inferred measurement statements are not equally valid in all systems under investigation" (PRZEWORSKI/TEUNE 1970:104). One hundred injured and dead in a political demonstration in a Western country would probably stir up the actors and the public much more and, under normal conditions, would have a much stronger impact than a similar case in a highly populated country like India. Thus, a similar event may have different consequences (cf. also DREW 1974) in a different context.[34] In general, the reaction to events like the one mentioned will be determined partly by the frequency of such occurrences in the particular contexts.

What can be done to be certain that indicators are equivalent? There are several strategies to follow:

1. The use of *experts* in particular countries, possibly those whose knowledge extends to several countries so that there are additional checks on the quality of indicators chosen.

2. *Correlation strategy* (cf. PRZEWORSKI/TEUNE 1970:120-31): a sample of indicators is collected. Some of these items are universally employed, some are nation- or culture-specific. After performing a correlation analysis, those indicators are retained which highly intercorrelate in all societies[35] as well as those which highly intercorrelate in the specific context from which they are chosen. If this strategy is to be employed constructively, other conditions (especially 3 and 4) must be met as well.

3. *Discriminant validity*: theoretically related indicators should not only intercorrelate highly (convergent validity, see strategy 2), but also should not intercorrelate, or only do so to a lower degree, with phenomena theoretically distinct from those under study (discriminant validity).

4. *Multitrait-multimethod strategy*: this is an extension of strategies 2 and 3 calling for replication of measurement in the sense that various characteristics of the respective phenomena be measured, and that different instruments be used (for some methodical intricacies of this technique, see ALTHAUSER/HEBERLEIN 1970).

5. *Replications*: in general, the more the better to see whether prior results are indeed stable. Researchers, instruments, countries, time periods, and indicators all could and should vary, either singly, in combinations, or altogether.

6. *Predictions* which in a way are replications extended into the future.

In general, the more of these strategies used, the more the researcher can be confident of his results. Equivalence of indicators is, of course, a theoretical matter and thus ultimately not measurable. One can only try to find better measurement approximations to the particular theoretical concepts. The issue is not so much whether the indicators chosen show high intercorrelations, but rather whether the units of counting are comparable (or, in the case of a more developed theory, functionally equivalent) across countries. These problems are pertinent to cross-national research in general and not just to the studies mentioned here.

To return to GURR's works, there are at least three more theoretical issues which should be mentioned briefly. As TILLY (1971:419; 1975) has pointed out, the building of coalitions[36] among groups of protesters is a much neglected subject in GURR's theory, as is the role of the *tertius gaudens*[37] (a third noninvolved party gaining from the conflict), be it the state or other parties to the conflict. Moreover, "an important portion of collective violence pits contenders for power against one another, rather than rebels against regimes. GURR's scheme eliminates such conflicts in principle, while his data include them in practice. No category in the scheme, furthermore, deals with the probability or the effect of agitation, organization, mobilization,[38] leadership, pooling of resources, development of internal communications among potential rebels [but see also chapter 9 of GURR 1970a which deals with some of these issues]. We have only the gross differences combined in Social and Structural Facilitation" (TILLY 1975:495; see chapter 8.4.6.6.1 for more details on this critique and for TILLY's own approach).

Furthermore, tactical elements in the use of strife are certainly discussed in GURR's *Why Men Rebel* (even if more or less passim); the measures, however, do not reflect tactical elements. Obviously, it is extremely difficult to find appropriate measures for tactics at a higher level of aggregation, yet it should be kept in mind that political violence is a phenomenon where strategy plays perhaps the dominant role (see also some of the theoretical arguments in chapter 2.1). Strategic elements are also of great importance in the process of coalition formation.

Lastly, and equally important, political violence is analyzed in terms of protest against the state or its agents. The question of state violence is often neglected in these works (although not so much in GURR 1970a and certainly not in his forthcoming analysis of the period 1966–70; as to the role of state violence, cf. also chapter 8.4.6.6.1). Some of GURR's critics, however, overdraw the point when they maintain that GURR's aim is in the end to provide state agents with recipes "how to keep them down" (on this see the history of project Camelot in HOROWITZ 1967). If his theory is valid, it may be interpreted and used from various points of view, e.g., for the purposes of controlling protest potentials on behalf of the state or for mobilizing and using them as a vehicle for achieving radical societal changes in the long run. Employing WEBER's distinction, there are clear implications of Wert*beziehungen* (value relations) in GURR's works, since he limits the analysis of political violence to "collective attacks . . . against the political regime, its actors . . . or its policies" (GURR 1970a:3-4; cf. chapter 2.1), but this is not to be confused with Wert*urteile* (value judgements). Nevertheless, NARDIN (1971:59) has reminded us that the state's role in violent political conflicts is "Janus-faced": on the one hand, the state[39] acts to prevent the outbreak of political violence or to keep it under control once

it has occurred; on the other hand, the state itself is a party to conflict—
and increasingly so (cf. the results for France, Germany, and Italy in TILLY
et al. 1975; see also chapter 8.4.6.6.1). A more recent example is the political
scene in Northern Ireland where the intervention of British troops led to the
current escalation (cf. BELL 1976; also ENLOE 1978). Yet, rather than
accepting the verdict of NARDIN criticizing GURR for having taken over the
"point of view of the authorities" (NARDIN 1971:20), one may simply state
that much of the present research in political violence is rather limited in
scope since the strong contribution that state violence makes to political
violence is mostly excluded in these analyses (exceptions being found in
HIBBS 1973; GURR 1970a, and especially in GURR et al., forthcoming).
If one were to compare the number of victims of state violence with those
affected by dissidents' use of political violence, one probably would come up
with a figure several times higher in the former case, at least for the nineteenth and twentieth centuries[40] (a conclusion also corroborated for the
period 1966-70; see GURR et al., forthcoming), but probably also for the
periods where so-called pre-industrial crowds (cf. also chapter 8.4.6.6.2)
prevailed. "Destruction of property, then, is a constant feature of the preindustrial crowd; but not destruction of human lives. . . . From this balance
sheet of violence and reprisal, it would appear, then, that it was authority
rather than the crowd that was conspicuous for its violence to life and limb"
(RUDÉ 1964:225-26). One has only to think of the pogroms and persecu-
tions in Czarist and communist Russia (especially 1936-38; cf. also DALLIN/
BRESLAUER 1970; JUVILER 1976), in Turkey, and under National Socialism in Germany, of the Hsiao-Minh campaign in China (1950-55, with several
million victims), or, more recently, of Uganda under Idi Amin (with the number of deaths approaching 300,000, according to Amnesty International), or,
less known, of the terrorist regime of Francisco Macías Nguema in Equatorial
Guinea (his opponents claim that he has killed about 50,000 of the nation's
population of 324,000; see *Newsweek*, Eur. ed. [20 June 1977] 28) or,
finally, of the Red Khmers in Cambodia (cf. SHAWCROSS 1978 for a discussion of the evidence). TILLY, MOORE and other conflict researchers, on the
basis of "informed guesses," tend to agree with such an interpretation. A
comprehensive theory of political violence would have to include statements
on the conditions and consequences of state violence as well. Furthermore,
it should specify how dissidents and state agents interact (cf. also chapter
5.1.2.5 and chapter 9).

5.1.1.1.3.2. Some General Methodological Issues

GURR uses aggregate economic, political, and social indicators for inferring
psychological states of mind. As SCHEUCH shows in a general discussion of
this and other strategies of measurement (for a classic treatment of fallacies
see ALKER 1969), there are always problems of analysis if the level of
measurement is not identical with the level of theoretical statements, in short,

if the principle of direct measurement is violated. "The danger of committing [the group fallacy] is always present when the unit to which the inference refers is smaller than the unit either of observation or of counting" (SCHEUCH 1966:164). In GURR's theory discrepancies between expectation levels and reality are said to cause feelings of relative deprivation. GURR uses only objective data and does not measure subjective reactions to these circumstances. Thus, there is no direct relationship between GURR's four forms of relative deprivation (see Figure 4.1) and his later analyses. Neither expectations nor the evaluation of one's own or the state's capabilities (the number and significance of alternatives; chapter 5.1.1.1.1) to fulfill these demands, both central components of GURR's psychological gap hypotheses, have been directly measured. Actually, the *same* measures are used to make inferences as to the *two* components of the gap hypotheses (i.e., expectations and capabilities). Even if, at the measurement level of nations, one were to use the GINI index of social inequality (see chapter 5.1.2.7) to measure feelings of relative deprivation *between* groups, there still would be a danger of inferential fallacy if one were to relate violent protests to deprivational circumstances. Relative deprivation is used as a dispositional concept. "Discontent is a psychological variable which is difficult to assess except by reference to its collective outcomes" (GURR 1970b:129). If one were to follow this line to an extreme, circular reasoning would be the result. More adequately formulated, GURR's empirically testable statements should read something like this: nations, whose GNP, rate of inflation, terms of trade, etc. change in a certain way, nations where political and economic discrimination exists to a certain degree, nations which had a violent past and command coercive forces, nations with these attributes show a particular form of political violence within the period 1961-65. There would be no danger of group fallacy if the statements were phrased at the nation level. "We do not even have the data whereby we could test whether hypothetically deprived *strata* of the population are those who engage in conflict behavior. Data, however, indicate that there is strong presumptive evidence that this is the case" (NESVOLD 1971:36). Yet, in spite of GURR's claims for his theory (GURR 1968a:1123), there is no way around collecting data on groups of *protesters themselves* if we are to be assured of more than highly inferential statements. The problem is not so much how GURR treats his data (he has developed many ingenious measures)[41] but the type of data he has at hand. Generally, the data of other pioneers in research on political violence are not better, as far as general theoretical statements at the level of individuals or groups are concerned. It should be emphasized, however, that much of the criticism directed at GURR's theoretical work (GURR 1970a) and at his empirical analyses reflects fundamental differences in paradigms. GURR, as a political scientist, is basically interested in *nation-specific patterns* ("world patterns") of civil conflict (see GURR et al., forthcoming), despite his strong emphasis on the relative deprivation variable. TILLY, as a sociologist, focuses on the *group approach* to violent political conflict; this has consequences on the methods chosen, the units of observation, and the analyses carried out (cf. also chapter 8.4.6.6.1 and chapter 9 as well as ZIMMERMANN 1980).

Another basic methodological argument is more ambivalent in nature. As briefly pointed out, GURR uses highly complex indexes as final measures of his ten independent variables. He tries to avoid idiosyncracies of specific measures by using a whole battery of carefully devised indicators. This so-called multiple indicators approach or multiple operationism, which goes back to LAZARSFELD (cf. LAZARSFELD/ROSENBERG 1955:15-18; see also CURTIS/JACKSON 1962), has been highly successful in social science. In recent years there is a growing methodological literature dealing with the relationships between background theories and so-called auxiliary theories which "consist of statements connecting abstract dimensions and their empirical indicators, statements which will be treated like other theoretical propositions" (COSTNER 1969:245-46). The strategies of theory construc-tion and control of measurement errors proposed by COSTNER (cf. BLA-LOCK 1971, pt. 4; BLALOCK 1974, pt. 2 for a critique and further develop-ments) have not yet been taken up in cross-national research on political violence[42] but undoubtedly will fascinate researchers in the future[43] as they try to find more precise parameter estimates of determinants of political violence. Going back to GURR's studies, at least at one point one may argue that his multiple index strategy may lead to distorted results. In GURR (1970b) the coercive resources of the regime and those of the dissidents are compared with each other. The same is done for the institutional resources. The "difference" score between coercive and institutional resources (using the former two difference scores) is then inserted in the multiple regression equation. Yet two countries could have considerably different numeri-cal values on these components, while the total balance score would re-main the same. Obviously, important theoretical differentiations would be obscured through such a procedure, unless institutional and coercive resources could be treated as functional equivalents (which they cannot, neither in theory nor in measurement).[44] Interestingly enough, GURR abandons this kind of summary score in later works for this and similar reasons (GURR 1972a). In a recent paper GURR/DUVALL (1973:140-41) themselves point out that three of the four balance variables had to be "deleted on various theoretical and empirical grounds" (due either to self-canceling effects or to interrelationships with other independent variables; cf. also chapter 5.1.1.1.4).

There is another more general drawback of GURR's use of index measures. If one wishes to apply the theory to public policy, one could scarcely tell agents of the state or rebels which variable would be of prime importance or what the *specific* impact of a distinct variable would be. "For example, riots involve violence, whereas antigovernment demonstrations, by definition in the coding, do not. The former may call for some contingency planning involving paramilitary requirements; yet this type of preparation for and display of force utilization would be little more than inefficient 'overkill' at best in the latter instance" (CHADWICK/FIRESTONE 1972:28). Conse-quently, these authors attribute "very low social utility to the findings in their present form" (ibid.). Thus, the high degree of data reduction in many of GURR's measures increases the amount of variance explained but reduces the applicability of the results in social situations. Interestingly, in a later work (GURR/DUVALL 1973; see the next chapter) mostly raw and untransformed measures are used rather than the former highly complex measures which were often difficult to interpret (cf. also the methods of transformation employed in GURR/LICHBACH 1979).

Finally, there are a number of technical arguments directly referring to the causal modeling procedures GURR uses. He obviously has made use of the so-called SIMON-BLALOCK technique when presenting his causal models for civil strife and for turmoil. There is much debate in the literature over whether this causal modeling technique or path analysis is more efficient. (Both are related; cf. the remarks in BLALOCK 1971:73ff.). In general, one may say: "the SIMON-BLALOCK procedure provides a basis for rejecting theories, but it is not in any way an inductive procedure for developing viable new theories" (HEISE 1969:64). Thus, insofar as GURR follows deductive reasoning (which, however, holds only to a lesser degree as far as the auxiliary theories and the selection of some of the indicators are concerned), his use of the SIMON-BLALOCK technique may be justified, since it allows him to test the relations of *one* independent variable to another. (However, this does not hold in the case of his model for turmoil; see chapter 5.1.1.1.2.3). On the other hand, path analysis would do this job much more elegantly and also provide a firmer basis as to the amount of variance directly or indirectly explained through an independent variable.[45] Unfortunately, GURR has not presented *explicit* causal models in his later papers, with the exception of GURR/DUVALL (1973; see the next chapter).

In most of his studies, regression analyses using ordinary least-squares are performed. Numerous assumptions[46] must be made if this technique of analysis is to be used in an efficient way. In later chapters some of these assumptions will be taken up. Here it may suffice to note that GURR claims to have found enough evidence in his studies to accept the assumption of linear relationships between variables (GURR/DUVALL 1973:144). However, one may raise the question of whether transformations of variables to achieve normal distributions have changed the *structure* of the relationships among variables (if not in GURR's works, then perhaps in other instances).[47]

When so many independent variables are used in a single analysis, multicollinearity effects[48] obviously inflate some of the causal coefficients. When orthogonality of independent variables is absent (cf. also chapter 5.1.2.4) "partial correlation coefficients ... will be highly unstable and sensitive to sampling errors. This means that we can be badly misled if we use partial correlations to measure the degree of relationship between the dependent variable and each of the (highly correlated) independent variables in turn" (BLALOCK 1970:420; for a discussion of some control strategies see ROCK-WELL 1975; cf. also FARRAR/GLAUBER 1967; SCHMIDT/MULLER 1978).

Furthermore, employing multiple regression analysis presupposes interval measurement of variables (but cf. also the recent discussion in KIM 1975 and SMITH 1978 for a critique). "These studies have been characterized by extensive use of sophisticated statistical sledgehammers to crack half-ripe chestnuts. Interval-order correlation and multiple regression techniques have repeatedly been applied to ordinal and nominal data, on the generally but not universally accepted rationalization that [somewhat] suspect results are better than mathematically-self-righteous ignorance" (GURR 1972b:34). The issue here is whether the use of strong statistical techniques (interval or even ratio level of measurement) is justified or whether weak statistical techniques (ordinal and nominal levels of measurement) are more adequate to the (ordinal?) structure of the data. Perhaps not surprisingly, using GURR's data and model of civil strife, BLOM (1973) reports a reduction of the explained variance from 65% to 34% when a rank-ordinal measure (KEN-DALL's tau is used (cf. also the findings reported in O'BRIEN 1978). (The *structure* of results is not changed.) What is needed, then, is more information on the robustness[49] of various measures, i.e., to what degree violations of strong measurement assumptions can be tolerated without leading to invalid inferences (cf. the debate between LABOVITZ 1967, 1972; BAKER et al. 1966; BOHRNSTEDT/CARTER 1971; ZELLER/LEVINE 1974 pleading for the use of strong statistics vs. various critics like WILSON 1971, 1974; HENKEL 1975; VIGDERHOUS 1977. For a brief overview see ACOCK/MARTIN 1974; cf. also the recent developments in SMITH 1974).

Some of the theoretical and methodological points mentioned here are taken up in a recent paper by GURR/DUVALL (1973) which will be discussed in the next section.

5.1.1.1.4. "Civil Conflict in the 1960s": Some Model Revisions

GURR/DUVALL (1973) examine the determinants for "variations in magnitudes of political conflict" (MPC) in eighty-six countries[50] (for the period 1961-65). "We deleted 28 countries for which data were dubious or missing; they were mostly the smaller, undeveloped countries of black Africa and also Afghanistan, Cambodia, China, Honduras, Nepal, Saudi Arabia, and Yemen" (ibid., p. 142). Man-days (once again including only nongovernmental participants) are used as the measure for the *extent* (pervasiveness), and deaths (including deaths of regime personnel) are used as the measure for *intensity* of political conflict. Both indicators are combined to measure the total extent of political violence. In addition, the dependent variable is divided into turmoil and rebellion: "We somewhat arbitrarily classified all riots, political demonstrations, general strikes, political clashes, and localized uprisings as turmoil. All other events, ranging from plots and coups through terrorism to civil war, were classified rebellion" (ibid., p. 143).

Following the criticism of ABELL (1971; cf. also chapter 5.1.1.1.3.1), the basic model of political violence is now presented in this form:

$$\text{Magnitude of political violence} = \text{RD} + (\text{RD} \times \text{JUST} \times \text{BALANCE}) + \epsilon$$

where RD is relative deprivation, JUST is justification (for details see preceding chapters) and ϵ stands for an error term. "The term in parentheses indicates that justifications and balance have no significant effects on violent conflict independently of RD; they act rather to amplify or inhibit its effects" (GURR/DUVALL 1973:137). Thus, in contrast with GURR's prior analyses, here these variables are indeed employed as mediating conditions, as implied in GURR's theory, and not simply in an additive manner.

Several of the independent variables are constructed and named differently than in previous studies, notably relative deprivation, now divided into *strain* (mainly denoting the former persisting deprivation measures)[51] and *stress* (denoting some of the former short-term deprivation measures) as well as into indicators referring to the coercive potential. One reason for choosing these new concepts instead of the psychological deprivation concept is to reduce the danger of group fallacy mentioned above.

Conflict traditions (TRAD), used to index the justification concept, are measured through the "durability of regime," the "relative scope and success of internal wars," the "frequency and success of coups," the "recency of last military intervention in civil politics," and the "union opposition status" (ibid., p. 146). *Dissident institutional support* (DIS) and *regime institutional support* (RIS) are two further highly complex independent variables which are negatively and reciprocally related.

In addition, two variables previously used are now *explicitly* taken into consideration: *economic development* (ECDEV using only one indicator: GNP per capita) and *external intervention* (EXINT) to support dissidents (support to governments has not been measured): EXINT stands in a reciprocal and reinforcing relationship to the magnitude of conflict. Conflict is also incorporated as a lagged endogenous variable (past MPC)[52] in the model. Consistent with their hypotheses, the authors report a strong positive relation between this variable and stress and, not surprisingly, conflict traditions. To measure the mediating effects explained in the revised causal model above, a composite term *Social tension* is formed (incorporationg some of the strain and stress measures x conflict traditions x dissident institutional support).[53] Finally, two dichotomous political system variables are used to measure "the existence or nonexistence of competitive, multiparty democracy (DEMOC) and, a mutually exclusive set, the existence of institutionalized autocracy or 'centrism' (CENT). (A number of countries are in neither category.)" (GURR/DUVALL 1973:141).[54]

Lack of space precludes a detailed description of the various steps taken in the authors' analyses. The reader is urged to consult their highly sophisticated study for more details. After estimating the parameters through two-stage (see MILLER 1971 and HIBBS 1973:206–33 for a description)[55] and three-stage least squares procedures, the authors come up with the following eleven variable, block-recursive, simultaneous equation model which accounts for about 75% of the variance in magnitude of political conflict[56] (see Figure 5.3).

Among the determinants of regime institutional support (RIS), dissident institutional support (DIS) has consistently (i.e., for all of the five dependent

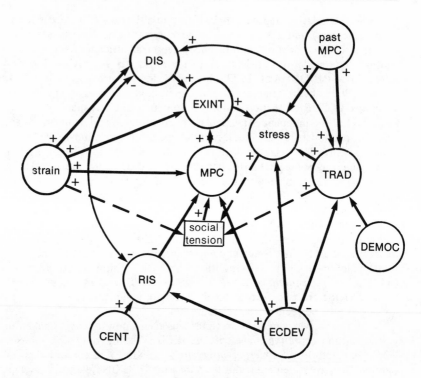

Figure 5.3.   Revised Model of Conflict Linkages
Source: GURR/DUVALL (1973:149)

variables: man-days, deaths, MPC, turmoil, and rebellion) had the greatest
negative influence, whereas economic development (ECDEV) and governmental centralization (CENT) have a comparable, but less strong, positive
effect on the dependent variable MPC. "In brief, regime institutions are
strongest in countries in which dissidents are organizationally weak, economic
development is high, and the political system is autocratic. The USSR is
typical of such high-RIS countries; Uganda in the mid-1960s was typical
of low RIS countries" (GURR/DUVALL 1973:154). Taking dissident institutional support (DIS) as the dependent variable, there is a strong and consistent
negative effect of RIS as well as a small and consistently positive influence
of strain. In the case of the dependent variable deaths, there is a notable
positive influence of both strain and conflict traditions (TRAD). Generally
the effect of RIS on DIS is smaller than vice versa. "Greater regime support
dampens dissident strength, but not as potently as dissident strength inhibits
support for the regime" (GURR/DUVALL 1973:154).

    Among the determinants of TRAD, economic development (ECDEV) is
consistently the most important, being negatively related to the dependent
variable, as is multiparty democracy (DEMOC), albeit to a considerably

smaller degree. Previous conflicts (past MPC) show a positive relation to the dependent variable, being strongest in case of turmoil and man-days. The predicted reciprocal influence between DIS and TRAD (see Figure 5.3) should be omitted. "But this challenges our common-sense observation that dissident groups are often the carriers of traditions of conflict" (GURR/ DUVALL 1973:155). Specification error[56] may be occurring here since in these equations much less variance is explained than in others.

Looking at the dependent variable societal stress, ECDEV (negative sign) and past strife (positive sign, but slightly weaker in the case of turmoil) are the strongest determinants. There is also a consistently positive influence of TRAD and STRAIN in the case of turmoil. A fourth and, except for turmoil, stronger positive determinant than TRAD is external intervention (EXINT). "When we compare the stress-turmoil equation with that for stress-rebellion, we are drawn to the conclusion that the extent of foreign intervention and conflict traditions determine whether stress leads to turmoil or to rebellion" (GURR/DUVALL 1973:156). EXINT is strongly and consistently influenced by strife (MPC). "Pronounced social strain and strong dissident organizations also increase the probability of intervention, particularly where conflict is pervasive" (ibid., p. 157).

Turning to the equations to predict the five ultimate dependent variables, the first remarkable finding is that each equation is distinct, though some more general relationships do emerge. The authors present this summary of findings:

> Tension (the multiplicative term incorporating stress, strain, and TRAD) is the primary driving force behind manifest conflict. It is relatively least important as a determinant of turmoil, but is by far the most potent source of pervasive and intense conflict. In addition, social strain has an independent and direct effect on the magnitude of conflict, except in the case of rebellion and, marginally, man-days. The third of the three major variables that exacerbate overt conflict is external intervention. There is no evidence that foreign involvement serves to reduce the severity or pervasiveness of conflict; quite the contrary.
>
> The principal inhibiting variable in the conflict equation is regime institutional support, whose effects are especially significant on turmoil and man-days. Strong dissident support, on the other hand, acts to make strife more deadly. . . . It simply reflects the fact that the more organized are dissidents, the more they are both source and target of deadly force.
>
> The only anomalous effects are those of economic development. As observed in other studies [see chapter 5.1.2.1 and passim], it tends to reduce magnitudes of *deadly* conflict. But it has a significant positive effect on turmoil and man-days.
>
> Finally, in the case of turmoil (but only in the case of turmoil), TRAD makes an independent and direct contribution to conflict apart from its interaction with stress and strain (GURR/DUVALL 1973: 157-58).

A plausible explanation for the positive influence of economic development on the various forms of political violence (with the exception of the dependent variables deaths and rebellion) may be that in these societies there are not only more resources to fight over or to use in conflicts, but also that the legitimacy of the political order in these nations leads their citizens to have higher expectations as far as performance of the state and the rights of citizens are concerned. Thus, only slight violations of these expectations may lead to *milder* forms of protest in these countries, because people expect their governments to be efficient or to provide them with opportunities for being efficient themselves. They have much higher standards for evaluating performance than would people in nations much less developed economically. However, one must consider that there are strongly inhibiting, albeit indirect (i.e., through RIS, stress, and TRAD), influences from economic development.

Using the language of path analysis, there are a number of important paths to consider. In some cases these paths are reciprocal, thus adding considerable insight to prior unidirectional models still dominant in conflict research (see also the following chapters). There is, for example, strong positive interdependence between the magnitude of political conflict and external intervention (see chapter 5.1.2.6). Another reciprocal relationship is more indirect, passing from MPC through EXINT which, in turn, increases the amount of stress, one of the determinants of the multiplicative term social tension.

Regime institutional support (RIS) clearly decreases the amount of political conflict directly, but there is also a more indirect decrease through DIS and EXINT. Looking at some of the exogenous variables, one sees evidence of the strong and positive impact of strain (with the exception of rebellion) which apparently finds its outlet through many channels, i.e., through dissident institutional support, external intervention on behalf of dissidents, the multiplicative term social tension, or most important, through acting directly on the magnitude of political conflict.

Finally, there is evidence that past strife is one of the background conditions of strife, thus supporting one of GURR's major hypotheses, the culture-of-violence hypothesis (cf. also chapter 5.1.2.8), in short, that strife breeds strife. (Yet stable implicit variables and autocorrelated residuals may contribute to these empirical correlations). Past violent political conflicts also exert influence through various other channels, i.e., stress, TRAD, DIS, RIS, etc. Furthermore, since none of the direct or indirect effects is greater than unity, the authors reach the conclusion that "the model is not explosive. Instead, the positive feedback is of successively dampened increments in strife" (GURR/DUVALL 1973:159; italics omitted here).

One must bear in mind that the results are based on cross-sectional analyses. Thus, different causal paths could emerge if one were to study the history and conditions of political violence in various countries *over time*. In some countries the variance explained is far below the average. In these cases it is likely that important causal influences are not considered. As the authors themselves point out (GURR/DUVALL 1973:163–64), regime type is a variable whose influence has not been sufficiently specified.

There is also an interesting correction of the components of social tension, since dissident institutional support must be deleted on the basis of empirical results. Yet, this changes the theoretical background formula for the magnitude of political violence (see the beginning of this section). It appears that GURR's balance notion proves to be much more complex than stated in earlier theoretical writings. In any case, the theory developed from the results of this study would look considerably different from the one outlined in *Why Men Rebel* (GURR 1970a). The psychological bias in GURR's theoretical writings has been eliminated, and, moreover, the concept of mediating variables has been much more specified, apparently rendering the dichotomizing of variables into deprivational background variables and mediating variables (i.e., sociostructural, traditional, and balance conditions) less useful than at earlier stages of development.

Finally, the model in Figure 5.3 thus far holds only for the period and sample under study. Obviously, replications employing different measures, if possible, or focusing at least on different time periods are necessary.[57] When applying the GURR/DUVALL model to twenty-five black African nations (there are only seven African nations in their sample) and using mainly the *World Handbook of Political and Social Indicators* (TAYLOR/ HUDSON 1972) and *Black Africa* (MORRISON et al. 1972) as sources, WELFLING (1975) is able to show that there are sampling errors, measurement errors, and specification[58] errors in the GURR/DUVALL analysis, though in general the model does well. She summarizes some of her results as follows:

> First, it is clear that the general model suffers from sampling error. An inspection of correlations across samples suggests that at least three concepts—strain, economic development, and regime institutional support—have weaker effects in Africa than in the 86-nation sample. . . . Dissident institutional support and perhaps past conflict have stronger effects in the African sample.
>
> Second, measurement error is clearly present in the African data sets, although the *Black Africa* data appear less erroneous. The extent of error varies considerably across concepts, and both random and systematic error are inferred to exist. . . .
>
> Third, the omission of certain potentially relevant concepts from the general model suggests some error in theoretical specification. The existence of institutionalized linkages [party systems] between publics and governments seems to reduce stress, while in new nations the length of time independent influences the extent of external intervention. In addition, there was evidence that different forms of conflict affect each other, but interpretations must be extremely tentative due to measurement error in turmoil. This third form of error appears the least severe and is perhaps the most easily remedied (WELFLING 1975: 887–88).

All in all, GURR (as the senior author) has developed an impressive and empirically tenable theoretical model that is more deductive in nature than any other thus far applied to research on political violence (perhaps with the exception of the works of MULLER; cf. chapter 5.3.2.3). In many instances, of course, GURR's efforts clearly show the fruitfulness of a reciprocal deductive-inductive approach to theory construction in the field of politimetrics,[59] to use the "new"[60] term. For paradigmatic reasons (i.e., as far as theory integration is concerned) and due to limitations typical of the kind of research under study here, we have described GURR's works and commented on them in detail. Another important strategy or paradigm that seems to be successful in research on political violence is exemplified in HIBBS's study (1973; see chapter 5.1.1.3). Before we turn to that work, however, a look at the studies of other pioneers in cross-national research on political violence is in order.

5.1.1.2. The Study of Systemic Aggression (FEIERABEND/FEIERABEND and Coworkers)

The studies of the FEIERABENDs and their coworkers are based on the frustration-aggression nexus, which the authors subscribe to somewhat uncritically, and on modernization theories. The former variants of theorizing have been extensively dealt with in chapter 3. Here we will comment on the body of modernization theories. We intend to list several trends as well as complications of this kind of research which provides for one of the background theories in research on political violence. There are many more references to these studies throughout this book.

5.1.1.2.1. A Note on Modernization Theories

"The dimensions of modernization (technological, organizational and attitudinal)[61] are frequently associated with a supporting complex of more specific changes—urbanization, the growth of literacy, the spread of mass communications, and political participation" (BILL/HARDGRAVE 1973: 63). LERNER was probably the first, apart from classic authors like MARX, to propose a causal model of these modernization processes. Actually, there are at least two different models discernible in his writings: "the Western model of modernization exhibits certain components and sequences whose relevance is global. Everywhere, for example, increasing urbanization has tended to raise literacy; rising literacy has tended to increase media exposure; increasing media exposure has 'gone with' wider economic participation (per capita income) and political participation (voting)" (LERNER 1958: 46). Elsewhere he writes: "Within this urban matrix develop both of the attributes which distinguish the next two phases—literacy and media growth. There is a close reciprocal relationship between these, for the literate develop the media which in turn spread literacy. But, historically, literacy performs the key function. . . . The capacity to read, at first acquired by relatively few people, equips them to perform the varied tasks required in the modernizing society. Not until the third phase . . . does a society begin to produce newspapers, radio networks, and motion pictures on a massive scale. This, in turn, accelerates the spread of literacy. Out of this interaction develop those institutions of participation (e.g., voting) which we find in all advanced modern societies" (LERNER 1958:60).

In the meantime numerous "LERNER models" have emerged from modernization studies (cf. ALKER 1966:22; McCRONE/CNUDDE 1967; TANTER 1967; SMITH 1969; SIGELMAN 1971; BRUNNER/BREWER 1971; KENT et al. 1971; SCHMITTER 1972a; see FREY 1973:400-18 for a useful overview). While there are a number of differences to be found in these studies there is, nevertheless, a basic consensus, summarized in the following statement which also indicates several shortcomings found in these approaches:

All view urbanization[62] –essentially an economic variable in LERNER's mind– as the independent, causal variable in the political development process. All trace the causal path from urbanization through categories of social and cultural development. And all analyze political development purely in terms of its dependence upon these ecological factors. But by the same token, the primary faults of these ecological renderings of the political development process are also shared. . . . The first concerns the data used in testing the ecological theory; these are invariably cross-sectional[63] measures of national levels of attainment on the selected variables–data not particularly well suited for the testing of development theory. A second, and more fundamental, flaw resides within the ecological theory itself. It is evident that the earlier systemic emphasis on subsystem interdependence has been replaced by a radically deterministic view of the development process–a view which consistently asserts the primacy of socioeconomic factors and the wholly derivative nature of political development (SIGELMAN 1971:11-12).

Political participation (defined as "activity by private citizens designed to influence governmental decision-making," HUNTINGTON/NELSON 1976:4) is also the ultimate dependent variable in the theoretical analysis of HUNTINGTON/NELSON (1976) who develop several models of how to achieve socioeconomic modernization, socioeconomic equality, political development (cf. the discussion in chapter 5.1.2.3), and political participation: "While the technocratic model leads to governmental repression in order to prevent political participation, the populist model leads to civil strife as a result of political participation. In both cases, and in a comparable manner, the dynamics of the relationships among the critical variables tend to produce a vicious circle in which the dominant tendencies are toward the maximization of the value of each variable"[64] (HUNTINGTON/NELSON 1976: 23-24). The HUNTINGTON/NELSON study develops numerous fruitful hypotheses. However, we find many of their conclusions to be based on insufficient or at least not representative empirical evidence. What seems to hold for several countries in Latin America and elsewhere does not necessarily apply to countries in other regions as well. Furthermore, the authors start from the assumption that political organization of the poor will only result "if mobility is blocked" (HUNTINGTON/NELSON 1976:113). While this might be true for definitional and theoretical reasons, it rarely is demonstrated on an empirical basis (cf. also chapter 5.1.2.4). Once again there is evidence of how tacit "Western" assumptions (in this case, the assumption that social mobility will do away with conflict potentials accumulating in the absence of social mobility) find their outlet in analyses of Western scientists. These remarks notwithstanding, the HUNTINGTON/NELSON analysis does for the cross-national perspective what VERBA/NIE (1972) have done for the United States perspective (at least with respect to political participation), namely to bring together a variety of theoretical streams and available empirical evidence and to relate them to each other in a more coherent theoretical approach, or at least to point out more clearly the alternatives which seem to exist in each case. After all, political participation is an umbrella concept comprising many different forms of political activity (cf. also chapter 9).

Another classic approach to the study of modernization is found in DEUTSCH's notion of social mobilization. He defines *social mobilization* as "an overall process of change, which happens to substantial parts of the population in countries which are moving from traditional to modern ways of life . . . in which major clusters of old social, economic and psychological commitments are eroded or broken and people become available for new patterns of socialization and behavior" (DEUTSCH 1961:493-94). Basically, his list of variables encompasses many of the determinants of political violence to be analyzed in greater detail in the coming chapters. DEUTSCH also makes an interesting prediction concerning the protest potential of different segments of the mobilized population (see chapter 5.1.2.4).

Before we return to the discussion of the FEIERABENDs' studies on political violence, a few caveats as to modernization theorizing should be mentioned. Without going into detail here (see BILL/HARDGRAVE 1973: 43-83 for a summary of some of the main points; cf. also EISENSTADT 1976; PALMER/THOMPSON 1978:chapter 2), the following shortcomings found in most modernization studies should at least be mentioned. Moreover, most of these errors also pertain to many studies on political development to be discussed in chapter 5.1.2.3.

1. Modernity and tradition are treated as opposites (see the summary of the various dichotomies in BILL/HARDGRAVE 1973:50-57; PALMER 1973:16-17), or, in GUSFIELD's (1967) phrase, as "misplaced polarities." As BENDIX puts it, "many attributes of modernization, like widespread literacy or modern medicine, have appeared, or have been adopted, in isolation from the other attributes of a modern society. Hence, modernization in some sphere of life may occur without resulting in 'modernity'" (BENDIX 1966/1967:329, italics omitted). In HUNTINGTON's words: "The cultural, psychological, and behavioral continuities existing within a society through

both its traditional and modern phases may be significantly greater than the dissimilarities between these phases" (HUNTINGTON 1971b:297).

2. Furthermore, the traditional end of the scale of comparison remains undefined: "The tribes of camel herders in the Arabian desert; the villages of Tropical Africa; and the imperial civilizations once governed by the Manchus in China and the Ottomans in Turkey—all become similar only as they are confronted in fact or contrasted in concept with modern civilizations" (RUSTOW 1967:12).[65]

3. Modernization is seen as a basically homeostatic, unidirectional, and universal[66] process of development (cf. ROSTOW's stages of economic growth, 1960, or ORGANSKI's stages of political development, 1967). Only in recent times have crises (see chapter 6), breakdowns, and decay (EISENSTADT 1964; HUNTINGTON 1965) during these processes gained attention. Interestingly enough, more historically oriented social scientists like BENDIX confine the modernization concept to quite limited historical periods: "By 'modernization' I refer to a type of social change which originated in the industrial revolution in England, 1760-1830, and in the political revolution in France, 1789-1794" (BENDIX 1966/1967:329; italics omitted).

4. In addition, modernization is treated as a quasi-deterministic process that, once under way and fulfilling certain conditions, is largely determined by endogenous factors and will automatically follow the Western example[67] of economic growth and political democracy. External influences are unduly neglected.

5. As pointed out already, the impact of political decisions or coalition formation processes—in short, of more decisional elements—is generally neglected in this body of research. A recent notable change is found in ALMOND et al. (1973; see also chapter 6.3.3).

6. More complex theoretical models of modernization processes[68] encompassing the interplay of socioeconomic and political variables as well as internal and external[69] influences either have not been developed yet to a sufficient degree or have not been adequately tested.

The different versions of dependency theory (dependencia theory), for example, those proposed by FRANK (1972; for a critique cf. NOVE 1974; HALPERIN 1976:59ff.), CARDOSO, SUNKEL, DOS SANTOS, and others (see CHILCOTE 1974 for an overview), have been criticized on various theoretical, methodological, and empirical grounds (cf. LALL 1975; O'BRIEN 1975; SMITH 1979; DUVALL 1978; JACKSON et al. 1979; DUVALL et al., forthcoming, with an effort to state "the" theory more precisely to allow for testing).[70] More recent evidence (e.g., WALLERI 1978a), evaluated by WALLERI (1978b; cf. also BORNSCHIER et al. 1978), however, leads to the conclusion that the majority of studies support dependency theory (cf. also RUBINSON 1976, with emphasis on state strength as an intervening variable; WEEDE 1980 for a critique of this study; and the sophisticated analysis by SNYDER/KICK 1979). Yet, adequate testing of dependency theory requires the use of longitudinal data and the rigorous control of outlying cases (as to their strongly disturbing effects see RAY/WEBSTER 1978). However, if cross-sectional data are employed, a possible alternative explanation cannot be ruled out, namely that "economic growth leads to dependency" (RAY/WEBSTER 1978:417) by attracting trade and foreign investment.[71] It should be apparent that an adequate understanding of modernization requires the joint analysis of social and political change at the world system level (cf. WALLERSTEIN 1974), at the national sociostructural level (cf. chapter 5.1), at the local level, and at the individual level. These criticisms notwithstanding, modernization theories and studies have provided an array of theoretical explanations which can be used in cross-national research on political violence. There are several applications of modernization theories in the studies of the FEIERABENDs to which we now turn again.

5.1.1.2.2. Basic Concepts and Operationalizations

FEIERABEND/FEIERABEND (1966, 1971, 1972; see also FEIERABEND/ FEIERABEND/NESVOLD 1969) collected data on internal conflict behavior (N=84 nations) for a period of fifteen years, 1948-62. Their dependent variable is political instability which they define as "the degree or the amount of aggression directed by individuals or groups within the political system against other groups or against the complex of officeholders and individuals and groups associated with them. Or, conversely, it is the amount of aggression directed by these officeholders against other individuals, groups, or officeholders within the polity" (FEIERABEND/FEIERABEND 1966:250). In contrast to GURR's earlier definition of political violence, state violence as well as conflicts among contenders other than the state are included in the object of explanation. In the empirical analyses of the FEIERABENDs, however, no distinctions between these various conflict constellations, distinctions important to a general theory of political violence, are made.

The dependent variable political instability is scaled along the intensities of conflict from zero (extreme stability, e.g., general election) to six (extreme instability, e.g., civil war). It should be noted that "indicators of official, and often violent, coercion—for example, mass arrests, imprisonments, repressive action against specific groups, martial law, executions . . .—are *also* included in national violence profiles. Therefore, estimated relationships between [coercion and political violence, to be discussed later on] reflect statistical, via definitional, artifacts rather than any true association" (SNYDER 1976: 288-89). The reliability (validity?) of the scaling procedure was checked through comparing the coding of independent raters. This consensual validation technique "by asking judges to sort the same events along the same continuum" (FEIERABEND/FEIERABEND 1966:252) was apparently successful ($r \approx .9$).[72] Stability profiles were constructed for seven years, 1955-61. "Countries were assigned to groups on the basis of the most unstable event which they experienced during this seven-year period" (FEIERABEND/ FEIERABEND[73] 1966:252). The FEIERABENDs wanted to give equal weight to the intensity of events and the frequency of events. "However, my decomposition of their conflict scores . . . shows that intensity is the only important component of national instability scores" (SNYDER 1976: 289 and note 10 ibid. for details).

The basic independent variable systemic frustration is again taken from the frustration-aggression research and defined as:

$$\frac{\text{social want satisfaction}}{\text{social want formation}} = \text{systemic frustration}$$

(FEIERABEND/FEIERABEND 1966:250). This is fundamentally the famous want/get formula[74] of LERNER (1958, 1963:333–35). "The higher (lower) the social want formation in any given society and the lower (higher) the social want satisfaction, the greater (the less) the systemic frustration and the greater (the less) the impulse to political instability" (FEIERABEND/ FEIERABEND, here with Betty A. NESVOLD 1966:256). For measuring want satisfaction, the following indicators are used: "GNP and caloric intake per capita, physicians and telephones per unit of population were singled out as indices of satisfaction. Newspapers and radios per unit of population were also included" (ibid., p. 258). Literacy and urbanization are chosen as indicators of want formation. "Exposure to modernity was judged a good mechanism for the formation of new wants, and literacy and city life were taken as the two agents most likely to bring about such exposure" (ibid.).

In the model of DEUTSCH, urbanization is an indicator of growing capabilities of the polity, whereas literacy indicates growing demands. In LERNER's model, urbanization, literacy, and the mass media indicate higher demands which may lead to a "revolution of rising frustrations"[75] (LERNER 1963:330f.) if the capacities of the state do not keep up with these demands. While both models consider literacy to be an indicator of demands, they diverge as far as the role of urbanization is concerned. Probably each of the indicators used in modernization research has been chosen at least once for indicating either demands or capabilities. The FEIERABENDs, however, take too many liberties. As there is a strong relationship between literacy and newspaper circulation,[76] one may ask why the latter indicator has been chosen to measure "want satisfaction" (or, with DEUTSCH, "capabilities") and the former to indicate "want formation" ("demands"). Furthermore, using radio distribution as an indicator of want satisfaction reverses the common theoretical rationale that the radio (as well as the cinema[77] and, increasingly, television) is one of the main transmitters of new ideas in underdeveloped countries (cf. the data in RUSSETT et al. 1964:293-303, and FLORA 1972:100-101; both, however, use only cross-sectional data; see also DEUTSCH 1974:544). It would be interesting to see whether the results reported by the FEIERABENDs would remain unchanged if they chose indicators more consistent with contemporary evidence and theory.

5.1.1.2.3. Some Empirical Results

In Table 5.2 several of the basic results of the FEIERABENDs are listed. In later chapters further results of their studies as well as some of the underlying theoretical questions will be considered. Note that the authors work with time lags between the independent and dependent variables; note as well that there are some inconsistencies where the independent variable occasionally outlasts the dependent variable (if only for a short time span).

In the first group of studies, modernity is measured according to the eight indicators listed, whereas only six of these are used to measure want satisfaction. Systemic frustration is indexed as the ratio of these six want satisfaction indicators to the higher of the two want formation indicators. The modernity index should be valid; the systemic frustration index, however, should be called into question (see the discussion above). Thus, the following result should be read carefully: The greater the systemic frustration within a polity, the greater the systemic aggression (YULE's Q=.9653). Contrary to prediction, there is no curvilinear relationship between level of modernity and political instability (η as the appropriate measure for curvilinearity differs only slightly from r, .667 vs. .625; on this issue see also chapter 5.1.2.1). However, there are only a few traditional societies (i.e., societies before the take-off phase; ROSTOW 1960) in the sample of the FEIERABENDs, thus making a linear negative relationship more likely.[78] There seem to be clear distinctions between modern and transitional societies: "It is at this middle stage that awareness of modernity and exposure to modern patterns should be complete, that is, at a theoretical ceiling, whereas achievement levels would still be lagging far behind" (FEIERABEND/FEIERABEND 1966:257). What is questionable, however, is the strategy of reinterpreting the modernization index into an index of frustration "indicating the extent to which these measured economic satisfactions are present within a society which may be presumed to have already been exposed to modernity" (FEIERABEND/ FEIERABEND 1966:262).

When relating the rate of modernization (see also chapter 5.1.2.2) to the dependent variable, there is a clear covariation (r=.66) supporting the hypothesis of the authors: "The higher the rate of change of the indices [of modernization], the greater the increase in instability" (FEIERABEND/ FEIERABEND, here with Wallace R. CONROE 1966:265; see also FEIERA-BEND/FEIERABEND/NESVOLD 1969:665), the rate of change in primary education being the strongest and the rate of change in literacy the weakest predictors. Whereas literacy may be a good predictor of the stability of a political system, this does not hold for the rate of change of this variable. Interestingly, the positive rate of change in national income predicts greater stability. As the authors maintain, income may be an item *without* ceiling effect, thus calling for a different explanation. In any case: "The most detrimental combination of factors appears to be a rapid increase in proportion of the population receiving primary education, but a slow rate of percentage change in GNP per capita. This set of circumstances is most conducive to political unrest among the transitional group of countries" (FEIERABEND/FEIERABEND/NESVOLD 1969:666–67).

In another study FEIERABEND/FEIERABEND (1971) examine the relationship between systemic frustration, political coercion (repression), and political instability. Following BUSS (1961:58) they postulate that "low levels of punishments do not serve as inhibitors; it is only high levels of punishment which are likely to result in anxiety and withdrawal. Punishment at mid-levels of intensity acts as a frustrator and elicits further aggression, maintaining an aggression-punishment-aggression sequence" (FEIERABEND/FEIERABEND 1971:420–21). Thus, the FEIERABENDs predict a curvilinear[79] relationship between political coercion and instability. When combining the two independent variables they state the following hypothesis: "The greatest tendency to political instability will result from a high level of socio-economic systemic frustration in combination with mid-level coerciveness of political regime. This combination, in fact, pools two sources of systemic frustration, one socio-economic, the other political" (ibid., p. 421).

The predicted curvilinear relationship between political coercion and systemic aggression is supported by the fact that η (.72) varies considerably from r (.409). Whereas two-thirds of all nations which make strictest use of coercive means are stable, there is a 3:1 probability that nations with a medium level of coercion will be unstable. In line with MACHIAVELLI the authors state: "Nothing less than a full-fledged totalitarian regime seems sufficient, over time, to keep the populace from expressing dissatisfaction in high levels of systemic aggression; then only if totalitarianism is unambiguously pursued will it be successful" (ibid., p. 429). Taking political coercion as the dependent variable, there is a negative relation (r=–.699) between modernity level and coercion. Transitional societies are much more likely to make use of coercive means than modern countries (no η reported here, though there is some evidence of a slightly curvilinear relationship; for further results and discussion see chapter 5.1.2.5). All in all, there is some evidence that more modern nations (except for communist and some autocratic countries) may be less coercive and produce less systemic frustration than nations on their way to modernization.

The curvilinear relationship between coercion and political violence is again supported when the dependent variable is turmoil (see second study in Table 5.2), though the difference between η (.69) and r (.58) is only slight[80] (FEIERABEND/NESVOLD/FEIERABEND 1970). More interesting, perhaps, is another result of their study, namely that there is a *linear* relationship (r=.67; η=.66) between *fluctuations* in the level of political coercion and the level of political violence. Apart from LeVINE who found for African colonies that "policies arousing conflicting expectations . . . lead to anti-European violence whereas relatively consistent policies do not" (LeVINE 1959: 427), this is the first systematic study of the impact of fluctuations in the use of coercive means.

Table 5.2. Summary of Results of Feierabend/Feierabend and Coworkers

Author	Dependent Variable	Indicators	Independent Variables	Indicators	Sample	Period	Results
(1) Feierabend/ Feierabend 1966, 1971	political instability (systemic aggression)	7-point conflict scale, 0 denoting extreme stability and 6 civil war	systemic frustration	ratio of want satisfaction (GNP and caloric intake per capita, physicians, telephones, newspapers, radios per unit of population) and want formation (literacy, urbanization)	84	1948-55 dependent variable 1955-61	Q = .9653
Feierabend/ Feierabend/ Nesvold 1969			modernity	GNP and caloric intake per capita, physicians, telephones, newspapers, radios per unit of population, literacy, urbanization			r = .625
			rate of modernization	rate of change in: caloric intake, literacy, primary and post-primary education, national income, cost of living, infant mortality, urbanization,	67<N<20	1935-62 dependent variable 1948-65	r = .66

	Dependent variable		Independent variable		$62<N<84$	1948–55	see first line
			systemic frustration	radios per 1,000 population as above			
			political coercion	7-point scale, 0 denoting "civil rights present and protected" and 6, denoting "civil rights nonexistent, political opposition impossible," etc.		1948–60	$r = .409$
						dep. var. 1955–61	$\eta = .72$
	political coercion	7–point scale (as above)	modernity	as above			$r = .699$
(2) Feierabend/ Nesvold/ Feierabend 1970	turmoil (political instability)	as above	political coerciveness	as above	73	1945–66	$\eta = .69$ $r = .58$
			use of coercive means (inconsistent/ consistent)			dep. var. 1948–65[+]	$r = .67$
			– – – – both indep. variables				$R = .76$

[+]Inaccuracies such as this (the independent variable includes a time slice subsequent to that of the dependent variable) can be observed occasionally in research on political violence.

There are several possible explanations for the relationship found, *none* of which can be sufficiently refuted by the indicators used:

1. Fluctuations in the level of coercion may come as a surprise to the population. As they were not expected, they may lead to a credibility gap and eventually to a further loss in legitimacy of the regime. In the case of tightening coercive measures, this explanation seems immediately plausible; in the case of lessening coercive restrictions, however, an additional assumption is made, namely that
2. Fluctuations (or in this case, simple changes in coerciveness) are exceeded by changes in expectation, i.e., the population expects even greater steps toward liberalization than those taken so far.
3. There may be another, and perhaps a priori more plausible, reason why turmoil (meaning systemic aggression; not in the sense of previous chapters) should be more likely despite a reduction in the level of repression: "it means the removal of the inhibitory mechanism, but not necessarily the removal of the instigation to violence that still may linger as the heritage of previously coercive regime" (FEIERABEND/NESVOLD/FEIERABEND 1970:102). Previous instigation to protest against the regime may not be reduced by a lowering of the state's grip on society. This explanation and all the others presuppose, of course, data on individuals or on specific groups collected over time.
4. A theoretical principle taken directly from research on learning behavior could be considered: activities intermittently reinforced are especially resistant to extinction. This would mean that the negative consequences of coercive means applied against the protesters are lower than the gains they made while the state used its coercive power in an inconsistent manner.
5. (Directly related to the previous mechanism.) Occasional repressive measures may lead to very intense frustrations, thus strongly increasing the protest potential.

There are dramatic historical examples that shed some light on the hypotheses mentioned (e.g., the Hungarian uprising and the Poznan rebellion in 1956, the Czech uprising in the first half of 1968, and events in the Dominican Republic after the removal of the Trujillo clan, FEIERABEND/NESVOLD/FEIERABEND 1970:115, and most recently the fall of the Shah in Iran). In chapter 8 more will be said on some of the theoretical explanations listed here. It may seem paradoxical that less coercion or more freedom should lead to protest; however, from the protesters' point of view things look different, since they interpret concessions as weakness of the hated regime. Once again, MACHIAVELLI's advice seems pertinent: "Undoubtedly, if high coerciveness is applied, it should be applied consistently" (FEIERA-BEND/NESVOLD/FEIERABEND 1970:115). The more successful tyrants in history realized this.

If one relates the two independent variables,[81] level of coerciveness and fluctuations in coerciveness, to the dependent variable, 58% of the variance is explained. "Permissive nations with a low level of fluctuation of coercion (high consistency) are overwhelmingly stable, while countries at mid-coercive levels with a high level of fluctuation (inconsistency) are predominantly unstable. It is especially among highly coercive countries that the notion of consistency adds a particular refinement" (FEIERABEND/NESVOLD/FEIERABEND 1970:110). This study (see also the reanalysis of the FEIER-ABEND data using multiple regression technique in PARANZINO 1972) lends support to a result appearing in a number of divergent studies (see chapter 5.1.2.5): coercive measures inhibit political violence only under very *specific* conditions. Yet, to make the point clear once again, these results are based mostly on cross-sectional data. In some cases, the causal relation may be just the reverse or, if time sequences within polities are studied, it may vanish or have to be specified through other variables. More-over, in some cases "inconsistent" application of coercive means may indicate consistent reactions to varying attacks of protesters, thus demonstrating strength rather than weakness of a regime. So far, only a climate of coerciveness has been measured. The question of theoretical and practical interest is, of course, whether these relationships hold if one looks not at *systemic coercion* but at *event coercion* (see chapter 5.1.2.5).

Finally, upon considering some of the results in FEIERABEND/FEIERA-BEND (1972; N=53 states, excluding the superpowers), several of the relationships mentioned emerge once again. Modernity shows consistently negative correlations with political instability (1948-62: r=-.71; 1955-61: -.66), external conflict (-.46), and systemic frustration (-.80). Rate of change in indicators of modernization also shows consistent relations (somewhat lower in the case of external aggression, .30 vs. $\approx$ .69 in the other cases), with the exception of the relationship to modernity (-.85). Coerciveness once again correlates positively with political instability (1948-62: .70; 1955-61: .54) and systemic frustration (.58) and negatively, as expected, with modernity (-.65).

Using systemic frustration, modernity, rate of modernization, and coercion as predictors, more than half of the variance in political instability can be explained in both periods (1948-62 and 1955-61). (In the case of external aggression, R^2 is only .37). Modernity and rate of change (modernity and political coercion during the longer period) are the best predictors of political violence. Thus, there is strong evidence that theories about modernity and modernization processes (see chapter 5.1.2.1 and 5.1.2.2 for a brief summary of evidence) indeed provide a useful guide-line in evaluating background conditions of political violence. Explanations would, however, be far too general if this were all that could be said about the determinants of political violence (cf. also chapter 9).

5.1.1.2.4. A Critique of the Studies of the FEIERABEND Group

Here we will merely give a short, general evaluation of the various studies of the FEIERABEND group (for a summary of these works cf. also FEIERA-BEND/FEIERABEND/NESVOLD/JAGGAR 1971; FEIERABEND/FEIERA-BEND 1973; FEIERABEND/FEIERABEND/NESVOLD 1973). The more specific critical arguments raised thus far will not be repeated. A brief comparison of the FEIERABENDs' studies with those of GURR will indicate some strengths of the latter's research. It should be noted that many of the critical arguments raised against GURR's studies (see chapter 5.1.1.1.3) apply here as well, sometimes even a fortiori.

One of the basic arguments against the work of the FEIERABENDs concerns the rather simple use the authors make of the frustration-aggression nexus. Even if they refer to systemic frustration as leading only to an "impulse to political instability," their procedure and their data no longer reflect this intermediate condition. Their coerciveness variable taps some of the aspects of GURR's theoretical rationale, but, in general, GURR has provided for much better integration of his various subtheories. The FEIERABENDs basically use bivariate theoretical reasoning, their occasional attempt at multivariate analysis notwithstanding. It is the mediating conditions which contribute to GURR's fascinating studies, whereas most of the theoretical ideas in the FEIERABEND studies are simpler in nature (though not necessarily wrong; however, many more controls are necessary). In studying their work, we learn little of how protest potentials are mediated so that they may lead to protest behavior, are subverted to other activities or even suppressed. Strictly speaking, we do not know about these processes from GURR's studies either. Yet in his studies the context wherein political violence takes place is more closely described than in the works of the FEIERABENDs.

As in GURR's analysis, state violence is largely excluded from the study, even if the definition of systemic aggression would allow for a separation of the categories (according to FEIERABEND/FEIERABEND 1973:198, a new data bank along these and other lines is currently being built up). However, considering the concept of systemic frustration and its alleged relation to systemic aggression, one may argue that political violence against state institutions rather than political violence in general was the universe of discourse. The labels chosen for the dependent variable vary from "turmoil" (being more comprehensive than the term as used in chapter 5.1.1.1.2.3) to "systemic aggression" to "political instability," though the measures remain the same. In chapter 6 there will be a more detailed discussion of whether a term like "political instability" is appropriate when political violence is occurring. For reasons given passim, it is not. Moreover, political violence could even be an indicator of the legitimacy of the political system, in the sense that *milder* forms of political violence may focus the attention of the public on social problems. In the event that these problems are solved, long-term stability of the political system may result. (This statement does not, of course, imply a functional relationship between political violence and long-term stability).

A comparison of the dependent variables in GURR's study (political violence scores of nations) and in the analysis of the FEIERABENDs (using national instability profiles) leads to an r=.7 (FEIERABEND/FEIERABEND/ NESVOLD 1969:682). This degree of overlapping may come as a surprise, since the categories of the dependent variables were differently chosen in the two studies. (Consequently, GURR/DUVALL, forthcoming, object to comparing their measures of *properties* of conflict with mere event counts which, furthermore, are not very reliable, especially in the case of protests.) The FEIERABENDs conceive of the dependent variable as one-dimensional, whereas GURR uses various groupings of the dependent variable, some of which are based on factor analytic studies (cf. Table 5.1). Given the current limited knowledge of the interrelationships among various forms of political violence, it may be a more useful strategy to use separate measures of the dependent variable(s) than to rely on one general theoretical explanation for a broad range of dependent variables. ADAMS gives an example illustrating the confusion likely to arise in the latter case: "A country having no events other than five years of guerrilla warfare would have an instability score of 420, while a country having four small demonstrations per year for five years and one week of guerrilla warfare would have a score of 424" (ADAMS 1970:28). (The FEIERABENDs themselves break down their dependent variable to see whether relationships are stable; cf. the tables in FEIERA-BEND/FEIERABEND/NESVOLD 1969:684–85; cf. also NESVOLD 1969).

To return to the basic criticism, there is no integrated theory in the works of the FEIERABENDs. Rather, they rely on rudimentary explanatory mechanisms borrowed from psychology (frustration-aggression nexus and learning principles) which are not, however, elaborated as far as an interdependent theoretical structure is concerned. The fascination of GURR's and HIBBS's studies stems partly from the fact that several plausible bivariate relationships (not unlike those of the FEIERABENDs) change considerably and often unexpectedly when control variables are introduced. The FEIERA-BENDs, however, make almost no use of such measures as grouping nations to control at least some of the variance.[82] Considering the full range of GURR's background and intermediating variables[83] and HIBBS's elaborate causal model (see chapter 5.1.1.3), the limits of the FEIERABENDs' approach become apparent. However, the greater time span covered in their data collection does give them some advantage over GURR (though his sample is larger).[84] In short, the FEIERABENDs deserve full credit as pioneers in cross-national research on political violence, but their work also suffers from a number of drawbacks which should not be overlooked.

If one compares some of the independent variables in GURR's studies with those of the FEIERABENDs, another interesting difference emerges. Although both have a similar background conceptualization (i.e., the notion of a discrepancy between aspirations and real possibilities, or between demands and capabilities), there are clear divergences on the operational level. Due to the ceiling character of many of their indicators, the operationalizations of the FEIERABENDs may be more useful for modernizing (transitional) countries where political and social mobilization has not yet reached the ceiling, whereas GURR's measures contain many more references to short-term and long-term changes in "money affairs," obviously indicators without ceiling character. His measures show sufficient variability to be more applicable on a universal basis than are the modernization indicators of the FEIERABEND group. In part, of course, this is still an open question calling for further systematic comparisons of indicators chosen. Moreover, the FEIERABENDs' indicators (or more precisely, the frustration index formed from these indicators) are probably of limited use even in transitional societies, as the following rigorous argument makes clear:

> There are a number of such "frustration ratios" which might emerge from reconstruction of the FEIERABENDs' study and their Table 4 [1966:260] indicates that any ratio constructed with two of their indicators in the numerator and six in the denominator would yield a significant relationship of independent to dependent variables. This leads us to doubt that the FEIERABENDs' findings show anything about the relation of frustration to instability at all. Instead the findings are probably an artifact of their rather loose speculative association of economic and social indicators with psycho-cultural concepts, and of the consistent relationships between developmental (modernity) indicators and instability (low modernity, high instability) they find throughout their study. . . . For clearly what they are involved in is no more than speculation which reinterprets economic and social indicators in psycho-cultural terms and here the speculation is, if anything, even more free-wheeling than their first associations of literacy, urbanization, etc., with want formation or want satisfaction. Their study, in short, shows empirical relationships between economic and social indicators and political instability measures. Their attempt to infer from such relationships a relation between frustration and instability fails because their model connecting frustration to their empirical indicator is only vaguely outlined and hence is unpersuasive (CHADWICK/FIRESTONE 1972:25).

5.1.1.3. The Study of "Mass Political Violence" (HIBBS)

Apart from the study of GURR/DUVALL (1973), HIBBS's analysis of mass political violence is the most elaborate study to date in research on political violence. In contrast to GURR, HIBBS does not start from a complex theoretical model. Instead he makes use of various partial theories which are often tested in several variants. His "eclectic and incremental model specification" (HIBBS 1973:3) strategy leads to some important results, only a few of which can be discussed here. In this chapter we will focus on HIBBS's final causal model of mass political violence. HIBBS uses the event data collection of the second edition of the *World Handbook of Political and Social Indi-*

cators (TAYLOR/HUDSON 1972), probably the most comprehensive data collection on political violence that has been published. He draws on a number of other sources as well. The sample comprises 108 nations. The period of investigation is divided into two parts, 1948-57 (D 1) and 1958-67 (D 2), allowing for specification of time-lagged effects. The dependent variable, mass political violence, denotes violent activities which are (1) aimed *against the system*, (2) *political*, and (3) *collective* in nature. ("An exception . . . is the inclusion of assassinations, which typically are not actually carried out by collectivities, but frequently are sponsored by dis- affected groups," HIBBS 1973:7). On the basis of factor analysis (cf. chapter 5.1.1.1.2.1) the dependent variable is divided into "Collective Protest" ("Riots, Antigovernment Demonstrations, Political Strikes") and "Internal War" ("Assassinations, Armed Attacks, Deaths").[85] In addition, coups d'état and government repression ("Negative Sanctions") are included as dependent variables. Coups are separated from the factor analysis, because they represent elite activities and not mass activities as do the other variables.

HIBBS first specifies a number of exogenous and endogenous variables whose theoretical importance is derived from various partial theories and occasional empirical evidence. We will discuss some of these important results in subsequent chapters. In his final causal model he distinguishes between simultaneously determined block variables (the "final" dependent variables), endogenous and lagged endogenous variables, and exogenous variables. "Equations are arrayed in functional sectors or 'blocks' that can be isolated for estimation purposes—all cross-sector causal influences are unidirectional (recursive) and all simultaneous (nonrecursive) relationships and feedback loops operate within blocks" (HIBBS 1973:135–36). Like GURR/DUVALL, HIBBS makes use of two-stage least square procedures to obtain consistent parameter estimates. In Figure 5.4 the four final dependent variables have been framed.

Starting with the relationships among the four simultaneously determined dependent variables, the following conclusions are reached: collective protest is more likely (p=.483; all coefficients are paths coefficients) to lead to nega- tive sanctions than is internal war (.182). Negative sanctions (including "acts of censorship against mass media, political publications . . . as well as restrictions on the political activity and participation of the general public, or specific persons, parties, and organizations," HIBBS 1973:89) may not be a promising device in the case of internal war where some of the elites have defected already. Incumbent elites may weaken their own position even more when applying negative sanctions. Another explanation may be that the measures employed do not adequately consider the reactions of elites in situations of internal wars. HIBBS himself mentions the possibility that in cases of internal war the elites react by employing military means of coercion.

Within the block of simultaneously determined variables, two causal sequences deserve special attention. The path from collective protest through negative sanctions to internal war is more important than the reverse path. Depending on the reactions of the elites, collective protests may lead to a stronger form of political violence,[86] i.e., internal war. Considering the

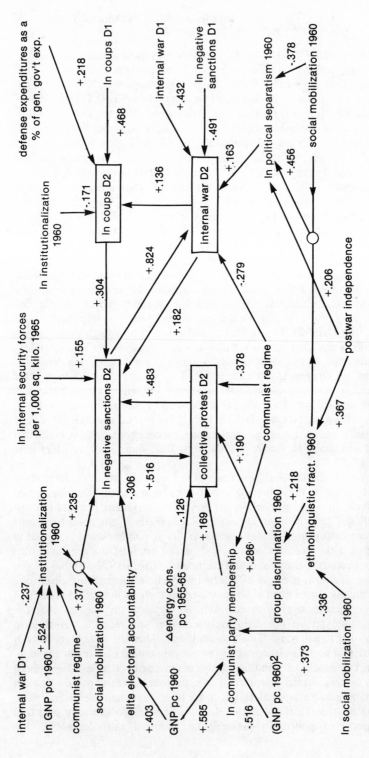

Figure 5.4. HIBBS's Final Causal Model of Mass Political Violence (O represents an interaction term)

Source: HIBBS (1973:181)

other three final dependent variables and omitting collective protest for a moment, there is clear evidence for HUNTINGTON's hypotheses on the determinants and impact on "praetorian polities": Negative Sanctions on behalf of the elites strongly increase (.824) the likelihood of internal war. This leads to coups (.136) and in turn to negative sanctions (.304) of the new elites (on this sequence cf. also the study of BWY 1968a and chapter 7). Both causal paths could also be combined. Thus, collective protest leads to negative sanctions which increase the likelihood of internal war, etc. (cf. also the evidence in LICHBACH/GURR 1980 who, however, use lagged measures; period: 1961-70). Since the path coefficients are smaller than unity, these loops are nonexplosive in nature.

One should, of course, be aware of the fact that these causal sequences are highly inferential in nature, as HIBBS has only cross-sectional data and no time series data available. Considering the inhibiting conditions, negative sanctions D 1 (i.e., in the prior period) is of primary importance (-.491) for internal war. Thus, the *short-term* effect of political repression (negative sanctions) on behalf of the elites may be an *increase in political violence*. In the *long run*, however, there is a greater probability of a *mitigating effect*.[87] On the other hand, in the case of the dependent variable collective protest there is no such dampening effect. "These findings firmly support the proposition that 'organized' and purposeful kinds of mass violence are more easily discouraged by sustained repression than are 'spontaneous' and nonpurposeful expressions of discontent" (HIBBS 1973:185). This interpretation is consistent with several other results (but cf. note 87 in this chapter; see BWY 1968a for the reverse rationale; cf. also chapter 5.1.2.5).

The second most important inhibiting influence works through a communist regime (.-378 on collective protest and .-279 on internal war). HIBBS interprets these results by referring to the police-state climate in communist countries. (However, his measures are quite indirect as to this point.) Another variable inhibiting collective protest (-.126) is "rate of change in energy consumption per capita" (1955–65). Yet, this variable, being in part shorthand for rate of economic development, has no comparable influence on internal war.

Elite electoral accountability also has a negative effect on collective protest. Assuming that elections are a means of controlling elites in democratic societies, there is at least an indirect effect (working through less negative sanctions, -.306) by which democratic political conditions lead to a reduction in the amount of political violence. Institutionalization ("Direct Taxes as a Percentage of General Government Revenue, 1960; Age in Decades of Present National Institutional Form, through 1968; Union Membership as a Percentage of the Nonagricultural Work Force, 1960; General Government Expenditures as a Percentage of the Gross Domestic Product, 1960; Age of the Largest Political Party Divided by the Number of Parties, circa 1965;[88] and the Age of the Largest Political Party, 1965," HIBBS 1973:99) acts to inhibit (-.171) coups. When using institutionalization in interaction with other explicative variables, more complex relationships emerge. If social mobilization ("Population in Cities of 100,000 or more residents per 1000 population [1965]; Economically Active Males in Nonagricultural Occupations per 1000 population [1960]; Newspaper Circulation per 1000 population [1960]; Radios per 1000 population [1966]; and Literacy per 1000 adults [1960]," ibid., pp. 56–57) is larger than institutionalization, a condition of major importance in HUNTINGTON's theory (see chapter 5.1.2.4), this structural imbalance increases the probability of negative sanctions (.235) and, in turn, the likelihood of both forms of political violence. "This suggests that in nations where the burdens generated by social mobilization outrun the capabilities of sociopolitical institutions, political elites tend to resort to repression as an alternative means of social control" (HIBBS 1973: 187).

An analysis of some of the "second-removed effects," reveals the following results: GNP per capita shows a positive relationship (.403) to elite electoral accountability (lending some credit to LIPSET's hypothesis linking economic and democratic political development, cf. chapter 5.1.2.3) and thus indirectly leads to a reduction in negative sanctions and political violence. A similar effect is found when GNP per capita is related to institutionalization: economically more developed nations have more stable institutions (.524) which impede the likelihood of coups (–.171) and, in combination with a comparatively lower degree of social mobilization, the amount of negative sanctions.

The variable communist regime has a similar indirect influence via institutionalization (.377, but see below for a critical evaluation of this result), whereas there is a negative relationship between internal war 1 and institutionalization (–.237). There is also a direct effect of internal war 1 on internal war in the later period (.432). This provides strong evidence for one of the better established hypotheses in research on political violence: the culture-of-violence thesis (cf. chapter 5.1.1.1 passim and especially GURR/DUVALL 1973, chapter 5.1.1.1.4, where this hypothesis is even stronger in the case of turmoil). There are a number of interesting results as to the determinants of coups also providing support to the culture-of-violence hypothesis; these will be taken up later in chapter 7.2.3.

The last direct effect (.163) on internal war originates in political separatism ("percentage of the population inferred to be 'dissatisfied with the closeness of their political association with the polity of which they are formally members,'" GURR 1966:75, quoted in HIBBS 1973:74) which, in turn, is influenced by postwar independence (.206). "This result indicates that recently independent ex-colonies, whose national boundaries were often determined by European imperialists without regard for ethnolinguistic or cultural composition, have higher separatism than one would otherwise anticipate [cf. also chapter 5.1.2.6]. What this [p=.367 between postwar independence and ethnolinguistic fractionalization] suggests is that the legacy of European imperialism has indirectly promoted Internal War through its effect on differentiation as well as through its impact on subsequent separatism" (HIBBS 1973:191; cf. also GEERTZ 1963). The strong influence of the interaction term *ethnolinguistic fractionalization* ("derived from data reported in the authoritative *Atlas Narodov Mira* on the numbers of people in distinctive cultural, ethnic, and linguistic groups. . . . the larger the number of groups and the smaller the proportion of the total population in each of them, the more fractionated or differentiated is the population," HIBBS 1973:68) x *social mobilization* is especially noteworthy (.456), thus strongly supporting DEUTSCH's contention (see chapter 5.1.2.4) that mobilized and differentiated segments of the population are most likely to constitute protest potentials.[89] There is additional evidence for the DEUTSCH rationale since social mobilization alone has a negative impact on political separatism (-.378). Social mobilization by itself seems to lead to more integration (note also the negative path to ethnolinguistic fractionalization, -.336), whereas mobilization *and* retained differentiation lead to more disruptions.

Finally, the other determinants of collective protest, group discrimination (.190) and communist party membership (.169), both have a positive effect. The discrimination of population segments ("the percentage of the population 'which is substantially and systematically excluded from valued economic, political, or social positions because of ethnic, religious, linguistic, or regional characteristics,'" GURR 1966:71, quoted in HIBBS 1973:74) thus leads to milder forms of violent protests. Depending on the elites' reactions to these protests (i.e., the degree of negative sanctions), more violent protests may or may not arise. If political separatism is involved, however, the likelihood is much greater that more intense forms of political violence (internal war) will occur.

The "double meaning" of social mobilization (in the sense of having positive or negative influences on other variables in the causal model) appears again as it shows a positive relationship to communist party membership (.373) but a negative one to cultural differentiation. There is no other explicative variable in this type of research on political violence whose causal influences are so diverse.

Another interesting independent variable is economic development which leads to a reduction in political violence (through the effects on elite electoral accountability and institutionalization). There is, however, a curvilinear relationship between this explanatory variable and communist party membership which in itself has a positive impact on collective violence (.169).[90]

The variance explained is, on the average, around .5, but considerably lower (or much too low) in the cases of elite electoral accountability (.163) and group discrimination (.047). (HIBBS, however, is more interested in finding consistent parameter estimations than in maximizing explained variance.) He reports that the various analyses of residuals, the deviations from the predicted scores of collective protest and internal war, provide no evidence as to systematic errors.

Since the merits of HIBBS's sophisticated approach are apparent even in this sketch of his results, we will concentrate on other aspects neglected in his study. HIBBS points out that socioeconomic inequality may be an important causal variable (see chapter 5.1.2.7) omitted from his equations. Furthermore, he mentions having neglected external interference (in political and economic terms) in internal conflict. Judging from the results of GURR/

DUVALL (1973), this is a serious shortcoming (cf. also chapter 5.1.2.6). Moreover, in several cases endogenous variables are not sufficiently specified. HIBBS aims first at finding determinants of political violence; thus these background determinants are only of secondary importance to him. The most serious weakness, however, stems from his use of essentially cross-sectional data (even if several lags are incorporated into the measures) for testing causal statements. As time series data were not at hand, this procedure was the only viable alternative. In some cases the use of cross-sectional data may even be justified. "Short-duration time series simply cannot pick up the effects of such variables as regime type, levels of institutionalization, cultural differentiation, and democratization. These variables, which have important effects on levels of mass political violence, do not change much in the short run; and without variance, estimation precision and causal inference are not feasible" (HIBBS 1973:201). Yet, the argument does not always hold, e.g., in the case of the relationships between collective protests and negative sanctions. Here we are interested in *event coercion data* (and reciprocal reactions) which were not available.

If one examines in detail the rationale for some of the variables, several questions remain. We doubt, for instance, that the measures of the welfare level or of the degree of institutionalization are directly applicable to communist states. (HIBBS actually adds a positive dummy term for communist regime, but this is not the point here.) In these countries the indicators of institutionalization (see above) may perhaps be better used for indexing totalitarianism. One might also wonder why "political authorities" should be "less inclined to apply 'Negative Sanctions' just because the Left has significant legislative political representation." As it turns out, they are not less inclined to do so (HIBBS 1973:163).[91] Even if the degree of prediction in some of these dubious cases is sufficient, we maintain that there are marked changes involved if the same indicators and the same rationale are used in very different contexts. Furthermore, at various points indexes are formed by additive combinations (means) of various indicators without sufficiently demonstrating that this theoretical assumption is empirically justified. At least there is no such evidence in HIBBS's book.[92]

Comparing the HIBBS study with those of GURR (and leaving the more rudimentary studies of the FEIERABEND group aside), interesting differences emerge. Many of HIBBS's statements unambiguously refer to macro-structures and not to the behavior or reactions of groups, etc. HIBBS does not use indexes as complex as those in GURR's works.[93] His theoretical interpretations are therefore much more easily comprehensible than those of GURR on the basis of his "conglomerate" theoretical variables. HIBBS's strategy of incremental model specification allows him to test for various partial theories (which, to a lesser degree, also holds true for GURR; cf. GURR et al., forthcoming). On the other hand, one is impressed by the strong and successful deductive reasoning found in GURR's works; his major weakness, however, is that, on the empirical level, there are too many, often too divergent, aspects subsumed under too few theoretical concepts. It is interesting to note that GURR/DUVALL, apart from incorporating some new variables, have reconstructed GURR's theoretical model in order to be more explicit on causal effects of specific theoretically important variables. HIBBS's strategy, on the other hand, clearly demonstrates how various partial theories (e.g., HUNTINGTON's hypotheses as well as DEUTSCH's social mobilization hypotheses) to explain political violence can be integrated and also more *precisely* (but cf. also chapter 5.1.2.4) tested than GURR's much more complex theoretical variables. In general, however, one is impressed by the convergence of theoretical reasoning found in the two works. Even if there are many differences in specific relationships, the overall picture leaves the reader with the impression that there is a basic consensus about those variables on the aggregate and/or global level that are important if phenomena of political violence are to be explained.

Finally, HIBBS reports that his dependent variables, collective protest D 2 and internal war D 2, intercorrelate to a considerable degree (r=.63), yet he does not pretend to have a theoretical explanation for this. Here as in almost all other works on political violence, we do not find an answer to the important question of how various forms of political violence are *causally* related to each other (even if HIBBS can point to some suggestive results, such as the causal loops between different forms of political violence; see Figure 5.4). However, his cross-sectional data are not sufficient to reach any direct conclusions as to causal relationships between various forms of political violence.[94] We have considerable evidence as to the long-term effects of political violence on further political violence (cf. the culture-of-violence hypothesis and also chapter 5.1.2.8), but hardly any systematic knowledge[95] as to sequences likely to exist in the short run (i.e., how often which form of political violence produces, substitutes, or merely precedes which other form of political violence).

Having considered the works of three pioneers in cross-national research of political violence in greater detail, the following sections will be much briefer. We shall focus on a number of bivariate and multivariate relationships between theoretically important variables and various forms of political violence. At the same time, there will be a discussion of some alternative theoretical approaches to the study of political violence.

5.1.2. Some Bivariate and Multivariate Determinants of Political Violence

Throughout this study a number of results bearing upon the relationships discussed here have been reported. In general, these results will not be repeated. In this section we try to give a somewhat more systematic (though not necessarily comprehensive) evaluation of the impact of some key variables in cross-national research on political violence. Throughout the following paragraphs the reader should keep in mind the difference between mere correlations and causal relationships. Unfortunately, at times it will be difficult to draw a line between suggestive correlations and causal relationships, especially since multivariate evidence is often lacking. Thus, when we speak of determinants in this study, we do so only with the usual reservations as to probabilistic statements in social science.

5.1.2.1. Socioeconomic Development and Political Violence

In background theory one of the most important determinants of political violence is socioeconomic development. There are, however, a number of results which partly contradict each other and render simple predictions derived from modernization theories incorrect or insufficient. Most researchers treat socioeconomic development and change as a whole and do not distinguish between the social and economic aspects which are often interrelated and therefore difficult to disentangle. However, for theoretical reasons (cf. the approach of HUNTINGTON in chapter 5.1.2.4), one should distinguish between the two aspects, as in separating socioeconomic development and change from political development and change; (cf. chapter 5.1.2.3).

One could easily cite a long list of authors, ARISTOTLE being one of the first, who relate socioeconomic development to political stability (cf. LIPSET 1960; CUTRIGHT 1963; McCRONE/CNUDDE 1967; NEUBAUER 1967; PRIDE 1970; HURWITZ 1971; FLANIGAN/FOGELMAN 1971a, 1971b; CNUDDE 1972). There is considerable empirical evidence from various samples, periods, and indicators that "modern" nations (cf. chapter 5.1.1.2.1) tend to have less political violence than do underdeveloped countries. There are, however, several partly modern countries with widespread political violence, but in general the violence is less intense (in terms of the recent analyses of GURR et al., forthcoming: "protest" rather than "rebellion") than that in underdeveloped areas. In simplest terms, poverty is often considered a cause of political instability and political violence, or, as Napoleon put it, "C'est le ventre, quit fait les révolutions." BANKS (1972:48-49) reports (N=51 nations) that "nonrevolutionary" states (which cluster on a factorial dimension) show moderately high correlations with various indicators of economic development $(.4 < r < .6)$, whereas "revolutionary" states load negatively on these variables $(-.3 > r > -.8)$. TANTER (1965:175) finds (N=70 nations; 1955-60) moderately negative correlations between GNP per capita and various conflict variables (with the exception of demonstrations). Comparable results can be found in TERRELL (1971:337; N=68), PARVIN (1973; N=26); FEIERABEND/FEIERABEND/NESVOLD (1969:684-85; N=68; but see also VON DER MEHDEN 1973 for a subsample of 40 nations of the FEIERABENDs' collection, years: 1960-65, and considerably different results) and ALKER/RUSSETT (1964:272, 288, 307; N=74). Contrary to some of GURR's earlier results, GURR et al. (forthcoming) report significant negative relationships between GNP per capita and their five political violence variables. "Per capita GNP has a weaker, -.42 correlation with mandays of conflict, which is consistent with our observation that wealth helps transform civil conflict—by making it less deadly [$r=-.55$ with conflict deaths per 10 million in 1961-65]—but is not so likely to reduce its extent"

(GURR 1979:62). Studying political and economic development in sixty-five nations from 1800 to 1960, FLANIGAN/FOGELMAN (1970) report the following result, after grouping their countries into four types according to the level of development and period of the developmental process: "countries which began their development relatively early and have reached high levels of development by the mid-twentieth century are less likely to experience domestic violence than those which have been developing only in the current century; and both groups of countries experience less violence than countries which began to develop only recently" (FLANIGAN/FOGELMAN 1970:14).

More differentiated results are found in a study by ADAMS (1970). He uses a much larger sample (N=130 countries) and reports a curvilinear relationship[96] between GNP per capita in the early 1960s and the extent of political violence during the period 1946-65. When more closely examining the seventy-one least-developed countries, a negative linear relationship is found when the Asian and Arabian countries ("poor but relatively deprived") are analyzed together with the developed countries, and a positive relationship is generally found in African countries (characterized as "poor and unaware" in GURR 1972b:37-38).

Thus, there is evidence for a negative relationship between socioeconomic development and political violence as well as for a curvilinear relationship (with a negative sign; see ALKER/RUSSETT 1964:307). As the "traditional" end of the modernity continuum is often insufficiently defined in these studies (cf. chapter 5.1.1.2.1), some of these results may be artifacts. Testing for various possible relationships between socioeconomic development and political violence, HIBBS found some evidence for a weak curvilinear relationship: "societies at middle ranges of economic development [measured through energy consumption per capita] typically experience slightly greater magnitudes of Collective Protest and Internal War than those at low or high development levels" (HIBBS 1972:28, 31). This result seems to be consistent with those of GURR/RUTTENBERG (1967:66-68; N=119 nations, period: 1961-63) and the speculations of the FEIERABENDs. It should be recalled, however, that socioeconomic development (GNP per capita) loses its explanatory power in the multivariate case (cf. the preceding chapter), where it only exerts a positive influence on institutionalization and democratic political conditions (elite electoral accountability), thus contributing quite indirectly to a reduction in the amount of political violence. In other respects, however, it increases the amount of political violence, since communist party membership is stronger in more developed nations (but less strong in the most developed nations, thus supporting the hypothesis of a curvilinear relationship between economic development and communist party strength; see BENJAMIN/KAUTSKY 1968),[97] and this, in turn, correlates directly with the amount of collective protest.[98]

If there is one basic finding in this chapter, it is that economically developed countries, in general, experience less intense forms of political violence. Economically underdeveloped countries are not only characterized by a higher degree of political violence, but also by social immobility and various other forms of strain in GURR's sense (see GURR et al., forthcoming). The relationship between being a poorer nation and having a comparatively greater amount of political violence does not necessarily imply that it is the poorest groups (MARX's "Lumpenproletariat") in these countries which rely on means of political violence. Furthermore, within poorer nations acts of political violence may very well occur in the more prosperous regions (for some evidence see HUNTINGTON 1968:44ff.).[99] Once again, one must avoid the danger of group fallacy (on the national, regional, or other levels) so easily subscribed to in interpretations of cross-national research.

5.1.2.2. Socioeconomic Change and Political Violence

There are a number of hypotheses linking different facets of socioeconomic change with political violence. OLSON (1963), for example, proposes the hypothesis that rapid economic change leads to a "social dislocation" which, in turn, creates alienation and a susceptibility to political radicalism in large portions of the population (cf. KORNHAUSER 1959; FROMM 1955; HOFFER 1951; LEDERER 1940; for a critique cf. GUSFIELD 1962; PINARD 1968).

Yet, a number of recent—not necessarily representative—studies, bearing on the effects of migration and urbanization and thus indirectly on alienation theory, lead NELSON to the following conclusion: "The assumptions that migrants are uprooted and isolated in the city are grossly overdrawn. The assumption that most are disappointed and frustrated by economic conditions is simply wrong. Some migrants undoubtedly are disillusioned, but lack of widespread contacts plus political inexperience and traditional patterns of deference makes it most unlikely that newcomers' frustrations will be translated into destabilizing political action" (NELSON 1970:399; see also NELSON 1969 and 1976 for a manifold picture drawing on examples from many developing countries; CORNELIUS 1969, 1971 with detailed results from Latin America, 1973, 1974; finally cf. WEINER 1967; OBERSCHALL 1969, and chapter 5.1.1.2.1). In the context of rapid urbanization, two causal processes are expected to work (cf. also TILLY 1973a:103), each increasing the likelihood of conflicts: the new environment would mean austerity for the newly arrived. It calls for increased discipline, thus breeding discontent; in addition, it creates a higher level of aspirations than can be realized due to contacts with the mass media and more modern social groups.

The first hypothesis cannot be supported with the data currently available. The "revolver approach" (WHITE 1973:49, following PYE) must be replaced by the notion of the "supportive migrant" who is more interested in finding out about his new environment and adjusting to it than he is willing or able to command the resources necessary to carry out political protest.[100] If political violence is to occur in mobilized segments of the population, it may be expected more from the second or later generations[101] of migrants who have been "mobilized" but remain "differentiated," in DEUTSCH's terminology (see chapter 5.1.2.4). There is more evidence for the latter argument (but cf. also NELSON 1969:35–44; CORNELIUS 1971:107-8 for some counterevidence) than for the more popular and stereotypic urbanization → alienation → radicalization hypothesis[102] (see chapter 5.3.2). A more detailed analysis, however, suggests that the following qualifications be made:

> While the historical evidence from Europe and North America lends considerable support to this 'second generation' hypothesis, it has not as yet been confirmed by evidence from the contemporary Third World cities. Indeed, in some respects, the slight evidence available tends to call the theory into question or to demand its qualification. CORNELIUS' work on Mexico City shows the second generation to have higher levels of political knowledge and awareness than the first. . . . But they also 'participate in politics significantly less than their parents.'[103] . . . A common sequence, particularly for Latin America, is as follows: *first*, mobility in the form of urban migration; *second*, for those migrants who become squatters—organization in the form of neighborhood associations to secure home ownership and urban services; *third*, mobility in the form of search for more skilled and higher paying jobs; *fourth*, possibly—if middle-class mobility is blocked—organization in the form of working-class unions, parties partially oriented to working-class problems, or populist movements. Where many migrants are temporary, as in Africa and parts of Asia, different patterns will appear, particularly in the first and second phases. And where politics is organized largely on communal lines, issues and loyalties are likely to cut across both urban-rural boundaries and class differences, so that the categories of peasant, migrant, and worker are less likely to provide a basis for collective political action, although there may still be a salient interplay of opportunities for mobility and collective organiation (HUNTINGTON/NELSON 1976:111, 113).

Thus, even the second generation hypothesis might prove to be a gross simplification of reality. "In those countries where urban participation rates are higher, the apparent direct relationship is spurious, a result of differences in education and occupation. When these factors are held constant, locality, size and length of urban residence appear to have no significant independent effect on political participation" (ibid., p. 47, drawing on results of the six-nation study of INKELES 1969). In any case, this is one of the central areas in modernization theory where much more research is needed.

Any kind of monocausal approach leads to questionable interpretations of socioeconomic and political modernization processes (cf. chapter 5.1.1.2.1). There are several conditions that must be specified if it is to be proven that rapid socioeconomic change leads to political violence or to political instability. A number of empirical results refute the idea that rapid socioeconomic change would directly lead to such violence and instability. TANTER/MIDLARSKY (1967) found a negative relationship[104] between economic growth rate (GNP per capita) and "revolutions" (for a critique of this study, see chapter 8.4.6.2) in four Latin American countries (period:

1955–60), whereas a positive relationship emerges for ten countries in the Near East and Asia. For more prosperous Latin American countries, BWY (1968b:46–47) reports a negative relationship between the rate of economic growth (GNP per capita, 1950–59) and his two dependent variables: "organized" (r=−.63) and "anomic" (−.33) violence (both for 1958–60). In countries at a lower level of economic development, however, this relationship is reversed. FLANIGAN/FOGELMAN (1970) find a negative relationship between rate of economic development ("rates of change in agricultural employment in the twentieth century") and political violence, as do ALKER/ RUSSETT (1964:321), using change in GNP per capita as one of the independent variables. Actually, it proved to be the strongest predictor (in a multivariate analysis as well) of "deaths from domestic group violence" (N=33). However, it should be recalled from chapter 5.1.1.2.3 that FEIERABEND/FEIERABEND/NESVOLD (1969) reported a linear correlation (r=.67) between their rate of modernization measure and political instability, with the notable exception of national income. HIBBS (1973) found a weak negative relationship between rate of economic change (change in energy consumption per capita, 1955–65) and political violence, but only in the case of collective protest (this relationship also holds in HIBBS's multivariate analysis; see Figure 5.4).

When using rate of change of urbanization ("% change in population in cities of 20,000 or more residents per 1000 population 1955–1960," HIBBS 1973:37) as the independent variable, contrary to much speculation no "significant" relationships emerge (N=58). Thus, there is no consistent positive or negative relationship between rapid urbanization and political violence on the nation level or on the group level. TILLY (who studied the relationship between urbanization processes and political violence in nineteenth-century France) also provides evidence against the urbanization → alienation → radicalization hypothesis. "There is, if anything, a negative correlation over time and space between the pace of urban growth and the intensity of collective violence" (TILLY 1969:33; cf. chapter 8.4.6.6.1).[105] GURR et al. (forthcoming) found significant positive relationships between the growth of the total population and the growth rate of the urban population (both for 1950–60) and their various dependent variables. After controlling for geocultural areas, however, somewhat inconsistent patterns emerge. There is evidence for a negative (yet insignificant) relationship between new city dwellers (1950–60) and political violence (except for the Euro-modern countries). Nevertheless, there may be some truth in the proposed relationship between rapid urbanization and political violence: in some cities, possibly those with relatively fewer resources, there may be an effect on political violence, whereas in more affluent cities no relationship or even a negative one may emerge, pointing to the integrative power of these cities. Once again, additional variables will have to be introduced into the analysis.

In HIBBS's study, population growth (average annual percent change in population, 1955–65), which normally, due to still high levels of birth rates but lowered death rates (see DEUTSCH 1974:539 for some data), takes place at an intermediate level of socioeconomic development, also proves to be a positive and significant determinant of both collective protest and internal war. In the final model specification processes, however, it no longer provides an adequate explanation. Nevertheless, in some countries a high rate of population growth could be a variable with impact on political violence. Better data on how population growth actually affects the resources of people must be collected.[106] For instance, in animal research there are numerous studies on the effects of crowding, whereas we know of only one cross-national study where the impact of crowding on political violence has been studied. Using various measures of crowding conditions and studying their relationship to two forms of political violence (GURR data for 1961-63; N=65 nations) WELCH/BOOTH report the following result: "After entering industrialization, urbanization, discrimination and security forces, crowding accounted for 14 percent of the variance in the incidence of civil disorder and 19 percent of the variance in whether or not there were casualties as a result of disorder. People per room accounts for the bulk of the variation in civil aggression. This variable is strongly related to both incidence and intensity of political violence" (WELCH/BOOTH 1974:155). The authors are, of course, aware that data at the individual level will have to be collected, especially as to how objective crowding conditions (i.e., spatial density) are reacted to socially, before any definite judgement about the impact of this variable can be made. We would assume that cultural regulations[107] play an important part if objectively defined crowding conditions emerge as subjective conditions contributing to political violence (cf. also STOKOLS 1976:50). There is also some highly suggestive evidence from a study by SPILERMAN (1970; see chapter 5.3.2.4) who reports that the absolute number of blacks in a city is the best ecological predictor of the riots of American blacks in the 1960s.[108]

Another popular hypothesis as to the effects of rapid socioeconomic change links increases in mass media exposure and education with instability. Some authors, however, such as GURR (1968a:1110 and GURR/ RUTTENBERG 1967:76 with some empirical findings contradicting their original assumption ibid. on p. 58), postulate a negative relationship between educational opportunities and political violence. Interestingly, sometimes the same indicators are used to index conflicting theoretical notions. We shall deal first with the alleged effects of increased mass media exposure.

It has often been stated that modernization starts with communication processes (in the widest sense, not in terms of the various "LERNER models"). "In the oral, traditional society the provisions for wide-horizon communication are inefficient: the traveler and ballad singer come too seldom and know too little. A modernizing of society requires mass media" (SCHRAMM 1963:38; also quoted in ROGERS 1969:96). Others, especially LERNER (see chapter 5.1.1.2.1), attribute a certain regularity to these communication processes. "The regularity is structural in the sense that it is built into any situation where communication *leads* development. This is because communication, especially via the mass media, accelerates rising expectations and multiplies consumer wants. Where communication leads in the formation of modernizing attitudes, as it now does everywhere, expectations are bound to outrun satisfactions and wants are bound to exceed gets. The communication nexus tends regularly to disequilibrate development by producing highly imbalanced want: get ratios that result in widening, ultimately disruptive and even revolutionary, frustration" (LERNER 1969:190-91).[109] Or, as HUNTINGTON puts it: "Urbanization, increases in literacy, education, and media exposure all give rise to enhanced aspirations and expectations which, if unsatisfied, galvanize individuals and groups into politics" (HUNTINGTON 1968:47).

The empirical evidence as to the effects of mass media exposure, however, is inconclusive. PARVIN (1973), for example, reports a positive relationship between the number of radios per capita and political violence (N=26 countries). TAYLOR (1969; N=117), on the other hand, found no relationships (except in European countries) between level and rate of communications development (newspaper circulation and radios per 1,000 population, ca. 1960, rates of change 1960-65) and the dependent variables turmoil, internal war (data from *World Handbook of Political and Social Indicators*, TAYLOR/ HUDSON 1972, ca. 1958-65) and political stability (defined in terms of changes of government). In the case of the European countries, there are negative ($\gamma \approx$ -.40, level) as well as positive ($\gamma \approx$ .35, rate of change) relationships. GURR et al. (forthcoming) found a negative or negligible relationship between expansion of the mass media (increases in radio audience and in daily newspaper circulation, both for 1953-63 and weighted for population) and political violence.

There is, of course, an important alternative to the hypothesis that increased mass media coverage leads to rising expectations. The rival hypothesis predicts that retreat rather than protest is the more likely reaction to the new stimulus "mass media." "Through the media[110] the masses can retreat into fantasy or a more successful vicarious existence. Rather than being stimulated and then frustrated by the media, the masses are seen to be lethargized and then diverted from more constructive activities" (FREY 1973:387). As of now, cross-national evidence bearing on this rival hypothesis does not seem to be available.

The underlying hypothesis as to the effects of increases in education can be stated as follows: "The expansion in the educational system and the comparatively limited growth in the economy and in the occupational structure ... [lead to] a vast and nearly uncontrollable increase in the number of unemployed and underemployed school leavers, whose political orientation toward the polity is marked by disaffection and alienation, and whose behavioral disposition is basically anomic" (COLEMAN 1968:29). In the forthcoming study of GURR et al., there is evidence for a significant relationship between the expansion in primary school enrollment ratios from the 1930s to 1960, the proportion of males between five and nineteen in primary and secondary schools from 1950 to 1960, and the more violent forms of political conflicts like rebellion, but less evidence when man-days and turmoil are used as dependent variables. For Latin American as well as African countries MORRISON/STEVENSON (1974) report several positive relationships between educational facilities and various indicators of political instability (either indicators of political violence or socioeconomic indicators).[111] Mass media participation and education are also employed in more complex theoretical notions. Yet, once again the evidence is inconclusive (see chapter 5.1.2.4).

Before ending this section two additional hypotheses must be considered briefly. Theorists including Marxists have suggested that an economic downswing (not only economic growth) will cause acts of instability and political violence (as to the nexus with revolution, cf. chapter 8.4). HIBBS, however, found no indication for this contention. GURR/DUVALL (1973), on the other hand, report considerable evidence as to the effects of economic downswings on political violence.

In general, it seems that rapid socioeconomic change cannot be considered an important direct determinant of political violence. Neither the rate of economic growth nor that of economic decline are *consistent* predictors of the dependent variables. This summary conflicts with much that has been written concerning these variables. However, this negative evidence should not be considered to disclaim these hypotheses in toto. Rather, one should look for time series data, for data on the history of specific protesting groups. Moreover, one should concentrate on the intervening conditions (some of which will be considered in chapter 5.1.2.4) between these independent variables and phenomena of political violence.

HUNTINGTON's summary of some aspects of the preceding discussion is suggestive, even if the results listed in the last two sections do not necessarily support his general conclusion. This may, in part, be due to the indicators chosen, to sampling differences, and to the fact that important theoretical links have not yet been specified. The hypothesis is that there are negative relationships between socioeconomic changes and political violence in more developed countries, and positive relationships in less developed countries. These contrarotating processes may have led to many inconclusive overall results as far as relationships between various facets of social change and political violence are concerned. Taking these aspects into consideration, HUNTINGTON's summary remains to be invalidated on a more rigorous basis: "In fact, *modernity breeds stability*, but *modernization breeds instability*. . . . It is not the absence of modernity but the efforts to achieve it which produce political disorder. If poor countries appear to be unstable, it is not because they are poor, but because they are trying to become rich" (HUNTINGTON 1968:41, our italics; cf. also ALKER/RUSSETT 1964:307). HUNTINGTON claims the relationship between poverty and instability on the nation level to be spurious or rather to lead to spurious inferences (HUNTINGTON 1968:39-59). The level of socioeconomic development[112] as well as the degree of stability of political institutions (see chapter 5.1.2.4) must be controlled if more valid conclusions about the impact of socioeconomic change are to be drawn.

HIBBS also fails to find systematic evidence that political violence impedes the rate of economic growth (HIBBS 1973:160). A similar result based on cross-sectional data is reported by FEIERABEND/FEIERABEND/HOWARD (1972; N=76 nations). The use of time series or process data, however, may very well lead to rather different results, namely that there is a reduction of the rate of economic growth as long as political violence persists (for evidence in this direction cf. ADELMAN/MORRIS 1967; 1973; ANDRESKI 1968; HUNTINGTON/DOMÍNGUEZ 1975). Over a longer time span, however, a period of rapid reconstruction might lead to an increase in the rate of growth. In answering this question one must be extremely careful as to the periodization of the dependent and independent variables.

5.1.2.3. Political Development and Political Violence

Since it is much more difficult to define and measure political[113] than socio-economic development, the evidence in this chapter will be less conclusive. However, throughout this study are numerous results as to the effects of political conditions on political violence, one of the most important being that democratic political conditions do not eliminate milder forms of political violence, partly because dissidents can use civil liberties (absent in totalitarian and most of the autocratic systems) to build up their organizations and to carry out their policies.[114] More intense forms of political violence, however, are unlikely to occur in democratic political systems. There is additional evidence for this in the recent study of GURR et al. (forthcoming). Coding procedures more elaborate and more flexible (GURR 1974a) than those previously employed (BANKS/GREGG 1965)[115] reveal significant positive relationships between anocracy[116] and GURR's measures of political violence and insignificant negative relationships between autocratic or democratic political systems and the dependent variables. In the particular country clusters, a less consistent picture emerges. In centralistic autocracies the outbreak of political violence apparently is much more successfully prevented than in any other form of government. On the other hand, anocratic, centristic, and neocolonial regimes provide conditions furthering political violence. However, according to GURR, characteristics of the political authority structure generally seem to have no immediate and more indirect effects on political violence.

The discussion of the "fads and foibles," to use SOROKIN's term, in political development research has many parallels with our critical evaluation of some of the premises in modernization research. There are, in fact, many writers who tend to equate political development and socioeconomic development, although there are strong reasons for separating socioeconomic modernization, political modernization, and political development (see HUNTINGTON's approach in chapter 5.1.2.4). Here we will not repeat in detail the shortcomings already mentioned in chapter 5.1.1.2.1. There is also no space for a discussion of the vast literature on political development. However, a few points should be mentioned.

1. Even though there is some basic consensus as to the meaning of political development (see 2 below), there is little agreement as to its precise definition. After an extensive review of the literature, PYE (1966) lists ten differ-

ent definitions,[117] "at least nine too many," according to RUSTOW (1969a: 1-2, quoted in HUNTINGTON 1971b:303, and also in BILL/HARDGRAVE 1973:66). Other authors come up with various theoretically and empirically derived criteria (e.g., ALMOND/POWELL 1966:105, "the increased differentiation and specialization of political structures and the increased secularization of political culture," or, stated differently, "The significance of such development is in general to increase the effectiveness and efficiency of the performance of the political system: to increase its capabilities," or COLEMAN 1971:74, italics omitted, "the political development process is a continuous interaction among the processes of structural differentiation, the imperatives of equality, and the integrative, responsive, and adaptive capacity of a political system"; see also WARD/RUSTOW 1964:6-7; BLACK 1966: 67-68; HOPKINS 1969:89; DOORNBOS 1969; HUNTINGTON/DOMINGUEZ 1975:53). The definitions of political development often include statements as to the "functions" which it may serve. ALMOND's approach is probably best known (cf. the quotation above and ALMOND 1960:17). Obviously, these are propositions which must be tested in reality (if they are testable at all as stated; cf. the criticism of HEMPEL 1959; see also the general discussion in BILL/HARDGRAVE 1973:212-17).

2. If one were to analyze the vast majority of studies on political development, it would probably be explicitly or implicitly equated with political development as reached in the Western hemisphere (see DENTON 1969 for a critique; cf. also O'BRIEN 1972). Defined in this way, political development would be "identified with one type of political system, rather than a quality which might characterize any type of political system" (HUNTINGTON 1965:389). The conceptual confusion would be reduced only slightly if one were to follow the rule to use political *modernization* to refer to the degree of political development reached in the West and political *development* as a concept not bound by time and space coordinates. In this sense, ancient Athens would have been a politically developed community, but not a politically modern one (cf. BILL/HARDGRAVE 1973:66-83 as well as HUNTINGTON 1968, passim, for a discussion of the various facets of the two concepts).

3. In the vast majority of studies, political development is seen as a product of socioeconomic development processes (see the references below), whereas there are probably reciprocal influences between socioeconomic and political development. (Thus, political development is not merely a cause of socioeconomic development,[118] as theorists including WEINER 1965:63-64 and PACKENHAM 1970:179, seem to maintain in reversing the original hypothesis, but one of its effects as well.) Apparently it was much less difficult to measure socioeconomic development and socioeconomic change. Perhaps this has led researchers to see the prime historical impetus[119] in these socioeconomic processes and not in political decisions or external influences[120] which are often neglected in this body of research.[121] The importance of political variables is underscored in PRIDE's longitudinal study of development processes (ca. 1840-1960 data) in twenty-six nations (two-thirds of them "Western" nations): "First, and most striking, virtually all the

countries which accomplished democratization[122] before significant social change are classified as stable democratic systems in the twentieth century; or to put it in another way, fully eight of the nine countries which became stable democratic regimes in the twentieth century were those that became democratic early in the mobilization phase, before significant social and economic change began. . . . The second striking finding is that where substantial mobilization occurred first the countries became nondemocratic without exception" (PRIDE 1970:703-4; italics omitted here). Studying thirty-six Amer-European and Latin American nations during a period of 102 years (1865-1966), BANKS (1970) also found considerable evidence of political development preceding mobilization (as in the former group of nations), if democratic political systems were to result (but cf. also BOLLEN's 1979 analysis questioning the existence of a relationship between the timing of development and democracy).

There have been various attempts to measure political development. Unfortunately, these efforts have been more successful as far as democratic political development[122a] is concerned, whereas the concept of political development in general has remained rather nebulous. What was to be a universal approach to political development turned out to be a form of Western ethnocentrism.[123] The discussion about CUTRIGHT's scale of political development (1963) being based on LIPSET's fundamental work (1959a) and, in fact, measuring democratic political development rather than political development in general is well-known (cf. SIMPSON 1964; McCRONE/CNUDDE 1967; SMITH 1969; CNUDDE/NEUBAUER 1969; CUTRIGHT/WILEY 1969/70; JACKMAN 1973; THOMAS 1974; but see also NEEDLER 1968 and OLSEN 1968b for some evidence in favor of the LIPSET-CUTRIGHT approach of linking socioeconomic development[124] with political development). Here we concentrate on those studies where aspects of political development (and not necessarily democratic political development) are directly related to political violence.

FLANIGAN/FOGELMAN (1970) report a negative relationship between democracy[125] and political violence on any level and at any rate of economic development. ADAMS (1970:137) also found a negative relationship between political development (using the CUTRIGHT index as a measure; N=75 polities, period: 1946-60) and political violence.

Using elite electoral accountability and electoral turnout as indicators as well as an interaction term of both, HIBBS comes to the conclusion that LIPSET's and other authors' hypotheses linking democracy with stability are not supported. "Democratic nations have nearly as high levels of Collective Protest and Internal War as nondemocratic ones. It appears, then, that democracy conceived as a framework for formal political activity simply does not pacify the behavior of significant segments of the mass public, however well it serves to establish regularized rules and mechanisms . . . through which competing political elites secure public office" (HIBBS 1973:118). When the CUTRIGHT index of political development (N=67) is used, there is, however, a negative relationship between democratic political conditions and political violence,[126] but only in the case of Internal War. Yet, upon controlling for

Energy Consumption per capita (degree of economic development) this relationship disappears.

The impact of communist political systems and of large communist parties in noncommunist countries is summed up by HIBBS as follows: "Communist societies have considerably less violence than non-Communist ones. . . . This deterrence effect of 'totalitarianism' is more effective vis à vis organized Internal War than it is for spontaneous Collective Protest [but see also the final causal model in Figure 5.4]. Sizable Communist parties in non-Communist nations serve to promote mass protest but have no systematic impact on the incidence of Internal War. Large-scale Communist movements are typically 'destabilizing,' but only up to a point"[127] (HIBBS 1973:130-31).

The last result is somewhat contrary to the widespread assumption found in KORNHAUSER (1959:46) and also in GURR's various writings, i.e., that communist organizations are among the primary agents for organizing violent political discontent. GURR et al. (forthcoming) report significant relationships between the size x status of the respective communist parties and their five dependent variables. In other words, whereas the sheer number of communist party members per 10,000 of population is not related to political violence, there is a clear relationship between large, illegal, or suppressed communist parties[128] and political violence. In the case of neocolonial and Latin American nations, however, there are no such relationships. The results for dissident unions' size x status are similar though much less pronounced, Euro-modern countries being the notable exception as there exists a highly significant relationship between this variable and political violence.

More results as to the effects and the determinants of political development will be mentioned in the next section when more complex interrelationships between various independent variables and political violence are discussed.

5.1.2.4. Structural Imbalances and Political Violence

Social scientists are fascinated by explanations of political violence via structural imbalances. The reason for this seems to be that in these explanations one can, indeed, find structural arguments rather than one-variable explanations (which, in any case, are only a first step towards more comprehensive explanations). Of the various structural imbalances considered relevant for the occurrence of political violence, we shall study here only the major ones. HIBBS (1973) discusses a number of other structural imbalances but does not find empirical support for their alleged causal impact on the dependent variables. For example, he found that, in general, neither a higher degree of urbanization (population in cities of 100,000+ residents per 1,000 population 1965) compared to the level of economic development (GNP per capita 1960), nor a level of social mobilization greater than those of governmental performance (nondefense activities as a percentage of gross domestic product 1960) or social welfare[129] (arithmetic mean of infant live births per 1000 births, calories per capita per 10 days; and physicians per million population, all 1960) are strong and consistent predictors of political violence.[130] (Both factors would be expected to lead to discontent of large portions of the population which could manifest itself in political violence.) However, in the study of DUFF/McCAMANT (1976:71, 79, 131; see note 129 for details and some caveats), the explanatory power of a related interaction term is demonstrated several times. Thus, the *rate of increase* in social mobilization correlates consistently with political violence (r between .30 and .44 and, in any case, higher than the level of social mobilization). Economic growth, on the other hand, correlates slightly negatively with political violence, and the excess of economic growth over the increase in social mobilization more negatively (years: 1950-70, r=-.57) with the dependent variable. In a multivariate analysis the latter explanatory variable turns out to be the most important one.

Likewise, the discrepancy between a higher level of education (literacy per 1,000 adults 1960) and a lower degree of economic development does not prove to be a good predictor of political violence. Similarly, SOFRANKO/BEALER (1972) report (N=74 nations) that the imbalance[131] between the educational sector and other societal sectors does not explain political violence (using data of the FEIERABEND group, 1955-61, and of GURR/RUTTENBERG, 1961-63).[132] In specific countries, however, an imbalance between high educational training and low economic opportunities may be a strong predictor of political violence, but apparently not on a cross-national basis.[133]

Thus, on the whole, theoretical notions much cherished in modernization literature (cf. some of the references in past chapters as well as in HIBBS 1973) are not supported[134] when tested on a cross-national basis.

> However, this does not mean that *theoretically*, taken in the abstract sense, such theories are unsound. If it were possible experimentally to manipulate nations so that, for example, there was little correlation between social mobilization and social welfare, then we could observe more satisfactorily the (interactive) effects of the conjunction of high social mobilization, low social welfare, and so on, and thereby draw definitive theoretical conclusions. Yet collinearity is in itself produced by some causal process that is responsible for variables "moving together." Therefore, unless these causal processes were to be disrupted in some fundamental and improbable way, such that the variables became no longer highly correlated, we never need to know the potential consequences of such interaction effects (HIBBS 1973:62-63).

Perhaps there is a less "dramatic" solution to this problem than HIBBS's pessimistic conclusion might suggest: improved measures, instead of the generally rather crude measures of the particular structural imbalance, might lead to more promising tests of these structural explanations, which remain plausible ideas after all.

When using more complex causal models, however, two imbalance terms, which at first failed to show the alleged effect, fare somewhat better. The first is based on a previously mentioned hypothesis of DEUTSCH who differentiates between an "underlying population" (total population minus mobilized population); a "mobilized population," which is more likely to become assimilated to the dominant cultural patterns of the particular community; and a population that is mobilized, yet retains its cultural distinctiveness:

"The share of *mobilized* but *differentiated* persons among the total population . . . is the first crude indicator of the probable incidence and strength of national conflict" (DEUTSCH 1966b:130; italics added). DEUTSCH distinguishes among several dimensions of assimilation: "(1) language; (2) culture; (3) ethnicity with its social associations, organizational memberships and family connections; (4) aspirations; (5) capabilities; (6) attainments; (7) civic compliance; and (8) political loyalties" (DEUTSCH 1974:545). A *simultaneous* assimilation in all of these dimensions, or at least in the more important ones, will be unlikely. Rather "other things assumed equal, the stage of rapid social mobilization may be expected, therefore, to promote the consolidation of states whose peoples already share the same language, culture and major social institutions; while the same process may tend to strain or destroy the unity of states whose population is already divided into several groups with different languages or cultures or basic ways of life" (DEUTSCH (1961:501).[135] "The integrative revolution does not do away with ethnocentrism; it merely modernizes it" (GEERTZ 1963:154). How such processes of assimilation and/or differentiation come into being and how elites and masses at large react to such processes are shown by ARMSTRONG (1976) who uses many instructive examples. At the same time he derives some new hypotheses as to the conditions of equilibrium between elites, population, and "mobilized and proletarian diasporas" (this being the title of his work). Social mobilization thus leads to an increased awareness of one's own cultural identity and at the same time of its distinctiveness from other cultural identities. Referring to Third World countries, GEERTZ expresses these theoretical considerations in the following terms:

> [A large portion of] modern political consciousness . . . takes the form of an obsessive concern with the relation of one's tribe, region, sect, or whatever to a center of power that, while growing rapidly more active, is not easily either insulated from the web of primordial attachments, as was the remote colonial regime, or assimilated to them as were the workaday authority systems of the "little community." Thus, it is the very process of the formation of a sovereign civil state that, among other things, stimulates sentiments of parochialism, communalism, racialism, and so on, because it introduces into society a valuable new prize over which to fight (GEERTZ 1963:120; cf. also BATES 1974 for an analysis of various other mechanisms as to how and why tribes remain important in modernization processes in contemporary Africa).

In simpler words and quite to the point, as put by a reporter in Ethiopia: "Lack of communications helped hold this empire together. New developing communications and the political awareness they encourage are straining its unity" (quoted in CONNOR 1972:329).

In the multivariate analysis of HIBBS, the variable percentage of mobilized but differentiated persons exerts a strong impact on the dependent variable internal war via the intervening variable of political separatism (see Figure 5.4 in chapter 5.1.1.3).[136] In their study of black African countries, MORRISON/STEVENSON (1972a:925) also report evidence which might be interpreted in favor of the DEUTSCH hypothesis. However, they do not use a multiplicative combination of two independent variables to represent the interaction term. Instead they rely on a theoretically inappropriate additive combination. DEUTSCH himself has pointed out that there may be strong reasons promoting the attraction of and adherence to one's own cultural identity, even at a very high level of social mobilization. It remains to be pointed out that with this interaction term one of the basic explanatory variables in comparative analyses of political violence has been considered. This is true at least at the macrolevel of analysis. What remains to be done is to study the impact of this variable on the group level. Such a strategy would also allow for statements as to the causes of protest behavior and protest readiness of groups which remain culturally distinct.[137]

The following hypotheses are more complex theoretically as well as empirically. HUNTINGTON's hypothesis about the significance of the balance between the degree of *social mobilization* (more precisely *political participation*) and *political institutionalization* as inhibiting political violence is not supported in HIBBS's study. HIBBS uses the following indicators of institutionalization: "Direct Taxes as a Percentage of General Government Revenue, 1960; Age in Decades of Present National Institutional Form, through 1968; Union Membership as a Percentage of the Nonagricultural Work Force, 1960; General Government Expenditures as a Percentage of the Gross Domestic Product, 1960; Age of the Largest Political Party Divided by the Number of Parties, circa 1965; and the Age of the Largest Political Party, 1965" (HIBBS 1973:99; cf. also the criticism in chapter 5.1.1.3), whereas HUNTINGTON proposes the following four general criteria: adaptability, complexity, autonomy, and coherence (see the rather general discussion in HUNTINGTON 1968:12-24 and BEN-DOR 1975 for a critique; cf. also below). HIBBS's measure of political participation, however, is open to serious criticism, since he uses electoral turnout as a measure of political participation, whereas HUNTINGTON, though not precise about this variable,[138] seems to refer to noninstitutionalized forms of political participation.[139] In the final multi-equation formulation, however, a higher degree of social mobilization compared to the degree of political institutionalization increases the number of negative sanctions and thus indirectly contributes to the amount of political violence (cf. Figure 5.4 in chapter 5.1.1.3).

These more negative results notwithstanding (they may in part be attributed to insufficient measures; cf. below), HUNTINGTON's conceptualization of political instability and political decay (HUNTINGTON 1965) which builds on several structural imbalances merits close attention. He starts from the assumption that "social mobilization is much more destabilizing than economic development"[140] (HUNTINGTON 1968:53). This is due to the discrepancy between rising demands (attributed to social mobilization processes) and insufficient capabilities to fulfil these demands (economic development), said to be a characteristic of transitional societies.[141] "The ability of a transitional society to satisfy these new aspirations, however, increases much more slowly than the aspirations themselves" (HUNTINGTON 1968:53–54). This gap, then, is said to lead to social frustration. Depending on two intermediating conditions, namely "opportunities for social and economic mobility and adaptable political institutions" (ibid., p. 54), social frustration may lead to political instability. If mobility opportunities are insufficient, people will turn to politics "to enforce [their] demands" (ibid., p. 55). Finally, (p. 55),

> the political backwardness of the country in terms of political insti
> tutionalization . . . makes it difficult if not impossible for the
> demands upon the government to be expressed through legitimate
> channels and to be moderated and aggregated within the political
> system. Hence the sharp increase in political participation gives rise
> to political instability. The impact of modernization thus involves
> the following relationships:

(1) $\dfrac{\text{Social mobilization}}{\text{Economic development}}$ = Social frustration

(2) $\dfrac{\text{Social frustration}}{\text{Mobility opportunities}}$ = Political participation

(3) $\dfrac{\text{Political participation}}{\text{Political institutionalization}}$ = Political instability

These relationships recall "the paradox that modernity produces stability and modernization instability" (ibid., p. 47). "Political systems can thus be distinguished by their levels of political institutionalization and their levels of political participation" (ibid., p. 78). HUNTINGTON stresses the point that it is neither the level nor the rate of political participation or political institutionalization but rather the ratio between the two which predicts political instability. In chapter 7.2.3, when "civic" polities are distinguished from "praetorian" polities, these criteria will be considered.

The most important aspect of HUNGTINGTON's work is his suggestion to separate socioeconomic modernization from political development, which manifests itself in strong political institutions and in modern political systems, particularly in a strong and adaptable party system (cf. chapter 6.3.5 and 7.2.3). "Rapid increases in mobilization and participation, the principal aspects of modernization, undermine political institutions. Rapid modernization, in brief, produces not political development but political decay" (HUNTINGTON 1965:386).

> By broadening the gap between aspirations and capabilities, social-economic modernization increases the *probability* of civil violence. By broadening the range of political participation, political modernization increases the *scope* of civil violence, unless broader institutional channels for peaceful participation also come into being. The combined effect of both social-economic and political modernization, however, is to undermine traditional political institutions and to make it most difficult to create broad-based political party systems and other forms of participatory political institutions. . . . The idea of "peaceful change" or "development without violence" thus becomes almost wholly unreal. There may well be violence without development; but there is virtually no development without violence[142] (HUNTINGTON 1971a:3).

Thus far political decay, political instability, and political violence have been issues of concern. HUNTINGTON (1968) uses the first and the second concepts synonymously, but he considers political violence to represent one aspect of political decay, and military coups another (cf. the discussion in chapter 7.2.3). Political corruption as well is an important indicator of political decay.

> The functions, as well as the causes, of corruption are similar to those of violence. Both are encouraged by modernization; both are symptomatic of the weakness of political institutions; both are characteristic of what we . . . call praetorian societies; both are means by which individuals and groups relate themselves to the political system and, indeed, participate in the system in ways which violate the mores of the system. Hence the society which has a high capacity for corruption also has a high capacity for violence (HUNTINGTON 1968:63).[143]

In later chapters (6.3.5 and 7.2.3) more will be said about HUNTINGTON's praetorian states. At this point it suffices to stress their main characteristic, the absence of strong and adaptable political institutions.

HUNTINGTON's controversial theory whereby various aspects of modernization, such as rapid socioeconomic change, social and political mobilization, and political institutionalization, are related to *each other*, explains political stability (or political development) and political instability (or political decay) by employing the *same* set of variables. This can be seen in that the theory explains "the anomaly that by many standards the relatively peaceful richer countries are also the faster changing" (TILLY 1973:431), precisely because of their greater institutional capacities. Yet, in spite of this achievement which contributes to the comprehensive and fascinating character of HUNTINGTON's theory, the critiques of RUSTOW (1969), KESSELMAN (1973), NARDIN (1971) and others merit attention. They feel that there is an inherent bias toward political order and stability in HUNTINGTON's theory (a bias which at times even seems to neglect the "costs" of political order). "Illuminating what political order is not,[144] HUNTINGTON fails to resolve a number of ambiguities in the implied account of what it *is*. Is political order *synonymous* with governmental authority, effectiveness, and legitimacy—or is the existence of this kind of government a *precondition* of political order?" (NARDIN 1971:26). Furthermore, HUNTINGTON in his institutionalization concept does not take account of the fact that political groups (in his terminology "social forces") can de facto act like institutions. "A given group may be regarded as a social force, insofar as it pursues interests common to its members which conflict with the interests of other social forces; but to the extent that it resolves conflicts of interest and manages conflict behavior among individuals and factions within the group, it functions as a political institution" (NARDIN 1971:27). HUNTINGTON is most strongly criticized for his tendency to equate political institutions with governmental institutions or institutions of the state, with the consequence that "disorder that results because of rulers and ruling institutions who exert coercion falls outside the definition" of political decay (KESSELMAN 1973:143).[145]

SANDERS's analysis (1973) as well calls the following assumptions of HUNTINGTON into question (cf. also the explication and critique of HUNTINGTON's theory by SIGELMAN 1979).

1. Do better mobility channels really lead to a reduction in political participation? HUNTINGTON apparently starts from the premise of a citizen too well fed to care about politics.[146]
2. Social frustration may, on the contrary, lead to withdrawal, to forms of alienated behavior, rather than to mobilization of discontent into the political arena. The vast proportions of the politically apathetic *Lumpenproletariat* in a great number of underdeveloped countries stress the point.
3. There may be other interdependencies among HUNTINGTON's variables than those specified in his theory. Actually, there is some, albeit very weak, empirical evidence of such alternative formulations (cf. below).

HUNTINGTON's insufficient explication of his concept of institutionalization has been strongly criticized. He does mention several possible indicators of his four basic dimensions of institutionalization:

Adaptability can be measured by chronological age, leadership successions, generational changes, and functional changes. Complexity can be measured by the number and diversity of organizational subunits and by the number and diversity of functions performed by the organizations. Autonomy is perhaps the most difficult of the criteria to pin down: it can, however, be measured by the distinctiveness of the norms and values of the organization compared with those of other groups, by the personnel controls (in terms of cooptation, penetration, and purging) existing between the organization and other groups, and by the degree to which the organization controls its own material resources. Coherence may be measured by the ratio of contested successions to total successions, by the cumulation or non-cumulation of cleavages among leaders and members, by the incidence of overt alienation and dissent within the organization, and, conceivably, by opinion surveys of the loyalties and preferences of organization members (HUNTING-TON 1965:404-5).

However, he does not specify the interrelationships among these components. Without such a specification (cf. also the attempt of WEEDE 1977a) one could always, in cases of instability or political violence, argue that some conditions of institutionalization have not been met. Furthermore, the danger of overinstitutionalization has been pointed out. As KESSELMAN writes in his case study on France: "If in transitional societies it is easier to destroy old institutions than to build new ones, the problem is reversed in developed polities, where established institutions may be outmoded [not adaptable] but still able [autonomous] to withstand challenge" (KESSELMAN 1970: 44; cf. also BEN-DOR 1974:81 and the additional empirical results in chapter 6.3.5).

Critics of HUNTINGTON's theory have focused largely on the question of value relations (*Wertbeziehungen*) in his approach. More substantial criticisms included empirical tests by SANDERS (1973; see below) and theoretical explanations like that of WEEDE. For a critique going beyond HUNTINGTON's position one must show "that or where there is no contradiction between more participation and stability or where such a contradiction cannot exist, that and why participation is a more important determinant [than others], if instability is to be avoided, that and for what reason an accelerated [in original, "too fast"] increase in participation does not lead via political decay, for example, to military intervention" or to other forms of political violence (WEEDE 1977a:424; my translation). Even if empirical research has not yet reached such a stage, there are some interesting results emerging from those few studies which test HUNTINGTON's theory.

SCHNEIDER/SCHNEIDER (1971) have tested some of HUNTINGTON's hypotheses (N=10 mostly Western European nations). One of their basic conclusions is that "rapid social mobilization can occur without disruptive effects [indexed by an eleven-point GUTTMAN scale ranging from political demonstrations to civil war] . . . if there is no severe gap between social mobilization[147] and institutionalization[148] or between social mobilization and the level of economic development" (SCHNEIDER/SCHNEIDER 1971: 85). Moreover, the "gap between social mobilization and the level of institutionalization has a more dramatic impact on political violence in the economically less-developed nations included in this study than in the more highly developed ones" (ibid., p. 87). Due to the limited size of the sample, these results should be treated with caution. The R^2 values (often reaching more than .90) also seem to be inflated.[149]

SANDERS (1973) uses cross-sectional data from the *World Handbook of Political and Social Indicators* (TAYLOR/HUDSON 1972) for up to 136 nations (base year 1965). After extensive testing of various alternative models (linear, nonlinear, recursive, nonrecursive, path models) of HUNTINGTON's gap hypotheses, he arrives at the following conclusion.

> In terms of the empirical analysis undertaken here . . . the Gap Hypothesis appears to be little more than a series of ill-conceived and unfounded assertions: (i) supposedly linear relationships are shown demonstrably to be *non*linear (between political participation and instability and between economic development and social frustration); (ii) relationships between variables which are predicted to be negative are in fact positive (mobility opportunities[150] and political participation); (iii) linkages between variables which should be strongly related if the internal consistency of the theory is to be confirmed, are not even nearly significant in terms of the data (social frustration and political participation); (iv) the role of frustration [here measured in terms of the relationships outlined by HUNTINGTON] in the theoretical scheme is completely misspecified, and consequently so too is the role of social mobilization; (v) there is a heavy and largely misplaced theoretical emphasis on institutionalization, a variable which (even conceptualized in the way HUNTINGTON suggests) rarely has a significant parameter; and (vi) partly because of the amorphous nature of the concept of institutionalization itself, there is a complete failure not only to adequately differentiate between what constitutes "participation" and what constitutes "instability," but also to provide a satisfactory explanation of what the relationship is between the two (SANDERS 1973:91-92).

As a matter of fact, SANDERS tentatively proposes to reverse in part HUNTINGTON's conceptualization of institutionalization. He finds a curvilinear relationship between political participation and political instability while controlling for institutionalization.[151]

As long as political participation (measured here in terms of antigovernment demonstrations and strikes) is below the threshold value (here the mean is used as a cut-off point), there is a positive relationship between political participation and political instability (riots, assassinations, political attacks, deaths from political violence, and the ratio of irregular [1965] to regular transfers of power [1960-65]).[152] Beyond this threshold, however, there is a negative relationship, suggesting that more frequent occurrences of antigovernment demonstrations and strikes do not lead to political instability, but rather to a reduction in political instability. Yet, there may be a number of uncontrolled variables involved in these relationships (i.e., on the level of indicators, when nonviolent protests are frequent, violent protests are not as frequent, whereas, with less nonviolent political protest, a positive relationship with violent protests seems to result). SANDERS offers this highly tentative interpretation: "In those countries where increases in participation serve to reduce instability . . . , by acting as a 'safety valve' for social frustration . . . we can say that protest *has* been institutionalized, and characterize

the political system as 'mature'" (SANDERS 1973:89) or "immature" in
the opposite case. SANDERS does not provide further evidence with nations
belonging to either group.

Putting aside these ambiguous results and their interpretation, there is still
criticism to be raised against HUNTINGTON's conception of the institutionalization variable. While HUNTINGTON distinguishes between institutionalization and participation, SANDERS points out that both are or can
be[153] aspects of the same thing, more frequent forms of political participation gaining the quality of institutionalized behavior and thus not leading to
political instability. This may be true even in situations of protest, as long as
nonviolent forms of political protest prevail.

LEHTINEN (1974) examines the relationships between modernization,
political development, and stability for eighty-three countries. He finds
that modernization[154] correlates negatively with political violence (FEIERA-
BEND data, 1948-62, granted that they represent a measure of political
instability; cf. the critique in chapter 5.1.1.2.4) as does political development.[155] Political development turns out to be a stronger predictor of political violence (r=-.55) than the interaction term between modernization and
political development (-.203). This is no surprise, considering the high intercorrelation between modernization and political development as measured
in this study (r=.82). A structural imbalance effect is thus hardly evident.

Serious criticism raised against this study has rendered it almost useless.
For example, adaptability as an indicator of political institutionalization is
measured through one or two indicators which actually could represent
aspects of the dependent variable political instability (namely, governmental
stability and stability of the party system). Political enculturation does not
seem to capture any of the facets of coherence stressed by HUNTINGTON.
Finally, LEHTINEN does not distinguish between modernization and social
mobilization (cf. the indicators chosen for indexing modernization) thus
obscuring one of the basic ideas in HUNTINGTON's theory and consequently
preventing a successful test of subsequent steps in the theory.

YOUGH/SIGELMAN (1976) have studied the relationships between
modernization (1966 levels of per capita GNP and energy consumption),
social mobilization,[156] political institutionalization[157] and political instability
as the dependent variable.[158] The sample comprises sixty-one underdeveloped nations in Latin America, Asia, Africa, and the Middle East.

> The correlations between instability and rate of social mobilization
> are uniformly low and—more damaging to the HUNTINGTON
> thesis—inverse. That is, political instability is *less* likely in systems
> undergoing rapid mobilization. Institutionalization and economic
> development have somewhat greater predictive power, but for each
> this power is greatest in the case of collective protest, where the
> anticipated directions of the relationships are reversed; statistical
> prediction in these instances is out of tune with theoretical expecta-
> tions. Only the mobilization gap consistently operates in the pre-
> dicted direction, and its correlations with instability are quite

moderate in magnitude [.207 < r < .381] (YOUGH/SIGELMAN 1976:226-27).

Only in the case of power transfers does the predicted gap between social mobilization and political institutionalization operate significantly and in the predicted direction. YOUGH/SIGELMAN draw several conclusions from their results. Firstly, their "analysis suggests that rapid social mobilization itself is far less politically destabilizing than had previously been supposed. Indeed, we would argue that HUNTINGTON and others have focused so single-mindedly on the dysfunctional aspects of rapid social change that they have overlooked the potential of such change for creating higher levels of political support" (ibid., p. 229). Data on the individual or group level might provide for some answers to these alternative predictions as to the effects of the very same theoretical variables. The authors also recommend taking into consideration that instability, violence, and, at least in part, social mobilization, and political institutionalization are multifaceted phenomena. Thus, there may be some relationships in accord with HUNTINGTON's (one-dimensional) theoretical predictions, while other facets of the same theoretical notions might operate in different ways. While the suggestions of YOUGH/SIGELMAN are worth further research, it should be stressed that their own study—like almost all studies bearing on HUNTINGTON's theory—suffers from severe operational weaknesses. Apart from the weaknesses mentioned above, political violence is their only indicator of political instability. Ironically, while YOUGH/SIGELMAN plead for a multifaceted approach, their own study still shows the limits of a one-dimensional approach.

DUFF/McCAMANT (1976:115ff.) report results which may be interpreted in favor of HUNTINGTON's theory (if one is willing to neglect the criticism brought forward in note 129). They use the strength of the Catholic Church, the level of institutionalization of the party system, and military subordination under civil leadership as indicators of institutionalization, from which they subtract their measures of social mobilization (as pointed out before, they do not use the theoretically indicated ratio formulation of the two independent variables) and come up with a negative relationship to political violence (r=-.35, 1950s, and -.56, 1960s). In a multivariate analysis, however, another interaction term turns out to be a better predictor of the scores on the dependent variable: political violence is inhibited above all if economic growth is sufficiently high to allow for coping with the degree of social mobilization. This new explanatory variable, which has the greatest explanatory power,[159] correlates rather strongly, however, with the other independent variables. This may have contributed to the disappearance of the first mentioned "interaction term" in the final regression equation.

Finally, there are tests of HUNTINGTON's theory based on somewhat arbitrary reinterpretations of the theory, but nevertheless leading to interesting results. Thus, RUHL (1975) studying political instability (1958-60; 1962-64 using BWY's 1968b data on organized political violence; cf. chapter 5.1.2.5) in eighteen Latin American countries reports better predictions if economic development is replaced by various measures of inequality;[160]

inequality is then used as the denominator of the first interaction term. HUNTINGTON emphasizes that, compared to the level of economic development, a relatively higher level of social mobilization[161] (in the absence of sufficient mobility opportunities and strong political institutions) increases the probability of political instability. Holding political institutionalization constant,[162] RUHL considers that social mobilization has an effect only if it is not compatible with the degree of inequality. (A related hypothesis will be taken up in chapter 5.1.2.7). RUHL finds that an additive combination of the variables mentioned leads to a somewhat better prediction (.79 for 1958-60) than the interaction term suggested by HUNTINGTON (variance explained 63.1%). This holds even for the second period (.54 for 1962-64), although the variance explained is low (28.7%). Thus, while political institutionalization consistently acts as a strong negative predictor of political instability and social mobilization as a less strong (or in the second period slightly stronger) positive predictor, the alleged interaction effect does not show up in its expected strength. It fares somewhat better, however, if the modifications suggested by RUHL are taken into consideration (change from .30 to .63 in the first period, and from .41 to .48 in the second period). Of the various speculations that build on HUNTINGTON's original formulation, that of RUHL seems to be more promising, even though his results should not be taken too seriously, considering the operationalization of the dependent variable (one form of political violence as standing for political instability), the circularity introduced by some of the institutionalization indicators, the neglect of HUNTINGTON's second of three interaction terms, inconsistencies in the periods of observation, etc.

Another variant is introduced by WAYMAN (1975) who replaces social mobilization by the "relevance of modernizing cleavages." His dependent variable, military involvement in politics, will, however, be dealt with in a later chapter (7.3). Here let it suffice to point out that his data seem to provide some highly indirect[163] empirical support for his modification of the original theory. There are also, however, numerous other explicative variables that will have to be incorporated into the analysis if military involvement in politics is to be explained to a sufficient degree.

Intensive modernizing (or *political*) cleavages may be caused by grievances of socially mobilized, but differentiated populations. Thus, DEUTSCH's hypothesis could be incorporated into the following reformulation of HUNTINGTON's original theory:

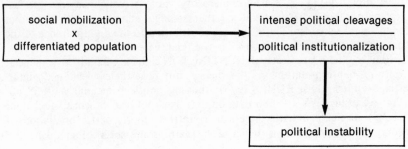

In any case, the routes and mechanisms eventually leading to political instability are not sufficiently specified at all, neither in HUNTINGTON's theory nor in any of the alternative formulations (cf. chapter 6).

Reviewing largely the same works we review in this study, SIGELMAN conveniently summarized some of the arguments against HUNTINGTON's theory: "The question remains of whether social mobilization is, as DEUTSCH supposed, a unidimensional process" (SIGELMAN 1979:217). As a consequence, "those who view politics from a 'social engineering' perspective might suggest that HUNTINGTON reversed the true flow of causality, because he ignored the extent to which the structural aspects of social mobilization, e.g., increased educational enrollments and broader access to mass media, follow from *deliberate* regime attempts to modernize in response to mass demands to do so" (ibid., p. 214; emphasis added). In sum, "HUNTINGTON either failed to acknowledge the multidimensionality of his concepts [such as political participation and social frustration], or having acknowledged it, nonetheless treated them in his explanation of political instability as though they were unidimensional. And finally, most of the concepts employed in the social mobilization approach are sadly lacking in empirical referents" (ibid., p.220).

It should be clear by now that much further explication of HUNTINGTON's theory is required. The theory in its simple structure greatly appeals to social scientists. It is now necessary to develop more adequate indicators and carry out detailed tests, if possible using time series data. Perhaps HUNTINGTON's theory fares somewhat better when some of the disturbing factors have been controlled. At present, however, the assumption should be that political instability is caused by more factors than simply an imbalance between political participation and political institutionalization (for a further discussion cf. chapter 6).

It might be argued that HUNTINGTON's formulation of the relationships among several theoretically important explanatory variables of political violence provides for a more promising starting point, at least on the level of comparative aggregate data analyses, than GURR's "excursions" into sociopsychological theorizing (e.g., frustration-aggression theory, theory of relative deprivation, learning theories) which cannot adequately be operationalized and tested with the data currently available.

Before concluding this section, the causal interdependencies among some of the key variables referred to here and more closely studied in DUVALL/WELFLING (1973a) deserve a brief comment. It is interesting to note that, contrary to HUNTINGTON's writings, DUVALL/WELFLING (1973a) in their study of the causal interdependencies of "social mobilization,[164] political institutionalization,[165] and conflict in Black Africa" (N=28; 1960-64 and 1965-69) found that social mobilization has little effect on conflict (turmoil, internal war, and elite conflict; cf. MORRISON/STEVENSON 1972a:908 and chapter 5.1.1.1.2.1), whereas conflicts do have effects on mobilization and the development of political institutions. There is, however, no convincing theoretical explanation as yet (neither in DUVALL/WELFLING 1973a nor in POPPER 1971; cf. also SCHMITT 1974:33 with respect to Northern Ireland and HIRSCHMAN 1963:256ff. referring to Latin America) as to *why* there should be such a relationship.

Summarizing this section, there is contradictory evidence as to whether the imbalance between political participation and weak political institutionalization predicts political violence. Another structural imbalance effect is found when the proportion of the population which has been mobilized but has also retained its distinctiveness is related to political violence.[166] It would be particularly interesting to combine the structural imbalance analyzed by DEUTSCH with those imbalances sugggested in HUNTINGTON's theory and to propose a general explanation of political violence. Probably HUNTINGTON's approach would turn out to be the more general. Yet, even in his broad conceptualization, not all cases of social mobilization will be captured. The following summary evaluations of some case studies provide some negative examples: "The crucial feature in Rwanda, Burundi, and southern Peru–northwestern Bolivia is that the social mobilization hypothesis does not apply. These are pre-social-mobilization revolts. They occur when the patterns of *institutionalization* are changed, with sharp, drastic consequences for those near the bottom of the ethnic hierarchy. Hierarchical ethnic structures exhibit the paradox of normative support for inequality for long periods of time and then large-scale, bloody social revolutions when the system's normative bases are eroded" (HUNTINGTON/DOMÍN-GUEZ 1975:75). With respect to many other instances of social mobilization of culturally distinct groups, however: "Social mobilization . . . does not necessarily freeze the traditional system at the preexisting level of social cleavage. It may reinvigorate a social cleavage at a higher level of interest aggregation" (HUNTINGTON/DOMÍNGUEZ 1975:69).

As to the various other structural imbalances which have been considered and were not supported empirically, many other variables (such as the legitimacy of the political system and its coercive resources) must be considered before the theoretical importance of these structural imbalances is "definitely" evaluated. The tendency of those countries en route to modernity to political instability or political violence is documented once again in the next section.

5.1.2.5. Coercion and Political Violence

In section 2.3 we defined coercion as force applied by the state against its population. Force denotes the actual or threatened use of violence. Obviously, the concept of coercion may refer to many other phenomena as well: "Coercion may be physical or nonphysical (psychological, spiritual, intellectual, aesthetic), violent or nonviolent, public (official) or private, individual or collective, overt or covert, legitimate or illegitimate, positive (rewards or promise of benefits) or negative (punishment, threat of deprivation), formal or informal, etc." (COOK 1972:116). In this study the term coercion is reserved for repressive activities of the state against parts of its population. These activities may be characterized by the actual or threatened use of violence or they may even be nonviolent. In any case, state coercion denotes here "(a) the application of actual physical violence, or (b) the application of sanctions [thought to be] sufficiently strong to make an individual [or a group] abandon a course of action or inaction dictated by his [its] own strong and enduring motives and wishes" (BAY 1958:93), the extreme case being physical elimination as in pogroms. Considering some of the empirical results which follow, we had to modify BAY's definition through the addendum "thought to be." The assessment of state agents may and often does prove wrong in reality. There are three aspects to be discussed in this section:[167]

1. The relationship existing between the two variables must be determined. A curvilinear and a linear relationship (with a positive or negative sign) have been predicted equally often. Or is there some other more complicated form of covariation?

2. The indicators chosen for indexing coercive measures of the state agents will deserve special attention because there seems to be less agreement about them than about other indicators, e.g., those for measuring economic development.

3. Finally, it often remains highly dubious whether the stated theoretical relationships have been measured at all.

There are two alternative hypotheses as to the effects of coercive means. Firstly, coercion will act as a *deterrent* to the use of means of political violence. Secondly, coercive means will be an *instigation*[168] to use violent means of protest. All the other relationships theoretically postulated or empirically found are interpreted as combinations of these two basic possibilities. A brief overview of some of the relationships between coercion and political violence is given in Table 5.3. Here we have listed only those studies where statistical coefficients have been explicitly stated (without repeating studies mentioned earlier). As SNYDER (1976:289) shows, however, artifacts resulting from the method used might lead or at least contribute to a positive relationship between coercion and political violence in the case of the FEIERABEND group's findings and to a negative one in the case of some of GURR's results. Before discussing some additional results, it should be pointed out that there seems to be no more evidence for either hypothesis (i.e., that there is a positive linear relationship or a curvilinear relationship between coercion and political violence). However, the deterrence hypothesis suggesting a negative relationship between coercion and political violence is not supported (but see below).

In a different sense, however, all three hypotheses are supported, *if* the relationship proves to be curvilinear. On a lower level, coercion is positively related to political violence which reaches its maximum at mid-level coercion. Beyond this turning point, as coercion reaches its maximum, there is a clear decrease in political violence. The rationale for a curvilinear relationship has been discussed in detail in chapter 5.1.1.2.3. There were a number of possible explanations for this curvilinear relationship, one of the more important ones being that insufficient (and inconsistent) use of coercion serves as additional instigation to aggression rather than as a deterrent, thus establishing an aggres-

Table 5.3. Coercion and Political Violence: Some Bivariate Relationships

Author	Dependent Variable	Indicators	Independent Variables	Indicators	Sample	Period	Results linear relationships
Markus/ Nesvold 1972	political instability	7-point scale (see chapter 5.1.1.2.2)	coercion	7-point scale, 0 denoting "civil rights present and protected" to 6 denoting "civil rights nonexistent, political opposition impossible," etc.	10	1959–61	$\gamma = .62$
Feierabend/ Feierabend 1972a	revolution	deaths from domestic group violence, duration (from Tanter/ Midlarsky 1967)	coercion (1948–60)	as above	18 Latin American countries	1958–60	$r = .58$
Jacobson 1973a	general conflict	from Gurr 1968a (see below)	coerciveness (early 1960s)	size of internal security forces (from Gurr 1968a), role of the police in political activities (from Banks/Textor 1963)	75	1961–65	$p = .10$ (.84 in economically developed countries)

						N	period	*curvilinear relationships*
Bwy 1968b	anomic violence	various indicators of internal conflicts on the basis of a factor analysis (cf. chapter 5.1.1.1.2.1)	force (1959–60)	defense expenditure as % of GNP		20 Latin American countries	1958–60	curvilinear relationship (but no relationship if organized lence is the dependent variable)
Gurr 1968a	civil strife	complex index of the pervasiveness, duration, and intensity of turmoil, conspiracy, and internal war (cf. chapter 5.1.1.1.1)	military/internal security forces	military and internal security forces per 10,000 adults (1960)		114	1961–65	curvilinear relationship (even more pronounced when considering 69 countries only and omitting countries with protracted political violence and those being externally threatened)
Markus/Nesvold 1972	political instability (lag: 1 month)	7-point scale (see above)	coercion	7-point scale (see above)		10	1959–61	(low-high-medium) $\gamma = .65$

sion → punishment → heightened aggression sequence. GURR (1970a:238–51) sums up the results of a number of case studies and of comparative analyses from various parts of the world covering different time periods. The majority of these studies provide evidence in favor of a curvilinear relationship. In their extension of GURR's original study, however, GURR/DUVALL (1973) reach different conclusions. When discussing some possible policy implications of their highly complex study (see chapter 5.1.1.1.4), they write: "Coercive elite policies breed civil conflict more often than civil peace. Some (measures of) institutionalized coercion contribute to order, but policies as diverse as punitive acts of coercive control and maintenance of costly military establishments tend to exacerbate future conflict" (GURR/DUVALL 1973: 160). Following their data more closely, they report self-cancelling effects of coercion: "Coercive capacity when used by regimes tends to have self-cancelling effects on magnitude of conflict. . . . For example: government acts of coercion tend quite systematically to increase subsequent magnitude of conflict; the size of military expenditures are consistently positive correlates of conflict in our 86 countries; yet the size of internal security forces weakly inhibits conflict in all but Western nations. There is no basis here for a 'regime coercion' variable that consistently reduces conflict magnitudes" (GURR/ DUVALL 1973:141). These results are not to be interpreted in the sense of "event coercion," i.e., actual conflict-repression sequences (cf. below), but only as correlates on the basis of cross-sectional data.[169]

Other studies reveal a wide range of additional results. MARKUS (1970: 28–30, as quoted in MARKUS/NESVOLD 1972:236) finds a strong linear relationship between "governmental coercion" and "political instability." The same holds true when coercion and minority-related hostilities are studied, r=.71 (FEIERABEND/FEIERABEND 1973:211; N=25 nations; period: 1955–59). In their study of integration and instability in thirty-two African countries, MORRISON/STEVENSON (1972a:921) also found positive relationships between their measures of coercive potential (such as military spending, foreign military aid, number of parties banned, number of arrests for political offensive, percent change of defense budget as percent of GNP) and "the likelihood of elite and communal instability."[170] A possible explanation for these relationships may be the "lack of institutionalization in police and armed forces, which have inherited the distasteful record of colonial repression" (ibid.).

The analysis of MARKUS/NESVOLD (1972) shows that different results may emerge when time lags are taken into account. In their study (see Table 5.3) a positive linear relationship between coercion and political violence emerges when both variables are simultaneously measured, and a curvilinear relationships occurs, when a time lag of one month is considered. Obviously, one would have to test for other time lags as well. There is as yet no theoretical reason why a time lag of one month should be of special importance. Nevertheless, the significance of time-lagged analyses is once again stressed in the study of ANDERSON/NESVOLD (1972; N=22 nations with 20 or more turmoil events in 1959; periods: 1948–58 for turmoil and 1945–58 for the independent variables; operationalizations basically similar to the FEIERABENDs' studies): "(1) High past fluctuation in coercion, (2) high past mean coercion, (3) low past instability, (4) relatively high recent coercion, and (5) relatively low recent instability, successfully predict to higher turmoil [here denoting general political violence] levels. Conversely, low past fluctuation in coercion, low past mean coercion, high past instability, relatively low recent coercion, and relatively high recent instability successfully predict future lower turmoil" (ANDERSON/NESVOLD 1972:907; numbers added). If the five independent variables are additively combined, the "turmoil" values for 1959 can be quite accurately predicted.

In several of the studies on the effects of coercion, indicators such as military expenditure as a percentage of gross domestic product or as a percentage of central government expenditure and military manpower per population are used, whereas, in the studies of the FEIERABENDs and their coworkers, censorship, lack of personal and political freedom, etc. are chosen to index coercion. The former indicators are often of a dubious nature since that type of coercive potential may be much more influenced by international conditions[171] than the following indicators proposed by HIBBS, GURR and others: internal security forces per 10,000 people or adults, and internal security forces per 1,000 square kilometers. In addition, the "loyalty, training, and technological sophistication" of these forces should be assessed, as GURR has attempted. "Moreover, the current size of these forces may in part be a *response to* the magnitude of previous mass violence, raising the problem of what causes what?"[172] (HIBBS 1973:86, both quotations ibid.). In his own study HIBBS reaches the conclusion that: "Neither the linear nor the curvilinear hypothesis is consistently supported by the empirical data. The most we can conclude, therefore, is that the strength of coercive forces available to governing elites does not seem to bear a marked curvilinear relation to mass violence, as previous analyses have suggested, and that the strength of such forces also fails to exert a substantial linear 'deterrence' effect" (ibid., p. 87). Internal security forces have a significant positive impact on negative sanctions which in turn are interrelated with the two main forms of political violence, collective protest and internal war. When negative sanctions such as censorship and political restrictions are used as independent variable, there is a significant positive relationship to both forms of political violence in the short run (actually, simultaneously measured indicators are used), whereas in the long run (lag: ten years) there is a negative relationship between these variables (being significant only in the case of internal war; see Figure 5.4).

As pointed out, two further hypotheses about the relationship between coercion and political violence have been studied on a cross-national basis. When the size of the *coercive potential* is weighted by its past *loyalty*, GURR finds a distinct negative relationship, as expected.[173] Employing the same procedure but using a different sample (N=130; period: 1946-65), ADAMS (1970:147) also reports a negative relationship. There is further evidence as to the importance of a loyal military. The "desertion of the intellectuals" (cf. BRINTON 1952), often quoted as a major condition of revolutionary activity, is probably much less important than the defection of elite military personnel (see chapters 7 and 8).

Whereas loyalty of the military and the internal security personnel is a variable referring to the behavior of potential anti-elite groups, *fluctuations in use of coercive means* once again refer to the population suffering from such uses of coercive power. In chapter 5.1.1.2.3 there was cross-national evidence for a linear relationship between fluctuations in coercion and political violence. MARKUS/NESVOLD (1972; see above) also found results in support of the hypothesis that "regime coercive control varies strongly with the consistency of regime-administered negative sanctions" (GURR 1970a: 256). GURR mentions several reasons (ibid., p. 255) why the inconsistent use of force on behalf of state agents (but also on behalf of protesters, see ibid., p. 260–73) leads to an increase and not a decrease in actual protests. For example, only some of the protesters are captured or punished. Others may think that they have a fair chance of succeeding in carrying out future protests. Nonparticipants are often indiscriminately affected by the use of coercive means, leading to resentment among them as well, resentment against such measures or against state officials directly. On the basis of learning principles[174] and inferred expectation states, we listed a number of possible explanations (see chapter 5.1.1.2.3) why the observed relationship between inconsistent use of coercive means and political violence is likely to hold. Additional aspects are mentioned by ECKSTEIN who admirably sums up the discussion:

> Unless it is based upon extremely good intelligence, and unless its application is sensible, ruthless, and continuous, its effects may be quite opposite to those intended. Incompetent repression leads to a combination of disaffection and contempt for the elite. Also repression may only make the enemies of a regime more competent in the arts of conspiracy; certainly it tends to make them more experienced in the skills of clandestine organization and *sub rosa* communication. No wonder that botched and bungled repression is often a characteristic of pre-revolutionary societies. The French *ancien régime*, for example, had a political censorship, but it only managed to make French writers into masters of the hidden meaning, and whet the appetite of the public for their subversive books (ECKSTEIN 1965: 154).

Thus far only *systemic* coercion has been measured. Theoretically (cf. chapter 5.1.1.2.3), however, we are more interested in finding out how "*event* coercion" (ANDERSON/NESVOLD 1972:807) affects political violence. In the preceding discussion repression has been used in a more general sense rather than in an action-related sense. Actually, however, we wish to find answers to both questions: (1) which consequences do actual repressions have (or, in the case of more comprehensive sequences, which are the preconditions of repression) and (2) is there an inhibiting or threatening effect resulting from the existence or imminent use of a repressive potential, and, if so, how strong are these effects? We shall return to these questions below. In the study of ANDERSON/NESVOLD there is evidence that the majority of violent protests are quite limited in time. Furthermore, the reaction of the state agents usually follows on the same day. In a majority of cases overreactions occur (in terms of the means employed compared to those of the protesters). Their study provides the first such systematic cross-national results. The authors ultimately stress the necessity of turning around the prevalent way of viewing coercion: "This 'turning around' would involve viewing turmoil behavior by a polity as a reinforcement schedule for government punitive responses" (ANDERSON/NESVOLD 1972:908). GURR et al. (forthcoming) report that there is a reciprocal relationship between governmental sanctions and political violence (cf. also HIBBS's final causal model in Figure 5.4 in chapter 5.1.1.3). LICHBACH/GURR (1980) discuss many hypotheses and present empirical evidence for 1961-70 (N=86 countries) on conflict-escalating processes, emphasizing the impact of past rebellion and protest, on the one hand, and the influences of coercive reactions of state authorities, on the other. NESVOLD/MARTIN (1974) provide additional evidence for an interdependency between coercion and political violence. In a study of 130 nations (1955–64), they found a positive correlation (r=.66) between coercion and political violence (using the operationalizations and coding procedures of the FEIERABENDs described in chapter 5.1.1.2.2). This relationship also holds after controlling for geocultural region, economic development, and levels of coercion (only in the case of Eastern European nations is there a slightly lower correlation, r=.55). Furthermore, they also found conflicts (coercion) to be persistent from one year to the next, r=.73 (.66). The correlations between coercion and political violence one year later, or between political violence and coercion a year later, differed only slightly in the various geocultural groupings. The general trend, however, is for "coercion to occur in the same year as conflict" (NESVOLD/MARTIN 1974:10). Finally, they report evidence from some countries that higher than normal levels of coercion may lead to subsequent peaks in political violence. However, their bivariate analyses are clearly insufficient for answering the underlying theoretical questions derived from BANDURA (1973). Some other possible key variables in line with GURR's writings are suggested in the following quotation: "If a group of dissidents perceives the legitimacy of its cause, has the resources to challenge authority effectively, and perceives government police action as excessive, we should have an explosive situation. We are attempting to develop other such prototypical situations in order to test for their predictive efficiency" (NESVOLD/MARTIN 1974:10).

Linking coercion or repression and violent protest provides some of the most fundamental hypotheses in research on political violence. "Perhaps most common of all, regimes challenged by serious rebellion often adopt unpopular policies (e.g., restriction of civil liberties, increased taxation and conscription) that stimulate protest by other challenging groups irrespective of their sympathies for or against the rebels" (LICHBACH/GURR 1980). Yet, it became clear in this section and in earlier ones that quite often the various hypotheses have been tested rather insufficently. Furthermore, when considering the results mentioned in this chapter, it should be kept in mind that data about coercive potentials and the way they are applied are frequently error-laden (see the discussion in chapter 5.1.3).

In summary, there is once again contradictory evidence as to the exact form of the relationship between coercion and political violence. Perhaps more consistent results may be obtained if (1) data about the military resources and the internal security forces, about their loyalty, training, experiences, and past behavior, (2) data on repressive measures such as censorship, political restrictions, and other forms of repression, and (3) information as to how these resources are actually applied, are employed in one and the same analysis. (4) In addition, an attempt should be made to collect less inferential data on the degree of deterrence of repressive potentials. This could create considerable difficulties, but, nevertheless, it is an important theoretical link in the relationships under study (cf. also the relevance of anticipated social consequences in the social learning theory of BANDURA 1973; see chapter 3.3 and Figure 3.1). If this were done, the level of explanation would no longer be the system level, but rather the group level. What we are calling for here, however, is treating both aspects jointly, i.e., combining system-level explanatory variables with group-level variables. Taking such variables explicitly into account would reduce the common danger of circular reasoning. We speak of circular explanations insofar as the existence of any coercive potential is used as a direct explanation of whatever score on the dependent variable political violence is encountered. However, the strategic considerations which occur during such a process are not at all captured. The result is rather that contradictory empirical findings as to the deterrent effect or instigation effect of repression can be "explained" without great difficulties simply by drawing on one of the many hypotheses in learning theory. What is needed is detailed information as to how a very specific result is arrived at. (Due to the complexity of such data, cross-national approaches do not seem to be a promising device here.) Only then will there be a chance of empirically refuting some of the equally plausible hypotheses derived from learning theory and referred to many times in this chapter. (5) Finally, we need to know how many deaths and injuries, apart from other damage, are caused by state agents (cf. the appropriate coding in GURR and Associates 1978:56-57), how this would affect those likely to protest, and how the state agents would react in turn. "A large portion of the European disturbances we have been surveying turned violent at exactly the moment when the authorities intervened to stop an illegal but nonviolent action.[175] This is typical of violent strikes and demonstrations. Furthermore, the great bulk of the killing and wounding in those same disturbances was done by troops or police rather than by insurgents or demonstrators. The demonstrators, on the other hand, did the bulk of the damage to property" (TILLY 1969:42).[176] Indirect, highly aggregated evidence about interaction sequences between agents of state repression and protestors is also found in the factor analysis of GURR/BISHOP (1976). A new protest and internal war emerge as distinct factors; if one includes acts of state violence in the factor analysis, the same dimensions again appear, now containing high-loading variables which measure political violence on behalf of state institutions and on behalf of dissidents. Some authors (BUSS 1961:31; O'LEARY/ DENGERINK 1973) expect attacks to be a stronger determinant of aggression than frustration.[177] Consequently, it will be of special importance to collect data on who caused the outbreak of conflict or who provoked it. The distinction among four types of governmental coercion suggested by SNYDER (1976:285-88) is quite useful in the context of the preceding discussion. He differentiates between preemptive and responsive coercion and between violent and nonviolent means. The discussion and the five items above might easily be rephrased in these terms.

Gathering data on event coercion would also mean that the groups engaging in political violence could be better identified, thus reducing the dangers of group fallacy (cf. also the summary remarks in chapter 9). There is probably no other variable in cross-national aggregate research on political violence as unsatisfactorily measured as state coercion, perhaps with the notable and notorious exception of the relative deprivation variable.[178]

The learning theories from which the underlying causal explanations in this chapter are taken may be considered a repository of hypotheses (see the brief overview in BERKOWITZ 1973:166ff.) to be considered in research on political violence. For example, the analysis of so-called reinforcement schedules (where one distinguishes between the frequency, intensity, duration, consistency, contiguity or delay, and the rates of change of rewards and punishments) would easily lead to the development of hypotheses not yet discussed in cross-national research on political violence (but see also the hypotheses in MARKUS/NESVOLD 1972; ANDERSON/NESVOLD 1972; NESVOLD/MARTIN 1974). Are direct[179] or vicarious (indirect)[180] punishments (i.e., coercive acts) or rewards equally effective? Is there a symmetry between punishment effects and reward effects (same slope, but different signs)? Are vicarious punishments less effective and vicarious rewards as effective as direct rewards? Or (even more complicating) are there additive or interactive effects between direct and vicarious forms of punishments or rewards? What about forms of violent political protest that do not occur for some time (extinction) but then recur again? There is a vast body of literature on these questions in animal research as well as a considerable amount in human psychological research (for an overview see BOE/CHURCH 1968; JOHNSTON 1972; WALTERS et al. 1972; BANDURA 1973:221-43; WALTERS/GRUSEC 1977). The results of these studies are, of course, only indirectly relevant to political violence research. However, this research does provide a number of interesting hypotheses which should be considered by researchers trying to explain violent political protest.[181] Other hypotheses may be drawn from criminological research (cf. TITTLE/LOGAN 1973), including the empirically corroborated hypothesis (TITTLE 1969; see also TITTLE/ROWE 1974; cf. also SILBERMAN 1976; for a critique and qualifications see GRASMICK/McLAUGHLIN 1978) that the *certainty*[182] of impending long-term imprisonment acts as a deterrent of criminal behavior (or, at least, of some forms of criminal behavior, see GEERKEN/GOVE 1977, and only for smaller cities, cf. BROWN 1978).

For a review of the evidence on general deterrence (i.e., "the symbolic effect that punishment may have on potential criminals") see NAGIN (1978: 96). He reports generally negative relationships between clearance rates, arrest probabilities, police expenditure per capita, and two measures of probability of imprisonment and crime rates, although there are some conflicting results, in particular concerning the relationship between sentence severity and crime rates. In general, however, the evidence is far from definitive because of limitations in the data on crimes and sanctions (e.g., the use of cross-sectional data). In addition, the incapacitation hypothesis ("the crime rate will . . . be reduced by physically constraining [through imprisonment] a greater proportion of the criminal element from committing crimes," NAGIN 1978:98) must be considered one of the more important rival hypotheses to the general deterrence hypothesis.

All of these research questions indicate the importance of collecting data over time (process data) to provide the researcher with detailed information on specific groups, their genesis, and eventual success or failure when carrying out protests (cf. GAMSON 1975 for a first notable effort along these lines; see chapter 9). Undoubtedly plenty of such data already exists. What is lacking is its systematic collection and refinement for the purposes of comparative research. If one conceives of theory as eventually providing instruments for mastering life situations, much more information on the transactions between various opponents taking part in acts of political violence is needed (cf. also the action-reaction model of "Conflict and Coercion in Dependent States" by JACKSON et al. 1978). We need to know not only whether a repressive climate is created by various coercive measures of the state authorities, but also how this effects the evaluation of available resources. We need information on how "objective" data are translated into strategic operations by the opponents in question. An interesting example, with which we will end this section, is the raw figures used for comparing and evaluating guerrilla resources and coercive resources: the ratio between guerrilla warriors and government troops has varied from 1:8 in Greece to 1:23 in Algeria and even 1:30 in Malaya (cf. GREENE 1974:84 and AHMAD 1971:148). Yet, even such a great "superiority" in Algeria did not prevent the victory of the insurgents, as opposed to events in Malaya and Greece. Obviously, more is at stake than mere military power in evaluating the political strength of opponents.

5.1.2.6. External Conflicts and Political Violence

Since political violence has been defined here solely as violence occurring within states, the broad field of external conflicts has not been considered. Even if the empirical evidence thus far does not favor this point of view, we believe (cf. also GURR 1973a) that both areas of concern should be incorporated into a broader frame of reference. There are innumerable, generally qualitative references as to the impact of external conflicts on internal conflicts (see ROSENAU 1964), but little systematic and consistent evidence (see the recent review by STOHL 1980). Furthermore, in the studies to be considered, external conflicts are often nonviolent, since violent international conflicts occur less frequently than violent internal conflicts.

In his study of internal and external conflicts in eight European countries over several centuries, SOROKIN presents this conclusion: "Contrary to expectation, the data [grouped in time intervals of quarter centuries and centuries] do not definitely show a positive association between unsuccessful wars and big disturbances nor between victorious wars and the absence of such. At best they yield only a very slight association between unsuccessful wars and disturbances" (SOROKIN 1957:597). Studying the period 1800–1960 FLANIGAN/FOGELMAN have this to say: "there is no general pattern of either positive or negative interrelationship between war and domestic political violence for all sixty-five of the countries" (FLANIGAN/ FOGELMAN 1970:5). Using factor analytic and multiple regression results, RUMMEL (1963) and TANTER (1966) *in general* found no evidence for interrelationships between external and internal conflict (cf. also TANTER 1969).[183] Using the same data base but with confirmatory factor analysis, EBERWEIN et al. (1979) do report some relationships between external and internal conflict behavior among nations in the period 1966–67. Yet, when controlling for population size in regression and partial correlation analyses, these relationships disappear.

In the various studies of WILKENFELD (see WILKENFELD 1974 for a summary) and WILKENFELD/ZINNES, however, there is some evidence of a relationship between external conflicts (using the RUMMEL-TANTER data for 1955–60; cf. also chapter 5.1.1.1.2.1) and internal conflicts, after controlling for *previous levels of conflicts* and after grouping nations according to type of *political system* (using the dichotomous and therefore insufficient classification of BANKS/GREGG 1965; for a critique see note 115; see also STOHL 1976:42 who points out that the grouping of nations should have been done before carrrying out the factor analysis). WILKENFELD/ZINNES (1973; N=74 nations) report, for instance, that there are relationships between external conflicts and less intense internal conflicts. Yet, this is the case only in personalist and polyarchic political systems, not in centrist political systems which seem more capable of insulating internal politics from external political influences. If one assumes polyarchic nations to be democracies, one may speculate that even in times of external crises the rights of the internal opposition to voice its protests are not curtailed. In personalist political systems, however, one can see the instability of the government whose resources are apparently overdrawn in external affairs as well as internal challenges. It has also been suggested that "higher information levels [of the population] and inadequate elite justifications of [external conflict] behavior may help to explain the higher association between foreign and domestic conflict behavior found in polyarchies and personalist nations" (STOHL 1976:43).

There are several, albeit not consistent, positive correlations between external conflicts and subsequent internal clashes.[184] Yet, the data at hand do not allow for a test of any of these possible explanations. In the writings of WILKENFELD/ZINNES there is no attempt at a general theoretical explanation of the results they found, but only ad hoc speculation. Furthermore, the number of cases often becomes too small for results to be reliable. This holds true in spite of WILKENFELD's efforts to increase the number of cases by using the conflict scores for each year and adding them up, thus neglecting the possible effects of prior conflicts on subsequent conflict scores (WEEDE 1970:235).

Using an interrupted time series design and building on the *New York Times Index* as data source, STOHL (1975, 1976) has analyzed whether there are relationships between the external wars of the United States (Spanish-American War, the two world wars, the Korean War, and the war in Vietnam) and subsequent violent tensions in the economic, social, and political spheres. While the patterns differ in all five cases, there is at least some evidence in favor of STOHL's three hypotheses: external war mobilizes subordinate groups into the internal political arena, leading to an intensification of economic conflict and to political violence (quite frequently in the form of government acts against subordinate segments, STOHL 1976:124). At the same time, the social status of these groups is raised in comparison with that of dominant social groups; this also contributes to an increase in the intensity of violent conflicts between these groups. Thirdly, the economic and social changes precipitated by external war lead to demands for the redistribution of power and rewards; this again is said to intensify conflicts. In all the cases studied, however, the theoretical links have not been further specified so that a rigorous test of these hypotheses still must be carried out (even though at least in the case of the United States after World War I, other evidence seems to corroborate the theoretical explanations of STOHL).[185]

In studies of this kind one should also take into consideration who is attacking and who is being attacked. Is the legitimacy of a regime greater when it is attacked than when it is the attacker? There are as well those cases where external attacking creates a climate of enthusiasm in the attacking country, often overshadowing internal conflicts. However, if there are strong dissident resources, *any* involvement in violent external conflicts may create conditions perceived by rebels as increasing their chances of revolutionary takeover. Moreover, one must distinguish between countries that initiate external hostilities and those that are attacked, if cases where internal conflicts are "pushed" into the external sphere (to increase internal cohesion) are to be differentiated from those where internal conflicts "pull in" or attract external interference (cf. CHITTICK/JENKINS 1976:287 and below).

In the literature on political violence, the external war → internal revolution connection probably has gained the greatest attention (cf. chapter 8.4.2). The scapegoat mechanism (more generally, the safety-valve explanation, whereby external conflicts supposedly take the steam out of internal conflicts[186] is the hypothesis most often advocated as far as the relationship between internal conflicts and subsequent external disturbances is concerned.[187]

In both cases, whether external conflicts cause internal conflicts or the converse, it is absolutely necessary to specify the various *linkage groups* ("group[s] with links to the domestic system and with some particular links to the international or foreign input," DEUTSCH 1966a:12) as well as other strategic internal groups. It is interesting to note that, in a study of thirty-three African countries (1963-65), relationships between internal conflicts and milder forms of external conflicts (and possibly between external and internal conflicts?) have been found (COLLINS 1973). African state boundaries often overlap with ethnic (linguistic or other social) ties, creating various types of *irredenta* (cf. WAI 1978; also ANDERSON et al. 1967: 67-74 for a worldwide overview, excluding Europe, of irredenta; on ethnic problems in Europe see the excellent summary by KREJCI 1978).[188] These results seem to be quite substantial in that these ethnic (linguistic or other) minorities or even majorities make for large protest potentials:

> Among those larger antagonisms which cut across nation-state boundaries are those between: Malays and Chinese (Malaysia and to a lesser extent Thailand, Indonesia, and the Philippines); Hindus and Moslems (India, Pakistan); Arabs and Jews (Palestine); Arabs and Blacks (Sudan, Chad, Ethiopia, Cameroons); Blacks and Whites (Rhodesia, South Africa, Angola, Mozambique, the United States); Latin and North Europeans (Belgium, Canada); Blacks and East Indians (Guayana, Trinidad); Protestants and Catholics (Northern Ireland). In addition, countries like Burma, Thailand, Ceylon, Pakistan, Iraq, Cyprus, Yugoslavia, and most of the countries of Black Africa have communal differences which are often no less likely to produce violence for being peculiar to the individual country (HUNTINGTON 1971a:11; cf. also the discussion in chapter 5.1.2.4 and the list of communal dissident groups in GURR and Associates 1978:181-85).[189]

According to VON DER MEHDEN (1973:17), in the period following World War II, 44% of the political violence must be viewed in connection with separatist movements. (Asian countries are counted only from their date of independence after World War II.) In Africa and the Middle East, including North Africa, the figure is 25%, in Europe 13%, and in Latin America 4%. The categories, however, do not preclude multiple classification of cases; the absolute figures are more conclusive, e.g., nineteen in Asia vs. thirty-five in Africa (cf. also chapter 5.1.2.8).

These findings are important in terms of both method and theory. SCHEUCH has persistently argued—and there is a rapidly growing literature on African nations in this respect[190]—that counting nations as units of observation may easily be misleading in cross-national analyses. "No amount of checking will reduce erroneous conclusions in a cross-national comparison that result from treating as polities in a substantive sense those units which are polities only in a purely formalistic sense, and which by no stretch of the imagination refer to units that are usually meant when discussing polities" (SCHEUCH 1966:145; cf. also BURROWES 1970:478). The Western idea of a nation may not mean much to tribes or people largely bound by "primordial ties" (GEERTZ 1963), which after all were and are quite important in many Western countries as well. Thus it is even more important that we go beyond national boundaries in the analysis of political violence,[191] as GURR (1973a) has argued. "Scholars studying 'internal' conflict largely fail to examine the supranational manifestations of their variables that might tell us whether local conflict is truly 'local,' or a manifestation of a much larger conflict. And those studying conflict among nations seldom look to the intra-national conditions that might inform us about when and how large-scale conflict will effect local conflicts" (GURR 1973a:10). GURR proposes examining whether there are aspects common to all forms of internal and external conflicts. "What is the nature of the leaders, and what are the common properties and attitudes of their followers, of *all* prospective conflict groups, whether intranational, national, or international?" (ibid.; cf. also the list of analytical questions and research hypotheses, ibid., p. 10–13).

There are many common examples besides the classic French and Russian revolutions of how internal and external conflicts might interrelate: "Many elites . . . encourage their citizens to riot and demonstrate against the resident agents and entrepreneurs of foreign foes: these techniques are those of 'internal' strife, whereas objectives and repercussions are international" (GURR 1973a:9). Success in internal war may stimulate related activities in another country which may lead to the mobilization of other nations on the international scene.

In his own studies GURR tried to take into account the external support given either to rebels or incumbent elites. He found that "external support for dissidents correlated .62 with total magnitude of strife, .70 with revolution (but only .14 with turmoil); external support for regimes was similarly correlated with the strife measures, .72 with revolution for example" (GURR 1972b:43; as to the definition of the dependent variables see chapter 5.1.1.1.1). Moreover, "the close connection between support for dissidents and countervailing support for the regime (and vice versa) is evident from the fact that their correlation is .83" (GURR 1970a:270–71). In the factor analysis of GURR/BISHOP (1976; see chapter 5.1.1.1.2.6 for further details), support of rebels and support of the regime load on the same intervention dimension and correlate (man-days) with rebellion. Building on the earlier study of GURR/DUVALL (1973), the authors interpret these results to mean that "internal war attracts intervention, intervention exacerbates internal war" (GURR/BISHOP 1976:98; for similar findings see below). The victims or, more neutrally, objects of interventions of this kind are mainly to be found in countries of the Third World.

In his study of ninety-five "local wars" between 1944 and 1969 KENDE reports these summary results, not unlike those of GURR/DUVALL (1973; see chapter 5.1.1.1.4; see also GURR 1970a:271): "As opposed to the wars prior to the Second World War the predominant type of war in our days is the internal war fought within the boundaries of one country . . . and of these, wars fought with foreign participation stand out as the greatest in number. . . . Since 1963 no political war has been fought without overt foreign participation" (KENDE 1971:12, 22). Being the victim of military intervention (i.e., external conflict fought out on internal territory) often causes long-term conflict potentials, even though in the short run internal conflicts may diminish (but cf. PEARSON 1974a and below). However, "intervention [may also directly] exacerbate civil conflict in the target country. Governments favored by interventions [may] repress opposition groups, who in turn [may raise] their number of armed attacks" (STOHL 1980: 320). An extension of KENDE's study to the period 1967–76 reveals related findings. Between 1945 and 1976, "120 wars were waged on the territories of 71 countries. . . . Eighty-four countries were involved in the 120 wars." During the last ten years "relatively more countries have become involved in the wars . . . than in the previous period" (KENDE 1978:227).

After studying thirty-three civil wars between 1910 and 1967, LUARD (1968:142–43) presents this conclusion: "Civil war is almost twice as common in the postwar as in the interwar period. Outside intervention is much more frequent than before. In the former period the result was more often that the government was overthrown, especially when there was outside intervention. In the later cases governments were often maintained; and again this was specially so where outside intervention took place. . . . In only two of the eighteen post-1945 cases did rebel forces succeed in overthrowing the government and establishing their own (China and Cuba)" (LUARD 1968: 142–43).[192]

In summary, external conflicts apparently are not *the* determinant of internal conflicts (and this holds when reversing the independent and dependent variables). Nevertheless, in the studies thus far, which favor considering the two domains of conflict as separate, the true relationships between the variables have either been superimposed upon by other, thus far neglected variables (cf. the discussion of linkage groups) or are mediated by other variables. Thus, some of the present results must be interpreted as spurious noncorrelations or, better stated, as having led to the spurious inference that there is no relationship between the two realms of conflict. This argument is somewhat bolstered in studies showing that external interventions (directly or through material aid) represent the link between external and internal conflicts. This is particularly striking after World War II and after the stabilization of the blocks and spheres of influence of the superpowers (cf. WEEDE 1975b). As several scholars have put it, the "internationalization of civil wars" seems to have become a predominant form of conflict in our time (cf. the figures in SMALL/SINGER 1979:100). Thus, in causal analysis the question is: Which is the dependent and which is the independent variable? Do internal wars or the imminent outbreak of internal conflicts attract external intervention? (See BLAINEY 1973:71 for at least thirty-three cases of this kind between 1823 and 1937; cf. also PEARSON 1974a and WEEDE 1975b:250 for some results, and WEEDE 1978 who reports a positive relation between internal conflicts and instability and American intervention on behalf of the incumbents between 1958 and 1965; for comparable results see PEARSON 1976 and GIRLING 1980:140–42.)[193] Or does one have to reckon with much more complicated causal chains and feedback processes? External interventions might serve a number of goals at the same time. The promise of latter massive support of rebels might encourage them to start fighting, and stronger external aid will come or not, depending on their initial successes and future chances. PEARSON considers internal conflicts as both independent and dependent variables. More precisely, his data do not show a clear pattern in either direction. Of his many interesting results, only a few are mentioned here (period: 1960–67): "while successful or unsuccessful coups did not seem very likely to bring intervention, social unrest capped by organized violence (armed attacks, deaths) seemed the most likely domestic conflict triggers of military intervention by foreign powers interested in propping up target governments" (PEARSON 1974a:282).

> One of the most important findings in the present study is that intervention breeds civil conflict in the target. Specifically, governments seem to suppress opposition groups in the midst of increased armed attacks from such groups and in the midst of foreign military intervention; in the process, many deaths result. While interveners and factions which invite intervention may seek 'stability,' the result of intervention is all too frequently *prolonged* (for as long as a year or more) violence and bloodshed (ibid., p. 285).

As the bulk of military interventions has been carried out by major powers, it is no wonder that geographic proximity is unrelated to the occurrence of such intervention (PEARSON 1974b). However, "the pattern of major power interventions is quite distinct from that of minor powers. Major power interventions generally concern strategic power balances, ideology, economic, diplomatic, and military interests, while minor powers have been more concerned with regional disputes over territory or social grievances, with regional ideology, or with security of immediate border areas" (PEARSON/BAUMANN 1974:277 for the period 1948–67). And finally, "long-standing hostile relations, such as border disputes, lead to hostile interventions even when force ratios are less than favorable to the intervener" (ibid., p. 275).

At this point, it is apparent that an analysis of political violence without consideration of supranational (inter)dependencies (cf. also KERBO 1978) can lead to premature conclusions. One is probably right in drawing this conclusion since recent works in conflict research seem to bear witness to this trend: scholars working in international conflict relations look more closely at internal conflicts as well, whereas researcher working on internal conflicts, whether on a cross-national basis or not, take global constellations into consideration.[194]

5.1.2.7. Socioeconomic Inequality and Political Violence

"At least since ARISTOTLE[195] theorists have believed that political discontent and its consequents—protest, instability, violence, revolution—depend not only on the absolute level of economic well-being, but also on the distribution of wealth" (NAGEL 1974:453). Yet a high degree of socioeconomic inequality may not contribute at all to political violence, provided that there is a norm integration justifying inequality within the society in question or that the repressive measures of the authorities are efficient to keep down any protests. However, one faces serious data problems if one tries to test hypotheses on the effects of socioeconomic inequality, because sufficiently reliable data on socioeconomic inequality exist only for a minority of nations. Data on inequality could easily become an explosive political issue. Consequently, elites, particularly in less egalitarian and/or more repressive societies, have an interest in not collecting the figures. Furthermore, there are various strategies of tax avoidance and evasion to consider when gathering data on inequality.[196] Thus, formal measures of inequality need not correlate highly with the effective degree of inequality. Nevertheless, some interesting and suggestive results will be mentioned here. Since data on the various forms of socioeconomic inequality are scarce or have not yet been put together in cross-national data banks, we focus here on inequality in land distribution.

RUSSETT (1964) relates inequality in land tenure (using the GINI index) in forty-seven nations to a cumulated score of violent political deaths per million from 1950 to 1962 and finds a relationship of r=.46 (or r=.29 when ECKSTEIN's [1962] internal war measures for 1946-61 are used). When controlling for percentage of labor force in agriculture,[197] a much stronger relationship emerges for agricultural nations (r=.70), thus lending strong support to the hypothesis "that a prosperous peasantry, a sturdy yeomanry, is especially likely to support the existing regime, but that a deprived peasantry . . . is a particular source of political discontent" (RUSSETT et al. 1964:320). The relationship is also upheld in a multiple regression analysis (N=33) employing several other socioeconomic variables (ibid., p. 321).[198]

Similarly, TANTER/MIDLARSKY (1967), employing data from the *World Handbook of Political and Social Indicators* (RUSSETT et al. 1964), find a positive relationship between inequality in land tenure and "revolutions" in 1950-62 (N=10).[199] PARVIN (1973; N=26 predominantly Western nations; no period specified) reports inequality of income distribution to be related to deaths resulting from domestic group violence but less important than other socioeconomic variables employed.

BARROWS (1976) has analyzed the determinants of political instability measured along the dimensions elite instability, communal instability, and turmoil (drawing on MORRISON et al. 1972a:122-24) in thirty-two black African nations during the 1960s. In a multiple correlation analysis he finds that inequality is a consistent predictor of all three of the dependent variables when measured along a scale of ethnic group inequality, mid-1960s (i.e., "the degree of disproportionality between the size of ethnic groups and their share of political power and/or other values [wealth, education, etc.]" (p. 154-55). Level of social mobilization (measured by a composite index based on factor score coefficients of various indicators on urbanization, education, mass communication, etc.) and ethnic pluralism turn out to be weak and inconsistent predictors of the dependent variables, with the exception of a constant negative relationship between social mobilization and communal instability and a positive one between ethnic diversity and turmoil (with correlation coefficients around ±.30 on the average in both cases). BARROWS's study appears particularly noteworthy since he makes an effort to consider various facets of ethnic diversity, such as ethnic distribution (linguistic fractionalization, ethnic fractionalization, ethnic polarization)[200] and ethnic pluralism (by running a factor analysis and using the loadings "as the basis for assigning weights to each of the indicators," BARROWS 1976:152). His final analysis, however, seems unconvincing and implausible to me. A high degree of statistical explanation notwithstanding, there is simply no reason why the ratio between civil servants and wage earners should be treated as the background variable and ethnic diversity as an intermediate variable. On the theoretical level, however, BARROWS's final remarks make more sense and should be tested for in future studies: "The more fundamental factors seem to be unequal access to the benefits of modernity and the incentive to political mobilization held out by expanded government. These factors conspire to activate the ethnic group competition that often erupts into violence" (BARROWS 1976:166).

Finally, there is a recent study by NAGEL (1974) who argues for a curvilinear relationship between inequality and discontent. He starts from FESTINGER's hypothesis that "the tendency to compare oneself with some other specific person decreases as the difference between his opinion or ability and one's own increases" (FESTINGER 1954:120) and combines this tendency to compare with the grievance resulting from comparison. This leads to the general hypothesis that discontent due to inequality is a function of the tendency to compare × grievance resulting from comparison. Mathematically he derives a curvilinear relationship between inequality and discontent: "discontent which, ceteris paribus, begins at zero in a perfectly egalitarian system, increases with inequality up to a maximum at some intermediate level of inequality, and then decreases again as complete inequality is approached" (NAGEL 1974:455). However, two empirical tests of this proposition provide only limited evidence in favor of NAGEL's theory. First, taking up the debate (see ibid. for details and PAIGE 1975:327-33 for an empirically based correction of some of the rather adventurous original theoretical formulations) over whether inequality in 1960 landholdings is positively, negatively, or otherwise related to the Saigon government controlling this area in 1965, he finds from a multiple regression analysis that, controlling for region, GNP, and other variables, the inclusion of the GINI index (using a squared term to test for curvilinearity and not just a linear term) significantly increases the amount of variance explained. In a second study data on inequality of land distribution in fifty-four nations (taken from TAYLOR/HUDSON 1972) are related to GURR's three indexes of conspiracy, internal war, and turmoil (1961-65) and to four other political violence variables again taken from TAYLOR/HUDSON and covering the period 1948-67. When GNP (which consistently is negatively related to the dependent variable and also the stronger determinant) is controlled for, the inequality measures do not show the predicted curvilinear relationship.

NAGEL discusses various possible explanations for his failure to find the expected relationship: the small N (also disturbing the other studies mentioned in this chapter) perhaps preventing a curvilinear relationship from showing up, other sources of wealth besides land tenure, mediating variables, and other explanations. Additional tests, however, do not improve his results.[201] Only in the case of conspiracy in agriculture-based societies (N=38) do the inequality measures prove to be significant predictors. The curvilinear relationship is reversed, as predicted on the basis of GURR's hypothesis: "The likelihood of conspiracy varies directly with the intensity and scope of elite relative deprivation and *inversely* with the intensity and scope of mass relative deprivation" (GURR 1970a:325; emphasis by NAGEL). Depending on the empirical variant, a combination of these two hypotheses of GURR can lead to the curvilinear relationship observed by NAGEL. Yet, R^2 is comparatively low (.32).

Apparently inequality and level as well as rate of economic development must be considered simultaneously (cf. WARD 1978:167 and passim for a critical evaluation of the literature) for an adequate analysis. Other variables such as the countries' histories and ideologies must also be taken into account. In some of the studies mentioned, economic growth variables were stronger predictors of political violence than inequality. There is, however, persuasive theoretical reasoning for a curvilinear relationship between inequality and political violence (cf. also chapter 5.3.2.4). "Economic development increases economic inequality at the same time that social mobilization decreases the legitimacy of that inequality. Both aspects of modernization combine to produce political instability" (HUNTINGTON 1968:58–59). Inequality should be curvilinearly related to economic development, reaching its peak at a mid-level of development as indirectly suggested by OLSON (1963) and empirically "demonstrated"[202] by ADELMAN/MORRIS (1973) and PAUKERT,[203] using a sample of fifty-six noncommunist states[204] (PAUKERT 1973; see also ibid. and in LOEHR 1977 for references as to the literature, especially the works of KUZNETS 1955; 1963; cf. the similar finding and the analyses by AHLUWALIA 1976 for sixty-two countries and AHLUWALIA 1976a for sixty countries; finally see JAIN 1975 for individual and household level data on income inequality for eighty-one countries). The interrelationships between these two independent variables used in explaining political violence may account for inequality not showing the predicted relationship. Apparently there is also an important causal connection between socioeconomic inequality and political participation.

> But, contrary to assumptions of the liberal model,[205] the flow of causal influence is stronger from political participation to socio-economic equality than in the reverse direction. In its early phases, the expansion of political participation along the lines of the bourgeois model tends to promote greater socio-economic inequality, thus reinforcing the effect of economic development. In its later phases, the expansion of political participation tends, in accordance with the operations of the populist model, to promote greater socio-

economic equality through governmental action to redistribute
income and wealth (HUNTINGTON/NELSON 1976:78).

Moreover, discontent, the inferred psychological reaction to socioeconomic inequality, has not been measured at all. As NAGEL himself suggests:
"Further tests are needed, but cross-national data may not be suitable for the
task. Instead, researchers should seek units (a) of reasonable cultural homogeneity, (b) exhibiting a full range of variation in inequality (c) along a
dimension of major importance to most members of the units. In addition,
they should (d) employ as a dependent variable a direct measure of discontent, or else try to incorporate other variables believed to mediate between
discontent and the dependent variables used" (NAGEL 1974:469). Thus,
data on how socioeconomic inequalities are perceived by various social
groups must be gathered,[206] if the inequality variable is to be employed in
a fruitful manner in studies on political violence or revolutionary activities.[207]

These latter recommendations are particularly important, because there
seems to be good reason to postulate a relationship between inequality and
political violence that is quite contrary to the one outlined by NAGEL. In
what is perhaps the most brilliant theoretical analysis of the consequences of
income inequality, HIRSCHMAN (1973) compares the tolerance for an
initially increasing inequality, i.e., others getting richer than oneself, to a
situation in a traffic jam in a tunnel. If others advance, much like drivers
in such a traffic jam, one expects the same for oneself at the beginning. This
hope factor makes for a greater tolerance as far as increased inequality is
concerned. If, however, there is no such betterment of the situation for a
person still hoping and/or if social advances are reacted to with "discrimination against nouveaux riches," the tunnel effect levels off with time. Supporters turn into enemies of the social order. HIRSCHMAN goes on to suggest that the "tunnel effect," which runs counter to NAGEL's theorizing
(and, in fact, seems to suggest a curvilinear relationship of a shape exactly
the opposite to that predicted by NAGEL), prevails only in ethnoculturally
homogeneous societies.

The most recent study (SIGELMAN/SIMPSON 1977; N=49 nations),
albeit still based on aggregate data, leads to the conclusion that there is no
V-curve relationship between economic inequality (using measures of personal income inequality taken from PAUKERT 1973) and political violence
(1958–67, internal war measure of HIBBS 1973; cf. chapter 5.1.1.3), as
might be expected on the basis of works by DAVIS (1948) and HIRSCHMAN
(1973; see above). The inverted V-curve hypothesis of NAGEL also goes
unsupported. If anything, there is a moderate positive linear relationship
between economic inequality and political violence, a relationship that
persists if control variables are added referring to the rate of social change
("between 1950 and 1960 percentages of population residing in cities of
100,000 or more"), to social mobility ("breath of national educational
enrollment," 1965), to sociocultural heterogeneity (a measure of ethnolinguistic fractionalization is employed), and to affluence (1965 per capita
GNP). While several of these measures are highly indirect in nature, once

again economic development proves to be a much stronger predictor of political violence than economic inequality. As far as the other test variables are concerned, the forty-nine nations are shown to be representative of a larger universe. A final and perhaps most important point is that only cross-sectional data were available; admittedly, such data are insufficent for testing a theoretical notion building on dynamic interrelationships.

5.1.2.8. Some Other Determinants of Political Violence

There are a number of variables which are of primary importance in the study of political violence, yet for various reasons these variables and their effects have been or will be discussed at other points in this study.

Legitimacy is a key variable in cross-national research on political violence, but thus far evidence as to the nature and effects of legitimacy have been quite indirect. Yet, considerable evidence does exist testifying to the "preventive" nature of legitimate political order. It may inhibit at least the more deadly forms of violent political conflict *without* undermining civil liberty. Autocratic regimes, however, may succeed to some extent in preventing the occurrence or spreading of either protest or rebellion, but the costs are shared by the population at large, not just by potential dissidents. In chapter 6.3.4 in the discussion of relationships between political crises and political violence, we will deal with efforts to incorporate the legitimacy variable into research on political violence or, more generally, into research on protest behavior.

Another important variable is *conflict traditions*, lending some support to the biblical *violence-begets-violence*. However, there is a danger that stable implicit variables and autocorrelated residuals contribute to correlations between prior and later levels of violent political conflicts, thus making this hypothesis extremely difficult to test.[208] Studying internal conflicts between 1948 and 1965, GURR et al. (forthcoming) found evidence in favor of the violence-breeds-violence hypothesis, yet with notable differentiations (cf. also LICHBACH/GURR 1980) since conflict traditions seem much stronger in European and Latin countries than in neocolonial nations which have more erratic conflict patterns. They also report that past success (defined in terms of gains by rebels) in internal wars (1850-1960) and in turmoil (1940-60) is related to later magnitudes of the same types of conflicts. In the case of conspiracy as well, positive but much less significant relationships are found. The culture-of-violence hypothesis, whose importance has been stressed repeatedly by GURR in his theory of political violence (cf. GURR 1970a:168-77) and which he has empirically corroborated (in addition cf. HIBBS 1973; chapter 5.1.1.3; ADAMS 1970:198 and passim), is also demonstrated in DUVALL/WELFLING's study of conflicts in twenty-eight black African nations:

> Turmoil [which is considerably underspecified in their causal
> model] appears to be a function of itself; that is, tumultuous Afri-

can countries tend to remain tumultuous over time. . . . Internal war,
however, is affected by all forms of previous conflict. No single
causal mechanism predominates. Both prior internal war and turmoil
are positively related to later internal war—evidence that sporadic
and anomic conflict can be, in fact tends to be, translated into more
organized and perhaps more deadly conflict in Africa. On the other
hand, elite conflict reduces the likelihood of later internal war. . . .
it might reflect in part the suppressive character of post-coup military regimes (DUVALL/WELFLING 1973:692).

Finally, *religious, regional, ethnic, racial, linguistic,* and *other communal-*
or *custom-based ties* (GEERTZ 1963 refers to them as "primordial attachments") must be mentioned but will not be studied again as to their impact
on political violence (see chapter 5.1.1; 5.1.2.4; 5.1.2.6).

Of a total of 132 contemporary states, only 12 (9.1 per cent) can be
described as essentially homogeneous from an ethnic viewpoint. An
additional 25 states (18.9 per cent of the sample) contain an ethnic
group accounting for more than 90 per cent of the state's total
population, and in still another 25 states the largest element accounts
for between 75 and 89 per cent of the population. But in 31 states
(23.5 per cent of the total), the largest ethnic element represents
only 50 to 74 per cent of the population, and in 39 cases (29.5 per
cent of all states) the largest group fails to account for even half of
the state's population. Moreover, this portrait of ethnic diversity
becomes more vivid when the number of distinct ethnic groups
within states is considered. In some instances, the number of groups
within a state runs into the hundreds, and in 53 states (40.2 per cent
of the total), the population is divided into more than *five* significant groups. . . . [CONNOR 1972:320; cf. also the various case
studies in HUNT/WALKER 1974] The 132 units include all entities
that were generally considered to be states as of January 1, 1971,
with the exception of a few microunits such as Nauru and Western
Samoa. However, East and West Germany, North and South Korea,
and North and South Vietnam were treated as single entities in the
belief that such treatment would minimize their distorting effects
(CONNOR 1972:320–21).

VON DER MEHDEN (1973:17) reports the following primordial forms of
political violence (out of all forms of political violence) in various regions,
allowing for multiple classification of events: 8% in Latin America, 27% in
Europe, 56% in the Middle East and Northern Africa, 63% in Africa, and
74% in Asia. These data refer to the period after World War II or after gaining
independence. However, the absolute figures are definitely too low: 23 (Latin

America), 30 (Europe), 16 (Middle East and Northern Africa), 35 (Africa), and 19 (Asia). As the study of VON DER MEHDEN apparently was not intended to be a study of all the cases of primordial political violence, these results should be read with care. (The same holds for the study by HEWITT 1977 on violent conflict in nineteen multiethnic societies.) GURR et al. (forthcoming) report additional evidence in favor of the hypothesis that the "possibility of an insurrectionary movement arising and then employing organized violence depends upon the existence of sharp divisions within the society created by regional, ethnic, linguistic, class, religious, or other communal differences that may provide the necessary social and geographic basis for supporting the movement" (PYE 1966:136). This class of variables, which frequently denotes a zero-sum structure of conflict lines, is of major importance for an understanding of the determinants and outcomes of some forms of political violence. Economic issues might be settled via bargaining, i.e., reaching a solution which entails at least *some* gains for *all* of the participants in conflict. In contrast, communal conflicts (which can be based on ethnic, linguistic, racial, religious, or other communal criteria of division) are often symbolic in nature and are perceived as matters of principle, as non-negotiable, and as touching on the sense of identity of one's own group. Therefore, they acquire the characteristics of conflicts with a zero-sum structure: each side automatically gets what the other loses and vice versa, thus leading to irreversible settlements (cf. OBERSCHALL 1973:50–51). As ESMAN puts it: "there are painfully few cross-cutting loyalties or multiple group memberships in communally divided societies. Those that exist tend to be far less important to the individual than his communal identity. And unless the multiple cleavages are both 'equally salient' and 'simultaneously experienced,' [NORDLINGER 1972:96] the cross-cutting hypothesis breaks down" (ESMAN 1973:71). It is the absence of cross-cutting cleavages (cf. also chapter 6.3.5 and the analysis of the classic example—or counter-example depending on the point of view[209]—namely Switzerland, in STEINER 1969, 1974) which often causes the development of a strong potential for violent political conflicts, a readiness to engage in political conflicts in a win-or-lose mood. As ZOLBERG writes with respect to black African countries: "Often, by the time of independence, one tribe or group of tribes had become more urban, more educated, more Christian and richer than others in the country. Hence, at the mass level, old and new cleavages tend to be consistent rather than cross-cutting; camps are clear-cut and individuals can engage wholeheartedly in the disputes that occur" (ZOLBERG 1968:73; see also the empirical results in MORRISON/STEVENSON 1972b).

The discussion of empirical results as to the determinants of political violence will conclude at this point. In the next section some general methodological problems arising in these cross-national aggregate analyses of political violence will be considered. In subsequent sections there will be numerous other theoretical and empirical arguments, some of them referring to a different level of explanation, bearing on the sociology of political violence.

5.1.3. Further Methodological Issues

Before concluding this discussion of cross-national research on political violence, a few remarks concerning further methodological problems may be in order. We will not repeat the methodological issues discussed thus far (see especially chapter 5.1.1.1.3). We shall instead focus on problems of collecting data on political violence, on coding procedures, and on some other issues. In short, this will be a discussion of errors likely to occur in this type of research and of some of the strategies employed to control these sources of errors.

The strongest threat to the reliability and validity of cross-national results on political violence probably arises from the *limited coverage of* the various *sources* used. There are three general sources of error in this respect:

1. *Violent political conflicts are not reported.* There are two reasons for this: (a) News about internal conflicts is suppressed (or distorted, cf. also 2) due to *censorship*[210] and is thus not reported or reported incorrectly in the sources used for cross-national analyses of political violence. (b) Only the *most important* events are reported, with less important conflicts left out. Insufficient means of communication and/or low interest in events in certain countries may be responsible for this type of error. One must consider that space for reporting is normally limited. Consequently, criteria of selection used by news agencies or newspapers[211] may cause distortions.[212]

2. *Incorrect data are reported.*[213] The magnitude of violent political conflicts may be *inflated* or *suppressed* or even—though rarely—fabricated. Some possible reasons have been mentioned in 1b.

3. There are also errors when *transforming data*, the so-called clerical errors (cf. RUMMEL 1972:143f.). These errors may originate during the coding, the punching of data cards, or at other occasions of data handling. They are comparatively easy to control, provided that further coders and punchers are working *independently*[214] of each other. Unfortunately, researchers in political violence often do not inform their readers to a sufficient degree about any reliability tests performed (see TAYLOR/HUDSON 1972:391–412 for a notable exception; cf. also GURR/RUTTENBERG 1967:37; and HARDISTY in GURR et al., forthcoming).

More complex sources of error are introduced when indexes are constructed which presuppose reported events to be *comparable*. In a more general sense, these are also errors due to transformation of data. The attribution of numbers to specific conflict events may already have caused some errors. The same holds for the transformation of data, a rather common procedure in this type of research. The models of factor analysis as well as regression analysis presuppose linear, interval-scaled relationships between normally distributed variables, an assumption which is not necessarily fulfilled in conflict research. If transformations (usually logarithmic) are performed, there is not always safeguarding against distorting the *structure* of the data (cf. KRUSKAL 1968). In some cases (as in the case of internal war in the study of GURR 1968a), the distribution remains skewed even after transformations have been carried out. Furthermore, there is no guarantee that comparable conflicts in different countries are equally scored in government reports and/or news articles. Conversely, there may be substantial differences, e.g., with respect to the political system, between apparently similar protests in different countries (see chapter 5.1.1.1.3.1 where the issue of equivalence has been dealt with at greater length).

Thus far we have described only *possible* sources of error[215] in this type of study. Information as to how these errors affect the relationships under study would be more significant. Whereas *random error* leads to an attenuation of the particular correlations[216] and thus to stricter tests[217] of the underlying hypotheses, *systematic* error may either lower or inflate relationships. Further distinctions are introduced when errors are considered not only in the *univariate* but also in the *bivariate* and the *multivariate* case (see RUMMEL 1972:441-45 for a brief discussion).

Whereas most researchers doing comparative studies in political violence perform some controls to prevent random or systematic distortions of their results, there are few studies in which the coverage of various sources has been analyzed as to whether different coverage affects the results in a random or systematic manner. DORAN et al. (1973) have performed one such analysis (for further studies along these lines cf. SCOLNICK 1974:486-89). They applied the coding procedures of the FEIERABENDs to reports of conflict phenomena in thirteen Caribbean countries between 1948 and 1964. In addition to the FEIERABENDs' global data source, *Deadline Data*, they made use of the *Hispanic American Report*. They found that the global source reports far fewer oppositional activities and the regional source is in general more detailed. In this case, three times as many events were reported in the regional source. When performing a factor analysis of various conflict variables (years 1955-57), results based on the local source are much more interpretable than those relying on the global source.

Obviously, when collecting conflict data one should use more than one source to control for potential *single vs. multiple* source differences (for a similar conclusion based on African studies, see COPSON 1973:211; cf. also BURROWES/SPECTOR 1970:4-5; AZAR 1970; AZAR et al. 1972; AZAR 1975:4; DORAN et al. [forthcoming]; BURROWES 1974; HOGGARD 1971:10-11; 1974; as well as PETERSON 1975:302ff.)[218] and at least one regional or local source to take care of *global vs. regional* differences. Furthermore, coders should have extensive knowledge of the events and countries with which they are dealing.

A conclusion similar to that in DORAN et al. must be drawn if the coverage of the *New York Times* (for some researchers the best general source available)[219] is compared to that of more regional sources, as TAYLOR/ HUDSON (1972) have done. They rely mainly on the *New York Times Index*,[220] which gives more condensed information than is found in the paper itself. In addition, they consult various other sources, notably the

Associated Press card file for Latin America and Europe, the *Africa Diary* for African countries (apparently the only area[221] for which the *New York Times Index* is inadequate), and the *Middle East Journal* for the Middle East. After performing controls to check the reliability and coverage of their various sources, they arrived at these general conclusions: "First, using secondary sources tends to compensate for deficiencies and gaps in the primary source rather than to accentuate them. Second, although there is variation from country to country and from variable to variable, this variation occurs as much within a second source as between them so that the different second sources used do not constitute a barrier to cross-regional comparison. Finally, although using data from third sources would have increased the total number of events by perhaps as much as 15 percent, it would not have substantially altered the overall picture" (TAYLOR/HUDSON 1972:422).

There is, however, a study by HAZLEWOOD/WEST (1974) who report results leading to less sceptical conclusions than those of DORAN et al. (but cf. also the criticism in JACKMAN/BOYD 1979: fn. 1). While also finding that the regional source (*Hispanic American Review*) reports more intensely (years 1955–60; N=20 Latin American countries; indicators taken from studies by RUMMEL, TANTER, FEIERABEND/FEIERABEND 1966, BOROCK 1967, and BANKS, 1971) than do the global sources (*New York Times Index, Deadline Data, New International Yearbook, Britannica Book of the Year, Facts on File*) HAZLEWOOD/WEST nevertheless did not find distortions of *relationships* among variables. However, they tested only for two hypotheses. A similar result emerged after performing factor analyses: "Despite the low bivariate correlations, the correlations between the global data and the regional data factor structures demonstrate the basic similarity of the data patterns regardless of their collection source(s)" (HAZLEWOOD/WEST 1974:330).

The most recent and most ambitious test of the effects of the use of multiple sources on the analysis of political violence was performed by JACKMAN/BOYD (1979) who studied the patterns of conflict in thirty black African countries. Basically, their results repeat those of TAYLOR/HUDSON (1972). In particular, JACKMAN/BOYD report that in comparing their data sources (*Keesing's Contemporary Archives, Facts on File,* and *African Recorder*) with the *World Handbook of Political and Social Indicators* (sources for Africa: *New York Times Index* and *Africa Diary*) "the benefits of reliance on multiple sources [seem to] outweigh the costs." Thus, differences in source coverage may have an effect on the findings, yet "these differences [may] stem at least as much from variations across data sets in event definitions and coding procedures." To test for these explanations, which they developed while comparing the coverage of their three sources with that of the *World Handbook* and *Black Africa* (MORRISON et al. 1972), JACKMAN/BOYD disaggregated their data on numbers of antigovernment demonstrations and political strikes by source. When testing the correlations of these variables with measures of social mobilization and multipartyism, they found no source coverage effects, in spite of the expectation that collective protest events, as compared to acts of rebellion, might be underrepresented in global sources. Although there were some differences in the various test results, the conclusion was basically the same when a second test on the effect of differential source coverage was performed relating coups d'état in twenty-nine African countries to four explicative variables. Even though the findings of JACKMAN/BOYD may not hold in other contexts and for other variables, their two tests lend support to the argument "that the cost-benefit ratio from using multiple sources may be unnecessarily high." This conclusion is strengthened if one considers that African countries are underreported in most of the data sources currently available. It will be of interest to find out whether similar conclusions are reached if property measures of conflict rather than mere event counts are used (cf. note 34).

One should not confuse the two questions dealt with here. In the case of whether conflict data are *descriptively* correct (univariate findings), the answer is, "obviously not." Yet, this need not necessarily have an effect on the *structure* of results (bivariate or multivariate findings). Conflict analyses can still be correct, as far as the structure among variables is concerned, even though they may be somewhat incorrect descriptively. Conflict data as found in current data sources may be *representative*, even though they may be lacking in descriptive accuracy. Yet, contrary to the interpretations of HAZLEWOOD/WEST and JACKMAN/BOYD, we maintain that the burden of proof rests with the individual researcher who is making a selection from a more comprehensive collection of sources.

Strategies for detecting other possible systematic errors have been devised by RUMMEL. He assumes that no country wants to report more internal conflicts than actually occurred.[222] There may be three reasons for countries having lower conflict scores than appropriate: (1) news censorship; (2) political disinterest of the rest of the world concerning events in certain countries; (3) conflict events are superseded by more interesting events, leading to a systematic underrepresentation of the former. If one correlates these variables with the political violence scores, one may detect the occurrence of any systematic errors. A censorship scale[223] is usually employed in the first case, whereas the number of foreign embassies and legations in a country (RUMMEL), the number of index cards in the particular data bank (TANTER), or the population size (FEIERABEND/FEIERABEND/NESVOLD) is used for indexing the second source of error. The third[224] possible distortion, however, has not been controlled in RUMMEL's study or, to our knowledge, in other studies.

If one continues to assume that countries do not want to report inflated conflict scores, then systematic distortions may be present only in the case of a *negative*[225] correlation between censorship and political violence. However, this is only a necessary and not a sufficient condition for systematic errors to take place, since countries with stricter censorship may indeed have lower conflict scores (cf. the results in TANTER 1965:164-65).[226] Similar reasoning applies in the case of the second possible distortion: If the number of foreign embassies and legations correlates positively with the political violence score, this may indicate that the country in question is better represented rather than that its conflict score is indeed higher than that of other countries. On the other hand, more prominent nations may also have more internal conflicts. In the case of a negative correlation between international interest and the political violence scores, one cannot speak of a distorting influence of the variable international interest. The same holds if there is no correlation at all. (In that case, all three of the sources of distortion mentioned above will be negligible.) RUMMEL (1963) reports "insignificant" positive correlations between the international interest and the conflict variables. Similar results are found in the studies of COLLINS (1973), TANTER (1966),[227] and FEIERABEND/FEIERABEND/NESVOLD (1969).[228] Many researchers are confident that their results are not seriously flawed by systematic distortions. However, sceptical readers will keep in mind the results of DORAN et al. (1973) and TAYLOR/HUDSON (1972). There are many roads to progress in cross-national research on political violence (cf. chapter 9). In any case, systematic comparisons of the reliability of available data sources will mark the road.

Another methodological and theoretical point deserving attention is the collection of data more adequately reflecting on the underlying theoretical questions. In many cases, we are not so much interested in cross-sectional or even *time-series* data (cf. BURROWES 1970 for a general treatment and HIBBS 1974; OSTROM 1978 for methodological discussions of problems arising in the use of time-series data):

1. Many of our theoretical questions require, not cross-sectional or even time-series data, but information on *sequences* or *processes* recording actions and reactions of conflicting groups at some length (in this respect cf. also the materials reprinted in the appendixes of TILLY 1978). This will also have consequences for the units[229] of inferences because "the unit or units for which the longitudinal relationship is hypothesized cannot be the same as those for which the cross-sectional relationship is established" (DUNCAN et al. 1961:166).[230] Nothing but the collection of truly sequential data will go beyond the educated guesswork so prevalent in cross-national research on political violence (as well as in many other areas of social research). In the near future this may not be possible at the broad cross-national level. Yet, in more homogeneous and better covered regions, efforts of this kind may lead to an enormous theoretical and practical reward[231] (cf. WRIGHT 1978 for time-series analyses on the processes of escalation and de-escalation during the conflict in Northern Ireland).

2. Especially if policy implications are at stake (cf. chapter 9), sequential data are a must, unless the underlying theoretical questions allow for other kinds of data.

3. Collecting data of this type would allow for much better specification of the contexts in which political violence is taking place. The researcher is often more interested in the immediate reactions to certain events, i.e., he is concerned with the context in a narrower

than usual sense, where the context is inferred from global data or aggregate data at the nation level. The ideal strategy, of course, is to look for both types of context in one and the same study.

4. Moreover, sufficiently dense time series data could be used for various tests, i.e., not only whether levels or rates of change of a variable have an impact, but also whether variations in rate of change affect the dependent variables, thus allowing for much more sophisticated tests of the theories discussed, for example, in chapter 5.1.2.5 (as to these and other advantages[232] of time series data, see also HAGE 1975; cf. also KIMBERLY 1976).

Finally, there are a number of guidelines which should be followed when performing tests as to the causes of political violence. Tests should be done for (1) nonlinear relationships, (2) threshold effects, (3) nonadditive relationships, (4) the stability of observed relationships in different geocultural regions and in other clusters of nations, (5) intranational differences, and (6) different time slices. (7) Different indicators as well as (8) different ways of combining them should also be employed. (9) Especially worthwhile would be the replication of some of the more prominent studies discussed here, either in different settings or with different indicators (see WELFLING 1975 for a remarkable example, chapter 5.1.1.1.4, and the reconsideration of BWY's study, 1968b, by SNOW 1968). (10) Furthermore, different facets of the dependent variables should be studied. (11) Finally, residuals should be analyzed in greater detail (see DRAPER/SMITH 1966:86–103 for a description of various techniques of analysis), especially where there is reason to expect alternative theoretical explanations to hold for a number of nations (cases).

Having discussed cross-national research on political violence rather extensively, we now turn to some other approaches to the study of political violence. From chapter 6 onward the cross-national perspective will once again predominate.

5.2. Case Studies on Political Violence

As political violence often touches on the vital issues of a polity, it comes as no surprise that there are literally hundreds of case studies on the causes and consequences as well as on the control and the prevention of political violence. Since the present study emphasizes the cross-national perspective, only a few case study examples will be dealt with here. The objects analyzed in case studies are often rather unique phenomena, rendering cross-national approaches somewhat difficult if not impossible. Nevertheless, new propositions may be derived from some of these studies and subsequently be tested on a cross-national basis. Case studies may also provide useful tests of cross-national theories (see ECKSTEIN 1975 for a comprehensive discussion of the merits and weaknesses of such forms of inquiry). The conditions and the historical context of political violence may be considered in much greater depth, thus supplying evidence as to whether cross-national theories (1) hold when studying more specific phenomena, (2) must be supplemented by culture- or context-specific explanations, or, depending on the number and type of cases, (3) must be totally rejected. (Chapter 5.3.2 on the American black riots of the 1960s is a good example in this respect. Yet, for reasons explained below, we have placed it in the next main chapter.)

The studies of HOBSBAWM (1959, 1969, 1974) on *social bandits*, or *primitive rebels* as he sometimes calls them, are among the major examples of case studies in research on political violence. In a way, the label "case study" is somewhat inappropriate, as HOBSBAWM is clearly interested in a cross-national perspective. He maintains that social banditry is a phenomenon universal in space and time. It arises in times of economic crisis and pauperization (or, to use GURR's conceptualization, it is a product of decremental deprivation, GURR 1970a:49; cf. chapter 4.3) and is likely to vanish as modernization proceeds, depriving the social bandits of the conditions under which their activities flourish. Social bandits usually can count on the support of their local community in their efforts to defend or restore the "traditional order of things 'as it should be.' . . . They right wrongs, they correct and avenge cases of injustice, and in doing so apply a more general criterion of just and fair relations between men in general, and especially between the rich and the poor, the strong and the weak" (HOBSBAWM 1972:26). A dual system of government, with the central government operating at some distance and a local government to which people are attached by loyalty and primordial ties (cf. chapter 5.1.2.8), is a condition typical of social banditry. HOBSBAWM refers to the Sicilian mafia, at least in its earlier stages, as a case in point (HOBSBAWM 1959: chapter 3; on the mafia cf. also PANTA-LEONE 1966; BLOK 1974).

Classic instances of social banditry are found in southern Italy from the eighteenth through the twentieth centuries and in Spain. Other examples come from numerous parts of the world (HOBSBAWM 1969) and refer generally to the same period. Basically, HOBSBAWM distinguishes three types of social bandits: "the *noble robber* or Robin Hood, the primitive resistance fighter or guerrilla unit of what I shall call the *haiduks*[233] and possibly the terror-bringing *avenger*" (HOBSBAWM 1972:20). Interestingly, he characterizes social banditry as a pre-political phenomenon, not only disappearing with the advance of industrialization but also being conversely related to agrarian revolutionary organizations. The social bandit is a "reformer" or a reactionary, but not a revolutionary (HOBSBAWM 1972:26). He is also different from millenarian activists who may turn up under similar conditions. (See chapter 8.2 for some references.) Nevertheless, revolutionary activities may originate from social banditry or from those conditions causing the social banditry. The label "pre-political"[234] is intended to designate the primitive and reactionary character of political violence typically found in social banditry. Drawing on HOBSBAWM's and RUDE's (cf. chapter 8.4.6.6.2) writings, TILLY (1969) has constructed a typology where he distinguishes between the relationship of protest groups to the structure of power and the organizational bases of protesters.[235] Primitive violence is characterized by the attributes "small-scale, local scope, participation by members of communal groups as such, inexplicit and unpolitical objectives" (TILLY 1969:13-14), whereas reactionary violence is described as "backward-looking, local in scope, resistent to demands from the center" (TILLY 1970:145).[236] Finally, as far as patterns of recruitment are concerned, "social bandits are normally both young and unmarried. Men marginal to the rural economy, or not yet absorbed or reabsorbed into it, will be drawn to banditry; notably ex-soldiers, who, with herdsmen, form probably its largest single occupational component. So will certain occupations which maintain a man outside the framework of constant social control in the community, or the supervision of the ruling group—e.g., herdsmen and drovers" (HOBSBAWM 1974:152).

In KÜTHER's work *Räuber und Gauner in Deutschland* (1976) (on "Robbers and rogues in Germany") social banditry is contrasted with mere robbery in the period from 1700 to 1820. As opposed to social bandits, rogues drew most of their numbers from farmers who had lost their homes, deserters, beggars, workers from the vast number of occupations considered dishonorable such as knackers, scissors-grinders, charcoal-burners, shepherds, and from groups suffering discrimination, e.g., Jews and gipsies. KÜTHER estimates their proportion to be as high as 10 to 15% of the whole population. State authorities, obviously, had great difficulties in controlling such a large rural *Lumpenproletariat*. The criminal bandits formed vagrant robber gangs. Due to the lack of support from the rural population, they had to change their locus of activity quite frequently, although each of the large gangs acted only in specific parts of Germany, e.g., the *große Niederländische Bande* ("great Dutch gang") along the middle and lower Rhine valley, Anton Lautner's gang of post robbers in Hesse, and the *Westphälische Bande*. Social bandits acted for some moral reasons; as HOBSBAWM said, they "right wrongs"; however, the motive of robbers was merely looting. It should be stressed that for most of these socially neglected and brutally repressed persons this was the only means of survival. (Many a vagrant carried a mark of burning on his forehead signifying the punishment awaiting him if he should be caught again.) With the arrival of the industrial proletariat and the gradual centralization of state authorities, however, vagrancy and robbery disappeared. Thus, social banditry must clearly be conceived of as communally based, social (and at times political) violence, whereas robbery could be described as anomic violence.

Some criticism has been voiced against the studies of HOBSBAWM. BLOK (1972; see also the reply of HOBSBAWM 1972a) maintains that HOBSBAWM has set up an ideal picture of the social bandit who can freely draw on the support of his communal fellowmen. BLOK argues that, on the contrary, social bandits often use means of terror to make the population comply with their goals. In addition, BLOK tries to argue "that brigandage and banditmyths, each in their own way, reinforce the existing distribution of power on various levels of society, and thus inhibit rather than promote the development of peasant mobilization" (BLOK 1972:11). HOBSBAWM's description of the conditions and consequences of social banditry may on occasion be too idyllic and stereotyped, the material being apparently too diverse to summarize in a few categories. The clear advantage of his type of case studies, however, lies in broadening our frame of reference. HOBSBAWM draws our attention to a phenomenon of political or pre-political violence thus far neglected (pre-political in the sense of not affecting the state level of politics). At the same time he makes it clear that these phenomena can be studied on a cross-national basis, if not quantitatively at present, then at least qualitatively.

Analyses of preindustrial crowds are largely descriptive in method. At best, bivariate statistical analyses are presented, and higher-order techniques of analysis are rarely used. This may be due largely to the limited data available, but it is also due in part to the fact that these analyses, apart from those of the TILLY group (see chapter 8.4.6.6.1), have been done by social historians rather than quantitatively trained social scientists.

Many other phenomena of political violence have been analyzed on a case study basis by social scientists and historians. *La violencia* in Columbia is one of the more intensely studied examples. It occurred in a zero-sum political culture (cf. HOSKIN/SWANSON 1973) where political institutions were weakly developed and where cross-cutting of social cleavages was rather low. Since the assassination of the politician Gaitán in 1948, more than 200,000 deaths have been blamed on this type of political violence which started in the rural provinces and later reached the cities as well (for analyses cf. GUZMÁN et al. 1962, 1964; HOBSBAWM 1963; WEINERT 1966; FRANCES 1967; BAILEY 1967; ANDERSON et al. 1967:109-20; PAYNE 1968; FALS BORDA 1969 and BOOTH 1974 for a factor analysis). Similarly, the protracted religious, social, and political conflicts in *Northern Ireland*, dating back to the seventeenth century, have attracted scholars interested in doing intensive case studies of phenomena of political violence. Again, one of the basic determinants of these conflicts seems to have been the minimal degree of cross-cutting of lines of social cleavage (cf. the general discussion in chapter 5.1.2.8 and the references in chapter 5.1.1.1.2.6). Other examples of persistent violent political conflicts will be referred to briefly in later chapters (mainly in chapter 8.4.4).

5.3. The Explanation of Specific Objects or Classes of Objects

5.3.1. Introductory Remarks and Some Illustrations

This final section dealing with approaches to the study of political violence focuses on explanations of specific dependent variables rather than on summary measures of political violence, as do large portions of chapter 5.1. However, even in that more general section numerous results as to the determinants of more specific dependent variables were reported.

Political assassinations[237] constitute a class of more specific phenomena of political violence (for another, military coups d'état, see chapter 7). Some studies on the determinants of political assassinations have been cross-national in nature (KIRKHAM et al. 1969; HAVENS et al. 1970; CROTTY 1971; FEIERABEND et al. 1971; GROSS 1974:161-75). The bulk of studies, however, have focused on the individual characteristics of assassins (cf. TAYLOR/WEISZ 1970 with their emphasis on pathological characteristics; also WILKINSON 1976) as well as on political constellations. FEIERABEND et al. (1971) present this summary of some of their results from cross-national analyses (period: 1948-67):

> Assassinations show a similar patterning as internal political violence and instability [p. 128]. . . . A high rate of assassination is positively related to systemic frustration, external conflict, minority tensions, and homicide rates, as well as to political instability and violence. The higher the levels of systemic frustration, external conflict, minority tension, homicide rates and general political violence within a society, the higher the assassination rates.—A high rate of assassination is inversely related to measures of modernity and suicide. . . . Frequency of assassination is curvilinearly related to coerciveness of political regime [p. 129]. . . . The United States is the fifth highest country among the eighty-four in terms of the total number of assassination events experienced. . . . Among the group of Western democracies, it has a score of sixteen assassinations, where ten countries have a score of zero [p. 136]. . . . Among the sixteen assassinations that occurred in the United States during the last twenty years, seven can be attributed to the [level of tension that exists among ethnic, racial, linguistic, religious and other groups within society]. Furthermore, of the twelve assassinations occurring in the 1960's, six stem from the minority problem [p. 138].

It should be noted that the newspapers apparently cover assassinations more consistently than other conflict events (cf. the discussion in chapter 5.1.3). FEIERABEND et al. write: "When one compares the *New York Times Index* data on total assassination events with that recorded from *Deadline Data*, the correlation coefficient is .80. When only successful assassinations are compared, the coefficient is .83" (ibid., p. 79).

Peasant wars form another class of important phenomena of political violence. While there are numerous case studies on the hundreds of local peasant wars that have occurred in history, cross-national analyses of peasant warfare (as distinguished from phenomena of social banditry; cf. chapter 5.2) have emerged only recently (cf. the analyses in chapter 8.4.4).

Subjects like *internal wars* [238] and *guerrilla warfare*, whose data have been incorporated in the general analyses discussed in chapter 5.1.1, will not be dealt with separately here. The reader is urged to consult chapter 5.1.2.6, and 8.4.4. Finally, *pre-industrial crowds*, as studied particularly in the works of RUDÉ (1964, 1970; see chapter 8.4.6.6.2) and of TILLY (see chapter 8.4.6.6.1) are also of interest here, but will be taken up in the context of chapter 8.

Following these dispositional remarks, we turn now to analyses of one of the best-documented phenomena of political violence.

5.3.2. The Riots of American Blacks during the 1960s as an Example of the Study of Riots

There are several reasons for including a section on the riots of American blacks in this study. First of all, these riots have been the most intensively studied of all violent political protest phenomena thus far, but several theoretical and methodological problems still are unresolved. Secondly, the study of the riots of American blacks[239] allows us to see whether those theories employed in most of the cross-national research can explain equally well, better, or not at all in the case of a comparatively homogeneous phenomenon. In addition, several other theoretical notions, focusing mainly on characteristics of individual participants in acts of political violence, will be discussed. There is a vast number of studies on the riots among American blacks. Rather than treating the empirical evidence in detail, we shall rely on summary references. Our interest is in finding out which theoretical explanations fare well and which do not.

The relative deprivation (cf. chapter 5.3.2.3) of many American blacks has been documented in numerous studies. Although blacks have made considerable gains in politics (cf. VERBA/NIE 1972:149-73 as to increases in conventional forms of political participation among blacks, and recently KUO 1977), they were and still are lagging very much behind in a number of areas. (Our period of reference is the late 1950s and the 1960s, unless otherwise specified.):

Housing. "The median central city in the United States in 1960 would require 88 percent of its black households to move from Negro blocks to predominantly white blocks to achieve racially random residential patterns" (PETTIGREW 1971a:430, following TAEUBER/TAEUBER 1965). There are even some signs that segregation was increasing (FARLEY/TAEUBER 1968), but the sample in this study comprised only thirteen different places. A recent more comprehensive study comes to this conclusion: "Doubtlessly there were declines from 1960 to 1970 if we consider changes occurring in SMSAs generally" (VAN VALEY et al. 1977:841; the sample comprises 237 metropolitan areas in 1970). "Nevertheless, the conclusion seems warranted that residential segregation persists in the seventies and as yet shows little indication of significant decline in response to other racial improvements" (ibid., p. 843; for a path analysis of determinants of residential segregation in American cities cf. MARSHALL/JIOBU 1975). VAN VALEY et al. also note that there is "no systematically analyzed evidence available on levels of suburban segregation" (ibid., p. 843; cf. also the discussion in VAN VALEY/ROOF 1976 and the arguments of WINSHIP 1977; 1978).

Schooling. In the majority of cases, blacks attend segregated schools or at least schools with a large portion of blacks. In the South this portion is almost 100%. There seems to be some evidence that cognitive skills of blacks are greater when the students are educated in desegregated schools (for many other results see COLEMAN et al. 1966[240] and more recently the controversy over JENCKS's book on inequality, 1973).

Economic aspects. Blacks have an unemployment rate about twice as high as that of whites. Although the proportion of blacks in various occupations has increased considerably, it still holds that the more qualified the job require-ments are, the greater is the underrepresentation of blacks (for some recent qualifications cf. below). "Nonwhites were consistently more likely to be operatives, service workers, nonfarm or farm laborers, and to be out of the labor force" (HAUSER/FEATHERMAN 1974a:259). Blacks are also gener-ally underpaid compared to whites. The average income of white families in 1969 was about \$9800 as opposed to \$6200 for black families (U. S. Depart-ment of Commerce 1971:60). PETTIGREW writes: "Between 1963 and 1973, the percentage of employed black males in white-collar jobs rose from 15 to 23 and those in skilled blue-collar jobs from 11 to 15. But these figures still trail far behind those of employed white males, of whom 42 percent were in white-collar jobs and 22 percent were in skilled blue-collar jobs. Consequently, the median black family income has remained between 50 and 61 percent of the income of the median white family since 1950" (PETTI-GREW 1976:478).

Detailed studies suggest the following general conclusions as to more recent trends: "In the past decade [between 1962 and 1973] blacks gained ground on whites in schooling, occupational status, and income, but the improvements were relatively greater for the young [cf. also JOHNSON/ SELL 1976] and in some instances occurred only among women [and in the South, FARLEY/HERMALIN 1972:357; McCRONE/HARDY 1978; for a detailed analysis of the causal processes bearing on the North-South differen-tiation, see HOGAN/FEATHERMAN 1977]. With respect to occupations, both black and white men experienced net upward status shifts in both the manual and nonmanual categories of the experienced civilian labor force" (FEATHERMAN/HAUSER 1976:624). "Indeed, in 1973 there was no difference in the average length of schooling between black and white men with the same socioeconomic background" (ibid., p. 631). Blacks, however, seemed to be "less successful than whites in converting their schooling into employment in better-paying occupations" (STOLZENBERG 1975:314).[241] As put by another scholar: "labor-market discrimination is much more impor-tant than differences in education as an explanation for the black-white income gap" (MASTERS 1975:99). "Of the total gap of \$3790, the compo-nents that can be labeled discrimination in employment (occupation and income) account for \$2260 (or about 60 percent) while the components for family background and years of school account for only \$1530" (MASTERS 1975:100–101; cf. also HAUSER/FEATHERMAN 1974b). In short, "although the racial gap narrowed over the decade, black men in 1973 had not matched the occupational standing of white men in 1962" (FEATHER-MAN/HAUSER 1976:621); "blacks were at a disadvantage when compared to whites both at the start and at the end of this decade, and very large racial differences remain" (FARLEY/HERMALIN 1972:353).[242] Yet, contrary to some statements in the literature, there is no simple pattern. It was found that "white representation increased relative to that of nonwhites in the four lowest-status occupation groups, yet nonwhites increased relative to whites among persons outside the labor force at younger ages and among persons still in the labor force at older ages. Likewise, the situation of non-whites improved relative to that of whites in some higher-status occupations (salaried professionals, self-employed managers, clerks, and craftsmen), but not in others (salaried managers and salesmen)" (HAUSER/FEATHER-MAN 1974a:259). These figures could be extended in many directions (for further evidence see the bulletin of the U. S. Department of Labor 1966; LEVITAN et al. 1975; NEWMAN et al. 1978; and chapter 5.3.2.3). We now turn to the various theories proposed for explaining the black riots in the 1960s, riots which generally can be defined as: "Events involving relatively spontaneous, shortlived but violent activity, in which the generalized aims of the insurgents or the objects of their aggression are *not coherently* specified" (MORRISON/STEVENSON 1971:350; emphasis added).[243]

5.3.2.1. Riffraff Theory

The Report of the Governor's Commission on the Los Angeles Riots (1965), [the McCONE Report], explains the riots as follows: Rioters are said to be "the criminal element," "wretched, vulgar men," killers of children," badly educated, unskilled, unemployed, young, and uprooted. They are said to form only a small minority (at the most 2%) of the black communities. It is maintained that the black majority does not approve of their rioting activities. A further argument refers to "outside agitators,"[244] said to instigate the riffraff and unite with it in rioting.[245]

If this picture were true (cf. RUSTIN 1966; BLAUNER 1966; FOGEL-SON 1967; CONOT 1967 for critiques; cf. also LIPSKY/OLSON 1977: 64-70), the consequences would be obvious: "Such an interpretation makes it easier for the public and its officials to deal with the dark, to rationalize the otherwise inexplicable, and to obviate the necessity to feel guilty about the society's failure to deal with the underlying causes of the violence in the ghetto" (MASOTTI 1967:1).[246] Accordingly, the Report judges violent acts to be an "explosion—a formless, quite senseless, all but hopeless violent protest." Actual evidence corroborates the McCONE report only in that unemployed, poorer, younger, unmarried black men are indeed somewhat overrepresented among rioters (cf. McCORD/HOWARD 1968; SEARS/TOMLINSON 1968; CAPLAN/PAIGE 1968a; 1968b; SINGER et al. 1970; FOGELSON/HILL 1968; Report of the National Advisory Commission on Civil Disorders (1968), [the KERNER Report][247]; ABUDU et al. 1972; FEAGIN/HAHN 1973:268-70; SEARS/McCONAHAY 1973). All other statements based on the riffraff theory (equated occasionally with the *absolute deprivation theory*, assuming the *Lumpenproletariat* to be the source of violent protests) are either dubious or refuted.[248] In general, the following summary seems to hold: "First, that a substantial minority of the ghetto population, ranging from roughly 10 to 20 per cent, actively participated in the riots. Second, that the rioters, far from primarily the riffraff and outside agitators, were fairly representative of the ghetto residents. And third, that a sizable minority (or, in some cases, a majority) of blacks who did not riot sympathized with the rioters" (FOGELSON 1971:30; cf. also BRINK/ HARRIS 1964 and the evidence in EISINGER 1973; 1974; 1976 pertaining also to nonviolent protests).

A close cousin of the riffraff theory, BANFIELD's (1970) theory of rioting for "fun and profit," also cannot be sustained in light of the evidence. BANFIELD stresses the hedonistic nature of these riots and maintains that other explanations frequently were post hoc rationalizations of prior behavior in terms of calculated efforts to change certain social structural arrangements. Empirical studies, however, do not corroborate BANFIELD's view (see SEARS/McCONAHAY 1973:106-25 for an explication of this viewpoint and for a detailed refutation using data from their 1965 study in Watts[249]).

5.3.2.2. Psychological Explanations (with Some References to Structural Aspects)

Several of the characteristics of rioters mentioned in the McCONE Report are also reported in a number of other studies which could be designated *alienation approaches* (for an extensive discussion of variants in psychological alienation theories see SEEMAN 1972; 1975; cf. also FINIFTER 1972; WRIGHT 1976 and LUDZ 1973 for a more general account).[250] In these studies, *social isolation, powerlessness,* and *states of anomie* (see WARREN 1969; GESCHWENDER/SINGER 1971; BULLOUGH 1967, but cf. also WILSON 1971; and the perspectives in KAPSIS 1978) are invoked to explain riot participation. Yet, there is also evidence to the contrary (MARX 1967; TOMLINSON 1968; SEARS 1969; MURPHY/WATSON 1970; SEARS/ McCONAHAY 1973). As summarized by CAPLAN:

> The militant . . . is the better educated but underemployed, [the] politically disaffected but not the politically alienated. He is willing to break laws for rights already guaranteed by law, but under ordinary circumstances he is no more likely to engage in crime than his nonmilitant neighbor. He is intensely proud of being black, but neither desires revenge from whites nor is socially envious of them. He has little freedom or resources to effectuate his personal goals, but strongly desires freedom and ownership of his own life. Indeed, this new man of the ghetto is also the man of paradox" (CAPLAN 1970:71; cf. also the profiles in FORWARD/WILLIAMS 1970:88 and in the KERNER Report 1968:73-77 and appendix 4).

This *"new ghetto man"* of CAPLAN's (or "new urban black" of SEARS/ McCONAHAY 1973) may be *the* new personality type in the ghetto. While he is perhaps the most prominent type, he is not the only one (see also the

empirical critique in MILLER et al. 1976, below). The powerlessness-aliena-
tion-unemployment results are not totally consistent with this ideal type
of the rioter. Using ROTTER's conceptualization, one may describe the new
ghetto man as a person who is convinced he will be able to control the
outcomes of his behavior (internal control) rather than feeling subjected
to incalculable external events (external control) (cf. FORWARD/WILLIAMS
1970, but see also CRAWFORD/NADITCH 1970; cf. also GURIN et al.
1969). ROTTER's "internal-external locus of control" variable is one of the
main theoretical elements used for explaining riot participation. In some
studies (see below) the extent of explanation is increased if this variable is
incorporated into various interaction terms.[251]

A reanalysis of the SEARS/McCONAHAY (1973) data and those from the
National Advisory Commission on Civil Disorders (KERNER Commission
1968), however, leads to a conclusion contrasting with the theory of the new
urban blacks or the new ghetto man. In addition to using too small numbers
per cell and tabulating in the wrong direction, SEARS/McCONAHAY are
criticized for not having distinguished sufficiently between active rioters and
mere spectators. Criticism is also raised against the construction of one of the
dependent variables in the KERNER Report (CAPLAN/PAIGE are the
authors of the table). A more appropriate data analysis drawing on survey
data on racial attitudes in fifteen American cities (CAMPBELL/SCHUMAN
1968) leads to the conclusion that rioters, in general, were rather less educated and had lower occupational positions than the theory of the new urban
blacks suggested. Counter-rioters, on the other hand, definitely were better
educated than activists. According to MILLER et al., their analyses sustain
neither the riffraff theory nor the theory of the new urban blacks nor the
concept of the new ghetto man. They also found that rioters did not overwhelmingly come from a Northern background.[252] Rather there was an
interesting relationship between the interaction term "poor education X
16-29 years of age x longer residence in Northern cities" and riot participation, a construct explanatory variable quite at variance with the theory of
the new urban blacks.

> There does appear to be a new urban black, and he is clearly not a
> rioter. He is a militant, but his militancy is directed toward avenues
> of nonviolent protest. In contrast to the potential rioter, he is more
> likely to come from the 44+ age group than from the 16-29 year old
> group. While the rioter is more likely to be unmarried, the protester
> is more likely to be married. The protester is more likely to come
> from a home that is intact; the rioter from a broken home. The pro-
> tester is more likely to come from the top of the occupational
> hierarchy; the rioter from the bottom. Given the combined thrusts
> of age and occupation, the combined effects of these two variables
> are best appreciated by the fact that 71% of individuals at least 44
> years of age and in the highest occupational category were pro-
> testers, but only 2.4% of the same group were rioters. Similarly 22%
> of the 16-29-year-olds who were unskilled workers were rioters but

only 15.2% were protesters. . . . The group most likely to riot is the 16-29-year-olds with incomes between $0 and $4999 (33.6%), but the individuals most likely to protest are those with incomes above $15,000 and over 45 years of age (67.9%) (MILLER et al. 1976: 362-63).

If science lives by the dialogue among scholars, the findings of the reanalyses of MILLER et al. (1976) should certainly stir up a prolonged discussion. Clearly they contradict many of the usual ("stereotyped," as MILLER et al. would say) notions about the participants in the black riots and the causes of their participation. Common sense considerations and some observations lead to the expectation that the *bulk* of violent protesters should come from the proportionally largest group within the (respective) population at large. Not all of the researchers dealing with the analysis of participation in the black riots seem to have kept in mind that "informing us what percentage of rioters are from the various social classes or from the various educational ranks tells us virtually nothing about what percentage of each of the social classes or educational groupings participated in the riot. Such miscalculation of percentages results in the twin errors of population and composition fallacy" (MILLER et al. 1976:343-44).[253]

5.3.2.3. Sociopsychological Explanations

According to the *blocked opportunity theory* employed by researchers including CAPLAN/PAIGE (1968b), MURPHY/WATSON (1969), and FORWARD/WILLIAMS (1970), persons most likely to participate in riots are individuals with high aspirations and beliefs in their own abilities to achieve their goals (internal control). At the same time these persons, to a greater extent, perceive discriminations which hinder them (at least in their own perception) to realize their goals. In this well-supported theory, the focus is no longer on individual characteristics, as in some of the approaches mentioned so far, but rather on structural attributes, in this case, discriminations. However, if this theory is to be valid in a more specific sense, then it must be demonstrated that there is more discrimination against these people who become rioters or that rioters perceive discriminations in their ghetto more than nonactive members of the black population (for some evidence cf. MURPHY/WATSON 1969).

Compared with that of other black groups, the socioeconomic standing of these portions of the black population has improved, resulting in the formation of new levels of social comparison which previously did not exist. At the same time these people are especially sensitive to the more subtle discriminations occurring at a higher socioeconomic level. Obviously, the blocked opportunity theory can be understood as a subcase of MERTON's general theory of anomie (MERTON 1957:121-94). In terms of the theoretical notions mentioned before, the interaction term, internal control x perceived discriminations, is considered a major explanatory variable in the blocked opportunity theory (for some findings consistent with this theory, cf. LIESKE 1978; N=334 disorders, 1967–69).

A similar interaction term is constructed when *political efficacy*[254] is related to *political distrust*.[255] Thus, drawing on GAMSON's (1968) theoretical outline, PAIGE (1971) found: "In sum, there is no independent linear relationship between political trust and riot participation—the alienated are no more likely to have participated in riots than are the confident. But when this variable is combined with efficacy, trust is extremely important in explaining the behavior of those who are high in efficacy" (as summed up in GAMSON 1971:51; CAPLAN 1971:152–56 and more generally ABERBACH/WALKER 1973).[256] There is probably a strong relationship between the extent of discrimination endured and political distrust. Taking into consideration that discrimination (blocked opportunities) is noticed particularly by individuals with higher socioeconomic characteristics who are usually persons with higher political efficacy as well, one may hold that the extensions of the blocked opportunity theory and the combination of the variables, political efficacy x political distrust, are comparable, though the theoretical background differs.

The theory of *relative deprivation* provides a more general theoretical framework for the blocked opportunity theory as well as for the explanatory variable, political efficacy x political distrust. In most studies, however, the implications of relative deprivation theory are little tested,[257] since economic indicators are used for indexing states of mind. Verification that the researcher's definition of the situation is the same as the definition of the subject is rarely done. In a *more general sense*, however, the black American riots of the 1960s are phenomena that can be explained by referring to the consequences of relative deprivation, and probably less in terms of the internal colonialism analogy proposed by BLAUNER (1969; cf. also CRUSE 1968). We maintain this even in light of the criticism raised by McPHAIL (1971) who, in reviewing the literature, reports that of 173 analyzed relationships between deprivation or frustration variables and five dependent variables only 1% were above .40 (Cramer's V). "These results require careful re-examination of the assumption that the DFA [deprivation → frustration → aggression] relationship is, . . . 'as fundamental to understanding civil strife as the law of gravity is to atmospheric physics' (GURR 1968b:50)" (McPHAIL 1971:1064). Insufficient working out of the relative deprivation theory as well as sampling errors may have contributed to these results. However, one may argue that different objects are being explained, when general discontent (cf. the summary results at the beginning of chapter 5.3.2) among the black population and participation under specific circumstances in specific forms of protest are being considered. There are strong reasons for using relative deprivation theory for the former; however, proponents of the theory still carry the burden of proof[258] in the latter case (as was true when applying relative deprivation theory to cross-national aggregate data, cf. chapter 5.1.1.1).

Dealing with relative deprivation theory in a more general sense, PETTI-GREW specifies four relative deprivation conditions prevailing in the case of American blacks:

> This pattern derives from four revolt-stirring conditions triggered by long-term improvements:
> (a) living conditions of the dominant group typically advance faster than those of the subordinate group;
> (b) the aspirations of the subordinate group climb far more rapidly than actual changes;
> (c) status inconsistencies among subordinate group members increase sharply; and
> (d) a broadening of comparative reference groups occurs for the subordinate group (PETTIGREW 1969:44).

There seems to be a consensus in the literature that conditions (b) through (d) are fulfilled in the case of the black riots. Only with respect to condition (a) is there some disagreement, although the majority of results seems to favor this condition (but not if *relative* gains are considered; see FARLEY/HERMALIN 1972[259] and the evidence quoted at the beginning of chapter 5.3.2). One must only bear in mind the difference between absolute and relative levels of improvement for blacks: "In spite of a general reduction in white-nonwhite income differences within educational levels, the overall gap between white and nonwhite income has *increased* during the 1960-70 decade. Although nonwhite income expressed as a proportion of white income has increased, suggesting improvement in the situation in one sense, the decomposition . . . indicates that while the differences due to white-nonwhite social position in terms of education, occupation, and region of the country have decreased, the labor force has shifted upward to an educational level at which the gap between whites and nonwhites within educational levels, occupational categories, and regions of the country is large" (JOHNSON/SELL 1976:189-90). There are contradictions between findings mentioned here and certain results, especially those of FEATHERMAN/HAUSER, reported at the beginning of chapter 5.3.2. These differences may stem from variations in sampling and/or operations used (cf. the methodological critique in VILLEMEZ/ROWE 1975). In any case, there is agreement among scholars over remaining differences[260] large enough to cause the build-up of discontent among blacks. Also there is evidence that "in the industrial non-South, decreasing black-white inequality has been accompanied by increasing inequality among blacks" (VILLEMEZ/WISWELL 1978:1019).

The second condition, that the expectations of the subordinate group are rising faster than actual improvements, is much better supported (cf. CANTRIL 1965:43 and the results of a national survey in 1963 in BRINK/HARRIS 1964:238).[261] The third condition posits an increase in status inconsistencies among subordinate group members. Without discussing the methodological (BLALOCK 1966) or theoretical (cf. ZIMMERMANN 1978) intricacies of the theory of status inconsistency, it can be maintained that, if any form of status inconsistency has an effect, it is likely to be the discrepancy between ascribed and achieved ranks which will lead to stress and affect the particular dependent variable. Since the 1940s blacks have made great gains in education (achieved characteristic). Yet, if one relates the occupational prestige and income in specific occupations to education, there is clear evidence of a high degree of discrimination against blacks. Attributes normally achieved or considered as achievable, like occupation and income, are associated by many American whites with an ascribed characteristic, namely skin color or race, and thus refined into ascribed characteristics. Consequently blacks are having lower outcomes for comparable inputs[262] (cf. ADAMS's 1965 inequity theory, chapter 4.2). For many blacks this results in the undercutting of their expectations to reach a certain status in society on the basis of various achievement criteria because of discriminatory practices of other persons.[263] This recalls the hypothesis of DAVIS, cited in chapter 4.3: "If a given social categorization is correlated with objective deprivation, relative deprivation will be more frequent among the deprived in the *more* favorite category" (DAVIS 1959:286, but cf. also the results of the study of PORTER/NAGEL 1976 in chapter 5.3.2.4). Indirect statistical evidence for this is found in FARLEY/HERMALIN (1972).

The fourth condition provides the general cognitive framework for the first three conditions. The above conditions may be summarized aptly as "actual gains, psychological losses" (PETTIGREW 1964:178-201) or, using GURR's conceptualization, as "progressive deprivation."[264] Expectations are increasing faster than the possibilities to fulfill these aspirations. Through increased aspirations the cognitive frame is widened, leading to more intensive comparisons with whites. At the same time large portions of the black population perceive themselves as "non-members," to use MERTON's terminology. In addition to the studies already mentioned, see COOK (1970), HOROWITZ (1970), RAINE et al. (1971), CATALDO et al. (1968), MURPHY/WATSON (1971), DIZARD (1970), BOWEN et al. (1968), GRINDSTAFF (1968), and SEARS/McCONAHAY (1973:87).[265] The theory of relative deprivation is usually tested rather loosely in these studies. ABELES's recent study of black militancy employs measures of "favorable attitudes towards violent and nonviolent tactics, Black Power, separatism, and of ambivalent attitudes towards whites" (ABELES 1976:123-24) and uses representative samples in Cleveland and Miami. His study leads to the conclusion that fraternal deprivation (measured by the CANTRIL ladder scale; cf. below) is a more potent predictor of the dependent variable than personal deprivation ("egoistical deprivation," to use RUNCIMAN's terminology; cf. the discussion in chapter 4.3). Furthermore, relative deprivation provides more successful explanations of black militancy among leaders, but not among followers. However, the independent variables altogether do not explain more than about 20% of the variance.

The best evaluation of DAVIES's J-curve hypothesis (another variant of relative deprivation theory) for explaining black rioting behavior during the 1960s has been given in a study by MILLER/BOLCE/HALLIGAN (1977). They employ three *objective* indicators: (1) the DAVIES measure, cf. note

262, relying on the same raw data for the second and third indicators; (2) "the difference between predicted income for blacks subtracted from predicted income for whites, when income is regressed against education"; (3) "subtracting a black individual's actual income from the income he would expect if he were white" (MILLER et al. 1977:970). In addition, they make use of three *perceptual* indicators of progressive relative deprivation (1956-68) using the following items: "(1) whether the respondent (R) perceived his financial situation as being better or worse than the year before; (2) R's expectation of his future financial prospects; and (3) R's perception of his financial satisfaction" (ibid., p. 972). In their explication of DAVIES's theory one basic assumption is that future expectations are tied to the evaluation of the present situation. While there is some empirical evidence for this on the part of white respondents, this does not hold for blacks in the North or in the South. Sampling errors or other alternative explanations can also be ruled out by the authors. Rather they report that "the black community generally, and the northern black community particularly, experienced extreme fluctuation and ambiguity in its perceptions of the trend of its finances, its financial satisfaction, and its expectations of financial improvement. These extreme fluctuations and ambiguities of black perceptions might have led to the urban riots of the 1960s" (MILLER et al. 1977:980). Consequently the authors propose a fluctuation-change hypothesis (instead of DAVIES's J-curve hypothesis), pointing out some comparable results reported in the literature (especially GROFMAN/MULLER 1973; cf. below). Although details of the relationship are omitted due to lack of data, MILLER et al. apparently invoke something like the following raw causal mechanism:

fluctuations → perceptual instability → discontent → . . . rioting behavior.

Drawing on a communication from GURR, they also suggest that the degree to which future expectations are tied to current attained values may vary from group to group (possibly according to their current relative standing). "Some preliminary analyses that we have undertaken demonstrate that for blacks, those at the lowest end of the continuum have the highest expectations" (MILLER et al. 1977:977). Compared to other writings on DAVIES's J-curve hypothesis (cf. especially chapter 8.4.6.1, but also below), there are two clear advantages in the study of MILLER et al.: firstly, they use both objective and subjective perceptual indicators for testing this hypothesis, and, secondly, they disaggregate the population according to distinct social categories. In this instance, both of these strategies lead to a strong rejection of DAVIES's hypothesis (cf. also chapter 8.4.6.1 and passim). In her critique of this study, CROSBY (1979) maintains that they have misrepresented the theory of relative deprivation. She objects strongly to the assumption that future expectations are tied to the evaluation of one's *own present* situation and claims that this is a gross misrepresentation of main streams of relative deprivation theory. She objects as well to some of the comparisons made and conclusions drawn by the authors: "If MILLER et al. had *aggregated their own data* [instead of the Michigan election survey data], would the resultant pattern have resembled DAVIES' aggregated data or their own individual-level data?" (CROSBY 1979:110).

Thus far, we have mainly discussed studies and theories which focus on *who* participated in the riots and *why* this might have been the case. In the next section we will be concerned with detecting some of the *structural* conditions and ecologial settings of the black protests, in short, *where* these protests were to occur. However, before concluding this discussion of socio-psychological explanations of the black riots, a look at the highly complex approach followed by MULLER (1972, 1973; see also GROFMAN/MULLER 1973) is appropriate. These works are characterized by a theoretical and methodological stringency thus far not found in research on political violence at the individual level (but cf. also MARSH 1977). The GUTTMAN-scaled dependent variable in these studies is *potential* for political violence (measured by approval of political violence and intention to engage in political violence).[266] Only attitudinal data are gathered; nevertheless, some inferences as to behavior are made. The sample is drawn from the population in Waterloo, Iowa, a small but quite typical town as far as rioting patterns are concerned. In fact, two samples are drawn, a random sample of the total population (disproportionately stratified to provide for a sufficient number of black respondents) and a sample of group influentials chosen by means of the reputational technique. One of MULLER's early conclusions is that potential for political violence cannot be explained by the variable relative deprivation (as measured by the CANTRIL self-anchoring striving scale). The data "suggest that the readiness to engage in revolution against the state will be greatest when a very low degree of trust in political authorities[267] is combined with a very high degree of belief that the use of violence by dissident groups in the past has helped their cause [efficacy of past violence]" (MULLER 1972:954). On conceptual grounds, however, the term revolution is clearly inadequate for what MULLER has actually measured. It should be noted that relative deprivation does not account for variation in the dependent variable once the other two variables are taken into consideration. If the variables short-term welfare gratification (to index relative deprivation) and efficacy of past violence are controlled, trust in political authorities is negatively related ($r=-.318$) to the dependent variable. Once the other two variables are controlled, efficacy of past violence correlates $r=.305$ with the dependent variable potential for political violence. The zero-order correlation of trust in authorities with efficacy of past violence is, as MULLER expected, negative ($r=-.419$). These measures are significant at the $p < .001$ level, while the relationship between short-term welfare gratification and the dependent variable is not even significant at the $p < .05$ level (holding constant trust in political authorities and efficacy of past violence).

In one of his most ambitious papers thus far, MULLER aims at constructing a nonalienation interaction theory of political protest, described as follows: "The basic theory predicts that protest attitude is a function of reinforcement learning for protest, inconsistency between alienated political attitude and nonalienated political behavior, politicized frustrative nonreward, and intense dissatisfaction with specific political personnel and policies" (MULLER 1973:116). His basic premise, supported by considerable evidence, is that "in most instances, alienation is not sufficient in and of itself to affect protest, but, rather, must occur in conjunction with a nonalienation state" (p. 7), whereby nonalienation signifies "variables which either are not classifiable under any of the dimensions of alienation or, while classifiable under the alienation[268] concept, are predicted to affect protest attitude by virtue of interaction between a nonalienation state on such a variable and an alienation state on some other variable" (p. 132).

Without going into detail here, a few remarks concerning his highly complex operationalizations and results are in order. In Table 5.4 the theoretical concepts and corresponding aspects at the operational level have been listed.

There are a number of variables not yet described. Anomia, political powerlessness, and political isolation are implemented as in other studies cited in preceding chapters. Nonalienated political behavior, denoted as conventional political participation (such as voting, attending election meetings), is combined with distrust of political authorities to form a new predictor of protest potential. The rationale is that citizens who share in conventional forms of political participation but also distrust political authorities are likely to experience feelings of dissonance which may result in protest activities.

Table 5.4. Summary of Main Variables Used by MULLER (1973:89-90)

		Abstract Level	Operational Level
V	=	protest attitude	potential for political violence
L	=	vicarious reinforcement learning for protest	efficacy of past violence
D	=	political trust/diffuse support for the authorities	distrust political authorities
B	=	nonalienated political behavior	conventional political participation
R	=	perceived level of politicized relative deprivation	present relative deprivation
M	=	locus of control of reinforcement	personal mastery
[C]	=	rate of change in politicized relative deprivation[+]	expected change in politicized relative deprivation
S	=	specific dissatisfaction	dissatisfaction with specific authorities
A	=	diffuse alienation	anomia
P_p	=	responsiveness of government to citizen influence	political powerlessness
P_i	=	internalization of widely shared political norms	political isolation
I	=	political trust/diffuse support for regime institutions	legitimating ideology
E	=	ethnic group standing[++]	race

[+]Absolute rate; cf. the results in GROFMAN/MULLER (1973; below).

[++]This variable is introduced as a substitute for other, here not explicitly incorporated, "attitudinal alienation variables" (MULLER 1973:91).

After having performed numerous tests, leading, in part, to confirmation and, in part, to denial of his hypotheses, and after having developed additional hypotheses (often incorporating interaction terms which increase the amount of variance explained), MULLER proposes the following model for explaining the potential for political violence.

$$V = \beta_0 + \beta_1 L + \beta_2 D{\times}B + \beta_3 R{\times}M + \beta_4 |C| + \beta_5 S + e$$

In addition to the citizens sample and the sample of group influentials, a sample of attentive citizens (defined in terms of scoring on dissatisfaction with specific authorities) is selected. Though his theoretical model in general does well, a number of differences between the three predictive equations are showing up. Efficacy of past violence (L) is the strongest predictor in all three equations, followed by the interactive term $D{\times}B$, i.e., the joint occurrence of distrusting the political authorities and participating in conventional forms of political behavior. Distrust (D) alone is also of some importance in the citizens sample (as is expected change in politicized[269] relative deprivation; on this see GROFMAN/MULLER 1973 and below). In the case of attentive citizens, $R{\times}M$ is also retained in the equation, signifying that present relative deprivation in conjunction with feelings of personal mastery creates some kind of stress increasing the potential for political violence. On grounds of theoretical reasoning, this interaction term should be a much more powerful predictor. MULLER earlier in his paper refers to AMSEL's conceptualization of frustrative nonreward, defined as "a hypothetical, implicit reaction elicited by nonreward after a number of proper rewards" (AMSEL 1958:103).[270] The mechanism touched upon in AMSEL's theory, i.e., a withdrawal (or in this case reduction) of a continuous reinforcement causing frustration, has been known to other authors as well, e.g., TOCQUEVILLE (see chapter 8.4.2). In the words of BERKOWITZ: "Poverty-stricken groups who have never dreamed of having automobiles, washing machines, or new homes are not frustrated because they have been deprived of these things; they are frustrated only after they have begun to hope" (BERKOWITZ 1969:15).

MULLER is somewhat dissatisfied with the results of his first attempts to test AMSEL's and other theories, because he wishes to explain two-thirds of the variance but reaches "only" about 50% (except for the citizens sample where: $R^2 = .37$), an astonishing figure nevertheless. Obviously, many more tests of the highly complex theoretical notions invoked are needed (multicollinearity of independent variables being perhaps another issue). Furthermore, continuous data may be more appropriate when testing such dynamic theories as AMSEL's theory of frustrative nonreward. Finally, there are so far no specifications of the causal interdependencies among the independent variables.

Not quite as complicated as MULLER's nonalienation interaction theory of political protest[271] but still highly sophisticated is the study of GROFMAN/MULLER (1973) who devote attention to a number of hypotheses neglected thus far in theorizing on relative deprivation. The independent variable under review here is C (from Table 5.4 and the preceding discussion) which is defined as "rate of change in politicized relative deprivation." To operationalize this concept,[272] CANTRIL's self-anchoring striving scale[273] is used. The empirical referents here are: "career satisfaction, economic well-being, satisfactory living conditions, and children's welfare" (GROFMAN/ MULLER 1973:518). In contrast with other authors, GROFMAN/MULLER do not speak of relative deprivation but of "relative gratification," "since the top of a Self-Anchoring scale is a condition of complete congruence between achievement optimum and achievement" (GROFMAN/MULLER 1973:520). It is the differences and the rates of changes in the *optimum* (not the maximum) level and the level of actual achievement on which GROFMAN/ MULLER are basing their study.[274] As the authors themselves make clear, one must distinguish this version of relative deprivation from GURR's version (cf. chapter 5.1.1.1.1) where *just deserts* and not an optimum level is the referent. A third alternative already mentioned (e.g., chapter 4.3) is defining relative deprivation in terms of the achievements of reference *individuals* or *groups* with whom the respondent identifies. Taking the differentiations below and those listed in CROSBY (1976) into consideration, there are many possible referents for social comparison processes. Much work of theoretical integration and empirical testing remains for researchers before any systematic knowledge as to the relative impact of these multiple referents will become available.

Differentiating between three points in time (past, present, future; intervals of 5 years), the following basic patterns of relative gratification are derived (see Figure 5.5). In the case of the so-called *rise* and *drop* hypothesis (also erroneously called the J-curve hypothesis; cf. chapter 8.4.6.1), the particular situation in each field is said to have improved at the beginning but later to have changed for the worse (patterns 3, 4, and 5).

In the study of GROFMAN/MULLER, respondents with these patterns score higher on the dependent variables, potential for political violence (MARSH 1977:147, however, fails to find support for the J-curve hypothesis; cf. chapter 9). On the other hand, in the reverse *drop* and *rise* cases (6–8), the respondents also attain higher scores on the dependent variable.[275] "Thus, the findings tend to support an *Absolute* J-Curve hypothesis, to the effect that individuals experiencing either a Rise-and-Drop or a Drop-and-Rise pattern of relative gratification will be more likely to show high potential for political violence than individuals experiencing a No-Change pattern of relative gratification" (GROFMAN/MULLER 1973:536). When studying the rate of change hypotheses,

> the data provide no support . . . that as degree of relative gratification increases over time, potential for political violence will tend to decrease. However, if we convert the rate-of-change scores into absolute magnitudes, the data consistently support an *Absolute* Change hypothesis that as absolute magnitude of relative gratification increases over time, potential for political violence will show a

Figure 5.5.   Patterns of Shift in Relative Gratification over Time

Source: GROFMAN/MULLER (1973: 524; following figures
          ibid.)

1.   no-change deprivation

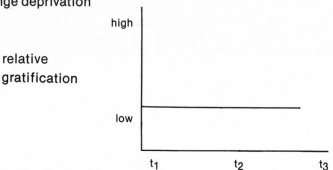

2.   no-change gratification

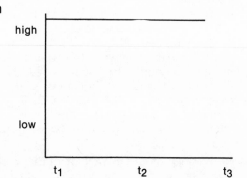

In the case of the so-called *rise* and *drop* hypothesis (also erroneously called the J-curve hypothesis; cf. chapter 8.4.6.1), the
particular situation in each field is said to have improved at the
beginning but later to have changed for the worse (patterns 3, 4,
and 5.)

3.

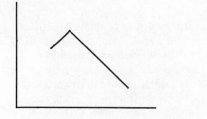

4.

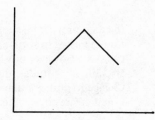

5.

In the study of GROFMAN/MULLER, respondents with these patterns score higher on the dependent variable, potential for political violence (MARSH 1977:147, however, fails to find support for the J-curve hypothesis; cf. chapter 9).

On the other hand, in the reverse *drop* and *rise* cases (6-8), the respondents also attain higher scores on the dependent variable.[275]

6.

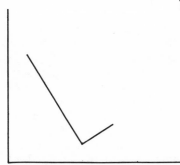

7.

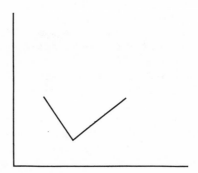

8.

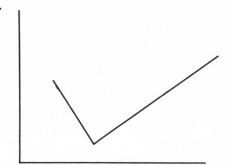

tendency to increase. Of the rate-of-change variables, the best predictor of potential for political violence is the absolute magnitude of present to future shift (ibid.).

A linear relationship between the absolute rate of change in relative gratification and protest potential is also found when control variables like political trust, efficacy of past political violence, race, age, and education are introduced.

As there is only one study in the literature which parallels this result (BOWEN et al. 1968, also quoted in GROFMAN/MULLER), the authors may have had reason to entitle their work "The strange case of relative gratification and potential for political violence: the V-curve-hypothesis." If negative rate of change, no rate of change, and positive rate of change are placed along the x-axis and y is the potential for political violence, distinct V-relationships emerge in all four of the areas to which the CANTRIL scale was applied.

How are these results to be interpreted? That protests (or here, increases of protest potential) are a reaction to a deterioration in one's overall standing (negative rate of change in relative gratification) should not come as a surprise. What is called for are interpretations of the relationship between positive rate of change in relative gratification and protest potential. Thus far in the present study (and in later chapters as well) there has been some evidence that protests occur against the background of recent improvements. Expectations as to the future are far ahead of the realities, leading to a more negative evaluation of the actual situation (*rising expectations* hypothesis). TOCQUEVILLE (see in chapter 8.4.2) has already provided the rationale for this relationship.

"A second explanation, labelled *Present Value of the Past*, is predicated on the assumption that, since a person's level of achievement in the present is based in part on past costs, the degree to which past costs are perceived as having been intolerable will vary proportionately with the magnitude of perceived positive change over time, resulting in the actual devaluation of utility of present achievement by an amount proportionate to the magnitude of positive change" (GROFMAN/MULLER 1973:537; see WOLF 1969 for details of this effort at explanation). This "backward-looking discount rate" or "decay rate" (WOLF 1969:3; GROFMAN/MULLER 1973:538) leads to the consequence that recent improvements are looked at as payments on account, with the rest still to come. In short, recent but insufficient improvements lead to an increase of the protest potential.

Neither explanation can be corroborated with the data at hand. There is even a third suggestive explanation: "Since a person who perceives positive change has more and *more to lose* (until such a positive change becomes stabilized over a period of time), positive change will produce a readiness to ensure that such change is maintained, by acts of dissent against the state if necessary, among persons who believe that such change could be threatened" (GROFMAN/MULLER 1973:537; emphasis added here). The more recent the gains, the greater the likelihood of protest to defend these gains. In the third explanation the focus is on the present state (credit), whereas in the other two explanations a debit-state is invoked.

We stress once again (cf. also chapters 4.3 and 5.1.1.1.3) that data should be collected relative to the *evaluation* of changes in the socioeconomic standing of respondents. Otherwise, one is left with a number of equally plausible alternative explanations, none of which can be refuted with the data at hand. Moreover, "there have been no investigations of whether the optimum level of achievement as defined by a Self-Anchoring scale is treated by individuals as a constant, or whether the past, present, and future comparisons are based on different optimum achievement levels" (GROFMAN/ MULLER 1973:520). As results like those of GROFMAN/MULLER may have policy implications[276] (some of which are touched upon by the authors themselves), much better data along the lines suggested in this study must be collected. Also replication is called for to avoid premature conclusions.

In sum, the works of MULLER and GROFMAN/MULLER are of great significance for the analysis of political violence on the individual and group levels, their importance perhaps resting not so much in specific results but in the strategies employed. In these works, carefully derived theoretical notions are tested in various forms and in numerous multivariate analyses, the focus always being on results that may be theoretically meaningful. Furthermore, notions based on learning theories are incorporated here to a greater extent than in many other studies (though the essentially cross-sectional data provide only for an insufficient test of such propositions). It remains to be seen whether MULLER's results are stable when other objects of explanation and/or contexts are chosen. In any case, at this stage of research on political violence on the individual and group levels, MULLER's works provide a yardstick[277] against which to evaluate forthcoming results.

There are also several reports on a study of a probability and quota sample of West German citizens (2,663 adults from four rural communities, two large cities, and six of the major universities are selected) also carried out by MULLER.[278] His results lead in part to a confirmation of some of his earlier findings but also to an extensive reformulation of earlier theoretical statements.[279] Even though the dependent variable and the setting in this new inquiry are beyond the scope of this chapter on the American black riots of the 1960s, a quasi-excursus on this recent work of MULLER's may be justified here on the basis of tracing continuities in theory construction. More general theories in the field of political violence and protest behavior should comprise statements on a variety of dependent variables in quite different settings. As MULLER's work may be considered an important step in that direction, a few words on these new developments seem in order here. The dependent variable aggressive political behavior[280] is defined as "political behavior that is illegal, disruptive of the normal functioning of government, and may entail the use of violence" (MULLER 1975:30), thus only in part comprising violent political protests (as holds for MULLER's earlier studies). In contrast to GROFMAN/MULLER (1973), here all three of the variants of relative deprivation theory (i.e., optimum deprivation, just deserts deprivation, and reference group deprivation) are tested for at the same time.

Whereas the CANTRIL scale was used for indexing relative deprivation in the sense of optimum deprivation and reference group deprivation, in the just deserts version of relative deprivation a list of fifteen items is employed. These items refer to goods in life which the respondent thinks are due to him. For example, one of the items reads: "Are your housing conditions very much worse, much worse, or only somewhat worse than those which are properly due to you?" (MULLER 1975:22).[281]

Empirically, the other two relative deprivation measures were not strongly correlated with the just deserts version. For example, 56.3% of the "people who are presumably quite frustrated or dissatisfied with respect to their just deserts, nevertheless, do not see themselves as standing farther than about half-way from their best conceivable rewards in life" (ibid., p. 28). Thus, "these results indicate that the Self-Anchoring scale is not a good measure of dissatisfaction. This is because (1) medium-sized or large discrepancies registered on the Self-Anchoring scale are not at all frustrating in a just deserts sense to quite a few people, and (2) even medium-sized or small discrepancies registered on the Self-Anchoring scale *can* be highly frustrating in a just deserts sense to some people" (ibid., p. 29). Interestingly, just deserts deprivation, if combined with the already familiar structural blame variable, proves to be a strong predictor of aggressive political behavior, even when the other two deprivation variables have been introduced as controls.[282] Considered in dynamic terms, "the condition of negative value anticipation [as predicted] enhances the relationship between the Aggressive Behavior Index and Structural Just Deserts Deprivation" (ibid., p. 38). These results favor an elaborated relative deprivation theory, yet it should be stressed that "relative deprivation, even in the sense of just deserts discrepancy, is *not* the necessary condition of aggressive political behavior [as stated by GURR; cf. chapter 5.1.1.1.1]. When it is absolutely not present, fairly sizeable rates of participation in aggressive political behavior still occur if political support is not high and if community context [as in the university milieu] facilitates aggressive action motivated by lack of political support" (ibid., p. 47–48; emphasis added). Yet MULLER does not claim that "relative deprivation in the just deserts sense, *per se*, would be related to aggressive political behavior independently of political support. . . . But when just deserts discrepancy *interacts* with structural blame and value anticipation, the resulting structurally-directed frustration, intolerable in the sense that the future is anticipated to be even worse, should provide motivational impetus sufficient to have an effect on aggressive behavior, given that political support is not positive" (ibid., p. 49).

Concerning the role of frustration or relative deprivation as such, much more evidence has been gathered in the meantime. Drawing on his data from a West German sample and a sample of New York City residents, MULLER is able to show that

> just-deserts frustration is clearly different from the reference group
> and aspirational varieties; in particular, the Cantril ladder scale
> measure should not, as it has been in the past, be interpreted as a

measure of relative deprivation in the sense that GURR defines the term. Second, people appear to have a tendency to set their just deserts below the achievement attained by the best-off members of their reference group, and below their aspirations (best possible solution); as a consequence, even those who perceive a great discrepancy between their own achievement and that which they would attain if their highest aspirations were realized do not feel that there is any great discrepancy between what they now have and what they are rightfully entitled to (MULLER 1980:78).

Thus, "the relationship between frustration in the aspirational sense and individual propensities for political protest and violence is, at best, quite weak" (ibid., p. 81). Further "results indicate that [while it is the strongest candidate among frustration concepts] just deserts frustration is most likely only an indirect cause of participation in political protest and violence in West Germany—hardly a necessary condition" (ibid., p. 93). In sum, "belief in the justifiability of aggressive action on utilitarian grounds, arising out of expectancy that aggressive action will be beneficial (weighted by its value), and belief in the normative justifiability of aggressive action, arising out of broad-based alienation from the political system and ideological approval of political aggression, are the psychological variables that predispose individuals in general to participate in protest and violence. More simply and tritely put, people rebel when they believe it is right to rebel and that rebellion will pay off" (ibid., p. 97).

A final noteworthy result of the study by MULLER (1975) is that the V-curve relationship of GROFMAN/MULLER (1973; cf. above) is found once again but disappears when structural just deserts discrepancy is used as a control variable. As was true in MULLER's Waterloo sample, the V-curve variant of relative deprivation is not a strong predictor of the dependent variable.

It will be fascinating to hear the results obtained when the findings of this paper of MULLER are related in detail to those found in MULLER/ JUKAM (1977; cf. also briefly chapter 6) where system support is the dominant independent variable being related to the same dependent variable (see already MULLER 1980). Finally, differentiating between local and national levels of distrust and support might be a useful addendum to a theory of individual protest behavior.

5.3.2.4. Structural and/or Ecological Explanations

In Table 5.5 some of the ecological conditions of black rioting behavior have been listed.[283] Obviously, there is a wide range of social conditions associated with the occurrence and intensity of riots. Yet, in causal terms a substantially different picture emerges upon controlling a number of independent variables. Probably the most ambitious multivariate analysis in these

Table 5.5. Structural and/or Ecological Determinants of Violent Black Protest Behavior

Author	N	Period	Sources	Dependent Variables	Independent Variables	Results Bivariate	Multivariate
1. Lieberson/ Silverman (1965)	76 riot cities	1913–63	N. Y. Times, Negro Yearbook, local newspapers, etc., census	race riots between blacks and whites	pop. changes in cities, unemployment rate, income differences between whites and blacks, poor housing conditions black store owners, proportion of blacks in service occupations number of black policemen, responsiveness of local gov. structure	matched pairs (N varying according to data available) no consistent relationships slightly negative relationships negative relationships	
2. Bloombaum (1968)	24 riot cities	1925–63	as in (1)	as in (1)	as in (1)	matched pairs (multidimensional scalogram analysis) no strong relationships, all relationships jointly considered: differences between riot cities and calm cities	
3. Downes (1968)	676 cities, incl.	1964–5/68	N. Y. Times, Congress. Quart., 1960	riots occurrence	more likely in larger cities, less growing cities, densely popu-	percentage based comparisons only	

129 riot cities	census, 1963 *Municipal Yearbook*	lated areas, cities with a 15% or more proportion of non-whites, with a higher death rate, greater unemployment, less educational achievement, lower family income, low % of sound housing units		
		intensity	pop. 1960	$\gamma = .75$ (all significant .70 at .05 level)
			% nonwhite 1960	.65
			change in % non-white 1950–60	– .47
			% housing units owner occupied 1960	.43
			population per sq. mile 1960	.41
			per capital general gov. expenditure 1963	
			% persons 25 years and over who have completed 4 years of high school or more 1960	– .41

Table 5.5. Structural and/or Ecological Determinants of Violent Black Protest Behavior (continued)

Author	N	Period	Sources	Dependent Variables	Independent Variables	Results Bivariate	Multivariate
4. Ford/ Moore (1970)	135 SMSAs incl. 60 with riot occ.	1965– 8/9/67	Permanent Subcom. on Invest. of Com. on Gov. Op. of U.S. Sen. (McClelland Comm.) 1960 census	riots occurrence	income nonwhite pop. 1960 median number of school years completed by nonwhite pop. 1960 % whites owning their homes minus analogous figure for nonwhite pop. 1960 % blacks in SMSAs, 1960		reverse sign (+) predicted sign (–) } R²=.44 predicted sign (+) reverse sign (–) } R²=.36 (all significant at .05 level)
				intensity	income nonwhite pop. 1960 % nonwhite pop. owning their homes 1960 % whites owning their homes minus anal. fig. for nonwhite pop. 1960		reverse sign (+) predicted sign (–) } R²=.46 predicted sign (+) reverse sign (–) } R²=.26 (all significant at .05 level)
5. Downes (1970)	676 cities incl. 149 riot cities	1963-68	as in (3)	riots occurrence	% nonwhite pop. 1960 population change in % nonwhite, 1950-60 % occupied housing units owner occupied 1960 pop. growth, 1950-60	γ = .74 (all significant at .05 level) .70 .54 – .49 – .41	

Study	No. of cities	Years	Sources	Dependent variable	Independent variables	Results
	149 riot cities			intensity	pop. 1960	γ = .62 (r = .57)
					change in % nonwhite, 1950–60	.45 (all signif-icant at .05 level)
					pop. per sq. mile, 1960	.38 (r = .35)
					number of councilmen	.35 (r = .35)
6. White (1968)	262 cities incl. non-riot cities	1963–67	mostly newspapers, 1960 census	occurrence of riots	% nonwhite pop.	partial correlation coefficient
					total pop.	= .280
					density	.170 $R^2 \approx$ .22
						.164
7. Spilerman (1970)	673 cities incl. non-riot cities (413 for multiple regres-sion)	1961–68	Lemberg Center *Cong. Quart.* Rep. of Nat. Adv. Com. on Civ. Disorders, *N.Y. Times Index,* 1960 census, *1965 Municipal Yearbook*	occurrence of riots	nonwhite pop. (log x)	r = .586 (all significant at .01 level)
					pop. per councilman	.485
					% nonwhite ($\sqrt{x}$)	.221
					% nonwhite males employed in tradi-tional black occupa-tions	− .215
					South (dummy)	− .198
					presence of mayor-council government	.184

% variance explained by each cluster of variables acting alone:
nonwhite pop. 46.8
rel. deprivation 20.4 (ratio nonwhite/white re occup., fam. income, unemp., educ.)
pol. structure 28.5 (pop. per councilman, % council members elected at large, partisan vs. nonpartisan election, mayor-council form of city gov. vs. other)
all clusters (exc. nonwhite pop.) 42.0

Table 5.5. Structural and/or Ecological Determinants of Violent Black Protest Behavior (continued)

Author	N	Period	Sources	Dependent Variables	Independent Variables	Results	
						Bivariate	Multivariate
							all clusters 51.3 % add. total variance expl. by nonwhite pop. when entered after *all* clusters and South. 9.3 % add. total variance expl. by all clusters except nonwhite pop. when entered after nonwhite pop. and South 4.5
8. Spilerman (1976)	322 events	1967–68	as above	intensity of riots	nonwhite pop. (log x) pop. per councilman % nonwhite ($\sqrt{x}$) % nonwhite males employed in traditional black occupations	r = .270 (figures .175 > .139 are .148 signif. at -.139 .01, < .139 at .05)	part. correl. controll. for region, nonwhite pop., temporal effects, no. of previous disturbances
					% nonwhites living in housing with substandard plumbing	.130	South (dummy) –.151 nonwhite pop. .339 (log x) (both significant at .01)
					presence of mayor-council government	.110	

Study	N	Years	Sources	Dependent variable	Independent variables	Findings
9. McElroy/ Singell (1973)	64 SMSAs with riot occurrence	1965–68	*N. Y. Times,* Cong. Hear., Rep. of Natl. Adv. Com., *Wanderer* (1968)	occurrence of riots (measured in terms of property damage and economic loss)	pop. per sq. mile 1965 / % change in tot. pop. 1950–60 / median school years completed 1960 / % change in professional and technical workers 1950–60 / median family income / income skewness / nonwhite median education divided by white education .109	all positively related to dep. var. (no coeff. of association reported)
10. Jiobu (1974)	74 riot cities	8/65 –1969	*Christ Sci. Monitor, Cong. Quart.,* Rep. of Natl. Adv. Com., *N.Y. Times,* etc.	occurrence of riots	city centrality (total pop. size, national headquarters) / black deprivation (poverty, traditional occupations)	$R^2 = .38$ using a multiplicative combination of the 2 ind. variables (black deprivation correlating negatively with the dep. variable)

respects is SPILERMAN's study of the determinants of spontaneous outbreaks during 1961-68 in "cities in the contiguous United States with populations exceeding 25,000 in 1960" (SPILERMAN 1970:630). One of his early
conclusions based on bivariate analyses seems to be in accordance with
predictions from the theory of relative deprivation: "it is evident that racial
disorders are more likely to occur where the level of life for the Negro is least
oppressive according to objective measures. There are more disturbances
where Negro disadvantage, relative to white residents, is small and where
Negro attainment surpasses that of Negroes living elsewhere. Moreover,
disorder-prone communities tend to have stable populations and better
quality housing" (SPILERMAN 1970:642-43).

After a multiple regression analysis, however, the theory of relative deprivation must be considered as just one of the victims of more powerful causal
analysis:

> Hypotheses were considered which attribute disorder-proneness to
> weak social integration, to alienation from the political system, and
> to the frustrations stemming from deprivation or unattainable aspira-
> tions. In all instances, upon controlling for Negro population, the
> explanation failed to account for the distribution of disorders. More
> generally, we conclude that the differences in disorder-proneness
> among communities cannot be explained in terms of variations in
> the objective situations of the Negro. . . . The susceptibility of an
> individual Negro to participating in a disorder does not depend upon
> the structural characteristics of the community in which he resides.
> As for the community propensity, it is the aggregate of the indi-
> vidual values—the larger the Negro population, the greater the like-
> lihood of a disorder. Little else appears to matter (SPILERMAN
> 1970:645).

All zero-order correlations are considerably reduced after introducing the
control variable, absolute size of the black[284] population. For Southern cities
a small correction (dummy term) seems to be indicated to take different
cultural traditions into consideration.[285] "Racial violence is more likely
where Negroes are better situated in occupational status, in education and
income, and where the rate of population growth is small. However, these
conditions have little to do with a community being prone to racial disorder, and are instead the incidental characteristics of cities with large Negro
populations" (ibid., p. 645).[286]

This result seems to agree with a general remark from TOMLINSON, also
referred to by SPILERMAN, "What produces riots is the shared agreement of
most Negro Americans that their lot in life is unacceptable. . . . What is unacceptable about Negro life does not vary much from city to city,[287] and the
differences in Negro life from city to city are irrelevant" (TOMLINSON
1968:29). According to SPILERMAN (and others, e.g., OBERSCHALL
1968:335-36; JANOWITZ 1968:32-33) it is the media, and mainly television, bringing about this common definition of the situation:

the extensive media coverage accorded to many of the incidents, with the actions of participants depicted in full relief, served to familiarize Negroes elsewhere with the details of rioting and with the motivations of rioters. Observing the behavior of persons who face similar deprivations and must contend with the same discriminatory institutions as oneself—in short, individuals with whom the viewer could identify—provided a model of how he, too, might protest the indignities of his circumstance. By conveying the intensity and emotion of a confrontation, television provided an essential mechanism for riot contagion; also, as a result of its national network structure, the provocations which arose in diverse settings were made visible in the ghettos of every city (SPILERMAN 1976:790).

Of course, SPILERMAN's interpretations are not necessarily valid at the individual level (danger of the ecological fallacy). SPILERMAN is able to show that some of the often proposed explanations lose their predictive power at the aggregate level after controlling for other explicative variables, notably the absolute number of blacks (the zero-order correlation between nonwhite population [log x] and number of disorders is r=.586),[288] yet he cannot show that individual values are indeed the major determinants of riot activities. Furthermore, there is no answer as to how individual and structural processes of mobilization are taking place, before as well as during the riots.

In the meantime SPILERMAN has extended his analyses to the determinants of the intensity of rioting. The study comprises 322 events, using the same criteria for the dependent variable as in the earlier study (at least thirty participants, primarily black aggression). The period now is limited to 1967-68,[289] as information prior to those years was insufficient to allow classification according to the operational criteria of intensity (ranging from 0: "Low intensity—rock and bottle throwing, some fighting, little property damage. Crowd size <125; arrests <15; injuries <8," to 3: "High intensity—major violence, bloodshed and destruction. Crowd size >400; arrests >65; injuries >35," SPILERMAN 1976:774). "Breaching the barriers against collective violence may require a precipitant of immense significance. Indeed, 168 of the 341 racial disturbances can be associated with one of two extraordinary events: the massive Newark riot of 1967 (which received extensive television coverage) or the assassination of Martin Luther King" (ibid., p. 773). Actually, SPILERMAN is interested in finding out whether the "frustrations felt by Negroes which derive from their local situations are salient to other aspects of the disturbance process. In this regard, there is certainly reason to expect community differences to exist in the level of Negro discontent" (ibid., p. 772). If these conditions are important causes of the black riots, perhaps they might account for the differences in intensity of rioting, notwithstanding their failure to account for the mere occurrence of rioting. Differences in grievance level between cities have been widely documented in the literature (cf. ROSSI et al. 1974 in note 287). Some researchers even report a direct relationship between these sociostructural or sociopsychological conditions and riot intensity (DOWNES 1968;MORGAN/

CLARK 1973; see note 288). SPILERMAN comes up again with basically the same results as in his earlier study (cf. Table 5.5; also the partly comparable evidence in HOPKINS/FEIERABEND 1971).

PORTER/NAGEL (1976) as well found some support of SPILERMAN's nonwhite population variable in their attempt to test whether a curvilinear relationship exists between various measures of inequality and the black riots during two periods, 1965 and 1968 (N=72 cities), and in fifty-nine cities with a riot in 1967.[290] While their results do not confirm the effects of housing inequality ("ratio of black to white percentages of crowded units") and educational inequality ("ratio of median school years completed among black males over age 25 to the same figure for whites"), at least in the instance of income inequality (logarithm of the difference score of black and white median incomes) they report that, for the 1967 data, the degree of variance explained is enhanced if a nonlinear term is added to the equation (R^2 reaching .46 vs. .32 without a quadratic figure), "with severity greatest at intermediate levels of inequality" (PORTER/NAGEL 1976:34). "For Detroit the ratio and difference of medians were .78 and $2,410; for Newark, .75 and $2,210" (ibid., p. 35). In the case of the larger sample "there was weak but significant evidence of a curvilinear parabolic pattern when we entered our income inequality measure without including other inequality variables. The income terms, however, were overwhelmed by occupation[291] and housing inequality when we added the latter variables to the regression equation" (ibid., p. 33). They argue that as "dissimilars converge," i.e., as the discrepancies between whites' and blacks' positions decrease, black discontent (in GURR's terminology, "progressive relative deprivation"; cf. chapter 4.3) rises rather than falls: "the expectations of the lower group will rise explosively, as the standards of the privileged exert a magnetic pull on the hopes of the deprived" (ibid., p. 9). They also refer to TOCQUEVILLE who proposed a similar argument (cf. chapter 8.4.2), namely that discontent is a function of relative prosperity and not of poor circumstances. In the study of GROFMAN/MULLER (1973; cf. chapter 5.3.2.3), evidence has been reported that readiness to engage in violent political protest behavior results not only when things change for the worse but also against a background of recent achievements for which several possible explanations were given (but could not be tested).

PORTER/NAGEL discuss some possible political implications of their results, e.g., that one might have to reckon with an increase in political violence as the degree of inequality between blacks and whites decreases up to a turning point (in this case .69). They claim to have provided enough evidence for their theoretically derived curvilinear relationship (drawing on psychological mechanisms already considered in chapter 5.1.2.7; cf. also the mixed evidence, ibid., as to such a relationship). Yet, one should point out that the data at hand hardly allow any rigorous test of the relationship postulated. Data will have to be collected over time on how income and other inequalities are perceived (cf. also the arguments in chapter 5.1.2.7). Psychologically, what makes for a lower and upper limit in inequality? The theoretical rationale may indeed be a sound one and basic to groups in the social comparisons they make, once their situation starts to improve. However, any judgement on the strength of this hypothesis at the present stage would be premature, since only insufficient data are available for a test. In addition, the measures of inequality in income, education, and occupation correlate to a degree of r=.60, raising the fundamental question of disturbances due to multicollinearity effects and the additional question of whether the measures of inequality are subjectively equally important and could be treated as functional equivalents (which is done in the aggregate statistical analysis of the authors). There are as well other possibly important factors neglected in the theoretical outline of these authors, e.g., repressive capacities, behavior of repressive forces, and some of the demographic factors tested for in the analyses of authors mentioned earlier. PORTER/NAGEL claim, however, that their measure of the dependent variable[292] "allows some tolerance for differences in unmeasured variables such as the police responses to a disturbance" (PORTER/NAGEL 1976:28). The authors also point out that they have been careful in looking only at black riots (and not including other types of riots), a precaution which has not always been followed.[293] Finally, as is true for the analyses of SPILERMAN and others as well, the predicted relationships will have to be studied on lower levels of aggregation (e.g., city bocks or even on the individual level) than those used at present.

Besides the results reported by PORTER/NAGEL (1976), there is another issue that might bear on the evaluation of the analyses of SPILERMAN. DANZGER, who reports (1968, with a quite different sampling of events) results similar to those of SPILERMAN (cf. also BUTTON 1978), in a more recent study (1975) has raised the question whether distorted wire reporting of conflict behavior might have introduced some errors into his own analyses as well as those of SPILERMAN and others. Studying the coverage of political protests (N=644) related to civil rights activities in the *New York Times* during 1955–65, DANZGER reports that in cities with wire services (Associated Press, United Press International) more conflicts are reported on than in other cities. The possibility that these cities also exhibit relatively higher conflict levels is discussed and not entirely ruled out after some control factors have been introduced. The presence of AP/UPI offices turns out to be the strongest predictor of conflict reports and even contributes an additional R^2: .054 to the degree of explanation reached, if entered as fourth and final variable in a step-wise regression analysis. DANZGER's results are said to indicate "that utilizing newspaper reports of conflict as the basis for analysis is likely to be misleading as these data are contaminated by the factor of wire service office location. But they also show if one uses only those cities which have already reported *some* conflict, there seems to be no such contamination" (DANZGER 1975:581). (It deserves to be noted that only in a later comment of DANZGER's is the reader informed that riot behavior constitutes less than one percent of my cases," DANZGER 1976:1067.)

The conclusion of DANZGER's analysis has been challenged by SNYDER/ KELLY (1977) in a study on "(1) racial disorders across 673 cities from 1965 to 1969 and (2) largely nonviolent collective protests occurring in 43 U.S.

cities during 1968" (ibid., p. 105). They develop and successfully test a model of news reporting wherein conflict intensity and media sensitivity are two interacting explicative variables. Thus, in opposition to DANZGER, they treat conflicts as heterogeneous phenomena. Unfortunately, their model is more suited for retrodictions than for predictive purposes. In any case, both conclusions reached might have some bearing on the validity of some of the results reported on in this chapter. From a cross-national point of view, these results should be seen as a serious warning against treating data drawn from standard references (cf. the discussion in chapter 5.1.3) as generally reliable. As already discussed in the context of cross-national research, the news coverage of sources has hardly drawn the attention it deserves from scholars.

To return to SPILERMAN's findings, his analyses and those focusing on the discrepancy between expectations and capabilities need not preclude each other. The absolute number of blacks has several structural implications:

> Population size relates to the origin and seriousness of riots in that larger ghettos seem likely to have
> (1) a greater number of violence-oriented residents, those viewing violence as a legitimate political tactic,
> (2) a greater resource potential for mobilizing and sustaining riots (e.g., more weapons, more potential participants, more ghetto organization of a formal and informal nature), and
> (3) more numerous frictional encounters between ghetto residents and white police and merchants, events historically likely to precipitate a ghetto riot (FEAGIN/HAHN 1973:122-23).

A result noteworthy in this context is reported by MIDLARSKY (1978) who analyzed the impact of "the interactive variable 'police force size multiplied by size of the black population'" on disorder frequency in cities with a black population of over 70,000. A correlation coefficient of r=.78 is found. "Further, in a step-wise multiple regression analyses including this variable and the variables, size of the total population, size of the black population, and size of the police force, no significant variance was added to the equation beyond the first variable included, namely, the interactive effect" (MIDLARSKY 1978:1005; see also the results on precipitants in the next section).

The likelihood of whether an individual will participate in rioting depends not only on these structural conditions (whose implications as specified by FEAGIN/HAHN must still be checked empirically) but also on explanatory variables discussed above, variables which focus on the individual level.

In terms of preventing the occurrence of further riots, there seems to be a clear implication of SPILERMAN's analysis: the absolute size of the nonwhite population in the area in question must be limited (but at what point?). However, one must remember that about 50% of the variance is unexplained in his analyses. There are two variables which seem to be of major importance in explaining the occurrence and intensity of riots, neither incorporated into the analyses of SPILERMAN:[294] the role and behavior of *white ghetto merchants* and that of the *police*. We cannot go into detail here (see the discussion of the literature in ALDRICH 1973; cf. also BERK/ALDRICH 1972; STURDIVANT/WILHELM 1968; STURDIVANT 1969). There can be no doubt that, in CAPLOVITZ's (1963) terms, "the poor pay more." Yet, contrary to widespread beliefs, there are apparently no clear-cut patterns as to *why* specific shops were looted during the black riots. A systematic account of looting events in fifteen cities in 1967 and three cities in 1968 by BERK/ALDRICH (1972; cf. also ROSSI et al. 1968) leads to the conclusion that some targets are chosen because of their familiarity or exposure to ghetto inhabitants or because they are negative symbols to the rioters. Only in cases where targets are chosen as objects of retaliation, could it be maintained that ghetto merchant practices are unambiguous causes of certain forms of black rioting behavior. Yet, taken together, these explanations account for no more than 20% of the variance.[295] Thus, one could say that ghetto merchant behavior, while being a general context factor,[296] is considerably less important than the class of variables referring to police behavior.

The black population generally complains about brutal and arrogant behavior on the part of the police, mostly whites at that time (for evidence see U. S. President's Commission on Law Enforcement and Administration of Justice, Task Force Report: Police [1967]; LEVY [1968]; FOGELSON [1968]; ROSSI et al. [1968]; GAMSON/McEVOY [1970]; GROVES/ROSSI [1970]; MARX [1970b]; HAHN [1971]; FEAGIN/HAHN [1973: 130–32; 151–59]; SEARS/McCONAHAY 1973:98]; ROSSI et al. [1974]). Besides resenting this "over-control" (CONANT 1968:427), blacks are concerned with "under-control," for instance, when personal security within the ghetto is at issue (cf. also HAHN/FEAGIN 1970). Many policemen, on the other hand, apparently judge the rioters as conspirators aiming at undermining the American constitution, a gross misunderstanding if one recalls that these protests served to point out how greatly the constitution was violated as far as equal opportunities for all are concerned.

Statements about the functions of the black riots easily become value judgements under the guise of science. Yet, taking the consensus of various surveys, one arrives at the following evaluation: The riots did serve to indicate legitimate claims of parts of the population and the lack of appropriate means to realize these expectations. Seen in this way, riots are, quite to the contrary of the riffraff theory, acts of rational behavior (in the sense of a warning strike), calling attention to conditions perceived as unjust.[297] This does not mean, however, that the interpretation of any phase or any riot as a pure bargaining process is justified. Conversely, there is no evidence for denouncing the riots as irrational. One should, however, make a clear distinction between the actual occurrences (cf. also the definition of riots in chapter 5.3.2) and the hopes and wishes later on associated with these events (cf. CAMPBELL/SCHUMAN 1968).[298]

5.3.2.5. Precipitating Events

Taking up the question of the *time* coordinates of the riots, the police once again play an important role. A comparison of the events which precipitated riots in earlier periods with the precipitants during 1964-68 shows some clear differences: whereas in the period between 1913 and 1963 21% of the precipitating events were interracial fights (LIEBERSON/SILVERMAN 1965:889), this category is now practically meaningless. In the 1960s the police were involved in precipitating events in more than one-third of all the cases (in half of the cases during 1964-67, according to FEAGIN/HAHN 1973:145). Typical events included the arrests of a youth because of driving offenses in Watts, a taxi driver in Newark, and a black found drinking after closing time in Detroit. The black riots of the 1960s have replaced the interracial riots which occurred during the first half of this century.[299] If there are casualties among whites, then they occur mostly among the police and the National Guard. The KERNER Commission which studied twenty-four major riots in 1967 concisely states: "Almost invariably the incident that ignites disorder arises from police action" (1968:93). A statistic on the precipitants of the most severe 1967 riots in forty riot cities shows that "killings, arrest, interference, assault, or search of Negro by police" (32.5percent) and "interracial rock throwing or fight, no mention of lethal weapons" (17.5 percent) constituted the two dominant categories apart from unknown precipitants (35 percent) (BUTTON 1978:18-19). The behavior of the police takes on cue qualities (cf. chapter 3.2), thus releasing a potential for protest that has accumulated over time.

What, then, are the characteristics of a precipitating event? Its symbolic nature is not called into question.[300] However, there is disagreement as to what creates this symbolic nature and whether precipitating events are random in nature or typically nonrandom. In what respects do situations with precipitating character differ from those without these attributes? What makes for a change in the definition of the situation? To our knowledge, there is no systematic study along these lines. Usually, the circumstances of the events in question are only loosely studied: If these circumstances are extraordinary, then they must be the source of what follows. Similar events at the present (in other areas or cities) or past are not systematically scrutinized for additional discriminating conditions that make for mobilization or demobiliziation (cf. TILLY 1978). Thus, there is no scale of comparison.

Much less debated than the kind and nature of precipitating events is the following causal chain: (1) Insufficient housing in big agglomerations leads to (2) a large number of people (the critical mass) assembling on the streets in the case of averse conditions (high temperature).[301] (3) This, in turn, increases the likelihood that certain symbolic events acquire cue character and become precipitants.

Thus, it is possible to list a number of necessary conditions for the outbreak of riots, but no sufficient condition. There are no systematic quantitative studies in which variables relating to the socioeconomic structures in the particular cities, the type and degree of social contacts, or the chances to take up other activities such as attending a sports event,[302] relating to similar occurrences in the past and, last but not least, relating to the legitimacy of the local political leadership are employed at the same time.

Some authors (SPILERMAN 1970; cf. also the KERNER Report) assume that precipitants are singular events random in nature. We believe, however, that this is a logically and empirically questionable assumption. In the KERNER Report itself there is evidence against the assumption of randomness of precipitants (randomness meaning in fact that the particular events could be "substituted" for by other random events). The KERNER Commission reports that in almost all cities *similar* events, serving almost as precipitants, have occurred in the past.[303] Thus, there is a priori a greater probability that some classes of events will become precipitants (cf. also FEAGIN/HAHN 1973:150). A formalization using Markov processes may be indicated. However, before this could be done in a useful manner, further detailed information as to the circumstances (build-up, etc.) of precipitating events is needed. Data will also have to be collected about comparable past events (whether acting as precipitants or not) so that it will be possible to test some propositions about the causes and features of precipitating events.[304] Failure to develop an explicit theory of precipitating events would result in purely descriptive or even tautological statements. The KERNER Report then, has the last word in that the "final incident" in a long chain of events became the precipitant.

5.3.2.6. Some Theoretical and Methodological Consequences

There are no cross-level analyses on the causes of the black riots linking attributes of the ghettos with characteristics of the participants. There are also no comparative longitudinal studies dealing with situational characteristics as well as reciprocal effects of the behavior of rioters and state agents. One should rely much more on information about actual behavior[305] as a guideline for future studies on riots. This could be collected through screened observation, content analysis of film materials, and the use of multiple interviews in crowd situations, new methods employed by McPHAIL (1978; WOHLSTEIN/McPHAIL 1979; cf. also WRIGHT 1978a). In simple terms, crowds differ and the techniques for analyzing crowd behavior must be varied as well.[306]

Employing *process approaches* (cf. also chapter 9) would sometimes allow for reconciling seemingly contradictory results as to the characteristics and causes of riot participation. Contradictory results may be attributed to the fact that the riot has gone into a different stage or that different types of riots are under study. To take just one example, MUELLER's (1978) factor analysis of twenty-four riot variables in seventy-seven riot cities for 1967 and 1968 leads to the detection of six factors, i.e., size, civilian assault, duration, police assault, arson, and gun fight. Furthermore, alienated persons as well as individuals with a strong sense of political efficacy and political distrust may participate in one and the same riot, but, contrary to SMEL-SER's (1963) requirement of generalized beliefs, for different reasons. The relative frequency of certain constellations of individual characteristics may also vary from phase to phase during a riot (cf. the general theoretical discussion of possible interrelationships between risks, rewards, and resources in OBERSCHALL 1973:157-72) and also from block to block within the same area.[307] In this context one should differentiate between the core (initiators) and fringe (followers). Moreover, one should differentiate according to the intensity of engagement (cf. also the theoretical distinctions in TILLY 1978, especially chapters 3 and 4). Followers need not be less active rioters than initiators. Even more complicated, one and the same individual may act quite differently due to his availability for certain activities. As McPHAIL points out: "Within a one-hour period of time, a person might walk from a bar or residence to the scene of a street arrest; chat with friends and acquaintances; curse the police; make a pass at a girl; throw a rock at a departing police car; light someone's cigarette; run down the street and join others in rocking and overturning a car; watch someone set the car on fire; drink a can of looted beer; assist firemen in extinguishing a fire as it spreads to an apartment house;[308] and so on" (McPHAIL 1971:1068).

In the literature there are classification schemes only for riot stages and processes (FEAGIN/HAHN 1973:160). One notable exception is a study by STARK et al. (1974) who have collected some data along the lines suggested here.[309] After analyzing 1,850 instances of rioting activities during the Watts 1965 riot, they report evidence against unilinear models of rioting processes as well as against contagion hypotheses.

> In only 21 percent of the instances of riot spread to a new geographical area did contagion involve a geographically contiguous area, a finding which provokes us to question possible mechanisms of riot spread and indicates a level of complexity in the contagion of riot behavior not adequately treated in the literature. Moreover, the fact that the phenomenon of adjacent spatial spread decreases as the riot progresses through time hints of even greater subtleties relating to the extent to which the mechanisms and agents of contagion change over time (STARK et al. 1974:874-75).

They interpret these and other results in terms of "differential changes over time in the mechanisms aiding and impeding riot spread, or possibly the successful legitimizing of riot norms over time and through variegated populations" (ibid., 875; cf. also BURBECK et al. 1978).

Several suggestions to be followed in the future have been made by McPHAIL: "The first strategy is to identify specific behavior patterns for concentrated and systematic observation and recording. The behavior patterns discussed . . .—the direction, frequency and velocity of assembling, focusing, further aligning, dispersing—represent one attempt to break up the complex composite which existing schemes have referred to as 'the crowd' into smaller, and therefore more manageable, units[310] of behavior for systematic investigation" (McPHAIL 1972:13; cf. also the appendix on "simple and complex forms of elementary collective behavior" in McPHAIL/PICKENS 1975).

Notwithstanding the vast amount of money and talent poured into studying the black riots of the 1960s, great gaps in research have been identified here. The black riots in which more than 200 persons lost their lives, about 8,000 were injured, some 50,000 arrested, and more than 200,000 individuals (not counting the coercive forces) participated,[311] are nevertheless one of the best studied examples of violent collective protests, documenting that quantitative studies on collective protest phenomena can be successful. Perhaps such studies will be even more successful if some of the earlier shortcomings are mastered in future studies. Theories for explaining turmoil in other parts of the world and/or at other times may vary, but not the analytical questions focused on here in chapter 5.3.2: (1) who is (2) how likely to participate with (3) what intensity in (4) what kind of activity under (5) what circumstances at (6) what point of time for (7) what reason?[312] Thus, researchers studying phenomena of political violence as well as other forms of collective behavior may benefit from the research efforts to unravel the causes of the black riots in the 1960s.

Chapter 6

Crises and Political Violence

In cross-national analyses of political violence, quite often political violence is equated with political instability or crises phenomena, yet no justification for such a juxtaposition is given. Consequently, our aims here will be (1) to define crises phenomena and discuss several general approaches to the study of crises, (2) to differentiate analytically between crises and political violence and show possible interrelationships between the two, and (3) to list and discuss those cross-national analyses bearing on crises phenomena, the relationships between crises and political violence, and other major theoretical variables. Finally, (4) a causal model of crises or, more precisely, legitimacy crises and other key variables will be developed (with persistence of a polity becoming the final dependent variable), and other theoretical suggestions as to the development of a cross-national crises science will be made. This chapter draws on ZIMMERMANN (1979a) where we have moved to a design-oriented theoretical synthesis, apart from emphasizing additional theoretical aspects. The focus here is still on dealing in some depth with materials important for the development of a cross-national crises science.

Many authors equate political violence with political instability without acknowledging the fact that the two phenomena should be kept apart, theoretically as well as empirically. FEIERABEND/FEIERABEND are quite frank as to why they chose the instability concept to denote phenomena of political violence, namely, for "lack of a better term" (FEIERABEND/FEIERABEND 1973:188). Similar examples of conceptual confusion are found in MORRISON/STEVENSON (1971:348) and BWY (1968b). (Admittedly, at various points in our previous discussion of the literature, purity in terminology has likewise been lacking.) There are many other instances where the concept of crisis has been used as an implicit variable invoked to close a causal chain, e.g., rapid socioeconomic change (cf. chapter 5.1.2.2) leading to crises situations (as an implicit intervening variable) which in turn lead to the occurrence of political violence. On closer examination of the preceding paragraph, another conceptual inadequacy is revealed, i.e., the equation of political crises with political instability. Actually, political instability seems to be a less dramatic and less emotionally laden term than political crisis (for definitional aspects see section 6.1). Several other terms, such as breakdown (EISENSTADT 1964), political decay (HUNTINGTON 1965), and low performance of the (party) system are often used in the literature to denote phenomena of political instability and political violence. Obviously, something must be done about this babel of voices. Although we cannot give a rationale or distinguish among all of these phenomena, at least a few of them may be more adequately studied if first findings and suggestions synthesized in this chapter are taken seriously in designing studies on interrelationships between crises phenomena, political violence, and other variables.

6.1. Crises: Definitions, Typologies, and General Approaches

What exactly is a crisis? In everyday language the term is frequently used. "Crisis," originating from the Greek and signifying a turning point, a crucial situation calling for decisions[1] was a fairly common term in medicine before it was introduced into the political realm, possibly in the eighteenth century[2] (cf. JÄNICKE 1971:53, and STARN 1971 for a general historical discussion of the crisis concept). Over the last decades social scientists have done surprisingly little analysis of the determinants and consequences of crisis phenomena, considering the fact that sociology is partially rooted in the industrial crisis that followed the European revolutions from 1800 onwards, and that crises have been a standard theme of many classical writers in the nineteenth century (as well as during the 1930s). While a number of case studies do exist, much remains to be done as far as the development of a cross-national perspective in the science of political crises is concerned.

There are various reasons for the underdevelopment of crises research, one being the diffuse quality of the concept crisis. Obviously, crises phenomena are often difficult to determine.[3] Self-fulfilling prophecies and other perceptual effects seem to be particularly important in the case of crises, rendering cross-national analyses extremely difficult and thus perhaps deterring researchers from studying such intricate phenomena. It may also be difficult to obtain a sufficient number of comparable cases[4] for cross-national, quantitative, studies. As a large number of diverse data sets must be collected in cross-national crises research, the capacities of one researcher are easily exhausted. Cross-national research on crises phenomena definitely calls for international cooperation of scholars.

Here we are concerned with internal crises, disregarding the influences of external crises (cf. chapter 5.1.2.6) or of other external factors, although they may be an important determinant of internal crises (cf. chapter 8 passim). Crises with political relevance, i.e., *political crises*, are the proper subject of this chapter.[5] Political crises are here understood in a wider sense than mere government crises; they call for and possibly lead to *substantial* changes in policies or the political order, not merely a replacement of personnel.[6] There are many forms of crises, from natural disasters to economic crises, which may occur without leading to a political crisis. The recent past of West Germany provides some examples in this respect. At present there is an economic crisis, or at least a relatively severe economic recession, yet no immediate political crisis. During the economic recession in 1966-67, however, the economic deterioration led to a political crisis, one indicator being the simultaneous gaining in strength of the National Democratic Party (NPD, the right extremist party). On the other hand, political crises (e.g., crises of political parties, constitutional crises) may also occur simply for political reasons (contrary to Marxist theory). It would be interesting to know how often the various types of crises (cf. below) have political consequences on the elites or at the system level and how often political and other types of crises are really unrelated.

According to VERBA crisis is "a change that requires some governmental innovation and institutionalization if elites are not seriously to risk a loss of their position or if the society is to survive" (VERBA 1971:302).[7] In VERBA's definition (used here as a working definition) either dysfunctioning elites (*crisis of an elite*) or dysfunctions of the *system*[8] are significant (cf. also ROSENAU 1964; RITTBERGER 1971; JÄNICKE 1973:37 who speaks of a"crisis of performance" and a "crisis of authority").[9] In contrast to many other crisis definitions (for an overview cf. JÄNICKE 1971:533ff.), in VERBA's definition, definitional criteria are not intermingled with possible causes of crises. In addition to an elite or government crisis and a system crisis, many other types could be listed, a *crisis of legitimacy* being the most important for present purposes (cf. chapter 6.3.4). In fact, each of the possible explanations of political crises referred to later has been used for labeling crises, e.g., performance crisis, crisis of the political institutions or of the party system, segmental crisis.

Another useful general differentiation is that between regime, government, and societal instability, the first two being related to political crisis, whereas the societal label embraces a number of other crises types not necessarily leading to political crises (for a useful first effort to delineate these three concepts, cf. JACKSON/STEIN 1971:195-211). This differentiation may, however, be much less applicable to nondemocratic political systems, since the political and societal spheres are much more intertwined in such societies and may not show much independent variation. Nevertheless, it may be helpful, for understanding such phenomena as the 1970 riots in Poland (or more recently the strike events in 1980) where an economic crisis immediately led to a political crisis or, to use the terms discussed, a societal crisis led to a government crisis ending (at least in 1970) with the replacement of some of the elites and with the proclaiming of new economic measures.

In terms of *general* theoretical approaches to explain political crises phenomena, three groups of theories can be distinguished: the *elite approach* (cf. below and also chapters 7 and 8), the *systems approach*, and the *decision-making approach*. According to the systems approach, dysfunctions in various main and sub-sectors of society cause crises phenomena. A crisis in a central sector of society is, by definition, more relevant to the survival of the system or the elites than a crisis in a peripheral sector. A crisis in a sub-system normally has little or no impact on the total system, unless crises in several subsystems, possibly with overlapping populations (cf. the religious and social cleavages in Northern Ireland where Catholics have lower social positions), create multiple dysfunctions (cf. JOHNSON 1964). On the other hand, in most political communities the state has increased its scope and intensity of activities over the last decades. Consequently, in times of crises and especially in times of multiple crises (cumulation of crises), the probability of *Staatsverdrossenheit* (a rough equivalent might be "weariness of the state") should increase due to the fact that the factor seen as source of discontent frequently is represented by state bureaucracies (and other state agents). Discussion of the ungovernability or the governmental overload of political systems (cf. HUNTINGTON 1975 and ROSE 1975; cf. also the criticism in SCHMITTER 1977; ROSE 1979; and ETZIONI, 1977-78, for a summary discussion of some of the more practical issues involved) must be seen in this context.

Many of the structural-functional systems approaches to crises phenomena rely on tautological reasoning,[10] for as the term crisis is merely replaced by the term dysfunction (or dissynchronization, cf. FLANAGAN 1973:49). JOHNSON (see also chapter 8.4.2) provides a good example: "Dysfunctional conditions are caused by pressures (whether they are external or internal is a distinction that is relevant only in a historical case) that compel the members of a substructure to do their work, or view their roles, or imagine their potentialities differently from the way they did under equilibrium conditions. The pressures that cause dysfunction (e.g., technological discoveries, imperialism, and many others . . .) we call sources of dysfunction" (JOHNSON 1964:5; italics omitted).[11] In this definition we are actually told that a dysfunction is not a function (although JOHNSON does make an effort to list some fairly general determinants of dysfunctions). Rarely do writers adhering to this kind of structural-functional approach discuss and provide evidence as to the specific conditions of types and, even more important, as to the degrees of dysfunctions.

In the decision-making approach some of these difficulties may be avoided. Yet, there seems to be only one cross-national study thus far in which the decision-making approach (or, more appropriately, the decisional challenges approach) has been applied to internal crises,[12] as will be discussed in chapter 6.3.1. This decisional challenges approach seems to be very promising but hardly sufficient for explaining political crises phenomena.

Obviously, the elite approach, the systems approach, and the decision-making approach to internal crises phenomena are interrelated in various ways (for some empirical evidence cf. chapter 6.3; a fairly general theoretical effort to relate these approaches to each other is found in JÄNICKE 1973a). Before we turn to some empirical and theoretical studies on crises phenomena, a few brief reflections on relationships between crises and political violence are in order.

6.2. Some Possible Relationships between Crises and Political Violence

Normally, the more frequent the occurrence and the greater the intensity of political violence, the more serious the crisis. One could scale crises according to (1) the absence of political violence, (2) the threat to use political violence, and (3) the use of political violence. Empirical illustrations[13] could easily be provided, for example, the crisis of the Weimar Republic from 1930 onward and the economic and political crisis in the Federal Republic of Germany at the end of 1966 which was characterized, in contrast to the earlier crisis, by the absence of political violence.

Another plausible hypothesis is that, as crises situations persist, the probability of political violence increases as well, depending on other variables such as the reactions of the state's coercive potential, the political alternatives open to dissidents, etc. Political violence, however, does not automatically lead to a crisis,[14] much to the regret of anarchists and other political protesters who assume that assassinating a key political figure will lead to a breakdown of society. Nevertheless, it may contribute at times to a collapse, as historians have noted, especially with respect to some of the assassinations in European countries before World War I.

Thus, there are three alternatives concerning the connection between crises and political violence:[15]

1. there is no relationship between political violence and crises;
2. political violence leads to or contributes to the occurrence and/or intensification of crises; and
3. crises lead to political violence.

In a dynamic analysis, of course, there may be reciprocal and quite indirect relationships between crises and political violence, as is documented in the fate of the Weimar Republic. Nevertheless, political violence in itself is neither a necessary nor a sufficient condition for a crisis to occur.

SANDERS (1979) has recently traced the relationships between challenges (i.e., violent political protests including riots, assassinations, guerrilla warfare, deaths from political violence), peaceful protests (strikes, demonstrations), changes in regime (changes in norm, party system, military/civilian status), and changes in government (changes in chief executive, cabinet composition) for 136 countries in 1948-67, drawing on the *World Handbook* (TAYLOR/HUDSON 1972) as a data source. He finds little support for the syndrome model (presupposing positive correlations among the four variables), the safety valve model (presupposing negative correlations), or a model building on HIBBS's (1973) analysis. In addition, the pattern of results remains stable if the region is controlled. On the basis of annual[16] time series data, SANDERS reports:

> (1) In the Atlantic area, peaceful challenges tend to precede regime changes; violent challenges tend to precede governmental changes;
> (2) in the Middle East, peaceful challenges tend to precede governmental changes; (3) in Eastern Europe, government changes tend to precede peaceful challenges; (4) in the Far East, peaceful challenges tend to precede violent challenges; violent challenges tend to precede regime changes; governmental changes tend to precede regime changes; (5) in sub-Saharan Africa, violent challenges tend to precede regime changes; (6) in Latin America, peaceful challenges tend

to precede violent challenges; violent challenges tend to precede governmental change (SANDERS 1979:30; for further results see also SANDERS 1981).

"Despite this general tendency for challenge behaviors to precede government or regime change, however, the specific pattern of significant lagged relationships varies from region to region.... In each of the Third World regions (Middle East, Far East, Sub-Saharan Africa and Latin America) there is a marked tendency for 'less severe' forms of instability ... to generate an internal dynamic of their own and to *escalate* into 'more severe' forms of instability" (ibid., p. 29–30), which seems to be due to the lack of institutional safeguards (cf. also chapter 7.2.3).

In his study on crisis, breakdown, and the reequilibration of democratic regimes in twentieth-century European and Latin American countries, LINZ (1978) provides several examples of this lack of institutionalization or, more precisely, of escalating processes of political protest and regime breakdown. "It is the dynamic characteristics [of polarized pluralism as a system of five or more parties with "coalition use" or "power of intimidation"] that account for the potential for breakdown in these systems: specifically, the polarization, the centrifugal drives, and the tendency toward irresponsibility and outbidding" (ibid., p. 26). In addition, "some of the delegitimizing consequences of violence can be found in the area of decisions made in response to violence" (ibid., p. 57).

6.3. Cross-national Studies of Crises Phenomena: Theoretical Outlines and Empirical Evidence

The three approaches to the study of crises discussed in chapter 6.1 were general in nature, focusing on different levels of explanation for understanding crises phenomena. The approaches to be discussed briefly here are, however, substantive and quite heterogeneous in nature. In several instances these theoretial efforts are quite impressive, although, in general, cross-national empirical evidence is rather meager.

6.3.1. An Operational Approach to Crises Phenomena (GURR)

One of the most useful approaches (GURR 1973) to crises analysis in the literature is based on the general assumption that crises are characterized by "all kinds of *intensive demands on behalf of large or strategic groups* of a national system that the government take action to protect or enhance their own or others' value positions"[17] (GURR 1973:68, using a quotation from GURR/McCLELLAND 1971:49). GURR equates *decisional challenges* with manifest[18] crises. He specifies his definition by terming challenges intensive if they are repeatedly stated, connected with intense emotions, and likely to lead to consequences in case no actions are taken.

A group is said to be large if at least one tenth of the whole population can be counted as followers, and strategic if it comprises at least one-tenth of the governmental or nongovernmental elites (GURR 1973:69). The question remains as to how to identify governmental and nongovernmental elite positions. The least distorting strategy would probably be to use several techniques, like the positional, the reputational, and the decision-making approaches, in a combined effort. Like many other authors, GURR also differentiates between a segmental crisis (only partial goals are the object of action) and a systemic crisis (the general values of the system are threatened). Among the operational criteria GURR mentions are: kind and object of decisional challenge, the percentage of the population that can be mobilized by the particular challenge, and the degree to which the participants perceive the system as being threatened. The degree of decisional challenge varies with five stages from low (challenges are mainly articulated by nonelites) to high (challenges are articulated by elites inside as well as outside the government and by nonelites). The degree to which the population is mobilized is estimated along a percentage scale. System threat is measured by assigning weights according to whether a mild or severe change of one or more important institutions is either impending or has happened in the past. The degree to which values are threatened is assessed in a basically similar way.

An example of systemic challenges (GURR 1973:76) is a challenge concerning the independence of the country or the international position or the economic system. Segmental challenges include claims for constitutional change, claims for more political participation or for basic changes of government policies. ECKSTEIN (1965:143–45) presents another hypothetical list of sources of internal crises.

A pretest with data for the United States from 1960 to 1967 (Civil Rights Movement), for France from 1957 to 1963 (Algerian war of independence) and for Cuba from 1910 to 1940 was apparently successful. Although GURR thinks that his operational criteria could be worked with on a larger scale, dealing with many crises all over the world, he seems to have run into some difficulties in his inquiry (GURR 1973:78–79). He himself states that he has given up collecting data on manifest crises. One of the difficulties in this kind of research may be that different types of crises may be found in different types of political systems. The degree of systemic interference seems to be greater than in other instances of cross-national research. Some political systems react so fast that there may at most be only signs of crises. There may be other difficulties, too, if the capabilities of governments to react to crises are to be assessed: the necessary variability in the independent and dependent variables may be lacking, calling into question the use of quantitative techniques. Moreover, the specification of time boundaries of the phenomena under study may cause trouble (in these respects cf. also the list of arguments in ECKSTEIN 1971:71). Another difficulty is that systems experiencing or having experienced fewer crises may be heading for a more fundamental crisis. If one were able to assess the legitimacy of the system directly, i.e., to ask the people themselves what they think about the system and what should be done about it, such cases could be detected. Thus, a system having *successfully* mastered a *Reinigungskrise* ("cleansing crisis," or more properly a "catharsis;" cf. also chapter 6.3.3) may be a more successful system, according to the degree of legitimacy attributed to it, than a system which experienced less manifest crises. Generally speaking, in GURR's approach elite, mass, and system elements are all combined in an extended variant of the decision-making approach.

GURR is also one of the contributors to another group of approaches to crises analyses called political performance approaches. With their emphasis on substantial sources of crises phenomena, performance approaches, in general, seem to cut across the three general approaches to crises phenomena discussed so far. (Unfortunately, from the point of conceptual clarity, many other theoretical approaches in this study could be placed under the political performance label, if defined in a broader manner.)

6.3.2. Political Performance Approaches

Even though the works mentioned in this chapter deal only indirectly with crises phenomena, we maintain that they are meaningful for the development of a cross-national crises science. Yet it should also be pointed out from the beginning that the relationship between these performance approaches and crises phenomena is quite complicated. As will become clearer, equating low political performance with crises phenomena is often unjustified on several grounds. A number of other variables may bear on the prediction of such a relationship.

6.3.2.1. Theoretical Exposition, according to ECKSTEIN

The dependent variable in the studies to be taken up here is political performance which unfortunately has not been explicitly defined.[19] Several dimensions are instead developed to exhaust the theoretical concept. In later stages, however, these dimensions actually function as independent variables, thus leaving open the meaning of that seductive term, political performance.

In political sociology and political philosophy, especially since the writings of Plato and Aristotle, various currents of thought concerning political performance are found. The studies on the relationships between socioeconomic and political development mentioned in chapter 5.1.2.3 also bear on this topic. Political performance should not be equated with political development or, more precisely, with democratic political development, because authoritarian or totalitarian polities at times may score high in some areas of performance although they may not necessarily be successful in acquiring legitimacy among the population at large. Political performance seems to be a technical output- or, more precisely, outcome-oriented standard, whereas democratic political development seems to have more input connotations (input with respect to politically active, selfdeterminate, non-regimented citizens). Performance and legitimacy may vary independently from each other, at least in the short run, although in the long run performance seems to be one of the requirements of system legitimacy (see chapter 6.3.4.1).

Here we are concerned mainly with the works of ECKSTEIN. Basically, ECKSTEIN's interests are centered on whether authority relations (or, more precisely, the congruence of authority patterns) in society have an impact on *governmental* performance (cf. ECKSTEIN/GURR 1975 for the most recent summary of this approach).[20] In his writings relevant to the present context, however, the variable authority relations becomes less important. Rather *political* performance now is at issue. One would expect governmental performance and political performance to be intercorrelated (cf. the discussion in chapter 6.3.4). In a 1969 study, ECKSTEIN (1969:287ff.) developed six dimensions of performance:[21] durability, legitimacy, strife-avoidance, output efficiency, permeation, and authority. In a later work (1971) only four basic dimensions are listed, allowing stricter formulation of the underlying theoretical questions. Consequently, we shall only focus on the revised version, which specifies:

1. durability— "persistence of a polity over time. The longer it persists the higher its performance" (ECKSTEIN 1971:21);
2. civil order— the absence of "actual" or "latent" collective violence (ibid., p. 32);
3. legitimacy— "refers to the extent that a polity is regarded by its members as worthy of support" (ibid., p. 50); and
4. decisional
   efficacy— "the extent to which polities make and carry out prompt and relevant decisions in response to political challenges" (ibid., p. 65).

In general, all four dimensions should positively intercorrelate: the degree of correlation may, of course, vary. ECKSTEIN has settled on these four basic criteria, because alternative conceptualizations, such as a capability approach or functional variants, might lead to even greater operational problems than those incurred when using these four theoretically derived dimensions.

6.3.2.2. The Twelve-Nation Study of GURR/McCLELLAND, as a Prestudy to GURR's "Persistence and Change in Political Systems"

GURR/McCLELLAND (1971) make a first attempt at testing ECKSTEIN's theory, using a sample of twelve countries (Canada, Columbia, France, Germany/West Germany, Italy, Mexico, the Netherlands, the Philippines, Spain, Sweden, Tunisia, Yugoslavia). The sample is formed on the basis of the expertise of the collaborators in this study, rather than on systematic sampling. The data are mostly taken from the *New York Times Index*. In addition, numerous monographs on the historical development in each country were consulted. The periods 1927–36 and 1957–66 were chosen for study, the basic assumption being that in both cases the consequences of the two world wars would have lost their immediate impact. All four of ECKSTEIN's theoretical variables are used, but, contrary to ECKSTEIN's view of these variables as being interdependent, durability is assumed to be a function of the other variables (even if there may be feedback influences in the long run). The unit of study is a polity defined as "the basic political arrangements by which national political communities govern their affairs, not the political communities themselves" (GURR/McCLELLAND 1971:11). "Examples of single but nonetheless fundamental changes from countries included in this study are the institutionalization of the Mexican Revolution in a dominant party, 1929–1934 (president-dominant to one-party dominant) and the establishment of the French Fifth Republic, 1958–1962 (legislature-dominant to president-dominant)" (ibid., p. 12). To obtain some long-range information about the histories of the particular polities, durability was also assessed for the period 1840-1970, and, when necessary, for other reference points in time. Short-term vs. long-term relationships between durability and performance differ in that in the long run durability and performance should covary positively, whereas in the short run other relationships may be possible.

The three independent variables are measured as follows: Civil order is divided into turmoil, conspiracy, and internal war, from GURR's earlier studies (for details cf. ibid., p. 22ff.). When the strife scores are compared with those of GURR's earlier study (GURR 1968a; 1961–65 data) and those of FEIERABEND et al. (1969), "significant" intercorrelations are found. Legitimacy is defined as "extent that a polity is regarded by its members as worthy of support" (ibid., p. 30), and community, regime, and incumbents (following EASTON 1965, cf. also chapter 6.3.4.1) are chosen as empirical referents. Quite elaborate measures of legitimacy[22] are used, but the empirical results do not seem to be satisfactory.

Even more problematic than the operations for indexing legitimacy are those for measuring decisional efficacy. Originally the authors had in mind the conceptualization discussed in chapter 6.3.1. But instead of measuring decisional challenges, they decided to measure efficacy of budgetary decisions and authority maintenance. Efficacy of budgetary decisions is indexed in a totally unconvincing way, since polities with no change in budgetary processes from one year to the next are given a high score (supposedly indexing stability).[23] With this type of scoring procedure, budgetary inflexibility and not performance is likely to be measured. One could even argue to the contrary, i.e., that budgetary changes occurring as responses to certain demands are an indicator of efficiency. In any case, a mere formal measurement without reference to budgetary substance is likely to be misleading. The other indicator is whether the budget has been approved of in time. However, in countries like West Germany there is almost a tradition for the budget to be passed late in parliament. The efficiency score is thus low. In reality, however, there hardly seems to be a parallel to what the authors actually wanted to measure.[24]

The other main indicator, maintenance of authority, is indexed through a number of highly complex measures which refer to legal procedures and their fulfillment in the political process. Rules of the game are contrasted with possible dissension over authority maintenance processes.

Only a few of the many interesting results of this prestudy (cf. also GURR 1974a below) can be mentioned in this context. In general, the durability of the polities studied seems to have increased from the first to the second period. Yet, polities with low performance scores in the past did not do much better in the more recent period, although some countries (e.g., Columbia, Spain) did show drastic improvements.

When a multiple regression analysis is performed, some interesting results emerge. Yet the dubious nature of some of the indicators chosen should again be pointed out. Furthermore, the small number of cases and the occasionally varying periods of observation may have introduced additional errors. Looking at the intercorrelations of some of the variables, one finds, for example: "legitimacy I [= 1st period] strongly affects durability I also and has a moderate time-lagged relation with durability II [= 2nd period]: its effects appear to be primarily short-term, secondarily long-term" (ibid., p. 76).

The multiple regression analysis leads to the following results: "The multiple relation between the era II performance dimensions and durability II is moderate, $R^2 = .56$ and less than the .66 obtained in the first era" (ibid., p. 77). After performing various controls, the following causal model is most consistent with the observed relationships:

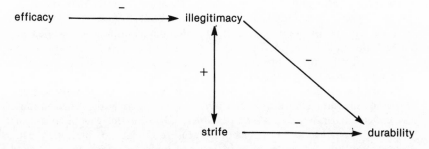

Figure 6.1.   Empirical Causal Model among Performance
              Dimensions, Showing Dominant Relationships Only

Source: GURR/McCLELLAND (1971:79)

When confronting these quantitative results with the qualitative evidence for the countries under study, a generally satisfactory degree of correspondence apparently was found. This strategy of combining quantitative techniques with detailed case study materials seems to be especially promising for the development of an autonomous crises science.

One could, of course, argue that the performance of a polity should be assessed through socioeconomic indicators in the first place (and then perhaps through [thoroughly refined] measures GURR/McCLELLAND suggest for indexing efficacy). Furthermore, one should carefully test for artifacts of measurement when the time boundaries of polities are to be determined. There is historical evidence for calling into question clear delimitations between different polities. A polity may formally cease to exist, yet nevertheless have a strong impact on its successor (cf. the conservative impact of the monarchist-oriented bourgeoisie and nobility in the Weimar Republic).

Most recently, GURR (1974a) has presented results building in part on the earlier study of GURR/McCLELLAND (1971). The sample now covers 336 polities ("as they have functioned in 91 nation states between 1800 and 1970," GURR 1974a:1500).[25] Lack of space precludes a description of the complicated measures used in this study. The basic research premise is "that the most important feature of any political system, for purposes of description, is its pattern of authority relations" (GURR 1974a:1484). The descriptive results provide evidence as to the *persistence of polities* (the mean lifespan of historical polities is thirty-two years, of continuing polities in 1971, forty-two years); the *"infant mortality"* (50% of the European [Third-World, nineteenth-century, twentieth-century] polities do not survive beyond an average of 12.2 [12.3; 19.9; 9.0] years); and the *survival probabilities* of polities, once they have attained a certain age (e.g., the probability of polities fifty years of age to reach seventy-five years is .60).

These are all interesting and new results. Yet, in terms of explanation a different picture emerges. When the five authority dimensions chosen (executive recruitment, decision constraints, participation, directiveness, centralization) are related to the dependent variables and when clusters of polities are formed according to region (European, Latin, Afro-Asian) and date of establishment (nineteenth century, twentieth century, continuing in 1971), rather inconclusive or inconsistent results are found. This is also true if authority systems (autocracy, democracy, and anocracy,[26] formed along the original authority dimensions and allowing for mixed types of authority systems as well) are related to the two dependent variables of this study, persistence and adaptability, both of which are subsumed under the general heading durability. Probably the most noteworthy exception is that "highly—consistently—democratic *and* highly autocratic political systems . . . have been more durable than systems of 'mixed' authority traits. . . . The evidence is unmistakable that the more closely a polity resembles a pure democracy *or* pure autocracy, as defined here, the longer it is likely to have persisted" (GURR 1974a:1502). Thus, there is some indirect evidence in favor of ECKSTEIN's congruence hypothesis (quoted in chapter 6.3.2.1).

It remains to be seen whether the introduction of intervening variables, such as the usual socioeconomic variables, will lend some support to the original formulation[27] or whether other variables, perhaps the conventional socioeconomic indicators, fare better in explaining the two dependent variables. One of the results of GURR's efforts is an enormous amount of highly suggestive descriptive results. Yet, in theoretical terms a pay-off may be harder to come by.

In their study on *Crises and Sequences of Political Development*, BINDER et al. (1971) also touch on the dimensions of performance and legitimacy.

6.3.3. "Crises and Sequences of Political Development" (BINDER et al.)

One of the most stimulating theoretical approaches to the cross-national study of crises phenomena is found in the essays by BINDER et al. (1971) who take "crises to represent situations in which the society moves in a new direction. They are the major decisional points at which the society is redefined, and are therefore relevant to sequential changes" (VERBA 1971:306). Clearly their efforts should have an impact on empirical research in the long run. The authors (BINDER, COLEMAN, LaPALOMBARA, PYE, VERBA, and WEINER) distinguish five different forms of crises which at times may be difficult to disentangle in empirical studies,[28] since several of these crises may occur at the same time (VERBA 1971:297). Especially in the case of legitimacy, such covariation seems to be likely. The five crises are summarized in Table 6.1.[29]

Originally, they considered a sequence of crises through which countries had to pass on their way to modernity (cf. also HUNTINGTON 1968, and chapter 5.1.2.1, 5.1.2.2 and passim). Yet, a "natural" sequence of crises is difficult to imagine or to establish historically (cf. GREW 1978), even if there may be some interdependencies (i.e., the probability of certain crises may be greater or smaller if they are preceded by other types of crises; cf. the list of a few paired sequences in VERBA 1971:311 and the historical examples in GREW 1978:33; cf. also RUSTOW 1967:126-32).[30] Empirically, causal sequences may be expected as well as causal loops signifying that conflicts not solved in the past constitute a permanent threat to a polity (cf. also the approach of LIPSET/ROKKAN 1967, below). While one would expect a solution to these crises in the long run if a polity is to survive, in the short run imbalances may exist (VERBA 1971:310). VERBA himself sees no clear logical structure (VERBA 1971:299) in this list of five crises[31] and stresses the potential ubiquity of the crises. Even if one crisis or critical item is solved at a certain point of time, it may arise again at a later point. He writes: "At some points [these items] are merely aspects of decisions; at others they become *problems*; at others they become *crises*" (VERBA 1971:300).

These possibilities notwithstanding, a *branching tree model* may be employed. VERBA describes this as a "sequence of choice points (not necessarily points of conscious decision, but points where development can go one way or the other). At any point in a sequence of development, there may be alternative next stages. But which one is chosen closes the options for others. Closely related to this is the notion of irreversibilities—choices of one branch which once chosen does not allow backtracking" (VERBA

Table 6. 1. Paradigm of the Modernization Syndrome and the Crises of Political Development

	Syndrome Components		
Crises	Equality	Capacity	Differentiation
Identity	politicization of identity	productive and administrative integration	individual adjustment, specificity of interests
Legitimacy	democracy, psychological legitimacy	definition of goals and implementation	spheres of political, administrative and judicial validity; divergent doctrines
Participation	voting, deliberating, self-regulation	information, access	decision-making structures, representation, interest groups
Distribution	equality of opportunity, achievement, standardization of welfare level	resource base, education, capital accumulation, allocation to general and particular goals	redistribution, equalization, incentives
Penetration	equalization of obligation and duties, individualization of citizenship	mobilization, rationalization, scope, range	technical, legal, intellectual specialization and coordination

Source: BINDER et al. (1971:65)

1971:308). The branching tree model is one of the more useful heuristic devices among the various types of causal sequence modeling for dealing with these problems.

It should be noted, however, that the importance of the five crises differs in different groups of countries (but cf. also the critical remarks in TILLY 1975a:610). For instance, participation and/or distribution crises are probably much more important in more developed countries, whereas crises of identity are predominant in underdeveloped and recently independent countries. Moreover, none of these crises seems to be permanently solved, even in modern nations, perhaps with the exception of the penetration crisis ("establishment of a co-ordinated network of territorial administrative agents independent of local power resources and responsive to directives from the central decisionmaking organs," ROKKAN 1970:670) and, much less so, the crisis of national identity. Also this list of crises may not exhaust the types of relevant crises. As long as there are no systematic data,[32] one typology is as good as another, if distinct analytical categories are applied.

Whereas BINDER et al. focus on modernizing countries and propose a paradigm of crises which might stimulate empirical research, there is at least one impressive study on crises phenomena in developed countries, i.e., the study of LIPSET/ROKKAN (1967; for a critical evaluation cf. MERKL 1969), on the development of political party systems in various European countries. Going back to the beginning of the Renaissance, they distinguish four critical historical cleavages:

> Two of these cleavages are direct products of what we might call the *National* Revolution: the conflict between *the central nation-building culture* and the increasing resistance of the ethnically, linguistically, or religiously distinct *subject populations* in the provinces and the peripheries (1); the conflict between the centralizing, standardizing, and mobilizing *Nation-State* and the historically established corporate privileges of the *Church* (2). Two of them are products of the *Industrial* Revolution: the conflict between the *landed interests* and the rising class of *industrial entrepreneurs* (3); the conflict between *owners* and *employers* on the one side and *tenants, labourers, and workers* on the other (4) (ROKKAN 1970a:102).

Depending on how these conflicts have been solved and whether prior conflicts are influencing later conflicts, different political cleavages are likely to persist and emerge, leading finally to a consolidation of the political party system in the early 1920s (but see the counterevidence in SHAMIR's sophisticated 1979 analysis). Here LIPSET/ROKKAN end their stimulating historical study which focuses on only one variable, yet a variable highly central for understanding crises phenomena at least in democracies: the institutionalization of political and other cleavages in party systems. It should be pointed out that in this study crises are de facto used as both independent and dependent variables.

It would be fascinating to speculate on similar studies in what HUNTINGTON calls "praetorian polities" (cf. chapter 7.2.3). How will the sequences of critical junctures and the overlapping of cleavages affect the fate of the polities in question? There is a host of interesting hypotheses on these issues, especially in HUNTINGTON (1968), but systematic comparative studies over time are still lacking.[33] The feasibility of a cross-national crises science is once again demonstrated in the study of LIPSET/ROKKAN. Though their study is generally qualitative in nature, one could imagine quantifying at least some of the dimensions used in their analyses.

Before ending this section, one final look should be taken at the qualitative analyses of seven historical crises situations (Britain, 1832, 1931; France 1870-75; Germany, Weimar Republic; Mexico under Cárdenas; Japan, Meiji Restoration; India, mid-1960s) in ALMOND et al. (1973). Using various data sets, they focus on perceived issue distances and resources of potential coalition partners, trying to make predictions as to the likelihood of certain coalitions, and even go so far as to speculate on alternative scenarios in the respective historical crises situations.[34] *Crisis, Choice, and Change* in its efforts to transform "historical episodes into analytical episodes" (ibid.,

p. 24) is still another major achievement en route to the development of a comparative crises science. This holds true in spite of the criticism raised.[35]

In the studies of ECKSTEIN (1971), GURR/McCLELLAND (1971), BINDER et al. (1971), and others as well, legitimacy has been a recurrent variable. It is considered in greater detail in the following section.

6.3.4. Legitimacy and Legitimacy Crises

The literature on the concept of legitimacy and possible empirical referents is endless. In terms of systematic empirical evidence, however, almost the reverse is true. There is also lack of agreement as to which *specific* features constitute legitimacy. Will MERELMAN's dictum of the "diffuse, largely irrational nature of political legitimacy" (MERELMAN 1966:548) prove right? Perhaps the question must be left open. Nevertheless, there are some promising efforts at determining some of the empirical referents of legitimacy. First, however, definitional and conceptual problems must be discussed.

6.3.4.1. Conceptual Aspects

Many internal crises bear on the legitimacy of particular political systems and/or incumbent elites. Or, conversely, a loss in legitimacy will lead to an intensification of other forms of crises. Accordingly, a crisis of legitimacy is the most important of all the crises mentioned in previous chapters (cf. also GREW 1978:25ff.). NIEBURG's definition of legitimacy is in accord with those of many other social scientists (cf. GRAHAM/GURR 1969:xxxii-xxxiii; PYE 1971:136): legitimacy "reflects the vitality of underlying consensus which endows the state and its officers with whatever authority and power they actually possess, not by virtue of legality, but by the reality of the respect which citizens pay to the institutions and behavior norms. Legitimacy is earned by the ability of those who conduct the power of the state to represent and reflect a broad consensus" (NIEBURG 1968:19). Or in terms of LIPSET's well-known definition which takes up some of the propositions from the preceding section: "Legitimacy involves the capacity[36] of the system to engender and maintain the belief that the existing political institutions[37] are the most appropriate ones[38] for the society. The extent to which contemporary democratic political systems are legitimate depends in large measure upon the ways in which the key issues which have historically divided the society have been resolved" (LIPSET 1960:77).[39]

Legitimacy is "indeed an attribute of the system" (KELMAN 1969:279; see also KELMAN 1970:228-29). Yet, at the same time, it is a genuine sociopsychological concept denoting the feelings, dispositions, and beliefs of individuals toward or about certain objects, in this case, the political system, elites, certain policies, specific institutions or symbols (for empirical results, cf. MULLER 1970a; 1970b), and the "outcomes of ongoing events and policies" (CITRIN 1974:987, emphasis omitted) as well.

There are a number of typologies of the dimensions of legitimacy and of other relevant dimensions (cf. also YANKELOVICH 1974; ANDRAIN 1975:150). KELMAN, for one, distinguishes between "sentimental attachments"("system's representativeness of group identity") and "instrumental attachments" ("system's effectiveness in meeting needs and interests," KELMAN 1970:231) to the system. He calls these two forms of attachment "sources of perceived legitimacy" (ibid., p. 231). His second basic dimension is called "processes generating perceived legitimacy within system members or subgroups" (by "sharing of system values," "participation in system roles," or "adherence to authoritative norms," e.g., law and order). On the basis of these two dimensions he identifies six different responses to the system. The two basic dimensions seem fruitful, yet the empirical referents remain to be specified in detail. Other forms of legitimacy are perhaps much more relevant as to individual behavior. In any case, this typology provides hypotheses that help in differentiating the very broad concept of legitimacy (and thus possibly further the construction of a cross-level theory of legitimacy).[40]

Apart from WEBER's (1964:157–222) typology of forms of legitimate authority (which is of less use in the present context),[41] EASTON's discussion of various types of legitimacy is probably referred to most often. Without going into detail here (for some empirical works starting from EASTON's outline, cf. chapter 6.3.4.2), EASTON's theory-oriented conceptualization of legitimacy may be briefly characterized as follows: firstly, there is usually an interdependency[42] between input into the political system and system output. Input may occur in the form of support and/or demand, support being further subdivided into overt (actions) support and covert (attitudes) support. A second perhaps more salient distinction is made between *diffuse support* and *specific support.* "Specific support flows from the favorable attitudes and predispositions stimulated by outputs that are perceived by members to meet their demands as they arise or in anticipation" (EASTON 1965:273). In short, outputs are said to act as "regulators of specific support" (ibid., p. 341). While there is a clear feedback loop between output and specific support, diffuse support is not attached to specific output conditions. It represents "a reservoir of favorable attitudes or good will" (ibid., p. 273), "a type of support that continues independently of the specific rewards which the member may feel he obtains from belonging to the system" (EASTON 1965a:125). "Indeed, no regime or community could gain general acceptance and no set of authorities could expect to hold power if they had to depend exclusively or even largely on outputs to generate support as a return for specific and identifiable benefits" (EASTON 1965: 269). In the long run, however, "diffuse support is [not] independent of the effects of daily outputs" (ibid., 273). "Even though the orientations derive from responses to particular outputs initially, they become in time dissociated from performance. They become transformed into generalized attitudes towards the authorities or other political objects. They begin to take on a life of their own" (EASTON 1975:446).[43] Thus, it may be true that "long-run political stability may be more dependent on a more diffuse sense of attachment or loyalty to the political system—a loyalty not based specifically on system performance" (ALMOND/VERBA 1963:246; cf. also their interpretations of the results of their five-nation study[44] and the specifications made below). In the case of West Germany, DEUTSCH/NORDLINGER (1968:352-53) estimate the "all-weather" democrats at about 25% of the population. According to ALMOND/VERBA (1963:64) 33% of the West Germans show pride in their economic institutions, whereas only 7% do so with respect to their governmental and political institutions (as opposed to 46% in the United Kingdom and 85% in the United States). These figures have changed during the 1970s, but basically this asymmetry between pride in economic institutions and pride in political institutions, with the latter connoting the more diffuse aspects of political support, persists. Thus, in large segments of the West German population efficiency is still more highly rated than democratic legitimacy. CONRADT (1980:221-25 especially) has investigated these questions using older and more recent survey data for the Federal Republic of Germany. He raises the question of how diffuse support is to be measured adequately as a component of affect and a variable that influences behavior. Thus, with respect to developments in West Germany, one could ask whether it is "not possible for a system to develop a reserve of 'support capital' from an extended period of high-level system performance" (ibid., p. 221). According to CONRADT this has indeed been happening (on the relationship between diffuse support and specific support see also MULLER/WILLIAMS 1980).

There is probably also a symbolic component in diffuse support. However, the nature of this component remains to be determined. Generally speaking, symbolic attachments play their part in strengthening diffuse support and serve as objects of this support at the same time.[45] For instance, in Mexico the "regime which is skillful in the dispensation of symbolic rewards may generate a greater amount of popular acceptance than the material performance of the same regime might seem to warrant. Those beliefs in 'regime responsiveness' which define 'the externally efficacious[46] individual' may be very much a product of symbolic outputs in authoritarian or poor regimes, while more a function of material outputs in either affluent or pluralist regimes" (COLEMAN/DAVIS 1976:203; cf. also CORNELIUS 1975:223; DAVIS 1976). In short, what may work in Mexico (i.e., the continuous generation of diffuse support for the Partido Revolucionario Institutional and its control over the mobilization resources of rival groups) may not work in more highly developed societies or may work under quite different circumstances (cf. below and EDELMAN 1964 who puts great emphasis on the symbolic component and outcomes of politics). In their analysis of four "poor people's movements" in the United States, PIVEN/CLOWARD (1977; for critiques of their main political implications see JENKINS 1979; MAJKA 1980; ROACH/ROACH 1980) also emphasize that symbolic concessions may deradicalize protest movements, apart from the often pursued strategy of co-opting the less radical leaders of protest movements. (However, the generalization of PIVEN/CLOWARD 1977 that organizing political dissent reduces the political impact of such disruptive behavior as strikes, sit-ins, and other collective activities is not warranted thus far. As critics have pointed out, their four case analyses are not conclusive even in themselves. Moreover, their theory conflicts with much of what has been written on this subject, from successful revolutionaries like LENIN [1902] to TILLY [1978], to name only a few authors. There are, in fact, many observations that belie the hypothesis of PIVEN/CLOWARD, especially if one considers successful revolutions or failed peasant attacks. However, it must be emphasized that PIVEN/CLOWARD's dependent variable often differs from those referred to in critiques of their study. Nevertheless, they have invited criticism by over-generalizing their findings from only four cases.)

Diffuse support "may be generated through responses of the following types: first, those that seek to instill a deep sense of legitimacy in the members for the regime as a whole and for individuals who act on behalf of it; second, those that invoke symbols of the common interest; and third, those that promote and strengthen the degree to which members identify with the political community" (EASTON 1965:277). The three types are said to be "interrelated but at least analytically separable" (ibid.). Thus, in EASTON's systems theory legitimacy is only a subset of diffuse support, yet probably the most important one.[47] Trust (or cynicism as the opposite) is the other subset. EASTON more likely speaks of trust if the incumbents rather than the political order as such are referred to. Even though legitimacy and trust may vary independently of each other, it is, as EASTON assumes

> very likely that those who consider a system legitimate will also have considerable confidence in it [and conversely]. Nonetheless, people may lose their trust in the ability of authorities to run the country yet not be prepared to deny the authorities in general the moral right to rule and to expect obedience to outputs. There is likely to be a wide abyss between feeling distrustful or cynical about authorities in general and refusing to accept outputs as binding. Yet both sentiments—trust and legitimacy—are alike in that they represent a kind of support which is theoretically important to view as independent of attitudes towards immediate outputs (EASTON 1975:453).

To return to the feedback model EASTON proposes, if a political system is under stress, there are three responses to such a threatening situation: "outputs, coercion, and the stimulation of good will" (EASTON 1965:275). "Whether the basis of acceptance [of the decisions of the authorities] is legitimacy, fear or force, habit, or expediency is irrelevant. In practice . . . we can expect every system to employ a combination of these and other measures as well, to improve the probability that outputs will be accepted as binding. The particular mixture will vary from system to system and time to time within any one system" (ibid., p. 285; cf. also the typology of ETZIONI 1968:480-82).[48]

Having defined the two types of support, specific and diffuse, EASTON goes on to develop an elaborate typology (ibid., p. 287). He distinguishes three[49] sources and two objects of legitimacy. Legitimacy may derive "from underlying *ideological principles*, from attachment to the *structure* and norms of the regime as such, or from devotion to the actual authorities themselves because of their *personal qualities*"[50] (ibid., p. 287; italics ours). It may be focused on two objects: *regime* ("that part of the political system that we may call its constitutional order in the very broadest sense," EASTON/ DENNIS 1969:59) or *authorities*, i.e., the incumbent elites. Six types of legitimacy are constructed from the two basic dimensions. Unfortunately, the delineations between the six types of legitimacy are not always clear. Furthermore, one may add "policies"[51] to the list of objects of legitimacy (cf. ECKSTEIN 1971:31), thus introducing specific support into EASTON's typology, which is by no means totally convincing, albeit suggestive for empirical research. The most comprehensive typology of objects and forms of legitimacy has been proposed by CITRIN (1977; cf. also MILLER 1979a for some first results in this respect). He differentiates according to the objects of legitimacy such as the national government, the political system, the constitution, the presidency, the supreme court, congress, the parties, politicians, the incumbent president, and local government. Together with evaluations like trustworthiness, honesty, competence, responsiveness, fairness, right to loyalty or identification, these objects of reference form a matrix of "beliefs about the political system." Yet, CITRIN points out that some of the cells in this matrix will have to be left empty, as "for example we might not choose to obtain a rating of the country's level of competence" (CITRIN 1977:388).

Distinguishing between diffuse and specific support, the latter being dependent on certain outputs, EASTON already pointed to some possible relationships between legitimacy and other major variables likely to be of relevance for the study of political protest phenomena and the persistence of political systems. First of all, *legitimacy* does not necessarily depend on *system performance* or output in the short run. In the long run, however, both should covary. If a regime and/or elites have been highly successful in the past, they may have acquired a certain amount of credit among the population (ALMOND 1969:464–"political capital accumulation"; cf. also MERELMAN's 1966 understanding of legitimacy as reinforcement learning) possibly allowing the system and/or the elites to survive in times of comparatively low output.[52] However, although somewhat less likely empirically, high performance of the system and/or the elites in the past may have led to higher expectation levels. If these standards are not reached because of low performance or because elites violate the rules of the game (as in the Watergate case), protests may result *because of* (and not despite) high legitimacy in the past. "Illegitimate policies or incumbents in otherwise highly legitimate polities are especially likely to inspire sharp protests at those policies and leaders, because they threaten people's general sense of identification with the polity" (GURR/McCLELLAND 1971:32; cf. also the empirical results in SIGEL/HOSKIN 1977:124). For new states, on the other hand, it might hold that effectiveness "as a sole foundation for legitimacy, is tenuous. Any government can become involved in crises; major groupings will oppose specific policies, sometimes to the point of alienation. Consequently any government which persists must have ascriptive grounds for support—i.e., a sense of traditional legitimacy. Where a polity does not have such legitimacy to begin with, as in the case of new states or postrevolutionary governments, it is inherently unstable" (LIPSET 1967:281). MERELMAN's (1966:552) dictum that "legitimacy comes late and may be late in leaving" sums up here what is probably one of the basic findings in research on political legitimacy. EASTON's concept of diffuse support is perhaps even more to the point: "This type of evaluation tends to be more difficult to strengthen once it is weak and to weaken once it is strong" (EASTON 1975:444).

The four basic combinations of presence or absence of legitimacy and performance ("effectiveness," LIPSET) have already been analyzed in LIPSET's typology (1960:81–83) and illustrated with some historical examples (cf. the quotation in note 39). In any case, if the survival of the system and/or the elites is at stake, legitimacy, as it reflects on the values of a political system, is more important[53] than performance which is "primarily instrumental" (LIPSET 1960:77). In the long run, however, there should be a rather close covariation of the two. Yet, even if performance and legitimacy are low, the *coercive potential* of the incumbents may prevent[54] the outbreak of political protest.[55] Systems and/or elites with low legitimacy may survive for quite some time. Historically some of the most autocratic political systems, such as czarist Russia[56] and the Ottoman Empire, have survived for several centuries, longer in fact than some of the early democracies so far. "A coercive regime stands firm; it has no problem of 'ungovernability,' in the sense of non-compliance; it is characterized by too much power and too little support" (ROSE 1977:4). Moreover, even if there were no strong coercive potential and legitimacy as well as performance were low, still another requirement is necessary for *protest* to become likely, i.e., the awareness of alternatives perceived as less burdensome. Counterelites, alternative ideologies, the mass media, and increased world-wide communications in general will make such situations less likely in the future, although various examples may still be found in isolated places in the world.

The basic causal model arising from the discussion above could be represented as in Figure 6.2 (omitting feedback relationships[57] between the ultimate dependent variable and prior variables).[58]

We expect only a weak relationship between illegitimacy and the occurrence of strong political dissent or political violence. This relationship, however, increases in the case of a low- or mid-level of repression (coercion).[59] Strong repression, in any case, reduces or inhibits political violence (in the sense of violence used against the system). In the present discussion we speak of a high coercive potential and high coercion and at times substitute one for the other. One must, of course, differentiate between the potential and the actual use of coercion. However, in the context here we are mainly interested in the *consequences* of a *high* coercive potential or of high actual coercion. Results from cross-national studies suggest that the consequences are likely to be comparable, i.e., political violence is less likely to occur, whereas on other levels of coercion and through inconsistent use of coercive means the amount of political violence is likely to increase (see chapter 5.1.2.5). High coercion is directly related to the dependent variable persistence, yet in terms of sub-

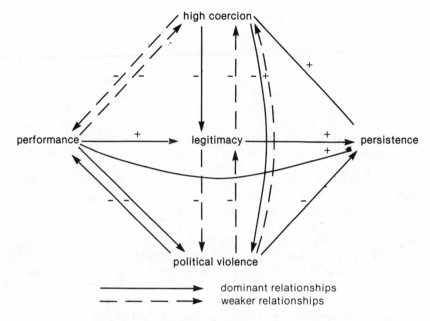

Figure 6.2.   A Long-term Causal Model of Relationships among Key Variables Explaining the Persistence of Political Systems (Model 1)

stantial explanation the more relevant path would be indirect: high coercive potential affects political violence negatively and thus reduces one of the major threats to persistence. Note that another threat to persistence, namely illegitimacy, is increased at the same time, yet the net effect of high coercive potential on persistence should still be positive. Finally, we predict a weak relationship between political violence and high coercion (not repression as such) (cf. also in connection with Figure 6.3).

In our model of political crises, legitimacy, or decline in legitimacy, is of central importance. It must be considered (even though not always in the short run) in connection with socioeconomic output and in itself, apart from political protest behavior, such as political violence, and repressive measures, one of the central determinants of the survival of polities.

Actually the underlying rationale of this causal model is common sense.[60] One may add the various possible sources of low performance, loss of legitimacy, and, as EASTON would say, "decline of support" discussed thus far in this study and below (chapter 6.3.5). The proposed causal model may be applicable to the persistence of both authorities and regimes.

In the case of advanced democratic industrial societies, the global model in Figure 6.2, which also refers to totalitarian, autocratic, and, in HUNTINGTON's (1968) sense, praetorian polities, would have to be modified. The variable high coercion would probably lose in explanatory power. Relationships between variables described thus far remain fairly general and must be specified in greater detail with respect to concrete conditions of decline in legitimacy and possible consequences for the mobilization of political dissent (cf. also below).

Note that in model 1 a linear relationship between performance and persistence has been postulated. However, a curvilinear relationship between system performance and persistence might also be expected in some cases: to acquire some basic stability in the short run, there must be system output. Once citizens have come to regard their political system as generally effective, diffuse support might develop and lead to maintaining the political system in spite of temporary setbacks in performance. We have seen already that this process of "legitimation" and "delegitimation" (VAN DOORN 1975:91ff; HARRIES-JENKINS/VAN DOORN 1975:8) is a permanent aim and threat to young, recently independent states and even to some older ones.[61] In the very long run, however, performance seems to be a requirement if diffuse support and specific support are not to be withdrawn from the political system. Thus, we predict a convergence between specific and diffuse support in the long run. However, the basic question remains as to how to delineate the turning points of this curvilinear relationship between performance and persistence and the points of convergence between specific and diffuse political support. Whereas specific support can be conceived of as varying linearly with performance, the relationship between performance and diffuse support should be nonmonotonic, except in the very long run.

The role of expectations which mediate[62] between output and support has not yet been discussed. In the end, it is not so much the output which is decisive but rather how it compares to the expectations attached to it. High output falling short of expectations will not be met by the same amount of specific support (and not at all of diffuse support) as output of the system and/or the elites that goes beyond expectations.[63] EASTON himself mentions that withdrawal of loyalty may also be caused by the "sudden frustration of expectations" (EASTON 1975:445; cf. also GURR's "progressive deprivation" in chapter 4.3).

To return to model 1 (Figure 6.2), we are concerned with *long-term* relationships. Thus legitimacy here is conceived of as a theoretical variable and *both specific and diffuse support* are said to be "cause"-indicators (cf. the distinction between cause indicators and effect indicators in NAMBOODIRI et al. 1975:597–605; cf. also below with respect to EASTON).[64] As indicated above, persistence of a political system may be achieved in the absence of legitimacy and in the presence of a high coercive potential and consistent use of coercion.[65] "Men may, of course, have order without liberty, but they cannot have liberty without order" (HUNTINGTON 1968: 7–8). Moreover, many a polity said to possess legitimacy might be more adequately characterized on closer scrutiny by a rather *specific mixture* of, to use the terminology of WRIGHT (1976), "consent," "assent," and "dissent." A political system which persists in spite of low performance may, under nonrepressive political circumstances, owe its survival to widespread diffuse support. Recalling LIPSET's arguments, this may be due to the following factors: (1) "the continuity of important traditional integrative institutions during a transitional period in which new institutions are emerging" (LIPSET 1960:79), or, more generally phrased, (2) "to have done great things together in the past, to wish to do more of them, these are the essential conditions for being a people.... The existence of a nation is a daily plebiscite"[66] (Ernest Renan in a lecture in 1882 as quoted in LIPSET 1967:19). Yet, empirical testing must determine whether *diffuse support* is indeed *the* causal variable or some other variable intervening between performance and persistence. To avoid circular reasoning, the notion of diffuse support must be tested in great detail against other possible theoretical constructs[67] proposed for explaining the relationship between low performance and persistence (cf. Figure 6.3, below). Recent analyses suggest some *alternative explanations* to those proposed by EASTON and taken up in our discussion and in Figure 6.2.

The subsequent paragraphs can in part be understood as a critique and modification of the EASTON model. The major attack on EASTON's systems theory of political support has been carried out by WRIGHT (1976). In opposition to most other critics of EASTON's systems analysis, who mostly object to the "black boxes" in his model, WRIGHT bases his arguments on a series of reanalyses of U. S. survey data while at the same time taking up some of the results of the debate between MILLER (1974a, 1974b) and CITRIN (1974). As the issues involved are rather complicated, some longer quotations may be appropriate here. Later on the analytical substance of the partial findings will be presented.

In an analysis of national survey data from the United States for 1964-70, MILLER (1974a) demonstrated that diffuse support is *not* "independent of the effects of daily outputs"[68] (EASTON) and, moreover, that "massive declines in the level of public allegiance *do* apparently leave the stability of the regime intact" (WRIGHT 1976:76). These findings call into question the theoretical scheme of EASTON: "If the 'reservoir of diffuse support' itself depends on the quality of the political product, then how can it sustain the regime through periods when quality declines?" (WRIGHT 1976:77). Obviously, the controversial Vietnam war and lower economic performance were major causes of this decline in support. These results are inconsistent with predictions derived from EASTON's theoretical scheme.[69] MILLER interprets his findings as indicating that "if present policy is maintained in the future . . . , trust of the government would continue to decline, increasing the difficulty for leaders to make binding political decisions, as well as raising the probability of the occurrence of radical political change" (MILLER 1974a: 971). Yet, "the political implications of MILLER's analysis depend on the discriminant validity of the Trust in Government scale as an indicator of attitudes toward the political regime" (CITRIN 1974:974). CITRIN presents a number of arguments and evidence not in line with MILLER's interpretations. In his reply MILLER himself (1974b) points out that his cumulative trust in government scale is not strictly comparable to the additive measures used by CITRIN. Nevertheless, CITRIN's points deserve attention.

First, "a diffuse sense of pride in and support for the ongoing 'form of government' can coexist with widespread public cynicism about 'the government in Washington' and the people 'running' it"[70] (CITRIN 1974:975).[71] One might, however, argue to the contrary as well:

> We find these conceptual exercises [cf. also MULLER/JUKAM 1977, below] to be largely beside the point. It is unlikely that the *mass public*[72] entertains any such niceties in their own political thinking, or that they distinguish between incumbents and the institutions[73] that they represent in meting out punishment for real or imagined excesses. In other words, "It is possible to have a fair amount of consensus approving the main characteristics of the formal system but still have considerable potential for insurgency. The 'man on the street' may be saying, 'The system is OK, it's just the guys running it.' When he undertakes insurgency against those 'guys,' however, the system is also likely to suffer some damage" [HAMILTON and WRIGHT 1975:25] (WRIGHT 1976:73; emphasis added).

Secondly, there may be a general Zeitgeist component "which legitimizes, even encourages, the expression of anti-political rhetoric, makes it fashionable to denigrate politicians and to criticize established institutions" (CITRIN 1974:975). This argument, while important for evaluating the rise and decline in trust over much longer periods of time, in this instance may actually be read in favor of MILLER's interpretation. Thus, the decline in the standards of the political language may serve as an additional indicator of political decay even though the behavioral implications suggested in MILLER's analysis may not come into being (due to a number of other factors such as high individual costs of participating in protest activities).

In the third argument of CITRIN, attention is once again drawn to some structural complexities: "A diffuse opposition to the 'government in general' does not preclude support for its authority in specific instances" (CITRIN 1974:978). In short, "Low scorers on the Trust in Government scale appear to form a heterogeneous group" (CITRIN 1974:978) which has serious consequences concerning predictions as to behavior. "The weak and unsystematic relationships between scores on the Trust in Government scale and support for an activist behavioral orientation belie the contention that a diffuse mistrust of political authorities intervenes between political cynicism and approval of disruptive sit-ins or mass demonstrations" (CITRIN 1974:982). In his rejoinder to CITRIN, MILLER provides some empirical evidence in favor of his interpretation, namely that the "trust scale does correlate with political actions and support for illegal protest behaviors *under appropriate conditions*" (MILLER 1974b:1000; emphasis added).

Building on the results of MILLER and providing some additional evidence as to the decline of political efficacy—besides political distrust the other major component of political alienation research[74]—WRIGHT points out: "Efficacy and trust, far from being independent of outputs, seem to be rather sensitive to them: Their level appears to rise and fall *precisely* in response to these 'disappointments' against which the reservoir of diffuse support is supposed to protect the system" (WRIGHT 1976:196). He then makes an important distinction among alienated groups, namely between the "recently alienated" and the "always alienated," drawing on the wide negative empirical evidence that, contrary to much speculation in alienation theory and in the theory of the mass society as well (cf. also chapter 5.1.2.2), those always politically alienated participate less in politics, be it conventional political behavior or protest behavior. If there are to be disruptive consequences of alienation, they should be expected among the recently alienated [a theoretical notion more adequate than the alienation concept might perhaps be relative deprivation (cf. chapters 4.3 and 5.3.2.3)] and not among the permanently alienated, among those for whom "powerlessness and distrust are the normal and natural state of affairs. There might also be some feeling that, bad as it is, the on-going system is no worse than any available alternative" (WRIGHT 1976:264). Moreover, "persons experiencing their alienation [as a loss] are probably far outnumbered by those whose alienation has been a part of their political thinking. Without some empirical procedure for separating the two groups, the disruptive potential of political alienation can never be definitely assessed" (ibid., p. 265).[75] Consensus theory, then, building strongly on the notion of diffuse support, may not be false so much as misdirected: "It falls short as a theory of *mass* politics," since "democracies apparently function even without large reservoirs of unconditional [i.e., diffuse] ... trust" (ibid., p. 259). But consensus theory with its stress on long-term socialization experiences "does apparently offer a viable account of that one group in the society whose mood and disposition might conceivably have an impact on stable democratic government" (ibid., p. 109). This group of "consenters [occupies] a key role in the 'two-step-flow' of political influence and information, not only in the upper middle class, but nearly everywhere in the society" (ibid., p. 270). The always alienated form another group (the "unorganized" and "underrepresented") among whom "assent" rather than "dissent" is to be found and expected. Assenters are mainly "preoccupied with the day-to-day humdrum of life." For them politics is "somebody else's game" (ibid., p. 276). Perhaps acquiescence is a more appropriate, though somewhat evaluative, term than assent. Survey data show, quite contrary to many a variant of relative deprivation theory, that the demands of assenters are anything but insatiable. Neither is there a strong coherence of problems that government should solve and of goals that it should achieve. Other writers describe part of the political behavior of assenting masses by invoking the notion of behavioral constraint, i.e., conventional political behavior that persists even if issue beliefs have changed and are now at variance with such a behavior (cf. SEARING et al. 1973:418 and their model on p. 419). Real danger for the existence of the political system is only to come from the "dissenters" and from their ability to increase their resources by converting assenters into dissenters (in this respect the failure of the French student revolt in May 1968 to sustain and enlarge dissent is instructive; cf. also the discussion in chapter 6.3.5).

Thus, assent is perhaps basic to stability (cf. similarly LIPSET 1960:

pt. 2; HUNTINGTON 1975:114; also DENNIS 1970; LEHMBRUCH 1975): "By depressing participation, alienation lessens 'demands' on the system, reduces 'strain,' and contributes to the 'mainly passive electorate'" (WRIGHT 1976:267). "The only firm conclusion that can be drawn from the evidence is that the consent of half the population is sufficient" (ibid., p. 269). Moreover, "if the nonconsenters fall into the ranks of assenters, then there is little reason to think that pure consent would be required of more than, say, 10% or 15% (enough, for example, to 'cover' the military, business, industrial, and financial establishments). These, however, are arbitrary guesses" (ibid., p. 269; cf. also the discussion in chapter 8.4.7). If "democracies apparently function even without reservoirs of unconditional [i.e., diffuse] trust" (ibid., p. 259), a worthwhile alternative explanation to that favored by EASTON might be to conceive of alienation as an effect, as the dependent variable and not as an independent variable. "Since . . . most people are not all that interested in politics anyway, alienation, in many cases, might well be experienced as a 'relief,' as an attitude that relieves one of democratic responsibilities" (ibid., p. 264). More realistically (and much more in line with major portions of WRIGHT's book), however, might be a feedback conceptualization of alienation, at least among the persistently alienated.

As long as assent does not drop markedly below 50% of the population and as long as dissent does not rapidly grow beyond, say, 30 to 35%, the system still may be expected to remain stable. Thus, one might assume that the assenting population in a way acts as a veto power (or, perhaps more appropriately, as a buffer), even though its acting consists largely of inactivity and disinterest. If dissenters increase their share at the expense of assenters, the passive veto power exerted thus far on behalf of assenters is converted into a threat to the survival of the elites and/or the political system (cf. also the analysis by LINZ 1978:78ff.).[76] In any case, what PINARD (1967) and others have pointed out should be kept in mind: Poor masses are, if anything, the followers in great social movements and rarely among the initiators of these movements.

WRIGHT's theory, which in some respects has been extended here, must be tested in other countries and for other periods as well. Western European electorates participate in the act of voting to a larger extent than do Americans (VERBA/NIE 1972:31). Americans, in turn, have higher rates in other forms of political participation. Thus, the forms assent takes in individual contexts need to be spelled out in much greater detail. Nevertheless, WRIGHT offers a more realistic[77] model of actual political behavior in many Western countries than EASTON does with his theoretical scheme which leaves the linkages between inputs and outputs rather unspecified. Various models will have to be developed and tested, for instance, long-term as suggested in our model 1 and more short-term as suggested in model 2 where we try to summarize the preceding discussion (see Figure 6.3). While in model 1 some predictions are made as to relationships between key variables over longer spans of time, on the left side of model 2 up to the variable dissent, greater emphasis is laid on *process changes* within a polity. Instead of performance, decline in performance now becomes the prior independent variable. According to WRIGHT's analysis (1976), a decline in performance will reaffirm dissenters in their point of view (therefore a plus sign has been added to the path). However, another group, in which diffuse support prevails, will not react with dissent to the decline in performance,[78] at least not in the short run. If it is to take place at all, first another group has to change its opinion and behavior from assent to dissent. In the short run, again, there is reason to expect assenters to react constantly *even* to declines in performance, but perhaps less so as this decline continues. In this case there could be a landslide transforming assent into dissent. These relationships are indicated by the dotted line and the dashed line. Dissent, then, is specified according to various possible components (cf. MULLER/JUKAM 1977). Here dissent with respect to the political system is considered as the most important threat to the survival of a polity (cf. the minus sign at the particular path; all other instances, where the system as such still commands some loyalty, will be less threatening). The dashed and positively marked path from dissent to strong and consistent repression represents the hypothesis that weak dissent might cause strong and consistent repression (it *does* so in a variety of countries). However, if dissent has reached a certain level, elites will not be able or willing to employ strong repressive measures. Or, if they do so, this will have a boomerang effect and lead to an increase in dissent (cf. the discussion in chapter 5.1.2.5). Thus, one might conceive of a curvilinear relationship between the two variables. If, however, repression precedes dissent, we predict that strong repression will reduce at least open dissent. Finally, in model 2 (as in model 1) nothing is said about mobilizing conditions. Both models would have to be extended in these respects (cf. the discussion in chapter 9). Illegitimacy and dissent do not automatically lead to political violence, but only if mobilization processes occur in a certain direction. Political violence as such and in itself does not always threaten the persistence of a polity. Only if political violence takes place with strategic groups participating is the survival of the polity in danger.

Whereas WRIGHT distinguishes mainly between the consenters, the dissenters (the "recently alienated"), and the assenters, SNIDERMAN (1978) is concerned with establishing further distinctions among "consenters." He wants to draw a line between the "committed" and the "supporters," the latter coming "closer to being good citizens in a democratic society than the committed," because their "orientation toward government is balanced" (ibid., p. 36, 37). Committed individuals are somewhat less educated than supporters, but in other social respects there is not much difference between them. According to SNIDERMAN the difference that separates the two groups is that the "faith of the committed is totalistic" (ibid., p. 41), whereas supporters are said to be more critically minded, to give positive evaluations of the government and negative ones as well. While SNIDERMAN's empirical findings (he uses two samples drawn from the San Francisco-Oakland Bay

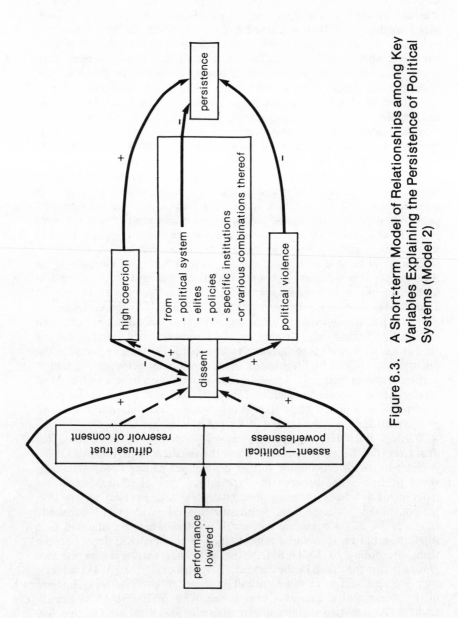

Figure 6.3. A Short-term Model of Relationships among Key Variables Explaining the Persistence of Political Systems (Model 2)

Area) confirm this theorizing in some instances, in other respects differences between the two groups do not seem to be too strong (cf. Table 2 ibid., p. 29).

Drawing on the works of EASTON, WRIGHT, SNIDERMAN, and others, a classification of various population subgroupings could be derived distinguishing their beliefs and behavior in normal times from those during times of crises (see Table 6.2). These suggestions in Table 6.2 may be speculative in some respects. Thus, future research should concentrate on drawing sharper boundaries between these various subgroups than has been done in SNIDERMAN's (1978) study.

Table 6.2. The Political System, Its Supporters and Opponents

	Grouping	Normal Times		Times of Crises	
		Beliefs	*Behavior*	*Beliefs*	*Behavior*
Compliance	committed	+	+	+(?)	+(?)
	supporters	+(±)	+	±	+
	diffuse	+	+	+	+
	specific	+	+	−	−(?)
	assenters	↔	+	−(?)	−(?)
	coerced	−(↔)	+	−	+
	dissenters	−	−	−	−

+ : pro-system
− : anti-system
↔ : ambivalent
in brackets: alternatives, doubts

Strictly speaking, adaptability is the ultimate dependent variable researchers (and politicians) want to know more about. What is needed is knowledge about the efficiency of a political system, not merely about its continued existence. The ultimate goal would be to use persistence and adaptability (cf. GURR 1974a and chapter 6.3.2.2) as measures of successful coping with changing environments. It is this idea of persistence which researchers ultimately have in mind,[79] not the mere persistence of regimes and/or elites which suddenly may find their end in rapid dissolution.[80]

The works of EASTON and WRIGHT will also be considered in the next section which puts a greater emphasis on how to measure legitimacy, whereas the present one was more concerned with how to define legitimacy in theoretical terms. Nevertheless, questions of measurement have been dealt with in the present context as well. EASTON conceives of trust (object of reference: generally incumbents) and legitimacy (object of reference: political system) as components or dimensions of diffuse support. In our model, however, diffuse and specific support are said to be cause-indicators of legitimacy. MULLER/JUKAM (1977; see the next section) treat political trust like EASTON as a property of incumbents and political support as a system property. This variety of conceptualizations is anything but desirable (apart from the negative findings of WRIGHT which would call into question any models of this sort). At present there is no answer to a host of questions: Is *support in general* a *multidimensional*[81] concept (breaking down into specific and diffuse components, and perhaps others as well)?[82] Which are the appropriate indicators to capture fluctuations in legitimacy and support? Should these indicators be conceived of as cause- or effect-indicators? What kind of errors in measurement will turn up? Finally, which behavioral consequences will result from a decline in legitimacy and a diminishing degree of support?

6.3.4.2. Some Empirical Attempts at Measuring Legitimacy

Throughout this study a host of results bearing on legitimacy as an independent or intervening variable and political violence as a dependent variable have been reported. Yet, in most cases, legitimacy of a political system and/or of the incumbents has been measured rather indirectly (for some exceptions cf. the preceding section).

> LIPSET (1960: chapter 3), for example, equates legitimacy with one of its presumed consequences, political stability, and BWY (1968b),[83] in a study of Latin America, indexes the concept with a measure of one of its presumed causes, the degree of political democracy in a society. A recent study by the senior author [GURR 1968a] combines measures of presumed causes *and* consequences of feelings of legitimacy: legitimacy is assumed to vary positively both with the degree to which political institutions are of indigenous rather than foreign origin, and with their durability (GURR/ McCLELLAND 1971:32).

Moreover, there are the usual cross-national designs which relate socioeconomic variables to political violence, the inference being that socioeconomically more successful nations will also be higher in legitimacy.[84]

Probably the most sophisticated, yet still fairly indirect, aggregate measures of legitimacy have been employed by GURR/McCLELLAND (1971: 30-48) who (1) use measures of illegitimacy manifestations (such as "overt strife, organized extremist oppositional activity [nonviolent], governmental repressive measures, symbolic oppositional activity") and (2) distinguish between three objects of illegitimacy sentiments (political community, regime, incumbents) as well as (3) between the intensity ("type of sentiment or objective expressed [and] the form in which it is expressed"), persistence ("number of years in which manifestations directed against a particular object occur in the period"), and scope ("proportion of a population *inferred* to share the feelings of illegitimacy manifest in it"; italics ours) of such sentiments. For further details, especially as to the weighting procedures, the reader is referred to this pioneering study. While various degrees of indirect measurement may be distinguished among the indicators of legitimacy used in these cross-national studies, the fact remains that all of these measures are indirect.

In general, the evidence resulting from these indirect measures of legitimacy was as expected, i.e., legitimacy tends to be negatively related to political violence. (In democratic political systems, however, slightly positive relationships between legitimacy and political protest were found [see the summary findings and the discussion in ZIMMERMANN 1980]). In chapter 5.3.2 additional and less indirect evidence as to the negative relationship between legitimacy and political violence was reported. Distrust, structural blame, alienation, social isolation and many other variables were related to various political violence variables. However, those constructs employed in research on aggregate data are often plagued by insufficient theoretical and empirical specification, i.e., researchers doing cross-national research on political violence seem to have chosen whatever they thought appropriate for indexing legitimacy. Perhaps many a rationale does indeed hold, yet efforts to cross-validate the measures used are rarely undertaken.

There is no way around treating legitimacy at the individual level. Legitimacy is a sociopsychological concept denoting the evaluation by an individual or by groups of states of various empirical referents, in the context here, of political macrophenomena. There is, of course, a vast number of studies bearing on different facets of legitimacy[85] in various areas of political research (cf. WRIGHT 1976 and the extensive discussion in the preceding chapter). With respect to the dependent variable political violence, however, efforts at directly measuring legitimacy are rather rare occurrences (but cf. also BARNES, KAASE et al. 1979). One of the best examples found in the literature is a study by MULLER/JUKAM (1977). Again the sample (cf. chapter 5.3.2.3) is drawn from rural, urban, and university communities in Germany. The dependent variable also remains the same, namely "aggressive political behavior: that is, political behavior that is illegal, disruptive of the normal functioning of government, and may entail the use of violence" (MULLER/JUKAM 1977:1573). Their measure of aggressive political behavior is based on two questions, one dealing with behavioral intentions, the other with actual behavior. The research procedure and the results of this study are highly suggestive for the development of an empirical theory of legitimacy, but too complex to be discussed here in detail. The best brief overview may be gained from quoting a few summary lines (italics added): "The data indicate that the theory of the behavioral consequences of the incumbent-system distinction suggested by the work of LIPSET and EASTON must be qualified according to whether ideology and community context are inhibitory or facilitative. The theory should be reformulated to take into account the effect of *ideological commitment* and *community context*, for each has a separate role to play in the explanation of aggressive political behavior, and the nature of this role does *not* appear to be linear additive" (ibid., p. 1589).

Affect for the system of government [political support][86] is a more powerful explanatory variable than affect for an incumbent administration [political trust] .[87] It is generally related to aggressive political behavior regardless of whether incumbent affect is positive or negative (though the relationship is depressed or heightened depending especially on whether ideological commitment[88] is non-Left or Left). Incumbent affect is unrelated to aggressive political behavior when system affect is controlled for. . . . All indications point to the conclusion that trust in government is . . . more sensitive to incumbent than to system affect[89] and should be classified in the same category as such variables as evaluation of public policy outputs and general approval–disapproval of the performance of an incumbent administration.[90] Incumbent affect, while probably not of much consequence in any direct causal sense does appear to condition modestly the relationship between system affect and aggressive political behavior such that when the incumbents are trusted and their policies are regarded in a positive light, the relationship is weaker than it is when the incumbents are not trusted and their policies are not regarded positively. The relationship between system affect and aggressive political behavior is most strongly specified by ideology: the relationship generally holds up well among persons with a leftist ideological orientation; but it is sometimes erratic and considerably weaker among persons with a centrist or rightist ideological orientation (ibid.).

MULLER/JUKAM present the following summary of their findings:

1. There is a specific effect due to incumbent affect, as predicted by the theory of the behavioral consequences of the incumbent-system distinction, but this effect is relatively minor compared to that which results from ideology.
a) Among the Left, regardless of the level of policy and trust, moderate-to-strong correlations are observed except in the instance of high policy and trust levels in the nonuniversity milieu.
b) Among the non-Left, regardless of the level of policy and trust, either (1) almost all persons are in the Inactive zone on the Aggressive Behavior index . . . or (2) the observed correlation between Political Support and the Aggressive Behavior index is very weak or else has a theoretically implausible sign. . . .
2. Although ideology appears to have the major specification effect on the relationship between Political Support and the Aggressive Behavior index—inhibiting it (or producing a change in sign) among centrists and rightists, facilitating it among leftists—a slightly stronger strength of relationship is observed among leftists in a facilitative community context [i.e., in the university environment] [91] than in an inhibitory community context. More importantly, community context affects the likelihood of participation in aggressive action, given varying degrees of political support among those with leftist ideological commitment.

a) When support is in the positive range, leftists in a nonuniversity context are practically certain to score in the Inactivity zone on the Aggressive Behavior index. This is much less true of leftists who reside in a university milieu.

b) When support is in the negative range, leftists in a university context are extremely likely to score at other than Inactive on the Aggressive Behavior index. This is much less true of leftists who reside in a nonuniversity milieu.

3. These generalizations apply to the Aggressive Behavior index as ranging from Inactivity (no participation in aggressive behavior and negative intention toward its performance) to High Civil Disobedience (participation in nonviolent aggressive action and positive intention toward political violence). Political violence occurs only under the following set of circumstances: (1) university context; (2) leftist ideological commitment; (3) low policy and trust; and (4) negative or very negative Political Support. But even under these conditions civil disobedience is a far more likely outcome than violent action (ibid., p. 1588).

As pointed out, the study of MULLER/JUKAM contains numerous findings of interest in the present context. Reasons of space, however, forbid a more detailed treatment. Perhaps some general comments will suffice here. In their study at first it seemed difficult to disentangle the specific effects of incumbent legitimacy and system legitimacy on the dependent variable; after the introduction of additional variables, however, it became evident that system legitimacy is the more important causal variable (at least in this sample and at this point of time) whereas incumbent legitimacy is relevant as a mediating condition. This study could serve as a paradigm of how to approach the study of legitimacy empirically in that it takes up most of the relevant theoretical distinctions made thus far in writings on legitimacy, tests for various interaction effects on various levels, and takes complex interrelationships between individual variables and context variables into account. A number of possible extensions are already suggested by MULLER's other works. Thus, one may wonder what the impact of the various forms of legitimacy will be if, for example, structural just deserts deprivation (denoting feelings of relative deprivation which are blamed on the social structure; MULLER 1975) is incorporated into the analysis, apart from considering the usual individual socioeconomic status variables and perhaps the social networks of the respondents as well. At the same time one also "must know what is happening to personal political influence and belief in the efficacy of past collective political aggression" (MULLER 1977a:467). Furthermore, the study of changes over time in the various forms of legitimacy (and this may include a substitution of the incumbent government by the present political opposition)[92] would provide extremely useful evidence as to the fever curve of the political system or of other elements of the political community. The least which could be said at the present point of time is that there is reason to hope that EASTON's question may eventually be answered on a more solid empirical basis: "Without discriminating in some way between specific and diffuse support, could we explain adequately the occurrence of extreme political tension, conflict, and discontent in some systems, especially democratic ones, without all these giving rise to serious threats to the stability of the regime or political community?" (EASTON 1975:443-44).[93] Much in the same vein, MILLER (1979) distinguishes between two theories of trust, one explaining "the long term decline in trust as the result of incumbents who were unpopular and perceived as untrustworthy." The other, focusing on "government policies and performance, provides a substantially different explanation of the long term trend." If the former were correct, ratings of the Carter administration should be higher than they are at present, since Carter's evaluation as a person has not changed significantly, as opposed to the public's current lack of confidence in the capacity of the incumbent government to solve the present economic problems. MILLER cites other evidence demonstrating that the trust in government variant of the two trust theories is the more powerful in explaining current political dissatisfaction in the United States.[94] However, as stressed by MILLER/LEVITIN (1976:227): "Trust in government, as measured by the items used in the Michigan studies as well as in the polls, is primarily based on satisfaction with how well the government is performing. The items do not tap feelings of loyalty or patriotism, abstract philosophical theories about government, or existential states of alienation or helplessness as directly as they indicate satisfaction with the performance of the party in power." While the incumbent government may rate poor, the basic loyalty to the American political system still exists.

More recent data from the 1978 National Election Study, however, lead MILLER (1979a) to the following conclusions:

> Distrust of authorities is the single most important explanation of low public confidence in the president and congress (betas of .38 and .51 respectively) thereby suggesting that accumulating dissatisfaction with the policies and actions of several leaders may have resulted in public discontent directed at the institutions of the political regime. . . . Finding that distrust of authorities had an independent effect on institutional confidence after controlling for public support of specific incumbents implies, contrary to what CITRIN (1974) and MULLER (1977a) argue, that it reflects accumulating discontent with a series of authorities and not necessarily those currently in office. . . . Evidently, distrust of authorities acts as an intervening variable which translates negative evaluations of government performance into institutional distrust. [More generally], discontent with the actions and policies pursued by a series of leaders may accumulate and eventually undermine respect for the political regime (ibid., p. 44-46).

In two more recent papers EASTON (1976; also COLEMAN/EASTON 1976) has made some useful suggestions as to further developments of an empirical theory of legitimacy. The question he raises is whether the various

forms and objects of reference of legitimacy can be most adequately represented through a *saliency model*, a *sequential model*, an *additive model*, or
a *combinatorial model*. Yet, these models need not preclude each other.
The third model, for example, is a special case of the fourth one. According
to the findings of MULLER/JUKAM (1977; cf. also CITRIN 1977:398) a
saliency model (the most important component in their study is loyalty to
the political system) could be combined with a sequential model specifying
the decline of legitimacy that is to infect other objects of legitimacy, once
a serious loss in legitimacy at a more important level has occurred. The third
alternative model, wherein a total additive score of legitimacy is formed on
the basis of the individual components of legitimacy,[95] could also be of
relevance in some instances (e.g., in federal systems, cf. KORNBERG et al.
1978). In general, we would expect such a model to hold more likely in
"normal times," whereas in times of crises findings as reported by MULLER/
JUKAM seem to be more probable. We would expect a combination of the
saliency model and the sequential model to be the most promising starting
point for further empirical studies on the question of legitimacy. Perhaps
two further models (actually sub-cases of the sequential model) and their
empirical correlates can be established on a broad empirical basis: (1) *the
erosion model*, where distrust focusing on a lower object level eventually
leads to feelings of illegitimacy vis-à-vis objects of higher levels; (2) *the
breakdown model* operating just the opposite way. A polity experiencing
this alternative—in reality one would expect some feedback relationships
between both models—does not have much of a chance of survival in times
of crises.

A final alternative might be to test for interaction terms as predictors
incorporating a distrust variable and other variables (such as resource measures) as well (cf. MARSH 1977 and some of the works by MULLER, especially 1979).

Whereas WRIGHT's results (1976) call for a correction of EASTON's
theoretical scheme, the findings of MULLER/JUKAM stemming from a
non-American context seem to be reconcilable with EASTON's propositions.
Two further variables must be considered when dealing with the distinction
between system and incumbents: firstly, conservatives might be less inclined
to denigrate the system as such (CITRIN et al. 1975:29) even if they may
be highly critical of incumbents, the reason being simply that the system
still guarantees them some of their privileges. Certain of the findings of
MULLER/JUKAM might perhaps be interpreted in this direction. More
generally put, one should always test whether a variable like party identification has an effect on zero-order relationships between measures of support
and explicative variables (MULLER 1978). Thus, KORNBERG et al., in a
nationwide survey of the Canadian electorate in 1974, found that "both
partisan object support and the direction and intensity of party identifica-
tions had powerful independent effects on regime support which persisted
under a variety of controls" (KORNBERG et al. 1978:213).[96] A second
question is whether the distinction between system and incumbents is of
varying importance (SIGEL/HOSKIN 1977). Is it of major importance in

times of crises? In the case of stable economic growth might incumbents and the system be treated alike? Conversely, one might argue that, especially in the case of a crisis, specific groups will consider the incumbents and the system to stand for the same evil. Thus, many more replication studies are needed to distinguish singular findings from more invariant results.

In any case, MULLER/JUKAM with their focus on the individual and/or group level of political legitimacy have made an important contribution to an empirical theory of legitimacy. A substantial theory of legitimacy will have to be developed *across both levels*, the *system level* and the *individual or group level*. Ultimately, it is the individuals and groups which attribute legitimacy to a political order.[97] Thus, legitimacy as a system property emerges from the sentiments of the people. "Legitimacy deals with whether or not the citizens accept the moral right of the political leaders to make binding decisions over them; only the citizens can grant legitimacy. . . . legitimacy proceeds not from the top downward but from the bottom upward; the nonleaders consent to the justifications proclaimed by the leaders" (ANDRAIN 1975:150). Another vital question to be answered in this context is how people come to *use* the notion of legitimate political order when describing or dealing with their political environment. This certainly is much less of a question to historically long-established democratic political systems, but of vital importance to fairly new polities (cf. also ZIMMERMANN 1981b with respect to the Federal Republic of Germany) which are still struggling to form a widely supported political order.

Future studies along the lines suggested here should answer not only the questions (1) *who* is how likely to react to a decline in the various dimensions of legitimacy, (2) *where* and (3) *why* is this possibly violent reaction to occur, but also (4) *when* is it to occur, thus increasing our knowledge of four basic research and political questions underlying most of the works dealt with in this study.

6.3.5. Further Theoretical Suggestions

A number of theoretical explanations or at least suggestive variables somewhat neglected thus far should be briefly mentioned here. To start, there are some noteworthy *political* explanations of crises and political instability. Most prominent are probably those explanations that claim the stability and adaptability of parties and/or the party system to be of vital importance for the stability of a political system. LIPSET (1960), for example, uses the size of antisystem *movements* (in fact, the percentage of *votes* gained is measured) as an indicator (predictor?) of the instability of democratic political systems. Yet, contrary to this rather rough measure there is evidence that so-called antisystem parties, such as the communist party in Italy or France, must be dealt with at a more differentiated level (for some cross-national evidence cf. HIBBS 1973; see chapter 5.1.1.3; see also the discussion in TANNAHILL 1978). Even though these parties may pursue long-range antisystem goals, their actual behavior often deviates from this end (although some party strategists might deny this).

In a classic and highly suggestive study, HUNTINGTON has stressed the salience of a stable and adaptable party system. While his hypotheses, aphorisms, etc. are far too numerous to be covered here, several quotations will outline his theoretical position: "In terms of political development . . . what counts is not the number of parties, but rather the strength and adaptability of the party system. The precondition of political stability is a party system capable of assimilating the new social forces produced through modernization. From this viewpoint, the number of parties is important only insofar as it affects the ability of the system to provide the institutional channels necessary for political stability" (HUNTINGTON 1968:420-21). HUNTINGTON discusses the modality and the impact of four types of party systems (one-party system, the dominant party system, the two-party system, and the multiparty system) in these assimilation processes. In general, two-party systems or dominant party systems are said to be better suited for the task (cf. also PRIDE 1970 for a study based on twenty-six nations). Multiparty systems provide "insufficient incentive for any established element within the political system to mobilize the peasants. . . . Once such mobilization does take place [the multiparty system] cumulates political and social cleavages so as to obstruct the easy assimilation of the peasant political movement into the political system" (ibid., p. 446).[98] "The party and the party sytem which combine [mobilization and organization] reconcile political modernization with political development" (ibid., p. 402).[99] Three criteria for the institutional strength of a political party are suggested: its "ability to survive its founder or the charismatic leader who first brings it to power" (ibid., p. 409), its "organizational complexity and depth, particularly as revealed by the linkages between the party and socio-economic organizations" (ibid., p. 410), and "the extent to which political activists and power seekers identify with the party" (ibid.). Or, more generally, "organization is the road to political power, but it is also the foundation of political stability and thus the precondition of political liberty. . . . In the modernizing world he controls the future[100] who organizes its politics" (ibid., p. 461).

HUNTINGTON's basic hypothesis that "a high level of participation combined with low levels of political party institutionalization produces anomic politics and violence" (ibid., p. 402)[101] has already been theoretically and empirically evaluated to a certain extent (see chapter 5.1.2.4). In the chapter on coups d'état this hypothesis will be encountered once again. While HUNTINGTON illustrates his hypotheses with many suggestive examples, the question nevertheless remains whether the relationships predicted will also hold on a more systematic basis. There are some further results loosely bearing on HUNTINGTON's hypotheses. GURR (1970a:286-87) reports (N=119 countries during 1961-1963) a slightly negative correlation between "party system stability"[102] and total magnitude of political violence (r=-.34), the relationship being lowest in polyarchic countries (-.21) and highest in centrist political systems (-.47).

There are, however, compelling theoretical reasons why parties or party systems may also allow for the mobilization of radical political elements, thus lowering the chances of stability (cf. PINARD 1971, below). Finally, GURR in his study of "persistence and change in political systems" (1974a; cf. also chapter 6.3.2.2) found that "the more Complex, Directive, and democratic system did prove to be consistently more persistent and adaptable *in the European culture zone and in the 20th century*" (GURR 1974a:1501). Yet, when looking at all historical polities and all regions combined, "autocratic and [somewhat contrary to HUNTINGTON] anocratic authority trends proved to *enhance* durability while democratic traits *reduced* it" (ibid., p. 1502).[103]

HUNTINGTON's theory has been criticized for theoretical reasons as well as for implicit value positions taken (cf. the arguments already dealt with in chapter 5.1.2.4). In particular, his concept of institutionalization has come under attack. KESSELMAN (1970) points out that the four criteria of institutionalization HUNTINGTON proposes, namely, adaptability, complexity, autonomy, and coherence, may vary independently from each other,[104] or even in opposite directions. BEN-DOR (1975) draws attention to HUNTINGTON's mixing of behavioral and structural aspects in his conception of institutionalization (cf. also the critique by SANDERS, 1973, in chapter 5.1.2.4). Finally, and in line with results GURR et al. have found recently (cf. note 103), overinstitutionalization, and not just underinstitutionalization, may lead to political decay. Using France for a case study, KESSELMAN comes to this general conclusion (already quoted in chapter 5.1.2.4): "If in transitional societies it is easier to destroy old institutions than to build new ones, the problem is reversed in developed polities, where established institutions may be outmoded [not adaptable] but still able [autonomous] to withstand challenge" (KESSELMAN 1970:44). Thus, HUNTINGTON's trichotomization of political systems according to the relationship of political participation to political institutionalization (cf. chapter 7.2.3) must be supplemented by a fourth type, that of overinstitutionalization.

In short, HUNTINGTON has produced perhaps the longest list of persuasive hypotheses in the cross-national literature on political instability and political violence, yet explications and *exact* tests of his numerous theoretical insights are lacking. The few empirical tests of his propositions are inconclusive and/or deficient in a number of ways. Thus, HUNTINGTON's theory has still to be refuted by rigorous cross-national tests. Perhaps it will prove to be a valid theory for modernizing countries (and only at specific points in their development), but less so for economically and politically more developed societies (but see also HUNTINGTON 1975 for an analysis of the United States).

An empirical test of some propositions on the effects of parties and party systems has been performed by TAYLOR/HERMAN (1971; cf. also DODD 1974; 1976; and SANDERS/HERMAN 1977) who studied the determinants of the duration of "196 governments which have occurred in all those countries of the world that have experienced competitive elections and uninterrupted parliamentary government in the post-war period . . . up to January

1st, 1969" (ibid., p. 28). Two criteria for evaluating the duration of governments are used: the government must be "headed by the same prime minister" and must rely "on the support of the same party or parties in the Chamber" (ibid., p. 29 citing a definition from BLONDEL 1968:190). Some of their basic results can be summarized as follows: "The proportion of seats held by anti-system parties was the best single indicator of governmental stability. Even more of the variance in stability was explained by the combined linear influence of the size of the anti-system parties and the fractionalization of the government. Further, the fractionalization of the pro-system parties significantly affects stability and, finally, our best explanation of government stability was the combined linear influence of the size of the anti-system parties and the fractionalization of the pro-system parties" (ibid., p. 37; for somewhat different results from India see BRASS 1977).[105]

The duration of government is, of course, not the same as the duration of the system of government. Stability within instability[106] may very well occur, as SIEGFRIED (1956; also quoted in TAYLOR/HERMAN) has pointed out, referring to the Fourth Republic in France. Moreover, a recent study of SULEIMAN (1977) on the self-image of graduates of the Grandes Ecoles leads to the conclusion that the stability in the administrative personnel might have been even more important in explaining the relative stability of the system during the Fourth Republic (the consequence being a rather positive self-image on the part of this administrative elite). Yet, there is

> some systematic evidence that cabinet instability is closely related to the breakdown of European parliamentary democracies in the interwar years, and to the intensity of the crises. Obviously, this is not a cause-and-effect relationship, since government instability is a reflection of the political and social crisis, but we have little doubt that frequent changes in government also contribute to that crisis. . . . Taking the average duration of interwar cabinets before the depression and after it . . . , we see that in only one of the countries in which governments lasted less than nine months on the average did democracy survive, and that was France. On the other hand, within that group of countries, in which governments lasted longer than nine months, only one experienced a regime change. That was Estonia, with its preemptive authoritarianism in which a democratically elected leader broke with democratic legality in a crisis situation. In most of the countries that had stable governments before the depression—the Netherlands, the United Kingdom, Denmark, Sweden, Norway, and Ireland—all of whom had governments with an average duration of one year or more, the post-depression governments were more stable (LINZ 1978:110-11; cf. also VON BEYME 1970; 1971 for some long-term evidence on cabinet instability and a systematization of possible causes).

The study of TAYLOR/HERMAN lends some credit to formal-legal theorizing on the negative impact of party systems with proportional representation on governmental stability. Yet, criteria (e.g., performance) other than mere stability and/or durability of governments must also be considered, rendering the solution of merely introducing a system of majority vote as a sufficient safeguard against instability (HERMENS 1941) too simple.[107] Furthermore, "it is perhaps no accident that when a two-party format is subject to maximal ideological distance and centrifugal competition, it is either destroyed or paves the way to a confrontation that takes the shape of civil war. This was the case in Columbia and perhaps in other Latin American countries" (LINZ 1978:24). WARWICK (1979) has done further research in this vein, studying nine parliamentary democracies (Belgium, the Netherlands, France—excluding the Fifth Republic, the four Scandinavian countries, Germany, and Italy—excluding the fascist period) for the periods 1918-39 and 1945-76. After redefining the dependent variable, cabinet durability, in three important ways,[108] he reports three major results: first, using rather crude dichotomous measures, political cleavages of the socialist/bourgeois, ethnic, and clerical/secular type are important in explaining the durability of coalition governments. Also, but less so, ideological cleavages are an important predictor. "It also means that game theoretical approaches can no longer be allowed to dominate theoretical or empirical work on coalition behavior" (WARWICK 1979:490). However, he, too, found "that majority (winning) coalitions last longer, although this follows from the rules of the game. More important, . . . minimal winning status is a very powerful independent influence on durability [for similar findings for fifteen European states during 1918-72 see DODD 1976:159]: even ideologically diverse coalitions that might be expected to experience internal dissension will last longer if they cannot afford to lose a member-party without losing their majority. Politicians thus appear to be under twin, and by no means compatible, motivations of pursuing their beliefs and pursuing power, and causal approaches that ignore either one of these motivations are likely to prove deficient" (WARWICK 1979:490).

ARIAN/BARNES (1974) try to show in their study of Italy and Israel that it is not only the two-party system (or the multiparty system under conditions of accommodative rule; see note 98) that furthers democratic stability, but the dominant-party system as well. Italy, however, has in recent years clearly shown the long-term costs one might incur under such a party system.

Another group of studies strongly alludes to the importance of historical antecedents in the explanation of present stability and instability (cf. HUNTINGTON 1977:282). The culture-of-violence hypothesis (cf. chapter 5.1.2.8), claiming that strife breeds strife, as well as the approach of BINDER et al. (1971) who stress the likely effects of specific sequences in political development (as do LIPSET/ROKKAN 1967), have been dealt with already. A third group of approaches which may be considered political culture explanations is much more general, if not holistic, in nature.[109] The lack of correspondence between the theoretical terms invoked and the level of measurement in many of these studies has often been noted (cf. ALMOND/ VERBA 1963 who rely on survey data). Using the dialectical formulation that "legitimacy comes late and may be late in leaving," MERELMAN (1966: 552) probably states *the* basic result of these studies.

There are also a number of *sociological* explanations which often overlap[110] with economic explanations (stressing explicative variables such as recessions, unemployment, slow economic growth, etc.).[111] Empirical evidence and theoretical reasoning lead to the prediction that at least the following two sociological explanations will be of major importance in the explanation of political crises. In the first approach the consequences of blocking certain groups from fully participating in politics and/or the economy[112] are stressed. However, it is not the mere fact that ethnic, racial, religious, linguistic, or other cultural groups are discriminated against which accounts for instability. The probability of political instability is heightened if these groups also possess resources to make their discontent known. The same interaction of variables, no access × resources, already proved to be of importance in explaining participation in rioting behavior among American blacks (cf. chapters 5.3.2.3 and 8.4.2). This interaction term should possess even greater predictive power if measured on the elite level, i.e., if counterelites are entirely blocked from gaining leading positions in society yet possess resources for risking an open conflict with the incumbents. "The closer a group is to the central communications channels, the more organized it is, the more it controls significant resources, the more likely is a particular problem to be converted into a political crisis. In this sense, it becomes clear that crises are more likely to start within the governing elite than out of it" (VERBA 1971:302). The same rationale applies if "the status of major conservative groups and symbols is ... threatened" (LIPSET 1960:78). PARETO's (1901) circulation of the elites, due to incompetent elites unable either to coopt counterelites or use strict repressive measures, as well as BRINTON's (1952) desertion of the intellectuals, usually occurring earlier in the process, also must be mentioned in this context (cf. the more detailed discussion in chapter 8.4.2).

In short, empirical evidence (although still awaiting more systematic treatment) and theoretical reasoning clearly recommend a research strategy wherein one differentiates between "ins" and "outs" (sometimes the former "ins") or, more generally, between various subgroups as to the legitimacy of the political community, the political system, the political institutions, the incumbents, and/or their policies. Rather than invoking global crises notions, possibly at the aggregate level, researchers should pay attention to the questions, crises for whom and crises in what respects?

In the other sociological approach of major importance in the explanation of crises phenomena, emphasis is laid on intermediate structures, or, more precisely, on the absence of such structural conditions. We will speak of intermediate structures as the most general concept, treating intermediate institutions (e.g., legal regulations such as voting laws), organizations (e.g., parties), or simply groups as subcases. Unfortunately there is no clear and generally accepted definition of intermediate structures. Usually they are defined according to their function, namely to mediate between individuals and elites. The broader framework for the theory of intermediate structures (if there is such a theory at all) can be found in the theory of the mass society (KORNHAUSER 1959). Briefly, the theory predicts that intermediate structures will prevent the destabilizing conditions of mass society from arising.[113] "If elites are relatively inaccessible to direct intervention by non-elites and/or if non-elites are relatively unavailable for mobilization by elites, then mass movements are less likely than if elites are readily accessible *and* if non-elites are relatively available" (KORNHAUSER 1959:114-15). If people are not sufficiently attached to these intermediate structures, alienation results, which in turn means greater potential for political radicalism (for another line of reasoning cf. WRIGHT 1976 above).

In theory, intermediate structures control and balance each other to neutralize or reduce conflict potentials (cf. the notion of cross-pressures). There are, however, several drawbacks to the theory in its present form. Quite often the conceptualization of intermediate structures is used in the sense of a "pre-stabilized harmony" (see PINARD 1968, 1971 for an empirically grounded major critique; cf. also HALEBSKY 1976).[114] Yet, one must differentiate *between* the impact of *various* intermediate structures and also allow for coalition building among intermediate organizations or groups if a more realistic adaptation of the theory of intermediate structures is to result. Moreover, there are no precise conditions as to when groups/ organizations act or function as intermediate groups/organizations, and when not. Quite frequently the concept of intermediate structures is invoked as a residual explanation. The question of groups, organizations, and institutions being intermediate or not depends, of course, on the subject under study. Thus, although the theory of intermediate structures focuses on a theoretically plausible general notion, nevertheless its present status is rather vague due to insufficient theoretical explication and lack of systematic empirical evidence.[115]

This conclusion does not hold for the more limited theory of cross-cutting (or criss-crossing) cleavages which is related to the theory of intermediate structures. "Multiple and potentially inconsistent affiliations, loyalties, and stimuli reduce the emotion and aggressiveness involved in political choice" (LIPSET 1960:88). Or as put somewhat more precisely with respect to crises: "Severity of crises, therefore, seems to be explained by some combination of salience, multiplicity, and cumulativeness of issues, so that the same political elites and support groups are polarized on one highly salient issue or combination of issues. The key is salience and intensity of antagonism, rather than number of issues. Multiple issues can accentuate polarization or reduce it, depending on their incidence" (ALMOND/MUNDT 1973: 626).

Several variables relevant for determining the amount of cross-cutting have been assembled by DAHL (1967:279-81). To list just a few of these variables, conflict is more likely to be severe if "attitudes of citizens, leaders and activists are divergent," if "lines of cleavages are non-overlapping," and if institutions provide no "agreed processes for negotiating consent and arriving at decisions." There are, however, severe difficulties in empirically determining the degree of cleavages and cross-cutting (for measurement suggestions see RAE/TAYLOR 1970). Whereas cross-cutting cleavages have been success-fully used as explanatory factors in various areas of political research, in research on political violence only strongly inferred measures of cross-cutting cleavages have been employed. What is necessary is information on how much and what kind of cross-cutting is needed among which social groups to make them engage in violent political protest or abstain from it.[116]

Distinguishing between the loyalty, disloyalty, and opposition of large portions of the population to the political system and the loyalty of inter-mediate organizations/groups to the political system,[117] the following typol-ogy of crises situations may be derived (see Table 6.3).

Table 6.3. A Typology of Crises Situations

		Loyalty of Larger Population Segments to the Political System	
		+	−
Loyalty of Organizations/ Groups to the Political System	+	1	2
	−	3	4

+ : condition met
− : condition not met

Neither case 1 nor case 4 should be difficult to analyze. Case 1 would denote a stable political system, whereas case 4 would signify a high potential for political instability within a political community. Case 2 would represent a medium potential for instability. An example can be found in the May 1968 events in France: large portions of the population, especially workers and students, were willing to protest for a short time. Yet, there were no pro-tracted protests, because intermediate organizations such as the Communist Union (CGT) and the Communist Party (CPF) which could have served as transmission belts of the dissenters did not lend their support to a sufficient degree (cf. DUVERGER 1968; GORZ 1970; JOHNSON 1972a; BROWN 1974). Neither did a people's front exist nor did a charismatic oppositional leader emerge who might have generated support from all protesting groups. Thus, the state authorities could easily step in after having ascertained the army's allegiance.

A typical example for case 3 is party crises or crises within particular elite groups possibly leading to a change in the leadership personnel, either by decision-making processes among the elites or by efforts on the part of the population. A number of questions may be derived from Table 6.3. For example, whereas a change from 1 to 4 will be most dramatic, will instability be reached more quickly if the path $1 \to 2 \to 4$ is chosen or the path $1 \to 3 \to 4$? Is a change from 1 to 2 less serious than from 1 to 3, or conversely so? The table may also be read in reverse, i.e., means of gaining stability in a political system. It would be interesting to study under which conditions (variety of conflict partners and their resources, role of the coercive forces, legitimacy of the system in the past, etc.) which kinds of reactions are likely to follow the "inconsistent" cases 2 and 3.

6.4. Concluding Remarks

(1) Combining various theoretical approaches such as those of GURR (1973; 1974a), GURR/McCLELLAND (1971), and the more qualitatively oriented ALMOND et al. (1973) seems promising in crises analysis. In a discussion of approaches to the study of political stability, HURWITZ (1973), too, has argued for a multifaceted approach.[118] Indicators of the forms and extent of political violence, the stability and adaptability of the party system and governments, the legitimacy and efficiency of the political and economic order, authority characteristics, the solutions to conflicts in the past, and various other societal attributes should be incorporated into a multidimensional approach. (2) Time series data or, even better, process data are needed for an adequate analysis of crises conditions. (3) Conventional analyses of aggregated socioeconomic and political variables may provide a *general* description of crises conditions. (4) In addition, data on decisional challenges must be collected. (5) Furthermore, loss of legitimacy can be measured adequately only on the individual level, then aggregated to legitimacy scores of specific subgroups, and perhaps later related to system level data. Having determined the legitimacy scores of various objects among various groups (6), policy processes (cf. also under 4) still remain to be considered. A useful first effort has been taken in the qualitative studies in ALMOND et al. (1973) which analyze the conditions and the impact of coalition formation.

As is true of other chapters in this study, there are policy implications (cf. also chapter 9) to be derived from a comparative study of the determinants and consequences of crises. Before that stage is reached, however, a barometer of crises situations must be developed, a yardstick to enable one to distinguish major crises from smaller ones and allow for better judgement as to which resources should be mobilized. The goal is to achieve what economists have already at least in part attained. Just as they have been able to devise various (at least in theory) efficient instruments, political scientists should be able to develop guidelines as to anticrises strategies. Measuring crises situations according to their scope and intensity[119] (by following the procedures already described in GURR 1973 and ZIMMER-

MANN 1981a) would reduce the danger of circular reasoning inherent in certain crises approaches since many more cases would become available to test the theoretical statements.

It is obvious that a crises science is not free of *Wertbeziehungen* (value relations). "Is political instability something of which the less the better? Or is there a critical or significant level of political instability? Critical for what? How is this critical level of political instability determined? Is it the same for every political system?" (AKE 1974:591). In the short run, it may be necessary to avoid certain crises situations, whereas in the long run the opposite strategy may be more fruitful, leading to a permanent settlement of certain conflict issues and thus creating value consensus and new structural arrangements.[120]

A rather long list of implicit and explicit hypotheses has been presented in the discussion of various approaches to crises phenomena. The fragmentary, prestudy character of many of the approaches listed here and of our discussion as well should have become apparent. It is not that scholars have not reflected upon crises phenomena. What is lacking is systematic, quantitative evidence on the determinants (and the outcomes) of crises phenomena.[121] Hopefully we have pointed out where to look for such evidence. Rather than waiting for "late capitalism," the last hope of an "overloaded" bourgeoisie, to die in a nightmare of crises and turmoil and explaining everything until then by notions of "latent crises," "wrong consciousness," etc., as some neo-Marxists do, we plead for multilevel, cross-national empirical research along the lines suggested here. Of course, if such research is to acquire scientific status, it must take the "historical cure" (ALMOND et al. 1973:22).

A sample of countries with comparable but divergent developments in the twentieth century would comprise countries like Norway, Sweden, Denmark, Belgium, the Netherlands, the United Kingdom, France, Germany, Austria, Italy, Canada, and the United States. *Performance* as the general label for socioeconomic output of a political system might be indexed through data on the level of economic growth, decline in the rate of economic growth, or economic depression; rate of unemployment; degree of social security or welfare level during times of crises; socioeconomic inequality; status of minorities; and forms of relative deprivation. Data on *political violence* have been collected by various scholars. Yet event sequences have rarely been studied. Instead of process data or time-series data, mostly cross-sectional data have been collected (see chapter 5.1 for a discussion of these works). Thus new types of data will have to be collected as well. Survey data on *legitimacy* in most instances have only recently been collected and generally fall short of the standards set by MULLER/JUKAM (1977); nevertheless, they are still of some interest. To estimate the degree of specific and diffuse support for earlier periods, a variety of indirect indicators could be employed, some of which have been mentioned passim, such as protest voting, industrial clashes, nonviolent demonstrations, infringements of the law, as well as indicators like growing dissent in newspapers, the content of mass media,[122] etc. A discussion of the design of such a study and the kinds of indicators one might seek, has been left to other more detailed papers (ZIMMERMANN 1979a; 1981a).

Briefly, the variables of importance for analyzing crises and crises outcomes in democratic industrial societies (from 1900 to about 1979) can be grouped into three categories: (1) determinants of crises, (2) reactions to crises, and (3) consequences for the persistence of the polity. We start from the assumption that political systems must show some economic efficiency if they are to survive. However, economic success in itself is not a necessary but a sufficient condition of survival of the polity. Economic failure, on the other hand, is not a sufficient but a necessary condition for a major crisis endangering the persistence of the political system. One also must look at the political transformation of economic and other demands into the political process, i.e., one must take into consideration the reactive capacity of the party system or the elites altogether. Economic distress hitting large portions of the masses and elite dissent form a necessary and sufficient combination of variables to threaten to bring down the polity. Strongly fractionalized parties and party coalitions engaged in the preservation of the political order in times of crises and faced by less fractionalized challenging forces represent the most unfavorable alternative, if the survival of the political order is at stake. In addition, one must think of dissident forces outside parliament which might unite with the parliamentary opposition to challenge the prevailing political system. Crises can therefore be operationalized as decisional challenges on behalf of large population segments, possibly including elite groups (strategic groups) from outside or from within the governmental apparatus.

More precisely, starting from GURR's (1973) suggestions, we develop a complex interaction term of decisional challenges: *intensity of decisional challenges* × *pervasiveness of decisional challenges* × *political transformability*. This signifies that decisional challenges represent a greater threat to the survival of the incumbent elites and the political order, (1) the more intense the political demands of the challengers are, i.e., the higher the level addressed and the more radical the demands; (2) the more widespread these challenges are, i.e., among anti-elites within and outside the state apparatus and among the population at large; and (3) the more means challengers possess to enter the arena of politics, i.e., parliament, with their demands. Thus, as already noted, a strong and little fractionalized opposition party or coalition attacking the system and fighting against fractionalized and weak incumbent parties defending the system represents the strongest means of transforming radical decisional challenges into a threat to incumbent political elites and the system. Decisional challenges that load high on only one or two of these dimensions a priori have a much lower probability of success than those with high scores on all three dimensions. The third dimension is of particular importance here.[123] As pointed out by PIVEN in her article on the "social structuring of protest" in the United States: "The main point, however, is simply that the political impact of institutional disruptions depends upon electoral conditions. Even serious disruptions such as industrial strikes will force concessions only when the calculus of electoral instability favors the protesters" (PIVEN 1976:322).

Provided that data can be collected along these lines, we believe that the prospects for empirical cross-national crises research will be good. With respect to reactions to crises, we have in mind variables referring to the cooptation of counterelites, forms of grand coalitions, budgetary changes, degree of support on behalf of intermediate organizations, repressive measures, etc. Measures of the ultimate dependent variable, persistence, could be constructed by starting from the coding suggestions of GURR (1974a).

However, there is another problem involved here, namely, how to define the ultimate dependent variable, persistence, and how to delineate it from reactions of the incumbent elites. In theory, persistence is enhanced, the more flexible the reactions of the incumbents are. Thus, these two theoretical variables are often dependent on each other. Since persistence in part depends on the reactions to crises, there may be only limited variation in these variables; this could endanger causal analysis. However, there are situations where incumbents react to decisional challenges as in Weimar Germany, but their policies fail and the system collapses in the end. LINZ's argument clearly shows the need to distinguish between crises reactions (efforts at reequilibration) and the persistence or failure of the polity as the ultimate dependent variable: "Reequilibration can be the outcome of near-breakdown in a democratic regime. Unfortunately, few of the crises of democracy have been studied from this perspective. In fact, it could be argued that several of the democracies that ultimately failed had overcome *previous* crises, and that scholars should therefore place more emphasis on the positive aspects of the way those crises were surmounted" (LINZ 1978:86; emphasis added).

In the present context it seemed important to reflect on basic theoretical relationships touched upon in the literature but never brought together in a coherent model as suggested here (especially in Figure 6.2). Persistence of political systems thus might be interpreted as the mastering of crises, as a failure due to the impact of crises, or perhaps, in some cases, as the postponing of crises. Statements on the *relative* impact of those variables combined in model 1 (or of others which might have been left out) will have to be derived from detailed empirical work. Perhaps some of the theoretical specifications, some of the paths predicted, will prove incorrect. If countries other than advanced industrial countries are selected for study, one almost certainly will have to reckon with other combinations of variables than that specified here. There is no reason to expect the paths outlined to be of equal importance. Is legitimacy indeed so relevant or is it only of secondary importance, i.e., will repression have a stronger impact, as we have in *general* predicted? What about more legitimate political systems with a long tradition of authority? How do coefficients change in these instances? Any appropriate analysis of crises will have to be based on cross-level analysis and also on process data. This may be illustrated with what is here the most important variable, legitimacy. Some groups might immediately claim that the political order is illegitimate. If the system legitimacy indeed decreases, other groups might be affected and a vicious circle might be formed. A good example can be found in the fears of segments of the middle class toward the end of the Weimar Republic, when the republic as a political order had lost any legitimacy in the minds of various groups, and this in turn had a strong contagious influence on large portions of the middle class.

In cross-national crises research there are many important questions[124] to be answered in order to uncover the causes and consequences of crises phenomena. Here we have only dealt with some basic variables that seem to provide a framework in which to deal with crises research. With scholars everywhere now talking about the ungovernability of our world (cf. CROZIER et al. 1975), social scientists should not join this choir of elated singers, but rather sit down, turn to historical factors shaping the development of societies in the twentieth century, and try to determine some of the causes of variability in crises and crises outcomes. LINZ and his coworkers (see LINZ/STEPAN 1978) have contributed significantly to the development of a cross-national crisis science. LINZ's work (1978), in particular, combines numerous analytical statements with rich historical insight. What is needed now is settling on a few key variables and gathering the necessary data on a systematic cross-national basis. In a way LINZ has done for the study of crisis and breakdown of democratic regimes what HUNTINGTON (1968; see chapter 7) has achieved for the analysis of "political order in changing societies" (i.e., Third World countries): to develop a basic set of theoretical arguments that may guide future research in a fruitful direction.

Many of the theoretical notions discussed in this chapter will be implicitly present in the following two chapters, both of which center on specific outcomes of the political process. There is much overlapping—in theory as well as empirical substance—of crises phenomena, coups, and revolutions. Coups are nevertheless, only a special kind of crisis and sometimes they occur even without major crises symptoms.

Chapter 7

Military Coups d'État in Cross-national Perspective [1]

Studies on coups are legion. Here we will be concerned mainly with some of the more recent, quantitative cross-national analyses of the determinants of coups d'état. More precisely, it is the military coups d'état (mostly after World War II) with which we are almost exclusively dealing here. The concept of military coup d'état is narrower than that of military intervention which may be defined as "the armed forces' constrained substitution of their own policies and/or their persons, for those of the recognized civilian authorities" (FINER 1962:23).[2] Coups are a subject of study which has attracted scholars for a variety of reasons. One reason is that coups occur frequently. For instance, 274 military coups[3] in 59 states between 1946 and 1970 have been listed in one comprehensive study on coups (coups being defined as "the removal or the attempted removal of a state's chief executive by the regular armed forces through the use or the threat of force," THOMPSON 1973:6).[4] Another study reports that "a coup or attempted coup occurred once every 4 months in Latin America (from 1945 to 1972), once every 7 months in Asia (1947 to 1972), once every 3 months in the Middle East (1949 to 1972), and once every 55 days in Africa (1960 to 1972)" (BERTSCH et al. 1978:431).

Among those countries not included in Table 7.1 which have experienced coups or coup attempts during the 1970s are Afghanistan, Angola, Bangladesh, Benin, Ceylon, Chad, Chile, Comoro Islands, Cyprus, Ivory Coast, Kenya, Lesotho, Liberia (again in April 1980), Madagascar, Malagasy Republic, Malaysia, Mauretania, Morocco, Mozambique, Niger, Oman, Qatar, the Philippines, Rwanda, Saudi Arabia, the Seychelles, Swaziland, Tanzania, and Uruguay (as well as Surinam early in 1980).

We have rearranged THOMPSON's data and compared them with data on coups reported by JANOWITZ (1977:51-56; period: 1945-75, excluding Europe) and FINER (1976:269-73; period: 1958-73; including Europe). JANOWITZ only lists coups that have been successful, whereas FINER includes unsuccessful coups as well. Thus, not only differences in the data sources used,[5] but also different definitions,[6] and different periods of observation have affected Table 7.2.

The most detailed coding procedures seem to have been followed by THOMPSON. He distinguishes between successful coups, aborted coups, and compromise coups.

Table 7.1. A Summary of Military-Coup Frequency (1946–70)

Coup Frequency	Number of States	States
1	17	Cambodia, Costa Rica, Equatorial Guinea, Ethiopia, Gabon, Iran, Jordan, Lebanon, Libya, Mali, Nepal, Nicaragua, Oman, Senegal, South Yemen, Uganda, Upper Volta
2	9	Burma, Central African Republic, Egypt, France, Ghana, Greece, Somalia, South Korea, Togo
3	7	Burundi, Zaire, Cuba, Pakistan, Portugal, Sierra Leone, Turkey
4	3	Colombia, El Salvador, Nigeria
5	6	Algeria, Congo (Brazzaville), Dahomey, Indonesia, Panama, Yemen
6	2	Dominican Republic, Honduras
7	2	Haiti, Sudan
8	2	Paraguay, Thailand
9	5	Brazil, Guatemala, Laos, Peru, South Vietman
11	1	Iraq
12	1	Ecuador
14	1	Syria
16	1	Argentina
18	2	Bolivia, Venezuela

Source: THOMPSON (1973:7)

The post-coup ruling arrangement must also survive for at least a week (n=124 [45.3%]). Unsuccessful coups must involve a recorded and recognizable physical attempt to seize control (n=131 [47.8%]). Without this criterion, it would be impossible to differentiate failures from plots that were crushed, never executed, or manufactured by the regime. Compromise coups may come about in two ways: (1) a chief executive may be removed successfully but resistance to the coup group (as distinguished from [insufficient] defense of the target incumbent) is sufficiently strong to dictate a post-coup ruling arrangement other than that originally envisioned by the coup makers; or, (2) both attacking and defending forces may lack sufficient strength to decide the immediate contest and some interim solution is accepted usually until one or the other gains the upper hand at a later date (n=19 [7.0%])" (THOMPSON 1973:53).

FINER reports a much lower failure rate, namely that 39 (30%) of his 130 coups were unsuccessful, whereas the failure rate given by KENNEDY (1974: 337–44; period: 1945–72) is closer to that in THOMPSON's study (136 coups, or 47.9%, out of 284 coups are said to have failed).[7] In regional terms, however, a number of differences emerge between the tabulations of KENNEDY and the data provided by THOMPSON. The former reports

Table 7.2. Regional Patterns in the Occurrence of Military Coups d'État

	FINER 1976 (period 1958-73)			JANOWITZ 1977 (period 1945-75)			THOMPSON 1973 (period 1946-70)		
	Coups (N)	Countries (N)	Percentage	Coups (N)	Countries (N)	Percentage	Coups (N)	Countries (N)	Percentage
Latin America	31	13	23.8	59	18	46.1	136	17	49.6
Sub-Sahara	38	14	29.2	32	17	25.0	38	17	13.9
Arabian countries	40	11	30.8	27	10	21.1	53	13	19.3
Asia	14	9	10.8	10	7	7.8	40	9	14.6
Europe	7	4	5.4	not reported			7	3	2.6
Total	130	51	100.0	128	52	100.0	274	59	100.0

Note the differences in definition underlying this table. See the text for a discussion.

absolutely and relatively more coup attempts in Arab countries (83 or 29.2%) and in sub-Saharan countries (78 or 27.5%), about the same figure for Asian countries (42 or 14.8%), but apparently misses a number of coup attempts in Latin America (81 or 28.5%).[8] KENNEDY relies on "books, articles, newspapers, and notes" (KENNEDY 1974:337) as sources. FINER draws on the *Annual Register*, the *Encyclopaedia Britannica*, the *Encyclopedia Illustrada Universel*, the *Middle East, 1961*, *Keesing's Contemporary Archives*, the *Statesman's Year Book*, and periodicals like the *Daily Telegraph*, the *Economist*, the *New York Times*, *Time Magazine*, the *Times*, and the *World Today*. THOMPSON uses "171 political histories and country/case studies, eight regional and nonregional news summaries, and the *New York Times* and the *Times* (London)" (THOMPSON 1976:274). JANOWITZ (1977:51-58) presents the most extended list of coups so far, even though he includes only successful attempts.[9] Despite some variations from study to study, his conclusions nevertheless seem to underscore the general trend:

> We have documented, in our sample of seventy-eight nation-states, 128 successful coups for the three decades since the end of World War II, that is, from 1945 to 1975. In statistical terms, this would mean slightly more than 1.5 coups per nation-state. However, the frequency is not equally distributed. There are twenty-two developing nations that did not experience a successful military coup between 1945 and 1975. (Since 1975 successful coups have occurred in some of these nations.) On the other hand, four countries, in different regions, account for [29] of the successful military coups, or [22.7] percent of the total number. (The coup-prone nations are Syria, 11; Bolivia, 7; Dahomey, 6; and Haiti, 5. These nations tend to be small; examining the largest fifteen, we find greater stability.) By region, Central and South America have had the highest frequency of successful military coups. The rank order of the other regions, roughly speaking, would be Sub-Sahara Africa, the Middle East, and Asia, if one takes into account the number of nations and the population base (JANOWITZ 1977:51-52; my recalculation).

In short, in the four regions mentioned "the coup is a more widespread way of changing governments than elections" (FINER, introduction to LUTT-WAK (1969:9). Leaving out India as an outlying case, it might even be said that at present more people live under governments which acquired power through coups than under regularly elected governments. "Of the entire range of 112 Third World Nations, only a comparative handful (Mexico, Venezuela, Sri Lanka, Tanzania, Kenya, and Tunisia) can be said to have faced successfully the challenges of governing a large, rapidly developing country under a more or less open and constitutional process and, at the same time, have managed to avoid giving the military a reason and an opportunity to intervene" (BERTSCH et al. 1978:434). THOMPSON (1972:5) shows that the cumulative proportion of independent states that have experienced military coups increased linearly from 21% in 1950 to 45% in 1970, comprising then 27% of the world's population.

A second reason for the extensive scholarly research on coups is that, compared to other topics in the field of macropolitical analysis (i.e., revolutionary attacks, protest, turmoil), coups are relatively homogeneous phenomena; this facilitates the performance of cross-national multivariate analyses. Coups may occur outside the military or, much more frequently, within the military (80% of all coups during 1951–1970, McKINLAY/COHAN 1974:2). They may or may not involve the use of violence.[10] "If violence is categorized in terms of none, incidental, substantial, extensive (i.e., civil war), the relative incidence of coups falling under these categories is 63, 18, 13, and 6 percent. Thus, some 80 percent of coups represent largely non-violent means of governmental change" (ibid.).[11] Whereas in chapter 5.1.1.1.2.3 and chapter 5.3.2, we have analyzed violent mass protests, in this chapter the subject is elite protest behavior.[12] In the following chapters on revolutions, the determinants of *both* mass and elite protests will be ascertained. Coups, as a form of elite protest behavior, must be distinguished clearly from revolutionary phenomena, a requirement many researchers have not complied with in their empirical studies (cf. the critique in chapter 8.4.6). Considered from a dynamic point of view, however, the different types of violent protest behavior may be related to each other. What begins as a coup may end in a revolutionary overthrow of the societal order.

7.1. Definitions and Typologies

Some of the relevant criteria of coups are listed in HUNTINGTON's definition (cf. also REJAI 1973:18; MORRISON/STEVENSON 1971: 351).

> The distinguishing characteristics of the coup d'état as a political technique are that: (a) it is the effort by a political coalition illegally to replace the existing governmental leaders by violence or the threat of violence; (b) the violence employed is usually small; (c) the number of people involved is small; (d) the participants already possess institutional bases of power within the political system. Clearly a coup can succeed only (a) if the total number of participants in the political system is small, or (b) if the number of participants is large and a substantial proportion of them endorse the coup [the latter condition is rarely met][13] (HUNTINGTON 1968:218).

Some further definitional criteria of coups,[14] namely suddenness and decisiveness, are found in the definition proposed by RAPOPORT: "The coup d'état is an unexpected, sudden, decisive, potentially violent, illegal act, dangerous for plotter as well as for intended victim, and needing great skill for execution. Its professed purpose is to alter state policies" (RAPOPORT 1966:60; italics omitted).

In most states of the world, the army represents the social body with the greatest potential of violence. Therefore it is not surprising that the army will become an important actor in situations "in which violence is the ultimate determinant, even if it is not used" (FIRST 1970:19). Or, as HOBBES put it: clubs become trump when no rule of trump is established. However, violence is not a necessary ingredient of coups. The most important characteristics of coups are that they take place rapidly and that only elite personnel are involved in the central planning agencies (for some qualifications cf. below).[15] Other things being equal, the more violence occurs in a coup, the more costs are incurred by the new power-holders (cf. also the general discussion as to interrelations of concepts like authority, power, force, violence, and others in chapter 2.3), but these costs do not necessarily seem to affect the duration of new military regimes (cf. note 11 for some results).

The military is not only the most powerful administrator or agent of violence; in many underdeveloped and transitional societies of the world it is also "the most modern institution[16] in terms of its advanced technology, educated elite, absorption of rational norms, division of labor, and exposure to western influence"[17] (BIENEN 1968a:xv; cf. also PAUKER 1959; J. JOHNSON 1962:76; 1964a; SHILS 1962; PYE 1961; HALPERN 1963; JANOWITZ 1964:42ff.; LISSAK 1967; 1973; DAALDER 1969:12-20; LEFEVER 1970). LEVY (1966:597) thus feels compelled to speak of "the universal presence of armed force organizations" in societies undergoing modernization. However, the existence of military forces should not automatically be associated with these characteristics. McWILLIAMS (1967a:19), for one, stresses the point (though he does not provide data) that the military exhibits the said characteristics only if it is confronted with external threats (cf. also HOPKINS 1966:172).[18]

One must be aware of the pitfall of generalizing when speaking of the modern qualities of the military: "The body of evidence weighs heavily in the direction of African armies which are neither 'complex structures,' nor national, westernized, or modern" (DECALO 1973:116; 1976). Systematic empirical evidence leads rather to reservations as to the performance of "these new armies in preindustrial societies [armies which are said to be] modeled after industrial-based organizations" (PYE 1962:75). Looking at all Latin American regimes from 1950 to 1967, SCHMITTER draws this conclusion: "How much Latin American countries invest, industrialize, increase their GNP, raise their cost of living, increase their school enrollment and/ or engage in foreign trade seems more the product of environmental or ecological factors than the willful acts of politicians grouped according to their competitiveness or civilian/military status" (SCHMITTER 1971:492). McKINLAY/COHAN (1974:12-13; 1975) also fail to find evidence (N=115 noncommunist countries; period: 1951-70) for the military being "significantly" better performers with respect to growth rates of exports and GNP. There is, however, one exception, the GNP growth rates in countries at the lowest level of economic development. In terms of expanding primary education, military regimes even lag behind civil-military regimes (yet, there is no such relationship after area and GNP controls have been introduced).[19] In Latin America, however, "there is some evidence to indicate that . . . military regimes perform somewhat better than the civilian regimes" (McKINLAY/

COHAN 1975:21), for "in both Central and South America, military regimes have better aggregate performance rates than the civil regimes [cf. also SCHMITTER 1971:441; but cf. also the mixed evidence in DICKSON 1977]. In Central America, the military regimes have much higher GNP and primary education growth rates" (McKINLAY/COHAN 1975:20). Results differing from these are reported in JACKMAN (1976; cf. also the more extensive discussion in chapter 7.2.3).

These results by and large call into question FINER's (1962:242) summary statement that "by any world standards military régimes have shown less than average capacity for statesmanship or economics."[20]

More recent analyses of McKINLAY/COHAN lead to a number of interesting findings, some of which seem to be at variance with their earlier results. They compare military regimes with several kinds of nonmilitary regimes and summarize their evidence as follows:

> The two types of system are clearly different from one another in what might be termed a political dimension and, to a lesser degree, they differ in terms of their international trading position, but they cannot be differentiated from one another by military, background economic, or economic performance criteria. Thus, systems which have experienced military regimes are not restricted to the weaker economic systems of the world once the small group of high income systems are removed. Their economic performance rates compare favorably with nonmilitary regime systems and, despite military rule, they do not, in general, have larger armed forces or greater military expenditure. While military regime systems do not have as firm a commitment to international trade, they are most clearly distinct from nonmilitary regime systems only in their lower levels of political activity and higher levels of political change (McKINLAY/COHAN 1976b:863).

In general, these results also hold after GNP and area have been controlled for, although some interesting differentiations emerge.

> African military regime systems have weaker background and international trade positions and do not perform as well as the equivalent nonmilitary regime systems.[21] Asian military regime systems have weaker background and international trade positions, but perform as well as the low-income nonmilitary regime systems. Latin American military regime systems are marginally weaker on background factors, have similar international trade positions, but perform slightly better than the nonmilitary systems.[22] Both types of system in the Middle East and North Africa are generally similar across all three categories of economic variables (ibid., p. 862).

The sample in this study comprises 101 political systems, of which only 37 are military regimes,[23] rendering the more detailed tabulations somewhat risky. For reasons of third factor control wealthier nations are excluded from the analysis. Furthermore, the period under study is limited to 1961-70. Thus, one may not be surprised to discover that results reported in McKINLAY/COHAN (1976a), referring again to the longer period (1951-70), lead to slightly different conclusions: "Military regimes are not associated with countries that have either lower levels of economic development or lower economic performance rates. Further, military regimes are more likely to be associated with an improvement rather than a deterioration in economic performance, through this association is not sufficiently strong to support the image of the military as a major force for economic development" (McKINLAY/COHAN 1976a:310).[24]

In short, results reported are not entirely consistent for different samples and periods. These inconsistencies notwithstanding, the general evidence as to the performance of military regimes vs. nonmilitary regimes is still summarized adequately in the following quotation:

> It would appear in general that the main parameters of absolute economic performance are set by existing levels of development and previous levels of economic performance. The form of the coup and the subsequent structure of the military regime do not have a major impact on performance. Whenever any evidence of some influence does appear, it generally indicates an association between *civilianization* and higher performance levels. However, the relationship between current and past performance is not wholly deterministic so that it is possible to examine the relative performance of military regimes *vis-à-vis* their predecessor civilian regimes. While the evidence indicates that military regimes are more likely to perform better than their preceding civilian regimes, this finding is not universally true. Unfortunately there is little about the form of the coup or the structure of the military regime that can explain the variation in the levels of relative performance (McKINLAY/COHAN 1976a: 309-10).

All these results and warnings notwithstanding, there is some truth in the statement that "the soldier is constantly called upon to look abroad[25] and to compare his organization with foreign ones. He thus has a greater awareness of international standards and a greater sensitivity to weaknesses in his own society" (PYE 1966:178). Yet, goals and outcomes of coups must be distinguished from each other. While the military usually refers to national glory, unification, redress of grievances, and socioeconomic development (or even austerity in the short run) when giving a public rationale for a coup,[26] the long-term outcome may be and often is clearly different. "Of the 229 coups of the 1946-70 period for which sufficient information was available, only 19, or 8 percent, were considered to be strikingly reformist in the sense that coup-makers were acting primarily to correct socioeconomic injustices and abuses of the political system" (PALMER/THOMPSON 1978:143).

"Furthermore, six of the nineteen were not even successful" (THOMPSON 1972:111).

Implicitly in the above discussion, the military has been linked to other political and social forces. Yet, rather than dealing with the numerous typologies of coups and civil-military relationships[27] that have been suggested in the literature (see GERMANI/SILVERT 1961; McALISTER 1961; FINER 1962:164-204; HUNTINGTON 1962a:23-24; JANOWITZ 1964:10-11; 1975:169 ff.; RONNEBERGER 1965; PETTEE 1966:15-16; PERLMUTTER 1969; 1974:132-38; 1977:16 and passim; LUCKHAM 1971; McKINLAY/ COHAN 1974:4; COCHRAN 1974; HAGOPIAN 1974:3-9; WELCH/SMITH 1974; BRIER/CALVERT 1975; TANNAHILL 1975; DECALO 1976: 249-54; BÜTTNER et al. 1976:90-91, 469-75; KIM/KIHL 1978, and FINER 1970:548-68 for one of the most elaborated typologies comprising many of the aspects to be discussed below), we are concerned here with hypotheses linking characteristics of the military, as well as economic, social, political, cultural, and other conditions, to the occurrence of coups d'état. Various types of coups will thus emerge as we proceed in evaluating the evidence bearing on the hypotheses suggested.

One possible objection to the numerous typologies of civil-military relationships found in the literature is that formal rule may considerably differ from actual rule. The so-called "other face of power" (BACHRACH/ BARATZ 1962; 1963) may seriously distort analyses which rely on formal definitions of authority relations. "Indeed when a government is influenced by the military, without its actual physical intervention, it may be the case that the military exercises even more power than it does where observable 'military intervention' exists" (O'KANE 1971:1-2).[28] In most of the societies lacking clearly established procedures for civilian rule, the army must be considered as the most important veto power. Even in communist nations which are under rigid control of the dominant communist party, the army may at times play a significant role, either by refusing consent to a designated future leader or by insisting on reshuffling government personnel to attain greater compliance with the military's demands (cf. also ALBRIGHT 1980 on the conditions of the relations between military and civil government in communist states). Since these political processes are extremely difficult to measure, researchers interested in the determinants of coups d'état or military intervention usually have left communist regimes out of their analyses. There is another justification for this procedure since coups or military interventions seem to be rarer phenomena in communist regimes than in authoritarian or personalist regimes. Usually "communist politicians have turned towards military activities (as in China, Vietnam, Yugoslavia, and in post-revolutionary Russia) rather than military leaders toward communism" (DAALDER 1969:11). Furthermore, control of the military through political officers or the secret police seems to be much tighter in communist regimes (see KOLKOWICZ 1967) than in other types of regimes (for a partial critique of the position taken by KOLKOWICZ see ODOM 1978; cf. also HERSPRING 1978 and COLTON 1979 who presents evidence that the relationship between army and party is much less conflict-prone than suggested by KOLKO-

WICZ). Among the rare instances of military coup conspiracies in communist countries are those in North Korea (1956), Albania (1961), and Bulgaria (1965). All of them failed.

7.2. Explaining Military Coups d'État

There are a vast number of hypotheses proposed for explaining military coups. Unfortunately, many of these determinants overlap with other determinants referred to in later chapters. We shall discuss each of them in light of the empirical evidence presented thus far. No claims as to comprehensiveness are being made. There is always the danger of spurious relationships or spurious noncorrelations among the various bivariate results reported. Some of these spurious results (or more appropriately, spurious inferences; cf. note 24 in chapter 5) will become apparent in the few multivariate analyses performed thus far.

Earlier approaches to the study of coups have focused on characteristics of the military as an explanatory factor. These conditions were said to "push" the military into politics. Later explanations stressed "pull" conditions, i.e., conditions lying outside of the direct sphere of the military, such as economic, sociostructural, or political factors. As will become apparent, the only way around this "hen-and-egg" type dichotomy lies in truly relational analyses linking military *and* other conditions for explaining coups.

7.2.1. Characteristics of the Military as Determinants for the Occurrence of Coups d'État

Military forces are said to "possess five characteristics not found in combination to anything like the same degree elsewhere: a highly centralized command, strict hierarchy, formidable discipline, extensive intercommunication and an *esprit de corps*. In addition, they have a symbolic character: they represent the guardian and custodian of the state against its external enemies; and with this goes an atavistic popular sentiment for the so-called military virtues of self-sacrifice, austerity, self-discipline, valour and the like. And finally, in all but a very few cases, they have a near monopoly of arms and a monopoly of heavy weaponry" (FINER 1970:542), or, in short, "a marked superiority in organization, a highly emotionalized symbolic status,[29] and a monopoly of arms" (FINER 1962:6). There are two basic classes of variables to be dealt with here: objective characteristics of the military and grievances of the military which may, but need not, be related to these objective characteristics.[30]

MILITARY GRIEVANCES

Using numerous data sources (world news digests, regional news digests, the *London Times*, and the *New York Times* as well as studies of specific

countries and cases) and covering the period from 1946 to 1970, THOMP-
SON (1973) found some evidence of various military grievances being related
to the occurrence of coups.[31] It should be noted, however, that there is
considerable overlapping of different classes of military grievances.

> The *corporate* dimension encompasses *positional resource*[32] con-
> flicts arising within the context of military organizational claims to
> support, privilege, and boundary maintenance. Ninety-nine coups
> involved this first issue dimension. The second dimension, the *not-
> so-corporate*, encompasses the *positional/resource* conflicts arising
> within the context of *suborganizational (individual/factional/
> sectional)* claims and subsumes an important subelement: the
> generalized forms of political warfare exhibited by personnel adjust-
> ments. Approximately three of every four coups entailed some
> form of this second dimension. However, while these dimensions are
> separable for the purposes of an analytical inventory, in an increas-
> ing number of cases, the two general categories overlap in complex
> and *interdependent grievance packages* (THOMPSON 1973:46;
> emphasis added).

In terms of regional breakdowns, "Arab coup-makers have been twice as
likely to reflect corporate interests as their Latin American counterparts.[33]
Yet, if one examines the change in dimensional mix over time, a slightly
different picture emerges. The not-so-corporate element has made relative
'gains' in both Latin America and in the Arab world, while the opposite
trend is clearly demonstrated by Asian coups" (ibid., p. 49). Unfortunately,
there is no theoretical explanation of such trends, except for the circular
statement that "one would expect the corporate factors to become distinc-
tively more common in situations where military corporate interests are in
the process of being consolidated" (THOMPSON 1973:49). While the "not-
so-corporate motivations virtually are inevitable to coup politics and are not
likely to wither away as long as coups continue" (ibid., p. 49), they are less
likely to lead to successful coups than corporate grievances, since the latter
are "more potent and thus, in this respect, more salient to the military coup
process. That corporate grievances are more potent is additionally supported
and partially explained by the fact that the coups in question are more likely
to be planned at the highest military levels and to encounter less military
resistance" (ibid., p. 50). These results notwithstanding, there is reason (and
some empirical evidence to be discussed later, cf. chapter 7.2.3) to believe
that grievances of the military are only important *ingredients* to rising discontent preceding a coup. Other conditions must be met as well, "regime
vulnerability" (ibid., p. 50) being probably the most important one here.
THOMPSON himself stresses the fact that his analyses are rather crude, lacking the precision of quantitative analyses. Furthermore, apart from area, no
control factors have been introduced.

In a recent article THOMPSON (1980) distinguishes between coups aimed
at the overthrow of civil governments and those aimed at military govern-

ments. Two hundred and twenty-nine coups with roots in corporate griev-ances of the military are studied for 1946–70. With the exception of Asia where coups of this category are more frequently directed against civil regimes, there are no distinctive results when this differentiation of the dependent variable (see also the theoretical discussion in chapter 7.3) is employed. Thus, NORDLINGER's (1977:78) contention that civil regimes are more frequently the victims of this type of coup is not corroborated.

One additional result of THOMPSON's many findings deserves to be mentioned here. Interestingly, defense allocations or fluctuations are of minor relevance in the occurrence of coups. The evidence, on the contrary, is "that years in which military coups occurred were more likely to coincide with years in which relative defense expenditures increased, not decreased" (THOMPSON 1973:20). Yet, at least three caveats should be brought forward against directly relating this finding to the original hypothesis. The number of cases studied is limited; defense allocations may be determined by some other, possibly international, factor and thus not be subject to much fluctua-tion; and "there is always the good possibility that a threat to severely reduce defense spendings would provoke remedial action prior to any actual reduc-tion" (ibid., p. 22).

SIZE OF THE MILITARY

Another variable said to be causal for the occurrence of coups is the size, absolute or relative, of the military. Interestingly, FEIT (1973) postulates that smaller armies would show a greater proclivity for intervention due to their better communication facilities, their better established corporate identity, and their availability to participate in internal politics (smaller armies may be less inclined to get involved in foreign politics).[34] Systematic cross-national tests (N=88 nations; period 1960s) by SIGELMAN (1975), however, lead to the conclusion that there is no negative relationship between absolute or relative size of the military and military intervention (cf. SIGEL-MAN 1974 for operationalizations) as predicted by FEIT on the base of his six case studies. Instead, positive, albeit generally small, relationships exist between the two variables. Similar results are also found after area controls have been introduced. BIENEN reports that no correlation can be established between coup propensity in Africa and the size of the army, the defense budget, or the source, character, or amount of external military aid (BIENEN 1969). STEPAN (1971) also failed to find a relationship between the size of the military and military intervention. The measures used were taken from PUTNAM (1967) and slightly modified by STEPAN (period: 1951-65).[35]

JANOWITZ, on the other hand, contends that the size and sophistication of the military establishment are positively[36] related to the propensity for intervention in politics (JANOWITZ 1964:40ff.), a hypothesis indirectly supported by PUTNAM (1967:100) who finds a correlation of r=.55 between defense expenditures as a percentage of GNP[37] and military intervention (N=20 Latin American countries during 1956-65).[38] PUTNAM, however, claims this to be "circular" causation (which may be avoided if lagged relationships are considered). Or, in the words of HIBBS, "A military establishment which has intervened in the past is very likely to have secured for itself a generous share of social resources, and civilian political elites anxious to avoid antagonizing the 'colonels' are unlikely to diminish the share substantially. Conversely, a well-financed or privileged military has a great deal at stake in political life, and this makes future intervention more probable" (HIBBS 1973:107). Lagging size (defense expenditures as a percentage of general government expenditures, 1960), HIBBS found a positive relationship with coups (1958-67; N=108 countries) that also stands out as significant in multivariate analyses (cf. Figure 5.4 in chapter 5.1.1.3). HIBBS's hypotheses appear confirmed in a study on Latin American countries during 1950-67 carried out by SCHMITTER. Performing various cross-sectional and longitudinal analyses, SCHMITTER found that the "military in power definitely tend to spend more on themselves—on defense spending—above all, when they are on-again, off-again rulers"[39] (SCHMITTER 1971:493). In a later study SCHMITTER (1973a:131) comes up with a slightly negative relationship between cumulative domestic military spending and military intervention (using PUTNAM's index) during 1945-61, and a positive relationship (r=.245) for 1962-70. Yet, he also notes that Gross Domestic Product (GDP), rather than external military aid or military rule, is the strongest correlate of domestic military spending (1960).[40] WEAVER (1973:96-97), however, criticizes the construction of the military intervention index by PUTNAM (1967) who averages out the year-by-year differences. In his own time series analysis of six Latin American countries (Argentina, Brazil, Chile, Columbia, Peru, Venezuela) during 1960-70, WEAVER found no clear-cut increases of military appropriations as percent of GDP after military take-over.

The evidence, then, is somewhat mixed. Furthermore, rather crude measures have been used for testing relationships between the size of the military and military intervention: "Even if we discuss merely the numbers of military men, it is extremely important to disaggregate this figure and examine such questions as the dispersion of the military, which units are strategically located in terms of internal political power, which units are best equipped and therefore have a comparative advantage over other units, and what is the command and control relationship between different units" (STEPAN 1971:26).

Pointing to the small numbers of soldiers required to seize power in a military coup d'état (cf. chapter 7.2.4 for some examples), FINER dismisses altogether the efforts to link the size of the military to the occurrence of coups. "The size of the armed forces is of major importance in deciding whether it can police a country and how it can govern, *after* it has taken over" (FINER 1976:225). Evidence from a number of studies seems to bear out FINER's point of view. In a study of African countries, DOLIAN (1973, as quoted in WELCH 1976:26) found a rise in military spending after the military had taken over. In his multivariate analysis of the determinants of military coups (cf. chapter 7.3), WAYMAN (1975) also dismisses size as a major explanatory variable. SOLAUN/QUINN (1973:100; cf. also ATKINS

1974:235) report equivocal results for Latin American countries if the size of the military budget is related to their dependent variable. SMALDONE (1974:212) finds little relationship between either the size of the army or the military budget and the occurrence of coups in sub-Saharan Africa from 1965 onwards.[41] Comparable results are reported by McKINLAY/COHAN (1976b: 856). Furthermore, from their study of 101 countries during 1961-70, the hypothesis must also be ruled out that "military size and expenditure tend to be higher in nonmilitary regime systems because civilian governments wish to inhibit the initiation of military coups through favorable allocations to the armed forces, thus giving higher mean values to the nonmilitary regime systems" (ibid.). There is, however, one exception, namely that military regime systems with low GNP levels "have higher expenditure and higher levels of diversification than low income nonmilitary regime systems. But this higher rate of expenditure must be qualified by the lower rates of growth of expenditure in the military regime system" (ibid.). It should be noted that we have interchangingly used data on military manpower and military budget allocation. Even though there are some variations if either indicator is employed, most of the evidence leads to the conclusion that neither of these indicators seems to be strongly related—at least not on a bivariate basis—to the dependent variable. Following JANOWITZ (1977), an interesting new development deserves attention, namely the development of paramilitary forces (cf. also ZURCHER/HARRIES-JENKINS 1978) defined as "essentially including the different types of national police forces and those militia personnel who have internal security functions" (JANOWITZ 1977:29). JANOWITZ attributes the relatively greater stability of many a military regime after 1965 to the rapid build-up of these forces (among other factors). Yet, what may hold in a variety of cases may not necessarily lead to a strong relationship on a wide empirical basis. (There are no correlational results of this sort reported in JANOWITZ 1977). In any case, evidence will probably be more in line with FINER's sceptical remark referred to above than with relating either a small or a large military force to the occurrence of coups. Size in itself is nothing more than a formal indicator which needs to be supplemented by substantial explanations. The recent exchange between THOMPSON (1978a; 1978b) and SIGELMAN (1978) also leads to the conclusion that "military size, albeit an intuitively appealing indicator of organizational strength, does not appear to be a particularly potent 'circumstance'" of military coup behavior (THOMPSON 1978a:98).

PROFESSIONALISM

To end this section, mention should be made of a hypothesis which bears some resemblance to arguments presented in chapter 7.2.3 yet which must be rejected in its present form,[42] i.e., the professionalism hypothesis advocated by HUNTINGTON in his earlier study (1957; cf. also ABRAHAMSSON 1972 and KOURVETARIS/DOBRATZ 1976:75-79 for a discussion of the professionalism literature).[43] The theory states that, as the military becomes more professionalized, i.e., acquires greater expertise, responsibility, and corporateness, the likelihood of coups diminishes.[44] Assuming that the capacities of the military establishment for modernization should correlate with its degree of professionalism, this proposition actually reverses the rationale mentioned earlier (cf. also FINER 1962:25; NUN 1965; EINAUDI/STEPAN 1971:123). Military officers

> may also be deterred from intervention by fear for the fighting capacity of their forces, fear of dividing the military forces against themselves, and fear for the future of their institution if their intervention should fail. In addition, FINER argues that professionalism by itself may spur the military to political intervention because they may see themselves as the servants of the state rather than of the government in power, because they may become so obsessed with the needs of military security that they will act to override other values, and because they object to being used to maintain domestic order (HUNTINGTON 1968b:493).

Apart from the fact that time-series data would be needed for an adequate test of the professionalism hypothesis, one may also argue, as FINER (1962: 25) does, that HUNTINGTON has presented an "essentialist" argument by describing a highly professional officer corps as standing "ready to carry out the wishes of any civilian group which secures legitimate authority within the state" (HUNTINGTON 1957:84).[45] Direct and cross-national tests of HUNTINGTON's professionalism hypothesis are lacking. (But cf. also the results as to corporate grievances of the military mentioned above and many other results as well, which seem to bear indirectly on this hypothesis). At least for underdeveloped countries, the empirical evidence does not seem to be in line with HUNTINGTON's argument: "If one considers 'social responsibility,' another defining characteristic of professionalism which for military professionals includes an acceptance of civilian supremacy, according to HUNTINGTON, one finds a number of instances (e.g., Pakistan, South Korea, Ethiopia, Ghana) in which forcible intervention by the military in politics came *after* a moderate level of professional expertise had been acquired, not during the period when expertise was lowest" (LOVELL 1974: 21; cf. also GREENE 1966:11; NUNN 1975). In addition, professionalism did not prevent military intervention in South America (CORBETT 1973: 930). In his later work HUNTINGTON (1968) actually provides a more complicated explanation for the occurence of coups (cf. chapter 7.2.3). Also of relevance is a distinction proposed by STEPAN:

> I call the professionalism HUNTINGTON alludes to, the 'old professionalism of external defense' and concur that the nature of military professionalism is of cardinal importance. However, it is my contention that the 'new professionalism of internal security and national development' that is dominant in such countries as Peru, Brazil, and Indonesia . . . is very different from 'old professionalism' in its content and consequences. . . . In a political context where the

military conclude that civilian leaders cannot carry out the development policies they deem necessary for internal security, the new professionalism contributes to a military role expansion that, in some circumstances, leads to seizure of power and the use of the state apparatus to impose a policy of internal security and national development (STEPAN 1978:129-30).

Thus, by and large, there is some mixed evidence for hypotheses linking coups to characteristics and/or grievances of the military. Yet, on theoretical as well as empirical grounds, truly military explanations of coups seem to be insufficient. Other explanations, emphasizing certain characteristics of the military *as well* as other factors, will have to be considered if substantial explanations of military coups d'état are to be developed.

7.2.2. Economic Determinants

Two broad classes of economic determinants may be distinguished, one referring to the situation of the military itself,[46] the other describing the economic situation of the polity and/or of other strategic groups within the polity. As there is considerable overlapping with political determinants, e.g., with those mentioned in HUNTINGTON's theory of praetorianism, some economic conditions will be jointly discussed with other variables in the next chapter.

ECONOMIC DEVELOPMENT

Military intervention in politics has been said to be more likely in poorer countries (FINER 1970:532-33; ADELMAN/MORRIS 1967:282 and passim). Yet, if one were to generalize from some of the results of cross-national studies on summary measures of political violence (see chapter 5.1.2.1), one might expect a curvilinear relationship between level of economic development and occurrence of coups d'état, with states at intermediate levels of economic development most likely to experience coups. Generally, the empirical evidence seems to be in favor of a negative relationship between level of economic development and coups without, however, unequivocally ruling out the possibility that a curvilinear relationship[47] may sum up more adequately the relationship between the two variables:

> Although military regimes and civil-military regimes generally have lower GNP than the civil regimes within areas, the overrepresentation of military regimes and civil-military regimes in higher-income areas [i.e., Latin America] could account for the absence of any significant variation in the aggregate analysis of variance. . . . Military regimes and civil-military regimes are not located in weaker economic systems. The indication is that, if adjustments are made for

area, then military regimes and civil-military regimes have significantly lower GNP than civil regimes (McKINLAY/COHAN
1975:16).

Military regimes and civil-military regimes are also characterized as "having
higher levels of primary production."[48] Distinguishing five levels of economic
development, FINER (1965:7; cf. also HOPKINS 1966) finds a negative
relationship between GNP per capita in 1957 and the percentage of states
experiencing military intervention during 1958-65[49] (taking all states in the
world as the basis, data from RUSSETT et al. 1964). Negative relationships
are also found in two studies on Latin American countries (FOSSUM 1967,[50]
period: 1907-66, N=20; and PUTNAM 1967,[51] period: 1956-65, N=20),
and in a study using the most comprehensive data set so far (THOMPSON
1975b:473; cf. also LUARD 1968:153). There are also two replications of
FOSSUM's study, one (HOADLEY 1973 and more detailed 1975) reporting
congruent results from sixteen Asian countries (period: after World War II
or after independence until the time of the study), the other (MORRISON/
STEVENSON 1974a), however, providing some slight evidence for a positive
relationship between economic development and coups in African countries
(thirty-two black African nations from independence until 1973), thus underlining the possibility of a curvilinear relationship between economic development and the incidence of coups. KENNEDY, however, finds a negative
relationship between economic development and military intervention for
seventy-seven nations during 1960-72, using only countries which had
experienced coups, and not civil regimes as well, as do McKINLAY/COHAN
(1975). "Excluding the smaller island countries and those landlocked in
southern Africa, which all have special characteristics. . . , military intervention is increasingly likely in a developing country, but more likely still in the
lower-income developing countries" (KENNEDY 1974:28).

JANOWITZ (1964:18-23), however, found that there is a positive, albeit
small, relationship between level of economic development and probability
of military oligarchies. Yet, he studied only African and Asian countries
(N=51), leaving out countries with higher levels of economic development.

ECONOMIC DECLINE

Another frequently proposed hypothesis (cf. also the next chapter) is that the
military will step in as the economic situation of the polity deteriorates. It
seems obvious (though hardly sufficiently tested) that a shrinking economic
pie in economically underdeveloped countries should lead to an intensification of conflicts. Some evidence[52] in favor of this hypothesis is presented in a
study of Latin American coups during 1823-1966 by DEAN (1970) who
found that economic downswings (as well as other forms of economic fluctuations) are covarying with the occurrence of coups. DEAN stresses the point
that coups are interrelated with international trade cycles, although no
detailed explanations of these relationships are given. NEEDLER (1968a:

61-62) also refers to deteriorating economic conditions as a determinant of the occurrence of coups, but his evidence is by no means conclusive (but cf. also the additional findings in NEEDLER 1974:149). FOSSUM (1967:237) reports for Latin American countries (1907-66) that military coups occurred twice as frequently during years of economic deterioration as in years of economic improvement. AMES also found that "coups occur at the bottoms of economic downturns" (AMES 1977:167, N=17 Latin American countries for 1948-70).[53] In another hypothesis (cf. chapter 7.2.3) NEEDLER relates economic development to political variables, creating interaction terms which, in turn, are related to the frequency of coups. Finally, THOMPSON (1975b:475-76) found that "Arab and African coups are the most likely to be linked to conditions of economic decline" (whereas worldwide only one in every six coups is attributed to a worsening of the economic situation). It seems noteworthy, however, that "thirty-eight of the forty-five coups (nearly 85 percent) . . . were successful" (ibid., p. 476). Thus, "while economic adversity may not be as commonly related to military coups as the literature would have us believe, deterioration may well be a factor highly facilitative for coup success. . . . This datum notwithstanding, economic difficulties should in general be viewed as conditions promoting regime vulnerability rather than as direct motivations for military coup makers" (THOMPSON 1972:145). (For a somewhat different causal ordering see Figure 7.1)

In general, relationships between economic variables and coup-making activities are *not* very pronounced (i.e., "deterministic"). Nevertheless, there is reason and evidence to believe that internal as well as external (international) economic conditions have an impact on the political structures of coup-prone countries. With respect to the United States and Latin American countries, for example, it has been stated that "so massive is this hegemony, that were accurate measures available, we would probably find that no two Latin American nations are as directly linked politically, economically, technologically, militarily, and culturally with each other as with the United States. Expressed differently, for all Latin American nations (including Cuba in a special sense) the 'most significant *other*' is the United States" (FAGEN/ CORNELIUS 1970:407, also quoted in DAVIS 1972:26). Yet, underdeveloped nations do not depend only on major powers; there is a general dependency of those countries whose export is made up of one or very few products which are severely affected by slumps in the world market. THOMPSON (1975b:473) lists some evidence indicating that countries with a few major export goods are more likely the victim of military coups.

Economic determinants are intertwined with societal and political determinants. Substantial explanations of the occurrence of coups seem much more likely to be generated if economic determinants *plus* other classes of determinants are jointly considered, thus providing linkages between framework conditions (economic and societal factors) and the political process (political conditions).[54] In order to link theoretical elements, a number of explanations which could have been treated in preceding chapters will be dealt with here under the general heading "sociopolitical determinants."[55] In contrast to the class of determinants discussed in chapter 7.2.1 where the military was directly affected[56] or at least may have felt directly affected, in this case the military feels affected because it perceives other objects as being in danger. Or, in other words, whereas in chapter 7.2.1 the military was said to be pushed to intervene, the paradigm here is that the military is pulled into the political arena.[57] Needless to say, both explanations may be relevant in the same instances.

7.2.3. Sociopolitical Determinants

HUNTINGTON has been the most ardent proponent of explaining coups in terms of the polity. "The effort to answer the question, 'What characteristics of the military establishment of a new nation facilitate its involvement in domestic politics?' is misdirected because the most important causes of military intervention in politics are not military but political and reflect . . . the political and institutional structure of the society" (HUNTINGTON 1968:194; cf. also RUSTOW 1967:176; GERMANI/SILVERT 1961). Before we go into a broader discussion of HUNTINGTON's protean concept of praetorianism, a few less elaborate but basic hypotheses and the empirical evidence for them must be considered. We start with a theoretical variable closely related to economic development:

SOCIAL MOBILIZATION

PUTNAM (1967), for example, assumes that polities in which the population has been socially mobilized will quite likely resist coup undertakings, thus increasing the costs for coup-makers. Looking at Latin American countries between 1956 and 1965, he comes up with an $r=-.53$ between social mobilization (percent of population in cities over 20,000, percent of adults literate,[58] newspaper circulation per 1,000 population, university students per 1,000 population, and radios per 1,000 population) and military intervention.[59] There is also a negative relationship between various indicators of economic development[60] and the dependent variable ($r=-.37$) which, however, becomes positive upon controlling for social mobilization ($r=.26$, or $p=.52$, respectively).[61] Negative relationships between indicators of social mobilization and the incidence of coups are also reported in several other studies.[62] FOSSUM (1967) for twenty Latin American countries and HOADLEY (1973) for sixteen Asian countries found indicators of social complexity to be negatively related to the dependent variable, a relationship that is also found to exist, though much less pronounced, for black African nations (MORRISON/STEVENSON 1974a:346). THOMPSON (1975b:477) reports a slight negative relationship between social mobilization and the occurrence of coups, on a world-wide basis as well as for specific regions.[63] However, a *positive* relationship between social mobilization and the occurrence of military coups, predicted in HUNTINGTON's (1968) theory of praetorianism, is reported in JACKMAN's (1978) multivariate analysis (see below).

Also using the social mobilization concept but relating it differently to the level of economic development, NEEDLER has proposed this hypothesis: "One is thus presented with a dialectical tension: if mass participation rises faster than the level of economic development, then constitutional functioning breaks down, usually with the imposition of a military regime, as the conservative forces in the society react against the attempts of constitutional governments to gratify desires of the newly participant masses through drastic social change" (NEEDLER 1968a:95; cf. also LIEUWEN 1964:107). NEEDLER claims to have found some evidence in favor of his hypothesis; yet, as HIBBS makes clear, his tests are inadequate. One must test for an *interaction* effect of level of social mobilization and economic development, the result of HIBBS's broader study (1973; period: 1958-67, N=108 countries) being that NEEDLER's hypothesis is not supported. In view of the high intercorrelation between social mobilization and economic development (r=.84), however, there is hardly a possibility for an interaction effect to show up, leaving the question whether NEEDLER's interaction hypothesis is indeed valid still unanswered.

Among the various other hypotheses NEEDLER proposed and tested, there is one being confirmed to an astonishing degree. The hypothesis reads: "Interventions increasingly occur to forestall the election and inauguration of reforming presidents" (NEEDLER 1968a:64; cf. also SOLAUN/QUINN 1973:46). The evidence drawn from Latin America is that each of the sixteen coups during 1935-44, each of the twenty-two coups during 1945-1954, and each of the eighteen coups during 1955-64 occurred around *election time* (NEEDLER 1968a:65; 1974:159 with similar evidence for 1955-64; cf. COLLIER 1978:74 for black African countries).[64] Furthermore, reform coups became less frequent during the same period. Commenting on FOSSUM's study and then presenting his own results, THOMPSON draws more reserved conclusions:

> In his study of successful Latin American coups (1907-1966), FOSSUM (1967:235) found that 38% took place either six months before or after an election. FOSSUM's method of determining election years, however, was rather crude. He assumed that elections occurred on the average every six years and derived his percentage figure from this assumption. In the 1946-1970 period, coups were not quite so commonly associated with elections. Rather than assume the frequency of elections, each coup was coded positively or negatively for motivations reputedly connected to electoral decisions, before or after the fact. It is interesting to note that the proportional distribution of preemptive processes seems to be perfectly correlated with regional propensities to indulge in elections. Thus, if elections become more common in non-Latin-American areas, it is quite possible that more preemptive coups could be expected in the future (THOMPSON 1973:37).

Still, in THOMPSON's study only twenty-six of 136 coups in Latin America occurred around election time (but cf. also the somewhat higher figures in THOMPSON 1975a:447).

Extending NEEDLER's universe from 1966 to 1970 (leaving out the period from 1935 to 1945) and using slightly different definitions, THOMPSON (1975a) provides evidence that after 1966 there is a greater tendency to reform coups in Latin American countries, possibly due to the Cuban lesson. However, the evidence is somewhat sketchy, as only eight coups have been added to the population. THOMPSON also stresses the need to study the military's perceptions of the sociopolitical environment more directly.

When speaking of elections, parties as well as party systems have been implicitly touched upon. Once again, the party system, as the most important characteristic of institutionally developed polities, is of primary importance in the writings of HUNTINGTON[65] who has suggested a theoretical framework that may serve to integrate the various partial explanations referred to thus far.

PRAETORIANISM

HUNTINGTON's theory of praetorianism[66] or, more generally, of praetorian polities, rests on one basic hypothesis that needs to be elaborated: "Political systems with low levels of institutionalization and high levels of participation are systems where social forces using their own methods act directly in the political sphere. . . . Conversely, political systems with a high ratio of institutionalization to participation may be termed civil polities" (HUNTINGTON 1968:80). It is not the level but the ratio of participation to institutionalization which decides on whether praetorian polities are to result or not. This basic hypothesis must immediately be linked with two rather far-reaching hypotheses, the first providing a description of some other features (besides coup activities) of praetorian polities, the second linking praetorian polities to level of socioeconomic changes.

> Military explanations do not explain military interventions. The reason for this is simply that military interventions are only one specific manifestation of a broader phenomenon in underdeveloped societies: the general politicization of social forces and institutions. In such societies, politics lack autonomy, complexity, coherence, and adaptability. All sorts of social forces and groups become directly engaged in general politics. Countries which have political armies also have political clergies, political universities, political bureaucracies, political labor unions, and political corporations. Society as a whole is out-of-joint, not just the military (ibid., p. 194).

Corruption[67] in a limited sense refers to the intervention of wealth in the political sphere. Praetorianism in a limited sense[68] refers to the intervention of the military in politics, and clericalism to the participation of religious leaders. As yet no good word describes extensive student participation in politics. All these terms, however, refer to different aspects of the same phenomenon, the *politicization of social forces*. Here, for the sake of brevity, the phrase *"praetorian society"* is used to refer to such a politicized society with the understanding that this refers to the participation not only of the military but of other social forces as well (ibid., p. 194–95; italics added).

Or as put in one of HUNTINGTON's many aphorisms: "The wealthy bribe; students riot; workers strike; mobs demonstrate; and the military coup" (ibid., p. 196). There are, of course, important distinctions between these social forces, the most important being that "colonels can run a government; students and monks cannot" (ibid., p. 239). "In a praetorian system social forces confront each other nakedly; no political institutions, no corps of professional political leaders are recognized or accepted as the legitimate intermediaries to moderate group conflict.[69] Equally important, no agreement exists among the groups as to the legitimate and authoritative methods for resolving conflicts" (ibid., p. 196). "In all stages of praetorianism social forces interact directly with each other and make little or no effort to relate their private interest to a public good" (ibid., p. 197). In short, the praetorian society resembles HOBBES's *bellum omnium contra omnes*, or, put more fashionably, conflict lines are perceived as possessing zero-sum character, the gains of one faction automatically being the loss of other factions.

The basic characteristic underlying praetorian societies, namely the "absence of effective political institutions" (ibid., p. 196), reoccurs when the concept of praetorianism is broadened by being related to socioeconomic change: "As society changes, so does the role of the military.[70] In the world of oligarchy, the soldier is a radical;[71] in the middle-class world he is a participant and arbiter; as the mass society looms on the horizon he becomes the conservative guardian[72] of the existing order" (ibid., p. 221). And lastly, an even more audacious set of hypotheses:

The instability and coups associated with the emergence of the middle class are due to changes in the nature of the military; those associated with the emergence of the lower class are due to changes in the nature of society. In the former case, the military are modernized and develop concepts of efficiency, honesty, and nationalism which alienate them from the existing order. They intervene in politics to bring society abreast of the military. They are the advance guard of the middle class and spearhead its breakthrough into the political arena. They promote social and economic reform, national integration, and, in some measure, the extension of political participation. Once middle-class urban groups become the dominant elements in politics, the military assume an arbitral or stabilizing role.

If a society is able to move from middle class to mass participation
with fairly well-developed political institutions..., the military
assume a nonpolitical, specialized, professional role characteristic of
systems with "objective" civilian control.... If, however, a society
moves into the phase of mass participation without developing effective political institutions, the military become engaged in a conservative effort to protect the existing system against the incursions of
the lower classes, particularly the urban lower classes. They become
the guardians of the existing middle-class order. They are thus, in a
sense, the door-keepers in the expansion of political participation in a
praetorian society: their historical role is to open the door to the
middle class and to close it on the lower class.[73] The radical phase
of a praetorian society begins with a bright, modernizing military
coup toppling the oligarchy and heralding the emergence of enlightenment into politics. It ends in a succession of frustrating and
unwholesome rearguard efforts to block the lower classes from scaling
the heights of political power (ibid., p. 222).

The broadening of political participation is also said to affect the durability of praetorian societies:

Praetorian oligarchies may last centuries; middle-class systems,
decades; mass praetorian systems usually only a few years. Either the
mass praetorian system is transformed through the conquest of
power by a totalitarian party, as in Weimar Germany, or the more
traditional elites attempt to reduce the level of participation through
authoritarian means, as in [Chile 1973 after the coup against
Allende]. In a society without effective political institutions and
unable to develop them, the end result of social and economic
modernization is political chaos (ibid., p. 198).

The concept and theory of praetorian polities remain vague in some
respects. Without repeating other criticisms against HUNTINGTON's scheme,
especially against his institutionalization concept (cf. chapters 5.1.2.4 and
6.3.5), the following general points may be raised here:

1. If praetorian polities are basically characterized by the politicization of
"social forces" acting "directly in the political sphere," then what about
American congressmen or senators, for example? Are they not representing
social forces, sometimes even quite directly, even if there are barriers to direct
intervention of social forces in politics? Is it the formal procedure which
counts or rather the actual outcome in the political process? To give another
example, do churches in West Germany have to worry, as long as a number of
leading politicians, being multifunctionaries at the same time, are watching
over religious issues in politics? While one is willing to give credit to HUN-
TINGTON's theory in general, there is nevertheless the harassing issue of
the yardstick that allows for empirically separating direct from indirect participation in politics. Unless one is willing to beg the question, distinctive and
independent[74] indicators for channeling social forces into the political process
are needed. In this context a number of important points have been made by

BIENEN (1974a) who maintains that "it is necessary to be explicit about what is meant by participation"[75] (BIENEN 1974a:11). Furthermore, political participation may have to be differentiated regionally. "Political participation may not stress national institutions if major arenas of politics are local ones. Political participation can also be reined in at various points without necessarily a regime becoming unresponsive to its population" (ibid., p. 195). Finally, extreme ethnic tensions, population pressures, and a fragmented ruling party, i.e., a political institution lacking in strength, have not led to political instability in Kenyan politics. "This suggests that perhaps it makes no sense to look at ratios of institutionalization and participation without emphasizing the content of policies formulated at the center and the way they are received throughout the country" (ibid., p. 195). In any case, "demands and participation must be kept analytically separate [and also be measured separately]. Increased participation need not lead to increased effective demands. There are tradeoffs between participation and the satisfaction of social and economic demands that have been apparent in Kenya. And leaders have received good information both at the center and in the rural areas by not closing off participation" (ibid., p. 194). Yet, what may hold under specific circumstances, i.e., in Kenya or in Mexico, where the direct participation of social forces is institutionalized in the political system (cf. PURCELL/PURCELL 1980) may not necessarily stand out in cross-national tests of HUNTINGTON's propositions which remain to be carried out. At any rate, the transmitter *and* the receiver of politically relevant stimuli must both be considered (cf. also JACKMAN 1978; below). SELIGSON/BOOTH (1979:4) also maintain that "different forms of participation [may have] different objectives." Participation "may create resources and hence serve to enhance infrastructure development and individual life chances" (ibid., p. 3).

2. A related, although grossly overdrawn, argument reads that "there is a strong tendency to tautology" (McKINLAY/COHAN 1974:17) in HUNTINGTON's writing. If his theory is simply used to tell us that praetorian polities exhibit one or all of the features mentioned above, indicating the absence of strong and adaptable institutions, and if, in turn, the absence of these institutions is used as explanation, the criticism would be sound (see SOLAÚN/QUINN 1973:23 for just such a negative example). Yet a thorough study of HUNTINGTON's writings reveals that one can hardly speak of circular reasoning, even if, at various points, precision is somewhat lacking in his paragraphs (which occasionally seem to be written for the sake of joining a number of highly stimulating "theoretical aphorisms"). Again, the development of precise indicators is a must if HUNTINGTON's theory is to be fruitfully applied. Ex ante analyses should provide a safeguard against circular reasoning in following HUNTINGTON's theoretical outline.

3. In its present form HUNTINGTON's theory seems to be too mechanistic. Must soldiers be "progressive" when their society is severely underdeveloped, and "conservative" when a medium stage of development has been reached? The cases of Peru and Brazil,[76] for instance, draw attention to another pattern: the military is trying to modernize the society (through

rural, industrial, and political reforms in Peru, or via forced economic growth in Brazil) while at the same time fighting rather harshly against internal guerrilla movements, the rationale being to do away with conditions in some ways comparable to those that eventually led to the outbreak and success of the Cuban Revolution.[77] (For a discussion of these policies, their implications, and impact see STEPAN 1971; 1973; 1978; EINAUDI/STEPAN 1971; EINAUDI 1973; ROUQUIÉ 1973; LOWENTHAL 1974a; 1975; PALMER 1974; MIDDLEBROOK/PALMER 1975; FIECHTER 1975; and CHAPLIN 1976.) "In both Peru and Brazil, changes in military perspectives may thus be said to have originated from within the military institutions themselves, and to have then been confirmed by the latter's interaction with society" (EINAUDI/STEPAN 1971:124).[78] It becomes evident, then, that systematic data collected over time are needed for an adequate evaluation of HUNTINGTON's hypothesis that the clue to military intervention lies in the political structure and not in the military itself.

Recent developments in Chile may serve as another example. Political participation strongly increased during the Allende years, yet students of Latin America (and also HUNTINGTON himself, 1968:222) from their historical and comparative knowledge would have judged the Chilean political institutions or the party system a priori as being rather stable. Following FINER (1970:554, 588) Chile has been cited as a rare example[79] of a civilian political culture in Latin America. Relying on HUNTINGTON's theories may have led to rather distorted interpretations of the subsequent developments in Chilean politics (cf. NUNN 1975; MICHAELS 1976; NORTH 1976, but see also LANDSBERGER/McDANIEL 1976 on "hypermobilization in Chile"; most recently see VALENZUELA 1978), not to mention external political influences, such as the involvement of the U. S. Central Intelligence Agency and the White House in Chilean politics (cf. MORLEY/SMITH 1977; ROXBOROUGH et al. 1977; KERBO 1978). Other examples from Latin America and elsewhere could be given: "HUNTINGTON's persuasive argument does not fully explain ... why military participation in different 'praetorian' societies varies so much in duration, intensity, and style. Why do officers in Peru and Panama seem to go way beyond middle-class civilian politicians in their reformist zeal, for instance? Or, why is military involvement in the politics of Santo Domingo, Haiti, or Nicaragua so much closer to gang plunder than to institutional exercise of national responsibility?" (LOWENTHAL 1974:129).

4. HUNTINGTON's treatment of the middle classes, of its interests and policies, deserves a comment. Firstly, one has to keep in mind "that military officers of middle-class origin [acting] compatibly with general middle-class interests does not prove that the officers are protecting the middle class" (LOWENTHAL 1974:123). Secondly, short-term vs. long-term impact may introduce another vital differentiation here. Thirdly, "the 'military-as-guardian-of-the-middle-class' hypothesis is simply too indiscriminate about what constitutes the middle class and what guardianship implies in policy terms to be a useful predictor of the outputs of military rule" (WEAVER 1973:82).[80] The guardian role of the military may imply that only the older

portions of the middle classes, the longer established middle classes, will be protected and want to be protected. Yet, do the middle classes really want to be protected? Survey data, diachronic data on capital transfers, on going into exile, on consumer habits, etc., should definitely be incorporated into the analysis. It remains highly doubtful (cf. the discussion in WEAVER 1973:81) whether the middle classes can be treated as homogeneous (cf. also NUN 1968). Should the new middle class, the industrialized middle class, not profit from further developments, in economics and in terms of political participation as well? Perhaps even worse for HUNTINGTON's theory, how likely are chances that parts of the middle classes form a coalition with parts of the lower classes against other middle class and upper class groups? In short, reducing social cleavages to a dichotomous confrontation may lead to an empirically rather ill-founded social structural model. Furthermore, a number of military regimes have recently followed policies not very much in line, at least in the short run, with the alleged interests of middle classes, who may not be inclined to appreciate austerity policies which will hit them badly. Perhaps a so-called guardian coup is against the interests of the new middle classes as well. And even if they might favor a coup for ideological reasons, the outcome of coup policies may actually be to their detriment.

These criticisms notwithstanding, there can be no doubt that HUNTING-TON has presented a highly stimulating theoretical tour de force pointing out what to look for. Yet the empirical evidence in favor of his theory is meager, to say the least. Nevertheless, the negative or inconclusive evidence found thus far can hardly be considered as an adequate test of HUNTINGTON's far-reaching propositions. In short, detailed explication of his propositions and elaborate empirical testing are largely lacking. To our knowledge there is no test of HUNTINGTON's theory of praetorianism, or, more narrowly, of military coups d'état, that not only relies on the use of adequate indicators but also employs measures of change in order to capture the dynamic elements in HUNTINGTON's set of predictions. Tests of his propositions have either treated praetorianism in the narrower sense, i.e., military intervention (dependent variable) or have looked at the policies of military regimes (independent variable) compared to those of other forms of government. The test actually required by HUNTINGTON (and similarly by NEEDLER) would call for considering both aspects in one analysis.[81] One would have to test first for whether the said conditions of the different forms of military intervention do hold in reality, and, second, for whether the military is carrying out the policies HUNTINGTON predicts in his propositions about the military as modernizers or as guardians of the existing middle class order (see below).

To start, a brief look at HUNTINGTON's own efforts to find empirical evidence for his theory may be in order. While he presents a number of suggestive cases for his various propositions, systematic evidence clearly is lacking,[82] especially as to the essentially diachronic nature of his theory. Stressing the importance of strong and adaptable party systems[83] (cf. also chapter 6.3.5), HUNTINGTON reports that the percentage of modernizing countries with coups since independence linearly increases from 0% in communist countries, 11% in one-party systems,[84] 43% in two-party systems, 68% in multiparty systems, to 83% in systems with no effective parties at all (HUNTINGTON 1968:408; N=83, data from VON DER MEHDEN 1964:65).[85] Bivariate relationships are, of course, rather inadequate for testing whether HUNTINGTON's basic interaction terms are indeed explanatory variables. In his study of military intervention in Latin American countries, PUTNAM (1967:99-100) found negative relationships between the stability of the party system ($r=-.36$) and the interest aggregation by parties ($-.63$), and the dependent variable military intervention.[86] Interest articulation by parties ($.04$) and interest articulation by associations ($-.19$) correlated less consistently with the dependent variable.[87] Analyzing conflict in twenty-eight sub-Saharan countries during 1960-64 and 1965-69, DUVALL/ WELFLING (1973a:690) report a strong negative relationship between institutionalization of the party system (see WELFLING 1973 for a discussion of the measurement procedure[88] and ibid., pp. 44-45, for similar results) and elite conflicts. The latter, however, are somewhat more broadly defined than military coups d'état, as "unregulated attempted removal of persons from the command positions they hold in governmental institutions" (DUVALL/ WELFLING 1973a:685). In the same multiple regression analysis, social mobilization (urbanization, primary education, radios) is found to be inversely yet only weakly (and not strongly as in PUTNAM's study) related to elite conflicts (cf. also note 61).

Other empirical tests of HUNTINGTON's theory are also insufficient, even though more elaborate measures have been employed. Using seven indicators of economic change (taken from ADELMAN/MORRIS 1967; general period: 1950-62) and relating them to the strength of the military in seventy-four non-Western, non-communist countries (1957-62), NORDLINGER claims to have found some support for the following hypothesis: "We would expect soldiers in mufti to act differently according to variations in the social structure and the distribution of political power. Where modernizing changes and mass political participation are not perceived as threats to the middle class' material and political privileges we would not necessarily expect the military to oppose them, and other factors may even lead the officers to allow such changes. Soldiers in mufti will protect the status quo only where the middle class' interests are seen to be threatened" (NORDLINGER 1970:1143). Mostly consistent, albeit low, positive correlations between the strength of the military and the dependent variable are found in nations with the smallest middle classes (less than 10%)[89] and in tropical African nations. Small and mostly consistent negative correlations are reported for Latin American,[90] Middle Eastern (cf. also the results in THOMPSON 1974:245)[91] and Northern African states as well as for Asian countries, thus perhaps testifying to the guardian role of the military in these countries.

Yet a number of serious objections must be raised against this study (some of them also mentioned by NORDLINGER himself [1968:1144] who at times speaks of "at least plausible" data). The periodization of the independent and dependent variables is rather inconsistent, apart from the fact that cross-sectional data, as in this case, are insufficient for a test of the underlying propositions, which are essentially HUNTINGTON's. The strongest criticism has been raised by WEAVER: "Since economic growth affords the middle class new jobs, consumer goods, improved social services, and overall higher standards of living, the finding that increased military strength is inversely related to economic development seems to attenuate the guardianship hypothesis. But NORDLINGER arrives at the opposite conclusion" (WEAVER 1973:89). The studies by McKINLAY/COHAN (1974; 1975; 1976a; 1976b; cf. previous chapters) who have collected their data on an annual basis as well as JACKMAN's study (1976) seem to be less open to criticism than NORDLINGER's efforts.

The ADELMAN/MORRIS data have been reanalyzed by JACKMAN (1976) in a way more appropriate methodologically.[91] In addition, JACKMAN looks for relationships between socioeconomic data (N=77 countries during 1960-70) and indicators of the duration of military rule, taken from several other sources. Testing for various alternative explanations, JACKMAN comes up with this conclusion: "Military intervention in the politics of the Third World has no unique effects on social change, regardless of either the level of economic development[93] or geographic region"[94] (JACKMAN 1976:1096). As implied by HUNTINGTON himself (1968:219ff.), his theory of praetorianism (in the narrow sense) may also be tested on a regional basis. Unfortunately the data available to JACKMAN (ibid., p. 1091f.) as well as to NORDLINGER fall short for a number of reasons. Thus, the negative results of these additional tests are not directly bearing on the evaluation of HUNTINGTON's theory. However, military rule in Africa[95] does seem to have a positive impact on GNP per capita growth rates (but cf. also chapter 7.1).

In at least a few cases, one may wonder whether the periods under study are simply not long enough for differences to emerge in the data. Furthermore, as put by AMES, "We are still left with the possibility that military governments may try to modernize their societies, but the environmental constraints they face may make all efforts hopeless" (AMES 1973:13). It remains a question of further systematic analyses whether JACKMAN's conclusion will indeed be the final word: "The civilian-military government distinction appears to be of little use in the explanation of social change" (JACKMAN 1976:1097). Perhaps some of the variables in HUNTINGTON's theory are superimposed by other variables, such as the degree of cooperation on the side of civilian technocrats, the existence of an efficient bureaucracy,[96] minimal infrastructure resources, and international cooperation. "It appears that nations desiring to achieve a rapid rate of economic growth will not accomplish this goal by adopting a military form of government unless other economic, social, and political factors likewise favor rapid growth" (BERTSCH et al. 1978:437).

The neglecting of the simultaneous analysis of causes and consequences of praetorianism, as implied in HUNTINGTON's theory, renders all these empirical tests inadequate. HIBBS's empirical test (1973:96-102) also falls under this verdict. He uses his social mobilization index (population in cities, economically active males in nonagricultural occupations, newspaper circulation, radios, literacy), compares it with the level of sociopolitical institutionalization (direct taxes, age of present national institutional form, union membership, general government expenditures, age of the largest political party divided by the number of parties, age of the largest party)[97] and relates the ratio scores to the occurrence of coups during 1958-67 (aggregated values; N=108 countries). None of the various relationships tested for, including the interaction term political participation/institutionalization, reaches significance; institutionalization (1960), however, exerts a significant negative impact[98] (p=-.171 in the final multivariate causal model; see Figure 5.4 in chapter 5.1.1.3) on the likelihood of coups.

JACKMAN's recent study (1978) also bears on HUNTINGTON's theory although his explanation of military coups d'état in thirty black African countries from 1960 through 1975 differs from HUNTINGTON's approach. JACKMAN draws on four explanatory variables: social mobilization ("the sum of the percentage of the labor force in nonagricultural occupations, c. 1966, and the percentage of the population that is literate, c. 1965"), ethnic dominance ("a binary variable that equals one when the largest ethnic group comprises at least 44 percent of the population, and zero otherwise"), party dominance (" at independence, in terms of the percentage of the vote won by the largest party"), and turnout ("a binary variable that equals one when turnout in the last election before independence[99] was more than 20 percent of the population, and zero otherwise") and explains more than four-fifths of the variance. He tests for various interaction terms (but not those specified in HUNTINGTON's theory), the most noteworthy results probably being the following: "First, social mobilization has a strong, linear destabilizing effect. It is important to remember that this pattern was found among countries that achieved political independence quite recently"; this is "consistent with DEUTSCH's and HUNTINGTON's hypothesis concerning the destabilizing effects of social mobilization in countries whose governments lack political capacity." Second, "cultural pluralism has important consequences for political instability. However, in contrast to the usual view..., it appears that ethnic diversity (that is, cultural pluralism) is a *stabilizing* force. Political instability seems to result when one group's size (at least 44 percent of the population) makes it dominant. This implies support for the MADISONian view that the presence of such dominant groups prevents the formation of countervailing power centers that help inhibit political instability." The effects of social mobilization and the presence of a dominant ethnic group are additive. "Thus, the present study affirms the centrality of ethnicity to the study of African politics; it suggests that the presence of a large and potentially dominant group has destabilizing results. Note, however, that no support was found for the view that variations in ethnic pluralism alter the effect of social mobilization on coups. Third, the results show that party dominance is stabilizing (while multipartyism has the opposite effect). This suggests that one-party dominance is probably an integrative force. Such an interpretation is strengthened by the analysis of the *combined* effects of party dominance and ethnic dominance. The size of the already pronounced stabilizing effect of party dominance is more than doubled as we move from plural societies to those in which there exists a dominant ethnic group (the coefficient for party dominance changes from -.202 to -.519). This pattern indicates that multipartyism is particularly destabilizing when coupled with the presence of a dominant ethnic group. Fourth, the results indicate that increased electoral turnout *decreases* the probability of coups. This is consistent with DEUTSCH's emphasis on the stabilizing effects of political participation" (JACKMAN 1978:1273). Note that political participation is conceived of here as institutionalized behavior in the form of turnout and not as uninstitutionalized political behavior, as seems to be implied in HUNTINGTON's analysis (cf. the discussion in chapter 5.1.2.4).

Impressive as his analysis may be in statistical terms, one nevertheless might object to JACKMAN's data trimming (e.g., in terms of dichotomizing the ethnic dominance variable just below the median to produce smaller residual sums of squares) done in earlier steps and to his theoretical eclecticism. JACKMAN quite often argues both ways: e.g., if the coefficient of cultural pluralism were positive, it would have been consistent with a well-established theoretical argument, i.e., the chances for consociational democracy in black African countries are very low. Since in fact the coefficient is negative, the MADISONian argument is favored as an explanation (which is, of course, modified in view of the other important findings in JACKMAN's analysis). Other theoretically important variables (cf. our summary in Figure 7.1 below) are not incorporated into JACKMAN's analysis.

> In short, the analysis suggests that both social mobilization and the presence of a potentially dominant ethnic group have destabilizing consequences, at least in the context of the new nations of black Africa. The first of these variables is one that changes relatively slowly, while the second is even less responsive to conventional political action. However, the results indicate that the destabilizing results of these two "social" variables, especially ethnic dominance, are substantially reduced by two "political" factors (mass participation and party strength). My emphasis on the role of strong political parties is hardly original. More novel is the clear implication of this analysis that the stabilizing impact of *mass* political participation may generally be as important as is the consolidation of political parties (an activity that is primarily in the hands of political elites). This suggests that besides its uncomfortable normative implications, the common argument that restricted participation brings stability may be more myth than fact (JACKMAN 1978:1274).

Some of JACKMAN's findings are supported in LATOUCHE's (1973) analysis of the determinants of the level of military intervention in thirty-two states of tropical Africa during 1960–71. "For each country and for each year, the level of military involvement in politics is assessed in the following way: full control = 4 points; veto right = 3 points; important role = 2 points; occasional influence = 1 point; no role = 0 point. The final index is the sum of all the annual scores for each country" (LATOUCHE 1973:209). (The critique raised against PUTNAM's 1967 index of military intervention applies to LATOUCHE's measure as well.) Political participation (indicators: turnout and percentage of votes cast for ruling party in the first election after independence) again reduces the level of military intervention. With respect to the role of party institutionalization (e.g., number of parties with legislative representation, number of parties not banned for the 1960-69 period), LATOUCHE's findings seem to be in line with JACKMAN's results and HUNTINGTON's theorizing. The negative relationship between high political participation and military intervention can be explained through the restraining influences exerted by institutionalized forms of political participation on the military's inclination to intervene. The positive relationship between party institutionalization and military intervention becomes understandable if one keeps in mind that the indicators chosen for party institutionalization actually index the fractionalization of the party system and not political institutionalization in HUNTINGTON's sense: "Thus in Tropical Africa political life, at least as it is demonstrated in political parties and electoral practices, tends to increase rather than inhibit social conflict and a high level of military intervention. The existence of a well-developed party sytem only serves to intensify the social tensions caused by the process of economic development and social mobilization by providing leaders, ideological platforms and instruments where tensions can reveal themselves and expand" (LATOUCHE 1973:392). Again HUNTINGTON's interaction term between the level of political participation and the level of political institutionalization is not tested for. Altogether LATOUCHE explains 40% of the variance with his five independent variables (economic development, social mobilization, political participation, party institutionalization, and internal conflict). Whereas the relationship between economic development and social mobilization (e.g., secondary school enrollment, automobiles per capita) remains unanalyzed in causal terms, economic development has a positive impact on political participation (dependence coefficient .41; see BOUDON 1965). Social mobilization has an even stronger impact on party institutionalization (.65) which is, however, negatively influenced (-.54) by political participation. Political participation also reduces the level of internal conflict (-.35). Party institutionalization increases it (.40). Internal conflict (e.g., demonstrations, rioting, civil wars, deaths in conflict, number of recorded instability events) has a consistent and relatively strong positive impact on military intervention (.58). While there are numerous additional (and often contradictory, e.g., on p. 392) findings and models in LATOUCHE's study, the present one (ibid., p. 353) seems to underline the general structure of some of his more important results.

Clearly, the theoretical statements by BIENEN (1974a; see further above), the impressive empirical evidence from JACKMAN, and the inconclusive findings of LATOUCHE as well as his efforts at explaining them call for intensified research. How strong are findings if various indicators of social mobilization, political participation, and party institutionalization as well as military intervention (see SIGELMAN 1974; TANNAHILL 1975; LATOUCHE 1973) are employed? LATOUCHE, like many other researchers, uses indicators of social mobilization which might index both aspects: want formation and want satisfaction (e.g., automobiles per capita) at the same time. DEUTSCH conceives of social mobilization in a different sense than HUNTINGTON. In the latter's theorizing (see chapter 5.1.2.4), social mobilization stands for increased demands on the system and not for system capacities. Better interpretive evidence on the roles of social mobilization, political participation, and political institutionalization and their impacts on military intervention will only be gathered if variability of theoretical findings is reduced through more controlled and consistent use of indicators.

In short, HUNTINGTON's theory still remains to be refuted or refined since the empirical evidence gathered so far is either not relevant to his theory or lacking in various respects.[100] WEEDE has aptly indicated the additional criteria to seek if HUNTINGTON's theory is to be falsified: One must show "that or where there is no contradiction between more participation and stability or where such a contradiction cannot exist, that and why participation is a more important determinant [than others], if instability is to be avoided, that and for what reason an accelerated [in original, "too fast"] increase in participation does not lead via political decay, for example, to military intervention" (WEEDE 1977a:424, quoted also in chapter 5.1.2.4; my translation).[101]

DEMOCRACY AND POLITICAL CULTURE

Less explicit than HUNTINGTON's theory of praetorianism is the explanation of military intervention proposed by FINER (1962; 1970). Whereas HUNTINGTON tries to be more specific as to the mechanisms within each type of polity, FINER is more concerned with fairly general political background conditions, namely with the roles of democracy and political culture.[102] Apart from these differences, however, there are some parallels[103] between HUNTINGTON's and FINER's analyses. The latter proposes this explanation:

> Where public attachment to civilian institutions is strong, military intervention in politics will be weak. . . . Where civilian associations and parties are strong and numerous,[104] where the procedures for the transfer of power are orderly, and where the location of supreme authority is not seriously challenged: the political ambit of the military will be circumscribed. Where the parties of trade unions are feeble and few, where the procedure for the transfer of power is irregular or even nonexistent, where the location of supreme authority is a matter of acute disagreement or else of unconcern and indifference: there the military's political scope will be very wide (FINER 1962:21).

Thus, strength of sociopolitical associations, regularity (legitimacy?) of power transfer, and regime legitimacy are used as definitional criteria of developed political cultures (cf. his typology of regimes according to the level of political culture achieved, FINER 1976:243).[105] FINER does not, however, specify the interrelationships among these three basic independent variables. He only stresses that all three of these conditions are met in democratic polities.[106]

Even more than in the case of HUNTINGTON, the evidence presented by FINER is qualitative and historical in nature, providing for vivid illustrations of FINER's propositions yet hardly for systematic evidence. Nevertheless, throughout this work numerous studies as to a negative relationship between economic development (one of the background variables in FINER's explanation) and political violence have been listed (cf. chapter 5.1.2.1). HIBBS (1973:106) also reports a negative relationship between GNP per capita in 1960 and coups during 1958-67, yet in his multivariate analyses other variables become more important. In their study of socioeconomic and political variables in seventy-four less-developed countries between 1950 and 1964, ADELMAN/MORRIS (1967:282 and passim) found low negative relationships between the degree of administrative efficiency (-.32), strength of democratic institutions (-.42), degree of freedom of political opposition and press (-.41), predominant basis of the political party system (-.23), degree of competitiveness of political parties (-.16), extent of political stability (-.44), extent of leadership commitment to economic development (-.22), and strength of the labor movement (-.42) and the dependent variable political strength of the military. There are, however, no consistent results when economic variables are correlated with the dependent variable. Several of the indicators in this study are merely based on estimations and are, therefore, dubious. Other, albeit very indirect, empirical evidence about the importance of illegitimacy as a determinant of political violence has been assembled in chapter 5.1 and elsewhere.

That FINER's theoretical explanation of military interventions remains somewhat vague has been pointed out before, the most common objection being that there is some circularity in the argumentation when using the principle of civil supremacy and the level of political culture as explanatory factors for phenomena which are clear expressions of the absence of just these conditions. Applying time-lagged specification, however, would allow for controlling this threat to validity.

CONTAGION

Before turning to the development of a more complex theoretical model of the determinants of coups, a number of other variables, said to be causally related to the occurrence of coups, deserve comment. For example, it has been suggested (LIEUWEN 1962:134; PITCHER et al. 1978) that coups may follow a contagion (diffusion) process, i.e., the likelihood of a coup becomes significantly greater in a country where the military or factions of it are watching successful coup-making activities in a neighboring country or region. Systematic empirical evidence, however, does not lead to a clear answer. WELLS, for example, found "two contiguous areas [within sub-Sahara Africa] in which coups have occurred. The western block is composed of Togo, Dahomey, Ghana, Nigeria, Upper Volta, and Mali. A central block consisting of the Central African Republic, Sudan, Congo, Burundi, and Congo Brazzaville—recently joined by Uganda—is also discernible. Both blocs experienced coups during 1966 and in the earlier wave of military take-overs" (WELLS 1974:875). A look at the map of the political world as of 1980 may also bolster the assumption that there may be contagion effects in coup-prone areas like South America, various parts of Africa and Southeast Asia (even though the distribution of military regimes does not say anything about the dynamics of the processes involved; cf. also below). PUTNAM (1967:102), however, failed to find support for the diffusion hypothesis in his data on Latin American countries.[107] Yet, he tested for contagion effects only in terms of the spreading of outside military training programs. When extending the period of observation, however, there does seem to be some evidence in favor of a contagion hypothesis. Thus, MID-LARKSY (1970) reports contagion effects for Latin American countries[108] during 1935-49 and 1935-64, but neither for 1950-64 nor, contrary to WELLS, for sub-Saharan countries during 1963-67. "Unfortunately, both analysts restrict themselves to an inspection of only successful events and their data universes are not restricted to military coups" (LI/THOMPSON 1975:67).

The most thorough examination thus far comes from a study of LI/THOMPSON who summarize some of their results as follows:

> A comparison of expected Poisson[109] and contagious Poisson distributions with observed coup frequency distributions indicated that the contagious Poisson provided a slightly superior prediction in most of the cases examined. Further testing on the potentially complicating influence of coup-proneness heterogeneity[110] produced results which suggest that the coup contagion hypothesis is best supported in terms of data from Latin America (1955-1970) and the Arab world (1955-1970, 1962-70) and least supported by 1962-1970 data from Latin America, Sub-Saharan Africa,[111] and the world. Alternatively, applications of the Gaussian model, offering the advantage of avoiding the interdependence/heterogeneity problem, indicated first-order Markovian dependence processes were at work in the 1946-1970 data for the world and Latin America. The data series of Southeast Asia (1946-1970) and of the Arab world 1946-1970, 1955-1970) failed to reveal the presence of Markovian dependence (LI/THOMPSON 1975:78, 80).

Even though these results are not always compatible with each other, there is at least more than random evidence that contagion processes may be at work, leaving still unanswered the question of what causes these contagion effects.

Obviously, some form of learning or imitation processes are at work. While several explanations are considered possible (e.g., coup-making as a model, as a disinhibition, as an example of conditions to be avoided through coups, and as reference group behavior, i.e., here "the action of one group member [creating] new status aspirations for the other members,"[112] ibid., p. 66), LI/THOMPSON (ibid., pp. 80–81) are much more cautious in their conclusions. They consider the disinhibitory effect "a much likelier candidate and a more general explanation" than other alternative explanations.

At present several analytical problems remain to be solved if the contagion hypothesis or, perhaps more adequately, the contagion hypotheses, are to be realistically evaluated. Firstly, even if contagion appears to be present, the same conditions in the model country and in the imitating country may, in effect, be the cause of the co-occurrence of events ("situational similarity" vs. "event interdependence," ibid., p. 65). "It does appear that Argentina, Chile, Peru, and Uruguay have experienced an element of diffusion. In each of these countries, however, the military has adapted to its immediate political environment" (JANOWITZ 1977:69).[113]

In their article on "GALTON's problem in cross-national research"[114] ROSS/HOMER have taken up the issues mentioned here: "Our starting point is that all cross-national researchers need to build into their designs ways of testing for the effects of both diffusion and function,[115] as these constitute either rival or partial explanations of their results" (ROSS/HOMER 1976:9). They perform a test of this kind using three sets of data (e.g., on black Africa, MORRISON et al. 1972, and on political instability, FEIERABEND/ FEIERABEND 1966). Via partial correlation analysis and regression analysis, the conclusion is reached that diffusion seems to have an effect, in that the zero-order correlations between socioeconomic variables and their dependent variables are suppressed to a noteworthy extent upon the introduction of diffusion as a control variable. Yet, even if diffusion effects might be at work (whether independently of or jointly with internal sociostructural effects), there is still the possibility of an underlying third variable explaining away the contagion hypothesis. Thus, more rigorous cross-national studies in this field (and in other areas as well) should incorporate two standard tests: (1) whether external conditions are better suited to explain portions of the phenomena under study, and (2) whether these external conditions, in turn, depend on some common factors (which may be domestic factors; cf. also the additional analytical distinctions in KLINGMAN 1980:128). The most recent (and perhaps best) overview of conditions, consequences, and possible controls of the problems raised by GALTON is found in KLINGMAN (1980). One of his results is obvious, namely that adequate conclusions about diffusion effects between states or about alternative interpretations are possible only on the basis of longitudinal data.

In the analysis of ROSS/HOMER the interesting finding emerges that, in the case of the FEIERABENDs' study, "the diffusion scores are higher for the socioeconomic variables than for the measure of instability" (ROSS/ HOMER 1976:21). Yet, several points of criticism must again be raised. As the authors themselves note: "The identification of diffusion . . . is not an explanation in itself, only a start toward developing one" (ibid., p. 17). Second, even if internal factors as well as diffusion effects seem to be present, the researcher still needs to specify the linkage groups or, more generally, the mechanisms (e.g., the mass media, MIDLARSKY 1975:163) via which diffusion takes place. There still might be a "functional" explanation (cf. note 115) within the broader framework of diffusion. Third and most important, a matrix of diffusion processes must be established (cf. also ROSS/HOMER 1976:25), as otherwise the particular dyads chosen for analysis will not necessarily form a random sample of all dyads. In the tests of ROSS/HOMER, each country is paired with its neighbor with which it shares the largest border, the major language (which turns out to be the strongest agent of diffusion in their study), and the highest volume of trade. A much more demanding test would have required incorporating as many neighbors as possible and determining whether diffusion indeed drops as the scores on the earlier chosen criteria of similarity become more and more dissimilar. Other things being equal, tests of the relative causal impact of diffusion processes, i.e., external factors vis-à-vis internal sociostructural factors, become more conservative, the more sociopolitical cultural differences (internal factors) and the geographical distance (external aspect) increase. The fallacy of attributing to external conditions (i.e., contagion) what, in fact, might more adequately be explained through internal conditions is a priori much greater in coup-prone Latin America than in Southeast Asia or the Mediterranean countries.

Secondly, unsuccessful as well as successful coups should be compared with each other. There may be some truth in the contagion hypothesis, yet other factors could prevent it from becoming true more often. The fact that some African statesmen seem to live with the fear of coups against their governments or, in this case, with the fear of contagion effects, became quite apparent when a number of them hastily left the 1975 Organization of African States conference in Kampala after it became known that General Gowon of Nigeria, also present, had just been ousted. Would there also be negative contagion processes, i.e., an absence of coups, if coups failed in some areas? What about the likelihood of coups in neighboring countries if coups are only partially successful or lead to protracted internal conflicts or to the involvement of other countries?

As of now, the contagion hypothesis "cannot predict when and where an initial wave of coups will begin, nor which countries will follow the example of the first" (WELLS 1974:876). In all of these studies it has been assumed "that whatever evidence was found would relate to interstate contagion. But it is quite plausible that military coups are interdependent within each state as well. . . . Unfortunately, it would be extremely difficult to attempt to control for these within-nation influences" (LI/THOMPSON 1975:82).[116] When dealing with contagion effects the underlying research question has changed already. Whereas the discussion thus far and for several paragraphs to follow centered around the questions of *where* and *why* coups are occurring, in the final sections some implicit answers as to *when* coups take place may have been given. We shall return to that question again.

COLONIAL LEGACY

Another variable more justifiably grouped under the label "sociopolitical determinants" refers to Third World states which became independent only recently.[117] There are numerous explanations why younger postcolonial states experience coups more often and only after some years under civil rule (cf. ZOLBERG 1968a:74-79). While some of these explanations overlap with explanations mentioned previously, the following may be singled out here: (1) As a legacy of colonial dependence, strong and adaptable political institutions may be lacking. (2) The failures of politicians (who may be incapable from the beginning) may show up only after some time has elapsed. Corruption and external dependencies may also increase in this period. (3) Similarly, the army may wait until the inefficiency of civil government or divisions among incumbent elites become apparent, thus rendering resistance to military takeover much less likely. The army, then, may appear as the organization able to "clear up the mess" politicians have left. (At the same time, it may take some years to build up an army able to carry out a coup; cf. RUSTOW 1963:10 for the Middle Eastern context). (4) After a few years of independence, factionalism within the army may be growing and lead to coup activities.

While there is some evidence that coups are becoming more likely after a few years of independence (cf. also note 113 above), there is no test allowing for separating or combining these and other explanations. FINER reports that "of the states that were over 150 years old at the end of [November 1969], only twenty-eight percent were affected [by military intervention]; of those between 149 and fifteen years old, thirty-seven percent; but of the states created in the last fifteen years, no less than fifty-two percent" (FINER 1970:532; cf. also FINER 1965; JANOWITZ 1964:16 and WELLS 1974:876 for an even higher percentage among African countries independent for more than ten years). THOMPSON (1975b:479) presents evidence that "systems with colonial backgrounds tend to be more prone to military coups" (lambda asymmetric, .26, period:1951-70).[118] Thus, in general, there is evidence supporting the legacy-of-the-past hypothesis (at least for African and Asian countries). Yet, although a number of explanations have been suggested, there is not enough systematic evidence about the mechanisms and the causes of such a relationship.

Furthermore, as THOMPSON makes clear, there is no general legacy factor: "The Arabist emphasizes Islamic political theory and the conditioning of Muslim religion and culture. The Latin Americanist delves into the societal consequences of the reconquest of the Iberian Peninsula, the ever-present *machismo*, and the historical supremacy of the *caudillo*. The Africanist cannot overlook the shortcomings and effects of colonial rule" (THOMPSON 1972:83). Thus, "military coup explanations do not actually deal with a legacy factor, but rather with a Latin American legacy factor, an Islamic legacy factor, and so forth" (ibid., p. 89). In our causal model (see Figure 7.1), part of the legacy factor is captured by the variable past military coup, whereas the explanatory variable colonial legacy and its consequences are conceived of as being of special importance in the African context.

MILITARY AID

As in other parts of this study, external influences have been rather neglected in the present analysis of determinants of coups. Military aid is one of the external variables assumed to be influential. Yet, neither HUGHES (1967; period:1961-4/65) nor WOLF (1965; sample: Latin American countries 1950-60, cf. also SANDOS 1973 for 1952-71), PUTNAM (1967:102), BAINES (1972; period: 1961-6/69) nor WEEDE (1978; period: 1958-65; cf. also McKINLAY 1979 on the impact of bilateral economic aid of the United States, the United Kingdom, France, and West Germany during 1960-70) find evidence that U. S. military aid was positively related to attempts at military coups.[119] Similarly, BIENEN (1969) concludes that there is no relationship between U. S. military assistance and coups of the military in Africa. A more thorough study (N=85 countries, studied at various periods during 1948-72) of the impact of U. S. military aid by ROWE (1974), however, leads to different, though not always unambiguous, results. He reports that military assistance (U. S. military aid/GNP; U. S. training per capita) has different effects depending on the form of government of the receiving country: controlling for preexisting levels of coup-making activities, the likelihood of such activities is increased in civil countries, whereas in military regimes the already dominating military becomes even stronger, thus reducing the likelihood of further instability through coup-making.[120] The differences in influence of U. S. military aid depending on the receiving country are also shown in a study of SCHMITTER (1973a) who, on the basis of cross-sectional analyses (N=19 Latin American countries during 1945-70) and serial regressions for six countries (Argentina, Brazil, Chile, Columbia, Peru, and Venezuela) during 1950-70, reports that "the military assistance-military rule relationship is by no means as clear" (SCHMITTER 1973a:145). There are many possible theoretical links between external military aid, domestic military spending, and coup-making activities (SCHMITTER 1973a:121-24). SCHMITTER's analyses thus far lead him to conclude that only in Argentina, Brazil, and Bolivia is there a positive relationship between military aid and military rule, whereas in Panama and the Dominican Republic a negative relationship prevails until 1966. In the other cases there seems to be no impact from military aid. In yet another study WOLPIN (1972:125 and passim) found that U. S. military aid has some effects on counter-revolutionary activities (i.e., here policies favorable to the United States), be it successful anti-guerrilla fighting or bolstering the political position of the conservative military (cf. also the case studies in WOLPIN, n.d.).[121]

Several problems must be solved before an adequate test of the external military aid → coup-making activities hypothesis can be devised. The United States is the most important provider of military aid, yet other industrialized countries of the world also have their share in the international weapons trade. Furthermore, data on external military aid and military training are hard to acquire and probably error-laden, apart from the possibility that it is not so much the quantity but the quality of the material that counts. Thus, indicators used so far are at best rather rough estimates of the measures one would like to have.

> What may be more important than the *absolute magnitude* of foreign military assistance are such things as: 1) the *type* of aid proffered (e.g., training, grants, credit-assisted sales or surplus stocks); 2) its *timing* (e.g., before, after or during a change of regime, in time of penury or prosperity); 3) its *distribution* (e.g., whether to army, navy, air force, state militia, even cavalry, artillery or staff school); 4) its *content* (e.g., the ideological thrust of training, the policy implications of different strategic doctrines; or 5) the *sheer fact that any aid at all is given* (e.g., indicating policy approval or symbolic moral support). If these qualitative and/or micro-quantitative aspects are so important, seeking to associate changes in spending or intervention with changes in the dollar magnitude of *total* military assistance will simply be "beside the point" (SCHMITTER 1973a:126-27).

FOREIGN VETO POWER

There are, of course, other forms of external influences, sometimes coming jointly with military aid. For example, a number of allegations have been made that the coup of the Greek junta in 1967 could not have occurred[122] or would have incurred greater resistance if the military intervention had not been backed by Washington (as well as by the North Atlantic Treaty Organization?). While in this case external support for internal coup-making activities could be reckoned with, there are also cases where external influences exert some form of veto power, e.g., France with her *forces d'intervention* in some of her former sub-Saharan colonies. The most notable form of such veto powers rests with the two superpowers, the United States and Russia, with respect to their own blocs and spheres of influence, to use the terminology and the results of WEEDE (1975b; see also the categories of countries in LUTTWAK 1969:44-45; cf. also McKOWN 1975). A vivid illustration may be found in the stepping up of American support in the Dominican Republic for the oligarchs and conservatives during the short civil war in 1965 following the coup to reinstall the leftist politician Juan Bosch (cf. SLATER 1970; MORENO 1970a; DAVIS 1972 for an account), whereas in the Communist bloc and sphere of influence the situation never got that far.[123]

There are other forms of external dependencies (i.e., economic dependencies, as in Latin America and elsewhere), which may lead to influences on coup-making activities more subtle than the alleged effects of military aid. Ideological boosting by external leaders such as Ghaddafi in Libya or

Nkrumah in Ghana, or in various countries in the Near East as well as in South East Asia may also contribute to the often closely intertwined phenomena of guerrilla movements, revolutionary struggles, coup-making activities, and internal wars.

PAST MILITARY COUPS

A further explicative variable cutting across several of the other explanations discussed above must be considered. There is empirical evidence that the likelihood of coups is severely increased if coups have occurred in the past (even though some of the coefficients may be inflated due to stable implicit variables; cf. also chapter 5.1.2.8). For instance, in 150 years of Bolivian history, approximately 200 coups have been counted thus far. Perhaps the strongest evidence comes from HIBBS (1973) who finds that coups during 1958–67 are strongly related (in fact, the strongest determinant in the multivariate analysis, cf. Figure 5.4 in chapter 5.1.1.3: p=.468) to coups during 1948–57 (N=108 countries). Further support (cf. also McKINLAY/COHAN 1974:2) can be found in studies on Latin America[124] (PUTNAM 1967: 104;[125] THOMPSON 1975b:471) but considerably less in studies on sub-Saharan Africa[126] (THOMPSON 1975b:471) and on Asia (THOMPSON 1975b:471).

Contrary to HUNTINGTON's suggestion that "a succession of military coups thus eventually tends to undermine the possibility of coups" (HUNTINGTON 1968:230), there is instead a positive feedback process between prior and later coups. JANOWITZ (1964:88) even speaks of a "cycle of distrust." Besides those factors already mentioned, there are several additional explanations of the occurrence of these feedback processes.[127]

Nevertheless, it is HUNTINGTON who once again has worked out a general framework in which to analyze sequences of coups. In his theoretical outline there are two basic reasons for coups to occur in succession. Firstly, coups are related to the stages of the modernization process. "Modernization is not the product of any one particular group, however 'modernized' that group may be in comparison with the rest of society. Rather it is the product of coup and countercoup in which military elements play important roles in inaugurating both conservative and radical regimes" (HUNTINGTON 1962a:36). Secondly, coups are the result of divisions within the new elites or of problems unresolved in prior coups. Both types seem to be interrelated in many ways. HUNTINGTON speaks of anticipatory,[128] breakthrough,[129] and consolidating[130] coups. "This complex pattern of anticipatory, breakthrough, and consolidating coups has characterized most of the shifts from traditional or oligarchical to middle-class praetorian regimes" (HUNTINGTON 1968:205). As political participation and social mobilization broaden, the military becomes inclined to use its veto power[131] against further expanding political participation. Parallel to these modernization processes HUNTINGTON perceives a division between moderates and radicals among the military once a coup has been staged.[132] "The division between moderates and radicals [as often found among the junior officers; cf. LIEU-WEN 1964:126; GUTTERIDGE 1969; and below] means that veto coups, like breakthrough coups, often come in pairs, the initial coup followed by a consolidating coup in which the hard-liners attempt to overthrow the moderates and to prevent the return of power to the civilians" (HUNTINGTON 1968:232). As THOMPSON writes, "the military personnel may have access to the sword, but it is a two-edged sword," since "military regimes are no more secure from military coups than their civilian counterparts. Slightly more than half of all Arab coups (1958-1970) were directed against chief executives who were or who had been military officers" (THOMPSON 1974: 238-39; cf. also BEN-DOR 1973:65; BILL 1969:56-57, but cf. also PERL-MUTTER 1970:291-92). Similar results will probably hold for other underdeveloped areas (cf. FOSSUM 1968:275 for Latin America), Argentina, Bolivia, Ecuador, Syria, Iraq, and Indonesia being some of the better known examples here.[133] Perhaps HUNTINGTON exaggerates the modernization perspective in coup sequences.[134] FINER puts it in simpler and perhaps more adequate terms: "The temporarily victorious elements find themselves under threat from other, rebellious, units,[135] and this goes far to explain why coup is so often followed by counter-coup, and why in so many instances what was erected by one military coup is pulled down by another" (FINER 1976:228).

MILITARY FACTIONALISM

Besides dissension over whether to follow radical or moderate policies after a coup has been carried out, another cleavage (often overlapping with the first) frequently arises, that between generals and the younger military. To our knowledge, there are only a few systematic cross-national studies subdividing the military into various branches[136] and ranks and relating these, in turn, to the outcome of coups. Analyzing coups in Latin America from 1907 to 1966, FOSSUM (1968) found that in economically more developed countries[137] coups are more likely to be carried out by top-ranking officers. Furthermore, if generals rather than lower-ranking officers are carrying out a coup, there is less need to form a coalition with other social groups. The colonels in revolt are thus often compelled to join forces with other groups, i.e., either to form a coalition with civilians or to find a high-ranking officer, such as General Ankrah in Ghana, to take over provisionally, or (perhaps the most radical solution) to retire senior officers after a coup (RUSTOW 1967:189). Lower-ranking officers are also much less likely to be successful when undertaking a coup, at least in African nations (WELCH 1974:133; N=19 countries, mostly during the 1960s).

THOMPSON (1976) has carried out the most comprehensive analysis of the impact of organizational factions among the military (N=274 military coups in fifty-nine states during 1946 and 1970). His main conclusions are: "Military coups reflecting greater organizational cohesion [senior leadership-headquarters-planned coups versus nonsenior leadership-headquarters-planned coups is used 'as a measure of the degree of organizational cohesion reflected by military coup attempts,' ibid., p. 261] are more likely to be successful and more likely to result in post-coup collective military executives. Collective executives are generally less likely to survive as long as single executives [but much less so in Latin America and Asia]. Military coups reflecting less organizational cohesion, then, are probably somewhat more likely to lead to more coups. These findings . . . reinforce the analytical position that the study of the military subsystem is a worthwhile approach to improving our knowledge of military political behavior" (THOMPSON 1976:272). Yet, features of the military subsystem must definitely be seen in the political context that HUNTINGTON, for instance, has so sweepingly outlined. Conversely, "like societal conditions will not produce like rates of military intervention unless intramilitary organizational factors are constant, which will not often be the case" (MOSKOS 1976:69).

While several authors (e.g., JANOWITZ 1964:68) have made the point that higher internal cohesion of the military will increase its capacity to intervene in politics, this condition, nevertheless, should not be confused with the mere frequency of military coups. Other things being equal, the evidence seems to lead to the conclusion that greater sectionalism, i.e., lower cohesion of the military, will lead to increases in coup frequency, since various groups will be competing for power and likely be in and out of office. "JANOWITZ (1964:68) has suggested a possible curvilinear quality by observing that a higher degree of cohesion strengthens the military *capability* to act in politics, while a low degree of cohesion may lead to a greater *propensity* to act in politics" (THOMPSON 1976:257, emphasis added).

THOMPSON also presents some other interesting findings which may be compared to those of FOSSUM (1968, see above), for example: "Military coup leadership is predominantly and approximately equally divided between middle and senior-ranking officers" (ibid., p. 259) which underlines the middle-level officers' strategic position in communication networks.

> Restricting attention to Latin America and Southeast and East Asia, the following findings . . . seem particularly pertinent: (1) the greater the number of services participating, the greater the proportion of successful outcomes; (2) approximately 75% of the cases where all three services participated involved senior rank leadership and headquarters planning; (3) 75% or more of the senior leadership headquarters planned cases with all three services participating were successful; and (4) in Latin America, 65% of the successful coups involving all three services installed post-coup regimes which survived more than two years. These findings could be interpreted as suggesting that coups involving all three services reflect greater organizational cohesion than those coups involving one or two services (ibid., p. 270; cf. also the similar findings in LUTTWAK 1979:195-207).

Yet even more successful than coups carried out by all three services are coups planned at senior leadership headquarters, since in these plots the "political resource advantages of the military organization" are maximized (ibid., p. 262).

Considering the impressive evidence for a positive feedback process between prior and later coups, a number of analytical questions still remain to be answered. Are coups less likely if the probability of carrying out a coup successfully has been less than about 50% (or so) in the past? Are coups less likely if resistance has been incurred in the past or if violence did occur? What about the impact of the fate of coup-makers? In sum, while there is much data on coup-prone political cultures in various areas of the world,[138] our knowledge of the causes of the particular sequences is much less developed. There are a number of theories, such as HUNTINGTON's theory of praetorianism, yet hardly any have been sufficiently tested.

PERSONAL MOTIVES

Last but not least, personal motives seem to be of major relevance in a number of coups. THOMPSON (1973:27), for example, provides evidence that individual interests can be discerned in roughly one-third of all coups (cf. also DECALO 1973:110ff.; the discussion in WELCH 1974; also McKOWN 1975; POTHOLM 1979:200–201). As DECALO says in summarizing his case studies of coups in Dahomey, Togo, Congo/Brazzaville, and Uganda:

> Except for the 1963 coups in Dahomey and Congo, personal factors have played an important, and at times dominant, role in propelling the armed forces into the political arena. Notwithstanding enduring structural, ethnic, and economic factors also conducive to the breakdown of political order (and present in all African systems), the interpersonal dynamics of the officer corps and interpersonal clashes between civil and military elites have been primary causes of political intervention by the armed forces. . . . The prevalence and importance of the idiosyncratic variable in military upheavals can be correctly assessed only after more empirical work has been done and the data evaluated. Studies to date have been quite inadequate, and the literature on military coups in Africa is cluttered with unfounded theories on the corporate integrity, professionalism, and nationalist credentials of armed forces (DECALO 1976:232-33).

EXTERNAL WAR

To end this rather long section on sociopolitical determinants, a number of other explanatory variables found in the literature will be discussed briefly. In general, these variables have either gained less attention than most of the variables discussed here or have been touched upon in part when dealing with other theoretical approaches or variables. Several scholars have turned their attention to the variable defeat in war (cf. also chapter 8.4). There are several reasons for expecting a link between external defeat and internal coup-making. To give only some examples: "An army that is too weak to beat a foreign enemy still has ample strength to cow its unarmed domestic antagonists. Defeat in war, moreover, is likely to undermine popular confidence in the existing government. The army itself—partly as a result of the psychological law that links frustration to aggression—is tempted to clear its tarnished record by finding a civilian scapegoat" (RUSTOW 1963:11). Examples may be found in some of the coups in Iraq, Egypt, Syria (cf. in THOMPSON 1973:25, but cf. also ibid., p. 55), as well as in Turkey in 1913 and 1919 and in Greece in 1922. However, JANOWITZ has argued to the contrary, but he does not present data for the new nations he is speaking about: "Either victories or defeats can serve as a basis of social cohesion, although numerically speaking, in new nations, military success has preceded intervention in domestic politics more frequently than has military defeat" (JANOWITZ 1964:36). Yet THOMPSON (1972:159) reports that "wars have only rarely been linked to military coups since 1946, perhaps largely because international warfare has not been very common since World War II. The major exception is the Arab-Israeli conflict."

INTERNAL DISRUPTIONS

Another variable is internal disruptions (RUSTOW 1963:11-12), in the form of collective protest or internal war (cf. also the study of DUVALL/WELFLING 1973a mentioned further above in this chapter; see also BIENEN 1968a; SOLAÚN/QUINN 1973:47; McDONALD 1975). In one of the most systematic studies of this hypothesis, HIBBS, on the basis of cross-sectional data (1948-67), found that collective protest "does not directly spur coups" (HIBBS 1973:161; for related findings for seventeen Latin American states during 1959-67 see FENMORE/VOLGY 1978; also THOMPSON 1972: 157-58). Reversing the hypothesis, there is also no evidence that coups "directly elicit Collective Protest" (ibid.).[139] Yet, internal war (1958-67) is directly[140] related (p=.136, cf. Figure 5.4 in chapter 5.1.1.3) to coups (1958-67).[141] TANNAHILL also finds "no appreciable difference in political unrest in military and civilian regimes" (TANNAHILL 1976:238-39) in South American countries during 1948-67 (for a related conclusion cf. DUFF/McCAMANT 1976:111). More adequate tests of these hypotheses, however, require the use of truly sequential data.[142]

CULTURAL PLURALISM

Racial, ethnic, linguistic, and religious differentiations or, more generally, cultural pluralism, have also been suggested as important for the occurrence of coups. The rationale is that either military groups differing in some of these respects are carrying out coups or that other military groups are fighting such forms of factionalism by staging a coup. Systematic evidence,[143] however, does not support this hypothesis:[144] "the ultimate political expression of primordial groups, separatism, is extremely rare in connection with military coups. Only five coups have had separatist goals and these have been confined to Indonesia, Zaire, Nigeria, and Syria" (THOMPSON 1973:55; cf. also FINER 1970:547-48, the very indirect influence of these variables in HIBBS's final causal model, and the mixed evidence in THOMPSON 1975b:478; only in Arab countries are racial, linguistic, and religious cleavages consistently and positively related to military coup proneness).

7.2.4. A Few Tactical and Analytical Considerations

Successful participation in politics presupposes having answers to tactical as well as substantial questions. Thus far most of the discussion has centered around the question of *where* coups are taking place. In general, the inference has been that characteristics of the particular polity also provide some clues as to the *why* of coup-making activities. Moreover, at times (for example, when dealing with variables like deteriorating economic conditions, impending elections,[145] external veto power, or coup contagion), implicit answers as to *when* to stage a coup have been given. Yet, well-grounded knowledge as to the latter question still seems to be lacking. Nevertheless, a few fairly general remarks can be made.[146]

GOODSPEED (1962:208ff.) distinguishes three stages of coups: preparation, attack, and consolidation. During preparation and attack a number of strategies must be planned and carried out, the most important being whom to win over for an attack[147] (cf. HUNTINGTON's 1968:214-15 analysis in terms of labor, government, and military) and whom to neutralize. How great are the costs of joining the conspirators (cf. TULLOCK 1974:60-86 for a formalization)? Does RIKER's "size principle," stating that "in n-person, zero-sum games, where side-payments are permitted, where players are rational, and where they have perfect information, only minimum winning coalitions occur" (RIKER 1962:32), indeed apply (even if some of the conditions may not be applicable in reality)?[148] For some related results see the study of THOMPSON (1976), discussed in the preceding chapter. There are other factors to be considered, such as the political climate (e.g., public opinion), military and political resources on both sides, international influences, and costs of repression even if a coup is successful. While the preparation phase may take quite a while, often years,[149] actual operations must be run within a few hours. Potential counterelites must be isolated (e.g., through exiling) or otherwise eliminated; the mass media as well as strategically or symbolically important places must be captured. LUTTWAK (1969: 55) even suggests that coups can be successful only in countries with one or a few political centers,[150] i.e., power centers (in this respect cf. the results of a multivariate analysis in WELLS 1974:884).[151] "Most military coups do originate in the ostensible political center, the capital. As for the element of success, fifty-seven percent of all center military coups have been successful compared to a low fourteen percent for non-center military coups. Furthermore, ninety-two percent of all successful coups and nearly ninety-nine percent of the headquarters level coup, the type most likely to succeed, have taken place in capitals" (THOMPSON 1972:149). As already pointed out in defining coups (cf. chapter 7.1), the perfect timing of a coup is of vital importance.[152] If some troops are a few minutes late, the rebels may miss their chance, since loyal troops may have been mobilized in the meantime. The importance of timing coups is underlined by a number of examples in which only a few hundred men (sometimes even less) have captured a whole country[153] (cf. also the classic analysis of MALAPARTE 1932). In several cases, the absence of the head of state (e.g., Nkrumah of Ghana in 1966, King Idris of Libya in 1969, Prince Sihanouk of Cambodia in 1970, Obote of Uganda in 1971, Busia of Ghana in 1972, or Gowon of Nigeria in 1975) triggered off a coup. Yet, the absence of the head of government is neither a necessary nor a sufficient condition for a successful military coup.

In terms of politics, the consolidation phase is often much more complicated than the preparation and attack phases. During this process of consolidation, more widespread violence may occur, especially if the attack has partly failed in that elites and portions of the army are remaining loyal and fighting for the ousted incumbents. Furthermore, even if coup-makers are totally successful in the short run, their strongest enemies may be found among their former colleagues (cf. the preceding section), since military factionalism (developing after a successful coup) may lead to a subsequent coup.

There probably will never be entirely reliable statistics as to the proportion of coups that failed.[154] Whereas aborted coups leave some traces discernible even to foreign newsmen or researchers, plots may often be alleged. "It would be interesting, for example, to determine whether more coup plots are revealed during the peaks of coup activity than during the troughs" (LI/THOMPSON 1975:82). Another question concerns the degree (cf. McKINLAY/COHAN 1974:2, already quoted above) and significance of violence[155] during coup-making activities.

7.3. A Causal Model of Military Coups d'État

In the following section we attempt to synthesize those variables which might be of major importance for explaining the occurrence of military coups d'état. The empirical results are not always comparable, since attempted but failed coups were included in some analyses and excluded in others. In spite of this shortcoming, we have treated the evidence available in toto rather than setting up separate causal models for successful coups and coups that failed. When our knowledge is more advanced, this will have to be done. At present, however, we still find ourselves in a heuristic stage which may require the setting-up of a model as broad as theoretically justifiable. It is also by no means clear that causal models of successful coups and of coups that failed will differ in their basic structure (cf. the discussion below, also pertaining to other aspects of the dependent variable). In general, there is evidence that both push and pull characteristics, i.e., characteristics of the military and society, are important for explaining coups. Unfortunately, there are only a few multivariate analyses of coup determinants (and sometimes of coup consequences). Yet, there is no study that would sufficiently fulfill the theoretical requirements that became apparent when discussing a host of potentially[156] important variables. Putting aside for the moment the constraints of data shortage, lack of cases, and methodological requirements of parameter estimation, a plausible multivariate causal model of coup determinants might look like the one in Figure 7.1.

There are a number of things to be said about the causal model in Figure 7.1. Firstly, variables said to be related to the occurrence of military coups d'état but deficient on theoretical or empirical grounds have *not* been added to the model. Relative and absolute size of the military (in terms of manpower and/or proportion of budgetary spending) belongs to this class of variables. Professionalism is another of these variables. As BIENEN (1978: 205) states: "The type of coup [is] not linked to . . . the level of professionalization of the army, or the career experience of the officers taking power. Nor [are] military coups related to social characteristics such as level of urbanization . . . or economic growth rates. Military coups in Africa were made by large and small armies and were led by both junior and senior officers. . . . Relatively cohesive armies carried out coups, as did fragmented armies." Furthermore, the factor "class or regional origins of the military corps taken as a whole" (MIGUENS 1975:105) does not reliably predict military coups.

Secondly, there are other variables, e.g., impending elections and absence of the head of government, which more appropriately might be classified as precipitating variables.

Thirdly, almost all of the variables referred to in the model show only weak or moderate relationships with their dependent variable (see THOMPSON 1972:247). Yet, there is some consistency in the findings reported. However, low or high zero-order correlations should not be interpreted as ruling out causal influences of the specific variable under study or as corroborating such influences. Since diverging trends are recognizable in different areas of the world due to different socioeconomic and political circumstances, one must reckon with the possibility that the development of causal models to explain the occurrence of military coups may be a viable strategy only for specific areas.

Fourthly, several of the predicted relationships require some explanation. In relating variables like *colonial legacy, ethnolinguistic fractionalization x social mobilization, political separatism, internal war,* and *past military coup* to one another and to the dependent variable, we relied mainly on the findings of HIBBS's (1973) multivariate analysis. "Recently independent ex-colonies, whose national boundaries were often determined by European imperialists without regard for ethnolinguistic or cultural composition, have higher separatism than one would otherwise anticipate. What this suggests is

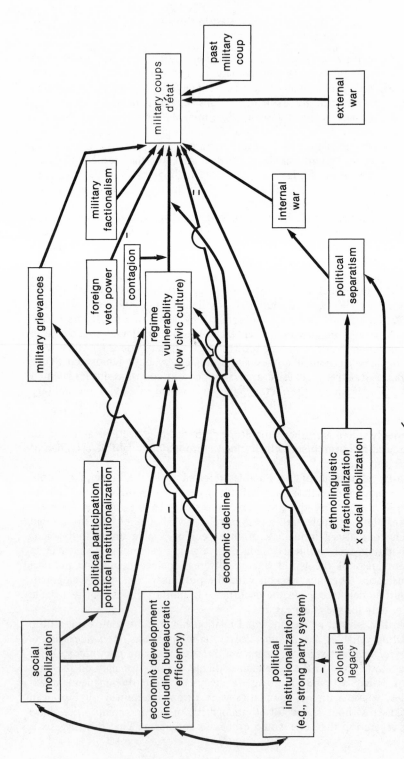

Figure 7.1.   A Causal Model of Military Coups d'État

that the legacy of European imperialism has indirectly promoted Internal War through its effect on differentiation as well as through its impact on subsequent separatism" (HIBBS 1973:191). In his analysis the path from internal war to coups is, however, much weaker (p=.136) than some of the other effects, e.g., that of ethnolinguistic fractionalization × social mobilization on political separatism (p=.456).

Taking another bloc of variables into consideration, if the *degree* of *political participation* exceeds the *degree* of *political institutionalization* (according to HUNTINGTON [1968] that is the case if there is either no party system at all or if it lacks strength and adaptability), regime vulnerability is expected to increase. *Institutionalization* alone, however, exerts an inhibiting effect on military coups. (It also might have a direct negative impact on regime vulnerability, a path not included in Figure 7.1).

Economic decline has a *catalytic* effect on military coups, i.e., it does not automatically lead to military coups or to regime vulnerability. Yet, in vulnerable regimes (cf. below) it should have an effect on the dependent variable. Economic decline also increases *military grievances* (be they of a corporate-positional resource nature, not-so-corporate in nature, or forming interdependent grievance packages). Military grievances, in turn, have a positive effect[157] on the occurrence of military coups, as does *military factionalism* (between the generals and the younger military and/or between moderates and radicals), whereas *economic development* has a direct negative effect on the dependent variable as well as an indirect effect through reducing the degree of *regime vulnerability*. PALMER/THOMPSON (1978:140) state that vulneraability "develops when the government or its leadership is without, has lost, or is in the process of losing alternative (to the military) support" which often is the case if several (or all) of the conditions of social mobilization (× ethnolinguistic fractionalization), colonial legacy, high political participation vs. low political institutionalization, and low economic development occur at the same time in a polity. "But as governments and their leadership become increasingly dependent on force and its managers (the military), it is unlikely that they will retain their control over the military" (PALMER/THOMPSON 1978:141). With HUNTINGTON (1968:34) we assume here that "*social mobilization* involves changes in the aspirations of individuals, groups, and societies" which, if not met by economic development (increased capacities), will have a positive effect on regime vulnerability.

Finally, there are the explanatory variables *foreign veto power* (or high probability of external intervention) and *external war* whose impact has been discussed above. Undoubtedly, there are numerous other variables, e.g., internal disruptions and external economic dependencies, that will have to be considered when testing more elaborate causal models of military coups. However, we believe that for the present we have combined the most "urgent" variables which should be submitted to tests with the specifications made here and in the next section.

The fourth interaction term incorporated into the model tries to capture the *joint* effect of *contagion* and *regime vulnerability*. Contagion, i.e., military coups occurring in neighboring countries, is believed to have an influence on the occurrence of coups in those political systems characterized as vulnerable.

SOME IMPLICATIONS

How can one determine the *vulnerability of political systems* without succumbing to circular reasoning? A possible solution would be to scale the vulnerability of political systems according to the determinants mentioned in the model (and perhaps according to other indicators of low legitimacy as well, drawing, if possible, on survey data) and to determine whether political systems with *ex ante* greater vulnerability scores do indeed have higher frequencies of military intervention. The notion of regime vulnerability (from THOMPSON 1975b and FINER 1962) is only then of some use, if these multiple correlations better predict states of the dependent variable than does directly relating the determinants of regime vulnerability to the ultimate dependent variable. Provided that adequate data and scaling procedures are available, a test could easily be performed by following path analytic procedures of breaking down causal paths into direct and indirect effects. In other words, even if independent variables like social mobilization, low economic development, low political institutionalization, economic decline, and colonial legacy show no strong bivariate variation with the dependent variable under study, one still might expect correlations of some degree, once the *in*vulnerable regimes are removed from the equations. In short, we expect multiple measures of regime vulnerability to lead to more adequate predictions of the dependent variable. However, there are strong technical and theoretical objections to such a procedure. If regime vulnerability is constructed as some kind of a combination of prior variables, coefficients are somewhat inflated and thus have to be interpreted in part as circular reasoning. If, however, the differences between the multiple predictions of the dependent variable and the separate measures are of *considerable* size, we would argue that the notion of regime vulnerability is indeed of use in explaining military coups d'état. The next step would then be to collect independently some further data[158] bearing on additional characteristics of vulnerable regimes and to relate these to the ultimate dependent variable.

In the meantime THOMPSON/CHRISTOPHERSON (1979) have carried out a first test as to the impact of the variable regime vulnerability. They do not, however, use many of the variables emphasized here but rather indicators of economic development, social mobilization, trade dependency, relative strength of the military subsystem, government spending as a proportion of GNP, etc. (Moreover, by using *all* of their predictors of the dependent variable as indicators of regime vulnerability, they conceptualize regime vulnerability in a different sense than that suggested here.) The period of observation covers the years from 1966 to 1970 (N=93; the independent variables are measured for 1965). On a world-wide basis there are no noteworthy relations between this conceptualization of regime vulnerability and the dependent variable, although relations were found to exist in Latin America (R^2=.507, N=19, significant predictor variables: size of the student body, literacy) and sub-Sahara Africa (R^2=.334, N=23, significant predictor variable: size of the student body). Yet, apart from mention of demands on the system resulting from social mobilization, there is no further explanation of these findings. There is also no question that such a test is insufficient in view of the theoretical and empirical relationships worked out in this chapter. The authors themselves acknowledge that their R^2 values are relatively low.

What are the next steps to be taken? One could test whether the causal model outlined here is valid in different regions of the world and for various periods of observation. The effects of error in measurement of variables and of multicollinearity may, however, prevent the in toto testing of such a model. Actually, longitudinal analyses of the preconditions and consequences of military coups are required rather than cross-sectional analyses which allow comparisons of economically more developed countries with underdeveloped countries in respect to the occurrence of coup behavior but do *not* answer the question of whether coup behavior declines as nations become economically more affluent and create stronger political institutions.

Another basic step is to compare how different definitions of military coup behavior (or military intervention, cf. SIGELMAN 1974) affect the number of cases under study and to determine what effect this has on the reliability of data.[159] In general, data on attempted but failed coups are less reliable (e.g., alleged plotting of internal political enemies) than data on successful coups. Comparing different indicators of successful coups leads to correlations varying between .68 (KENNEDY vs.KORNBERG/PITTMAN collection) and .80 (THOMPSON vs. KORNBERG/PITTMAN collection) at the maximum (DUVALL/SHAMIR 1978:Table 8). Correlations between more judgemental measures of military intervention generally do not go beyond .5 (SIGELMAN 1974). These results lead DUVALL/SHAMIR to construct a more direct measure of military influence, i.e., the proportion of top formal governmental positions held by military officers, a measure that needs further validation (and neglects the "other face of power," cf. BACH-RACH/BARATZ 1962).

A related and ultimately more important question is whether different coverage of sources used and different definitions of the dependent variable(s) have an effect on the *structure* of results. JACKMAN/BOYD (1979) report that in comparing event counts from their data sources (*Keesing's Contemporary Archives, Facts on File,* and *African Recorder*) with data from the *New York Times Index, Africa Diary,* and *Black Africa* (MORRI-SON et al. 1972) these effects are of minor importance in the explanation of military coups in twenty-nine African countries. Their tests lend support to the argument "that the cost-benefit ratio of multiple sources may be unnecessarily high" (JACKMAN/BOYD 1979:434). This conclusion is strengthened if one takes into consideration that occurrences in African countries are generally underreported in most of the data sources currently available and that distortions therefore should be most apparent in this case. But clearly more replication studies are called for before this issue is considered settled.

Another question is whether to conceive of the dependent variable as a binary coup propensity (experienced coup or not) or as a frequency measure with the 0-category included or not (cf. THOMPSON 1978a:95). This classification may be crossed with the one discussed above (i.e., whether the dependent variable is to include failed coups as well). In addition, coups against civilian regimes may have to be distinguished from coups against military regimes. This is an important theoretical distinction, raising the question of whether polities which experience their first deviation from the "democratic path of virtue" must be separated from polities where military factionalism manifests itself in permanent coup behavior. Table 7.3 summarizes these possibilities.

Most of the variables likely to explain the incidence of coups, whether failed or not, are also likely to be important in the explanation of the frequency of such forms of behavior.[160] However, just as some of the precipitating conditions of successful coup behavior and/or some of the required states of antecedent variables have not been met in the case of failed coups, some variables might be of relatively greater importance in explaining the frequency of coups. Military factionalism is one such variable and regime vulnerability another. "But there is no reason to assume that the *same* set of

Table 7.3. Some Possible Dependent Variables in the Analysis of Military Coups D'État

		Coups			
		Successful		Failed	
		Against Civilian Regimes	Against Military Regimes	Against Civilian Regimes	Against Military Regimes
	Never				
Occurrence	Once				
	Often				

variables and attributes will predict *equally* well to the extent that a state is likely to experience several coups or an extended sequence of coup and countercoup in a relatively short time period" (THOMPSON 1978b:103; emphasis added). Thus, one must distinguish carefully between the incidence of coups, their frequency, their outcome, and the type of regime against which they are directed (cf. THOMPSON 1980 as a recent example, for details see chapter 7.2.1), until we know whether these distinctions have a definite effect on the structure of results.[161] We doubt that combining successful coups (weighted 5), unsuccesful coups (weighted 3), and plotted coups (weighted 1) into one index as JACKMAN (1978) has done following MORRISON et al. (1972:128) will be an adequate strategy in the long run. Such a procedure is justifiable on the grounds of distinguishing polities as to their total amount of coup behavior. Yet, in terms of understanding the different processes leading to success or failure of different types of coups, nothing is gained.[162]

Apart from works by HIBBS (1973), THOMPSON, LATOUCHE (1973), and more recently JACKMAN (1978), there are very few multivariate studies on the determinants of military coups d'état.[163] In addition to the factors outlined in our causal model, consequences of coups must also be considered for a thorough understanding of military coups. In the past they have not always been separated sufficiently from alleged causes of coups (and vice versa). Only portions of the voluminous literature on coups could be used here; nevertheless most of the relevant quantitative cross-national literature has been covered.[164] There are numerous other works, such as case studies[165] and qualitative analyses of coups that we could not include.

In several respects, conclusions similar to those in some previous chapters must be drawn.

1. Time series data (and sequential data with respect to the immediate conditions of coup-making activities and their immediate impact) should be collected, as in some case studies.

2. The sociostructural analysis must be broader than in the past. Data on the social background of the military and, if possible, on their political and social attitudes,[166] should also be incorporated into the analysis. Whether and how backgrounds and attitudes are related to military intervention should be tested.

3. The forms and degrees of civil-military cooperation should be studied more closely. For example, is ethnic membership or class the basis of military-civil contacts (cf. LEMARCHAND 1974)? Infrastructural capacities and bureaucratic efficiency should be considered as variables deserving separate treatment in elaborate causal modelling and testing.

4. Not only broader international conditions but also the "mutual interactions and national security policies of individual . . . countries are an important, although largely neglected, topic for research" (EINAUDI/STEPAN 1971:131).

5. Returning to the theoretical considerations, HUNTINGTON's theory of praetorianism still seems to provide the best and most encompassing theoreti-

cal starting point. In particular, his characterization of praetorian polities as polities in which conflict lines are perceived according to the zero-sum notion is still not sufficiently tested, apart from other difficulties with HUNTINGTON's theory.

What do we actually know about the virtues and vices of military rule in underdeveloped countries and the chances of military retreat[167] from internal politics (cf. also PERLMUTTER 1970; WELCH 1971a; 1974a; 1976; the typology in FINER 1974; BIENEN/MORELL 1976; LAMBERG 1979)? We have a lot of data but little that allows for a clear answer to propositions such as the following by HUNTINGTON: "In those countries which are less complex and less highly developed,[168] the military may . . . be able to play a constructive role, if they are willing to follow the Kemalist model"[169] (HUNTINGTON 1968:261; as to the Kemalist model cf. also LERNER/ ROBINSON 1960 and WARD/RUSTOW 1964:352-88; on the period from 1945 to 1973 see also WEIHER 1978). "To move their society out of the praetorian cycle [the military] cannot stand above politics or attempt to stop politics. . . . If the military fail to seize that opportunity, the broadening of participation transforms the society into a mass praetorian system. In such a system the opportunity to create political institutions passes from the military, the apostles of order, to those other middle-class leaders who are the apostles of revolution" (HUNTINGTON 1968:262). It seems as if TALLEYRAND's well-known aphorism must be amended: You can do everything with bayonets but sit on them—or govern highly complex social systems.[170] Yet, even less complex social systems might not be led as successfully by the military as the Kemalist model suggests. (The assumptions of the Kemalist model were again violated by the Turkish coup of 1980.) FINER's summary may very well be a realistic appraisal of the present situation: "The most likely outcome of one military coup and one military régime in the Third World is a second coup and a second military régime, separated by bouts of indirect military rule, monopartism and feebly functioning competitive party politics—an alternation of these three types for a considerable age to come" (FINER 1970:573). Other studies are pertinent here as well. For instance, LASSWELL's "garrison state hypothesis" predicting a domination of politics by elites specialized in the management of violence, the causes of which are both social pressures and technological developments (LASSWELL 1941; cf. also HUNTINGTON 1957:346-50 for a critique), may indeed provide "a reasonably accurate image of the development of civil-military relations throughout much of the world" (WELCH/SMITH 1974:259).[171] (However, reviewing the evidence, ARON [1979:355] states that the "industrialized world is more removed than ever before from the garrison state." From his point of view, the thesis also does not hold for African states. It is perhaps true only for China during the Cultural Revolution and for post-victory communist Vietnam.)

Several of the determinants of coups will appear again in the final chapter on patterns of political violence which bears on a classic subject in social science, the study of revolutions. In fact, some revolutions started as revolutionary coups (e.g., the Russian October Revolution of 1917 and the Cuban Revolution). Without going into detail at this point, the attitudes or, more precisely, the behavior of the military are again among the most important determinants[172] of the success of revolutions.

Chapter 8

The Cross-national Study of Revolutions: Toward a Critical Assessment

8.1. Introductory Remarks

"History has not normally been kind to revolutions" (HUNTINGTON 1971a:5). There have not been many revolutions;[1] so-called Grand Revolutions or "Great social revolutions" (EDWARDS 1927), such as the French Revolution, the Russian Revolution, and the Chinese Revolution, have been even rarer. History has been somewhat kinder, however, to revolutionary activities, even if the eventual outcome was not revolution but another form of social change or even social restoration. Social scientists interested in developing a causal science of revolutions are thus confronted with an almost impossible task. A broader definition of the dependent variable, i.e., revolutionary phenomena as opposed to revolutions, to increase the number of cases under study, does not solve the problem since, first, we are interested in finding determinants of successful revolutionary overthrow, determinants which differ from those of unsuccessful overthrows (even if not in all respects), and, second, we do not know how such a *definition* will affect the results obtained (see also chapter 8.5 on the question of an adequate research design). As of now, there is no study providing the scholar with guidelines as to the price he pays for relying on either a narrow or a wider definition of revolution.[2]

Here we are concerned with, in GREENSTEIN's (1967) words, clearing away some underbrush that has impeded the cross-national study of revolutionary phenomena. There is a flood of publications with the word "revolution" in the title. If only a fraction of these works were useful for our purposes, this inventory could achieve much more conclusive results. Unfortunately, that is not the case. We will first comment on several definitions, typologies, and theories.[3] Later we will confront several of the theoretical statements with the qualitative and quantitative empirical evidence gathered thus far. We will leave it to other scholars to elaborate, on a systematic cross-national basis, on our results (e.g., the causal model in chapter 8.4.7).

In general, the results and the discussion in the preceding chapters on crises and coups d'état will not be repeated here, although both chapters are important for the study of revolutions, especially the portion on crises of legitimacy (6.3.4). Furthermore, philosophical systems such as Marxist interpretations[4] of revolution are also excluded from the discussion since we are concerned here with tested or testable hypotheses rather than with philosophical or ideological[5] systems.[6] For example, when MARX states that "a revolution is only possible as a consequence of a crisis. . . . Yet, the former is just as certain as the latter" (my translation),[7] he probably is right as far as the first half of his proposition is concerned, but not with respect to the second half (not even during the 1850s; see STADLER 1964). There have been crises in a number of industrialized societies which have not led to a revolution. There is no predetermined relationship between crises and revolution as MARX assumes. There are, of course, other variables and hypotheses to be derived from the works of MARX and other writers that are worth testing, such as LENIN's (1902) stress on the decisive role[8] of a closely knit and strictly organized vanguard party of revolutionary professionals, or MAO's emphasis on the difference it makes whether or not revolutionaries win the peasants to their cause (cf. chapter 8.4.4), or even MARCUSE's claims (1968; 1972) that there is a revolutionary potential among students and other minorities in industrialized societies which might be stronger than the revolutionary consciousness of ordinary workers. Some of these variables will be taken up in later parts of this chapter. In general, however, we are interested in the social and political conditions that make for successful revolutions rather than in philosophical or ideological systems.[9]

Other areas worthy of study but not dealt with here include the theoretical writings, pamphlets, and memoirs of revolutionaries themselves (and of counterrevolutionary writers like BURKE with his *Reflections on the Revolution in France*. 1790; cf. COBBAN 1971:29ff. for a critique): the analyses of, in some respects, related phenomena such as millenarist movements or sects; and historical and philosophical literature on the conditions and justifications of tyrannicide (cf. JÁSZI/LEWIS 1957) or regicide (cf. VON BEYME 1973:7-11). Finally, historical monographs on various aspects of the English Revolution (cf. HILL 1965; 1967; 1972; STONE 1970; 1972; cf. also STONE 1967),[10] the French Revolution (cf. the references in chapter 8.4.6.6),[11] the Russian Revolution (cf. CARR 1950-53; CHAMBERLIN 1952; DAVIS 1922), the Chinese Revolution[12] (see BIANCO 1971; SCHURMANN 1966), or other revolutions are not dealt with in detail here although they do contain valuable information for scholars interested in developing a cross-national science of revolutions. We are, however, dealing with some of the comparative and, at times, even quantitative historical studies on revolutionary activities, mostly during the eighteenth and nineteenth centuries (cf. chapter 8.4.6.6). It is this "history from below" (LEFEBVRE) that has pointed the way to some of the more fruitful studies of revolutionary conditions and activities.

In the following chapters, an effort is first made to define revolutions more precisely than is often done in the cross-national literature. Secondly, several typologies of revolutions and other forms of violent political protest behavior are discussed. Thirdly, a number of theories or "explanation sketches,"[13] as HEMPEL (1965) has called them, are very briefly presented, the emphasis being on isolating some key[14] variables to be employed in more rigorous cross-national tests. Fourthly, there is an analysis of several quantitative cross-national studies of revolutionary phenomena. To be honest, the systematic empirical evidence used to support the various theoretical positions and approaches is meager, to say the least. The largely negative results encountered in these early cross-national studies will be contrasted with findings from sociohistorical approaches (which, in part, share the cross-national perspective). Richness in historical detail can successfully be matched with more general theoretical statements, provided that a number of requirements (dealt with throughout this chapter) are met. Fifthly, a preliminary causal model of revolutions is developed on the basis of theories and evidence available thus far. Finally, there are some considerations which are important if more successful systematic analyses of the conditions of revolutions—or, more generally, of revolutionary activities—are to be carried out in the future.

8.2. Definitions of Revolution

The definition and analysis of revolutions has persistently led to disagreement among participant observers, historians, and social scientists alike, perhaps the most famous example being the dialogue (cf. in GRIEWANK 1969:189ff. and in ARENDT 1964:40ff.) between King Louis XVI of France and the Duc de La Rochefoucauld-Liancourt during the night after the capture of the Bastille: "C'est une révolte"—"Non, sire, c'est une révolution."

Apparently there is no unequivocal origin of the term revolution. On the contrary, there seem to be several roots.[15] "Only during the late Christian period did the concept 'revolutio' appear (as the substantive to 'revolvere') denoting turning around and circular movement, the orbit of the moon and, finally, in a figurative sense (in Augustin's writings) the idea of reincorporation or return of the times" (GRIEWANK 1969:17; my translation). For Dante revolution similarly meant the change of the stars. A famous example of one of the original meanings of the term is found in the main work of Copernicus, *De revolutionibus orbium coelestium*, appearing two centuries later in 1543.

In the middle of the fourteenth century the concept of revolution is used for denoting political phenomena. The merchant brothers Villani of Florence speak of *rivoltura* and *rivoluzione* (or *revoluzione*): "Both concepts are almost synonymously used as an expression for restless and tumultuous times, confusion and conflicts—probably not uninfluenced by the astronomical use of the concept 'revolutio' (turning of the stars around a center), which is also found in Dante's writings. Yet, the Villanis give no further delineation of the political meaning of these concepts. Giovanni Villani describes the popular turmoil of 1343 in a moralizing manner as 'reformation' of the country . . . and notes that within a short time 'so many new and varied revolutions' [tante novità e varie rivoluzioni] have occurred, thus not *one* revolution as turning over the state, but various restless, one might say turbulent, events" (GRIEWANK 1969:104-5; my translation; cf. also MARTINES 1972).

Later in the seventeenth century the concept of revolution acquires a different meaning. During the times of the "Glorious Revolution" it denotes the reinstitution of prior states expected by large portions of the English aristocracy upon the arrival of William III in England. The goal of this "revolution" was not totally new political and social circumstances, but rather the restoration of former, more "moderate," political conditions, "similar to the old notion of 'reformation' as renunciation of misuses, distortions and wrong ways" (GRIEWANK 1969:145; my translation; but cf. also JONES 1972 for a reinterpretation of the Glorious Revolution). Thus, ROSEN-STOCK-HUESSY (1951:8) rightly stresses that the Glorious Revolution was a revolution "without revolutionaries" (cf. also STRAKA 1973). Revolution still denotes a "quasi-objective" phenomenon, somewhat like a natural phenomenon (cf. also the uses of the concept of revolution as discussed in GOULEMOT 1967; MAZAURIC 1967; BENDER 1977:107ff.; cf. also the old doctrine of [Aristotle and] Polybius on the circulation of constitutions—πολιτείων ἀνακύκλωσις—see SNOW 1962).

Only during the later phases of the Enlightenment does a "subjective component"[16] in the interpretation of revolutions emerge, leaving a strong impact on political thinking and political history in Europe and elsewhere in the world.

The millenarism of the late Middle Ages and Calvinist Puritanism (cf. WALZER's *The Revolution of the Saints* 1965; 1963; as well as GRIEWANK 1969; CAPP 1972; cf. also the historical overview in CALVERT 1970a) have left their traces on revolutionary thinking as well. Millenarian (chiliastic, millenial, nativist, transformative, messianic, revitalistic, etc.) movements are interpreted in a variety of ways, "as predominantly Western by the European historian, as a reaction to culture-shock by the anthropologist, as instances of mental stress by the psychiatrist, as sects by the sociologist of religion, as revolutionary movements by the political scientist" (BARKUN 1974:3). In other words, "movements with an apparently religious character tend to be classified as millenarian, while those that are professedly secular are regarded as movements of political revolution" (ibid., p. 23). As to the causes of these movements, "there must be multiple rather than single disasters [natural and/or social]; a body of ideas or doctrines of a millenarian cast must be readily available; a charismatic figure must be present to shape those doctrines in response to disaster; and the disaster area must be relatively homogeneous and insulated. The combination of necessary and sufficient [?] conditions suggests that millenarian movements are essentially rural-agrarian rather than urban-industrial" (ibid., p. 6). Nevertheless, in BARKUN's opinion various twentieth century examples can be given as well. Actually, he is here following the conclusion drawn by COHN (1970) in his study on medieval millenarism. Of questionable value, however, is the direct inference from medieval experiences to modern times that is often made in this type of studies.

Many authors tend to equate revolution and the excessive use of violence. TIMASHEFF writes: "Revolutions are *violent* conflicts" (1965:12; cf. also REJAI 1973:8; HAGOPIAN 1974:1).[17] Other authors (cf. GROTH 1972: 32), however, justly stress that it is not the use of violence which is characteristic of revolutions as opposed to other forms of conflict, but rather the consequences revolutionary activities have for the particular social structure.[18] The example of Cuba demonstrates that revolutionary change may occur under conditions involving less use of violence than is characteristic of, for example, major internal wars. DOMÍNGUEZ estimates that "approximately 2000-2500 persons (or two to three times the 898 reported in the only detailed account ever published, which itself was demonstrably understated) were killed on both sides during the insurrection against Batista" (DOMÍNGUEZ 1974:216-17). The fact that Marxist and other authors[19] frequently stress the necessity of violence for revolution to occur[20] is in itself interesting. The definition of revolutions, however, does not become more precise through suggestions of this kind. The use of violence is not the characteristic of revolutions, yet violence often is an unavoidable ingredient in carrying out a revolution. However, it would be senseless to equate a potential means with a minimal definitional criterion.

The replacement of the previous leadership is also not a decisive criterion of revolution. WELCH/TAINTOR claim that: "What distinguishes political revolution from these other quick and violent forms of political change is the institutionalization and consolidation of a new political order" (WELCH/ TAINTOR 1972:2-3). In reality, however, it sometimes may be difficult to draw such distinctions. AMANN accordingly feels justified in proposing a rather different definition of revolution, namely as "breakdown, momentary or prolonged, of the state's monopoly of power, usually accompanied by a lessening of the habit of obedience" (AMANN 1962:38-39). Here the breakdown of the monopoly of power of prevailing elites is the central definitional criterion, no matter how and by what means this breakdown takes place.[21] Thus, AMANN's definition lacks the characteristic which distinguishes between various forms of power takeover (cf. also KAMENKA 1966:131-32).[22] What are the boundaries within which these criteria may be used? Was France in May 1968 in a momentary breakdown of the state's (the elites') monopoly of power? (And how does one measure the state's monopoly of power?).[23] One must recall that one resource of power, namely the army, was not used at all, the reason perhaps being that the leading military did not consider the situation grave enough.[24] Bearing this in mind, was there really a breakdown of power (cf. also the critique of AMANN's definition in GILLIS 1970:347)?

Again, for revolution to take place, it is less important that power is turned over (normally by the use or threat[25] of some form of violence) than that a fundamental change of the social structure occurs. The latter aspect is noted by ARENDT (1964:27ff.),[26] although in a one-sided manner. It is her conviction that revolutions must produce something new to merit the label "revolution": "Only where this pathos of novelty is present and where novelty is connected with the idea of freedom are we entitled to speak of revolution" (ARENDT 1964:27). Yet, the class of revolutionary objects is once again delineated in an unfruitful way, since revolutions aimed at establishing values and some structures of a former epoch would not here be counted.[27] We must also criticize the idea of historicism inherent in this conception of revolution. Is there indeed more freedom to be expected with new revolutions looming on the horizon?[28]

A central definitional criterion of revolutions is that *fundamental* changes occur, no matter whether the particular conditions sought have already occurred in the past or not. The criterion of fundamental changes allows for distinguishing revolutions from coups, e.g., from those coups carried out by political opponents with the mere promise to return to former ("better") states. In the sense of our definition (cf. below), this type of coup cannot be treated as a revolution. It would, however, qualify as revolution (or at least as revolutionary coup), if there were indeed fundamental changes in the prevailing political and social structures.

HUNTINGTON's elaborate definition of revolutions (HUNTINGTON 1968:264 with notable addenda from HUNTINGTON 1971a:5 in brackets)[29] may be helpful in summarizing part of the preceding discussion:

> A revolution is a rapid, fundamental, and violent domestic change in
> the dominant values [concepts of legitimacy] and myths of a
> society, in its political institutions, social structure [economic rela-
> tionships], leadership, and government activity and policies [in
> short, the demolition of the existing social, economic, and political
> order and the effort to substitute an entirely new one]. Revolutions
> are thus to be distinguished from insurrections, rebellions, revolts,
> coups and wars of independence.[30]

HUNTINGTON adds that revolutions are a product of the West, or more generally: "Revolution is thus an aspect of modernization" (ibid., p. 265). HUNTINGTON here apparently uses a definitional criterion similar to that of ARENDT whom he also quotes in his book.

To repeat and to take up another possible definitional criterion, neither the criterion of novelty nor that of violence is a necessary definitional criterion of revolution, nor is rapid speed of the turnover (cf. GURR 1973b: 360f.).[31] The duration of such events is, however, of some importance. Yet, how long a period of turnover must last in order to qualify as a revolution remains one of the many unanswered questions in research on revolutions. Must there be the same elite personnel (thus one generation at the maximum) for the event to qualify as revolution? How great is the probability that successors to "true" revolutionaries will be "true" revolutionaries themselves?

Following are other definitions found in the literature,[32] definitions which do not always fulfill the criteria outlined above. WELCH/TAINTOR, for instance, propose four definitional criteria of revolutions (which in part transcend the preceding discussion):

1. a change in the means of selecting political leaders, and the creation of new political elites, usually by extraconstitutional or non-systemic means;
2. new and expanded channels for access to positions of political power;

3. expanded political participation, possibly temporarily; and
4. the creation and solidification of a new political order on a different basis of political legitimacy (WELCH/TAINTOR 1972:2).[33]

In other definitions (LEIDEN/SCHMITT 1968:3ff.; cf. also POLLOCK/RITTER 1973:4-7; RUSSELL 1974:6),[34] the same points are generally stressed, even if not always as clearly as by WELCH/TAINTOR. SKOCPOL (1979:4, 33) proposes a definition of revolution that has much in common with ours. Summing up the preceding discussion, we have arrived at the following working definition of revolutions (emphasizing that revolution is an outcome and not a goal state): *A revolution is the successful overthrow of the prevailing elite(s) by a new elite(s) who after having taken over power (which usually involves the use of considerable violence and the mobilization of masses) fundamentally change the social structure and therewith also the structure of authority.*

It does not seem necessary to introduce the criterion of illegality into the definition. Illegality is already implied by the word overthrow. The incumbents of key positions in a society usually are interested in stabilizing the state of the society (or changing it in their direction) by legal and other means. Knowing that revolutions are illegal (yet not necessarily illegitimate) acts does not enlarge our understanding of them. A change in the structure of authority is an important definitional criterion of revolutions since the replacement of previous elites does not mean that a new *structure* of authority is established. A fundamental change of the social structure, however, does imply a concomitant change in the structure of authority as well.

The mobilization of the masses seems to be another important definitional criterion. GUEVARA (1966) in his elite-centered theory of the *foco* had to pay a high price for a wrong theory in the wrong place at the wrong time, for the Bolivian peasants resented the revolutionaries who were largely foreigners and intellectuals. Not even the Bolivian Communist Party supported Guevara. This outcome is clearly contrary to the experience in Cuba where the breakdown of the Batista army, the power deflation of his regime, and the withdrawal of U. S. support to Batista (cf. DRAPER 1962; THOMAS 1963; GOLDENBERG 1965) allowed for a rather easy victory by the rebels. Furthermore, it should not be forgotten that Castro gained support from many other social groups as well, mostly from the middle strata (cf. also the analysis in chapter 8.4.6.5). In Bolivia, however, "Barrientos' political response was to isolate the guerrillas by emphasizing their alien character and by drawing attention to his own solidarity with the Bolivian peasants. The government also cracked down on various opposition groups, especially those in the mining region" (DAVIS 1972:17). Increased U. S. military aid and training in counter-guerrilla activities and the so-called *acciones cívico-militares* contributed significantly to the failure (cf. MOSS 1971; 1972; MORENO 1970) of this type of guerrilla strategy, also observable in a number of other Latin American countries (cf. GOTT 1973 for an analysis of guerrilla movements in Guatemala, Venezuela, Columbia [MAULLIN 1973], and Peru; for movements in other countries cf. LAMBERG 1972; DAVIS 1972; MERCIER 1969; ALLEMANN 1974; KOHL/LITT 1974; and some of the articles in ALEXANDER 1976). It is perhaps no accident that, after the total failure of elite-instigated rural guerrilla movements in Latin America and after the death of their proponent Guevara (and the capture of DEBRAY),[35] rebels and theoreticians (MARIGHELLA[36]—see MOSS 1971; and more differentiated: GUILLÉN—see HODGES 1973) have turned to urban guerrilla activities to a greater extent (cf. also HODGES 1974). Yet, with the exception of the Tupamaros in Uruguay (cf. PORZECANSKI 1973 for an analysis; see also LAMBERG 1972:201-24; ALLEMANN 1974:277ff.) who at one point were close to acquiring a kind of Robin Hood image (cf. the analysis in chapter 5.2) among large parts of the population but who suffered a severe loss in legitimacy through a series of political murders, all of these movements have failed (the death of one of the theoretical leaders, Marighella in Brazil, being an additional indicator). These urban guerrilla activities (kidnappings, bombings, robberies, etc.) have increased considerably in the late 1960s and during the first half of the 1970s, spreading throughout the world. Two of the more prominent examples are the Symbionese Liberation Army in California and the Baader-Meinhof gang and their successor groups in West Germany. Yet it remains highly doubtful whether urban guerrilla activities will escalate to revolutionary fighting on a larger, mass-based scale. In effect, urban guerrilleros are lacking one of the vital requirements of successful guerrilla activities: a strategic *hinterland*. Accordingly, the death rate among urban guerrillas is rather high. If the urban environment provides any strategic advantages,[37] they are for students (or youth in general) and professionals from which urban guerilleros are largely drawn. For other groups and in other respects, however, strategic advantages are more likely to be found in a larger and more remote base area (cf. chapter 8.4.4). Yet these largely negative results may not preclude a quite different evaluation in the future if the present rate of urbanization in some Third World countries continues. Perhaps HUNTINGTON is right with his intermediate predictions: "Urban terrorism, in short, is easy; urban revolution extremely difficult. . . . In most Third World countries, it indeed may be too late for a peasant revolution; but it could also be too early for an urban one" (HUNTINGTON 1971a:9-10).

If the masses are not mobilized in favor of a revolutionary overthrow, they must at least remain neutral or be neutralized if the insurgents are to win (cf. also BLACKEY/PAYNTON 1971:284). Our definition of revolution does not imply that changes are caused solely by the new elites but simply that it is the elites who normally initiate these changes which are then taken up or varied by other population segments. The (re)construction of a social system is understood as an interactive process of revolutionary elites and revolutionary masses.[38] Furthermore, one probably must consider opponents of the revolution as having some sort of influence which may at times be strong enough to leave an impact on the pace revolutionary efforts will eventually take (in this respect cf. the slowing down of the Mexican Revolution; see the analyses of CLINE 1962; ECKSTEIN 1977).

In any case, by using this definition the delicate differentiation between progress and reaction or between revolution and counter-revolution is avoided (cf. also BRACHER 1976a:137–38).[39] If one takes this definition as a starting point for a cross-national analysis of revolutions, the number of cases, lies somewhere in between that of HUNTINGTON, who would score less cases, and AMANN, who would list the greatest number of cases.

8.3. Typologies of Revolutions

Actually, not only revolutions but also other forms of political protest behavior will be dealt with here.[40] If, in a more formal sense, revolution is to be distinguished from other forms of political protest behavior, the concept of revolution should be applied only in the singular. In terms of substantial typologies, in terms of causes and outcomes of revolutions, however, the plural is adequately used. (Yet, typologies of the latter kind are lacking, although some efforts can be found in the literature.) As may be expected in a field as underdeveloped as the comparative analysis of revolutions, typologies abound where systematic empirical knowledge is rather scarce. Unfortunately, in many works revolutions are not distinguished clearly enough from other forms of political protest behavior; this is probably one of the reasons why there is no developed social science of revolution. Examples of this flaw are given throughout the following sections.

In the literature one of the basic distinctions among types of revolutions is the distinction between political and social revolution (cf. e.g. LASSWELL/KAPLAN 1952:272–84). "Political" normally denotes something like a simple coup d'état which ends with the replacement of the former elite(s) by a new one but does not lead to marked changes in the social structure. Yet, one should be cautious (cf. chapter 7 passim) of a simple equation such as this: revolution = social and political revolution; coup d'état = political revolution. As we shall see, there may be more intricate relationships between coups and revolutions. GROSS (1958) has stated that all social revolutions are political revolutions as well, whereas the opposite does not hold. The aborted German revolution of 1918, for instance, was a political revolution, furthered by external defeat, but not a social revolution (see KLUGE 1978 for a recent review of the literature). At this point it may be helpful to go back to our definition of revolution developed in the preceding section. Leaving other criteria aside here, revolution was defined as a fundamental change of the social structure which implies an according change in the structure of authority. In GROSS's terminology social revolutions represent the more extensive type of revolution, of which political revolutions are a subcase (cf. also HUNTINGTON 1968:308). (Yet, why use the term political revolution at all? We would prefer leaving this term out of a science of revolutions and would rather speak of some more precisely described form of political change.)

The terminological confusion created by inflating the term revolution can be observed in a typology proposed by KORNHAUSER (1971). He uses three basic criteria for distinguishing revolutions: "*transformation* of whole societies," "*polarization* of social forces,"and "*mobilization* of large numbers of people" and comes up with eight types of revolutions depending upon whether the three criteria are met. Yet, it remains highly speculative what distinguishes an orderly revolution (with only the transformation criterion fulfilled), for example, from a mass revolution (with all three criteria met). According to the prevalent use of the term revolution, the latter would qualify as an orderly revolution. Additional criticism, especially as to the types communal revolution, coopted revolution, and nationalist revolution, could be raised. Actually, it is not the three basic criteria from which KORN-HAUSER starts but rather the mechanical use he makes of them in devising his eight types of revolution which must be rejected.

Our own conceptualization of revolutions resembles that of the Marxists in that the importance of fundamental social changes is underlined. However, it clearly differs from Marxism in that it considers political factors (rather than social factors alone) in the inception of a revolution. There is, in fact, evidence (cf. below) that some revolutions (revolution in our sense, social revolution in GROSS's terminology) started from mere changes in the political elites. Such an approach is consistent with LENIN's pragmatism, but certainly not with MARX's dogmatism as far as the theoretical analysis of conditions of revolutions is concerned. Our point may be illustrated by an admittedly difficult case, the takeover of power by the Nazis in 1933. The Nazis came to power legally, a fact often overlooked by writers on revolutionary phenomena. Once in power, they made extensive use of it or, to use GROSS's term, they carried out a political revolution. Some writers (DAHRENDORF 1965c:431–48) even suggest that they carried out a social revolution as well in that, following the 20 July 1944 assassination attempt, hundreds of aristocratic and other opponents were eliminated.[41] In any case, when using GROSS's and other writers' distinction between political and social revolution, it would make much more sense to apply it to the *outcome*[42] of the Nazi reign (cf. also MAZLISH et al. 1971:456) than to most of the coups in Latin America or elsewhere in the world. However, we would suggest *not* using this dichotomy, since it creates connotations to be avoided. One should use the term revolution in the stricter sense specified in the preceding section and denote other phenomena of political protest and political violence by different concepts rather than by inflating the term revolution.

These more general remarks are directly applicable to the typologies found in the literature. Many typologies listing various forms of revolution do not distinguish sufficiently between different forms of political protest and their outcomes. (There is only one class of typology which does not fall victim to this verdict, namely typologies of revolution which specify the causes of revolution, the participants, the forms of organization, the goals, and the outcomes.) The most common general mistake is that the concept of revolution is attached to phenomena which are actually coups. The disastrous consequences of such a classification can be observed in the few empirical analyses claiming to be comparative studies of revolution (cf. chapter 8.4.6).

These general considerations may suffice here. Additional weaknesses will become apparent as we turn to the discussion of several of the better-known typologies of revolution.

To start, PETTEE (1966:15-16) distinguishes between a "private palace revolution," a "public palace revolution" (cf. also LASSWELL/KAPLAN 1950:261-68), a "rebellion of an area against rule by the government of another country," and the "great national revolutions." He considers these forms as grouped along a continuum whose underlying criterion may be the use of violence, as VON BEYME (1973:23) has noted. Yet, PETTEE's somewhat unsystematic text does not thoroughly justify such an explication. HUNTINGTON has proposed at least two typologies relevant in the present context. One has been quoted in note 30 in the preceding section and will be considered again below; the other is somewhat dated (HUNTINGTON 1962a: 23-24). Here he proposes the following types: "internal war," "revolutionary coup," "reform coup," and "palace revolution."

Using internal war as the most general term, ROSENAU (1964:63-64) developed an often quoted typology in which three forms of internal wars[43] are distinguished: *"Personal wars* . . . are perceived as being fought over the occupancy of existing roles in the existing structure of political authority. . . ." *"Authority wars* . . . are being perceived as being fought over the arrangement (as well as the occupancy) of the roles in the structure of political authority, but with no aspiration on the part of the insurgents to alter either the other substructures of the society or its major domestic and foreign policies. . . ." *"Structural wars* . . . are perceived as being not only contests over personnel and the structure of political authority, but also as struggles over other substructures of the society . . . or its major domestic and foreign policies." We find this typology, especially the definition of structural wars and their delineation from authority wars, lacking in stringency.

A much more elaborate typology has been developed by JOHNSON (1964:26ff.) who uses four criteria for distinguishing revolutions:

1. targets of revolutionary activity [government, regime, or community];
2. identity of the revolutionaries (masses, elites-leading-masses, and elites);
3. revolutionary goals or "ideology"; and
4. whether or not the revolution is spontaneous or calculated.

JOHNSON then goes on to identify six types of revolutions:

1. the jacquerie[44] (mass peasant uprising);
2. the millenarian rebellion (the jacquerie plus charismatic leadership);
3. the anarchistic rebellion (revolutionaries "seek to relieve dysfunctions caused by a previous attempt within the system to relieve other dysfunctions");

4. the jacobin communist revolution[45] (the "great" revolutions such as in France and Russia);
5. the conspirational coup d'état; and
6. the militarized mass insurrection ("calculated, mass, revolutionary wars on the basis of guerrilla warfare and nationalistic ideologies such as in China 1937-1949, Algeria 1954-62, and North Vietnam, 1945-1954").

JOHNSON himself (1964:30) points out that in his typology he did not take sufficient note of the particular social systems. Also he did not specify the causes of the various forms of protest behavior. (Furthermore, of the four criteria suggested, the third, revolutionary goals or ideology, is at least partially contained in the first, targets of revolution.) Using JOHNSON's four criteria in a formal manner several other types of protest activities could be derived. Thus far there is not sufficient empirical evidence as to whether the six elaborated types are indeed the most important. The three other criteria (goals, identity of the revolutionaries, spontaneous vs. calculated protest), however, seem to be useful for constructing a typology. They need only be supplemented by two criteria taken care of in the typology of TANTER/MIDLARSKY (1967:265): the degree of violence and duration. TANTER/MIDLARSKY distinguish four dimensions: mass participation, duration, degree of domestic violence, and intentions of the insurgents, and derive the following four types (wording is for the most part as in original):[46]

Mass revolution: long duration, high degree of domestic violence; goal—fundamental changes in the structure of political authority and the social system;

Revolutionary coup: low mass participation, short to moderate duration, low to moderate degree of domestic violence; goal—fundamental change in the structure of political authority and possibly some change in the social system;

Reform coup: goal—moderate changes in the structure of political authority;

Palace Revolution: no mass participation, very short duration, virtually no domestic violence and virtually no change.

Some of the criteria helpful in distinguishing revolutions from other forms of (violent) political protest are taken up in Figure 8.1, which in part borrows from HUNTINGTON's earlier typologies (1962a;1968). The most important differentiation in this typology is that between elites and masses. Mass-led violent uprisings are usually bound to fail if revolutionary overthrow is the goal. Wars of independence tap an additional dimension, namely external dependencies. In general, wars of independence are nonrevolutionary[47] in character (thus the term colonial revolution [see BROCKWAY 1973] would be misleading in the context of this chapter); yet there are several examples of revolutionary wars of independence,[48] including

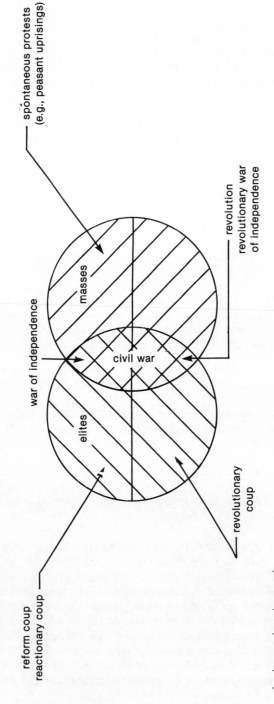

Figure 8.1. Revolutions and Other Forms of (Violent) Political Protest

+ This presupposes either a cooperating or at least not actively hostile (or otherwise rigidly coerced) population.

those in China during the 1940s and in Yugoslavia following the occupation by Nazi Germany. As can be seen in our figure, in the latter case civil warfare, warfare against foreign intruders, and revolutionary activities intersect each other.

If the regime is seriously weakened, especially by dissension among the elites, a revolution may be impending, provided that political and social discontent has grown to a high level, masses are mobilized by the elites, and this mobilization is accompanied by strong demands for radical social change (neglecting some other variables for the moment; cf. chapter 8.4). There is another partly overlapping alternative, i.e., civil war, which is most likely to occur if resources on both sides reach parity. Thus, not only elites but the masses as well are split (cf. the theoretical models in GURR 1970a:333, 341ff. and the interesting theoretical modifications by KORPI 1974a).[49]

To conclude this discussion of the advantages and disadvantages of typologies of revolution and other forms of political protest, we will mention briefly one of the more recent examples. RUSSELL (1974:56–59) stresses that revolutions refer to outcomes[50] and not to goals. It is important to note that "extremely revolutionary situations do not necessarily produce extremely revolutionary outcomes" (TILLY 1978:199; cf. also his Figure 7-3, ibid., p. 198). Furthermore, RUSSELL differentiates between short-term and long-term consequences. The two revolutionary upheavals in Russia in 1905 and 1917 may serve as an example. Short-term failure did not demoralize revolutionaries. In some respects it actually was a clear signal that the old regime could be attacked, perhaps with greater success, some time in the future. Other short-term failures easily come to mind, among the better-known examples the experience of the Chinese communists during the 1920s and Castro's early attacks on the Moncada barracks (1953).

Typologies generally convey a static image. Yet in reality there are several noteworthy examples of interrelationships of these various types, the question here being how they are related to revolutions. The relationship most often observed apparently exists between coups and revolutions. "Coups may occur within revolutions,[51] for they are a very efficient way of bringing a revolutionary government to power, but crucially they are not the revolution itself, but only a particular type of strategy employed by the revolutionary government to bring it to power and so enable it to carry out a revolution over the following years through laws which result in the revolution of the society" (O'KANE 1971:7). Ethiopia (cf. e.g., WOLDE-GIORGIS 1978 and OTTAWAY/OTTAWAY 1978) and Afghanistan before the Soviet invasion provide two recent examples; in contrast, developments in Portugal[52] seem to have led to a parliamentary system revoking some of the revolutionary measures taken earlier. The ubiquity of coups is stressed in GOODSPEED's summary of case studies including coups in Belgrade (1903), Dublin (Easter 1916), Saint Petersburg (1917), and Berlin (Kapp-Putsch 1920), as well as Mussolini's March on Rome (1922) and the attempt on Hitler's life (1944): "The coup d'état is seen in isolation, as the forerunner of civil war, as the climax to a successful revolution, as an attempt at counterrevolution, as the aftermath of foreign war, and as an attempt to mitigate defeat in war"

(GOODSPEED 1962:xii). Coups may not only precede revolutions but also end revolutionary activities, as in Chile. In this special case, however, one might even use a contradiction in terms and speak of an evolutionary-revolutionary way, pursued by the legally elected government of Allende, to be swept away by the rightist coup in 1973. Some other patterns are noted by RUSTOW: "All military revolutions begin as coups, and most coups claim to be revolutions. Once power is attained, some coups develop into revolutions: the difference is not in the promise but in the performance. The regimes established by Mustafa Kemal in Turkey after 1919, in Mexico under a succession of presidents between 1920 and 1940, and by Nasser in Egypt[53] since 1952 probably furnish the best empirical examples of such a development" (RUSTOW 1967:200). In fact, this latter pattern of "revolution from above" (the so-called "white" revolution) is frequently employed in order to prevent more serious and uncontrolled forms of revolutionary activities by the masses.

Revolution from above, or elite revolution, as a type of revolutionary change is also the subject of the comparative analysis of military bureaucrats and developments in Japan, Turkey, Egypt, and Peru by TRIMBERGER (1978).[54] She emphasizes that in order to succeed, elite reformers (perhaps a more appropriate term) or gradual revolutionists must prevent mass participation or otherwise neutralize the masses and must succeed in destroying the economic and political base of the upper class or aristocracy.[55] "The Meiji Restoration,[56] Nasserism, and military government in Peru after 1968 all meet this criterion of a revolution. The Ataturk regime was only marginally revolutionary. Ataturk destroyed the political, but only part of the economic, base of the notables of the Ottoman Empire" (TRIMBERGER 1978:3). The minimal use of violence furthers this extralegal takeover of political power. "Why and under what conditions do state bureaucrats become relatively autonomous in precapitalist or early capitalist societies? . . . Such autonomy is likely to occur when there is no consolidated landed class, as in nineteenth-century Japan and Turkey, or when a landed oligarchy is in economic and political decline. In the latter case, the rising bourgeoisie must also be weak and/or dependent on foreign interests, as in twentieth-century Egypt and Peru" (ibid., p. 5). With respect to late-developing nation-states TRIM-BERGER maintains:

> Military elites may stage coups and intervene in politics when one or more of [the following] conditions are absent, but such political action will either maintain the given social and economic structure or attempt to restore a declining order. A military coup will promote revolutionary change only when a significant segment of the military bureaucracy is: (a) autonomous (in recruitment and structure) from those classes which control the means of production; (b) politicized around an ideology of nation building; (c) threatened by nationalist movements from below; and (d) faced with contradictions in the international power constellation which can be exploited to increase national autonomy (TRIMBERGER 1978:156).

TRIMBERGER claims these four conditions are necessary and sufficient "to generate revolutionary action by military bureaucrats in a late-developing nation-state" (ibid.). GURR, however, points out a major shortcoming of this study: "A flaw in TRIMBERGER's analysis is that autonomy of industrial development is treated as a dichotomous variable: an economy is either autonomous (which is good) or dependent (which is bad), and any restriction on autonomy means failure. The overriding desirability attributed to economic autonomy is TRIMBERGER's position, not necessarily the ultimate objective of the revolutionary bureaucrats she analyzes" (GURR 1980a: 294).

In addition to the relationships specified thus far, there are other sequences between forms of political protest behavior and revolutions (cf. passim below), for example, between internal (civil) wars and revolution. Revolutions may not be entirely successful and thus be fought out in a civil war as in Russia, or a civil war may be won and thus pave the way to revolution later on as in China.[57]

In conclusion, systematic empirical results are more important than typologies of revolutions[58] and loosely gathered empirical evidence in determining likely sequences of the various forms of political protest and their eventual outcomes. Consequently, we now turn to an evaluation of the manifold causes suggested in theories of revolution.

8.4. Attempts at Explaining Revolutions

It is not difficult to dismiss explanations of revolutions such as the following by TIMASHEFF: "If, within a state, tension (or a cluster of tensions) has arisen between the government and an opposition and has reached such proportions that the symptoms of plasticity have become apparent, and if the conflict has not been resolved either by reform or reaction, a revolution is most likely to follow" (TIMASHEFF 1965:160). This "final formula of the causation of revolution" (ibid.), in fact, is a tautology. Looking at the literature, one finds that such "explanations" are anything but rare, even if they may not be as easily detected as in this case.

In the following sections a brief review of some theories and "explanation sketches" (HEMPEL 1965) is given. In some cases only key variables will be dealt with. Firstly, there will be a discussion of studies dealing basically with personality aspects of revolutionaries. Secondly, sociostructural as well as political factors will be considered in greater detail. And finally, more elaborate approaches to the study of revolutions will be taken up and confronted with empirical evidence.

8.4.1. Personality Approaches

Quite a few authors concentrate on the personality structures of revolutionaries when explaining revolutions. Personality approaches are useful in connection with other explanations focusing on higher level objects of explanation. If taken separately, however, their limitations should be kept in mind. Thus, neither the structure of the particular form of group revolutionary behavior nor its temporal and local incidence may be explained by analyzing personality aspects of revolutionaries.[59] GREENSTEIN (1967) in his analyses of the pros and cons of personality approaches has already dealt with the specific arguments. In the literature, WOLFENSTEIN (1967) proposes a rather questionable explanation when he tries to show that Lenin, Trotsky, and Gandhi (as to the latter cf. also ERIKSON 1969) had to act as they did simply on the basis of unresolved oedipal constellations (cf. also MAZLISH's "revolutionary ascetic," 1976, and JOHNSON's highly critical 1977 review of MAZLISH.) Other works sharing related teleological perspectives of explanation are ELLWOOD (1905), RIEZLER (1943), HOFFER (1951), LIFTON (1970), and PYE (1976)[60] (for a critique see REJAI/PHILLIPS 1979:25ff.).

In the study of DOWNTON (1973) relations between charismatic revolutionary leaders and revolutionary followers are discussed (cf. also the works by CALVERT 1970; DALY 1972; TAINTOR 1972; WELCH/TAINTOR 1972:197ff.; see also the stereotypes as to characteristics of the crowds in the French Revolution found in LeBON 1913 and chapter 8.4.6.6.2 for some works leading to rather different conclusions). Only qualitative empirical evidence is found in these studies. Furthermore, none of them meet the methodological and analytical requirements worked out by GREENSTEIN (1967). Less far-reaching but more substantial in nature is a study by STRAUSS (1973) who analyzes data on Russian revolutionaries who participated in the revolutionary attack in 1905 and were still alive in 1917. Data on the socioeconomic background of revolutionaries as well as on their participation in various revolutionary activities were factor-analyzed (Q-type), leading to six types of revolutionaries:[61] "(a) Rebel; (b) Striker; (c) Propagandist; (d) Party organizer; (e) Upper-level politician; (f) Intelligentsia" (STRAUSS 1973:300ff.). About 80% of the total variance is explained by these six factors. Moreover, individuals from middle and upper class social background were strongly overrepresented in the sample. Thus, there is some evidence for the hypothesis that the desertion of elites is an essential precondition if revolutionary undertakings are to be at all successful. Finally, Jews (about 25% in the sample versus 4% in the total Russian population) were overrepresented among revolutionaries (also among Hungarian revolutionaries after World War I; see McCAGG 1972). In the long run, methodologically solid studies such as this provide more substantial evidence[62] than the "great personality" interpretations whose empirical basis is often rather thin. (Monographs on revolutionaries are important, but there should be no misunderstanding as to their explanatory power.) A comprehensive review and critical evaluation of theory and research in the study of revolutionary personnel is found in REJAI (1980).

8.4.2. Toward the Development of a Sociostructural and Political Explanation: Tracing Some Key Variables

In one way or another, all of the explanations of revolutions dealt with in the remainder of this section could be classified as sociostructural and/or political explanations. In contrast to subsequent sections where we put greater emphasis on more complex explanations of revolutions (with the exception of some of the empirical explanations discussed in chapter 8.4.6), here the focus is on unravelling and, step by step, bringing together a set of theoretically important variables. After having dealt separately with more elaborate explanations of revolutions in some of the subsequent sections, these key variables and others will be included in a synthetic sociostructural and political model of revolutions.

As held true in the previous section, theoretical promise is one thing, empirical performance another. Dissension among elites; politically inept and corrupt upper social strata; frustrated expectations (resulting from blocked political, economic, and social aspirations; cf. below and passim in this study); antagonisms between social strata; a general feeling of malaise; the role of the army; foreign influences; resources available to the competitors—these and other variables (cf. the list of hypotheses in ECKSTEIN 1965:143-45 and his own paradigm ibid., p. 159-63) are frequently mentioned in theoretical studies on revolutions (cf. PETTEE 1938; EDWARDS 1927; MEUSEL 1934; KUMAR 1971:40-52; for a critique see RITTBERGER 1971:505-6). GOTTSCHALK (1944), for example, stresses the following five general factors: a provocation on behalf of the government or an external power leads to discontent; this, in turn, spreads among the population; a counterprogram raising hopes is devised (role of the intellectuals; cf. below); leadership personnel must be available if protest is to be successful; finally, as the "immediate cause" of revolution (GOTTSCHALK 1944:7) there is a "weakness of the conservative forces"or, in other words, a crisis in political leadership (cf. PARSONS 1964, "power deflation").

As CARR, perhaps somewhat too strongly, has said with respect to the Russian Revolution: "The contribution of LENIN and the Bolsheviks to the overthrow of Tsarism was negligible. . . . Bolshevism succeeded to a vacant throne" (CARR 1960:25).[63] However, a more balanced account reads:

> Rather, the government literally committed suicide by alienating
> every conceivable source of popular support. By blocking wage
> increases and factory reforms, by continually postponing any new
> land settlement, and by its attempts to renew the war effort the
> Provisional Government discredited itself in the eyes of the workers,
> peasants, and soldiers of Russia. Similarly the moderate socialist
> leaders of the Petrograd Soviet were swept into the "refuse pile of
> history" because by late summer they had clearly lost touch with

the masses.[64] The election results in the Soviets, trade union organizations, factory committees, and city councils from August onwards clearly demonstrate a growing rejection of Menshewik[65] and Socialist Revolutionary leadership (ULDRICKS 1974:410-11; cf. also ROSENBERG 1974 for an analysis of the unrealistic policies of the liberal Kadets and their fate later on; cf. also PEARSON 1977).

The importance of developments in the Petrograd garrison in the summer of 1917 lies less in the garrison's positive military contribution to the Bolshevik victory than in the disastrous effect that the demoralization of the garrison had upon the attempts to reestablish public order and governmental authority and ultimately in the elimination of garrison troops as a significant military force on the side of the Provisional Government. Had the Bolsheviks been opposed by a few well armed and disciplined military units, it is not at all certain that they could have seized power;[66] the crucial point is that by October there were almost no troops upon which the government could rely. That a similar process of disintegration had occurred in the provinces and the front sealed the fate of the Provisional Government. . . . At the same time the Bolsheviks must be credited with having been the only major Russian political group to recognize the enormous potential significance of the garrison[67] and to make a serious effort to obtain its support (RABINOWITCH 1972:191;[68] cf. also PIPES 1968).

Some of the very same explicative variables noted above have already been described by TOCQUEVILLE in his classic *L'Ancien Régime et la révolution* (1856; see also the critical discussion in RICHTER 1966; ZEITLIN 1971; cf. also LINDNER 1972:19-30 and GEISS 1972). TOCQUEVILLLE's central hypothesis has become one of the most famous propositions in the study of revolutions. "Revolution does not always come when things are going from bad to worse. It occurs most often when a nation that has accepted, and indeed has given no sign of even having noticed the most crushing laws, rejects them at the very moment when their weight is being lightened. The regime that is destroyed by a revolution is almost always better than the one preceding it, and experience teaches us that usually the most dangerous time for a bad government is when it attempts to reform itself" (TOCQUEVILLE 1856 as quoted in RICHTER 1966:119—as to the rationale of this hypothesis, cf. the discussion and the indirect evidence in chapter 5.1.2.5). TOCQUEVILLE points out that "it was precisely in those parts of France where there had been most improvement that popular discontent ran highest." The causal mechanisms making for such a relationship have been discussed at length in chapter 5.3.2.3. Note that the statement refers to regions and not to individuals. Thus, we are still left with the possibility of an aggregate fallacy (but cf. also the evidence in chapter 8.4.6.6.2).

TOCQUEVILLE's observation reappears in BRINTON's 1952 summary of his comparative analysis of revolutions in England, the United States,[69] France, and Russia:

First, these were all societies on the whole on the upgrade economically before the revolution came, and the revolutionary movements seem to originate in the discontents of not unprosperous people who feel restraint, cramp, annoyance, rather than downright crushing-oppression. . . .

Second, we find in our prerevolutionary society definite and indeed very bitter class antagonisms, though these antagonisms seem rather more complicated than the cruder Marxists will allow. . . . Strong feelings, too, as James C. DAVIES suggests, are roused in those who find an intolerable gap between what they have come to want—their "needs" and what they actually get. Revolutions seem more likely when social classes are fairly close together than when they are far apart. . . .

Third, there is what we have called the desertion of the intellectuals [cf. EDWARDS 1927]. This is in some respects the most reliable[70] of the symptoms we are likely to meet. . . .

Fourth, the governmental machinery is clearly inefficient, partly through neglect, through a failure to make changes in old institutions, partly because new conditions . . . laid an intolerable strain on governmental machinery adapted to simpler, more primitive, conditions.

Fifth, the old ruling class—or rather, many individuals of the old ruling class—come to distrust themselves, or lose faith in the traditions and habits of their class. . . . [as to the latter see also BRZEZINSKI 1971:504-5; cf. KIRCHHEIMER 1965].

The dramatic events that start things moving, that bring on the fever[71] of revolution, are in three of our four revolutions intimately connected with the financial administration[72] of the state. In the fourth, Russia, the breakdown of administration under the burdens of an unsuccessful war is only in part financial. . . .

Yet one is impressed in all four instances more with the ineptitude of the governments' use of force than with the skill of their opponents' use of force (BRINTON 1965:250ff.).

There are clear merits in BRINTON's qualitative analysis, particularly in that he seeks a comparative analysis of the conditions of revolution (for some similar results see also SOULE 1935:1-71). Yet one must also point out that the social substratum in the four revolutions has not been analyzed in sufficient detail by BRINTON, as RUDÉ has undertaken in his studies on the French Revolution (cf. chapter 8.4.6.6.2). The desertion of the intellectuals or of the elites is probably one of the central variables for the genesis of revolutions. PARETO (1901, 1963) some years earlier had noted the same phenomenon when speaking of the "circulation of elites" (see LOPREATO 1973 for a "formal re-statement"). The lions of yesterday are the foxes of tomorrow or, in the metaphorical language of PARETO, history is nothing but the "graveyard of aristocracies."[73] For PARETO, there seem to be several reasons for this circulation of elites, one being that the incumbent elites miss the opportunity to coopt those elites who may otherwise form an opposition,[74] another consisting in the general weakness of the foxes, in their inability to suppress opposition by force.[75] PARETO perceives elites to be worn-out and decadent after having reigned for some time. "When simultaneously the upper strata are full of decadent elements and the lower strata are full of elite elements, the social equilibrium becomes highly unstable and a violent revolution is imminent" (PARETO 1965:84, as quoted in HAGOPIAN 1974:53).

Needless to say in this context, revolutionary leaders come by and large from middle-class origin, are better educated, have better occupations and generally more resources available than do rank and file revolutionaries (cf. the brief overviews in REJAI 1973:31ff. and 139; 1980:113-14; see also LASSWELL/LERNER 1966; LAQUEUR 1968:503; OBERSCHALL 1973: 150ff.; DONALDSON/WALLER 1970; GREENE 1974:16-32; PUTNAM 1976:193ff.; NAGLE 1977; and REJAI/PHILLIPS 1979). In line with these characteristics, elite revolutionaries generally come from large cities (but cf. also REJAI/PHILLIPS 1979:107 for a slight qualification), Mao and Ho Chi Minh being notable exceptions here.[76] For further information on personality and social background characteristics of sixty-four revolutionary leaders (the sample comprises leaders from the English, American, French 1789, Mexican, Russian, Chinese, Bolivian, Vietminh, Hungarian, Cuban, Algerian, and French 1968 "revolutions"), see REJAI/PHILLIPS 1979. They underline in greater detail many of the findings briefly summarized here. Furthermore, they report that "well over half of [the revolutionary leaders] turn out to have led a rather tranquil [family life]" (ibid., p. 80); that "a large number of leaders are prolific publishers" (ibid.); that most of the contemporary revolutionary leaders are adherents of Marxism and nationalism; that "middle children are underrepresented among revolutionary elites" (ibid., p. 192), but "that there is no single pattern in the radicalization of revolutionary elites [n=32 here]. Since each revolutionary will encounter a different constellation of experiences, the particular 'mix' among the radicalizing agents will vary from revolutionary to revolutionary" (ibid., p. 197). Consequently, they propose a situational theory of revolutionary leadership emphasizing the "close interplay between three variables in the emergence of revolutionary leaders: a revolutionary situation, a mental set or psychology, a range of skills. Taken together, the three variables demonstrate why it is that: (1) not all revolutionary situations give rise to revolutionary leaders, and (2) not all persons with the appropriate psychology and skills emerge as leaders of revolution" (REJAI/PHILLIPS 1979:59; see also p. 60 for their model). They also indicate the next step (thus answering some of the present criticism), namely a comparison of revolutionary leaders with political leaders in general.

Revolutionary elites not only organize the potential for mass rebellion but also formulate a new ideology.[77] The role of the intelligentsia[78] in developing new social ideas has often been stressed. Well-known examples include the Puritan ministers during the seventeenth century, the French *philosophes* during the eighteenth century, and the Russian intellectuals during the nineteenth century. Students as a kind of future elite at times also have their share in revolutionary protest activities, the Chinese Cultural Revolution during the second half of the 1960s[79] and the demonstrations against Reza Shah Pahlevi providing recent examples. (The student revolt of the 1960's, in general, does not qualify as revoluntionary in character, the turbulent events in France during May 1968 perhaps being a more questionable case.) Yet one should clearly distinguish between the desertion of the elites and the impact of the intellectuals (who, in fact, often do not have direct access to the mass media). In our opinion, the former is of greater significance in the occurrence of revolution,[80] while a change in the intellectual climate may be one of the more long-term influences on revolutionary outbreaks. Thus, it comes as no surprise that the desertion of the intellectuals is usually the first step in the revolutionary process.[81]

As already stated, the desertion of certain of the elites is often caused by blocked opportunities of mobility (as to the impact of this variable see chapter 5.3.2.3; cf. also the analytical differentiations in OBERSCHALL 1973:160 who distinguishes between horizontal and vertical aspects of integration). GESCHWENDER (1968) and other authors interpret this process in the context of status inconsistency theory.[82] Yet not only elites but larger masses as well may be affected by blocked mobility channels. The aspiring French bourgeoisie, for instance, was not able to achieve a place in society equivalent to its economic resources (cf. BARBER 1955). The impermeability of the social system led to the build-up of considerable frustrations. "Thus, the 'winners' who benefit most from economic growth are likely to be 'marginal men' who have often proven susceptible to revolutionary appeals" (HAGOPIAN 1974:176). Status inconsistency theory (or, more precisely, the combination of high achievement dimensions and low ascriptive dimensions; cf. also chapter 5.3.2.3) sheds some light on one of the mechanisms likely to have an effect (but see also the methodological warnings of BLALOCK 1966) in such a situation (cf. also the evidence on revolutionary leaders in REJAI/PHILLIPS 1979:167-70). In a narrower sense, however, elite dissent would *presuppose* status *con*sistency among all members of the elite, since, by definition, "elite" would imply holding a top position in a hierarchy. If one uses a less restrictive definition of elites, namely persons holding central positions in one or several hierarchies important to the functioning of the political and economic system, status inconsistency may indeed be one determinant of dissent among the elites. This dissent is in itself one of the most important variables, apart from the mobilization of discontented masses and disloyalty of the army, if the success of revolutionary attempts is to be explained.[83]

The preceding brief discussion and the results in chapter 5 should make it clear that economic indicators (in the sense of the economic deterioration → revolutionary attack hypothesis) are sufficient for explaining neither revolutionary activities nor—a fortiori—successful revolution. Nevertheless, economic causes remain very important determinants[84] of attempts at revolutionary overthrow, as will be shown for the French Revolution in chapter 8.4.6.6.2.

Some of the conditions of revolutions stated thus far may be summarized using a slightly different terminology:

> Feelings of frustration and discontent ["deprivation"], widespread in society, must be focused upon political institutions ["structural blame" or "system blame"]. These institutions, in turn, must be viewed as rigid and unyielding, as inaccessible and unconcerned. Inconsistent use of force by the political elite may deepen the grievances harbored against political institutions. The growth of a myth of economic, social and political betterment provides an opportunity for the full transfer of allegiance and legitimacy to new institutions.[85] It is with the emergence of alternative political institutions that revolution comes to public attention (WELCH/TAINTOR 1972:13).

To return to the role of elites, they must lead mass protests if attempts at revolutionary overthrow are to be at all successful. This means that they must create organizations for mass mobilization, i.e., some kind of a revolutionary party.[86]

LENIN's (1967) "What is to be done?" of 1902 contains a classic formulation of the problem. There must be a small centrally organized and controlled party consisting of professionals (cf. also the analyses of SELZNICK 1960; the historical account of the Communist Party of the Soviet Union by SCHAPIRO 1970; see SCHURMANN, 1966, and HARRISON, 1972, with respect to the Chinese Communist Party; cf. also the brief overview given by PAGE 1968). LENIN's model of the Bolshevik party is not entirely new. There are various precursors, yet they were much less successful in carrying out their revolutionary ideas. "Lenin's model of the Bolshevik party had its umbilical cord attached to Tkachev's theory and model. Tkachev in turn was probably influenced by Blanqui, and Blanqui by the French conspirators Buonarrotti and Babeuf, who originate ideologically from the late Jacobins" (GROSS 1974:56-57; cf. also VON BORCKE 1977). In early 1917 the Bolshevik Party had no more than 25,000 party members (even though by August 1917 it had grown to about 240,000 members; cf. RIGBY 1968). Compared to other groups, however, the Bolsheviks were the best organized group at that point,[87] as is often the case with communist insurgents. HAMMOND (1975:642) reports that only in the case of the Hungarian Soviet Republic of Béla Kun[88] have communists been overthrown (1919) after having been in control of a country as a whole. "Once a Communist regime is fully ensconced, it is almost impossible to remove it, except perhaps by foreign intervention" (HAMMOND 1975:642). The rebels' relative advantage of commanding better organized resources becomes even greater if prevailing elites can no longer rely on institutionalized forms of behavior. In such a society, oppositional elites can directly mobilize revolutionary masses against the incumbent government (cf. KORNHAUSER's 1959 theory of mass society; cf. also chapter 6.3.5).[89]

Two major explicative variables have not as yet been dealt with: the existence and the role of the army and whether or not the army is unsuccessfully engaged in external warfare. Both aspects may, of course, be related. "Defeat and/or demobilization provide especially favorable circumstances for revolution because they combine the presence of substantial coercive resources with uncertain control over their use" (TILLY 1978:211). There are several examples in history that unsuccessful engagement in external warfare[90] has led to the disintegration of the army (and the political leadership), thus eventually paving the way for rebels to take over the political system.[91] SETON-WATSON (1951), for example (cf. also HUNTINGTON 1968:304-8; ARENDT 1964), maintains that the revolutions in China, Russia, [92] and Yugoslavia would not have been possible without the armies' external defeat causing a loss in legitimacy and eventually the internal defeat of the government.[93] Thus, HAGOPIAN is quite right when speaking of "war [as] the midwife of revolution" (HAGOPIAN 1974:163).[94] STEIN/RUSSETT (1980:411) report that in all nine instances of a major power losing a war since 1850 a regime change occurred, whereas there was no regime change at all among the winners of sustained war between major powers.

Attempts at revolutionary overthrow do not succeed in the face of a strong, loyal, and readily available army. Cuba provides perhaps the most interesting example here, since comparatively few rebels (not more than 6,000 even on the day of victory) could win against an army which, though highly superior in terms of military equipment, had almost completely broken down (see THOMAS 1963). Many observers have noted parallels to the events in Nicaragua in summer 1979 when the (partly Cuban-supported) Sandinistas won against the National Guard of Somoza. Another parallel was the withdrawal of U. S. financial support from the incumbent government for violations of human rights. In Iran, as soon as the army, the key figure, declared itself neutral, power was taken over by Ayatollah Khomeini in February 1979. "Whatever government or party has the full allegiance of a country's armed forces is to all intents and purposes politically impregnable" (CHORLEY 1943:16). If this condition is not met, however, various outcomes, such as a civil war with army sections fighting on both sides or a successful revolution, are possible (cf. the causal model in chapter 8.4.7). In the words of CHORLEY who was the first to treat the army's role in a detailed historical study:

> Insurrections cannot be permanently won against a professional
> army operating its technical resources at full strength. They can be
> won only when the introduction of some extraneous factor cripples
> the striking power of the professional fighting forces for one reason
> or another. . . .[95] The supreme solvent for the disintegration of the
> rank and file is an unsuccessful war. . . . There can be little doubt
> that under modern conditions the last stages of an unsuccessful war
> provide the surest combination of circumstances for a successful
> revolutionary outbreak (CHORLEY 1943:23, 108).

The validity of CHORLEY's analysis is clearly underlined by a recent study of HAMMOND (cf. also SETON-WATSON 1951; STRAUSZ-HUPÉ et al. 1963; BLACK/THORNTON 1964; SCALAPINO 1965; MOSS 1975) who sums up the evidence as to the determinants of successful communist takeovers:[96]

> Military force has been the key to success in almost every case, and usually this has meant the Red Army. Out of a total of twenty-two Communist takeovers beginning in 1917, the Red Army played some role in fifteen and played the leading role in twelve. Where the Red Army was not decisive, native armed forces generally were used, as in Yugoslavia, Albania,[97] China, Vietnam, and Cuba. Indeed, there were only three instances in which armed force was not the crucial element—in the tiny states of San Marino, Kerala, and West Bengal. Moreover, in each of these three states the Communists were subsequently removed from office. Thus it can be said that armed force was the determinant of victory in *all* cases in which Communists have not only seized power but have managed to retain it. . . .
> Almost all communist takeovers have occurred either during international wars or in the aftermath of such wars—wars which undermined the old political, economic, and social order and which, in many cases, provided an opportunity for a foreign Communist army (usually the Red Army) to intervene (HAMMOND 1975:640-41).

However, "the history of communism has by no means been a steady succession of unmitigated triumphs. In fact, more Communist revolutions have been defeated than have not" (HAMMOND 1975a:xv). These results are, of course, no news to successful revolutionaries: "Political power grows out of the barrel of a gun. . . . Whoever wants to seize and hold on to political power must have a strong army" (MAO Tse-tung; *Problems of war and strategy*, Peking: n.p., 1954:14-15, here as quoted in HAMMOND 1975:640-41).

RUSSELL (1974:12ff.) cites other authors concurring with CHORLEY in her analysis but also a number of writers who subscribe to the view of MAO (and GUEVARA) that "popular forces can win a war against the army." Obviously, these counter-hypotheses do not refer to the same object. What is meant by MAO is that popular forces, if united, can successfully fight an army that is not at the height of its strength.[98] GUEVARA's own disaster may once again be recalled here. RUSSELL's analysis of the role of the army in twenty-eight mass rebellions[99] after 1906 (in twenty-two countries) leads her to conclude that "in no case of successful rebellion did the regime retain the loyalty of the armed forces" (RUSSELL 1974:77).[100] Yet, an unloyal[101] army in itself is only a necessary, but not a sufficient condition of revolutions.[102] In this context a longer quotation from TROTSKY may be helpful:

> There is no doubt that the fate of every revolution at a certain point is decided by a break in the disposition of the army. Against a numerous, disciplined, well-armed and ably led military force, unarmed or almost unarmed masses of the people cannot possibly

gain a victory. But no deep national crisis can fail to affect the army to some extent. Thus along with the conditions of a truly popular revolution there develops a possibility—not, of course, a guarantee—of its victory. However, the going over of the army to the insurrection does not happen of itself, nor as a result of mere agitation (TROTSKY 1957, here as quoted in RUSSELL 1974:81).

Thus, the following rudimentary causal model may be developed.[103] Note that population disloyalty, elite leadership and army disloyalty must occur interactively (not additively) for attacks to lead to revolutionary overthrow.

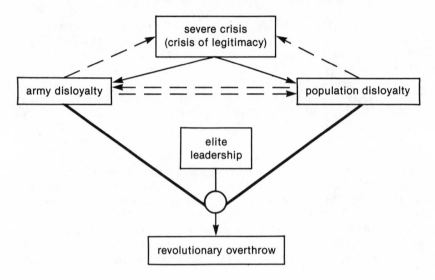

Figure 8.2. A Basic Model of Revolutionary Overthrow

Several authors (e.g., TIMASHEFF 1965) perceive a direct relationship between war and revolution. SOROKIN (1925; 1937; 1957), however, on the basis of far-reaching historical studies (cf. also HUNTER 1940) and several case analyses, comes to this conclusion (also dealt with in chapter 5.1.2.6): "Contrary to expectation, the data do not definitely show a positive association between unsuccessful wars and big disturbances nor between victorious wars and the absence of such. At best they yield only a very slight association between unsuccessful wars and disturbances" (SOROKIN 1957:597). And furthermore: "War, as such, no matter whether successful or not, is neither a necessary nor a sufficient condition for starting or reinforcing internal disturbances" (ibid., p. 598). His "disturbances," are, however, not to be equated with revolutions. They comprise many other forms of violent political protest as well. (Actually he ends up with more than 1,000 "revolutions.") Furthermore, with superpowers emerging in the twentieth century, SOROKIN's historical generalizations[104] may not necessarily provide an answer valid today.

Considering the preceding discussion, one might posit a rank order of importance for the three major causal variables in the explanation of revolutions:

1. disloyalty of the army (and the internal security forces) or, more generally, a breakdown of the monopoly of coercion;
2. desertion of the elites;
3. discontent among the population at large.[105]

In concluding this discussion of some major sociostructural and political variables explaining the occurrence of revolutions, a look at JOHNSON's (1964; 1966) purely macrosociological approach may be of interest. He distinguishes between dysfunctional sociostructural factors and "accelerators" (usually called precipitants; cf. below). Dysfunctionality is said to occur when the social system is out of balance, with "power deflation"[106] or "loss of authority" being likely causes of such dysfunction. In short, JOHNSON offers this explanation: "Multiple dysfunctions plus elite intransigence cause revolution" (JOHNSON 1964:22). More generally, he distinguishes four kinds of "pressures . . . which may destroy a system's equilibrium": "(1) exogenous value-enhancing sources; (2) endogenous value-enhancing sources; (3) exogenous environment-changing sources; and (4) endogenous environment-changing sources" (JOHNSON 1966:64). However, it remains totally unclear what is meant by dysfunctionality.[107] If one looks at JOHNSON's indicators of dysfunctionality (e.g., suicide rate, criminal activities, size of police departments, JOHNSON 1966: chapter 6), one wonders what they might have to do with revolutions directly. At best, the materials presented are illustrative in nature.

Besides the so-called dysfunctions which denote the "preconditions" (ECKSTEIN 1965:140) for the buildup of protest potentials, precipitants are needed to spark off a revolutionary potential: "Accelerators [or precipitants] are occurrences that catalyze or throw into relief the already existent revolutionary level of dysfunctions. They do not of themselves cause revolutions; but when they do occur in a system already bearing the necessary level of dysfunctions . . . , they will provide the sufficient cause of the immediately following revolution" (JOHNSON 1964:12). Tracing the use of the term in chemistry, HAGOPIAN (1974:166) rightly describes a precipitant as promoting "a drastic and immediate reaction amongst preexisting ingredients." HAGOPIAN (ibid., p. 167) also distinguishes accidental precipitants from planned precipitants, the latter being more characteristic of revolutions in the last two centuries. In literature there seems to be no agreement about the events belonging to the class of precipitants. The reader is referred to the discussion of precipitants in chapter 5.3.2.5. Mutatis mutandis, the arguments presented there hold here as well (cf. also OVERHOLT 1977:317). They lead one to call into question a description of revolutionary precipitants as "phenomena . . . almost always unique and ephemeral in character" (ECK-STEIN 1965:140).

JOHNSON claims to have specified necessary and sufficient conditions of revolutions. Yet this is true only in a purely formal sense. In terms of substance, his theorizing remains rather vague although he goes into much greater detail when presenting his typology of revolutions (JOHNSON 1964:26ff.; cf. also chapter 8.3).

The discussion thus far has centered on isolating variables which may be important for explaining revolutions. The arguments presented have generally been based on a mixture of theoretical justification and some kind of qualitative empirical evidence. This procedure will also be followed in some of the sections below. For the moment it may be helpful to deal with three theoretical explanations of revolutions in toto. They are related in some respects although basically they explain different aspects of revolutions. To start, HUNTINGTON's less ambitious yet still far-reaching explanatory sketch of revolutions will be taken up. MOORE's sociohistorical analysis provides a broader theoretical and historical framework to analyze the phenomenon of revolution, followed by a look at SKOCPOL's recent comparative analysis of three social revolutions.

8.4.3. The Theoretical Approaches of HUNTINGTON, MOORE, and SKOCPOL

8.4.3.1. HUNTINGTON

For HUNTINGTON a revolution is an "aspect of modernization." "Like other forms of violence and instability, it is most likely to occur in societies which have experienced some social and economic development and where the processes of political modernization and political development have lagged behind the processes of social and economic change" (HUNTINGTON 1968:265). The process of mobilization leads to the entrance of new groups into the political arena. If the political structure (political institutionalization) does not provide for a sufficient number of possibilities to realize the claims and aspirations of these new groups including new elites and other social forces, this in the end will lead to revolution. "The great revolutions of history have taken place either in highly centralized traditional monarchies (France, China, Russia), or in narrowly based military dictatorships (Mexico, Bolivia, Guatemala,[108] Cuba), or in colonial regimes (Vietnam, Algeria).[109] All these political systems demonstrated little if any capacity to expand their power and to provide channels for the participation of new groups in politics" (HUNTINGTON 1968:275).[110]

This hypothesis certainly is not new. It is one of the general hypotheses in this study on theories and empirical research on political violence, crises, and revolutions. Yet HUNTINGTON leaves conventional ground when proposing a series of additional hypotheses, worth quoting in full:

> Two general patterns [of revolution] can be identified. In the
> "Western" pattern, the political institutions of the old regime
> collapse; this is followed by the mobilization of new groups into
> politics and then by the creation of new political institutions. The
> "Eastern"[111] revolution, in contrast, begins with the mobilization
> of new groups into politics and the creation of new political institu-
> tions and ends with the violent overthrow of the political institu-
> tions of the old order. . . . The French, Russian, Mexican, and, in its
> first phases, Chinese Revolutions approximate the Western model;
> the latter phases of the Chinese Revolution, the Vietnamese Revolu-
> tion, and other colonial struggles against imperialist powers approxi-
> mate the Eastern model. In general, the sequence of movement from
> one phase to the next is much more clearly demarcated in the
> Western revolution than in the Eastern type. In the latter all three
> phases tend to occur more or less simultaneously. One fundamental
> difference in sequence, however, does exist between the two. In the
> Western revolution, political mobilization is the consequence of the
> collapse of the old regime; in the Eastern revolution it is the cause of
> the destruction of the old regime (ibid., p. 266-67).

Thus, HUNTINGTON in part agrees with PETTEE's observation that revolution "begins simply with a sudden recognition by almost all the passive and active membership that the state no longer exists" (PETTEE 1938:100, as quoted in HUNTINGTON 1968:267; for a theoretical and empirical elaboration along these lines cf. also chapter 8.4.6.6.1).

> The distinguishing characteristic of the Western revolution is the
> period of anarchy or statelessness after the fall of the old regime
> while moderates, counterrevolutionaries, and radicals are struggling
> for power. The distinguishing characteristic of the Eastern revolution
> is a prolonged period of "dual power" in which the revolutionaries
> are expanding political participation and the scope and authority of
> their institutions of rule at the same time that the government is, in
> other geographical areas and at other times, continuing to exercise
> its rule. In the Western revolution the principal struggles are
> between revolutionary groups; in the Eastern revolution they are
> between one revolutionary group and the established order. . . . In
> the Western revolution the revolutionaries come to power in the
> capital first and then gradually expand their control over the
> countryside. In the Eastern revolution they withdraw from central,
> urban areas of the country, establish a base area of control in a
> remote section, struggle to win the support of the peasants through
> terror and propaganda, slowly expand the scope of their authority,
> and gradually escalate the level of their military operations from
> individual terroristic attacks to guerrilla warfare to mobile warfare

and regular warfare. Eventually they are able to defeat the government troops in battle. The last phase of the revolutionary struggle is the occupation of the capital (ibid., p. 271-72).[112]

In the Western model the beginning of the revolutionary struggle can be clearly marked, but not the end, whereas in the Eastern model the opposite holds true. "The end of the revolutionary process . . . can be precisely dated symbolically or actually by the final conquest of power by the revolutionaries in the capital of the regime: January 31, 1949, January 1, 1959"[113] (ibid., p. 272), April 30, 1975, or July 19, 1979.

In the following longer quotation some further differences between the two types of revolution are elaborated:

> The Western revolution is usually directed against a highly traditional regime headed by an absolute monarch or dominated by a land-owning aristocracy. The revolution typically occurs when this regime comes into severe financial straits, when it fails to assimilate the intelligentsia and other urban elite elements, and when the ruling class from which its leaders are drawn has lost its moral self-confidence and will to rule. The Western revolution, in a sense, telescopes the initial "urban breakthrough" of the middle class and the "green uprising" of the peasantry into a single convulsive, revolutionary process. Eastern revolutions, in contrast, are directed against at least partially modernized regimes.[114] These may be indigenous governments that have absorbed some modern and vigorous middle-class elements and that are led by new men with the ruthlessness, if not the political skill, to hang on to power, or they may be colonial regimes in which the wealth and power of a metropolitan country gives the local government a seemingly overwhelming superiority in all the conventional manifestations of political authority and military force. In such circumstances no quick victory is possible and the urban revolutionaries have to fight their way to power through a prolonged rural insurrectionary process. Western revolutions are thus precipitated by weak traditional regimes; Eastern revolutions by narrow modernizing ones (ibid., p. 273).[115]

Apart from these differences between Western and Eastern revolutions, there seem to be a number of conditions underlying successful revolutions in general, the first being that successful revolutionary overthrows presuppose coalitions between different social groups.

> One social group can be responsible for a coup, a riot, or a revolt, but only a combination of groups can produce a revolution. . . . In 1789, PALMER observes, "Peasant and bourgeois were at war with the same enemy, and this is what made possible the French Revolution." [PALMER 1959:484] . . . The probability of revolution in a modernizing country depends upon: (a) the extent to which the urban middle class—intellectuals, professionals, bourgeoisie—are alienated from the existing order; (b) the extent to which the

peasants are alienated from the existing order; and (c) the extent to which urban middle class and peasants join together not only in fighting against "the same enemy" but also in fighting for the same cause. This cause is usually nationalism (ibid., p. 277).

And this, in turn, is reinforced by "foreign war and foreign intervention. Nationalism is the cement of the revolutionary alliance and the engine of the revolutionary movement" (ibid., p. 308).

It must be added here that HUNTINGTON does not consider all of the social forces participating in revolutionary coalitions to be of equal importance. Rather, it is the peasants who play the decisive role. If they join the revolutionary coalition, i.e., are won over by urban intellectuals and middle class members, revolutionary success becomes much more likely. "Each of the major revolutions in Western, as well as non-Western societies, was in large part a peasant revolution. This was true in France and in Russia as it was in China" (ibid., p. 293). Peasants thus seem to have some kind of veto power (which certainly is not consciously exerted by them). "The role of the city is constant: it is the permanent source of opposition.[116] The role of the countryside is variable: it is either the source of stability or the source of revolution. For the political system, opposition within the city is disturbing, but not lethal. Opposition within the countryside, however, is fatal. He who controls the countryside controls the country" (ibid., p. 292; cf. also GURR 1970a:266). Quite in line with this analysis, HUNTINGTON suggests that "urban migration is, in some measure, a substitute for rural revolution" (ibid., p. 299).[117] The results of the impact of urban migration (cf. chapter 5.1.2.2) should be recalled here. Recent migrants to the city are anything but ardent revolutionaries.

In short, a revolutionary peasantry is a necessary condition for attempts at revolutionary overthrow to succeed, but not a sufficient one. Leadership by the urban middle classes must also be present[118] as well as neutralization of the army and the internal security forces. In any case, there is evidence enough to refute MARX's theory of a greater likelihood (or, more precisely, his definitive forecast) of revolution in industrially more advanced countries. Twentieth century revolutions predominantly took place in backward agricultural societies (or in partially modernizing ones), whereas earlier revolutions occurred in economically and culturally advanced countries (cf. also the analysis of MOORE in the next section).

To return to a previously mentioned variable, the energizing role of nationalism becomes immediately clear when viewed in the proper context: "No society can carry out a revolution in isolation. Every revolution is, in some measure, against not only the dominant class at home but also against the dominant system" (HUNTINGTON 1968:306). "The stimulus to nationalist mobilization may be furnished either by a foreign political, economic [cf. also chapter 8.4.6.3], and military presence in a country before the collapse of the old order or by foreign political and military intervention after that collapse. In Mexico, China, Vietnam, Cuba, Guatemala, the presence of foreign business, foreign bases, or foreign rule, furnished a target against which the masses could be aroused. All these countries except Vietnam [on the "revolution" in Vietnam, see WOODSIDE 1976] were formally independent when their revolutions began but all of them also were economically and militarily subordinate to foreign powers" (HUNTINGTON 1968:304-5). In the case of China, war against the Japanese invaders created better conditions for the communist revolutionaries in that the incumbent regime was weakened through external fighting. Being successful defenders of the fatherland, insurgents at the same time gained in legitimacy. Moreover, they also came to be seen as the only power likely to guarantee stability after the end of war (cf. C. JOHNSON 1962; BELL 1973:108; SMITH 1973:108-10).[119]

Even in the case of the two great revolutions carried out in the absence of major foreign intervention or penetration, namely the French Revolution and the Russian Revolution, there were serious international attempts at counter-revolution *after* the collapse of the old order. With respect to the former, it has been noted that "the war revolutionized the Revolution ... making it more drastic at home and more powerful in its effects abroad" (PALMER 1959:2, 4, as quoted in HUNTINGTON 1968:305-6).[120] The Bolivian Revolution, which in comparison[121] to the Mexican Revolution (cf. HUNTINGTON 1968:315-34; and ALEXANDER 1958:271ff.) must be considered as at least partly abortive,[122] also testifies to the importance of international dependencies. "The Bolivian Revolution[123] thus raises the issue of whether a complete revolution is possible in the absence of both a significant prerevolutionary foreign presence and a significant post-revolutionary foreign intervention. It raises the question but does not answer it" (HUNTINGTON 1968:333).

In summary, revolutions are won by coalitions of social forces, coalitions in which the peasants play a major part. Revolutions must be seen in the international context as well (cf. also chapter 7.2.3). Finally, success in revolutionary activities presuppposes organization above all. HUNTINGTON's reminder at the end of his fascinating book deserves to be quoted again: "Organization is the road to political power. . . . In the modernizing world he controls the future who organizes its politics" (ibid., p. 461). Probably the best conditions for developing the said revolutionary organizations exist in situations of external warfare when insurgents are taking over the role of defenders of the country or of liberation forces, in short, when they are acting as nationalists fighting for their country in the first place, while also pursuing their long-term political, social, and ideological goals.

While the empirical evidence for each of the hypotheses mentioned above is limited by historical circumstances, HUNTINGTON's hypotheses do seem testable to a certain degree on a quantitative basis. At present these hypotheses are fascinating yet much too encompassing. We need more systematic data on the kind and intensity of social cleavages, on the processes of mobilization, on the build-up of revolutionary coalitions, etc. What kind of coalitions occur in which areas at what point in time? Is there always a dichotomy between city and countryside,[124] or is there a continuum with thresholds? Moreover, is this dichotomy altogether too simple since there are many kinds of cities with different occupational structures and perhaps different cleavages? The countryside as well is not an invariate factor. There are many different types of soils and crops cultivated and accordingly quite different social relations between lords and peasants in the country (cf. the next section as well as the analysis of PAIGE 1975 in chapter 8.4.4). Finally, the density of the rural population may also have an effect on the conditions of mobilization. Thus, the urban-rural scene should best be studied along a number of continua, not just one or two. How do revolutions like the English Revolution fit into the broad East-West dichotomy? Are peasants so important themselves (cf. also chapter 8.4.4) or only as a vehicle which is later on led by other social groups, such as the Bolsheviks in Russia?[125] Do peasants indeed perceive a coalition in times of revolution, a coalition between themselves and the cities, or do they simply act on their own behalf trying to handle their own affairs without much interference from the outside?

Lastly, in some cases the sequence of events in the Western[126] model of revolutions has not been stated correctly. GILLIS (1970) points out that in the case of the French Revolution and the aborted revolution in Germany in 1848 (cf. also GILLIS 1971) quite substantial modernization efforts were undertaken in both regimes not only after but *before* the revolutionary outbreak (cf. also TOCQUEVILLE's hypothesis quoted in the preceding section). HUNTINGTON is correct, however, when writing that in the case of the Western revolutions rebels took the country from the central cities, whereas in the Eastern revolutions first the countryside had to be won before the cities could be captured.[127]

8.4.3.2. MOORE

The basic dichotomy between city and countryside is encountered again in the study of MOORE (1966) which takes its start from a much broader conceptualization and focuses on conditions as well as consequences of revolutions. In addition, a number of other cleavages besides city and country are brought to attention. Yet, rather than starting with this earlier publication,[128] we first want to have a basis from which to trace MOORE's extensive historical analyses (much beyond the scope of this study). Several of the basic differences between HUNTINGTON and MOORE have been summarized by SALAMON. Since we will go into some detail, they may serve as a guideline. "Where HUNTINGTON concentrates simply on the basic dichotomy between urban and rural sectors of a society, MOORE concentrates on the complex set of interrelations among four critical sets of actors in the premodern society: the landed upper class, the peasantry, the urban bourgeoisie, and the governmental bureaucracy. Where HUNTINGTON tends to stress political relations, MOORE focuses instead on economic relations" (SALAMON 1970:97).

England, France, the United States, Germany, Russia, China, Japan, and India—these are the countries MOORE chooses for his comparative analyses. MOORE attempts "to discover the range of historical conditions under which either or both of these rural groups [the landed upper classes and the peasantry] have become important forces behind the emergence of Western parliamentary versions of democracy, and dictatorships of the right and left, that is, fascist and communist regimes" (MOORE 1966:viii). The following conditions seem to be of prime importance in this venture, namely

> two major variables, the relationships of the landed upper classes with the monarchy [or more generally the preindustrial bureaucracy; cf. ibid., p. 417] and their response to the requirements of production for the market. There is a third major variable that has already crept into the discussion: the relationship of the landed upper classes with the town dwellers, mainly the upper stratum that we may loosely call the bourgeoisie. The coalitions and counter-coalitions that have arisen among and across these two groups have constituted and in some parts of the world still constitute the basic framework and environment of political action, forming [a] series of opportunities (ibid., p. 423).

Put another way, if a liberal democratic society is to develop, the following conditions must be met: "the development of a balance to avoid too strong a crown or too independent a landed aristocracy" and "a turn toward an appropriate form of commercial agriculture either on the part of the landed aristocracy or the peasantry" (ibid., p. 430). Two additional conditions must also be fulfilled: "the weakening of the landed aristocracy and the prevention of an aristocratic-bourgeois coalition against the peasants and workers" (ibid., p. 431). Finally, "commercial and industrial leaders must be on their way to becoming the dominant element in society. . . . All these things can happen, it seems, only at an early stage in economic development. That they will be repeated anywhere in the twentieth century also seems highly unlikely" (ibid., p. 425).[129]

Apart from the road to Western liberal democracy, there are two other roads to modernity: Where the commercial impulse is weak among the landed upper classes, "the result will be the survival of a huge peasant mass that is at best a tremendous problem for democracy and at worst the reservoir for a peasant revolution leading to a communist dictatorship. The other possibility is that the landed upper class will use a variety of political and social levers to hold down a labor force on the land and make its transition to commercial farming in this fashion. Combined with a substantial amount of industrial growth, the result is likely to be what we recognize as fascism" (ibid., p. 420). In England, "commercial farming by the landed aristocracy removed much of what remained of its dependence on the crown. . . . Likewise the form commercial farming took in England, in contrast to eastern Germany, created a considerable community of interest with the towns. Both factors were important causes of the Civil war and the ultimate victory of the parliamentary cause," whereas "east German Junkers reduced formerly free peasants to serfdom in order to grow and export grain" (ibid., p. 420), the cities being bypassed in the exportation.

British development beginning in the seventeenth century remains unique, yet there are two other routes to the development of Western liberal democracy:

> The English Civil War checked royal absolutism and gave the commercially minded big landlords a free hand to play their part during the eighteenth and early nineteenth centuries in destroying peasant society. The French Revolution broke the power of a landed élite that was still mainly precommercial, though sections of it had begun to go over to new forms requiring repressive mechanisms to maintain its labor force. In this sense . . . the French Revolution constituted an alternative way of creating institutions eventually favorable to democracy. Finally, the American Civil War likewise broke the power of a landed élite that was an obstacle in the way of democratic advance but, in this case, one that had grown up as part of capitalism (ibid., p. 426; as to the interpretation of the American Civil War cf. also the harsh critique by BENSON 1972 who considers it a separatist war rather than a social revolution).

In summary,

> The taming of the agrarian sector has been a decisive feature. . . . It was just as important as the better-known disciplining of the working class and of course closely related to it. Indeed the English experience tempts one to say that getting rid of agriculture as a major social activity is one prerequisite for successful democracy. The political hegemony of the landed upper class had to be broken or transformed. The peasant had to be turned into a farmer producing for the market instead of for his own consumption and that of the overlord. In this process the landed upper classes either became an important part of the capitalist and democratic tide, as in England, or, if they came to oppose it, they were swept aside in the convulsions of revolution or civil war. In a word, the landed upper classes either helped to make the bourgeois revolution or were destroyed by it (ibid., p. 429-30).

So much for the development of the "bourgeois-democratic revolution."

A different set of conditions emerges for twentieth century revolutions. "The most important causes of peasant revolutions have been the absence of a commercial revolution in agriculture led by the landed upper classes and the concomitant survival of peasant social institutions into the modern era when they are subject to new stresses and strains" (ibid., p. 477).[130] "Twentieth century peasant revolutions have had their mass support among the peasants, who have been the principal victims of modernization put through by communist governments. Nevertheless I shall remain candidly and explicitly inconsistent in the use of terms. In discussing peasant revolutions we shall be speaking about the main popular force behind them, well aware that in the twentieth century the result was communism" (ibid., p. 428-29).

Much of MOORE's analysis is based on consensus among scholars, his special discovery being lord and peasant as gate-keepers to modernity. Actually, an important third social group is added, the urban bourgeoisie which must be vigorous and politically as well as economically independent if liberal democracy is to be successfully established. There is no need to stress the merits of MOORE's stimulating cross-national analysis. Instead a few shortcomings will be mentioned here (cf. also WIENER 1975).

Firstly, the selection of countries is somewhat erratic (though not untypical as far as major historical currents are concerned). Smaller countries are almost totally neglected in his analysis. Although he gives reason[131] for not going into detail with developments in such countries as Switzerland or in Scandinavia, these cases nevertheless might provide useful additional evidence on MOORE's broad historical explanatory sketch. TILTON (1974) lists the following historical and political conditions underlying the origins of the liberal Swedish democracy:

> (1) the availability of parliamentary institutions in which concessions could be extracted;
> (2) the absence of a professional standing army available for repressive purposes;
> (3) the presence of massive unrest and some minor outbreaks of violence; and
> (4) the conviction among the elite of the possibility of revolution and also of the possibility of a peaceful resolution of grievances"
> (TILTON 1974:568; for a somewhat different account cf. CASTLES 1973).

TILTON thus believes he has refuted MOORE's analysis (and DAHRENDORF's as well; cf. TILTON for a discussion) in this particular instance.

Other countries in the "middle belt" (ROKKAN 1973:81) between the European seaward powers, England and France, and the landward powers, Prussia and Russia, might also serve as test cases (for more elaborated analyses cf. the various works of ROKKAN, e.g., 1973, and below). Another question is whether MOORE's results are applicable to Third World countries, particularly to those with a colonial heritage. His own analyses of India are suggestive in a variety of ways, but India is probably not a very typical example of likely developments in the Third World. The absence of relatively cohesive and strong institutions at the village level in part accounts for the absence of peasant revolution in India.

Not only the sampling of countries but other aspects as well in MOORE's comparative analysis have come under attack. Some critics have pointed to the fact that, in carrying out his analysis, MOORE actually focuses on many social groupings in addition to the four dealt with thus far; this is used as evidence against MOORE's theoretical scheme.[132] Yet, one may concur with MOORE that he has indeed concentrated on the most important groupings, with one exception: the army.

The strength and also the pitfalls of his study may result from the same factor, his almost total reliance on economic factors, although he does stress at various points that political factors (cf. MOORE 1966:422) should also be taken into consideration (whereas he has clear reservations as to the explicative power of cultural or ideological factors).[133] Thus, not much is said about either political strategies (on this cf. the analyses in ALMOND et al. 1973:641-43 and passim) or international influences and other variables such as population growth. "The international dimension remains implicit: he talks of the wool, wine, and grain trades, of the differential timing of industrialization, and of war, but these are not raised to an explicit theoretical level. Both ANDERSON [1974a; 1974b][134] and WALLERSTEIN [1974] do so, albeit in different ways with varying degrees of success" (GOUREVITCH 1978:436). Geographical-political factors are also of considerable importance in explaining the phenomena under study. MOORE himself makes this point: "At a deeper level of causation, England's whole previous history, her reliance on a navy instead of an army, on unpaid justices of the peace instead of royal officials, had put in the hands of the central government a repressive apparatus weaker than that possessed by the strong continental monarchies. Thus the materials with which to construct a German system were missing or but feebly developed" (MOORE 1966: 444).

Other criticism refers to MOORE's interpretations of specific historical developments, e.g., the enclosure movement in England. There are a number of statements in MOORE's book (ibid., p. 426) which do correspond with the views of his critics. Yet, STONE (1967a)[135] as well as ROTHMAN (1970; cf. ibid. for some other disagreement on historical matters) have stressed that the modernization process in the agrarian sector in England, especially the enclosure movement, proceeded much less violently than is suggested at times by MOORE (on the role of violence cf. also below).

ROKKAN (1975) has perhaps provided the most fruitful criticism and extension of MOORE's analysis. His points of disagreement, as far as the French case is concerned, are summarized as follows:

> How could this "seaward empire-nation" with its strong bonds
> between the rural and the urban economies build up an absolutist
> regime so very different from the representative rule prevailing in
> Britain? None of MOORE's arguments from the differences in the
> character of the rural-urban alliances in the two countries carries
> decisive weight: the contrast between labor-reducing wool produc-
> tion in England and labor-intensive wine production in France,
> the direct links between the city elite and the estate owners in
> England, the important role of the French monarchy in linking the
> urban bourgeoisie with the rural nobility through the *vénalité des
> offices*. Clearly, to account for the differences between England
> and France, it is necessary to go further in the differentiation of
> variables: we would have to consider a variety of indicators such as
> the *openness vs. exclusiveness in the class structure* (England: open-

ness ensured through primogeniture rule; France: large but socially exclusive nobility), the *equalization of tax burdens* (England: no exemptions for peers; France: extensive exemptions), *the ease of resource extraction for the state* (England: customs collection in the harbors; France: greater cost of controls, exemptions a necessary strategy in the reduction of organized resistance against taxation) and, last but not least, the *geopolitical loads and their consequences for the actual fiscal requirements of the state* (England an island, consequently lower defense requirements; France a larger territory with open borders to the North and the Northeast). In our reformulation of the conceptual map we have given pride of place to this geopolitical dimension. France was *closer* to the central trade belt and had to build up a much stronger apparatus to define its national territories; England was *at a safe distance* from the central area and did not have to build up a monolithic apparatus to delimit a distinctive system (ROKKAN 1975:586-87).

ROKKAN continues with a paired comparison of developments in two so-called smaller countries (MOORE; "smaller," once again, from his point of analysis).

Perhaps the closest parallel to the English-French contrast is the Swedish-Danish: Sweden was able to keep up its estate representation through most of the era of absolutism and moved very gradually, step by step, toward mass democracy; Denmark, by contrast, was an absolute monarchy from 1660 to 1839 and moved quite suddenly to near-manhood suffrage already in 1849. Historians who have compared the developments of the two states during the crucial seventeenth century have been struck by the similarities between Sweden and England on the one hand, Denmark and France on the other. The Danes shared with the French a highly exclusive nobility; the owners of the large estates not only kept the peasantry in a state of near-serfdom, but maintained a posture of aloofness from the urban bourgeoisie. The nobility had for centuries kept the monarchy under control through the institution of the *Haandfaestning*, a contract sworn by the King on the accession to the Throne, guaranteeing the maintenance of privileges. With the increase in commercial activity, notably the greater revenues from the Sound dues, the King was gradually able to strike an alliance with the bourgeoisie and the clergy against the nobility: the result was the coup of 1660 and the introduction of absolute rule. In Sweden there was also a strong nobility, but it was much more open to cooperation both with the Monarchy and with the burgeoning bourgeoisie of the cities. Of major importance in the linking of rural and urban interests were the great iron and copper mines: it is tempting to argue that this trade developed linkages in Sweden similar to those the wool trade did in England. As a result, the Swedish nobility and their bourgeois allies

could resist much more efficiently the tendencies to absolute rule
which had been strengthened through the successes of the Swedish
Kings in building the Baltic Empire. The Estates in fact succumbed
for a brief period, from 1680 to 1719, but the decline of the Empire
brought back the rule of the Estates: the great Era of Liberty in
Sweden is the nearest parallel anywhere in Europe to the era of
parliamentary supremacy opened up by Walpole in England.

Again, the factor of geopolitical distance looms large. Denmark
was at the tail end of the central trade belt and controlled a crucial
thoroughfare in the European commercial system, the Sound.
Sweden had been heavily entangled in the affairs of the trade belt
during the Thirty Years War, but later lost out against the Prussians
and withdrew to the homeland territories to the north: the Sound
and the Baltic isolated it from the central network of continental
cities much in the way the Channel did Britain (ROKKAN 1975:
588–89).

These results and suggestions might be read both ways, either as basically
underlining MOORE's argument that the findings are not too different from
those he is coming up with when analyzing only "significant power[s] in
world politics" or as pointing to additional important differentiations such
as those arising from geopolitical distances. Given the present state of knowledge, it is difficult to tell which are really the underlying variables and how
precisely they interrelate with the other classes of variables mentioned.

One of ROKKAN's most recent theoretical contributions consists in
adapting the "exit, voice, and loyalty" paradigm of HIRSCHMAN (1970)
to the conceptual map of Europe which ROKKAN has developed over the
years (cf. also ROKKAN 1974). Depending on the power of the territorial
centralizers, either *exit* was closed or controlled, thus increasing the likelihood of greater internal protests at a later point (*voice*), or the cities were
able to form alliances keeping the exit option open to them. "But the absolu-
tist-centralist states not only tried to close their borders, they also choked
the channels of representation within the territory. In HIRSCHMAN's model
[cf. BIRCH 1975 for some theoretical extensions] you cannot reduce both
the *exit* and the *voice* options at the same time without endangering the
balance of the system. This is what happened in the absolutist-mercantilist
states" (ROKKAN 1975:589). These are some of ROKKAN's results:

> [One] can expect a smooth transition to [mass democracy] *either*
> when the teritory is sufficiently remote from the exit promptings of
> the trade belt to have allowed the early growth of distinctive legal,
> religious, and linguistic standards (the English, Swedish, Norwegian,
> and Icelandic cases) *or*, within the central belt, whenever the cities
> have been able to establish strong enough consociational ties to

thwart the development of a centralizing state apparatus (the Dutch and the Swiss cases).

Conversely you should expect difficult, often violent, transitions in all other cases: whenever a strong center had been built up at the edges of the trade belt and had had to develop a national political system through constant struggles to limit the multiple exit options kept up in the trade belt (the Danish, French, Spanish, Prussian, and Austrian cases); whenever center-building, nation-building, and the opening up of the channels of mass politics followed closely on each other (the Italian, Irish, Finnish, Czechoslovak, Polish, and Hungarian cases) (ibid., p. 591).

ROKKAN's pioneering work[134] has opened a whole set of new questions. Whereas MOORE has broadened the analysis of revolutions by going back to earlier historical developments, ROKKAN, in turn, has enlarged the setting for understanding these historical and revolutionary developments. Yet, while ROKKAN's analyses are indeed fascinating, they are not the theme of this chapter or of this study.

To conclude the analysis of MOORE's work, a number of other points of criticism must be mentioned. One point of disagreement arises in connection with MOORE's analysis of revolution from above and national socialism. Some of the long-term causes of national socialism have been specified in MOORE's analysis, but there are still more short-term causes to be considered.[137] What would have happened if there had been a majority voting system in the Weimar Republic, if the treaty of Versailles had been somewhat more favorable to the German people, and if economic policy in the early 1930s had followed the policies of economic crises management (e.g., deficit spending)? At best, we are given a rough sketch by MOORE, leaving much to be explained. Moreover, at least at some points, MOORE seems to share the questionable interpretation of fascism as "an attempt to make reaction and conservatism popular and plebeian, through which conservatism, of course, lost the substantial connection it did have with freedom" (MOORE 1966:447).[138] In other instances (e.g., MOORE 1966:448), however, he uses different characteristics of fascism. Moreover, BLACK has put MOORE's three paths to modernization into an even broader context:

> In what sense have democracy, fascism, and Communism succeeded each other? The introduction of Communism, in fact, preceded that of fascism. In what sense did the conservative route taken by Germany and Japan "culminate" in fascism? In neither country did fascism survive for more than a dozen years. If MOORE would maintain that the natural course of developments in Germany and Japan was interrupted by war and defeat, he would also have to acknowledge that war and near defeat had to do with the success of Communism in Russia and China (BLACK 1967:1338).

Otherwise put, events, sequences, and outcomes in MOORE's scheme are not independent from each other, rendering simultaneous cross-national analyses risky. Conditions are simply not equivalent: "The commercialization of sixteenth-century English agriculture is equivalent to similar processes in nineteenth-century Japan only if the international setting of both is neglected, and yet this setting contributed materially to the democratic development in one case and the dictatorial development in the other" (BENDIX 1967:626).

Other scholars (e.g., SALAMON 1970:98ff.) have noted that there is a danger of circular reasoning in MOORE's analysis, stemming from the many post hoc, ergo propter hoc conclusions he is forced to make. Although MOORE is, of course, aware of these dangers, the difficulty remains in assessing, for example, "the degree of cultural autonomy of the bourgeoisie, the degree to which the bourgeoisie adopts or rejects the cultural norms and traits of the landed elite" other than "by looking at what that bourgeoisie does" (SALAMON 1970:99). "Nothing is said about criteria for determining [the relative strength of a commercial or bourgeois impulse] independently from knowledge of the political outcomes (democracy, fascism, communism) to be explained" (SKOCPOL 1973:12). The same kind of fallacy may have clouded MOORE's rather far-reaching conclusion as to the role of violence. Thus, STONE (1967a:34) rejects MOORE's conclusion that a violent destruction of the peasantry is a prerequisite to democracy (cf. also ROTHMAN 1970). (Perhaps MOORE has fallen victim to his conviction that traditional peasants cannot be good democrats in a world oriented toward modernity. Again, the study of the smaller countries, not taken up in MOORE's analysis, may provide extremely useful evidence on this issue.) There are even somewhat euphoric statements as to the "functionality" of violence in the process of development: "In the Western democratic countries revolutionary violence (and other forms as well) were part of the whole historical process that made possible subsequent peaceful change. In the communist countries too, revolutionary violence has been part of the break with a repressive past and of the effort to construct a less repressive future" (MOORE 1966:506; cf. MOORE 1968 for a more differentiated view). However, as TILTON has shown in the case of Sweden, "a radical reform [in a late developing country] can substitute for revolutionary violence" (TILTON 1974:569; cf. also CASTLES 1973 for the same conclusion).[139] Several critics of MOORE object to his alleged neo-Marxist analysis. Yet, it would be easy to prove his critics wrong, since MOORE is anything but orthodox, perhaps his only orthodoxy consisting in his stress on economic factors. However, there is one additional parallel to MARX, namely in the interpretation of the role of violence in the process of development.[140] If one wants to criticize MOORE for his "neo-Marxism," his functional interpretation of political violence would indeed be his most vulnerable point.

In a review of MOORE's book, SKOCPOL presents two basic counterarguments. "First the independent roles of state organization and state elites in determining agrarian societies and landed upper classes' responses to challenges posed by modernization at home and abroad must be acknowledged and explained. Second, one must break from a focus on exclusively intrasocietal modernizing processes" (SKOCPOL 1973:30). As SKOCPOL herself points out, MOORE at various times makes use of either form of argument, but he excludes both categories of variables from the main sets of determinants upon which he builds his investigation. Focusing on the English route to modernization, SKOCPOL raises the question, "in what sense were English landlords—the *only* landed upper class that MOORE identifies as market-commercial—landlords who employed Parliamentary decrees to enclose lands, and who used control of parish political offices to regulate the movements of agricultural laborers via administration of justice and the Poor Laws, *less dependent upon political mechanisms* for extracting a surplus from producers than, say, prerevolutionary Chinese landlords, or nineteenth-century Prussian landlords, or post-Restoration Japanese landlords?" (ibid., p. 14). From her point of view, "what really made England special was the lack of a bureaucratic central authority and the extent to which landlords dominated both Parliament and the very important local administrative and sanctioning machineries" (ibid., p. 16).

What does MOORE's analysis really prove? In the strict sense, nothing, as he deals with very few cases, covers an enormous time span, and employs rather broad social categories.[141] The danger of post hoc fallacies, of mixing causes, consequences and functions, is a permanent threat to his conclusions. However, MOORE has pointed to a number of variables to look for in the historical context mentioned. Whether the same set of variables will be helpful in understanding the contemporary world remains to be seen. MOORE himself leaves this question open. Actually, a set of variables useful in this respect has already been discussed by HUNTINGTON (cf. the preceding chapter and passim in this study) who, in a way, has extended MOORE's analysis into the middle of the twentieth century. He has also freed it—perhaps even too much—from its economic determinism. In any case, MOORE's explanatory sketch surely has provided scholars with work for at least a decade. Even if not all of the options implied in his set of variables are open in the present world, MOORE's basic variables may nevertheless be of importance for understanding contemporary phenomena as well (cf. also the analysis of PAIGE 1975 in chapter 8.4.4).

As we have had to say many times in this study, there are many theories, some apparently quite powerful, in the comparative analysis of revolutions. Yet, much remains to be done before the bare theoretical bones provided by HUNTINGTON and MOORE will carry the flesh of quantitative historical analyses. As FLORA has put it with respect to MOORE's analyses: "As far as the *kind* of empirical reasoning is concerned, there is no essential progress to be found in comparison to TOCQUEVILLE's analysis of the French Revolution more than a hundred years ago" (FLORA 1974a:88; my translation). Thus, quantification is necessary, even if it will not answer all (or perhaps even the most important) questions (cf. some of the caveats in MOORE 1966:509–23). Quantification could proceed on MOORE's sociostructural analyses, the time sequences and coalition junctures specified, the costs of modernization and violence, and many other questions as well.[142]

8.4.3.3. SKOCPOL

MOORE's comparative analysis of revolutions or, more generally, of routes to modernization has been taken up and broadened by SKOCPOL (1979) in her comparative analysis of "States and Social Revolutions." She deals extensively with the French, Russian, and Chinese Revolutions but also looks at other revolutionary events to work out the contrasting conditions prevalent in each instance. Her approach is based on ideas borrowed from Marxist and political conflict perspectives. She stresses the importance of international structures and world-historical developments. Furthermore, as already suggested by the title of her book, she distinguishes between the state as an actor and dominant socioeconomic factors. "Currently prevalent theories of revolution instead either analytically collapse state and society or they reduce political and state actions to representations of socioeconomic forces and interests" (SKOCPOL 1979:14). This is also her basic criticism of TILLY's approach (cf. chapter 8.4.6.6.1), even though in TILLY's explanatory scheme such a distinction does not seem to be necessary. SKOCPOL, however, justly maintains that there is the "possibility that fundamental conflicts of interest might arise between the existing dominant class or set of groups, on the one hand, and the state rulers on the other" (ibid., p. 27). In short, "such factors as state administrative efficiency, political capacities for mass mobilization, and international geographical position are also relevant" to the explanation of revolutions (ibid., p. 22). Compared to prior comparative analyses of revolutions, the new focus in her study is the emphasis "upon the relationships of states to military competitors abroad and to dominant classes and existing socioeconomic structures at home" (ibid., p. 31). This framework of analysis leads her to conclusions such as the following:

> If . . . politically organized and administratively entrenched landed classes were present, as they were in France and China, then the reactions of these classes against autocratic attempts to institute modernizing reforms deposed the monarchies and precipitated breakdowns of administrative and military organizations. This meant that externally induced political crises developed into potential social-revolutionary situations. But if, as in Japan and Prussia, politically powerful landed classes were absent, so that the old-regime states were more highly bureaucratic, then foreign-induced crises could be resolved through political struggles confined, broadly speaking, within the established governing elite and administrative arrangements. And this precluded the possibility for social revolution from below (ibid., p. 110-11).

On the internal side of the equation, the important question is what makes for peasant mobilization. Variables of importance here are "rentier agriculture, peasant community structures, and the breakdown of the repressive apparatus" (ibid., p. 128). The core of the argument then reads: "As soon as —and only when—[the dominant class], under international pressure in a modernizing world, had backed itself into a revolutionary political crisis, did the peasantry become able to achieve long-implicit insurrectionary goals. The conjunctural result was social revolution" (ibid., p. 117).

> Just as the socio-economic basis of the French peasant community explained the accomplishments and limits of the peasant revolution in France, so did the qualitatively different basis of the *obshchina* provide the key to the content of the peasant victory in Russia. French peasant communities, based as they were simply upon the coordination of the agricultural cycle and the management of residual common lands, supported the antiseigneurial revolts of 1789. But then they disintegrated in the face of the conflicting interests of richer and poorer peasants over private property rights. In contrast, the Russian *obshchina*, though it recognized and made possible landholding and cultivation by individual peasant households, did not legitimate private landed property as such (ibid., p. 139).

In sum, SKOCPOL proposes a tripartite causal scheme for explaining the origin and the outcomes of the French, Russian, and Chinese Revolutions. First, she speaks of conditions for political crises which reside in the structural features of the monarchy/dominant class and the agrarian economy. International pressures are also important. Defeat in war, imperialist intrusions, and, more generally, external modernization challenges are key concepts in the context of the latter bloc variable. Second, she speaks of conditions for peasant insurrection, distinguishing here between agrarian class structures and local politics. And third, she views the societal transformations, the outcomes of revolutions, as a result of the first and second factors.

Her analysis has already been praised by students of revolution like WOLF and TILLY, and, in fact, there is much to recommend her study as one of the dominant paradigms in the comparative analysis of revolutions. She incorporates a vast amount of information on the historical circumstances in the countries she deals with and combines this with a lucid structural argument which brings together a variety of preconditions and outcomes, while at the same time demonstrating that the absence of crucial conditions in other instances made for a failure of revolutionary undertakings or for different structural outcomes.

> Variations in the revolutionary conflicts and outcomes have been explained partly in terms of the specific features of each revolutionary crisis: exactly how each old-regime state broke apart; exactly what kind of peasant revolts were facilitated by existing agrarian structures. And variations have also been explained partly by reference to the specific socioeconomic structures and international situations carried over, more or less, from each Old to New Regime. Social revolutions accomplish major transformations, to be sure.

But they effect such transformations only within the confines of historically given domestic and international situations (ibid., p. 280).

There is much to be commended in SKOCPOL's analysis. Nevertheless, in my opinion, the broad argument she suggests is at the same time also the major weakness of her approach. In other words, much more research is called for to break down such aggregate notions as the state and the international system. At present she treats them as if they were unified monolithic actors. Both are incorporated into the analysis as some kind of a deus ex machina, without really showing concretely how state structures and international factors *interacted* with revolutionary conditions. Perhaps we over-emphasize this criticism here, but more research along these lines is needed. Her framework allows for handling a wide variety of phenomena, but the argument in itself frequently is supplemented by additional factors and aspects which make her framework appear less cohesive than it had at first glance. In this respect, there is a clear parallel to MOORE's theoretical scheme here: the broad framework allows for an elegant handling of diverse developments, but it is still a very loose framework, working with highly aggregated "actors."

Lord and peasant were key figures in MOORE's causal scheme for explaining the social origins of dictatorship and democracy. The literature and research on peasants and peasant revolutions has been growing enormously during recent years.[143] Consequently, a few remarks on this body of research may be in order.

8.4.4. Some Notes on Peasants and Peasant Revolutions (including Some Additional Remarks on Guerrila Warfare and Political Terrorism)

One of the initial difficulties lies in defining a peasant. LANDSBERGER presents a useful list of definitional criteria. The peasant might be regarded as "rural cultivator," seeing "himself as ... part of a familial household" rather than as relating primarily to the market. Another characteristic of the peasant is "his subordinate position in a hierarchical economic and political order" which means "that a greater or lesser share of his effort is appropriated by others." Furthermore, peasants have "relatively little education and organizational ability, with the result that [effective] leadership often comes from outside the peasantry" (LANDSBERGER 1969a:1-4). Unfortunately, there is no agreement—some authors even debate the worth of the definitional criteria listed thus far—as to whether hired labor must be excluded from the category of peasants, whether "peasants would include only those rural cultivators who own the land on which they work" (ibid., p. 3). "Finally there is the problem that 'laborer,' 'tenant,' and 'owner,' are statuses which individuals may and do occupy simultaneously, making it impossible to place them in one or another category exclusively" (ibid., p. 4). Numerous other definitional characteristics are discussed in the literature (WOLF 1966; POTTER et al. 1967:2-13; HALPERN/BRODE 1967:46-56; ROGERS 1969:19-41; STAVENHAGEN 1970; SHANIN 1971; MINTZ 1973; HILTON 1975:13), some of which are correlates or consequences of peasant status. Perhaps the most important notion in this respect is FOSTER's (1965) characterization of peasants as sharing the "image of limited good": "Peasants view their social, economic, and natural universes—their total environment—as one in which all of the desired things in life such as land, wealth, health, friendship and love, manliness and honor, respect and status, power and influence, security and safety, *exist in finite quantity* and *are always in short supply*, as far as the peasant is concerned" (FOSTER 1965:296).[144] Even though this hypothesis has been debated in the literature (see, e.g., KENNEDY 1966), there seems to be some evidence (cf. ROGERS 1969:28) that peasants frequently perceive zero-sum constellations in their environment.[145]

Peasants producing almost exclusively for mere subsistence must be differentiated first, from "primitives" who are not "subject to the dictates of a superordinate state" but "live outside the confines of such a political structure" (WOLF 1973:xviii) and second, from farmers who enter the "market fully" (ibid., p. xix). WOLF's explanations of peasant warfare and revolutionary activities, like those of TILLY and other authors (cf. chapter 8.4.6.6.1), must be seen in this context. "The change-over from peasant to farmer . . . is not merely a change in psychological orientation; it involves a major shift in the institutional context within which men make their choices. Perhaps it is precisely when the peasant can no longer rely on his accustomed institutional context to reduce his risks, but when alternative institutions are either too chaotic or too restrictive to guarantee a viable commitment to new ways, that the psychological, economic, social, and political tensions all mount toward peasant rebellion and involvement in revolution" (ibid., p. xix).

Categories like peasant and lord may, however, be too heterogeneous for the particular questions under study. A number of more specific typologies (cf. STINCHCOMBE 1961; PAIGE 1975) have been developed in the literature, yet consensus as to how to differentiate among peasants and among lords seem to be lacking. The definitional problems briefly referred to here have plagued various researchers in their efforts to establish a cross-national approach to the study of peasant rebellions and revolutions. Variation within the concepts proposed is probably too great to allow rigid empirical tests of the propositions developed. However, as PAIGE's (1975) penetrating work shows, greater conceptual clarity can be achieved even in cross-national research on agrarian revolutions.

In the following paragraphs several explanations as to social and political conditions of peasant rebellions will be dealt with. WOLF's (1973) theoretical outline is perhaps the most prominent thus far, whereas PAIGE's (1975) elaborate theory represents the most complicated approach. In addition, several other variables mentioned in other publications will be discussed briefly here. WOLF (1969, 1969a) in his influential *Peasant Wars of the Twentieth Century* contends that protest comes more from the "middle peasantry" than from poor peasants.

> Poor peasants and landless laborers . . . are unlikely to pursue the course of rebellion, *unless* they are able to rely on some external power to challenge the power that constrains them.[146] Such external power is represented in the Mexican case by the action of the Constitutionalist Army in Yucatán, which liberated the peons from debt bondage "from above"; by the collapse of the Russian army in 1917 and the reflux of the peasant soldiery, arms in hand, into the villages; by the creation of the Chinese Red Army as an instrument designed to break up landlord power in the villages. . . . The rich peasant, in turn, is unlikely to embark on the course of rebellion. . . . Only when an external force, such as the Chinese Red Army, proves capable of destroying [the] other superior power domains, will the rich peasant lend his support to an uprising. . . . There are only two components of the peasantry which possess sufficient internal leverage to enter into sustained rebellion. These are (a) a land-owning "middle peasantry" or (b) a peasantry located in a peripheral area outside the domains of landlord control (WOLF 1971: 268-69).

As middle peasants normally are rather conservative in their general outlook on society, a number of conditions must be met before rebellion or even revolutionary activities result. Two factors are basic here, according to WOLF. One is the impact of modernization, the other is how strong existing traditional ties and organizations remain with regard to the challenge of modernization. In wondering about the radical spirit of the middle peasant, one must consider "that it is also the middle peasant who is relatively the most vulnerable to economic changes wrought by commercialism, while his social relations remain encased within the traditional design" (ibid., p. 270).[147] "This is perhaps best seen in Russia where successive land reforms threatened the continued peasant access to pasture, forest and plowland. Yet it is equally evident in cases where commercialization threatened peasant access to communal lands (Mexico, Algeria, Vietnam), to unclaimed land (Mexico, Cuba), to public granaries (Algeria, China), or where it threatened the balance between pastoral and settled populations (Algeria). . . . Finally, both the demographic crisis [population explosion] and the ecological crisis converged in the crisis of authority" (ibid., p. 266-67). Revolutionary potential among the peasantry is made up of a so-called "tactically mobile peasantry" which comprises the middle peasants with their comparatively greater resources and the "'free' peasants of peripheral areas" (ibid., p. 269). Evidence for the latter statement comes from "Morelos in Mexico; [the] Nghe An province in Vietnam; Kabylia in Algeria; and Oriente in Cuba"[148] (ibid., p. 271). However, there is no course leading inevitably to rebellion or even revolution, as "demonstrated by Barrington MOORE (1966) who showed how traditional feudal forms were utilized in both Germany and Japan to prevent the formation of such a gap in power and communication during the crucial period of transition to a commercial and industrial order" (ibid., p. 267).

WOLF's theoretical explanation of peasant rebellions rests on an "interactive effect of peasant traditionalism and the penetration of market forces in agriculture" (CHIROT/RAGIN 1975:428): "the old is not yet overcome and remains to challenge the new; the new is not yet victorious. . . . Traditional groups have been weakened, but not yet defeated, and new groups are not yet strong enough to wield decisive power" (WOLF 1973:283). "Thus it is the very attempt of the middle and free peasant to remain traditional which makes him revolutionary" (ibid., p. 292). "Throughout history peasant revolts and jacqueries have typically aimed at the elimination of specific evils or abuses" (HUNTINGTON 1968:374), not at the destruction of society as such.[149] Revolutionary goals were only envisaged by the peasants when the reinstallment of their ancient rights proved to be impossible.

Yet, revolutionary attempts on the part of peasants remain unsuccessful if the peasants are not joined by other social forces,[150] e.g., urban elements that bring in organizational and political resources. "In the Mexican case, final victory was won neither by Zapata's guerrillas[151] nor by Villa's cowboy *dorados*. The palm of success went to a civilian-military leadership in control of a specialized army—separate and distinct from any *levée en masse* of the peasantry" (WOLF 1973:296). In Mexico and Algeria,

> the peasant rebellions of the hinterland set fire to the pre-existing structure; but it fell to the army and its leadership to forge the organizational balance wheel which would enable the postrevolutionary society to continue on its course.
>
> In Russia, China, and Viet Nam, however, we must note that the roles of army and party were reversed. In these cases, it was the political parties of middle-class revolutionaries who engineered the seizure of power and created the social and military instruments which conquered the state, and ensured transition to a new social order. It is probably not an accident that these are also three countries which were characterized by patterns of conspiratorial and secret societies before the advent of revolution (ibid., p. 297).

Main support of the Russian Revolution came from "industrial workers in key industrial regions, and not from the peasantry" (ibid., p. 300). Reviewing largely the same cases as WOLF, LANDSBERGER comes up with this conclusion: "The peasantry did not begin to act until after the more general revolution had already begun, initiated by middle class and working class elements, not by the peasantry" (LANDSBERGER 1974a:60; with respect to the Russian Revolution, however, see the more balanced account by KEEP 1976;[152] cf. also GILL 1979; ROEDER 1979).

Actually, the role of the Russian peasants has been more important than suggested in the two quotations from WOLF and LANDSBERGER. In opposition to the political program of the various rival factions and parties, the Bolsheviks were willing to sanction the peasants' seizure of large land-holdings and their redistribution during the late summer and fall of 1917 (cf. KINGSTON-MANN 1972). The peasants had thus made one important move toward revolution, even if they did not necessarily have revolution in mind (cf. KEEP 1976). In Petrograd, the place where the decisive battle was fought,

> the more militant units of the Petrograd garrison were practically begging the party to lead an uprising and the Bolsheviks were quite literally pushed into action by radical elements in the streets and in the lower party organs. In almost all cases radicalization preceded "Bolshevization." . . . The post-February period in Russia shows that the masses, however mobilized, in fact rapidly outran the militancy and radicalism of all revolutionary elites. It was only by a conscious and difficult effort that one elite, the Bolsheviks, "caught up" to the masses and thus assumed "leadership" of the October revolution. In this instance the conclusion is inescapable that the masses mobilized an elite! Similarly, the populace of Petrograd can be said to have followed (indeed, actively to have sought) charismatic leadership. But, this statement is misleading unless it is coupled with the realization that the masses developed their own distinctive political program, encompassed in the slogan, "bread, land, and peace" (ULDRICKS 1974:412; cf. also KELLER 1973).

Thus, for revolutionary activities to be successful, other social forces must join with the peasants in a revolutionary coalition (apart from the numerous other conditions which must be met; cf. throughout this chapter). "In all of our six cases [Mexico, Russia, China, Viet Nam, Algeria, Cuba] we witness . . . a fusion between the 'rootless' intellectuals and their rural supporters" (WOLF 1973:289).

The extensive quotations from WOLF's writings clearly demonstrate a number of parallels to MOORE's and HUNTINGTON's analyses. Again new market relations and coalition formation are key variables for an understanding of peasant rebellions and revolutionary activities and their eventual outcomes. At various points in MOORE's writing (1966:460, 473) there are clear signs of congruence with WOLF's basic interaction term. In his own study, however, MOORE has moved further ahead in analyzing options for coalition-making and their later pay-off. The exceptionally broad framework in MOORE's penetrating study becomes evident again in the following quotation which brings up another major hypothesis in research on revolutions: "The great agrarian bureaucracies of royal absolutism, including China, have been especially liable to the combination of factors favoring peasant revolution. . . . By taming the bourgeoisie, the crown reduces the impetus toward further modernization in the form of a bourgeois revolutionary breakthrough. This effect was very noticeable even in France. Russia and China, in escaping bourgeois revolution, became more vulnerable to peasant revolutions" (MOORE 1966:478).[153] WOLF's interaction hypothesis may be a powerful explanatory hypothesis once the relevant quantitative analyses have been performed on a broader scale.[154] Further-more, it may prove useful for explaining counterrevolutionary activities as well, such as those in the Vendée (cf. TILLY 1964 and chapter 8.5).

The coalition argument in WOLF's theory seems to be rather well sup-ported throughout this whole chapter on revolutions. The long list of unsuc-cessful peasant revolts carried out without support from other social strata— e.g., "the Jacquerie of 1358, which lent its name to many later peasant rebellions; Wat Tyler's popular rebellion of 1381; the German peasant wars of 1525,[155] the astonishing provincial insurrection against Henry VIII in 1536 and 1537, which came to be known as the Pilgrimage of Grace; the bloody revolt of the Don Cossacks in the 1660's" (TILLY 1969:5)—testifies to the futility of autonomous peasant rebellions. Whether the middle peasant is indeed the key figure among the peasantry and, if so, for what reasons, remain to be seen in more detailed future research (cf. also GENELETTI 1976:62).[156] PINARD (1967) has collected evidence from a number of social movements documenting that middle class members are indeed early joiners of movement activities, at least earlier than "lower class" members ("the masses"). In his analysis of the Chinese experience ALAVI (1965) reaches a parallel conclusion: "Our hypothesis . . . reverses the sequence that is sug-gested in Maoist texts—although it is in accord with the Maoist practice! It is not the poor peasant who is initially the leading force, and the main force of the peasants' revolution with the middle peasant coming in only later when the success of the movement is guaranteed, but precisely the reverse" (ALAVI 1965:275). "After peasant associations had been established, ini-tially under middle peasant leadership, Communist Party cadres encouraged poor peasants to press their demands, both through their representatives on the peasant associations as well as collectively through demonstrations" (ibid., p. 261). The failures of autonomous peasant uprisings notwithstanding (cf. also DAVIES 1973), there is no doubt that peasants have been one (if not *the*)[157] reservoir of revolutionary masses, which is perhaps no wonder considering the fact that they make up the "majority of mankind" (SHANIN 1971a:238). "The peasants have provided the dynamite to bring down the old building. To the subsequent work of reconstruction they have brought nothing; instead they have been—even in France—its first victims" (MOORE 1966:480).

The strong involvement of peasants in revolutions is surprising in at least two respects. Firstly, as pointed out earlier, peasants are usually rather conservative in their outlook. This is also demonstrated in that peasant discontent quite frequently leads them to demand a return to what they consider their original rights. Rarely do they have in mind entirely new revolutionary goals. Secondly, contrary to MARX[158] and ENGELS, the bulk of revolutionary fighters has not come from the urban industrial proletariat but rather from the more backwards rural areas. MAO's revisions of the Marxist doctrine are highly instructive here. Drawing partly on LENIN's work, he distinguished between no less than eight categories of peasants and devised strategies to win them over for his revolutionary cause (see the *Report on an Investigation of the Peasant Movement in Hunan* 1927; cf. also

HOFHEINZ 1977:29ff., 310ff.; McDONALD 1978).[159] As has been pointed out by JOHNSON (1962; 1965),[160] the Chinese communists had a chance to seize power only once they had won the support of the Chinese peasants (cf. also the longitudinal ecological study of HOFHEINZ 1969 and CHAN/ ETZOLD 1976 for analyses of the communists' defective strategy during the 1920s; see also HOFHEINZ 1977:284ff. on the legacies of the Chinese communist peasant movement). The Japanese invasion made it possible for the communists to present themselves as real nationalists (in contrast to the Kuomintang), defending their homeland together with the peasants against foreign intruders (see also KATAOKA 1974). Appeal to peasant nationalism thus proved to be an effective weapon in the communist struggle for power. Related constellations have been shown to exist in other cases as well: "The three victorious communist revolutions of the twentieth century—the Russian, Yugoslav[161] and Chinese—depended in crucial stages of their struggle on peasant support. Yet in all three the communists became a force capable of seizing and maintaining power only when the old regime had been smashed by external force. It was only after defeat in war, and disintegration of the State machine, that the communists were able to mobilize the peasants for their purposes" (SETON-WATSON 1966:129-30). Vietnam (cf. McLANE 1971) might perhaps be mentioned as a fourth example. The causal connection, external defeat → loss of internal authority (power deflation) → breakdown of army loyalty, has been discussed before here in the section on revolutions. Several other links which might occur in this context have been summarized by ZAGORIA (1974).

> In a word, agrarian revolution can come either from below, as in Russia in 1917, or from above, as in China, Yugoslavia, and Vietnam. In both instances, one of the crucial intervening variables is a lessening of the repressive capacity of the government.
> But many other events contribute to agrarian revolution during a war. Peasants are conscripted and gain access to arms. Peasants are forced to give an increased share of their food and other resources to the state in order to supply the army and to pay for the costs of war. Peasants are uprooted from the normal patterns of village life. . . . An extraordinary opportunity is created during war for a revolutionary party to establish links with the peasantry, to organize it, and to join forces with it against the rural elite. One of the main obstacles to peasant mobilization, isolation within the village community, is eliminated (ZAGORIA 1976:324).

GUERRILLA WARFARE

If LENIN has been credited with modifying Marxian analysis with respect to the role of leadership and organization, it is MAO who developed a strategy (cf. KAU 1974) of how to win over the peasants (cf. HOFHEINZ 1977), a segment of the population which was also of vital importance in the Russian Revolution[162] and in other revolutions as well. Part of MAO's skill consisted in devising "new"[163] political and military strategies and tactics[164] for guerrilla warfare (see MAO Tse-tung 1961a and SARKESIAN 1975:205ff.). Some of his rules for winning over the population are as succinct as they are successful, for example: "The three disciplinary rules were: (1) Obey orders in all your actions; (2) Don't take a single needle or a piece of thread from the masses; and (3) Turn in everything captured. The eight points of attention were: (1) Speak politely; (2) Pay fairly for what you buy; (3) Return everything you borrow; (4) Pay for anything you damage; (5) Don't hit or swear at people; (6) Don't damage crops; (7) Don't take liberties with women; and (8) Don't ill-treat captives" (MAO 1961:155-56, as quoted in JOHNSON 1965:51). Two of his most prominent slogans are "learn from the masses, unite with the masses" and "the populace is for the revolutionaries what water is for the fish," the latter being a consequence of the former.

Successful guerrilla warfare requires a hinterland, a strategic and remote base area (cf. McCOLL 1967) for training guerrilleros and building up administrative facilities.[165] Guerrilla warfare is not in itself a technique, but rather must be seen in a broader context.[166] "Guerrilla warfare does not have the capability of deciding the outcome of a war. Final victory has to be won by means of regular warfare. However, the regular warfare phase in the Chinese revolutionary war was the outgrowth of the long period of irregular guerrilla warfare. . . . From little to big, from weak[167] to strong—that is the general law of the expansion of revolutionary strength" (JOHNSON 1965:52). Viewed in this connection, guerrilla warfare becomes a tactic of waging a protracted war. There are many reasons (that indicated by JOHNSON [1962; cf. above] being perhaps the most important) why Mao was successful in carrying out his decisions, which were, above all, motivated by political as well as military considerations. It is precisely the political component in guerrilla and protracted warfare which Guevara neglected in his Blanquist undertaking in Bolivia. "Following the Maoist logic, the protracted quality of people's war will undermine the old regime in two ways. In the first place, the revolutionary army will *outfight* the government's army; in the second and more important place, the revolutionary infrastructure will *outadminister* the government's bureaucracy" (HAGOPIAN 1974:372, drawing on AHMAD 1971:145). "The main differences between the rural guerrilla *foco* and the Maoist people's war lie in the rather scanty numbers in the guerrilla bands, the absence . . . of a strong revolutionary party or of close relationships to professedly revolutionary parties, and the reluctance to build up a political-administrative structure going beyond the immediate logistical needs of the military effort" (ibid., p. 373).[168]

Guerrilla fighting techniques and terrorist measures are often employed by ethnic and cultural minorities[169] (many of whom are supported by external powers). There are many examples of guerrilla warfare in the world at present and in the recent past, e.g., Burundi, Sudan, Zaire, Ethiopia (Ogaden) and Somalia, Eritrea, the Ivory Coast, Nigeria, Rwanda, Dhofar, Palestine (e.g., Fatah, Saiga, Palestine Liberation Organization), and in areas settled by the Kurds. The Muslim-led Moro National Liberation Front in the Philippines (on western and southern Mindanao), the Front de la Libération du Québec (FLQ), separatist groups in the Spanish Basque areas[170] as well as in Catalania are further examples[171]. Guerrilla warfare is also being waged in many other places, such as in some former Portuguese African territories. Yet, as of now there is no detailed cross-national quantitative analysis[172] of the conditions under which such warfare occurs and the outcomes to which it may lead: success, failure, or partial arrangement.

The comprehensive analysis of LAQUEUR (1976) who deals with historical as well as contemporary forms of guerrilla warfare comes closest to such an undertaking. He examines the many forms of guerrilla warfare that have occurred in history (e.g., to mention only some of the incidents during the nineteenth and early twentieth centuries here, the anti-Napoleonic wars in Spain, southern Italy, the Tyrol, Russia; the Boer War; the guerrilla warfare during the Mexican Revolution waged by Pancho Villa and Zapata; the activities of Lawrence of Arabia; the guerrilla tactics of Lettow-Vorbeck in East Africa; the warfare in Palestine; the communist-led guerrilla warfare in Malaya; the Mau Mau uprising in Kenya) emphasizing that, "in actual fact, guerrilla warfare is as old as the hills and predates regular warfare. Primitive warfare was, after all, largely based on surprise, the ambush and similar tactics" (LAQUEUR 1976:ix).[173]

"The theory of small warfare (*petite guerre*) has its origins in the seventeenth-century. It was mainly based on the experiences of the Thirty Years' War (which, perhaps more than any other, had been a 'war without fronts'), of the Spanish War of Succession, and the wars of Frederick the Great.... The concept of a national war . . . emerged only in the Napoleonic age" (ibid., p. 100–101). "The term 'guerrilla' was originally used to describe military operations carried out by irregulars against the rear of an enemy army or by local inhabitants against an occupying force" (ibid., p. viii).[174]

"Throughout the nineteenth and twentieth centuries there have been three main species of guerrilla wars. They have been directed against foreign occupants, either in the framework of a general war[175] or after the defeat of the regular army and against colonial rule.[176] Secondly, guerrilla warfare has been the favorite tactic of separatist, minority movements fighting the central government. . . . And thirdly, guerrilla warfare against native incumbents has been the rule in Latin America and in a few other countries" (ibid., p. 395;[177] cf. also ELLIOTT-BATEMAN et al. 1974).

LAQUEUR emphasizes that one of the conditions for successful guerrilla warfare is that the guerrilleros act in close cooperation with regular armies and be supported with arms.[178] Yet, even in those cases where partisans or guerrilla fighters were successful, some caveats must be noted. "It is, of course, true that but for their military involvement in Russia and on other fronts, the Germans could have crushed the partisans with the greatest ease, just as the Chinese Red Armies could not have won their war but for Japan's many preoccupations elsewhere. But this does not detract from the partisans' achievements" (LAQUEUR 1976:219). Moreover, as holds true of warfare in general, charismatic figures are of great importance if a guerrilla war is to be carried out successfully. "It is doubtful whether the Chinese Communists would have won if Mao had indeed been killed in the late 1930s, as the Soviet press announced at the time. It is almost certain that the Yugoslav partisans would not have lasted beyond winter 1941 but for Tito, and the Cubans were the first to admit that without Castro the invasion of Cuba would have failed"[179] (ibid., p. 379).

As far as participation of social groups in guerrilla warfare and acts of terrorism is concerned, according to LAQUEUR hardly any generalization is possible. However, several patterns do seem to emerge: "Usually the smaller the guerrilla army, the larger the middle-class element" (ibid., p. 398). It has frequently been noted that terrorists often come from middle-class occupations (e.g., law or medicine), apart from the general recruiting of students. A sizable portion of the Narodniki and Bakunite anarchists were of noble and/or affluent origin. However, numerous terrorists were and are also drawn from lower social classes (e.g., "Nechayev came from a serf's family," PARRY 1976:526).

In his evaluation of the chances of successful guerrilla warfare in general (and of urban guerrilla warfare in particular) LAQUEUR reaches a conclusion very much in line with those of other analysts: "History has demonstrated that guerrilla war stands a better chance of success against foreign domination than against one's own kind—nationalism is, by and large, the single most potent motive force. But nationalism per se, pure and unalloyed, is an abstraction; in the real world it appears only in combination with other political and social concepts, and programs. It is in this context that the infusion of radical—not Marxist—ideas takes place" (LAQUEUR 1976:381). "During the last fifteen years some hundred and twenty military coups have taken place whereas only five guerrilla movements have come to power; three of them as the result of the Portuguese military coup in 1974; Laos and Cambodia fell after the collapse of Vietnam. . . . The prospects for conducting successful guerrilla war in the postcolonial period have worsened, except, perhaps, to a limited extent in the secessionist-separatist context" (ibid., p. 408–9). Finally, "What Regis Debray said about the Tupamaros applies *mutatis mutandis* to guerrillas and terrorists operating in democratic societies in general; that digging the grave of the 'system' they dig their own grave, for the removal of democratic restraints spells the guerrilla's doom" (ibid., p. 496–97).

As noted above, in many instances guerrilla warfare must be seen in a much broader context (cf. HUNTINGTON 1962a), i.e., from an international point of view (cf. BERES 1974 for some model-building with respect to international politics). JOHNSON (1973), for instance, has recently given an evaluation of the Chinese and others' experiences with strategies of people's war.[180] "If, in fact, the evidence proves accurate that the Chinese are now ending their period of active revolutionary ecumenicism, then we must conclude that the Chinese revolution generated no longer nor more destructive a period of such activity than the American revolution did in Latin America, the French revolution in western Europe, or the Russian revolution in eastern Europe" (JOHNSON 1973:114).

POLITICAL TERRORISM

There are great variations among the numerous guerrilla movements active at present or in the recent past.[181] Many of these movements, some of which have been listed above, definitely fall short of the conditions met in the Chinese model. There is also considerable variation among these groups in the use of terror as a means of political conflict.[182] Terrorism can serve many goals. It can be employed as a means within other forms of fighting, such as civil warfare, revolutionary attacks, wars of secession, anticolonial warfare, fighting for greater cultural autonomy, etc., and as an end in itself. In any case, "terrorism is a weapon of the weak" (CROZIER 1960:159; cf. also the case study of the revolutionary terrorism of the Front de Libération Nationale [FLN] in Algeria by HUTCHINSON 1978 which demonstrates the multifold uses made of terrorism).

Most definitions of terrorism (cf. ALEXANDER 1976; ALEXANDER/ FINGER 1977; *Disorders and Terrorism* 1976:3) stress the "systematic use of murder, injury and destruction or the threat of such acts [for] political ends" (LAQUEUR 1977b; cf. also MICKOLUS 1978:44). WILKINSON (1977:52) points out that terrorism is inherently indiscriminate, arbitrary and unpredictable, "both in the minds of its victims and audience and in its effects upon individuals and society." GURR (1979a:24) correctly notes that "intrinsically, terrorism is a state of mind."[183] Some authors distinguish between *national* terrorism (sometimes including counterterrorism or *state* terrorism), *transnational* terrorism (stressing the links between various terrorist groups in different countries), and *international* terrorism where the targets lie in a different country or "belong" to a country different from the nationality of the terrorist (cf. e.g., DOBSON/PAYNE 1979; FRIEDLANDER 1979). "International terrorism can be a single incident or a campaign of violence waged outside the presently accepted rules and procedures of international diplomacy and war; it is often designed to attract worldwide attention to the existence and cause of the terrorists and to inspire fear" (JENKINS/JOHNSON 1975:3; for a comprehensive bibliography on international terrorism see LIVINGSTON et al. 1978; cf. also TUTENBERG/POLLAK 1978).

In his broad overview of terrorism in the nineteenth and twentieth centuries, LAQUEUR (1977b) emphasizes that terrorism comes in many guises, is influenced by many factors, and cannot be traced to a single cause or constellation of causes. Terrorism takes place in a variety of ways and in quite different political systems. It has been used by nationalist, leftist, rightist, religious, and other groups and movements. Also different types of personalities have engaged in acts of terrorism. Only the totalitarian states of the twentieth century (and some democracies) have been largely free from acts of terrorism (but not from state terrorism in the former case). Terrorism occurs in "mature" democracies as well as in succumbing autocracies. What was often the last resort against autocratic societies in the nineteenth century frequently has become the first resort of today's young terrorists. Democracies are probably most vulnerable as targets that could be attacked by terrorists. GURR (1979a:30) reports for the 1960s[184] (N=87 countries) that "unlike most other forms of political violence, terrorist campaigns and episodes . . . were more common in European and Latin countries than in Afro-Asian ones; in democratic states rather than in autocratic or new Third-World political systems; and in the most prosperous rather than the poorer countries." "This is the regional location of 2690 international terrorist incidents recorded between 1968 and 1977: the Atlantic Community, 46 percent; Latin America, 28 percent; the Middle East, 16 percent; the rest of the world, 10 percent. Though few of the attacks occurred in the United States itself, American property and citizens were victimized in 43 percent of all incidents" (BELL/GURR 1979:333). As LAQUEUR (1977b)[185] says, if, according to MAO, the guerrillero is like the fish in the water, the terrorist needs just as much the permissiveness of democratic society. One must acknowledge in this connection that "there are no solutions [to terrorism] in open societies" (BELL 1978:278). WILKINSON (1977) gives a similar analysis, but he also advocates firm reactions within the existing laws (cf. also the discussion in KUPPERMAN 1977). Yet, according to data referred to by LAQUEUR (1977b), the vast majority of international terrorists captured in a third country were released very soon afterwards. Those terrorists who were sentenced received only eighteen months of imprisonment on the average. Moreover, as is also documented in a study by the Rand Corporation (cited in LAQUEUR 1977b), "political terrorism has been a relatively low-risk tactic for those who use it. Rioting and guerrilla warfare—two alternative forms of violent political action—can be shown to cause disproportionately large numbers of casualties among rioters and guerrillas by comparison with either the security forces or, usually, non-combatants" (GURR 1979a:38). As disturbing as these figures might be, "in fact one cannot identify even one unambiguous instance in the last 18 years of a campaign of political terrorism that led directly or indirectly to revolutionary change of the kind championed by the Left"(ibid., p. 24). Moreover, if democracies mobilize against terrorism, its chances of success are slight, as has been documented in European countries and in the United States in the second half of the 1970s when terrorist activities declined from the peak reached in 1973-74 (especially with respect to hijacking; cf. also the figures in MILBANK 1976, but also FRIEDLANDER 1979:xii who cites data which belie the decline of these activities in the first half of 1978; see also RUSSELL 1979). In his account of *trans*national terrorism during 1968-75, MICKOLUS (1978) shows that such activities reached their peak in 1974 (330 out of a total 831 deaths) but declined slightly afterwards, without, however, falling to the level of the early 1970s.[186] About half of the incidents occurred in Western countries which shared an even higher proportion of victims (769 out of 1,322, or 58.2%). Yet, events in Western countries could have been better reported in MICKOLUS's sources. Moreover, only some of the events in the Middle East have been coded as transnational terrorism. *International Terrorism in 1977* (U. S. Central Intelligence Agency 1978), however, reports a rising rate of terrorist activities until 1976 and then a decline.

LAQUEUR maintains that sociologists are better equipped to explain social movements than the activities of relatively small and often "voluntaristic" groups. However, we do not believe that the statement that there is no general explanation of terrorism is in itself a sufficient "explanation." It is likely that different types of terrorist groups require different explanations. In addition, the role of the state authorities in the particular contexts must be taken into account for adequate assessments of the likelihood of future terrorism.[187]

Due to increased mass media coverage,[188] to better communication networks in general, to arms proliferation to all sorts of groups, to strong financial backing by foreign powers, and, in some cases, to persisting causes of discontent, terrorism on the international scene is likely to become more complex in the years to come unless countermeasures by state authorities prove more successful than they have been in the past. Yet, as has been noted before, against *desperados* there is no safe countermeasure at all. These new developments may lead to an intermingling of terrorism employed by dissidents as one weapon in ethnic strife with gang terrorism serving ends which are not shared by people other than the terrorists themselves. Third party interests (e.g., political goals of a foreign country) further complicate the analysis. In any case, for political reasons and for reasons of scientific political analysis, it may prove useful to distinguish between political terrorists[189] (who must be fought on political grounds if there is to be success), criminal terrorists, and merely insane people (cf. BELL 1975:10ff.). The issues and costs apparently differ in each of these cases. Social scientists apparently have not yet taken up these rather complicated matters on a more than casual basis (cf. HOROWITZ 1973; cf. also the discussion of the many historical shades of terrorism[190] in WILKINSON 1974).

Two of the many prominent Russians in the nineteenth century who have gained recent attention are Morozov who proclaimed a permanent terrorist revolution and Tkachev (see GROSS 1958). Among other famous precursors of today's terrorists are Bakunin and his disciple Nechayev who in his *Catechism of the Revolutionist* (1869; see CONFINO 1973) called for rather indiscriminate use of terror.[191] Having failed to achieve their political goals with peaceful efforts, the Russian *narodniki* after the formation of the *Narodnaya Volya Party* in 1880 turned to violent terrorist means, killing the czar and high public officials. After their failure to reach the peasantry, they saw this as a means to stir up the Russian societal order (for historical accounts of this time cf. VENTURI 1966; ULAM 1977; GEIERHOS 1977; VON BORCKE 1977; LAQUEUR 1977b).[192] There are clear parallels with several contemporary terrorist organizations (e.g., in West Germany and in Uruguay where the Tupamaros substituted more or less indiscriminate terrorist means for more limited strategies followed earlier). What is likely to happen, judging from Russian history and from the experiences of the urban guerrilleros in Latin America, is that the application and indiscriminate use of more coercive means will lead to eventual failure of these groups,[193] even though there is the danger that in digging their own graves terrorists might dig the grave of democracy as well. In their fanatic fight many of today's terrorists, especially the Arab/Palestinian group with its worldwide networks (supported by such countries as Libya, Algeria, Yemen, North Korea, Iraq, and, indirectly, Russia), seem to have fully subscribed to the famous statement of Emile Henry who replied to the court interrogation on his throwing a bomb into a café in 1894: "Il n'y a pas d'innocents." Castro's much more "benevolent" guerrilla strategy, whereby even soldiers captured from Batista's army were treated in a kindly manner and thus converted into advertising agents of the "Twenty-sixth of July Movement," provides the maximum contrast to the behavior of many of today's premature and self-proclaimed revolutionaries.

"The propaganda of the deed" (a slogan apparently coined by Paul Brousse more than one hundred years ago; cf. also LAQUEUR 1977b on precursors) favored by many of today's terrorists may lead to a success if governments or societies at large fail to understand the basic tenet of terrorism: "Terrorism is the indirect strategy that wins or loses only in terms of how you respond to it" (FROMKIN 1975:697; cf. also PRICE 1977). The point is that adequate reactions become more difficult, the more international actors are involved in the events. It has often been noted that the kidnapping of foreign diplomats ("diplonappings," BAUMANN 1974:35) and the hijacking of airplanes filled with tourists are ideal tactics because vulnerability of the target government(s) is high in these instances. International terrorism has thus been defined as "warfare without territory, waged without armies as we know them. It is warfare that is not limited territorially: sporadic 'battles' may take place worldwide. It is warfare without neutrals, and with few or no civilian innocent bystanders" (JENKINS 1975:21; BELL 1975). "'An operation can be planned in Germany by a Palestine Arab, executed in Israel by terrorists recruited in Japan, with weapons acquired in Italy but manufactured in Russia, supplied by an Algerian diplomat financed with Libyan money'" (PARRY 1976:537 quoting SEGRE/ADLER 1973:21-22).

Many of the contemporary generally ultra-leftist[194] terrorist groups will continue to plague[195] governments and peoples around the world[196] if the present rate of conviction is not considerably increased (cf. also the figures quoted above). Among these groups are the Weathermen (see DANIELS 1974 for an account), their more recent subgroup (Weather Underground), and the Symbionese Liberation Army in the United States (see the biographical account by McLELLAN/AVERY 1977), the Baader-Meinhof gang (the Red Army Fraction, see BECKER 1978) and successor bands in West Germany, the Brigate Rosse and Prima Linea in Italy (cf. the brief analysis in RONCHEY 1979), the Rengo Sekigun in Japan, the FLQ in Quebec, the Turkish Liberation Army, the Ejército Revolucionario del Pueblo (ERP) and the "Peronist" Montoneros in Argentina (controlled now by the army's coercive measures), the (almost totally defeated) Tupamaros in Uruguay, and groups elsewhere in Latin America. As SLOAN/KEARNEY report in a study of forty-four nominally distinct terrorist organizations during 1968-76: "In only 41 incidents (37%) were terrorists killed or captured. In 61 incidents (55%) the terrorists either escaped or were released by authorities" (SLOAN/KEARNEY 1976:10).[197] They also report that diplomats (or foreign representatives in a broader sense) were the most frequent victims of terrorism.

Perhaps not surprisingly but surely contrary to many headlines, they find that women terrorists made only for 13 (or slightly less than 4%) of their sample of 359 terrorists.[198] Finally, "the average age of those terrorists for whom descriptive data was available was 24 years" (ibid., p. 5). Thus, it is mainly youth who are recruitment material for terrorists "though even that rule has its exceptions: the Brazilian theorist of the 'armed struggle,' Marighella, was in his fifties when he began his work" (THOMAS 1977:1338). (We would suspect the average age of leading actors in genuine guerrilla warfare to be considerably higher, but we do not know of any comparison in this respect.) Other evidence of importance here comes from a study by RUSSELL/ MILLER.

> Statistics compiled on over 350 known terrorists from eighteen
> Middle Eastern, Latin American, West European and Japanese groups
> [active during 1966-76] revealed the composite terrorist as a single
> male, aged 22 to 24, with at least a partial university education,
> most often in the humanities. Terrorists who have practiced voca-
> tions have generally been in law, medicine, journalism, teaching
> and—in only Turkish and Iranian groups—engineering and technical
> occupations. Today's terrorist comes from an affluent middle- or
> upper-class family that enjoys some social prestige. The university
> served as the recruiting ground for all but one of the groups sur-
> veyed, and it was there that most terrorists were first exposed to the
> ideas of Marxism or other revolutionary theories (RUSSELL/
> MILLER 1977:17; cf. also LAQUEUR 1977b).[199]

One of the most interesting questions in the study of political terrorism is to what extent—and what kinds of—contagion mechanisms are at work. A recent longitudinal study by KOLLER (1979) on terrorist activities in Argentina, Chile, Bolivia, Paraguay, Brazil, and Uruguay during 1968-75 suggests that the occurrence of these events in Argentina can be more adequately explained on the basis of a social learning model, i.e., here the information provided by Argentina's neighboring countries. In fact, the diffusion curve resembles the S-shape predicted in the Gompertz equation. Yet, as KOLLER himself points out, the exact process of geographical contagion cannot be explained with his current design (cf. also the discussion in chapter 7.2.3). MIDLARSKY et al. (1980:295) report that "the presence of the contagion of international terrorism has been demonstrated in the world and two regions [N=136 at the maximum; period: 1968-74] using probability theory, the theory of hierarchies[200] in Latin America, analysis of the behavior of radical groups in Western Europe, and finally significant autocorrelation effects both within and between regions. Bombings demonstrate the strongest contagion effects, with kidnappings as a contagious process found most significantly in Latin America. Hijackings also were found to be contagious in Latin America but not to the same extent." Moreover, "Asia and Africa were relatively immune to skyjacking, and kidnapping was practiced little outside Latin America, Western Europe, the Middle East, and southern Africa" (ibid., p. 281). HEYMAN/MICKOLUS (1980), however, point to several shortcomings of this study. Primarily, effects of diffusion may occur only at the group level, neglecting other factors. Terrorism cannot diffuse at the state level. Even though this objection is correct, nevertheless it is somewhat superfluous, as is demonstrated in the case of Nicaragua, where the success of the Sandinistas has led to the fear in neighboring states that terrorism and increased guerrilla activities will spread throughout the region, especially in Guatemala and Honduras. The military coup d'état that took place in October 1979 in El Salvador must be viewed as an as yet unsuccessful effort to keep society under control in the face of increased dissident activities.[200a] At present the coup seems instead to have furthered a civil war.

From the discussion of the forms, conditions, and chances of success of the varieties of guerrilla warfare and terrorism,[201] it should be apparent that guerrilla warfare cannot automatically be equated with terrorism (cf. also the discussion in MÜNKLER 1980). The greater the aims of a guerrilla movement, the more controlled use it should make of terrorism as a means[202] to attain those ends. In most instances, bombing is easier than attempting to reach a solid, empirically grounded analysis of the political situation from which the "correct" conclusions may be derived.

To return to peasant warfare, there are some other variables which have been said to influence the likelihood of peasant rebellion. In Russia, *absentee ownership*, was widespread (but cf. MOORE 1966:454-55); when visiting the country the nobility would display its distinctiveness by speaking French rather than Russian (cf. PAIGE 1975:106 for some contemporary empirical evidence on the impact of absentee ownership). In Prussia, on the other hand, the noblemen usually resided in the country and associated to a greater extent with their subordinates which helped make for the greater conservatism of the Prussian peasantry (cf. also the further references in GREENE 1974:130).

In theory *inequality in land* has frequently been associated with peasant revolutionary attacks. Unfortunately, on a worldwide basis there is a serious shortage of reliable data on inequality. The few systematic quantitative cross-national studies performed thus far have yielded inconclusive results (see chapter 5.1.2.7) as have a number of national studies which have been hotly debated for scientific and political reasons.

Studying the social conditions of governmental control in Vietnam at the end of 1965, MITCHELL (1968) arrived at the conclusion that support for the Saigon regime was greatest in areas where land ownership was low and tenancy high. A possible causal link for this seemingly implausible result may be that: "It can be argued that an external threat to the community in the form of a disciplined guerrilla force can best be handled when the structure of authority is simple. Landlords, with clear interests in defending the village, may be able to efficiently organize their tenants and debtors into a resistance. A more democratic community of small independent farmers may prove indecisive and incapable of organizing a defense" (MITCHELL 1969:1170). This study has been severely criticized by PAIGE (1975:327-33; 1970; cf. SANSOM 1970:230ff., and AHMAD 1971:200-01 for some additional points of criticism). By the same token, some of WOLF's (1969) arguments about the role of the middle peasant are refuted. WOLF, in fact, uses MITCHELL's results for bolstering his own theory. Through extensive tabular analysis PAIGE shows "that in both the current war in South Vietnam and in the Communist uprisings of the colonial period the pattern of relationships between Communist control and land tenure and commercial agriculture are precisely the opposite of those suggested by MITCHELL" (PAIGE 1975:332; see also PARANZINO 1972a; McALISTER 1969; McALISTER/MUS 1970).

Performing a similar analysis on the determinants of support for the Hukbalahap (HUK) guerrilleros in the Philippines, MITCHELL (1969) this time finds the expected relationship, namely that a high tenancy rate is positively related to guerrillero support (the HUK activity being concentrated in areas of rice share-cropping in central Luzon; cf. also AVERCH/KOEHLER 1970; LACHICA 1971; KERKVLIET 1977). These scant empirical results (cf. HUNTINGTON 1968:58, 382ff. for some additional positive evidence) are by no means sufficient for evaluating the hypothesis: inequality in land distribution → increased discontent of the deprived section of the population → greater likelihood of revolutionary attacks.[203] Many additional variables (mentioned in our discussion throughout) should be considered if an adequate evaluation is to be reached. Inequality in itself may be rather insignificant (cf. also MOORE 1966:455), as shown in the long history of inegalitarian land distribution and short periods of revolutionary attack all over the world. Yet, once combined with other conditions, e.g., those considered by PAIGE, a causal connection to revolutionary events may be found. PAIGE's study deserves our attention before ending this discussion of determinants of peasant revolutions.

WOLF's basic analytical categories are taken up and considerably broadened by PAIGE (1975) in his quantitative and qualitative analysis of "agrarian revolution," which may become one of the paradigms for research on peasants in the coming years. His theory rests on a number of highly complicated interaction terms. These are derived (1) from the size and type of income upper classes and lower classes receive, which depend on (2) the agricultural product raised and the social organization of the sphere of production, and from (3) the type of political organization likely to be the result of conditions (1) and (2). "The theory of rural class conflict [predicts] that the social movements associated with various types of agricultural organization are fundamentally a result of the interaction between the political behavior associated with the principal source of income of the upper and lower agricultural classes. Combinations of income sources are associated with particular types of agricultural organization and lead to particular forms of social movement"[204] (PAIGE 1975:70). Widening or constant market relations are once again important as suggested by the subtitle of PAIGE's work, *Social Movements and Export Agriculture in the Underdeveloped World*. WOLF's "middle peasant," however, loses in prominence.

Probably the best summary of PAIGE's complex theory can be found in the following set of hypotheses (the hypotheses under D being the most important in the present context):

A. A combination of both noncultivators and cultivators dependent on land as their principal source of income leads to an *agrarian revolt*. This combination of income sources is typical of *commercial haciendas* and closely related systems. An agrarian revolt is directed at the redistribution of landed property and typically lacks broader political objectives. The typical tactic of such movements is the *land invasion*. An agrarian revolt is most likely when a socialist or reform party has weakened landed-upper-class control of the state and provided the organization framework lacking among cultivators dependent on land.

B. A combination of noncultivators dependent on income from commercial capital and cultivators dependent on income from land leads to a *reform commodity movement*. Such a combination of income sources is typical of *small holding systems*. The reform commodity movement is concerned with the control of the market in agricultural commodities. It demands neither the redistribution of property nor the seizure of state power. The typical tactic of such movements is a *limited economic protest*. The greater the sensitivity to markets in small holdings systems, the greater the probability of a reform commodity movement.

C. A combination of noncultivators dependent on income from capital and cultivators dependent on income from wages leads to a *reform labor movement*. Such a combination of income sources is typical of *plantation systems*. The reform labor movement is concerned with limited economic demands for higher wages and better working conditions. It demands neither the redistribution of property nor the seizure of state power. The typical tactic of such movements is the *strike*. Reform labor movements are most likely in *industrial plantation systems*.

D. A *combination* of *noncultivators* dependent on *income from land and cultivators* dependent on *income from wages* leads to *revolution*. Such a combination of income sources is typical of *sharecropping* and *migratory labor estate systems*. The revolutionary movement demands the redistribution of landed property through the seizure of the state. The typical tactic of such movements is *guerrilla war*. In *sharecropping systems* the dominant ideology is likely to be *Communist*, while in *migratory labor systems* the dominant ideology is likely to be *nationalist*. *Revolutionary socialist movements* are most likely in *decentralized sharecropping systems*, and *revolutionary nationalist movements* are most likely in *colonial settler estate systems* (PAIGE 1975:70-71; italics added).

Carrying out a "cross-national statistical study of 135 agricultural *export* sectors [the unit of analysis] in 70 underdeveloped nations[205] and colonies in the period from 1948 to 1970" (ibid., p. 4, italics added), with data taken mainly from the *New York Times*, the *Times* of London, the *Hispanic Ameri-*

can Report, the *Africa Diary*, and the *Asian Recorder*, PAIGE in general found support for his propositions. Three detailed country studies—Peru ("hacienda and plantation"), Angola ("migratory labor estate"), and Vietnam ("sharecropping")—lead to results generally in accord with the quantitative evidence.

Reviewing PAIGE's book, WOLF (1977), however, points to a number of shortcomings in the three case analyses performed and calls into question the (in his opinion) too abstract coding procedures which were missing important information in countries like Columbia, Malaya, Vietnam, and the Indian state of Kerala. He also draws attention to the fact that "real social movements, in contrast to theoretically constructed types, frequently involve coalitions of disparate social elements, ranged against other coalitions of disparate social elements and operating with very different economic, social, political, and ideological resources. Thus simplifying assumptions may tend to obscure important realities" (WOLF 1977:744).

PAIGE's study is the most ambitious analysis of peasant revolutions or, more appropriately, of revolutionary attacks[206] performed thus far. Actually, the dependent variables are not only rebellion and revolutionary protest but also reform movements[207] and nationalist movements. He has devised a bold and in many respects new theory of agrarian revolution which needs much more systematic and explicit testing in the future. Interestingly enough, the notion of zero-sum conflict constellations, characteristic of most research on relationships between lord and peasant, is found here again as a major background variable. In short, then, one of PAIGE's basic results reads: "Of all the major types of agricultural organization considered in this analysis only the decentralized sharecropping systems show this potential for class-based agrarian revolution" (PAIGE 1975:375). An explanation for this (first stated in the negative) can be found in the following remarks:

> The income sources of the cultivating and noncultivating classes should have a series of economic and political consequences for both. An upper class dependent on industrial capital should, first, be economically powerful and therefore less dependent on political concessions and privileges than an upper class dependent on land. Second, the industrial upper class should make greater use of free wage labor and therefore be less [?] opposed to granting limited political or economic rights to workers. Third, the increasing productivity associated with mechanization should provide an increasing share of agricultural production to be used to grant benefits to workers, eliminating the zero-sum conflict situation typical of landed estates. Overall these political characteristics tend to focus conflict on the distribution of income from property rather than property itself (ibid., p. 350; for a critique of partially "mechanistic" assumptions of PAIGE cf. also SCHULMAN 1978:753).

In Vietnam, however, to take one example,

> the landlords of the Mekong were economically weak and dependent on outside military and political power, required a legally impotent labor force produced by a landlord-dominated political system, and discouraged any productivity gains which might have increased the share of agricultural production going to the tenants. Like the *hacendados* of the Peruvian sierra or the *fazenda* owners of Angola, the landlords of the Mekong combined economic and political characteristics which should lead to political conflict over economic issues and force laborers to either violent opposition or inaction (ibid., p. 371; cf. also the analysis in ZAGORIA 1974).

Building on previous steps in the analysis, PAIGE reaches the following conclusion in line with other analyses in this chapter on revolutions: "Revolutionary movements are most likely to occur when cultivators [upper class members] are unable to grant political and economic concessions because they must rely on legal or extralegal force to maintain their position. . . . It is only when strong working-class[208] political organizations [are] combined with a weaker upper class dependent on force that revolution is likely"[209] (ibid., p. 57–59).

PAIGE's sweeping generalizations have, of course, met considerable criticism. Thus, DISCH, for one, points out that "not only does PAIGE isolate the export sector from the rest of rural society, but he also neglects the importance of the urban sectors, and the role of the state. The only external linkage the sector has is to the world market through commodity exchange" (DISCH 1979:248). "It is unclear *why* PAIGE restricts himself to export agriculture: which characteristics does he believe are so particular to this sector as to warrant its distinction from the rest of the agricultural sector, and why do they facilitate the analysis of revolts in this system? There is no systematic analysis of the impact of the world market on the export sector, which one suspects would have been the reason in the first place for singling out this part of agriculture for analysis. One also gets the feeling that PAIGE is equating export agriculture with market-oriented production. If PAIGE had looked at the differences between market-oriented and locally subsistence-oriented production, this might perhaps have been more meaningful" (ibid., p. 250). In short, the *differentiating characteristics* are lacking.

Concentrating on a few key variables, PAIGE has left out other variables which could be of some importance, such as whether there is a colonial legacy or not. ADAS (1977), among others has brought up this issue; he also points out that there are in reality more types than just "peasants" and "lords" as suggested in PAIGE's dichotomy (cf. also LANDSBERGER 1977:277). Moreover, what about the middle peasants, so important in WOLF's explanation? SOMERS/GOLDFRANK (1979:447) have objected to "untheorized parametric conditions [that] make an appearance: urban radical parties increase the likelihood of agrarian revolts in commercial hacienda systems; and without colonial regimes, migratory labor estates fail to give rise to revolutionary nationalism." OBERSCHALL (1978a:297) takes up the latter argument: "The loosening social control in overseas empires after World War II and the much greater likelihood of outside support, both domestic and international, for rural movements, must have been decisive." Moreover, "in some cases PAIGE identifies an outside party with the very meaning of an indigenous movement (other cases, such as regional secession movements, are excluded from the analysis). Bringing in an external factor here entails the creation of phenomena, meant to be derived from the theory, that the theory itself cannot explain" (SOMERS/GOLDFRANK 1979:448–49). Apparently PAIGE also does not distinguish strictly enough between *movements* and one of their *outcomes*: revolution (ibid., p. 450; cf. also the definitional chapter 8.2). Furthermore, in two of the three case studies, PAIGE's unit of analysis creates some problems: "PAIGE's reliance on parties to define a revolutionary movement is internally inconsistent, since the revolutionary parties in both Vietnam and Angola arose not from the export sectors but from elsewhere" (SOMERS/GOLDFRANK 1979:451; cf. also the criticism in SKOCPOL 1980). PAIGE's "monocausal" approach, which stresses the importance of income source, overlooks a number of other important variables. Neglecting "mobilization and collective action makes the explanation of many of the dimensions of conflict (e.g., magnitude, duration, timing, forms, outcomes) difficult" (OBERSCHALL 1978a:297). In short, "PAIGE has imposed a static conceptualization conducive to quantifiable measurements on an historically constituted and reconstituted reality" (SOMERS/GOLDFRANK 1979:457).

The results of PAIGE's study refer to the period from 1948 to 1970. One prediction as to the likelihood of peasant revolutionary attempts in the future (to be distinguished from the more harmless peasant rebellions which have occurred frequently and will continue to take place in many areas of the world, including more industrialized states such as France) has already been cited: "In most Third World countries, it indeed may be too late for a peasant revolution, but it could also be too early for an urban one" (HUNTINGTON 1971a:10).[210] Unless peasant discontent is mobilized and/or supported by an outside elite, i.e., today largely an urban elite, substantial gains on behalf of the peasantry will be rather unlikely.[211] Furthermore, the repressive capacities of the state agents seem to improve much faster than the economic conditions of peasants, rendering revolutionary attempts unlikely unless major defections occur among the coercive state apparatus. For the past two or three hundred years, however, a different conclusion must be drawn. As much as the formula "no bourgeoisie, no democracy" (MOORE 1966: 418)[212] seems to hold true, the similarly derived formula "no revolutionary attacks on behalf of the peasantry, no revolution at all"[213] seems to capture one of the basic results in analyses of revolutions (cf. also chapter 8.4.6.6.2 and ROEDER 1979 for the twentieth century).

Lord and peasant are two protagonists—the bourgeois being the third—in MOORE's revolutionary drama. They appeared again (albeit in an occasionally somewhat different fashion) in HUNTINGTON's theorizing on conditions of revolution, and in WOLF's study of peasant warfare in the twentieth century. Thus, there is consensus among a number of leading scholars—one being a social historian, the other a political scientist, and the third an anthropologist—as to what constitutes an essential condition of (past) revolutions. There are, of course, a number of other essentials, some of which we have already dealt with and some of which are still to come.

8.4.5. Natural History Approaches

MOORE and other authors describe historical processes in their individuality although their aim is to find general patterns. The same may be said of the following group of approaches. Their contribution to our understanding of revolutions is of a rather dubious nature, however. In natural history approaches,[214] in a sense, the "astronomical" conceptualization of revolution is taken up again: there is a primary state, some deviations from this state, revolutionary events, and finally a return to the primary state (though perhaps on a "higher" level, at least in natural history variants of enlightenment philosophy). On the basis of the history of the French Revolution, BRINTON (1952) delineates the following stages through which revolutions must pass:[215] The inefficiency of the incumbent government is followed by the desertion of the elites. Then mass mobilization is likely to take place, followed by the overthrow of the prevailing regime which, in turn, is succeeded by the rule of the moderate revolutionaries. The moderates find themselves torn between the conservatives and the radicals. Finally, more radical elements take over ("reign of terror[216] and virtue") until they also have to cede to the more moderate elements again ("Thermidor") which bring back institutionalization and bureaucratization to the community.

HOPPER (1950) distinguishes between a "preliminary stage" (mass excitement and unrest, yet still on an "individual" basis), a "popular stage" (the discontent becomes collective discontent), a "formal stage" of the "formulation of issues and formation of publics," and an "institutional stage." This classification may not be very precise; nevertheless, there are a number of stimulating hypotheses to be found in HOPPER's writing.

The third of the better-known examples of "natural stages models" comes from EDWARDS (1927) who actually was the first to propose such a model. He distinguishes the following phases: "preliminary symptoms of unrest"; "advanced symptoms of revolution"; "transfer of the allegiance of the intellectuals"; development of a "social myth"; "development of the revolutionary mob"; "rule of the moderates"; "rise of the radicals"; "the Reign of Terror"; and "the return of normality" (a further example of a natural history approach is found in PETTEE 1938; for a famous nineteenth century instance cf. BURCKHARDT 1905).[217]

However, considerable criticism may be raised against these approaches which often subscribe to inappropriate organizational analogies. The logic of such backward reasoning is generally rather weak. Among the many questions raised but hardly answered by natural history approaches are: How many stages will have to be distinguished? Are there periods of gradual change between stages, or are abrupt changes much more likely? What about fluctuations between stages (instead of unilinear developments)? In most cases, simply a description of the particular phenomena is given. More precise criteria as to the specific stages are lacking.[218] If different stages can indeed be determined, then one also must watch for additional conditions which explain the phenomena typical of each stage of a revolution. (Seemingly contradictory theoretical statements might thus be reconcilable if it could be shown that they refer to different stages of a revolutionary process.)

Needless to say, each stage model would have to be tested in a number of cases if any gain in terms of theory is to be expected. To my knowledge no one has seriously embarked on such an undertaking which might indeed provide us with valuable insights if *all* of the modern revolutions were studied, or otherwise might settle the question for some time to come just by pointing out that there are no natural stages[219] through which revolutions must pass.[220]

8.4.6. Some Further Empirical Studies of Revolutions

Previous chapters have presented numerous empirical findings. Yet, these findings were generally discussed in an effort to list variables probably of theoretical importance in the explanation of revolutions. In this chapter the empirical side of the argument will be stressed. Nevertheless at various points in the following paragraphs important theoretical arguments will be made as well. Some of the empirical studies to be dealt with are quantitative, some qualitative in nature. In several of the quantitative studies to be discussed first (which deal mostly with revolutions in the twentieth century), other events besides revolution (e.g., coups) have been included in the same analysis. This procedure will, of course, come in for some harsh criticism. The second group of partly quantitative, partly qualitative studies is concerned with revolutionary phenomena and phenomena of collective violence in general mainly during the nineteenth century. Once again heterogeneity among the objects of explanation is considerable. Still we hope to demonstrate that, in spite of all the shortcomings encountered, a cross-national quantitative approach to the analysis of revolutions is a promising venture. The listing of numerous variables, typical of analyses of single cases (cf., e.g., DUNN 1972), is not our intention. We are seeking to settle on a number of key variables and to examine how well they explain revolutionary phenomena in the presence of other important variables. Yet, to be fair to the reader, the latter is still the goal (cf. also the causal model in chapter 8.4.7), the studies under review here being first steps to achieving that goal. Quantitative cross-national analyses of the conditions of revolutions have obviously been less successful than cross-national analyses of military coups d'état (cf. chapter 7), but they do not seem to be impossible, as is apparent in the discussion below.

Before analyzing studies by DAVIES, TANTER/MIDLARSKY, CAL-VERT, ZEITLIN and other writers, a brief look at some statistics related to the analysis of revolutions may be useful here. MODELSKI (1964a:123f.) found that out of one hundred internal wars between 1900 and 1962, thirty-nine ended with the victory of the incumbents and thirty-nine with the victory of the rebels. The other cases were as follows: eleven separations, six compromises, and five unresolved conflicts. However these results cannot be generalized, since MODELSKI did not start from a theoretically derived sample,[221] even though he claims to have included most of the better-known cases of internal violence. Among his so-called internal wars are the power takeovers by Hitler and de Gaulle as well as the Stalinist purges. As GURR conjectures, in recent decades the resources of the powerholders apparently have improved. GURR thus reports on the basis of his own data that between 1961 and 1965 chances of winning were much less for the rebels than indicated in MODELSKI's study: of forty-four internal wars (coups are not included here) only "four led to greater concessions or a takeover of power by the rebels, whereas twenty-five obviously ended without any gain for the dissidents. The chances of success thus were four in twenty-nine or about 1:7" (GURR 1973:83; my translation; see also GURR 1980a:266 for slightly different figures and a success rate of 1:4). (Only guerrilla activities with more than 1,000 rebel participants were counted by GURR. TINKER et al. [1969: 374-75], however, reported that in twenty-four internal wars after World War II, the rebels won in 25% of the cases, whereas 29% of the clashes were in dispute). Probably the rate of failure is even higher if smaller rebel units are involved. However, one might expect a less massive reaction of the state to small rebel groups than to large groups of protesters of immediate danger to the incumbent government. "Furthermore, two out of four successful cases involved traditional groups protesting against 'modernity': the Kurds in Iraq[222] and the Royalists in Yemen. In both cases, these were victories of colonialized people over the dominance of vanishing European colonialism" (GURR 1973:83; my translation). These and the following results should not be interpreted as relevant to the outcome of revolutionary attacks in general, because the periods under study are much too short and/or heterogeneity among the events considered is too great by far to allow for such inferences. TAYLOR/HUDSON (1972; cf. also GURR 1973:80) report only one case of an irregular takeover of power (France) in ten selected Western countries during 1948-67, although more than 2,000 "armed attacks"[223] were counted during this period. BANKS (1972:44-45) reports that nine of the ten nations scoring high on the dimension of "revolution"[224] are Latin American countries (the top scorer is China), the Russian Revolution not being included in the period of observation (from 1919 on). These results are confirmed in a Q-factor analysis showing that thirteen of the "revolutionary states" are Latin American states (ibid., p. 48). In a last step BANKS uses the factor loadings for correlating revolutionary and nonrevolutionary states with a number of welfare measures for the year 1963 (e.g., consumption of energy per capita, number of physicians per capita, GNP per capita). It turns out that the revolutionary states, on the average, correlate negatively ($r \approx -.6$) with these indicators (and the nonrevolutionary states positively as expected). These findings underline many of the results reported throughout this study, yet the issue of what they have to do with revolution remains totally open, the nomenclature of BANKS/RUMMEL notwithstanding.

8.4.6.1. The J-Curve Hypothesis (DAVIES)

At various points in this study, the J-curve hypothesis has been mentioned (e.g., chapter 5.3.2.3). DAVIES writes: "The J-curve is this: revolution is most likely to take place when a prolonged period of rising expectations and rising gratifications is followed by a short period of sharp reversal, during which the gap between expectations and gratifications quickly widens and becomes intolerable. The frustration that develops, when it is intense and widespread in the society, seeks outlets in violent action" (DAVIES 1969: 690; originally formulated in DAVIES 1962:6).

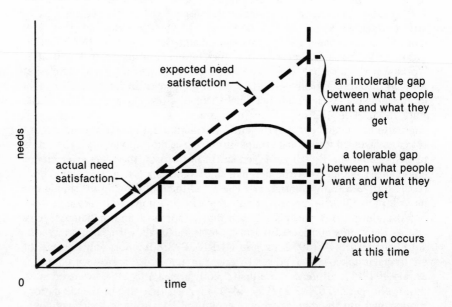

Figure 8.3. Need Satisfaction and Revolution (the J-Curve hypothesis)

Source: DAVIES (1962:6)

DAVIES relies on precursors such as TOCQUEVILLE, MARX,[225] William JAMES, LERNER (as to the latter two, see also chapter 5.1.1.2.2), and BRINTON; their hypotheses, however, are not fully congruent with his own.[226] Actually, DAVIES aims at combining the "rise" hypothesis of TOCQUEVILLE (cf. chapter 8.4.2) and the "drop" hypothesis of MARX (denoting the absolute deprivation hypothesis and not the relative deprivation hypothesis as quoted in note 225, the former being of greater importance in MARX's theoretical system). As DAVIES himself notes, one has only to put these hypotheses in the right order to arrive at the J-curve hypothesis.

It has already been stated that the designation "J-curve"[227] is slightly incorrect, since the J-curve has been inverted. DAVIES uses the following examples[228] for illustrating his hypothesis: Dorr's rebellion of 1842 (a local conflict in Rhode Island with one person killed!); the Russian Revolution of 1917; the Egyptian revolution (more precisely, the coup d'état of 1952); and, for further illustrative purposes, the American "Revolution," the French Revolution, and some riots. The reaction of the American population to the depression during the 1930s is treated as a negative example.[229] The revolutionary activities in the Dominican Republic in 1965 (cf. HUNTINGTON 1968:373; also LOWENTHAL 1972) serve as another positive example of DAVIES's J-curve hypothesis.[230] Other empirical patterns, however, are somewhat more ambiguous. The Mexican Revolution, for example, was preceded by economic growth,[231] thus providing evidence in favor of TOCQUEVILLE's hypothesis (cf. chapter 8.4.2), yet also by growing inequality (HUNTINGTON 1968:316). Finally, there seems to be enough evidence to prove that the Chinese Revolution rather firmly contradicts the hypotheses of DAVIES and TOCQUEVILLE (cf., e.g., WERTHEIM 1974: 187). (Additional counterexamples[232] may be found in the reactions of several Western nations to the great economic depression of the 1930s). Obviously, many other variables must be considered for an appropriate evaluation of the J-curve hypothesis, the more important ones being the past legitimacy of the political system and the effectiveness of incumbent and opposition leadership.

In short, the issue of whether TOCQUEVILLE, DAVIES, or even GROFMAN/MULLER (cf. chapter 5.3.2.3) is coming closer to empirical reality has not been settled. Several additional variables will have to be tested. Until then, all of these hypotheses on the origins of revolutions are somewhat plausible, that of DAVIES appearing a priori most likely. "A proper verification that the phenomenon exists will require comparisons of periods of J-curve, U-curve, M-curve and no curve, as well as between revolutions and nonrevolutions, in order to see whether there is in fact an affinity of one for the other" (TILLY 1975:529). It should be stressed once again that several of the cases DAVIES refers to as supporting his J-curve hypothesis could be debated on empirical grounds (cf. the discussion in WERTHEIM 1974:186ff.), a notable example being found in HOBSBAWM's (1962: 60–61) analysis of the economic conditions preceding the French Revolution (cf. also PALMER 1959:482ff.; chapter 8.4.6.6.2).

In a more recent article DAVIES applies his theoretical scheme to the American Civil War, the takeover of power by the Nazis, the student movements during the 1960s, and the riots of American blacks during the 1960s (DAVIES 1969).[233] If one uses our definition of revolution, from the various examples suggested by DAVIES only the French and the Russian Revolutions may justly be called revolutions, the others representing various forms of violent protest activities or, in the case of the Nazis, even a legal change of power (but as to the *impact* of Nazi authority cf. also the remarks in chapter 8.2).

There are, in fact, further objections to DAVIES's analysis, which is very often referred to or dealt with in an uncritical manner:[234]

1. How are the states of mind which DAVIES presupposes actually transmitted? In some cases, DAVIES covers periods of fifty and more years. Is there really something like a collective consciousness or a psychological time? If so, this should be shown by independent measures[235] and not merely inferred.

2. As argued in chapter 5.3.2.6, quite different motivations may be congruent with the same activity: protest behavior. The degree of satisfaction of individual needs is nowhere assessed in DAVIES's article (cf. also the critical arguments in chapter 5.1.1.1.3). (How important are economic, social, and political determinants of satisfaction of needs? How do they interact?). In his more recent contribution, however, DAVIES (1969:723-25) develops more sensitive, although still indirect, measures for assessing the degree of frustration among American blacks (cf. also chapter 5.3.2.3).

3. A further objection refers to the uncritical acceptance of the MASLOW conception of a hierarchy of needs: "The MASLOW need hierarchy is a necessary part of psychological explanation of the causes of revolution. MARX to the contrary, revolutions are made not only by economically depressed classes and their leaders but by the joint effort of large numbers of those people in all social groups who are experiencing frustration of different basic needs" (DAVIES 1969:694). If this hypothesis does hold in reality (it is formulated as a truism), it is difficult to understand how DAVIES is able to draw a single line representing the degree of need fulfilment. Either he draws numerous lines for the degree of need fulfilment of particular groups[236] or he considers the curve as an average score.

4. As holds true for many other authors as well, DAVIES cannot explain *when* a revolutionary outbreak is to take place (as he himself acknowledges, 1974:609). A threshold condition such as that indicated in the J-curve hypothesis is rather useless, unless more precise conditions are stated. Accordingly the theoretical rationale DAVIES gives for his hypothesis remains indeterminate: "The crucial factor is the vague or specific fear that ground gained over a long period of time will be quickly lost" (DAVIES 1962:8). Clearly DAVIES falls victim to the (possibility of the) aggregate fallacy in assuming that those hit worst by economic reversals are most likely to be revolutionaries. Critics need only contrast DAVIES's crude measures with the rich wording of his hypothesis: What is a "prolonged period of rising expectations" or a "short period of sharp reversal"? What are the rates of improvement and of decline like?[237] How is an "intolerable gap between expectations and gratifications" measured independently of the factor under study? What is meant by "widespread frustrations" in society?

5. Finally, there is no explanation of mobilization processes in DAVIES's theory of revolution, and mobilization processes are necessary conditions if revolutionary attack is to occur at all.[238]

8.4.6.2. "A Theory of Revolution" (TANTER/MIDLARSKY)

TANTER/MIDLARSKY study seventeen "successful revolutions" between 1955 and 1960. Actually, however, there is only one revolution in their sample, the Cuban Revolution. All others were forms of coups d'état (cf. chapter 7). Counting de Gaulle's takeover of power in France in 1958 as a revolution, as TANTER/MIDLARSKY do, leads to rather grotesque results. Once again, the claim to present an empirically based theory of revolution is hardly well-founded.[239]

The seventeen "revolutions" are indexed by "duration and deaths from domestic violence."[240] Reviewing our discussion in previous chapters, there is no need to comment on such measures of the dependent variable. TANTER/MIDLARSKY test whether there is a relationship between education (the "primary school ratio-number enrolled in primary school divided by the total population aged 5-14"; data mostly for 1950-54) and revolution.

In addition, the DAVIES hypothesis is tested as follows: "Achievement and aspirations are defined by the rate of change of GNP/CAP over time. Expectations are defined by the drop or reversal in the rate of change of GNP/CAP" (TANTER/MIDLARSKY 1967:272). More specifically, the two hypotheses read: "(1) The higher the rate of increase of GNP/CAP preceding the revolution and the sharper the reversal *immediately* prior to the revolution, the greater the duration and violence of the revolution. (2) The lower the level of educational attainment prior to the revolution, the greater the duration and violence of the revolution" (ibid., p. 272).

Concerning the first hypothesis, in the case of Asian countries (n=6) and Middle Eastern countries (n=4) there are positive correlations (r>.90); however, a slightly negative correlation (r=-.12) emerges for Latin American countries (n=7). Including all countries studied, there is a relationship of r=.22 between independent and dependent variable. The education measure correlates negatively with the dependent variable (r=-.31); in the case of Latin American countries (here data for n=9 countries) a positive coefficient (.33) is found. In the case of the two other groups, negative correlations (Asia: -.76, Middle East: -.92) are reported. The authors conclude from these results that Latin American revolutions must be different from those in the other two areas. Interestingly, in the case of Cuba, they find some evidence in favor of a J-curve pattern. Yet, the two turning points (from which the rise-and-drop phase begins) are not more than three years apart. More seriously, one and the same indicator (GNP/CAP) is used for indexing two theoretical concepts: achievement and aspirations. At best, there is only one, albeit very indirect, measure of achievement. Aspirations are not measured at all. It is assumed that they are slightly higher than the level of achievement but will not be adapted to a reversal in capabilities. Since there are no independent measures, there can be no mention of a "revolutionary gap."[241] The same held true for DAVIES's operationalization. Once again, rules of correspondence have been violated (cf. also the criticism in CHADWICK/FIRESTONE 1972:23).[242]

In conclusion, employing just two variables to explain revolutions is indeed an audacious undertaking (granted that there were none of the additional problems entirely discrediting the empirical study by TANTER/MIDLARSKY). Furthermore, the number of cases is rather small. The empirical portion of the TANTER/MIDLARSKY study has little to do with revolutions. At best, this piece of research demonstrates how an empirically based comparative sociology of revolutions should *not* proceed.

8.4.6.3. "Toward a Theory of Political Instability in Latin America" (MIDLARSKY/TANTER)

A second study by the same authors again raises a number of questions yet is not as misleading as their theory of revolution. Here the aim is to develop a theory of political instability in Latin America. The dependent variable revolutions is defined according to TANTER (1966). Again, in fact, it is mostly coups that are measured. In the causal model of the authors, economic presence of the United States (measured as product of the percentage of external trade of the country in question with the United States and the size of American direct investments per capita in that country) is the basic independent variable. In addition, two other independent variables are considered: level of economic development (measured as in the preceding study) and hostility to the United States (measured by the number of protests, accusations, negative sanctions, ambassadors expelled; see TANTER 1966: 63 for details). The degree of political violence is also ascertained and treated as a correlate of the dependent variable. The sample comprises eighteen countries, fourteen "nondemocratic" and four "democratic." All variables are measured for 1958–60, with the exception of American economic presence (1956).

The basic hypothesis is that the economic presence of the United States will lead to a hostile attitude against Americans, this being the case, however, only in nondemocratic countries. Even if there is no theoretical rationale[243] for such an assumption, empirically there is some support for it (disregarding the small number of cases for a moment). Interestingly, there is a positive relationship between economic development and the frequency of revolutions. In the preceding section, we saw that the authors found a negative relationship between *rate* of change of economic development and intensity of "revolutions." The two results should not be confused. Furthermore, here they have also counted countries in which revolutionary violence has not been successful.

In the final causal model of the authors the following positive relationships emerge: economic presence of the United States has an impact on degree of economic development which, in turn, influences the likelihood of revolutions. A weaker causal influence is said to occur via hostility, which also influences the dependent variable revolutions. If this model (the authors consider their study a prestudy) could be corroborated in further tests, a number of political implications would follow immediately (as to that, cf. MIDLARSKY/TANTER 1967).[244]

8.4.6.4. The Study of CALVERT

CALVERT (1970) analyzes 363 "revolutionary" events between 1901 and 1960. He uses a power model of revolutions and tries to take into consideration the resources (especially armed units) which the rival factions have at hand. Unfortunately, his model is not tested in an adequate manner.

He collected data on the following aspects: periodicity of revolutions, duration, participating personnel, goals, structure of authority of the attacked government (WEBER's criteria); strength of the revolutionary forces; number of deaths; kinds of weapons used; governmental reactions; external aid; and others (for further details see CALVERT 1970:86–93). CALVERT uses the following definition of revolution: "A complete overthrow of the established government in any country or state by those ... who are previously subject to it; a forcible substitution of a new ruler or form of government" (ibid., p. 5). This definition includes other forms of protest behavior, like coups, as well as wars of independence. Furthermore, peaceful secessions from colonial powers also fall under the definition. This explains the comparatively high portion of so-called civil revolutions. On the average, there were six successful overthrows per year (unsuccessful efforts have not been considered by CALVERT). One hundred seventy, almost half of the cases, were carried out without the help of the military, one hundred twenty-three with some participation of the military, and seventy through the military alone (ibid., p. 209). Revolutions were most frequent after World War I. Before and after World War I there is a constant five-year frequency, apart from some minor deviations (lower peaks during the early 1930s and at the end of the 1940s, ibid., p. 203, and around 1965, BRIER/CALVERT 1975:4). That a vast number of coups are included in the cases under study is also documented by the fact that about 37% of these revolutions lasted less than one day and 37% 30 days, and only 7% took longer than one year (ibid.).[245]

The reader who expects results in line with the categories suggested by CALVERT gets the impression that CALVERT, who looks at numerous cases in detail, has not fully analyzed his material. The recent contribution by BRIER/CALVERT (1975), in which the analysis is extended to the 1960s (ninety-three additional cases), does not modify this conclusion. Only some bivariate analyses are carried out and they rarely take up basic theoretical questions (as to further details cf. CALVERT 1970).

8.4.6.5. A Study on Cuban Workers (ZEITLIN)

ZEITLIN (1966; 1966a; 1970) interviewed 202 Cuban workers in 21 factories dispersed over the whole island. The interviews were held in 1962, two years after the nationalization of industry and more than one year after the proclamation of the socialist revolution. He reports that he was able to pose his questions uncensored (he was helped, as he writes, through a recommendation letter by Guevara himself) to an apparently representative sample of workers.[246]

ZEITLIN starts from alienation theory and takes occupational alienation to represent alienation in a more general sense. Overall, he finds that the workers sympathetic to the Cuban Revolution were generally those whose occupational position[247] had improved. Apart from the unemployed and black workers, older workers supported the revolution, as did workers who were about the same age as Castro himself. Communists were less well thought of than the revolution in general. This is demonstrated in a number of tabular breakdowns. Only workers in the sugar industry (or their sons) were highly sympathetic toward the communists[248] as well.

The results of ZEITLIN's study are probably not too enlightening for understanding other revolutionary situations. Yet it is remarkable that such a study could have been performed in a country which had just experienced a revolution. Even if one does not subscribe to ZEITLIN's final conclusion[249] (or to some of his more dogmatic positions; cf. also the review of ZEITLIN's work by GREENSTONE 1970), his study stands out as one of the few sociological empirical studies on revolutions worth being read. Although we are mainly concerned here with cross-national analyses of revolutions, we felt compelled to deal briefly with ZEITLIN's work, since it contrasts so strongly with the pompous rhetoric in certain theoretical cross-national studies which are actually only embellishments of rather poor empirical work.

The empirical insights into the causes of revolutions gained in sections 8.4.6.1 through 8.4.6.5 have been meager, to say the least. While there will be a number of caveats as far as the studies in the next section are concerned, there can be no doubt that in terms of empirical and, at times, theoretical substance, a very different conclusion will have to be drawn.

8.4.6.6. Sociohistorical Analyses of Revolutionary Protests

At various points in the preceding discussion, references to historical events and/or analyses have been made. In this chapter we try to be more systematic in concentrating on two paradigms of analyses of revolutions. While their techniques of analysis may differ, they both share a common focus: "history from below" (LEFEBVRE). Over the past twenty-five years and particularly in recent years, this type of research has grown extensively. There is now a respectable and still vastly expanding body of research on revolutionary activities in Europe during the eighteenth and nineteenth centuries.

A broad cross-national outlook, an extensive dependent variable comprising not only revolutionary attacks but also collective violence and collective protest in general, ambitious theory construction with its background in sociological modernization theory as well as complex statistical testing—

these are some of the characteristics of the first group of studies, the quantitative analyses of TILLY and his coworkers. The second group comprises the sociohistorical analyses of RUDÉ whose works excel in rich historical detail, presenting not only a number of important historical insights but also much material that could be used for more rigorous statistical analyses. Both approaches have considerable merits, but also some shortcomings. These works are dealt with in detail here, because they have set standards of how to approach the cross-national study of revolutions on a fruitful empirical basis. The fact that their work is not to be seen in isolation will become apparent later on in this chapter.

8.4.6.6.1. Analyses of Collective Violence in France, Italy, and Germany from 1830 to 1930 (TILLY and Coworkers)

TILLY claims that revolutions depend on "four proximate conditions: (1) the emergence of coalitions of contenders making exclusive alternative claims to control of the government; (2) the expansion of commitment to those claims by members of the population under control of that government; (3) the formation of coalitions[250] between members of the polity and members of the revolutionary bloc; (4) repressive incapacity [or unwillingness, p. 521] of the government's agents" (TILLY 1975:546-47). These conditions[251] have already been encountered in our discussion. Less emphasized had been the consideration of "exclusive alternative claims to control of the government" as *the* definiens of revolutionary situations. Actually, the idea is not new. AMANN, for instance, explicitly defines revolutions as "breakdown, momentary or prolonged, of the state's monopoly of power, usually accompanied by a lessening of the habit of obedience" (AMANN 1962:38-39; cf. chapter 8.2 for a discussion of this approach). TROTSKY with his notion of "dual sovereignty" also should be mentioned.

In TILLY's set of conditions, no reference is made to fundamental social change and certain other characteristics of revolution mentioned in chapter 8.2. Thus, rather than emphasizing a specific sociostructural outcome of a process when defining revolution, TILLY's formulae of revolution as "fragmentation of a single polity" (RULE/TILLY 1972:54), as "emergence of an alternative polity" (TILLY 1975:523), or as situations of "multiple sovereignty" focus on what is probably the main determinant[252] (cf. the discussion in TILLY 1975:522) for such processes of change taking place later on.[253] In essence, TILLY's theoretical analysis has something in common with BRINTON's "key" variable, the desertion of the intellectuals, and with PARETO's analysis (as to these cf. chapter 8.4.2). In the words of TILLY: "An outpouring of new thought articulating objectives incompatible with the continuation of the existing polity is probably our single most reliable sign that the first condition of a revolutionary situation is being fulfilled" (TILLY 1975:526).

Thus, there are predecessors of this approach to the study of revolutions. In explicating his particular model, however, TILLY introduces a number of variants that deserve special attention. (Only the more important will be mentioned here.) He stresses the merits of his own group-centered approach in opposition to deprivation theories and what he calls "breakdown" theories.[254] Breakdown theories are based on the "idea that collective violence appears as a by-product of processes of breakdown in society. Large structural rearrangements in societies—such as urbanization and industrialization— in this view tend to dissolve existing controls over antisocial behavior just as the very fact of rearrangement is subjecting many men to uncertainty and strain" (TILLY et al. 1975:4). In general, TILLY claims breakdown theories to be invalid (for an empirical test cf. below); in respect to tension release models and deprivation models he notes: "They neglect the struggles among classes and power blocs which constitute the bulk of political conflict" (TILLY 1975:488).

In his own work TILLY starts from a rather broad definition of revolutions.

> Theoretically, I am not convinced that revolutions in the narrow
> sense of violent, excessive transfers of power are phenomena sui
> generis. On the contrary, I am impressed with the carry-over of
> routine forms of political action into revolutionary situations, the
> apparently small initial differences separating "successful" from
> "unsuccessful" revolutions, and the apparent contingency of the
> degree of violence itself. Yet, multiple sovereignty does seem to
> mark out a domain of situations which have a good deal of homo-
> geneity by comparison with all cases of single sovereignty (TILLY
> 1975:522–23).

There is also a practical argument, since multiple sovereignty, the definiens of revolutions, is "rather easier to identify than is, say 'fundamental social change'" (ibid., p. 523; but cf. also the critique below). However, contenders for power "are almost always with us in the forms of millenial cults, radical cells, or rejects from positions of power. The real question is when such contenders proliferate and/or mobilize" (ibid., p. 525).

As will become clearer, TILLY's theory of revolution or, more adequately, of collective violence[255] is somewhat more complicated than the explanatory sketch above would seem to indicate. He and his coworkers are concerned with changes in the forms and determinants of collective violence from the end of the eighteenth century onwards, mainly in France but also in Germany and Italy (and other European countries as well). TILLY's numerous publications are mostly based on French data. While the dependent variables have varied at times, for present purposes it will suffice to concentrate on the most recent publication by TILLY/TILLY/TILLY (1975) and to refer to some other publications of this group only in passing. Many of their previous results are reanalyzed and interpreted in greater detail in this publication. "This book deals mainly with changes in the form, frequency, locus, and personnel of collective violence in three European countries over a substantial period of industrialization and urbanization" (TILLY et al. 1975:13). The authors focus on "unbiased samples of all violent events—events in which more than some minimum number of persons [fifty persons, or twenty in Germany] took part in seizing or damaging persons or property—occurring in certain periods: several decades in Italy; 1830-1930 in Germany; 1830-1960 in France.[256] This did not in any sense exclude the study of nonviolent strikes, demonstrations, or political crises" (ibid., p. 15). Operationally the dependent variables are defined as incidents, participation, man-days, and/or arrests. Two national daily newspapers were scanned for the whole period in France (in the earlier period most commonly *Le Constitutionnel, Le Moniteur, Le Siècle,* and *Le Droit*; later on most commonly *Le Temps, Le Monde,* the *Journal des Débats,* and *Combat*) and Germany (*Augsburger Allgemeine Zeitung* for 1816-1871, *Kölnische Zeitung* for 1871-1913). In addition, many other sources were consulted. In Italy detailed political histories were used for data collecting. Various controls of source coverage and other reliability checks were performed, leading the authors to the following conclusions (cf. also the discussion in chapter 5.1.3):

> (1) Every source omits some of the events we are interested in and some crucial details of other events; the smaller the event, the greater the omissions. (2) All the comprehensive sources pay dispro-portionate attention to those events which occur in central locations or have wide political impact. (3) Published sources are less reliable for details of the events than for the fact that an event of a certain kind took place. (4) For the two purposes combined, a continuous run of a national newspaper is a somewhat more reliable source . . . than any major archival series we have encountered, a much more reliable source than any combination of standard historical works, and superior to any other continuous source it would be practical to use (ibid., p. 16).

To stress the point, much more than revolutionary events is under study in TILLY's broad approach.

> At the start, we failed to see that the central phenomenon we were tracing was collective action, that only some collective action had a significant component of conflict, and that only some of those conflicts would turn violent.[257] . . . The great bulk of such [collec-tive protest] events in a given period did *not* end in violence: for example, our best estimate is that, of the 20,000 strikes which took place in France from 1890 through 1914, only 300 to 400 produced any violence beyond the scale of minor pushing and shoving (SHORTER and TILLY 1971b). From 1915 through 1935, the figure is 40 or 50 violent strikes out of 17,000. . . . [Furthermore,] the violent events did not begin much differently from the non-violent ones; for the most part, the presence or absence of resistance by a second party to an action stating a claim by a first party deter-mined whether violence . . . resulted (ibid., p. 248, 249).[258]

In an earlier publication TILLY reports these results: "Demonstrations were more common contexts for collective violence than strikes were. About 10 percent of the nineteenth-century disturbances, and about 20 percent of the twentieth-century disturbances, grew directly from demonstrations. . . . In the later period the government more often deployed its repressive forces in anticipation of a disturbance, and protesters often prepared deliberately for a violent showdown. Each learned to anticipate—and, in a curious sense, coordinate itself with—the other's action" (TILLY 1972:223).

The revolutionary events in the 1830s and 1840s (as well as the early 1870s in France) comprise only a small portion of this data collection. Consequently we will focus here on some of the more general results the authors arrive at in their time series analyses. Their data base is one of the most comprehensive in the field of political violence. It is certainly the richest for France, Italy, and Germany. Even though dealing only partly with revolutions, TILLY's approach aptly demonstrates which road to follow if the comparative analysis of revolutions is to be led out of the current deadlock. The work of TILLY and his coworkers is extremely important in the context of this inventory of revolutionary analyses, although his own data and analyses do not convincingly "prove" the superiority of his approach over deprivation approaches (cf. below). Some of the main descriptive and explicative results of their various studies are briefly listed here. For more detailed quantitative analyses of systematically refined historical data, the reader is referred to the various works of TILLY and coworkers, especially the book by TILLY et al. (1975).

Three groups of results may be distinguished, the first two directly linked with each other: firstly, some notable changes in the forms of collective violence and among the participating groups have been noted, the turning point being roughly around 1850 in France and Germany, and somewhat later in Italy. Secondly, there are numerous efforts to relate these changes to other, perhaps causally relevant variables. Some of these efforts fail, while others are more successful. Thirdly, at least in the case of France, there are some interesting correlates of collective violence, while other correlates which might have been expected on theoretical grounds again do not show up.

To start, TILLY and coworkers distinguish three types of collective violence: competitive, reactive, and proactive. *Competitive* collective violence "once produced a good deal of violence [including] feuds, acts of rivalry between adjoining villages, recurrent ritual encounters of competing groups of artisans" (TILLY et al. 1975:50).[259] "The predominant forms of collective violence in France during the first half of the nineteenth century were *defensive*: tax rebellions[260] fended off state employees; food riots[261] beat back outside merchants; attacks on machines repelled technical innovations. The demonstrations, strikes, and rebellions which grew in importance over the century had a much larger *offensive* component; their participants reached for recognition, for a larger share, for greater power" (ibid., p. 49). The defensive forms were *reactive* forms of protest. From the mid-nineteenth century on, however, the latter "*proactive* forms of collective action became the standard settings for collective violence. They are 'proactive' rather than 'reactive' because at least one group is making claims for rights, privileges, or resources not previously enjoyed" (ibid., p. 51).[262]

"Primitive forms of collective violence gave way to reactionary ones, which in turn ceded their place to modern forms of collective violence" (TILLY 1979:113). It must be emphasized that these and some other types[263] are not to be conceived of as clearly separating historical periods (cf. also the modifications in TILLY 1979, especially with respect to the prior overemphasis on the role of violence). They should, at least to a certain extent, be viewed as overlapping for several centuries (cf. the estimation in TILLY et al. 1975:54). BLICKLE (1979:237) also questions the applicability of TILLY's typology to the late-medieval revolts which, in his opinion, showed some clear signs of proactive collective action and were not merely reactive in nature. Moreover,

> ingenious as it is, this typology fails to support TILLY's largest claim—to explore all forms of collective action as they change during industrialization and nation-state building—above all because the typology neglects many conceivable forms of class-based conflict. For example, the typology has no place for peasant seizures of land-lords' estates such as those that occurred in Russia during 1917, for these were communal, yet pro-active (and not a defense against state encroachments). Nor would the scheme allow for something like a work stoppage to defend against an employer's encroachment on contract provisions by workers in a single factory, for this would be associational, yet reactive (and not a demand for political inclusion). Class conflicts such as these are constantly important in history, not only as major forms of collective action in their own right, but also because they directly and indirectly structure political struggles (SKOCPOL/SOMERS 1978:486).

There seem to be two basic related sources of these changes in the forms of collective violence, the more general being industrialization, the more specific being changes in organization. On the basis of various correlation and multiple regression results, it turns out that, contrary to much theorizing, urbanization's inducing deprivations and/or transmitting rising deprivations does not seem to have a strong effect on collective violence (cf. also the similar results reported in chapter 5.1.2.2). There seems instead to be a negative, albeit small, relationship between rapid urbanization and collective violence (TILLY et al. 1975:83, 322 and passim; cf. also RUDÉ 1973a), at least in the short run. There are, however, more indirect long-term links between the urban environment and the dependent variable. In terms of demography, there can be no doubt that "violence urbanized. It moved toward the large industrial concentrations. It gravitated toward the centers of power" (TILLY et al. 1975:68).[264] Furthermore, the "figures show a considerable rise in the mean number of participants and a drop in the mean days the average participant spent in a violent encounter" (ibid., p. 68). "The typical violent event became shorter, and bigger" (ibid., p. 70). These results are found for all three countries, some notable differences notwithstanding.

In France, "the curve of incidents for the thirty-one years from 1830 to 1860 peaks in 1832, 1848, and 1851. The year 1832 brought a crisis; it eliminated the major enemies of the regime which had come to power in the Revolution of 1830. . . . The violent conflicts of 1851 . . . occurred mainly in the course of the resistance to Louis Napoleon's coup d'état (ibid., p. 62). The absolute peak in events of collective violence in France during the whole period occurred in 1848, immediately followed by the number of events in 1934-37, a third period of great violence being 1904-07. "Italy had many more peaks: 1843-1849, with the Revolutions of 1848 at the center; 1859-1863, the first great period of struggles around Unification; 1868-1870, the completion of Unification; 1897-1898, when the conflicts were more heavily concentrated in the North and Center (Milan's Fatti di Maggio[265] being the most dramatic series of events); 1913-1915, a period of massive strikes, demonstrations, and antiwar actions; 1919-1922, the postwar left/right conflicts which brought the Fascists to power" (ibid., p. 245-46). "The striking contrast between Italy and Germany . . . appears in the periodicity of collective violence: a few well-defined peaks around major transitions in Germany; a much larger number of incomplete transitions and a much larger number of violent surges in Italy" (ibid., p. 246). France stands in between: "More clusters than Germany, fewer than Italy" (ibid.). Whereas France experienced more collective violence during her first wave of industrialization between 1830 and 1850 and Italy between 1848 and 1896, "Germany[266] experienced far less violence during the initial growth spurt attributed to her (1850-1870) than earlier (1830-1850)" (ibid., p. 268).[267]

Thus industrialization and modernization in general had an impact on the likelihood and the forms of collective violence. Yet, "there is no tendency for recent migrants to Italian, German, and French cities to become exceptionally involved in movements of protest or in collective violence; on the contrary, we have some small indications of their *under*involvement" (ibid., p. 269). Recent migrants apparently must first develop social bonds before they can acquire the necessary resources for carrying out acts of collective violence. Thus, whereas urbanization as such is slightly negatively related to the dependent variable, urbanity must nevertheless be considered as an indirect determinant of the ultimate dependent variable. It is true that recent migrants when coming to the cities quite often lack the contacts and facilities to engage in protests.[268] Yet it is also true that expanding cities in the wake of industrialization become the locus where new organizations are formed representing claims that had previously gone unheard. The change in the composition of participants is remarkable: "The men who took part were, by and large, politically alert, organized, integrated into the life of the city" (TILLY 1973a:116), working predominantly in ordinary metals, construction, food, leather, and printing industries (these French data referring to "persons arrested for taking part in June Days of 1848," ibid., p. 117). The groups represented varied from case to case and country to country, yet the general picture shows that participants were "integrated into the life of the city" (cf. also the next chapter).

This conclusion is also upheld if one looks at other important events of collective violence in France, although there are some remarkable changes in the groups participating and in their degree of involvement in these events. In the revolutionary crowd in Paris in the 1830s artisans, skilled workers, younger workers, and immigrants to the city dominated. There is no evidence in favor of the conspiracy hypothesis, since a "comparison of the names and other identifying data of persons included in the lists of arrested, charged, convicted and dead shows a striking lack of continuity" (PINKNEY 1972: 519).[269]

TILLY/LEES (1974) seem to have made the most thorough study of the Paris revolutionary crowds during June 1848; they used data on the entire 11,616 persons arrested. Only a few of their interesting results can be mentioned here (see also PRICE 1972:164-89 for basically similar findings). Drawing on the acts of official inquiry, on police and prefects' reports, on judicial and other records (which might have biased their results to adopt the perspective of the authorities) they report: "The typical insurgent was a male worker employed in the metal, building or clothing trades. He had a wife and children and was between the ages of twenty and forty. Although he lived in eastern Paris, he probably had not been born there. In addition, our typical participant was very likely to be a member of either the National Guard or the National Workshops. The specific occupational titles one encounters most frequently in the dossiers of the June Days are the 693 *journaliers*, 570 *masons*, 474 *menuisiers*, 448 *marchands*, 446 *cordonniers*, 317 *ébénistes*, 295 *tailleurs,* 268 *mécaniciens* and 261 *serruriers*" (TILLY/ LEES 1975:190). "Most of the insurgents were well settled in Paris. After several years of residence, they had joined local institutions and had established families. The contribution of migrants such as these to the political struggles of the Second Republic is a sign of the integration of the Parisian working class, rather than proof of a threat to public order coming from disoriented outsiders" (ibid., p. 197). Having carried out a multivariate analysis of area characteristics, the authors report that "the geography of the rebellion corresponded, in a general way, to the geography of poverty and the geography of working-class political and economic organization" (ibid., p. 201). Thus, workers' organizations seem to have facilitated participation in militant acts of political protest, whereas a different conclusion must be drawn with respect to the impact of the clubs: "While the clubs were certainly militant in many ways, their militancy was closer to the existing structure of power and their alliances with the bourgeoisie much stronger, than in the case of the workers' societies" (ibid.; cf. also AMANN 1975 for a detailed account of the role of clubs in the 1848 revolution and GOSSEZ 1967 for an analysis of the workers' associations and newspapers).

The Paris insurrection of June 1848 appears to be the best documented of the series of revolutions or revolutionary attempts in 1848 and the years thereafter. Perhaps it is even "one of the best documented rebellions to occur anywhere" (TILLY/LEES 1975:186; for a critique of their study see also TRAUGOTT 1980a). Yet, this very advantage has also contributed to a result peculiar in research on revolution thus far. TRAUGOTT (1980) reports farreaching parallels in his analysis of the social substratum of the French Revolution of 1848; however, his data, in contrast to TILLY/LEES, refer to members of the Mobile Guard as well. Thus, any explanation drawing on occupational membership or social categories of participants in revolutionary activities lacks the *differentia specifica*. Other more specific explanations are called for then, for example, the collective experiences in organizations during the time from February until June 1848 (for details cf. TRAUGOTT 1980). In another article TRAUGOTT (1980a) also shows "that the Mobile Guard, far from comprising a 'predominantly' lumpenproletarian body 'sharply differentiated' from the working class [as MARX maintained], in fact constituted a reasonable cross-section of the Parisian population of the times and, in its class composition, differed little from the insurgents themselves" (TRAUGOTT 1980a:710). The riffraff theory is also once again refuted. (The first to use the Mobile Guard enlistment records to test propositions set forth by MARX and ENGELS is Pierre CASPARD rather than TRAUGOTT, as the latter frankly admits.)

Placing the French Revolution of 1848 (cf. also the narrative account by DUVEAU 1965; also PRICE 1975) in the international context of the revolutionary attacks it catalyzed in Germany (cf. also NAMIER 1946; STADELMANN 1948; HAMEROW 1958; NOYES 1966 for an analysis of the disunited working-class associations; SCHIEDER 1974), Italy, Austria, Hungary and Bohemia, Eastern Europe, and elsewhere, STEARNS (1974a; cf. also ROBERTSON 1952; LANGER 1966; DROZ 1967; FASEL 1970; and the documentary account by EYCK 1972) arrives at this general conclusion: "The fundamental flaws in each of the risings consisted of the liberal mentality of the revolutionary leaders and the profound social cleavages between the liberal and lower-class forces involved in the revolution" (p. 225). Apart from the liberals' inability to maintain an alliance with the lower social strata, they also underrated the question of military strength (cf. CALLIES 1976 for an analysis of a pertinent case, the role of the Bavarian army during 1848/49): "They were often misled by their initial success, and their own belief in persuasion, to think that this was not necessary; it was easy to pretend that the old order had seen the light and would not use the regular military force in a repressive way. The typical liberal desire to establish a civil militia, which was manifest in every major center, was not an adequate substitute" (STEARNS 1974a:227). "The risings of 1848 proved to be a spectacular climax to the age of revolution in Western and Central Europe. After more than sixty years of recurrent revolt, revolution in the classic sense dropped out of the experience of much of the European continent. Only *defeat in war* would bring an occasional echo of the revolutionary experience" (ibid., p. 247; emphasis added).

Considering the June 1848 events from a diachronic point of view, the following synopsis may be given: "The largest single group of participants— over 2,000 men—came from the construction industry. The metalworking industries and the clothing trades came next; every major category supplied a number of recruits. What sets off June 1848 from the insurrections of 1830, 1834, 1839, or even February 1848, however, is the diminished role of shopkeepers and skilled artisans like goldsmiths or printers as compared with factory-based mechanics and semi-skilled workers like those in the construction industry" (TILLY 1972:229). Three years later, the 1851 insurrection

> comes out as substantially more bourgeois in character than the June Days, yet far from devoid of workers. Whereas only 2 or 3 percent of the arrestees of 1848 came from the professions or finance, they provided almost a fifth of the 1851 contingent. The shares of textiles and clothing, metals, transportation, and construction—especially, that is, those industries which were new to insurrection in 1848—shrank significantly. Food production and the shoe industry, however, contributed larger shares than before. Calculated as rates based on the current labor force, participation ran about a quarter of its previous level (ibid., p. 231-32).
>
> [The] working-class character was much more marked in 1871 than it had been in 1851, when the professions, *rentiers*, wholesale and retail merchants, and office workers comprised 27.4% of the total as compared with 15.6% during the Commune. Nonetheless one notices the substantial place of the office workers among the insurgents, and even more so among the deportees. That is an important fact: it was the first time [that] those that were not quite white-collar workers joined a workers' insurrection. In June, 1848, the office workers fought on the side of the establishment.
>
> Insurrection of which workers? The categories most strongly represented are the ones we have called Metal, Construction and Day-Labor. They are represented in greater proportion than in 1851. . . . That growth came to a large extent from the rapid development these new industries underwent in Paris during the Second Empire (ROUGERIE 1964:128, as quoted in TILLY 1972:233-34; for some additional data cf. also ROUGERIE 1971).[270]

Additional studies on collective violence in France[271] and England during the eighteenth and nineteenth centuries will be dealt with in the following section.

To return to TILLY on the effects of modernization, state formation, and industrialization processes: "So urbanization, industrialization, and state-making are by no means irrelevant to collective violence. It is just that their effects do not work as breakdown theories say they should. Instead of a short-run generation of strain, followed by protest, we find a long-run transformation of the structures of power and of collective action" (TILLY et al. 1975:254). "Our political process model fits the observations much better: instead of being a direct response to hardship, normlessness, or rapid change, collective violence is a by-product of contention for power and of its repression" (ibid., p. 252). Or as put in TILLY (1975:545): "The mediating variables are political ones: the nature of repression, the established means for acquisition and loss of power, the predominant modes of mobilization, the possibilities for coalition-making, the concentration or dispersion of government." The causal model would then look like that in Figure 8.4.

> The structure of power, alternative conceptions of justice, the organization of coercion, the conduct of war, the formation of coalitions, the legitimacy of the state—these traditional concerns of political thought provide the main guides to the explanation of revolution. Population growth, industrialization, urbanization, and other large-scale structural changes do, to be sure, affect the probabilities of revolution. But they do so indirectly, by shaping the potential contenders for power, transforming the techniques of governmental control, and shifting the resources available to contenders and governments. There is no reliable and regular sense in which modernization breeds revolution (TILLY 1973:447).

In fairness to TILLY and colleagues it must be said that they consider Figure 8.4 to be only an explanatory sketch developed from their research thus far.[272] The reader should keep this in mind when reading the next paragraphs.

Actually, neither organization nor contending for power are adequately measured (cf. below). Consequently, for the present, the following statement, and other similar ones, is no more than a largely untested hypothesis (if not a truism): "So the number of violent incidents is a function of the intensity of the political struggle and the tactics of the contenders" (TILLY et al. 1975:71).

Having dealt with some determinants of collective violence and of changes in the forms of collective violence, there are more interesting results if one considers some of the correlates of collective violence. We are now concerned with relationships between other forms of collective action and collective violence, the question being whether collective violence is indeed a "byproduct of collective action" (TILLY et al. 1975:243). For strikes which "were illegal in France until 1864 and poorly reported before 1885" (ibid., p. 73), this is largely true (there are no results reported for the other two countries): "Strikes also became big, but short of duration. The timing is different from that of the transformations of collective violence, but the processes are surely related. In both cases complex organizations, not only capable of mobilizing people for protest but also fairly effective in demobilizing them once the issue was decided, assumed a larger and larger role in the preparation of encounters between contenders and authorities" (ibid., p. 71; cf. SHORTER/TILLY 1974 for a detailed analysis of strikes in France). At least after 1890 strikes and collective violence are positively related, whereas between 1870 and 1890 a slightly negative correlation appears. Indicators of social cohesion (indicators which do *not necessarily* stand for forms of *collective* action) such as suicide, vagrancy, and criminal convictions, are, by and large, all unrelated to collective violence. There is, however, some evidence for the plausible "inference that repression [in the form of criminal conviction] tends to *follow* major upheavals" (ibid., p. 78).

LODHI/TILLY report additional interesting correlates of collective violence: "Cross-sectional comparisons of the 86 French departments at five-

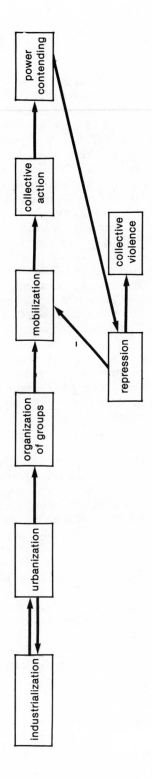

Figure 8.4.   The General Causal Model of TILLY et al.

Source: TILLY et al. (1975:244; slightly modified here)

year intervals from 1831 to 1861 bring out a strong relationship of property crime to urban population, a highly variable relationship of collective violence to urban population, and no reliable relationship of personal crime to urban population. The relationships with the pace of urban growth in all these regards are weak or non-existent" (LODHI/TILLY 1973:296). Collective violence is not an alternative to criminal violence, which would presuppose a negative relationship between the two. Again, riffraff theories (cf. chapter 5.3.2.1) do not bear out. Even so, riffraff theorists might suggest that one form of "criminality" is quite likely to influence the other. There is, however, reasoning as well as evidence for a definite refutation of such pseudo-explanations. To stress only two points: the repressive capacities of the state have broadened over the later decades of the nineteenth century, thus preventing many criminals from successively engaging in all of these activities. Secondly, unions have had an interest in preventing criminals from participating in their strikes and demonstrations. It should be stressed that several of the preceding results are based on bivariate analyses alone, the data coming solely from France. More detailed multivariate tests must still be carried out.

Looking at the causal model in Figure 8.4 and knowing what the authors actually studied (according to their 1975 book), the reader may have the feeling that perhaps too much theoretical force has gone into this model and not enough into the systematic construction of indicators and indexes for measuring the theoretical concepts used. One gets the impression that the political process model, while being there from the beginning in its basic features (documented in TILLY's various publications: 1970; 1972; 1972a; 1973), actually has developed through the stages of research (see TILLY 1978 for the most suggestive formulation thus far) without leading to more refined and thus theoretically more adequate measures. The final model seems to have been superimposed on the data. To take some examples: the notion of power struggle is never precisely (i.e., operationally) defined. Rather, power is used in a general, somewhat metaphorical, sense. If TILLY objects to the ever-present and applicable notion of deprivation, the same holds true for his notion of power struggles. Actually, only a very general framework is posited wherein various forms of collective violence are found, forms that change over time. At least at times[273] this has been noted by the authors themselves: "Despite a number of trials, we have not so far been able to develop a reliable procedure for enumerating contenders, measuring their mobilization,[274] and characterizing their relationship to the existing structure of power which is truly independent of the conflicts we are attempting to explain" (RULE/TILLY 1972:57; cf. also SNYDER 1978 and the recent discussion and suggestions in TILLY 1978). What does power mean? How can it be measured? How does it affect the contending partners or the rest of the political system? How are gains and losses in power to be assessed? "If we can't be sure who the members of a polity are, it will also be difficult to distinguish between the challengers and polity members. . . . Are [military coup phenomena] manifestations of intrapolity member conflict, polity member-challenger conflict; government-polity member conflict, or government-challenger conflict? Arguments can be made for all four categorizations, but it is difficult to pick and choose among the possible categorizations without more precise guidelines" (PALMER/ THOMPSON 1978:308). Secondly, "if we do not have indicators which measure fluctuations in the success of group access to governmental allocations and services (the distinguishing criterion of polity membership), we cannot be sure that fluctuations are taking place or how much fluctuation is taking place. If we do not have this sort of information, how are we to predict the probability of violence?" (ibid., p. 309). In short, "TILLY and collaborators have never succeeded in solving a crucial problem . . . : finding 'reliable procedures' for enumerating contenders, measuring mobilization, and specifying the relationship of groups to existing structures of power" (ECKSTEIN 1980:150). Claims-to-power theorists must either specify the level of power[275] (e.g., in the case of revolutionary attacks, the power of the state as such) or otherwise risk the danger of using this theoretical notion in an extremely vague sense.

A second point is related to this criticism: Organizational strength, a key variable in TILLY's mobilization-organization-power contending theory of collective violence, is mainly assessed by the number of union members; this is clearly insufficient for indexing a theoretical variable of such importance in TILLY's causal model. As HAUPT has noted (1977:250), there is no further differentiation between various forms of organization, e.g., between unions, parties, or associations, and the specific impact these might have on the forms of collective action (but cf. also the study by TILLY/LEES 1975, mentioned further above, for some noteworthy evidence in favor of TILLY's theoretical position). In any case, what is needed are indicators referring to behavioral aspects of organizational strength which are, of course, independent of the behavioral aspects to be explained. There are additional points of criticism if one looks at the model in Figure 8.4. A third problem is that the causal nature of the relationship between collective action and collective violence is not sufficiently specified in the theoretical model. How and when does collective action lead to collective violence? Is collective violence a last resort and/or a reaction to intensified repression by state agents? What is the causal nexus between the two variables? Contrary to the prediction of the causal model, power contending might have a direct effect on collective violence. Repression might also affect the organization of groups. More rigorous and truly cross-national testing of the causal model (e.g., through path analysis) is thus called for.[276]

When elaborating a power contending model to explain collective violence and revolutionary activities, TILLY may have been influenced too much by French experiences, by political developments in a state whose high degree of political, economic, and social centralization has been noted by numerous authors, TOCQUEVILLE and MARX being only the most renowned examples. It remains to be seen whether, on the basis of more systematic historical data on other European countries, different models emerge, perhaps more in line with reasoning suggested in variants of relative deprivation theory. As to Spain and Britain, TILLY et al. have this to say: "Spain displays some interesting parallels with Italy. In Spain the transition from the classic reactive forms of collective violence—the food riot, the tax rebellion, and so on—came late and on a schedule which varied markedly with the modernity of the region. In Spain agricultural proletarians (especially the *braceros* of the south) played a major part in nineteenth- and twentieth-century political conflicts. In Spain there were many crises, each surrounded by its own array of collective violence" (TILLY et al. 1975:274).

> [In Britain the] years from 1830 to 1832 . . . resembled the time of the French and German revolutions of 1848 in two important respects. First, they brought a great swelling of both proactive and reactive collective action on the part of many different segments of the population, often in some sort of alliance with middle-class reformers. Second, they marked the transition from predominantly reactive to predominantly proactive popular movements; after that point, the food riot, the tax rebellion, machine-breaking, and kindred actions faded fast away. From the 1830s on, petitions, demonstrations, strikes, mass meetings, special-purpose associations predominated in British collective action [see STEVENSON 1979 for a useful summary of the changes in popular disturbances in England from 1700 to 1870].[277] Essentially the same transition occurred in France and Germany two or three decades later (ibid., p. 275-76).

One should take into consideration, however, that "England of the 1820s and 1830s happens to be an exceptionally well analyzed case.[278] Elsewhere, we know less of the detail. In general, all we can be sure of is that (1) organizational nuclei existed before the great bursts of working-class association—England in the 1830s, France and Germany in 1848, and so on—and played significant parts in them; (2) the extension of the vote tended to accompany and encourage the legalization of working-class associations; (3) legalization gave a great boost to the strength and prevalence of associations" (ibid., p. 280).

As to the individual hardships of protesters—their relative deprivation in the sense of GURR and MULLER—there is no operation in the works of TILLY which comes near to a test. Thus, while TILLY is perhaps right with his attacks on primitive forms of breakdown and deprivation theories, more refined variants, developed especially by MULLER (see MULLER 1979 for a summary), have never been put to test and will probably be rather difficult to evaluate on such a grand historical scale without survey data. Contrary to TILLY, relative deprivation may lead to the forming of organizations and then to mobilization. (We refer to theories of relative deprivation here and not to breakdown and dissolution theories). Our argument is consistent with the second half of the following quotation: "On the face of it, we have no good reason to expect marginal and desperate populations to mount violence-producing collective actions. Unless breakdown and dissolution lead desperate and marginal populations to *reorganize* themselves around new beliefs and claims, the observed sequence of actions leading to collective violence casts serious doubt on the classic breakdown-dissolution theory" (TILLY et al. 1975:251). The causal sequence would then look like that in Figure 8.5.

TILLY himself has shown possible ways of combining both approaches:

> [The] emergence of an alternative polity . . . may possibly be related to rising discontent, value conflict, frustration, or relative deprivation. The relationship must be proved, however, not assumed. Even if it is proved that discontent, value conflict, frustration, and relative deprivation do fluctuate in close correspondence to the emergence and disappearance of alternative polities— a result which would surprise me—the thing to watch for would still be the commitment of a significant part of the population, regardless of their motives, to exclusive alternative claims to the control over the government currently exerted by the members of the polity (TILLY 1975:523-24; cf. also the remarks in TILLY et al. 1975: 8-9).

Although TILLY et al. would probably not interpret their results as supporting a model like that in Figure 8.5, their tests of deprivation models have been insufficient. Following conventional methods in their study of disturbances in France from 1830 through 1960, SNYDER/TILLY (1972) employ indexes of food prices, prices of manufactured goods, and industrial production for measuring deprivation, thus running the same risks of fallacies of aggregation that imperil cross-national efforts to test deprivation theories (cf. also TILLY et al. 1975 passim; cf. the discussion in chapter 5.1.1.1.3.2). Although harsh, DAVIES is correct when noting: "Without other data, these indexes say only that there were fluctuations in food prices, manufactured goods prices, and industrial production" (DAVIES 1974:608). SNYDER/TILLY find only "insignificant" results when relating these deprivation measures to collective violence (changes in the number of participants in disturbances), whereas their own measures of repression (excess arrests, size of national budget, man-days of detention in jail) fare considerably better, at least for the period 1886-1939 ($R^2 = .49$). For 1830-1960 some changes in the predictive equation are introduced. R^2 drops to .17, leading the authors to conclude "that there are other variables acting on this system which we have not been able to grasp" (SNYDER/TILLY 1972:529). Their measure for indexing power struggles (elections held or not), however, turns out to be less powerful, although the signs are positive as predicted. They interpret their findings as being generally more favorable toward their power-contending model, even if the chain of inference is rather long. Size of national budget is not necessarily an indicator of degree of repression used by incumbents against likely contenders. Incidentally, HALABY (1973), in his critique of this study, stresses the lack of correspondence between theoretical concepts and empirical measures employed, as well as pointing to several other methodological shortcomings. SNYDER/TILLY (1973; cf. also TILLY et al. 1975:81) report, however, that using real wages as a

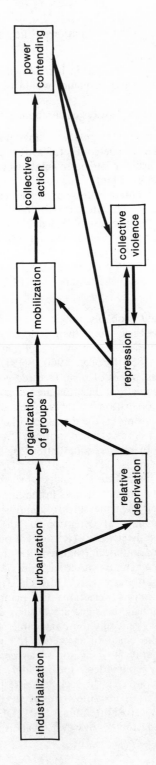

Figure 8.5. A Revised Version of TILLY's Power-Contending Model

more direct measurement of deprivation leads to insignificant results.[279] In a review of the TILLYs' book, ELWITT also questions some of Charles TILLY's conclusions:

> The statistics on violence that he cites . . . refute his own argument by showing that political upheaval occurred precisely at those times when social tensions reached intolerable levels (the late 1840s, 1897–1910) or when the entire nation was gripped by a general economic crisis (the 1930s). Charles [TILLY] also fails to take full advantage of his chosen approach. He would be less confident about the autonomy of politics were he to consider such measurable quantities as work speed-ups, the relation of wages to profits, the rate of the concentration of capital, and the subordination of independent craftsmen to capital—to suggest only a few (ELWITT 1976: 577).[280]

Breakdown theories (i.e., theories of discontent) and solidarity theories, as the authors like to call them (TILLY et al. 1975:7), need not be exclusive. States of relative deprivation might be considered a background factor which in the presence of additional conditions leads to the formation of organizations. These in turn strengthen the solidarity among population segments which judge their states of deprivation to be intolerable and therefore call for changes. Elsewhere (ZIMMERMANN 1980) these questions have been dealt with in greater detail (see also ibid. for a direct comparison of TILLY's approach with GURR's works; cf. also USEEM 1980). Let it suffice here to draw on the words of AYA whose analysis parallels ours: "Run backwards, that is to say retrospectively, theories that explain revolutions and collective violence by shared frustrations, discontents, deprivations, and so forth are invariably true—true by definition. Run forwards, or prospectively, however, such theories are powerless to distinguish political watersheds from business as usual" (AYA 1979:58). "If, by the volcanic model [as he calls it], revolutions and collective violence are eruptions of rage, then people suffering the worst grievances should make the readiest rebels. . . .[281] The political model, on the other hand, predicts the opposite: that displaced, disfranchised groups would be under-represented in the census of popular activism. Why? Because people with the meanest grievances to fight about have often the fewest resources to fight with" (ibid., p. 73–74). And finally:

> The volcanic model . . . makes two inferential leaps—from social change to mass anger, and from mass anger to collective violence— thereby vaulting the problem of how change stirs up grievances among specific groups, and how said discontent converts into concerted protest. The political model [of TILLY], on the other hand, implies two analytic links to span these gaps: one, an indelible but indirect relation between the economic and political structure of a social setting, the changes it undergoes over time, and the genesis of conflict; two, an organizational and tactical nexus between the

advent of grievances and collective action to repair them. It suggests, in short, a political power analysis of both grievances and opportunities to act upon them (ibid., p. 75–76).

Perhaps the most useful confrontation between theories of collective action and of relative deprivation is found in ECKSTEIN (1980) who suggests many important qualifications and tests to be carried out for both theories. Partly on purpose, ECKSTEIN overlooks many details dealt with here and elsewhere; yet the strength of his arguments may in fact be due to his bold eclecticism (see ECKSTEIN 1980:esp. p. 149ff.).

Before ending this section on the works of TILLY and his co-workers, we will briefly consider KORPI's (1974) theoretical effort to combine features of GURR's approach with those of TILLY's. KORPI aims at a causal ordering of those variables likely to be of major importance in whether or not a power-contending faction will mobilize, in itself a multiplicative function of expected success and utility of reaching the goal. In brief, KORPI claims that his power balance model modifies TILLY's political process model in a number of respects, the "central prediction of the power balance model of conflict [being] that between parties with unequal power resources, decreases in the difference in power resources will increase the probability of conflict, while increases in the power difference will decrease the probability of conflict" (KORPI 1974:1577). It should be noted that KORPI expects conflicts to be more likely if one group gains new power resources, whereas TILLY claims that conflict would be as probable in the case of parties losing power resources. The main difference between KORPI's model and GURR's model of internal war (GURR 1970a:234, 277) is summarized in the following hypothesis:

> We can expect a curvilinear relationship between on the one hand the difference in power resources between the parties and on the other hand the probability of manifest conflict between them. The probability of manifest conflict is thus low when parties have greatly unequal power resources but will normally increase when the difference in power resources begins to decrease. In contrast to other models of conflict, which usually assume maximum probability of conflict at the point of parity in power resources between the parties, a bimodal distribution of the probability of manifest conflict on the difference in power resources between the two actors is predicted here (KORPI 1974:1574; italics omitted).

KORPI rather skillfully derives this theoretical conclusion; however, it will be extremely difficult to specify what is meant by power resources or such terms as expectancy of success. Even more complicated data sets would be needed than in the case of the other two theoretical models. KORPI agrees with TILLY in that political factors (in his case, differences in power resources) are of prime importance. Accordingly, there are two causal paths (see Figure 8.6) leading from perceived differences in power resources—via expectancy of success or via expected costs of reaching goal and utility of

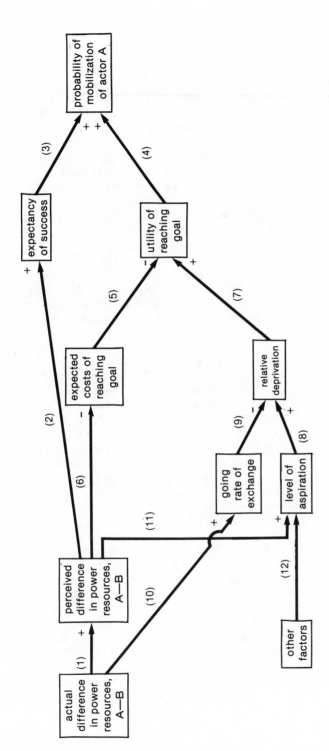

Figure 8.6. Causal Model of Major Variables "assumed to affect the probability of mobilization of actor A in a situation of potential conflict with actor B"

Source: KORPI (1974:1573).

reaching goal—to the dependent variable. There is also a third causal path which leads first to relative deprivation (in itself partly a function of the level of aspiration) and from there through utility in reaching goal to the dependent variable. Thus, some of TILLY's main propositions as well as GURR's central variable relative deprivation have been combined in one complex model.

Whether such a basically political model of the probability of mobilization or the model in Figure 8.5 is valid remains to be seen from future research. Both could, of course, be combined. A number of causal variables would then have to be added on the left side in Figure 8.5 to determine in a more calculative sense whether mobilization is to occur or not. (For better readability we have omitted such a complex drawing from this text.)

Compared with GURR's theoretical model, the works of TILLY and KORPI have considerably more to say on the importance of mobilization and some of its likely determinants. In this respect most cross-national studies on political violence have lacked common sense. *How* do people, whether feeling relatively deprived or not, come to join in acts of collective violence? By what means and at what point? In the final chapter we will attempt further to answer these questions.

To summarize the contribution of the TILLY group to the cross-national study of revolutions (and not of collective violence), our knowledge of the causal conditions of revolutions has not been substantially enlarged,[282] although TILLY has provided the reader with valuable criticisms of other approaches to the study of political violence. The various references to his works throughout this study testify to this fact. In addition, if one considers the paths to follow if the comparative analysis of revolutions is to develop, the TILLY group clearly has paved a way. In short, the goal of developing a cross-national quantitative science of revolutions has still not been attained, but we have a route to follow.

8.4.6.6.2. Analyses of Revolutionary Crowds (RUDÉ)

While the studies of TILLY and coworkers are dominated by a cross-national and quantitative perspective, the highly praised works of RUDÉ (1959; 1964; 1970) are less rigidly quantitative in character,[283] yet do provide us with numerous insights into the forms and dynamics of protests in the eighteenth century and the first half of the nineteenth century in France and Britain. RUDÉ is basically interested in finding out who participated in what kind of violent protest for what reason and with what effect. He is concerned with preindustrial crowds[284] prominent in a particular period "—it may extend over a hundred years or it may be more or it may be less—during which a society is adapting itself to the changes brought about by rapid industrialization and at the end of which that society has (as in Britain in the nineteenth century) become radically transformed, so that we may speak of a new society—an 'industrial' society—as having come into being" (RUDÉ 1970:17).

The "distinctive hall-marks of the 'pre-industrial' crowd (at least, in its Western European manifestations) are: (1) the prevalence of the rural food riot; (2) the resort to 'direct action' and violence to property; (3) its 'spontaneity'; (4) its leadership from 'without' the crowd;[285] (5) its mixed composition, with the emphasis on small shopkeepers and craftsmen in the towns and weavers, miners, and labourers in the village; and (6) its concern for the restoration of 'lost' rights"[286] (ibid., p. 23).

With respect to France he in part anticipates the results of TILLY, yet only as far as the period before 1850 is concerned. Only a few of the many findings in RUDÉ's works will be mentioned here. The following statements concerning groups participating in violent protest activities before and during the French Revolution mostly speak for themselves. According to RUDÉ's results "the ordinary people of Paris were bound together by one common aim—to ensure adequate supplies of food at a steady and reasonable price" (ibid., p. 157; cf. also KAPLAN 1976 for an analysis of the "political economy" of bread in the reign of Louis XV); "it is, in fact, no mere coincidence (as LEFEBVRE and LABROUSSE[287] have both pointed out) that the Bastille should have fallen on the very day that the price of grain throughout France reached its cyclical peak" (ibid., p. 165). These so-called *menu peuple*[288] comprised "wage-earners, craftsmen, small shopkeepers, workshop masters, clerks and others" (ibid., p. 133-34). "Our study has indicated, too, how responsive the popular movement was, at every stage, to any shortage or upward fluctuation in the price of essential consumer goods, particularly of bread" (ibid., p. 196). "It is, in fact, significant that the most substantial of [the movements for higher wages]—the movements of April-June 1791 and of January-July 1794—took place at times of a shortage of labour and of falling or stable prices; and that the latter movement collapsed when the Thermidorians relaxed controls and reverted to a policy of high prices and inflation" (ibid., p. 197). RUDÉ stresses that "on balance, it may be claimed that the particular demands of the wage-earners—for higher wages and better working conditions—were comparatively unimportant as a stimulus to revolutionary activity and that the wage-earners were more inclined to be drawn into participation in these events by the need for cheap and plentiful bread, a motive which they shared with the *menu peuple* as a whole" (ibid., p. 161). However, RUDÉ notes that "the main social movements of the spring and summer of 1794 were wages movements rather than movements in shops and markets over food supplies" (ibid., p. 187).

Turning to the *vainqueurs de la Bastille*,[289] there were only a few persons from bourgeois background among the eight or nine hundred participants. "The rest . . . are almost all small tradesmen, artisans, and wage-earners. Of these, about two-thirds are small workshop masters, craftsmen, and journeymen drawn from about thirty petty trades; the remainder are engaged in manufacture, distribution, building, the professions, and general trades" (RUDÉ 1959:57). More generally, one has "to note the sustained militancy of members of certain trades such as furnishing, building, metal-work, and dress. Most conspicuous of all were the locksmiths, joiners and cabinet-makers, shoemakers, and tailors; other frequently in evidence were stone-masons, hair-dressers, and engravers; and, of those engaged in less skillful occupations, wine-merchants, water-carriers, porters, cooks, and domestic servants. Workers employed in manufactories (textiles, glass, tobacco, tap-estries, porcelain) played, with the exception of the gauze-workers, a rela-tively inconspicuous role in these movements" (ibid., p. 185). RUDÉ also notes that "at the Bastille, the unemployed country-workers,[290] whose influx into the capital had been one of the more striking manifestations of the economic crisis which heralded the Revolution, played little or no part;[291] and wage-earners in general, even workshop journeymen, appear to have been in a distinct minority" (ibid., p. 180).

Apart from the *menu peuple* or *sans-culottes*, as they were called after June 1792, other social groups had their share in the French Revolution. "MATHIEZ, in particular, has made us familiar with the picture of the origins of the great Revolution as a gradual 'unfolding' of minor revolutions— first the 'révolte nobiliaire'; then the 'révolution bourgeoise' and, finally, the popular revolution" (RUDÉ 1970:64).[292] Commenting on this view, RUDÉ (ibid.) emphasizes what turns out to be one of the major points of his studies: "While such a presentation is convenient and has more than a grain of truth in it, it tends to reduce the intervention of the masses to one of secondary importance and fails to show that the popular movement, while intensified and accelerated by the revolutionary crisis, had its origins in the Old Régime and, in fact, preceded by many years the revolutionary activity of the *bourgeoisie*" (ibid.). However, "it was, in fact, to be one of the great lessons of the French Revolution that the popular movement, how-ever militant and widespread, could only succeed and survive as an effective revolutionary force as long as it was allied to an important section of the *bourgeoisie*; conversely, that the *bourgeoisie* could only carry out its histori-cal task of destroying feudal property relations as long as they, or a substan-tial part of them, maintained their links with the broad masses of town and countryside" (ibid., p. 80-81). "The main lesson of 1775 was, in short, that in the conditions of eighteenth-century France, no isolated movement of wage-earners, artisans and village poor[293] could hope to yield revolutionary results. This truth was to be realized on more than one occasion both before and during the Revolution" (ibid., p. 67).

> It was only when the *bourgeoisie* entered the revolutionary struggle, as it did in the winter of 1788–89, that the popular masses were able to acquire a political direction and a set of political aims and con-cepts[294]—such concepts as Third Estate, Nation, "complot aristocra-tique" and the Rights of Man—without which they would have expended their energies on actions limited to economic ends. This is not to underrate the importance of their contribution; without their intervention, the *bourgeois* revolutionaries of July 1789—many of whom were stricken by panic at the crucial moment of insurrec-tion—would have been doomed and the recently constituted National Assembly dispersed by royal troops (ibid., p. 80).

Or as put in another variant of the theme,

> [The popular movement] grew from a movement concerned, in the
> first place, with purely economic ends into one with more or less
> clearly defined political aims; it developed a common bond of
> interest between the wage earners, craftsmen, wine-growers and
> small tradesmen of town and countryside against monopolists,
> hoarders and grain-speculators; this movement, in turn, began to
> "merge" with that of the small peasant proprietors against feudal
> game laws, tithes and dues; and, finally (though not always in point
> of time), the movement of townsmen and villagers "merged" with
> the political action of the *bourgeoisie* against feudal privilege and the
> whole apparatus of government of the Old Régime (ibid., p. 75).[295]

The role played by the army during the French Revolution (cf., e.g.,
SCOTT 1978) as well as in 1830 and in February 1848 may briefly be summarized by relying again on RUDÉ:

> In Paris, the Gardes Françaises were loyal enough to shoot down the
> Réveillon rioters in April; but, by June, they were parading to shouts
> of *Vive le tiers état!*, and in July they played a crucial part in the
> capture of the Bastille. After this, a new national army emerged,
> which proclaimed its allegiance to the nation and the new revolu-
> tionary authorities; but it was kept out of Paris, whose defense was
> entrusted to the National Guard. The Guard, at first solidly *bour-
> geois*, was effective . . . in suppressing the demonstration of July
> 1791; but it gradually became the instrument of the sans-culottes as
> much as of the Assembly; and it was only when the army was called
> in again, in May 1795, that the long series of popular disturbances
> that had marked the whole course of the Revolution in Paris was
> brought to a close.
>
>   In 1830 and 1848, the defection of the armed forces was once
> more decisive in assuring the defeat of the royal government and the
> success of the revolutionary challenge. Yet the pattern was not the
> same as that of 1789. The outbreak of 1830 was a short-lived affair
> and, after three days' street-fighting, Charles X was driven out and
> Louis Philippe was installed for the next eighteen years. In February
> 1848, it was the defection of the National Guard in Paris, even more
> than that of the army (which was passive rather than openly rebel-
> lious), that drove Louis Philippe, in his turn, into exile. This time,
> the popular forces that challenged the authority of the new revolu-
> tionary government and Assembly were far stronger and more
> efficiently organized than they had been in 1789. Yet they were
> brought to heel not after six years but after a mere four months.
> This was due partly to the building of railways, which made it
> possible to summon troops more quickly to the capital; and it
> was due, perhaps even more, to the loyalty of the bulk of the

National Guard and the Mobile Guard, who were the real victors of the June insurrection (RUDÉ 1964:265-66).

There are some other interesting comparisons:

If we examine the occupations of the 11,693 persons[296] who were charged in the [June revolt of 1848], we find a remarkable similarity to the trades of those who stormed the Bastille and captured the Tuileries sixty years before. We find among them no fewer than 554 stonemasons, 510 joiners, 416 shoemakers, 321 cabinet makers, 286 tailors, 285 locksmiths, 283 painters, 140 carpenters, 187 turners, 119 jewelers, and 191 wine merchants; and most of these occupations are among the dozen largest categories to which the prisoners belonged. . . . Striking as certain of the similarities between the crowds in 1789 and June 1848 are, however, the differences are equally great. . . . In the earlier revolution, the initiative was generally taken by the workshop masters, who were more literate and more highly politically educated than their apprentices and journeymen, and the traditional crafts played the major role in popular insurrection. This time the case was somewhat different. The initial impetus . . . came from the workers in the national workshops: this in itself was something new, as when similar workshops were closed down in Paris in 1789 and again in 1791 it hardly caused a ripple in the struggle of the political parties. . . . It was the workers in the railway workshops of La Chapelle, already a thriving industrial suburb to the north of the old city, who built some of the first barricades in the Faubourg Poissonnière; and we find railwaymen also joining port and riverside workers in manning the barricades on the Island of the Cité. These workers had since February been among the most highly organized and militant in the capital; GOSSEZ describes them as forming "the vanguard of the insurrection."

The railways therefore played an ambivalent role. On the one hand, by bringing in trainloads of troops and provincial volunteers to swell the forces of order, they played a substantial part in crushing the insurrection; on the other hand, by creating a new type of industrial worker, they set a new stamp on the workers' movement that would have important consequences for the future (ibid., p. 175-77).

This set of quotations clearly underscores the more general analyses arrived at in previous chapters: successful attempts at revolution require (1) that several key issues in society remain unresolved, (2) that various social groupings—among them elite elements blocked from attaining the aspired social positions and/or desiring for ideological reasons to overthrow the prevailing political order—form a revolutionary coalition, and (3) that major parts of the state's coercive forces defect or are at least neutralized.

Some parallels have been noted for Britain with respect to the participation of social groups in violent protests. Yet, the political and social impact of these events is much less dramatic than in France. A few summary quotations dealing with the best known samples of preindustrial rioting in Britain will suffice here. "Of some 275 disturbances that I have noted between 1735 and 1800, two in every three are [riots occasioned by a shortage or a sudden rise in the price of food] ;[297] and it is unlikely that the proportions are any different for the remaining years of the century" (RUDÉ 1964:35-36).[298]

> Two general points apply to all the food riots of the century and are perhaps worthy of mention here. One is the large numbers of industrial workers that took part in these disturbances. We constantly read, in this connection, of the activities of Kingswood colliers, Cornish tinners, Staffordshire potters, Tyneside keelmen, and Wiltshire and Somerset weavers. It is another reminder that in England as in France the typical form of social protest at this time, even among wage earners, was the food riot rather than the strike. Another point to note is that food riots tended to break out more frequently in the north and west than in the south and east. This is not really surprising, as the main wheat-growing areas lay in the south and east while their produce, when the export of grain was permitted, was more often shipped from northern and western ports (ibid., p. 37).

A much greater variety prevailed in the city riots during the eighteenth century. "In the anti-Irish riots of 1736, as we might expect from their nature and origins, wage earners formed [a larger] portion; whereas in 1768 the Wilkite rioters [see RUDÉ 1962; cf. also HAYTER 1978 on the role of the army during this and other disturbances in 1756-80] appear again to have been a similar mixture of wage earners, small employers, and independent craftsmen. Such elements, too, although rarely reappearing on the lists of householders assessed for the parish poor rate, were rarely vagrants, rarely had criminal records of any kind, generally had settled abodes, and tended to be 'respectable' working men rather than slum dwellers or the poorest of the poor" (ibid., p. 61). "The Rebecca riots in Wales [1839; 1842-43], like the Swing riots in England [1830; see HOBSBAWM/RUDÉ 1969], owed their origins to a variety of causes, but all were associated with the dissolution of old village ties" (ibid., p. 156).

As to labor disputes, it is noted that

> Far more frequent . . . than assaults on persons and private dwellings were attacks on industrial property, workshops, and machinery. This form of "collective bargaining by riot" . . . is to the eighteenth-century industrial dispute what popular price fixing, or *taxation populaire*, is to the contemporary food riot. Both forms of direct action, the one by small producers, the other by small consumers, appear over a similar span of years: attacks on machinery are recorded at least as early as 1663 and as late as 1831. Such attacks,

in turn, were of two kinds and had two different (though related)
purposes in view: the one to protect the worker's livelihood against
wage cuts or rising prices; the other to protect his livelihood against
the threat, or the believed threat, of new machinery. They have
often been confused and placed under the common label of
"Luddism," a term which applies more particularly to the English
machine-wrecking riots of 1811–17; though even these . . . were by
no means confined to protests against technical innovation (ibid.,
p. 70).

There is a third type of riot which RUDÉ (ibid., p. 135ff.) calls the
"Church and King" riots, taking place during the 1790s. "In contrast with all
these other movements, a distinctive feature of 'Church and King' riots and
demonstrations is their political conservatism. Where other movements, in-
spired by liberal, democratic, republican, or anticlerical ideas, are concerned
to destroy privilege or absolute monarchy, or to enlarge the frontiers of
religious toleration, these rioters proclaim their attachment to the established
order and traditional way of life against their disruption by 'Jacobins,' 'un-
believers,' 'foreigners,' or other alien elements" (ibid., p.135).

Apart from information on the occupations of rioters RUDÉ's sources
(mainly police records) also contain information about the age and sex of the
participants. Leaving aside such special events as the march of the market-
women to Versailles in October 1789, the crowd was mainly composed of
men, although women did, of course, take part (cf. HUFTON 1971), especially in the food riots. "The average age of the 662 *vainqueurs de la Bastille*
was 34, of those killed and wounded in the assault on the Tuileries in 1792,
38; and of those arrested after the insurrection of May 1795, 36. Such men
were appreciably older than those arrested for taking part in the French grain
riots of 1775 (average age 30), in the pro-*parlement* disturbances (23) and
Réveillon riots (29) on the eve of the Revolution, and in the Champ de
Mars affair of 1791 (31). The proportion of persons who may be termed
literate from their ability to sign the police magistrate's report on similar
occasions also varied considerably from one disturbance to another: from
33 percent in the grain riots of 1775 to 62 percent in the Réveillon riots,
to 80 to 85 percent respectively in the case of the *journées* of July 1791
and May 1795" (ibid., p. 209).

According to life expectancy rates at that time, rioters must be considered middle-aged. Thus, there is strong evidence against the riffraff theory,
with respect to variables like occupation and age (see chapter 5.3.2.1 for an
extensive discussion). The selection of targets provides further evidence
against the riffraff theory:

The Gordon rioters in London[299] and the "Church and King" rioters
in Birmingham, having carefully earmarked their victims, took
meticulous care to avoid destroying or damaging the properties of
their neighbors. The machine wreckers of 1830 appear to have discriminated between one type of farmer and another; the Réveillon
rioters in Paris looted shops, but only foods shops; Ned Ludd [on

the Luddism of the years 1811-17, cf. THOMIS 1970; see also
STEVENSON 1979:155-62] and Rebecca[300] invariably chose their
targets with deliberate care; the crowds that burned the Paris customs posts spared those belonging to the Duc d'Orléans; the September "massacres" despatched only such victims as had been found
guilty by improvised tribunals; . . . In fact, the study of the preindustrial crowd suggests that it rioted for precise objects and rarely
engaged in indiscriminate attacks on either properties or persons
(ibid., p. 253-54; the findings of STEVENSON 1979 for England
from 1700 to 1870 underscore RUDÉ's conclusions).

In fact, if deaths occurred during acts of political violence, they were
mostly due to activities of state agents. "Because a number of events we have
studied in Germany, Italy, and France would not have been violent if troops
and police had not attacked, it is likely that some of the apparent difference
between Great Britain and other countries results from greater British constraints on military and police violence" (TILLY et al. 1975:280; cf. also
GURR et al. 1977:81 and passim). TILLY and coworkers are led to even
harsher conclusions:

> Forms of collective action do vary in the probability that they will
> lead to the damage or seizure of persons or objects, but (1) practi-
> cally no common forms of collective action which we have en-
> countered are intrinsically violent; (2) for most common forms of
> collective action the probability of violence is far closer to zero than
> to one; (3) the great bulk of collective violence emerges from much
> larger streams of essentially nonviolent collective action; (4) a sub-
> stantial part of the violence we observe consists of the forcible
> *reaction* of a second group—often of specialized repressive forces
> in the employ of governments—to the nonviolent collective action
> of the first (TILLY et al. 1975:282).

In any case, these authors are among the very few who have clearly distinguished between deaths caused by protesters in acts of political violence and
by state agents. As pointed out earlier (cf. chapter 5.1.1.1.3.1), this is another
field where research on political violence should provide further information
in the future.

There is also no basis for considering rioters as instigated by conspirators
or representing criminal elements or "classes dangereuses" (CHEVALIER
1958; see in particular RUDÉ 1973a). Thus, there is ample evidence against
the various stereotypes emerging from riffraff theories, particularly in the
works of BURKE, LEBON, TARDE, PARETO, MOSCA, and MICHELS
(see NYE 1977 for a discussion; cf. also the critical assessment of some of
these works in COBBAN 1971a). "In short, the crowd was violent, impulsive,
easily stirred by rumor, and quick to panic; but it was not fickle, peculiarly
irrational, or generally given to bloody attacks on persons. The conventional
picture of the crowd painted by LEBON and inherited by later writers is not

lacking in shrewd and imaginative insight; but it ignores the facts of history and is, in consequence, overdrawn, tendentious, and misleading" (RUDÉ 1964:257).

In his studies RUDÉ has set new standards of research in a number of ways (see PALMER 1960 for a brief critical evaluation). Nevertheless, at times the question arises (disturbing many other researchers as well) whether the activists reported on in the records are representative of their particular populations (e.g., with respect to their occupations). As put by TILLY: "SOBOUL's and RUDÉ's investigations have shown that the existing records are very rich and that a bright historian can do wonders with them; they have not erased the suspicion that the people who get into the record differ from those who do not. That suspicion can only be confirmed or spiked through much closer comparison of sources generated in different ways (for example, dossiers of arrestees vs. records of persons killed and wounded vs. eye-witness accounts for the June Days or the Commune)"[301] (TILLY 1972b:100). Furthermore, BLUMER noted in a review of RUDÉ (1964) that analyses of the crowds themselves as they develop over time are not performed:[302] "We are given no explanation of why under the same set of specified conditions crowds form at given places and times but not at other places and times. Nor does he explain why, again under the same conditions, some crowds are strong and persistent while others are weak and easily disintegrated" (BLUMER 1965:43; cf. also the discussion in chapter 5.3.2.5).

Going through RUDÉ's numerous studies one hardly comes to the conclusion that deprivation theories are meaningless. Rather, one gets the impression that deprivation theories as *background* theories could be combined with TILLY's power-contending notion. Deprivation theories may, for example, provide an answer to the question of why there was turmoil in 1775 in France yet give no information as to the differential conditions making for revolution in 1789 (cf. also the quotations above). Considering the variety of causes suggested by RUDÉ,[303] the J-curve hypothesis as an explanation of the French Revolution again appears to be rather insufficient.

The data TILLY collected or, more appropriately, the way they were collected, allow for causal modelling procedures of a much more powerful kind than holds true of RUDÉ's data. There is a variety of data scattered throughout RUDÉ's works (e.g., the statistical appendix in RUDÉ 1959: 242–52), yet compared to TILLY the degree of quantification is rather rudimentary at present. Although it may be somewhat unfair to say, considering the work RUDÉ and others have done, the reader has the feeling that there is much ad hoc theorizing in the works of these scholars who consider themselves primarily social historians rather than sociologists or political scientists. Yet, tests of complex hypotheses are possible even when dealing with such remote occurrences as the French Revolution. This is demonstrated, for example, by SHAPIRO/DAWSON (1972; cf. also SHAPIRO et al. 1973) who take up a question already dealt with theoretically in chapter 8.4.2. They measure "as the independent variable, local differences in the opportunities for ennoblement provided by the institutional structure. We measure, as the dependent variable, local differences in radicalism in the grievance lists

[*Cahiers de Doléances*] [304] drawn up at the electoral meetings to choose deputies for the Estates-General of 1789. We seek to discover whether, in places where ennoblement opportunities were plentiful, the bourgeoisie was more or less radical than where ennoblement opportunities were scarce" (SHAPIRO/DAWSON 1972:169). The sample consists of the general *cahiers* of the Third Estate and the Nobility. The dependent variables were indexed by "demands for equality," "demands for change," "similarity to the decree of 4 August 1789," "similarity to the Declaration of the Rights of Man," and "total number of grievances" as found in these *cahiers*. Without going into detail as to results of these tests of the blocked-opportunity → political discontent hypothesis, it might be said that the authors found some support for another hypothesis of TOCQUEVILLE. He "explains bourgeois antipathy to the nobility by referring to the visible possibility of deserting the bourgeois class to enter a noble class distinguished, with an intolerable clarity, from the rest of the populace" [305] (ibid., p. 185). "In the Third Estate, small but consistently positive correlations are found between the number of ennobling offices in the electoral circumscriptions and the five scores measuring radicalism [306] in the *cahiers*. In the Nobility, generally, negative correlations are found between the number of ennobling offices and the scores on radicalism" (ibid., p. 180).

One may ask whether the number of ennobling offices is an adequate indicator of mobility opportunities (or of aspirations of mobility). Real opportunities for mobility might differ from those perceived. After some additional controls the authors found "that obstacles to real opportunities for ennoblement were, in general, unimportant in generating radicalism in the Third Estate *cahiers*" (ibid., p. 183). Rather, "population of the principal town in each electoral circumscription" exerts a strong controlling influence on the original relationships. The population figures in themselves correlate around .30 with the number of ennoblement offices (after Paris has been removed), yet in 4 out of 5 cases they correlate stronger with the dependent variables than number of ennoblement offices. Apparently there is some kind of an "urbanization" effect which is, however, difficult to detect, since urbanization "includes all kinds of mobility, social as well as geographic, together with an array of economic and psychological variables" (ibid., p. 185). Due to the aggregate nature of their data the final conclusion of the authors is not sufficiently corroborated: results "permit us to conclude that the social system was affected politically by the ennoblement process, that the effects operated through the *spectators* of this process more than through frustrated, would be beneficiaries of it, and that, as between the TAINE-DOLLOT hypothesis [stressing the radicalizing effects of blocked channels of mobility] and the TOCQUEVILLE hypothesis [relating radicalization to increased opportunities of upward social mobility], we should choose the latter because of its superior value in explaining the politics of the social system as a whole" (ibid., p. 185; italics added). Only individual (e.g., biographical) data will allow ruling out an explanation like the following (which overlaps with TOCQUEVILLE's): those who stay behind, for whom there are real and/or apparent opportunities for ennoblement but who do not attain it, resent the nobility much more strongly than those "spectators" who rarely have an opportunity of participating in such upward-mobility processes but see others leaving the bourgeois class.

Having emphasized the works of TILLY and RUDÉ in the last two sections, one must not forget the giants on whose shoulders these authors stand, namely LEFEBVRE with his studies *Les Paysans du nord pendant la Révolution française* (1924), *La Grande Peur de 1789* (1932), "La Révolution francaise et les paysans" (1933; cf. also the review by PALMER 1959a), and "Foules révolutionnaires" (1954); his disciple SOBOUL (1958) with his dissertation thesis on the sans-culottes during the year II (cf. also MARKOV/ SOBOUL 1957; MARKOV 1956;[307] 1976; and the critical review of this type of study in PALMER 1960);[308] LABROUSSE (1933; 1943); and, among the older social historians, MATHIEZ (1928) as well as many others (see TILLY 1964a for a brief overview of some of these studies).

For treatments of the French Revolution in general (as well as the historical circumstances and the international impact) see also the following works: LEFEBVRE (1947; 1962/1964; 1963), LEFEBVRE et al. (1930); HAMP-SON (1963); SOBOUL (1964); GODECHOT (1965); FURET/RICHET (1965–1966); JONES (1967); MAZAURIC (1970); PALMER (1971); GRIE-WANK (1972); MARKOV/SOBOUL (1973); ROBERTS (1978); DOYLE (1980); RUDÉ (1973) covering the period up to 1815; HOBSBAWM (1962) covering the years up to 1848 as well; FURET (1971; 1978) for a critique of simplified pseudo-Marxist interpretations of the French Revolution; SCHMITT (1976) for a useful summary of various interpretations, controversies, and gaps in research in connection with the French Revolution; and RUDÉ (1961) for another discussion of various interpretations of the French Revolution.[309]

COBBAN has argued that the French Revolution was, contrary to dogmatic Marxist theories or various claims by SOBOUL and others, "to an important extent one *against* and not *for* the rising forces of capitalism" (COBBAN 1971:168; cf. also the review article by HUNECKE 1978). The revolution was "a triumph for the conservative, propertied, land-owning classes, large and small" (ibid., p. 170). COBBAN (ibid., p. 61) comes to the conclusion that the French Revolution was a political revolution led by the "*officiers* and the men of the liberal professions"[310] (not by the landholding bourgeoisie) rather than a social revolution. Actually, he claims his social interpretation of the French Revolution to be only a hypothesis, aimed at drawing researchers into more detailed analyses of the various social strata or social classes found under the Ancien Régime, during the French Revolution, and afterwards. What he says with respect to the Ancien Régime, namely that the structure of society "was a good deal more complex than was allowed for in the simple pattern of bourgeois and feudalism" (ibid., p. 166; in these respects cf. also the results in TAYLOR 1967 and the study by LUCAS 1973)[311] holds for other periods as well. In short, much remains to be done—even after SKOCPOL's (1979) impressive comparative analysis— with respect to terminology and study of social structure. (For a critique of COBBAN's interpretation see LEFEBVRE 1956 and the more dogmatic objections by SOBOUL 1976a; see also the reply by COBBAN 1971a: 270-82, and CAVANAUGH 1972 and DAWSON 1972:1-27 for a review of studies bearing on COBBAN's thesis).

In his *The Age of Democratic Revolution: A Political History of Europe and America: 1760-1800,* PALMER (1959; 1964; cf. also GODECHOT 1965) contends that the French Revolution falls into the much broader pattern of what he calls the "democratic revolution":

> [This revolution] emphasized the delegation of authority and the removability of officials, precisely because . . . neither delegation nor removability were much recognized in actual institutions.
>
> It is a corollary of these ideas that the American and the French Revolutions, the two chief actual revolutions of the period, with all due allowance for the great differences between them, nevertheless shared a good deal in common, and that what they shared was shared also at the same time by various people and movements in other countries, notably in England, Ireland, Holland, Belgium, Switzerland, and Italy, but also in Germany, Hungary, and Poland, and by scattered individuals in places like Spain and Russia (PALMER 1959:5).

Critics (e.g., AMANN 1963; LEFEBVRE 1966), however, have emphasized the specific features of the French Revolution, denying that it fits neatly into the Atlantic (or Western) pattern as suggested by GODECHOT and PALMER. "It has been objected, in fact, that it is only possible to conceive of a general 'Western' or 'World' revolution during this period in terms of a purely ideological-constitutional movement from which the *sans-culottes,* the *levée en masse,* the peasant risings, the food crisis, and even the constitutional experiments of 1792-1794 are excluded or glossed over" (RUDÉ 1961:28).

It remains for us to explain why we chose to examine in detail the French Revolution along with other eighteenth and nineteenth century periods in France and England. The answer is obvious: RUDÉ, TILLY, and others have demonstrated that even historical matters can eventually be studied with modern computer facilities, allowing for more precise empirical testing of more elaborate theories. As put by one of the leading scholars of the Bolshevik revolution: "The more sociological history becomes, and the more historical sociology becomes, the better for both" (CARR 1961:60; cf. also the perspectives on future developments in TILLY 1979a). Considering the state of knowledge of the French Revolution,[312] one realizes that other Great Revolutions in history have been studied in much less detail, at least as far as the topics of the present study are concerned. We have been rather didactic in our focus on TILLY's and RUDÉ's works; one of our aims was to demonstrate how fascinating social science analyses of revolutions can be and are becoming,[313] a fact all the more noteworthy because these works contrast so positively with many of the sterile approaches we explored in earlier chapters on analyses of revolutions.

8.4.7. A Raw Causal Model of Revolutions

After the excursus into more historical matters and the lengthy discussion of theories on revolution, it may be useful to summarize in a rudimentary causal model those variables important in the analysis of revolutionary phenomena—important either on the basis of theoretical analysis or of some systematic empirical knowledge (see p. 400-401).

Compared to the numerous variables mentioned in this chapter—which might easily add up to one of the shopping lists ECKSTEIN (1965) critically commented on—rather few variables remain.[314] Yet, this model is still quite complex even if most of the postulated relationships are apparent from the preceding discussion. It is interesting to note that in several instances the same general theoretical notions as in the causal model of crises research (cf. Figure 6.2 in chapter 6.3.4.1) reappear in this model, albeit occasionally under different names. This reflects the broad consensus scholars have reached as to conditions underlying crises and one of their eventual but rare outcomes, revolution. Compared to the crises model, where only the main theoretical block variables were listed, the present model is somewhat more specific, for example, as to the antecedent conditions and likely consequences of loss of regime legitimacy. It should be stressed that not all of the requirements mentioned in the model must be met for revolution to occur. The more important conditions *necessary* for revolution to take place have been put in capital letters. There are at least three critical junctures in this model which bears some resemblance to a "branching tree model," i.e., a "sequence of choice points (not necessarily points of conscious decision, but points where development can go one way or the other). At any point in a sequence of development, there may be alternative next stages. But which one is chosen closes the options for others. Closely related to this is the notion of irreversibilities—choices of one branch which once chosen does not allow backtracking" (VERBA 1971:308). Whether some decisions prior to revolution are indeed irreversible is, of course, an empirical matter. The branching tree model might be a useful heuristic device for developing causal models of revolutions, but it should not necessarily be understood in a literal sense. The decisions occurring around any of the three critical junctures are made under much greater constraints than is typical of each preceding phase. In addition, the constraints accumulate until the final critical juncture is reached. While the idea of constraints or of a branching tree model precludes *feedback* influences, such forms of influence nevertheless could have been added to the present model (cf. also Figure 8.2). In fact, there are feedback influences between loss of regime legitimacy and the desertion of elites. For reasons of economy,[315] however, the model has been restricted to the more dominant causal directions.[316] (Following the theoretical approach outlined by SKOCPOL 1979, one might also add a factor dealing with international influences other than external defeat. This might have an effect on loss of regime legitimacy, on the desertion of elites, and on other variables in the model. Finally, HUNTINGTON 1968 has emphasized the role of nationalism as a defense against external modernizing threats, a factor which in effect may contribute to revolution in Third World countries.)

The *first critical juncture* exists in the complex variable *loss of regime legitimacy*. Recalling the discussion in chapter 6.3.4, this denotes not only loss of specific support of the regime but also the withdrawal of diffuse support. Building on the results of MULLER/JUKAM (1977), loss in regime legitimacy should be expected to be a greater threat than loss in incumbents' legitimacy to the survival of a political system. The latter is, however, an important determinant of whether or not loss in regime legitimacy occurs. (Empirically it seems rather unlikely that a crisis in political leadership will be preceded by loss of regime legitimacy. The reverse causal sequence can be expected to be more frequent.) Both crisis in political leadership (= loss of incumbents' legitimacy) and loss of regime legitimacy (with emphasis on withdrawal of diffuse support) have an effect on the desertion of elites, a direct one in the latter case, and an indirect one in the former. The desertion of elites is also preceded by the early withdrawal of support on the part of a subgroup of the elites, the intellectuals. Elites who have withdrawn their allegiance to the regime quite likely will conceive of an alternate political order. As a consequence, they might engage in forming new organizations supporting their claims or in winning and redefining existing ones, thereby increasing the probability of successful mobilization of large discontented sections of the population. One should also expect a direct, though weaker, impact of loss of regime legitimacy on successful mobilization of discontented masses (success not yet measured in terms of final revolutionary outcome but *ex ante* in terms of organizational strength). Yet, as OBERSCHALL points out: "It is the un- or weakly organized collectivities, especially if they are economically dependent upon the groups they seek to revolt against, that find it difficult to produce their own 'inside' leaders for sustained social movements. Here the availability of outside leaders and resources for mobilization is a necessity" (OBERSCHALL 1973:160; cf. also McCARTHY/ZALD 1973:17-18).

Expressed in different theoretical terms, diffuse support may be one of the most important conditions for institutions to be strong and adaptable to crises situations. Thus, strong and adaptable political institutions[317] may be conceived of as acting like filters and thus deciding on whether the variables mentioned to the left in Figure 8.7 do indeed lead to a loss of regime legitimacy. For theoretical reasons, the quality and performance of political leadership must be treated independently from the strength and adaptability of political institutions, as we have done in the model. Their function, however, is the same: If neither institutions nor political leaders, as those in the position to draw on institutionalized political resources or to be called to act by institutions themselves, are capable of reaching adequate decisions in the sense of reducing the threat resulting from the antecedent conditions, then the "flood," i.e., the revolutionary potential, will pass the first gate.

The *second critical juncture* has already been mentioned while discussing the first (loss of regime legitimacy) of which it is a consequence: *desertion of*

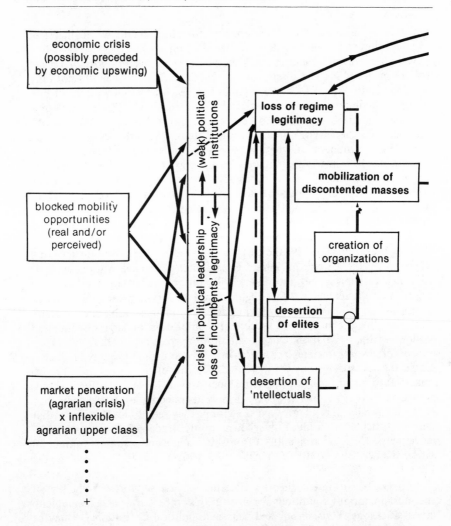

Figure 8.7. A Raw Causal Model of Revolutions

As pointed out in the text, additional feedback loops are left out in the model. — ⟶ represents weaker relationships, ⟶ symbolizes stronger relationships. O is the symbol for an interaction term. Dotted lines within the little boxes stand for catalyzing or inhibiting influences of those variables that affect the particular dependent variable. Precipitants have been omitted from the model (cf. also the discussion in chapter 5.3.2.5). Finally, the model takes into consideration most of those factors which have

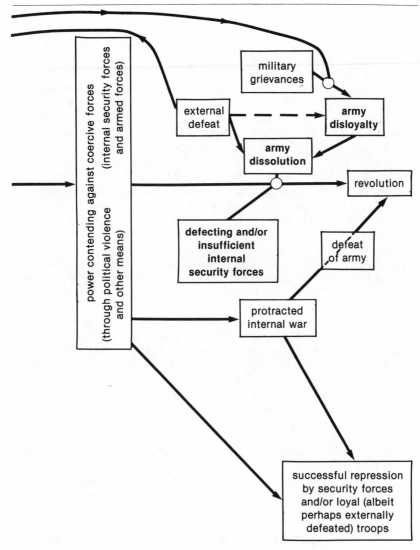

been found to explain revolutions in the past. It does not necessarily make predictions concerning future periods of observation.

In this model we aim at systematizing necessary conditions of revolutions. Consequently we have refrained from listing on the left hand side of the model "all" those conditions that have contributed to revolutionary activities on behalf of specific population segments. In general, there is much less consistent empirical evidence as to these factors than as to those outlined in the model.

the elites. Once they have withdrawn their attachment to the existing political structures and become engaged in making claims to an alternative political order and in building up organizational facilities, the threat of mobilized masses bringing about the downfall of the existing political system becomes considerably enlarged. Mobilization without elite support, i.e., spontaneous mass rebellion, is likely to lead to failure. Mobilized discontented segments of the population led by qualified personnel bringing together and building up resources have a much better chance of standing up against the prevailing system.

Whether they will indeed be successful depends on the *strength and loyalty of incumbents' coercive forces* (internal security forces and/or armed forces), the *third critical juncture* (or fourth, if one counts the successful mobilization of discontented masses as the third). If they are affected by the crisis in political leadership which may lead to a withdrawal of their loyalty, or if they are out of function either for external (e.g., defeat in war) or internal (e.g., military grievances) reasons, the chances of the rebels are increased almost to the point of victory. (All three of these general conditions might, of course, occur interactively or even by means of feedback processes.) The dashed line from external defeat to army disloyalty represents a weaker causal connection than is assumed to exist between external defeat and army dissolution. There are various examples of externally defeated armies which were in the process of dissolution but were still strong enough to battle the internal radical opposition. Whether these hypotheses (and others in the model) and the importance attributed to them will hold is, of course, a question of systematic quantitative research.

More generally, when the phase of contending for power, based on elite-led mass mobilization, has been reached, there are three "options," depending on the behavior of the coercive forces:

1. Immediate revolutionary success in the presence of disloyal and/or insufficient[318] armed forces and internal security forces (as well as external support for the rebels).

2. A phase of protracted internal warfare which may lead to success of the rebels, if parts of the coercive forces get worn out. External support for the rebels or the incumbents may again be an important condition of ultimate victory for either side.

3. Successful repression by loyal security forces and/or armed troops (and/or external support), success depending, in part, on the harshness and consistency of the measures used (cf. the discussion and the results in chapter 5.1.2.5). Thus, there is a direct path from the mobilization of discontented masses to revolution if the coercive forces have become dissolved and/or disloyal as well as a more indirect path via protracted internal war which might lead to either successful repression of the revolutionary coalition or to ultimate revolutionary overthrow, depending on the balance of resources and their use in combat.

Most of the variables referred to in the model are macrovariables thus reflecting the kind of cross-national research generally carried out. Several of these variables could, of course, be rephrased on the individual or group level (cf. also the discussion in chapter 9). Empirical evidence along these lines, however, is only beginning to come in.

Expressed somewhat differently, there are at least three "crisis strata" (Sigmund NEUMANN) that must form a coalition if revolutionary protests are to be at all successful: bourgeois, middle social strata elements must combine with peasant groups and groups of workers (although the latter have been of less importance than the peasantry[319] in actual revolutions) if the first critical juncture, that of strongly calling into question the legitimacy of the prevailing order, is to be passed. Such a coalition, in turn, depends on elite support (second critical juncture) if it is to reach the third critical juncture: contending for power against internal security forces and/or armed forces. In Figure 8.2, early in the theoretical discussion (chapter 8.4.2), these various conditions have been combined to form one complex interaction term. From an empirical point of view, one should reckon with various sequences and combinations as to how such a final constellation might build up (our outline here providing only a base model). Thus, while we were able to specify at least three critical junctures (i.e., necessary conditions) for revolution to occur, obviously there is no set of sufficient conditions that would allow diagnosing revolutions. Taking the complexity of conditions of revolutions into consideration, one almost certainly would be safe in predicting that there is no set of sufficient conditions to be detected (except for circular explanation).

Such a causal model may be used in analyses of successful and unsuccessful revolutionary attacks. What is lacking in research on revolution is evidence as to the relative importance of the variables mentioned in the model and those mentioned throughout this chapter. To what extent must mobility channels be blocked or perceived as blocked so that widespread discontent will amass? How important in statistical terms is the influence of incumbent elites as well as defecting elites in the presence of other variables? At what point are major political failures still correctable (and at what price)? Is it largely before the first critical juncture is passed because potential counterelites have not yet entered the stage actively? How efficient are co-optation measures and other strategies to deal with defecting elites? All these questions could, of course, be considered from the opposite point of view. What must be done to make rebellion against the system more powerful and probably more successful? The results of science can be treated in both ways: how to affect antecedent conditions to increase or to decrease the score on the dependent variable under study. The responses to the challenges along the first critical juncture are probably most important for the margins in behavior which remain. A wrong decision at this point may increase the "overload" (see HUNTINGTON/DOMÍNGUEZ 1975:15) of the political system and thus prevent the employment of resources otherwise perhaps available. Depending on the options (e.g., strict internal repression) chosen here, the third critical juncture may be either completely avoided or soon reached. Adaptable, not merely persisting, political systems (cf. the discussion and the results in chapter 6.3.2.2) use their remaining options (e.g., reforms for improving the output of the economic and political system) to prevent a coalition of dissidents from passing this very first critical juncture, oppressive regimes use theirs by bringing in the option available at the third juncture (i.e., the direct employment of the army) or by relying on the army as a permanent threat when deciding on reactions demanded at the horizon of the first juncture. What precisely are the conditions out of which revolutionary demands (power contending demands) are raised as opposed to previous demands for reform? How much inconsistent use or inefficiency of the internal security forces and/or the army is suffcient for rebels to win?

What are typical paths found in more than one revolution? While it seems as if the three critical junctures must be passed in any revolution, the sequences leading to them and through them seem to display considerable variety.

1. There are clear variations as to the crises strata engaged in revolutions (cf., e.g., the aristocratic-urban-rural coalitions during the English Revolution with the agrarian–small-urban–elite coalition in the Chinese Revolution; for other examples, cf. passim in this chapter).

2. Another important set of variations has been emphasized by HUNTINGTON (cf. chapter 8.4.3.1): the differences between those revolutions starting from the central city (such as in France and Russia) and leading to increased fighting against the revolutionary forces later on, and the revolutionary attacks beginning in the countryside, where fighting is intense from the beginning (Chinese Revolution, most of the revolutions after the Second World War and certainly most of the colonial "revolutions") and decreases once the capital has been taken. "Center-out has been the standard pattern in modern European revolutions. . . . Twentieth-century guerrilla doctrine, however, has called for periphery-in revolutions. Asia has the prime example of China to pull it in this direction. It also has the models of the Huks in the Philippines, the Vietminh in Vietnam, and the Malayan People's Anti-Japanese Army. . . . No doubt the overwhelmingly rural character of the Asian population has something to do with it" (TILLY 1974:289-90).

3. One may perhaps add a third type to the distinction proposed by HUNTINGTON, i.e., a mixed type important in its own right. This type would comprise revolutions in which the contention for power stretches over a number of years with different factions holding parts of the center and the periphery at various points of time. The course of the English Revolution as well as the Mexican Revolution may serve as examples here.

4. A fourth interesting difference emerges in the form of political takeover, basic distinctions here being whether takeover occurs relatively easily and decisively (once the particular preconditions have been met), as in the Russian and Cuban Revolutions, or whether the breakdown of the old regime leads to a prolonged period in which the contenders for power fight among themselves to determine who will succeed in power. The French Revolution, perhaps the English Revolution, the Mexican Revolution, and in recent

times the developments in Portugal starting from a revolutionary (or at least reform) coup serve as examples.

Recalling that "history has not normally been kind to revolutions" (HUNTINGTON 1971a:5), what may be done to make such a model more than a graphic summary of more or less plausible, yet hardly statistically evaluated, relationships? Data on the variables on the left hand side of the model have been collected in the past. It has at least been demonstrated that workable data bearing on these variables can be collected (if level of analyses problems are neglected for the moment). Data on withdrawal of support for regime are much more difficult to obtain. What is required here are individual data or equivalent sets of data allowing for inferences as to how segments of the population have felt about their government and their regime (cf. MULLER/ JUKAM 1977 in chapter 6.3.4.2). Measures of the degree of mass defection and elite defection have already been proposed by GURR (1973; cf. in chapter 6.3.1). At this point they need much more refining. GURR has also suggested a number of measures pertaining to the mobilization phase and the organizational resources upon which rebels might rely. Yet, rather than incorporating aggregate measures here, sequential measures as to the formation and growth of organizations (or, more precisely, as to the conditions of such organizational changes and their consequences) are to be derived (cf. also the discussion in chapter 9). Great difficulties may be anticipated if the loyalty of the army and its "psychological" (not merely numerical) strength are to be assessed in advance (to avoid circular reasoning). GURR's scoring procedures may be helpful as a starting point. The measurement of resources in a wider sense (e.g., population sympathizing and supporting but not actively engaged; advantages of terrain, etc.) will also be difficult (again cf. some of GURR's measures discussed and partly criticized in chapter 5.1.1.1). Finally, how can the dependent variable revolution be measured? Useful indicators to look for include major changes in leadership, in the economic and/or political system, in social mobility, in cultural standards and dominant ideological systems, in laws and law-making procedures, in emigration, in the degree of property transfer; number of people physically eliminated; changes in income distribution; changes in political participation or restrictions thereon, etc.

In many respects revolutions appear to be a subject too complex to be handled in plain quantitative analyses. Accordingly, historians and monographers will have their special objects of study for decades to come. What we have been arguing for, on the other hand, is to draw more fully on the capacities of quantitative cross-national research and thus to enrich our understanding of revolutions. If in the long run there is little success along the lines suggested here, theorizing on the conditions of revolutions will likely be as heterogeneous as documented in this entire chapter. In such a case, there will be a large number of more or less plausible theories, yet hardly any systematic knowledge.[320] This may be disappointing yet perhaps inescapable.

8.5. The Cross-national Study of Revolutions: Some Final Remarks and Some Consequences

Several analytical questions have been touched upon in the preceding discussion, sometimes implicitly and sometimes explicitly. Other questions which are also of importance in the analysis of revolutions have been omitted. A few remarks are thus in order here.

To start, probably the most intriguing problem in the cross-national study of revolutions is whether or not to include failed attempts at revolutions and revolutions that succeeded initially but were later unsuccessful (aborted revolutions).[321] Naturally, the value of such a strategy depends on the kinds of questions one asks. Furthermore, additional data problems may occur when dealing with attempts at revolution that failed. For example, one does not know whether the rebels would have carried out their revolutionary program if they had been successful. However, if one wants to avoid some of the logical pitfalls plaguing conventional cross-national analyses of revolutions, one must include unsuccessful revolutionary attempts in the study: "An explanation of protest, rebellion, or collective violence that cannot account for its absence is no explanation at all" (TILLY et al. 1975:12). If the question is what the conditions of successful revolutions are, this implies a comparison with unsuccessful revolutionary attempts since otherwise there would be no yardstick of measurement.[322] It should be noted, however, that in proposing such a strategy we are not calling for greater variability in the dependent variable or for an extension of the definition of revolutions to (other) forms of political violence.[323]

One of the basic questions on revolutions to be answered is whether some of the independent variables accounting for successful revolutions also explain the outbreak of unsuccessful revolutionary attacks. If there is some overlapping in the conditions promoting revolutionary attempts regardless of their outcomes, what are the variables making for success in one case and for immediate or later failure in other cases (following MILL's method of differences or the more up-to-date logic of canonical analysis [cf., e.g., LEVINE 1977])?[324]

> If, for example, attempts to make revolutions differed fundamentally from all other sorts of political conflicts, but successful and unsuccessful attempts differed only through the intervention of chance, then a lifelong study of successful revolutions alone would probably yield nothing but shaky hypotheses about the causes of revolution. This is an argument not for abandoning the analysis of the so-called Great Revolutions, but for trying to link their study with that of the larger set of events to which they belong. Then we can preserve the distinctness of the Great Revolutions by treating revolutionary character—the extent to which the particular series of events at hand produced class realignments, transformations of governments, further structural change, etc.—as a variable (TILLY 1975:489).[325]

Building on these arguments, other questions of interest come to mind. Why have there been no attempts at revolution in situations where some, though not all, of the major determinants have been met?[326] Why were some revolutions successful without meeting the entire list of variables mentioned in preceding chapters, while other revolutions required a comparatively larger set of conditions to be fulfilled? Or are these only superficial differences while the basic underlying constellation of variables is always more or less the same?

Second, another major shortcoming of this chapter on revolutions is that the study of revolutionary ideas and their impact on society has been neglected. These topics are of great importance, especially in determining long-term explanations of revolutions. The general emphasis in this study has been on sociostructural conditions, yet revolutionary ideas in a sense constitute the lubricating oil without which no revolutionary machine could run.[327] One should recall that social scientists interested in sociostructural analysis or in history from below do not advocate entirely neglecting the impact of revolutionary ideas and ideologies but wish to place them in the right context.[328]

Third, the impact of (charismatic) revolutionary leadership has been grossly neglected in the present discussion.[329] Once again, this may be a topic less accessible to computer-based analyses. However, a somewhat helpful paradigm has already been suggested and used, albeit in a different field, by ALMOND et al. (1973) in their analyses of the coalition options in times of crises and the resulting consequences. There is probably a close connection between leadership and the duration of revolutions. Do revolutions which become institutionalized[330] (i.e., endure longer than one generation of revolutionary leadership) differ from revolutions influenced more strongly by charismatic first-hour revolutionaries? A number of possible comparisons come to mind here, e.g., Sun Yat-sen[331] and Mao vs. Kerensky-Lenin-Stalin vs. the entirely different form of leadership in the Mexican Revolution.[332] What about the fate of revolution if the leader or one of the leaders dies?[333] Cromwell (see HILL 1970) and Mirabeau are only two of several notable examples here.

Fourth, who makes the revolution and who profits from its outcome?[334] The French Revolution may serve here to illustrate this differentiation. While there can be no doubt, after the studies of SOBOUL, RUDÉ, and others, that the sans-culottes were a strong force in the revolutionary venture, the outcome of the French Revolution was nevertheless much less to their advantage than their degree of participation might have suggested.[335] Certain portions of the bourgeoisie actually seem to have profited most from the French Revolution (SOBOUL 1956; COBBAN 1971a:62-63). Perhaps even more than the sans-culottes, the rural proletariat suffered from the Revolution (LEFEBVRE 1924; cf. also COBBAN 1971:170), not only in the French case but in other revolutions as well.

Fifth, what is the role of violence—or more pronouncedly, terror—in the revolutionary process? Is it, as MARX (and ENGELS in his "Anti-Dühring" 1960:225) maintains, really "the midwife of every old society which is pregnant with the new; [is it] the instrument with the aid of which social movement forces its way through and shatters the dead, fossilized, political forms"? Is terror a necessary ingredient of revolution, or does it only occur at times of (allegedly) increased counter-revolutionary activities (cf. below)? Does it pay[336] (and for whom)[337] to rely on violent means when carrying out revolutionary activities? One must distinguish among the various forms and goals of terror—prerevolutionary terror (aiming at weakening government resistance and/or at winning or neutralizing parts of the population), terror during the actual process of revolution, and postrevolutionary terror (often between incumbent factions). Somewhat detailed accounts of revolutionary terror are available for the French Revolution, less for other revolutions. GREER (1935) in his study of the geographical and social incidence of terror during the French Revolution[338] has set up a paradigm which might be applied to other revolutions as well (provided there were no problems of data availability). For some other treatments of terror during the French Revolution, see COBB (1961; 1963 considering the role of the revolutionary army in these matters; 1965), PALMER (1970), and earlier treatments, for example, MATHIEZ (1928).

An interesting hypothesis has been suggested by TILLY (1975:535; cf. also SOULE 1935:21) who, in his power-contending model of revolution, proposes that violence becomes more extensive *after* the outbreak of revolution and not before as stated in the typical tension-release models. TILLY proposes several explanations for his proposition:

> First, the appearance of multiple sovereignty puts into question the achieved position of every single contender, whether a member of the polity or not, and therefore tends to initiate a general round of mutual testing among contenders. . . . Second, the struggle of one polity against its rival amounts to war: a battle fought with unlimited means. . . . Third, the revolutionary coalition is likely to fragment once the initial seizure of control over the central government apparatus occurs. . . . Fourth, the victorious polity still faces the problem of reimposing routine governmental control over the subject population, even after multiple sovereignty has ended (TILLY 1975:535–36).

In each of the four cases the result is said to be a likely increase in violence. There should be evidence in support of TILLY's hypothesis,[339] partly because it captures reality, partly because in his model the point of multiple sovereignty comes *early* in the revolutionary process, thus making the proposition true by definition to a certain extent.

Sixth, one should consider in detail the counter-measures of incumbent elites. It is by no means sufficient to speak of a mere breakdown of the old order. Propositions as to the interrelationships between actions of both sides must be developed and systematically tested. Furthermore, there seems to be no cross-national work focusing on the counter-revolutionary activities of those portions of the population unwilling to live under a new revolutionary regime. In his analysis of the Vendée counter-revolution TILLY (1964; cf.

also 1963) has once again shown how such a cross-national study might be undertaken. The basic framework is similar to that found in his later works, with urbanization and new market constellations as major underlying causes of various forms of protest activities and of changes in protest activities. In this context TILLY shows that support for the French Revolution was greatest in the most urbanized sectors of the west (Val-Saumurois), whereas in less urbanized areas where the bourgeoisie had come to power only recently or where "recent social change had been both turbulent and uneven" (in the Mauges, TILLY 1964:37), rather strong opposition was met. Counter-revolutionaries were found mainly among the nobility, the clergy, peasants, and rural artisans. Disagreement over religious matters and conscription policies were other vital issues in the counter-revolutionary protests in the Vendée (for a discussion of the works of TILLY, BOIS 1960, and others, see, e.g., MITCHELL 1968a; cf. also MITCHELL's later study 1974).[340] It remains to be seen in further cross-national studies whether a summary like HAGOPIAN's does indeed hold for other counter-revolutions as well: "Thus, for the English and French revolutions, rural regional characteristics and economic backwardness are highly correlated with counter-revolution" (HAGOPIAN 1974:343).

Counter-revolutionary attempts must often be viewed in a broader historical and international perspective. In his study of the French counter-revolution GODECHOT comes to this general conclusion: "Attention [of the counter-revolutionary theorists] was focused, above all, on the political and religious aspects; they did not understand that by satisfying the basic demands of the peasants they could have won them over with them" (GODECHOT 1971:384-85). Again the failure to form a political coalition proved to be a deadly mistake in (counter-)revolutionary activities. From a long-term perspective, however, a somewhat different evaluation is more appropriate: "Thus the counter-revolutionary doctrines themselves had a long-term[341] rather than a short-term influence" (ibid., p. 385), i.e., after 1814 and not between 1789 and 1804. External powers may fear the diffusion of revolutionary activities in neighboring countries, in rival countries, or in countries considered to be under their own sphere of political and military influence. Thus:

Seventh, the international aspects of revolution and revolutionary attacks deserve attention. With respect to the French Revolution, it has been said: "As the war itself was a product of a revolutionary situation in France, the latter was to be influenced in turn by its own product. The war was revolutionized as a result of what is called the 'Second Revolution' in France, an event which was in itself a product of the war. A vicious cycle of war and revolution could not have a more telling illustration than in the case of the French Revolution" (KIM 1970:36). "The French Revolution and the Napoleonic wars in turn laid the basis for the independence movements in Latin America between 1810 and 1830 [see LYNCH 1973]. The successful Paris Revolution of July 1830 against the restored Bourbon monarchy touched off nationalist movements in Poland (against Russian domination), in Belgium (against Dutch domination), and appears to have been the accelerator of largely liberal revolutionary movements in Italy, Switzerland, Germany, Spain, and Portugal. In 1848 Paris was again the powder keg for revolutionary explosions throughout Europe, from Copenhagen through Berlin to Vienna, Budapest, Lombardy, and Palermo" (GREENE 1974:117). Concerning the Bolshevik Revolution: "After the Bolshevik Revolution in November of 1917 there were a number of Soviet-style abortive revolutionary drives in Berlin in 1919, Munich in 1923 [in style, but not in political orientation], and Italy in 1919-20. With the exception of Béla Kun's Hungarian Soviet Republic in the spring and summer of 1919, all such attempts seem to have been superficial and futile" (HAGOPIAN 1974:111). More recent examples are found in the increased attempts at revolutionary overthrow that could be observed after the success of the Cuban Revolution and the fall (or "liberation") of South Vietnam. Another aspect of linking internal and international factors is brought up by GOLDFRANK (1979) in his attempt at a "structural explanation of the Mexican Revolution." He stresses the importance of a "permissive world context." Underlining our conclusions from the preceding chapter, GOLDFRANK claims to have "identified four conditions as necessary and sufficient for revolution in general and the Mexican Revolution in particular: a favorable world context, an administrative and coercive crisis of the state, widespread rural rebellion, and dissident elite movement(s)" (GOLDFRANK 1979:160).

Eighth, and perhaps the most significant question, but also a question rather difficult to answer at present: Is HUNTINGTON right in his sweeping argument that "the truly helpless society is not one threatened by revolution but one incapable of it" (HUNTINGTON 1968:262;[342] for a similar summary see MOORE 1966:457-58), or are there additional aspects to reckon with before this hypothesis can be considered empirically grounded?

Finally, given that we do not have sufficient empirical knowledge as to the conditions of revolutions, what about the *point in time* of their occurence? Do we know more about this question, as DAVIES (1971:foreword) maintains? This statement by a scholar, one of the few to have carried out empirical analyses of revolutions, contrasts with the confessions of many revolutionaries who admit to having been surprised by the sequence of events (cf. the references in KUMAR 1971:68-69), even if they themselves were there at the right time. (If the present state of knowledge were *strictly* evaluated, one would have to admit that we do not know much about revolutions, neither their causes nor the point in time of their occurrence; cf. also TILLY 1975:525). The rapid political changes in Iran during 1978 and 1979 until the fall of the Shah at the beginning of 1979 (for many "experts" unexpected), and, even more so, the signs under which this development took place, underscore this point dramatically.

These questions of study have taken us far beyond the aim of this chapter. There is no need to sum up again what has been said here. It is sufficient to point out that, at present, the cross-national study of revolutionary phenomena is not yet fully established. Hopefully, the possibilities of such an undertaking have been illustrated in this chapter, largely a criticism of existing studies. Yet, at various points, we have dealt with studies which seemed particularly notable either because they contained promising hypotheses not found in other works (e.g., HUNTINGTON 1968) or because they manifested to a remarkable degree the advantages of a broad, comparative, albeit qualitative, analysis (MOORE 1966; SKOCPOL 1979). A third noteworthy group of studies includes the works of TILLY and associates which indicate the direction in which future cross-national studies should proceed. Also of note are the works of scholars like RUDÉ, SOBOUL, and LEFEBVRE in the field of social history, and the many other researchers who have done remarkable studies on which a discipline such as the cross-national analysis of revolutions might build.

While the social historical analyses of LEFEBVRE, RUDÉ and others provide us with a great richness in detail, we can derive a broad theoretical framework from the works of MOORE and SKOCPOL, supplemented by a set of more specific conditions from HUNTINGTON (or more general conditions from ROKKAN). Finally, as TILLY and his coworkers have partially demonstrated, even revolutionary activities may be handled fruitfully on a quantitative cross-national basis, provided the necessary time series data collections have been established. Thus, while all these studies differ in their objects of explanation, not to mention the means of providing us with explanations, there is nevertheless some relationship among them, be it only that the scholar approaching revolutions cross-nationally here finds some scholars to whom he might look or whose shoulders he might stand upon.

Chapter 9

Political Violence, Crises, and Revolutions: Theories and Research—Some Concluding Remarks

"Everything that exists exists in quantity," Lord KELVIN is said to have remarked (cf. MOORE 1966:519). There is no need to enter the philosophical debate as to whether this statement is true or meaningful. It simply represents a premise to which most of the scholars whose works we have considered would probably subscribe. Yet a scientific creed is one thing, substantial results another. After all that has been said at various points in preceding chapters, it comes as no surprise that the aspirations of the researcher interested in quantitative cross-national research in the fields of political violence, crises, and revolutions remain unfulfilled. These difficulties notwithstanding, the goal of developing "universally" valid theoretical explanations which are more general and at the same time more precise than those typically found in qualitative analyses of phenomena of political violence, crises, and revolutions will continue to be sought. No doubt there may be limits to a cross-national quantitative approach to these fields, but such an approach also has distinct advantages. The aim is not to substitute a badly reasoned quantitative approach for a well-reasoned qualitative one but rather to combine good reasoning with as much precision as possible, precision in the nomothetic rather than in the idiographic sense. By now, the drawbacks as well as the promises of a cross-national approach to the fields of political violence, crises, and revolutions should be evident. The drawbacks, i.e., insufficent data material for far-reaching theoretical statements, bad theoretical reasoning for the indicators chosen, or simply questionable statistical manipulations, have been indicated throughout this study. The virtues might be found in many a substantial result that has been commented on in prior chapters.

We began this study with a discussion of some basic conceptual and theoretical notions. Considering the conceptual confusion that can be found in portions of the literature, it was our aim in chapter 2 to suggest some ways of ordering basic ideas recurring in conflict research. While it appeared that there are numerous definitions of political violence, there certainly was none sufficient to cover all the aspects of political violence to be considered in the course of our study. Nevertheless, we maintain that the definition of NIEBURG with its stress on bargaining aspects is a useful starting point. However, this is not the case as far as more violent and more escalated forms of political protests, i.e., revolutionary actions, are concerned. Yet, even revolutionary actions do not spring immediately from the social ground; they gradually build up through a number of less violent activities, as documented in almost all of the revolutions covered later in the study.

In chapter 3 we dealt with the theoretical and empirical status of some basic sociopsychological theories. We were especially concerned with refuting simple frustration-aggression hypotheses (as found, for example, in the macrostudies by FEIERABEND/FEIERABEND, see chapter 5.1.1.2). Furthermore, the social learning theory of aggression, as formulated by BANDURA and taken up in recent research, must be considered a basic extension (if not rival) of earlier sociopsychological explanations of aggressive behavior.

Chapter 4 brought the preliminary section to an end. Here basic theories of social comparison processes were discussed. Later on important extensions of relative deprivation theory were brought up. In general, it was our aim in these first chapters to equip the reader and ourselves with a conceptual and theoretical yardstick, before we delved into the rather complicated theoretical and empirical studies discussed throughout the following sections.

Chapter 5 contained the first comprehensive block of theories in this study. The works of GURR and HIBBS in particular were treated as paradigms for cross-national macropolitical research on political violence. While the merits of GURR's extensive studies (i.e., his efforts at integrating a vast number of theoretical notions, his sometimes ingenious operationalizations, and his effort to be as universal in testing as the theoretical questions and the data allowed for) were acknowledged at various points, there were also a number of shortcomings found in his studies. The inferential gap resulting from the discrepancies between his measures and the basic theoretical relative deprivation variable has often been commented on in the literature. But there were other shortcomings as well, for example, the complex construction of some of the indexes used which often does not allow for separation of effects of specific theoretically important variables or the inferential limits set by cross-sectional data. However, some of these earlier shortcomings were corrected for in GURR's more recent works (partly in collaboration with DUVALL) on political violence. The other paradigm for cross-national research on political violence can be found in HIBBS's study which is much less deductively oriented than GURR's works in general but still leads to highly interesting theoretical results. At the present stage of knowledge, his strategy of incremental model specification has proven very fruitful. Like the works of GURR and HIBBS, the studies of the FEIERABENDs are pioneering works as well, yet they are open to all sorts of theoretical and methodological criticism. Should there be a warning against uncritical reception of research results on political violence, it should be raised against most of the FEIERABEND studies. Their basic frustration-aggression nexus is much too simple. Their procedures of index construction are also vulnerable to a number of theoretical and methodological attacks.

In dealing with the cross-national approaches of three pioneers in the study of political violence, a vast array of hypotheses was revealed, some of them deserving a second look. This was done in chapter 5.1.2 where several theoretically important determinants of political violence were evaluated, drawing on numerous other cross-national studies as well. Data aggregated at the level of nations and/or global data were used in these studies. In some instances, a consensus as to basic relationships was found, but there were also a number of studies providing different results as to the impact of socio-economic development, socioeconomic change, political development, structural imbalances, coercion, external conflicts, and socioeconomic inequality on the very same dependent variable, political violence.

Some critics of these broad cross-national studies of political violence may have felt more comfortable with the section that followed (5.2), where we dealt with the usefulness of case studies on political violence, the fascinating studies of HOBSBAWM on social banditry serving as a master case.

Chapter 5.3 took us back to some of the theories already encountered in the cross-national analyses but now applied to within-nation phenomena, specifically to a category of events of political violence extensively studied, the riots of American blacks during the 1960s. In addition to theories already dealt with, numerous other theoretical notions were introduced here. Most of these were to explain the participation of blacks in these riots. Thus, they focused on the individual and/or group level of explanation. It turned out that, in general, there was considerable active support of the riots among somewhat better-off sections of the black population, loosely speaking, among those relatively deprived as compared to whites with similar "inputs" of education or occupational training. However, engagement in riot activities was found among numerous other sections of the black population as well, especially among young male adults with a low level of political trust, and, at times, high feelings of efficacy. On the ecological level it turned out that cities with the greatest number of blacks were the ones most likely to experience riots, and more intense riots as well. Apparently a higher aggregation of dissatisfied population segments creates facilitative conditions for discontent. At the same time it was found that police-black relations are an important determinant for the growth of black discontent and, in a great number of cases, even for the outbreak of hostilities. The black riots were dealt with fairly extensively in this study, since we thought it useful to reflect on the societal background against which cross-national theories on political violence must be evaluated. In part, this theoretical work got its impetus (and its financial support) from the political shock that occurred after rioting became extensive in the middle 1960s. Thus it was perhaps no surprise that theories which worked well for explaining American black rioting behavior were encountered again in cross-national research on political violence.

While a vast body of empirical research could be drawn on in the early chapters, a rather different situation emerged in the chapter on the cross-national study of crises (chapter 6), crises meaning here political crises that might threaten the survival of the political order. Actually, this second major block in our study derives its origin from our dissatisfaction with research in the field of political violence equated with crises or political instability, without elaborating what crises are and how to study them. In short, political violence may be one of the major determinants of political crises (and one of its consequences as well), but there are numerous other variables to be taken into consideration before a cross-nationally oriented crises science is to work successfully. Several suggestions were made in our review of the literature. Decision-making approaches apparently proved superior to functional or systems approaches to the study of crises. We then looked at studies dealing conceptually with various forms of crises, crises of legitimacy being the most dangerous for any political system. Building on explanation sketches and some empirical results scattered throughout the literature, several suggestions for the development of a cross-national crises science were made. Some of these suggestions could even be incorporated into a causal model, which might be useful in further cross-national empirical research. The ultimate dependent variable, however, was no longer crises, but persistence and adaptability of political systems. Legitimacy, in turn, was considered the basic mediating variable of all the other theoretical relationships considered in the model. Crises were incorporated into the model in a twofold way: low political, social, and economic performance may lead to a crisis (severe loss of legitimacy), the result of which may be examined in the persistence of polities. (There were, of course, several other variables to be discussed in this context.) Many of the variables and theoretical notions elaborated on in the crises chapter were to occur again in the analysis of revolutions, a subject immediately related to crises research, even though the connection between crises and revolutions is anything but deterministic.

To avoid some of the theoretical pitfalls of studies inquiring into the causes of revolutions, military coups d'état were dealt with first (chapter 7). It cannot be emphasized strongly enough that military coups are not revolutions (even if, considering the category of revolutionary coups, there may be some overlap in the long-term consequences). Moreover, coups are not necessarily a form of political violence, albeit violence is the ultimate determinant in almost any military coup. Coups are invariably carried out by elite members. They are short in duration, their aims usually differing from those of revolutions. The cross-national research on military coups has made considerable progress during recent years. Thus, there was once again a sizeable body of empirical findings derived from a number of cross-national studies. Most of these results were summarized in the causal model in Figure 7.1.

Having dealt with military coups in a separate chapter, the chapter on revolutions (chapter 8) could be more homogeneous (while still heterogeneous in itself) than many of the cross-national aggregate data analyses of "revolutions." We conceived of revolution as the successful overthrow of the prevailing elite(s) by a new elite(s) who after having taken over power (which usually involves the use of considerable violence and the mobilization of masses) fundamentally change the social structure and therewith also the structure of authority. Violence may be an important feature in revolutions (and often this is the case), but it is not a necessary condition for revolution to occur. Bearing this in mind, some efforts were made in structuring the vast literature on revolutions. Several typologies of revolutions and of forms of protest behavior were evaluated, but even the most elaborate and useful of these fell short in one or more respects. In the theoretical portions of this chapter it was seen that the literature provides many theoretical suggestions as to the causes of revolutions yet hardly a body of systematically derived theory. Nevertheless, on the basis of theoretical analyses some vague "uniformities" were found.

The more systematic evaluation focused on three groups of studies. The first group, which included works by DAVIES, TANTER/MIDLARSKY, and CALVERT, was flawed because of its lack of substantial (e.g., its monocausal) theorizing and because of its often rather incompetent use of statistics. From the second group of analyses several important studies could be drawn on. The broad sociohistorical analyses by MOORE, who emphasizes the economic and political relationships between lords and peasants, between the bourgeoisie and the state bureaucracies and the resulting coalitions, were extended by HUNTINGTON who stresses the conditions of center-periphery as well as urban-rural connections in his theoretical work on revolutions. Both authors as well as SKOCPOL underline the importance of winning the peasantry if revolutionary attacks are to be successful, a question taken up in a separate chapter on peasant revolutions. Peasant rebellions only turn into successful revolutions if the peasants are joined by an urban coalition or by supportive army forces. Above all, the army is a major determinant in any revolutionary attempt. The army either must be exterminated by external defeat or come to sympathize with the rebels for internal reasons if their attempt at power is to be successful. Numerous other variables, such as elite defection, the desertion of intellectuals, and the creation of revolutionary organizations furthering the mobilization of discontented masses, were suggested throughout the chapter which eventually culminated in a rudimentary causal model of revolutions. The third group of studies considered at some length included basic results of RUDÉ's sociohistorical analyses on revolutionary crowds during the eighteenth and nineteenth centuries and of TILLY's quantitative studies of the impact of urbanization and new market constellations on peasants, artisans, and workers. It was stressed that different causal paths may occur in the case of revolutions. However, there do seem to be several necessary paths through which any successful revolution must pass.

Finally, several other aspects of revolution were briefly taken up. In general, the conclusion was similar to that in the crises chapter. There is not yet a sufficiently elaborated cross-national science of revolutions. There are a number of highly promising ventures, but they must be brought together in one way or another and systematically confronted with data. It is hoped that our work is a first step in that direction.

There is no need to repeat here in greater detail what has been said in chapters 2 through 8. Thus, for summaries of findings, criticisms, and caveats the reader is referred to the conclusion of each major chapter. At this point, we will touch upon some neglected aspects in the study of political violence, crises, and revolutions. Furthermore, there are some relationships to other social phenomena that come into focus once the narrow frame of reference of the present body of research is enlarged.

Part of the essence of this study can be found in the causal model on revolutions (Figure 8.7) discussed in chapter 8.4.7, in the model on crises and persistence of political systems (Figure 6.2) in chapter 6.3.4.1, and in the model on military coups d'état in chapter 7.3 (Figure 7.1). As we have pointed out, there are a number of important links between crises, military coups d'état, and revolutions. The more important theoretical relationships—particularly those elaborated in the model on crises and persistence—have been incorporated into the causal model on revolutions. Additional variables of importance have been mentioned in the causal model on military coups d'état and elsewhere in the text. Certainly, one could extend the model on revolutions by adding some of these variables, which, in a broader sense (not as in chapter 7.2.1), might be conceived of as causing military grievances. If revolutions were defined solely in terms of social and political changes induced after the fact, both variants of "revolutions," i.e., revolutionary coups and the so-called mass revolutions, would have to be combined in one model. The definition of military coup as behavior of an elite group and of revolution as an outcome of the joint behavior of elites and masses (which reflects the use made of these concepts in political science), however, precludes such an undertaking. In any case, a causal model of revolutionary coups could rely on fewer explanatory variables than a model of mass revolutions.

One might also want to add some of the more important determinants of political violence to the model of revolutions. It should be kept in mind, however, that political violence is neither *the* determinant nor *the* definitional criterion of revolutions. Consequently, it would be difficult to locate political violence and its predetermined causes in Figure 8.7. Political violence is one of several means of achieving revolutionary or other political goals. It could be conceived of as a consequence of market penetration, of blocked mobility opportunities, of an economic crisis, etc., or as causing, in turn, the weakening of political institutions and a crisis in political leadership, thus in a way acting as intermediate variable. Political violence could be a consequence as well as a cause of loss of regime legitimacy. Such violence could occur prior to or subsequent to the mobilization of discontented masses. It could take place during the phase of power contending as well as after the takeover of political power.

A recently established discipline like the cross-national study of political violence, crises, and revolutions entails a considerable number of shortcomings. Some of these have been indicated in earlier chapters, others will be taken up in these final remarks. Thus, most of the results mentioned are based on *cross-sectional data* analyses, placing harsh restrictions on causal inferences, even if one might argue—as HIBBS (1973:201) does— that such analyses might be quite appropriate when dealing with variables like type of political system, degree of institutionalization, cultural differentiation, and democratic political conditions. However, cross-sectional data by their very nature do not capture, for instance, the interrelationships among various forms of political violence over time.[1] On the basis of cross-sectional data analyses, HIBBS has presented various noteworthy hypotheses as to the transition or escalation from one form of political violence to another, in this case, from the relatively weaker form of collective protest via repressive reactions (negative sanctions) of state authorities to internal war. Yet it remains to be seen *how* one form of political violence actually influences subsequent ones,[2] be they stronger or weaker forms.[3]

TILLY and coworkers have developed a viable alternative here. His detailed data on conflict in European countries seem to allow for statements as to the circumstances making for either nonviolent or violent forms of protest behavior. GAMSON (1975) has followed him in his investigation of the determinants of group outcomes for fifty-three "randomly" selected American protest groups between 1800 and 1945.[4] The unit of analysis thus changes *from the national level to the group level*[5] which, in general, should lead to theoretically and empirically more fruitful statements in this area of research than are found in the present cross-national literature on political violence. Empirically grounded statements referring to groups and their activities would approach the principle of direct measurement in the study of protest. They might extend to the history of groups, to their rise and decline, to processes of group mobilization and other aspects (see below), as well as to strategic aspects in the use of violent means. This is a perspective that so far has been largely missing from cross-national aggregate analyses.

Incidentally, the title of GAMSON's book is *The Strategy of Social Protest*, one of his major findings being that a group which is not a member of the pluralist group taking part in the exchange of political power (according to SCHATTSCHNEIDER [1960:35], the "heavenly chorus" that "sings with a strong upper-class accent") may gain access to the political process[6] and attain the status of a respected association by following a strategy of calculated employment of political violence[7] while, at the same time, building up centralized bureaucratic organizational resources. Acceptance was found to be more likely, if the group in question did not insist on displacing other groups, was pursuing a single goal, was comparatively large, and provided incentives for member participation.

"One effect of GAMSON's analysis is to blur the boundary between movement politics and normal politics; another is to define more clearly the boundary between the politics of the represented and the unrepresented" (ZELDITCH 1978:1514). Of course, it remains to be seen whether GAMSON's results also hold for other countries or other political systems. Moreover, in a generally favorable review ZELDITCH (1978) points out four shortcomings in this work: (1) The sample may not be representative, especially since almost a third of the cases involve unions. "I have some doubts, therefore, about just how many cases GAMSON really has and about just how much of his story is merely the union history of America" (ibid., p. 1517). In short, there may be interlocking groups and "constituencies." (2) "The effectiveness of a particular movement organization usually cannot be uniquely attributed to its own incentives, organization, issues, or tactics. . . . How seriously would we take GAMSON's conclusions about violence if one of the effects of a movement organization's violence were to increase the acceptability and effectiveness of its less violent competitors?" (ibid.) To broaden the argument, GAMSON's data do not provide unambiguous answers as to whether violent and nonviolent protests are to be considered as alternative or as reinforcing forms of protest behavior. (3) "There is a theoretically important gap in the results. There is no distinction between mobilization of the unpeople of a polity and mobilization of those who *are* members for other purposes" (ibid., p. 1518; emphasis added). (4) Finally, one may object to the mostly dichotomous tabular analysis. "GAMSON appears to have underemphasized the complex interaction between and among the variables he has chosen for analysis" (WALSH 1978:174). For instance, due to the lack of a multivariate analysis, "it is not at all clear whether violence alone has positive effects" (GURR 1980a:262) or works only in conjunction with the factors determined by GAMSON.

Reanalyzing GAMSON's data and partially recoding the dependent variables, GOLDSTONE (1980) questions the positive impact of organization on the success of protest groups. According to GOLDSTONE, GAMSON considered successor groups inadequately and accordingly found a lower success rate than actually holds true. The American political system is said to be characterized not so much by limited pluralism, as GAMSON would have it, but by its great flexibility and permeability. In his reply, GAMSON (1980) criticizes GOLDSTONE (1980) for bringing together things which ought to be distinguished, e.g., with respect to the dependent variables. Also the period for attributing success to a challenging group was unduly extended in GOLDSTONE's analysis (far beyond the fifteen-year limit in GAMSON's study; cf. also the useful discussion of possible measures of outcomes to protest behavior in SNYDER/KELLY 1979; and especially the variety of research perspectives suggested by GURR 1980a:250ff.).

Another reanalysis of GAMSON's data using techniques of multivariate analysis has led to the following conclusions: "We found that the forces that lead to protest group success are, in order of relative importance, a desire on the part of the protest group not to replace an established member of the polity, the number of alliances a group has with other groups, the absence of factional disputes, quite specific and limited goals, and a willingness to use sanctions against other groups" (STEEDLY/FOLEY 1979:12, 14). In their study of 281 incidents of collective violence in Canada from 1963 to 1975, FRANK/KELLY (1979) also found some results that support GAMSON's conclusions. Their model specifies the factors mediating between type of group (organization), political status, goals of action, specific form of action, and the intensity of repression. In sum, there is some (ambiguous) evidence that the better organized a group, the higher its political status. The more specific the goal of action and the more specific the form of action pursued, the less intense is the repressive reaction. In some instances, however, results varied between Ontario (n=145) and Quebec (n=136), especially with respect to the relationships between political status and repression (acceptable groups showed a relatively high rate of arrests in Ontario), goals and repression (groups with specific goals showed a relatively high rate of arrests in Ontario), and between specific form of action (strike, demonstration, or random) and repression. Other studies (MIROWSKY/ROSS 1979; WEISBURD 1979) drawing on GAMSON's data set have also led to conclusions which are, by and large, reconcilable with GAMSON's interpretations (cf. also ZIMMERMANN 1982 for a sketch of a study meant to replicate and extend GAMSON's work in the European context).

Neither the problems[8] of *organization building*,[9] fund raising, and organization maintenance nor the question of continuity in leadership and membership structure nor the related question of goal displacement have received the necessary attention of most of the scholars engaged in cross-national research on violent protest behavior (see ZALD/ASH 1966 and ZURCHER/CURTIS 1973 for some useful hypotheses in these respects). As several authors (e.g., WILSON/ORUM 1976; McCARTHY/ZALD 1977; see also ZALD/McCARTHY 1979) emphasize, some of the problems of organizational coordination of resources, division of labor, winning a large member base, etc. might be solved by mobilizing and combining already existing core groups, quasi-groups, or transitory teams (see OBERSCHALL 1973; 1978b). The importance of the organizational focus has been well captured in the argument by USEEM: "Since central conditions in American life cannot be resolved short of massive transformation of major institutions, the primary sources of organizational collapse of protest efforts in the United States can usually be traced to organization and mobilization problems rather than changes in originating conditions. This hypothesis runs counter to the models of GURR, SMELSER, and others; as the primary source of protest demise, these schemes would focus on reversals in the trends originally responsible for the protest, such as decreased subjective deprivation and lessened strain" (USEEM 1975:51). All this would, of course, only be relevant in the context of enduring political violence and not—almost by definition—in the presence of spontaneous violent protest.

Another research design worth following involves comparisons within *specific regions*,[10] frequently with reference to smaller countries—a strategy successfully used by ROKKAN in his many comparative analyses. In selecting France, Italy, and Germany for a closer study TILLY has in a way pursued the same strategy.

Comparative aggregate data analyses could provide the structural framework within which comparative analyses of political groups could achieve more fruitful theoretical and empirical results. These analyses could refer to the effects of various degrees of cross-cutting cleavages and of the openness of the social structure for certain groups (e.g., what are the institutionalized or noninstitutionalized alternatives open to potential protest groups to voice their protests?).[11] They might bear on subjective reactions (definitions and perceptions of legitimacy, definitions of the situation) to objective circumstances (thus introducing some *cross-level theorizing* and measures), and on the behavior of these groups as well.

At present one could group the theories on the conditions of violent political protest behavior roughly into three categories:

1. macrotheories, e.g., HUNTINGTON's gap hypotheses;
2. macrotheories standing proxy for group-level or microtheories,
   e.g., GURR's relative deprivation theory;
3. microtheories.

What is lacking[12] is true cross-level theorizing and cross-national empirical theory-building on the *individual level* (as to the latter, cf. MULLER 1977, 1980 for an evaluation of present knowledge). Apart from MULLER's survey analyses (see chapter 5.3.2.3), the sophisticated study by MARSH (1977), using a representative sample of the British population and a student sample, could serve as a paradigm for the third category of theories. He aims at a psychological theory of protest behavior. Actually, the dependent variable is protest potential (to measure "people's readiness to engage in examples of unorthodox political behavior," ranging from signing petitions to occupying buildings and blocking traffic). As it turns out, MARSH's psychological explanations prove to be better predictors of the dependent variable than social or structural explanations. His explanation entails the "'three levered trigger' of political aggression: the coalescence of political efficacy, capacity for [ideological] conceptualization and distrust. This combination of cognitive skill and affective feeling states forms the core of the basic disposition of *disrespectful or aggressive political competence* that we hold to be the most important psychological component of protest potential" (MARSH 1977:224). Among the population segments most prone to protest he includes young educated middle-class people with leftist political sympathies, younger male trade unionists, older middle-class Labour supporters, and young working-class Tories, the latter two groups being the "most susceptible to the mobilizing effects of relative deprivation" (ibid., p. 145). Contrary to the findings of CITRIN/ELKINS (1975) which stem from their not entirely representative study of 1968 and show British students, in general, to be not much more critical of government performance than the population at large, MARSH found among his student sample (in 1974) "an integrated syndrome of aggressive leftwing post-materialist ideological dissatisfaction [that] is clearly responsible for the ultra-high levels of student protest" (MARSH 1977:212). His explanation of the protest potential is most strongly corroborated in the case of these students. The final conclusion that "there appears to be a movement of British political life away from a quiet and respectful participatory democracy towards a noisy and disrespectful participatory democracy" (ibid., p. 234) is perhaps a realistic forecast of developments to expect in continental democracies.[13]

The most far-reaching study in this vein is the cross-national analysis of "mass participation in five Western democracies" (United States, United Kingdom, Netherlands, Austria, and West Germany) by BARNES/KAASE et al. (1979). The measures of their dependent variable refer to behavioral intentions and reported past behavior and ask for participation (or willingness to participate) in a whole battery of conventional and unconventional forms of political participation. Among their most important findings are the following (underlining some of the results reported in this chapter and elsewhere in this study): Younger respondents are more liberal in their political attitudes and more protest-prone. Increasing level of education turns out to be one of the most powerful predictors of unconventional political involvement. Yet, they still report a lot of political agreement between parents and their offspring. There is a relationship between unconventional and conventional political participation, i.e., those who engage in the former also make use of conventional means of political participation (but not vice versa). There is also a group of protesters (the activists) which favors the use of nonconventional forms of political participation. Although some variation from country to country is found, these patterns are generally confirmed for the five countries studied. Post-materialist values (cf. also note 13) are becoming *relatively* more important, in comparison to material values. "One element of the 'New Politics' is a strong emphasis on broadening opportunities for political participation beyond the established sphere of electoral politics, which integrates to a large extent conventional and unconventional politics" (BARNES/KAASE et al. 1979:531). Finally, relative deprivation fails to be a strong predictor of the dependent variable. In their political recommendations the authors partly go beyond their data base and call for broader patterns of political institutionalization and accommodation rather than for limiting political participation which might undermine the legitimacy of democratic polities.

The most rigorous analysis of survey data dealing with protest potentials has been presented by MULLER (1979) who in his book *Aggressive Political Participation* sums up his prior results (cf. chapters 5.3.2.3 and 6.3.4.2) and joins them to some new findings and interpretations. In his expectancy-value-norms model, aggressive political participation is a function of utilitarian justification for aggression; normative justification for aggression; normative justification for aggression among persons from a facilitative social context, in this case the university; facilitative social norms, in this instance exposure to the university milieu; and availability. MULLER develops and tests numerous variants of his basic expectancy-value-norms model, most of which operate with complex multiplicative terms. More than half of the variance is explained in his model, an astonishing figure for any survey researcher. (Since a more detailed summary of MULLER's complex findings would take up undue space here, the reader is referred to MULLER 1979). Other variables, e.g., specific political performance dissatisfaction, internal-external control of reinforcement, personal and political resources, or other measures of individual self-esteem and competence do not change the basic explanatory model when included in the predictive equations. Testing various models, MULLER also shows that frustration has only a facilitative indirect role in the expectancy-value-norms theory. In both instances (BARNES/ KAASE et al., and MULLER) the predictive validity of their findings and theoretical explanations remains to be demonstrated (cf. the discussion in MULLER 1979:246ff.).

Moving from the individual level to the group level in the study of political protest behavior, attention should also be focused on processes of *coalition formation* by the dissidents[14] as well as the incumbent elites. The studies in ALMOND et al. (1973; cf. also the brief remarks in chapter 6.3.3) are of major importance here. FLANAGAN (1973:67–98), one of the editors of *Crisis, Choice, and Change* (ALMOND et al. 1973), has much to criticize as far as the applicability of current models of coalition formation to real politics is concerned. In their own approach which they conceive of as an effort at combining system-functional theory, social mobilization theory, rational-choice–coalition theory, and leadership theory, ALMOND et al. soften some of the rigid assumptions in older coalition theories (cf. the overviews in BROWNE 1973 and BRAMS 1973 and the works in the *American Behavioral Scientist* 18, no. 4 [April 1975] and in GROENNINGS et al. 1970; furthermore cf. RIKER/ORDESHOOK 1973:176–201; KOMORITA 1974; KOMORITA/MOORE 1976) while adding some new inductively obtained criteria to their analyses. One of their interesting hypotheses stemming from their case studies in coalition making reads: "The stability of a crisis outcome may be directly related to the size of the emergent coalition in the short run, but inversely related to it in the long run" (ALMOND et al. 1973:637). And yet, after having carried out their analyses, they must admit: "Human choice, bargaining, risk-taking, skill, and *chance* must be thrown in to explain the actual outcome. The weakness in our capacity for prediction comes out most dramatically in those cases in which the winning option did not even appear in our set of options that had 'reasonably' good chances of winning" (ALMOND/MUNDT 1973:648–49). What is needed, then, is the development of multicausal models of coalition behavior and coalition payoff, in the field of political protest behavior as well as in other areas, to find out whether models confirmed in laboratory settings (such as that of LAWLER/YOUNGS 1975 which stresses perceived utility, anticipated conflicts, and attitudinal agreement among coalition partners, payoff, and probability of success as basic determinants of coalition choice) are of importance in a variety of contexts.

Bargaining processes[15] (cf. the summary discussion in RUBIN/BROWN 1975; cf. also WILSON 1961; LIPSKY 1968; APFELBAUM 1974; YOUNG 1975; DRUCKMAN 1977; MORLEY/STEPHENSON 1977; FRIEND et al. 1977) among potential coalition groups and between these and state institutions, as well as the *policies of recruitment* (see ZYGMUNT 1972) and *organizational differentiation* followed by these groups, also deserve closer attention of scholars interested in developing theories on political violence or other forms of protest behavior.

Finally, the study of the *elite* personnel and its behavior must be incorporated into the analysis.

> The leader as a figure omnipresent in any political process, as the maker of decisions, originator and recipient of messages, performer of functions, wielder of power, and creator or operator of institutions can bring these disparate elements into a single, visible focus. The study of leadership, moreover, can readily be supplemented with an examination of the social and political organization that he founds and transforms, with an analysis of the psychological appeals and political sanctions that give leader and organization a hold on their mass following. In short these may be the elements for a new theoretical view,[16] both comprehensive and dynamic, of the political process as a whole (RUSTOW 1970:7; also quoted in ALMOND et al. 1973:17).

As ALMOND/MUNDT put it: "Coalition analysis yields the options; leadership and choice analysis gives us the decision" (ALMOND/MUNDT 1973: 630). In the long run, many of these efforts are bringing political factors back into social science analyses (cf. e.g., FLANAGAN 1973:44; see also TILLY et al. 1975:298).

If one were to follow the strategy proposed here, empirically grounded statements as to *mobilization processes*[17] might also be derived. Mobilization processes are not considered in most of the studies dealt with here. According to TILLY, mobilization can be conceived as "reducing the competing claims on resources controlled by members, developing a program which corresponds to the perceived interests of members, building up a group structure which minimizes exit and voice"[18] (TILLY 1978:71-72). There is little in the literature bearing on these processes (cf. MARX/WOOD 1975 for a useful overview). Promising approaches start from the assumption that collective behavior does not differ fundamentally from other forms of non-institutionalized behavior[19] and incorporate *game theoretic elements* (*benefits/costs*) or *resources/risks* considerations into their analyses, as OBERSCHALL (1973:162 and passim) has done in his "resource management theory" (cf. also BERK 1974; BRAMS 1975; TILLY 1978). To a considerable extent these theoretical considerations might explain the readiness of individuals to join certain groups[20] and the strategic alternatives open to these groups (as to the latter cf. KORPI 1974, as well as LAWLER/YOUNGS 1975; cf. also the general theory in BANDURA 1973; see chapter 3.3). Systematic empirical findings directly bearing on theories about mobilizing conditions of violent protest behavior have not yet been reported. However, several possibly important variables have been mentioned in the literature, such as *availability* (in terms of space and/or time) of certain alternatives (cf. the analyses in McPHAIL 1971 and McPHAIL/MILLER 1973; see also SNOW et al. 1980)[21] and *supporting vs. nonsupporting context* (cf. MULLER/JUKAM 1977).

TILLY (1978) has developed several new ideas on how to study the mobilization of contending groups. He conceives of mobilization as a function of organization which is defined as the product of "catness × netness" (TILLY 1978:84). "Solidary organization is a product of catness and netness, called catnet for short. Catness refers to the strength of a shared identity in a group and to the sharpness of social boundaries that comprise all those who share a common characteristic. Netness refers to the density of networks among group members that link them to each other by means of interpersonal bonds. Solidarity increased with catness. Mobilization in turn can be measured by the amount and kind of resources in a group multiplied by the probability that these will be delivered for the pursuit of group goals, when needed" (OBERSCHALL 1978a:308). Mobilization, then, in TILLY's formulae is the product of the quantity of resources collectively controlled multiplied by the probability of their delivery (TILLY 1978:84). OBERSCHALL (1973; 1978a; 1978b) also points out that the chances of mobilization of protest groups are strongly enhanced if they can rely on pre-existent networks (e.g., quasi-groups, solidary groups, transitory teams, associations) that can be linked to a common cause (cf. also SNOW et al. 1980). In this context ROGOWSKI/WASSERSPRING (1971:21; cf. also ROGOWSKI 1974) have emphasized the mobilizing qualities of segmented (stigmatized) groups or, in more general terms, of distinctive sociocultural groups. Drawing on OLSON's (1965) logic of collective action (see also FIREMAN/GAMSON 1979 for an explication and partial critique of the utilitarian logic in the resource-mobilization perspective), OBERSCHALL also emphasizes the role of incentives in the mobilization of protesters and in the maintenance of protesting organizations. He points out (cf. also GRANOVETTER 1978) that costs of participation decrease with the number of participants (OBER-SCHALL 1978b:509).[22] Thus, it is not the sheer number of individuals with grievances but the distribution of grievances in segments within a societal order that is important (WEEDE 1975a:421).

In part these new analyses contradict SMELSER's (1963) theoretical approach that generalized beliefs are a requirement for collective behavior to take place. At the same time, seemingly contradictory results as to the social and personal characteristics of rioters (cf. the typologies in HAGOPIAN 1974:314-15, 329-32; TILLY 1978:89; LIPSET/RAAB 1970; COUCH 1970) might be reconciled in these new approaches in so far as the reward-cost ratios of participation might differ for various groups (e.g., among initiators vs. followers; cf. McCARTHY/ZALD 1973; 1977; OBERSCHALL 1978a: 309).[23] Results contradictory at first glance (cf. also ORUM 1974) would not automatically lead to the falsification of other, perhaps likewise "mono-causal," efforts at explanation.[24] They may instead serve as a clue that the explanandum might vary. There might be different *phases*[25] during a riot just as there might be great variation from one riot to the next in terms of participation by certain socioeconomic groups.

Third parties[26] which might act as mediators[27] between the fronts of protest as well as the *tertius gaudens* (as to further roles cf. FISHER 1972; RUBIN/BROWN 1975:54-64; WILKINSON 1976; WILLIAMS 1977:351ff.; and the *locus classicus* SIMMEL 1968:75-100) have also been neglected in these studies. The same holds true for the criteria making protest groups appear legitimate or illegitimate in the eyes of the *public*. "Force and violence can be successful techniques of social control and persuasion when used for purposes which have extensive popular support. If such support is lacking, their advocacy and use are ultimately self-destructive, either as techniques of government or of opposition. The historical and contemporary evidence of the United States suggests that popular opinion tends to sanction violence in support of the status quo:[28] the use of official violence to maintain public order, the use of private violence to maintain popular conceptions of social order when government cannot or will not" (GURR 1979b:499). In this context TURNER (1969) has developed some theoretical notions of interest.[29] According to his analysis, protest must come from members of a group "whose grievances are already well-documented, who are believed to be individually or collectively powerless to correct their grievances, and who show some signs of moral virtue that render them 'deserving'" (TURNER 1969:818). SCHUMAKER has developed a causal model of *policy respon-*

siveness[30] to protest groups in which he distinguishes between protester-controlled variables (e.g., demand dimensions, leadership dimensions, organization dimensions, and action dimension, i.e., unconventionality of actions) and variables located in the environment (degree of support or hostility of the following sectors: agency officials, elected officials, the media, active groups, community as a whole). Using two nonrandom samples, the first comprising ninety-three cases with data taken from the *New York Times* and from local sources, the second based on the responses of 119 officials in forty-six cities, period: 1966-71, he finds out that the environment of social support is more strongly[31] related to policy responsiveness. Nevertheless, protester-controlled variables might have an effect, albeit small, on the dependent variable and/or an indirect impact via gaining social support through the adoption of appropriate forms of behavior. In a follow-up article drawing on the same data base, SCHUMAKER reaches these conclusions: "Constraint utilization will be most effective when third parties are either uninvolved in the protest or when they are involved and unsupportive of protester demands. Under these conditions, constraints may be effective resources enabling protesters to coerce targets into being responsive to their demands. Constraint utilization will be least effective when third parties are involved and supportive of protester demands or are attentive but initially neutral or divided in their support of the protesters" (SCHUMAKER 1978: 168). "Public hostility to protesters is enhanced when groups make zero-sum demands. And, at least in contemporary American society, the use of constraints by protesters is frequently viewed as being illegitimate and enhances public hostility toward the protesters. Thus, in a context where protesters depend on public support to attain their policy goals, constraints are not effective resources available to protesters" (ibid., p. 182; cf. also the analysis in WILLIAMS 1977:235-36).

The analysis of protests becomes even more complicated if one keeps in mind that *target groups* and *social control agents* might have to be distinguished (cf. the analysis in WILSON 1977). Demonstrators occasionally confound the two and thus diminish their chances of winning over third parties or the *media*. The latter could be said to represent the fourth contending party. The fourth rank, of course, does not imply that the media is the least important factor to be reckoned with. Moreover, as third parties to conflict might have access to the media, there might be accelerating processes in winning outside support once the cause of a protesting group has been accepted by such a third party. Conversely, if a third party withdraws its support from a protesting group this could lead to a more hostile or at least less favorable presentation of the group's claims in the media, thus contributing to the demobilization of resources.

All this leads back to the *labeling* aspect (dealt with in chapter 2.1), the process of defining protest phenomena in one way or another. This is an area of research to which a science of protest behavior should devote priority.[32] As BLUMENTHAL et al. (1972) have shown for a representative sample of American men, the approval or rejection of the behavior of specific groups (black or students) or of representatives of specific institutions influences the designation of what the respondent thinks violence is or is not. For example, to staunch supporters of violence for social control (e.g., police violence), nonviolent forms of student protest or even merely deviating opinions are held to be violence, whereas adherents of violence for social change consider the use of violence a legitimate means of political conflict. Generally comparable results[33] were found with a smaller and nonrepresentative sample (N=283, drawn from the Detroit metropolitan area and from four Southern sampling units) in 1972.[34] Again, "identification [with the persons or groups involved in the violence] was a major variable in explaining attitudes toward violence" (BLUMENTHAL et al. 1975:195). Numerous other relationships are tested for in the two volumes by the BLUMENTHAL group, e.g., relationships between various sociodemographic measures, attitudinal measures, and the particular indexes of violence. Especially noteworthy is their failure to find support for various measures of relative deprivation to show a close variation with their particular dependent variables. Furthermore, political distrust leads to a greater willingness to engage in protest activities only among blacks and "those who were politically oriented to the left" (BLUMENTHAL et al. 1975:84).

The question remains as to the *outcomes of political violence.*[35] According to GAMSON (1975) violence is a useful means[36] (but not the only means) for groups to achieve access to the political process. (The most successful[37] groups reached their goals without using violence). Almost certainly this statement will have to be refined, if other space and/or time coordinates are chosen.[38] "Evaluating the success or failure of outcomes may vary between leaders, followers, third parties, and targets" (MUELLER 1978:51) as well as between observers. Real success must be distinguished from symbolic reassurances, and short-term gains may perhaps be judged long-term losses. "Protest groups are inherently more effective in raising issues and establishing their importance than in participating in the formulation or adoption of solutions to the problems they dramatize" (HAWLEY 1970:1257). We cannot comment extensively, not even with GAMSON's data, as to the effectiveness of protest and turmoil, as this would require cost/benefit calculations which require data on the costs of alternative (e.g., nonviolent) strategies of protest. As LIPSKY (1968:1155-56) has pointed out, there are many ways in which target groups may thwart the demands of protesters, e.g., via symbolic or material satisfactions, by a reorganization of target groups "to blunt the impetus of protest efforts," by appearing to be "constrained in their ability to grant protest goals," via using their "extensive resources to discredit protest leaders and organizations," or simply by postponing action. Target groups may ignore protest groups or they may give community-based protesters "the appearance of authority without its substance, thereby forcing them to discredit themselves through attempting actions that they cannot carry out" (FAINSTEIN/FAINSTEIN 1974:193).

PIVEN/CLOWARD (1971) try to show that in case of the blacks' riots there were manifest short-term gains (cf. also the partly supportive evidence in BETZ 1974; see also WELCH 1975; and the more ambiguous findings in BERKOWITZ 1974a; COLBY 1975; and the comprehensive review by

GURR 1980a, especially his Table 2). In her detailed analysis of twenty-four different kinds of riot events in seventy-seven cities for 1967 and 1968, MUELLER (1978) detects two factors of official response, namely *symbolic reassurances* (high loadings: recognition; meetings with representatives of protesters; tokenism; and setting up of investigating committee) and *long-term commitment* (diplomacy, i.e., visits to the riot area by high level officials; appointment of blacks to a visible community position; advantages). A noteworthy finding is that "number of injuries has a positive influence on long term commitments" (ibid., p. 59). But she considered only a two-week period starting with the first day of rioting. From a more long-term perspective,[39] however, PIVEN/CLOWARD (1977) note a pattern of reaction similar to that experienced by other protesting groups in American history: symbolic concessions deradicalize political protest movements and the less radical leaders of protest movements are often coopted.[40] To return to the most prominent hypothesis thus far, a reanalysis of the riot-social welfare nexus devised by PIVEN/CLOWARD (1971) has been performed by JENNINGS (1978). Carrying out analyses of national trends as well as comparative state analyses, he arrives at the following results:

> Analyses indicated that the welfare rolls did expand in response to the urban riots of the 1960s,[41] however, the data also indicated that the rolls can increase substantially in the absence of civil turmoil and that they did not decline in the aftermath of disorder. We also found strong evidence that the relief rolls respond to labor market conditions. Changes in the unemployment rate are accompanied by changes in welfare recipients rates. A multiple regression analysis indicated that changes in unemployment explained more of the variance in welfare roll change from 1938 to 1976 than did the urban riots of the 1960's. In addition, the graphs present a picture of a welfare system with a built-in tendency to expand over time (JENNINGS 1978:18).

Moreover, in a reanalysis of the data of PIVEN/CLOWARD (1971), ALBRITTON (1979) claims that the temporal sequence was just the reverse; thus, one needs to find another explanation. One possible explanation is that the states had an interest in increasing their lists of welfare recipients in order to receive additional federal money. In reply, PIVEN/CLOWARD (1979) accuse ALBRITTON of various methodological errors and criticize his conclusions. Finally, to conclude this brief and highly eclectic overview of findings bearing on the outcomes of the black riots of the 1960s, the response of the urban criminal justice system must be considered. BALBUS (1973) found that the justice system clearly wanted to keep the rioters "off of streets." He also reached the "paradoxical" conclusion that "court sanctions following minor revolts were generally *more* severe than those following major revolts" (BALBUS 1973:252).[42]

One of the most comprehensive studies on the outcomes of the black riots of the 1960s is BUTTON's (1978) macrolevel analysis of the responses to the black turmoil in forty riot cities. In addition, BUTTON collected interview data from influential people in two riot cities, Rochester and Dayton, and from fifty high federal officials. "Expenditure increases for total Housing and Urban Development, Urban Renewal, and Housing programs are all significantly correlated statistically with riot characteristics and, based on ... path models, are *directly* and *positively affected* (except for Urban Renewal) to a highly significant degree by the number of riots" (BUTTON 1978:89). Moreover, "although the president [Nixon] attempted to apply some braking efforts to the growth of these programs, the Great Society thrust of the previous decade had gained an inertia of its own and continued to escalate. By early 1973, however, President Nixon declared a moratorium on all federally subsidized housing in order to cut costs in a period of serious inflation" (ibid., p. 101). Thus, BUTTON notes a movement from riot prevention to riot control. "Urban black upheavals of the 1960s had a greater impact upon the Department of Justice than upon perhaps any other federal department or agency" (ibid., p. 152).[43] In terms of theory, BUTTON's most significant finding is perhaps: "Violence seems to be more of an impetus to change when it is utilized in conjunction with other, nonviolent, conventional stategies as a means of asserting the demands of the politically powerless. The early riots occurred almost simultaneously with the peaceful protests of the civil rights movement, intensive lobbying campaigns on behalf of major civil rights legislation, increased black electoral participation, and other conventional political activities. By late in the decade, however, the riots appeared to have pre-empted other strategies. Urban violence assumed the position of primary tactic of urban blacks, and it proved to be noticeably less successful" (BUTTON 1978:176).[44]

To turn to another important question: Do weaker forms of violent protest, such as strikes, sit-ins, and demonstrations, because they frequently occur in democratic societies, serve as a safety valve, thus preventing the build-up of protest potentials of a much larger size (cf., e.g., MARSH 1977: 231; SANDERS 1973)? The French fruit-grower who dumps his surplus products, with a certain regularity, on the *routes nationales* might express his discontent in what he considers to be the appropriate form of protest; the state or the political order as such, however, will hardly be perturbed by such forms of quasi-institutionalized ritualized protests. Structurally comparable examples could be reported from many other Western democracies. "As Stanley HOFFMANN argues, 'The protest movement is both the safety valve of a society divided by deep conflicts and the traditional French form of democracy" (HOFFMANN 1962:79, quoted in ROTH/WILSON 1976:456).

The empirical evidence at hand, however, does not yet allow for *functional statements* of the kind mentioned, e.g., what do "in the short run" and "in the long run" mean? Far-reaching interpretations, such as considering a certain degree of criminal behavior as a normal pathology of societies (DURKHEIM 1895), would run a much higher risk of leading to distorted interpretations of reality in the case of political violence[45] than in the case of criminal behavior[46] (cf. also NELSON 1971:52-56 on the question of integrative or disruptive consequences of social conflicts; cf. also BRICKMAN

1974:22-23; and GRUNDY/WEINSTEIN 1974:18-21 for an overview of other functional statements in this context).[47] DURKHEIM attributes two main functions to deviant behavior: First, it has a boundary-maintaining function. Second, deviant behavior can play its part in the "gradual evolution of the social collective" (SUCHAR 1978:24) or, more generally, in bringing about social change. Note, however, that "DURKHEIM never specifies how much of a deviation from the average rate is necessary for social disorganization to be indicated" (ibid., p. 22). For political violence to indeed be a *normal* pathology of societies, one would have to show that more or less all societies have some political violence but still manage to survive. A statement of such a general nature is obviously untenable. More specifically, if political violence were indeed functional for the survival of polities, one would have to demonstrate that those polities which have survived for a long time also show relatively high rates of political violence. Again, this statement obviously proves to be incorrect.

However, perhaps there is some truth in DURKHEIM's reasoning, if two additional tests are carried out: (1) Are nonviolent forms of protest (cf. also below) a functional alternative for violent forms of protest? (2) Is political protest a functional alternative for internal war (cf. also GURR/LICHBACH 1979)? In the words of HIRSCHMAN: A society (even the communist variant of totalitarian society) "needs *minimal* or *floor* levels of exit and voice in order to receive the necessary feedback about its performance. Every [society] thus navigates between the Scylla of disintegration-disruption and the Charybdis of deterioration due to lack of feedback" (HIRSCHMAN 1974:16). The question is whether the handling of protest by protesters and authorities alike provides the necessary feedback. While a business firm has an objective indicator of success that can be easily ascertained (profit), an adequate measure for democracies or, more generally, polities (long-term survival rate?) is much more difficult to derive. For (1) and (2) to be true, one would have to show that there is a long-term empirical covariation between polities who show higher scores on each of the first alternatives and their survival rates. Yet, even if this were true, numerous other factors of importance are probably still omitted. There may be some truth in the proposition that protest, as the weaker dimension of political dissent, via *voice* (HIRSCHMAN 1970) indicates some minimum loyalty to the polity, whereas internal war means fighting over the polity and thus stands for *exit* or, in TILLY's framework, for the "fragmentation" of the polity. To demonstrate this on a solid empirical basis, however, will require much more data accumulation and measurement over longer periods.[48]

There may be other, more serious consequences arising from results mentioned in this study. In GAMSON's work one of the research questions was whether it pays to use violence, i.e., what can one do *with* violence. Now the question is what can be done *against* political violence. The restriction of the concept of political violence to attacks against the state or its representatives, as found in chapter 5 in particular, might lead to the erroneous conclusion that this kind of research has only one goal, namely the development of strategies for keeping rebels down. The results of science may be read both ways, i.e., to increase the score of a dependent variable or to decrease it. Bearing this in mind, the question of what could be done to reduce political violence might also imply that something is done against the social and political conditions (the "causes") making for political violence and not merely against the actual occurrence of political violence (the "symptoms") or against the impending outbreak of political violence. Whether the reduction of political violence is a goal that should be pursued is, of course, a question of value preferences. To us, the answer is yes, but it should be kept in mind that the reduction of political violence might also imply harsh repression and considerable social injustice. Thus, political violence cannot be seen in isolation from other phenomena. It is difficult or perhaps impossible to argue about the moral qualities of violence from a scientific point of view. There simply is no rule, either for deciding on manichean interpretations of political violence (cf., e.g., ZINN 1968; BROWN 1969) such as labeling political violence as good or bad, progressive or reactionary or for evaluating the hypothesis that the state shows its real face when employing force and repression against its citizens. Most of these formulae come from the nineteenth century (cf. VAN DEN HAAG 1972:75–86, and the discussion in chapter 8.4.4). These questions and aspects of political violence have been neglected in our discussion here (cf., e.g., GRUNDY/WEINSTEIN 1974). The assertions by SOREL on the myth of violence (in his *Réflexions sur la violence* 1908), by FANON (1967 and in less plainly apologetic terms CAMUS 1949) on the allegedly therapeutic ego-forming value of violence,[49] and by MARCUSE that if "oppressed and overpowered minorities . . . use violence, they do not start a new chain of violence but try to break an established one" (MARCUSE 1969:130–31)[50] might have their own peculiar effects. To the researcher they seem difficult to test or likely to be proven questionable or wrong when rigorously evaluated.[51]

To turn to the question of policy implications, the "therapy" derived from results presented in this study should not look like HUNTINGTON's policy recommendations for South Vietnam. They relied on insufficient empirical evidence and poorly applied theory, not to mention the misunderstanding of the causes of the opponent's political strength: "If the 'direct application of mechanical and conventional power' takes place on such a massive scale as to produce a massive migration from countryside to city, the basic assumptions underlying the Maoist doctrine of revolutionary war no longer operate. The Maoist-inspired rural revolution is undercut by the American-sponsored urban revolution" (HUNTINGTON 1968a:656). From the results described here, one may derive various courses of action: (1) that the degree of social mobilization or of aspirations which have been enlarged by increases in education and possibly by the mass media should be reduced (or channeled via symbolic means of political participation) and brought into balance with the rate of expansion of institutional capacities or even with the present institutional capacities (which, in general, would mean that social injustices would be cemented); (2) that, in case of emergency, the use of repressive measures should be as harsh and consistent as possible,[52] (3) that ethnic, linguistic, racial, and other cultural minorities should be kept at a lower level of social mobilization in order to prevent the build-up of a protest potential; or (4) that the institutional capacities[53] should be increased while at the same time allowing for social mobilization and forms of *accommodation*[54] (cf. NORDLINGER 1972; LIJPHART 1968; 1977 and the works in McRAE 1974; cf. also PINARD 1976 for a useful discussion of related, but partly different approaches), i.e., of arrangements among the specific elites, including those which have most recently been mobilized, arrangements acceptable to the specific clienteles. All of these are political questions. The results of these studies, provided they stand further tests,[55] can be read in both ways. A devoted revolutionary hoping for revolution in stable democracies might do more for his professional career by joining guerrilla movements somewhere in the Third World. This prediction is based on the assumption that established democratic regimes will continue to engender beliefs of legitimacy and that the forces of repression will be used in a wise manner. "The long-range effectiveness of public force in maintaining civil peace seems to depend on three conditions: public belief that governmental use of force is legitimate, consistent use of that force, and remedial action for the grievances that give rise to dissidence" (GURR 1979b:502). Ultimately, the use of coercive means deserves closest attention from those in command of such means. If the employment of repressive measures were an easy task, one would have to ask why political regimes do not persist much longer than they in fact do (for the moment neglecting external factors). Increased repression pays only where it is employed harshly and consistently; even then, one would have to ask: Pays for whom and for how long? However, hazardous use of repressive measures easily produces a boomerang effect, i.e., an aggravation of the original situation. This is the consensus emerging from a large body of studies,[56] some cross-national and quantitative, others more historical-monographic in orientation.

Apart from policy implications[57] and other questions mentioned above, there are additional aspects which have been purposely neglected in this study, e.g., the impact of ideas and belief systems on protest behavior. At times we dealt with variables trying to extract theoretical notions from this block of influences, but in general we focused on sociostructural analyses of conditions causing violent political behavior. Furthermore, *nonviolent* forms of protest behavior have not been considered here, quite contrary to TILLY's important dictum that "to understand and explain violent actions, you must understand nonviolent actions" (TILLY 1978:182). Most of the literature and many historical cases have been thoroughly evaluated by SHARP in his *The Politics of Nonviolent Action* (1973) which summarizes his earlier writings on this subject. He defines nonviolent action as "covering dozens of specific methods of protest, noncooperation and intervention, in all of which the actionists conduct the conflict by doing—or refusing to do— certain things without using physical violence. As a technique therefore, nonviolent action is not passive" (SHARP 1973:64). Thus, nonviolent protests are only one category of the variants of nonviolent action. Others include persuasion, social noncooperation, economic noncooperation (boycott and strikes), political noncooperation, and nonviolent intervention. Nonviolent action is also a more general term than civil disobedience (defined by one author as "a public, nonviolent, conscientious yet political act contrary to law usually done with the aim of bringing about a change in the law or policies of the government," RAWLS 1971:364 following BEDAU 1961; cf. MACFARLANE 1971:13 for a similar definition and BAY 1968 for a slightly different view and a useful summary article), also the subject of a rather extensive literature (cf., e.g., ZINN 1968; ZASHIN 1972). From the incumbents' point of view, political violence also represents acts of civil disobedience. Following historical precedents like the resistance of the Gueux to Spanish rule from 1565 to 1576, the classic example of nonviolent protest is that of Gandhi who described his doctrine of *satyagraha* as "Force which is born of *Truth* and *Love* or non-violence" (as quoted in LEWY 1974:298); its most important feature is the use of nonviolence (*ahimsa*). (As to GANDHI cf. the psychoanalytic interpretation by ERIKSON 1969; the attempt at systematizing his doctrine by NAESS 1958; the analyses in LEWY 1974:297-323 who focuses on the religious background of GANDHI's doctrine; and BONDURANT 1965). Another notable example of nonviolent protest is the resistance in Norway and Denmark against the German intrusion in World War II. Many of the better known examples of nonviolent resistance were efforts at defending one's own country against foreign intruders (cf. also the articles in ROBERTS 1967 and in EBERT 1970). Following World War II there have been many examples of nonviolent resistance and extensions of its repertoire of techniques, especially in the United States, the two best known cases being the Civil Rights Movement and the Student Movement.

Are there thresholds between nonviolent and violent forms of protest? If so, where and when do these occur? Are there typical sequences as nonviolent forms of protest turn into violent actions, e.g., in cases where authorities do not respond to demands raised? What is needed is information on the "repertoires of contention" (TILLY 1979). Focusing on the development of protests in America and Britain between 1750 and 1830, TILLY distinguishes between the similarity of forms of protest behavior to known forms of actions and the probability of their use; he goes on to develop several different variants of collective action repertoires. Among the research problems lying ahead in this field, he mentions that: "The first is to establish whether the existing repertoire itself constrains the pattern of collective action; after all, whatever recurrence of contentious forms exists could well result from the recurrence of the interests, organizations, and opportunities that produce contention. The second part is to explain the variation and change. What are the relative contributions of repression, tactical experience, and organizational changes? How do they interact?" (TILLY 1979:154-55). It would be extremely interesting to see how well nonviolent vs. violent methods of protest behavior, or violent vs. nonviolent reactions of the incumbents, would fare[58] if the available historical evidence were systematically taken into consideration. As of now, research activities have concentrated on either domain (as has been the case in the study of both internal and international political violence) without crossing the border. There is reason and some evidence for treating them together.

Perhaps this study should have carried the subheading "Trends Report." It is hoped that some of the various trends covered in this inquiry will converge into larger trends, thus advancing our knowledge significantly beyond the present state by organizing our theoretical view of empirically observed relationships and thus contributing to an understanding of what otherwise might be "hitherto unconnected things" (POPPER 1972:241). In the end, however, the scientist must be interested not only in doing his work for the sake of pure knowledge but also in contributing to a reduction of human suffering through the application of better corroborated theories.

Notes

Chapter Two: Conceptual Problems

1. It may be of interest to note that there is no separate keyword for violence either in the *International Encyclopedia of the Social Sciences* or in the widely used dictionary of GOULD/KOLB (1964).

2. We regard the political issues in any social system as those which concern the structure and exercise of authority at the most inclusive levels. In the nation-state the most inclusive levels are the political regime and its subordinate elements; in universities they are usually the governing administrative and faculty bodies; in tribal societies they are the chief and his supporting institutions; and so forth. Any demands or disagreements about the structure or procedures of these bodies, or about the identity of those who staff them, or the policies that they carry out, constitute *political* conflict. Or, in other terms, political conflict is distinguished from other types of conflict by the particular goods over which there is contention—for political conflict contention takes place over the nature, occupancy, and outputs of socially inclusive authority patterns (GURR/DUVALL 1976:141).

   Thus, for GURR/DUVALL the term political denotes contentions over authority structures. When indexing this concept, however, the indicator stressed in our discussion, namely the sheer number of participants, again will be an indicator of prime importance because indicators on the intentions of rebels or insurgents or other contenders are harder to come by than data on the size of contending factions.

3. The labeling approach has gained great attention in the literature. Critics, however, have pointed to numerous shortcomings, e.g., that primary acts of deviance cannot be explained by labeling (cf. also the modifications proposed by LEMERT 1967, who speaks of "secondary deviance"). For a recent summary of the weaknesses of the labeling approach, see GOVE:

   The evidence consistently indicates that it is the behavior or condition of the person that is the critical factor in causing someone to be labeled a deviant. Furthermore, the evidence indicates that with most forms of deviance the role played by social resources is relatively minor. Perhaps even more devastating to the labeling perspective is that with some forms of deviance, most clearly with

(3)

mental illness and physical disability, the evidence indicates that
the effect of individual resources is directly counter to that
posited by labeling theory. For these forms of deviant behavior,
and sometimes for other forms, social resources facilitate
entrance into a deviant role (GOVE 1976:224).

Cf. also the contributions to GOVE (1975) and the more balanced
evaluation given by CONOVER (1976); GIBBS/ERICKSON (1975);
MONTANINO (1977:279–88); and in Part 1 of *Social Forces* 56, no. 2
(December 1977).

4. In a representative survey of American men in 1969 BLUMENTHAL et
   al. (1972) found that different parts of the population advocate the use
   of violence either for social control or for social change. Thus, definitions of legitimacy of violence vary. For instance, respondents strongly
   approving of the resolute use of public authority consider nonviolent
   forms of student protests or even deviant opinions as violence. Conversely, adherents of more radical social change consider violence a
   legitimate means in political confrontation. One may also speculate
   that the philosophies of violence of subpopulations vary in degree of
   constraint, e.g., persons with more education hold to more consistent
   philosophies (cf. CONVERSE 1964; for some evidence along these lines
   see BLUMENTHAL et al. 1972:217, for example).
5. Cf. also TILLY/RULE (1965:4) and VAN DEN HAAG: "violence is
   coercive only when used instrumentally to control the future actions
   of people; it is politically so when used to control or influence collective policies or the distribution of power. Violence by such individuals
   is political only when it has such aims" (VAN DEN HAAG 1972:60).
   HAAG also notes the distinction between violence and violation
   (simply breaking rules) as do other authors (e.g., GRUNDY/WEIN-
   STEIN 1974:8).
6. Moreover, if protesters use milder forms of violence this does not necessarily imply a bargaining strategy but may rather stand for tactical
   behavior as long as their own resources are too limited to achieve more
   radical goals.
7. Following is a list of terms often treated as equivalents or conceptual
   cousins of violence: Gewalt, potestas, maiestas, Macht, Kraft, violentia,
   facultas, auctoritas, coercio, potentia, vis, vehementia, impetus, Stärke,
   Zwang, forza, vehemenza, potesta, potenza, commando, pouvoir,
   puissance (excerpted from *Deutsches Wörterbuch*, comp. Jacob Grimm
   and Wilhelm Grimm, IV.1.3., [Leipzig 1898], p. 4952).
8. "Threats are forms of social influence that attempt to affect another's
   behavior by altering the perceived gains and costs of his alternative
   courses of action through linking an externally imposed reward or
   punishment to his relevant alternatives" (M. DEUTSCH 1973:140; see
   also the useful list of characteristics of threats ibid., p. 124ff.).
9. Again the labeling perspective is of importance if one thinks of the
   efforts of groups or individuals to change the definition of criminal

violence into one of political violence (or conversely so). In the present context it is not the legalistic perspective that counts, but rather the social determinants of labeling.

10. In this study all italics are used as in the originals, unless otherwise noted.

11. In this respect the study of GURR/BISHOP (1976) remains unsatisfying as well. See chapter 5.1.1.1.2.6.

12. Actually WEBER speaks of *Gewaltsamkeit* (rather than *Gewalt*) which has a slightly different and rather diffuse meaning. WALTER translates *Gewaltsamkeit* as "extreme coercion and forcefulness" (WALTER 1969:50; see ibid. the discussion as to whether to translate *Gewaltsamkeit* as "force" or "violence"; see also below).

13. As to the intricate relationships between legality and legitimacy in Max WEBER's writings, see, e.g., WINCKELMANN (1952).

14. "In the perfect social order all acts judged legal would be regarded as legitimate by the community, all illegal acts would be illegitimate. No such clear-cut distinction holds in the United States [or in other countries] as far as violence, force, and protest are concerned nor has it ever. Our nation was founded in a revolutionary war that was illegal but widely regarded as legitimate. It survived civil war whose competing causes most Northerners and Southerners thought both legal and legitimate" (GRAHAM/GURR 1969:xxxi).

15. There are additional concepts in the literature that would deserve attention, e.g., social unrest which includes both violent and nonviolent forms. Furthermore, some of the concepts discussed in chapter 2.1 should be recalled. For the concept of political instability see the discussion in chapter 6.

16. "Power is purposive influence; it may be coercive but it need not be. Coercion is only one of several forms of power" (M. DEUTSCH 1973:87; see also the typology of power, ibid.).

17. "'Power' is the probability that one actor within a social relationship will be in a position to carry out his own will despite resistance" (WEBER 1947:152). A more adequate translation would be: "Power is the capacity to carry through one's will in a social relation against resistance, irrespective of the sources of that capacity."

18. "The probability that certain commands (or all commands) from a given source will be obeyed by a given group of persons" (WEBER 1947:324).

19. In his effort to formalize the concept of power, PASSIGLI (1973) seems to have started from considerations similar to those presented here. For a recent attempt at delineating the concept of power in a more precise way (i.e., by means of path analytic considerations) see NAGEL (1975). A somewhat dated discussion is found in LASSWELL/ KAPLAN (1952). Cf. also the classification of variables in KIPNIS (1974).

20. This type of system can be characterized by a relatively low degree of violent political protests, a result which hardly astonishes considering

(20)

the degree of prevention usually taken in these political systems (cf. also some of the results in chapter 5.1 and in GURR/DUVALL, forthcoming).

21. For a more philosophical overview and discussion of many of the issues involved here, cf. the articles in PENNOCK/CHAPMAN (1972).

Chapter Three: Experimental Studies of Aggressive Behavior

1. "Can we really learn anything valid about human behavior—in this case, aggression and conflict—from the results of animal behavior? The growing consensus, based upon increasingly sophisticated work in several fields, is a carefully qualified no" (NELSON 1974:313; cf. also NELSON 1975). See also FISCHER (1975) for a short summary of important arguments as to the relevancy of ethological research for understanding human aggressive behavior. FISCHER strongly objects to a number of propositions put together in a somewhat provocative article by VAN DEN BERGHE (1974).

2. Although FROMM criticizes the drive conceptions of FREUD and other writers as well as various other approaches, his own study nevertheless builds on psychoanalytic ideas, even if he tries to merge them with a more sociological perspective. Generally, he distinguishes between "biologically adaptive, life-serving, benign aggression and biologically nonadaptive, malignant aggression" (FROMM 1973:187).

3. Neither genetic deviations nor sexual arousal (cf., e.g., the studies referred to in JOHNSON 1972:104-6 as well as BARON 1974b; 1977) have proved to be consistent predictors of aggression.

4. For a third case, *accidental aggression*, see below.

5. It should be pointed out, however, that in most experimental studies intentions concerning behavior are *not* measured (cf. the criticism in STONNER 1976:249). For additional criticism see below.

6. A list of criteria useful in this context has been given by FESHBACH:

> The moral evaluation of a violent act is a function of the lawful status of the act, the extent of personal versus social motivation and the degree of personal responsibility as reflected in the role of authority, the options available to the individual, the defensive or initiated basis of the violence, the degree of emotional disturbance, the amount of force employed, and the intentionality of the act. To these criteria must be added normative considerations of fair play, the degree and manner of the violence, the age and sex of the victim, and, more generally, the appropriateness of the target. Last to be mentioned, but probably most important, is one's attitude toward the objectives of the violence (FESHBACH 1971:290).

See also the recent chapter of RULE/NESDALE (1976).

7. Researchers "have expressed the view that the term drive, to be useful, must be given a sound physiological basis. However, the more I investi-

gate the physiological basis of behavior, the less need I find for the concept of drive" (MOYER 1969:104). Cf. also the intensive discussion in MOYER (1976).

8. The point is brought up in a similar way in the following quotation: "Anger tends to lower the threshold for aggressive responses, and in the absence of imminent punishment, a stimulus that would ordinarily not elicit an aggressive response, would lead to aggression" (BUSS 1961:59).

9. For an interesting failure in replicating the setting of BERKOWITZ/ LePAGE (1967), see ELLIS et al. (1971). In their experiment a large portion of the subjects did not believe the cover story. Apparently the ecological validity of this kind of setting is quite limited (cf. also the discussion in GEEN 1976:202ff.). According to ELLIS et al. weapons (in the presence of a policeman) can also serve as inhibiting stimuli for some subjects. Operant conditioning may be a more appropriate explanation than classical conditioning as favored by BERKOWITZ. Furthermore, the experimental design used by BERKOWITZ/LePAGE may cause demand effects, as PAGE/SCHEIDT (1971; cf. also SCHUCK/PISOR 1974) try to show (but see also BERKOWITZ's, 1971, answer). Yet, see also the evidence from a field experiment in line with the reasoning of BERKOWITZ/LePAGE (1967), namely, that "the presence of an irrelevant aggressive cue can increase aggressive behavior" (HARRIS 1976:35). Other alternative explanations of the experimental results found may be that "the subject in such studies may view himself as helping the confederate learn rather than harming him (CHERRY/MITCHELL/NELSON 1973) or as acting defensively and legitimately rather than aggressively (KANE/DOERGE/TEDESCHI 1973) and that he may respond differently in such a situation where he knows that his behavior is being observed than if it were measured unobtrusively" (HARRIS 1974:561–62). Additional explanations of the very same experimental behavior observed have been suggested by GOLDSTEIN et al., namely "the subject may adapt to a particular reinforcement, thus requiring a more intense level on subsequent trials to maintain the same subjective intensity" (GOLDSTEIN et al. 1975: 169). Still another variant of explaining the aggressive behavior may be seen in the tendency to devaluate the victim. In short, there is growing evidence that "previously unaccounted for variables produce the behavior exhibited by subjects in the BERKOWITZ paradigm. . . . the norm of reciprocity is one of these mediating variables" (KANE et al. 1976:672).

Thus, researchers should be very sensitive to a variety of serious threats to their favorite theoretical explanation. All that can be said at present is that the original setting serving as a paradigm for the bulk of experimental studies on aggression has come under vigorous attack. Even though it may be difficult in experimental research on aggression to substitute on a large scale for the BUSS/BERKOWITZ paradigm, it probably will be a safe prediction that researchers in the near future will develop a variety of alternative settings to measure aggressive behavior in the laboratory (cf. BARON 1977: chapter 2).

(10)

10. In general, one should not expect that these mediating variables might be combined on an additive basis. In almost any experiment on aggressive behavior, highly complex interaction effects have been reported instead. Furthermore, these interaction effects are rarely stable from one series of experiments to another performed by a different researcher. The multitude of ad hoc explanations in experimental research on aggression underlines this observation.

11. "In short, people do not have to be angered or emotionally aroused to behave aggressively. A culture can produce highly aggressive people, while keeping frustration at a low level, by valuing aggressive accomplishments, furnishing successful aggressive models, and ensuring that aggressive actions secure rewarding effects" (BANDURA 1973:59).

12. See also chapter 5.1.1.2.3 and 5.1.2.5.

13. Spontaneous acts of aggression are, of course, a different class of aggressive behavior.

14. Experimental subjects which have been *frustrated* by a model may simply imitate the model's behavior when there is an opportunity to behave aggressively toward another person. Thus, one might have to reckon with model effects in experiments which were merely designed to make the subjects angry and not to provide for an aggressive model as well (cf. BANDURA 1973:134–35).

15. If one were to summarize the discussion about the mass media producing cathartic effects (i.e., reducing aggression by displaying aggressive behavior) or increasing the probability of aggressive behavior, *in general* the evidence so far refutes the cathartic model of aggressive display. There are several studies which report some cathartic effects (KONEČNI 1975; MANNING/TAYLOR 1975; KONEČNI/DOOB 1972; DOOB/WOOD 1972; FESHBACH 1970; FESHBACH/SINGER 1971), but a number of objections have been raised against various of these studies, e.g., those by FESHBACH (cf. in GEEN 1976:228; cf. also the discussion of alternative arguments in KONEČNI/EBBESEN 1976:363ff.). At times theoretical explanations other than interpretations via cathartic effects have been suggested (e.g., BERKOWITZ 1973:111). Carrying out a series of field experiments, MILGRAM/ SHOTLAND (1973) also found no significant evidence that the behavior of an aggressive model is being imitated. Once again, however, the dependent variable (breaking of a charity box) seems to lack in ecological validity. The counterargument seems to be somewhat better corroborated (cf. the overview in ANDISON 1977 with respect to television violence), namely that models in the mass media—and it is mainly the impact of television which has been studied—have an effect on *specific* persons with specific predispositions or structures of personality ("selective exposure") and would lead to aggressive behavior only under a set of additional conditions ("selective reinforcement"). Yet hardly any evidence based on intensive long-range studies is available. For a survey of results obtained thus far, see also the *Report to the Surgeon General's Scientific Advisory Committee on Television and Social Behavior* (Washington: U. S. Department of Health, Education, and Welfare, 1972) 5 vols. (Leading researchers on aggression, however,

such as BANDURA or BERKOWITZ, were *not* appointed as members of the consulting board due to interventions of the television corporations). See also BANDURA et al. (1963a, 1963b); LANGE et al. (1969); GORANSON (1970); ERON et al. (1971) for a longitudinal study; GEEN/STONNER (1972); POWERS/GEEN (1972); HANRATTY et al. (1972); MURRAY (1973); BANDURA (1973:273 ff.); LIEBERT et al. (1973); COMSTOCK (1975); COMSTOCK et al. (1975); GEEN (1975, 1976); GEEN et al. (1975); QUANTY (1976); KAPLAN/SINGER (1976); BELSON (1978). Finally, even modified hypotheses such as the following have not been sufficiently confirmed (cf., e.g., HARTMANN 1969): "When aggression occurs in the absence of anger, there is an *increase* in the tendency to aggress. When aggression occurs in the presence of anger, there is a cathartic effect, i.e., a decrease in the tendency to aggress. Thus the most important determiner of the cathartic effect is the presence or absence of anger" (BUSS 1961:89).

16. *Acquisition* and *activation* of a behavioral response may be determined by similar conditions, but often additional conditions hold, if learned behavior is to be activated.

17. *Guilt* is one of these variables (cf., e.g., the study of KNOTT et al. 1974).

18. Furthermore, there is a clear need for devising experimental settings controlling for more than four variables at a time and for ordering them afterwards in multivariate analyses. Partly, however, such a claim contradicts the call for greater ecological validity of experimental settings. (Nevertheless, experimental settings of this type might generate important information on causal conditions of aggressive behavior.)

Chapter Four: Theories about Social Comparison Processes

1. For a slight correction of HOMANS's formula on the basis of balance theory (imbalances as creating costs), see ALEXANDER/SIMPSON (1964).

2. Concerning this point, compare the attack of EKEH (1974:158ff.) who, on the basis of autobiographical statements by HOMANS, judges the idea of investments to be rather conservative and status-preserving in nature. Accordingly, he tends to do away with it as an ideological "justification of inequality in society" (ibid., p. 163; cf. also RUNCIMAN 1967).

3. For a slightly incorrect representation, see the formula in JASSO (1978:1401). JASSO's article contains a critique of existing formulae of justice (including those of ADAMS [cf. in the next chapter] and WALSTER et al. 1973) and the derivation of a new, apparently more adequate formula to measure the "justice of earnings." The formula given is a "more extensive and precise representation of the model proposed by BERGER et al. [1972]" (JASSO 1978:1416).

4. For a more philosophically oriented discussion of conditions of justice, see the much debated work of RAWLS (1971). For critiques, see

(4)

COLEMAN (1974); *Theory and Decision* 4, no. 3/4 (February/April 1974); and the *American Political Science Review* 59, no. 2 (June 1975):588 ff.

5. BLAU (1964) points to additional problems when working with the concept of investment. Investments themselves, such as expertise, may contain elements of costs. Power influences which may distort the principle of distributive justice are not taken into consideration. Thus, due to imperfections of the particular exchange markets, the going rate of exchange may be different from the fair rate of exchange.

6. Empirical evidence, however, is scant so far in any case (but see the discussion concerning the "free rider position" in economics, e.g., OLSON [1965], where some evidence can be found which may be in favor of EKEH's position).

7. For further theoretical differentiations of the concept of distributive justice, see BERGER et al. (1972) who differentiate, e.g., between "local" and "referential" (i.e., generalized) comparisons (cf. also the further developments in TÖRNBLOM 1977).

8. Cf. also AUSTIN (1977:290–95) for a discussion of dimensions of equity comparisons, e.g., proximity, similarity, and instrumentality.

9. "Equity theory," rather than "inequity theory" as originally proposed by ADAMS, by now has become the more common label in the literature.

10. There are also several studies which report overrewarded individuals developing feelings of guilt which are, however, rather indirectly measured (cf. the overview in ADAMS/FREEDMAN 1976:45). In other studies (PRITCHARD 1969) there is some evidence that persons profiting from inequity relationships react less sensitively than victims of such relationships (cf. also AUSTIN 1977:285).

11. As LEVENTHAL (1976a:113–14) notes in an overview of several studies (which report somewhat contradictory results): the rule of equality seems to be used more often in group decisions than in individual decisions. Rewards distributed through third persons also often do not follow the equity rule (cf. the studies mentioned ibid., p. 107).

12. HOMANS stresses the point that these conceptual variants of justice do not necessarily exclude each other: "If the persons are equal in contributions, then their equality in reward meets the conditions of distributive justice; the ratio of contributions is still equal to the ratio of rewards" (HOMANS 1976:232).

13. To cite WEICK: "Man does not live by equity alone" (as quoted in HOMANS 1976:237).

14. He states the hypothesis that the latter form of relative deprivation will be more important than the former, but does not find sufficient empirical support for this in his survey on various attitudes of respondents in England and Wales (see RUNCIMAN 1966).

15. A similar hypothesis is derived from another theoretical conceptualization, the theory of power equalization. See MULDER et al. (1973) and the partial experimental evidence they have provided. Cf. also MULDER (1977).

16. But cf. also some of the analyses of revolutions in chapter 8.
17. The concept of decremental deprivation is somewhat similar to AMSEL's concept of "frustrative nonreward" (AMSEL 1962; cf. also chapter 5.3.2.3) and to the notion of "extinction-induced aggression" (cf. the review in KELLY 1974). In case of decremental deprivation the discrepancy between expectations and capabilities is caused by decreasing capabilities vs. constant expectations, whereas in AMSEL's theory an actual reward lags behind the expected level of rewards which is anticipated to remain constant. (Actually, the term decremental deprivation is somewhat misleading, as the degree of deprivation is not decreasing, but increasing.)
18. If this were done, we would know more about determinants for selecting reference groups (e.g., similarity vs. proximity) than at present. But cf. also the empirical evidence accumulated in SULS/ MILLER (1977).
19. The theory of relative deprivation generally can be conceived of as a subcase of reference group theory. One of the interesting differences between the two theories, however, seems to be that positively evaluated reference groups are either membership groups or groups in which an individual aspires membership. In cases of relative deprivation, however, different mechanisms seem to apply. To stress the point made here: a reference group, normally viewed negatively or neutrally, temporarily could become a positively evaluated reference group. If the conditions of relative deprivation are eliminated, however, one's own membership group will be more positively evaluated. (However, feelings of relative deprivation may lead, on the contrary, to a downgrading of the comparison group and to a better evaluation of one's own group).
20. Cf. the concept of "structural just deserts" as theoretically developed and empirically corroborated by MULLER (1975; cf. also chapter 5.3.2.3). The shorthand stands for relative deprivation whose cause is perceived as structural in nature and blamed on the political system, on the elites, or on other groups. A precursor of this concept can be found, e.g., in PORTES/ROSS (1974). Cf. also the recent explication of the theory of relative deprivation in CROSBY (1976) and COOK et al. (1977).
21. In accordance with what has been said above about the concepts of HOMANS and ADAMS (cf. also chapter 9), collective discontent does not imply that there is only one factor, such as a certain violation of the rule of distributive justice, causing discontent, but rather that there is a multitude of very different sources of collective discontent.

Chapter Five: Approaches to the Study of Political Violence

1. As we do not carry out secondary analyses ourselves, the thrust of our arguments will derive either from showing inconsistencies in the theoretical arguments used or from demonstrating an unusually low

(1)

    correspondence between operationalizations and theoretical rationale applied. Moreover, the empirical and theoretical findings of each study will be contrasted with empirical and/or theoretical results from other studies. For a shorter discussion dealing mainly with political protest (and not political violence in general) see ZIMMERMANN (1980). Topics for future research are also stressed in that contribution, whereas here the emphasis is more upon a discussion of the wide variety of findings reported in the literature.

2. Viable operationalizations of this aspect might be derived from tracing the discussion of the social comparison approaches in chapter 4.

3. GURR defines institutionalization, one of the major variables in his analysis, in more general terms than is usually done in social sciences. The same holds for the concept of values (see above).

4. GURR does not always make consistent use of his terms. Turmoil and protest are occasionally used synonymously, and on other occasions they are distinguished from each other. In this study, if not otherwise specified, political violence is used as the general concept which at times is replaced by the term violent protest behavior. There must be some flexibility in the use of these concepts, not only for reasons of stylistic elegance, but also because different authors make different use of these concepts.

5. Similar indicators have already been used in the studies of SOROKIN (1957:373–407), i.e., social area, duration, and intensity.

6. For a more detailed discussion of factor analytic studies of conflicts within nations, cf. ZIMMERMANN (1975, 1976); STOHL (1980).

7. See, e.g., RUMMEL's definition of revolution (which more strongly denotes—amongst other phenomena—coups d'état or such attempts rather than revolutionary activities): "any illegal or forced change in the top governmental elite, any attempt at such a change, or any successful or unsuccessful armed rebellion whose aim is independence from the central government" (RUMMEL 1963:5).

8. The data used in this factor analysis were partly collected by GURR and his coworkers and partly taken from TAYLOR/HUDSON (1972) and other sources. The authors aimed at finding empirical evidence for a rather broad, theoretically derived typology of political violence. Availability of data, however, placed some limits on this undertaking. After having carried out a factor analysis in which eight factors emerge, their theoretically derived typology had to be somewhat modified. Among the factors representing physical violence are three factors referring to internal political violence, i.e., *protest* (high loading variables—protest, turmoil, arrests; percent total variance explained: 7.6%), *repression* (relative strength of police and/or internal security forces, sanctions: 3.8%), *internal war* (deaths from political violence, coups, intensity of domestic political conflict: 5.6%). Two additional factors are *external war* (battle death, war participation: 5.4%), and external *intervention* (rebel aid, intervention, regime aid, rebellion: 9.0%). Three factors are identified and labeled as structural violence (cf. the criticism of this concept in chapter 2.2). Two of these are summarized as "structures

of denial": *discrimination* (in economic and political terms: 7.2%) and *social violence* (murder, mortality, suicide, proportion of elementary school age children not in school: 19.9%). The third factor referring to structural violence is *militarism* (military spending, military personnel: 6.3%). Some overlapping of the militarism factor with the intervention factor is also reported (the last two factors are brought together under the label of "structures of coercion"). In chapter 5.1.1.1.2.6 and 5.1.2.6 some further results of GURR/BISHOP will be discussed.

9. "Significance" in connection with these and numerous other results in this study is used only in a figurative, i.e., heuristic-pragmatic, sense, not in the sense of the model of probability sampling. For a justification of such a use of terminology, see GOLD (1969), for example. But see also MORRISON/HENKEL (1969). In comparative aggregate data analyses on political violence, generally coefficients more than twice the value of the particular standard error are accepted as significant.

10. When Western nations are analyzed as a separate group, similar results emerge: "the immediate determinants of magnitudes of strife are historical levels of strife, long-term deprivation, facilitation, and legitimacy, in that order of importance" (GURR 1969a:622). Unfortunately, GURR does not give further details here. As to the "nations of the Western community" see the next chapter.

11. Moreover, in GURR's causal model of turmoil the alleged positive causal influence of short-term deprivation (measured through economic indicators referring to the 1950s and early 1960s) on past strife (1946–59) as well as the negative influence on coercive force loyalty totally lack in plausibility. The positive effect of coercive force loyalty on legitimacy also rests on weak assumptions. As put by SCHUCK (1976:188): "How . . . could the loyalty of coercive forces in 1960 affect the origin of [a country's institution, the latter representing part of the measurement of legitimacy]?" SCHUCK, however, fails in his effort to develop more plausible explanations (he performs a path analysis on GURR's original data) because he treats facilitation as an exogenous variable which is clearly contrary to GURR's theoretical intention.

12. COOPER's rationale is mainly based on the idea of criss-crossing of social conflict potentials (see also chapters 5.1.2.8 and 6.3.5), leading him to predict that associational groups "such as labor unions, chambers of commerce" are more heterogeneous than, e.g., institutional groups "such as the military, major churches" (COOPER 1974:271) and thereby contribute to a reduction of turmoil.

13. Strife is used here in a broader sense than in previous chapters.

14. "Rebellion includes events previously characterized as conspiracy (highly organized strife with limited participation) and internal war (highly organized strife with widespread popular participation)" (GURR 1970b:131).

15. "Our findings . . . suggest that in the modern and Western clusters, short-term swings do not affect the balance of expectations and reality.

(15)

There would appear to be enough confidence in the system to overcome the effects of short-term deprivation" (COOPER 1974:284).

16. There is theoretical reason (see chapter 5.1.1.1.1) for GURR's balance
variables, yet one of the indicators for measuring the dissidents' resources, "remote-area concentration of dissidents," apparently is used
either to measure the coercive control or the institutional resources
without explaining the particular use of the very same indicator.

17. As GURR puts it: "The more effective a political system has been in
resolving past problems the greater are popular expectations that it will
do so in the future, and the greater the likelihood that its discontented
citizens will feel justified, on both normative and utilitarian grounds, in
resorting to political violence to compel attention to unresolved problems" (GURR 1970a:182).

18. These measurement problems, in turn, stand only for a variety of
theoretical questions. See chapter 5.1.1.1.3.1.

19. In this study, and generally in the pertinent literature as well, concepts
like nation, state, and sometimes political systems will be used as
synonyms. It is well-known, of course, that there are important
differences between these three concepts, yet so far there has been no
agreement whether to follow the suggestion of CONNOR (1972:
333ff.), for example, who differentiates between political unit
(state) and unit of culture and language (nation), a distinction which
represents common European traditions. (As to these problems see also
the discussion in NETTL 1968.) CONNOR pleads for more distinct use
of these concepts and shows the present resulting confusion: "In this
Alice-in-Wonderland world in which nation usually means state, in
which nation-state usually means multi-nation state, in which nationalism usually means loyalty to the state, and in which ethnicity, primor-
dialism, pluralism, tribalism, regionalism, communalism, parochialism
and sub-nationalism usually mean loyalty to the nation, it should come
as no surprise that the nature of nationalism remains essentially
unprobed" (CONNOR 1978:396). For a useful discussion of criteria
distinguishing between ethnic categories and ethnic groups cf. McKAY/
LEWINS (1978).

20. These nations, in turn, only represent a sample of larger nations and
colonies between 1961 and 1965.

21. A high level of economic development is also attributed to countries
like Venezuela and the Philippines as well as to the Eastern European
communist countries. Being based on raw classifications like this, some
of the following results should be evaluated rather carefully. The
grouping according to the geocultural region is probably the least
heterogeneous.

22. The classification of BANKS/GREGG (1965) is questionable, too, as it
does not allow for mixed types of political systems. Nations are
grouped according to the highest factor they are loading on, disregarding other factors. But see chapter 5.1.2.3 for another procedure. As to
a discussion of the concept of polyarchy, cf., e.g., WARE 1974.

23. BUDGE/O'LEARY (1973), for instance, report that the degree of
cross-cutting cleavages in Belfast is much less than in Glasgow. On this,

cf. also the remarks of LIJPHART (1975:97ff.) and chapter 9.

24. As has been noted by various authors before, strictly speaking there are no spurious relationships but only spurious inferences from observed correlations.

25. "In the decade of the 1960s in 87 countries our data show that an estimated one and three-quarter millions people met their death in violent group conflict. More than a million of them died in Vietnam, some 300,000 in Indonesia, more than 150,000 in Nigeria, and about 75,000 in the Congo. In the remaining 83 countries the death toll was 90,000 — a large number but one which gains perspective from the fact that about one and one-quarter million people died in traffic accidents in the developed Western nations during the same decade" (GURR et al., forthcoming).

26. For results referring to the period 1945–65 and sixty-three nations see HUDSON (1970:285). Cf. also TAYLOR/HUDSON (1972: 94–95).

27. Rap Brown notes that violence "is as American as cherry pie."

28. Cf., e.g., NEWTON/ZIMRING (1970) and chapter 3.2. Cf. also KENNETT/ANDERSON (1975) on "the origins of a national dilemma."

29. On the basis of data for the 1960s for eighty-seven states, GURR (1979:73) reaches this conclusion: "The United States is unique among contemporary Western democracies in nurturing an enduring tradition of private political murder in resistance to change. The other side to this example of American exceptionalism is the violence with which authorities respond to some kinds of protest."

30. FEIERABEND/FEIERABEND/NESVOLD (1969:660; for further details see chapter 5.1.1.2) reach a similar conclusion (period 1948–65; N=68 nations): African, Asian, and Latin American countries which are not democracies (and do not belong to traditional African or Asian oligarchies) show a greater amount of political violence than Western nations. Cf. also TAYLOR/HUDSON (1972:94ff.) and GURR/DUVALL (forthcoming) for the 1960s (N=87 countries).

31. Being involved in only 7% of all the strife events, economic groups seem to be of least importance. This may be due in part to the definition chosen ("percentages of events in which initiators acted primarily as members of organizations of workers, the unemployed, craftsmen, traders, or employers," GURR 1969a:585).

32. "Of fifty-six internal wars . . . identified, forty-nine were directed toward overthrowing or drastically modifying political systems; seven were 'private wars,' protracted and widespread violence among members of hostile ethnic or in several cases political groups" (GURR 1970a:177).

33. To quote only two summary findings from this body of work: "Public protest cuts across class lines to mobilize discontented people whatever their social status" (GURR 1979:64). "The supposition that communal groups are the major source of dissidence in the poorer countries while associational groups are most important

(33)

in developed countries proves accurate, to a degree. The archtypical [*sic*] associational groups—economic and open political organizations—were distinctly more important in the most-developed countries, where they mobilized just over 50 percent of all political dissidence compared with only 30 percent in the least-developed countries" (ibid., p. 68) where dissidence was more likely to have its origins with communal and clandestine groups. GURR also notes the protest activities of communal and regional dissidents in Western democracies, including, e.g., the Québecois in Canada, Scottish and Welsh nationalists in Britain, Catholics in Northern Ireland, South Tyrolese people in northern Italy, Bretons in France, "and even advocates of autonomy for Switzerland's Jura region" (ibid., p. 68).

34. The basic procedure to reduce some "noise" in this respect is to relate particular figures to units of population, for example, as GURR does. He touches on the issue raised here in another article: "The essential research question is whether it is more appropriate to measure the *properties* of conflict, such as its duration, intensity, scale, and impact, either in single events or at the national level; or to concentrate on the *incidence* of conflict, i.e., on the number of distinguishable events which occur" (GURR 1974b:250–51). He is critical of the fact that compilers of data handbooks "repeatedly— and mistakenly, I think— . . . treat counts of conflict events as though they were conflict properties" (GURR 1974b:251).

35. If the means and variances are also similar, the evidence would be much more conclusive, of course. For the related strategy of *criterion validation*, see chapter 5.1.1.1.4.

36. Actually, GURR's definition of political violence (see chapter 2.1) provides for this aspect, but his measures are too implicit by far on the issue of coalition formation.

37. Since the analysis of SIMMEL, this is a classic case in conflict analysis. Yet, when studying violent conflicts within nations, the tertius gaudens should be a rarer phenomenon than, for example, in case of international warfare.

38. Mobilization is defined as "the extent of resources under the collective control of the contender; as a process, an increase in the resources or in the degree of collective control (we can call a decline in either one *demobilization*)" (TILLY 1978:54; cf. also chapter 9).

39. Here and elsewhere the concept of state is used as shorthand. However, one should not necessarily treat the state as a monolithic partner in conflicts. The state may disintegrate into factions hostile to each other. The antecedent conditions of revolutions provide a classic example here (cf. chapter 8).

40. There is a rather "profane" reason for this: the state, in general, commands more qualified resources and consequently is able to do more damage to the enemy through the use of troops or internal security forces.

41. In a few cases, however, some doubts remain: when discussing the indicators of facilitation, GURR himself notes (GURR 1968a:1114) that data concerning right extremist parties were not available to the same

extent as those on communist parties. His analysis therefore might be biased as far as the influence of this indicator is concerned. There may also be a flaw in the rationale for the scoring of communist party status. GURR assumes that more factionalized groups provide for "more numerous organizational foci for action" (ibid.), but he tends to overlook the fact that more factionalized parties may be more involved in sectarian warfare against each other and thus destroy some of the potential resources of dissidents.

42. But see JACOBSON (1973a) for a start, albeit insufficient, and COSTNER/SCHOENBERG (1973) for a reanalysis of data first analyzed by OLSEN 1968b (as to the latter author cf. also chapter 5.1.2.3). Cf. also the recent account by SNYDER (1978).

43. Apart from other questions discussed in chapter 9, for example.

44. There is evidence for our argument because the multiple correlation coefficient between these four balance indicators and various forms of strife is higher than the criticized arithmetic combination of these independent variables (GURR 1972a:189). Thus, these variables are not equally well suited to predict political violence.

45. Another issue is whether one ought to use standardized coefficients, as in path analysis, or unstandardized coefficients. The latter would allow for comparisons of strength of relationships in *different* samples, whereas the former (as the scales of measurement have been standardized) facilitate comparison of effects of various independent variables on the same dependent variable within the *same* sample (see SCHOENBERG 1972 for a summary discussion of these issues; see also KIM/MUELLER 1976 and HARGENS 1976 for a diverging point of view).

46. "(1) The true structural equations are actually linear in form; (2) there is no measurement error in any of the independent variables in any given equation and only strictly random error in the measurement of the dependent variable; (3) the expected value of ϵ_i is zero, that is, $E(\epsilon_i)=0$; (4) the independent variables in any equation are uncorrelated in the population with the disturbance term of that equation [cov $(X_i,\epsilon_j)=0$, for $i < j$]; (5) each disturbance term has a constant variance $\sigma_{\epsilon_i}^2$; and (6) sampling has been random" (NAMBOODIRI/CARTER/BLALOCK 1975:445–46).

47. Research reports on cross-national studies of political violence are ofte too brief to clear up the reader's doubts in this respect.

48. "Multicollinearity refers to the intercorrelation of independent variables. It produces high variances (and thus standard errors) for parameter estimates. Thus, although R^2 may be high, the estimated effects of individual independent variables are not sharp, and it is impossible to reject hypotheses concerning them" (HIBBS 1973:47).

49. "Robustness refers to the ability of a statistic to maintain its logically deduced interpretation even when its assumptions have been violated. . . . Robustness studies are actual tests for the interpretations of a statistic" (LABOVITZ 1972:19).

50. In GURR (1979) and GURR et al. (forthcoming) results on N=87 countries are reported, the reason being that "in the 'Civil Strife Events'

(50)

data set, Northern Ireland is treated as an entity separate from Great Britain, while in all other data sets they are reported as a single entity, the United Kingdom" (GURR and Associates 1978:2; see ibid. for a description of these different data sets).

51. There are, however, some objections to be raised against the construction of this variable. As put by WEEDE:

> In the particular index nine standardized indicators are employed of which two or three measure economic discrimination, political discrimination, religious or potentially separatist cleavages, and economic dependence on foreign countries. Yet, the explicative variable strain is constructed as being dependent on protest and violence: 1. Only correlates of internal conflict are accepted as indicators of strain. 2. Likewise the weighting of each facet of strain is determined only ex post facto, after having regressed internal conflict on these four aspects. This procedure increases the degree of statistical explanation but hardly contributes to that of theoretical explanation (WEEDE 1975a:415; my translation).

52. Estimated for 1955–60 on the basis of regressing MPC measures for 1961–65 on population-weighted political violence event data as reported in the *World Handbook of Political and Social Indicators* (TAYLOR/HUDSON 1972), and using these regression equations for "'best' estimated strife scores" of the former period (GURR/ DUVALL 1973:143).

53. See the rationale for using only DIS as balance indicator (GURR/ DUVALL 1973:140–41).

54. For a detailed description of the construction and modifications of the dependent and independent variables as well as the criteria of validity applied (the authors mainly employ criterion validation, thus expecting measures to correlate in the predicted direction in the total sample as well as in subsets, to have the predicted time-dependent relationships, and to have similar effects on the dependent variables), the reader should consult GURR et al. (forthcoming). There will be many more interesting results in this book, especially as to the effects of forming nation clusters (cf. also GURR/ DUVALL, forthcoming).

55. Ordinary Least Squares is not an appropriate technique for estimating blocks of structural equations that incorporate simultaneous interdependencies, since least-squares regression assumes that disturbances are uncorrelated with independent variables. . . . This fundamental assumption is always violated in simultaneous specifications—the jointly determined endogenous variables (Y_m) are by definition of the model correlated with the disturbance terms. Hence, to proceed with Ordinary Least Squares regression would yield incorrect (inconsistent) estimates of the true causal parameters.

An alternative estimation procedure, Instrumental Variables— Two Stage Least Squares (IV–2SLS), resolves this problem in the following way. In the "first stage" the simultaneously deter-

mined, endogenous Y_m variables are regressed on all the predetermined endogenous X and exogenous Z_i which are known or
assumed to be uncorrelated with the disturbances. The fitted
values or "systematic parts" of the Y_m generated by these first-
stage regressions are thus linear functions of ("instrumental")
variables that are uncorrelated with the disturbance terms and,
therefore, are themselves uncorrelated with the disturbances.
Hence the fitted values are used as surrogates for the original Y_m
variables in a "second-stage" regression estimation of the model.
If the theoretical specification of the system incorporates the
required a priori information concerning the equations to be estimated (the identification problem), then these second-stage
regressions are solvable and yield correct (consistent) estimates
of the causal parameters (HIBBS 1973:157).

56. In GURR/DUVALL (1973) there are no causal models as to the determinants of the other dependent variables, although there are some
references of this type in the authors' text (and here as well).

57. See GURR/LICHBACH (1979) for a forecasting of properties of conflict for ten countries (selected out of the eighty-six countries on the
basis of a stratified random sample) for the period 1971–75. Values
predicted on the basis of a model to explain political conflict for
eighty-six nations during 1961–65 (the model is a variant of that
present in GURR/DUVALL 1973) match quite well with the observed
scores.

58. "When one has mistakenly either omitted or included variables in an
equation assumed to capture the true causal structure to Y, or when the
functional form chosen to represent the variables is incorrect, we say
that one has made a specification error" (BOHRNSTEDT/CARTER
1971:128).

59. "'Politimetrics' is the quantitative study of political groups, institutions, nations, and international systems" (GURR 1972a:1).

60. There are a number of related concepts, the most notable perhaps being
William PETY's "political arithmetick" of 1676. For a historical
review of other early efforts, cf. FLORA (1974). ALKER (1975;
cf. also ALMOND 1969:454) has perhaps suggested the most har-
monious term of all, namely "polimetrics." See ibid., pp. 146–47 for
a definition and some further concepts. Cf. also FREY/LAU 1968.

61. LERNER (1958), for example, speaks of "empathy" feelings which are
created in and necessary for the process of modernization (cf. also
LASSWELL/LERNER/MONTGOMERY 1976). Using survey data from
Costa Rica, ARMER/ISAAC (1978:332), however, provide strong
counterevidence against this proposition: "Our evidence suggests that
psychological modernity has, at best, limited influence on social change
through its impact on behavior." There are numerous other studies
employing individual measures of modernity such as those of INKELES
(see INKELES/SMITH 1974 for a summary; cf. also the discussion of
some measurement problems in this kind of studies in KAHL 1970;
ARMER/SCHNAIBERG 1972, 1977; COUGHENOUR/STEPHENSON
1972; COHEN/TILL 1977). Using data from the five-nation study by

(61)

KARSH (1971) RAU (1980) finds that modernity is not unidimensional and accordingly calls for reanalyses of existing data sets.

62. FLORA, however, reports (N=94 nations) that literacy is primary in the *old* developed countries, whereas in the *new* countries there is quite often an *over-urbanization* compared to the degree of literacy reached. "Today the average rate of urbanization in the Islamic countries is five times higher than it was in the Protestant countries around 1850, but the average rate of literacy is still less than one third" (FLORA 1973: 227; cf. also ZAPF/FLORA 1971:73–77). Elsewhere FLORA summarizes his results as suggesting "that the differences in the sequences of various developmental processes in Western Europe are so striking that one should no longer search for a general model. Instead it may be more meaningful to think in terms of different types and to specify the structural and historical context with which they are associated. The fact that LERNER's model does not describe 'the' path of Western modernization . . . implies that one has also to give up the idea of an 'optimal' sequence . . . which would provide a basis for the prediction of instability" (FLORA 1975:92). On the basis of data from 1961 SCHRAMM/RUGGELS (1967) also found a number of results which deviate substantially from LERNER's basic model(s), especially as to the prime influence of urbanization. Furthermore, when controlling for geocultural regions, additional differences emerge. The authors also disagree on the threshold values given by LERNER in his theory. For more differentiated considerations, however, cf. also LERNER (e.g., 1957:269).

63. However, see WINHAM (1970) for a study of developmental processes in the United States using longitudinal data (1790–1960). His results are basically in accord with LERNER's writings, but see also MARQUETTE (1974, 1976).

64. "In the overall process of development, the expansion of political participation can conceivably be: (a) a primary goal of the political elites, social forces, and individuals involved in the process; (b) a means by which elites, groups, and individuals achieve other goals that they value highly; or (c) a by-product or consequence of the achievement of other goals, either by societies as a whole, or by elites, groups, and individuals within those societies. Or, and we do not mean to be facetious, it could also quite conceivably be none of the above" (HUNTINGTON/ NELSON 1976:40).

65. "Whichever the sophistication, whatever the gains in specification about subsystems, contemporary convergence theorists argue in effect the relatedness of four revolutions which come to engulf the globe. These are the industrial, the democratic, the integrative eventuating in a flexible status system, and the cultural, where a kind of Protestant Reformation fall-out comes to rationalize all symbolic universes. The detail has changed since the 19th century but the essence has not; for the sum of these four revolutions is still the universal endproduct of a movement from status to contract, or from *Gemeinschaft* to *Gesellschaft*" (BAUM 1974:226).

66. "Modernization is [generally characterized as] a revolutionary, complex, systemic, global, lengthy, phased, homogenizing, irreversible and progressive process" (abridged quotation on the basis of HUNTINGTON 1971b:288–90).

67. For an interesting summary sketch of historical observations contrary to much written in modernization studies on the United States, the United Kingdom and Germany, see WEHLER (1975:31–33).

68. For some analytical guidelines, see, e.g., VERBA (1971:308).

69. "The picture is less than complete if one treats developing countries as isolated and autonomous, without reference to foreign military assistance, covert external political intervention and overt military invasion, the power of multinational corporations over the political and economic processes of third-world countries, dependency relationships more generally, and the manipulation of the international monetary system and trade relationships to favor the interests of the wealthy and powerful nations" (KESSELMAN 1973:149).

70. Cf. also KOBRIN (1976) for much more complicated quantitative cross-national results as to the impact of direct foreign investment on industrialization and social change, as well as the perspectives drawn by PORTES (1976:80–82).

71. The Yale Dependency Project (Director: Bruce RUSSETT) currently in progress will provide more rigorous findings. Cf. also the references and the caveats in note 204.

72. See also the scalogram analysis of NESVOLD (1969) which leads to comparable results, except for the eleven communist countries in the sample. Concerning the procedure followed by the FEIERABENDs, however, the question may be raised as to whether the presentation of a scale along which the events had to be placed might have caused some artifacts of measurement.

73. Here with NESVOLD/HOOLE/LITELL.

74. Actually, numerator and denominator have been changed. When using the explicit formula (given in LERNER 1963:333, and, in fact, based on William JAMES, 1890), there are no divergences.

75. Somewhat earlier, STALEY used the term: a "revolution of rising expectations" (STALEY 1954:15–21). There is good reason, however, for considerably divergent predictions (cf. also chapter 5.1.2.2). "The effect of these processes of social change is that while there are demands, sometimes even very strong ones, even in remote rural areas, for material improvements, for consumer goods, and for jobs, these demands often occur within a still viable traditional context in which provision of a minimum of economic, social, and psychological security dampens whatever frustrations unfulfilled demands generate" (OBERSCHALL 1969:9; cf. also MIGDAL 1974). Other authors such as FREY (1973:387) point out that one may speak of a "revolution of rising expectations or frustrations" only with respect to members of the elites and not as bearing on the masses in general.

76. OLSEN (1968b:705), e.g., reports an r=.83 for over one hundred countries (year: 1960).

77. There is additional empirical evidence for our argument from a study of forty-nine poor countries carried out by DELACROIX/RAGIN (1978). Contrary to the theory proposed by INKELES/SMITH (1974) and in line with the critique of modernization theory and research by PORTES (1973; 1976), they argue that "the school must have a positive effect on development and exposure to the Western cinema a negative one" (DELACROIX/RAGIN 1978:131). For INKELES/ SMITH (1974) the "school and the mass media create modern individuals who staff the modern institutions that are necessary for economic growth" (DELACROIX/RAGIN 1978:125). PORTES, on the other hand, stresses that modernizing forces exogenic to a society are largely detrimental to economic development, a proposition borne out by the analysis of DELACROIX/RAGIN. Their study is, of course, open to criticism because many other possible explanatory variables have not been controlled for. Consequently their conclusions go much beyond the evidence currently provided: "The advancement of the culturally diverse countries of the Third World does not require the uniform establishment of modernizing institutions aimed at the eradication of traditional mentalities. A central part of the modernization process entails, instead, the selection of the proper weapons from an arsenal that includes 'traditional' ideologies (for example, the cult of the emperor), 'modern' ones (for example, Marxist-Leninism), as well as many syncretic ones (for example, Arab socialism)" (ibid., p. 147). In any case, the cinema should be even less used as an indicator of want satisfaction than the radio.
78. In grouping nations according to their level of modernity, a rather arbitrary procedure has been followed: the twenty-four nations with the highest modernity scores are contrasted with those with the lowest scores. The remainder are summed up in the middle category.
79. There are, however, several sociopsychological experiments which demonstrate a positive linear relationship between attack and aggressive behavior (e.g., KNOTT/DROST 1972) and not the curvilinear relationship predicted by BUSS (1961:29). In addition, BUSS has not specified the coordinates of the turning point.
80. WALTON (1965) reports a large difference between η (.72) and r (.41), quoted in FEIERABEND/NESVOLD/FEIERABEND (1970:113).
81. The level of coerciveness in part predetermines the probability of fluctuations occurring. Thus, these two independent variables are more strongly interrelated than would be desirable for more reliable parameter estimation.
82. For an exception see FEIERABEND/FEIERABEND/NESVOLD (1973:422) where the authors report, for example, that only polyarchic political systems (see BANKS/GREGG 1965) show a negative relationship with political instability (r=-.48). When using CUTRIGHT's index of political development (CUTRIGHT 1963; see also chapter 5.1.2.3) they find a correlation of r=-.41.
83. Occasionally (see, e.g., FEIERABEND/FEIERABEND/NESVOLD 1973:423) there are references to variables that are theoretically more intriguing and prove powerful predictors in other studies as well. For

example, "there is a correlation of .56 between unrest and minority
conflict in the sample of twenty-five states" (ibid.). Finally, it should
be mentioned that the FEIERABENDs relate their political violence
data to several other variables, such as need achievement (actually,
increases in the level of need achievement between 1925 and 1950
prove a better predictor of political violence during 1948–54, r=.53),
homicide, and suicide (FEIERABEND/FEIERABEND/NESVOLD/
JAGGAR 1971). However, these variables rarely seem to touch upon
those theories that prove to be more important in many other studies
on political violence.

84. As to the quality of the FEIERABEND data, however, see the results
of HAZLEWOOD/WEST (1974) who report relatively low correlations
between the RUMMEL/TANTER data (1955–60) and the FEIERA-
BEND data for twenty Latin American countries and higher correlations between the RUMMEL/TANTER data and BANKS's data set.
Cf. also chapter 5.1.3.

85. Some of the definitional ambiguities in HIBBS's study are brought up in
the critique of SMALDONE: HIBBS's "selection of certain domestic
event variables as measures of mass political violence is questionable.
For example, the inclusion of *nonviolent* antigovernment demonstrations as an indicator of political violence is hardly appropriate. Additionally, assassinations are also dubious measures of *mass* political
violence, especially when the assassination of opposition leaders and
newspaper editors is subsumed in the definition of *antisystem* behavior.
The death of persons in opposition is more likely to be regime-inspired,
and more accurately indexes elite repression. Riots are also questionable indicators of mass political violence, unless they are specifically
directed against the incumbent authorities. It is possible, for instance,
that rioting may be more a measure of ethnic or sectarian conflict than
antisystem violence" (SMALDONE 1976:153–54). Such ambiguities
are likely to be found in almost any cross-national study on political
violence (cf. throughout this study).

86. These results seem to parallel in part those DORAN reports, after
having carried out factor analyses of numerous conflict variables (using
the conflict variables of the FEIERABENDs which are more comprehensive than those of RUMMEL and TANTER [cf. chapter 5.1.1.1.2.1]
and employing regional data sources, namely the *Hispanic American
Report* and the Spanish-language newspapers *Vision* and *Tiempo*) for
eight Caribbean countries during 1948–64 (Costa Rica, Dominican
Republic, El Salvador, Guatemala, Haiti, Honduras, Nicaragua, and
Panama). DORAN designates these nations as members of the "American sphere of influence" which is determined through the techniques
of hierarchical clustering and factor analysis:

> Solid support for the cyclical contagion hypothesis emerges from
> this analysis. Large scale violence first arises (factor III) as spon-
> taneous communal insurrections or riots. It is then transformed
> into elite challenges to establishment rule associated with the
> election process (factor IV), possibly involving succession crises,

(86)

alleged irregularities, and corruption. In the following year
violence shifts to the mass level (factor V) in the form of organized strikes and channeled protest. The pattern of this instability does not follow the simple "trickle-down" path from elite
to mass. Instead, the original stimulus seems to arise in communal
revolt or rebellion. When opposed by governmental sanction,
violence appears to be adopted by members of the elite who in
turn may have a hand in subsequent organized mass unrest.

No inevitability is attached to these cycles of violence. Nonetheless the consistency of the patterns is undeniable. The first
begins in 1949 and ends in 1951; the second begins in 1955 and
stretches over a four-year period with a slightly longer elite phase
in the years 1956–1957. But violence in the 1960s departs completely from these patterns (DORAN 1976:38–39).

This appears due in part to the variety of effects triggered by the Cuban
Revolution. The factor structure emerging in this study bears some
resemblance to that in the analyses of RUMMEL and TANTER, but
also to those carried out by MORRISON/STEVENSON for Africa
(see chapter 5.1.1.1.2.1 for details): "instability within the American
sphere of influence appears to include turmoil and subversion, dimensions common to other regions and the system as a whole. Additionally,
sphere countries display communal, elite, and mass conflict forms
paired with peculiar combinations of government sanctions best
described as modalities of repression. A significant point is that these
factors represent a fragmentation of the 'revolution' dimension
observed at the global level, a dimension which is otherwise missing
from this analysis" (DORAN 1976:36).

87. TILLY et al., however, come up with a somewhat different result:
repression "works in the short run. It works even better in the long
run: so far as we can tell, it is not true that a population beset by consistent tyranny eventually becomes so frustrated that it will do anything to throw off the yoke; in fact, repressed populations demobilize,
work through the approved channels of collective action, and seek non-
collective means of accomplishing their ends" (TILLY et al. 1975:285).
However, there are other results in this study (see chapter 5.1.2.5)
which are more in line with the interpretation of HIBBS. But see also
WEEDE (1977c:passim) who performs a reanalysis of the HIBBS data,
regroups the data into different periods of observation, and reports
results more in favor of the TILLY et al. position. The strategy of disaggregation is also employed by SANDERS (1978:126) who reports
"several significant regional effects . . . which HIBBS' analysis fails to
specify." Also he presents results not in accord with the relationships
between HIBBS's four ultimate dependent variables.

88. The theoretical rationale given reads: "The fewer the parties and the
older they are, the more adaptable they must be as political institutions, and the more adaptable the party system as a whole must be to
changing conditions" (HIBBS 1973:99). There is, however, the possi-

bility of a curvilinear relationship as well. For example, see the results in GURR (1974a). The theoretical justifications for using direct taxes and union membership as indicators of political institutionalization (the latter is familiar from GURR's studies) are that direct taxes are much more difficult to collect than indirect ones and that a high degree of union membership stands for the political representation of certain demands and thus exerts a negative impact on the degree of political violence.

89. GEERTZ suggests this explanation: "it is the very process of the formation of sovereign civil state that, among other things, stimulates sentiments of parochialism, communalism, racialism, and so on, because it introduces into society a valuable new prize over which to fight and a frightening new force with which to contend" (GEERTZ 1963:120).

90. However, Communist party membership has no effect on internal war, for which HIBBS suggests this explanation: "Although large Communist parties may advocate revolutionary change, they nevertheless do not consistently engage in activities that seriously and directly threaten the structure of the existing political system. This probably reflects the 'parliamentary mentality' that characterizes, with some significant exceptions, large, mass-based parties on the radical left" (HIBBS 1973:192 omitting the italics in original). The reactions of the communist party and the communist union in France to the May 1968 revolt and the opposition of the communist party in Bolivia to the activities of Ché GUEVARA are examples given by HIBBS. There is, of course, a great danger of premature generalization of such findings, e.g., as far as the alleged "Euro-communism" is concerned. For a discussion of the latter phenomenon, see BLACKMER/TARROW (1975).

91. In HIBBS's comparative analyses (as well as in GURR's) political movements of the extreme right were not considered.

92. The study of JACOBSON (1973a) is an example of the errors which occur when rather unrelated indicators are summed up in one index (for more details cf. chapter 5.1.2.4).

93. Even when defining the dependent variable, GURR chooses the more complex alternative. Cf. the following operationalizations: "To obtain combined magnitude scores for turmoil, conspiracy, internal war, and all strife, the three component logged scores were added, divided by eight to obtain their eighth root, and the anti-log used as the polity magnitude-of-strife score" (GURR 1968a:1109). "The (natural) logarithm of the sum of the events distinguishing each dimension is used as the operational measure of Collective Protest and Internal War" (HIBBS 1973:16).

94. As WEEDE (1977c) has discovered, there are, starting from the premises of HIBBS, several alternative causal models which can be at least partially confirmed with the data available.

95. WELFLING comes up with this result: "the best African equations . . . suggest that past rebellion may reduce future turmoil, indicating an additional failing of the GURR-DUVALL model, which treats each form of conflict as a separate and unrelated phenomenon" (WELFLING 1975:887).

(96)

96. A similar relationship exists between the level of technological development (measured through the BERRY index, 1960) and political violence (ADAMS 1970:136).
97. HIBBS (1973:193) points out, however, that time-series data are needed for an adequate evaluation of the BENJAMIN/KAUTSKY hypothesis.
98. Yet RUMMEL (1969) maintains that economic development and political violence are not related at all since they load on different dimensions when jointly factor analyzed. On the basis of regression results HUDSON (1971; period 1948–65) draws a similar conclusion. Both studies are also cited in HIBBS (1973:24).
99. As PINARD (1967) is able to show in a summary of various studies, members of the lower social strata join new social movements only after these movements have attained a certain degree of publicity, whereas members of the middle strata, having more resources at hand, are much more likely to join at an earlier point of time. Yet, social movement activities are a different (though sometimes overlapping) form of collective behavior than acts of political violence.
100. After all, for the "first generation migrant" *actual* personal living standards in the city may still be higher than in the countryside.
101. Cf. also the analysis in HUNTINGTON (1968:278–83).
102. One also should be aware of the possibility that migrants move back to their village. However, the more prestigious the city is, the less likely this becomes. Furthermore, one must control for chances of upward social mobility if the urbanization → alienation → radicalization hypothesis is to be adequately evaluated.
103. But consider the following remark of CORNELIUS summarizing his study of the "migrant poor in Mexico City": "Of far greater potential importance as a source of opposition to the regime are the more highly educated, city-born off-spring of migrants and native-born city dwellers in general, who may even find themselves at a disadvantage vis-à-vis recent migrants in competition for certain kinds of jobs" (CORNELIUS 1975:229). Fear of the power of local landlords or of the repressive capacities of the police, in many instances, may contribute to the low level of participation in activities of violent political protest. In Mexico City, however, different mechanisms seem to work, the most important, according to CORNELIUS, being the belief and experience that nonviolent forms of raising demands on behalf of the poor in general lead to "successful" outcomes (but cf. also the more critical issues raised in chapter 6.3.4.1).
104. As do PARVIN (1973) for twenty-six nations (dependent variable: deaths resulting from domestic group violence; no period specified) and MORA Y ARAUJO (1972:230) for one hundred nations (1948–62; FEIERABEND/FEIERABEND data).
105. However, collective violence is somewhat more generally defined by TILLY than in this study (cf. chapter 2.1).
106. For a discussion of various measures of urban population density and results as to various dependent variables, see CARNAHAN/GUEST/GALLE 1974; cf. also BOOTH 1975; 1976. Overviews of the literature

can be found in FISCHER et al. 1975, FRIEDMAN 1975, and in *The American Behavioral Scientist* 18, no. 6 (July–August 1975); FISCHER (1976:154–69); BAUM/EPSTEIN 1978; and, mainly with respect to international conflicts, in CHOUCRI 1974.

107. Cf. the perceptive analysis of RAPOPORT who defines crowding as "excessively high affective density, i.e., undesirably high perceived density, when the various mechanisms for controlling unwanted interaction with other people are no longer working. . . ." (RAPOPORT 1975:153).

108. Interestingly, WELCH/BOOTH found in another study (1975) that various crowding conditions lose their predictive power once the absolute number of blacks has been taken into account (676 U.S. cities; period: 1961–68).

109. The last terms in this quotation are probably somewhat too strongly worded, at least in the context of the present discussion.

110. Depending, of course, on the content of the media, another variable which should be considered.

111. In the latter case, however, some circular reasoning is introduced, as the indexes used also include indicators for the educational sector.

112. HUNTINGTON appears to make a correct prediction in stating that "the relation between the rate of economic growth and political instability varies with the level of economic development." When specifying his hypothesis, however, he seems to overdraw the point. At least there is no sufficient evidence for his hypothesis that "at low levels [of economic development] a positive relation exists, at medium levels no significant relation, and at high levels a negative relationship" (HUNTINGTON 1968:53). The evidence rather seems to suggest that there is a greater probability of a positive relationship between socioeconomic rate of change and political violence at a *medium* level of economic development, the fate of the government of the Shah of Iran providing a recent example here.

113. Which at times is superficially equated with political performance. On the latter see chapter 6.3.2.

114. "Thus we encounter the paradox that the more committed the society and the regime are to the normal politics of persuasion and bargaining, the more vulnerable they are to short-term, tactically skillful exployment of violent or otherwise coercive direct action" (WOLFINGER et al. 1976:575–76). "The typical democracy in the 1960s had approximately twice the extent [man-days of participation] of conflict as the typical autocracy, but only half the rate of conflict deaths. The crux of the matter is that peaceful protest is tolerated in democracies and serious rebellion is uncommon. In the autocracies, conflict is more likely to be manifest in violent forms, including rebellion, and the authorities use greater force to suppress it" (GURR 1979:61). "Both democratic and autocratic governments have the institutional means to 'deliver' reforms, if and when they make the commitment to do so. None of these conditions is likely to be found in the typical underdeveloped, elitist country. . . . Their rulers . . . often see conflict as a zero-sum game in which the only victory is total political victory"

(114)

(ibid., p. 71). Finally, "conflict was distinctly more brutal and one-sided in autocratic regimes, where dissidents made up 85 percent of the fatalities, than in the democratic regimes [59 percent]. There was a similar disparity between the highly developed countries and the moderately developed ones. Since the armies and police forces of all these groups of countries are relatively large and well-equipped, the differences are almost surely attributable to policies of restraint on the part of the authorities of the developed democracies—restraint that has its counterpart in the preference of dissidents in these countries for protest over rebellion" (GURR et al., forthcoming).

115. See the reference in chapter 5.1.1.1.2.6. Whereas in the study of BANKS/GREGG the political systems of nations were classified according to the factor with the highest loadings of variables, i.e., on the basis of dichotomies (for example, either being a polyarchy or not), the coding procedures of GURR allow for multidimensional classifications of characteristics of political systems.

116. Referring to a "state . . . which has minimal functions, an uninstitution-alized pattern of political competition, and executive leaders constantly imperiled by rival leaders" (GURR 1974a:1487; cf. HUNTINGTON's "praetorian polities," chapter 7.2.3).

117. "1. The political prerequisite of economic development; 2. the politics typical of industrial society; 3. political modernization; 4. the operation of a nation-state; 5. administrative and legal development; 6. mass mobilization and participation; 7. building of democracy; 8. stability and orderly change; 9. mobilization and power; 10. one aspect of a multi-dimensional process of social change" (PYE 1966:33–45). Cf. also the differentiations in HUNTINGTON/DOMÍNGUEZ (1975:3–5).

118. Cf. also CAMERON (1974) who criticizes that political factors have not been considered in the processes of social mobilization: "mobilization is not simply socially determined but, rather, the result of policy conflict" (CAMERON 1974:146). In this perspective the impact of mobilizing groups, parties, and elites (cf., e.g., the results in COULTER 1971–72:45, 61, and passim) is stressed (cf. also chapter 9 and NETTL 1967).

119. There is, of course, another perhaps more telling reason for these developments, i.e., the evolutionary tradition of European and American social philosophy in the nineteenth century (cf. NISBET 1969 for a broad overview covering periods as early as that of classical Greece).

120. "American political scientists may have avoided external influences because they themselves were, in some measure, one of those influences. Third World radical theorists may have exaggerated the role of external influences, on the other hand, in order to rationalize and justify their own failures to develop their societies" (HUNTINGTON/DOMÍNGUEZ 1975:94). For a critique of the literature on political development with respect to Latin America see, e.g., O'DONNELL (1973). For a critique and extension of O'DONNELL's perspective see COLLIER (1978a).

121. More recently there seem to have been some changes. One of the particularly important research questions in this respect is: "To what

extent, for instance, does the probable impact of the foreign versus domestic environment vary inversely with political participation, institutionalization, and integration? In the early 1970s these were the type of question toward which students of political development were beginning to turn" (HUNTINGTON/DOMÍNGUEZ 1975:94). As to HUNTINGTON's approach referred to in this quotation, cf. chapter 5.1.2.4.

122. Measured according to FLANIGAN/FOGELMAN who distinguish four aspects: "(1) a democratically elected chief executive (2) universal suffrage (3) the absence of political suppression (4) political competition between parties" (PRIDE 1970:687).

122a. For a new index of political democracy derived from confirmatory factor analysis that has the advantages of greater reliability, sample size (N=113 and 123), and temporal coverage (1960 and 1965) than other indexes, see BOLLEN (1980).

123. As put by a leading scholar in the field:

> The European sequence simply cannot be repated in the newest
> nations; the new nation-builders have to start out from funda-
> mentally different conditions, they face an entirely different
> world. But they can learn to develop new combinations of
> policies from a detailed analysis of the many facets of the Euro-
> pean experiences of state-building and national consolidation.
> They may learn more from the smaller countries than from the
> large, more from the multiculturally consociational polities than
> from the homogeneous dynastic states, more from the European
> latecomers than from the old established nations: what is impor-
> tant is that these experiences be sifted and evaluated, not just
> case by case, but within an effort of cross-regional systematiza-
> tion (ROKKAN 1975:600).

124. See also COULTER (1975) who establishes quantitative relationships between social mobilization and liberal democracy both on the global level and on more regional levels. Yet his results may be affected by multicollinearity.

125. Measured through an "eight-point Index of Democracy based on combinations of four basic characteristics of the political system: form of selection of the chief executive; political competition; extent of suffrage; and degree of political suppression" (FLANIGAN/FOGEL-MAN 1970:15).

126. For similar results cf. WILEY (1967).

127. The reaction of the French Communist Party to the rebellion of May 1968 provides a good example. See also note 90.

128. The assumption being that potential protest is greater when there are several factions in communist party organizations and not just one. But cf. also the critique in note 41.

129. The rationale is that government performance and social welfare might reduce the costs created by rapid social mobilization. GURR et al. (forthcoming) report consistently negative relations when government spending as a percentage of GNP is correlated with political violence. After grouping nations together, however, the negative relationship

(129)

remains only in centrist nations (it even increases to –.39). A positive relation holds for Latin countries (.51), a modestly positive one for neocolonial, and a weakly negative one for Euro-modern nations. DUFF/McCAMANT (1976:71) report a correlation of r=.60 (–.37) between welfare minus social mobilization and political violence (standardized indexes for armed and unarmed forms of political violence were added up, weighting the former by 1.5) for twenty Latin American states during 1960–70 (1950–60). Compared with the study of HIBBS, three points of their study are worth noting here: their indicators of welfare (GNP per capita, literacy, calorie consumption, medical doctors and hospital beds per 10,000, with the first indicator treated as equivalent to the other three) to a considerable extent tap other aspects like economic development as well. They probably also show high intercorrelations with the indicators of social mobilization (newsprint per capita, radios per 1,000, televisions per 1,000, percent urban) calling into question the validity of the reported relationship. Moreover, the independent variable, the interaction term, is not constructed as a quotient, but rather as a difference (thus, in a stricter sense, being no interaction term at all). These points of criticism also bear on the other results of DUFF/McCAMANT referred to in this chapter. Some of their results, nevertheless, sound plausible. For example: "In 1955 Cuba's level of social mobilization was far higher than its welfare relative to all other Latin American countries, and mobilization continued to change faster than did welfare in the 1950s" (DUFF/McCAMANT 1976:94). One should not, however, use this finding as a direct explanation of the Cuban Revolution at the end of the 1950s (cf. also chapter 8.4). Yet, it is a noteworthy result.

130. The basic imbalance between demands (measured as rate of population change and change of numbers of radio receivers) and *capacity* or *support* of a regime (government stability; deaths due to domestic group violence [the choice of this indicator, however, leads to circular reasoning]; executive turnovers) is also employed in JACOBSON's path model (1973a; N=75 nations). He does not, however, use an interaction formulation when relating demands and capacity (or support) to the dependent variables (GURR's civil strife variables, 1961–65). Nevertheless, his results are consistent with prevalent theoretical reasoning: support of a regime decreases the amount of political violence, demands increase it. Altogether, only one third of the variance is explained in JACOBSON's path model (41% in the case of conspiracy). Yet, the amount of variance explained increases if economic development is controlled for. It should be stressed, however, that the study of JACOBSON (1973a) provides a good example of how *not* to manipulate indicators. Apart from the already criticized operationalization of support, one must point out that central government spending as a percentage of GNP is a dubious indicator of the performance dimension.

131. Measured through a technique used by CUTRIGHT (1963), i.e., by regressing the score of the particular sector on those of the other sectors. The size and the sign of the residuals provide information as to the type of imbalance.

132. Only when the imbalances among the political, the economic, the educational, the welfare, and the communication sectors (measured largely for the end of the 1950s and the early 1960s) are taken together ("total magnitude of imbalance"), does a notable relationship emerge (r=.55); however, it is inflated due to the intercorrelations of the independent variables (R=.18; ibid., p. 50).

133. Once again it seems noteworthy that similar indicators are chosen for indexing opposite theoretical assumptions. For example, in opposition to other authors and in agreement with GURR, DUFF/McCAMANT consider increases in education as an indicator of want satisfaction and not of want generation and they report consistently low negative relations to political violence when education (percentage of children in schools) is relatively higher than the degree of mobilization (DUFF/McCAMANT 1976:123). Economic development should, however, be an important third variable here.

134. But cf. also some of the works in HEINTZ (1972) which are, however, quite often too abstract. Rather few indicators are taken into consideration when measuring the theoretical constructs in question.

135. This sense of personal cultural identity might be even further strengthened through *rapid centralization*, a variable that should be separated from social mobilization for analytical and perhaps empirical reasons (cf. also the analysis of "social cleavages and partisan conflict" in Switzerland by KERR 1974).

136. Cf. also the results of INGLEHART/WOODWARD (1967–68; N=81 nations) which also lend some indirect support to DEUTSCH's hypothesis.

137. In this context GURR has suggested an interesting hypothesis: "It is highly likely that increases in economic well-being and popular political participation for majority groups in European nations exacerbate the hostilities of regional and ethnic minorities that do not have what they regard as a fair share of those benefits" (GURR 1969a:587).

138. Contrary to HIBBS, one may also argue that the indicator "union membership as a percentage of the non-agricultural work force" could be used to index political participation instead of political institutionalization.

139. Accordingly, the critique of HAGOPIAN does not hit the mark: "the very concept of participation implied in HUNTINGTON's analysis is a rather weak one. Is the closeness of the Soviet citizen to the apparatus of party and state really participation or regimentation? Or is there no distinction between the two?" (HAGOPIAN 1974:63). In HUNTINGTON/NELSON (1976) political participation is explicitly dealt with, but somewhat differently than in HUNTINGTON's earlier formulation (1968).

140. This is an important distinction (or rather assumption) not made by the FEIERABENDs in their inductive proceeding. Cf. the criticism in chapter 5.1.1.2.3.

141. "Social mobilization involves changes in the aspirations of individuals, groups, and societies; economic development involves changes in their capabilities. Modernization requires both" (HUNTINGTON 1968:34).

(142)

142. The latter opinion is shared by several other prominent social scientists who are more strongly influenced by MARXist positions (such as MOORE 1966; cf. chapters 8.4.3 and 9).

143. For a critique of HUNTINGTON's analysis of corruption, the reader is referred to AKE (1974). Apparently the links between modernization and corruption are not yet sufficiently specified by HUNTINGTON. Nevertheless, he develops a number of hypotheses about the determinants and consequences of corruption (see HUNTINGTON 1968: 59–71) which are worth testing on a systematic cross-national basis. Cf. also the discussion and the references in chapter 7.2.3.

144. Critics (cf. RIGGS 1967:335) have, however, objected that HUNTINGTON does not specify the degree of political decay.

145. However, if one looks at the subsequently described indicators HUNTINGTON suggests as indexing his institutionalization concept, KESSELMAN's objections are not necessarily justified.

146. At another place a general explanation is suggested: "Economic development thus may produce greater pressures and stimuli to participate in politics but may also, other things being equal, lessen the incentive to do so by opening up more appealing opportunities to participate in other things" (HUNTINGTON/DOMÍNGUEZ 1975:43). See also HUNTINGTON/NELSON (1976:79–115).

147. "The percentage of economically active males engaged in nonagricultural occupations; the percentage of urban population . . . ; the extent of mass communications . . . and the percentage of the population enrolled in higher education" (SCHNEIDER/SCHNEIDER 1971:75).

148. Index formed of four subindexes measuring the adaptability, coherence, legitimacy, and complexity of political institutions.

149. WEEDE (1977b:662) also notes that in using the z-transformation for building the interaction term, social mobilization/economic development, SCHNEIDER/SCHNEIDER (1971) have implied a comparison with other countries as to the relative position of each country. However, this seems to be neither justified on the basis of HUNTINGTON's writing nor explained by the authors.

150. However, these opportunities are only extremely indirectly measured through the degree of urbanization and the proportion of the male working population in nonagricultural occupations. As SANDERS himself notes, no other data on mobility were available on a broad cross-national basis, so these fairly indirect measures had to be relied on. HUNTINGTON's theoretical conceptualization is definitely not captured by these operationalizations.

151. Measured additively on the basis of age of current institutional form, age of current constitutional form, number of years since independence, number of years since the beginning of the period of consolidation of modernizing leadership.

152. The periodization of the last mentioned indicator is not very convincing, however.

153. As HUNTINGTON has used ambiguous formulations, there is even some evidence for such an interpretation. Thus, HUNTINGTON writes: "Institutions are stable, valued, recurring *patterns of behavior*" (HUNTINGTON 1965:394; italics added).
154. Percentage of the labor force employed in nonagricultural activities, GNP per capita, literacy, percentage of population living in cities over 20,000, newspaper circulation per 1,000 population.
155. Here used as representing HUNTINGTON's concept of political institutionalization and measured as interest articulation by political parties, current status of the legislature, character of the bureaucracy, vertical power distribution, horizontal power distribution (all five to measure complexity), interest articulation by anomic groups, political participation of the military, role of police (all three to measure autonomy), governmental stability, stability of the party system (both to measure adaptability), political enculturation, and sectionalism (both to measure coherence). The indicators of political development (political institutionalization) are drawn from BANKS/TEXTOR (1963) and based largely on estimates.
156. School enrollment per capita, literacy rate, radios per capita, and newspaper circulation per capita, all measured in terms of annual percentage change, 1955–66.
157. Rather insufficiently indexed through administrative efficiency, legislative effectiveness, the age of national political institutions and, introducing a facet of the dependent variable and thus some circularity into the argument, military intervention.
158. Riots, protest demonstrations, antigovernment demonstrations, general strikes, assassinations, guerrilla warfare, armed attacks, coups d'état, and revolutions were factor-analyzed, leading to the usual (cf. chapter 5.1.1.1.2.1) first two factors, collective protest and internal war, accounting for 33.6% and 24.4% of the explained variance, and to the third factor, power transfers, with the high loading variables coups and revolutions (explained variance=24.4%).
159. The result of their multivariate analysis reads: "Violence increases when economic growth fails to keep up with the change in social mobilization, where the military is not institutionalized, and where primary education does not match the demand for it" (DUFF/McCAMANT 1976:127). Comparable results (but reverse signs, with subordination of the military under civil leadership as the most important, are found, if the expenditures for education per capita as second most important, and the interaction term as the third most important) are found, if the dependent variable is social cohesion. The authors use social cohesion as a summary notion for political violence and repression (suspension of constitutional rights; arrests, exiles, and executions; restrictions on political parties; censorship of the media). In many instances, repression is determined by the same variables as political violence. In the final multiple regression analysis, spending on education and institutionalization are found to be the most important (and at the same time

(159)

inhibiting) conditions of repression. Thus, there are once again some findings in the study of DUFF/McCAMANT which provide evidence as to the theoretical conceptualization of HUNTINGTON. In his terminology political systems with low cohesion were to be called praetorian states (cf. chapter 7.2.3).

160. Two referring to the agricultural component, namely percentage of farmers owning 50% of the land and the Gini index of land tenure inequality taken from TAYLOR/HUDSON 1972 and combined into one index (cf. RUHL 1975:10 for details), and one referring to the nonagricultural component, namely inequality in income distribution.

161. In RUHL's study, percent urban, percent literate over fifteen years of age, percent in nonagricultural occupations, number of university students per 100,000 population, mean of radio and newspaper distribution per 1,000, using the loadings of these indicators on a single unrotated factor for determining their individual weights.

162. Again somewhat insufficiently measured through only four indicators: legislative effectiveness, percent presidential vote going to parties active prior to 1945, number of regular executive transfers minus number of irregular transfers (1948–59), number of full years from 1933 through 1959 during which a constitutionally elected and constitutionally acting chief executive was in office. These indicators are said to capture the adaptability, autonomy, and coherence of institutionalization, while complexity has not been measured at all.

163. E.g., WAYMAN uses urbanization and literacy in a combined index to measure "urban-rural divisions."

164. Indexed in terms of urbanization, education, and mass media exposure.

165. Using marker variables which load high on one of the four dimensions of institutionalization factored out by WELFLING (1973): stable interactions, adaptability, boundary, and scope.

166. However, the question may be raised whether the impact of ethnolinguistic fractionalization has been adequately captured by HIBBS who maintains that "the larger the number of groups and the smaller the proportion of the total population in each of them, the more fractionated or differentiated is the population" (HIBBS 1973:68) or whether in *some cases* it is not so much the sheer number of groups, but rather a *special combination* of the number of groups multiplied by population size which accounts best for the political violence and political instability observed. We would hypothesize that this is true at least in several of the more spectacular current instances of political violence. After all, people seem to react to perceived threats, and these very well might be related in some curvilinear way to the number of ethnolinguistic groups, reaching perhaps the maximum value if only two to four groups are competing for dominance (or, more generally, for societal goods).

167. A discussion showing many parallels to ours here is found in a recent article by SNYDER 1976.

168. For other than cross-national evidence see chapter 5.3.2.

169. Only in the case of political discriminations do GURR/DUVALL (1973:167) find a consistent negative effect on the extent of political

violence, while economic discriminations contribute to violent conflict if there are opportunities for political activity.

170. "The joint effects, therefore, of greater pluralism, centralization and coercive potential exacerbate, rather than inhibit, the incidence of both communal and elite instability" (MORRISON/STEVENSON 1972a: 924; cf. also note 135).

171. TERRELL (1971) found (N=75 nations) that political violence in the past (turmoil, internal war; cf. TANTER in chapter 5.1.1.1.2.1; period: 1955–60) is only weakly related to coercion (indicators: defense expenditure as a percentage of GNP; percent of population under arms; early 1960s) in a later period, thus suggesting that other, probably international factors influence the coercive potential much more strongly. He also found that systemic frustration, as operationalized by the FEIERABENDs, is only weakly related to political violence (r=.18 for turmoil, .42 for internal war).

172. BWY (1968b), for example, finds (N=20 Latin American countries) no relationship between coercion (defense spending as percentage of GNP) and organized political violence (see Table 5.3). (The curvilinear relationship he reports for anomic violence [again see Table 5.3] is not corroborated in the analysis of political violence in twenty Latin American countries between 1950 and 1970 by DUFF/McCAMANT 1976:121–22, who use defense expenditure and strength of military personnel as indicators.) Yet, a linear relationship (r=.416) is found if organized violence (1958–60) is correlated with change in defense expenditures (1958–63). However, BWY himself has interpreted the data in a rather speculative manner (SNOW 1968; WEST 1973:73ff.).

In a further work BWY (1968a) studies forms of political violence in twenty-one provinces in Brazil and Cuba (1956–59 and 1960–64) as well as in the Dominican Republic and Panama (1958–61 and 1962–66). The sample is highly biased since there are thirteen Brazilian provinces in the sample. The divergences in the periods of study are caused by the availability of survey data which are from 1960 in the former case and from 1962 in the latter. In these studies the CANTRIL scale was used for measuring feelings of deprivation. Only a few of the results of the multivariate analysis of BWY will be mentioned here: there is a positive relationship between elite instability at an earlier point of time (t_1 —the variable was constructed on the basis of results of a factor analysis) and internal war at a later point (t_2). If one assumes that internal wars require thorough organization, elite dissent might very well be considered a necessary condition for the outbreak of internal war. Other results of this study suggest the following causal connection: if violent protests in the past lead to a dissent among the elites, the probability of subsequent internal war is increased. However, there is a negative relationship between elite instability (t_1) and turmoil (t_2); positively stated, stable elites do not prevent the outbreak of spontaneous violent activities. In the case of turmoil, there is a stronger impact from earlier violent reactions of the incumbent government. In this case, an explanation easily comes to mind, namely the violence-breeds-violence explanation. Yet, surprisingly, there is no such relation

(172)

in the case of internal war, the stronger form of political violence. While criticism has been raised against BWY's study (WEST 1973:92ff.), for the first time in the literature on political violence, aggregate data and survey data have been combined in one and the same cross-national study. Due to large divergencies in the periodization of variables, however, most of these results (given the present state of knowledge) appear speculative.

173. But see also COOPER (1974:283) who found less consistent results in a multivariate analysis after controlling for geocultural regions and level of economic development. In his study the Latin American countries clearly stand out as a deviant case. GILMAN (1971:127–28) reports no effect of the loyality of military personnel in his sample of twenty-one African, Asian, and Latin American high-conflict countries (period: 1948–68). He also fails to find support for a curvilinear relationship. Once again, there is a positive relationship between coercion and political violence.

174. "Whatever the intensity of the punishment, it should be applied consistently. A given disapproved action once punished should always be rebuked. Above all, it should never be rewarded. This punishment, moreover, should be administered early, right after the action is initiated, in order to lessen the possibility that the goal of the disapproved behavior is reached and the behavior reinforced" (BERKOWITZ 1973:119).

175. At another place TILLY writes (somewhat too subtly?): "there is an intimate dependency between violent and nonviolent forms of collective action—one is simply a special case of the other—rather than some moral, political, or tactical divide between them" (TILLY 1974: 283).

176. One must add that TILLY's data refer mostly to the period between 1830 and 1930 and mostly to France (partly to Italy and Germany). Cf. TILLY et al. (1975) and the detailed discussion in chapter 8.4.6.6.1.

177. As already pointed out by BANDURA: "Aversive stimulation, in the form of personal insult or physical assault, is in fact a much more potent elicitor of aggression than some environmental cue that has merely been previously associated with anger-arousing experiences. Thus, people often counteraggress when insulted or struck without requiring additional stimulus prompts; they aggress on slight provocation when they see that such actions are effective in gaining desired outcomes" (BANDURA 1973:135–36; see chapter 3.3).

178. But cf. also GROFMAN/MULLER (1973) and chapter 5.3.2.3 for a more successful approach.

179. The failures of a protesting group need not lead to retreat or dissolution of this group, but rather might cause a concentration process and a doubling of efforts. The early history and eventual success of the Russian, Chinese and Cuban Revolutions are equally instructive here.

180. A review of the literature leads to the conclusion that vicarious punishment has rather inhibiting effects, whereas vicarious reinforcement

leads to less articulate effects. Following BANDURA, these possible explanations are suggested: "Perhaps vicarious punishment carries more information concerning the modeled behavior than does vicarious reward. Another possibility is that vicarious punishment is much more salient than vicarious reward" (THELEN/RENNIE 1972:103). A test of these hypotheses would require data at the individual or group level.

181.   See HAMBLIN et al. (1963) for an interesting example. In experimental analyses they found an exponential relationship in the form of the J-curve (see chapter 8.4.6.1) between degree of interference and aggressive reactions.

182.   A prior question would be to what degree potential "punishments" are credible, a question calling for data at the individual level. See also the extensive discussion and the reformulations suggested in the recent review of the literature in GIBBS's (1975) book on *Crime, Punishment, and Deterrence*. He stresses that the concept of deterrence is used in a rather unclear manner, leaving out of consideration numerous important factors, e.g., perceptual factors and extralegal influences. Consequently, measurement of deterrence, in general, has been insufficient in past research. GIBBS proposes several new strategies to follow and derives numerous additional hypotheses, one of the more prominent being: "The greater the celerity, certainty, and severity of punishment, the less the crime rate" (GIBBS 1975:222). The study of ERICKSON et al. (1977) is one of the first to take up some of the issues described by GIBBS. While their findings are still somewhat ambiguous, they nevertheless seem to suggest that the deterrence relation "could reflect differential social condemnation of crime" (ibid., p. 305). "Until defenders of the doctrine show that the relation between properties of legal punishments and the crime rate holds independently of the social condemnation of crime, then all purported evidence of general deterrence is suspect" (ERICKSON et al. 1977:316; italics omitted). Such a confirmation of deterrence doctrine would, of course, require data at the individual or group level. Furthermore, it may be the case that "the perceived certainty of punishment and perceived seriousness are so highly collinear that their effects on the rates cannot be differentiated" (ibid., p. 305). For another study bearing on these problems, see TITTLE (1977). Cf. also the more general discussion in ZIMRING/ HAWKINS (1973).

183.   Cf. also OTTERBEIN (1968) who found no relationship between external and internal conflicts when studying fifty of those societies listed in MURDOCK's *Ethnographic Atlas*.

184.   There is another interesting result found in an analysis of conflict interactions of the People's Republic of China during 1950–70. Surprisingly, there is a stronger relationship between external conflicts and subsequent internal conflicts than vice versa (ONATE 1974; but cf. also LIAO 1976).

185.   Cf. also MURRAY (n.d.) who reports strong bivariate relationships between American participation in a major foreign war and various measures of racial riots with concentrations in 1919, 1943, and 1968.

(186)

186. And, at the same time, increase the internal cohesion. Cf. the overview of respective empirical findings in various fields of study in STEIN (1976).
187. For a discussion of the cross-national evidence and a systematization of various possible explanations of *these* relationships, see HAZLEWOOD (1975) and ZIMMERMANN (1975, 1976). Cf. also EBERWEIN et al. (1978, 1979).
188. "One indication of the extent of fragmentation in Africa is that one-half of the 2,000 languages of the world are indigenous to Africa, with more languages spoken per unit of population in Africa than in any comparable portion of the world" (SMOCK/BENTSI-ENCHILL 1975: 4). It is no wonder, then, that the official policy of the Organization of African Unity is to control these conflict potentials. Cf., e.g., Resolution 16 passed in 1964 and calling for "respect [of] borders existing on their achievement of national independence" (as quoted in COPSON 1973:199). See also TOUVAL (1972).
189. Some additional countries are referred to in a list given by CONNOR: "Among the states currently or recently troubled by internal discord predicated upon ethnic diversity are [naming mainly the nations given in addition to HUNTINGTON and leaving out some others] Albania, Algeria, Burundi, Cambodia, the Chinese People's Republic, Congo, Czechoslovakia, Dahomey, Equatorial Guinea, France, Greece, Iran, Italy, Ivory Coast, Ghana, Kenya, Laos, Liberia, Malagasy, Nigeria, Romania, Rwanda, Sierra Leone, Spain, the Soviet Union, Thailand, Tanzania, Togo, Uganda, the United Kingdom, the United States, Yugoslavia, Zaire, and Zambia" (CONNOR 1973:2).
190. As put in a longer passage of ZOLBERG which is worth quoting:

> Although we can refer to the existence of "states" and "regimes" in Africa, we must be careful not to infer from these labels that their governments necessarily have authority over the entire country, any more than we can safely infer from the persistence of these countries as sovereign entities proof of the operations of endogenous factors such as a sense of community and the ability of authorities to enforce cohesion against people's will. Persistence may only reflect the initial inertia, which keeps instruments of government inherited from the colonial period going, as well as the inertia of claimants which assures in most cases that all the problems will not reach the center simultaneously; it may reflect also the absence of effective external challenges and even to a certain extent the protection provided by the contemporary international system which more often than not guarantees the existence of even the weakest of sovereign states born out of the decolonization of tropical Africa (ZOLBERG 1968:72).

Cf. also the critical, albeit somewhat unsystematic, work of BOZEMAN (1976) on *Conflict in Africa: Concepts and Realities*.

(Chapter Five)

191. Cf., e.g., BARROWS (1976) who uses ethnic identity groups as the units of analysis in his study on political instability in Black Africa. See the next chapter for some details of this study.
192. DENTON/PHILLIPS (1968:92) find clear evidence of a relationship between external and internal wars when grouping their data into twenty-year periods between about 1500 and 1950. For a comprehensive list of internal wars from 1816 onwards see WALLACE/SINGER (1973: appendix).

193. Military aid to countries suffering from severe domestic disruption, or severe disruption in countries highly economically dependent on the United States (as compared to other states of the region) tended to precede U.S. interventions. . . . Patterns of U.S. intervention also seemed to change over the years. Strategic military (aid) and diplomatic (foreign service) interests best predicted U.S. interventions in the 1950s, while economic dependence, internal violence, and U.S. economic aid became better predictors in the 1960s. Indeed, regionally high levels of U.S. economic penetration were present in some form (trade, aid, or percentage of imports) in nine of thirteen intervention targets in the 1960s, and seemed threatened by high domestic violence in five (PEARSON 1976:58).

There seems to be no general explanation of U.S. military interventions abroad over the entire period studied (1950–67). In spite of the generally small portions of variance explained in PEARSON's analysis, "there is evidence that at least two sets of factors apply in various circumstances: (1) factors associated with dependence on the United States— especially economic and military dependence; (2) factors associated with U.S. competition with major and/or Communist powers. One group of interventions took place in U.S. 'client states,' and another group took place in states still subject to U.S.–USSR–PRC contention" (ibid., p. 58; PRC = People's Republic of China). "A recent study by the Brookings Institution (paid for by the Pentagon) shows that the U.S. military was involved in a 'show of force' in other countries 215 times since 1945 (OBERDORFER 1977). This compares to the 115 interventions by the Soviet Union (who was second in number of interventions) in the same period" (KERBO 1978:375). Cf. also KENDE 1978. However, the pattern for the United Kingdom is somewhat different: "United Kingdom military intervention after World War II was generally limited to a particular set of places and circumstances; countries within the bounds of the Empire, in the immediate vicinity of an Army base, experiencing political violence, whose authorities might officially request action of Britain. Most interventions, twenty-three [out of thirty-four military interventions between 1949 and 1970], met all of these requirements" (VAN WINGEN/TILLEMA 1980:296).
194. The new phenomenon of worldwide political terrorism provides for another dramatic example, apart from external interventions elaborated on here.

(195)

195. Cf. KORT (1952) for an effort of "quantification of Aristotle's theory of revolution" in which he draws on the works of PARETO and of the American mathematician Harold T. DAVIS.

196. For a methodological discussion of various indexes of inequality, see ALKER/RUSSETT (1966); cf. also COWELL (1977); ALLISON (1978); PEREIRA/SALINAS (1978). For the development of a new index of land inequality, see PROSTERMAN (1976).

197. Incorporating this variable additively, but not multiplicatively as suggested in NAGEL's formulation (NAGEL 1974:467; see below).

198. In RUSSETT et al. (1964:239ff.) results for N=50 countries are reported. RUSSETT (1964) also mentions that the correlation between land inequality and violent deaths increases to .71 if variables such as GNP per capita, percentage of the population in agriculture, and tenancy are controlled. Yet there is no theoretical discussion of this result (cf. CHADWICK/FIRESTONE 1972:6). There is also the possibility of another third factor interfering. "If RUSSETT had, for example, included only rural areas in his measures of civil disorder, explanations which relied on spurious correlation between tenure forms and urban characteristics would have been ruled out" (PAIGE 1975:73). Testing a revised formulation of HUNTINGTON's theory of political instability on eighteen Latin American nations, RUHL (1975:15; see chapter 5.1.2.4 for details) also reports a negative relationship between income distribution, circa 1960, and organized political violence (which represents the measure of political instability). Yet, in a multivariate analysis this relationship persists only for the years 1962–64.

199. Actually, seventeen nations form the sample of the study of TANTER/ MIDLARSKY (1967). For the remaining seven countries no data are presented. Thus, it is unclear whether this result holds in general (CHADWICK/FIRESTONE 1972:12). The latter authors also point out that there is no theoretical interpretation of the GINI index ("revolutionary gap," increased expectations, or both?) in this study (see also the severe criticism in chapter 8.4.6.2).

200. The measure "attempts to locate societies along a continuum which ranges from unipolar through bipolar to multipolar configurations of ethnic groups" (BARROWS 1976:150).

201. NAGEL also fails to find results in support of RUSSETT's earlier study but withdraws what he has said after carrying out additional analyses using transformed (and not, as originally done, untransformed) data. Thus there are no fundamental differences between the results in the two studies (NAGEL 1976:315). One must also interpret with some caution a result of DUFF/McCAMANT (1976:83) who report an r of only .13, since data were available for only sixteen Latin American countries. This delimits the variability of inequality in land distribution much more than in RUSSETT's study.

202. The sample of the authors consists of *less* developed nations. However, a rigorous test of the hypothesis would require longitudinal rather than cross-sectional data. Furthermore, JACKMAN (1975) and RUBINSON (1976) fail to find evidence in favor of a curvilinear relationship

between economic development and inequality. But see also WEEDE (1980) who confirms the curvilinear relationship.

203. "To generalize, one might say that the greatest inequality of income is to be found among the somewhat richer African countries (Gabon and the Republic of South Africa, but also Senegal and Sierra Leone) and the poorer Latin American countries (Columbia, Peru, Brazil, and Bolivia), as well as in two middle eastern countries (Iraq and the Lebanon). There are no Asian countries among those with the greatest inequality of income" (PAUKERT 1973:121).

204. For a recent effort to detect the determinants of inequality (actually the dependent variable is social equality) in sixty noncommunist countries, see JACKMAN (1975, especially pp. 27–60 for the relationships between economic development and various measures of equality). Cf. also the theoretical extensions found in HUNTINGTON/NELSON (1976:66ff.) who, after carrying out some tabular reanalyses, come up with the conclusion that the "evidence presented so far shows that at the national level a broad correlation exists between economic equality and political democracy, a relation that generally holds up even when economic development is held constant" (HUNTINGTON/NELSON 1976:67). Cf. also the reanalysis of CUTRIGHT's and JACKMAN's data by RUBINSON/QUINLAN (1977:611), supporting the "hypothesis that inequality has a negative effect on democratization, but there is less empirical support for the original hypothesis that democratization negatively affects inequality." For comparative analyses of the impact of foreign economic dependence on inequality of internal income distribution, see CHASE-DUNN (1975) and RUBINSON (1976). In both cases, however, only a few varibles are employed, so that the alleged connection between the two variables is not yet sufficiently specified. Moreover, using second order polynomial regression analysis, WEEDE (1980) accuses RUBINSON (1976), RUBINSON/ QUINLAN (1977), STACK (1978), and many others of poor specification of the role of economic development. In another article WEEDE/ TIEFENBACH (1981; N=71 countries) fail to find support for three versions of dependency theory. Communist rule and military participation ratio prove to be consistent predictors of income equality. There are, however, other forms of inequality in communist states which may be more important than income inequality. One of the possible variables to reckon with when analyzing the relationship between dependency and inequality may be growth of the tertiary sector (cf. EVANS/TIMBERLAKE 1980 for evidence of a positive link of this variable to income inequality for forty-nine underdeveloped countries). STACK's (1978; N=32 states) finding that direct government involvement is the most important negative explanatory variable (independent of economic development and the rate of economic growth), if the degree of income inequality is to be explained, thus must be treated with caution (for other criticism see JACKMAN 1980 who questions the inclusion of communist countries in the analysis, since the role of the state is different in those cases; see also the reply by STACK 1980).

(204)

In the most comprehensive review of the literature thus far and also on the basis of some new analyses, BORNSCHIER et al. (1978:651) report for various samples and periods: "Flows of direct foreign investment and aid have had a short-term effect of increasing the relative rate of economic growth of countries. Stocks of direct foreign investment and aid have had the cumulative, long-term effect of decreasing the relative rate of economic growth of countries," the latter relationships being much stronger in richer countries. Cf. also the references and the caveats in chapter 5.1.1.2.1.

205. In the "benign" *liberal* model socioeconomic development is directly (and indirectly via greater socioeconomic equality) to lead to political stability and to democratic political participation which are expected to stand in a feedback relationship. However, since development according to this model is extremely rare, four other models are suggested: in the *bourgeois* model (in opposition to the restrictive *autocratic* model, both referring to phase 1) limited political participation is granted to the bourgeoisie which leads to more socioeconomic development and to less socioeconomic equality. This, in turn, opens phase 2 where the lower socioeconomic strata are demanding political participation; two basic models here are the *populist* model allowing for such participation with the consequence of greater instability and less growth, and the *technocratic* model repressing participation for the sake of more socioeconomic development but also causing greater socioeconomic inequality and perhaps instability, thus possibly initiating another vicious circle (HUNTINGTON/NELSON 1976:17–25).

206. Consequently, measurement at the group level is called for.

207. Furthermore, in a more comprehensive causal model of the determinants of political violence one should also study the input variables of socioeconomic inequality, such as socioeconomic opportunities or even political violence (cf. JACKMAN 1975; see note 204). Cf. also HUNTINGTON/NELSON (1976: chapter 3).

208. Moreover, a violent solution of a conflict in the past might open the road to more peaceful developments, as in the case of the American Civil War (cf. also the analytical considerations in BINDER et al. 1971).

209. While there are several quite distinct communal groups in Switzerland, cross-cutting of religious, linguistic, and other characteristics is nevertheless rather considerable. For *the* deviant case, the Jura separatists, see, e.g., HENECKA (1972).

210. Censorship may, of course, affect other variables, as well, such as those referring to the coercive capacity of a political system.

211. "Since the wire services report far more conflict acts than appear in newspapers (WYNN/SMITH 1973:4), it definitely appears to be the editorial policies of newspapers which are the major factor in their non-reporting of events. In short, for a number of reasons, newspapers do not present the public with 'all the news that's fit to print'" (SCOLNICK 1974:487), the latter being the motto of the *New York Times* (cf. also note 219).

212. On the local level of reporters, these problems may read like this: "(1) Foreign newsmen may not have access to a troubled area. . . .

(Chapter Five)

(2) A newsman's stay in a country may be partially contingent on his willingness to withhold information about events considered sensitive by the host government. (3) Reporters are changed from time to time. . . . (4) Some reporters may feel it desirable to give detailed reports of events while others consider it a virtue to keep their reports brief. . . . (5) The difference in knowledge of a country may affect the views. . . . (6) Their ideologies or beliefs may cause foreign newsmen to stress or deemphasize reports of conflict in their assigned country" (SCOLNICK 1974:487).

213. Some researchers such as RUMMEL (1963) speak of "errors of omission" (in part under the first source of error) and "errors of commission" (see below).

214. In reality, however, the senior researcher frequently transmits his screen of coding to his coworkers (cf., e.g., chapter 5.1.1.2.2) so that in the end no control of errors will be achieved by employing additional coders (SCOLNICK 1974:498–99).

215. The various estimation procedures (see e.g., GURR 1968a:1108) used in the case of missing data may cause numerous other errors which may be difficult to detect.

216. A high correlation between two variables, on the other hand, indicates the absence only of random error but not of systematic error.

217. It would then be natural to lower the level of significance in order to avoid type 2 fallacies (hypothesis is rejected, albeit correct).

218. For discussions of data problems in international event data analyses, see, e.g., the works in AZAR/BEN-DAK (1975).

219. But see LICHTHEIM (1965) for some impressions as to the "fit"-ness of the *New York Times*.

220. "The common practice of utilizing the *New York Times Index* rather than the paper itself as a data source places an additional editorial layer between the events and the researcher. . . . It would be interesting to know the type and quantity of the information lost through using only the *Index*. In this regard, AZAR et al. (1972:377) report that in their source comparison of events of Israel and Egypt for two months in 1957, they found that the *Index* reported 78% of the events in the newspaper" (SCOLNICK 1974:489). For a brief critical overview of the range of several sources, *Keesing's Contemporary Archives, Facts on File, Deadline Data on World Affairs*, and the *New York Times*, see SCOLNICK (1974:489–91; cf. also GURR 1972a:66–84 and GURR 1974b).

221. Cf. also the results obtained when correlating GURR's measures of civil strife with the data sets collected in the handbook on Black Africa (MORRISON et al. 1972:125): the turmoil indicators correlate only weakly (r=.40), whereas the general civil strife measure is much more strongly related to the particular instability measure (r=.82). GURR/ DUVALL (forthcoming) point out, however, that their combined measures of *properties* of conflicts are not directly comparable with mere event counts.

222. However, there may be peculiar exceptions, e.g., in the case of a country wanting to obtain external support against internal rebels.

(223)

223. Cf., e.g., NIXON (1965) who presents a nine-point censorship scale to estimate press freedom in the particular countries to four general experts and to one country expert. He finds that economic development is one of the strongest correlates of press freedom (1960: r=.64; 1965: r=.70 for 117 countries). Cf. also GASTIL (e.g., 1977).

224. Furthermore, there is also a fourth danger, that of over-reporting: "event data drawn from newspapers tend to exaggerate periods of intensive international or domestic conflict, and to underemphasize periods of low or 'normal' activity." Weekly journals seem to be less distorting in this respect than daily journals (according to BURROWES/ SPECTOR 1970:5, here quoted in SCOLNICK 1974:448; cf. also TAYLOR/HUDSON 1972:65).

225. GURR (1968a:1108), for one, generally reports slightly positive relationships between censorship and his measures of strife (FEIERABEND/FEIERABEND/NESVOLD 1969:682 even found an r=.51; see also GILMAN 1971:75 and LOWENSTEIN 1967). "The results almost certainly reflect the association of high levels of economic development and press freedom in the Western nations, which tend to have less strife than the developing nations" (GURR ibid.).

226. Cf. TANTER (1966:44–45) for different reasoning, although elsewhere his arguments are in line with our presentation; see TANTER (1965:163).

227. In some studies the number of index cards of a country in the particular data bank is used as an indicator of international interest. TANTER (1965:164) reports that 4% (1955–60) or 8% (1948–62) of the variation in the conflict variables was caused by the card error variable (data source: *Deadline Data*). For similar results cf. TANTER (1971:90, 105). Only in the case of strikes (TANTER 1965:163–65) is 29% of the variance shared with the international interest variable (years: 1948–62, N=66 countries; for further details see also RUMMEL 1963; 1971:42; in general, cf. also the discussion in GURR 1972a:49–59).

229. FEIERABEND/FEIERABEND/NESVOLD (1969:688) use population size as a control variable. They report no indications that the conflict scores of "more interesting" nations are distorted by systematic errors.

229. And some other consequences as well: for reasons specified in measurement theory, in feedback models strong effects often cannot be separated from weaker ones. Parameter estimates on the basis of multiple measures of the same variable over time lead, in the case of positively autocorrelated residuals (cf. HIBBS 1974 and WEEDE 1977c:40ff.), to inflated coefficients.

230. There is also the question of the point at which a process may be considered to have ended. Especially in the case of less dramatic sequences, such a determination might create difficulties, whereas identification becomes easier when the events under study are more dramatic. One also must raise the question as to the criteria used for denoting the beginning of a process.

231. The consequence would be that no general theoretical statements were sought at this point. However, the validity of the statements might be

increased. Thus, requirements of equivalence and sampling considerations may be at variance.

232. For example, deviant cases are not discussed on the basis of "one shot measurements" as in the case of cross-sectional data, but rather on the basis of several points of comparison.

233. There is, however, a variant of banditry which, however ineffective by modern standards, is or was more overtly a movement of protest and revolt. We may call it *haidukry*, after the Balkan outlaws of this name, though it is also found in East and South-east Asia, and possibly elsewhere. What distinguishes haidukry from other kinds of social banditry is that its social function is consciously recognised, permanent, and to this extent it is much more institutionalised and structured than the common type of brigandage, in which men become bandits because they happen to fall foul of the official law, and bands form casually around prestigious outlaws (HOBSBAWM 1974:154).

234. BENDIX points out that the term prepolitical is "marred by a schematic Marxist interpretation which characterizes all types of premodern social protest as 'primitive'" (BENDIX 1964:45). Cf. also the critical remarks in TILLY et al. (1975:289).

235. See chapter 8.4.6.6.1 for a discussion of TILLY's own approach.

236. *If* the terms primitive and reactionary were used to connote more than implied here, then the criticism of FREIBERG (1971:51–52) may, indeed, be in order: "the issue of local power was 'reactionary' yesterday and yet 'progressive' today (it would seem), as in the separatist movements involving the Welsh, Scottish, Breton, Basque, Slovak, and Flemish." Cf. also the selfcriticism in TILLY/TILLY/TILLY (1975:49–50). For more details on TILLY's typology see chapter 8.4.6.6.1.

237. Generally defined as the "politically motivated murder or attempted murder of a prominent government official or politician, or other public figure, domestic or foreign" (GURR and Associates 1978:35).

238. Ten of the world's thirteen most deadly conflicts in the past 160 years have been civil wars and rebellions . . . according to data collected by Lewis F. RICHARDSON [1960:32–43] to which events after 1948 are added here. The conflicts most destructive of life were World Wars I and II. Of the other eleven all but one were primarily internal wars and all caused more than 300,000 deaths each; the Tai-P'ing Rebellion, 1851–64 [cf. YU-WEN 1973; KUHN 1970]; the American Civil War; the Great War in La Plata, 1865–70; the post-revolutionary Civil War in Russia, 1918–20; the first and second Chinese Civil wars, 1927–36 and 1945–49; the Spanish Civil War; the communal riots in India and Pakistan, 1946–48; the Vietnam War, 1961–[75]; the private war between Indonesian Communists and their opponents, 1964–66 (casualty figures are problematic); and the Nigerian Civil War,

1967–[70] (GURR 1970a:3; for some further data cf. ORLAN-
SKY 1970; cf. also the largely historical account of revolutionary
civil wars by WILKINSON 1975).

GURR (1979:52) reports data on internal wars (guerrilla wars, civil
wars, local rebellions and revolts, private wars) for eighty-seven countries in the 1960s. Civil wars occurred in thirty-three countries (none of
them being a Western democracy). The mean number of dissidents was
10,000. The annual death figure was 200 (median). Total deaths are
estimated at over 1,500,000 ("including dissidents, governmental
personnel, foreign troops and advisors, and people killed accidentally
or incidentally. People executed by governments for taking part in civil
conflict also are counted"). More recent events overlapping in part with
the categories of civil wars and rebellions have taken place in Cambodia,
ending with the takeover of the Red Khmers (1975), in a variety of
African countries, largely those under former Portuguese colonial rule,
and most recently in Lebanon.

239. Since both terms can be found in the scientific literature, we use the
words "blacks" and (rarely) "Negroes," being aware that in everyday
language the term "Negro" carries with it some rather unfriendly
connotations.

240. For a critique of this study, the so-called COLEMAN Report, see, e.g.,
the contributions to MOSTELLER/MOYNIHAN (1972). Cf. also the
counterevidence in TenHOUTEN's study (1970) using data from Los
Angeles.

241. These substantial gains have not eliminated the racial difference
in returns to schooling, but neither have blacks experienced the
downward shift in education-specific occupational status which
has occurred among whites. . . . The racial gap in mean socioeconomic status has declined, and similarities in the process of
status allocation for young men of both races are greater, but
blacks still experience occupational discrimination. . . . differentials in returns to education and family resources remain, as do
gaps in average occupational status, especially among older men
(FEATHERMAN/HAUSER 1976: first quotation on p. 646, the
latter quotations on p. 647).

242. In 1972 as in 1962 there are large differences in the educational
attainment, occupational status, and income of black and white
men in each of the age groups 35 to 44, 45 to 54, and 55 to 64.
In 1962 the racial differential in educational attainment ranged
from 3 to 4 years of schooling, and in 1972 it ranged from 2.25
to 3 years. In 1962 the occupational differential between the
races was 21 or 22 points on the Duncan scale at every age, and in
1972 it was about 18 points. In 1962 the income differential
between the races ranged from $3200 to $3800, and in 1972 it
ranged from $2900 to $3200 in constant (1961) dollars
(HAUSER/FEATHERMAN 1974b:329).

243. This definition agrees with the riot definition given in the *World Handbook of Political and Social Indicators*: "A riot is a violent demonstration or disturbance involving a large number of people. . . . Riots in comparison with demonstrations and armed attacks, are characterized by spontaneity and by tumultuous behavior" (TAYLOR/HUDSON 1972:67). Cf. also the definition of REJAI: "A riot is a nonlegal, nonroutine, generally spontaneous group action, transitory in time, indefinite in place, voluntary or semivoluntary in membership, undertaken to express specific grievance and frustration" (REJAI 1973:17).

244. Another unsupported hypothesis is that recent immigrants from the South are most likely to be participants in rioting (cf., e.g., SEARS/McCONAHAY 1973:31; LUPSHA 1969:280–81). Cf. also the general cross-national aggregate analyses in chapter 5.1.2.2.

245. This list of attributes (Los Angeles police chief Parker even spoke of "monkeys in the zoo" [OBERSCHALL 1972:250]) resembles European fin de siècle stereotypes of collective behavior, as found, e.g., in the writings of LEBON, SIGHELE, TARDE, and later ORTEGA Y GASSET.

> There are many historical examples of [criminal and individualistic looters] being drawn into a riot, unconcerned and perhaps even unaware of the broader issues. Riots clearly offer a cover for normally prohibited behaviour. Yet such people are always present, while riots occur infrequently and are very much related to broader social, political, economic, religious, and racial issues. An explanation that seeks the source of riots in the nature of man, or of certain men such as those of the lower social classes, cannot explain their variation (MARX 1970:350B).

246. "The underclassed theory was neither popular with black leaders nor with liberal intellectuals. It clearly undermined the political significance of the riots and could be used for justifying a policy of nonresponse, except for increasing police efficiency. Relegating the riots to the actions of a few pathological and deviant individuals meant that the political, social, and economic problems of the black community could be considered as irrelevant to the riots" (MILLER et al. 1976:339).

247. For a critique cf., e.g., the review symposium in the *American Political Science Review* 63, no. 4 (December 1969): 1269–81; LIPSKY/OLSON 1977; and many other works cited in chapter 5.3.2.

248. "The rioters are not the poorest of the poor. They are not the least educated. They are not unassimilated migrants or new-comers to the city. There is no evidence that they have serious personality disturbances or are deviant in their social behavior. They do not have a different set of values. None of these factors sets the rioter off from the rest of the community in a way that justifies considering him a personal failure or an irresponsible person" (CAPLAN/PAIGE 1968b:19–20).

249. On the Watts riot cf. also the studies in COHEN (1970).

250. Cf. also the causal analysis of determinants of self-estrangement and powerlessness among a cohort of Wisconsin men in OTTO/FEATHERMAN (1975).

251. There are, however, a number of serious methodological flaws in many
of the studies employing alienation or internal-external control concepts. The scales employed often call for agreement response set,
measure only attitudes and not behavior (cf. also note 305), are generally not one-dimensional, and do not fulfill the criterion of "discriminant validity" (CAMPBELL/FISKE 1959; GURIN et al. 1978). See
ROBINSON/SHAVER (1973:161–210) for a general overview and
PHARES (1976) for a review of research on "locus of control in personality" (cf. also LEFCOURT 1976). In the case of ROTTER's
internal control variable, a high score may express feelings of personal
guilt or resignation rather than feelings of personal mastery (cf. also
COLLINS 1974). "Some of these studies suggest externals are more
socially and politically active, especially in the case of black subjects,
whereas internals generally have been more active. Other work suggests
that if you divide the ROTTER I–E scale items into subscales you may
get results different from those based on total I–E scores" (PHARES
1976:97). Perhaps the answer to these problems may be found in
"using only the Personal Control factor among Negroes. The reason for
this is probably because whites show a much higher relationship
between personal and ideological beliefs than do Negroes. For without
the same experiences of discrimination and racial prejudice, whites are
less likely to perceive an inconsistency between cultural beliefs and
what works for themselves" (LAO 1970:269; cf. also GURIN et al.
1969).

GURIN et al., using data from a national survey in 1972, address
the issue more specifically: "Personal control was clearly personal in
nature and control ideology was politically toned for liberals and
blacks. In contrast, among conservatives, both control dimensions
tapped a personal expectancy, and neither was related to political attitudes. The results for the conservatives therefore support the original
assumption of unidimensionality of the I–E scale. Conservatives apparently read both sets of questions as asking about their own situation,
assuming that what works for them also works for people in general.
The distinction between personal control and an ideology about the
role of control in the culture at large is particularly striking among
liberals and blacks" (GURIN et al. 1978:288). "Clarification of the role
of internal and external control in political behavior thus requires two
distinctions that have only rarely been drawn. One is the political perspective of the actors either as challenging or as accepting the status
quo. The other is externality either as personal powerlessness or as an
ideology that stresses social determination and awareness of system
barriers. The importance of the second depends on the first" (ibid.,
p. 289). Among his student population, RENSHON also fails to find
evidence of high personal control as a predictor variable of political protest participation. Instead, "individuals with low personal control are
more likely to have participated than individuals with high personal
control" (RENSHON 1974:194; cf. also the findings from ten black
colleges in GURIN/EPPS 1975). To give another example, a high score
on an alienation scale may reflect a *realistic* evaluation of one's own

resources and not so much a psychological state of mind with all the connotations referred to in psychological alienation theories.

252. Cf. also the results of the ecological studies of SPILERMAN in chapter 5.3.2.4 which are based on a larger data base than any of the studies referred to here (although his data are aggregate data).

253. There is, however, one caveat against the study of MILLER et al.: Does it make sense to label a determined *non*violent protester a militant?

254. Here generally defined as "the belief that the ruled in a political system have some capacity for exercising influence over the rulers" (MULLER 1970a:792).

255. Here generally defined as the reversal of: "trust can be defined as the probability . . . that the political system (or some part of it) will produce preferred outcomes, even if left untended" (GAMSON 1968:54).

256. There are, however, some methodological problems to contend with. As RANSFORD puts it: "Although the distinction between efficacy and trust is important, the problem is to develop a measure of efficacy/ powerlessness that is not contaminated by distrust" (RANSFORD 1972:336). Moreover, it should be noted that PAIGE's measure of trust contains only one item. Cf. also BLUMENTHAL et al. (1975:82–84) for mixed results as to GAMSON's prediction of an interactive effect between low trust and high efficacy. FRASER (1970), HAWKINS et al. (1971), WATTS (1973), and KONING (1978) in four nonrepresentative studies, failed to find support for the hypothesis that mistrustful but efficacious individuals show higher rates of political participation. Yet, they measured mostly conventional and not unconventional political participation (but cf. also DUBEY 1971). MARSH (1977:122), however, was able to replicate PAIGE's findings with data from British respondents.

257. One of the many variants of rather indirect testing of the theory of relative deprivation is found in McELROY/SINGELL (1973) who relate riot occurrences and intensities to the discrepancy between "the high levels of economic performance and social development in the larger SMSA" and the "inferior levels in the central city and the ghetto" (McELROY/SINGELL 1973:289). For a summary of some of their results see Table 5.5 in chapter 5.3.2.4. Cf. also the extensions in DOTSON (1974).

258. As MULLER, one of the leading researchers who have worked with variants of relative deprivation theory (cf. below), puts it: past microtests of relative deprivation may have measured a discrepancy "that many people may not find particularly frustrating" (MULLER 1975:7).

259. "Rises in family income were greater [in the sixties] among blacks than among whites. Median family income among whites rose about 25 percent while that of blacks went up 40 percent, and as an outcome, the ratio of nonwhite to white income rose" (FARLEY/HERMALIN 1972:354). Actually, a slightly more complicated picture must be drawn:

> Over the decade of the 1960's, the median family income of blacks just about doubled. The figure for these families in 1969

(259)

was $5,999, compared with $9,794 for whites. In 1959, median
income was $3,047 for blacks and $5,893 for whites. The ratio of
black to white median income rose from .52 in 1959 to .61 in
1969. In absolute terms, however, black families in 1969 received
an average of $3,795 less than their white counterparts, whereas
they had received $2,846 less in 1959. By 1972, the median
income of black families had climbed to $6,864 compared to
$11,549 for white families, but the black/white income ratio
declined to .60 in 1971 and to .59 in 1972—the level at which it
had been in 1967. So the 1969–70 recession—like the recession in
1960–61—resulted in a widening of the white/black income gap,
which in absolute terms amounted to $4,685 in 1972 (BRIMMER
1974:148–49).

260. FARLEY (1977) in an attempt to answer the question whether the
"gains of the 1960s have disappeared in the 1970s" confirms many
of the results mentioned so far, his overall summary being that "indeed,
racial differences attenuated in the lean 1970s just as they did in the
prosperous 1960s" (FARLEY 1977:189). Large differences remain,
however: "For instance, a higher proportion of white men in 1940 than
black men in 1976 held white-collar jobs (U. S. Bureau of the Census,
1943: Table 64; U. S. Bureau of Labor Statistics, 1976: Table A–21).
The purchasing power of the typical black family in 1974 was equivalent to that of a white family twenty years earlier (Table 3), and the
earnings of black men lag far behind those of white men (Table 4)"
(FARLEY 1977:206).

261. See also the discussion of the empirical evidence as to sociopsychological changes (mainly during the 1960s) in HYMAN (1972).

262. See DAVIES (1969:726) who constructs a weighted index of relative
deprivation when relating the ratio

$$\frac{\text{average family income of nonwhite population}}{\text{average years of schooling for nonwhite population}}$$

to that of the total population. The following values are reported:
1940: 57.5%, 1952: 85.5% (highest score) and 1967: 81.2%. Cf. also
FARLEY/HERMALIN (1972) and the study of MILLER et al. (1977)
who use a variety of indicators and report results strongly diverging
from those of DAVIES.

263. "The median wage or salary of nonwhite high school graduates 16 to 21
years old in February 1963 was about 15 percent below wages of white
dropouts in the same age group" (U. S. Department of Labor 1966:
129). See also the data in ABERBACH/WALKER (1973:42).

264. GRAHAM/GURR draw a parallel to a result often found in modernization studies: "So far as the United States is concerned, it has the socioeconomic and political characteristics associated with civil peace in
most other nations. But some specific groups are caught up in cycles of
social change that resemble those of transitional societies both in their
nature and in their violent consequences" (1969:571). Cf. also LIESKE
(1978).

265. In their study of blacks in Los Angeles, SEARS/McCONAHAY report that feelings of relative deprivation were greatest among the objectively most advantaged, native, and young population. Subjective status deprivation caused a doubling of the participation rate (SEARS/ McCONAHAY 1973:87–94). As to their study cf. the reanalysis of MILLER et al. (1976) leading to several conclusions quite contrary to those in the original study (see the preceding chapter).

266. Both measures intercorrelate at .53 (SOMER's d).

267. Measured through twelve items referring to "three categories of political authorities–government officials, the police, and judicial personnel–at both national and local levels of government" (MULLER 1972:958).

268. It should be noted, however, that MULLER occasionally speaks of alienation in too broad a sense; for example, relative deprivation is treated as a subcase of alienation, thus obliterating important differences between the two conceptualizations.

269. "According to the *politicized deprivation* version, it is only when deprivation-induced frustration is accompanied by attribution of responsibility for the condition to sociopolitical structural arrangements that men are sufficiently motivated to engage in protest behavior" (MULLER 1973:3).

270. As to the history and theoretical localization of this conceptualization, especially with respect to the theoretical system of HULL and the works of SPENCE, see AMSEL (1962, 1958) and YATES (1962:182–97). Cf. also the parallels to the notions of "extinction-induced aggression" and "decremental deprivation" (GURR) discussed in chapter 4.3.

271. Which he calls a "psychological" theory, but we think that the general heading "sociopsychological" under which it has been grouped here is equally justified. Interestingly, MARSH (1977:125, cf. chapter 9) finds support for a nonalienation interaction theory also as far as orthodox political participation is concerned.

272. In terms of operationalizations actually employed, the attribute "politicized" is rather inappropriate.

273. "A person is asked to define on the basis of *his own* assumptions, perceptions, goals, and values the two extremes or anchoring points of the spectrum on which some scale measurement is desired–for example, he may be asked to define the 'top' and 'bottom,' the 'good' and 'bad,' the 'best' and the 'worst.' This self-defined continuum is then used as our measuring device" (CANTRIL 1965:22). In survey research a number of scales of this type have been used in recent years. There are several difficulties, however, when applying such a scale. The best *possible* position need not be identical with a position defined as *justified* on the basis of the individual's own criteria. The high and low levels on the particular dimensions may not be constantly defined over time (cf. GROFMAN/MULLER 1973, below). In cross-national studies problems arise as to whether the metrics of such a scale are equivalently evaluated by respondents in different countries. Furthermore, interval comparisons on the basis of a CANTRIL type scale may be highly misleading, as, in general, only ordinal level of measurement is reached. Finally,

(273)

in at least one study the use of such a scale for predicting the likelihood of protest behavior led to disappointing results (see FREE 1971 for Brazil and Nigeria). For additional criticism see below.

274. There is a parallel to the FEIERABENDs' concept of systemic frustration (see chapter 5.1.1.2.2): "Systemic frustration at any given time is a function of the discrepancy between present social aspirations and expectations, on the one hand, and social achievements, on the other" (FEIERABEND/FEIERABEND/NESVOLD 1969:636). But see also GROFMAN/MULLER (1973:517–18) for a list of hypotheses as to how "aspirations" could be explicated.

275. The other patterns, not important for the subsequent analysis, are (GROFMAN/MULLER 1973:524):

‹ decreasing gratification

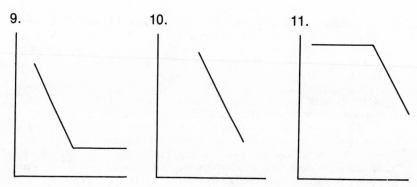

increasing gratification

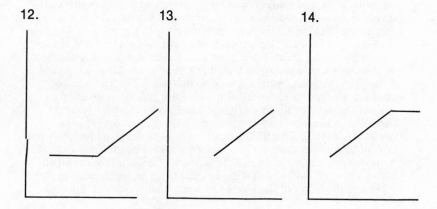

(Chapter Five)

276. It should be recalled, however, that in the multivariate analyses the impact of |C| is small (see preceding paragraphs).
277. Other noteworthy efforts in the analysis of individual protest behavior (and protest potential) can be found in the exploratory studies of MARSH (1974). He reports approval, justification, behavioral intentions and evaluation (such as "effectiveness") of protest activities to be scalable along a GUTTMAN scale ranging from nonviolent to violent means of protest. There is still another parallel to MULLER's studies, as MARSH also found no support in favor of relative deprivation theory. The test samples of fifty persons each were drawn from students, young workers, older workers, and older middle-class groups in England. Also see MARSH's representative study (1977; cf. chapter 9) confirming the relevancy of several of MULLER's interaction terms (cf. also the preliminary results from surveys in Britain, Germany, Holland, Austria, and the United States in KAASE/MARSH 1976, and the final book version BARNES/KAASE et al. 1979). For an analysis of conditions perceived as justifying the use of different forms of violence among American men, see BLUMENTHAL et al. (1972; representative sample drawn in 1969; cf. also the refinements in BLUMENTHAL et al. 1975 and in chapter 9).
278. In a recent paper, MULLER analyzes the same German data in terms of "expectancy-value-norms theory." "The explanatory terms . . . are utilitarian incentive for aggressive action, normative incentive for aggressive action, and social norms about the desirability of aggressive action" (MULLER 1978:555). Again MULLER is able to explain a large amount of the variance in "aggressive political participation." See also MULLER (1979).
279. It should also be pointed out that in these studies MULLER restricts his analyses to ordinal level statistics avoiding the (unjustified? cf. the discussion in chapter 5.1.1.1.3.2) use of higher order statistics.
280. "To measure this, respondents were given a set of ten cards on which ten different behaviors were listed. . . . Respondents were asked to indicate (1) whether or not they approved of each behavior; (2) how large a percent, in their opinion, of citizens in the Federal Republic would approve of such behaviors; (3) whether or not they would engage in each behavior; and (4) whether or not they had done each behavior" (MULLER 1975:30–31).
281. Measuring relative deprivation in the sense of just deserts by asking people what they feel may be due to them may not be a good operationalization or may at least lead to distortions in the following cases: (1) some people may have to be told what may be due to them; (2) demagogues or popular oppositional leaders may arise and cause rapid increases in the level of just deserts aspirations among larger segments of the population. The presently employed measure, if used for predictive purposes, may thus lag considerably behind actual developments.
282. The reference group version of relative deprivation may, however, have an influence on what an individual perceives as being his just deserts, a possibility which is not captured in the measures used and

(282)

which may adequately be tested only with diachronic data. Also, the questions used to find out about possible reference groups may not have gone sufficiently into detail. MULLER asked for a comparison of one's own standing to that of the "respondent's circle of acquaintances" (ibid., p. 9). Yet, a reference group may very well comprise individuals with whom one is not directly acquainted.

283. A more detailed yet somewhat dated discussion of some of these studies may be found in ZIMMERMANN 1974a.

284. Actually only the nonwhite population figure is available and used accordingly. In many other studies as well, data on the nonwhite population are employed as a substitute for data on the black population. Usually this appears justified as both highly intercorrelate (but see, e.g., JIOBU 1971:513 for one of several exceptions).

285. "A southern city tended to have fewer and less violent outbursts, possibly because Negroes in that region held lower expectations regarding improvements in their circumstances and were more fearful of retribution from participation in racial protest" (SPILERMAN 1976: 789–90).

286. In addition, the following hypotheses must be rejcted: (1) The probability of the occurrence of riots is the same in every city. (2) Cities with violent protest(s) in the past are more likely to have violent protest(s) in the present (reinforcement-hypothesis). (3) Geographical proximity explains the distribution of riots (contagion-hypothesis). Using a lognormal model (and not the negative binomial as SPILERMAN did), MIDLARSKY, however, reports that there is a strong hierarchical contagion effect operating "in the period coterminous with the Newark and Detroit disorders [July 1967]." He finds a "dependence of small cities upon the behavior of large ones, and the accelerated occurrence of disorders in small cities when larger ones are experiencing disturbances. . . . The approximate value of 40,000 black population size differentiates between behaviors in the two city size categories" (MIDLARSKY 1978: all quotations on p. 1,005). "The onset of disorders in large cities is far more a consequence of interaction between the police and black city residents than are disorders in smaller cities which are subject to contagion effects" (MIDLARSKY 1977:47).

287. But cf. also the study of ROSSI et al. (1974) who interviewed policemen, educators, social workers, political workers, retail merchants, and personnel officers in fifteen major metropolitan areas where extensive rioting occurred in 1967. The authors report a number of differences between these cities. Cf. also SPILERMAN (1976), dealt with below.

288. MORGAN/CLARK (1973) in a study of black riots in forty-two cities with more than 50,000 and less than 750,000 inhabitants (thus leaving out the biggest cities, but including twenty-three riot cities) also find size of the nonwhite population to be an important determinant of the incidence of violent black protests in 1967 (the dependent variable differs somewhat from that of SPILERMAN). Even more important,

however, are two other variables: "First, total population, not non-white population, was the single best predictor of disorder frequency. Second, the best theoretical explanation of disorder frequency requires using the number of both blacks and police as predictors" (MORGAN/CLARK 1973:617). Both variables taken together explain 34% of the variance. The authors then go on to test various predictors of the intensity of riot occurrence. Summing up their evidence they present this conclusion: "Cities with a greater confrontation probability (with respect to number of blacks and number of police) had more frequent disorders. Cities with a higher grievance level among blacks (with respect to ["housing inequality," but cf. also the opposite result in the study of PORTER/NAGEL 1976, below, and "job inequality"]) had higher rates of disorder participation and hence more severe disorders" (MORGAN/CLARK 1973:622). SPILERMAN (1976:788–89) reacts to this study by pointing to the small sample size, the differences in defining the dependent variable ("the disorders they analyzed include incidents in which the aggression was perpetrated by whites, as well as instances of Negro aggression [MORGAN/CLARK, 1973:612]," SPILERMAN 1976:789), and the insufficient use of control variables (e.g., city size instead of nonwhite population). In SPILERMAN's own analysis of the determinants of riot intensity, the absolute number of nonwhites again proves to be the strongest predictor.

289. "It is found that (1) disorder severity declined as a function of the number of prior outbreaks in a city and (2) there is evidence for a temporal effect, with the post-Martin Luther King-assassination disturbances having been unusually destructive" (SPILERMAN 1976:771).

290. Riots occurring in the two weeks following the assassination of Martin Luther King have not been considered, as, in the opinion of PORTER/NAGEL (1976:26), these events were "much more in the tradition of righteous indignation . . . than of rising expectations of frustration-aggression" (LUPSHA 1971:101). Thus, comparability of the results of SPILERMAN and those of PORTER/NAGEL is limited. Nevertheless, there are a few parallel findings (especially as to the impact of black population size). The year 1967 is chosen because correlations aggregated over several years might be ambiguous. However, using census data from 1970 again introduces some variance into the analysis which might lead to distorted findings. PORTER/NAGEL claim that the 1970 figures contain data closer to the actual year under study than those of 1960, whereas SPILERMAN would argue that the earlier census data are of more use as his "hypotheses refer to the impact of conditions which have been in existence for some period of time" (SPILERMAN 1976:784).

291. Aggregating differences in the proportions of whites and blacks in three occupational categories: craftsmen, nonfarm laborers, and nonhousehold service workers.

292. "Totals for each incident of police injuries, civilian injuries, arrests,

(292)

and arsons" using standard scores. "Because the resulting indicators . . . are highly skewed, we took their natural logarithms in order to approximate more closely the normality assumptions of least-squares regression and to maximize the linear relations between the index and our predictors" (PORTER/NAGEL 1976:28).

293. An error of this kind has been made by the Lemberg Center for the Study of Violence. This is one source the authors use, apart from the high quality data of the *Staff Study of Major Riots and Civil Disorders, 1965 through July 31, 1968* (U. S. Congress, Senate, Committee on Operations, 1968).

294. In SPILERMAN (1976:788, n. 24), the importance of the variable police organization and training is assessed and some results are presented. However, these are very tentative due to quite insufficient data.

295. The existence of patterns (and not of total chaos) in looting behavior is another blow to assumptions of traditional European mass psychology. See COUCH (1968) for a general critique.

296. It should be recalled from Table 5.5, however, that LIEBERSON/ SILVERMAN (1965) found Negro ownership of ghetto stores to have a slightly negative effect on the dependent variable (interracial riots).

297. Studies showing that feelings of relative deprivation exist could have a twofold function for the political system as a whole: (1) to indicate that the threat to the cohesion of the political community is not that decisive, since basic values are still shared; and (2) that, in case a remedy for blocked means (e.g., better housing, schools, jobs) is not provided for, a more radical form of collective behavior might result. This kind of thinking corresponds to the approach taken by SMELSER (1963). He states in his *Theory of Collective Behavior* that, when a problem is not solved on one level, the next higher level is addressed, thereby increasing the resources mobilized by all factions in the struggle (for a critique of this conceptualization, see, e.g., MARX/WOOD 1975: 406–13).

298. A comparison of survey data from Detroit blacks in 1971 with data from 1968 shows that "for those under age 33 (and to a lesser degree for the sample as a whole), Alienation is lowest for the middle educated groups and rises among *both* the most- and the least-educated" (SCHUMAN/HATCHETT 1974:120). In general, signs of suspicion and distrust against whites are widespread among blacks. Cf. also the evidence accumulated in ABRAMSON (1977).

299. JANOWITZ (1969) tries to capture this change in proposing the terms "communal riots" and "commodity riots," the latter label being somewhat inappropriate since more than commodities were at stake in the 1960s.

300. As SMELSER says within the framework of his theory of collective behavior: "These events may confirm or justify the fears or hatreds in a generalized belief; they may initiate or exaggerate a condition of strain; or they may redefine sharply the conditions of conduciveness. In any case, these precipitating factors give the general beliefs concrete, immediate substance. In this way they provide a concrete setting toward which collective action can be directed" (SMELSER 1963:17).

301. According to the KERNER Report (1968:66), 83% of the riots in 1967 (136 out of 164) occurred between June and August. Yet there has also been a decrease in hot summer rioting for the years 1967–71 (BASKIN et al. 1972). Experimental studies on the impact of high temperatures have also led to ambiguous results. Whereas GRIFFITT/ VEITCH (1971) found evidence in line with the present argument (the dependent variable being interpersonal liking), BARON/BELL report a more complicated result, namely "that high ambient temperatures facilitated aggression by nonangered subjects but actually inhibited such behavior by those who had previously been provoked" (BARON/ BELL 1975:825). The serving of a cooling drink may also reduce aggressive behavior (BARON/BELL 1976), a topic studied in an extension of their original experimental setting which, however, lacks ecological validity. Nevertheless, the hypothesis of a curvilinear relationship between negative affect (caused by hot temperature) and aggression, reaching its peak on a middle level of negative affect, should be taken up and tested for in nonlaboratory settings (for laboratory findings see BELL/BARON 1976). Due to the presence of other factors (possibly inhibiting factors, e.g., negative consequences for the aggressor himself in the case of very hot temperatures) escape from a situation of extreme discomfort may be a more likely reaction than aggressive behavior. Furthermore, apart from heat, "the longer hours of daylight, and the presence of teen-agers home from school may also play an important role" (BARON 1977:149).
302. Cf. McPHAIL/MILLER (1973) for a first systematic study of assembling processes in collective behavior. Unfortunately, their dependent variable is not riot occurrence.
303. LOCKE (1969:125), for instance, reports that rumors spread in Detroit during the days before the outbreak of the riot.
304. For an interesting catalogue of variables referring to these and other riot aspects, cf. MOMBOISSE (1967). The focus in this particular study is on riot control.
305. Actually, if attitudes relevant to behavior are appropriately measured, there is also some hope in the attitude vs. action controversy ("consistency controversy"; cf. FISHBEIN 1967a for one of the first attempts at redirection of attitude research and LISKA 1975 for a general overview of these issues). In more recent literature on the impact of attitudes on behavior, numerous suggestions have been made, e.g., that one should distinguish between attitudes toward an object and attitudes toward a situation (ROKEACH/KLIEJUNAS 1972). The attitude toward a situation (behavior) component has been studied in greater detail by FISHBEIN/AJZEN who suggest the following variables to be of major importance in predicting the likelihood of certain forms of behavior: attitude toward the act, social normative beliefs, motivation to comply with social normative beliefs, and beliefs about the consequences of the behavior (see FISHBEIN/AJZEN 1975:301ff. and passim for a recent summary of the various models they have suggested). WICKER's (1971) call for "other variables" to reduce the gap in predicting behavior from attitude measures has thus in part been

(305)

answered by FISHBEIN/AJZEN. Several other variables, however, deserve to be considered as well, such as object centrality, attitude extremity, attitude intensity (PETERSON/DUTTON 1975; cf. also the causal model of PERRY et al. 1976:237), degree of public exposure, situational factors, etc. Researchers have shown growing interest in measuring more precisely the attitude and the behavior with which they are concerned, as well as the circumstances of both (see AJZEN/ FISHBEIN 1977 for an evaluation of the evidence). There is also a growing interest in whether the prediction of the very same behavior will also hold in different contexts. A useful overview of these recent developments can be found in SCHUMAN/JOHNSON (1976). For a methodological discussion bearing on some of these questions see MERVIELDE (1977). Cf. also GROSS/NIMAN (1975) and others who recommend the use of repeated attitude measurements.

306. Besides the methodological weaknesses touched upon thus far, there are a number of other difficulties, such as: (1) time-space coordinates are often not directly comparable; (2) fear of punishment (or boasting behavior) may have led to incorrect answers to survey questions; (3) the instant of interviewing, e.g., whether immediately after a riot or considerably later, may have affected the results obtained; (4) samples are often not representative of the particular community; (5) third factor controls are frequently lacking.

307. Cf. the so-called zone-sector strategy as a means of collecting data on crowd behavior as described in SEIDLER et al. (1976).

308. Cf. ANDERSON/DYNES/QUARANTELLI (1974) for a typology of counter-rioters where the counter-rioter is not only described as being interested in preserving the status quo (the common stereotype found, for example, in the KERNER Report). ANDERSON et al. propose several other types of counter-rioters as well.

309. But cf. also WANDERER (1969) for an effort to scale riot events according to their intensity (N=75 cities with riots in 1967). Actually, he found evidence in favor of a GUTTMAN-type scale, yet there is no indication of whether the *succession* of events (not just the occurrence) also fulfills the criteria of GUTTMAN scaling. SPILERMAN (1976:774), moreover, raised some criticism against the procedure used by WANDERER. First, WANDERER employs qualitative measures. Second, variables like crowd size, number arrested, and number injured were not considered. Third, SPILERMAN tries to show that the calling of the state police and the national guard does not necessarily indicate riot severity, but may correlate with other causal variables that must be made explicit in the analysis. For another one-dimensional scale of riot activity (urban disorders from 1965 to 31 July 1968), cf. COLE (1974: 28–29).

310. Even with crowds one should reckon with the possibility that quite a few variants of behavior are determined by friendship or acquaintance groups. Cf. AVENI (1977).

311.   Total man-days of dissidence increased in the United States seven-fold between the early and late 1960's from 7 to 49 per 1000 population. Conflict deaths increased three-fold from 4.3 to 14 per 10 million population. The proportion of increase attributable to rebellion was inconsequential and the United States remained fourth in magnitude of rebellion among European democracies, after Northern Ireland, Greece, and Italy. The increase in protest was far greater, sufficient to move the United States into second place after Northern Ireland. The magnitude of protest in the United States during those turbulent years was of the same order as protest in such countries as India, Panama, and South Vietnam. Overall, the United States ranked 15th in protest among the 87 nations in the years from 1966 to 1970 (GURR et al, forthcoming).

312.   And (8) leading to which outcomes? (See chapter 9.)

Chapter Six: Crises and Political Violence

1.   Cf. the definition of ERIKSON who in his writings focuses on individual personality development ("identity crisis"): "Crisis . . . is a necessary turning point, a crucial moment, when development must move one way or another marshaling resources of growth, recovery, and further differentiation" (ERIKSON 1968:16).
2.   STARN (1976), however, provides evidence for the use of the crisis notion in British politics as early as 1659.
3.   Even though, as STARN (1971) points out, the notion of crisis may be more fruitfully employed than, e.g., the concept of revolution which seems to be plagued by historical precedents (cf. also the discussion in chapter 8.2).
4.   One must further reckon with self-destroying prophecies which also might reduce the number of cases available for comparison.
5.   At least in the first part. Later on, persistence of political systems becomes the ultimate dependent variable. Notions like political system, political regime, political order, and polity will be used interchangeably in subsequent portions of this chapter, whereas government will refer to the incumbents of office.
6.   Change is the important criterion, as stated in VERBA's definition (cf. below).
7.   Cf. also the following definition: "A crisis exists when reinstitutionalization within a performance area is needed if elites or the system are not to risk dissolution" (VERBA 1971:305).
8.   Apart from low economic performance, the denial of access to the political process to specific groups or their gross underrepresentation in elite posts may severely contribute to system crises. Some partly indirect cross-national evidence as to these effects may be found in GURR/DUVALL (1973).

9. RUMMEL (1965:205) limits his definition of crises to situations where-in the incumbent government is threatened. Usually the notion of government crisis is invoked when the position of the incumbent elites is endangered. However, an elite crisis is not necessarily to be equated with a government crisis, as antielites might also be subsumed under such a concept. In the literature, in general, elite crisis and government crisis seem to be treated as interchangeable.

10. Similar tautologies are found in the works of neoMarxist proponents of systems theory (another parallel being the almost total abstention from discussing empirical indicators for the specific theoretical positions taken). HABERMAS proposes this basic explanation of crises. "Crises occur when the structure of a societal system allows for less possibilities to solve problems than were to be used for the continuous existence of the system" (HABERMAS (1973:11; my translation). For HABERMAS there is a deep motivational crisis among individuals living under the conditions of "late capitalism." This decline of legitimacy arises from the value discrepancies of capitalism with its emphasis on individual efficiency and the growing Moloch of a state capitalist society within which this individual motivation no longer works. While sharing parts of this analysis BELL nevertheless notes that in the language of HABERMAS "systems become 'reified'; that is, the systems create or compel behavior, or manipulate persons, and the recalcitrances of individual societies, or the character of people or traditions, disappear under the monolithic weight of the term 'system' " (BELL 1976:249). MARCUSE's view on crises is not totally unrelated to that of HABER-MAS. "The centrifugal forces which appear in the emergence of trans-cending needs . . . are generated by the mode of production itself. . . . Capitalism has opened a new dimension, which is at once the living space of capitalism and its negation" (MARCUSE 1972:18–19). Other explanations are of no more help, e.g., that of AKE (1974:589): "Political change . . . becomes an instance of political instability only when it violates established expectations about how that particular type of change may legitimately occur."

11. An obvious advantage of vague formulations such as this seems to be that they fit excellently into post hoc explanations. Cf. also the follow-ing definition: "A crisis is a situation which disrupts the system or some part of the system (that is, a subsystem such as an alliance or an indi-vidual actor). More specifically, a crisis is a situation that creates an abrupt sudden change in one or more of the basic systemic variables" (HERMANN 1969:411).

12. In the field of international politics, however, numerous crises studies focusing on decisional elements can be found. Cf. HERMANN (1969) (and see also the works in HERMANN 1972, the discussion of crises concepts and theories in ROBINSON 1972 and in *International Studies Quarterly* 21, no. 1 [March 1977]). HERMANN tries to be explicit on definitional criteria of crises situations. For the subjects under study here, however, his efforts are not very helpful. Though external crises

may be related to internal crises, the characteristics of internal crises differ considerably from external crises.

13. The occasional success of nonviolent political protests, however, stands against this scaling operation (cf. the impact of Gandhi, under admittedly quite peculiar historical circumstances).

14. TILLY (1969) shows, for example, that collective violance occurred quite frequently in France during 1830–60 and 1930–60 without necessarily leading to crises of the political system. Cf. chapter 8.4.6.6.1 for a more detailed account of the works of TILLY and his associates.

15. For a similar discussion referring to relationships between crises and rebellions, see GURR 1973:79–82.

16. Disaggregating the data on a monthly base seemed to reveal little.

17. For the definition of value positions, see chapter 5.1.1.1.1.

18. There is reason for dealing only with manifest crises and not with so-called latent crises as well. This dichotomy, often proposed by writers with a Marxist orientation, renders itself rather useless for empirical studies. Crises are in the first place sociopsychological phenomena which must be *experienced* by individuals. This will become clearer as we continue. The critique raised against GALTUNG's notion of structural violence (cf. chapter 2.3) *mutatis mutandis* applies here, too.

19. But cf. also DEUTSCH: "Performance is the name we give to any outcome which is desired but is improbable without an effort to produce it" (DEUTSCH 1970:198). It "includes two dimensions: *effectiveness* — making an unlikely outcome more likely to happen—and *efficiency*—the ratio between change in the probability of the outcome and the costs incurred in producing it" (DEUTSCH 1974:230). GURR links political performance to political stability (which it has "partly replaced") and then goes on: "We speak of the 'stability' and 'performance' of political systems in ways analogous to physicians' concern with the health of a patient and economists' evaluations of the efficiency of an enterprise. But, whereas physicians are largely agreed about the characteristics of healthy people, there is much inconsistency and disagreement about what constitute the 'vital signs' of political systems" (GURR 1974a: 1483).

20. The congruence hypothesis of ECKSTEIN maintains that "high performance by a government requires congruence between its authority pattern and the authority patterns of other social units in the society" (ECKSTEIN 1969:283), "chiefly the units most instrumental in political socialization and in processes of recruitment of political elites" (ECKSTEIN 1979:17). (Cf. also his paradigmatic case study on Norway, ECKSTEIN 1966, and the opposite view in HUNTINGTON 1975). ECKSTEIN proposes two variants of congruence, "absolute congruence" and "relative congruence." Just recently, he added that "congruence should increase monotonically as a function of performance (support)" and that "it is considered a necessary condition for very high support" (ECKSTEIN 1979:17; cf. also our discussion below). So far, however, only a few empirical results bearing on the congruence

(20)

hypothesis have been reported (but see also GURR 1974a, below). The task of transforming such a global hypothesis into sensitive empirical operations seems to be rather demanding.

21. For a discussion of some other performance criteria, see ALMOND (1969:460–69).

22. These measures, in part, refer to overt strife, to organized extremist oppositional activities, to other kinds of oppositional activities, and to governmental repressive measures. One may argue that, despite the complex weighting procedures of the authors, there may be some circular reasoning in the subsequent causal analyses, since indicators of political violence are also used for one of the other independent variables (or, with respect to illegitimacy, dependent variables), i.e., strife. But see GURR/McCLELLAND (1971:48) for an empirically based justification of their procedure.

23. Cf. HURWITZ (1973:453) who also criticizes this assumption.

24. Afterwards the authors apparently took note of this deficiency in indicator selection (cf. GURR/McCLELLAND 1971:69, 71).

25. "(1) Countries like Liechtenstein and Bhutan, too small or peripheral to be 'in' the international system; (2) 'new nations' of the post-1940 era; and (3) states during periods of colonial rule, except for colonies which gained internal autonomy and then independence prior to 1940" (GURR 1974a:1488) are not included in the sample.

26. A system type "which has minimal functions, an uninstitutionalized pattern of political competition, and executive leaders constantly imperiled by rival leaders. . . . Anocracy . . . means literally the absence of power or control" (GURR 1974a:1487).

27. "Hypothesis 1: Persistence and adaptability tend to be greater in polities of high Directiveness and Complexity. . . . Hypothesis 2: Persistence and adaptability tend to be enhanced most by democratic authority traits, less by autocratic traits, and least by anocratic traits" (GURR, 1974a:1496), and hypothesis 3 referring to consistent authority patterns.

28. For an overview of some possibly useful indicators, see ROKKAN (1969:67–68; see also ROKKAN et al., 1971:30ff.).

29. It would not be too difficult to point to inconsistencies and lack of precision in some of the cells in this table. Furthermore, one should reckon with the possibility that efforts to fulfill one of the specific goals (listed under the three criteria of development relevant in each crisis: equality, capacity, and differentiation) may preclude successful attainment on another dimension.

30. "Countries that have clearly established their sense of national *identity* and achieved a broad recognition of the *legitimacy* of their system of government before they are confronted with the demand for universal *participation* in public affairs are, for example, significantly different from countries in which popular *participation* precedes either the *legitimization* of public institutions or the *penetration* of the governmental system into the mass of society" (PYE 1971a:ix). Cf. also HUNTINGTON's (1968) description of stable and unstable polities (see chapter 7.2.3).

31. Originally (see PYE 1963) there was also an integration crisis which was later dropped from the theoretical scheme. The original formulation seems to be well captured in a paraphrase by ROKKAN (which, however, was not checked with the authors):

> Three of the six crises arise out of conflicts in the extension and differentiation of the administrative apparatus of the nation-state:
> the *penetration* crisis—the crucial initial challenge of the establishment of a co-ordinated network of territorial administrative agents independent of local power resources and responsive to directives from the central decisionmaking organs;
> the *integration* crisis—clashes over the establishment of allocation rules for the equalization of the shares of administrative offices, benefits and resources among all the culturally-territorially-politically distinct segments and sectors of the national community;
> the *distribution* crisis—conflicts over the expansion of the administrative apparatus of the nation-state through the organization of services and the imposition of control measures for the equalization of economic conditions between the different strata of the population and between localities differing in their resources and levels of production.
> The other three crises arise out of conflicts between elites and counterelites in the definition and differentiation of the territorial population:
> the *identity* crisis—the crucial initial challenge in the establishment and extension of a common culture and the development of media and agencies for the socialization of future citizens into this community of shared codes, values, memories and symbols;
> the *legitimacy* crisis—clashes over the establishment of central structures of political communication, consultation and representation commanding the loyalty and confidence of significant sections of the national population and ensuring regular conformity to rules and regulations issued by the agencies authorized by the system;
> the *participation* crisis—the conflict over the extension of rights of consultation and representation to all strata of the territorial population and over the protection or rights of association, demonstration and opposition (ROKKAN 1970:670).

32. As TILLY puts it (in accordance with VERBA himself), "neither the crises, nor the sequences, nor the connections among them, have been reliably identified" (TILLY 1975a:611). The studies in GREW (1978) do not do away with this objection.
33. This holds true in spite of the various studies on coups d'état (see chapter 7).
34. Yet, interestingly there is no explicit crisis definition in this book which is strongly inductive in nature.

(35)

35. Critics have pointed to the use of imprecise and arbitrary measures, the cases selected for study and, as a consequence, the lack of a homogeneous explanandum, and the general subscription to zero-sum conflict analysis (cf. BARRY 1977a; 1977b; and the reply by ALMOND/ FLANAGAN 1978; cf. also the critique in HOLT/TURNER 1975).

36. There is disagreement as to whether this definition indeed captures central aspects of legitimacy. "Legitimacy is a quality attributed to a regime by a population. That quality is the *outcome* of the government's capacity to engender legitimacy; the capacity to produce legitimacy is not legitimacy itself" (MERELMAN 1966:548). We would maintain, however, that this point of disagreement will have to be settled empirically (cf. below the distinction between short- and long-term conditions and effects).

37. LIPSET's definition somewhat obscures the importance of charisma of political leaders in newly developing nations (but see also on this point LIPSET 1967). Leadership variables should be treated much more explicitly in crises research (cf., e.g., WILLNER 1968). "In Tanzania, Guinea, and Senegal the influence of a strong leader (Nyerere, Toure, and Senghor, respectively) may contribute to a more stable institutionalized party system and may minimize elite conflict. Similarly, the skillful leadership of Nyerere in Tanzania could have averted the magnitudes of internal war predicted on the basis of our model" (DUVALL/ WELFLING 1973a:695). One of the best indicators of the importance of these variables is the turbulence usually created through the death of a charismatic figure, the problem then being how personal charisma can be transferred to a successor or to the new political system as a whole (cf. also HUNTINGTON's approach in chapter 6.3.5).

38. A slightly more restrictive definition of legitimacy is suggested in another article of LIPSET: "Legitimacy involves the capacity of a political system to engender and maintain the belief that existing political institutions are the *best that could possibly be devised*" (LIPSET 1959:108; emphasis added). Cf. below for some additional aspects of LIPSET's treatment of legitimacy.

39. PYE, among many other authors, notes that a society (a regime, the elites) may avoid some crises the more it commands legitimacy: "Thus a dramatic resolution of a legitimacy crisis can set the stage for a society to be spared, for a time at least, the other crises" (PYE 1971: 137). "When the effectiveness of various governments broke down in the 1930s, those societies which were high on the scale of [inferred] legitimacy remained democratic, while such countries as Germany, Austria, and Spain lost their freedom, and France narrowly escaped a similar fate" (LIPSET 1960:82).

40. In another article KELMAN (1969:280) uses basically the same model, but speaks of "patterns of personal involvement in the national system." He calls his second dimension "manner of integration into the system," subdividing it into ideological, role-participant, and normative integration.

41. See EASTON (1965:301–2) for a more specific critique. As WEBER tends to equate legal authority with legitimacy (at least in the modern

state), he seems to miss a basic point of the discussion here (as to WEBER, cf. WINCKELMANN 1952; HUFNAGEL 1971; and BENSMAN 1979 for a useful explication of the various meanings WEBER attaches to legitimacy). For a brief overview of various jurisprudential views on legality-legitimacy, see D'ENTRÈVES (1963). RUSTOW's (1967:157) adoption of WEBER in defining political legitimacy as the sum of traditional, rational-legal, and charismatic legitimacy (cf. also ANDRAIN 1975:156) is not very helpful either. Nevertheless, once the *sociopsychological* qualities of legitimacy have been more precisely measured, it may be interesting to test RUSTOW's hypothesis, derived from his definition: "To obtain the same amount of political legitimacy, any decrease in one of the terms must be compensated by an increase in one or both of the others" (ibid.).

42. Critics, however, have frequently noted that the conversion process of inputs into outputs remains rather underspecified in EASTON's writings.

43. It remains to be tested empirically whether polities with diffuse support reach the same longevity as polities with diffuse and specific support. Yet a clear separation between the two independent variables might be impossible due to the transition phenomenon described. An interactive effect of diffuse and specific support on longevity might then be quite likely. If tests of these propositions are to succeed at all, great care must be taken when drawing time boundaries on the periods to be analyzed.

44. The mixed form of the "civic culture, which sometimes contains apparently contradictory political attitudes [e.g., active political participation and passive acceptance], seems to be particularly appropriate for democratic political systems, for they, too, are mixtures of contradictions" (ALMOND/VERBA 1963:340). According to their interview data, ALMOND/VERBA maintain that civil cultures are present only in Britain (the prime example) and the United States, but not in West Germany, Italy, or Mexico. For a discussion and critique of the notion of the deferential British implied here, see JESSOP (1971). Also "there is no evidence to indicate whether the civic culture is the source or the product of stable democracy. It is possible that the civic culture develops only after many decades of democratic experience" (ROTH/WILSON 1976:447). More recently see also *The Civic Culture Revisited* (ALMOND/VERBA 1980).

45. "Important segments of the German army, civil service, and aristocratic classes rejected the Weimar Republic not because it was ineffective, but because its symbolism and basic values negated their own" (LIPSET 1959:87).

46. The distinction between external and internal efficacy draws on an analysis of the Index of Political Efficacy of the Survey Research Center at the University of Michigan carried out by BALCH (1974). It was his aim to show that "diffuse system support is . . . linked with external efficacy . . . and individual ego strength is . . . linked with internal efficacy" (BALCH 1974:31). The scale of political efficacy seems to be composed of two discrete subscales. Performing a path

(46)

analysis on survey data from 1956 to 1960, McPHERSON et al. (1977) recommend to researchers using the Index of Political Efficacy "to consider using NO CARE and NO SAY items without the VOTING and COMPLEX items. The former two items are reliable, reasonably stable, and almost uncontaminated by systematic measurement error, while the latter items are relatively unreliable, unstable, and display systematic differences from each other and the NO SAY and NO CARE items" (McPHERSON et al. 1977:520; for some related conclusions see HOUSE/MASON 1975). The items read: "Sometimes politics and government seem so complicated that a person like me can't really understand what's going on (COMPLEX). Voting is the only way that people like me can have a say about how the government runs things (VOTING). I don't think public officials care much about what people like me think (NO CARE). People like me don't have any say about what the government does (NO SAY)." Cf. also the discussion below.

47. "The inculcation of a sense of legitimacy is probably the single most effective device for regulating the flow of diffuse support in favor both of the authorities and of the regime" (EASTON 1965:278). EASTON and DENNIS consequently made an effort to link their systems analysis with research on political socialization. Yet results have become available which "cast considerable doubt upon the importance of childhood data collected under allocative politics and system persistence models [i.e., the model favored by EASTON]" (SEARING et al. 1973:429).

48. A question of special interest in this context is how states which are not fully legitimate govern themselves (cf. ROSE 1969). What is their specific "mix" of strategies for obtaining compliance vis-à-vis more democratic polities, for example? "It is our contention that the conditions leading to semiloyalty, or even suspicion of semiloyalty, by leading participants in the political game, opposition and government parties alike, account for the breakdown process [of democratic regimes] almost as much as the role of the disloyal opposition" (LINZ 1978:38).

49. EASTON (1965:307) himself mentions an additional category, "omnibus legitimating responses," which simply denotes responses which do not fit exactly into one of the six proposed types as they overlap with others.

50. WEBER's (1964:179–201, 832–73) discussion of the charismatic leader and his followers comes to mind here. In EASTON's view, personal legitimacy is broader in scope than charismatic legitimacy (cf. the inconclusive discussion in EASTON 1965:303–4).

51. And, as EASTON does at times, political community as the most general object of reference (see EASTON 1965:320ff. for a general discussion).

52. On the other hand, "what, on purely theoretical grounds, might be less expected is that systems free from any visible threat of stress should find it continuously necessary to attend to the renewal of sentiments of legitimacy" (EASTON 1965:308).

53. In this chapter external factors have been totally omitted from the discussion. If they were taken into consideration, there might very well be cases where a regime gains in legitimacy as well as in performance but

(Chapter Six)

still fails due to external pressures. The fate of the Czech government in 1968 provides an example here.

54. No news to successful dictators: "Let them hate me as long as they fear me" (Caligula).

55. Recently, it has also been argued that in Western states increased state interventionism is to make up for deficits in performance on the part of the economy (the capitalist class) and thus to prevent further erosion of the legitimacy of the political order. O'CONNOR puts the arguments in this way:

> The capitalistic state must try ot fulfill two basic and often mutually contradictory functions—*accumulation* and *legitimization*. This means that the state must try to maintain or create the conditions in which profitable capital accumulation is possible. However, the state also must try to maintain or create the conditions of social harmony. A capitalist state that openly uses its coercive forces to help one class accumulate capital at the expense of other classes loses its legitimacy and hence undermines the basis of its loyalty and support. But a state that ignores the necessity of assisting the process of capital accumulation risks drying up the sources of its own power, the economy's surplus production capacity and taxes drawn from this surplus (and other forms of capital) (O'CONNOR 1973:6; cf. also OFFE 1973 for another variant of this theory).

> Yet, the problems of accumulation and legitimization are faced by *any* industrial and preindustrial society. As BELL notes: "The essential difference between so-called socialist states and the Western capitalist states is less the question of property relations (though private property has given a dominant economic class a disproportionate degree of political power) than the character of the polity, the way the citizenry conceives of the public household. . . . it is not the 'capitalist state' that runs [the risks mentioned above], it is the democratic polity" (BELL 1976:231). Other objections to this type of crisis analysis are that, to a large extent, concepts are left undefined and/or are presented without specific empirical referents; no attempts at falsification are made, and some kind of predetermined development apparently is subscribed to.

56. The argument just presented will, however, be somewhat weakened if one takes into consideration the unquestioned authority the czar had among large portions of the peasantry who spoke of him as the "little father."

57. We are aware of the problems of identification in such a model operating with so many feedback loops. Our heuristic exercise may nevertheless be of some use in that it might tell the researcher where to look first. Putting these theoretical matters to empirical tests in any case would require the making of bold assumptions if efforts at falsification are to succeed.

(58)

58. For one: "Under any circumstances, ineffectiveness in goal-achievement may undermine legitimacy, but differences of opinion about the legitimacy of any regime may conversely lessen its effectiveness" (WISEMAN 1971:183). Or: "The longer a system endures at internal peace, the more likely are the symbols and attitudes of legitimacy to be passed on unquestioningly from one generation to the next (see MERELMAN 1966)" (GURR/McCLELLAND 1971:32).

59. There is also the possibility of an interaction effect. For reasons of simplicity, however, we assume a mere additive effect here. Moreover, from a historical point of view, there is also the possibility of a positive effect of repression on performance. Historical latecomers such as Prussia, Japan, and Russia provide examples, even though in the former two instances repression occurred less in the economic sphere. Also in the case of Russia one would have to take into consideration the enormous numbers of victims when evaluating performance.

60. There are some parallels between our model 1 and the model developed by ECKSTEIN/GURR (1975:468). Their dependent variable is persistence and adaptability (which they subsume under the general label durability). In their comprehensive work ECKSTEIN/GURR discuss a number of feedback effects which have been left out here. Altogether, however, we believe that the present model, developed independently by us (apart from the impetus received from the works of GURR/ McCLELLAND 1971 and GURR 1974a) is simpler. The basic hypothesis of ECKSTEIN/GURR (1975:470) is that the durability of political systems "depends principally on congruence and complementarity on the most salient dimensions of authority," "chiefly the units most instrumental in political socialization and in processes of recruitment of political elites" (ECKSTEIN 1979:17). Recently ECKSTEIN added that "congruence should increase monotonically as a function of performance (support)," that "it is considered a necessary condition for very high support" (ECKSTEIN 1979:17), and finally that the x-variable and y-variable could be reversed. As to a theoretical position counter to congruence theorizing see, e.g., HUNTINGTON (1975). The work of LINZ (1978) also shows some clear parallels to our undertaking here, even though we focus only on a few theoretically important variables, whereas he deals with many more variables and adds historical insight to his discussion of the conditions and consequences of the breakdown of democratic regimes.

61. An interesting question in this context has been taken up by ROSE who asks "whether the techniques suitable for developing support and compliance differ from those maintaining them once full legitimacy is achieved. A century ago BAGEHOT argued that this was the case, and events since have supported his thesis" (ROSE 1971:38).

62. Apart from exceeding expectations, governments may be overloaded because of scarce resources available, inadequate governmental institutions, insufficient output, or output with less pay-off than expected. See the problem outline by ROSE (1975).

(Chapter Six)

63. There is also the possibility of a gap between what people experience personally and what they think is generally true. The two need not be consistent.

64. One must admit, however, that in terms of operationalization not much has been gained so far, since the concept of diffuse support in itself is difficult to index. Nevertheless, we would maintain that legitimacy should be conceived of as the more abstract theoretical notion. Cf. also the discussion below.

65. Compare also the following remarks underlining a rather different approach to the problems of crises, illegitimacy, and political instability than the one outlined, e.g., by EASTON: "Two elements predominate in concepts of political stability: order and continuity" (HUNTINGTON/DOMINGUEZ 1975:7). As to the approach taken by HUNTINGTON, who stresses the order component of stability rather than the legitimacy (consensus) component, cf. chapters 5.1.2.4, 6.3.5, and 7.2.3.

66. EASTON probably would deny this famous dictum of RENAN; in his version of systems theory, diffuse support is just the opposite of a daily plebiscite.

67. Alienation concepts are of special importance here. Following FINIFTER (1972), EASTON suggests considering alienation as a possible determinant (and effect, in turn) of lack of support (as to another important theoretical conceptualization, cf. GAMSON 1968). More complicated is EASTON's attempt to delineate the concept of compliance. He does not conceive of it as a component of support, but "as a determinant, consequence or possible indicator of support rather than as one of its dimensions" (EASTON 1975:455). For the sake of simplicity, compliance should not be conceived of as a dimension of legitimacy: in the case of voluntary compliance (an extreme case), legitimacy is given. Where compliance takes place under conditions of mere repression (the other extreme case) repression in itself might be a more appropriate term (see model 1). Other theoretical concepts which must be distinguished in this context include such notions as relative deprivation, discontent, and systemic frustration.

68. The confidence in political leaders decreased from 1964 to 1972 (MILLER 1974b:990). Trust in government strongly declined among whites during 1964–70, long before Watergate, and even more so among blacks, who showed an increase in trust from 1964 to 1966 (MILLER 1974a:955). In addition, "support of the federal government decreased substantially between 1964 and 1970" (MILLER 1974a:970).

69. SEARS et al. (1978) also believe they have found evidence against the behavioral relevance of the EASTON concept of diffuse trust. They report a lack of covariation between this variable and supportive reactions to energy-saving measures (sample: inhabitants of Los Angeles in 1974). Yet, rather than drawing on EASTON's framework, their result might perhaps be interpreted more adequately as a form of habitual reaction.

(70)

70. Conversely, the system may have lost all credit in the eyes of some individuals, while local representatives of the system are exempted from such a critique.

71. Compare, e.g., SNIDERMAN et al. (1975) for some data on the "stability of support for the political system" during the Watergate crisis. Compare also SEARING et al. (1973:420) who argue that one should differentiate between diffuse support with policy agreement and diffuse support of a political system without policy agreement.

72. On the *elite* level, however, the distinction between incumbent elites and political system as such is a rather important one, even though the masses are the *differentiating factor* as to the likelihood of success and the eventual outcomes of more intense forms of political dissident behavior. Cf. the analyses of coups and revolutionary attempts in chapters 7 and 8.

73. EASTON (1975:439ff.) has noticed this himself (cf. also LOEWEN-BERG 1971 and for empirical counterevidence SIGEL/HOSKIN 1977:119). Compare also CONVERSE's "The Nature of Belief Systems in Mass Publics" (CONVERSE 1964). One must also bear in mind, with respect to many American elections, that: "People are likely to be attracted to candidates more because of their personality or party identification than because of the stands they take on issues. It appears that even the presumed policy differences among party candidates themselves are less likely to influence political outputs than the level of economic development" (EASTON 1975:440 referring here to the work of DYE 1966).

74. Using representative American survey data and carrying out a factor analysis of some measures of political beliefs, CITRIN (1977:389) finds a third theoretically meaningful component, responsiveness of government. Yet, other authors at times subsume this dimension under the conceptual label of trust.

75. For comparable conclusions see CITRIN's San Francisco Bay Area studies of 1972 and 1973 (CITRIN 1977). He points out that alienation as such only very weakly predicts protest readiness. Alienation in interaction with variables like education, age, intellectual and political resources, however, substantially raises the accuracy of prediction.

76. Contrary to the beliefs and hopes of democrats, a democratic regime should never be allowed to approach the point at which its survival will depend on the readiness of its supporters to fight for it in the streets. Few citizens, even in a crisis, are ready to support those who might want to overthrow democracy, but in modern society they feel unable to do anything in such a situation. Only those on the extremes of the political spectrum are prepared to fight or are likely to have the organizational resources to do so. To resist the disloyalty of minorities, a democratic government must pevent their access to the means of violence by keeping them disarmed and politically isolated from mass support. Should such minorities be able to gain support from the levels of power

that would allow them to command the loyalty or neutrality of the instruments of coercion of the state, the fate of the regime is in serious danger (LINZ 1978:85).

77. ASHER (1978:730), however, contends that WRIGHT's indicators "may be overly sensitive to specific governmental outputs and current events. If so, then WRIGHT does not have adequate grounds for ruling out diffuse support as a source of stability."

78. "Outputs and beneficial performance may rise and fall while this support, in the form of a generalized attachment, continues. The obverse is equally true. Where support is negative, it represents a reserve of ill-will that may not easily be reduced by outputs or performance" (EASTON 1975:444). In general, whether the political system should be blamed for these breakdowns in performance or whether people simply blame them on the system does not make any difference in an empirically oriented crises science.

79. One may speculate that in such a model of adaptability, variables like coercion and political violence would carry less weight than in models explaining the persistence of political systems.

80. Note that we speak of persistence in a somewhat different sense than ECKSTEIN/GURR (1975) who start from the following definitional equation: Durability = persistence + adaptability. In another paper (ZIMMERMANN 1979a) we use persistence as the general dependent variable that can be measured dichotomously or continuously (durability).

81. This holds perhaps for performance as well. Thus, a total score of performance might hide countervailing trends in specific areas.

82. Perhaps elites as well can command diffuse support (even though, for reasons of conceptual clarity, the notion of diffuse support should be reserved for the system level, cf. EASTON 1975:445). In any case, one must reckon with support being a multidimensional concept.

83. Using FITZGIBBON's (1967) "democratic attainment index" which is based on sampling expert opinions on fifteen criteria every five years, BWY (1968b) reports strong negative relationships between legitimacy (using change as well as static measures, 1950–1955, 1955) and organized violence (1958–1960). Yet no strong relationship is found between legitimacy and anomic violence (N=20 Latin American countries). But see SNOW (1968) for a harsh criticism pointing to various contrary results and to other shortcomings as well. Cf. also chapter 5.1.2.5.

84. An interesting measure of legitimacy is suggested by KENNEDY. In the second part of the following quotation, however, once again problems of indexing legitimacy via indirect measures become apparent:

> The extent to which a regime is secure in its legitimacy could be measured by the relative size of its internal security budgets; the stronger the sense of legitimacy that a government has in the minds of its citizens the less it will need to enforce its rule by intensive sanctions against dissidents and would-be dissidents. It is

(84)

not entirely an accurate measure (nor are these budgets readily
available for measurement) because a well-organized and alienated
minority in a society, and particularly in the urban industrialized
societies, can disrupt the process of government to such an extent
that extraordinary measures of security are required to enforce
the will of the majority (KENNEDY 1974:21–22).

85. Among indicators commonly employed are decline in party identification, the rise of single-issue parties, and various measures of political
distrust and support. Decline in party identification need not, however,
indicate a loss of regime legitimacy, but, on the contrary, may document that the electorate is becoming more self-assured in view of the
insufficient performance of its former parties.

86. Eight items referring, for example, to the "evaluation of how well the
system upholds basic values, . . . is consonant with [the respondent's]
basic values, . . . operate[s] in such a way as to uphold presumably
consensual political values such as representation of citizens and protection of basic rights due to them" (MULLER/JUKAM 1977:1566).

87. Four items, two of them asking directly for the respondent's "evaluation of the trustworthiness of the national government" (MULLER/
JUKAM 1977:1569).

88. KLINGEMANN's (1972) left-right scale is used.

89. For comparable results see also SIGEL/HOSKIN (1977). They report
another finding perhaps of general importance: at first legitimacy might
be withdrawn from more local institutions (cf. the findings on the black
riots in chapter 5.3.2) before political institutions of a higher order will
be affected by a decline in legitimacy which then might lead to a
decline in diffuse support. They also propose the notion of comparative
pride, i.e., the evaluation of one's own political system, its incumbents,
institutions, policies, etc. compared to those in other countries.
Depending on the outcome of such comparison processes, the original
discontent might be enhanced or mitigated. The sample in their study
has been drawn from high school seniors in Pennsylvania.

90. Selection from eleven items which the respondent described as a task
of the incumbent government.

91. "Nearly one-sixth of those in the university milieu express very negative
support and almost one-third score at the 'negative' zone; by contrast,
outside of the university milieu, very few register in the 'very negative'
zone of Political Support, while only 9.1 percent of those in the urban
milieu and only 14.8 percent of those in the agrarian milieu register in
the 'negative' zone" (MULLER/JUKAM 1977:1580). They propose the
following explanation for this facilitative effect due to community
context: (1) students are easily available; (2) they probably risk less
than other groups; (3) the university climate facilitates participation in
protest activities.

92. One may, of course, call into question whether the results of MULLER/
JUKAM (1977) will be the same if the present conservative opposition is
elected to office.

93. Or as put by STOKES (1962:72, also quoted in MULLER/JUKAM
1977:1568): "Plainly we ought not to assume that the people expressing negative feeling toward government . . . were calling for fundamental change in the political order." In fact, it may work just the opposite
way: to preserve the political order in the long run by calling for
specific, less far-reaching changes in the short run.

94. Combining data on political trust (1974 American national election
survey) with data on the front-page content of ninety-four newspapers,
MILLER et al. (1979) found that political distrust (cynicism) seems to
be influenced not only by policy dissatisfaction (p=.25) and incumbent
support (Gerald Ford: p=–.13), but also by media criticism (p=.19),
which in itself is negatively related to incumbent support (r=.–17).
Cynicism, in turn, is positively related to inefficacy (p=.35). Exposure
to media, however, is negatively (p=–.18) related to inefficacy. "Our
analyses suggest a conceptual model that posits a structural explanation
of inefficacy as a result of accumulating distrust. As discontent with
government accumulates over time, we would expect, eventually, an
erosion of citizens' beliefs about political institutions. . . . Cynicism
evidently reflects general dissatisfaction with government performance
and not simply a lack of support for specific incumbents [cf. also
MILLER 1979]. It may therefore be considered a 'leading' indicator
of diffuse support" (MILLER et al. 1979:79).

95. Thus, an increase in legitimacy of specific political institutions might
take place, whereas other reference objects experience a decline in
legitimacy very much in the sense of "checks and balances." The
Watergate crisis, e.g., led to a sizeable increase in public esteem as far
as the judges and the courts of justice were concerned.

96. Yet, their instrument of measuring support (a thermometer scale
ranging from 1 to 100 with 50 reflecting neutral feelings) might have
introduced some errors of measurement, as "negative support" might
be a phenomenon to be captured more adequately through a separate
dimension going in another direction (cf., e.g., the study by SNIDER-
MAN 1978 mentioned before).

97. There is also an international attribution effect which we will not
take up in our discussion of internal crises: regimes with any degree of
autocracy will gain some international respect the longer they persist.
The history of diplomatic relations provides many instances in this
respect.

98. There are, of course, a number of well-known examples which testify
to the stability of multiparty systems, the Netherlands and Switzerland
being the most prominent. (For a discussion of the issues involved, such
as *Verzuiling* and elite consensus, cf. LIJPHART 1968, DAHL 1971:
105–23, STEINER 1974, and chapter 9; for a summary of critical
arguments see OBLER et al. 1977.) For some recent quantitative evidence along these lines from European states during 1918–72, see
DODD (1976). Multiparty coalitions were quite stable if they were
"minimum winning." HUNTINGTON, however, deals largely with
modernizing countries: "It would appear that a multiparty system is

(98)

    incompatible with a high level of political institutionalization and political stability in a modernizing country. In modernizing countries multiparty systems are weak party systems" (HUNGTINGTON 1968: 423). Results from a study of twenty-five black African countries (data taken from MORRISON et al. 1972) provide evidence in favor of HUNTINGTON in the sense that in 1963 "one-party states were better able to contain . . . general communal instability [revolts, civil wars, ethnic conflicts, rebellions, and irredentist conflicts]" (McKOWN/ KAUFFMAN 1973:64).

99.   In other words (but still in HUNTINGTON's sense): "A system is there-fore more likely to endure if it reduces its dependence on the avail-ability of outstanding leaders and maintains some balance between demands and capabilities" (KAVANAGH 1977:4). However, person-ality variables are of vital importance in times of crisis if the leadership personnel is exposed to increased stress (see also the analysis by LINZ 1978:90–91).

100. In this respect there are many parallels to various passages in the works of LENIN and other revolutionaries. Cf. also HUNTINGTON (1968: 334–43 and passim). The following comment from a review by RUS-TOW draws the attention to policy implications that may follow from these portions of HUNTINGTON's analysis (cf. also the criticism raised in chapter 5.1.2.4). He begins by quoting HUNTINGTON (1968: 402): "'Mobilization' and 'organization,' those twin slogans of commu-nist political action, define precisely the route to party strength. The party and the party system which combine them reconcile political modernization with political development." RUSTOW then continues his review:

> And yet in the final pages it is democracy, universal suffrage, and the two-party system that appear to have the last word. And sig-nificantly, it is the "conservatism of Democracy" through its tendency to "Ruralizing Elections" that HUNTINGTON praises (pp. 443, 448).
>
> The passages on Leninism are the core of the puzzle. Here is HUNTINGTON, the Harvard adviser on American foreign aid, giving his sympathetic accounts of traditional monarchs and military juntas, detailing the advantages of Tory democracy—and, like a latter-day Ludendorff, loading Leninism aboard a sealed compartment in his argument as his answer to the political prob-lems of the developing countries (RUSTOW 1969:124).

101. Put in very simple terms, this hypothesis is anything but new: "In some measure, governability and democracy are warring concepts. An excess of democracy means a deficit in governability; easy governability suggests faulty democracy" (CROZIER et al. 1975:173). JOSEPH (1979) provides a useful summary of arguments raised by neoconserva-tives like HUNTINGTON and SARTORI and by revisionist liberals like LINDBLOM and DAHL in the debate on the "crisis of pluralist democracy."

102. Employing a rather crude measure, "Party system stability was measured dichotomously, distinguishing between countries with large and persisting party organizations (including one- as well as multi-party systems), and those with parties that were predominantly ephemeral, personalistic, or nonexistent" (GURR 1970a:286).
103. Using cross-sectional data for 330 polities from 1800 to 1970, GURR et al. (forthcoming) report a third-degree polynomial relationship between national political institutions (largely measured as in GURR 1968a, using indigenous origins and longevity as basic dimensions) and magnitude of conflict: From 0 to 45 years of longevity, there is a negative relationship (the slope being rather large) with the dependent variable. From 45 to 160 years, however, a positive relationship between age of institutions and conflict is found, whereas beyond this point once again a negative relationship emerges (based on too few cases to be reliable). Thus, there is some slight evidence that institutions may "wear out" over time.
104. SARTORI (1976:267) even wonders whether adaptability does not refer to a different level. Perhaps it can best be conceived of as a function of the other three components: complexity, autonomy, and coherence. Cf. also ROBINS (1976) for an effort to explain and apply HUNTINGTON's criteria to "Political Institutionalization and the Integration of Elites." For the most part, however, ROBINS's book is disappointing, as it contains rather sweeping generalizations but no hard data.
105. In a recent paper SANDERS/HERMAN (1976; 1977) report similar results when dealing with government stability and survival in 329 cases. The relative size of antisystem parties and whether a government has a majority turn out to be the strongest predictors. Finally, the longer a government exists or survives, the more likely is the occurrence of riots (very weak positive correlations) and of protest demonstrations (slightly positive correlations), whereas a comparable negative relationship emerges with respect to political strikes.
106. For example, cabinet ministers may only circulate in and out of office.
107. In a study of democratic political stability (measured in terms of support for system parties as well as government persistence, see HURWITZ 1971; for an index of political stability in terms of changes of government, cf. TAYLOR 1969:560) in twenty Western nations (period: 1945–69), HURWITZ (1972) has tested the predictive power of the following variables: economic development (+); economic growth (–); Roman Catholicism as dominant religious belief system (–); degree of multiparty system (–); religious, linguistic, ethnic/racial homogeneity (+); and level of democratic attainment (+). In bivariate terms, the signs of the coefficients are as expected, with the exception of religious homogeneity and democratic performance where negative signs are observed. The individual hypotheses do not fare well in explaining variation in the dependent variable. "When examined as a group, [however,] they account for less than two-thirds of the variance in stability" (ibid., p. 485). For a new measure taking care of the rela-

(107)

tive size of parties and its impact on political instability (defined in terms of executive instability, following TAYLOR/HUDSON 1972) for 142 post-1944 elections in 15 Western European countries see LAAKSO/TAAGEPERA (1979). Using various indexes, they report no relationship between what they call the "effective number of parties" and political instability.

108. One-party majority governments and consociational systems were excluded, since as WARWICK shows, different causal processes are involved. Finally, "only those [governments] whose demise was the result of a loss of internal cohesion or parliamentary support were considered appropriate material, since terminations caused by such factors as regular elections or the death of a President are irrelevant to the issue at hand" (WARWICK 1979:489).

109. Critics of the concept of political culture have objected to the common practice of using the notion of political culture as a residual explanation of a large variety of phenomena.

110. For example, communication and integration are two global variables which have been suggested to explain political instability and political violence (cf. MORRISON/STEVENSON 1972a and AKE 1967). Yet, looking at the operationalizations used or proposed, much overlapping with other socioeconomic variables (and other classes of variables as well) takes place. For some interesting results as to the conditions of political instability in the African context, see MORRISON/STEVEN-SON (1972a).

111. An elaborate index comprising various socioeconomic variables (social welfare, social mobilization, economic growth, government extractive capability, and government distributive capability) for predicting system instability in nineteen Latin American countries has been devised by DUFF/McCAMANT (1968). Yet, as shown by MORRISON/ STEVENSON (1974), there is one basic component of this index: the difference between social welfare and social mobilization which predicts almost equally as well the scores on the dependent variable instability and on other dependent variables, namely organized violence and anomic violence. In general, similar results hold for black African countries. It should be noted, however, that the index does not explain more than 18% of the variance in political instability. Moreover, the original index used for measuring the dependent variable has not been independently validated. Finally, one may wonder whether similar results will be obtained if the social-welfare–social-mobilization variable is used in the theoretically more adequate form of a ratio (as, e.g., in HIBBS 1973; cf. chapter 5.1.2.4) instead of the present variant employing difference measures.

112. Cf. GURR/DUVALL (1973:167) on the relationship between political and economic discrimination. They found political discrimination to have causal priority in explaining the magnitude of political conflict. Or as put by ALMOND/VERBA: "Everything being equal, the sense of ability to participate in politics appears to increase the legitimacy of a system and to lead to political stability" (ALMOND/VERBA 1963:

243). The underlying rationale is that full political participation will lead to a reduction of discrimination in other areas as well.

113. There is, of course, an underlying parallel in the theories of HUNTINGTON and KORNHAUSER. What, according to their function, are termed intermediating groups in the theory of mass society are denoted as political institutionalization in HUNTINGTON's theoretical scheme. Both theories, however, remain insufficiently specified. Furthermore, the theoretical considerations following the presentation of Table 6.3 could also be linked to WRIGHT's (1976) ideas.

114. As other authors have done (cf. ECKSTEIN 1961:42–45; HEBERLE 1963), PINARD has pointed out that not only individuals but also organizations may be alienated from dominant developments within the society. Thus, they may not be able to fulfill the function they are said to fulfill, namely to dampen political radicalism, but may instead act as transmission belts for political radicalism (for further points of criticism against the theory of mass society, cf. PINARD 1971: 179–219).

> If the strains are severe and widespread, alienated groups will tend to be particularly active; moreover, either conformist groups will tend to move from a restraining position to a more neutral or even to a mobilizing position, or their members will tend to elude their restraining effects. Their communicating role, on the other hand, will be working fully. To the extent that this prevails, I would predict that integrated individuals and pluralist societies will be more prone to social and political movements than atomized people and mass societies. This prediction, of course, is just the opposite of that made by mass theorists.
>
> If, on the other hand, strains are not severe or widespread, then restraining effects will tend to predominate over mobilizing effects, and communicating effects will be weak since there is no need for a new movement. Under such circumstances, any new movement, if it should appear, will of course be weak; but to the extent that it succeeds in recruiting some people, the basic proposition of mass theory should hold: the lower the degree of integration, the greater the proneness to social movements. So far, therefore, mass theory appears to be sound, paradoxically, only when strains are limited, that is, when the success of a movement is highly problematic to start with (PINARD 1971:194).

Actually, SMELSER's (1963) scheme of analysis is used as the theoretical model in PINARD's analysis of the Social Credit Party in Canada. Strain is defined by PINARD in terms of economic hardship (crisis), whereas the party system is conceived of as a conducive variable, for there was no sufficiently strong alternative for discontented voters (the Conservatives were weak) who thus gave a third party, the Social Credit Party, a chance.

115. A notable effort to determine some of the conditions for intermediate groups and organizations to function as predicted in theory is found in

(115)

LEPSIUS (1968) who studies the conditions of the breakdown of intermediate structures at the end of the Weimar Republic and the beginning of the Nazi regime. Out of the various specific conditions worked out by LEPSIUS, we will mention only a few. He starts from the assumption that "intermediate groups are dependent in their legitimacy on the functioning of government" (ibid., p. 298). If an intermediate group or organization drops out, a power deficit among the system of intermediate groups and organizations is said to result, a vacuum which may be filled or reduced through coalition formation. If this does not occur, successively all of the other intermediate groups and organizations are said to be in danger. Intermediate groups should avoid the personalization of conflicts, as the charisma of a political leader might be strong enough to override the attachment individuals might have for these particular groups. While this set of conditions has been derived from an analysis of the coming to power of the Nazis in Germany these hypotheses are nevertheless interesting enough to merit testing on a wider scale.

116. Two further qualifications of the theory of cross-cutting cleavages should be mentioned here: "If a society is either too homogeneous or too heterogeneous over racial, linguistic, and religious [and other relevant] cleavages, then democratic political organization is not likely to be stable" (RAE/TAYLOR 1970:108). Another important specification is that the effects of cross-cutting may be different according to the "proportion of the population" that is "politically active" (HUNTINGTON 1968:417).

117. The additional differentiations as to objects of legitimacy discussed in chapter 6.3.4 may, of course, be applied here as well.

118. AKE (1967) also has listed a number of key variables (basically covered here) serving as predictors of political stability. His general theory is "that the political system undertaking social mobilization maximizes its capacity for carrying out the process and remaining stable despite the potentially disruptive short-run effects of social mobilization if it is authoritarian, paternal, 'identific,' and consensual. If any of these four structural characteristics is absent and to the extent that functionally compensating factors are also absent, the destabilizing effects of social mobilizations are increased" (AKE 1967:101).

119. Actual intensity is meant here and not intensity estimated along a scale of potential performance, as favored, e.g., in some functional or neo-Marxist approaches to the analysis of crises.

120. Cf., e.g., the structure and the experiences of the German labor movement during the Weimar Republic and afterwards with developments in the Federal Republic of Germany. The newly formed organizations of labor, as well as labor relations in general, have given the Federal Republic an economic advantage over some other Western countries where greater fractionalization of labor organizations seems to prevail.

121. Notwithstanding the stress on quantitative analyses in this study, pursuing a qualitative strategy at *this* point may, in some respects, be a more useful strategy in crises analyses. Perhaps substantial gains in the immediate future may be expected from studies in which a group of

highly comparable crises situations is focused on (and not crises as diverse as in ALMOND et al. 1973).

122. Cf., e.g., KRACAUER's (1947) famous analysis of movies in the Weimar Republic preceding the coming to power of the Nazis.

123. The pervasiveness of decisional challenges is, of course, not totally independent of their political transformability. A large segment of the population may express some demands and may also be represented in parliament with these demands. Yet this "double-weighing" by means of a multiplicative combination is intended to distinguish this type of challenge from decisional challenges on behalf of an *extra*parliamentary opposition (e.g., right now the West German anti–atomic-energy movement).

   Of course, our operationalizations may not make as much sense for all Western political systems, e.g., not in the United States where issue-coalitions among different wings of the major parties are possible.

124. What about the perception of conflict structures through elite and/or mass publics? Zero-sum political cultures, where the gains of certain groups are almost automatically perceived as losses of other groups, are unstable by definition. What are the conditions for zero-sum political cultures to develop? Who defines the point in time at which a crisis exists? The mass media? Parts of the elites? How do elite definitions of the situation and the general feeling of malaise interact over time? Are there time lags in the perception of "objective" crisis situations? Why do perceptions lead only at certain times to a spreading of crisis feelings? What are the relationships between the persistence of a crisis, its intensity, and the solutions finally reached? (For a study of power maintenance and transfers in and after crises years between 1949 and 1966, see HUDSON 1971; N=95 nations.) How often are crises situations perceived as zero-sum conflicts, and how often are other conflict models useful? What relationships exist between internal and external crises? Finally, successful crises managers must be distinguished from crises intensifiers (Brüning with his ill-conceived austerity policy at the end of the Weimar Republic providing an example of the latter type).

Chapter Seven: Military Coups d'État in Cross-national Perspective

1. Parts of this chapter are drawn from ZIMMERMANN (1979b).

2. Cf. also the discussion of the concept of military intervention in THOMPSON (1975b:467). In later portions of this chapter we will be less strict and use military coups and military intervention synonymously (as is often done in the literature).

3. "The definition of a military coup does not require that the coup effort be executed exclusively by regular military personnel; only that some regular military personnel participate. Between 1946 and 1970, about two out of every five military coups involved nonregular military actors (e.g., police, paramilitary, and civilians)" (THOMPSON 1973:52). Cf. also TAYLOR/HUDSON (1972:150–53) who report 147 "irregular

(3)

executive transfers" in fifty-three countries between 1948 and 1967, "irregular executive transfer" being defined as "a change in the office of national executive from one leader or ruling group to another that is accomplished outside the conventional legal or customary procedures for transferring formal power in effect at the time of the event and accompanied by actual or directly threatened violence." This definition is more general than the usual definitions of military coups d'état. Coups, however, constitute the most frequent subcategory of irregular executive transfers.

4. Altogether, some 81 states seem to have experienced some military coup behavior in the twentieth century by 1976 (PALMER/THOMPSON 1978:138). Worldwide data on coup behavior for three decades (1948–77) will be found in the forthcoming third edition of the *World Handbook of Political and Social Indicators*, edited by Charles TAYLOR et al. Writing at approximately the same time as THOMPSON, BLACK reports these findings: "A review of the 123 military regimes in the twentieth century . . . leads to the conclusion that 96 were concerned primarily with order and unity, and that 26 military regimes in 19 countries made a significant effort to transform their societies" (BLACK 1972:20). "The number of . . . military regimes has been growing steadily throughout the twentieth century. Four such regimes were established between 1900 and 1914, 14 in the 1920's, 19 in the 1930's, 14 in the 1940's, and 46 in the 1960's. Of these, 30 survived into the 1970's, and 6 new ones were added" (ibid., p. 16).

5. BIENEN (1978a:11), for one, lists unsuccessful coups for Kenya and Tanzania in 1964, both not included in THOMPSON's lists (but included in LATOUCHE's table, 1973:446 and, in the case of Tanzania, included in LUTTWAK's list, 1979:199). In other instances, however, the agreement between BIENEN, who does not specify his sources, and THOMPSON seems satisfactory.

6. There are not only differences in the definition of successful coups and, where appropriate, unsuccessful coups, but also as far as geographical clustering of nations is concerned. JANOWITZ, for instance, counts Somalia as an Arab country because of its religious and cultural bonds (99% of the population are Muslim), whereas we have opted here for the sub-Saharan group.

7. "The military coup, ignoring all other factors, has a roughly even statistical chance of either succeeding or failing" (THOMPSON 1972:27).

8. Interestingly, according to KENNEDY failure rates of coups seem to increase from Latin American countries (28 out of 81 or 34.6%), to Asian countries (20 out of 42 or 47.6%) and Arab countries (42 out of 83 or 50.6%) to the sub-Sahara region (46 out of 78 or 59.0%). Again the findings of THOMPSON differ considerably from these results. He reports the highest failure rate for European countries (5 out of 7 coups or 71.4%), and lower rates for, in declining order, Latin American countries (77 out of 135 coups; not out of 136 as suggested in Table 7.1 for in his more detailed listing THOMPSON 1973:68 reports

only 6 [instead of 7] coup attempts for Haiti, or 57.0%), Asian (16 out of 40 coups or 40%) and Arab countries (21 out of 53 coups or 39.6%), and sub-Saharan countries (13 out of 38 coups or 34.2%). The rates of compromise coups are between 3.7% (5 out of 135) of all coup attempts in Latin American countries and 11.3% (6 out of 53 coups) in Asian countries, discounting the somewhat higher figure in Europe which is difficult to interpret due to the small number of cases.

Figures for military intervention in black African countries during 1958–75 reported by ANTOLA (1975:208) are closer to THOMPSON's than to those of KENNEDY: ANTOLA lists 52 coups out of which 14 were unsuccessful (27%). According to his figures, the likelihood of unsuccessful military intervention has increased from 25% during the second half of the 1960s to 35% during the first half of the 1970s. LATOUCHE (1973:199) reports considerably different figures for 32 tropical African states during 1960–71: about 2 in 5 coups (18 out of 44) failed.

Finally, LUTTWAK's (1979:195–207) figures from 1945 to August 1978 are not entirely comparable, since he seems to include coups or attempted coups of nonmilitary actors. He reports 288 coups or coup attempts for 77 countries, the rate of failure being 46.5% (131). Following are the figures for the various regions: Africa 137 coups or coup attempts of which 70 (51.1%) failed; Latin America 95, of which 38 (40%) failed; Asia 39 of which 16 (41%) failed, and Europe 11 of which 7 (63.6%) failed. Thus, his figures differ from those of KENNEDY and THOMPSON although in some instances they do seem to be in accord.

9. JANOWITZ draws on THOMPSON (1973), WELCH (1974:125–45), SOLAÚN/QUINN (1973), ANDREWS/RA'ANAN (1969), and BE'ERI (1970:246ff.).

10. The conventional "code specifies that the deposed president shall not be subjected to unnecessary physical discomfort; exile, not the firing squad, is the lot that commonly [in Latin America, not necessarily in Africa or Asia] falls to forcibly unemployed chief executives. The violation of this code produces a sense of shock, as witnessed by the reactions to the assassination of President Villarroel during the 1946 Bolivian coup d'état" (SOLAÚN/QUINN 1973:7).

11. THOMPSON (1975a:452) found for Latin American countries that "some two-thirds of the successful coups (1946–1970) involved minimal or no resistance (71%) and the absence of bloodshed (67%)" and that "between 1946 and 1970, an average death toll of 926 lives per year[!] can be directly traced to military coups" (THOMPSON 1972: 250). It is interesting to note that "civilian involvement occurs in only 25 percent of coups but almost three quarters of these involve some degree of violence" (McKINLAY/COHAN 1974:2). The authors find neither a relationship between degree of violence and subsequent duration of a military regime nor between degree of violence and GNP level (however, GNP level was rather crudely, i.e., dichotomously, determined).

(12)

12. GURR's analyses of the determinants of "conspiracy" (cf. passim in chapter 5.1.1), while being instructive in several respects, nevertheless go beyond the subject of the present discussion.

13. It remains a question of empirical judgment, however, whether HUNTINGTON's (1968:241) hypothesis as to the conditions of *long-term* success of coups does hold: "The ability of the military to develop stable political institutions depends first upon their ability to identify their rule with the masses of the peasantry and to mobilize the peasantry into politics on their side." The urban intelligentsia, the labor movement, as well as factions within the military may be much more important determinants of long-term success of coups. It should be added that HUNTINGTON assumes the urban population to be hostile to coup-making.

14. "The origin of the word [coup] is not certain, but most authorities believe it derives from the Latin word *colaphus* meaning blow or cuff which, in turn, came from the Greek word *kolaphos*" (RAPOPORT 1966:59). GOOCH (1977) describes the change from the "positive" meaning of a coup as "a sudden, skillful stroke by a monarch in defiance of custom or law" (p. viii) to the current use which developed about two hundred years later, namely after the French Revolution.

15. On this point cf. also the definition of LUTTWAK: "A coup consists of the infiltration of a small but critical segment of the state apparatus, which is then used to displace the government from its control of the remainder" (LUTTWAK 1969:27).

16. Yet military leaders may also act as "traditionalizers" as pointed out by MAZRUI in his article on military rule and the re-Africanization of Africa: "the evidence from East Africa would seem to suggest that soldiers may be greater traditionalizers than the more westernized civilians they ousted. For better or worse, that is certainly true of Idi Amin as compared with Milton Obote, and true of Mobutu Sese Seko as compared with such figures as Kasavubu and Moise Tschombe" (MAZRUI 1976:271).

17. Frequently, the army is also the only institution in which all races and religions are represented and only one language, generally that of the former colonists, is spoken (cf. PYE 1961).

18. McWILLIAMS even maintains that the latter condition "existed in many Middle Eastern states, close to the centers of world politics and conflict, where military modernization was the price of the survival of the state. It has been less evident in Latin America, where external pressures for military change have been almost nonexistent, or in Africa, where modern armies, created by colonial powers, have been little more advanced than civilian groups" (McWILLIAMS 1967a:19). But results on the performance of military regimes in various areas (cf. below) do not seem to agree with the external threat → modernization of the military → modernization of society hypothesis.

19. On expanding educational facilities, cf. also the results of JACKMAN (1976), somewhat at odds with those of McKINLAY/COHAN. See also PLUTA (1979:476) who reports for South American governments during 1961–70 that "civilian governments spend more for education."

Like others, he also found that there is "little apparent relationship . . . between regime type and either level of defense spending or size of armed forces" (ibid.).

20. Inconclusive and, considering our aim here, rather indirect results are also found in a study of FEIERABEND/FEIERABEND/HOWARD (1972) on the potential impact of coerciveness (for a discussion of the indicators, cf. chapter 5.1.2.5) on socioeconomic change (N=76 countries; period for the dependent variable: 1935–62, whereas the independent variable, in part, covers later [!] time slices). A final point of criticism refers to the circular reasoning the authors employ when they introduce level of economic development as a control variable yet do not control for overlapping of indicators of economic development with indicators chosen for indexing the dependent variable.

21. This conclusion is corroborated for black African states during the 1960s in the analysis by ANTOLA (1975:214–15): "Military-ruled nations differ in all three dimensions from countries ruled by a civilian government. They have a slower growth rate of the GNP per capita, they have a lower level of the GDP per capita and they also have a slower rate of gross domestic capital formation than have civilian-ruled countries."

22. A study of ten South American countries during 1948–67 by TANNA-HILL (1976) confirms this conclusion. While, in general, there is not much difference in the economic performance of military and civilian regimes, in terms of industrial growth and currency stability, military regimes are more successful than nonmilitary regimes. "The chief differences between military and civilian governments, however, are political. In this area, military regimes prove more repressive [cf. also the figures in McKINLAY/COHAN 1976b:853ff.] and more conservative than civilian governments" (TANNAHILL 1976:233).

23. "A military regime system is any system in which the armed forces have made a coup and subsequently established a government whose main executive post is held by a military person and which lasts for at least the major part of one year" (McKINLAY/COHAN 1976b:850).

24. In this study of McKINLAY/COHAN (1976a) no controls for GNP and area are reported. Advocates of the military-as-modernizers position (cf. also subsequent portions of this chapter) might perhaps argue that it will take more than a decade for the economic policies of the military to succeed.

25. PRICE, however, points to dysfunctions likely to arise if armies or officers take their standards of reference entirely from abroad (cf. also WOLPIN 1975 for some empirical evidence on "External Political Socialization as a Source of Conservative Military Behavior in the Third World"): "It can be hypothesized that as a consequence of foreign reference-group commitments the military tends to be cut off from the expressive symbols that will have resonance in their own societies. They will tend to rely instead on the martial rituals and symbols of a foreign cultural milieu, and this deficiency in the area of indigenous symbol manipulation will seriously reduce their political leadership capacity" (PRICE 1971:428). Yet more successful armies or army leaders—suc-

(25)

cessful in drawing broad support for the army as a guardian of national unity and independence—only adopt certain external symbols and try to amalgamate them with native traditions: PRICE's hypothesis may hold only for rather feudal armies. Nevertheless, his warning that "the consequences for the behavior of organization and officer corps cannot be inferred from the formal organizational model" (PRICE 1971:401) deserves closer attention. Organizational models and reference groups models should, in fact, be considered together at this stage of knowledge instead of preferring one to the other.

26. FINER presents an instructive list of *official* regime styles:
    "Nasser: Presidential Democracy
    Ayub Khan: Basic Democrcay
    Sukarno: Guided Democracy
    Franco: Organic Democracy
    Stroessner: Selective Democracy
    Trujillo: Neo-Democracy
to which he simply adds; "The one style missing here is 'democracy,' without qualification" (FINER 1962:242).

27. Actually, there are three basic types: military government, civil-military government, and civil government (cf. FINER 1962:165), and perhaps these altogether more relevant types of military rule: "Direct and indirect; personal, factional, and institutional; intermittent and long-term; reformist and progressive" (LOWENTHAL 1974:122) as well as "reactionary." We find these terms more precise than expressions like "the military as rulers," "the military as guardians," or "the military as arbitrators" commonly used in the literature (cf. e.g., PALMER/ THOMPSON 1978:141–44).

28. In general, measures "are insensitive to the vibrations of brown oxfords walking to and from cabinet rooms, whispers in the ear of opposition legislators, rumbling from the strategic garrisons, and the sound of the *first* rather than just the other combat-shot dropping" (WEAVER 1973:95). Military involvement may be a generally more adequate term than the conventional notion of military intervention. On the distinction between stable and unstable military rule and military coups d'état see also the diagram in ZIMMERMANN (1981:493).

29. "The nation replaces the dynasty as the object of military loyalty. Nationalism provides the military with a civic religion and an overriding set of values. Because they have a unique role as guardian of the national territory, they regard themselves and are much regarded as the ultimate repositories and custodians of the nation's values" (FINER 1962:207).

30. Note that the word "characteristics" in the heading of this section is to have a wider connotation, i.e., encompassing military grievances as well.

31. "The military is jealous of its corporate status and privileges. Anxiety to preserve its autonomy provides one of the most widespread and powerful of the motives for intervention" (FINER 1962:47; cf. also LIEUWEN 1964). "Announcement of plans for a popular militia; drastic reduction in military budgets; denial of new weapons; 'interference' in promotions or elections to the officers' club; early retire-

ment of leading officers" (WELCH/SMITH 1974:16–17)–all of these may contribute to grievances of the military.

32. "Six extremely intertwined positional needs are identifiable among the host of attributed coup motivations: (1) autonomy, (2) hierarchy, (3) monopoly, (4) cohesion, (5) honor, and (6) political position" (THOMPSON 1973:12). THOMPSON considers political position as "the most common of the six corporate positional factors" (ibid., p. 17), yet one may argue whether autonomy would not be a more appropriate and less circular description of the military's motivation in deciding whether to stage a coup or not (apart from other conditions mentioned below).

> Positional conflicts are generally intermingled with another type of corporate grievance–the conflict over resources. These can be divided into four subtypes: (1) dissatisfaction over pay, promotions, appointments, assignments, and/or retirement policies; (2) dissatisfaction over budget allocations, training facilities-policies, and/or interservice favoritism; (3) dissatisfaction over general military policy and/or support for military operations (i.e., war, insurgency, and the maintenance of order); and (4) some combination of the first three subtypes" (ibid., p. 17).

33. Moreover, "Arab and African coups seem to be those most concerned with corporate positions while Asian and Arab coups are those most concerned with corporate resource standings and military factional/ethnoregional/sectional interests" (THOMPSON 1973:46–47).

34. The latter aspect is focused on in a somewhat different hypothesis proposed by WELCH/SMITH: "The likelihood of military intervention diminishes with the emergence of a clear-cut, external focus for national defense" (WELCH/SMITH 1974:11).

35. Another question is whether the occurrence of coups, in turn, affects the size of the military. McKINLAY/COHAN (1975:13) report these results: "Military rule does not lead to an increase in military expenditure or in the size of the armed forces." Area controls, however, lead to a slightly different evaluation of this hypothesis:

> The military regimes and civil-military regimes of Central America both have size and expenditure scores significantly higher than the civil regimes (at the .10 level); the military regimes and civil-military regimes of Africa have significantly higher expenditures than the civil regimes (at the .01 level); and the civil-military regimes, but not the military regimes, of Asia have higher expenditure than the civil regimes (at the .05 level). The only time a civil regime score greatly exceeds those of military regimes and civil-military regimes is in South America, where the size of the armed forces in the civil regimes is significantly higher (at the .01 level) (McKINLAY/COHAN 1975:13).

Drawing on NORDLINGER (1970), FINER (1976:238) reaches a more sweeping conclusion: "The proportion of G.N.P. devoted to defence was almost twice as large in countries ruled by the military 1957–62,

(35)

as in countries whose military were not politically involved." The conclusions of McKINLAY/COHAN have also been challenged by HILL
(1979) who studied the allocations for military activities (in terms of
military spending/Gross Domestic Product and the size of the armed
forces) in 101 nations during the mid-1960s. Using two control variables (economic development and international border conflicts) he
finds "that military influence in civilian politics has an important positive relationship to military policy allocations, even when the influence
of plausible alternative explanatory variables is taken into account.
Furthermore, military influence is most important in this regard for
poorer and less institutionally developed polities" (HILL 1979:375).
For some additional results cf. below.

36. "In spite of all precautions, a large army amidst a democratic people
will always be a source of great danger; the most effectual means of
diminishing that danger would be to reduce the army" (Alexis de
TOCQUEVILLE, *Democracy in America*, [New York: Schocken
Books, 1961] 2:324, here as quoted in STEPAN 1971:21). A related
view of the army as a potentially "preponderant force in a country" is
expressed by MOSCA in his *The Ruling Class* (New York: McGraw-Hill,
1939), p. 226.

37. PASSOS (1968:79) reports a positive relationship (r=.57) between military expenditure (percent of national budget) and "nonregular pattern
of governmental change" (twenty Latin American countries during
1945–65). WELLS (1974:883) also finds a positive relationship between military expenses as a percentage of government expenses and
military coups in thirty-one black African countries during the 1960s
(r=.36).

38. Other size indicators (such as military personnel as a percentage of
adults, total military personnel) were found to be very weakly related
to military intervention (PUTNAM 1967:100).

39. Somewhat different results are reported by NORDLINGER: "In those
Latin American countries [mostly during the second half of the 1950s
and the first half of the 1960s] with a politically non-involved military
the mean level of defense expenditures as a proportion of central
government expenditures is 9.3 percent; in countries with an officer
corps that has intermittently entered the political arena the percentage
is 14.1; while the figure reaches 18.5 percent in countries dominated by
the military circa 1960" (NORDLINGER 1970:1135).

40. SCHMITTER, moreover, points to a number of theoretical links
between these variables, an additional possible influence being military
spending in a neighboring country (cf. SCHMITTER 1973a:167–71).

41. McKOWN (1975), however, reports a negative bivariate relationship
between total defense budget, 1967 and military intervention in fourteen African countries as of end of 1969.

42. Perhaps there is a negative relationship between professionalism of the
military and military intervention, but only after a threshold level of
political development has been reached. HUNTINGTON (1957:32) also
stresses that his model of professionalism holds only where the military
develop their skills for warfare against foreign enemies. NORDLINGER

(1977:50–53) argues (as does FINER, see in the text) that greater professionalism may also lead to greater concern with developments in society and thus further military intervention, contrary to HUNTINGTON's hypothesis. Empirically these contradictory trends should contribute to a low correlation between military professionalism and military intervention. Cf. also the discussion in the text below; HUNTINGTON's renewed stress that professionalism, if appropriately classified, will prevent military intervention (see his preface to PERLMUTTER 1977:xi); and the extensions in PERLMUTTER (1977).

43. Cf. also LARSON (1974) for a comparative evaluation of the contrasting positions taken by HUNTINGTON (1957) and JANOWITZ (1960).

44. KOURVETARIS (1971), however, in his interview study of one hundred middle and upper ranking army officers in Greece during the winter months of 1968–69 finds no relationship between professionalism and disposition to intervene.

45. FINER's own proposition, however, is no less circular. He claims (FINER 1962:32) that the "armed forces' acceptance of the principle of civil supremacy" is the most important insurance against military intervention. Nevertheless, *ex ante* analyses might render this hypothesis useful.

46. These determinants have been discussed in the preceding section.

47. Possibly with more than one threshold level.

48. Actually, the evidence here is rather indirect, since nations with military regimes in most cases have already experienced coups whereas we are more concerned with determinants of the occurrence of coups. Assuming, however, that the level of economic development will not change too much in the short run, there is some argument for listing the results of McKINLAY/COHAN here. The determinants for the occurrence of coups should not be confused with the outcome or consequences of coups. For example, the evidence of McKINLAY/COHAN (1975; see above) that, on the lowest level of economic development, military regimes are more successful in their economic policies than other types of regimes, should not be taken for evidence that coups are therefore much more likely in these countries.

49. Two extensions of this study lead to similar conclusions (FINER 1968:28, extending the period of observation until the end of 1967, and FINER 1976:275–76 using data on, at the maximum, 126 nations for 1958–73), even though there are some slight variations in the categorization of the independent variable.

50. FOSSUM also claims to have found some evidence showing that status-inconsistent (large but poor) nations experience more coups. Yet status inconsistency theory is plagued by too many theoretical and methodological problems (cf. the summary in ZIMMERMANN 1978) to take this result as evidence for the theory (cf. also the criticism in HERNES 1969).

51. Cf. also the somewhat indirect evidence (the dependent variable political stability includes more than coups) in BANKS (1970) who studied Latin American countries in comparison with European countries during 1865–1966.

(52)

52. Cf. also WELCH (1970:29) and NELKIN (1967) for some observations referring to various African states and MERKX (1973) for evidence of a relationship between recessions and armed rebellions in Argentina during 1870–1970.
53. AMES's study (1977) tests a variety of hypotheses which have been suggested for explaining the cycles in government spending observed in the Latin American countries under scrutiny.
54. Which, in the long run at least, may also have an effect on the other classes of variables (cf. the discussion in chapter 5.1.2.3 as well as passim in this study).
55. Explanations referring to social stratification, social resource allocations, and social mobilization are probably the most important ones to be grouped under the labels social, societal, and sociostructural explanations. We here prefer sociopolitical as the most general label, since social factors seem to be relevant only insofar as they influence (or, from the point of view of certain groups, threaten to influence) the political process.
56. Unfortunately, this has not always been measured independently of the outcome, i.e., coups.
57. JANOWITZ presents the argument in a slightly different way. He speaks of "reactive militarism" which "results from the weakness of civilian institutions and the pressures of civilians to expand the military role" (JANOWITZ 1964:85).
58. WAYMAN (1975:23), however, reports a curvilinear relationship between literacy level and military intervention (1960) for ninety-one countries, with nations on an intermediate level of literacy reaching the highest score on the dependent variable (using the somewhat arbitrary classifications of ADELMAN/MORRIS 1967).
59. The index of military intervention is a "rating assigned to each country for each year . . . based on the extent of military intervention in the political life of that country for that year. This rating is on a scale from zero to three, from least to most intervention" (PUTNAM 1967:89). Some of the disadvantages of this operationalization of the dependent variable have already been noted. The same arguments hold for the study of LATOUCHE (1973) discussed in chapter 7.2.3. For the development of more flexible indexes see SIGELMAN (1974) and TANNAHILL (1975). The latter proposes a measure that allows for greater variability than the measure proposed by PUTNAM while at the same time reducing arbitrary decisions. Furthermore, it should be pointed out that at least half of the variance remains unexplained in PUTNAM's analysis.
60. Which itself highly correlates with social mobilization, r=.89.
61. The path coefficient between social mobilization and military intervention is p=−.99. Thus, "social mobilization clearly increases the prospects for civilian rule" (PUTNAM 1967:106). NEEDLER (1974:151ff.) argues similarly when explaining the high correlation (r=.615) between percentage of the population which is Indian and frequency of military coups in Latin America during the nineteenth century. (For 1930–65, r=.489, although the correlation becomes negative for the period

1900-29, r=-.254.) The "lack of social mobilization and integration [of the Indian population] into national society may *fail to inhibit* the occurrence of coups" (NEEDLER 1974:153), although "the most convincing structure of explanation linking the frequency of coups and the Indian character of a society lies not in these factors, but in the attitudes and behavior which the existence of a subject caste of Indians generated in the non-Indian sectors of society" (NEEDLER 1974:153). One must distinguish carefully what is meant theoretically *and* operationally when employing the social mobilization variable (cf. also the discussion concerning HUNTINGTON's theory below and in chapter 5.1.2.4). Moreover, in HIBBS's (1973:109) multi-variate analysis social mobilization albeit correlating negatively with coups, turns out to be an insignificant determinant in the presence of institutionalization and defense expenditures.

62. Cf. also FELDBERG (1970), although his operationalizations of concepts call for some criticism.

63. A refined hypothesis on the effects of social mobilization, more in line with HUNTINGTON's theory (cf. below), has been presented by WAYMAN: "In countries where civilian mobilization is widespread (and which are not engaged in external war), military involvement will be possible only when the legitimacy of the civilian regime is low, and when salient political cleavages make it possible for the military to gain the cooperation of one of the mobilized civilian coalitions" (WAYMAN 1975:31, omitting the italics from the original). He also lists some evidence in line with this hypothesis, but his dependent variable differs somewhat from military coups (cf. chapter 7.3). It should be noted, however, that WAYMAN (1981) has some reservations about my interpretation of his work, although I believe that his claims are not sufficiently warranted.

64. CANTÓN (1969:256-57) found for military interventions in Argentina between 1900 and 1966:

> Not one military intervention favourable to a "popular" tendency was ever successful. Of the revolts against a "popular" tendency all succeeded except two, and both of these (in 1951 and June 1955) were against Perón. The army never once intervened to redress an electoral injustice, i.e., to support a winning party which had illegally been declared the loser. It never once intervened to annul fraudulent elections when the fraud was used against a popular party. The most it ever did was to remain neutral where the polls favoured the continuation of the popular party *already* in office (as summarized in FINER 1976:264).

65. There are, of course, other authors who have stressed the vital importance of an autonomous party system (cf., e.g., HALPERN 1963: 283ff.), yet HUNTINGTON goes far beyond this when elaborating his theory of praetorianism. Kemal Ataturk as one of the successful military modernizers apparently has shared this perspective. "As long as officers remain in the Party we shall build neither a strong Party nor a strong Army" (as quoted in FINER 1962:31).

(66)

66. In historical terms a "quite misleading" term (FINER 1976:239).
67. "Corruption is behavior which deviates from the formal duties of a public role because of private-regarding (personal, close family, private clique) pecuniary or status gains; or violates rules against the exercise of certain types of private-regarding influence" (NYE 1967:419). In praetorian societies public norms are either nonexistent or not generally shared. Instead some kind of "amoral familism" (to use BAN-FIELD's, 1958:10 and passim, term; cf. also the critique of BAN-FIELD's *The Moral Basis of a Backward Society* by DAVIS 1970) is typical of praetorian polities. "If the joint membership of a large number of organizations in one society, that is, pluralism, is the hallmark of the representative society, then membership in monistic groups is the hallmark of the praetorian society" (FEIT 1973:4).

    In the literature there is a growing debate as to the conditions and consequences of political corruption (cf. SCOTT 1972; BEN-DOR 1974; LaPALOMBARA 1974:402–19; and the articles in HEIDEN-HEIMER 1970 for an overview; see also the recent, partly mathematical discussion by ROSE-ACKERMAN 1978). Rather than condemning political corruption in toto, some researchers have pointed to a number of "positive" functions it may have. RIGGS (1963), for example, conceives of corruption as having positive effects on the development of strong parties which are autonomous especially from the bureaucracy (cf. also the analysis in SCOTT 1969). NYE (1967) has broadened the discussion by pointing to a number of variables to be considered, yet his cost-benefit analysis still awaits empirical testing. One of the alleged benefits of corruption is that it may serve as an alternative (cf. also SMELSER 1971 for a structural-functional analysis) to political violence, i.e., it may contribute to conflict resolution (at least in the short run). "He who corrupts a system's police officers is more likely to identify wih the system than he who storms the system's police stations" (HUNTINGTON 1968:64).

    Yet critics of corruption also point to other connections, e.g., "Many developing societies are ruled by the gun, and bribery pays for the bullets. . . . In a world where money is all that is needed to assure access to superior arms technology with which to keep the exploited masses suppressed, corruption ceases to be functional in any but the most cynical meaning of the word" (HOOGVELT 1976:132). HUN-TINGTON (1968:71) also contends that as political institutionalization progresses, corruption is eventually reduced (cf. also the discussion in BAYLEY 1966). Yet empirical evidence again is lacking. Moreover, as BEN-DOR (1974:81) makes clear, there are a number of reasons for a "coexistence of clientelism and institutionalization." See also WID-MAIER (1978:141–52) for an interesting discussion of possible relationships between modernization, bureaucratization, and political corruption.

68. In this respect cf. also the description of the praetorian state in RAPO-PORT (1962:72): "In effect, a praetorian state is one where private ambitions are rarely restrained by a sense of public authority or com-

mon purpose; the role of power (i.e., wealth and force) is maximized."
For another explication of the theory see PERLMUTTER (1969;
1974:7 and passim; 1977).

69. The clear parallel to KORNHAUSER's theory of mass society (1959;
cf. chapter 6.3.5) is noted by HUNTINGTON himself: "A direct relationship exists between leaders and masses; in KORNHAUSER's terms,
the masses are available for mobilization by the leaders and the leaders
are accessible to influence by the masses" (HUNTINGTON 1968:88).

70. Some additional important characteristics, already dealt with in other
portions of this study, can be summarized in a late developers
syndrome.

> [In] late developers as compared with early developers: (a) the
> state normally plays a more important and more coercive role in
> the process of industrialization; (b) the bourgeoisie is likely to be
> weaker and hence, according to some theories, democracy is less
> likely to emerge; (c) exogenous influences on political develop-
> ment are likely to be more important; (d) rates of social mobiliza-
> tion are likely to be high compared with rates of industrialization;
> (e) overall rates of socioeconomic change are likely to be higher
> and hence social tensions sharper; (f) in part as a result of these
> earlier factors, mass participation in politics is broader and popu-
> lar demands on the political system more intense in comparison
> with the level of economic development and political institu-
> tionalization; and (g) in part as a consequence, violence, and
> instability are more likely to be prevalent (HUNTINGTON/
> DOMÍNGUEZ 1975:14).

71. An interesting corollary to this hypothesis may be found in ANDRE-
SKI (1961; cf. also WELCH/SMITH 1974:15) who, following MOSCA,
suggests that coopting the military into the dominant societal strata
contributes to the prevention of military intervention.

72. As to the guardian role of the military cf. also the typology in WELCH/
SMITH (1974:69–73).

73. NUN's largely theoretical analysis of the "middle-class military coup"
clearly parallels HUNTINGTON's and NEEDLER's propositions in this
respect: "Latin American middle classes are threatened by the oligarchy
or by the working classes, and voting is one of the principal instruments
of this threat. Therefore, the army—that in the majority of the countries represents the middle classes with all their contradictions—comes
to the defense of the threatened sectors and allows for political instability in the defense of a premature process of democratization" (NUN
1968:147).

74. Independent from the objects under study.

75. In his study of Kenyan politics, BIENEN starts from a rather broad definition of participation: Political participation "involves focusing on
the different modes of participation used by various groups and individuals as they try to influence each other and Government on public
and potentially public issues" (BIENEN 1974a:17).

(76)

76. During the 1960s reformist claims on behalf of the military have also been made, e.g., in Ecuador (cf. also FITCH 1977), Argentina, Panama, El Salvador, and Bolivia.

77. "The military institutions came to see existing social and economic structures as security threats because these structures were either so inefficient or so unjust that they created the conditions for, and gave legitimacy to, revolutionary protest" (EINAUDI/STEPAN 1971:124).

78. In the case of Peru, COTLER (1970–71) even speaks of "military populism," denoting leftist policies aimed at getting mass support without totally alienating the middle and upper social strata from the polity. (In this respect cf. also the coup in 1975 against General Velasco and STEPAN 1978 as well as PHILIP 1978).

79. Uruguay, Costa Rica, and Mexico being other examples. In Uruguay, however, the military in 1973 took over the affairs of government.

80. Furthermore, what about middle class *and* upper class segments uniting against the expansion of political participation on the part of the lower classes?

81. Problems of parameter estimation may,however, be insurmountable at present. In feedback models it may often be impossible to separate strong effects from weaker ones. Also parameter estimates of variables which have been repeatedly measured, in the case of positively auto-correlated residuals, lead to inflated coefficients (cf. HIBBS 1974).

82. For instance, do the wealthy bribe, do students riot, do workers strike, do mobs demonstrate, and does the military coup at the *same* time? Explicative variables of the *broader* features of praetorian polities have been tested for even less than potential determinants of praetorianism in the narrow sense. Perhaps there is no general theory of praetorianism at all?

83. "Corruption, division, instability, and susceptibility to outside influence all characterize weak party systems" (HUNTINGTON 1968: 405).

84. RIVKIN (1969:51ff., 259–61) reports a high frequency of coups in African one-party states during the 1960s. In her analysis of "patterns of political change in tropical Africa" COLLIER comes up with more refined findings: "Where a one-party regime was formed by election or merger, these regimes were based on parties that had fared well under the competitive elections introduced during the period of decolonialization. . . . Consequently, these regimes had relatively little opposition and greater legitimacy. They have generally not been susceptible to military overthrow. . . . Where one-party regimes were established by coercive means or where multiparty systems continued to exist . . . in the power struggle which followed, no acceptable solution could be reached, and the military intervened" (COLLIER 1978:73). "There is a remarkable difference in the frequency of military interventions between British and French ex-colonies [also noted by COLLIER 1978] : in French ex-colonies there have been twice as many domestic military interventions than in former British colonies. Similarly, more than half of all domestic interventions have taken place in former French colonies" (ANTOLA 1975:211).

Studying the frequency of parliamentary meetings (mostly during the 1960s) in Ghana, Nigeria, Tanzania, Uganda, Kenya, Malawi, and Zambia, HAKES draws the highly tentative conclusion that "the prospects for regime stability are better in Tanzania than in Kenya, Zambia, or especially Malawi, the other three countries in our analysis that have not experienced coups" (HAKES 1973:33). Finally, McKOWN/KAUFFMAN in their study of the role of party systems in African politics come to the conclusion that "the party system is not a relevant variable" due to the lack of "any apparent relationship between elite instability events and party system type" (McKOWN/KAUFFMAN 1973:69). A similar conclusion follows from the evidence gathered in FINER (1970:528; sample: African states during the 1960s).

85. HUNTINGTON (1968:423) also reports that *successful* coups occurred in 25% of the one-party systems, in 44% of the two-party systems, and in 85% of the multiparty systems between 1945 (or date of independence) and 1966 (N=80 nations). For less discriminating results in the African context between 1960 and 1966, cf. FINER (1967:506).

86. Cf. also DUNCAN (1968:190) for evidence on the negative impact of modern institutionalized parties on the frequency of coups in Latin American countries between 1945 and 1964.

87. The measures of the independent variables were taken from BANKS/TEXTOR (1963). As these figures are largely based on estimates, these results of PUTNAM's analysis should be considered as bearing only indirectly on HUNTINGTON's writing.

88. The rationale of HUNTINGTON's institutionalization variable differs somewhat from the operationalization chosen by WELFLING (1973), who uses marker variables loading highly on the four dimensions of institutionalization that turn out in a factor analysis, namely, stable interactions, adaptability, boundary, and scope.

89. Furthermore, "it is only at the very lowest levels of political participation and only in the context of a miniscule middle class that the officers sponsor modernizing policies, whereas HUNTINGTON is somewhat more generous in estimating the parameters within which this occurs" (NORDLINGER 1970:1144).

90. Results consistent with these are found by PUTNAM (1967:96): the percentage of population in middle and upper social strata correlates negatively ($r=-.48$) with his military intervention index. Cf. also PASSOS (1968) for Latin American countries (1945–65) and HOADLEY (1973:120) for sixteen Asian countries.

91. Cf. HALPERN (1963:9, 75, 253) for the contrary position, FINER (1976:263), JANOWITZ (1975:155ff.), PERLMUTTER (1967), and TIBI (1973) for critiques of HALPERN's optimistic speculations on the benevolent "new middle classes" of the Arab military. See also THOMPSON (1973:41) for some evidence and the recent discussion in BILL/LEIDEN (1979:123ff.).

92. In contrast to NORDLINGER's comparisons of "within-stratum coefficients across strata," JACKMAN used a covariance model: "comparisons across strata of the metric regression coefficients generated with a covariance analysis model are not subject to distortion from variation

(92)

in within-stratum variances, and they therefore offer a more meaningful basis for the comparison of the nature of the true effects" (JACKMAN 1976:1089–90).

93. "In two instances, however (involving the . . . dependent variables: GNP per capita growth rate and changes in human resources [two sets of data on school enrollment], respectively), the data are partly consistent with HUNTINGTON's hypothesis and NORDLINGER's conclusion. In these two cases, the parameter estimates for military rule are positive and statistically significant for countries in the low-development category" (JACKMAN 1976:1086). For further results partly along these lines and partly differing, cf. chapter 7.1. It should be added that using his second data base, JACKMAN (1976:1096) failed to find support for the relationship noted earlier between military government and changes in school enrollment ratios.

94. KIM/KIHL (1978:19–20) also report that the "civilian/military distinction of regimes in the aggregate makes little difference in accounting for levels of economic performance of Asian countries during the year 1960–75." Yet, they also found "some interesting differences . . . between the military-dominant and civilianized-military regimes in Asia. Such civilianized-military regimes as Indonesia, South Korea [which just recently experienced a change], and Taiwan, for instance, show considerably higher levels of economic performance as compared with most of the military-dominant Asian regimes. This observation holds true even when comparing those civilianized-military regimes with many of the civilian or Communist regimes in Asia. Significant exceptions to this generalization, however, include such high-performance civilian regimes in Asia as Japan and Singapore."

95. The results of WELLS (1974:883–84) are only of indirect relevance here due to inconsistencies in the time spans of indicators and to the fact that coups are used as dependent variable. He reports totally insignificant or negative relationships (except for literacy, r=.22, and mass media availability, r=–.24) between socioeconomic variables and his index of coup activity in black African nations (N=31) during the 1960s. In his multivariate analysis there is no relationship between economic growth and the dependent variable (whereas mass media availability and economic development are both strongly negatively related to coup activities). MORRISON/STEVENSON (1976), however, point out that for the variables WELLS has used data which lack reliability due to his neglecting of regional data sources. Therefore, they feel his results lead to distorted conclusions. Socioeconomic variables are important, contrary to WELLS's conclusion that military characteristics, i.e., the milieu of the military, more accurately predict the dependent variable. PHILLIPS/BA-YUNUS (1976) also point to much lowered values of R^2 if the R^2 formula is corrected, as must be done in the case of a relatively large number of independent variables compared to the number of observations.

96. Cf. SIGELMAN (1971) who has performed one of the very few cross-

national studies (N=115 nations) evaluating the role and impact of bureaucracies on political development. He performs a scalogram analysis based on cross-sectional (and not the required longitudinal) data, taken from BANKS/TEXTOR (1963). SIGELMAN claims to have provided "fairly convincing evidence that bureaucratic development is a necessary condition, a sine qua non of further modernization" (SIGELMAN 1971:46). Yet, he also admits that it is not a sufficient condition, thus lending some credit to RIGGS's counterhypothesis: "My general thesis is that premature or too rapid expansion of the bureaucracy when the political system lags behind tends to inhibit the development of effective politics" (RIGGS 1963:126). Employing rather crude organizational indicators, NORDLINGER (1970:1141) found his relationships between strength of the military and economic change unaffected when introducing efficiency of the bureaucracy as a test variable.

97. Cf. chapter 5.1.2.4 for a more detailed description and critique of these indexes.

98. Cf. THOMPSON (1975b:481) who finds comparable results when using measures of national government revenues.

99. "Regardless of the degree of *social* mobilization, *political* mobilization in the form of higher levels of mass electoral participation may reflect a higher degree of acceptance of conventional, nonviolent processes of elite succession. If this acceptance is in fact widespread at the time of independence, it may mean that subsequently the population and the politically relevant strata are less likely to respond favorably to violent and extraconstitutional attempts to seize power" (JACKMAN 1978: 1274).

100. One of the latest tests is also one of the poorest: RHODA (1978; N=51 nations from 1960 to 1965) leaves out the political participation variable and, in several instances, succumbs to circular reasoning. His "evidence" is in favor of HUNTINGTON's theory.

101. Or, to point to another possibility, "Does institutionalization inhibit the possibility of governmental instability under conditions of civil disorder?" (HUDSON 1970:246).

102. "Cuartelazos take place in countries with a relatively low level of political culture, precisely because it is in such countries that the military realize they can discount civilian hostility or even count on civilian support" (FINER 1962:162). The coup is "a technique which can *succeed* only so long as political participation remains limited. As societies modernize and participation broadens, the coup becomes a *less effective* and a *less frequent* form of political action. On a global level basis, coups are much more prevalent in countries at lower rather than higher levels of economic development" (HUNTINGTON 1971a:4; emphasis added).

103. These are the more interesting since HUNTINGTON (1968) does not take note of FINER (1962) and FINER (1970) does not build on HUNTINGTON's analysis. Clearly, a chance has been missed to have some

(103) firsthand comments from these two pioneers on each other's works (going beyond the acknowledgements in the second edition of FINER's book in 1976).

104. Cf. HUNTINGTON (1968, above) for a different argument as to the impact of numerous parties and for some evidence for the reverse hypothesis, at least in modernizing societies.

105. For a brief discussion of the ambiguous concept of political culture, cf. PYE (1972) who points to a number of shortcomings in the present use of this concept while still maintaining that it is a useful theoretical notion (cf. also the discussion in HUNTINGTON/DOMÍNGUEZ 1975: 15–32). In any case, FINER's use of the concept is broader than that of ALMOND/VERBA (1963:14–15): "The political culture of a nation is the particular distribution of patterns of orientation toward political objects among the members of the nation." "This political culture has been shaped by the nation's history and by the ongoing processes of social, economic, and political activity. The attitude patterns that have been shaped in past experience have important constraining effects on future political behavior. The political culture affects the conduct of individuals in their political roles, the content of their political demands, and their responses to laws" (ALMOND/POWELL 1978:25).

106. The ordering of the three basic determinants seems to lead to this causal model: "The political influence of the military is limited by the military's own incapacity to govern which is, firstly, a consequence of social differentiation and complexity in modern societies characterized by division of labor, and, secondly, the consequence of a lack in legitimacy on the part of military governments. The deficit in legitimacy, in turn, is a result of the level ('order') of political culture" (WEEDE 1977a:413; my translation).

107. FOSSUM (1967:238–41) provides some evidence for and against contagion effects among neighboring and non-neighboring countries in Latin America during 1907–66 (see also the negative evidence in THOMPSON 1972:215).

108. Variables like industrialization, communication, education, and transportation are said to have no significant effect on the occurrence of military coups in Latin America. MIDLARSKY even goes so far as to conclude that "the sources of [military intervention and of war as well] are to be found more readily in aspects of the international system than in domestic societal sectors" (MIDLARSKY 1975:185), a conclusion which makes sense only if one conceives of the international system as in a way preconditioning the behavior of national political systems. Yet, as will be noted in the text as well, notwithstanding a high degree of statistical explanation, a stress on external factors will *never* provide a satisfying *substantial* explanation of the occurrence of military coups, since only certain kinds of nations are affected by diffusion processes (and only at specific points of time), whereas other countries remain untouched by such events. Diffusion processes may perhaps provide an answer to the question of *when* military coups are taking place, but not necessarily of *why* this is the case (cf. also MIDLARSKY 1970:83).

109. The Poisson distribution assumes independence of events, in opposition to the contagious Poisson distribution.
110. I.e., the assumption that countries *differ* in their likelihood of experiencing coups.
111. This result somewhat contradicts the summary given by JANOWITZ: "The [sub-Saharan] region has the features of a historical and ecological entity—despite enormous diversity—and has displayed a pattern of diffusion of military intervention. One can almost speak of Francophone and Anglophone sequences of diffusion. In the Francophone area, the sequence started soon after the restructuring of France's relations with black Africa in 1960. In the British areas, the process was delayed" (JANOWITZ 1977:65).
112. "However, since reference groups also serve as evaluator check-points and aid in setting enforcing behavioral norms. . . . reference groups could presumably also function as a form of disinhibitor" (LI/THOMPSON 1975:66).
113. JANOWITZ also observes military coup contagion processes at work in areas affected by World War II and subsequent postcolonial independence.

> An important part of World War II was fought in the Middle East, and formal independence came there early. In fact, one may assert that the process of decolonization had already started in the Middle East during the aftermath of World War I. But by 1950 these politico-military movements were well under way. On the other hand, Sub-Sahara Africa was less altered by World War II and was more remote from the European center; and decolonization occurred there later. It was not until the second half of the 1960s that interventionist military politics became fully manifest there. The Asia region is between these two areas in tempo and is closer to the Middle East than to Sub-Sahara Africa. Of course, we are dealing with a much less clearly delimited region, and more with differing subregions, so that the process of diffusion is far less operative (JANOWITZ 1977:56–57).

With respect to coup contagion in sub-Saharan Africa, see also HUFF/ LUTZ (1974) and the discussion below.
114. "GALTON's problem is the problem of distinguishing whether the correlational support established for hypotheses in worldwide [studies] should be interpreted as evidence of nomothetic-functional, or of idiographic-diffusional relationships" (SCHAEFER 1974:1).
115. Considering the many weaknesses of functional explanations, however, the term "explanation by internal factors" might be more appropriate than "functions."
116. At present, this statement is definitely true. Yet, if systematic evidence is gathered over longer periods of time, at least some partial answers to the latter question may be expected.
117. FIRST (1970:14), however, argues that this hypothesis would lead to self-evident results, which would be true if only postcolonial experi-

(117)

ences were compared to colonial experiences. What *is* being compared is younger countries with older countries.

118. A related hypothesis, namely, that "'newer' systems tend to be more prone to military coups," "new" denoting "a state's length of membership in the international system" (THOMPSON 1975b:479–80), was supported for countries in Southeast and East Asia and in sub-Saharan Africa during 1955–70 and during 1961–70, respectively.

119. Using a larger sample, BRIER/CALVERT (1975:5) also do not consider foreign aid a special feature of coups.

120. The great majority of the less developed countries do not have regimes fully under the control of their military. For such countries to become recipients of U.S. assistance in the form of money, equipment, and training for their military forces appears to enhance the likelihood of regime instability—of successful and unsuccessful coups. On the other hand, for those poorer societies already under military rule, the evidence suggests that the position of the military is more firmly entrenched by U.S. aid and training. In short, U.S. military assistance appears to be a contributing factor in undermining civilian elements and increasing the incidence of praetorianism in the less developed areas of the world (ROWE 1974:253).

121. One may, however, raise the question of whether WOLPIN's conclusion does indeed hold, that the particular political regimes, e.g., Mossadegh in Iran, Arbenz in Guatemala, Allende in Chile, might have survived if they had been more radical. To us, the opposite seems more likely to hold true.

122. There are, of course, other factors as well. For instance, "in evaluating the role of the military in Greece. . . , one must take into account the 26 years of wars and successive military interventions (1909–24, 1936–47) resulting from this territorial and political instability, as well as the 32 years (1924–36, 1947–67) of relatively democratic, although frequently turbulent, civilian rule" (BLACK 1972:19).

123. Unless one wants to consider some of the efforts of liberalization in Eastern European countries as some form of coup, which, actually, they were not.

124. But cf. also DEAN (1970:71) who found no correlation between prior and later coups in the same country when studying a much longer time period (1823–1966). That the strength of the correlation varies if different periods of observation are related to each other is also documented in NEEDLER's analysis of Latin American countries: "The correlation between the frequency of coups, by country, in the period 1930 to 1965 and the frequency of coups during the nineteenth century (1823–1899) is only .184. But the frequency of coups after 1930 is not even predicted by the frequency of coups in the previous thirty years: the correlation is .025" (NEEDLER 1974:146).

125. There is even an r=.47 if military intervention during 1906–15 is correlated with military intervention during 1956–65.

126. However, DUVALL/WELFLING (1973a) provide evidence—stemming from a multivariate analysis of elite conflicts (defined somewhat more broadly than coups; cf. the definition in MORRISON/STEVENSON 1972a:908) in twenty-eight sub-Saharan countries—that elite conflicts during 1960–64 are unrelated to elite conflicts during 1965–69. Rather:

> Elite conflict is a function (inverse) of the prior institutionaliza-
> tion of the party system. That is, coups and attempted coups
> occur most frequently in systems that have poorly developed
> linkages between publics and government. In addition, the proba-
> bility of a coup is apparently promoted by high levels of turmoil
> but reduced by the existence of internal wars. It is as if severe
> conflict among identity or associational groups restricts group
> leaders or elite elements from direct conflict for positions of
> authority, perhaps by refocusing the attention and identity of
> elites to respective publics or by physically eliminating certain
> elites from the arenas of authority by drawing them into the
> conflict in some sense. Elite conflict is not a self-reinforcing
> phenomenon. Prior attempted coups contribute nothing to the
> explanation of subsequent coups when other variables are taken
> into account (DUVALL/WELFLING 1973a:692–93).

127. "LUCKHAM. . . , for example, has suggested that military forces with small officer corps are the most likely to suffer serious personnel losses and severe weakening of the hierarchical structure via coup politics and therefore more likely to experience repeated coups" (as referred to in THOMPSON 1978a:97).

128. Anticipatory coups are coup-like efforts, premature in the sense that they lead to failure in the short run. They are "part of the process of sounding out sources of support and opposition, testing the strength of the ruling monarchy or oligarchy" (HUNTINGTON 1968:204).

129. Breakthrough coups occur when "modernizing elements in the army depose the traditional ruler, seize power, and set forth goals of reform and social change designed to make their society approximate the model of what a modern system is supposed to be" (HUNTINGTON/ DOMÍNGUEZ 1975:57).

130. "The consolidating coup puts the final seal on the fate of the old regime; with it the new middle-class elements establish their dominance on the political scene" (HUNTINGTON 1968:205).

131. Namely, at two instances: "One is the actual or prospective victory at the polls of a party or movement which the military oppose or which represents groups which the military wish to exclude from political power. . . . Veto coups also occur when a government in power begins to promote radical policies or to develop an appeal to groups whom the military wishes to exclude from power" (HUNTINGTON 1968: 223–24).

132. Cf. also NEEDLER's conclusion for Latin American countries: "The tendency has emerged for a conflict to develop, following a coup d'état, between a more fundamentalist 'hard line' and a 'soft line' that shows

(132)

greater readiness to restore constitutional procedures and is normally represented by officers of higher rank, occupying positions of greater prestige in the provisional government" (NEEDLER 1968a:75).

133. Yet, when analyzing the causes of coups, one should keep in mind that "military intervention in politics is rarely the idealized Western image of military versus civilian, but rather is a matter of the armed forces coalescing with one group of civilians against another" (WELCH/SMITH 1974:262).

134. We would also call into question whether there is really such an underlying historical logic as described in JANOWITZ's "natural history of transformation." "The idea of a natural history of the sociopolitical movement helps clarify the societal transformation in the new nations after 1945 and in Latin America after 1960. The natural history perspective focuses on the ability of leaders to remain in power; it highlights the shift in an elite strategy from limited reform to marked interventionist aspirations and then to the emergence of a Thermidor—or of more pragmatic consolidation" (JANOWITZ 1977:70). The reign of Idi Amin in Uganda is a drastic yet premonitory counterexample to any claims as to historical functions of the military (cf. also the summary remarks at the end of chapter 7) or of military leaders.

135. This, in turn, is noted by HUNTINGTON himself: "Once the military are in power, the coup coalition begins to split" (HUNTINGTON 1968:231). Cf. also the results in THOMPSON (1976) and RIKER's size principle, taken up below.

136. As one might guess, the air force and the navy have only recently attained some influence in coup-making activities. For some other important results cf. FOSSUM (1968:284–86).

137. Assuming that in economically more developed countries the army will also be more developed, the following rationale appears sound: "Where large modern armies do intervene, it is the generals at the uppermost echelons of command rather than middle-grade officers who are the likely leaders" (WELCH/SMITH 1974:243). In these technologically more advanced armies it may be extremely difficult for young ambitious officers to keep under control the variety of professional groups likely to exist in such armies.

138. In Latin America, for example, a special vocabulary of coups or coup-like activities has developed. To give only a few examples (for additional ones cf., e.g., MIGUENS 1975:119): besides the actual coup, the *golpe de estado*, there are the *pronunciamento* wherein "a body of people—a section of the armed forces, a party, the people of a state or province—'pronounce' against the regime; that is, they openly raise the standard of revolt" (NEEDLER 1968b:81); the barracks revolt of *cuartelazo*; the *telegráfico*, consisting "in the telegraphic pronouncement of major provincial commanders against the incumbent government" (RUSTOW 1967:182); the *madrugonazo*, "a rising at dawn against the government" (THOMPSON 1972:122); the various means of imposing a special candidate, often the favorite of the military (*imposición* or *candidato único*); illegal retention of an office or *continuismo*. A more general term is *caudillismo*, defined as "(1) the repeated emer-

gence of armed patron-client sets, cemented by personal ties of dominance and submission, and by a common desire to obtain wealth by
force of arms; (2) the lack of institutionalized means for succession to
offices; (3) the use of violence in political competition; and (4) the
repeated failures of incumbent leaders to guarantee their tenures as
chieftains" (WOLF/HANSEN 1966-67:169).

    Zero-sum political cultures seem particularly prone to coup-making
activities. In these countries some scholars (cf. STOKES 1952:468;
ZOLBERG 1968:77–78; BIENEN 1971a:16; HUNTINGTON/DOMÍN-
GUEZ 1975:49) have suggested that coups may become a normal
form of governmental change. PAYNE even draws this conclusion: "In
the same way that elections are central components of a constitutional
democracy the military coup is considered essential to the functioning
of the system in Peru" (PAYNE 1972:360), without really specifying
why and in what respects a military coup is functional. HUNTINGTON
is somewhat more precise here: "Frequent reform coups d'état should
not be viewed as a pathological but rather as a healthy mechanism of
gradual change, the non-constitutional equivalent of periodic changes
in party control through the electoral process" (HUNTINGTON 1962a:
40). The metaphor of "democracy by violence" (PAYNE 1965:268–
83), however, is considerably overdrawn if we use the concepts of
political science in a clear manner. Many coups serve interests other
than those normally expressed via parliamentary opposition.

139. However, in his analysis of successful coups in Latin America (1907–
66), FOSSUM (1967:235) found that 61% of them occurred during
public disorders.

140. LATOUCHE (1973) also reports strong evidence for a direct relationship between level of internal conflict (e.g., demonstrations, rioting,
civil wars, deaths in conflict, number of recorded instability events)
and level of military intervention. See above for a more detailed discussion of his study.

141. Disaggregating the data of HIBBS, SANDERS even reports evidence for
seven out of nine "Southern African" countries that "coups generally
tend to *preceed* internal war in this region rather than follow it"
(SANDERS 1978:125; emphasis in original).

142. Leaving still unanswered the question as to *why* such coups take place.

> Of those coups that are actually associated with some form of
> disorder, six possibilities exist to link the coup to the unrest: (1)
> the timing is coincidental; (2) since the military is very much in
> demand, the regime is more vulnerable than usual, hence, it is a
> good opportunity for a coup; (3) the coup-makers are sympathe-
> tic to the grievances of the disorderly; (4) the coup-makers fear
> disorder per se and act to suppress it; (5) the unrest is intended to
> invite or to provoke a military coup; and (6) some combination
> of possibilities two through five (THOMPSON 1973:45).

> Moreover, there is also the possibility that internal disruptions are
> better reported before and after the occurrence of coups. Thus, com-
> parisons with other "quiet" periods could lead to erroneous conclusions.

(143)

143. In a variety of cases, however, "ethnic antagonism was clearly present," such as "in the two Nigerian coups (January and July 1966), the two Sierra Leone coups in March 1967 [see COX 1976 for a detailed case study], the Dahomey coups, the Uganda coup in January 1971, and the Rwanda coup in July 1973" (SMALDONE 1974:213). One might add the various coups against the dominant Amhara in Ethiopia to this list (see, e.g., OTTAWAY/OTTAWAY 1978). Cf. also BEBLER 1973 and the discussion in NORDLINGER (1977:42).

144. WILLNER nevertheless perceives the need of something like a consociational solution: "I would rather suggest that in multiethnic, multilingual and multiregional states, the ability of the military to act as an effective political force depends upon the retention of familial, ethnic, and regional attachments by a broadly based military elite whose members can serve as political brokers" (WILLNER 1970:270).

145. If the military stage a coup after a clear-cut victory of parties or politicians they oppose, their loss in legitimacy may be even greater.

146. However, this is not the major task in this chapter.

147. THOMPSON (1973:31) reports "alliances with opposition or ruling party factions" only in about one in six cases in the universe (slightly higher figures, 25%, are given by McKINLAY/COHAN 1974:2) and in approximately one in three cases in the Arab countries.

148. There are some indirect suggestions in the literature that RIKER's size principle might provide a useful explanation here. Cf. the so-called "swing man" who is defined as "the leading figure in the new government; yet he is the person who was least committed to the objectives of the coup, whose threshold to intervention was the highest of all the conspirators, and who was a last-minute addition to the conspiracy" (NEEDLER 1966:621). LANG, however, gives a somewhat different description of the swing man's position and role, seeing him as a "man whose support makes the difference, who often gains a major voice and may even emerge as the official leader" (LANG 1972:127; cf. also THOMPSON 1973:35). Finally, cf. THOMPSON (1974:245) for evidence from the Arab world that RIKER's size principle might also hold *after* a coup has been staged. "The process of post-coup coalition reduction may bring about further coups" (THOMPSON 1972:66). See also the results of THOMPSON (1976; chapter 7.2.3) which are partly reconcilable with the latter hypothesis.

149. Some eventually successful coup-makers repeatedly tried their fate in coups, Nasser and Castro being two of the better known examples.

150. JANOWITZ suggests another (overlapping?) pattern: "The coup-prone nations tend to be small. . . . paradoxically, the larger nation-states have developed greater stability" (JANOWITZ 1977:58).

151. LUTTWAK (1969:37–44) also discusses two other conditions, dealt with at greater length above: limited political participation and substantial independence from influences of foreign powers in the internal life of the target country.

152. Not just of coups, but of other phenomena of political violence as well. Yet, while chances for correcting earlier mistakes may exist in other forms of protests (cf. in this respect the highly instructive failures of

the Chinese communists during the twenties and thirties), there usually is no second try for an aborted coup. However, quite a few leading politicians or military men in these countries have been involved in a variety of plots and counterplots over the years.

153. "In Dahomey, General Soglo, who had come to power by a coup d'état, was overthrown by sixty paratroopers in December 1967. In Ghana 500 troops, from an army of 10,000, toppled supposedly one of the most formidable systems of political mobilization on the continent" (FIRST 1970:4). "It only took 150 paratroopers to overthrow President M'Ba of Gabon and President Olympio of Togo in 1963" (FINER 1970:542). "The entire Northern Region of Nigeria was subverted in the January 1966 coup by no more than some 500 men and thirty officers" (FINER 1976:225). Even General Pak in South Korea in 1961 did not need more than "3,600 out of an army numbering 600,000" (FINER 1962:159).

154. FINER (1962:160), for example, reminds us "that far more cuartelazos [coups also?] fail than succeed" without providing detailed statistical data, although his point seems highly plausible. But cf. also the evidence discussed at the beginning of this chapter.

155. Two interesting hypothesis being: "As participation broadens . . . and society becomes more complex, coups become more difficult and more bloody" (HUNTINGON 1968:230); and "where violence has occurred during the coup process, during the period of military rule, or within the military itself—the transition back to civilian rule is unlikely to be voluntarily undertaken by those elements who have been on top in the military" (BIENEN/MORELL 1974:10).

156. Or in several bivariate analyses, *actually* important variables.

157. One might also conceive of an interaction term here: military grievances in the presence of regime vulnerability, as THOMPSON (1973:50) argues.

158. Perceptual data of the military referring to how the military views the prospects of the political system and the economy would be of major importance here, but will not be available on a cross-national basis.

159. Coding procedures definitely call for tests of reliability. THOMPSON, for example, who has carried out the most systematic analyses thus far writes that his "project was entirely a one-researcher enterprise. Consequently, no reliability tests, formal or informal, were conducted. To the extent that such tests are necessary to detect disagreement among several coders and related coding instruction problems, reliability tests were not necessary. This does not imply that the data that were subsequently created are perfectly reliable" (THOMPSON 1973:54).

160. In another context (see chapter 5.3.2.4) SPILERMAN (1970; 1976) reports that the absolute number of the nonwhite population in "cities in the contiguous United States with populations exceeding 25,000 in 1960" (SPILERMAN 1970:630) is by far the best predictor of both the incidence and the frequency of spontaneous outbreaks in the black population during 1961–68.

161. There is an interesting inconsistency between HUNTINGTON's (1968:218) definition of a coup d'état which emphasizes that "a coup can

(161)

succeed only if the total number of participants in the political system is small" and his explanation of the occurrence of military coups which stresses the relatively high degree of political participation of social forces. The logical conclusion would be that a higher degree of political participation compared to the level of political institutionalization fosters the intervention of the military in the political process but endangers its success. As HUNTINGTON himself notes: "As participation broadens . . . and society becomes more complex, coups become more difficult and more bloody" (HUNTINGTON 1968:230).

162. The various strategies of disaggregation suggested here might be supplemented by a factor analysis of political system variables and other macropolitical variables to detect whether there are clusters of nations which experience no, one, or many failed or successful coups, before performing the type of causal analysis proposed here.

163. WAYMAN's (1975) analysis of the determinants of military involvement in politics in 110 countries during the 1960s deserves some attention as one of the very few multivariate studies on military coups. Actually, while not quoting HIBBS, WAYMAN uses many of the variables HIBBS has dealt with in his study. Some of WAYMAN's results seem to be in line with the theorizing of HUNTINGTON and other writers, yet they should nevertheless be treated with caution, as several of WAYMAN's operationalizations are open to criticism. For instance, like many authors before him, he misses the essence of HUNTINGTON's interaction term when constructing his respective independent variable. Furthermore, his dependent variable is military rule so that his results are not strictly comparable with results on military intervention discussed here (cf. also the exchange between WAYMAN 1981 and ZIMMERMANN 1981). Also his causal model does not fit well in the African context. Finally, in several instances disparate time periods are used. Cf. also the interesting study of O'KANE (1971) which, however, for a number of reasons (e.g., inconsistent periodization of indicators, too many dummy terms, and faults in the theoretical ordering of variables) must be considered a preliminary work.

164. Cf. McKINLAY/COHAN (1974; 1975) and the various articles of THOMPSON for a number of other questions already dealt with on a cross-national basis.

165. There is no need to stress the usefulness of case studies (cf., e.g., BÜTTNER et al. 1976; HADDAD 1965; 1971; 1973). Equally important may be analyses of "pairs of cases chosen to highlight theoretically significant differences [such as] : Peru and Brazil, Argentina and Chile, Panama and Nicaragua" (LOWENTHAL 1974:127).

166. Not only survey data, which may be impossible to collect in many countries, but data stemming from all forms of content analysis may be useful here.

167. Will TALLEYRAND's scepticism prove right: "On peut militariser un civil, mais on ne peut pas civiliser un militaire?" McKINLAY/COHAN have made some useful distinctions as to studying the termination of military regimes. "The agent responsible for the termination may be (a) the military alone, (b) a coalition of military and civilian forces,

or (c) civilians alone. The method of termination may be (a) an election, (b) a direct transfer to a civilian government, (c) a military coup, or (d) an uprising. The form of post-transfer government may be (a) another military government, (b) military leadership of a civilian regime, or (c) a civilian regime" (McKINLAY/COHAN 1976a:294). They also report some results which seem to be among the first of this kind in the cross-national literature on military regimes.

Elections tend to appear after tolerably short regimes, which in relative terms have been successful economically. Uprisings are also associated with successful relative economic performance, but the civilian dissatisfaction manifested in an uprising is produced probably by resentment toward the long duration of the military regime. To the extent that duration is related to certain types of civilianization, it seems to be the case that civilian unhappiness with a military regime is more a product of political than of economic factors. Finally, the coup method appears to be characteristic of less successful economic performance, greater importance of military resources and shorter duration. Thus, the armed forces would seem to be more likely to terminate a military regime when they are more powerful than civilian groups and when the regime is performing poorly in economic matters; political questions do not arise (ibid., p. 308–9).

In his analysis of the conditions of military retreat in Latin American countries, NEEDLER (1980) points to some parallel findings. He stresses that it is a process taking place in two steps, since the military personnel carrying out the transfer of power to the civilians in general is not the same as that having carried out a coup. Furthermore, the economic conditions prevailing during a military withdrawal from power frequently differ little from those that caused the military to intervene. NEEDLER makes clear that, at times, civilian politicians support the military on its way to power to eliminate civil opponents in the first round.

FINER, on the basis of data from McKINLAY/COHAN (1974), writes that "48 percent of [the military regimes] last fewer than two years and only 21 percent last longer than five years. Not only that; only about one eighth are brought down by the civilians (and one eighth are brought to an end by civilians and other military factions combined). But the vast bulk of regimes installed by the military—82 percent—are brought down by the military. Altogether, this combination of coercive repression with shortlived governments (installed and removed by other military factions), together with the likelihood that the economic performance will be much the same as if civilians had remained in office, seems a pretty poor option. But of course it is not the civilian populations who exercise this option. It is their armed forces that do it for them" (FINER 1975:299).

168. HUNTINGTON/DOMÍNGUEZ summarize several somewhat dated empirical studies as follows: "For the 49 countries in the world at the lowest levels of socio-economic development, authoritarian regimes

(168)

seem to have some positive results for more rapid economic growth. Once countries reach a somewhat higher state of development—roughly a 1961 per capita GNP of $250 or more—authoritarian government begins to lose its comparative advantage" (HUNTINGTON/DOMÍN-GUEZ 1975:62; cf. also ADELMAN/MORRIS 1967:197). More recent evidence comes from the study of McKINLAY/COHAN (1975:21).

169. Mexico is another noteworthy example "where parties came out of the womb of the army, political generals created a political party, and the political party put an end to political generals" (HUNTINGTON 1968: 258). This idea is actually much older: "Dans la naissance des sociétés ce sont les chefs des républiques qui font l'institution; et c'est ensuite l'institution qui forme les chefs des républiques" (MONTESQUIEU 1828:119–20). However, one of the recent examples HUNTINGTON deals with, General Pak in South Korea, illustrates how difficult it may be for the "political party [to] put an end to political generals" (cf. also FINER 1962:204 and the results in McKINLAY/COHAN 1974:2–4).

170. As once put in the British *Economist*: One should not expect the fire-brigade to run the factory it is to prevent from burning down.

171. Thus, there is little consistent evidence for what McALISTER (1961; 1965; 1966) has termed the "revisionist" position which claims that the military have the capacity for modernization and are successful in their policies. JANOWITZ's optimism does not seem to be proven by a great number of cases: "The most successful military regimes—if one can use this term [it seems to be "true" by definition] —are, or will be in the long run, those that are able to share political power with or even transform themselves into more civilian-based political institutions" (JANOWITZ 1977:73). The traditionalist argument which views the capabilities of the military outside of their proper domain much more sceptically seems, in general, to be closer to the point.

172. Yet military coups should not be confused with revolutions. Cf. chapter 8.3.

Chapter Eight: The Cross-national Study of Revolutions

1. At least with respect to the period under study in this chapter, i.e., from the Renaissance to the present, the emphasis being on the last three centuries.

2. There is, however, considerable illustrative material as to the nonsense that may be produced by using unsuitable operational definitions of revolutions; cf. chapter 8.4.6.

3. Or rather on key varaibles which have been suggested as being causal in nature.

4. For a discussion of Marxist, neo-Marxist, and socialist views, cf., e.g., BLACK/THORNTON (1964) who also provide an analysis of commu-nist revolutionary activities in various parts of the world, LINDNER (1972), LENK (1973), VON BEYME (1973:13–19); JAROSLAWSKI

(1973); WINKLER (1974); SCHISSLER (1976); DRAPER (1977).
Cf. also the excellent theoretical account in KASE (1968).

5. Or religious systems. Cf. LEWY (1974) for a detailed account and case
analyses of the connections between "religion and revolution." Religious
factors, in some cases, e.g., in the opposition against the modernizing
regime of the Shah of Iran (see note 27) or in the Hussite revolution
(see KAMINSKY 1967; KALIVODA 1976), may account for the
spreading of revolutionary ideas, whereas in other instances religious
beliefs might be of a preventive nature. In the latter sense, Methodism
may have contributed to the nonoccurrence of a revolution in England
in the nineteenth century (cf. also HEARN 1978:200ff.). To many
observers Hinduism is the most prominent example of religion as an
"opium of the people," to use MARX's extreme formulation. The
impact of religion has clearly been neglected thus far in the cross-
national analysis of revolutions.

An exception is perhaps the complex approach by EISENSTADT
(1978). Put in simple terms, he tries to establish a connection between
(1) the organization of authority or, more generally, of societal order,
(2) the religious tension (if present) between transcendental expectations and behavior in this world, and the occurrence of revolutionary
changes or not. Only where (1) and (2) take on special forms, e.g.,
when there is an imperial-feudal state (in opposition to a patrimonial
state whose authority is more isolated and therefore better protected)
as well as a religion with transcendental reference and a strong component of active salvation in this world, only under these circumstances
is a revolutionary change of society promoted. In imperial and imperial-
feudal societies, "various social strata enjoy a high degree of autonomy,
center and periphery mutually impinge upon one another, and efforts
to resolve the inevitable tension between the transcendental and the
mundane involve attempts to change the world rather than to escape
from it. Consequently, there is a close relationship between movements
of protest in the periphery and political struggles at the center, and a
high degree of convergence among changes in major social institutions;
[EISENSTADT] refers to this as a 'coalescent' pattern of change. None
of these features characterizes patrimonial societies" (SHEFTER 1980:
133). Yet, as WEEDE (1979a) notes, there are several historical cases
which do not correspond to this scheme or cannot be adequately categorized. In addition, EISENSTADT's terminology and his treatment of
data, particularly the ancient historical, is anything but precise.

6. "In any given work by a Marxist, the disentanglement of what we may
call the *scientific* elements from what we may call, with an equal desire
to use good rather than bad words, the *moralistic* elements is almost
as difficult as a similar operation on the work of the classical economists" (BRINTON 1965:288).

7. "Die Klassenkämpfe in Frankreich," in *Ausgewählte Werke* [Selected
works] (East Berlin: Dietz Verlag 1966) 1:211.

8. HUNTINGTON states this rather drastically: "Marx was a political
primitive. He could not develop a political science or a political theory,
because he had no recognition of politics as an autonomous field of

(8)

activity and no concept of a political order which transcends that of social class. Lenin, however, elevated a political institution, the party, over social classes and social forces" (HUNTINGTON 1968:336).

9. The futility of drawing on revolutionary ideologies and revolutionary intentions for explaining the incidence and the outcome of revolutions is demonstrated by AYA (1979:48 and passim): "In two key cases, Mexico and China, the ideological currents that emerged triumphant did not palpably exist as political reference points when the old régimes were toppled in 1911" (ibid., p. 64).

10. For a detailed review of the literature as to the peasantry and the English Revolution, cf. MANNING (1975; cf. also ROOTS 1966). As to the importance of the levellers, see BRAILSFORD (1961) and WEBSTER (1974). Concerning the importance of the middle sort of people, see MANNING (1976).

11. Cf. also the hypothesis of TREVOR-ROPER (1959) that there was a general (revolutionary) crisis between the (bureaucratic) state and society, i.e., the expanding state power, the nobility, and various other societal groups in several European countries during 1640–60. For debate on this thesis, cf. the works of HOBSBAWM, MOUSNIER, ROBERTS, and TREVOR-ROPER in ASTON (1965). Cf. also ELLIOTT (1969; 1963) who questions the applicability of the thesis to France and Spain (see the objections raised by KAMEN 1971:308). A general overview of the debate can be found in RABB (1975). For the most recent account see PARKER/SMITH (1978). For a detailed critique see also LUBLINSKAYA (1968).

12. When we speak of the Chinese Revolution, the reference is to the Communist Revolution (unless otherwise indicated). For some balanced accounts of the origins of the rather incomplete Chinese Revolution in 1911, cf. WRIGHT (1968), her conclusion being that "there was no class or group, articulate and well-formed, ready to replace the old elite" (ibid., p. 59; on the role of the bourgeoisie cf. also BERGÈRE 1968). There should be no doubt, however, that

> The 1911 Revolution was, despite its shaky aftermath, a revolution. It was, specifically, not one but two revolutions. One was the narrowly political revolution of 1911–12 that overthrew the system of monarchical rule. The other was the broader cultural revolution of 1895–1913 which destroyed the Confucian system of values. Both of these were permanent achievements as proven by Yüan Shih-k'ai's failure to revive either the monarchy or Confucianism. The 1911 Revolution, it is true, failed to bring forth a new society to replace the one it had swept aside. It was more successful at destruction than at reconstruction. Nevertheless, in its embrace of nationalism, egalitarianism, and popular participation in social and political affairs, it clearly pointed the way to the creative achievements of May Fourth and beyond (RHOADS 1975:277).

> Cf. also RANKIN (1971) for a study of the role of radical intellectuals in Shanghai and Chekiang, the useful brief account of the 1911

revolution by LIANG (1962) who stresses the importance of the uprisings before the revolution (see also KUHN 1970 for a more long-
term perspective), as well as CHENG (1973); LEWIS (1976);
ESHERICK (1976).

13. "Such a sketch consists of a more or less vague indication of the laws
and initial conditions considered as relevant, and it needs 'filling out'
in order to turn into a full-fledged explanation. This filling-out requires
further empirical research, for which the sketch suggests the direction"
(HEMPEL 1965:238).

14. Unfortunately, as ECKSTEIN (1965) has shown, in the flood of studies
on revolutions almost any factor has been termed causal in the occurrence of revolutions.

15. As to the following, cf. ROSENSTOCK-HUESSY (1951); GRIEWANK
(1969); KAMENKA (1966); KUMAR (1971:7–40). Cf. also KOSEL-
LECK (1969); LASKY (1976:240–59). For the history of the concept
of revolution and its precursors among Greek and Latin philosophers,
see also HATTO (1949) and the comprehensive study by SEIDLER
(1955). See also FUKS (1974) for an analysis of "patterns and types of
social economic revolutions in Greece from the fourth to the second
century B.C." For an interesting discussion of the development of the
concept of "révolution" in France from the Middle Ages until the
Enlightenment, see BENDER (1977). As to CONDORCET, cf., e.g.,
REICHARDT (1973).

16. ROSENSTOCK-HUESSY (1931) has summarized the change in the
concept of revolution in this tripartite distinction: "naturalistic,"
"romantic," and "realistic." Yet these terms bear a number of un-
desired connotations. Even if the Glorious Revolution may have been
considered a natural phenomenon in its time, the political events as
such were anything but natural (cf., e.g., the discussion in KENYON
1977).

17. The dubious statistics of "revolutions" found in a study of CALVERT
(1967; cf. chapter 8.4.6.4 for a critique) are taken up by KRAMNICK:
"If one takes as a criterion for revolution governmental change through
violent means, one finds, according to a recent account, 135 revolutions
between 1946 and 1965–367 between 1900 and 1965, or 5.56 per
year" (KRAMNICK 1972:29).

18. The example of Gandhi, sometimes mentioned in this respect, does not
fit here since his nonviolent protest occurred within the process of
building a nation-state. The then-dominant elites belonged to another
political and cultural context (cf. also the next chapter).

19. Following MARX, ENGELS considers violence the "midwife of any
ancient society which broods over a new one." Violence "is the tool
whereby the social movement makes its way and destroys torpid and
dead patterns" (Friedrich ENGELS, *Die Rolle der Gewalt in der
Geschichte* [East Berlin: Dietz Verlag, 1964] p. 43; my translation; cf.
also MARX: *Das Kapital*, vol 1, in MARX-ENGELS, *Werke*, [23:779]).
MAO puts it this way: "A revolution is not the same as inviting people
to dinner or writing an essay or painting a picture or embroidering a
flower; it cannot be anything so refined, so calm, and gentle, or so mild,

(19)

kind, courteous, restrained and magnanimous. A revolution is . . . an act of violence whereby one class overthrows the authority of another" (MAO Tse-Tung 1927, as quoted in VATIKIOTIS 1972:211). A perhaps more adequate explanation of the role of violence in revolutions is given by WINKLER (1974) who points out (cf. also the analysis of MOORE 1966, chapter 8.4.3.2, for some related aspects) that violence is more likely to play an important role in revolutions if a "labor revolution" has not been preceded by a "bourgeois revolution." However, MARX and ENGELS are quite correct in speaking of "revolution [as] the driving force of history" (Karl MARX and Friedrich ENGELS, *The German Ideology*, English trans. International Publishers (New York: 1939) p. 29.

20. But cf. also Rosa LUXEMBURG (1966–68:178) for the opposite view on this issue.
21. Cf. also the definition of TILLY: "A revolution begins when a polity becomes the object of effective, competing, mutually exclusive claims from two or more separate polities" (TILLY 1973:439).
22. GROTH in part seems to subscribe to a similar definition. For him revolution denotes "any non-systemic change either in the leadership or the institutions of a state, or both. By non-systemic is meant change which in its forms is not expressly, or by wide agreement, authorized by the constitutional legal provisions of an existing system, and one which redistributes the loci of political decision-making power" (GROTH 1972:32).
23. "It is impossible to fit any decentralized traditional society, or any modern federal society, into the model" (STONE 1966:174).
24. Or perhaps, as has also been suggested, because leading generals wanted to bargain with de Gaulle for a rehabilitation of high officers dishonored during the Algerian conflict.
25. The consequences of lack of definitional clarity can be seen in BRIER/ CALVERT (1975) who, starting from the definition that revolutions are "occasions on which governments were overthrown by physical force or convincing threat of it," count ninety-three such "revolutions" from 1961 to 1970 (and sixty-two during 1951–60). Their "checklist of transitions" is updated for 1971–79 in CALVERT (1979).
26. As to ARENDT's writings on revolution, see the devastating critique by HOBSBAWM (1964); cf. also JONAS (1969).
27. Examples of the latter type of revolution have been rare in modern times, unless one wants to count (some of) the varieties of "fascism" as revolutions. Especially in the case of German national socialism, old established elements of society were combined with more revolutionary elements (cf. BRACHER 1976b for a summarizing comparative analysis, and the additional discussion below).

A noteworthy exception is the on-going Shiite "Islamic Revolution" led by Ayatollah Khomeini in Iran (cf. GRAHAM 1978 for a background study up to 1977; cf. also HALLIDAY 1979). ARANI (1980), in his useful summary of Khomeini's revolution and its consequences thus far, points to the weakness and the corruption of the formerly governing middle classes and the regime. The Shah had missed the chance to create a real social and political base, for example, among the middle classes. When he could no longer stay in office, was no longer backed morally by the United States, and did not use the army which was already showing signs of disloyalty, the regime quickly collapsed. Buttressed by the encompassing element of anti-Western religious revival, Khomeini's support rests mainly on the alliance with the bazaar merchants who provide the money, on alienated students without career prospects, on other groups of the intelligentsia opposed to the Shah, and on the Lumpenproletariat. In the end, the policy of too rapid economic growth which violated all standards and caused a decline in real income among the lower social classes (a policy which also led from 1976 on to a recession except in the construction industry), the policy of urbanization, and the failed land reform were among the decisive factors for the revolution in Iran. Furthermore, the army was purposely recruited from divergent social groups, making it a loyal instrument as long as the Shah was present but hastening its collapse after the fall of the Shah. (There was also American pressure against a military coup d'état.) See also HOTTINGER (1979) as to the chances of the Islamic Revolution spreading to Saudi Arabia.

28. Strictly speaking, such criticism would not apply to ARENDT's definition (cf. also CONDORCET, "Sur le sens du mot 'révolutionnaire,'" in Oeuvres [Paris: Henrichs, 1847–1849] vol. 12, whom ARENDT is following here), since a gain in freedom must occur if an event is to qualify as revolution. It should be noted that ARENDT had the American Revolution in mind when developing her conceptualization of revolution. Concerning the revolutionary character of the American "Revolution" cf. also note 47, and DIPPEL (1976) for a comparative analysis of the French Revolution and the American Revolution with respect to the idea of novelty in revolution.

29. Cf. also HUNTINGTON (1971b:318) for a slight variant and STOKES (1952:461) for a definition in many respects similar.

30. HUNTINGTON (1968:264) continues as follows (cf. also the typologies in chapter 8.3):

> A coup d'état in itself changes only leadership and perhaps policies; a rebellion or insurrection may change policies, leadership and political institutions, but not social structure and values; a war of independence is a struggle of one community against rule by an alien community and does not necessarily involve changes in the social structure of either community. What is here called simply "revolution" is what others have called great revolutions, grand revolutions, or social revolutions. Notable examples are the French, Chinese, Mexican, Russian, and Cuban revolutions.

31. The latter characteristics are not only mentioned in HUNTINGTON's definition, but also, e.g., by OBERSCHALL (1973:91f.). Cf. also FRIEDRICH (1966:5): "Political revolution, then, may be defined as a sudden and violent overthrow of an established political order." TILLY aptly summarizes the consequences of defining revolutions according to the duration of events:

(31)

> The largest disparities in definitions of revolution came from the time spans the definers want to consider. In a short time span, we have definitions that concentrate on a central event: a certain kind of bid for power, a temporary dissolution of government, a transfer of power. In a medium time span, we have definitions that examine the population or government before, during, and after such a crucial event, and ask whether any significant change occurred; a coup d'état that substituted one military faction for another might qualify as a revolution under the short-run definition, but not under the medium-run definition. In a long time span, finally, we have definitions that relate the crucial event and the changes (if any) surrounding it to a reading of broad historical trends—for example, by restricting the name of revolution solely to those transfers of power that produce the durable substitution of one whole class for another (TILLY 1974:285).

32. Cf. also BLACKEY/PAYNTON (1971:280–313) for some additional examples as well as YODER (1926) for earlier efforts at definition.
33. Elsewhere, however, WELCH/TAINTOR (1972:21) propose a definition resting almost exclusively on the last definitional criterion. Cf. also CALVERT for whom revolution denotes:

> a) A *process* in which the political direction of a state becomes increasingly discredited in the eyes of either the population as a whole or certain key sections of it. . . .
> b) A change of government . . . , an *event*.
> c) A more-or-less coherent *programme* of change in either the political or social institutions of a state, or both.
> d) A political *myth* that gives to the political leadership resulting from a revolutionary transition short-term status as the legitimate government of the state (CALVERT 1970:4).

34. A revolution is "a popular movement whereby a significant change in the structure of a nation or society is affected. Usually an overthrow of the existing government and the substitution by another comes early in such a movement and significant social and economic changes follow" (GOTTSCHALK 1944:4).
35. "The vanguard party can exist in the form of the guerrilla base (*foco insurrectionál*) itself. The guerrilla force is the party in embryo. This is the staggering novelty introduced by the Cuban Revolution" (DEBRAY 1967:106; other italics omitted). Cf. also the highly critical evaluation of DEBRAY's work by MERCIER 1969. For a critique from a more orthodox communist point of view, cf. WODDIS (1972:179–276). See also the recent self-criticism of DEBRAY (1974): focism "was Leninism in a hurry" (DEBRAY 1975:100, my translation). For a slightly glorifying, but nevertheless informative account of the marxism of Regis DEBRAY, see also RAMM (1978).
36. However, sceptical remarks as to the possibilities of isolated urban guerrilla warfare may also be quoted: "The decisive struggle is the one in the strategic area (i.e., the rural area) and not the one that evolves

in the tactical area (i.e., the city)" (MARIGHELLA, as quoted in
KOHL/LITT 1974:83).

37. "Guillén argued that topography is only a passive element, that the
revolution is made by men, and that cities are jungles of cement in
which the guerrillas are both safer and logistically better supported than
in the mountains" (HODGES 1973:6–7).

38. It should be borne in mind, however, "that when we talk about the
mobilization for revolution of workers, peasants, or the middle classes,
we are talking about a small minority of activists within each of these
categories" (GREENE 1974:48).

39. Cf. the similar definition of internal war by ECKSTEIN (cf. chapter
2.3; also LEIDEN/SCHMITT 1968:6–7). As to counterrevolutions see,
e.g., MEUSEL 1934; MEISEL 1966; and MAYER 1971:86ff. Cf. also
chapter 8.5.

40. In addition, the reader is referred to chapter 5 passim and to chapter
2.2 for a number of other typologies in the field of political violence
(cf. also SOMBART 1924).

41. BRACHER (1976c) has, however, introduced an important distinction:
"One could reach the conclusion that not actually Hitler and national
socialism, but rather their failure led to the 'German Revolution' in the
sense of modernization. . . . In line with this argument one would have
to modify or to extend the modernization proposition of Ralf
DAHRENDORF" (my translation). In his article, BRACHER (cf. also
his recent books 1976a; 1976b) stresses a number of contradictions in
national socialism which obviate any simple theoretical formula for this
phenomenon. He also objects to considering national socialism the
German variant of fascism. Thus, he denies that there was such a thing
as a coherent fascism in Europe between the two world wars.
BRACHER stresses that, in terms of political goals, of ideology, of
means of mass mobilization, etc., the Nazis—and, of course, Hitler
himself—may very well be considered revolutionaries. The argument
rests on the following thesis:

> The undesired consequences of historical events also must be con-
> sidered in their evaluation. The Glorious Revolution, the Ameri-
> can Revolution—an unintended revolution, and the Napoleonic
> era, too, with its immeasurable effects, were unexpected conse-
> quences of historical crises. They were almost paradoxical,
> ambiguous revolutions: paradoxical in combining the irreconcil-
> able (for example, a legal revolution); ambiguous in their contrast
> between intention and result. Yet, their results are not to be
> belittled. This holds true also for the German, European, and
> worldwide political significance of national socialism and its
> catastrophe (BRACHER 1976a:137–38; my translation).

In Italy a related discussion seems to have been opened by DE
FELICE's book *Intervista sul fascismo* (1975) in which he distinguishes between "fascism-movement" and "fascism-regime," with the
latter more conservative variant winning in Italy. Events at the end of
June 1934 in Germany could be interpreted in the same vein. (The

(41)

consequences of the Second World War about which BRACHER is
partly arguing are, however, a considerably different matter.)

42. Cf. below for an elaboration of this point.

43. A parallel to Aristotle has been noted here by KELLY/MILLER (1970:
249).

44. "'Jacquerie' is a term applicable only to certain kinds of peasant revolt.
The term derives from 'Jacques Bonhomme,' a derisive nickname for
peasants employed by French nobles in the fourteenth century; and the
original Jacquerie itself was a month-long peasant revolt in north-
central France in the late spring of 1358" (HAGOPIAN 1974:14). Cf.
also HILTON (1973) who looks at medieval jacqueries from a comparative point of view, and studies in greater detail the English uprising of
1381. Much later examples of this type of peasant rebellion are the
Pugachov revolt in Russia (LONGWORTH 1975) in 1772-4, and the
peasant uprising in Rumania in 1907.

45. The term "Jacobin communist revolution" is criticized by STONE
(1966:163). One might also doubt whether the label "anarchistic rebellion" (3) is correct in the case of the example given, the Vendée revolt.
As to the latter, see TILLY (1964) who calls it a counterrevolution but
at times uses other terms as well. Cf. chapter 8.5.

46. Their examples, however, do not always fit the definitional criteria
given. Algeria (1962) and the United States (1776) hardly fall under the
category "revolution with mass participation."

47. This also holds true for the American War of Independence, in spite of
the claims of those who maintain that there are enough indications of
an American revolution (cf. most recently BECKER 1980). "The
American Revolution, JAMESON argued, substantially reduced the
prominence, role, and wealth of the colonial upper classes and accelerated the rise of a middle-class gentry which greatly benefited from the
confiscation of Tory estates, the emigration to Canada of British
Loyalists, the removal of the Crown's restrictions on land colonization,
and the abolition of primogeniture" (pp. 16–20, 32–35 in JAMESON
1956 [1926], as quoted in GREENE 1974:7). PALMER (1959:185–
90) even maintains that, in comparison with France, the amount of
emigration and property confiscation was relatively greater in the
American case (see GREER 1951 for France). Yet, this still would not
be a sufficient criterion for revolution to exist. Rather, overall changes
in the social structure and in values must be considered decisive. Furthermore: "The difficulty here, of course, is not only that it is hard
sometimes to tell the difference between genuine and spurious loyalist
refugees, but also that it was comparatively easy for the loyalists, by
moving to one of the remaining provinces of British North America, to
remain in an English-speaking, North American environment under the
old flag; French dissenters from the French Revolution had no such
option [but to join other sympathizers abroad], and so the relative
rates of emigration are not really comparable" (NELSON 1965:1007).

Much research (for a summary cf. TOLLES 1954) on JAMESON's
theses has led to the conclusion that "virtually nothing new on the
structure of society [has] been unearthed. Whoever possessed the

wealth of the country when the Revolution was over, the economic
class structure remained about what it had been; reforms in landholding
were mainly symbolic; the Industrial Revolution awaited a still later
generation" (BERTHOFF/MURRIN 1973:260; cf. also the sociostructural analysis in MAIN 1965). The position taken in this study is
shared, e.g., by MOORE (1966; but it should also be noted that for him
the real American revolution was the Civil War; cf. MOORE 1966:413
and passim) and HUNTINGTON (1968:7). The basic argument could
be phrased in this way:

> Even those political changes that must be regarded as revolution-
> ary—the separation from Britain and the establishment of a
> republican form of government under written constitutions,
> federal and state—involved no complete break with the past.
> Indeed, American historians have, in general, not yet sufficiently
> acknowledged the debt of the new United States to colonial and
> British institutions and practices. Not only was the political
> theory underlying both the Revolution and the Constitution
> mainly English, but most of the new republican institutions of
> the United States were, in various ways, derived from British and
> colonial precedent (NELSON 1965:1003; cf. also MAIER
> 1972:271).

As the focus in this study is on sociostructural factors accounting for
revolutions, there seems to be no need to take up in detail the various
debates on the correct interpretation of the American Revolution (nor
of the French Revolution; but cf. some of the references in chapter
8.4.6.6.2). GREENE (1973) gives a useful overview of various interpretations (cf. also the contributions in BERKHOFER 1971 and in
GREENE/MAIER 1976), including (1) the progressive view (e.g.,
BEARD, TURNER, PARRINGTON; cf. also the debate between
McDONALD and MAIN, for example, in MAIN 1960) stressing the
importance of social class and economic interests (cf., e.g., the recent
discussion in EGNAL/ERNST 1972) in the American Revolution; (2)
the traditional Whig interpretation (e.g., BANCROFT) or more recent
neo-Whig variants (e.g., MORGAN 1976), and (3) the approach favored
by BAILYN (1965; for a critique cf., e.g., ERNST 1973; 1976:166ff.,
and some of the contributions in YOUNG 1976) who emphasizes the
ideological and intellectual component in the American Revolution. As
interesting as these various alternatives (and many others; for useful
overviews cf. also the essays in KURTZ/HUTSON 1973) of conceiving
of the American Revolution may be in themselves, one should not
overlook the fact that there have been only minor social structural
changes resulting directly from the American Revolution. With respect
to value changes, quite a few scholars even maintain that "the upsurge
of reformist zeal . . . is a central part of the Revolution" (BAILYN
1973:15). In this respect, i.e., in the way revolutionaries conceived
of their behavior (cf., e.g., BROWN 1955:351 and passim), there even
seem to be some parallels between the Glorious Revolution a century
earlier and the American Revolution. Put in still another perspective:

(47)

"It is certainly indisputable that the world, when it contemplates the events of 1776 and after, is inclined to see the American Revolution as a French Revolution that never quite came off, whereas the Founding Fathers thought they had cause to regard the French Revolution as an American Revolution that had failed" (KRISTOL 1973–74:5). A much more hypothetical question is raised by NISBET: "Whether [the] social discontents, based on differential wealth and class inequality, would have reached revolutionary proportions in the colonies had there been no war with England is of course subject to debate" (NISBET 1977:68).

There has also been some argument as to the revolutionary character of the English Revolution. A longer quotation from one of its leading scholars may provide an answer here:

> Although the revolution ostensibly failed, there survived ideas about religious toleration, limitations on the power of the central executive to interfere with the personal liberty of the propertied classes, and a policy based on the consent of a very broad spectrum of society. They reappear in the writings of John Locke and find expression in the political system of the reigns of William and Anne, with well-developed party organizations, the transfer of far-reaching power to Parliament, a Bill of Rights and a Toleration Act, and the existence of a surprisingly large, active, and articulate electorate. It is for these reasons that the English crisis of the seventeenth century can lay claim to being the first "Great Revolution" in the history of the world, and therefore an event of fundamental importance in the evolution of western civilization (STONE 1970:108).

ZAGORIN emphasizes a different aspect: "Royalist and Parliamentarian did not correspond to a structural differentiation in English society nor were they the vehicle of contradictory class or economic interests. Both reflected, rather, the schism within the aristocratic order and the general political nation" (ZAGORIN 1969:336). See also RICHARDSON (1977) for an overview of changing interpretations of the concept of revolution and the outcome of the English Revolution (cf. also HILL 1968). The general point behind these examples is that the use of the term revolution is anything but consistent in the literature.

48. "War or revolution? Both. The same conjunction appears in [some of] the multiple rebellions of conquered territories against Napoleon" (TILLY 1973:445).

49. KORPI (1974a) predicts that the probability of manifest conflict is greatest when the power resources of one party approach those of the other but still fall somewhat behind (and not when both parties reach parity in power resources, as GURR would predict). This leads him to expect a "bi-modal distribution of the probability of manifest conflict" (KORPI 1974a:99), treating utility of achieving the goal, expectancy of success in conflict initiation and in defense, and relative deprivation as intervening variables (and leaving out other important variables, e.g.,

external support). A variant of KORPI's model is discussed in chapter
8.4.6.6.1.

50. REJAI's (1973:9) definition of revolution provides one of the many
examples where this criterion is neglected (but cf. also REJAI 1977:
7–8). See also AYA (1979) on definitions of revolution.

51. For instance: "The combination of the three estates in June 1789; the
coup d'état of June 1793; and those of Fructidor, An V; Floreal, VI;
Prairial, VII; and the 18 Brumaire; are only a few of the many coups in
the French revolution" (PETTEE 1971:28). (Yet PETTEE uses the
concept of coups rather loosely here.)

52. For analyses of the armed forces' coup and subsequent revolutionary
developments in Portugal, cf., e.g., RODRIGUES et al 1976); Fields
(1976); Harsgor (1976); and PORCH (1977). As SCHMITTER points
out, the coup in Portugal has to be seen in a broader historical context:
"The coup of 25 April 1974 can indeed be described as an inverted
national liberation movement, the product of a sort of domino effect
working in reverse. An imperial power sought to prevent the serial loss
of its colonial overseas dependencies and was itself progressively undermined and then suddenly overthrown by the effort" (SCHMITTER
1975:27).

53. Cf. ISSAWI (1963).

54. For Prussia cf., e.g., KOSELLECK (1967). See also GILLIS (1970).

55. A somewhat different pattern is exemplified in Stalin's highly coercive
revolution from above, manifesting itself in forced industrialization and
collectivization (cf., e.g., LAQUEUR 1968:506 and TUCKER 1973;
1977; forthcoming).

56. Cf., e.g., WHITE (1973a); AKAMATSU (1968).

57. See PEPPER (1978) for an account of the civil war in China during
1945–49.

58. Cf., e.g., BLANKSTEN (1962), NUN (1968), and BELL (1973:120–21)
for some additional examples. Perhaps the most ambivalent type of
revolution is the permanent revolution. The Chinese cultural revolution
(see PFEFFER 1971; HAH 1972; WERTHEIM 1974:333–51 and the
next chapter) may be understood as a recent example of this type
which has been of much concern to active revolutionaries and has
given rise to numerous philosophical writings. See TETSCH (1973) for
a useful historical review dealing with Trotsky, with his precursors,
and also with more recent authors. As to the relationship between
permanent revolution and totalitarianism, cf., e.g., NEUMANN 1965.

59. The most devastating argument is, of course, that there are always
many other people around who might have had comparable personal
experiences and also developed similar personality types but who never
turned into revolutionaries. Personality approaches are thus only on
safe ground if they can establish that there is indeed some statistical
relationship between specific experiences during the phases of socialization, personality development, and political behavior later on. As they
usually cannot fulfill this task (see the evidence in REJAI/PHILLIPS
1979), rather different roads should be pursued in the study of collective dissent and protest (cf., e.g., chapter 9).

(60)

60. This type of psychohistory (PYE 1976:ix) quite easily leads to conclusions like the following: "We have found . . . that in the case of Mao Tse-tung the critical developments were related to pre-Oedipal experiences and involved primarily Mao's relationship with his mother, a relationship which also gave him a sense of being unjustly treated when he could no longer command her undivided attention. Our hypothesis is that this range of primary experiences best explains Mao both as rebel and as charismatic leader" (PYE 1976:xiii). More restrained studies like that of RUSTOW (1970) on Atatürk may prove much more helpful in this context.

61. Another Q-factor analysis of revolutionary leaders has been carried out by REJAI/PHILLIPS (1979). They claim to have distinguished five different types of revolutionaries. Yet the labels attached to these types are highly questionable, since Giap, for one, is counted among the "scholars" and not among the "generals" (ibid., p. 134).

62. Personality studies must not be limited to revolutionary leaders. The personality profiles of revolutionary followers are of interest in themselves.

63. In this connection some writers like to point out that everyday life did not change much during those revolutionary events. In Petrograd streetcars were running and even the theaters were giving their daily performances.

64. Cf. also HAIMSON's (1964; 1965) controversial thesis that events during the summer of 1917 had accelerated only the "broad processes of polarization that had already been at work in Russian national life during the immediate prewar period" (HAIMSON 1965:17). For a general narrative account of the February revolution see KATKOV (1967).

65. See HAIMSON (1974) on the fate of the Mensheviks during and after the Russian Revolution.

66. Cf. also some of the more dated interpretations of the Russian Revolution in BILLINGTON (1966). For additional accounts see LAQUEUR (1967).

67. The impact of the sailors' revolt must, of course, be mentioned also (cf., e.g., MAWDSLEY 1978). "In any event the Baltic seamen had been a major factor in the Bolshevik success in October, not so much for their numbers as for their superior experience, discipline, and enthusiasm and for the impressive war equipment—from rifles to destroyers and cruisers—that they delivered to the cause of revolution" (SAUL 1978:192).

68. LENIN describes the same chain of events by drawing on a simple, almost tautological formula:

> The fundamental law of revolution, which has been *confirmed* by all revolutions, and particularly by all three Russian revolutions, and particularly by all three Russian revolutions in the twentieth century, is as follows: it is not enough for revolution that the exploited and oppressed masses should understand the impossibility of living in the old way and demand changes; it is essential

for revolution that the exploiters should not be able to live and rule in the old way. Only when the *'lower classes' do not want* the old way, and when the 'upper classes' *cannot carry on in the old way*—only then can revolution triumph (*"Left-wing" Communism, an Infantile Disorder* [Moscow: Foreign Languages Publishing House, n.d.] p. 81).

Actually, the incumbents should have been warned by the July 1917 events. The premature uprising of the Bolsheviks failed, however, not the least important reason being the fragmentation of the dissidents' power structure (e.g., the Central Committee, the All-Russian Military Organization, and the Petersburg Committee, "each with its own responsibilities and interests," RABINOWITCH 1968:5). The results regarding the impact of intensive and consistent use of coercive means (cf. chapter 5.1.2.5) also come to mind in the present discussion.

69. The American War of Independence would not qualify as revolution according to more restrictive definitions of revolution; cf. chapter 8.2 and note 47.

70. Yet, to avoid circular reasoning, the desertion of the intellectuals must be assessed independently of its consequences. In a later edition of his book, however, BRINTON argued that the "alienation of the intellectuals" is not a clear-cut sign of impending revolution, since intellectuals are usually alienated to a certain extent in modern societies (BRINTON 1965:vi).

71. This analogy (cf. also BRINTON 1952:16f.) might perhaps be appropriate in crises research but hardly in studies on revolutions (cf. also chapter 8.4.5).

72. The fiscal component of revolution has been emphasized especially by MANN (1947; cf. also ARDANT 1975). The American "Revolution" and the *Fronde* (cf., e.g., MOUSNIER 1970) serve as two well-known examples. For an instructive comparison of the tax systems in England and France (less abundant and more expensive to raise, moreover many exceptions creating discontent) and their consequences, see HARTMANN (1978).

73. Obviously this position is one-sided, even if one fundamental aspect of a sociology of revolution is stressed. Critics, and not only those of a Marxist persuasion, have objected to the "voluntaristic" qualities of this approach. Speaking more strictly, according to PARETO, the appropriate *ratio* between lions and foxes is important for the stability of elites.

74. In this sense, LASSWELL/KAPLAN (1952:281) have adapted MANNHEIM's well-known distinction between ideology and utopia to incumbent elites and counterelites, thus rendering this dichotomy more fruitful for the study of revolutions. For a broad and somewhat unsystematic discussion of the connections betwen utopian thinking in several fields and revolution, cf. LASKY 1976.

75. "The great revolutions have usually commenced from the top, not from the bottom. . . . It has been very justly said that governments are not

(75)

overthrown, but that they commit suicide" (LEBON 1913:29, 54).

76. In addition, revolutionary leaders, on the average, are between 35 and 45 years old (cf. the evidence assembled in REJAI 1973:31), i.e., relatively young, at least as compared to some postrevolutionary elites (cf. the evidence in PUTNAM 1976:195–201). Finally, the over-representation of racial, ethnic, or cultural minorities among revolutionary leaders has been noted many times.

77. As put by REJAI:

> Ideology may perform a number of crucial social-psychological functions. First, it articulates social ills, denounces existing ideas and institutions, and undermines the confidence and morale of the ruling regime while simultaneously offering an alternative set of values and a new vision of society. Second, ideology rationalizes, legitimizes, and justifies the grievances and demands of the revolutionaries: it lends dignity to revolutionary action. Third, ideology gives the revolutionaries a sense of unity, solidarity, and cohesion; it instills revolutionary zeal, commitment, devotion, and sacrifice. Fourth, ideology serves as an instrument of mass mobilization. . . . Finally, ideology may serve as a cover for personal motives and ambitions of the revolutionary leaders (REJAI 1973:33–34).

78. To take up MANNHEIM's phrase, there is some evidence that the "socially unattached" (*sozial freischwebend* in the original) intelligentsia plays its part in developing a revolutionary mind, but the data just briefly referred to in the text also speak to the contrary: revolutionary elites are to some degree well-adapted to society, yet still willing to change society drastically. In short, MANNHEIM's formula considerably overdraws the point. Interestingly, HIBBS (1973:48) failed to find support for the hypothesis that a positive difference between "university students or graduates and professional-technical employment opportunities" (which would contribute to the socially unattached intelligentsia) has an impact on mass political violence.

79. The Red Guards included many other groups in addition to students. "As a result of experiences gained during the Socialist Education Movement, Mao apparently concluded in 1966 that Party rectification was too important a task to be left to an increasingly bureaucratized and unresponsive Party establishment. Therefore he turned to the youth (Red Guards), the Army, and the worker-peasant masses ('revolutionary rebels') of China to carry out the struggle against bourgeois power-holders within the Party" (BAUM 1975:8–9). Later on, however, support by the army was needed to keep the Red Guards under control.

"The Cultural Revolution can thus be best described as Mao's attempt to resolve the basic contradictions between the egalitarian view of Marxism and the elitist tendencies of Leninist organizational principles. By drawing the Chinese masses into the political process, Mao wanted to reverse the trend toward restratification caused by the bureaucratization of the Party, and he also wanted to build a mass consensus on the future direction of the society" (LEE 1978:3). It should be noted that this "revolution" was started by incumbent elites (e.g., MAO himself) to strengthen their political position which had deteriorated following the failing social experiments during the 1950s. Perhaps the notion of purge is not totally inappropriate. The reader should at least take note of the inconsistency in using the term revolution here for political activities started by incumbent elites and not merely by counterelites or disloyal masses. As to the Chinese Cultural Revolution, cf. also, e.g., LEWIS (1970); BAUM/BENNETT (1971); ROBINSON (1971); KARNOW (1972); KAROL (1974); AHN (1976); BRUGGER (1978); MACFARQUHAR (1974) with a strong emphasis on the origins of the Cultural Revolution; DITTMER (1977) for an analysis of political symbolism during those years; and HINIKER (1977) for an analysis of the Cultural Revolution in terms of reducing the cognitive dissonance resulting from the failure of the Great Leap Forward. A useful sociohistorical account of the Cultural Revolution may be found in HOFFMANN (1977). Cf. also DITTMER (1974) as to an analysis of the fall of one of the leading politicians, President Liu Shao-ch'i.

80. HAGOPIAN (1974:156), in addition, distinguishes between "division and ineptitude in the 'Ruling Class,'" the former probably being the more important determinant. One might consider some of the earlier notes stating that, other things being equal, division among elites and equal resources available to both sides would likely lead to civil war, division among elites and inept incumbent elites more likely to revolution.

81. "The shifts in commitment by intellectuals which contribute most to hastening a revolutionary situation, in my view, consist of coalitions between revolutionary challengers and groups of intellectuals having membership in the polity" (TILLY 1978:214).

82. Cf. also GALTUNG (1964) who uses the term "rank-disequilibrium."

83. In a more general sense, the frustration of increased expectations which results from blocking channels of social mobility can also be dealt with in terms of the theory of relative deprivation (cf. chapter 4.3). The former is only one of the mechanisms working within the more general theory of relative deprivation (cf. also LUPSHA 1969:284).

84. Take, for example, the impact of tax quarrels (MANN 1947; ARDANT 1965) which stand for more than merely another form of economic grievance. In the case of the French Revolution, for example, they must be conceived of as "a chronic ill of the monarchy and principal of the immediate causes of the Revolution" (SOBOUL 1962:108, also quoted in HAGOPIAN 1974:166).

85. Cf. also KRAMNICK who aims at demonstrating parallels between scientific revolutions (cf. KUHN 1962) and societal revolutions: "A clear parallel between the scientific and political revolution exists . . . for once a scientific paradigm has been overthrown, it is quickly replaced by another which with equal zeal governs scientific research, enforcing the new canons of legitimacy and orthodoxy" (KRAMNICK 1972:59).

86. As TROTSKY once said: "Without a guiding organization the energy of the masses would dissipate like steam not enclosed in a piston-box. But nevertheless what moves things is not the piston or the box, but the steam" (TROTSKY 1957:xix). On TROTSKY's social and political thought, see the recent monograph by KNEI-PAZ (1978).

87. Even though RABINOWITCH (1976) argues that the party's "internally relatively democratic, tolerant, and decentralized structure and methods of operation, as well as its essentially open and mass character" (ibid., p. 311), that its "relative flexibility . . . as well as its responsiveness to the prevailing mass mood, had at least as much to do with the ultimate Bolshevik victory as did revolutionary discipline, organizational unity, or obedience to Lenin" (p. xxi; cf. also the critique by SCHAPIRO in *The New York Review of Books*, [31 March 1977]). Reviewing the work of KEEP (1976), SKOCPOL (1978:198) builds on the same argument: "It was not that a communist party created popular organizations, then came to power and ruled through them; rather, it first allied with spontaneously created or popularly supported bodies in order to ride an urban-based state power and then increasingly by-passed or destroyed all such popular organizations as it consolidated power in and through traditionally organized state bureaucracies." DENITCH (1978) also links the success of the FLN and the Yugoslav communists to their spontaneity *and* organization.

88. For an analysis of the 133 days of Bela Kun's regime cf. the essays in JANOS/SLOTTMAN (1971) and VÖLGYES (1971); see also TÖKÉS (1967) and JÁSZI (1924). "Bela Kun's regime survived as long as it did mainly because it seemed to cater to broad nationalist sentiments, not so much because of its 'proletarian' character; when it lost this broad support, it quickly collapsed" (HAGOPIAN 1974:112).

89. One important qualification needs to be added, namely that revolutionary parties, usually of the vanguard type, begin to change considerably under the impact of revolutionary processes. "The Bolshevik party at the beginning and until World War I was a vanguardist one. During the Russian Revolution of 1917, it was transformed or evolved into a cadre model, always with vanguardist and elitist leadership on various levels of command. The vanguardist model was frequently used in the past for conquest of political power, while the cadre was for consolidation of the political conquest" (GROSS 1974:103).

90. It should be noted that JOHNSON (1964:13) considers defeat in external war an accelerator, a rather unusual addendum to the list of precipitants (cf. the discussion below). Later on, however, he seems to be more in line with conventional reasoning (JOHNSON 1964:18).

91. These revolutions are, of course, to be distinguished from political and social changes imposed by the winner of an external conflict which may be revolutionary in character but are not to be called revolutions (cf. KORNHAUSER's 1971:389, "imposed revolutions"; cf. also SETON-WATSON 1961:xi; another term would be "interventionist revolution"; see also HAMMOND 1975a and below).

92. "The Bolsheviks had won the October Revolution of 1917 because the Officers' Corps of the Tsarist armed forces had been decimated by war

(Chapter Eight)

and the rank and file was already disaffected [cf., e.g., WETTIG 1967; FERRO 1967; 1971; WADE 1972; KEEP 1976; WILDMAN 1980]; whereas the Revolution of 1905 [cf. HARCAVE 1964; SCHWARZ 1967; and ASCHER 1978 for useful accounts] had been lost despite disaffection in the rank and file—the *Potemkin* mutiny in the navy, for example—because the Officers' Corps was still virtually intact" (CHOR-LEY 1973:ix). The impact of external defeat on revolutionary over-throws is also underlined by the Free Officers' coup against King Farouk following Egypt's defeat in the war against Israel in 1948. Bolivia's defeat in the Chaco war against Paraguay also left its imprint on Bolivian society which was to experience a revolution almost two decades later.

93.　Sometimes an elite has been able to mobilize enough loyal forces to put down a domestic insurrection even after a defeat in war, but the most important successful revolutions of the past century were all accelerated by the incapacitation of the armies of *status quo* elites in foreign wars. Examples include France, 1871; Russia, 1905 and 1917; Hungary, Germany, and Turkey, 1918; the overthrow of Mussolini, 1943; the anti-colonial revolts in French and Dutch colonies after World War II; and China and Yugoslavia during World War II (JOHNSON 1966:104).

(As pointed out before, not all of these examples would qualify as revolutions.)

One of the factors differentiating the two types of situations distin-guished here seems to be that, in one instance, usually an internal crisis precedes the external crisis which thus intensifies the societal overload (as, e.g., in Imperial Germany toward the end of the First World War), while in the other instance, the societal order and the army retain enough loyalty to survive attacks by dissenting groups even after an external defeat of the army. The case of Germany is ambiguous here, as KLUGE (1975), for example, has shown. Although the army had been defeated in the First World War, some army remnants retained enough power to crush, with the support of police forces, the so-called workers' and soldiers' councils (*Arbeiter- und Soldatenräte*) and other forms of revolutionary organizations. Yet, even though these activities contri-buted to the formation and consolidation of the new regime, most of these army officers were not firm supporters of the Weimar Republic. They were united in their vigorous anticommunism.

94.　Or as Heraclitus put it: "War is the father of all things."

95.　SKOCPOL recently suggested an explanation of revolutions which takes its departure from these notions of CHORLEY. For SKOCPOL revolu-tion is the result of "foreign pressures and administrative/military col-lapse" (SKOCPOL 1976:181). Cf. also chapter 8.4.3.3.

96.　The author has deliberately chosen this term instead of revolution which would be misleading here. "The twentieth century has seen fewer revolutions started by the populace than the nineteenth, and their fate in modern states has generally been defeat. The Communists and Nazis learned that lesson. Mussolini's combination of illegal action and legal

(98)

takeover became the new model for overthrow of democracies" (LINZ 1978:15).

97. The developments in Albania have not drawn the close attention of scholars of revolution. Even if the occurrences there may not fully qualify as revolution, they stand for more than an imposed revolution. Cf. the evaluation of PETERS:

> Neither Stalin nor Tito supplied any war material to the Albanian National Liberation Army, although . . . it was Tito's emissaries who supplied the ideological and technical advice and direction. The Communist seizure of power in Albania, therefore, was the most indigenous of all the Communist takeovers in Eastern Europe, because the Albanian Communist Party was the only one to seize power without direct military aid from foreign Communists. In this respect Albania differs from Yugoslavia, Czechoslovakia, and China, for in each of these countries the local Communists received substantial aid from the Red Army (PETERS 1975:292).

98. Three paths are possible: a) sheer insufficiency of the available means of coercion; b) inefficiency in applying the means; c) inhibitions to their applications. The starkest cases of insufficiency occur when the balance of coercive resources between the government and the alternative coalition swings suddenly toward the latter, because the government has suffered a sudden depletion of its resources (as in a lost war), because the alternative coalition has managed a sudden mobilization of resources (as in the pooling of private arms) or because a new contender with abundant coercive resources has joined the coalition (as in the defection of troops or foreign intervention) (TILLY 1978:209). Cf. also chapter 8.4.7.

99. Mass rebellion was measured by four complex indicators indexing "amount of violence," "number of active rebels," "social-geographical area involved," and "duration of the event."

100. RUSSELL also deals extensively with the likelihood of a mass rebellion in South Africa, but denies the success of it unless "external intervention on the side of the blacks" occurs (RUSSELL 1974:89). Furthermore, blacks at present seem to lack organizational facilities, partly due to harsh suppression by the South African government. Cf. also the studies of VAN DEN BERGHE (1976); R. W. JOHNSON (1977) and GANN/DUIGNAN (1978).

101. Measured through indexes of "degree of disloyalty," "time at which disloyal," and "proportion of armed forces disloyal at a particular time."

102. In a review of RUSSELL's book, MAYER/MAYER (1976) challenge several of RUSSELL's conclusions. They emphasize in particular that army disloyalty may be the consequence of mass rebellion rather than its cause. For a more extended theoretical model of revolution cf. chapter 8.4.7. Furthermore, basically only bivariate analyses have been

carried out with respect to the importance of a loyal army. For a critique of the sampling procedure, cf. also SOLAÚN (1976:638).

103. RUSSELL lists a number of additional variables (mostly referring to characteristics of the military itself) which may contribute to an army becoming disloyal:

> the social-class composition of the armed forces on both the officer and conscript level; the proportion of officers to men; the closeness of contacts between the armed forces and the civilian population; whether the army is a long-service, professional army or a short-service, conscript army, or something in between; the recruitment criteria, for example, political versus military; the pay, status, and promotion opportunities, and how these compare with opportunities outside of the armed forces; the emphasis in the training on discipline, courage, efficiency, and obedience; the existence of an ideology shared with the regime; and how well or badly the troops are treated. Lip service given to the important role of the armed forces must be replaced by thorough examination of the effect of factors such as these on their loyalty to the regime (RUSSELL 1974:81).

104. In his investigations SOROKIN covers several centuries, in some cases even more than a thousand years.

105. With respect to these variables cf. also the speculations of LEONHARD (1975) as to the likelihood of a revolution in the Soviet Union.

106. "'Power deflation' [denotes] a resort to force [on behalf of the incumbents as well as the opposition] because the usual channels of peaceful change are clogged" (WELCH/TAINTOR 1972:11 following PARSONS 1964).

107. "If one tells an automobile mechanic that the car's engine is dysfunctional, it is just about as clear and true as when one says it about an old society" (DAVIES 1967:253; cf. also NARDIN 1971:38).

108. Cf. SCHNEIDER (1959; 1975); WASSERSTROM (1975).

109. Cf. HUMBARACI (1966); O'BALLANCE (1967); QUANDT (1969); OTTAWAY (1970); HEGGOY (1972); JACKSON (1977); and the narrative account by HORNE (1978).

110. If one draws on this explanation for predictive purposes, it becomes crucial "to specify 'mobilization' and 'institutionalization' independently of each other" (TILLY 1973:434; cf. also the discussion in chapters 5.1.2.4 and 7.2.3).

111. As will become clear, the Western and Eastern patterns are not identical with geographical regions. Rather the terms have been borrowed from the historical precedents.

112. It is interesting to note that HUNTINGTON's distinctions are also found in Chinese documents. "For example, in 1965 Lin Piao wrote: 'The October revolution began with armed uprisings in the cities and then spread to the countryside, while the Chinese revolution won nation-wide victory through the encirclement of the cities from the rural areas and the final capture of the cities.' Long Live the Victory of

(112)

People's war!, Peking, 1966:43" (as quoted in HAMMOND 1975: 639).

113. The second date refers to Batista's going into exile, the third to the fall of Saigon, the fourth to the fall of Managua. Yet, one may wonder whether the Cuban Revolution does indeed fit as well into the Eastern model as, for example, the latter phases of the Chinese Revolution (former date mentioned in the quotation; see also SKOCPOL 1979:303 for the opposite argument). In the Cuban case, there seems to be some evidence that, at least in part, the following basic characteristics of Western revolutions were met: "The political institutions of the old regime collapse; this is followed by the mobilization of new groups into politics and then by the creation of new political institutions" (HUNTINGTON 1968:266). The argument is supported in greater detail by HAGOPIAN:

> The Cuban Revolution is in reality an intermediate type between the Eastern (Chinese) and Western models of revolution. Its retention of certain 'Western' features derives mainly from its relatively high level of urbanization, industrialization, and standard of living compared to most Third World countries [Cf. also chapter 8.4.6.2]. The chief deviation from the Eastern prototype is that Castro did not fight a truly protracted civil war that involved large conventional forces as well as small guerrilla units. There was no mass party tightly linked with a mass army in the Chinese or Vietminh manner. . . . Perhaps most significantly, the Batista regime was not really defeated: it *collapsed* for largely internal reasons, some of which had precious little to do with Castro's and Che Guevara's daring escapades (HAGOPIAN 1974:291).

Considering the small number of cases, any general statement as to (Western, Eastern or other) patterns of revolution is risky.

114. But cf. below for a critique of this point.

115. In addition, HUNTINGTON proposes a number of interesting hypotheses which should be tested on a systematic quantitative basis: "In the Western revolution, terror occurs in the latter phases of the revolution and is employed by the radicals after they have come to power primarily against the moderates and other revolutionary groups with whom they have struggled. In the Eastern revolution, in contrast, terror marks the first phase of the revolutionary struggle. It is used by the revolutionaries when they are weak and far removed from power to persuade or to coerce support from peasants and to intimidate the power reaches of officialdom. . . . Emigration . . . reaches its peak at the beginning of the revolutionary struggle in the Western model but at the end of the struggle in the Eastern pattern" (HUNTINGTON 1968:274).

116. Or more precisely: "The city is the center of opposition within the country; the middle class is the focus of opposition within the city; the intelligentsia is the most active oppositional group within the middle class; and the students are the most coherent and effective revolutionaries within the intelligentsia" (HUNTINGTON 1968:290). Yet, it

remains doubtful whether students are indeed the "most coherent and effective revolutionaries" (see also the opposite conclusion in another portion of HUNTINGTON's book, 1968:239). There is, however, wide empirical evidence showing that sizable portions of the students are in opposition no matter who is in government or what the incumbent government does.

Furthermore, as HUNTINGTON himself notes, "The image of the middle class as a revolutionary element clashes, of course, with the stereotype of the middle class as the keystone of stability in a modern polity" (HUNTINGTON 1968:289). The apparent contradiction might be reconcilable from a dynamic point of view: "As the middle class becomes larger, it becomes more conservative" (ibid.). Well-known examples of large conservative middle classes include Imperial Germany as well as Japan.

117. Forecasting some future trends, HUNTINGTON comes up with these projections:

> Rural reform and urban migration may provide alternative routes which the bulk of the Third World countries may follow. They may thus foreclose or severely reduce the probability of future revolutions along the lines of the urban middle-class–peasant revolutionary coalitions which have existed and succeeded in the past. Yet urbanization is only an element in modernization and the phenomenon of urbanization without industrialization may open up Third World countries to the possibility of new types of social revolution absent from the history of the early modernizers. Such revolutions may be necessary to complete the process of modernization which the urban migration began. . . . In most Third World countries, it indeed may be too late for a peasant revolution; but it could also be too early for an urban one (HUNTINGTON 1971a:10).

118. These ideas on the necessity of coalition-forming among revolutionaries are shared by numerous scholars in the field (and by revolutionaries themselves, of course). MEUSEL may be quoted as a good example: "The German peasant war of 1525 [cf. also note 155] was lost because it was restricted essentially to the *countryside*. The German revolution of 1848 was lost because it remained essentially confined to the *city*" (MEUSEL 1952:39; my translation). There are no data available as to the relative size of middle class elements (and perhaps even upper class members) in a revolutionary coalition and/or about the necessary degree of cleavage in the middle or upper classes to ensure the success of revolutionary attacks.

119. However, some qualifications must be added to such an analysis. SELDEN (1971), for example, tries to show that

> A land or agrarian "revolution" sponsored by the communists was the basis for developments. This "revolution" consisted of a considerable land reform that eliminated landlordism, limited rich (by Chinese standards) peasants' holdings, and increased

(119)

those of middle and poor peasants. Before the communists' intervention in the late 1920's, peasant social protest was vented through banditry and self-help cooperative movements [cf. the overview in CHESNEAUX 1973].... When war came they were in a good position to win the reputation of being the best defenders of China's sovereignty and pride—but the spadework had been done during the previous decade (HAGOPIAN 1974: 288–89).

"Their appeal to the peasant was rooted in an effective program of administration and reform [delivering land to the peasants]. The new nationalism in the countryside was linked to the revitalization of the social and economic life of the village" (SELDEN 1971:277). In a study in the T'aihang-Pingyuan region, THAXTON finds evidence for his revision of current interpretations: "Long before the arrival of the revolutionary army and the Japanese occupation, the peasants were ready to support a government that would help them recapture the basic elements of social justice they had lost. Exploitation, rather than the impact of the war *per se*, was what aroused the villagers as *potential* participants in the Communist Party's revolutionary war against the Japanese—a pattern not unlike that of Central Luzon before the rise of the Huks, or of Tonkin before the rise of the Vietminh" (THAXTON 1977:54). The result in the very end may perhaps best be described with SCHURMANN's words: "The Chinese Communists were finally able to achieve what no state in power in Chinese history had been able to do: to create an organization loyal to the state which was also solidly imbedded in the natural village" (SCHURMANN 1971:416, also quoted in HAGOPIAN 1974:290).

120. A directly related question is whether there is a tendency of revolutions to spread. There is no clear answer as yet, especially if one considers only successful revolutions. On the other hand, there is ample evidence that attempts at revolutionary overthrows come in waves at various times during the nineteenth century (1820, 1830, 1848) and after the two World Wars in this century. (BRACHER, 1976a:38, consequently calls the European turnovers during 1917/18 "antiwar-revolutions.") Diffusion is also encountered in the case of imposed communist takeovers. "Countries that have become Communist since 1917 have bordered on an established Communist state in every case except one— Cuba" (HAMMOND 1975:641).

121. The research strategy of paired comparisons seems to be quite useful at the present stage of knowledge about the conditions of revolution. Interesting examples, apart from HUNTINGTON, can be found in ÖZBUDUN (1970—Mexico vs. Turkey) and KAUTSKY (1975—Mexico vs. Soviet Union). Cf. also ECKSTEIN (1976).

122. Yet, on the basis of more rigorous standards, the Mexican revolution as well must be considered "incomplete," one indicator being the giving up of the program of landholding village communities (*ejidos*) after 1940. As to a general evaluation of the Mexican revolution cf. NEED-

LER (1970); ATKIN (1970); and MOLS/TOBLER (1975). Cf. also HELLMAN (1978).

123. Cf. also ALEXANDER (1958); PATCH (1961); ZONDAG (1966); KLEIN (1968); WESTON (1968); MALLOY (1970); MALLOY/ THORN (1971).

124. EISENSTADT (1978) in his generalizations on "Revolution and the Transformation of Societies" tries to interpret revolutions in ancient and in modern times in terms of confrontations between center and periphery. Yet, he often draws on this paradigm of explanation in an ad hoc manner and uses fairly common and at the same time abstract language, so that in terms of substance not much is gained for a cross-national analysis of revolutions. See also note 5.

125. If there was a coalition with urban elements, it consisted in the official approval of the land seizures initiated by the peasants themselves (cf. below).

126. Cf. above as to inconsistencies with respect to the Eastern model.

127. This aspect is also stressed by MOORE (1969) in an article where he analyzes the chances of revolution in the United States, which are—apart from the impossibility of creating and mobilizing revolutionary masses—almost nil, since rebels would have no chance for retreating into a territory not covered and controlled by the incumbents (cf. also chapter 8.4.4).

128. Incidentally, HUNTINGTON does not quote MOORE (but cf. also HUNTINGTON 1971b:311–12), although many of his ideas seem to be shared by MOORE.

129. Cf. also HUNTINGTON: "First, the earlier this development takes place in the process of modernization and the expansion of political participation, the lower the costs it imposes on society. Conversely, the more complex the society the more difficult it becomes to create integrating political institutions. Second, at each stage in the broadening of political participation the opportunities for fruitful political action rest with different social groups and different types of political leaders" (HUNTINGTON 1968:238). A suggestive hypothesis in this context has been presented by HUNTINGTON/DOMÍNGUEZ (following POWELL 1971:216ff.): "A sequence of politicization, commercialization, and urbanization leads to rural revolution, while a commercialization-politicization-urbanization sequence tends to produce agrarian reform" (HUNTINGTON/DOMÍNGUEZ 1975:15).

130. "The process of modernization begins with peasant revolutions that fail. It culminates during the twentieth century with peasant revolutions that succeed" (MOORE 1966:453). HUNTINGTON, as will be recalled, has expressed the same idea with these words: "The countryside . . . plays the crucial 'swing' role in modernizing politics. The nature of the Green Uprising, the way in which the peasants are incorporated into the political system, shapes the subsequent course of political development. . . . The role of the city is constant: it is the permanent source of opposition. The role of the countryside is variable: it is either the source of stability or the source of revolution" (HUN-

(562)

TINGTON 1968:292). Cf. also the analysis ibid. pp. 72–78, especially the table on p. 76 as well as the following summary: "Paradoxically, the Green Uprising has either a highly traditionalizing impact on the political system or a profoundly revolutionary one" (HUNTINGTON 1968:77).

131. The focus of interest is on innovation that has led to political power, not on the spread and reception of institutions that have been hammered out elsewhere, except where they have led to significant power in world politics. The fact that the smaller countries depend economically and politically on big and powerful ones means that the decisive causes of their politics lie outside their own boundaries. It also means that their political problems are not really comparable to those of larger countries. Therefore a general statement about the historical preconditions of democracy or authoritarianism covering small countries as well as large would likely be so broad as to be abstractly platitudinous (MOORE 1966:x).

Obviously, these are assumptions which could be definitively decided on only *after* these questions have been studied on a broad empirical basis.

132. SHAPIRO points to additional aspects worth noting in this context:

Note that England differs from Germany and Japan in that the crucial ends were those of the bourgeoisie rather than the landed upper classes. In order to account for such divergencies, MOORE calls upon a number of added explanatory variables such as the dependence of the English wool growing nobility on the towns for their markets, democratic traditions stemming from the theoretical equality of the parties to feudal contracts of vassalage, ethnic heterogeneity in parts of Russia, England's reliance on naval rather than military power, the early or late coming of industrialization, educational systems, caste and colonialism. Such variables enter each individual case from left field, so to speak. They dilute the book's theoretical claims and at times give it the appearance of a conventional historical survey (SHAPIRO 1967:821).

133. For a critique along these lines, see ROTHMAN (1970); LOWENTHAL (1968); cf. also the reply by MOORE (1970).

134. For a perceptive critique of ANDERSON's (1974a; 1974b) influential books see SKOCPOL/FULBROOK (1977). As others have done, they criticize ANDERSON's use of the concept of feudalism. Also "England diverges from ANDERSON's arguments in practically every important respect" (ibid., p. 295). Cf. also the review by TRIMBERGER (1976).

135. "My reservations are confined to a belief that he seriously exaggerates both the degree to which the landlord class had adopted commercial principles (in fact they were mostly *rentiers*, as he admits in a footnote) and the speed and the violence of the disappearance of the small peasant proprietor" (STONE 1967a:33).

(Chapter Eight)

136. See ROKKAN (forthcoming) for what is probably the best summary of his intentions and results. In this contribution he also makes an effort to link his own approach with WALLERSTEIN's (1974) capitalist world-system approach and the West-East dimension stressed by ANDERSON (1974a; 1974b).
137. In fairness to MOORE, he has, of course, noted this point as well as many of the other objections raised against his analysis.
138. It should be added that experts on the German variant of "fascism," national socialism, stress that it differed considerably from fascism, whatever is understood by this concept. See BRACHER (1976b) for a most recent statement and chapter 8.3.

139. Whatever the reasons for the anomalous development of the Swedish peasantry, its results, in MOORE's terms at least, seem to be clear. Unlike the situations in either Britain or France, there was no need to destroy by revolutionary violence either of the old rural classes in order to bring about industrialism. To a large extent the practices of the *independent* peasantry were irrelevant to an emerging industrialism, which found its impetus partly from foreign capital and partly from a very small class of indigenous, monopoly entrepreneurs, who after 1866 were united with the nobles' landed and bureaucratic interests in a plutocratic first chamber. That this plutocratic alliance was itself not the basis for the authoritarian variant of capitalism was a consequence of the already existing political power of the landed peasantry (CASTLES 1973:330; emphasis added).

140. Cf. also MARX: "Revolutions are the locomotives of history" ("Die Klassenkämpfe in Frankreich 1848 bis 1850." *Aus der Neuen Rheinischen Zeitung*, Preußisch-Hannoversche Revue, 1850, Berlin 1895:90; here quoted according to GRIEWANK 1969:218). Cf. also the hypotheses and the empirical results in GURR 1973b.
141. As other reviewers did before, SKOCPOL also criticizes the use of sometimes rather abstract theoretical concepts. For example: "Does it make sense to lump together under the rubric of 'political mechanisms' everything from 'customary' landlord/peasant relations to local government and central state functions?" (SKOCPOL 1973:14).
142. For an admittedly limited simulated data analysis of MOORE's study, see MOY (1971).
143. Actually, the peasant had been a largely neglected figure in cross-national research. "The peasant is an immemorial figure on the world social landscape, but anthropology [sociology] noticed him only recently" (GEERTZ 1972:1).
144. In this context, cf. also the notion of "amoral familism" (BANFIELD 1958) which could be conceived of as a consequence of "zero-sum" perceptions in peasant communities.
145. The characteristics of peasants listed here do not refer to peasants (or, perhaps more adequately, farmers) in industrialized countries.

(146)

146. Note that Mao (as well as Lenin) concluded that landless laborers could become revolutionaries, if only because of their availability in times of revolutionary protests. Cf. LANDSBERGER (1974a:39).

147. But see also STOKES (1978) for some counterevidence from colonial India against WOLF's middle peasant thesis.

148. Cf. ALROY (1967) for a discussion of the generally scarce evidence as to peasant support of the Cuban revolutionaries. For a partly conflicting view see USEEM (1977) who emphasizes the supportive role of the squatters.

149. Consequently, throughout most of the peasant rebellions in medieval Europe and during later rebellions as well, peasants believed that the true or just king was on their side. As put in the slogan of Wat Tyler's uprising of 1381 in England, "with King Richard and the commons." In Russia, the figure or the myth of the "true-Czar" or the "Czar-deliverer" has been a permanent feature of peasant rebellions, especially during the seventeenth and eighteenth centuries (cf. also SCOTT 1977:277). Cf. also AVRICH (1972) for a longitudinal analysis of the four major Cossack revolts (under the leadership of Bolotnikov, 1606–7; Razin, 1670–71; Bulavin, 1707–8, and Pugachev, 1773–74; on the latter cf. also LONGWORTH 1975). AVRICH emphasizes the continuity in both the underlying conditions of these revolts and their eventual outcomes.

150. As TILLY has said:

> The basic conditions for resistance are first, a focused threat to peasant survival, with well-defined agents having visible external connections, occurring simultaneously in a number of localities that are already in communication with each other; and second, a significant local framework for collective action in the form of mutual obligations, communications lines, and justifiable common claims on resources. From WOLF's accounts of twentieth-century peasant wars and from a general survey of modern European experience, it is reasonable to add an important facilitating condition: the availability of urban-based allies in the form of intellectuals, liberal bourgeois, labor leaders, military chiefs, professional politicos, or others (TILLY 1974:296).

The success of the Sicilian *mafia* or, more precisely, the lack of protest among peasants, may be understood in light of this explanation (see BLOK 1974).

151. Cf. WOMACK (1972), WHITE (1969), and HUIZER (1970) as to an evaluation of the Zapata movement. Cf. also WATERBURY (1975) for an analysis contrasting the conditions of peasant support for Zapata (in Morelos) with those making for nonrevolutionary peasants (in Oaxaca).

152. Studying seventeenth century peasant uprisings in France, Russia, and China, MOUSNIER reaches a similar conclusion: "In none of these three countries can it be said that the peasants took the initiative in these revolts. They were always begun by other elements, and, in France, a society with a greater diversity of estates than the other two, they were often begun to a greater extent than elsewhere, by the higher

social strata" (MOUSNIER 1971:327). Cf. also the critical evaluation of MOUSNIER's study by GATELY et al. (1971).

In his critique of PORCHNEV's study (1963) MOUSNIER (1958) also maintains, contrary to PORCHNEV, that there were were no autonomous peasant revolts in pre-Fronde France during 1623–48 which can be interpreted as class warfare. Rather a variety of conflict constellations can be detected, involving bourgeois elements and, at times, noble elements acting in most instances against the expanding central authority. For an effort to reconcile both interpretations, cf. MANDROU (1959). See also SALMON (1967) and MANDROU (1969) for useful reviews of the controversy (cf. also BERNARD 1964) and WALLERSTEIN (1974:283ff.) who places it in the context of his approach to the modern capitalist world-system.

Without outside support and leadership, peasant uprisings are bound to fail. This conclusion, reoccurring at various points in the entire chapter, must also be drawn if one looks at the late medieval revolts during the fourteenth and fifteenth centuries—cf. MOLLAT/WOLFF (1970) for a comparative analysis dealing with peasant revolts in France, Florence, the Netherlands, England, on the Iberian peninsula, in Catalania, in Bohemia, and elsewhere (cf. also HILTON 1973). MOLLAT/WOLFF also stress the reactionary character of most of these peasant revolts (cf. also chapter 8.4.6.6.1). For an analysis of revolts from the fifteenth through the seventeenth centuries, see, e.g., KOENIGSBERGER (1971), and FORSTER/GREENE (1970) for studies of sixteenth- and seventeenth-century revolts (cf. also KAMEN 1971). The phenomena dealt with in these comparative analyses are rather heterogenous (cf. also ELLIOTT 1969). In the case of FORSTER/GREENE, they include:

> (a) Great national revolutions, specifically the Dutch break with Spanish rule in the late 1500s and the English overthrow of the Stuarts in the 1640s; (b) national revolts such as the French Fronde of 1648–1653 and the almost contemporaneous Catalan rebellion against Spain, which according to FORSTER and GREENE had the potential of becoming genuine revolutions; (c) large-scale regional rebellions with limited revolutionary potential, as shown by Pugachev's movement; (d) secessionist coups d'état, exemplified by the Portuguese overthrow of Spanish rule 1640–1688; and (e) urban Jacqueries, such as those in mid-seventeenth century Sicily and Naples (MOOTE 1972:211, who provides a useful comparative analysis of the works of FORSTER/GREENE and KOENIGSBERGER).

153. This analysis seems to be partly shared by TROTSKY:

> If the agrarian problem . . . had been solved by the bourgeoisie, if it could have been solved by them, the Russian proletariat could not possibly have come to power in 1917. In order to realize the Soviet state, there was required a drawing together and mutual

(153)

penetration of two factors belonging to completely different historic species: a peasant war—that is, a movement characteristic of the dawn of bourgeois development—and a proletarian insurrection, the movement signalizing its decline. That is the essence of 1917 (TROTSKY 1932:51).

154. A first example of such studies can be found in an article by CHIROT/ RAGIN (1975) on the origins of the peasant rebellion in Romania in 1907 (cf. also the account in EIDELBERG 1974) which provides support for WOLF's explanation.

155. The failure of the German peasants' war of 1524–26 may be attributed to the inability of the peasants to win support at large from the towns. In the literature there is still much debate as to how to explain and interpret this rare event of revolutionary or reactive violence (in the sense of TILLY, cf. chapter 8.4.6.6.1) in German history. Marxist, mostly East German, scholars tend to view it in close connection with the German reformation and treat the whole series of events as kind of an early bourgeois revolution, whereas Western scholars are less inclined to subscribe to such functional historical interpretations. Consequently, there is still no agreement as to whether political factors (much emphasized in the classic study by FRANZ, 1933), religious, economic (e.g., economic and legal oppression by prelates and nobles), or social factors are most important, or how relatively important they are in explaining the peasant uprising. (It seems noteworthy that the more affluent peasants were strongly engaged in this war, thus providing some additional evidence for one of WOLF's hypotheses.) For some useful overviews of the controversies with Marxist scholars, cf., e.g., SCHULZE (1973); WOHLFEIL (1972; 1977). See also BLICKLE (1975; 1975a); NIPPERDEY (1975:85–112); WEHLER (1975a); WOHLFEIL (1975); BAK (1976) and SCRIBNER/BENECKE (1979) for some additional materials as well as the case study of the peasant war in southern Upper Swabia by SABEAN (1972). A most recent overview of research on the German peasant war is given by SCOTT (1979a; 1979b) and by BLICKLE who emphasizes that "the area with well-developed *Gemeinde* [community] coincides geographically—apart from the strip along the north-east sea coast—with the area of widespread rebellions" (BLICKLE 1979:236–37).

156. ZAGORIA (1974), for one, stresses the revolutionary potential among rural tenants and proletarians in contemporary Asia. Some additional hypotheses of interest in this context are suggested by GENELETTI (1976) who predicts different probabilities of agrarian radicalism according to the level of economic development, the degree of landownership, and the dependency of the peasants (but he does not provide sufficient empirical evidence for his theory).

157. Yet FANON (1961) clearly overdraws the point when proclaiming the poor African peasant the revolutionary subject par excellence (cf. COSER 1966; GROHS 1968; STANILAND 1969; WODDIS 1972: 54–66; PERINBAM 1973; JINADU 1973; and BLACKEY 1974 for critical evaluations).

158. Cf. HARRISON (1971) for a review of various Marxist (orthodox and non-orthodox) positions dealing with Chinese peasant rebellions. A differentiating analysis as to MARX's theorizing on peasants is found in DUGGETT (1975). See also WITTFOGEL (1960) on the "Marxist view of Russian society and revolution" as well as his *Oriental Despotism* (1957).

159. While stressing the importance of Mao, Ho Chi Minh (cf., e.g., FALL 1967) and his main strategist Vo-nguŷen-Giap, the other highly successful revolutionaries in Asia, should not be forgotten here.

160. Cf. also BIANCO (1971:155ff.) for an extension of the analysis along JOHNSON's lines.

161. Cf. also the analysis in DENITCH (1976; 1976a; JOHNSON 1962; SHOUP 1975) who points out that the new party cadre structure "was to revolutionize relationships within the villages and to transform the countryside *before* the cities were conquered" (DENITCH 1976:468). Yugoslavia may thus serve as another example of HUNTINGTON's Eastern model of revolution. Actually, historical events took a much more complicated path, as summarized in the quotation from SETON-WATSON:

> The Yugoslav Revolution of 1941–45 was made possible by war, which destroyed the old Yugoslavia. Within a few months of the occupation and partition of the defeated country, two new wars had started—a national war between Croats and Serbs in Bosnia and a war of resistance by Serbs against Germans in Serbia. This second war soon produced a third war, a civil war between royalist and communist Serbs. In the following years the three wars became fused, and took on new shapes. In the end there emerged a single war between two adversaries. On one side were the Partisans, led and fully controlled by the Communist Party, appealing with growing success to Serbs, Croats, Slovenes and Macedonians to unite as brother nations against a common enemy. On the other side were the Germans, assisted by the allied armies of Italy (until 1943), Bulgaria and Hungary, and by extreme nationalist Croats (Ustasha) and Serbs (Chetniks), whose hatred of the rival neighbouring nation outweighed their dislike of the foreign conqueror. During the "War of Liberation," which had acquired this comparatively simple form by the beginning of 1943, if indeed not earlier, the Yugoslav Communists established, in the "liberated areas" in the mountains and forests, the essential machinery of government which ultimately took over the whole country, the large cities, of course, last of all. The progress of the Yugoslav Communists to power in many ways resembles that of the Chinese (SETON-WATSON 1972:193).

162. As one writer put it, the communists were only sanctioning later what had been achieved by spontaneous activities of peasants tired of the war and their usually absent landlords (cf. also above).

(162)

Among the peasants, the Bolsheviks had no real following. But as the only party without ties to the existing order they could afford to give in temporarily to their demands for the sake of seizing power. This they did on taking over the government and again after the chaos of the Civil War. Subsequently of course the Bolsheviks found it necessary to turn on those who had brought them to power and to drive the peasants into collectives in order to make them the main basis and victims of the socialist version of primary capitalist accumulation (MOORE 1966:481). See KEEP (1976) for a detailed account.

163. MAO's tactic of guerrilla warfare was "adopted as a result of the *failure* of other tactics" (FAIRBAIRN 1974:88; cf. also CHESNEAUX et al. 1977:155ff.). "Mao claimed that these tactics 'are indeed different from any other tactics, ancient or modern, Chinese or foreign.' But neither for Sertorius nor for Viriatus two thousand years earlier [nor for the philosopher Sun Tzu who wrote 2,400 years ago] would these ideas have been startling revelations—nor for guerrilla leaders all over the globe throughout history. Although neither the strategy nor the tactics were novel, their use in the framework of a political doctrine was" (LAQUEUR 1976:245).

164. "Our strategy is to put one against ten, while our tactic is to pit ten against one—this is one of the fundamental principles on which we beat the enemy" (MAO as quoted in JOHNSON 1965:52).

165. "Once a territorial base has been established and secured, political violence tends to assume the character of war between nations" (GURR 1970a:266–67).

166. "Without a political goal, guerrilla warfare must fail as it must if its political objectives do not coincide with the aspirations of the people" (MAO Tse-tung 1961:43).

167. "Guerrilla warfare is a form of warfare by which the strategically weaker side assumes the tactical offensive in selected forms, times and places" (HUNTINGTON 1962:xvi). "Little warfare" is indeed the original notion of the Spanish word *guerrilla* (PARET/SHY 1962; ASPREY 1975; LAQUEUR 1976; PARRY 1976). The ratios of guerrilla fighters to normal troops trying to battle them have ranged accordingly from 1:8 in Greece to 1:23 in Algeria and 1:30 in Malaya (cf. GREENE 1974:84, and AHMAD 1971:148). Yet, even a superior relationship such as in the case of Algeria did not prevent victory of the guerrilla forces. Final victory must have been based on more than military factors alone. A satisfactory explanation of these cases will always have to refer to political factors (cf. also chapter 5.1.2.5).

Some writers (e.g., ZAWODNY 1962) also speak of "unconventional warfare." But at least since the early nineteenth century there is a "convention" of guerrilla warfare which reached its peak during World War II and in the period thereafter.

For useful historical reviews of guerrilla fighting, cf. LAQUEUR (1976); PARRY (1976); ELLIS (1976); ASPREY (1975); the informative study by HAHLWEG (1968); CAMPBELL (1967). One of the

(Chapter Eight)

classical analysts of the political components in warfare, CLAUSE-
WITZ, has also written on guerrilla warfare. His manuscripts on "small
war" have only been published very recently (CLAUSEWITZ 1966:
208–599).
168. "The dramatic failure of the 'military' theory of insurgency in Latin
America may have its parallels in the relative lack of success of the
'military' theory of counter-insurgency in South East Asia" (HUN-
TINGTON 1971a:7). Or put in another context:

> As a theory *Revolution in the Revolution?* is radical but wrong. It
> corresponds closely to the theory of revolutionary warfare
> favored in Washington. It views revolutionary war, "in its forma-
> tive stages," essentially in military terms. The civilian population
> is ignored until after a certain success has been achieved. Govern-
> ment's legitimacy is viewed in terms of coercion; hence military
> action becomes the chief instrument of subversion. The revolu-
> tionaries, considered "outsiders" by the population, tend to view
> the civilians as spectators who will join the winning side. . . .
> Debray's *foco*, I am afraid, is a tailor's fit for the American
> counter-insurgency program. Che Guevara's Bolivian campaign was
> an example of the pitfalls of the *foco* theory (AHMAD 1968:82).

For evaluations of DEBRAY's theory of the *foco*, see the articles (some
of them showing strong political engagement) in HUBERMAN/
SWEEZY (1968). As to a critique of DEBRAY's (and GUEVARA's)
revolutionary analysis and tactical conclusions, cf. also MARTIĆ
(1975); HALPERIN (1976); MOSS (1972); MORENO (1970); and
chapter 8.2.
169. But not only by them. Many of the so-called counter-insurgency techniques (cf. the bibliography in CONDIT et al. 1963; and the discussion
in, e.g., OSANKA 1962; GALULA 1964; SULLIVAN/SATTLER 1971;
KITSON 1971; 1977; for a critical evaluation cf. AHMAD 1971; WOLF
1966; see BLAUFARB 1977 for a critical appraisal of American counter-insurgency doctrine and performance, especially in Vietnam, Thailand, the Philippines, and Malaya) are in fact techniques of guerrilla
warfare which have been derived from the experiences gained in batt-
ling guerrilleros. (Cf. also the instructive analysis of techniques of partisan
warfare in HEILBRUNN 1962). In some instances (e.g., in some Latin
American countries) state authorities have not refrained from using
methods of torture to break the resistance of their terrorist groups. As
of now, some of the countermeasures have been "successful." Whether
this will be true in the long run or on the international scene where
terrorism has been spreading in recent years remains an open question,
even though the prospects of "victory" of international terrorism do
not seem to be good.
170. For a general background study, cf. the analysis of BLASCO (1974)
and more specifically DA SILVA (1975). Cf. also HEIBERG (1975)
and PAYNE (1975).
171. GURR (1979:52) counts 12 guerrilla wars in Western democracies and
120 in other countries, with a median number of 2,600 dissidents parti-

(171)

cipating during the 1960s (N=87 countries). The estimated total death figure is 1,300,000.

172. In the aggregate analyses of GURR, HIBBS, and others (cf. chapter 5.1), data on terrorism and guerrilla warfare have been combined for empirical reasons with data on other forms of conflict. What is called for here is a cross-national analysis that *distinguishes* among these forms of conflict.

173. There is also a parallel to social banditry (cf. also chapter 5.2): "The ecology of guerrilla war and banditry is identical to all intents and purposes. This applies to all the more recent major guerrilla wars—China, Cuba, Algeria, Vietnam, Greece, the Philippines, Malaya, and so on. Naturally both guerrillas and bandits looked for hideouts in difficult terrain. But there was also usually a regional tradition of 'young people taking to the hills'" (LAQUEUR 1976:96).

174. Language purists have also noted that, since *guerrilla* literally means "little war," the rather common use of notions like "guerrilla warfare" is a pleonasm.

175. "In World War I guerrilla tactics were hardly applied at all, in the second they played a certain limited role in some countries in the struggle against the foreign occupier" (LAQUEUR 1976:152).

176. Cf., e.g., BELL (1976a) for some instructive case analyses.

177. "A fourth category might have been added, that is, those revived right-wing terrorist gangs who in Argentina, Brazil, Italy, and mostly Spain have begun to carry the battle into the leftist enemy's territory, in most instances in collaboration with the local police. Perhaps the Ulster Protestant organizations might be included in this group" (THOMAS 1977:1338). THOMAS also emphasizes that in many instances there is also a "general responsibility of governments for what has happened" (ibid., p. 1340).

178. "There are but two cases in recent history in which major guerrilla armies survived and expanded without outside supply of arms—China and Yugoslavia" (LAQUEUR 1976:394).

179. The impact of these men is all the more astonishing considering that "the most important guerrilla leaders of our time, including MAO, Tito, Giap, Castro, Guevara, as well as the foremost theoreticians among them, were self-made men in the military field" (LAQUEUR 1976:397). Morover, "MAO and Ho Chi Minh, Castro [and] Guevara . . . were not in the least aware of the fact their ideas had been expounded before and even tried, albeit not very successfully" (LAQUEUR 1976:384).

180. See also VAN NESS (1970) for an earlier evaluation and for some data on various forms of Chinese support for national liberation movements.

181. "It must not be inferred that MAO is regarded as having said the last word on the subject. The fate of the Hukbalahaps in the Philippines, the Malayan Communists, the Indian guerrillas in Telingana, the Indonesian Communists, Guevara in Bolivia should at least teach us not to think in terms of a unitary 'third world' in which the same set of tactics is always applicable. All revolutions are unique but whatever general

(Chapter Eight)

rules can be discerned must come from a study of the widest range of historical experience" (ELLIS 1973:2).

182. Unfortunately, many definitions of terrorism subscribe to rather obvious circular formulations. A typical example can be found in the definition of the Convention for the Prevention and Punishment of Terrorism of the League of Nations of 1937: Terrorism is defined as all "criminal acts directed against a state and intended or calculated to create a state of terror in the minds of particular persons, or a group of persons or the general public" (as quoted in QURESHI 1976:152).

183. For a historical account of the origins of the word *terreur* in MONTES-QUIEU's *Esprit des lois* and its use during the French Revolution, see KESSLER (1973). According to LAQUEUR (1977b), the word "terrorism" appears for the first time in the *Dictionnaire de l'Académie française* in 1798 to qualify a regime according to its use of *la terreur*.

184. Comparable studies for the entire 1970s have not yet been published. "Regionally, terrorist attacks have been most frequent in Europe (50%) and Latin America (21%). North America (14%), the Middle East and North Africa (11%), Asia (2%), and subsaharan Africa (2%) round out the count. In 1970 there were twice as many operations in Latin America as in Europe. By 1978 (through September) the ratio was reversed. In the first three quarters of 1978, Europe counted at least 506 incidents, led by Italy, compared with 256 in Latin America. Distinct variances exist between regions in the use of specific tactics. For instance, 62% of all kidnappings have occurred in Latin America while Europe has witnessed 54% of all bombings and 44% of all assassinations. The data base lists, for North America, some 667 incidents, of which 575 or 86% have been bombings" (MILLER/RUSSELL 1979: 197; see RUSSELL 1979 for additional figures).

Altogether MILLER/RUSSELL report more than 5,000 terrorist incidents from January 1970 (excluding Northern Ireland, Israel, and some smaller African states) and 2,735 killed, 3,472 injured, and 3,286 hostages. Many of their findings are congruent with those of BELL/GURR (1979; see in the text).

For an application of GURR's (1968a) theoretical model to data for the years 1968–74 (data taken from MICKOLUS 1978), see OSMOND (1979). As one might expect, the theory of relative deprivation does not fare well (with the exception of Latin American countries, but here again the problem of inferential measurement of the theoretical concept arises). A data bank for analyzing assassinations of political leaders is being completed by SNITCH (1980) for the years 1968–78 (N=123 countries). He reports that, compared to the years 1947–67, political assassinations have increased considerably, that there is no relationship to indicators of economic development, that extremist groups participated in almost half of the cases, and that Argentina, Italy, Guatemala, the United States and Lebanon were the countries that experienced most assassinations.

The announced comprehensive study by MICKOLUS (1980) documenting more than 5,000 events and presenting further analyses (years:

(184)

1968–79) was not available to me when writing this note (December 1980).

185. Since I had only the German edition of LAQUEUR (1977b) available, I refrained from more detailed references here.

186. "A CIA study which counts all incidents with international targets or ramifications identifies 111 incidents in 1968, 282 in 1970, and a peak of 413 in 1976, followed by a decline to 279 in 1977. The tactics chosen varied considerably over time: political highjacking reached a peak with 21 incidents in 1970; by 1977 they had declined to eight. Bombings and kidnappings, on the other hand, reached their peak in the mid-1970s before beginning a decline" (BELL/GURR 1979:333).

187. On the problems and prospects of nuclear terrorism cf., e.g., BERES 1978; GREENBERG/NORTON 1979.

188. Thus multiplying what THORNTON (1964:82) has called the "advertising" function of terrorism. Or, in the words of BELL: "Most revolutionaries can bomb their way into the headlines but not into power. Their bombs are simply not big enough" (BELL 1977:486). As to the impact of the mass media on terrorism and vice versa, cf. also WÖRDE-MANN (1977). Television stations even went so far as to cover terrorist actions for a whole day as in Japan or to turn to live transmission when five young West German terrorists were flown out of the country in return for the promised release of the kidnappers' hostage. "Melvin J. Lasky notes pertinently that the state's television network 'was hijacked, in effect, to serve the kidnappers' master plan'" (PARRY 1976:520).

189. CROZIER speaks of "disruptive terrorism" and describes its aims as follows:

    – To gain publicity for the movement, and arouse admiration and emulation.
    – To secure funds and build up the movement's morale and prestige.
    – To discredit and demoralize the authorities.
    – To provoke the authorities into taking excessively harsh repressive measures, likely to alienate the population and force a rising spiral of official expenditure in arms, lives, and money, resulting in public clamour for the abandonment of counter-action (CROZIER 1974:127).

190. FAIRBAIRN distinguishes between revolutionary terrorism, disruptive terrorism "designed to advertise the movement," and coercive terrorism which "embraces both an attempt 'to demoralize the civilian population, weaken its confidence in the central authority, and instill fear of the revolutionary movement' and through exemplary acts of torture and/or executions to force obedience to the leadership of the revolutionary movement" (FAIRBAIRN 1974:350). "Terror is used as a deliberate strategy to demoralize the government by disrupting its control, to demonstrate one's own strength and to frighten collaborators. More Greeks were killed by EOKA than British soldiers, more

Arabs than Jews in the Arab rebellion of 1936–1939, more Africans than white people by the Mau Mau" (LAQUEUR 1976:401).

191. Another interesting case is that of the until recently almost forgotten Johannes Most who once was a member of the Social Democratic Party in the German *Reichstag* but later turned into a fanatical terrorist who eventually emigrated to the United States. LAQUEUR (1977b) calls him the "high priest" of American terrorism for many years.

192. Cf. also AVRICH's (1967) informative study on the fate of the Russian anarchists during the last decades of the Czarist empire and after 1920. Of course, bomb-throwing anarchists exemplify only one extreme of anarchism, to some writers a gross distortion of the real ideas of peaceful anarchism. For useful accounts of the origins and varieties of anarchism, see WOODCOCK (1977) and LÖSCHE (1977).

193. GURR, however, points to a gloomy future: "It is not likely but conceivable that some kinds of political terrorism will eventually become a functional equivalent, in the political arena, of strike activity in the economic sphere: a recognized, perhaps even ritualized means by which groups exert political influence when the now conventional methods of democratic political participation prove inadequate" (GURR 1979a:45).

194. "Terrorism always assumes the protective colouring of certain features of the *Zeitgeist*, which was fascist in the 1920s and 1930s but took a different direction in the 1960s and 1970s. . . . Many Latin American terrorists of the 1960s and 1970s, for instance, would almost certainly have been fascist, had they been born twenty years earlier" (LAQUEUR 1977:14–15).

195. Several authors (e.g., LAQUEUR 1977b; GURR 1979a) emphasize that, compared to events of war or even rates of traffic accidents, the number of terrorist victims is relatively low. In the period 1966–76 between 6,000 and 8,000 people are said to have been killed by terrorist activities, more than half of them in Argentina and Northern Ireland.

196. For a comprehensive list of terrorist groups and their current activities, cf. CROZIER (1976:219–30). Cf. also JENKINS/JOHNSON 1975; LAQUEUR 1977b. MICKOLUS (quoted by FRIEDLANDER 1979: 148) lists 158 terrorist groups around the world.

197. For other interesting materials bearing on these and related questions, cf. also *International Terrorism* (U. S. Congress, House, Committee on Foreign Affairs, 1974), *Hearings on Terrorism* (U. S. Congress, House, Committee on Internal Security, 1974), *Disorders and Terrorism* (National Advisory Committee on Criminal Justice, Standards, and Goals, 1976), with an extensive bibliography.

198. Evidence from another study on 350 terrorists leads to the following conclusion: "With few exceptions, the role of [terrorist] women was confined to intelligence collection, operations as couriers, duties as nurses and medical personnel, and in the maintenance of 'safe houses' for terrorists sought by police and for the storage of weapons, propaganda, false documentation, funds, and other supplies" (RUSSELL/ MILLER 1977:21). The terrorist scene among West German groups, then, seems to be a somewhat deviant case since women are in the majority, at least as far as the most wanted terrorists are concerned.

(199)

199. Drawing on his findings for the 1960s, GURR writes that "political terrorism appears to be a tactic of political activists who lack the broad base of support needed for large-scale revolutionary activity" (GURR 1979a:35). "Political terrorism in democratic societies, and in some others as well, is principally the tactic of groups that represent the interests and demands of small minorities" (ibid., p. 43), of "minorities of minorities" (BELL/GURR 1979:344).

200. "Patterns are hierarchical [when the] larger, more visible, and generally more respected units are the first to engage in a behavior actively and then the less highly ranked units imitate that behavior" (MIDLARSKY et al. 1980:272).

200a. In her analysis of terrorism in sub-Saharan countries, generally from their independence until 1969, WELFLING (1979) develops the hypothesis that terrorism is relatively rare in these countries because these very same regimes are more susceptible to coups. Yet, thus far she has presented only qualitative evidence. Moreover, events in several Latin American countries (see chapter 7 passim) would contradict her hypothesis (which actually is more complicated than as described here).

201. For further useful works on political terrorism, see STOHL (1979); ALEXANDER et al. (1979); for some data on the second half of the 1960s and the early 1970s, cf. SOBEL (1975).

202. As MAO put it in 1938: "Every Communist must grasp the truth, 'Political power grows out of the barrel of a gun.' Our principle is that the party commands the gun and the gun must never be allowed to command the party."

203. Or communist party support as another dependent variable; cf. ZAGORIA (1974) for empirical support from India, Indonesia, and the Philippines.

204. The ultimate dependent variable event type was coded according to "two sets of coding categories: (1) the specific demands of the event participants and (2) the ideology of any political party with which they are affiliated" (PAIGE 1975:94).

205. Excluding communist nations, but including "the peripheral, least industrialized areas of Europe" (PAIGE 1975:74). As DISCH (1979: 243) has noted, PAIGE's procedure allows for "several units of analysis within one nation-state."

206. Or of class conflicts as CHODAK (1977:415) notes in a review of PAIGE's book.

207. There are some interesting parallels between PAIGE's empirical results and HUNTINGTON's theory.

> If the substitute theory [reform as substitute for revolution] is generally right, the catalyst theory [reform as making revolution more likely] is generally wrong, and vice versa. More probably, one is right under some conditions and the other is right under other conditions. The relevant conditions include the *prerequisites* for reform and revolution and the *consequences* of reform for revolution. Undoubtedly, the single most important connection between reform and revolution is that the centralization of

power in the political system appears to be a precondition for both (HUNTINGTON 1968:366).

For reasons discussed elsewhere in this study, there seem to be opposite outcomes depending on where, when, and for whom reform is taking place: "Reforms directed at the urban middle class are a catalyst of revolution: reforms directed at the peasantry are [meant to be] a substitute for revolution" (ibid., p. 369). HUNTINGTON views land reform as leading to conflict because of the zero-sum perception of resources, unless high compensation is possible (as in Venezuela via oil money). Distinguishing land reform by foreign action, or through a dominant political party, from land reform by revolution, HUNTINGTON has this to say as to the latter type: "In land reform by revolution, the peasant uprisings normally eliminate much of the landowning elite by violence and death or by fear and emigration. The radical intelligentsia of the city assumes the political leadership roles in the society, brings into existence new political institutions, and ratifies the actions of the peasants by land reform decrees. More land reform has taken place by revolution than by any other means" (ibid., p. 385). As to the conditions and the consequences of land reform, cf. also the cross-national analysis of TAI (1974) dealing with Colombia, India, Iran, Mexico, Pakistan, the Philippines, Taiwan, and the United Arab Republic.

208.   The notion of working class in the context of PAIGE's study is not used in the sense typical for industrialized states.

209.   Or, as put in one of PAIGE's many variations:

> When landed property is the only source of income for the agrarian lower classes, conflicts over the ownership of property and the control of the state are the result. When industrial and financial capital are the major source of upper-class wealth, concessions can always be made and rural social movements diverted before they reach revolutionary proportions. Revolution begins not among the class-conscious proletariat of the industrial plantation, but among the proletarianized sharecroppers and migratory laborers of the landed estate (PAIGE 1975:122).

210.   It might be extended here by a thoughtful insight of BURCKHARDT (n.d.:127): "The urban population may be more open to *raisonnement* during crisis, be more susceptible to demagogues; but, depending on the kind of crisis, the rural population may still be the more frightful one" (my translation).

211.   In the absence of such outside mobilization and support, MARX's often quoted disdainful description will be realistic for some time to come. He spoke of the isolated, politically inexperienced, small French peasantry as "potatoes in a sack" (The Eighteenth Brumaire of Louis Bonaparte [1852] quoted in MARX-ENGELS; [Frankfurt/Main: Fischer Taschenbuch 1966] 4:113).

(212)

212. In greater detail: "A vigorous and independent class of town dwellers has been an indispensable element in the growth of parliamentary democracy" (MOORE 1966:418).

213. At least in the sense of revolutions dealt with in this chapter. Revolutionary *coups* which later lead to successful transformations of society may be carried out *without* backing from a revolutionary peasantry. The developments in Turkey and Japan provide examples of these so-called revolutions from above (cf. TRIMBERGER 1972; 1978; and chapter 8.3). See also SKOCPOL (1980) for a critical overview of works discussed in the present context and additional studies dealing with the question of what makes peasants revolutionary. Emphasizing her own approach (see chapter 8.4.3.3), she stresses the impact of imperialist activities on smaller or weakened states and less directly the consequences of increased commercialization of agriculture. Thus she speaks only indirectly about causes of peasant revolutionary activities. There are few other cases for which her argument would be valid beside her main cases, China and Vietnam.

214. SMELSER's (1963:313–81) constructivist theory of collective behavior in some respects bears resemblance to natural history approaches. Yet, in spite of all the criticism raised against SMELSER's pioneering study (cf., e.g., chapter 5.3.2.6), his theoretical scheme as well as his very many brief analyses contain valuable insights into the study of collective behavior phenomena.

215. In fairness to BRINTON, it should be pointed out that he also speaks of "first approximations to uniformities" only (BRINTON 1952:5, 26, and passim). However, his conceiving of revolutions as some kind of a fever led him astray when proposing his model of natural stages. For an effort to apply BRINTON's sequence of stages to the revolts of the Netherlands in the sixteenth century, cf. GRIFFITHS (1959–60).

216. A useful discussion of this as well as of natural history approaches in general can be found in HAGOPIAN (1974:194–250). Revolutionary terror is also the subject in chapter 8.5.

217. Cf. FRANÇOIS (1974) for another rather inexact (and therefore unsuccessful) effort aiming at incorporating counterrevolutionary activities as well. In her spiral model she deals with late medieval and early modern European revolts. As to the latter, cf. also note 152.

218. "Because of disagreement over just what constitutes a revolution and the revolutionary cycle, two stage theories have been proposed by SOROKIN; three by MEADOWS [1941]; four by HOPPER; five by EDWARDS; and six by BRINTON" (LIPSKY 1976:499).

219. For instance, the stages of extremism, terror, military dictatorship, and counterrevolution do not apply to the Mexican Revolution (cf., e.g., GREENE 1974:11).

220. Perhaps a more realistic idea would be to conceive of revolutions as "ups" and "downs" on a *number* of dimensions. Cf. also the somewhat inadequate diagrams in HAGOPIAN (1974:245).

221. The same holds true for the list of internal wars appended to ORLANSKY (1970).

222. Meanwhile they seem to have lost their war, too.

223. Using this definition: "An armed attack is an act of violent political conflict carried out by (or on behalf of) an organized group with the object of weakening or destroying the power exercised by another organized group" (TAYLOR/HUDSON 1972:67; for further details see ibid.).

224. It should be remembered (cf. chapter 5.1.1.1.2.1) that BANKS uses RUMMEL's definition of revolutions: "Any illegal or forced change in the top governmental elite, any attempt at such a change, or any successful or unsuccessful armed rebellion whose aim is independence from central government" (RUMMEL 1963:5), a definition only partly congruent with the definition of revolution followed here. In TANTER's (1965) study, revolutions correlate positively with guerrilla warfare in in both periods (1955–60: r=.60; 1948–62: r=.52). BANKS (1972), however, reports that guerrilla warfare is loading on the factor subversive rather than on revolutions.

225. A noticeable increase in wages presupposes a rapid growth of productive capital. The rapid growth of productive capital brings about an equally rapid growth of wealth, luxury, social wants, social enjoyments. Thus, although the enjoyments of the workers have risen, the social satisfaction that they give has fallen in comparison with the increased enjoyments of the capitalist, which are inaccessible to the workers, in comparison with the state of development of society in general. Our desires and pleasures spring from society; we measure them, therefore, by society and not by the objects which serve for their satisfaction. Because they are of a social nature, they are of a relative nature (MARX/ENGELS, "Wage Labour and Capital," in *Selected Works in Two Volumes*, [Moscow: Foreign Languages Publishing House, 1955] 1:94, here as quoted by DAVIES 1962:5).

226. Cf. also GESCHWENDER (1968) for an attempt to integrate several different hypotheses and theories: rise and drop hypotheses; the theory of relative deprivation; status inconsistency theory; and propositions about the effects of discrepancies between expectations and capabilities. The DAVIES hypothesis is only a special case of the latter. GESCHWENDER claims that all of these theories could be subsumed under the theory of cognitive dissonance, which may not come as a surprise considering the flexibility of FESTINGER's (1957) theory.

227. It is also not to be confused with F. ALLPORT's J-curve for measuring the degree of conformative behavior. DAVIES makes this clear himself.

228. Cf. also the overview in GERSCHENKRON (1964) and KROES (1966) as to the uprising in Hungary in 1956.

229. Cf. also the doubts raised by JOHNSON (1966:63). Yet he does not go into detail when mentioning possible counterexamples such as the Irish rebellion from 1916–23, the Spanish civil war, and the communist revolutions in China and Cuba. TANTER/MIDLARSKY (1967; cf. chapter 8.4.6.2), on the other hand, report that the Cuban Revolution does fit in the J-curve pattern (cf. also THOMAS 1963).

(230)

230. Cf. also long-term (1860–1930 vs. 1930–45) as well as some short-term (1945–54) developments in Mekong Delta Vietnam (NAGEL 1974:464, on the basis of a study by SANSOM 1970).
231. "The growth curves of both Mexico and Bolivia prior to their revolutions contradict the DAVIES J-curve theory" (DUFF/McCAMANT 1976:75). For some *indirect* positive evidence (the dependent variable is rebellions, not revolutions) from Argentina (1870–1970), see MERKX (1973).
232. "The relative calm of the industrialized nations in the mid-1970's appears to fly in the face of the [J-curve] hypothesis. After World War II, these nations experienced steady improvements in economic and social conditions until the oil embargo instituted by OPEC in late 1973; then a sharp reversal began. Yet the highest rates of violent civil conflict coincided with the zenith of the improvement trend, reached during the late 1960's and early 1970's, while the deterioration trend has coincided with decreasing rates of civil conflict—exactly the opposite of what the hypothesis predicts" (MULLER 1979:14).
233. However, MULLER could not confirm the DAVIES hypothesis (see chapter 5.3.2.3).
234. In fact, it is the article on revolution most often reprinted.
235. Cf. also the criticism of the CANTRIL scale in chapter 5.3.2.3 and ibid. passim.
236. "What is self-actualization to one person . . . may be perceived as a threat by another" (ZURCHER 1973:92).
237. See MORALES (1973) for an arbitrary application of DAVIES's theory. MORALES acknowledges some of these problems herself. Cf. also ZARTMAN et al. (1971).
238. "*Who* endures the frustrations in question, *who* makes revolutions, and what connection do the two actors have with each other?" (RULE/ TILLY 1971:8).
239. To us it simply does not seem to be a useful strategy to define revolution as follows: "A revolution may be said to exist when a group of insurgents illegally and/or forcefully challenges the governmental elite for the occupancy of roles in the structure of political authority. A successful revolution occurs when, as a result of a challenge to the governmental elite, insurgents are eventually able to occupy principal roles within the structure of the political authority" (TANTER/MIDLARsky 1967:267). The authors add: "This definition . . . sets a lower bound or minimum criterion for the existence of revolution" (ibid.). In simplest terms, the definition lacks in precision.
240. Data were collected for the period of 1950–62, since, from the authors' point of view, the degree of political violence before and after revolutions should be taken into account. This extension of the period of observation, however, may have seriously distorted the results reported (apart from the many other weaknesses in their study).
241. The indicator for education is also not very wisely chosen. Apparently modernization and subsequent increases in demand due to longer schooling are to be measured. Yet it would be much more consistent if the same indicator (and additional indicators, e.g., with respect to

secondary education) were used for the adult population, being a
potential from which revolutionaries might be recruited. The measures
used at present would be justifiable, albeit rather indirectly, if more
appropriately lagged measures were used (instead of those referring to
the periods 1950–54 vs. 1955–60).

242. In addition, CHADWICK/FIRESTONE point out that TANTER/MID-
LARSKY are not testing the DAVIES hypothesis, since their dependent
variable refers to the intensity of revolutionary events whereas DAVIES
is concerned with the occurrence of such events.

243. Unless one subscribes to the dogma that people in a democratic polity
cannot be against American economic presence. Actually, the causal
variable the authors seem to have in mind is socioeconomic inequality,
which well might be greater in nondemocratic societies.

244. There is, however, some additional serious criticism to be raised against
this study: "Investment per capita does not relate the foreign presence
to the size of the national economy, and what results is a combination
of U. S. investment and the wealth of the economy, not the importance
of the foreign presence. [Second], by multiplying the two figures [US
investment per capita times proportion of total trade with the US], the
distribution of the combined index becomes highly skewed, invalidating
any regression analysis used on that data" (DUFF/McCAMANT 1976:
88). Using more appropriate measures of Latin American economic
dependency during the 1950s and 1960s leads DUFF/McCAMANT to
conclude that

> All four nations—Cuba, Venezuela, Guatemala, and the Dominican
> Republic—where U. S. investment was high and then stagnated
> experienced high violence. Two of them—Cuba and Venezuela—
> showed exceptional scores on the welfare/mobilization differen-
> tial [cf. chapter 5.1.2.4]. This more complex view of economic
> dependency indicates a relationship with violence, which may be
> indirect through the welfare/mobilization differential. . . . One of
> the explanations for the development of a situation in which
> social mobilization has and continues to outrun societal welfare is
> that economic dependency tends to stimulate short-run growth as
> it tends to retard long-run growth. When new foreign investment
> slows down, stops, or is withdrawn, economic growth also slows
> down, but social mobilization is likely to continue (DUFF/
> McCAMANT 1976:92, 93).

> TANTER (1969a:177) also reports some relationships between
> several measures of American economic presence (1953–61) in eighteen
> Latin American countries and various measures of political violence
> (1961–63; data taken from GURR). Yet, as WEST (1973:116) points
> out, the time lags and measures used are rather arbitrary, just as in the
> study of MIDLARSKY/TANTER (1967).

245. Additional evidence along these lines comes from BRIER/CALVERT
(1975:4). For some related results, cf. KORNHAUSER (1971:381–82).
His definition of revolution is also rather broad, thus rendering his
figures somewhat useless in the present context.

(246)

246. FARBER, however, questions whether ZEITLIN's findings are truly representative. "His survey was conducted in 1962, *after* widespread purges of democratically elected trade-union leaders and the introduction of various other repressive measures. A great number of workers undoubtedly supported the revolution at that time, but ZEITLIN assumes that he was able to discriminate between those workers who were telling him the truth and those who were merely protecting themselves" (FARBER 1976:240).

247. Since questions sometimes referred to periods in the past, the answers are not always to be taken literally.

248. Since ZEITLIN studied only the responses of workers, some additional references as to the social class character of the Cuban Revolution might be appropriate here. GREENE, on the basis of various other studies, draws this conclusion:

> The more organized sectors of the working class supported Castro in the last stages of the revolution. It was really the urban middle classes, including business and the professions, that were the important source of money and supplies, responding to Castro's stated objective of resolving the economic difficulties associated with Batista. Pro-Castro support from the Catholic hierarchy and the urban middle classes, even tacit support from the Cuban upper classes, increased after Batista's resort to terror in 1958. . . .
> Thanks in part to the withdrawal of American support for Batista, the blunders and repression of his government, and the ambiguity of Castro's intentions, the core alliance of intellectuals, students, and a small part [cf. ALROY 1967; but see also USEEM 1977] of the Cuban peasantry mobilized support from all the major sectors of Cuban society (GREENE 1974:46; cf. also the figures reported in FAGEN 1965). Cf. also DRAPER (1962); KLING (1962); GOLDENBERG (1965; 1972); BLASIER (1967); (THOMAS 1967; 1971); AMARO (1969); GIL (1969); GUDE (1969); MASCHKE (1973); BONACHEA/MARTIN (1974); LLERENA (1978) and DOMÍNGUEZ (1978).

According to FARBER, Castro ought to be seen as a Bonapartist revolutionary (just as much as Batista is said to have acted like a Bonapartist conservative): "The opposition to Batista was not led either by any of the older parties or politicians or by working-class, peasant, or middle-class leaders and movements. Instead, an essentially déclassé nontraditional leadership organized a heterogeneous coalition which included conservatives, reformists, and revolutionaries. After Batista's overthrow, Castro easily dissolved this coalition, with the eventual aim of creating a fundamentally different power base and social system" (FARBER 1976:236). As has been stressed before in this chapter on revolutions, perhaps the most important factor contributing to the success of Castro (apart from his personal charisma; cf., e.g., GONZALES 1974) was the breakdown of Batista's army (cf. also PÉREZ 1976:152ff.) and the subsequent collapse of his regime.

249. "The revolution had abolished [the workers'] alienation from the means of production, from government, and from nation" (ZEITLIN 1970:295).
250. "This sort of coalition-formation is likely to occur, on the one hand, when a challenger rapidly increases the store of resources under its control and, on the other, when a member loses its coalition partners within the polity, or the polity is more or less evenly divided among two or more coalitions, or an established member is risking loss of membership in the polity through failure to meet the tests of other members" (TILLY 1973:444).
251. It should be added that, with the exception of the third, TILLY considers them to be necessary conditions of revolutions.
252. Taking up the discussion from chapter 6.3, one might also speak of a severe loss in regime legitimacy or of situations of multiple crises.
253. The breadth of TILLY's theoretical scheme becomes apparent if one takes into consideration that there are various possibilities for the multiplication of polities to occur.

    1. The members of one polity seek to subordinate another previously distinct polity; where one of the polities is not somehow subordinate to the other at the outset, this circumstance falls into a gray area between revolution and war.
    2. The members of a previously subordinate polity assert sovereignty.
    3. Challengers form into a bloc that seizes control over some portion of the governmental apparatus.
    4. A polity fragments into two or more blocs, each exercising control over some part of the government (TILLY 1974:286).

    Revolutions, then, form only a subclass among the various possibilities of multiple sovereignty. In the first case, if successfully carried out, a reduction, not a multiplication, in the number of polities actually results.
254. Deprivation theories and breakdown theories are not necessarily the same, a point to be taken up later on. TILLY at various points seems to treat them as two sides of the same coin.
255. In the following, we use the concept of collective violence as intended by TILLY. For the most part, it denotes what we have termed political violence. Thus, our usage of the concept of collective violence in chapter 2.1 is more restrictive.
256. "We can make fairly continuous observations for France from 1830 through 1960, for Germany from 1830 through 1913, but for Italy only for the decades beginning in 1850, 1880 and 1890" (TILLY et al. 1975:245).
257. "There is an intimate dependency between violent and non-violent forms of collective action—one is simply a special case of the other— rather than some moral, political, or tactical divide between them" (TILLY 1974:283).
258. Recall that in HIBBS's causal model (1973:181; cf. Figure 5.4 in chapter 5.1.1.3), negative sanctions on behalf of incumbents led to an inten-

(258)

sification of conflict as well, i.e., led from collective protest to internal war.

259. In this type of collective violence (and less so in the other types) the focus is on relationships between groups participating in acts of collective violence. The cross-national aggregate studies in chapter 5.1 showed that this aspect clearly had been neglected in the process of data collecting and analysis.

260. "The tax rebellion developed in the sixteenth century, flourished in the seventeenth, recurred in 1789, 1830, or 1848 as new revolutionary officials sought to reimpose the state's authority; it vanished after 1849. Its history traced the government's long struggle to secure both obedience and income" (TILLY et al. 1975:47).

261.   The name is misleading: most often the struggle turned about raw grain rather than edibles, and most of the time it did not reach the point of physical violence. The classic European food riot had three main variants: the *retributive action*, in which a crowd attacked the persons, property or premises of someone believed to be hoarding or profiteering; the *blockage*, in which a group of local people prevented the shipment of food out of their own locality, requiring it to be stored or sold locally; the *price riot*, in which people seized stored food or food displayed for sale, sold it publicly at a price they declared to be proper, and handed the money over to the owner or merchant (TILLY 1976:371; 1975b: 386).

See also L. TILLY (1971) as well as TILLY (1975b) for a broader historical background analysis.

The timing of the food riot's rise and fall is revealing. In England [see also STEVENSON 1979:91ff.], France and some other parts of western Europe, the food riot displaced the tax rebellion as the most frequent violent form of collective action toward the end of the seventeenth century. It declined precipitously in England just after 1820, in Germany and France just after 1850, only to linger on in parts of Spain and Italy into the twentieth century.... E. P. THOMPSON [1971] has called the entire process a decline of the old Moral Economy, a shift from a *bread nexus* to a *cash nexus*. People resisted the process so long as local solidarity and some collective memory of the locality's prior claims survived (TILLY 1976:372).

262. In a sense, MANNHEIM's distinction between ideology and utopia is found here again, although MANNHEIM was more concerned with idea systems and their dependency on social situs (*Soziallagen*) rather than with collective protest. Furthermore, MANNHEIM's use of the notion of ideology contradicts TILLY's formula of reactive violence in that in MANNHEIM's sense *privileged* classes would attach themselves to ideological thinking, conserving past social and cultural states, whereas here it is mostly *underprivileged* classes that fight for the restoration of

(Chapter Eight)

earlier times (cf. the next section for additional evidence; see also chapter 8.4.4).

263. Which are not always clearly distinguished from each other; cf. the typologies in TILLY et al. (1975:250); TILLY (1975:508; 1969: 39–40) for examples.

264. In France "violent conflict has moved northward, although the southern regions still have more than their share" (TILLY et al. 1975:67).

265. See L. TILLY (1972) for a detailed analysis.

266. As to Germany, cf. also R. TILLY (1970) and R. TILLY/HOHORST (1976).

267. Concerning the latter period, cf. also BLEIBER (1966; 1969). See also RUPIEPER (1978) for an analysis of participants in revolutionary protests in Saxony during 1848–49. Drawing on the records of convicted participants, he points out that artisans and journeymen as well as townsmen and people from the smaller towns were strongly represented among these protesters. VOLKMANN (1975) analyzes social protests in Germany during the *Vormärz* (period covered: 1830–32; main source: Augsburger *Allgemeine Zeitung*). As in 1848, the revolution in Paris (July 1830) preceded unrest in other European countries, this time in Belgium, England, Germany, Switzerland, Poland, Denmark, Italy, and other countries (for an overview of recent work on the revolutions of 1830 in European countries, cf. CHURCH 1977). With respect to the "forgotten revolution" (VOLKMANN) in Germany, VOLKMANN (1975) points out that members of occupations that were threatened by economic change were especially prone to protest. Political engagement (e.g., in a civil militia) and regional mobility (e.g., of journeymen, students) also contributed to participation. Lower-class participation was relatively stronger in the more severe cases of unrest, which the author attributes to the lack of organizational facilities at workers' disposal. For additional findings, see also VOLKMANN (1977), especially with respect to the connections between initiated reforms and relatively fewer protests as well as protests aggravated through a lack of reforms. Cf. also SCHIEDER (1978) on the liberal protest movement of 1832 in Rhineland-Palatinate. He reports that small tradesmen and craftsmen were overrepresented among the followers, whereas academics were overrepresented among their leaders.

268. There are, of course, various indications that recent migrants, as well as other social groups, do engage in acts of collective violence (cf. below; RUDÉ 1970 passim; the next chapter), but they cannot be considered *the* social segment carrying out acts of collective violence.

269. Furthermore, "among Parisians of 1830 were hundreds of veterans of revolutionary and Napoleonic armies" (PINKNEY 1964:15). Cf. also PINKNEY (1972a).

270. For a thorough evaluation of the Paris Commune of 1871, especially in the light of prior revolutions, see *Le Mouvement Social,* no. 79 (April/ June 1972). Cf. also HUNECKE (1974) for a discussion of the literature; the *International Review of Social History* 17, pt. 1–2 (1972); WILLIAMS (1969), as well as the excellent account by EDWARDS (1971). A most recent treatment is found in HAUPT/HAUSEN (1979).

(271)

271. In a study of working class participation in revolution and collective political violence in Marseille during 1830–71, AMINZADE reports the following findings: "It was the same occupations that were highly organized enough to launch several strikes during the Second Empire that contributed a disproportionate share of their workers to the insurrection of 1871. Bakers, tanners and curriers, coopers, cratemakers, and metal workers were the most strike-prone occupations, each of them experiencing three or more strikes during the period from 1848 to 1871" (AMINZADE 1973:26). Absolute deprivation and massive unemployment "did not lead to collective action on the part of unorganized workers. . . . On the other hand, [they] did activate groups of workers who were already organized and politically conscious" (ibid., p. 29).

272. Accordingly, the question remains whether curvilinear relationships exist between repression and collective violence (cf. the evidence in chapter 5.1.2.5) and mobilization as well as between power-contending and repression.

273. "The next step, we believe, is to introduce explicit models of the structure of power, and explicit statements of the rights and obligations of the participants, into the analysis" (TILLY et al. 1975:298).

274. As SNYDER, one of TILLY's collaborators, notes: "In these studies mobilization is usually measured by crude proxies, such as shifts in groups' size, and the strongest supporting evidence pertains to fluctuations in industrial strike activity—a phenomenon that, given the importance of unions, probably best fits the assumption of heavily centralized mobilization mechanisms and neglect of individual actor" (SNYDER 1978:507; cf. also ibid., p. 511).

275. Here again *differences* between various forms of collective (political) violence show up, differences which TILLY, for theoretical interests and methodological reasons, tends to obscure.

276. It is noteworthy that more refined measures lead to results which at times are contradictory to conclusions stated with some emphasis in the text. Cf. TILLY et al. (1975:83) for an example.

277. As to Britain, see also the next chapter as well as the works by HAMMOND/HAMMOND (1948); THOMPSON (1963); and LANGER (1969) for an encyclopedic account of developments in several European countries during 1832–52. On problems of social control in nineteenth-century Britain, cf. also DONAJGRODZKI (1977). TILLY and coworkers are now engaged in a broad study of "British contentious gatherings" around the "strategic" year of 1830 (1828–34) (for an overview of the project and some first results, see SCHWEITZER et al. 1980).

278. Cf. also PEACOCK (1965), STEVENSON (1974) for a recent summary of the literature on food riots in England, and BELOFF (1963) for an analysis of corn riots during an earlier period (1660–1714). See SHELTON (1973) for an analysis of the 1760s and BOOTH (1977) for the end of the eighteenth century.

279. Economic fluctuations (price swings, production indexes) are also not related to collective violence (SNYDER/TILLY 1972; TILLY et al.

1975). Furthermore (and of course noted by SNYDER/TILLY), there is the possibility of reciprocal causation between collective violence and repression. See figure 8.5.

280. ELWITT also objects to the inadequate treatment of the Paris Commune events by TILLY: "He casually remarks that he will not discuss the Paris Commune, because his model has no room for the massive arrests that took place after the Commune was suppressed and 'therefore did not enter into our statistics.' He judges that 1870–71 remains a 'doubtful case in the correlation between extent of violence and extent of political change (p. 60)'" (ELWITT 1976:577).

281. "It goes without saying that at the bottom of every protest movement there is a feeling of grievance. But this is no more than stating the obvious; there is no accounting for the fact that at one time a major grievance may be fatalistically accepted whereas elsewhere (or at another time) a minor grievance may provoke the most violent reaction" (LAQUEUR 1976a:363, also quoted in AYA 1979:82).

282. No wonder after all, considering the definition of the dependent variables.

283. For example, there are no correlation analyses in RUDÉ's studies, although they could be performed on the basis of his materials.

284. RUDÉ speaks of crowds, not of mobs as described in the writings of LEBON, for example. Cf. the discussion below.

285. Where the typical rioter or rebel is a craftsman, a labourer or a peasant, [the typical leader] may be a small nobleman, a lawyer, a journalist or a government official. Strictly speaking, there may be three types of leader: the leader-in-chief, in whose name the crowd riots or rebels; the intermediate leader—a sort of N.C.O.— who passes on the slogans or tells the rioters whose house has to "come down"; and the most articulate or militant among the rioters themselves, whose leadership is purely local and purely temporary. Of these three, the last alone emerges from the "crowd" itself. He may be an anonymous figure who rides on a white horse, brandishes a sword or blows a bugle; he may bear a pseudonym like the countless Rebeccas, Ned Ludds, and Captain Swings of the early nineteenth century, or like Tom the Barber who led the anti-Irish rioters in London in the 1730; or he may be known by his proper name like the local leaders of London's Gordon Riots. . . . with the rise of a working-class movement in both England and France in the 1830s . . . we find men emerging as leaders from the crowd itself, who are no longer occasional, sporadic and anonymous, but continuous and openly proclaimed (RUDÉ 1970:19–20).

286. "'Lost' rights, such as the 'just wage' and the 'just price' and even (later in the period) the right to vote" (RUDÉ 1970:23). "Preindustrial protest is not a function of rapidly rising expectations. For in learning about the nature of preindustrial protest we have learned a great deal about the values of preindustrial people, not all of it surprising to be sure. The absence of a belief in progress or in new rights—which of

(286)

course was quite compatible with a vigorous sense of justice—is one of their most striking features" (STEARNS 1974:4).

287. Cf. LABROUSSE (1933; 1943); and LABROUSSE et al. (1970:529–63; 693ff.). LABROUSSE also stresses that

> the rise of 1789–1790, although sudden, sharp and very much blamed for causing all the economic difficulties even though it carried prices to a new level, did not set a new record, or anywhere near it with respect to the amplitude of the spread between its high and low points. But it did strike an economy which was just recovering and still upset from a serious and persistent economic *malaise*, as well as from the shock of 1785. And the political shock of 1789 in turn complicated the crisis since it disquieted the manufacturer and business man, seriously disturbed the luxury trade, and caused the flight of both men and capital (LABROUSSE 1943, here quoted from the reprint in GREENLAW 1958:67).

288. "This term, borrowed from the contemporary manuscript journal of the Parisian bookseller Hardy, 'Mes Loisirs, ou Journal d'événements tels qu'ils parviennent à ma connoissance' . . . , cannot lay claim to any sociological exactitude. It has, however, been found convenient to use it in describing collectively wage-earners, small property owners and urban poor" (RUDÉ 1970:133).

289. As to the storming of the Bastille, cf. also, e.g., GODECHOT (1965a).

290. In general, however, a different conclusion is reached: "It may, in fact, be concluded that a remarkable feature of the early insurrectionary movements of the Revolution in Paris was the widespread participation of unemployed workers of every occupation; yet they rarely appear in the guise of beggars or vagabonds" (RUDÉ 1970:127).

291. In greater detail the statements read: "about 400 of the 653 captors of the Bastille whose origins are known were of provincial extraction. Yet the majority were *settled inhabitants* of the Faubourg St. Antoine" (RUDÉ 1970:109; italics added). In later revolutionary attacks during the nineteenth century, however, some changes seem to have occurred: "George RUDÉ . . . found, in the journées of the Revolution of 1789 for which data is available, a proportion of immigrants among the participants that is about the same as that in the 1830s. Rémi GOSSEZ [1956:448] has studied the insurgents of June 1848, and Jacques ROUGERIE [1964a:35] the activists in the defense of the Commune of 1871, and both have published preliminary results of their investigations. The former found a higher proportion of immigrants—about 85 percent of the insurgents were from outside the Department of the Seine, reflecting the influx of provincials seeking employment or relief in the depression years after 1846 [but cf. also TILLY/LEES 1974 for a lower figure; cf. the preceding chapter]. In 1871 the proportion dropped to near the levels of 1830 and 1834, to approximately 74 percent" (PINKNEY 1972:514–15).

292. "The French Revolution, in its first phase a revolution of the nobles, represented the climax of this rebirth of aristocratic opposition. . . .

The popular and peasant revolutions, culminating in the night of
August 4, broke the power both of the monarchy and the nobility.
Unlike the bourgeoisie which had not aimed for the ruin of the aristocracy, the popular revolution wiped the slate clean and soon completed the social revolution by nationalizing church property"
(LEFEBVRE 1966:81, 82). Or as put in a variant: "The first act of the
Revolution, in 1788, consisted in a triumph of the aristocracy, which,
taking advantage of the government crisis, hoped to reassert itself and
win back the political authority of which the Capetian dynasty had
despoiled it. But, after having paralyzed the royal power which upheld
its own social preeminence, the aristocracy opened the way to the bourgeois revolution, then to the popular revolution in the cities and finally
to the revolution of the peasants—and found itself buried under the
ruins of the Old Regime" (LEFEBVRE 1947:3; for some minor points
of disagreement with this work, cf. COBBAN 1971a:62–64 and
passim). See also the review article by DAVIES (1964) on the origins
of the French peasant revolution.

293. Cf. the thorough analysis by HUFTON (1974) on the deplorable life of
the poor in France during the second half of the eighteenth century.

294. It needed more than economic hardship, social discontent, and
the frustration of political and social ambitions to make a revolution. To give cohesion to the discontents and aspirations of
widely varying social classes there had to be some unifying body
of ideas, a common vocabulary of hope and protest, something,
in short, like a common "revolutionary psychology." In this case,
the ground was prepared, in the first place, by the writers of the
Enlightenment (RUDÉ 1973:74).

295. "Thus, peasants and urban craftsmen and workers were drawn together
in common hostility to government, landlords, merchants and specula-
tors, and these classes entered the Revolution in a context of increasing
poverty and hardship rather than of 'prosperity'" (RUDÉ 1964:74) as
maintained in TOCQUEVILLE's famous hypothesis (cf. chapter 8.4.2).
From a longterm perspective, however, the latter's hypothesis seems to
fare much better.

296. TILLY/LEES (1975; cf. the preceding chapter) present a slightly higher
figure.

297. "Food riots were more common in France than in England. In England,
there were provincial riots in 1727, (sporadically) in the 1730s, in
1740, 1756 and 1757, 1766 (by far the worst year of all), 1772 and
1773, and 1783. In France, Daniel MORNET has recorded them in
forty separate years between 1724 and 1789 and, according to his
figures, they occurred in twenty-two of the twenty-five years following
1763, the only exceptions being 1769, 1779 and 1780" (RUDÉ
1970:55).

298. Cf. also THOMPSON 1971.

299. The anti-Catholic Gordon riots took place in June 1780.

300. On the Rebecca riots, see also WILLIAMS 1955.

(301)

301. Furthermore, in the sources occupational terms are often used in a rather loose or general manner, thus rendering comparisons of occupational groups somewhat arbitrary.

302. RUDÉ himself brings up the question (cf. RUDÉ 1964:237ff.).

303. The French Revolution appears, then, to have been the outcome of a combination of factors, both long-term and short-term, that arose from the conditions of the *ancien régime*. The long-standing grievances of peasants, townsmen and bourgeoisie; the frustration of rising hopes among wealthy bourgeois and peasants; the insolvency and break-down of government; a growing "feudal reaction"; the claims and intransigence of aristocracy; the propagation of radical ideas among wide sections of the people; a sharp economic and financial crisis; and the successive "triggers" of state bancruptcy, aristocratic revolt and popular rebellion; these all played their part. Were these factors peculiar to France? Considered in isolation, the answer must be no (RUDÉ 1972:251–52).

304. As to the question of validity when using these *cahiers*, cf. also the discussion in SHAPIRO et al. (1973). Problems of working with the *cahiers* are dealt with extensively in ROBIN (1970).

305. In a way this hypothesis is a corollary to that of TOCQUEVILLE (see chapter 8.4.2), namely that discontent or revolution is more likely to occur when living conditions are generally improving yet old grievances against the prevailing order persist.

306. In a preliminary report on the results of a study on 741 of the *cahiers de doléances*, TAYLOR points out:

> Enlightenment political ideas were quantitatively insignificant in most sectors of French opinion before the Estates General met on May 5. Far more important than concepts of natural rights, popular sovereignty, and the separation of powers as mandates for change was tradition—legal, constitutional, and institutional—construed in a way that owed nothing to TOCQUEVILLE's "abstract, literary politics" [that was said to have created, over the last decades of the old regime, a revolutionary mentality]. But in addition we have had to recognize—and it is probably the most significant result of this study—that very few Frenchmen in March and April [1789] had any idea how radical the Revolution was going to be, or that there would be any alteration so fundamental that it might be called a revolution. In fact, we have not found the word "revolution" in these documents. But this is not remarkable. For France and for most of Europe it was the events of 1789 and the years that followed that gave the word "revolution" its modern meaning (TAYLOR 1972:481).

307. Cf. TØNNESSON (1959) for a follow-up study during the year III.

308. It is quite interesting that TILLY, commenting on SOBOUL's work, draws support for his own approach: "The shortage of bread mobilized a population already politically conscious, active, and organized. If SOBOUL's major conclusions are valid, it mobilized particularly those

segments of the population which were most conscious, active, and organized. And they were far from the most desperate or miserable segments of the population" (TILLY 1964a:114).

309. Cf. also the articles in KAPLOW (1965); KAFKER/LAUX (1968); ROSS (1971); SCHMITT (1973); and JOHNSON (1976). See also the various works of COBB, e.g., (1957); (1959); (1967); (1970).

310. It was this last group that was the most revolutionary, says COB-BAN. Certainly they were the most vociferous. But did they represent only their own interests? And what were those interests? Did the *officiers* constitute a class at all, much less a declining one, as COBBAN argues? Can decline be measured by a fall in the price of offices? And were the *gens de loi* as bad off as all that? Were they anticapitalist? Can their attitudes on this question be measured by their opinions on a given navigation law, as in the case of Brissot? Is the failure of the successive assemblies to change the system of colonial trade a sign of their traditionalism? Since Professor COBBAN fails to answer these questions, it seems a *non sequitur* for him to say that "the Revolution, in its economic consequences, seems indeed to have been the kind of Revolution we should expect if . . . it was led not by industrialists and merchants, but by *officiers* and professional men" (KAPLOW 1965a:1095).

311. ZEITLIN draws some interesting parallels between the analyses of TOCQUEVILLE and COBBAN: "TOCQUEVILLE observed many of the phenomena to which COBBAN calls attention: the similarities between noblemen and bourgeois (but also their differences); the fact that the bourgeoisie as well as the nobility gained at the expense of the peasantry; the town vs. the country; and, finally, the great gulf between rich and poor, generally" (ZEITLIN 1971:153).

312. But even here a number of important questions remain unanswered, as discussed in the text (and in other parts of the literature not referred to here).

313. In the meantime, RUDÉ's approach had a strong impact on younger scholars dealing with prerevolutionary and revolutionary crowds in the United States (cf., e.g., HOERDER 1977; COUNTRYMAN 1976; the review article by GREENE 1973a; cf. also MAIER 1970; RUDOLPH 1959). Cf. also some of the works mentioned in connection with the Russian Revolution (e.g., in chapter 8.4.2).

314. Recalling the discussion on the conditions of political violence, protest, internal war, etc. (cf. chapter 5.1), numerous additional independent variables could be added to the exogenous variables on the far left side of the model. We believe, however, that most of the *basic* explanatory variables underlying the discussion in this chapter have been captured in figure 8.7.

315. There are also technical reasons for keeping the number of feedback influences low, since the estimation of causal parameters will otherwise lead to grossly distorted results. (Yet, what to do, *if* an adequate theoretical model *were* calling for more feedback loops than are

(315)

allowed for in the rules of identification? This would seem to be the social scientist's squaring of the circle.)

316. One could think of a path going from external defeat (and also from protracted internal war) to military grievances. For reasons of simplicity, however, we have abstained from adding these paths to the model.

317. Still a rather vague notion; cf. also the discussion in chapter 6.3.5. See also the debate on the notion of assent in chapter 6.3.4.

318. Both components, the loyalty and the strength of the coercive forces, must be considered (as GURR has done in his empirical studies) for an adequate assessment of outcomes likely to be found.

319. Notwithstanding prolonged ideological statements as to the workers' importance and their revolutionary consciousness under appropriate conditions. The statement in the text does not lend itself to universal extrapolation as to the conditions of future revolutions.

320. To avoid some misunderstandings, we do not subscribe to any form of implicit or explicit historical "logic," an argument which is often prematurely raised by critics of a quantitative social historical science. Any researcher working with historical data, the quantitatively oriented scholar as well as the researcher concentrating on qualitative analyses, must avoid the poor logic of historicism (cf. POPPER 1957). We would, however, maintain that chances are greater in the case of the scholar relying more on quantitative techniques. The issue is not historical depth vs. superficial quantification (cf. also the discussion in chapter 9) but rather quantification *and* historical depth with the aim of testing theories (for discussions of some of the issues involved, cf. GOTT-SCHALK 1963 and WEHLER 1973).

321. "Abortive revolutions occurred [for example] in Hungary and throughout Germany in 1848, in Hungary in 1919, in Bavaria in 1923[?], and perhaps most impressively of all, in Spain in the 1930's" (HAGOPIAN 1974:102; on the Spanish anarchists' and anarcho-syndicalists' revolution in 1934–37, see, e.g., BRENAN 1969; BROUÉ/TÉMIME 1961; MALEFAKIS 1970; and BERNECKER 1978). Chile would be a most recent example. As to the abortive revolutions in 1848 and thereafter, cf. the references in chapter 8.4.6.6.1.

322. HAGE (1975) has summarized a whole canon of arguments relevant in cross-national research at the level of nation-states. The argument relevant in this context reads: "We find that BRINTON (1965) never examines countries that have an absence of revolution. No wonder he finds it difficult to locate the causes. He violated a basic canon of research—examining instances where the event does not occur" (HAGE 1975:144).

323. Defining revolutions more narrowly (yet also more adequately) may even prevent the development of a (metric) scale of revolutionary change. The basic definitional criterion of revolution, namely fundamental sociostructural change, at least from a logical point of view, defies such scaling.

324. Cf. GEISS (1975) for a general sociohistorical overview of successful revolutions (not all of them actual revolutions) and those which failed.

(Chapter Eight)

325. More generally: "A valid theory of collective action must explain the comings and goings. It must also explain why some groups never show up at all" (TILLY 1978:60).

326. RUDÉ (1970:67), for example, has raised the question (cf. chapter 8.4.6.6.2 for an answer) why there had not been a revolution in France before 1789, namely in 1775, when food riots were reaching a peak. Similarly, why were there no revolutions in 1830 and 1848 in England? There "was no revolution in 1832 not so much because the Tories or the Lords surrendered to the threats of Whigs or Radicals, as because nobody of importance wanted one and because the combination of political and material factors that alone would have made one possible was conspicuously lacking" (RUDÉ 1971:243). In 1848 the question was "hardly worth the asking" (RUDÉ 1971:244). For Britain during 1789–1848, cf. also THOMIS/HOLT (1977) who emphasize that the army and police forces remained loyal and that the rebels lacked in support and organizational facilities.

327. As characterized by one of the leading scholars of revolution who has considered the impact of both social structural conditions and philosophical ideas on the occurrence of the English Revolution: "Ideas were all-important for the individuals whom they impelled into action; but the historian must attach equal importance to the circumstances that gave these ideas their chance. Revolutions are not made without ideas, but they are not made by intellectuals. Steam is essential to driving a railway engine; but neither a locomotive nor a permanent way can be built out of steam" (HILL 1965:3).

328. In more general terms: "The weakness of the cultural explanation is . . . in the way they are put into the explanation. . . . To explain behavior in terms of cultural values is to engage in circular reasoning. If we notice that a landed aristocracy resists commercial enterprise, we do not *explain* this fact by stating that the aristocracy has done so in the past or even that it is the carrier of certain traditions that make it hostile to such activities: the problem is to determine out of what past and present experiences such an outlook arises and maintains itself" (MOORE 1966:485–86).

329. Cf. DOWNTON (1973:209–88) as to the importance of revolutionary charisma and a number of historical examples.

330. Cf. KÄSLER (1977) for a discussion of concepts drawing largely on WEBER's "routinization of charisma." Cf. also SKOCPOL (1976a) for a comparative analysis of old regime legacies in Communist Russia and China. She emphasizes that some of the diverging developments in both countries could be traced to earlier experiences of revolutionaries and to structural constraints of the old regime (cf. also CHENG 1979). Finally, cf. SUEDFELD/RANK for some empirical support for their hypothesis "that long-range success for a [revolutionary] leader would be associated with low conceptual complexity during the phase of revolutionary struggle (when it is desirable to have a categorical, single-minded approach to problems) and a change to high complexity during the poststruggle consolidation phase (when, as leaders of a government

(330)

in power, the former revolutionists would need a relatively graduated, flexible, and integrated view)" (SUEDFELD/RANK 1976:169; N=19 revolutionary leaders, eight of them leading figures of the American War of Independence).

331. Cf. SCHIFFRIN (1968); LEE (1970); BIANCO (1971); FRIEDMAN (1974).

332. Thus, it may be just as difficult to specify where a revolution ends as to determine when it starts.

333. Or is murdered like Robespierre (cf. RUDÉ 1975 for a recent evaluation of Robespierre's role in and contribution to the French Revolution; cf. also the review essay by SHULIM 1977).

334. A related question is whether revolutionaries indeed carry out the program they originally aimed at or, at least in part, something else. Judging from a number of cases, a gap between revolutionary promise and performance seems to be quite normal.

335. There seems to be agreement among many of the scholars quoted that part of the sans-culottes' failure stemmed from the incoherent positions for which they were fighting, i.e., more "progressive" political solutions (e.g., decentralization and egalitarian democracy) yet clearly "regressive" economic policies. Their calls for regulation of prices and regimentation of trade were swept away in the Thermidor reaction of the bourgeoisie.

336. As put by a satirical German writer (Peter STRUWWEL, alias Heinrich Hoffmann) in 1848: "Revolution. An article much in demand on the market of world affairs, but rather dear and expensive" (p. 33, my translation).

337. Obviously, mere body counts would often fall short of an adequate answer. Cf. HAGOPIAN's reply (1974:380) to MOORE's (1966) comparison of a projected death rate of the *Ancien régime* with the "35,000 to 40,000" (MOORE) victims of terror during the French Revolution.

338. On GREER's (1935) work see also the critique by LOUIE (1964) and SHAPIRO/MARKOFF (1975) for a more elaborate discussion of hypotheses on the incidence of terror that might be testable on an adequate statistical basis (depending on the data available).

339. To name only two historical examples: France in 1832 vs. 1830 (cf. also BEZUCHA 1974; 1975 for evidence on the Lyon uprisings during 1832–34 which he considers the protomodern rebellion) and in the terror years 1793–94. Cambodia after the takeover by the Red Khmers provides a more recent illustration. See PONCHAUD (1977) and SHAWCROSS (1978) for some sketchy evidence on the role of state terror there.

340. Cf. also the review of GODECHOT who mainly raises the question of study designing: "In France there are many regions which present the same geographic, social and economic differences which we have noticed between the Mauges and Val-Saumurois. And yet the political evolution has been the same. For example, the differences between the wooded regions of Limousin and Rouergue and the wide, spacious plateaux of le Quercy; between the massif of the Vosges and the plain of

Alsace. . . ." (GODECHOT 1967:468). For some minor qualifications by TILLY himself, cf. the preface to the new edition of 1976: "Cities and urbanization have fundamental roles in [the expansion of capitalism and the concentration of power in national states]. Too great a focus on urbanization (or too broad a definition of urbanization) nevertheless draws attention away from the independent effects of capitalism and statemaking. In the Vendée itself, it is valuable to learn the place of cities and city-based merchants in the growth of the cottage textile industry. It is also important to realize that the property relations which developed were not those of 'city' or 'country' but of classic mercantile capitalism" (TILLY 1976:x, preface to the enlarged edition of *The Vendée*). Cf. also LEWIS's (1978) study on the "second Vendée," i.e., "the continuity of counter-revolution in the department of the Gard, 1789–1815." LEWIS also discovers a relationship between recent social change and participation in counterrevolutionary activities.

341. From this perspective, HAGOPIAN's affirmation is perhaps warranted "that counterrevolution is an integral part of revolution" (HAGOPIAN 1974:381). However, there is no cross-national analysis of counter-revolutions or counterrevolutionary activities that would allow for making more general statements here. For early and somewhat questionable typological efforts, cf., e.g., MAYER (1971:86–116).

342. A more elaborate hypothesis by HUNTINGTON in this context reads: "Every revolution strengthens government and the political order. . . . It is a way of reestablishing violently and destructively but also crea- tively the balance between social and economic development, on the one hand, and political development on the other" (HUNTINGTON 1968:313). (The following somewhat difficult sentence has been left out of the quotation: "It is a form of political development which makes society more backward and politics more complex.") In terms of SKOCPOL's approach (cf. chapter 8.4.3.3): "If states are extractive organizations that can deploy resources to some extent independently of existing class interests, then it makes sense that revolutions create the *potentials* for breakthroughs in national economic development in large part by giving rise to more powerful, centralized, and autonomous state organizations. This was true for all of the revolutions from above and below that we studied, although the potential for state-guided or initiated national economic development was more thoroughly realized in Japan, Russia, and China than it was in France and Turkey" (SKOC- POL/TRIMBERGER 1978:130).

Chapter Nine: Political Violence, Crises, and Revolutions.
Some Concluding Remarks.

1. For a useful overview of methods of temporal analysis, see HANNAN/ TUMA (1979).
2. Technically, however, such an analysis might be endangered by the in- fluences of autocorrelated residuals and stable implicit variables.

(3)

3. There are a few studies which demonstrate that it is possible to order events of political violence according to the intensity of means employed (GUTTMAN scale type, cf. NESVOLD 1969 for seventy-one noncommunist countries and eleven communist countries in 1948–61, and SCHNEIDER/SCHNEIDER 1971 for ten Western nations in 1948–68). The basic assumption in this study, however, is that political violence in general is a multidimensional phenomenon, as shown in the various factor analyses in chapter 5.1.1.1.2.1 and in the recent factor analysis by GURR/BISHOP (1976). The procedures in the NESVOLD study and the SCHNEIDER/SCHNEIDER study must obviously be checked against (1) other categorizations of the data (one intriguing problem being to avoid scalability by definition) and (2) against other samples and time periods, before any general conclusions may be reached. MULLER (1976; 1977:73) also demonstrates that collective political aggression can be measured along a single dimension, but his measures partly refer to behavioral intention, not to actual behavior, even though his measures give greater weight to actual participation than to possible future participation. OLSEN/BADEN (1974) report unidimensionality of a scale to measure "willingness to grant legitimacy to several different kinds of social protest actions" in American and Swedish contexts. Using survey data, BLUMENTHAL et al. (1975), MARSH (1977), and BARNES (1977) also show that protest potential can be scaled along a single dimension varying from nonviolent unconventional means of political protest to more severe forms of political dissent. Yet, in a more refined reanalysis of aggregated event data (taken from TAYLOR/HUDSON 1972), SCHADEE (1976) reopens the question of GUTTMAN scalability of events of political violence and political protest. Finally, for one of several methodological corrections of GUTTMAN's formulae, cf. McCONAGHY 1975.

4. Yet GAMSON's data do not provide unambiguous answers as to whether violent and nonviolent protests are alternative or reinforcing forms of protest behavior (operating perhaps by means of feedback influences; cf. also below).

5. Thus, the focus could be on questions such as these: "How do the forms and levels of participation directed at local levels of government relate to, and compare with, those directed at national government? How is this balance affected by social and economic change?" (HUNTINGTON/NELSON 1976:16).

6. "Moreover, a history of accomplishment is an important asset, and as GAMSON (1975) shows for his sample of social movement organizations, longevity provides an edge in the attainment of legitimacy. Older organizations have available higher degrees of professional sophistication, existing ties to constituents, and experience in fund-raising procedures" (McCARTHY/ZALD 1977:1233).

7. GAMSON thus contradicts the widespread belief that violence is used as a last resort (cf. also chapter 2.3). "Violence grows from an impatience born of confidence and a sense of rising power. It occurs when the challenging group senses that the surrounding community will condone it, when hostility toward the *victim* renders it a relatively safe strategy. In

(Chapter Nine)

this sense, violence is as much a symptom of success as a cause" (GAM-SON 1974:39). GAMSON also maintains "that it is not the weakness of the user but the weakness of the target that accounts for violence" (GAMSON 1975:82).

8. Nor the control of such activities via *agents provocateurs* and informants. Cf. MARX (1974) for stimulating explorations along these lines.

9. In a study of a representative U.S. sample in 1972, USEEM/USEEM (1979) report some evidence that could indirectly be interpreted as underlining the importance of organizations if the incumbent regime is indeed to be threatened by a loss of public confidence. While they find that structural variables like unemployment, race, educational level, length of residence in the local community, etc., as well as political liberalism, correlate with low confidence in government and protest support ("respondent's endorsement of several types of protest tactics"; "respondent's feelings that the authorities should meet the demands"; "respondent's expressed affinity for radical students, black militants, urban rioters", etc.), they fail to find support for a direct covariation between low confidence in government and protest support. The higher correlation between "government disaffection and protest support among liberals is [perhaps] related to different expectations held. . . . It is also possible that liberals were more often members of political organizations sympathetic to the aims of existing protest movements" during the period studied (USEEM/USEEM 1979:849). BARNES's (1977) report on a national survey of Americans age sixteen and over also sheds some light on the kinds of results that might be expected once measures of organizational involvement (and appropriate controls) have been introduced:

> The strong contribution of organizational involvement to conventional political participation, which has been noted in many studies, is reconfirmed. The relationship holds even when controls for age, education, and left-right self placement are instituted. It was expected that organizational involvement would depress protest potential, and this was shown to be the case. However, when the same set of controls are employed, the relationship largely vanishes, for organizational activists tend to possess the demographic and political characteristics of the members of the population who are low on protest. The relationships between organizational involvement, on the one hand, and political dissatisfaction and distrust, on the other, are quite weak. Indeed, the variables that were strong predictors of conventional and unconventional participation explain little of the variance in dissatisfaction and distrust (BARNES 1977:11).

10. Also, in this type of study, the problem of finding equivalent indicators would not be as bothersome as in world-wide cross-national analyses. Even comparisons of carefully selected pairs may lead to the development of fruitful new hypotheses which might not be detected in broad-scale cross-national comparisons.

(11)

11. Cf. VERBA/NIE (1972) and VERBA et al. (1978) as to the determinants and consequences of *institutionalized* forms of political participation. Institutionalized channels of political participation (e.g., membership in communist parties) might act as catalyzing protest potentials or protest behavior, as documented in the analyses of GURR and HIBBS. Equating institutionalized means of political influence with a reduction of protest potential is neither theoretically nor empirically justified. Formally equivalent access might lead to rather different results, depending on the political goals pursued.

12. Cf. also DEUTSCH/SENGHAAS (1973:314) for some other possible perspectives of analysis omitted here.

13. There are many other interesting findings and explanations to be found in MARSH's study, e.g.: "Exactly in line with [INGLEHART's] 1970 findings, the postbourgeoise [*sic*] group are almost four times more likely than the acquisitives to favor nonlegal forms of protest. This finding is also independent of the powerful age effect in that postbourgeois over thirty years of age are almost twice as likely to favor protest than acquisitives *under* thirty. Combined with age, the effect is very impressive: Only 15 percent of young postbourgeoise [*sic*] would go no further than petition signing and more than half would engage in illegal forms of protest" (MARSH 1977:185; cf. also INGLEHART 1977a; 1977b; MULLER 1979:202). MARSH, however, interprets postbourgeois or postmaterialist political values less in terms of Maslowian self-realization, as INGLEHART does, than in terms of power-seeking. Furthermore, there is a positive relationship between protest potential and orthodox political participation which is especially strong on the left side of the political continuum (MARSH 1977:93).

   Critics of INGLEHART's work have objected to his operationalization which forces respondents into either a materialist or a postmaterialist category on the basis of their replies to two questions (WRIGHT 1978b) and, by so doing, leaves out numerous other respondents (HERZ 1979:301). Others have noted that both materialist and postmaterialist values may be shared by the same person at the same time (e.g., HERZ 1979:298–99). Moreover, in a multivariate analysis of data from the five countries studied in the BARNES/KAASE volume, INGLEHART (in BARNES/KAASE et al. 1979: chapter 12; cf. also INGLEHART 1978 for similar results with U. S. data from 1974) reports that the strongest predictor of protest potential is youth (beta on the average: .203) and that values, which in turn partially depend on youth (.193), are "only" the second strongest predictor of the dependent variable (.191). Finally, the crucial test for INGLEHART's findings and predictions is a severe economic downswing (HEISLER 1979:154). In such circumstances will there be fire behind the postmaterialist smoke? (For further comments and critiques, see, e.g., WRIGHT 1978b who questions INGLEHART's sampling procedures, data handling, and interpretations; see also FLANAGAN 1979 for an analysis and modifications of the relationship between value changes and partisan changes, drawing on data from Japan). Building on the theoretical work of MASLOW (1943) and on socialization theory, INGLEHART has pointed to some important value changes that have taken place after World War II in Western countries (and perhaps in others as well). Discounting the criticisms of INGLEHART's study, the breadth of his findings from more than half a dozen countries and from several panel studies appears impressive.

14. For example, organizational resources could be made available by social groups other than the one which is to benefit most from protest behavior. Cf., e.g., the liberal white community's support for the black civil rights movement in the United States.

15. It should be noted that, by definition, bargaining is possible only in conflict situations with non-zero sum constellations (cf. also the definitional considerations in chapter 2.1), i.e., bargaining should be excluded in cases of fundamental principles or values, in cases of indivisible goods which are not calculable by a common standard, and perhaps in instances where outcomes are irreversible (see PINARD 1976:38 on the basis of a paper by OBERSCHALL; cf. also OBERSCHALL 1973: 49–64).

16. This new theoretical view "tends to emphasize the instrumental aspects of the leader-follower relationship, based on the mutual benefit that each derives from it" (OBERSCHALL 1973:172). "Because [leaders] are involved full-time and because their activities entail higher risks and potentially higher rewards than for followers, leaders must be understood from the point of view of the individual incentives, gains, risks, and opportunities for advancement that participation in a social movement represents for them" (OBERSCHALL 1973:159). Leaders are thought to be strongly motivated by these aspects, and not by ideological considerations alone. As put by McCARTHY/ZALD: "Grievances and discontent may be defined, created, and manipulated by issue entrepreneurs and organizations" (McCARTHY/ZALD 1977:1215). Cf. also the conceptual and analytical efforts of McCARTHY/ZALD who attempt to construct a partial theory of resource mobilization and social movements, distinguishing among social movement sector, social movement industries, and social movement organizations. They stress that several organizations may represent or compete for the same social movement. Thus, individuals may sometimes be members of several protest organizations.

17. As RUDÉ asks with respect to the collective protests in eighteenth-century England: "Who acted as intermediaries between the leaders or the 'middling' strata and the rioters in the streets? Who organized them? Who passed on the slogans, or brought them, so constantly and continuously, into the streets?" (RUDÉ 1970:339).

18. See HIRSCHMAN (1970) on these concepts.

19. This new approach might be seen as a reaction to traditional studies on collective behavior which frequently start from the assumption that this form of behavior is irrational in nature. "Yet there is a danger here in substituting a super-rationalistic model for an irrational model" (MARX/WOOD 1975:387).

20. As put in another article by OBERSCHALL: "The larger the size of the protesters and the stronger the image of the movement, the greater the

(20)

anticipated benefits because the probability of success is higher. The larger the size, the lower are the anticipated costs from repression (safety in numbers) and the costs of movement activity (economies of scale). Decreasing costs and increasing benefits result in a bandwagon effect that increases size and thus decreases costs and increases benefits yet further" (OBERSCHALL 1978c:273). A negative bandwagon effect might also take place, especially when the mobilizing effect via attention of the media is breaking down.

21. But consider also the negative evidence as to the causal importance of such a variable, as reported in MULLER's analyses of his German sample (cf. chapter 6.3.4.2; see MULLER 1978, but also the more refined results in MULLER 1979). Apparently availability is not as unimportant a variable as it first appears.

22. As FROHLICH and coworkers say in their critique of OLSON (1965): "Whether individuals have dominant or contingent strategies has been shown to depend on the shape of their utility functions and of the production function governing the supply of the collective good. Only if one assumes that both are linear is it necessarily the case that individuals have dominant strategies. With decreasing marginal evaluation and S-shaped production functions, it is possible (though not necessary) that individuals will have *contingent* strategies, and thus their expectations about the decisions of others will be relevant to the choice of whether to contribute or not" (FROHLICH et al. 1975:328; emphasis added).

23. As to the points mentioned here, cf. also the analytical differentiations in SMELSER (1968:109). OBERSCHALL puts it in these terms: "The lower the risks and the higher the rewards for an individual and members of a group or social stratum, i.e., the lower [the] risk/reward ratio, the more likely are they to become participants in a social movement of opposition, of protest, or of rebellion. We assume, of course, that the individual or the groups under discussion have grievances to begin with. Because of individual differences in personality, motivation, social support, and so on, one would expect a certain amount of variation in the responses of group members even under the same conditions of risk, reward, and intensity of grievances" (OBERSCHALL 1973:162). Due to changes in the balance of forces, the risk/reward ratios may change one prediction stating: "The fastest way to produce high rates of social movement participation is to lower risks and to increase rewards *simultaneously*" (OBERSCHALL 1973:163; cf. also passim in this study). OBERSCHALL then goes on to discuss in an *ideal-type* manner the risk/reward ratios of various social groupings and the likelihood of conditions causing changes of these ratios. Thus, members of the free professions (or, more generally, people with discretionary work schedules) seem to run lower risks, whereas businessmen are more vulnerable if they participate in acts of collective protest (they might make higher profits by abstaining from participation). A somewhat different calculation may hold for small businessmen who might profit from joining the appropriate oppositional movement. Lower civil servants and white-collar employees run some risks if they participate, since they might be

replaced in their jobs by more obedient persons. Poor farmers with very few alternatives incur much greater costs than middle peasants (cf. also chapter 8.4.4). One might also raise the question of whether there is a point beyond which lowering the risks and increasing the rewards act as alternatives. Or does the lowering of risks always have to come first?

24. Like mobilization processes and impediments to mobilization *crowds themselves* have not yet been studied in sufficient detail. For an overview of some early conceptual efforts, cf. TURNER (1964) who compares imitation theory, the contagion hypothesis, and his preference, the "emergent norm theory" (which stresses the importance of specific norms as they develop during the processes of collective behavior). Yet he does not present precise conditions as to the temporal and analytical interdependence of the various conditions mentioned. Concerning the emergent norm approach, cf. also the theoretical extensions in WELLER/QUARANTELLI (1973).

25. Consequently, there must be a specific explanation for each distinct phase during a riot.

26. "The 'problem of the powerless' in protest activity is to activate 'third parties' to enter the implicit or explicit bargaining arena in ways favorable to the protesters. This is one of the few ways in which they can 'create' bargaining resources" (LIPSKY 1968:1145). One should keep in mind that "utilizing their excellent access to the press, public officials may state or imply that leaders are unreliable, ineffective as leaders ('they don't really have the people behind them'), guilty of criminal behavior, potentially guilty of such behavior, or are some shade of 'left-wing.' Any of these allegations may serve to diminish the appeal of protest groups to potentially sympathetic third parties" (LIPSKY 1970: 180). For a critique of LIPSKY's emphasis on the role of third parties, cf. PIVEN/CLOWARD (1977:23–24 and passim).

27. Mediators are particularly effective if they have not been identified previously with either side, if they speak with a united voice, and most crucial, if they have a mandate for representing the public whose interest and point of view have been drowned in the charges, countercharges, and staking out of positions by the adversaries. Mediators may thus possess considerable moral authority before which both sides are able to moderate their stand without losing face and giving an appearance of weakness (OBERSCHALL 1973:266).

28. "Most reformers in the United States have thought they had more to lose and less to gain from violence. This is one of the ironies of democracy as practiced in America: reformers have been hopeful enough of success to try to avoid violently antagonizing the Establishment, while the Establishment has often felt so threatened by the reformers' chances of success that coercion was necessary" (GURR 1979b:496).

29. Cf. also ALTHEIDE/GILMORE (1972) for a generally successful empirical validation of this theoretical scheme.

30. Cf. also SCHUMAKER/GETTER (1977) for an analysis of whether there is a responsiveness bias in American city politics. From their

(30)

> sample of fifty-one communities, the answer must be a yes in favor of
> upper SES membership groups.

31. In the case of the United Fruit Workers,

> Students had to contribute time to picketing grocery stores and
> shipping terminals; Catholic churches and labor unions had to
> donate office space for boycott houses; Railway Union members
> had to identify "scab" shipments for boycott pickets; Teamsters
> had to refuse to handle "hot cargo"; Butchers' union members had
> to call sympathy strikes when grocery managers continued to
> stock "scab" products; political candidates and elected officials
> had to endorse the boycott. The effectiveness of the boycott
> depended little upon the resources of mobilized farm workers;
> instead, they became a political symbol. It was the massive out-
> pouring of support, especially from liberals and organized labor,
> that made the boycott effective and, thereby, forced growers to
> the bargaining table (JENKINS/PERROW 1977:264).

> It is also noteworthy "that liberals directed their efforts toward sup-
> porting insurgents rather than pressuring government" (ibid., p. 265).
> In sum, "it was the interjection of resources from outside, not sharp in-
> creases in discontent, that led to insurgent efforts" (ibid., p. 266).
> However, "liberal support can fade and political elites shift their stance,
> as has happened to the UFW since 1972" (ibid., p. 267), thus endanger-
> ing even the gains of the past (cf. also the examples and the analysis in
> PIVEN/CLOWARD 1977).

32. An adequate and nontautological analysis of the impact of labeling on
    specific forms of behavior must, of course, include the "study of non-
    events" (WILSON 1977:479).

33. However, MARSH (1977: chapter 3) does not find this clear-cut dis-
    tinction between these two indexes of violence among his British
    respondents.

34. In addition, several criterion groups were selected for special study.

35. Outcomes are not the central topic of this study. Moreover, this section
    was written prior to GURR's (1980a) summary of research on the out-
    comes of violent conflict which now gives a comprehensive overview
    and provides useful analytical criteria for future studies. Thus, he differ-
    entiates, e.g., between the issues of conflict, the types of conflict, the
    levels of conflict, the targets of conflict, and the outcomes to both
    sides: dissidents (e.g., fate of groups, policies adopted, systemic change)
    and targets (authorities, respectively).

36. "It is worth noting that, with the exception of the Night Riders, none
    of the groups that used violence made it a primary tactic. Typically it
    was incidental to the primary means of influence—strikes, bargaining,
    propaganda, or other nonviolent means. It is the spice, not the meat and
    potatoes" (GAMSON 1975:82). The Night Riders are described as a
    "group that attempted to mobilize tobacco farmers of the black patch
    area to achieve control of the marketing of tobacco and to break the
    power of the tobacco trust" (GAMSON 1975:150). See also SCHU-
    MAKER (1975:517) who in his study on the outcomes of urban

policies in the United States provides some evidence that the use of violence may reduce the protesters' chances of success.

37. "A still more precise criterion is the extent to which the grievances which give rise to collective protest and violence are resolved" (GURR 1979b:497).

38. In an analysis of violent strikes in France between 1890 and 1935, SHORTER/TILLY (1971b:112) also find some indications in favor of GAMSON's hypothesis. In the case of industrial strikes in Italy (1878–1903), however, such a result does not emerge. Violent clashes among workers as well as with police forces turned out to be less successful in terms of goals achieved (SNYDER/KELLY 1976).

39. GURR (1980a:279) in this context points to an important gap in research: "Not one of the empirical studies reviewed here examines the impact of civil rights activities on social or economic programs at any level of government."

40. Another strategy of restabilization has been the setting up of riot commissions. In the words of LIPSKY/OLSON, "Riot commission politics is part of the process by which the United States purchases sytem stability at the expense of blacks and through explicit and implicit mechanisms [i.e., stressing localized dimensions of the problem, deflecting citizens' immediate concerns through short- and long-range assurances, lowering riot visibility and challenging the legitimacy of riot participants, ibid., p. 443] that substantially insulate the system from their political influence" (LIPSKY/OLSON 1977:455).

41. GRØNBJERG et al. (1978:26), however, argue "that almost the reverse took place: that a liberal presidential administration, by expanding welfare payments, promoted agitation for further expansion of benefits."

42. BALBUS even attaches a functional explanation to this finding: "American political authorities are thus forced to pay a price for their effort to adapt normal sanctioning mechanisms to the challenge of collective revolts, the price being minimal deprivation inflicted on the participants. But this is a price willingly paid, since the use of ordinary sanctioning mechanisms permits political authorities to define the revolts as 'ordinary crime.' And . . . this definition is consistent with their long-run interest in maximizing their legitimacy and minimizing the revolutionary potential of the revolts" (BALBUS 1973:255).

43. "In general, one cannot fail to be impressed more by the scope and intensity of the law enforcement or control response than by the relatively limited character of the social and economic reforms which came in the aftermath of rioting" (FEAGIN/HAHN 1973:260). Reviewing the evidence, GURR (1980a) clearly reaches the opposite conclusion.

44. Altogether, the outcomes of the student revolt of the 1960s have been more favorable, even though expectations of protesting students were frequently not met. Nevertheless, on many a campus students achieved "significant changes . . . [e.g., as to] curricular revisions and the introduction of new programs . . . , formation of new committees or study groups, granting [of] greater student representation on existing committees, establishment of special admissions policies for minority group

(44)

students, liberalization of parietal rules, reforms in the judicial process, alterations in the grading system and in graduation requirements, and hiring more black faculty or administrators" (ASTIN et al. 1975:146). Also in many countries the franchise has been lowered to eighteen years since 1968. However, the general liberal public was sympathetic (at least for a certain period) to many student demands. Other support frequently came from junior faculty members. Participation in university politics and in political and societal processes in general have become a permanent issue thanks to the student revolt and the general *Zeitgeist*. Perhaps it is fair to say that the student revolt definitely ended the quiet and internally peaceful period of reconstruction after World War II in Europe no less than in neo-isolationist and neo-conservative America. That it had an impact is undoubtedly true. Whether it was the major driving force behind these changes or just the "vehicle for the *Zeitgeist*," i.e., a catalyst, may be judged more adequately from a more distant vantage point. However, the impact of the student revolt should not be overemphasized. Roughly a decade after the student revolt, many student bodies, at least in the more industrialized countries, are relatively silent (cf., e.g., STATERA 1975 as to the decline of student movements in Europe).

45. Cf., e.g., NIEBURG (1963:43): "Violence is necessary and useful in preserving national unities."

46. One must also consider the relationships between political violence, voting behavior as an expression of protest behavior, nonviolent strikes, suicide, alcoholism, and other forms of deviant behavior. Do these phenomena vary independently of each other, do they influence each other, or do they act as substitutes for each other? Are they to be understood as expressing some underlying general conditions? An encompassing theory of anti-institutionalized behavior should provide an answer to these questions. Very few steps in this direction have been taken as yet.

> One of the most pervasive assumptions of theories of crime and conflict is that both are rooted in social tensions that are manifest in a prevailing sense of individual anomie, alienation, or discontent. It is plausible to suppose that such states of mind will motivate some to join in collective action and others, depending on their needs and opportunities, to take more individualistic courses of action. A second line of argument is that widespread and prolonged group conflict causes or increases the breakdown of moral order. People in disorderly times are more likely to do what they feel like doing than what others say is right and proper. A third factor is that elites faced with real or threatened resistance probably intensify efforts at social control across the board, increasing policing, prosecuting, and punishment (GURR 1976:82–83).

GURR and his collaborators report evidence from London, Stockholm, Sydney, and Calcutta during various periods of the nineteenth and twentieth centuries that seems to support these hypotheses (ibid., 83–91, and GURR et al. 1977:666–75). "The immediate conclusion to

be drawn from these comparisons is that sharp increases in indicators
of crime of violence and theft usually coincide with episodes of strife.
Objective criteria have been used to identify 29 substantial increases
in violent crime, measured mostly by reference to changes in conviction
rates. Nineteen of the 29, or 66 percent, coincided with serious internal
conflict. Of the increases in theft, thirteen of 25 also coincided with
civil strife" (GURR 1976:90).

See also SHORTER/TILLY (1974) for a first effort at discovering
the determinants of strikes in France (1830–1968) and relating strikes
to other phenomena of collective violence. Cf. also STEARNS (1974)
and HIBBS (1976) who has carried out the most sophisticated cross-
national analysis (cf. also SHORTER/TILLY 1971a) of "industrial conflict in [ten] advanced industrial societies" between 1950 and 1969.
HIBBS examines some theoretical explanations not found in analyses of
political violence. Several explanations from studies on political
violence are also taken up here, such as variants of the deprivation
approach. With the exception of long-run expectation-achievement gaps
(using indirect measures in terms of variations in the rates of change in
money earnings deflated by the consumer price index), none of the
deprivation approaches contributes significantly to the variation in the
volume of strikes. HIBBS favors an explanation by mechanisms of
"'memory' persisting several periods back through time, in the sense
that a change in real wages affects strike activity over a number of subsequent years"(HIBBS 1976:1057). It turns out that industrial conflict
"responds to movements in real wages" (ibid., p. 1057), occurs somewhat independently of the efforts of Labor-Socialist party elites to
deter industrial conflict, does not "drop-off during the tenure of
governments controlled by Labor or Socialist parties," but rather "does
appear to vary (nonlinearly) with the relative size of Communist Party
memberhip. This lends support to the earlier proposition that Communist parties in advanced industrial societies remain important agencies
for the mobilization of latent discontent and the crystallization of
labor-capital cleavages" (HIBBS 1976:1058). Finally, as the labor
market tightens and the percentage of the civilian labor force unemployed increases, there is a deterrent effect on the volume of strikes
(HIBBS 1976; 1978:157; TILLY 1978:166; for critical comments on
HIBBS's 1976 study, see WEEDE 1979).

47. There is a long list of authors who attribute *instrumental* functions to
the use of violence (rational aspect, cf. RUDÉ 1967; WALLACE
1970–71) and assign it a *communicative* function (SEARS/TOMLIN-
SON 1968:496–500; COSER 1967: part 1; DRAKE 1968; NIEBURG
1969; ETZIONI 1970:18 even considers demonstrations as an "interim
election tool"), that of *collective bargaining* (cf. HOBSBAWM 1952:59;
1959; WILSON 1961; LIPSKY 1968; NIEBURG 1969:40–45) or who
consider political violence an *integrative* force (cf. IGLITZIN 1970).
Most of these functions overlap, as in the case of violence serving a
rational function or representing a form of collective bargaining. For
COSER violence fulfills three functions: (1) "Violence as achievement"
(the formerly powerless demonstrate that they are able to concentrate

(47)

their resources; cf. also FANON and some other authors to be mentioned below); (2) "violence as a danger signal"; and (3) "violence as a catalyst" ("the use of extralegal violence by . . . officers may, under certain circumstances, lead to the arousal of the community and to a revulsion from societal arragements that rest upon such enforcement methods" (COSER 1967:87–88). Once again the alleged functions of violence overlap. Obviously, the differentiations proposed by COSER are not very precise. Furthermore, there is a striking absence of data in COSER's work (cf. also the criticism in BIENEN 1968:21–25). Riots are frequently viewed as a form of collective bargaining, i.e., both parties to conflict are willing to find a compromise through conceding in some respects and receiving compensations. The compromise on the part of the protesters is that only weaker forms of violent protest behavior are employed (and/or employed for a shorter period), whereas the dominant party shows its willingness to bargain by promising to act in an agreed-upon manner. In following such a view, two points are easily overlooked: it is assumed that protesters follow such a calculated strategy from the beginning. This might be true in some cases, yet in most instances, especially in escalated riots where heterogeneous populations participate, such forms of behavior become extremely unlikely. On the other hand, the course of events is interpreted after the fact as following the pattern of a bargaining process. In reality, however, quite different goals might have been pursued at the beginning. In any case, statements as to the functional qualities of political violence, which characterize violence as an independent and no longer as a dependent variable, at present go far beyond the range of empirically grounded statements.

48. Thus, at present it might be difficult to interpret the relatively high correlation HIBBS (1973) reports between collective protest and internal war ($r=.63$) in terms of the second alternative.

49. In SARTRE's preface to FANON's book we even read: "To shoot down a European is to kill two birds with one stone, to destroy an oppressor and the man he oppresses at the same time: there remain a dead man, and a free man" (SARTRE, preface to FANON 1967:19).

50. MARCUSE's concept of "repressive tolerance," a consciously chosen contradiction in terms, resembles the notion of "structural violence." An existing state of affairs is compared with an optimal one, which, however, is not described in detail.

51. For SOREL there is no falsification of the myth. One might, however, argue to the contrary since one could test whether the use of violence does indeed have a therapeutic effect or whether fear or stupor are more likely consequences.

52. In one of the more recent American textbooks in political science, one finds these recommendations (which might indeed prove valid):

1. Seek to maintain conventional channels of politics even during confrontations (for example, keep bargaining during strikes).
2. Maintain a high capacity for violence, but troops and police must be trained and equipped so that precisely the right amount

(Chapter Nine)

of counter-violence can be employed to stop violence without falling into vicious cycles where terrorism breeds counter-terrorism, which in turn further encourages terrorism.
3. Be willing to use the capacity for violence to protect the normal political mechanisms and individual rights, but employ the absolute *minimum* level necessary for success.
4. Use the conventional channels of politics quickly to grant those changes which enjoy broad popular support, do not freeze or become stubborn under threats and refuse to make desirable changes simply because their proponents have become abusive or violent (WOLFINGER et al. 1976:582).

GURR (1979b:504–6) focuses on "optimum strategies for civil peace," emphasizes that frequently "the optimum response must be a mix of control and remedial strategies" (ibid., p. 505) and arrives at conclusions not unlike those of WOLFINGER et al.

53. According to the cross-sectional analysis by GURR/DUVALL (1973), the following relations seem to hold: a regime enjoying institutional support will nevertheless exhibit a limited degree of violent protests. The inhibiting influence of strong regime-supporting institutions is severely weakened, however, once the dissidents have gained a certain degree of institutional support. In other words, once rebels have gained in institutional support and in other resources (elite dissension being a basic variable here), the inhibiting power of state institutions is rapidly reduced. One might possibly conclude from this that regime-supporting political institutions should be strong but flexible as well (cf. also the results in GURR 1974a and the preceding note).

54. Building on his earlier works, LIJPHART (1975; cf. also DAALDER 1974) presents three sets of conditions of vital importance for the functioning of "consociational democracies": *firstly*, the leaders of groups or parties formerly fighting against each other must develop rules of coalition and representation (usually on a proportional basis) and achieve consent for these arrangements among their own clienteles. *Secondly*, there should be a multiple base of power (and not two equally strong factions) with mutual or minority veto power. "The least favorable situation is the one exemplified by Northern Ireland: a dual division into political subcultures without equilibrium and with one subculture capable of exercising hegemonic power" (LIJPHART 1975: 100). Furthermore, there must be a normative attachment to grand coalitions as a form of government as well as a minimum of national solidarity (and traditions of elite accommodation; see LIJPHART 1977:99–103). *Thirdly*, such a model will function only (a) in culturally pluralistic societies with small populations, whose cleavages are clearly recognizable but not reinforced through everyday encounters, and (b) if some form of external threat is perceived by the community at large. Northern Ireland meets almost none of these conditions, which leads LIJPHART to propose a partition of Northern Ireland and to recommend a resettlement of the Catholic and Protestant populations into more homogeneous parts of the country as a possible (but still rather

(54)

unlikely and in the end problematic) solution (for discussions of other solutions cf. also ROSE 1976; SCHMITT 1976; BELL 1976b).

Theorists dealing with the conditions and the consequences of consociational democracy and political accommodation are not in agreement about either their respective conditions or, as a consequence, their cases under study. STEINER, for one, points out that "the following statement by LIJPHART does not seem to apply to Switzerland: 'Clear boundaries between subcultures have the advantage of limiting mutual contacts and, consequently, of limiting the chances of ever-present potential antagonisms from erupting into actual hostility.' What exactly does LIJPHART understand by limited mutual contacts? How numerous should the interactions among nonelite members of the various subcultures be to qualify as 'limited' in LIJPHART's sense?" (STEINER 1974:258). STEINER actually reports a considerable amount of interaction between nonelite members of various subcultures. He also points to some of the possible long-term consequences of amicable agreement which might—in the presence of perceived inequity among the subcultures, perceived incapacity of the system for innovation, and perceived opportunities for the articulation of dissent—lead to forms of intersubcultural hostility (STEINER 1974:276; cf. also STEINER/OBLER 1976; OBLER et al. 1977). Other matters of disagreement include the roles of the elites (cf., e.g., NORDLINGER 1972 who stresses the determinative role of political elites vs. ESMAN who believes that this "does not account for a number of reasonably successful cases of communal conflict management, e.g., India, Canada, Switzerland, which have not depended on the structured predominance of elites," ESMAN 1973:72). Another question is whether consociationalism requires a certain level of socioeconomic development to function. The recent failure of insufficiently implemented consociational policies (cf., e.g., HUDSON 1976; BILL/LEIDEN 1979:133) in Lebanon comes to mind here, even though several additional (partly external) factors had an impact on the destruction of the political system there. Finally, cf. also the critique by BARRY (1975) focusing on problems of concept formation (cf. also LORWIN 1971:144) and theory building. In the case of STEINER's (1974) analysis of consociationalism in Switzerland, BARRY (1975:485) points out that "the crucial point is that the institution of collective decision-making by simple majority of the popular vote is in itself the antithesis of 'amicable agreement.'" The most recent (and probably most extensive) comparative evaluation of the prospects of "democracy [and political stability] in plural societies" may be found in LIJPHART's new book (1977). In cases of noteworthy but not overwhelming pluralism (no quantitative assessment is given), LIJPHART (1978) predicts a greater probability of success for the consociational model of democracy as compared to majoritarian models (cf. also STEINER 1974:268). "It is nevertheless necessary to conclude that the chances for consociational democracy decrease as the degree of pluralism of plural societies increases" (LIJPHART 1978:36).

55. These should cover much longer periods where necessary. For example, one must study at least the last three hundred years in Northern Ireland to allow for an adequate evaluation of the present situation there. Cf. also the references in chapter 5.1.1.1.2.6.
56. Even if most of the evidence bearing on the employment of repressive measures is indirect in nature.
57. Cf. also M. DEUTSCH (1973:351ff.) for some more general strategies of conflict resolution.
58. E.g., third parties might be of primary importance in the case of non-violent protest movements. "In the case of Gandhi's and Martin Luther King's nonviolent campaigns, it was British home opinion and the parliamentary opposition in one case, and Northern public opinion, Congress, and the Washington administration in the other, that represented the crucial third party in the conflict whose reaction to the repression of peaceful protest campaigns was to swing their support to the side of the protesters" (OBERSCHALL 1973:321).

Bibliography

Abeles, Ronald P. 1976. "Relative deprivation, rising expectations, and black militancy." *Journal of Social Issues* 32, no. 2:119–37.

Abell, Peter. 1971. "Why do men rebel? A discussion of Ted Robert Gurr's 'Why men rebel.'" *Race* 13, no. 1 (July):84–89.

Aberbach, Joel D., and Walker, Jack L. 1973. *Race in the city: political trust and public policy in the new urban system*. Boston: Little, Brown & Co.

Aberle, David F. 1962. "A note on relative deprivation theory as applied to millenarism and other cult movements," in Sylvia Thrupp (ed.), *Millennial dreams in action: essays in comparative study*. Comparative Studies in Society and History, Supplement no. 2. The Hague: Mouton, 209–14.

Abrahamsson, Bengt. 1972. *Military professionalization and political power*. Beverly Hillls: Sage Publications.

Abramson, Paul R. 1977. *The political socialization of black Americans: a critical evaluation of research on efficacy and trust*. New York: Free Press.

Abudu, Margaret J. G.; Raine, Walter J.; Burbeck, Stephen L.; and Davison, Keith K. 1972. "Black ghetto violence: a case study inquiry into the spatial pattern of four Los Angeles riot event-types." *Social Problems* 19, no. 3 (Winter):408–27.

Acock, Alan C., and Martin, J. David. 1974. "The undermeasurement controversy: should ordinal data be treated as interval?" *Sociology and Social Research* 58, no. 4 (July):427–33.

Adams, Hebron Elliott. 1970. "The origins of insurgency." Ph.D. dissertation, University of Lancaster.

Adams, J. Stacy. 1963. "Toward an understanding of inequity." *Journal of Abnormal and Social Psychology* 67:422–36. Abridged in Henry Clay Lindgren (ed.), *Contemporary research in social psychology: A book of readings*. New York: Wiley (1969), 210–34.

Adams, J. S. 1965. "Inequity in social exchange," in L. Berkowitz (ed.), *Advances in experimental social psychology*, vol. 2. New York: Academic Press, 267–99.

Adams, J. Stacy, and Freedman, Sara. 1976. "Equity theory revisited: comments and annotated bibliography," in Berkowitz/Walster, 43–90.

Adas, Michael. 1977. Review of "Agrarian Revolution" (Paige 1975). *Journal of Social History* 10, no. 3 (Spring):373–76.

Adelman, Irma, and Morris, Cynthia Taft. 1967. *Society, politics and economic development: a quantitative approach*. Baltimore: Johns Hopkins Press.

Adelman, Irma, and Morris, Cynthia Taft. 1973. *Economic growth and social equity in developing countries*. Stanford: Stanford University Press.

Agulhon, Maurice. 1973. *1848 ou l'apprentissage de la République, 1848-1852*. Paris: Editions du Seuil.

Ahluwalia, Montek S. 1976. "Income distribution and development: some stylized facts." *American Economic Review* 66:128-35.

Ahluwalia, Montek S. 1976a. "Inequality, poverty and development." *Journal of Development Economics* 3:307-42.

Ahmad, Eqbal. 1968. "Radical but wrong," in Huberman/Sweezy, 70-83.

Ahmad, Eqbal. 1971. "Revolutionary warfare and counterinsurgency," in Miller/Aya, 137-213.

Ahn, Byung-joon. 1976. *Chinese politics and the Cultural Revolution: dynamics of policy processes*. Seattle: University of Washington Press.

Ajzen, Icek, and Fishbein, Martin. 1974. "Factors influencing intentions and the intention-behavior relation." *Human Relations* 27, no. 1 (January): 1-15.

Ajzen, Icek, and Fishbein, Martin. 1977. "Attitude-behavior relations: a theoretical analysis and review of empirical research." *Psychological Bulletin* 84, no. 5:888-918.

Akamatsu, Paul. 1968. *Meiji-1868:Révolution et contre-révolution au Japon*. Paris: Calmann-Lévy.

Ake, Claude. 1967. *A theory of political integration*. Homewood, Ill.: Dorsey Press.

Ake, Claude. 1967a. "Political integration and political stability: a hypothesis." *World Politics* 19, no. 3 (April):486-99.

Ake, Claude. 1974. "Modernization and political instability: a theoretical exploration." *World Politics* 26, no. 4 (July):576-91.

Ake, Claude. 1975. "A definition of political stability." *Comparative Politics* 7, no. 2 (January):271-83.

Alavi, Hamza. 1965. "Peasants and revolution." *The Socialist Register*: 241-77.

Albright, David E. 1980. "A comparative conceptualization of civil-military relations." *World Politics* 32, no. 4 (July):553-76.

Albritton, Robert B. 1979. "Social amelioration through mass insurgency? A reexamination of the Piven and Cloward thesis." *American Political Science Review* 73, no. 4 (December):1003-11.

Aldrich, Howard E. 1973. "Employment opportunities for blacks in the black ghetto: the role of white-owned business." *American Journal of Sociology* 78, no. 6 (May):1403-25.

Aldrich, Howard, and Reiss, Albert J. 1970. "The effect of civil disorders on small business in the inner city." *Journal of Social Issues* 26, no. 1:187-206.

Alessio, John C. 1980. "Another folly for equity theory." *Social Psychology Quarterly* 43, no. 3 (September):336-40.

Alexander, C. Norman, and Simpson, Richard L. 1964. "Balance theory and distributive justice." *Sociological Inquiry* 34, no. 2 (Spring):182-92.

Alexander, Robert. 1958. *The Bolivian national revolution*. Westport, Conn.: Greenwood Press.

Alexander, Robert J. 1978. *The tragedy of Chile*. Westport, Conn.: Greenwood Press.

Alexander, Yonah, ed. 1976. *International terrorism: national, regional, and global perspectives.* New York: Praeger.

Alexander, Yonah; Carlton, David; and Wilkinson, Paul, eds. 1979. *Terrorism: theory and practice.* Boulder, Colo.: Westview Press.

Alexander, Yonah, and Finger, Seymour Maxwell, eds. 1977. *Terrorism: interdisciplinary perspectives.* New York: John Jay Press.

Alexander, Yonah, and Kilmarx, Robert A., eds. (1979). *Political terrorism and business: the threat and response.* New York: Praeger.

Alker, Hayward R. 1965. "Measuring inequality," in *Mathematics and politics.* New York: Macmillan, 29–53.

Alker, Hayward R. 1969. "A typology of ecological fallacies," in Dogan/Rokkan, 69–86.

Alker, Hayward R. 1975. "Polimetrics: its descriptive foundations," in Greenstein/Polsby, vol. 7:139–210.

Alker, Hayward R., and Russett, Bruce M. 1964. "The analysis of trends and patterns," in Russett et al.: 259–364.

Alker, Hayward R., and Russett, Bruce M. 1966. "Indices for comparing inequality," in Richard L. Merritt and Stein Rokkan (eds.), *Comparing nations: the use of quantitative data in cross-national research.* New Haven: Yale University Press, 623–35.

Allemann, Fritz René. 1974. *Macht und Ohnmacht der Guerilla.* München: R. Piper & Co.

Allison, Paul D. 1978. "Measures of inequality." *American Sociological Review* 43, no. 6 (December):865–80.

Almond, Gabriel A. 1960. "Introduction: a functional approach to comparative politics," in Gabriel A. Almond and James S. Coleman (eds.), *The politics of the developing areas.* Princeton: Princeton University Press, 3–64.

Almond, Gabriel A. 1969. "Political development: analytical and normative perspectives." *Comparative Political Studies* 1, no. 4 (January):447–69.

Almond, Gabriel A., and Flanagan, Scott C. 1978. "Back to the barre, Brian Barry." *British Journal of Political Science* 8, no. 1 (January):119–27.

Almond, Gabriel A., and Mundt, Robert J. 1973. "Crisis, choice, and change: some tentative conclusions," in Almond et al.:619–49.

Almond, Gabriel A., and Powell, G. Bingham. 1966. *Comparative politics: a developmental approach.* Boston: Little, Brown & Co.

Almond, Gabriel A., and Powell, G. Bingham, Jr. 1978. *Comparative politics: system, process, and policy.* 2d ed. Boston: Little, Brown & Co.

Almond, Gabriel A., and Verba, Sidney. 1963. *The civic culture: political attitudes and democracy in five nations.* Princeton: Princeton University Press.

Almond, Gabriel A., and Verba, Sidney, eds. 1980. *The civic culture revisited.* Boston: Little, Brown & Co.

Almond, Gabriel A.; Flanagan, Scott C.; and Mundt, Robert J., eds. 1973. *Crisis, choice, and change: historical studies of political development.* Boston: Little, Brown & Co.

AlRoy, Gil Carl. 1967. "The peasantry in the Cuban revolution." *Review of Politics* 19, no. 1 (January):87–99.

Althauser, Robert P., and Heberlein, Thomas A. 1970. "Validity and the multitrait-multimethod matrix, in Edgar F. Borgatta (ed.), *Sociological methodology* (1970). San Francisco: Jossey-Bass (1970), 151–69.

Althauser, Robert P.; Heberlein, Thomas A.; and Scott, Robert A. 1971. "A causal assessment of validity: the augmented multitrait-multimethod matrix," in H. B. Blalock (ed.) *Causal models in the social sciences.* New York: Macmillan, 374–399.

Altheide, David L., and Gilmore, Robert P. 1972. "The credibility of protest." *American Sociological Review* 37, no. 1 (February):99–108.

Amann, Peter. 1962. "Revolution: a redefinition." *Political Science Quarterly* 77, no. 1 (March):36–53. Also in Welch/Taintor (1972), 42–55.

Amann, Peter, ed. 1963. *The eighteenth-century revolution. French or Western?* Boston: D. C. Heath & Co.

Amann, Peter H. 1975. *Revolution and mass democracy. The Paris club movement in 1848.* Princeton: Princeton University Press.

Amaro, Nelson. 1969. "Mass and class in the origins of the Cuban Revolution." *Studies in Comparative International Development* 10, no. 4 (April):547–76.

Ames, Barry. 1973. *Rhetoric and reality in a militarized regime: Brazil since 1964.* Sage Professional Paper in Comparative Politics Series, no. 01–042.

Ames, Barry. 1977. "The politics of public spending in Latin America." *American Journal of Political Science* 21, no. 1 (February):149–76.

Aminzade, Ronald. 1973. "Revolution and collective political violence: the case of the working class of Marseille, France, 1830–1871." Center for Research on Social Organization, University of Michigan. Mimeographed.

Amsel, A. 1958. "The role of frustrative nonreward in noncontinuous reward situations." *Psychological Bulletin* 55:102–119.

Amsel, A. 1962. "Frustrative nonreward in partial reinforcement and discrimination learning: some recent history and a theoretical extension." *Psychological Review* 69:306–328. Abridged in Lawson, 147–158.

Anderson, B.; Berger, J.; Zelditch, M.; and Cohen, B. P. 1969. "Reactions to inequity." *Acta Sociologica* 12, no. 1:1–12.

Anderson, Charles W.; Mehden, Fred R. von der; and Young, Crawford. 1967. (2d ed. 1974.) *Issues of political development.* Englewood Cliffs: Prentice-Hall.

Anderson, Clifford W., and Nesvold, Betty A. 1972. "A Skinnerian analysis of conflict behavior: Walden II goes cross-national." *American Behavioral Scientist* 15, no. 6 (July/August):883–909.

Anderson, Norman H. 1976. "Equity judgements as information integration." *Journal of Personality and Social Psychology* 33, no. 3:291–99.

Anderson, Perry. 1974a. *Passages from antiquity to feudalism.* London: NLB.

Anderson, Perry. 1974b. *Lineages of the absolutist state.* London: NLB.

Anderson, Thomas P. 1980. "The ambiguities of political terrorism in Central America." *Terrorism* 4:267–76.

Anderson, William A.; Dynes, Russell R.; and Quarantelli, E. L. 1974. "Urban counterrioters." *Trans-Action* 11, no. 3 (March/April):50–55.

Andison, F. Scott. 1977. "TV violence and viewer aggression: a cumulation of study results 1956–1976." *Public Opinion Quarterly* 41, no. 3 (Fall): 314–31.

Andrain, Charles F. 1975. *Political life and social change.* 2d ed. Belmont, Calif.: Wadsworth/Duxbury Press.

Andreski, Stanislav. 1961. "Conservatism and radicalism of the military."
    Archives Européennes de Sociologie 2, no. 1:53–61.
Andreski, Stanislav. 1968. *The African predicament: a study of the pathology
    of modernization.* London: Michael Joseph.
Andrews, William G., and Ra'anan, Uri, eds. 1969. *The politics of the coup
    d'état: five case studies.* New York: Van Nostrand Reinhold Co.
Antola, Esko. 1975. "The roots of domestic military interventions in Black
    Africa." *Instant Research on Peace and Violence* 5:207–21.
Apfelbaum, Erika. 1974. "On conflicts and bargaining," in Leonard Berko-
    witz (ed.) *Advances in experimental social psychology*, vol. 7. New
    York: Academic Press, 103–56.
Arani, Sharif. 1980. "Iran: from the Shah's dictatorship to Khomeini's dema-
    gogic theocracy." *Dissent* (Winter):9–26.
Ardant, Gabriel. 1965. *Théorie sociologique de l'impôt.* 2 vols. Paris:
    SEVPEN.
Ardant, Gabriel. 1975. "Financial policy and economic infrastructure of
    modern states and nations," in Tilly (1975a), 163–242.
Arendt, Hannah. 1964. *On revolution.* New York: Viking Press.
Arendt, Hannah. 1973. "On violence," in *Crises of the republic.* Harmonds-
    worth: Penguin (1973), 83–163.
Arian, Alan, and Barnes, Samuel H. 1974. "The dominant party system: a
    neglected model of democratic stability." *Journal of Politics* 36, no. 3
    (August):592–614.
Armer, Michael, and Isaac, Larry. 1978. "Determinants and behavioral conse-
    quences of psychological modernity: empirical evidence from Costa
    Rica." *American Sociological Review* 43, no. 3 (June):316–34.
Armer, Michael, and Schnaiberg, Alan. 1972. "Measuring individual modern-
    ity: a near myth." *American Sociological Review* 37, no. 3 (June):
    301–16.
Armer, Michael, and Schnaiberg, Allan. 1977. "Reply to Cohen and Till."
    American Sociological Review 42, no. 2 (April):378–82.
Armstrong, John A. 1976. "Mobilized and proletarian diasporas." *American
    Political Science Review* 70, no. 2 (June):393–408.
Aron, Raymond. 1979. "Remarks on Lasswell's 'The garrison state.'" *Armed
    Forces and Society* 5, no. 3 (Spring):347–59.
Artz, Frederick B. 1934. *Reaction and revolution, 1814–1832.* New York:
    Harper & Row.
Ascher, Abraham. 1978. *The revolution of 1905.* Stanford: Stanford Uni-
    versity Press.
Asher, Herbert B. 1978. "Partisan realignment. Survey essay." *Contemporary
    Sociology* 7, no. 6 (November):725–31.
Asprey, Robert B. 1975. *War in the shadows: the guerilla in history.* 2 vols.
    New York: Doubleday & Co.
Astin, Alexander; Astin, Helen S.; Bayer, Alan E.; and Bisconti, Ann S. 1975.
    The power of protest. San Francisco: Jossey-Bass.
Aston, Trevor, ed. 1965. *Crisis in Europe 1560–1660: essays from "Past &
    Present."* Introduction by Christopher Hill. London: Routledge &
    Kegan Paul.
Atkin, Ronald. 1970. *Revolution: Mexico 1910–20.* New York: John Day
    Co.

Atkins, G. Pope. 1974. "The armed forces in Latin American politics," in Cochran, 228–55.

Austin, William. 1977. "Equity theory and social comparison processes," in Suls/Miller, 279–305.

Austin, William, and Walster, Elaine. 1974. "Participants' reactions to 'Equity with the world.'" *Journal of Experimental Social Psychology* 10, no. 6 (November):528–48.

Austin, William, and Walster, Elaine. 1975. "Equity with the world: the transrelational effects of equity and inequity." *Sociometry* 38, no. 4 (December):474–96.

Aveni, Adrian F. 1977. "The not-so-lonely crowd: friendship groups in collective behavior." *Sociometry* 40, no. 1 (March):96–99.

Averch, Harvey, and Koehler, John. 1970. *The HUK rebellion in the Philippines: quantitative approaches.* Santa Monica: Rand.

Avermaet, Eddy van; McClintock, Charles; and Moskowitz, Joel. 1978. "Alternative approaches to equity: dissonance reduction, pro-social motivation and strategic accommodation." *European Journal of Social Psychology* 8, no. 4 (October-December):419–37.

Avrich, Paul. 1967. *The Russian anarchists.* Princeton: Princeton University Press.

Avrich, Paul. 1973. *Russian rebels, 1600–1800.* London: Allen Lane, The Penguin Press. (Original 1972.)

Ax, A. F. 1953. "The physiological differentiation between fear and anger in humans." *Psychosomatic Medicine* 15:433–42.

Aya, Rod. 1979. "Theories of revolution reconsidered: contrasting models of collective violence." *Theory and Society* 8, no. 1 (July):39–99.

Aya, Roderick, and Miller, Norman, eds. 1971. *The new American revolution.* New York: Free Press.

Azar, Edward. 1970. "Analysis of international events." *Peace Research Reviews* 4:1–113.

Azar, Edward E. 1975. "Ten issues in events research," in Azar/Ben-Dak, 1–16.

Azar, Edward E., and Ben-Dak, Joseph, eds. 1975. *Theory and practice of events research: studies in inter-nation actions and interactions.* New York: Gordon & Breach Science Publishers.

Azar, Edward E.; Cohen, Stanley H.; Jukam, Thomas O.; and McCormick, James M. 1972. "The problem of source coverage in the use of international events data." *International Studies Quarterly* 16, no. 3 (September):373–88.

Bachrach, Peter, and Baratz, Morton S. 1962. "Two faces of power." *American Political Science Review* 56, no. 4 (December):947–52.

Bachrach, Peter, and Baratz, Morton S. 1963. "Nondecisions: an analytical framework." *American Political Science Review* 57, no. 3 (September): 633–42.

Bachrach, Peter, and Baratz, Morton S. 1970. *Power and poverty: theory and practice.* New York: Oxford University Press.

Backman, Earl L., and Finlay, David J. 1973. "Student protest: a cross-national study." *Youth and Society* 5, no. 1 (September):3–46.

Bailey, Norman A. 1967. "La violencia in Columbia." *Journal of Inter-American Studies* 9, no. 4 (October):561–75.

Bailyr., Bernard, ed. 1965. *Pamphlets of the American Revolution, 1750–1776*, vol. 1: 1750–1765. Cambridge, Mass.: Belknap Press of Harvard University Press.

Bailyn, Bernard. 1973. "The central themes of the American Revolution" in Kurtz/Hutson, 3–31.

Baines, John M. 1972. "U. S. military assistance to Latin America: an assessment." *Journal of Interamerican Studies and World Affairs* 14, no. 4 (November):469–87.

Bak, Janos, ed. 1976. *The German peasant war of 1525*. London: Frank Cass.

Baker, Bela O.; Hardyck, Curtis D.; and Petrinovich, Lewis F. 1966. "Weak measurements vs. strong statistics: an empirical critique of S. S. Stevens' proscriptions on statistics." *Educational and Psychological Measurement* 26, no. 2:291–309. Also in Lieberman, 370–81.

Balbus, Isaac D. 1973. *Dialectics of legal repression: black rebels before the American criminal courts*. New York: Russell Sage Foundation.

Balch, George I. 1974. "Multiple indicators in survey research: the concept 'sense of political efficacy.'" *Political Methodology* 1, no. 1 (Spring): 1–43.

Bandura, A. 1963. "Aggression," in *Child psychology*, part 1. Chicago: National Society for the Study of Education, 364–415.

Bandura, A., ed. 1971. *Psychological modeling: conflicting theories*. Chicago: Aldine-Atherton.

Bandura, Albert. 1973. *Aggression: a social learning analysis*. Englewood Cliffs: Prentice-Hall.

Bandura, Albert. 1973a. "Social learning theory of aggression," in Knutson (1973), 201–50.

Bandura, Albert. 1974. "Behavior theory and the models of man." *American Psychologist* 29, no. 12 (December):859–69.

Bandura, Albert, and Walters, Richard H. 1959. *Adolescent aggression: a study of the influence of child-training practices and family interrelationships*. New York: Ronald Press.

Bandura, Albert, and Walters, Richard H. 1963. *Social learning and personality development*. New York: Holt, Rinehart & Winston.

Bandura, A.; Ross, D.; and Ross, S. A. 1961. "Transmission of aggression through imitation of aggressive models." *Journal of Abnormal and Social Psychology* 63:575–82.

Bandura, Albert; Ross, Dorothea; and Ross, Sheila A. 1963a. "Imitation of film-mediated aggressive models." *Journal of Abnormal and Social Psychology* 66:3–11.

Bandura, Albert; Ross, Dorothea; and Ross, Sheila. 1963b. "Vicarious reinforcement and imitative learning." *Journal of Abnormal and Social Psychology* 67:601–7.

Bandura, Albert; Underwood, Bill; and Fromson, Michael E. 1975. "Disinhibition of aggression through diffusion of responsibility and dehumanization of victims." *Journal of Research in Personality* 9, no. 4 (December):253–69.

Banfield, Edward C. 1958. *The moral basis of a backward society*. Glencoe: Free Press.

Banfield, Edward C. 1974. *The unheavenly city revisited (A revision of "The unheavenly city" 1970)*. Boston: Little, Brown & Co.

Banks, Arthur S. 1970. "Modernization and political change." *Comparative Political Studies* 2, no. 4 (January):405–18.

Banks, Arthur S. 1971. *Cross-polity time-series data*. Cambridge, Mass.: MIT Press.

Banks, Arthur S. 1972. "Patterns of domestic conflict: 1919–39 and 1946–66." *Journal of Conflict Resolution* 16, no. 1 (March):41–50.

Banks, Arthur S. 1974. "Industrialization and development: a longitudinal analysis." *Economic Development and Cultural Change* 22 (January): 320–37.

Banks, Arthur S., and Gregg, Phillip M. 1965. "Grouping political systems: Q-factor analysis of a cross-polity survey." *American Behavioral Scientist* 9, no. 3 (November):3–6. Also in Gillespie/Nesvold (1971), 311–20.

Banks, Arthur S., and Textor, Robert B. 1963. *A cross-polity survey*. Cambridge, Mass.: M.I.T. Press.

Barber, Elinor G. 1955. *The bourgeoisie in 18th–century France*. Princeton: Princeton University Press.

Barkun, Michael. 1974. *Disaster and the millenium*. New Haven: Yale University Press.

Barnes, Samuel H. 1977. "Some political consequences of involvement in organizations." Paper delivered at the 1977 Annual Meeting of The American Political Science Association, 1–4 September, in Washington, D.C.

Barnes, Samuel H.; Kaase, Max; et al. 1979. *Political action: mass participation in five Western democracies*. Beverly Hills: Sage Publications.

Barnet, Richard J. 1968. *Intervention and revolution: the United States in the Third World*. New York: World Publishing Co.

Baron, Robert A. 1971. "Aggression as a function of magnitude of victim's pain cues, level of prior anger arousal, and aggressor-victim similarity." *Journal of Personality and Social Psychology* 18, no. 1 (April):48–54.

Baron, Robert A. 1973. "Threatened retaliation from the victim as an inhibitor of physical aggression." *Journal of Research in Personality* 7:103–15.

Baron, Robert A. 1974a. "Aggression as a function of victim's pain cues, level of prior anger arousal, and exposure to an aggressive model." *Journal of Personality and Social Psychology* 29, no. 1 (January): 117–24.

Baron, Robert A. 1974b. "The aggression-inhibiting influence of heightened sexual arousal." *Journal of Personality and Social Psychology* 30, no. 3 (September):318–22.

Baron, Robert A. 1977. *Human aggression*. New York: Plenum.

Baron, Robert A., and Bell, Paul A. 1975. "Aggression and heat: mediating effects of prior provocation and exposure to an aggressive model." *Journal of Personality and Social Psychology* 33, no. 5 (May): 825–32.

Baron, Robert A., and Bell, Paul A. 1976. "Aggression and heat: the influence of ambient temperature, negative affect, and a cooling drink on physical aggression." *Journal of Personality and Social Psychology* 33, no. 3 (March):245–55.

Baron, Robert A., and Eggleston, Rebecca J. 1972. "Performance on the 'aggression machine': motivation to help or harm?" *Psychonomic Science* 26, no. 6:321–22.

Barrows, Walter L. 1976. "Ethnic diversity and political instability in Black Africa." *Comparative Political Studies* 9, no. 2 (July):139–70.

Barry, Brian. 1975. "Political accommodation and consociational democracy." *British Journal of Political Science* 5, no. 4 (October):477–505.

Barry, Brian. 1977a. "Review article: 'Crisis, choice, and change,' part I." *British Journal of Political Science* 7, no. 1 (January):99–113.

Barry, Brian. 1977b. "Review article: 'Crisis, choice, and change,' part II." *British Journal of Political Science* 7, no. 2 (April):217–53.

Baskin, Jane A.; Lewis, Ralph G.; Mannis, Joyce Hartweg; and McCullough, Lester W., Jr. 1972. "The long, hot summer? An analysis of summer disorders 1967–1971." Lemberg Center for the Study of Violence. Waltham, Mass.: Brandeis University.

Batatu, Hanna. 1978. *The old social classes and the revolutionary movements in Iraq: a study of Iraq's old landed and commercial classes and of its communists, Ba'thists, and free officers*. Princeton: Princeton University Press.

Bates, Robert H. 1974. "Ethnic competition and modernization in contemporary Africa." *Comparative Political Studies* 6, no. 4 (January): 457–84.

Baum, Andrew, and Epstein, Yakov M., eds. 1978. *Human responses to crowding*. Hillsdale, N.J.: Lawrence Erlbaum Associates.

Baum, R. C. 1974. "Beyond convergence: toward theoretical relevance in quantitative modernization research." *Sociological Inquiry* 44, no. 4:225–40.

Baum, Richard. 1975. *Prelude to revolution: Mao, the party, and the peasant revolution, 1962–1966*. New York: Columbia University Press.

Baum, Richard, with Bennett, Louise B., eds. 1971. *China in ferment: perspectives on the cultural revolution*. Englewood Cliffs: Prentice-Hall.

Baumann, Carol Edler. 1974. "The diplomatic kidnappings: an overview," in *International Terrorism*. Global Focus Series, no. 16. Institute of World Affairs. Milwaukee: University of Wisconsin.

Bay, Christian. 1958. *The structure of freedom*. Stanford: Stanford University Press.

Bay, Christian. 1968. "Civil disobedience," in *International Encyclopedia of the Social Sciences*, vol. 2, 473–87.

Bayley, David H. 1966. "The effects of corruption in a developing nation." *Western Political Quarterly* 19, no. 4 (December):719–32.

Bebler, Anton, ed. 1973. *Military rule in Africa: Dahomey, Ghana, Sierra Leone, and Mali*. New York: Praeger Publishers.

Becker, Howard S. 1963. *Outsiders: studies in the sociology of deviance*. London: Free Press of Glencoe.

Becker, Jillian. 1978. *Hitler's children? The story of the Baader-Meinhof gang*. London: Panther.

Becker, Robert A. 1980. *Revolution, reform, and the politics of American taxation, 1763–1783*. Baton Rouge: Louisiana State University Press.

Bedau, Hugo A. 1961. "On civil disobedience." *Journal of Philosophy* 58, no. 21 (October 12):653–65.

Be'eri, Eliezer. 1970. *Army officers in Arab politics and society*. London: Praeger/Pall Mall.

Bell, Daniel. 1976. *The cultural contradictions of capitalism*. London: Heinemann.

Bell, David V. J. 1973. *Resistance and revolution*. Boston: Houghton Mifflin Co.

Bell, J. Bowyer. 1971. *The myth of the guerrilla: revolutionary theory and malpractice*. New York: Alfred A. Knopf.

Bell, J. Bowyer. 1974. "The chroniclers of violence in Northern Ireland revisited: the analysis of tragedy." *Review of Politics* 36, no. 4 (October):521–43.

Bell, J. Bowyer. 1975. *Transnational terror*. Hoover Institution Studies, no. 53. Stanford University: Hoover Institute on War, Revolution, and Peace.

Bell, J. Bowyer. 1976. "Strategy, tactics, and terror: an Irish perspective," in Alexander, 65–89.

Bell, J. Bowyer. 1976a. *On revolt: strategies of national liberation*. Boston: Harvard University Press.

Bell, J. Bowyer. 1976b. "The chroniclers of violence in Northern Ireland: a tragedy in endless acts." *Review of Politics* 38, no. 4:510–33.

Bell, J. Bowyer. 1977. "Trends on terror: the analysis of political violence." *World Politics* 29, no. 3 (April):476–88.

Bell, J. Bowyer. 1978. *A time of terror: how democratic societies respond to revolutionary violence*. New York: Basic Books.

Bell, J. Bowyer, and Gurr, Ted Robert. 1979. "Terrorism and revolution in America," in Graham/Gurr, 329–47.

Bell, Paul A., and Baron, Robert A. 1976. "Aggression and heat: the mediating role of negative affect." *Journal of Applied Social Psychology* 6, no. 1 (January-March):18–30.

Bell, Wendell, and Freeman, Walter E., eds. 1974. *Ethnicity and nation-building: comparative, international and historical perspectives*. Beverly Hills: Sage Publications.

Beloff, Max. 1963. *Public order and popular disturbances, 1660–1714*. London: Frank Cass & Co.

Belson, William A. 1978. *Television violence and the adolescent boy*. Farnborough, Hampshire: Saxon House.

Bender, Karl-Heinz. 1977. *Revolutionen. Die Entstehung des politischen Revolutionsbegriffes in Frankreich zwischen Mittelalter und Aufklärung*. Munich: Wilhelm Fink Verlag.

Bendix, Reinhard. 1964. *Nation-building and citizenship: studies of our changing social order*. New York: John Wiley & Sons. New enlarged ed. 1977. Berkeley: University of California Press.

Bendix, Reinhard. 1966–67. "Tradition and modernity reconsidered." *Comparative Studies in Society and History* 9:292–346.

Bendix, Reinhard. 1967. "Review of Moore (1966)." *Political Science Quarterly* 82:625–27.

Ben-Dor, Gabriel. 1973. "The politics of threat: military intervention in the Middle East." *Journal of Political and Military Sociology* 1, no. 1 (Spring):57–69.

Ben-Dor, Gabriel. 1974. "Corruption, institutionalization, and political development: the revisionist theses revisited." *Comparative Political Studies* 7, no. 1 (April):63–83.

Ben-Dor, Gabriel. 1975. "Institutionalization and political development: a conceptual and theoretical analysis." *Comparative Studies in Society and History* 17, no. 3 (July):309–25.

Benjamin, Roger W., and Kautsky, John H. 1968. "Communism and economic development." *American Political Science Review* 62, no. 1 (March):110–23. Also in Gillespie/Nesvold, 353–72.

Benjamin, Walter. 1965. *Zur Kritik der Gewalt und andere Aufsätze*. Frankfort on the Main: Suhrkamp.

Bensman, Joseph. 1979. "Max Weber's concept of legitimacy: an evaluation," in Arthur J. Vidich and Ronald M. Glassman (eds.), *Conflict and control: challenge to legitimacy of modern governments*. Beverly Hills: Sage Publications, 17–48.

Benson, Lee. 1972. *Toward the scientific study of history*. Philadelphia: J. B. Lippincott.

Beres, Louis René. 1974. "Guerillas, terrorists, and polarity: new structural models of world politics." *Western Political Quarterly* 27, no. 4 (December):624–36.

Beres, Louis René. 1978. "The nuclear threat of terrorism." *International Studies Notes* 5, no. 1 (Spring):14–17.

Berger, Joseph; Zelditch, Morris, Jr.; Anderson, Bo; and Cohen, Bernard P. 1972. "Structural aspects of distributive justice: a status value formulation." in Joseph Berger, Morris Zelditch, Jr., and Bo Anderson, *Sociological theories in progress*. Boston: Houghton Mifflin Co., 119–46.

Bergère, Marie-Claire. 1968. "The role of the bourgeoisie," in Wright, 229–95.

Berghe, Pierre L. van den. 1965. "The role of the army in contemporary Africa." *Africa Report* 10 (March):12–17. Also in McWilliams (1967), 278–87.

Berghe, Pierre L. van den. 1967. *Race and racism: a comparative perspective*. New York: John Wiley & Sons.

Berghe, Pierre L. van den. 1974. "Bringing beasts back in: toward a biosocial theory of aggression." *American Sociological Review* 39, no. 6 (December):777–88.

Berghe, Pierre, van den. 1976. *South Africa: a study in conflict*. Berkeley: University of California Press.

Berk, Richard A. 1974. "A gaming approach to crowd behavior." *American Sociological Review* 39, no. 3 (June):355–73.

Berk, Richard A., and Aldrich, Howard E. 1972. "Patterns of vandalism during civil disorders as an indicator of selection of targets." *American Sociological Review* 37, no. 5 (October):533–47.

Berkhofer, Robert F., ed. 1971. *The American Revolution: the critical issues*. Boston: Little, Brown & Co.

Berkowitz, Leonard. 1958. "The expression and reduction of hostility." *Psychological Bulletin* 55:257–83.

Berkowitz, Leonard. 1962. *Aggression: a social psychological analysis*. New York: McGraw-Hill.

Berkowitz, L. 1964. "Aggressive cues in aggressive behavior and hostility catharsis." *Psychological Review* 71:104–22.

Berkowitz, Leonard, ed. 1965. *Advances in experimental social psychology*, vol. 2. New York: Academic Press.

Berkowitz, Leonard. 1965a. "The concept of aggressive drive: some additional considerations," in Berkowitz (1965), 301–29.

Berkowitz, L. 1968. "The study of urban violence: some implications of laboratory studies of frustration and aggression."*American Behavioral Scientist* 11, no. 4 (March/April):14–17.

Berkowitz, Leonard. 1969. "The frustration-aggression hypothesis revisited," in Berkowitz (1969a), 1–34.

Berkowitz, Leonard, ed. 1969a. *Roots of aggression: a reexamination of the frustration-aggression hypothesis.* New York: Atherton.

Berkowitz, Leonard. 1969b. "Social motivation," in Gardner Lindzey and Elliot Aronson (eds.), *Handbook of social psychology*, 2d ed., vol. 3. Reading, Mass.: Addison-Wesley, 50–135.

Berkowitz, L. 1970. "The contagion of violence: an S-R mediational analysis of some effects of observed aggression ," in William J. Arnold and Monte M. Page (eds.), *Nebraska symposium on motivation, 1970.* Lincoln: University of Nebraska Press, 95–135.

Berkowitz, Leonard. 1971. "The 'weapons effect,' demand characteristics, and the myth of the compliant subject." *Journal of Personality and Social Psychology* 20, no. 3 (December):332–38.

Berkowitz, Leonard. 1972. "Frustrations, comparisons, and other sources of emotional arousal as contributors to social unrest." *Journal of Social Issues* 28, no. 1:77–91.

Berkowitz, Leonard. 1973. "Control of aggression," in Bettye M. Caldwell and Henry N. Ricciuti (eds.), *Review of child development research*, vol. 3. Chicago: University of Chicago Press, 95–140.

Berkowitz, Leonard. 1974. "Some determinants of impulsive aggression: the role of mediated associations with reinforcements for aggression." *Psychological Review* 81, no. 2 (March):165–76.

Berkowitz, Leonard, and Alioto, Joseph T. 1973. "The meaning of an observed event as a determinant of its aggressive consequences." *Journal of Personality and Social Psychology* 28, no. 2 (November): 206–17.

Berkowitz, L., and Buck, R. W. 1967. "Impulsive aggression: reactivity to aggressive cues under emotional arousal." *Journal of Personality* 35: 415–24.

Berkowitz, L., and Geen, J. A. 1962. "The stimulus qualities of the scapegoat." *Journal of Abnormal and Social Psychology* 64:293–301.

Berkowitz, L., and Geen, R. G. 1967. "Stimulus qualities of the target of aggression: a further study." *Journal of Personality* 5:364–68.

Berkowitz, Leonard, and Knurek, Dennis A. 1969. "Label-mediated hostility generalization." *Journal of Personality and Social Psychology* 13, no. 3 (November):200–206.

Berkowitz, Leonard, and LePage, Anthony. 1967. "Weapons as aggression-eliciting stimuli." *Journal of Personality and Social Psychology* 7, no. 2: 202–7.

Berkowitz, Leonard, and Walster, Elaine, eds. 1976. *Equity theory: toward a general theory of social interaction. Advances in experimental social psychology*, vol. 9. New York: Academic Press.

Berkowitz, Leonard; Corwin, Ronald; and Heironimus, Mark. 1963. "Film violence and subsequent aggressive tendencies." *Public Opinion Quarterly* 27, no. 2 (Summer):217–29.

Berkowitz, William R. 1974a. "Socioeconomic indicator changes in ghetto riots tracts." *Urban Affairs Quarterly* 10, no. 1 (September):69–94.

Bernard, Leon. 1964. "French society and popular uprisings under Louis XIV." *French Historical Studies* 3, no. 4 (Fall):454–74.

Bernecker, Walther L. 1978. *Anarchismus and Bürgerkreig: Zur Geschichte der Sozialen Revolution in Spanien, 1936–1939*. Hamburg: Hoffmann und Campe Verlag.

Berry, Brian J. L. 1960. "An inductive approach to the regionalization of economic development," in Norton Ginsburg (ed.), *Essays on geography and economic development*. Chicago: University of Chicago Press, 78–107.

Berry, Brian J. L. 1961. "Basic patterns of economic development," in Norton Ginsburg, *Atlas of economic development*. Chicago: University of Chicago Press, 110–19.

Berthoff, Rowland, and Murrin, John M. 1973. "Feudalism, communalism, and the yeoman freeholder: the American Revolution considered as a social accident," in Kurtz/Hutson, 256–88.

Bertsch, Gary K.; Clark, Robert P.; and Wood, David M. 1978. *Comparing political systems: power and policy in three worlds*. New York: John Wiley & Sons.

Betz, Michael. 1974. "Riots and welfare: are they related?" *Social Problems* 21, no. 3:345–55.

Beyme, Klaus von. 1970. *Die parlamentarischen Regierungssysteme in Europa*. Munich: R. Piper.

Beyme, Klaus von. 1971. "Party systems and cabinet stability in European parliamentary systems," in Henry Steele Commager et al., (eds.), *Festschrift für Karl Loewenstein*. Tübingen: J. C. B. Mohr (Paul Siebeck), 51–70.

Beyme, Klaus von, ed. 1973. *Empirische Revolutionsforschung*. Opladen: Westdeutscher Verlag.

Bezucha, Robert J. 1974. *The Lyon uprising of 1834: social and political conflict in the early July monarchy*. Cambridge: Harvard University Press.

Bezucha, Robert J. 1975. "The revolution of 1830 and the city of Lyon," in Merriman, 119–38.

Bialer, Seweryn, and Sluzar, Sophia, eds. 1977. *Radicalism in the contemporary age*, vol. 1: *Sources of contemporary radicalism*. Boulder, Colorado: Westview Press.

Bianco, Lucien. 1971. *Origins of the Chinese revolution 1915–1949*. Stanford: Stanford University Press. (French original 1967.)

Bienen, Henry. 1968. *Violence and social change: a review of current literature*. Chicago: University of Chicago Press.

Bienen, Henry, ed. 1968a. *The military intervenes: case studies in political development*. New York: Russell Sage Foundation.

Bienen, Henry. 1968b. "Public order and the military in Africa: mutinies in Kenya, Uganda, and Tanganyika," in Bienen (1968a), 35–69.

Bienen, Henry. 1969. "Foreign policy, the military and development: military assistance and political change in Africa," in Richard Butwell (ed.), *Foreign policy and the developing nation*. Lexington: University of Kentucky Press, 67–111.

Bienen, Henry, ed. 1971. *The military and modernization*. Chicago and New York: Aldine/Atherton.

Bienen, Henry. 1971a. "The background to contemporary study of militaries and modernization," in Bienen (1971), 1–33.

Bienen, Henry. 1974. "Military and society in East Africa: thinking again about praetorianism." *Comparative Politics* 6, no. 4 (July):489–517.

Bienen, Henry. 1974a. *Kenya: the politics of participation and control.* Princeton: Princeton University Press.

Bienen, Henry. 1978. "Military rule and political process: Nigerian examples." *Comparative Politics* 10, no. 2 (January):205–25.

Bienen, Henry. 1978a. *Armies and parties in Africa.* New York: Africana Publishing Co.

Bienen, Henry, and Morell, David. 1974. "Transition from military rule: Thailand's experience," in Kelleher, 3–26.

Bienen, Henry, and Morell, David, eds. 1976. *Political participation under military regimes.* Sage Contemporary Social Science Issues, no. 26. Beverly Hills: Sage Publications.

Bigelow, Robert. 1972. "The evaluation of cooperation, aggression, and self-control," in James K. Cole and Donald D. Jensen (eds.), *Nebraska symposium on motivation.* Lincoln: University of Nebraska Press, 1–57.

Bill, James A. 1969. "The military and modernization in the middle East." *Comparative Politics* 2, no. 1 (October):41–62.

Bill, James A., and Hardgrave, Robert L., Jr. 1973. *Comparative politics: the quest for theory.* Columbus, Ohio: Merrill.

Bill, James A., and Leiden, Carl. 1979. *Politics in the Middle East.* Boston: Little, Brown & Co.

Billington, James H. 1966. "Six views of the Russian Revolution." *World Politics* 18, no. 3 (April):452–73.

Binder, Leonard. 1971. "Crises of political development," in Binder et al., 3–72.

Binder, Leonard; Coleman, James S.; LaPalombara, Joseph; Pye, Lucian W.; Verba, Sidney; and Weiner, Myron. 1971. *Crises and sequences in political development.* Princeton: Princeton University Press.

Birch, A. H. 1975. "Economic models in political science: the case of 'Exit, voice, and loyalty.'" *British Journal of Political Science* 5, no. 1 (January):69–82.

Birrell, Derek. 1972. "Relative deprivation as a factor in conflict in Northern Ireland." *Sociological Review* 20, no. 3 (August):317–43.

Black, Cyril E. 1966. *Dynamics of modernization: a study in comparative history.* New York: Harper & Row.

Black, C. E. 1967. "Review of Moore (1966)." *American Historical Review* 72:1338.

Black, Cyril E. 1972. "Military leadership and national development," in David McIsaac (ed.), *The military and society: proceedings of the Fifth Military History Symposium, USAF Academy.* Washington, D.C.: U.S. Government Printing Office, 16–35.

Black, Cyril Edwin, and Thornton, Thomas P., eds. 1964. *Communism and revolution: the strategic uses of political violence.* Princeton: Princeton University Press.

Blackey, Robert. 1974. "Fanon and Cabral: a contrast in theories of revolution for Africa." *Journal of Modern African Studies* 12, no. 2:191–209.

Blackey, Robert, and Paynton, Clifford T., eds. 1971. *Why revolution?*

Theories and analyses. Cambridge, Mass.: Schenkman Publishing Co.

Blackey, Robert, and Paynton, Clifford. 1976. *Revolution and the revolutionary ideal*. Cambridge, Mass.: Schenkman Publishing Co.

Blainey, Geoffrey. 1973. *The causes of war*. London: Macmillan.

Blalock, Hubert M. 1966. "The identification problem and theory building: the case of status inconsistency." *American Sociological Review* 31, no. 1 (February):52–61.

Blalock, H. M., Jr., ed. 1971. *Causal models in the social sciences*. London: Aldine-Atherton.

Blalock, H. M., Jr., ed. 1974. *Measurement in the social sciences: theories and strategies*. Chicago: Aldine Publishing Co.

Blalock, Hubert M., and Wilken, Paul H. 1979. *Intergroup processes: a micro-macro perspective*. New York: Free Press.

Blanksten, George. 1962. "Latin American revolutions," in *The 1962 Carolina Symposium: today's revolutions*. Chapel Hill: University of North Carolina Press, 71–79.

Blasco, Pedro Gonzalez. 1974. "Modern nationalism in old nations as a consequence of earlier state-building: the case of Basque-Spain," in Bell/Freeman, 341–71.

Blasier, Cole. 1967. "Studies of social revolution: origins in Mexico, Bolivia, and Cuba." *Latin American Research Review* 2, no. 3 (Summer):28–64.

Blau, Peter. 1964. *Exchange and power in social life*. New York: Wiley.

Blaufarb, Douglas. 1977. *The counter-insurgency era: U. S. doctrine and performance, 1950 to the present*. New York: Free Press.

Blauner, Robert. 1966. "Whitewash over Watts: the failure of the McCone Commission report." *Trans-Action* 3, no. 3: 3–9.

Blauner, Robert. 1969. "Internal colonialism and ghetto revolt." *Social Problems* 16, no. 4 (Spring):393–408.

Blauner, Robert. 1972. *Racial oppression in America*. New York: Harper & Row.

Bleiber, Helmut. 1966. *Zwischen Reform und Revolution: Lage und Kämpfe der schlesischen Bauern und Landarbeiter im Vormärz 1840–1847*. Berlin (East): Akademie-Verlag.

Bleiber, Helmut. 1969. "Bauern und Landarbeiter in der bürgerlich-demokratischen Revolution von 1848/49 in Deutschland." *Zeitschrift für Geschichtswissenschaft* 17, no. 3:189–309.

Blickle, Peter. 1975. *Die Revolution von 1525*. Munich: R. Oldenbourg Verlag.

Blickle, Peter, ed. 1975a. *Revolte und Revolution in Europa*. Munich: R. Oldenbourg Verlag.

Blickle, Peter. 1979. "Peasant revolts in the German empire in the late middle ages." *Social History* 4, no. 2 (May):223–39.

Blok, Anton. 1969. "Mafia and peasant rebellion as contrasting factors in Sicilian latifundism." *Archives Européennes de Sociologie* 10, no. 1:95–116.

Blok, Anton. 1972. "The peasant and the brigand: social banditry reconsidered." *Comparative Studies in Society and History* 14, no. 4 (September):494–503.

Blok, Anton. 1972a. "On brigandage with special reference to peasant mobilization." *Sociologia Neerlandica* 8, no. 1:1–13.

Blok, Anton. 1974. *The mafia of a Sicilian village 1860-1960: a study of violent entrepreneurs* (foreword by Charles Tilly). Oxford: Basil Blackwell.

Blom, Hans W. 1973. "Re-testing violence: a case study in theory-model interdependence." Rotterdam: Nederlandse Economische Hogeschool. Mimeographed.

Blondel, J. 1968. "Party systems and patterns of government in Western democracies." *Canadian Journal of Political Science* 1, no. 2 (June): 180-203.

Bloombaum, Milton. 1968. "The conditions underlying race riots as portrayed by multidimensional scalogram analysis: a re-analysis of Lieberson and Silverman's data." *American Sociological Review* 33, no. 1 (February):76-91.

Blumenthal, Monica D. 1972. "Predicting attitudes toward violence." *Science* 176 (June 23):1296-1303.

Blumental, Monica D. et al. 1972. *Justifying violence: attitudes of American men.* Ann Arbor: Institute for Social Research.

Blumenthal, Monica, D.; Chadiha, Letha B.; Cole, Gerald A.; Jayaratne, Toby Epstein. 1975. *More about justifying violence: methodological studies of attitudes and behavior.* Ann Arbor: Survey Research Center— Institute for Social Research.

Blumer, Herbert. 1965. "The justice of the crowd." *Trans-Action* 2, no. 6 (September/October):43-44.

Boe, Erling E. and Church, Russell M., eds. 1968. *Punishment: issues and experiments.* New York: Appleton-Century-Crofts.

Bogart, Leo. 1972-73. "Warning: the Surgeon General has determined that TV violence is moderately dangerous to your child's mental health." *Public Opinion Quarterly* 36, no. 4 (Winter):491-521.

Bohrnstedt, George W., and Carter, T. Michael. 1971. "Robustness in regression analysis," in Costner, 118-46.

Boice, Robert. 1976. "In the shadow of Darwin," in Geen/O'Neal, 11-35.

Bois, Paul. 1960. *Paysans de l'ouest: des structures économiques et sociales aux options politiques depuis l'époque révolutionnaire dans la Sarthe.* Le Mans: M. Vilaire.

Bollen, Kenneth A. 1979. "Political democracy and the timing of development." *American Sociological Review* 44, no. 4 (August):572-87.

Bollen, Kenneth A. 1980. "Issues in the comparative measurement of political democracy." *American Sociological Review* 45, no. 3 (June): 370-90.

Bonachea, Ramón L. and San Martín, Marta. 1974. *The Cuban insurrection, 1952-1959.* New Brunswick, N.J.: Transaction Books.

Bondurant, Joan V. 1965. *Conquest of violence: the Gandhian philosophy of conflict.* rev. ed. Berkeley: University of California Press.

Bondurant, Joan V., ed. 1971. *Conflict, violence and nonviolence.* Chicago and New York: Aldine/Atherton.

Booth, Alan, ed. 1975. "Human crowding." *Sociological Symposium* 14 (Fall).

Booth, Alan. 1976. *Urban crowding and its consequences.* New York: Praeger Publishers.

Booth, Alan. 1977. "Food riots in the North-West of England 1790-1801." *Past and Present* 77 (November):84-107.

Booth, John A. 1974. "Rural violence in Columbia: 1948–1963." *Western Political Quarterly* 27, no. 4 (December):657–79.

Borcke, Astrid von. 1977. *Die Ursprünge des Bolschewismus: Die jakobinische Tradition in Rußland und die Theorie der revolutionären Diktatur*. Munich: Johannes Berchmans Verlag.

Borgatta, Edgar F., ed. 1969. *Sociological methodology 1969*. San Francisco: Jossey-Bass.

Bornschier, Volker; Chase-Dunn, Christopher; and Rubinson, Richard. 1978. "Cross-national evidence of the effects of foreign investment and aid on economic growth and inequality: a survey of findings and a reanalysis." *American Journal of Sociology* 84, no. 3 (November):651–83.

Borock, D. M. 1967. "Universal and regional dimensions of domestic conflict behavior." Ph.D. dissertation, University of Cincinnati.

Botz, Gerhard. 1976. *Gewalt in der Politik: Attentate, Zusammenstöße, Putschversuche, Unruhen in Österreich 1918–1937*. Munich: Wilhelm Fink Verlag.

Boudon, Raymond. 1965. "A method of linear causal analysis: dependence analysis." *American Sociological Review* 30, no. 3 (June):365–74.

Bowen, Don R.; Bowen, Elinor R.; Gawiser, Sheldon R.; and Masotti, Louis H. 1968. "Deprivation, mobility, and orientation toward protest of the urban poor." *American Behavioral Scientist* 11, no. 4:20–24.

Bowles, Samuel, and Levin, Henry M. 1968. "The determinants of scholastic achievement—an appraisal of some recent evidence." *Journal of Human Resources* 3, no. 3:3–24.

Bozeman, Adda B. 1976. *Conflict in Africa: concepts and realities*. Princeton: Princeton University Press.

Bracher, Karl Dietrich. 1976a. *Die Krise Europas 1917–1975*. Propyläen–Geschichte Europas, vol. 6. Berlin: Propyläen Verlag.

Bracher, Karl Dietrich. 1976b. *Zeitgeschichtliche Kontroversen: Um Faschismus, Totalitarismus, Demokratie*. Munich: R. Piper.

Bracher, Karl Dietrich. 1976c. "Tradition und Revolution im National-sozialismus." *Frankfurter Allgemeine Zeitung*, no. 26 (January 31). Supplement: "Ereignisse und Gestalten."

Brailsford, H. N. 1961. *The levellers and the English Revolution*. London: Cresset Press.

Brams, Steven J. 1973. "Positive coalition theory: the relationship between postulated goals and derived behavior," in Cornelius P. Cotter (ed.), *Political Science Annual* 4:3–40.

Brams, Steven J. 1975. *Game theory and politics*. New York: Free Press.

Brass, Paul R. 1977. "Party systems and government stability in the Indian states." *American Political Science Review* 71, no. 4 (December): 1384–1405.

Brenan, Gerald. 1969. *The Spanish labyrinth: an account of the social and political background of the civil war*, 2d ed. Cambridge: Cambridge University Press.

Brewer, Marilyn B.; Campbell, Donald T.; and Crano, William D. 1970. "Testing a single-factor model as an alternative to the misuse of partial correlations in hypothesis-testing research." *Sociometry* 33, no. 1 (March):1–11.

Brickman, Philip. 1974. *Social conflict: readings in rule structures and conflict relationships*. Lexington, Mass.: D. C. Heath & Co.

Brier, Alan, and Calvert, Peter. 1975. "Revolution in the 1960s." *Government and Opposition* 23, no. 1 (March):1–11.

Brimmer, Andrew F. 1974. "Economic developments in the black community." *Public Interest* 34:146–63.

Brink, William, and Harris, Louis. 1964. *The negro revolution in America.* New York: Simon & Schuster.

Brink, William, and Harris, Louis. 1966. *Black and white: a study of U. S. racial attitudes today.* New York: Simon & Schuster.

Brinton, Crane. 1952. *The anatomy of revolution.* New York: Prentice-Hall. Rev. and expanded ed. New York: Vintage Books, 1965.

Brockway, Fenner. 1973. *The colonial revolution.* London: Hart-Davis, MacGibbon.

Brogan, D. W. 1951. *The price of revolution.* New York: Harper & Row Brothers.

Broué, Pierre, and Témime, Émile. 1961. *La révolution et la guerre d'Espagne.* Paris: Les Éditions de Minuit.

Brown, Bernard E. 1974. *Protest in Paris: anatomy of a revolt.* Morristown, N.J.: General Learning Press.

Brown, Don W. 1978. "Arrest rates and crime rates: when does a tipping effect occur?" *Social Forces* 72, no. 2 (December):671–82.

Brown, Judson S., and Farber, I. E. 1951. "Emotions conceptualized as intervening variables—with suggestions toward a theory of frustration." *Psychological Bulletin* 48, no. 6 (November):465–95.

Brown, Richard Maxwell. 1969. "Historical patterns of violence in America," in Graham/Gurr, 45–84.

Brown, Richard Maxwell. 1975. *Strain of violence: historical studies of American violence and vigilantism.* New York: Oxford University Press.

Brown, Robert E. 1955. *Middle-class democracy and the revolution in Massachusetts, 1691–1780.* Ithaca, N.Y.: Cornell University Press.

Browne, Eric C. 1973. *Coalition theories: a logical and empirical critique.* Sage Professional Papers in Comparative Politics Series, no. 01–043.

Brugger, Bill, ed. 1978. *China: the impact of the Cultural Revolution.* London: Croom Helm.

Brunner, Ronald D., and Brewer, Garry D. 1971. *Organized complexity: empirical theories of political development.* New York: Free Press.

Brunswik, E. 1949. *Systematic and representative design of psychological experiments.* Berkeley: University of California Press.

Brzezinski, Zbigniew. 1968. "Revolution and counterrevolution (but not necessarily about Columbia!)." *The New Republic*:23–25. Also in Harvey A. Hornstein et al. (eds.), *Social intervention: a behavioral science approach.* New York: Free Press (1971), 502–6.

Budge, Ian, and O'Leary, Cornelius. 1973. *Belfast: approach to crisis: a study of Belfast politics, 1613–1970.* London: Macmillan/St. Martin's Press.

Bühl, Walter L. 1970. *Evolution und Revolution: Kritik der symmetrischen Soziologie.* Munich: Wilhelm Goldmann Verlag.

Bullough, Bonnie. 1967. "Alienation in the ghetto." *American Journal of Sociology* 72, no. 5 (March):469–78.

Burbeck, Stephen L.; Raine, Walter J.; and Stark, M. J. Abudu. 1978. "The dynamics of riot growth: an epidemiological approach." *Journal of Mathematical Sociology* 6, no. 1:1–22.

Burckhardt, Jacob. [1905]. *Weltgeschichtliche Betrachtungen*. Berlin: Ullstein.

Burgess, Philip M., and Lawton, Raymond W. 1972. *Indicators of international behavior: an assessment of events data research*. Sage Professional Papers in International Studies, 1st series, no. 02–010.

Burgess, Robert L., and Nielsen, Joyce McCarl. 1974. "An experimental analysis of some structural determinants of equitable and inequitable exchange relations." *American Sociological Review* 39, no. 3 (June): 427–43.

Burke, Edmund. 1790. *Reflections on the revolution in France*. London: J. Dodsley.

Burnstein, Eugene, and Worchel, Philip. 1962. "Arbitrariness of frustration and its consequences for aggression in a social situation." *Journal of Personality* 30:528–41. Also in Berkowitz (1969a), 75–91.

Burrowes, Robert. 1970. "Multiple time-series analysis of nation-level data." *Comparative Political Studies* 2, no. 4 (January):465–80.

Burrowes, Robert. 1972. "Theory si, data no! A decade of cross-national political research." *World Politics* 25, no. 1 (October):120–44.

Burrowes, Robert. 1974. "Mirror, mirror, on the wall . . .: a comparison of event data sources," in Rosenau, 383–406.

Burrowes, R., and Spector, B. 1970. "Conflict and cooperation within and among nations: enumerative profiles of Syria, Jordan, and the United Arab Republic, January 1965 to May 1967." Presented at the meetings of the International Studies Association. Mimeographed.

Burrowes, Robert, and Spector, Douglas Muzio. 1971. "Sources of Middle East international event data." *Middle East Studies Association Bulletin* 5:54–71.

Burrowes, Robert, and Spector, Bertram. 1973. "The strength and direction of relationships between domestic and external conflict and cooperation: Syria, 1961–67," in Wilkenfeld, 294–321.

Buss, Arnold H. 1961. *A psychology of aggression*. New York: Wiley.

Buss, Arnold H. 1964. "Physical aggression in relation to different frustrations." *Journal of Abnormal and Social Psychology* 67:1–7. Also in Berkowitz (1969a), 61–74.

Buss, Arnold H. 1966. "Instrumentality of aggression, feedback, and frustration as determinants of physical aggression." *Journal of Personality and Social Psychology* 3, no. 2:153–62.

Buss, Arnold H. 1971. "Aggression pays," in J. L. Singer, 7–18.

Buss, Arnold; Booker, Ann; and Buss, Edith. 1972. "Firing a weapon and aggression." *Journal of Personality and Social Psychology* 22, no. 3 (June):296–302.

Büttner, Friedrich; Lindenberg, Klaus; Reuke, Ludger; Sielaff, Rüdiger. 1976. *Reform in Uniform? Militärherrschaft und Entwicklung in der Dritten Welt*. Schriftenreihe des Forschungsinstituts der Friedrich-Ebert-Stiftung, vol. 127. Bonn and Bad Godesberg: Verlag Neue Gesellschaft.

Button, James W. 1978. *Black violence: political impact of the 1960s riots*. Princeton: Princeton University Press.

Bwy, Douglas. 1966. "Social conflict: a keyword-in-context bibliography on the literature of developing areas, with supplementary references from Latin America." Evanston: Northwestern University.

Bwy, Douglas. 1968a. "Dimensions of social conflict in Latin America." *American Behavioral Scientist* 11, no. 4 (March/April):39–50.

Bwy, Douglas P. 1968b. "Political instability in Latin America: the cross-cultural test of a causal model." *Latin American Research Review* 3, no. 2 (Spring):17–66. Abridged in Gillespie/Nesvold (1971), 113–39; Feierabend/Feierabend/Gurr (1972), 223–41.

Cain, Maureen, E. 1968. "Some suggested developments for role and reference group analysis." *British Journal of Sociology* 19:191–205.

Calhoun, Daniel. 1970. "Studying American violence." *Journal of Interdisciplinary History* 1:163–85.

Calhoun, John B. 1972. "Population density and social pathology." *Scientific American* 206:139–48.

Callies, Jörg. 1976. *Militär in der Krise. Die bayrische Armee in der Revolution 1848/49*. Boppard/Rhein: Harald Boldt Verlag.

Calvert, P. A. R. 1967. "Revolution: the politics of violence." *Political Studies* 15, no. 1 (February):1–11.

Calvert, Peter. 1969. *Latin America: internal conflict and international peace*. London: Macmillan.

Calvert, Peter. 1970. *A study of revolution*. Oxford: Clarendon Press.

Calvert, Peter. 1970a. *Revolution*. London: Pall Mall Press.

Calvert, Peter. 1979. "Social conflict and revoutionary change." Presented to the Workshop on Social Conflict of the European Consortium for Political Research. Brussels. Mimeographed.

Cameron, David R. 1974. "Toward a theory of political mobilization." *Journal of Politics* 36 (February):138–71.

Campbell, Angus, and Schuman, Howard. 1968. "Racial attitudes in fifteen American cities," in *Supplemental Studies for the National Advisory Commission on Civil Disorders*. Washington, D.C.: U. S. Government Printing Office, 1–67.

Campbell, Arthur. 1967. *Guerrillas: a history and analysis*. London: Arthur Barker.

Campbell, Donald T., and Fiske, Donald W. 1959. "Convergent and discriminant validation by the multi-trait-multi-method matrix." *Psychological Bulletin* 56:81–105. Abridged in Fishbein (1967), 282–89.

Campbell, John P., and Pritchard, Robert D. 1976. "Motivation theory in industrial and organizational psychology," in Marvin D. Dunnette (ed.), *Handbook of industrial and organizational psychology*. Chicago: Rand McNally, 63–130.

Camus, Albert. 1949. *L'homme révolté*. Paris: Librairie Gallimard.

Cantón, D. 1969. "Military interventions in Argentina: 1900–1966," in Jacques van Doorn (ed.), *Military profession and military regimes: commitments and conflicts*. The Hague: Mouton, 241–68.

Cantril, Hadley. 1965. *The patterns of human concerns*. New Brunswick: Rutgers University Press.

Caplan, Nathan. 1970. "The new ghetto man: a review of recent empirical studies." *Journal of Social Issues* 26, no. 1:59–73.

Caplan, Nathan. 1971. "Identity in transition: a theory of black militancy," in Aya/Miller, 143–65.

Caplan, Nathan, and Paige, J. M. 1968a. "Survey of Detroit and Newark riots participants," in *Report of the National Advisory Commission on Civil Disorders*. New York: Bantam Books, 127–37.

Caplan, N. S., and Paige, J. M. 1968b. "A study of ghetto rioters." *Scientific American* 219, no. 2 (August):15–21.

Caplovitz, David. 1963. *The poor pay more: consumer practices of low-income families*. New York: Free Press.

Capp, B. S. 1972. *The Fifth Monarchy men: a study in seventeenth-century English millenarianism*. London: Faber & Faber.

Carlton, David, and Schaerf, Carlo, eds. 1975. *International terrorism and world security*. London: Croom Helm.

Carnahan, Douglas L.; Guest, Avery M.; and Galle, Omer R. 1974. "Congestion, concentration and behavior: research in the study of urban population density." *Sociological Quarterly* 15, no. 4 (Autumn):488–506.

Carr, Edward Hallett. 1950–53. *The bolshevik revolution, 1917–1923*. 3 vols. London: Macmillan & Co. Repr. 1966.

Carr, E. H. 1950–69. *A history of Soviet Russia*. 9 vols. London: Macmillan.

Carr, Edward Hallett. 1961. *What is history?* London: Macmillan & Co.

Carr, Edward Hallett. 1962. *Studies in revolution*. London: Frank Cass & Co.

Carthy, J. D., and Ebling, F. J., eds. 1964. *The natural history of aggression*. New York: Academic Press.

Castles, Francis D. 1973. "Barrington Moore's thesis and Swedish political development." *Government and Opposition* 8, no. 3 (Summer):313–31.

Cataldo, Everett F.; Johnson, Richard M.; and Kellstadt, Lyman A. 1968. "Social strain and urban violence," in Masotti/Bowen, 285–98.

Cater, Douglass, and Brickland, Stephen. 1975. *TV violence and the child: the evolution and fate of the surgeon general's report*. New York: Russell Sage Foundation.

Cavanaugh, Gerald J. 1972. "The present state of French revolutionary historiography: Alfred Cobban and beyond." *French Historical Studies* 7, no. 4 (Fall):587–606.

Chadwick, Richard W., and Firestone, Joseph M. 1972. "Intrastate sociopolitical and empirical conflict models: a selective review and appraisal." Research Paper no. 20. Center for Comparative Political Research. Binghampton: State University of New York.

Chadwick-Jones, J. K. 1976. *Social exchange theory: its structure and influence in social psychology*. London: Academic Press.

Chamberlin, William Henry. 1952. *The Russian Revolution, 1917–1921*, 2 vols. New York: Macmillan. (Original 1935.)

Chan, F. Gilbert, and Etzold, Thomas H. eds. 1976. *China in the 1920s: nationalism and revolution*. New York: New Viewpoints.

Chandler, David B. 1973. "Towards a classification of violence." *Sociological Symposium* 9 (Spring):69–83.

Chaplin, David, ed. 1973. *Peruvian nationalism: a corporatist revolution?* New Brunswick: Transaction Books.

Chase-Dunn, Christopher. 1975. "The effects of international economic dependence on development and inequality: a cross-national study." *American Sociological Review* 40, no. 6 (December):720–38.

Chenery, H. and Syrquin, M. 1975. *Patterns of development 1950–1970*. Oxford: Oxford University Press.

Cheng, Ronald Ye-lin. 1973. *The first revolution in China: a theory*. New York: Vantage Press.

Cheng, Ronald Ye-lin. 1979. "The effect of revolutionary values, beliefs, and social structures on revolutionary mobilization and success." *Sociological Inquiry* 49, nos. 2-3:168–90.

Cherry, F.; Mitchell, H. E.; and Nelson, D. A. 1973. "Helping or hurting? The aggression paradigm." Paper presented at the American Psychological Association Convention.

Chesneaux, Jean. 1973. *Peasant revolts in China 1840–1949*. London: Thames & Hudson.

Chesneaux, Jean; Bastid, Marianne; and Bergère, Marie-Claire. 1976. *China from the opium wars to the 1911 revolution*. New York: Pantheon Asia Library.

Chesneaux, Jean; Le Barbier, Françoise; and Bergère, Marie-Claire. 1977. *China from the 1911 révolution to liberation*. London: Harvester Press.

Chevalier, Louis. 1973. *Laboring classes and dangerous classes*. New York. French original: *Classes laborieuses et classes dangereuses à Paris pendant la première moitié du XIXe siècle*. Paris: Librairie Plon (1958).

Chilcote, Ronald H. 1974. "Dependency: a critical synthesis of the literature." *Latin American Perspectives* 1, no. 1:4–29.

Chirot, Daniel, and Ragin, Charles. 1975. "The market, tradition and peasant rebellion: the case of Romania in 1907." *American Sociological Review* 40, no. 4 (August):428–44.

Chittick, William O., and Jenkins, Jerry B. 1976. "Reconceptualizing the sources of foreign policy behavior," in James N. Rosenau (ed.), *In search of global patterns*. New York: Free Press, 281–91.

Chodak, Szymon. 1977. "Review of 'Paige: Agrarian revolution: social movements and export agriculture in the underdeveloped world' (1975)." *Sociology and Social Research* 61, no. 3 (April):412–16.

Chorley, Katherine. 1943. *Armies and the art of revolution*. London: Faber & Faber. New ed. Boston: Beacon Press (1973).

Choucri, Nazli. 1974. *Population dynamics and international violence: propositions, insights, and evidence*. Lexington, Mass.: D. C. Heath.

Church, C. H. 1977. "Forgotten revolutions: recent work on the revolutions of 1830 in Europe." *European Studies Review* 7:95–106.

Citrin, Jack. 1974. "Comment: The political relevance of trust in government." *American Political Science Review* 68, no. 3 (September):973–88.

Citrin, Jack. 1977. "Political alienation as a social indicator: attitudes and action." *Social Indicators Research* 4:381–419.

Citrin, Jack, and Elkins, David J. 1975. "Political disaffection among British university students: concepts, measurement, and causes." Institute of International Studies, Research Series, no. 23. Berkeley: University of California.

Citrin, Jack; McClosky, Herbert; Shanks, J. Merrill; and Sniderman, Paul M. 1975. "Personal and political alienation." *British Journal of Political Science* 5, no. 1 (January):1–31.

Clark, Terry N. 1972. "Structural-functionalism, exchange theory, and the new political economy: institutionalization as a theoretical linkage." *Sociological Inquiry* 42, nos. 3-4:275–98.

Clausewitz, Carl von. 1966. *Schriften–Aufsätze–Studien–Briefe*, vol. 1. Edited by Werner Hahlweg. Göttingen: Vandenhoeck & Ruprecht.

Clinard, Marshall B. 1974. *Sociology of deviant behavior*. 4th ed. New York: Holt, Rinehart & Winston.

Cline, Howard F. 1962. *Mexico: revolution to evolution, 1940-1960*. London: Oxford University Press.

Clutterbuck, Richard. 1978. "Northern Ireland: is there a way?" *Washington Review of Strategic and International Studies* 1, no. 2 (April):52–64.

Cnudde, Charles F. 1972. "Theories of political development and the assumptions of statistical models." *Comparative Political Studies* 5, no. 2 (July):131–50.

Cnudde, Charles F., and Neubauer, Deane E., eds. 1969. *Empirical democratic theory*. Chicago: Markham.

Cobb, Richard. 1957. "The revolutionary mentality in France, 1793-94." *History* 42, no. 146 (October):181–96.

Cobb, Richard. 1959. "The people in the French Revolution." *Past and Present* 15 (April):60–72.

Cobb, Richard. 1961, 1963. *Les armées révolutionnaires: instrument de la terreur dans les départements, Avril 1793–Floréal an II*. 2 vols. Paris: Mouton & Co.

Cobb, Richard. 1965. *Terreur et subsistances 1793-1795*. Paris: Librairie Clavreuil.

Cobb, Richard. 1967. "The police, the repressive authorities and the beginning of the revolutionary crisis in Paris." *Welsh History Review* 3, no. 4:427–40.

Cobb, R. D. 1970. *The police and the people. French popular protest 1789-1820*. Oxford: Oxford University Press.

Cobban, Alfred. 1964. *The social interpretation of the French Revolution*. Reprint. Cambridge: At the University Press, 1971.

Cobban, Alfred. 1971a. *Aspects of the French Revolution*. Frogmore, St. Albans: Paladin (Original 1968).

Cochran, Charles L., ed. 1974. *Civil-military relations: changing concepts in the seventies*. New York: Free Press.

Cohan, A. S 1975. *Theories of revolution: an introduction*. New York: John Wiley & Sons.

Cohan, Alvin S., and McKinlay, Robert. 1974. "Revolution, coups, and system change." Paper presented to the Annual Meeting of the American Political Science Association. August/September, in Chicago.

Cohen, Jere, and Till, Amnon. 1977. "Another look at modernity scales: reanalysis of the convergent and discriminant validities of the Armer, Kahl, Smith and Inkeles, and Schnaiberg scales." *American Sociological Review* 42, no. 2 (April):373–78.

Cohen, Nathan, ed. 1970. *The Los Angeles riots: a socio-psychological study*. New York: Praeger Publishers.

Cohen, Ronald L. 1979. "On the distinction between individual deserving and distributive justice." *Journal for the Theory of Social Behaviour* 9, no. 2 (July):167–85.

Cohn, Norman. 1970. *The pursuit of the millenium: revolutionary millenarians and mystical anarchists of the middle ages*. London: Temple Smith.

Colby, David. 1975. "The effects of riots on public policy: exploratory note." *International Journal of Group Tensions* 5, no. 3 (September):156–62.

Cole, Richard L. 1974. *Citizen participation and the urban policy process*. Lexington, Mass.: D. C. Heath & Co.

Coleman, James S., ed. 1965. *Education and political development.* Princeton: Princeton University Press.

Coleman, James S. 1971. "The development syndrome: differentiation-equality-capacity," in Binder et al., 73–100.

Coleman, James S. 1974. "Review essay: inequality, sociology, and moral philosophy." *American Journal of Sociology* 80, no. 3 (November): 739–64.

Coleman, James et al. 1966. *Equality of educational opportunity.* Washington, D.C.: U. S. Government Printing Office.

Coleman, Kenneth M., and Davis, Charles L. 1976. "The structural context of politics and dimensions of regime performance: their importance for the comparative study of political efficacy." *Comparative Political Studies* 9, no. 2 (July):189–206.

Coleman, William, and Easton, David. 1976. "The concept of support for the political community reconsidered." Presented to the Conference on Political Alienation and Support, 27–30 May, Stanford. Center for Advanced Study in the Behavioral Sciences. Mimeographed.

Collier, David. 1978a. "Industrial modernization and political change: a Latin American perspective." *World Politics* 30, no. 4 (July):593–614.

Collier, Ruth Berins. 1978. "Parties, coups, and authoritarian rule: patterns of political change in Tropical Africa." *Comparative Political Studies* 11, no. 1 (April):62–93.

Collins, Barry E. 1974. "Four components of the Rotter internal-external scale: belief in a difficult world, a just world, a predictable world, and a politically responsive world." *Journal of Personality and Social Psychology* 29, no. 3 (May):381–91.

Collins, John N. 1973. "Foreign conflict behavior and domestic disorder in Africa," in Wilkenfeld, 251–93.

Colton, Timothy J. 1979. *Commissars, commanders, and civilian authority: the structure of Soviet military politics.* Cambridge, Mass.: Harvard University Press.

Comstock, George A. 1975. *Effects of television on children: what is the evidence?* Santa Monica, Calif.: Rand Corporation.

Comstock, G. et al. 1975. *Television and human behavior: the key studies.* Santa Monica, Calif.: Rand Corporation.

Conant, Ralph W. 1968. "Rioting, insurrection and civil disobedience." *American Scholar* 37, no. 3 (Summer):420–33.

Conant, Ralph W., and Levin, Molly Apple, eds. 1969. *Problems in research on community violence.* New York: Praeger.

Condit, D. M. et al. 1963. *A counterinsurgency bibliography.* Washington, D.C.: Special Operations Research Office, The American University.

Confino, Michael. 1973. *Violence dans la violence: le débat bakounine-nečaev.* Paris: François Maspero.

Conn, Paul. 1971. *Conflict and decision making: an introduction to political science.* New York: Harper & Row.

Connery, R. H., ed. 1969. *Urban riots: violence and social change.* New York: Vintage Books.

Connor, Walker. 1972. "Nation-building or nation-destroying?" *World Politics* 24, no. 3 (April):319–55.

Connor, Walker. 1973. "The politics of ethnonationalism." *Journal of International Affairs* 27, no. 1:1–21.

Connor, Walker. 1976. "Ethnonationalism in the first world: the present in historical perspective," in Esman, 19–45.

Connor, Walker. 1978. "A nation is a nation, is a state, is an ethnic group is a . . ." *Ethnic and Racial Studies* 1, no. 1 (October):377–400.

Conot, Robert. 1967. *Rivers of blood, years of darkness.* New York: Bantam Books.

Conover, Patrick W. 1976. "A reassessment of labeling theory: a constructive response to criticism," in Coser/Larsen, 228–43.

Conradt, David P. 1980. "Changing German political culture," in Almond/Verba, 212–72.

Converse, Philip E. 1964. "The nature of belief systems in mass publics," in David Apter (ed.), *Ideology and discontent.* New York: Free Press, 206–61.

Cook, Karen S. 1975. "Expectations, evaluations and equity." *American Sociological Review* 40, no. 3 (June):372–88.

Cook, Karen S., and Parcel, Toby L. 1977. "Equity theory: directions for future research." *Sociological Inquiry* 47, no. 2:75–88.

Cook, Samuel Dubois. 1972. "Coercion and social change," in Pennock/Chapman, 107–43.

Cook, Thomas D.; Crosby, Faye; and Hennigan, Karen M. 1977. "The construct validity of relative deprivation," in Suls/Miller, 307–33.

Cook, Thomas J. 1970. "Benign neglect: minimum feasible understanding." *Social Problems* 18, no. 2 (Fall):145–52.

Cooper, Mark N. 1974. "A reinterpretation of the causes of turmoil: the effects of culture and modernity." *Comparative Political Studies* 7, no. 3 (October):267–91.

Copson, Raymond W. 1973. "Foreign policy conflict among African states, 1964–1969," in Patrick J. McGowan (ed.), *Sage International Yearbook of Foreign Policy Studies* 1:189–217.

Corbett, Charles D. 1973. "Politics and professionalism: the South American military." *Orbis* 16 (Winter):927–51.

Cornelius, Wayne A., Jr. 1969. "Urbanization as an agent in Latin American political instability: the case of Mexico." *American Political Science Review* 63, no. 3 (September):833–57.

Cornelius, Wayne A., Jr. 1971. "The political sociology of cityward migration in Latin America," in Francine F. Rabinovitz and Felicity M. Trueblood (eds.), *Latin American Urban Research*, no. 1. Beverly Hills: Sage, 95–147.

Cornelius, Wayne A. 1973. *Political learning among the migrant poor: the impact of residential context.* Sage Professional Paper in Comparative Politics Series, no. 01–037.

Cornelius, Wayne A. 1974. "Urbanization and political demand making: political participation among the migrant poor in Latin American cities." *American Political Science Review* 68, no. 3 (September):1125–46.

Cornelius, Wayne A. 1975. *Politics and the migrant poor in Mexico City.* Stanford: Stanford University Press.

Corning, Peter A. 1971. "The biological bases of behavior and some implications for political science." *World Politics* 23, no. 3 (April):321–70.

Corning, Peter A. 1973. "Human violence: some causes and implications," in Charles R. Beitz and Theodore Herman (eds.), *Peace and war*. San Francisco: W. H. Freeman and Co., 119–43.

Corning, Peter A., and Corning, Constance Hellyer. 1972. "Toward a general theory of violent aggression." *Social Science Information* 11, nos. 3–4:7–35.

Coser, Lewis A. 1956. *The functions of social conflict*. Glencoe: Free Press.

Coser, Lewis. 1966. "The myth of peasant revolt." *Dissent* 13 (May/June): 298–303.

Coser, Lewis A. 1967. *Continuities in the study of social conflict*. New York: Free Press.

Coser, Lewis A. 1968. "Conflict: social aspects." *International Encyclopedia of the Social Sciences*, vol. 3. New York: Macmillan and Free Press, 232–36.

Coser, Lewis A., and Larsen, Otto N., eds. 1976. *The uses of controversy in sociology*. New York: Free Press.

Costner, Herbert L. 1969. "Theory, deduction, and rules of correspondence." *American Journal of Sociology* 75, no. 2 (September):245–63. Also in Blalock (1971), 299–319.

Costner, Herbert L., ed. 1971. *Sociological methodology 1971*. San Francisco: Jossey-Bass.

Costner, Herbert L., and Schoenberg, Ronald. 1973. "Diagnosing indicator ills in multiple indicator models," in Goldberger/Duncan, 167–99.

Cotler, Julio. 1970–71. "Political crisis and military populism in Peru." *Studies in Comparative International Development* 6, no. 5:95–113.

Couch, Carl J. 1968. "Collective behavior: an examination of some stereotypes." *Social Problems* 15, no. 3 (Winter):310–22.

Couch, Carl J. 1970. "Dimensions of association in collective behavior episodes." *Sociometry* 33, no. 4 (December):457–71.

Coughenour, C. Milton, and Stephenson, John B. 1972. "Measures of individual modernity: review and commentary." *International Journal of Comparative Sociology* 13:81–98.

Coulter, Philip. 1971–71. "Democratic political development: a systemic model based on regulative policy." *Development and Change* 3, no. 1:25–61.

Coulter, Philip. 1972. "Political development and political theory: methodological and technological problems in the comparative study of political development." *Polity* 5 (Winter):233–42.

Coulter, Philip. 1975. *Social mobilization and liberal democracy: a macroquantitative analysis of global and regional models*. Lexington, Mass.: Lexington Books.

Countryman, Edward. 1976. "'Out of the bounds of the law': northern land rioters in the eighteenth century," in Young, 37–69.

Couzens, Michael. 1971. "Reflections on the study of violence." *Law and Society Review* 5, no. 4 (May):583–604.

Cowell, F. A. 1977. *Measuring inequality*. Oxford: Philip Allan.

Cox, Thomas S. 1976. *Civil-military relations in Sierra Leone: a case study of African soldiers in politics*. Cambridge, Mass.: Harvard University Press.

Crawford, Thomas, and Naditch, Murray. 1970. "Relative deprivation, power-lessness, and militancy: the psychology of social protest." *Psychiatry* 33, no. 2 (May):208–23.

Crook, Wilfried Harris. 1931. *The general strike: a study of labor's tragic weapon in theory and practice.* Chapel Hill: University of North Carolina Press.

Crosby, Faye. 1976. "A model of egoistical relative deprivation." *Psychological Review* 83, no. 2 (March):85–113.

Crosby, Faye. 1979. "Relative deprivation revisited: a response to Miller, Bolce, and Halligan." *American Political Science Review* 73, no. 1 (March):103–12.

Crotty, William J., ed. 1971. *Assassinations and the political order.* New York: Harper & Row.

Crozier, Brian. 1960. *The rebels.* London: Chatto & Windus.

Crozier, Brian. 1974. *A theory of conflict.* London: Hamish Hamilton.

Crozier, Brian, ed. 1976. *Annual of power and conflict, 1975–1976—a survey of political violence and international influence.* London: Institute for the Study of Conflict.

Crozier, Michel; Huntington, Samuel P.; and Watanuki, Joji. 1975. *The crisis of democracy.* New York: New York University Press.

Cruse, Harold. 1968. *Rebellion or revolution?* New York: William Morrow Co.

Curtis, Richard F., and Jackson, Elton F. 1962. "Multiple indicators in survey research." *American Journal of Sociology* 68, no. 2 (September): 195–204.

Cutright, Phillips. 1963. "National political development: measurement and analysis." *American Sociological Review* 28, no. 2 (April):253–64.

Cutright, Phillips, and Wiley, James A. 1969–70. "Modernization and political representation: 1927–1966." *Studies in Comparative International Development* (Monograph Series) 5, no. 2:23–41.

Daalder, Hans. 1962. *The role of the military in the emerging countries.* Publications of the Institute of Social Studies, Series Minor, vol. 1. The Hague: Mouton. (2d printing 1969).

Daalder, Hans. 1974. "The consociational democracy theme." *World Politics* 26, no. 4 (July):604–21.

Dahl, Robert A. 1966. "Patterns of opposition," in Robert A. Dahl (ed.), *Political opposition in Western democracies.* New Haven: Yale University Press, 332–47.

Dahl, Robert A. 1967. *Pluralist democracy in the United States: conflict and consent.* Chicago: Rand McNally.

Dahl, Robert A. 1971. *Polyarchy: participation and opposition.* New Haven: Yale University Press.

Dahm, Helmut, and Kool, Frits, eds. 1974. *Die Technik der Macht.* Olten: Olten Verlag.

Dahrendorf, Ralf. 1958. "Toward a theory of social conflict." *Journal of Conflict Resolution* 2, no. 2 (June):170–83.

Dahrendorf, Ralf. 1965. "Die Funktionen sozialer Konflikte," in Dahrendorf (1965b), 112–31.

Dahrendorf, Ralf. 1965a. "Elemente einer Theorie des sozialen Konflikts," in Dahrendorf (1965b), 197–235.

Dahrendorf, Ralf. 1965b. *Gesellschaft und Freiheit: Zur soziologischen Analyse der Gegenwart*. Munich: R. Piper & Co.

Dahrendorf, Ralf. 1965c. *Gesellschaft und Demokratie in Deutschland*. Munich: R. Piper & Co.

Dallin, Alexander, and Breslauer, George W. 1970. *Political terror in communist systems*. Stanford: Stanford University Press.

Daly, William T. 1972. *The revolutionary: a review and synthesis*. Sage Professional Paper in Comparative Politics Series, no. 01–025.

Daniels, David N.; Gilula, Marshall F.; and Ochberg, Frank M. eds. 1970. *Violence and the struggle for existence*. Boston: Little, Brown & Co.

Daniels, Robert Vincent. 1960. *The conscience of the revolution: communist opposition in Soviet Russia*. Cambridge: Harvard University Press.

Daniels, Stuart. 1974. "The weathermen." *Government and Opposition 9*, no. 4 (Autumn):430–59.

Danzger, Herbert M. 1968. "Civil rights conflict and community power structure." Ph.D. dissertation, Columbia University.

Danzger, M. Herbert. 1975. "Validating conflict data." *American Sociological Review* 40, no. 5 (October):570–84.

Danzger, M. Herbert. 1976. "Reply to Tuchman." *American Sociological Review* 41, no. 6 (December):1067–71.

Davies, Alun. 1964. "The origins of the French peasant revolution of 1789." *History* 49, no. 165 (February):24–41.

Davies, C. S. L. 1973. "Peasant revolt in France and England: a comparison." *Agricultural History Review* 21:122–34.

Davies, James C. 1962. "Toward a theory of revolution." *American Sociological Review* 27, no. 1 (February):5–19. Also in Davies (1971), 134–47.

Davies, James C. 1967. "The circumstances and causes of revolution: a review." *Journal of Conflict Resolution* 11, no. 2 (June):247–57.

Davies, James C. 1969. "The J–curve of rising and declining satisfactions as a cause of some great revolutions and a contained rebellion," in Graham/Gurr, 690–730.

Davies, James C., ed. 1971. *When men revolt and why: a reader in political violence and revolution*. New York: Free Press.

Davies, James C. 1974. "The J-curve and power struggle theories of collective violence." *American Sociological Review* 39, no. 4 (August):607–13.

Davis, Charles L. 1976. "The mobilization of public support for an authoritarian regime: the case of the lower class in Mexico City." *American Journal of Political Science* 20, no. 4 (November):653–70.

Davis, H. T. 1948. *Political statistics*. Evanston, Ill.: Principia.

Davis, J. 1970. "Morals and backwardness." *Comparative Studies in Society and History* 12:340–53.

Davis, Jack. 1972. "Political violence in Latin America." *Adelphi Papers*, no. 85. London: International Institute of Strategic Studies.

Davis, James A. 1959. "A formal interpretation of the theory of relative deprivation." *Sociometry* 22, no. 4 (December):280–96.

Davis, Jerome. 1922. "A sociological interpretation of the Russian Revolution." *Political Science Quarterly* 37:227–50.

Davis, Nanette J. 1972. "Labeling theory in deviance research: a critique and reconsideration." *Sociological Quarterly* 13, no. 4 (Autumn):447–74.

Dawson, Philip. 1972. *Provincial magistrates and revolutionary politics in France, 1789-1795.* Cambridge, Mass.: Harvard University Press.

Dean, Warren. 1970. "Latin American golpes and economic fluctuations, 1823-1966." *Social Science Quarterly* 51, no. 1 (June):70-80.

Debray, Régis. 1965. "Castroism: the long march in Latin America." *New Left Review* (September/October) 33:17-58. Slightly revised version in Kelly/Brown (1970), 442-81.

Debray, Régis. 1968. *Revolution in the revolution?* Harmondsworth, Middlesex: Penguin Books. American ed. New York: Grove Press (1967). French original. Paris: Librairie François Maspero (1967).

Debray, Régis. 1974. *La critique des armes.* Paris: Éditions du Seuil. German ed. quoted: *Kritik der Waffen: Wohin geht die Revolution in Lateinamerika?* Reinbek: Rowohlt (1975).

Decalo, S. 1973. "Military coups and military régimes in Africa." *Journal of Modern African Studies* 11, no. 1 (March):105-27.

Decalo, Samuel. 1976. *Coups and army rule in Africa: studies in military style.* New Haven: Yale University Press.

Deegan, John, Jr. 1974. "Specification error in causal models." *Social Science Research* 3, no. 3 (September):235-59.

Deegan, John, Jr. 1975. "The process of political development: an illustrative use of a strategy for regression in the presence of multicollinearity." *Sociological Methods and Research* 3, no. 4 (May):384-415.

Delacroix, Jacques, and Ragin, Charles. 1978. "Modernizing institutions, mobilization, and third world development: a cross-national study." *American Journal of Sociology* 84, no. 1 (July):123-50.

Denitch, Bogdan. 1976. "Violence and social change in the Yugoslav revolution: lessons for the Third World?" *Comparative Politics* 8, no. 3 (April):465-78.

Denitch, Bogdan. 1976a. *The legitimation of a revolution: The Yugoslav case.* New Haven: Yale University Press.

Denitch, Bogdan. 1978. "Spontaneity and organization: revolutionary party and modernization." Paper presented at the World Congress of the International Sociological Association, in Uppsala.

Dennis, Jack. 1970. "Support for the institution of elections by the mass public." *American Political Science Review* 64, no. 3 (September): 819-35.

Dennon, A. R. 1969. "Political science and political development." *Science and Society* 23 (Summer):285-98.

Denton, Frank H., and Phillips, Warren. 1968. "Some patterns in the history of violence." *Journal of Conflict Resolution* 12, no. 2 (June):182-95.

Derriennic, Jean-Pierre. 1972. "Theory and ideologies of violence." *Journal of Peace Research* 9, no. 4:361-74.

DeSchweinitz, Karl, Jr. 1970. "Growth, development, and political modernization." *World Politics* 22, no. 4 (July):518-40.

Deutsch, Karl W. 1953; 2d ed. 1966b. *Nationalism and social communication: an inquiry into the foundations of nationality.* Cambridge, Mass.: MIT Press.

Deutsch, K. W. 1961. "Social mobilization and political development." *American Political Science Review* 55, no. 3 (September):493-514.

Deutsch, Karl W. 1964. "External involvement in internal war," in Eckstein, 100–110.

Deutsch, Karl W. 1966. *The nerves of government*. New York: Free Press.

Deutsch, Karl W. 1966a. "External influences in the internal behavior of states," in R. Barry Farrell (ed.), *Approaches to comparative and international politics*. Evanston: Northwestern University Press, 5–26.

Deutsch, Karl W. 1970; 2d ed. 1974. *Politics and government: how people decide their fate*. Boston: Houghton Mifflin Co.

Deutsch, Karl W. 1973. "Zum Verständnis von Krisen und politischen Revolutionen," in Jänicke, 90–100.

Deutsch, Karl, and Nordlinger, Eric A. 1968. "The German Federal Republic," in Roy C. Macridis, and Robert E. Ward (eds.), *Modern political systems: Europe*. 2d ed. Englewood Cliffs: Prentice-Hall, 299–450.

Deutsch, Karl W., and Senghaas, Dieter. 1973. "The steps to war: a survey of system levels, decision stages, and research results," in Patrick J. McGowan (ed.), *Sage International Yearbook of Foreign Policy Studies* 1, 275–329.

Deutsch, Morton. 1964. "Homans in the Skinner box." *Sociological Inquiry* 34, no. 2 (Spring):156–65.

Deutsch, Morton. 1973. *The resolution of conflict: constructive and destructive processes*. New Haven: Yale University Press.

Deutsch, Morton. 1975. "Equity, equality, and need: what determines which value will be used as the basis of distributive justice." *Journal of Social Issues* 31, no. 3 (Summer):137–49.

Dew, Edward. 1974. "Testing elite perceptions of deprivation and satisfaction in a culturally plural society." *Comparative Politics* 6, no. 3 (January): 271–85.

Dickson, Thomas, Jr. 1977. "An economic output and impact analysis of civilian and military regimes in Latin South America." *Development and Change* 8, no. 3 (July):325–45.

Dippel, Horst. 1976. "The American revolution and the modern concept of 'revolution,'" in Erich Angermann, Marie-Luise Frings, and Hermann Wellenreuther (eds.), *New wine in old skins: a comparative view of socio-political structures and values affecting the American revolution*. Stuttgart: Klett-Cotta: 115–34.

Disch, Arne. 1979. "Peasants and revolts: review of Paige (1975)." *Theory and Society* 7, nos. 1–2 (January-March):243–52.

Disorders and terrorism. 1976. Report of the Task Force on Disorders and Terrorism. National Advisory Committee on Criminal Justice Standards and Goals. Washington, D.C.: U.S. Government Printing Office.

Dittmer, Lowell. 1974. *Liu Shao-ch'i and the Chinese Cultural Revolution: the politics of mass criticism*. Berkeley: University of California Press.

Dittmer, Lowell. 1977. "Thought reform and cultural revolution: an analysis of the symbolism of Chinese polemics." *American Political Science Review* 77, no. 1 (March):67–85.

Dizard, Jan. 1970. "Black identity, social class, and black power." *Psychiatry* 33, no. 2 (May):195–207.

Dobson, Christopher, and Payne, Ronald. 1979. *The weapons of terror: international terrorism at work*. London: Macmillan.

Dodd, Lawrence C. 1974. "Party coalitions in multi-party parliaments: a game-theoretic analysis." *American Political Science Review* 68, no.4 (December):1093–1117.

Dodd, Lawrence C. 1976. *Coalitions in parliamentary government*. Princeton: Princeton University Press.

Dogan, Mattei, and Rokkan, Stein, eds. 1969. *Quantitative ecological analysis in the social sciences*. Cambridge, Mass.: MIT Press.

Dolian, James P. 1973. "The military and the allocation of national resources: an examination of thirty-four Sub-Sahara African nations." Paper presented at the International Studies Association Meeting, 14–17 March, in New York.

Dollard, J.; Doob, L. W.; Miller, N. E.; Mowrer, O. H.; and Sears, R. R. 1939. *Frustration and aggression*. New Haven: Yale University Press.

Domínguez, Jorge I. 1974. "The civic soldier in Cuba," in Kelleher, 209–38.

Domínguez, Jorge. I. 1978. *Cuba: order and revolution*. Cambridge: Harvard University Press.

Donajgrodzki, A. P., ed. 1977. *Social control in nineteenth-century Britain*. London: Croom Helm.

Donaldson, Robert H. and Waller, Derek J. 1970. *Stasis and change in revolutionary elites: a comparative analysis of the 1956 party central committees in China and the USSR*. Sage Professional Paper in Comparative Politics Series, no. 01–011.

Donnenwerth, Gregory V., and Törnblom, Kjell Y. 1975. "Reactions to three types of distributive injustice." *Human Relations* 28, no. 5 (May): 407–29.

Doob, A. N. 1970. "Catharsis and aggression: the effect of hurting one's enemy." *Journal of Experimental Research in Personality* 4:291–96.

Doob, Anthony N., and Wood, Lorraine E. 1972. "Catharsis and aggression: the effects of annoyance and retaliation on aggressive behavior." *Journal of Personality and Social Psychology* 22, no. 2 (May):156–62.

Doorn, Jacques van. 1975. *The soldier and social change: comparative studies in the history and sociology of the military*. Beverly Hills and London: Sage Publications.

Doornbos, Martin R. 1969. "Political development: the search for criteria." *Development and Change*: 93–115.

Doran, Charles F. 1976. *Domestic conflict in state relations: the American sphere of influence*. Sage Professional Paper, International Studies Series, no. 02–037.

Doran, Charles F.; Pendley, Robert E.; and Antunes, George E. 1971. "Reliability of cross-national measures of civil strife and instability events: a comparison of indigenous and secondary data sources." Houston: Rice University. Mimeographed.

Doran, Charles F.; Pendley, Robert E.; and Antunes, George E. 1973. "A test of cross-national event reliability: global versus regional data sources." *International Studies Quarterly* 17, no. 2 (June):175–203.

Dotson, A. Bruce. 1974. "Social planning and urban violence. An extension of McElroy and Singell." *Urban Affairs Quarterly* 9, no. 3 (March): 283–301.

Downes, Bryan T. 1968. "Social and political characteristics of riot cities: a comparative study." *Social Science Quarterly* 49, no. 3 (December): 504–20. Also in Glenn/Bonjean (1969), 427–43.

Downes, Bryan T. 1970. "A critical reexamination of the social and political characteristics of riot cities." *Social Science Quarterly* 51, no. 2 (September):349–60.

Downton, James V., Jr. 1973. *Rebel leadership: commitment and charisma in the revolutionary process.* New York: Free Press.

Doyle, William. 1980. *Origins of the French Revolution.* Oxford: Oxford University Press.

Drake, St.C. 1968. "Urban violence and American social movements," in R. H. Connery (ed.), *Urban riots: violence and social change.* Proceedings of the Academy of Political Science 29, 13–24.

Draper, Hal. 1977. *Karl Marx's theory of revolution.* 2 vols. New York: Monthly Review Press.

Draper, N. R., and Smith, H. 1966. *Applied regression analysis.* New York: John Wiley & Sons.

Draper, Theodore. 1962. *Castro's revolution: myths and realities.* New York: Frederick A. Praeger.

Drew, Paul. 1974. "Domestic political violence: some problems of measurement." *Sociological Review* 22, no. 1 (February):5–25.

Droz, Jacques. 1967. *Europe between revolutions, 1815–1848.* London: Fontana/Collins.

Druckman, Daniel, ed. 1977. *Negotiations: social-psychological perspectives.* Beverly Hills: Sage Publications.

Druckman, Daniel, and Zechmeister, Kathleen. 1973. "Conflict of interest and value dissensus: propositions in the sociology of conflict." *Human Relations* 26, no. 4 (August):449–66.

Dubey, Sumati N. 1971. "Powerlessness and the adaptive responses of disadvantaged blacks: a pilot study." *Human Organization* 30, no. 2 (Summer):149–57.

Duff, Ernest A., and McCamant, John F. 1968. "Measuring social and political requirements for system stability in Latin America." *American Political Science Review* 62, no. 4 (December):1125–43.

Duff, Ernest A., and McCamant, John F. (with Waltraud Q. Morales). 1976. *Violence and repression in Latin America: a quantitative and historical analysis.* New York: Free Press.

Duggett, Michael. 1975. "Marx on peasants." *Journal of Peasant Studies* 2, no. 2 (January):159–81.

Duncan, Otis Dudley. 1975. *Introduction to structural equation models.* New York: Academic Press.

Duncan, Otis Dudley; Cuzzort, Ray P.; and Duncan, Beverly. 1961. *Statistical geography: problems in analyzing areal data.* New York: Free Press.

Duncan, W. Raymond. 1968. "Education and political development: the Latin American case." *Journal of Developing Areas* 2:188–210.

Dunn, John. 1972. *Modern revolutions: an introduction to the analysis of a political phenomenon.* New York: Cambridge University Press.

Durkheim, Emile. 1895. *Les règles de la méthode sociologique.* Paris: Presses Universitaires de France.

Duvall, Raymond, and Welfling, Mary. 1973a. "Social mobilization, political institutionalization, and conflict in Black Africa: a simply dynamic model." *Journal of Conflict Resolution* 17, no 4 (December):673–702.

Duvall, Raymond, and Welfling, Mary. 1973b. "Determinants of political institutionalization in Black Africa: a quasi–experimental analysis." *Comparative Political Studies* 5, no. 4 (January):387–417.

Duvall, Raymond D. 1978. "Dependence and dependencia theory: notes toward precision of concept and argument." *International Organization* 32, no. 1 (Spring):51–78.

Duvall, Raymond, and Shamir, Michal. 1978. "The coercive state: cross-national, time-series indicators." Paper prepared for Conference on Indicator Systems, June, in Berlin, Institute for Comparative Social Research. Mimeographed.

Duvall, Raymond; Jackson, Steven; Russett, Bruce; Snidal, Duncan; and Sylvan, David. (Forthcoming). "A formal model of 'dependencia' theory: structure and measurement," in Richard Merritt and Bruce Russett (eds.), *From national development to global community*.

Duveau, Georges. 1967. *1848: the making of a revolution*. London: Routledge and Kegan Paul. French original *1848*. Paris: Editions Gallimard (1965).

Duverger, Maurice. 1968. "An impossible revolution." Original in *Le Monde*, 12 July. English trans. in Kelly/Brown (1970), 507–11.

Dye, Thomas R. 1966. *Politics, economics and the public: policy outcomes in the American states*. Chicago: Rand McNally.

Dynes, Russell, and Quarantelli, E. L. 1968. "What looting in civil disturbances really means." *Trans-action* (May):9–14.

Easton, David. 1965. *A systems analysis of political life*. New York: John Wiley & Sons.

Easton, David. 1965a. *A framework for political analysis*. Englewood Cliffs: Prentice-Hall.

Easton, David. 1972. "Some limits of exchange theory in politics." *Sociological Inquiry* 42, nos. 3–4:129–48.

Easton, David. 1974. "The conceptualization of support." Paper presented at the Conference on Political Support, 24 April, in Chicago.

Easton, David. 1975. "A re-assessment of the concept of political support." *British Journal of Political Science* 5, no. 4 (October):435–57.

Easton, David. 1976. "Theoretical approaches to political support." *Canadian Journal of Political Science* 9, no. 3 (September):431–48.

Easton, David, and Dennis, Jack. 1967. "The child's acquisition of regime norms: political efficacy." *American Political Science Review* 61, no. 1 (March):25–38.

Easton, David and Dennis, Jack, with the assistance of Sylvia Easton. 1969. *Children in the political system: origins of political legitimacy*. New York: McGraw-Hill.

Ebert, Theodor. 1970. *Gewaltfreier Aufstand: Alternative zum Bürgerkrieg*. Frankfurt/M.: Fischer Taschenbuch.

Eberwein, Wolf-Dieter; Hübner-Dick, Gisela; Jagodzinski, Wolfgang; Rattinger, Hans; and Weede, Erich. 1978. "Internes und externes Konflikt-verhalten von Nationen, 1966–1967." *Zeitschrift für Soziologie* 7, no. 1 (January):21–38.

Eberwein, Wolf-Dieter, Hübner-Dick, Gisela; Jagodzinski, Wolfgang; Rattinger, Hans; and Weede, Erich. 1979. "External and internal conflict behavior among nations, 1966–1967." *Journal of Conflict Resolution* 23, no. 4 (December):715–42.

Eckstein, Harry. 1961. *A theory of stable democracy*. Research Monograph, no. 10. Princeton University: Center of International Studies. Also in Harry Eckstein, *Division and cohesion in democracy: a study of Norway*. Princeton: Princeton University Press (1966), 225–88.

Eckstein, Harry. 1962. *Incidence of internal wars 1946–1959*. Princeton: Center of International Studies.

Eckstein, Harry. ed. 1964. *Internal war: problems and approaches*. New York: Free Press.

Eckstein, Harry. 1965. "On the etiology of internal wars." *History and Theory* 4, no. 2:133–63. Also in Welch/Taintor (1972), 60–90, and slightly abridged in Feierabend/Feierabend/Gurr (1972), 9–30.

Eckstein, Harry. 1969. "Authority relations and governmental performance: a theoretical framework." *Comparative Political Studies* 2, no. 3 (October):269–325.

Eckstein, Harry. 1971. *The evaluation of political performance: problems and dimensions*. Sage Professional Paper in Comparative Politics Series, no. 01–017.

Eckstein, Harry. 1975. "Case study and theory in political science," in Greenstein/Polsby, vol. 7, 79–137.

Eckstein, Harry. 1979. *Support for regimes: theories and tests*. Research Monograph, no. 44. Princeton University: Center of International Studies.

Eckstein, Harry. 1980. "Theoretical approaches to explaining collective political violence," in Gurr, 135–66.

Eckstein, Harry, and Gurr, Ted Robert. 1975. *Patterns of authority: a structural basis for political inquiry*. New York: John Wiley & Sons.

Eckstein, Susan. 1976. *The impact of revolution: a comparative analysis of Mexico and Bolivia*. Sage Contemporary Political Sociology Series, no. 06–016.

Eckstein, Susan. 1977. *The poverty of revolution: the state and the urban poor in Mexico*. Princeton: Princeton University Press.

Edelman, Murray. 1964. *The symbolic uses of politics*. Urbana: University of Illinois Press.

Edelman, Murray. 1977. *Political language: words that succeed and policies that fail*. New York: Academic Press.

Edwards, Lyford P. 1965. *The natural history of revolution*. New York: Russell & Russell. Original Chicago: University of Chicago Press (1927).

Edwards, Steward. 1971. *The Paris Commune 1871*. London: Eyre & Spottiswoode.

Egnal, Marc, and Ernst, Joseph A. 1972. "An economic interpretation of the American Revolution." *William and Mary Quarterly Third Series* 29, no. 1 (January):3–32.

Eidelberg, Philip Gabriel. 1974. *The great Rumanian peasant revolt of 1907: origins of a modern jacquerie*. Leiden: E. J. Brill.

Einaudi, Luigi R. 1973. "Revolution from within? Military rule in Peru since 1968." *Studies in Comparative International Development* 8, no. 1 (Spring):71–87.

Einaudi, Luigi R., and Stepan, Alfred. 1971. *Latin American institutional development: changing military perspectives in Peru and Brazil.* Santa Monica: Rand Corporation.

Eisenstadt, S. N. 1964. "Breakdowns of modernization." *Economic Development and Cultural Change* 12, no. 4 (July):345–67.

Eisenstadt, S. N. 1973. *Traditional patrimonialism and modern neopatrimonialism.* Sage Research Papers in the Social Sciences Series, no. 90–103.

Eisenstadt, S. N. 1976. "The changing vision of modernization and development," in Schramm/Lerner, 31–44.

Eisenstadt, S. N. 1978. *Revolution and the transformation of societies: a comparative study of civilizations.* New York: Free Press.

Eisenstein, Elizabeth L. 1965. "Who intervened in 1788? A commentary on The coming of the French Revolution." *American Historical Review* 71, no. 1 (October):77–103.

Eisinger, Peter K. 1973. "The conditions of protest behavior in American cities." *American Political Science Review* 67, no. 1 (March):11–28.

Eisinger, Peter K. 1974. "Racial differences in protest participation." *American Political Science Review* 68, no. 2 (June):592–606.

Eisinger, Peter K. 1976. *Patterns of interracial politics: conflict and cooperation in the city.* New York: Academic Press.

Ekeh, Peter. 1974. *Social exchange theory.* London: Heinemann Educational Books.

Elliot, R. S. P., and Hickie, John. 1971. *Ulster: a case study in conflict theory.* London: Longman.

Elliott, J. H. 1963. *The revolt of the Catalans: a study in the decline of Spain (1598–1640).* Cambridge: University Press.

Elliott, J. H. 1969. "Revolution and continuity in early modern history." *Past and Present* 42 (February):35–56.

Elliott-Bateman, Michael; Ellis, John; and Bowden, Tom. 1974. *Revolt to revolution: studies in 19th and 20th century European experience.* Manchester: Manchester University Press.

Ellis, Desmond P; Weinir, Paul; and Miller, Louie. 1971. "Does the trigger pull the finger? An experimental test of weapons as aggression-eliciting stimuli." *Sociometry* 34, no. 4 (December):453–65.

Ellis, John. 1973. *Armies in revolution.* New York: Oxford University Press.

Ellis, John. 1976. *A short history of guerrilla warfare.* New York: St. Martin's Press.

Ellwood, Charles. 1905. "A psychological theory of revolutions." *American Journal of Sociology* 11 (July):49–59.

Elwitt, Sandford. 1976. "Review of Tilly et al. (1975)." *American Historical Review* 81, no. 3 (June):577–78.

Elwood, Ralph Carter, ed. 1976. *Reconsiderations on the Russian Revolution.* Columbus, Ohio: Slavia Publishers.

Engels, Friedrich. 1960. *Herrn Eugen Dührings Umwälzung der Wissenschaft ("Anti-Dühring").* Berlin (East): Dietz Verlag.

Enloe, Cynthia H. 1973. *Ethnic conflict and political development.* Boston: Little, Brown & Co.

Enloe, Cynthia H. 1978. "Police and military in Ulster: peacekeeping or peace-subverting forces." *Journal of Peace Research* 15, no. 3:243–58.

D'Entrèves, Alexander P. 1963. "Legality and legitimacy." *Review of Metaphysics* 16, no. 4 (June):687–702.

D'Entrèves, Alexander Passerin. 1967. *The notion of the state: an introduction to political theory*. Oxford: Clarendon Press.

Epstein, Seymour, and Taylor, Stuart P. 1967. "Instigation to aggression as a function of defeat and perceived aggressive intent of the opponent." *Journal of Personality* 35:265–89.

Erickson, Maynard L; Gibbs, Jack P.; and Jensen, Gary F. 1977. "The deterrence doctrine and the perceived certainty of legal punishment." *American Sociological Review* 42, no. 2 (April):305–17.

Erikson, Erik H. 1968. *Identity: youth and crisis*. London: Faber & Faber.

Erikson, Erik H. 1969. *Gandhi's truth: on the origins of militant nonviolence*. New York: W. W. Norton & Co.

Ernst, Joseph. 1973. "Ideology and the political economy of revolution." *Canadian Review of American Studies* 4, no. 2 (Fall):137–48.

Ernst, Joseph. 1976. "'Ideology' and an economic interpretation of the revolution," in Young, 159–85.

Eron, Leonard D.; Walder, Leopold O.; and Lefkowitz, Monroe M. 1971. *Learning of aggression in children*. Boston: Little, Brown & Co.

Eron, Leonard D. et al. 1972. "Does television violence cause aggression?" *American Psychologist* 27:253–63.

Esherick, Joseph W. 1976. *Reform and revolution in China: the 1911 Revolution in Hunan and Hubei*. Berkeley: University of California Press.

Esman, Milton J. 1973. "The management of communal conflict." *Public Policy* 21 (Winter):49–78.

Esman, Milton J., ed. 1976. *Ethnic conflict in the Western world*. Ithaca, N.Y.: Cornell University Press.

Etzioni, Amitai. 1968. *The active society*. New York: Free Press.

Etzioni, Amitai. 1970. *Demonstration democracy*. New York: Gordon & Breach.

Etzioni, Amitai. 1971. "Violence," in Robert K. Merton and Robert Nisbet (eds.), *Contemporary social problems*. 3d ed. New York: Harcourt Brace Jovanovich, 709–41.

Etzioni, Amitai. 1976. "Collective violence," in Robert K. Merton and Robert Nisbet (eds.), *Contemporary social problems*. 4th ed. New York: Harcourt Brace Jovanovich, 675–724.

Etzioni, Amitai. 1977–78. "Societal overload: sources, components and corrections." *Political Science Quarterly* 92, no. 4 (Winter):607–31.

Evans, Peter B., and Timberlake, Michael. 1980. "Dependence, inequality, and the growth of the tertiary: a comparative analysis of less developed countries." *American Sociological Review* 45, no. 4 (August):531–52.

Eyck, Franck. 1972. *The revolutions of 1848–49*. Edinburgh: Oliver & Boyd.

Fagen, Richard R. 1965. "Charismatic authority and the leadership of Fidel Castro." *Western Political Quarterly* 18 (June):275–84.

Fagen, Richard R. 1966. "Man mobilization in Cuba: the symbolism of struggle." *Journal of International Affairs* 20, 254–71. Also in Jackson/Stein (1971), 385–96.

Fagen, Richard R., and Cornelius, Wayne A. Jr., eds. 1970. *Political power in Latin America: seven confrontations*. Englewood Cliffs: Prentice-Hall.

Fainstein, Norman I., and Fainstein, Susan S. 1974. *Urban political movements: the search for power by minority groups in American cities*. Englewood Cliffs: Prentice-Hall.

Fairbairn, Geoffrey. 1974. *Revolutionary guerilla warfare: the countryside version*. Harmondsworth: Penguin Books.

Fall, Bernard P., ed. 1967. *Ho Chi Minh on revolution: selected writings, 1920–66*. London: Pall Mall Press.

Fals Borda, Orlando. 1969. *Subversion and social change in Columbia*. New York: Columbia University Press.

Fanon, Frantz. 1961. *Les damnés de la terre*. Paris: François Maspéro. English ed. *The wretched of the earth*. Harmondsworth: Penguin Books (1967).

Farber, Samuel. 1976. *Revolution and reaction in Cuba, 1933–1960: a political sociology from Machado to Castro*. Middletown, Conn.: Wesleyan University Press.

Farley, Reynolds. 1977. "Trends in racial inequalities: have the gains of the 1960s disappeared in the 1970s?" *American Sociological Review* 42, no. 2 (April):189–208.

Farley, Reynolds, and Hermalin, Albert. 1972. "The 1960s: a decade of progress for blacks?" *Demography* 9, no. 3 (August):353–70.

Farley, Reynolds, and Taeuber, Karl E. 1968. "Population trends and residential segregation since 1960." *Science* 159 (March 1):953–56.

Farrar, Donald E., and Glauber, Robert R. 1967. "Multicollinearity in regression analysis: the problem revisited." *Review of Economics and Statistics* 49, no. 1 (February):92–107.

Fasel, George. 1970. *Europe in upheaval: the revolutions of 1848*. Chicago: Rand McNally.

Feagin, J. R. 1968. "Social sources of support for violence and nonviolence in the Negro ghetto." *Social Problems* 15, no. 4 (Spring):432–41.

Feagin, Joe R., and Hahn, Harlan. 1973. *Ghetto revolts: the politics of violence in American cities*. New York: Macmillan Co.

Feagin, Joe R., and Sheatsley, Paul B. 1968. "Ghetto resident appraisals of a riot." *Public Opinion Quarterly* 32, no. 3 (Fall):352–62.

Featherman, David L., and Hauser, Robert M. 1976. "Changes in the socioeconomic stratification of the races, 1962–73." *American Journal of Sociology* 82, no. 3 (November):621–51.

Feierabend, Ivo K. 1971. "Cross-national analysis of political violence," in Douglas E. Knight, Huntington W. Curtis, and Lawrence J. Fogel (eds.), *Cybernetics, simulation and conflict resolution: proceedings of the Third Annual Symposium of the American Society for Cybernetics*. New York: Spartan Books, 97–117.

Feierabend, I. K., and Feierabend, R. L. 1965. "Cross-national data bank of political instability events (code index)." Public Affairs Research Institute. San Diego State College.

Feierabend, I. K., and Feierabend, R. L. 1966. "Aggressive behaviors within polities, 1948–1962: a cross-national study." *Journal of Conflict Resolution* 10, no. 3 (September):249–71.

Feierabend, Ivo K., and Feierabend, Rosalind L. 1971. "The relationship of systemic frustration, political coercion, and political instability: a cross-national analysis," in Gillespie/Nesvold, 417–40.

Feierabend, Ivo K., and Feierabend, Rosalind L. 1972. "Systemic conditions of political aggression: an application of frustration-aggression-theory," in Feierabend/Feierabend/Gurr, 136–83.

Feierabend, Ivo K., and Feierabend, Rosalind L. 1973. "Violent consequences of violence," in Hirsch/Perry, 187–219.

Feierabend, Ivo K.; Feierabend, Rosalind L.; and Gurr, Ted Robert, eds. 1972. *Anger, violence, and politics: theories and research*. Englewood Cliffs: Prentice-Hall.

Feierabend, Ivo K., and Feierabend, Rosalind L., with Norman M. Howard. 1972. "Coerciveness and change, cross-national trends." *American Behavioral Scientist* 15, no. 6 (July/August):911–27.

Feierabend, I. K.; Feierabend, R. L.; and Litell, N. G. 1966. "Dimensions of political unrest: a factor analysis of cross-national data." Presented to the Annual Meeting of the Western Political Science Association, March, in Reno. Mimeographed.

Feierabend, Ivo K.; Feierabend, Rosalind L.; and Nesvold, Betty A. 1969. "Social change and political violence: cross-national patterns," in Graham/Gurr, 632–87. Abridged in Feierabend/Feierabend/Gurr (1972), 107–24.

Feierabend, Ivo K., with Feierabend, Rosalind L. and Nesvold, Betty A. 1973. "The comparative study of revolution and violence." *Comparative Politics* 5, no. 3 (April):393–424.

Feierabend, Ivo K.; Feierabend, Rosalind L; Nesvold, Betty A.; and Jaggar, Franz M. 1971. "Political violence and assassination: a cross-national assessment," in Crotty, 54–140.

Feierabend, Ivo K., and Feierabend, Rosalind L., with Scanland, Frank W. and Chambers, John Stuart. 1969. "Level of development and international behavior," in Richard Butwell (ed.), *Foreign policy and the developing nation*. Lexington: University of Kentucky Press, 135–88.

Feierabend, I. K., and Nesvold, B. A., with Feierabend, R. L. 1970. "Political coerciveness and turmoil: a cross-national inquiry." *Law and Society Review* 5, no. 1 (August):93–118.

Feierabend, Rosalind L., and Feierabend, Ivo K. 1972a. "Appendix: Invitation to further research—designs, data, and methods," in Feierabend/Feierabend/Gurr (1972), 369–93.

Feierabend, Rosalind L.; Feierabend, Ivo K.; and Sleet, David A. 1973. "Need achievement, coerciveness of government, and political unrest: a cross-national analysis." *Journal of Cross-Cultural Psychology* 4, no. 3 (September):314–25.

Feit, Edward. 1973. *The armed bureaucrats: military-administrative regimes and political development*. Boston: Houghton Mifflin.

Feit, Edward. 1975. "A comment on Sigelman's 'Military size and political intervention.'" *Journal of Political and Military Sociology* 3, no. 1 (Spring): 101–102.

Feldberg, Roslyn L. 1970. "Political systems and the role of the military." *Sociological Quarterly* 11, no. 2 (Spring):206–18.

Felice, Renzo de. 1975. *Intervista sul fascismo*. Rome: Gins, Laterza and Figli Spa. (*Interpretations of fascism*. Cambridge: Harvard University Press 1977).

Felice, Renzo de. 1976. *Fascism: an informal introduction to its theory and practice*. New Brunswick: Transaction Books.

Fenmore, Barton, and Volgy, Thomas J. 1978. "Short-term economic change and political instability in Latin America." *Western Political Quarterly* 31, no. 4 (December):548–64.

Ferro, Marc. 1968. "The aspirations of Russian society," in Pipes, 143–57.

Ferro, Marc. 1971. "The Russian soldier in 1917: undisciplined, patriotic, and revolutionary." *Slavic Review* 30, no. 3 (September):483–512.

Ferro, Marc. 1972. *The Russian Revolution of February 1917*. Englewood Cliffs: Prentice-Hall. French original. *La révolution de 1917: la chute du tsarisme et les origines d'Octobre*. Paris: Aubier (1967).

Feshbach, S. 1956. "The catharsis hypothesis and some consequences of interaction with aggressive and neutral play objects." *Journal of Personality and Social Psychology* 24:449–62.

Feshbach, Seymour. 1961. "The stimulating versus cathartic effects of a vicarious aggressive activity." *Journal of Abnormal and Social Psychology* 63:381–85.

Feshbach, S. 1963. "The drive-reducing function of fantasy behavior." *Journal of Abnormal and Social Psychology* 34:849–67.

Feshbach, Seymour. 1964. "The function of aggression and the regulation of aggressive drive." *Psychological Review* 71, no. 4 (July):257–72.

Feshbach, Seymour. 1970. "Aggression," in P. H. Mussen (ed.), *Carmichael's manual of child psychology*. 3d ed., vol. 2. New York: John Wiley & Sons, 159–259.

Feshbach, Seymour. 1971. "Dynamics and morality of violence and aggression: some psychological considerations." *American Psychologist* 26, no. 3 (March):281–92.

Feshbach, S., and Singer, R. D. 1971. *Television and aggression*. San Francisco: Jossey-Bass.

Festinger, Leon. 1954. "A theory of social comparison processes." *Human Relations* 7, no. 2 (May):117–40. Also in Hyman/Singer (1968), 123–46.

Festinger, L. 1957. *A theory of cognitive dissonance*. Evanston: Row, Peterson.

Fidel, Kenneth. 1975. *Militarism in developing countries*. Edison, N. J.: Transaction Books.

Fiechter, Georges-André 1975. *Brazil since 1964: modernization under a military régime: a study of the interactions of politics and economics in a contemporary military régime*. New York: Halsted Press. (French original 1972.)

Fields, Rona M. 1976. *The Portuguese revolution and the armed forces movement*. New York: Praeger Publishers.

Finer, S. E. 1962. *The man on horseback: the role of the military in politics*. London: Pall Mall. Enlarged version. Baltimore: Penguin Books (1976).

Finer, S. E. 1965. "The military take-over bidders." *New Society* 162 (November):7-9.

Finer, S. E. 1967. "The one-party regimes in Africa: reconsiderations." *Government and Opposition* 2:491–509.

Finer, S. E. 1968. "Armed forces and the political process," in Julius Gould (ed.), *Penguin social sciences survey 1968*. Harmondsworth, Middlesex: Penguin Books, 16–33.

Finer, S. E. 1970. *Comparative government*. London: Allen Lane, The Penguin Press.

Finer, S. E. 1974. "The man on horseback–1974." *Armed Forces and Society* 1, no. 1 (Fall):5–27.

Finer, S. E. 1975. "The mind of the military." *New Society* 7 (August): 297–99.

Finifter, Ada W. 1970. "Dimensions of political alienation." *American Political Science Review* 64, no. 2 (June):389–410.

Finifter, Ada W., ed. 1972. *Alienation and the social system.* New York: John Wiley & Sons.

Fink, Clinton F. 1968. "Some conceptual difficulties in the theory of social conflict." *Journal of Conflict Resolution* 12, no. 4 (December):412–60.

Fink, Clinton F. 1972. "Conflict management strategies implied by expected utility models of behavior." *American Behavioral Scientist* 15, no. 6 (August):837–58.

Fireman, Bruce, and Gamson, William A. 1979. "Utilitarian logic in the resource mobilization perspective," in Zald/McCarthy, 8–44.

Firestone, Joseph M. 1971a. "Three frameworks for the study of violence: a critique and some suggestions for a new synthesis." Binghampton, N.Y.: Center for Comparative Political Research. Mimeographed.

Firestone, Joseph M. 1971b. "The causes of urban riots: a new approach and a causal model." Binghampton, N.Y.: Center for Comparative Political Research. Mimeographed.

Firestone, Joseph M. 1974. "Continuities in the theory of violence." *Journal of Conflict Resolution* 18, no. 1 (March):117–42.

First, Ruth. 1970. *The barrel of a gun: political power in Africa and the coup d'état.* London: Allen Lane, The Penguin Press.

Fischer, Claude S. 1975. "The myth of 'Territoriality' in Van den Berghe's 'Bringing beasts back in.'" *American Sociological Review* 40, no. 5 (October):674–76.

Fischer, Claude S. 1976. *The urban experience.* New York: Harcourt Brace Jovanovich.

Fischer, Claude S.; Baldassare, Mark; and Ofshe, Richard J. 1975. "Crowding studies and urban life: a critical review." *Journal of the American Institute of Planners* 41, no. 6 (November):406–18.

Fishbein, Martin, ed. 1967. *Readings in attitude theory and measurement.* New York: John Wiley & Sons.

Fishbein, Martin. 1967a. "Attitude and prediction of behavior," in Fishbein, 477–92.

Fishbein, Martin, and Ajzen, Icek. 1975. *Belief, attitude, intention, and behavior: an introduction to theory and research.* Reading, Mass.: Addison-Wesley Publishing Co.

Fisher, Ronald J. 1972. "Third party consultation: a method for the study and resolution of conflict." *Journal of Conflict Resolution* 16, no. 1 (March):67–94.

Fisher, Sydney Nettleton, ed. 1963. *The military in the Middle East.* Columbus: Ohio State University Press.

Fitch, John Samuel. 1977. *The military coup d'état as a political process, Ecuador, 1948–1966.* Baltimore: Johns Hopkins University Press.

Fitzgibbon, Russell H. 1956. "A statistical evaluation of Latin-American democracy." *Western Political Quarterly* 9, no. 3 (September):607–19.

Fitzgibbon, Russell H. 1967. "Measuring democratic change in Latin America." *Journal of Politics* 29, no. 1 (February):129–66. Also in Gillespie/Nesvold (1971), 383–416.

Flacks, Richard. 1969. "Protest or conform: some social psychological perspectives on legitimacy." *Journal of Applied Behavioral Science* 5, no. 2:127–50.

Flanagan, Scott C. 1973. "Models and methods of analysis," in Almond et al., 43–102.

Flanagan, Scott C. 1979. "Value change and partisan change in Japan: the silent revolution revisited." *Comparative Politics* 11, no. 3 (April): 253–78.

Flanigan, William H., and Fogelman, Edwin. 1970. "Patterns of political violence in comparative historical perspective." *Comparative Politics* 3, no. 1 (October):1–20.

Flanigan, William, and Fogelman, Edwin. 1971a. "Patterns of political development and democratization: a quantitative analysis," in Gillespie/ Nesvold, 441–73.

Flanigan, William, and Fogelman, Edwin. 1971b. "Patterns of democratic development: an historical comparative analysis," in Gillespie/Nesvold, 475–97.

Flora, Peter. 1972. "Historische Prozesse sozialer Mobilisierung, Urbanisierung und Alphabetisierung, 1850–1965." *Zeitschrift für Soziologie* 1, no. 2:85–117.

Flora, Peter. 1973. "Historical processes of social mobilization: urbanization and literacy, 1850–1965," in S. N. Eisenstadt and Stein Rokkan (eds.), *Building states and nations: models and data resources*, vol. 1. Beverly Hills: Sage Publications, 213–58.

Flora, Peter. 1974. "A new stage of political arithmetik." *Journal of Conflict Resolution* 18, no. 1 (March):143–65.

Flora, Peter. 1974a. *Modernisierungsforschung: Zur empirischen Analyse der gesellschaftlichen Entwicklung.* Opladen: Westdeutscher Verlag.

Flora, Peter. 1975. "Quantitative historical sociology." *Current Sociology* 23, no. 2.

Fogelson, Robert. 1967. "White on black: a critique of the McCone Commission Report on the Los Angeles riots." *Political Science Quarterly* 82, no. 3 (September):333–67.

Fogelson, Robert M. 1968. "From resentment to confrontation: the police, the Negroes, and the outbreak of the nineteen-sixties riots." *Political Science Quarterly* 83, no. 2 (June): 217–47.

Fogelson, Robert M. 1970. "Violence and grievances: reflections on the 1960s riots." *Journal of Social Issues* 26, no. 1:141–63.

Fogelson, Robert M. 1971. *Violence as protest: a study of riots and ghettos.* Garden City, N.Y.: Doubleday & Co.

Fogelson, R. H., and Hill, Robert. 1968. "Who riots? A study of participation in the 1967 riots." *Supplemental Studies for the National Advisory Commission on Civil Disorders.* Washington, D. C.: Government Printing Office, 221–48.

Fogelson, Robert; Black, Gordon S.; and Lipsky, Michael. 1969. "Review symposium: report of the National Advisory Commission on Civil

Disorders." *American Political Science Review*, 63, no. 4 (December): 1269–81.

Ford, William F., and Moore, John H. 1970. "Additional evidence on the social characteristics of riot cities." *Social Science Quarterly* 51, no. 2 (September):339–48.

Forster, Robert, and Greene, Jack P., eds. 1970. *Preconditions of revolution in early modern Europe*. Baltimore: Johns Hopkins Press.

Forward, John R., and Williams, Jay R. 1970. "Internal-external control and black militancy." *Journal of Social Issues* 26, no. 1:75–92.

Fossum, Egil. 1967. "Factors influencing the occurrence of military coups d'état in Latin America." *Journal of Peace Research* 4, no. 3:228–51.

Fossum, Egil. 1968. "Some attributes of the Latin American military coup." *Proceedings of the International Peace Research Association, Second Conference*, vol. 2. Assen: Van Gorcum & Co., 269–93.

Foster, George M. 1965. "Peasant society and the image of limited good." *American Anthropologist* 67, no. 2 (April):293–315.

Fraczek, Adam, and Macaulay, Jacqueline R. 1971. "Some personality factors in reaction to aggressive stimuli." *Journal of Personality* 39, no. 2 (June):163–77.

Frances, Albert S. 1967. "Structural and anticipatory dimensions of violent social conflict (an analytical study of 'La violencia' in Columbia)." Ph.D. dissertation, University of Pittsburgh.

François, Martha Ellis. 1974. "Revolts in late medieval and early modern Europe: a spiral model." *Journal of Interdisciplinary History* 5, no. 1 (Summer):19–43.

Frank, André Gunder. 1972. *Lumpenbourgeoisie and Lumpendevelopment: dependency, class and politics in Latin America*. New York: Monthly Review Press.

Frank, J. A., and Kelly, Michael. 1979. "'Street politics' in Canada: an examination of mediating factors." *American Journal of Political Science* 23, no. 3 (August):593–614.

Franz, Günther. 1933. *Der deutsche Bauernkrieg*. 10th ed. Darmstadt: Wissenschaftliche Buchgesellschaft (1975).

Fraser, John. 1970. "The mistrustful-efficacious hypothesis and political participation." *Journal of Politics* 32 (May):444–49.

Free, Lloyd A. 1971. "Gauging thresholds of frustration," in Davies, 251–58.

Freedman, Jonathan L. 1975. *Crowding and behavior: the psychology of high-density living*. New York: Viking Press.

Freeman, Michael. 1972. "Review article: theories of revolution." *British Journal of Political Science* 2, no. 3 (July):339–59.

Freiberg, J. Walter. 1971. "The dialectics of violence: repression and rebellion." Ph.D. dissertation, University of California, Los Angeles.

Frey, Bruno, and Lau, J. Lawrence. 1968. "Towards a mathematical model of government behavior." *Zeitschrift für Nationalökonomie* 28:355–80.

Frey, Frederick W. 1970. "Cross-cultural survey research in political science," in Robert T. Holt and John E. Turner (eds.), *The methodology of comparative research*. New York: Free Press, 173–294.

Frey, Frederick W. 1973. "Communication and development," in Ithiel de Sola Pool and Wilbur Schramm (eds.), *Handbook of communication*. Chicago: Rand McNally, 337–461.

Friedlander, Robert A., ed. 1979. *Terrorism: documents of international and local control.* 2 vols. Dobbs Ferry, N.Y.: Oceana Publications.

Friedman, Edward. 1974. *Backward toward revolution: the Chinese revolutionary party.* Berkeley: University of California Press.

Friedrich, Carl J., ed. 1966. *Revolution. Nomos VIII.* New York: Atherton Press.

Friend, Kenneth E.; Laing, James D.; and Morrison, Richard J. 1977. "Bargaining processes and coalition outcomes: an integration." *Journal of Conflict Resolution* 21, no. 2 (June):267-98.

Frohlich, Norman; Hunt, Thomas; Oppenheimer, Joe; and Wagner, Harrison R. 1975. "Individual contributions for collective goods: alternative models." *Journal of Conflict Resolution* 19, no. 2 (June):310-29.

Fromkin, David. 1975. "The strategy of terrorism." *Foreign Affairs* 53, no. 4 (July):683-98.

Fromm, Erich. 1941. *Escape from freedom.* New York: Farrar & Rinehart.

Fromm, Erich. 1955. *The sane society.* New York: Rinehart & Co.

Fromm, Erich. 1973. *The anatomy of human destructiveness.* New York: Holt, Rinehart & Winston.

Fuks, Alexander. 1974. "Patterns and types of social economic revolution in Greece from the fourth to the second century B.C." *Ancient Society* 5:51-81.

Funke, Manfred, ed. 1977. *Terrorismus: Untersuchungen zur Strategie und Struktur revolutionärer Gewaltpolitik.* Frankfort: Droste/Athenäum.

Furet, François. 1971. "Le catéchisme révolutionnaire." *Annales (Ecónomies. Sociétés. Civilisations)* 26:255-89.

Furet, François. 1978. *Penser la Révolution française.* Paris: Gallimard.

Furet, François, and Richet, Denis. 1965-66. *La révolution.* 2 vols. Paris: Réalités Hachette.

Fusfeld, Daniel R. 1973. *The basic economics of the urban racial crisis.* New York: Holt, Rinehart and Winston.

Galtung, Johan. 1964. "A structural theory of aggression." *Journal of Peace Research* 1:95-119. Abridged in Feierabend/Feierabend/Gurr (1972), 85-97.

Galtung, Johan. 1965. "On the meaning of nonviolence." *Journal of Peace Research* 2:228-57.

Galtung, Johan. 1965a. "Institutionalized conflict resolution: a theoretical paradigm." *Journal of Peace Research* 2:348-97.

Galtung, Johan. 1969. "Violence, peace, and peace research." *Journal of Peace Research* 6:167-91.

Galtung, Johan. 1978. "Der besondere Beitrag der Friedensforschung zum Studium der Gewalt: Typologien," in Röttgers/Saner, 9-32.

Galtung, Johan, and Höivik, Tord. 1971. "Structural and direct violence: a note on operationalization." *Journal of Peace Research* 8:73-76.

Galula, David. 1964. *Counterinsurgency warfare: theory and practice.* London: Pall Mall Press.

Gamson, William A. 1966. "Rancorous conflict in community politics." *American Sociological Review* 31, no. 1 (February):71-81.

Gamson, William A. 1968. *Power and discontent.* Homewood, Ill.: Dorsey Press.

Gamson, William A. 1971. "Political trust and its ramifications," in Gilbert Abcarian and John W. Soule (eds.), *Social psychology and political behavior: problems and prospects*. Columbus, Ohio: Charles E. Merrill Publ. Co. 40–55.

Gamson, William A. 1974. "Violence and political power: the meek don't make it." *Psychology Today* 7 (July):35–41.

Gamson, William A. 1975. *The strategy of social protest*. Homewood, Ill.: Dorsey Press.

Gameson, William A. 1980. "Understanding the careers of challenging groups: a commentary on Goldstone." *American Journal of Sociology* 85, no. 5 (March):1043–60.

Gamson, William A., and McEvoy, James. 1970. "Police violence and its public support." *Annals of the American Academy of Political and Social Science*, no. 391 (September):97–110.

Gann, Lewis H. 1971. *Guerrillas in history*. Stanford: Hoover Institution Press.

Gann, L. H., and Duignan, Peter. 1978. *South Africa: war, revolution, or peace?* Stanford: Hoover Institution Press.

Gasset, José Ortega. 1932. *The revolt of the masses*. New York: W. W. Norton & Co.

Gastil, Raymond D. 1977. "The comparative survey of freedom VII." *Freedom At Issue* (January-February):5–17.

Gately, Michael O.; Moote, A. Lloyd; and Willis, John E., Jr. 1971. "Seventeenth-century peasant 'furies': some problems of comparative history." *Past and Present* 51 (May):63–80.

Geen, Russell G. 1968. "Effects of frustration, attack, and prior training in aggressiveness upon aggressive behavior." *Journal of Personality and Social Psychology* 9, no. 4:316–21.

Geen, Russell G. 1975. "The meaning of observed violence: real vs. fictional violence and consequent effects on aggression and emotional arousal." *Journal of Research in Personality* 9, no. 4 (December):270–81.

Geen, Russell G. 1976. "Observing violence in the mass media: implications of basic research," in Geen/O'Neal, 193–234.

Geen, Russell G. 1976a. "Aggression," in Thibaut et al., 241–63.

Geen, Russell, and Berkowitz, Leonard. 1966. "Name-mediated aggressive cue properties." *Journal of Personality* 34, no. 3 (September):456–65.

Geen, Russell G., and Berkowitz, Leonard. 1967. "Some conditions facilitating the occurrence of aggression after the observation of violence." *Journal of Personality* 35:666–76. Also in Berkowitz (1969a), 106–18.

Geen, Russell G., and O'Neal, Edgar, eds. 1976. *Perspectives on aggression*. New York: Academic Press.

Geen, R. G., and Stonner, D. 1972. "The context of observed violence: inhibition of aggression through displays of unsuccessful retaliation." *Psychonomic Science* 27, no. 6:342–44.

Geen, R. G., and Stonner, D. 1973. "Context effects in observed violence." *Journal of Personality and Social Psychology* 25, no. 1 (January): 145–50.

Geen, Russell G., and Stonner, David. 1974. "The meaning of observed violence: effects on arousal and aggressive behavior." *Journal of Research in Personality* 8, no. 1 (June):55–63.

Geen, Russell G.; Stonner, David; and Shope, Gary L. 1975. "The facilitation of aggression by aggression: evidence against the catharsis hypothesis." *Journal of Personality and Social Psychology* 31, no. 4 (April):721-26.

Geerken, Michael, and Gove, Walter R. 1977. "Deterrence, overload, and incapacitation." *Social Forces* 56, no. 2 (December):424-47.

Geertz, Clifford. 1963. "The integrative revolution: primordial sentiments and civil politics in the new states," in Clifford Geertz (ed.), *Old societies and new states: the quest for modernity in Asia and Africa.* New York: Free Press, 105-57.

Geertz, Clifford. 1972. "Studies in peasant life: community and society," in B. J. Siegel (ed.), *Biennial Review of Anthropology 1971.* Stanford: Stanford University Press, 1-41.

Geierhos, Wolfgang. 1977. *Vera Zasulič und die russische revolutionäre Bewegung.* Munich: Oldenbourg.

Geiss, Imanuel, ed. 1972. *Tocqueville und das Zeitalter der Revolution.* Munich: Nymphenburger Verlagshandlung.

Geiss, Imanuel. 1975. "Bürgerliche und proletarische Revolution: Skizze zu einem vergleichenden sozialgeschichtlichen Überblick," in *Aus Politik und Zeitgeschichte—Beilage zur Wochenzeitung Das Parlament,* B 42/7 (October):3-47.

Geneletti, Carlo. 1976. "The political orientation of agrarian classes: a theory." *Archives Européennes de Sociology* 17, no. 1:55-73.

Gentry, William D. 1970. "Effects of frustration, attack and prior aggressive training on overt aggression and vascular processes." *Journal of Personality and Social Psychology* 16, no. 4 (December):718-25.

Gerassi, John, ed. 1971. *Towards revolution.* 2 vols. London: Weidenfeld & Nicolson.

Gerlach, Horst. 1969. *Der englische Bauernaufstand von 1381 und der deutsche Bauernkrieg: ein Vergleich.* Meisenheim am Glan: Anton Hain.

Germani, Gino, and Silvert, Kalman. 1961. "Politics, social structure, and military intervention in Latin America." *Archives Européennes de Sociologie* 2, no. 1:62-81. Also in McWilliams (1967), 227-48.

Germani, Gino, and Silvert, Kalman. 1966. "Politics and military intervention in Latin America," in Jason L. Finkle and Richard W. Gable (eds.), *Political development and social change.* New York: John Wiley & Sons, 397-401.

Gerschenkron, Alexander. 1964. "Reflections on economic aspects of revolution," in Eckstein, 180-204.

Geschwender, James. 1964. "Social structure and the negro revolt: an examination of some hypotheses." *Social Forces* 43:248-56.

Geschwender, James A. 1968. "Explorations in the theory of social movements and revolutions." *Social Forces* 47, no. 2 (December):127-35.

Geschwender, James A., ed. 1971. *The black revolt: the civil rights movement, ghetto uprisings, and separatism.* New York: Wiley.

Geschwender, James A., and Singer, Benjamin D. 1970. "Deprivation and the Detroit riot." *Social Problems* 17, no. 4 (Spring):457-63.

Geschwender, James A., and Singer, Benjamin D. 1971. "The Detroit insurrection: grievance and facilitating conditions," in Geschwender, 353-60.

Gibbs, Jack P. 1975. *Crime, punishment, and deterrence.* New York: Elsevier North-Holland.

Gibbs, Jack P., and Erickson, Maynard L. 1975. "Major developments in the sociological study of deviance." *Annual Review of Sociology* 1:21–42.

Gil, Federico G. 1969. "Antecedents of the Cuban Revolution," in Lazar/ Kaufman, 293–310.

Gilison, Jerome M. 1972. *British and soviet politics: legitimacy and convergence.* Baltimore: Johns Hopkins Press.

Gill, Graeme J. 1979. *Peasants and government in the Russian Revolution.* London: Macmillan.

Gillespie, John V., and Nesvold, Betty A. eds. 1971. *Macro-quantitative analysis: conflict, development, and democratization.* Sage Readers in Cross-National Research, vol. 1. Beverly Hills: Sage Publications.

Gillin, J. Christian, and Ochberg, Frank M. 1970. "Firearms control and violence," in David N. Daniels, Marshall F. Gilula and Frank W. Ochberg (eds.), *Violence and the struggle for existence.* Boston: Little, Brown & Co., 241–55.

Gillis, John R. 1970. "Political decay and the European revolutions, 1789–1848." *World Politics* 22, no. 3 (April):344–70.

Gillis, John R. 1971. *The Prussian bureaucracy in crisis 1846–1860: origins of an administrative ethos.* Stanford: Stanford University Press.

Gilman, Bernard. 1971. "Political violence: a comparative and longitudinal analysis." Ph.D. dissertation, University of North Carolina.

Giner, Salvador. 1976. *Mass society.* London: Martin Robertson.

Girling, John L. S. 1980. *America and the Third World: revolution and intervention.* London: Routledge & Kegan Paul.

Glazer, Nathan, and Moynihan, Daniel P. eds. 1975. *Ethnicity: theory and experience.* Cambridge: Harvard University Press.

Glenn, Norval D., and Bonjean, Charles M. eds. 1969. *Blacks in the United States.* San Francisco: Chandler Publishing Co.

Godechot, Jacques. 1956. *La grande nation: L'expansion révolutionnaire de la France dans le monde de 1789 à 1799.* 2 vols. Paris: Aubier.

Godechot, Jacques. 1965. *Les révolutions (1770–1799).* 2d. ed. Paris. English trans. *France and the Atlantic Revolution of the eighteenth century, 1770–1799.* New York: Free Press (1965).

Godechot, Jacques. 1965a. *La prise de la Bastille—14 Juillet 1789.* Paris: Gallimard. English trans. *The taking of the Bastille—July 14th 1789.* London: Faber and Faber (1970).

Godechot, Jacques. 1967. "On the sociology of the Vendée. Review of Charles Tilly: The Vendée." *Government and Opposition* 2:464–69.

Godechot, Jacques. 1971. *The counter-revolution: doctrine and practice 1789–1804.* New York: Howard Fertig.

Gold, David. 1969. "Statistical tests and substantive significance." *American Sociologist* 4, no. 1 (February):42–46.

Goldberger, Arthur S., and Duncan, Otis Dudley, eds. 1973. *Structural equation models in the social sciences.* New York: Academic Press.

Goldenberg, Boris. 1963. "The Cuban Revolution: an analysis." *Problems of Communism* 12, no. 5:1–9. Also in Welch/Taintor (1972), 300–313.

Goldenberg, Boris. 1965. *The Cuban Revolution and Latin America.* London: George Allen and Unwin.

Goldfrank, Walter L. 1979. "Theories of revolution and revolution without theory: the case of Mexico." *Theory and Society* 7, nos. 1–2 (January–March):135–65.

Goldstein, Jeffrey H.; Davis, Roger W.; and Herman, Dennis. 1975. "Escalation of aggression: experimental studies." *Journal of Personality and Social Psychology* 31, no. 1 (January):162–70.

Goldstone, Jack A. 1980. "The weakness of organization: a new look at Gamson's 'The Strategy of Social Protest.'" *American Journal of Sociology* 85, no. 5 (March):1017–42.

Gonzalez, Edward. 1974. *Cuba under Castro: the limits of charisma*. Boston: Houghton Mifflin Co.

Gooch, Herbert Elmer. 1977. "Coup d'état: historical and ideological dimensions of the concept." Ph.D. dissertation, Berkeley: University of California.

Goode, William J. 1972. "Presidential address: the place of force in society." *American Sociological Review* 37, no. 5 (October):507–19.

Goode, William J. 1978. *The celebration of heroes: prestige as a social control system*. Berkeley: University of California Press.

Goodspeed, D. J. 1962. *The conspirators: a study of the coup d'état*. London: Macmillan & Co.

Goranson, Richard E. 1970. "Media violence and aggressive behavior: a review of experimental research," in Leonard Berkowitz (ed.), *Advances in experimental social psychology*, vol. 6. New York: Academic Press, 1–31.

Gorz, André. 1970. *Die Aktualität der Revolution: Nachtrag zur "Strategie der Arbeiterbewegung im Neokapitalismus."* Frankfort on the Main: Europäische Verlagsanstalt.

Gorz, André. 1972. *Zur Strategie der Arbeiterbewegung im Neokapitalismus*, 7th ed. Frankfort on the Main: Europäische Verlagsanstalt.

Gossez, Rémi. 1956. "Diversité des antagonismes sociaux vers le milieu du XIXe siècle." *Revue Économique* 7, no. 3:439–57.

Gossez, Rémi. 1967. *Les ouvriers de Paris*. La Roche-Sur-Yon: Imprimerie Centrale de L'Ouest. Bibliothèque de la révolution de 1848, vol. 24 (1967).

Gott, Richard. 1973. *Rural guerrillas in Latin America*. Harmondsworth: Penguin Books. (Original 1970.)

Gottschalk, Louis. 1944. "Causes of revolution." *American Journal of Sociology* 50, no. 1 (July):1–8. Also in Welch/Taintor (1972), 176–82.

Gottschalk, Louis, ed. 1963. *Generalization in the writing of history*. Chicago: University of Chicago Press.

Gough, Kathleen, and Sharma, Hari P., eds. 1973. *Imperialism and revolution in South Asia*. New York: Monthly Review Press.

Gould, Julius, and Kolb, William L., eds. 1964. *A dictionary in the social sciences*. New York: Free Press.

Goulemot, Jean Marie. 1967. "Le mot révolution et la formation du concept de révolution politique (fin XVIIe siècle)." *Annales Historiques de la Révolution Francaise* 39:417–44.

Gourevitch, Peter. 1978. "The international system and regime formation: a critical review of Anderson and Wallerstein." *Comparative Politics* 10, no. 3 (April):419–38.

Gove, Walter R., ed. 1975. *The labelling of deviance: evaluating a perspective*. New York: John Wiley & Sons.

Gove, Walter R. 1976. "Deviant behavior, social intervention, and labeling theory," in Coser/Larsen, 219–27.

Governor's Commission on the Los Angeles riots. *Violence in the city–an end or a beginning?* (1965). McCone Commission Report. Los Angeles.

Governer's Select Commission on Civil Disorders, State of New Jersey. Report for Action. (1968). Trenton.

Graham, Hugh Davis. 1972. "The paradox of American violence: a historical appraisal," in Short/Wolfgang, 201–9.

Graham, Hugh Davis, and Gurr, Ted Robert, eds. 1969. *Violence in America: historical and comparative perspectives. A report submitted to the National Commission on the causes and prevention of violence*. New York: Frederick A. Praeger. Revised edition. Beverly Hills: Sage Publications (1979).

Graham, Robert. 1978. *Iran: the illusion of power*. London: Croom Helm.

Granovetter, Mark. 1978. "Threshold models of collective behavior." *American Journal of Sociology* 83, no. 6 (May):1420–43.

Grasmick, Harold G., and McLaughlin, Steven D. 1978. "Deterrence and social control: comment on Silberman (1976)." *American Sociological Review* 43, no. 2 (April):273–80.

Grazia, Alfred de. 1962. in *Political behavior*, in *Politics and government*, vol. 1. New York: Collier Books.

Greenberg, Martin H., and Norton, Augustus R., eds. 1979. *Studies in nuclear terrorism*. Boston: G. K. Hall.

Greene, Fred. 1966. "Toward understanding military coups." *Africa Report* 11, no. 2 (February):10–14.

Greene, Jack P., ed. 1973. *The reinterpretation of the American Revolution 1763–1789*, with an introduction by Jack P. Greene. New York: Harper & Row.

Greene, Jack P. 1973a. "The social origins of the American Revolution: an evaluation and an interpretation." *Political Science Quarterly* 86, no. 1 (March):1–22.

Greene, Jack P., and Maier, Pauline, eds. 1976. "Interdisciplinary studies of the American Revolution." *Journal of Interdisciplinary History* 6, no. 4 (Spring).

Greene, Thomas H.1974. *Comparative revolutionary movements*. Englewood Cliffs: Prentice-Hall.

Greenlaw, Ralph W., ed. 1958. *The economic origins of the French Revolution: poverty or prosperity? Problems in European Civilization*. Boston: D. C. Heath & Co.

Greenstein, Fred I. 1967. "The impact of personality on politics: an attempt to clear away underbrush." *American Political Science Review* 61, no. 3 (September):629–41.

Greenstein, Fred I. 1969. *Personality and politics: problems of evidence, inference, and conceptualization*. Chicago: Markham.

Greenstein, Fred I. 1975. "Personality and politics," in Greenstein/Polsby, vol. 2, 1–92.

Greenstein, Fred I., and Polsby, Nelson W., eds. 1975. *Handbook of political science*. 8 vols. Reading, Mass.: Addison-Wesley Publishing Co.

Greenstone, J. David. 1970. "Stability, transformation, and regime interests."
   World Politics 22, no. 3 (April):448–73.
Greer, Donald. 1935. *The incidence of the terror during the French Revolu-
   tion: a statistical interpretation.* Cambridge: Harvard University Press.
   New ed. Gloucester, Mass.: Peter Smith (1966).
Greer, Donald. 1951. *The incidence of the emigration during the French
   Revolution.* Cambridge, Mass.: Harvard University Press.
Greer, Scott, and Orleans, Peter. 1962. "The mass society and parapolitical
   structure," *American Sociological Review* 27, no. 5 (October):634–46.
Gregg, Phillip M., and Banks, Arthur S. 1965. "Dimensions of political
   systems: factor analysis of a Cross-Polity Survey." *American Political
   Science Review* 59, no. 3 (September):602–14. Also in Gillespie/
   Nesvold (1971), 289–309.
Grether, D. M., and Maddala, G. S. 1973. "Errors in variables and serially
   correlated disturbances in distributed lag models." *Econometrica* 41,
   no. 2 (March):255–62.
Grew, Raymond. 1978. "The crises and their sequences," in Raymond Grew
   (ed.), *Crises of political development in Europe and the United States.*
   Princeton: Princeton University Press, 3–37.
Griewank, Karl. 1969. *Der neuzeitliche Revolutionsbegriff: Entstehung und
   Geschichte.* 2d ed. Frankfort on the Main: Europäische Verlagsanstalt.
   [Original Weimar: Hermann Böhlaus Nachfolger (1955)].
Griewank, Karl. 1972. *Die Französische Revolution: 1789–1799.* 4th ed.
   Cologne and Vienna: Böhlau-Verlag.
Griffiths, Gordon. 1959–60. "The revolutionary character of the revolt of
   the Netherlands." *Comparative Studies in Society and History*
   2:452–72.
Griffitt, Williams, and Veitch, Russell. 1971. "Hot and crowded: influences
   of population density and temperature on interpersonal affective
   behavior." *Journal of Personality and Social Psychology* 17, no. 1
   (January):92–98.
Grimshaw, Allen D. 1963. "Government and social violence: the complexity
   of guilt." *The Minnesota Review* (Winter):236–45. Also in Grimshaw
   (1969), 515–25.
Grimshaw, A. D. 1968. "Three views of urban violence: civil disturbance,
   racial revolt, class assault." *American Behavioral Scientist* 11, no.
   4:2–7.
Grimshaw, Allen D., ed. 1969. *Racial violence in the United States.* Chicago:
   Aldine Publishing Co.
Grindstaff, Carl F. 1968. "The Negro, urbanization, and relative deprivation
   in the deep South." *Social Problems* 15, no. 3 (Winter):342–52.
Groennings, Sven; Kelley, E. W.; and Leiserson, Michael, eds. 1970. *The study
   of coalition behavior: theoretical perspectives and cases from four
   continents.* New York: Holt, Rinehart & Winston.
Grofman, Bernard N., and Muller, Edward N. 1973. "The strange case of relative gratification and potential for political violence: the V-curve
   hypothesis." *American Political Science Review* 57, no. 2 (June):
   514–39.
Grohs, G. K. 1968. "Frantz Fanon and the African revolution." *Journal of
   Modern African Studies* 6, no. 4:543–56.

Grønbjerg, Kirsten A.; Street, David; and Suttles, Gerald D. 1978. *Poverty and social change*. Chicago: University of Chicago Press.

Gross, Feliks. 1958. *The seizure of political power in a century of revolutions*. New York: Philosophical Library.

Gross, Feliks. 1969. "Political violence and terror in 19th and 20th century Russia and Eastern Europe," in Kirkham et al., 421–76.

Gross, Feliks. 1972. *Violence in politics: terror and political assassination in Eastern Europe and Russia*. The Hague and Paris: Mouton.

Gross, Feliks. 1974. *The revolutionary party: essays in the sociology of politics*. Westport, Conn.: Greenwood Press.

Gross, Steven Jay, and Niman, C. Michael. 1975. "Attitude-behavior consistency: a review." *Public Opinion Quarterly* 39, no. 3 (Fall):358–68.

Groth, Alexander. 1966. *Revolution and elite access: some hypotheses on aspects of political change*. Davis: Institute of Governmental Affairs, 1–22. Also in Welch/Taintor (1972), 31–41.

Groth, Alexander. 1979. "The institutional myth: Huntington's order revisited." *Review of Politics* 41, no. 2 (April):203–34.

Groves, W. Eugene, and Rossi, Peter H. 1970. "Police perceptions of a hostile ghetto: realism or projection." *American Behavioral Scientist* 13, nos. 5–6 (May-August):727–43.

Grundy, Kenneth W., and Weinstein, Michael A. 1974. *The ideologies of violence*. Columbus: Charles E. Merrill.

Gude, Edward W. 1969. "Batista and Betancourt: alternative responses to violence," in Graham/Gurr, 731–48.

Guevara, Ché. 1966. *On guerrilla warfare*. New York: Frederick A. Praeger.

Gurin, Patricia, and Epps, Edgar. 1975. *Black consciousness, identity, and achievement: a study of students in historically black colleges*. New York: John Wiley & Sons.

Gurin, P.; Gurin, G.; Lao, R.; and Beattie, M. 1969. "Internal-external control in the motivational dynamics of Negro youth." *Journal of Social Issues* 25, no. 3 (Summer):29–54.

Gurin, Patricia; Gurin, Gerald; and Morrison, Betty M. 1978. "Personal and ideological aspects of internal and external control." *Social Psychology* 41, no. 4 (December):275–96.

Gurr, Ted. 1966. *New error-compensated measures for comparing nations: some correlates of civil violence*. Research Monograph, no. 25. Center of International Studies. Princeton, N.J.: Princeton University.

Gurr, Ted Robert. 1968a. "A causal model of civil strife: a comparative analysis using new indices." *American Political Science Review* 62, no. 4 (December):1104–24. Also in Gillespie/Nesvold (1971), 217–49, and in Feierabend/Feierabend/Gurr (1972), 184–222.

Gurr, T. R. 1968b. "Urban disorder: perspectives from the comparative study of civil strife." *American Behavioral Scientist* 11, no. 4 (March/April): 50–55. Also in Masotti/Bowen (1968), 51–67.

Gurr, Ted Robert. 1968c. "Psychological factors in civil violence." *World Politics* 20, no. 2 (January):245–78. Also in Feierabend/Feierabend/ Gurr (1972), 31–57, and in Jackson/Stein (1971), 285–307.

Gurr, Ted Robert. 1969a. "A comparative study of civil strife," in Graham/ Gurr, 572–632.

Gurr, Ted Robert. 1969b. *Cross-national studies of civil violence*. Washington, D.C.: Center for Research in Social Systems, The American University.

Gurr, Ted Robert. 1970a. *Why men rebel.* Princeton: Princeton University Press.

Gurr, Ted Robert. 1970b. "Sources of rebellion in Western societies: some quantitative evidence." *Annals of the American Academy of Political and Social Science*, no. 391 (September):128–44.

Gurr, Ted Robert. 1972a. *Politimetrics: an introduction to quantitative macropolitics.* Englewood Cliffs: Prentice-Hall.

Gurr, Ted Robert. 1972b. "The calculus of civil conflict." *Journal of Social Issues* 28, no. 1:27–47.

Gurr, T. R. 1973. "Vergleichende Analyse von Krisen und Rebellionen," in Jänicke, 64–89.

Gurr, Ted Robert. 1973a. "Social change and the interplay of internal and international political conflicts." Presented to the Ninth World Congress of the International Political Science Association, August, in Montreal. Mimeographed.

Gurr, Ted Robert. 1973b. "The revolution-social change nexus: some old theories and new hypotheses." *Comparative Politics* 5, no. 3 (April): 359–92.

Gurr, Ted Robert. 1974a. "Persistence and change in political systems, 1800–1971." *American Political Science Review* 68, no. 4 (December): 1482–1504.

Gurr, Ted Robert. 1974b. "The neo-alexandrians: a review essay on data handbooks in political science." *American Political Science Review* 68, no. 1 (March):243–52.

Gurr, Ted Robert. 1974c. "Urban public order in the 19th and 20th centuries: a comparative study." Paper presented to the Seventh World Congress of Sociology, August, in Toronto.

Gurr, Ted. Robert. 1976. *Rogues, rebels, and reformers: a political history of urban crime and conflict.* Beverly Hills and London: Sage Publications.

Gurr, Ted Robert. 1978. "Burke and the modern theory of revolution: a reply to Freeman." *Political Theory* 6, no. 3 (August):299–311.

Gurr, Ted Robert. 1979. "Political protest and rebellion in the 1960s: The United States in world perspective," in Graham/Gurr, 49–76.

Gurr, Ted Robert. 1979a. "Some characteristics of political terrorism in the 1960s," in Stohl (1979), 23–49.

Gurr, Ted Robert. 1979b. "Alternatives to violence in a democratic society," in Graham/Gurr, 491–506.

Gurr, Ted Robert, ed. 1980. *Handbook of political conflict: theory and research.* New York: Free Press.

Gurr, Ted Robert. 1980a. "On the outcomes of violent conflict," in Gurr (1980), 238–94.

Gurr, Ted Robert, and Bishop, Vaughn F. 1976. "Violent nations, and others." *Journal of Conflict Resolution* 20, no. 1 (March):79–110.

Gurr, Ted Robert, and Duvall, Raymond. 1973. "Civil conflict in the 1960s. A reciprocal theoretical system with parameter estimates." *Comparative Political Studies* 6, no. 2 (July):135–69.

Gurr, Ted Robert, and Duvall, Raymond D. 1976. "Introduction to a formal theory of political conflict," in Coser/Larsen, 139–54.

Gurr, Ted Robert, and Duvall, Raymond. Forthcoming. *Conflict and society: a formalized theory and contemporary evidence.*

Gurr, Ted Robert, and Lichbach, Mark Irving. 1979. "A forecasting model for political conflict within nations," in J. David Singer and Michael D.

Wallace (eds.), *To augur well: early warning indicators in world politics.* Beverly Hills: Sage Publications, 153–93.

Gurr, Ted Robert, and McClelland, Muriel. 1971. *Political performance: a twelve nation study.* Sage Professional Paper in Comparative Politics Series, no. 01–018.

Gurr, Ted Robert, and Ruttenberg, Charles. 1967. *The conditions of civil violence: first tests of a causal model.* Research Monograph, no. 28. Center of International Studies. Princeton, N.J.: Princeton University. Abridged also in Gillespie/Nesvold (1971), 187–215.

Gurr, Ted Robert; Grabosky, Peter N.; and Hula, Richard C., eds. 1977. *The politics of crime and conflict: a comparative history of four cities.* London and Beverly Hills: Sage Publications.

Gurr, Ted Robert, and Associates. 1978. *Comparative studies of political conflict and change: cross-national data sets.* Ann Arbor: Inter-University Consortium for Political and Social Research.

Gurr, Ted Robert et al. Forthcoming. *World patterns of political conflict.* Beverly Hills: Sage Publications.

Gusfield, Joseph R. 1962. "Mass society and extremist politics." *American Sociological Review* 27, no. 1 (February):19–30.

Gusfield, Joseph R. 1967. "Tradition and modernity: misplaced polarities in the study of social change." *American Journal of Sociology* 72, no. 4 (January):351–62.

Gutteridge, William. 1969. *The military in African politics.* London: Methuen & Co.

Guzmán, Germán; Fals Borda, Orlando; and Umaña Luna, Eduardo. 1962 and 1964. *La Violencia en Columbia.* 2 vols. Bogotá: Ediciones Tercer Mundo.

Haag, Ernest van den. 1972. *Political violence and civil disobedience.* New York: Harper & Row.

Habermas, Jürgen. 1973. *Legitimationsprobleme im Spätkapitalismus.* Frankfort on the Main: Suhrkamp Verlag.

Haddad, George M. 1965. *Revolutions and military rule in the Middle East: the Northern tier.* New York: Robert Speller.

Haddad, George M. 1971. *Revolutions and military in the Middle East,* part 1: Iraq, Syria, Lebanon and Jordan. New York: Robert Speller & Sons.

Haddad, George M. 1973. *Revolutions and military rule in the Middle East: the Arab states,* part II: Egypt, The Sudan, Yemen and Libya. New York: Robert Speller & Sons.

Hage, Gerald. 1975. "Theoretical decision rules for selecting research designs: the study of nation-states or societies." *Sociological Methods and Research* 4, no. 2 (November):131–65.

Hagopian, Mark N. 1974. *The phenomenon of revolution.* New York: Dodd, Mead & Co.

Hah, Chong-Do. 1972. "The dynamics of the Chinese cultural revolution: an interpretation based on an analytical framework of political coalitions." *World Politics* 24, no. 2 (January):182–220.

Hah, Chong-Do and Schneider, Jeanne. 1968. "A critique of current studies of political development and modernization." *Social Research* 35, no. 1 (Spring):130–58.

Hahlweg, Werner. 1968. *Guerilla: Krieg ohne Fronten*. Stuttgart: W. Kohlhammer.

Hahn, Harlan. 1971. "Ghetto assessments of police protection and authority." *Law and Society Review* 6, no. 2 (November):183–94.

Hahn, Harlan. 1973. "The political objectives of ghetto violence," in Daniel Gordon (ed.), *Social change in urban politics*. Englewood Cliffs: Prentice-Hall, 225–56.

Hahn, Harlan, and Feagin, Joe R. 1970. "Riot-precipitating police practices: attitudes in urban ghettos." *Phylon* 31 (Summer):183–93.

Haimson, Leopold. 1964. "The problem of social stability in urban Russia, 1905–1917 (part one)." *Slavic Review* 23, no. 4 (December):619–42.

Haimson, Leopold. 1965. "The problem of social stability in urban Russia, 1905–1917 (part two)." *Slavic Review* 24, no. 1 (March):1–22.

Haimson, Leopold H., ed. 1974. *The Mensheviks: from the revolution of 1917 to the second world war*. Chicago: University of Chicago Press.

Hakes, Jay E. 1973. *Weak parliaments and military coups in Africa: a study in regime instability*. Sage Research Papers in the Social Sciences, Comparative Legislative Series, no. 90–004.

Halaby, Charles N. 1973. "'Hardship and collective violence in France': a comment." *American Sociological Review* 38, no. 4 (August):495–500.

Halebsky, Sandor. 1976. *Mass society and political conflict: toward a reconstruction of theory*. Cambridge: Cambridge University Press.

Halliday, Fred. 1979. *Iran: dictatorship and development*. Harmondsworth: Penguin.

Halperin, Ernst. 1976. *Terrorism in Latin America*. The Washington Papers IV, 33, no. 480033. Beverly Hills and London: Sage Publications.

Halpern, Joel M., and Brode, John. 1967. "Peasant society: economic changes and revolutionary transformation," in Bernard Siegel and Alan R. Beals (eds.), *Biennial Review of Anthropology 1967*. Stanford: Stanford University Press, 46–139.

Halpern, Manfred. 1963. *The politics of social change in the Middle East and North Africa*. Princeton: Princeton University Press.

Hamblin, Robert L.; Bridger, David A.; Day, Robert C.; and Yancey, William L. 1963. "The interference-aggression law?" *Sociometry* 26:190–216.

Hamerow, Theodore S. 1958. *Restoration, revolution, reaction: economics and politics in Germany 1815–1871*. Princeton: Princeton University Press.

Hamilton, Richard F., and Wright, James. 1975. *New directions in political sociology*. Indianapolis: Bobbs-Merrill Co.

Hammond, J. L., and Hammond, Barbara. 1948. *The village labourer*. 2 vols. London: Guild Books.

Hammond, Thomas T. 1975. "A summing up," in Hammond (1975a), 638–43.

Hammond, Thomas T., ed., and Farrell, Robert, associate ed. 1975a. *The anatomy of communist takeovers*. New Haven: Yale University Press.

Hampson, Norman. 1963. *A social history of the French Revolution*. London: Routledge & Kegan Paul.

Handberg, Roger B., Jr. 1972. "Violence and the fragile state: test of a model." *Review of Social Theory* 1, no. 1 (September):19–41.

Hannan, Michael T., and Tuma, Nancy Brandon. 1979. "Methods for temporal analysis." *Annual Review of Sociology* 5:303–28.

Hanratty, Margaret A.; O'Neal, Edgar; and Sulzer, Jefferson L. 1972. "Effect of frustration upon imitation of aggression." *Journal of Personality and Social Psychology* 21, no. 1 (January):30–34.

Harcave, Sidney. 1964. *The Russian revolution of 1905*. London: Collier-Macmillan.

Hargens, Lowell L. 1976. "A note on standardized coefficients as structural parameters." *Sociological Methods and Research* 5, no. 2 (November): 247–56.

Harries-Jenkins, Gwyn, and Doorn, Jacques van, eds. 1975. *The military and the problem of legitimacy*. Beverly Hills and London: Sage Publications.

Harris, Anthony R. 1975. "Imprisonment and the expected value of criminal choice: a specification and test of aspects of the labeling perspective." *American Sociological Review* 40, no. 1 (February):71–87.

Harris, Mary B. 1974. "Mediators between frustration and aggression in a field experiment." *Journal of Experimental Social Psychology* 10: 561–71.

Harris, Mary B. 1976. "Instigators and inhibitors of aggression in a field experiment." *Journal of Social Psychology* 98:27–38.

Harris, Richard J. 1976a. "Handling negative inputs: on the plausible equity formulae." *Journal of Experimental Social Psychology* 12:194–209.

Harrison, James P. 1971. *The Chinese communists and Chinese peasant rebellions: a study in the rewriting of Chinese history*. New York: Atheneum.

Harrison, James Pinckney. 1972. *The long march to power: a history of the Chinese Communist Party, 1921–72*. New York: Macmillan.

Harrod, Wendy Jean. 1980. "Expectations from unequal rewards." *Social Psychology Quarterly* 43, no. 1 (March):126–30.

Harsgor, Michael. 1976. *"Portugal in revolution."* Washington Paper Series, no. 33. Beverly Hills: Sage Publications.

Hartmann, Donald P. 1969. "Influence of symbolically modeled instrumental aggression and pain cues on aggressive behavior." *Journal of Personality and Social Psychology* 11, no. 3 (March):280–88.

Hartmann, Peter Claus. 1978. "Die Steuersysteme in Frankreich und England am Vorabend der Französischen Revolution: Ein Strukturenvergleich," in Hinrichs et al., 43–65.

Hartup, Willard W. 1974. "Aggression in childhood." *American Psychologist* 29, no. 5 (May):336–41.

Hatto, Arthur. 1949. "'Revolution': an enquiry into the usefulness of an historical term." *Mind* 58 (October):495–517.

Haupt, Heinz-Gerhard. 1977. "Zur historischen Anayse von Gewalt: Review of Tilly et al. (1975)," in R. Tilly, 236–56.

Haupt, Heinz-Gerhard, and Hausen, Karin. 1979. *Die Pariser Kommune: Erfolg und Scheitern einer Revolution*. Frankfort: Campus Verlag.

Hauser, Robert M., and Featherman, David L. 1974a. "White-non-white differentials in occupational mobility among men in the United States, 1962–1972." *Demography* 11:247–65.

Hauser, Robert M., and Featherman, David L. (1974b): "Socioeconomic achievements of U. S. men; 1962–1972." *Science* 185 (July 26th): 325–331.

Havens, Murray Clark; Leiden, Carl; and Schmitt, Karl. 1970. *The politics of assassination*. Englewood Cliffs: Prentice-Hall. Revised ed.: *Assassination and terrorism: their modern dimensions* (1975).

Hawkins, Brett W.; Marando, Vicent L.; and Taylor, George A. 1971. "Efficacy, mistrust, and political participation: findings from additional data and indicators." *Journal of Politics* 23, no. 4 (November):1130–36.

Hawley, Willis D. 1970. "Review of Michael Lipsky: Protest in city politics." *American Political Science Review* 64, no. 4 (December):1257–58.

Hayter, Tony. 1978. *The army and the crowd in Mid-Georgian England*. London: Macmillan.

Hazlewood, Leo. 1973a. "Concept and measurement stability in the study of conflict behavior within nations." *Comparative Political Studies* 6, no. 2 (July):171–95.

Hazlewood, Leo A. 1973b. "Externalizing systemic stress: international conflict as adaptive behavior," in Wilkenfeld (1973), 148–90.

Hazlewood, Leo. 1975. "Diversion mechanisms and encapsulation processes: the domestic conflict-foreign conflict hypothesis reconsidered," in Patrick McGowan (ed.), *Sage International Yearbook of Foreign Policy Studies*, vol. 3. Beverly Hills: Sage Publications, 213–44.

Hazlewood, L. A., and Paranzino, D. 1971. "Regions, regionalism, and violence: 'groups' of political systems as problems in comparative analysis." Presented at the International Studies Association Meetings. San Juan, Puerto Rico. Mimeographed.

Hazlewood, Leo A., and West, Gerald T. 1974. "Bivariate associations, factor structures, and substantive impact: the source coverage problem revisited." *International Studies Quarterly* 18, no. 3 (September):317–37.

Hearn, Francis. 1978. *Domination, legitimation, and resistance: the incorporation of the nineteenth-century English working class*. Westport, Conn.: Greenwood Press.

Heath, Anthony. 1976. *Rational choice and social exchange: a critique of exchange theory*. Cambridge: Cambridge University Press.

Heggoy, Alf Andrew. 1972. *Insurgency and counter-insurgency in Algeria*. Bloomington: Indiana University Press.

Heiberg, Marianne. 1975. "Insiders/outsiders: Basque nationalism." *Archives Européennes de Sociologie* 16, no. 2:169–93.

Heidenheimer, Arnold J., ed. 1970. *Political corruption: readings in comparative analysis*. New York: Holt, Rinehart & Winston.

Heilbrunn, Otto. 1962. *Partisan warfare*. London: George Allen & Unwin.

Heintz, Peter, ed. 1972. *A macrosociological theory of societal systems: 1 – with special reference to the international system*. Bern: Hans Huber.

Heise, David R. 1969. "Problems in path analysis and causal inference," in Borgatta, 38–73.

Heise, David R. 1970. "Causal inference from panel data," in Edgar F. Borgatta (ed.), *Sociological methodology 1970*. San Francisco: Jossey-Bass, 3–27.

Heisler, Martin O. 1979. "Review of Inglehart (1977a)." *Journal of Political and Military Sociology* 7, no. 1 (Spring):151–54.

Hellman, Judith Adler. 1978. *Mexico in crisis*. London: Heinemann.

Hempel, Carl G. 1959. "The logic of functional analysis,'. in Llewellyn Gross (ed.), *Symposium on sociological theory*. Evanston, Ill.: Row, Peterson, 271–307.

Hempel, Carl G. 1965. "The functions of general laws in history," in *Aspects of scientific explanation and other essays in the philosophy of science*. New York: Free Press, 231–43.

Henecka, Hans Peter. 1972. *Die jurassischen Separatisten: Eine Studie zur Soziologie des ethnischen Konflikts und der sozialen Bewegung*. Meisenheim am Glan: Verlag Anton Hain.

Henkel, Ramon E. 1975. "Part-whole correlations and the treatment of ordinal and quasi-interval data as interval data." *Pacific Sociological Review* 18, no. 1 (January):3–26.

Hermann, Charles F. 1969. "International crisis as a situational variable," in James N. Rosenau (ed.), *International politics and foreign policy: a reader in research and theory*. New York: Free Press, 409–21.

Hermann, Charles F., ed. 1972. *International crisis: insights from behavioral research*. New York: Free Press.

Hermens, Ferdinand A. 1941. *Democracy or anarchy?* South Bend, Ind.: Notre Dame University Press.

Hernes, Gudmund. 1969. "On rank disequilibrium and military coups d'état." *Journal of Peace Research* 6:63–72.

Herspring, Dale R., guest ed. 1978. "Civil military relations in communist countries: first steps toward theory." *Comparative Communism* 11, no. 3 (Autumn).

Herz, Thomas. 1979. "Der Wandel von Wertvorstellungen in westlichen Industriegesellschaften." *Kölner Zeitschrift für Soziologie und Sozialpsychologie* 31, no. 2 (July):282–302.

Hewitt, Christopher. 1977. "Majorities and minorities: a comparative survey of ethnic violence." *The Annals of the American Academy of Political and Social Science* 433 (September):150–60.

Heyman, Edward, and Mickolus, Edward. 1980. "Observations on 'Why violence spreads.'" *International Studies Quarterly* 24, no. 2 (June): 299–305.

Hibbs, Douglas A., Jr. 1973. *Mass political violence: a cross-national causal analysis*. New York: Wiley.

Hibbs, Douglas A., Jr. 1974. "Problems of statistical estimation and causal inference in time-series regression models," in Herbert L. Costner (ed.), *Sociological methodology 1973–1974*. San Francisco: Jossey-Bass Publishers, 252–308.

Hibbs, Douglas A., Jr. 1976. "Industrial conflict in advanced industrial societies." *American Political Science Review* 70, no. 4 (December): 1033–58.

Hibbs, Douglas A. 1978. "On the political economy of long-run trends in strike activity." *British Journal of Political Science* 8, no. 2 (April): 153–75.

Higham, Robin, ed. 1969. *Bayonets in the streets: the use of troops in civil disturbances*. Lawrence: University Press of Kansas.

Higham, Robin. 1972. *Civil wars in the twentieth century*. Lexington: University of Kentucky Press.

Hill, Christopher. 1965. *Intellectual origins of the English Revolution*. Oxford: At the Clarendon Press.

Hill, Christopher. 1967. *The century of revolution 1603-1714*. London: Nelson. (Original 1961.)

Hill, Christopher. 1968. *Puritanism and revolutions: studies in interpretation of the English Revolution of the 17th century*. London: Panther.

Hill, Christopher. 1970. *God's Englishman: Oliver Cromwell and the English Revolution*. London: Weidenfeld & Nicolson.

Hill, Christopher. 1972. *The world turned upside down: radical ideas during the English Revolution*. London: Temple Smith.

Hill, Kim Quaile. 1979. "Military role vs. military rule: allocations to military activities." *Comparative Politics* 11, no. 3 (April):371-77.

Hilton, Rodney. 1973. *Bond men made free: medieval peasant movements and the English rising of 1381*. London: Temple Smith.

Hilton, R. H. 1975. *The English peasantry in the later middle ages*. Oxford: Clarendon Press.

Himes, Joseph S. 1971. "A theory of racial conflict." *Social Forces* 50, no. 1 (September):53-60.

Himes, Joseph S. 1974. "Toward a theory of racial-ethnic conflict." Paper prepared for the eighth World Congress of Sociology, August, in Toronto.

Hiniker, Paul J. 1977. *Revolutionary ideology and Chinese reality: dissonance under Mao*. Beverly Hills: Sage Publications.

Hinrichs, Ernst; Schmitt, Eberhard; and Vierhaus, Rudolf, eds. 1978. *Vom Ancien Régime zur Französischen Revolution: Forschungen und Perspektiven*. Göttingen: Vandenhoeck & Ruprecht.

Hirsch, Herbert, and Perry, David C., eds. 1973. *Violence as politics: a series of original essays*. New York: Harper & Row.

Hirschman, Albert O. 1963. *Journey toward progress: studies of economic policy-making in Latin America*. New York: Twentieth Century Fund.

Hirschman, Albert O. 1970. *Exit, voice, and loyalty*. Cambridge, Mass.: Harvard University Press.

Hirschman, Albert O. 1973. "The changing tolerance for income inequality in the course of economic development." *Quarterly Journal of Economics* 87:544-66. (With a mathematical appendix by Michael Rothschild.)

Hirschman, Albert O. 1974. "'Exit, voice, and loyalty': further reflections and a survey of recent contributions." *Social Science Information* 13, no. 1 (February):7-26.

Hoadley, S. Stephen. 1973. "Social complexity, economic development, and military coups d'état in Latin America and Asia." *Journal of Peace Research*, nos. 1-2:119-20.

Hoadley, S. Stephen. 1975. *Soldiers and politics in Southeast Asia: civil-military relations in comparative perspective*. Cambridge, Mass.: Schenkman Publishing Co.

Hobsbawm, E. J. 1952. "The machine breakers." *Past and Present* 1 (February):57-70.

Hobsbawm, E. J. 1959. *Primitive rebels: studies in archaic forms of social movement in the 19th and 20th centuries*. Manchester: Manchester University Press.

Hobsbawm, E. J. 1962. *The age of revolution 1789-1848*. New York: Mentor Books.

Hobsbawm, E. J. 963. "The revolutionary situation in Colombia." *World Today* (19 June):248-58.

Hobsbawm, Eric J. 1964. "Review essay: 'On revolution,' by Hannah Arendt." *History and Theory* 4, no. 1:252–58.
Hobsbawm, E. J. 1969. *Bandits*. London: Weidenfeld & Nicolson. Here quoted after the Penguin Books edition, Harmondsworth (1972).
Hobsbawm, Eric. 1972a. "Social bandits: reply." *Comparative Studies in Society and History* 14, no. 4 (September):503–505.
Hobsbawm, Eric J. 1973. *Revolutionaries. Contemporary essays*. London: Weidenfeld & Nicolson.
Hobsbawm, E. J. 1974. "Social banditry," in Landberger, 142–57.
Hobsbawm, E. J., and Rudé, George. 1969. *Captain Swing*. London: Lawrence & Wishart.
Hodges, Donald C., ed. 1973. *Philosophy of the urban guerrilla: the revolutionary writings of Abraham Guillén*. New York: William Morrow & Co.
Hodges, Donald C. 1974. *The Latin American Revolution: politics and strategy from APRA-Marxism to Guevarism*. New York: William Morrow.
Hoerder, Dirk. 1977. *Crowd action in revolutionary Massachusetts, 1765–1780*. New York: Academic Press.
Hoffer, E. 1951. *The true believer: thoughts on the nature of mass movements*. New York: Harper.
Hoffmann, Rainer. 1977. *Maos Rebellen: Sozialgeschichte der chinesischen Kulturrevolution*. Hamburg: Hoffmann und Campe.
Hoffmann, Stanley. 1962. "Protest in modern France," in Kaplan, 69–91.
Hofheinz, Roy. 1969. "The ecology of Chinese communist success: rural influence patterns, 1923–1945," in A. Doak Barnett (ed.), *Chinese communist politics in action*. Seattle: University of Washington Press, 3–77.
Hofheinz, Roy. 1977. *The broken wave: the Chinese communist peasant movement, 1922–1928*. Cambridge, Mass.: Harvard University Press.
Hogan, Dennis P., and Featherman, David L. 1977. "Racial stratification and socioeconomic change in the American North and South." *American Journal of Sociology* 83, no. 1. (July):100–126.
Hoggard, G. 1971. "An analysis of the 'real' data: reflections on the uses and validity of international interaction data." Presented to the Meeting of the International Studies Association. Mimeographed.
Hoggard, Gary. 1974. "Differential source coverage in foreign policy analysis," in Rosenau, 353–81.
Høivik, Tord. 1977. "The demography of structural violence." *Journal of Conflict Resolution* 14, no. 1:59–73.
Holt, Robert T., and Turner, John E. 1975. "Crises and sequences in collective theory development." *American Political Science Review* 69, no. 3 (September):979–94.
Homans, George C. 1961. *Social behavior: its elementary forms*. New York: Harcourt, Brace & World. Revised ed. New York: Harcourt, Brace, Jovanovich (1974).
Homans, George C. 1976. "Commentary," in Berkowitz/Walster, 231–44.
Hoogvelt, Ankie M. M. 1976. *The sociology of developing societies*. London: Macmillan.
Hook, Ernest B. 1973. "Behavioral implications of the human XYY genotype." *Science* 179:139–50.
Hook, Sidney. 1934. "Violence," in *Encyclopaedia of the Social Sciences*,

vol. 15. New York: Macmillan, 264–67.

Hoole, F. W. 1964. "Political stability and instability within nations: a cross-national study." Master's thesis, San Diego State College.

Hoover, Calvin B. 1960. "Revolutions and tyranny." *Virginia Quarterly Review* 36:182–94.

Hopkins, Keith. 1966. "Civil-military relations in developing countries." *British Journal of Sociology* 17, no. 2 (June):165–82.

Hopkins, Phyllis, and Feierabend, Rosalind. 1971. "Correlates of United States riots, 1965–1967: a cross-city comparison." *Proceedings of the Annual Convention of the American Psychological Association* 6, 311–12.

Hopkins, Raymond. 1969. "Aggregate data and the study of political development." *Journal of Politics* 31, no. 1 (Feburary):71–94.

Hopmann, P. Terry. 1967. "International conflict and cohesion in the communist system." *International Studies Quarterly* 11, no. 3 (September):212–36.

Hopper, Rex D. 1950. "The revolutionary process: a frame of reference for the study of revolutionary movements." *Social Forces* 28, no. 3 (March):270–79. Reprinted in part in Turner/Killian (1957), 310–29.

Horchem, Hans Josef. 1975. *Extremisten in einer selbstbewußten Demokratie.* Freiburg/Breisgau: Herderbücherei.

Horne, Alistair. 1978. *A savage war of peace: Algeria 1954–1962.* New York: Viking Press.

Horowitz, Irving Louis. 1967. *The rise and fall of the Project Camelot.* Cambridge, Mass.: MIT Press.

Horowitz, Irving Louis. 1968. "Political legitimacy and the institutionalization of crises in Latin America." *Comparative Political Studies* 1, no. 1 (April):45–69.

Horowitz, Irving Louis. 1970. "'Separate, but equal': revolution and counter-revolution in the American city." *Social Problems* 17, no. 3 (Winter): 294–312.

Horowitz, Irving Louis. 1972. "The morphology of modern revolution." *Indian Journal of Sociology* 3, nos. 1–2 (March/September):3–34.

Horowitz, Irving Louis. 1973. "Political terrorism and state power." *Journal of Political and Military Sociology* 1, no. 2 (Spring):147–57.

Horowitz, Irving Louis; Castro, José de; and Gerassi, John, eds. 1969. *Latin American radicalism: a documentary report on left and nationalist movements.* New York: Random House.

Horton, Paul B., and Leslie, Gerald R. 1974. *The sociology of social problems.* Englewood Cliffs: Prentice-Hall.

Hoskin, Gary, and Swanson, Gerald. 1973. "Inter-party competition in Columbia: a return to La Violencia?" *American Journal of Political Science* 17, no. 2 (May):316–50.

Hottinger, Arnold. 1979. "Does Saudi Arabia face revolution?" *New York Review of Books* June 28:14–17.

House, James S., and Mason, William M. 1975. "Political alienation in America, 1952–1968." *American Sociological Review* 40, no. 2 (April): 123–47.

Huberman, Leo, and Sweezy, Paul M., eds. 1968. *Regis Debray and the Latin American revolution: a collection of essays.* New York: Monthly Review.

Hudson, M. C. 1970. *Conditions of political violence and instability*. Sage Professional Paper in Comparative Politics Series, no. 01–005.

Hudson, Michael C. 1971. "Political protest and power transfers in crisis periods: regional, structural, and environmental comparisons." *Comparative Political Studies* 4, no. 3 (October):259–94.

Hudson, Michael C. 1976. "The Lebanese crisis: the limits of consociational democracy." *Journal of Palestine Studies* 5, nos. 3–4, 19–20 (Spring-Summer):109–22.

Huff, David L., and Lutz, James M. 1974. "The contagion of political unrest in independent Black Africa." *Economic Geography* 50, no. 4:352–67.

Hufnagel, Gerhard. 1971. *Kritik als Beruf: Der kritische Gehalt im Werk Max Webers*. Frankfort on the Main: Propyläen Verlag.

Hufton, Olwen. 1971. "Women in the revolution 1789–1796." *Past and Present* 53 (November):90–108.

Hufton, Olwen H. 1974. *The poor of eighteenth-century France, 1750–1789*. Oxford: Clarendon Press.

Hugger, Paul. 1976. *Sozialrebellen und Rechtsbrecher in der Schweiz: eine historisch-volkskundliche Studie*. Zürich: Atlantis.

Hughes, David R. 1967. "The myth of military coups and military assistance." *Military Review* 47 (December):3–10.

Huizer, Gerrit. 1970. "Emiliano Zapata and the peasant guerillas in the Mexican Revolution," in Stavenhagen, 375–406.

Hull, Roger H. 1976. *The Irish triangle*. Princeton: Princeton University Press.

Humbaraci, Arslan. 1966. *Algeria: a revolution that failed: a political history since 1954*. London: Pall Mall Press.

Hunecke, Volker. 1974. "Die Pariser Kommune von 1871." *Neue Politische Literatur* 19, no. 1 (January):83–108.

Hunecke, Volker. 1978. "Antikapitalistische Strömungen in der Französischen Revolution: Neuere Kontroversen der Forschung." *Geschichte und Gesellschaft* 4, no. 3:291–323.

Hunt, Chester L., and Walker, Lewis. 1974. *Ethnic dynamics: patterns of intergroup relations in various societies*. Homewood, Ill.: Dorsey Press.

Hunter, Robert. 1940. *Revolution: why, how, when?* New York: Harper & Brothers.

Huntington, Samuel P. 1957. *The soldier and the state: the theory and politics of civil-military relations*. New York: Belknap Press of Harvard University Press.

Huntington, Samuel P. 1962. "Introduction," in Osanka, xv–xxii.

Huntington, Samuel P. 1962a. "Patterns of violence in world politics," in Huntington (ed.), *Changing patterns of military politics*. New York: Free Press, 17–50.

Huntington, Samuel P. 1965. "Political development and political decay." *World Politics* 17, no. 3 (April):386–430.

Huntington, Samuel P. 1966. "Political modernization: America vs. Europe." *World Politics* 18, no. 3 (April):378–414.

Huntington, Samuel P. 1968. *Political order in changing societies*. New Haven: Yale University Press.

Huntington, Samuel P. 1968a. "The bases of accommodation." *Foreign Affairs* 46, no. 4 (July):642–56.

Huntington, Samuel P. 1968b. "Civil-military relations," in *International Encyclopedia of the Social Sciences*, vol. 2:487–95.

Huntington, Samuel P. 1971a. "Civil violence and the process of development." *Adelphi Papers* 83:1-15.

Huntington, Samuel P. 1971b. "The change to change: modernization, development, and politics." *Comparative Politics* 3, no. 3 (April):283-322.

Huntington, Samuel P. 1975. "The United States," in Crozier et al., 59-118.

Huntington, Samuel P. 1977. "Remarks on the meanings of stability in the modern era," in Seweryn Bialer and Sophia Sluzar (eds.), *Radicalism in the contemporary age, vol. 3: Strategies and impact of contemporary radicalism.* Boulder, Colorado: Westview Press, 269-82.

Huntington, Samuel P., and Domínguez, Jorge I. 1975. "Political development," in Greenstein/Polsby, vol. 3, 1-114.

Huntington, Samuel P., and Nelson, Joan M. 1976. *No easy choice: political participation in developing countries.* Cambridge, Mass.: Harvard University Press.

Hurewitz, J. B. 1969. *Middle East politics: the military dimensions.* New York: Praeger. English ed. London: Pall Mall Press.

Hurwitz, Leon. 1971. "An index of democratic political stability: a methodological note." *Comparative Political Studies* 4, no. 1 (April):41-68.

Hurwitz, Leon. 1972. "Democratic political stability: some traditional hypotheses reexamined." *Comparative Political Studies* 4, no. 4 (January):476-90.

Hurwitz, Leon. 1973. "Review essay: contemporary approaches to political stability." *Comparative Politics* 5, no. 3 (April):449-63.

Hutchinson, Martha Crenshaw. 1978. *Revolutionary terrorism: the FLN in Algeria, 1954-1962.* Stanford, Calif.: Hoover Institution Press.

Hyman, Elizabeth H. 1972. "Soldiers in politics: new insights on Latin American armed forces." *Political Science Quarterly* 87, no. 3 (September):401-18.

Hyman, Herbert H. 1972. "Dimensions of social-psychological change in the Negro population," in Angus Campbell and Philip E. Converse (eds.), *The human meaning of social change.* New York: Russell Sage Foundation, 339-90.

Hyman, Herbert H., and Singer, Eleanor, eds. 1968. *Readings in reference group theory and research.* New York: Free Press.

Iglitzin, Lynne B. 1970. "Violence and American democracy." *Journal of Social Issues* 26, no. 1:165-86.

Iglitzen, Lynne B. 1972. *Violent conflict in American society.* San Francisco: Chandler Publishing Co.

Inglehart, Ronald. 1971. "The silent revolution in Europe: intergenerational change in post-industrial societies." *American Political Science Review* 65, no. 4 (December):991-1017.

Inglehart, Ronald. 1977a. *The silent revolution: changing values and political styles among Western publics.* Princeton: Princeton University Press.

Inglehart, Ronald. 1977b. "Political dissatisfaction and mass support for social change in advanced industrial society." *Comparative Political Studies* 10, no. 3 (October):455-72.

Inglehart, Ronald. 1978. "Value priorities, life satisfaction, and political dissatisfaction among Western publics," in Richard F. Tomasson (ed.), *Comparative Studies in Sociology* 1:173-202.

Inglehart, Ronald. 1979. "Value priorities and socioeconomic change," in Barnes, Kaase et al., 305–42.

Inglehart, Ronald F., and Woodward, Margaret. 1967–68. "Language conflicts and political community." *Comparative Studies in Society and History* 10:27–48.

Inkeles, Alex. 1969. "Participant citizenship in six developing countries." *American Political Science Review* 63, no. 4 (December):1120–41.

Inkeles, Alex, and Smith, David H. 1974. *Becoming modern: individual change in six developing countries*. Cambridge, Mass.: Harvard University Press.

International Review of Social History 17, parts 1–2, 1972. "1871."

Issawi, Charles. 1963. *Egypt in revolution: an economic analysis*. London: Oxford University Press.

Jackman, Robert W. 1973. "On the relation of economic development to democratic performance." *American Journal of Political Science* 17, no. 3 (August):611–21.

Jackman, Robert W. 1975. *Politics and social equality: a comparative analysis*. New York: Wiley-Interscience.

Jackman, Robert W. 1976. "Politicians in uniform: military governments and social change in the third world." *American Political Science Review* 70, no. 4 (December):1078–97.

Jackman, Robert W. 1978. "The predictability of coups d'état: a model with African data." *American Political Science Review* 72, no. 4 (December):1262–75.

Jackman, Robert W. 1980. "Keynesian government intervention and income inequality." *American Sociological Review* 45, no. 1 (February): 131–37.

Jackman, Robert W., and Boyd, William A. 1979. "Multiple sources in the collection of data on political conflict." *American Journal of Political Science* 23, no. 2 (May):434–58.

Jacknis, Norman J. 1973. "On the relation of regression analysis to congruence-consonance theories of governmental performance." *Comparative Political Studies* 6, no. 2 (July):251–54.

Jackson, Henry F. 1977. *The FLN in Algeria: party development in a revolutionary society*. Westport, Conn.: Greenwood.

Jackson, Robert J., and Stein, Michael B., eds. 1971. *Issues in comparative politics: a text with readings*. New York: St. Martin's Press.

Jackson, Steven; Russett, Bruce; Snidal, Duncan; and Sylvan, David. 1978. "Conflict and coercion in dependent states." *Journal of Conflict Resolution* 22, no. 4 (December):627–57.

Jackson, Steven; Russett, Bruce; Snidal, Duncan; and Sylvan, David. 1979. "An assessment of empirical research on dependencia." *Latin American Research Review* 14, no. 3:7–28.

Jacobson, Alvin L. 1973a. "Intrasocietal conflict, a preliminary test of a structural-level theory." *Comparative Political Studies* 6, no. 1 (April): 62–83.

Jacobson, Alvin L. 1973b. "Some theoretical and methodological considerations for measuring intrasocietal conflict." *Sociological Methods and Research* 1, no. 4 (May):439–61.

Jänicke, Martin. 1971. "Zum Konzept der politischen Systemkrise." *Politische Vierteljahresschrift* 12, no. 4:530–54.

Jänicke, Martin, ed. 1973. *Herrschaft und Krise*. Opladen: Westdeutscher Verlag.

Jänicke, Martin. 1973a. "Die Analyse des politischen Systems aus der Krisenperspektive," in Jänicke (ed.), *Politische Systemkrisen*. Cologne: Kiepenheuer & Witsch, 14–50.

Jaguaribe, Helio. 1973. *Political development: a general theory and a Latin American case study*. New York: Harper & Row Publishers.

Jain, Shail. 1975. *Size distribution of income: a compilation of data*. Washington: World Bank.

James, William. 1890. *The principles of psychology*, vol. 1. New York: Henry Holt & Co.

Jameson, J. Franklin. 1926. *The American Revolution considered as a social movement*. Princeton: Princeton University Press. New edition: Boston: Beacon Press (1956). Introduction by Arthur M. Schlesinger.

Janos, Andrew C. 1964. *The seizure of power: a study of force and popular consent*. Research Monograph, no. 16. Princeton: Center of International Studies.

Janos, Andrew C., and Slottman, William B., eds. 1971. *Revolution in perspective: essays on the Hungarian Soviet Republic of 1919*. Berkeley: University of California Press.

Janowitz, Morris. 1960. *The professional soldier: a social and political portrait*. Glencoe: Free Press.

Janowitz, Morris. 1964. *The military in the political development of new nations: an essay in comparative analysis*. Chicago: University of Chicago Press.

Janowitz, Morris. 1968. *Social control of escalated riots*. Chicago: University of Chicago Center for Policy Study.

Janowitz, Morris. 1969. "Patterns of collective violence," in Graham/Gurr, 412–44.

Janowitz, Morris. 1975. *Military conflict: essays in the institutional analysis of war and peace*. Beverly Hills and London: Sage Publications.

Janowitz, Morris. 1977. *Military institutions and coercion in the developing nations*. Chicago: University of Chicago Press. Expanded edition of *The military in the political development of new nations*.

Janowitz, Morris, and Doorn, Jacques van, eds. 1971. *On military intervention*. Rotterdam: Rotterdam University Press.

Jaroslawski, Jan. 1973. *Theorie der sozialistischen Revolution: Von Marx bis Lenin*. Hamburg: Hoffmann und Campe Verlag.

Jasso, Guillermina. 1978. "On the justice of earnings: a new specification of the justice evaluation function." *American Journal of Sociology* 83, no. 6 (May):1398–1419.

Jászi, Oscar. 1924. *Revolution and counter-revolution in Hungary*. London: King & Son.

Jászi, Oscar, and Lewis, John D. 1957. *Against the tyrant: the tradition and theory of tyrannicide*. Glencoe, Ill.: Free Press.

Jencks, Christopher et al. 1972. *Inequality: a reassessment of the effect of family and schooling in America*. New York: Basic Books.

Jenkins, Brian M. 1975. "International terrorism: a new mode of conflict," in Carlton/Schaerf, 13–49.

Jenkins, Brian M., and Johnson, Janera. 1975. *International terrorism: a chronology, 1968-1974*. Santa Monica, Calif.: Rand Corporation.

Jenkins, J. Craig. 1979. "What is to be done: movement or organization? Review of Piven/Cloward (1977)." *Contemporary Sociology* 8, no. 2 (March):222-28.

Jenkins, J. Craig, and Perrow, Charles. 1977. "Insurgency of the powerless: farm workers movements (1946-1972)." *American Sociological Review* 42, no. 2 (April):249-68.

Jenkins, Robin. 1971. "Why *do* men rebel? A discussion of Ted Robert Gurr's 'Why men rebel.'" *Race* 13 (July):89-92.

Jenkins, Robin, and MacRae, John. 1968. "Religion, conflict, and polarisation in Northern Ireland." in *Proceedings of the International Peace Research Association*. Second Conference. Assen: Van Gorcum and Co., 125-54.

Jennings, Edwart T. 1978. "Urban riots and welfare policy change: a test of the Piven-Cloward theory." Paper delivered at the Annual Meeting of the American Political Science Association, 31 August-3 September, in New York.

Jessop, R. D. 1971. "Civility and traditionalism in English political culture." *British Journal of Political Science* 1, no. 1 (January):1-24.

Jinadu, L. Adele. 1973. "Some aspects of the political philosophy of Frantz Fanon." *African Studies Review* 16, no. 2 (September):255-89.

Jiobu, Robert M. 1971. "City characteristics, differential stratification, and the occurrence of interracial violence." *Social Science Quarterly* 52, no. 3 (December):508-20.

Jiobu, Robert M. 1974. "City characteristics and racial violence." *Social Science Quarterly* 53, no. 1 (June):52-64.

Johnson, Chalmers A. 1962. *Peasant nationalism and communist power: the emergence of revolutionary China, 1937-1945*. Stanford: Stanford University Press.

Johnson, Chalmers. 1962a. "Civilian loyalties and guerrilla conflict." *World Politics* 14, no. 4 (July):646-61.

Johnson, Chalmers. 1964. *Revolution and the social system*. Hoover Institution Studies, no. 3. Stanford: Hoover Institution.

Johnson, Chalmers. 1965. "Building a communist nation in China," in Robert A. Scalapino (ed.), *The communist revolution in Asia: tactics, goals, and achievements*. Englewood Cliffs: Prentice-Hall, 47-81.

Johnson, Chalmers. 1966. *Revolutionary change*. Boston: Little, Brown.

Johnson, Chalmers. 1973. *Autopsy on people's war*. Berkeley: University of California Press.

Johnson, Chalmers. 1977. "Pregnant with 'meaning!' Mao and the revolutionary ascetic." *Journal of Interdisciplinary History* 7, no. 3 (Winter): 499-508.

Johnson, Douglas, ed. 1976. *French society and the revolution*. Cambridge: Cambridge University Press.

Johnson, Harry M. 1971. "Stability and change in ethnic-group relations," in Bernard Barber and Alex Inkeles (eds.), *Stability and change*. Boston: Little, Brown & Co., 311-53.

Johnson, John J., ed. 1962. *The role of the military in underdeveloped countries*. Princeton: Princeton University Press.

Johnson, John J. 1964a. *The military and society in Latin America*. Stanford: Stanford University Press.

Johnson, Michael P., and Sell, Ralph R. 1976. "The cost of being black: a 1970 update." *American Journal of Sociology* 82, no. 1 (July):183–90.

Johnson, Richard. 1972a. *The French Communist Party versus the students: revolutionary politics in May-June 1968*. New Haven, Conn.: Yale University Press.

Johnson, Roger N. 1972. *Aggression in man and animals*. Philadelphia: W. B. Saunders Co.

Johnson, R. W. 1977. *How long will South Africa survive?* London: Macmillan Press.

Johnston, James M. 1972. "Punishment of human behavior." *American Psychologist* 27, no. 11 (November):1033–54.

Jonas, Friedrich. 1969. "Hannah Arendts Theorie der Revolution." *Soziale Welt* 20:359–68.

Jones, Alfred W. 1969. "Contributions to a methodology for analyzing the internal behavior of nations." *General Systems* 14:151–56.

Jones, Ben R. 1967. *The French Revolution*. London: University of London Press.

Jones, J. R. 1972. *The revolution of 1688 in England*. London: Weidenfeld & Nicolson.

Joseph, Lawrence B. 1979. "The continuing crisis of pluralist democracy: neo-conservatism and revisionist liberalism." St. Louis: Washington University. Mimeographed.

Juviler, Peter H. 1976. *Revolutionary law and order: politics and social change in the USSR*. New York: Free Press.

Kaase, Max. 1972. "Political ideology, dissatisfaction, and protest." Presented at the Annual Meetings of the American Political Science Association, Washington, D. C. Mimeographed.

Kaase, Max. 1976. "Bedingungen unkonventionellen politischen Verhaltens in der Bundesrepublik Deutschland," in Kielmansegg, 179–216.

Kaase, Max. 1976a. "Political ideology, dissatisfaction and protest: a micro theory of unconventional political behavior." *German Political Studies* 2:7–28.

Kaase, Max and Marsh, Alan. 1976. "Pathways toward political action." Presented to the European Consortium Workshop Joint Sessions. Louvain, April, in Belgium. Mimeographed.

Käsler, Dirk. 1977. *Revolution und Veralltäglichung: Eine Theorie post-revolutionärer Prozesse*. Munich: Nymphenburger Verlagshandlung.

Kafker, Frank A. and Laux, James M. eds. 1968. *The French Revolution: conflicting interpretations*. New York: Random House.

Kahl, Joseph A. 1970. *The measurement of modernism: a study of values in Brazil and Mexico*. Austin: University of Texas Press.

Kalivoda, Robert. 1976. *Revolution und Ideologie: Der Hussitismus*. Cologne: Böhlau-Verlag.

Kaltefleiter, Werner. 1975. "Probleme der demokratischen Legitimation politischer Herrschaft." *Aus Politik und Zeitgeschehen, Beilage zu: Das Parlament*, B 47/1975, 29–38.

Kamen, Henry. 1971. *The iron century: social change in Europe 1550–1660.* London: Weidenfeld & Nicolson.

Kamenka, Eugene. 1966. "The concept of political revolution," in Friedrich, 122–35. Also in Kelly/Brown (1970), 110–21.

Kaminsky, Howard. 1967. *A history of the Hussite revolution.* Berkeley: University of California Press.

Kane, T. R.; Doerge, P.; and Tedeschi, J. T. 1973. "When is intentional harm doing perceived as aggressive? A naive reappraisal of the Berkowitz aggression paradigm." Paper presented at the American Psychological Association Convention.

Kane, Thomas R.; Joseph, Joanne M.; and Tedeschi, James T. 1976. "Person perception and the Berkowitz paradigm for the study of aggression." *Journal of Personality and Social Psychology* 33, no. 6 (June):663–73.

Kaplan, Lawrence, and Kaplan, Carol, eds. 1973. *Revolutions: a comparative study.* New York: Vintage Books.

Kaplan, Morton A., ed. 1962. *The revolution in world politics.* New York: Wiley & Sons.

Kaplan, Robert M., and Singer, Robert D. 1976. "Television violence and viewer aggression: a reexamination of the evidence." *Journal of Social Issues* 32, no. 4:35–70.

Kaplan, Steven L. 1976. *Bread: politics and political economy in the reign of Louis XV.* 2 vols. The Hague: Martinus Nijhoff.

Kaplow, Jeffry. 1965. *New perspectives on the French Revolution: readings in historical sociology.* New York: John Wiley & Sons.

Kaplow, Jeffry. 1965a. "Review of Cobban (1964)." *American Historical Review* 70, no. 4 (July):1094–96.

Kapsis, Robert E. 1978. "Black ghetto diversity and anomie: a sociopolitical view." *American Journal of Sociology* 83, no. 5 (March):1132–53.

Karnow, Stanley. 1972. *Mao and China: from revolution to revolution.* New York: Viking Press.

Karol, K. S. 1974. *The second Chinese Revolution.* New York: Hill and Wang. French original 1973.

Kase, Francis J. 1968. *People's democracy: a contribution to the study of the communist theory of state and revolution.* Leyden: A. W. Sijthoff.

Kataoka, Tetsuya. 1974. *Resistance and revolution in China: the communists and the second United Front.* Berkeley: University of California Press.

Katkov, George. 1967. *Russia 1917: the February revolution.* London: Longmans.

Katz, Irwin, and Gurin, Patricia, eds. 1969. *Race and the social sciences.* New York: Basic Books.

Kau, Ying-Mao. 1974. "Urban and rural strategies in the Chinese Communist Revolution," in Lewis, 253–70.

Kaufmann, Harry. 1965. "Definitions and methodology in the study of aggression." *Psychological Bulletin* 64, no. 5:351–64.

Kaufmann, Harry. 1970. *Aggression and altruism: a psychological analysis.* New York: Holt, Rinehart & Winston.

Kautsky, John H. 1969. "Revolutionary and managerial elites in modernizing regimes." *Comparative Politics* 1:441–67.

Kautsky, John H. 1975. *Patterns of modernizing revolutions: Mexico and the Soviet Union.* Sage Professional Paper in Comparative Politics Series, no. 01–056.

Kavanagh, Dennis. 1977. "Political leadership and overload." Paper presented at the European Consortium for Political Research Workshop, in Berlin.

Keep, John L. H. 1976. *The Russian Revolution: a study in mass mobilization.* New York: W. W. Norton & Co.

Kelleher, Catherine McArdle, ed. 1974. *Political-military systems: comparative perspectives.* Beverly Hills and London: Sage Publications.

Keller, Theodore. 1973. "To lead the people: notes on the Russian revolutionaries." *Journal of Contemporary Revolutions* 5, no. 3 (Summer): 94–121.

Kelley, Jonathan, 1974. "The politics of school busing." *Public Opinion Quarterly* 38, no. 1 (Spring):23–39.

Kelly, Dennis D. 1974. "The experimental imperative: laboratory analysis of aggressive behaviors," in Shervert H. Frazier (ed.), *Aggression*, vol. 52. Proceedings of the Association for Research in Nervous and Mental Disease, December 1972. Baltimore: Williams & Wilkins Company.

Kelly, George A., and Brown, Clifford W., Jr., eds. 1970. *Struggles in the state: sources and patterns of world revolution.* New York: John Wiley & Sons.

Kelly, George A., and Miller, Linda B. 1970. "Internal war and international systems: perspectives on method," in Kelly/Brown, 226–60.

Kelman, Herbert C. 1969. "Patterns of personal involvement in the national system: a social-psychological analysis of political legitimacy," in James N. Rosenau (ed.), *International politics and foreign policy.* 2d ed. New York: Free Press, 276–88.

Kelman, Herbert C. 1970. "A social-psychological model of political legitimacy and its relevance to black and white student protest movements." *Psychiatry* 33, no. 2 (May):224–46.

Kende, Istvan. 1971. "Twenty-five years of local wars." *Journal of Peace Research* 8:5–22.

Kende, István. 1977. "Dynamics of wars, or arms trade, and of military expenditure in the 'Third World' 1945–1976." *Instant Research on Peace and Violence* 2:59–67.

Kende, István. 1978. "Wars of ten years (1967–1976)." *Journal of Peace Research* 15, no. 3:227–41.

Kennedy, Gavin. 1974. *The military in the third world.* London: Duckworth.

Kennedy, John G. 1966. "'Peasant society and the image of limited good': a critique." *American Anthropologist* 68:1212–25.

Kennett, Lee, and Anderson, James LaVerne. 1975. *The gun in America: the origins of a national dilemma.* Westport, Conn.: Greenview Press.

Kent, Edward, ed. 1971. *Revolution and the rule of law.* Englewood Cliffs: Prentice-Hall.

Kenyon, J. P. 1977. *Revolution principles: the politics of party 1689–1720.* Cambridge: Cambridge University Press.

Kerbo, Harold R. 1978. "Foreign involvement in the preconditions for political violence: the world system and the case of Chile." *Journal of Conflict Resolution* 22, no. 3 (September):363–92.

Kerkvliet, Benedict J. 1977. *The HUK rebellion: a study of peasant revolt in the Philippines.* Berkeley: University of California Press.

Kerr, Henry H., Jr. 1974. *Switzerland: social cleavages and partisan conflict.* Sage Professional Papers in Contemporary Political Sociology Series, no. 06-002.

Kesselman, Mark. 1970. "Overinstitutionalization and political constraint: the case of France." *Comparative Politics* 3, no. 1 (October):21-44.

Kesselman, Mark. 1973. "Order or movement? The literature of political development as ideology." *World Politics* 26, no. 1 (October):139-54.

Kessler, Helmut. 1973. *Ideologie und Nomenklatur der revolutionären Gewaltanwendung in Frankreich von 1770 bis 1794.* Munich: Wilhelm Fink 1973.

Kielmansegg, Peter Graf, ed. 1976. *Legitimationsprobleme politischer Systeme.* Sonderheft 7/1976 of the Politische Vierteljahresschrift. Opladen: Westdeutscher Verlag.

Kim, C. I. Eugene, and Kihl, Young W. 1978. "The civilianized military regimes in Asia and their socio-economic performances." Prepared for presentation to the Research Committee on Armed Froces and Society, 9th World Congress of Sociology in Uppsala, Sweden, August 14-19. Mimeographed.

Kim, Jae-On. 1975. "Multivariate analysis of ordinal variables." *American Journal of Sociology* 81, no. 2 (September):261-98.

Kim, Jae-On, and Mueller, Charles W. 1976. "Standardized and unstandardized coefficients in causal analysis: an expository note." *Sociological Methods and Research* 4, no. 4 (May):423-38.

Kim, Kyung-Won. 1970. *Revolution and international system.* New York: New York University Press.

Kimberly, John R. 1976. "Issues in the design of longitudinal organizational research." *Sociological Methods and Research* 4, no. 3 (February): 321-47.

Kingston-Mann, Esther. 1972. "Lenin and the beginnings of Marxist peasant revolution: the burden of political opportunity, July–October 1917." *Slavonic and East European Review* 50, no. 121 (October):570-88.

Kipnis, David. 1974. "The powerholder," in James T. Tedeschi (ed.), *Perspectives on social power.* Chicago: Aldine Publishing Co., 82-122.

Kirchheimer, O. 1965. "Confining conditions and revolutionary breakthroughs." *American Political Science Review* 59, no. 4 (December): 964-74.

Kirkham, James F.; Levy, Sheldon G.; and Crotty, William J. 1969. *Assassination and political violence,* vol. 8. A report to the National Commission on the Causes and Prevention of Violence. Washington, D. C.: Government Printing Office.

Kitson, Frank. 1971. *Low intensity operations: subversion, insurgency, peace-keeping.* London: Faber & Faber.

Kitson, Frank. 1977. *Bunch of five.* London: Faber & Faber.

Klein, Herbert S. 1968. "The crisis of legitimacy and the origins of social revolution: the Bolivian experience." *Journal of Inter-American Studies* 10 (January):102-16.

Kline, F. Gerald; Kent, Kurt; and Davis, Dennis. 1971. "Problems in causal analysis of aggregate data with applications to political instability," in Gillespie/Nesvold, 251-79.

Kling, Merle. 1956. "Towards a theory of power and political instability in Latin America." *Western Political Quarterly* 9, no. 1 (March):21-35. Also in Petras/Zeitlin (1968), 76-93.

Kling, Merle. 1962. "Cuba: a case study of a successful attempt to seize political power by the application of unconventional warfare." *Annals of the American Academy of Political and Social Science* 341 (May): 42–52.

Kling, M. 1967. "Violence and politics in Latin America." *Sociological Review Monographs* 11:119–32.

Klingemann, Hans D. 1972. "Testing the left-right continuum on a sample of German voters." *Comparative Political Studies* 5, no. 1 (April):93–106.

Klingman, David. 1980. "Temporal and spatial diffusion in the comparative analysis of social change." *American Political Science Review* 74, no. 1 (March):123–37.

Kluge, Ulrich. 1975. *Soldatenräte und Revolution: Studien zur Militärpolitik in Deutschland 1918/19*. Göttingen: Vandenhoeck und Ruprecht.

Kluge, Ulrich. 1978. "Krisen des politischen und sozialen Wandels in Deutschland zwischen Kaiserreich und Republik: Bemerkungen zu jüngsten Beiträgen der neueren westdeutschen Revolutions– und Räteforschung." *Archiv für Sozialgeschichte* 18:610–32.

Knei-Paz, Baruch. 1978. *The social and political thought of Leon Trotsky*. Oxford: Oxford University Press.

Knopf, Terry Ann. 1975. *Rumours, race, and riots*. New Brunswick, N.J.: Transaction Books.

Knott, Paul D., and Drost, Bruce A. 1972. "Effects of varying intensity of attack and fear arousal on the intensity of counter-aggression." *Journal of Personality* 40, no. 1 (March):27–37.

Knott, Paul D.; Lasater, Lane; and Shuman, Rich. 1974. "Aggression-guilt and conditionability for aggressiveness." *Journal of Personality* 42:332–44.

Knutson, John F., ed. 1973. *The control of aggression*. Chicago: Aldine Publishing Co.

Kobrin, Stephen J. 1976. "Foreign direct investment, industrialization, and social change." *Journal of Conflict Resolution* 20, no. 3 (September): 497–522.

Köhler, Gernot, and Alcock, Norman. 1976. "An empirical table of structural violence." *Journal of Peace Research* 13, no. 4:233–55.

Koenigsberger, H. G. 1971. *Estates and revolutions: essays in early modern European history*. Ithaca, N.Y.: Cornell University Press.

Kohl, James, and Litt, John. 1974. *Urban guerrilla warfare in Latin America*. Cambridge, Mass.: MIT Press.

Kolkowicz, Roman. 1967. *The Soviet military and the communist party*. Princeton: Princeton University Press.

Koller, Douglas B. 1979. "The diffusion of political violence in Argentina: a domestic vs. an international context." Montreal: McGill University. Mimeographed.

Komorita, S. S. 1974. "A weighted probability model of coalition formation." *Psychological Review* 81, no. 3 (May):242–56.

Komorita, S. S., and Moore, Danny. 1976. "Theories and processes of coalition formation." *Journal of Personality and Social Psychology* 33, no. 4 (April):371–81.

Konečni, V. J. 1975. "Annoyance, type and duration of postannoyance activity, and aggression: the 'cathartic effect.'" *Journal of Experimental Psychology: General* 104:76–102.

Konečni, Vladimir J., and Doob, Anthony N. 1972. "Catharsis through displacement of aggression." *Journal of Personality and Social Psychology* 23, no. 3 (September):379–87.

Konečni, Vladimir J., and Ebbesen, Ebbe B. 1976. "Disinhibition versus the cathartic effect: artifact and substance." *Journal of Personality and Social Psychology* 34, no. 3 (September):352–65.

Koning, Steven M. 1978. "The trust-efficacy hypothesis revisited." Merrill-Palmer Institute, Detroit. Mimeographed.

Kornberg, Allan; Clarke, Harold D.; and Leduc, Lawrence. 1978. "Some correlates of regime support in Canada." *British Journal of Political Science* 8, no. 2 (April):199–216.

Kornberg, Allan; Clarke, Harold D.; and Stewart, Marianne C. 1979. "Federalism and fragmentation: political support in Canada." *Journal of Politics* 41, no. 3 (August):889–906.

Kornhauser, William. 1959. *The politics of mass society*. New York: Free Press.

Kornhauser, William. 1971. "Revolutions," in Roger W. Little (ed.), *Handbook of military institutions*. Beverly Hills: Sage Publications, 375–98.

Korpi, Walter. 1974. "Conflict, power, and relative deprivation." *American Political Science Review* 68, no. 4 (December):1569–78.

Korpi, Walter. 1974a. "Conflict and the balance of power." *Acta Sociologica* 17, no. 2:99–114.

Kort, Fred. 1952. "The quantification of Aristotle's theory of revolution." *American Political Science Review* 46, no. 2 (June):486–93.

Koselleck, Reinhard. 1967. *Preußen zwischen Reform und Revolution: Allgemeines Landrecht, Verwaltung und soziale Bewegung von 1791 bis 1848.* Stuttgart: Ernst Klett Verlag.

Koselleck, R. 1969. "Der neuzeitliche Revolutionsbegriff als geschichtliche Kategorie." *Studium Generale* 22:825–38.

Kossok, Manfred, ed. 1976. *Rolle und Formen der Volksbewegung im bürgerlichen Revolutionszyklus.* Berlin (East): Akademic-Verlag.

Kourvetaris, G. A. 1971. "The Greek army officer corps: its professionalism and political interventionism," in Janowitz/Doorn, 153–201.

Kourvetaris, George A., and Dobratz, Betty A. 1976. "The present state and development of sociology of the military." *Journal of Political and Military Sociology* 4, no. 1 (Spring):67–105.

Kracauer, Siegfried. 1947. *From Caligari to Hitler: a psychological history of the German film.* Princeton: Princeton University Press.

Kramnick, Isaac. 1972. "Reflections on revolution: definition and explanation in recent scholarship." *History and Theory* 11, no. 1:26–63.

Krane, Dale. 1974. "Economic development, political centralization, and political stability." Paper presented to the Annual Meeting of the American Political Science Association, August/September, in Chicago.

Kregarman, John J., and Worchel, Philip. 1961. "Arbitrariness of frustration and aggression." *Journal of Abnormal and Social Psychology* 63:183–87.

Krejci, Jaroslav. 1978. "Ethnic problems in Europe," in Salvador Giner and Margaret Scotford Archer (eds.), *Contemporary Europe: social structures and cultural patterns.* London: Routledge & Kegan Paul, 124–71.

Kristol, Irving. 1973–74. "The American Revolution as a successful revolution," in Tonsor, 3–21.

Kroes, Rob. 1966. "Revolution and scientific knowledge." Presented to the Working Group on Armed Forces and Society. Evian. Mimeographed.

Kruskal, Joseph B. 1968. "Transformation of data," in David Sills (ed.), *International Encyclopedia of the Social Sciences*, vol. 15. New York: Free Press and Macmillan, 182–93.

Küther, Carsten. 1976. *Räuber und Gauner in Deutschland: Das organisierte Bandenwesen im 18. und frühen 19. Jahrhundert*. Göttingen: Vandenhoeck und Ruprecht.

Kuhn, Philip A. 1970. *Rebellion and its enemies in late imperial China: militarization and social structure, 1796–1864*. Cambridge, Mass.: Harvard University Press.

Kuhn, Thomas S. 1962. *The structure of scientific revolutions*. Chicago: University of Chicago Press.

Kumar, Krishan, ed. 1971. *Revolution: the theory and practice of a European idea*. London: Weidenfeld & Nicolson.

Kunczik, Michael. 1975. *Gewalt im Fernsehen: Eine Analyse der potentiell kriminogenen Effekte*. Cologne: Böhlau-Verlag.

Kuo, Wen H. 1977. "Black political participation: a reconsideration." *Journal of Political and Military Sociology* 5, no. 1 (Spring):1–16.

Kupperman, Robert H. 1977. "Treating the symptoms of terrorism: some principles of good hygiene." *Terrorism* 1, no. 1:35–49.

Kupperman, Robert H., and Trent, Darrell M. 1979. *Terrorism: threat, reality, response*. Stanford: Hoover Institution Press.

Kurtz, Stephen G., and Hutson, James H., eds. 1973. *Essays on the American Revolution*. Chapel Hill: University of North Carolina Press.

Kuznets, Simon. 1955. "Economic growth and income inequality." *American Economic Review* 45, no. 1 (March):1–28.

Kuznets, Simon. 1963. "Quantitative aspects of the economic growth of nations, VIII: the distribution of income by size, part 2. *Economic Development and Cultural Change* 11, no. 2 (January):1–80.

Laakso, Markku, and Taagepera, Rein. 1979. "'Effective' number of parties: a measure with application to West Europe." *Comparative Political Studies* 12, no. 1 (April):3–27.

Labovitz, Sanford. 1967. "Some observations on measurement and statistics." *Social Forces* 46, no. 2 (December):151–60.

Labovitz, Sanford. 1972. "Statistical usage in sociology: sacred cows and ritual." *Sociological Methods and Research* 1, no. 1 (August):13–37.

Labrousse, C.-E. 1933. *Esquisse du movement des prix et des revenus en France au 18e siècle*. 2 vols. Paris: Dalloz.

Labrousse, C.-E. 1943. *La crise de l'économie française à la fin de l'Ancien Régime et au début de la Révolution*. Paris: Presses Universitaires françaises.

Labrousse, Ernst; Léon, Pierre; Goubert, Pierre; Bouvier, Jean; Carrière, Charles; Harsin, Paul. 1970. *Histoire économique et sociale de la France*, vol. 2: *Des derniers temps de l'âge seigneurial aux préludes de l'âge industriel (1660–1789)*. Paris: Presses Universitaires de France.

Lachica, Eduardo. 1971. *The Huks: Philippine agrarian society in revolt*. Praeger Special Studies. New York: Praeger Publishers.

Lall, Sanjaya. 1975. "Is 'dependence' a useful concept in analyzing underdevelopment?" *World Development* 3, nos. 11–12:799–810.

Lamberg, Robert F. 1972. *Die Guerilla in Lateinamerika: Theorie und Praxis eines revolutionären Modells*. Munich: Deutscher Taschenbuch Verlag.

Lamberg, Robert F. 1979. "Generäle als Retter? Ursprünge, Kennzeichen und Perspektiven der südamerikanischen Militärregime." *Neue Zürcher Zeitung* (June16-17):37.

Landsberger, Henry, ed. 1969. *Latin American peasant movements*. Ithaca, N.Y.: Cornell University Press.

Landsberger, Henry A. 1969a. "The role of peasant movements and revolts in development," in Landsberger (1969), 1-61.

Landsberger, Henry A. 1973. "The problem of peasant wars: review article." *Comparative Studies in Society and History* 15, no. 3 (June):378-88.

Landsberger, Henry A., ed. 1974. *Rural protest: peasant movements and social change*. London: Macmillan.

Landsberger, Henry A. 1974a. "Peasant unrest: themes and variations," in Landsberger (1974), 1-64.

Landsberger, Henry A. 1977. "The sources of rural rebellion," in Bialer/ Sluzar, 247-91.

Landsberger, Henry A., and McDaniel, Tim. 1976. "Hypermobilization in Chile, 1970-1973." *World Politics* 28, no. 4 (July):502-41.

Lang, Kurt. 1972. *Military institutions and the sociology of war: a review of the literature with annotated bibliography*. Beverly Hills: Sage Publications.

Lange, Alfred, and Nes, Ad van de. 1973. "Frustration and instrumentality of aggression." *European Journal of Social Psychology* 3, no. 2:159-77.

Lange, David L.; Baker, Robert K., and Ball, Sandra J. 1969. *Mass media and violence: a report to the National Commission on the Causes and Prevention of Violence*. Washington, D.C.: U. S. Government Printing Office.

Lange, Freddy. 1971. "Frustration-aggression. A reconsideration." *European Journal of Social Psychology* 1, no. 1:59-84.

Langer, William L. 1966. "The pattern of urban revolution in 1848," in Evelyn M. Acomb and Marvin L. Brown (eds.), *French society and culture since the old regime*. New York: Holt, Rinehart & Winston, 90-118.

Langer, William L. 1969. *Political and social upheaval 1832-1852*. New York: Harper & Row.

Lanning, Eldon. 1974. "A typology of Latin American political systems." *Comparative Politics* 6, no. 3 (April):367-94.

Lao, Rosina C. 1970. "Internal-external control and competent and innovative behavior among Negro college students." *Journal of Personality and Social Psychology* 14, no. 3 (March):263-70.

LaPalombara, Joseph. 1974. *Politics within nations*. Englewood Cliffs: Prentice-Hall.

Laponce, Jean. 1974. "Hirschman's voice and exit model as spatial archetype." *Social Science Information* 13, no. 2 (June):67-81.

Laqueur, Walter. 1967. *The fate of the revolution – interpretations of Soviet history*. London: Weidenfeld & Nicolson.

Laqueur, Walter. 1968. "Revolution," in *International Encyclopedia of the Social Sciences*, vol. 13. New York: Macmillan and Free Press, 501-507.

Laqueur, Walter. 1975. "In dubious battle." *Times Literary Supplement* (August 1): 862–63.

Laqueur, Walter. 1976. *Guerrilla: a historical and critical study*. Boston: Little, Brown & Co.

Laqueur, Walter. 1976a. "Coming to terms with terror." *Times Literary Supplement* (April 2):362–63.

Laqueur, Walter. 1977. "Interpretations of terrorism: fact, fiction and political science." *Journal of Contemporary History* 12, no. 1 (January): 1–42.

Laqueur, Walter. 1977a. *The guerrilla reader: a historical anthology*. New York: New American Library.

Laqueur, Walter. 1977b. *Terrorism*. Boston: Little, Brown. German edition: *Terrorismus*. Kronberg/Taunus: Athenäum (1977).

Laqueur, Walter, ed. 1977c. *The terrorism reader*. Bergenfield, New York: New American Library.

Larson, Arthur D. 1974. "Military professionalism and civil control: a comparative analysis of two interpretations." *Journal of Political and Military Sociology* 2, no. 1 (Spring):57–72.

Lasky, Melvin J. 1976. *Utopia and revolution: on the origins of a metaphor, or some illustrations of the problem of political temperament and intellectual climate and how ideas, ideals, and ideologies have been historically related*. Chicago: University of Chicago Press.

Lasswell, Harold D. 1941. "The garrison state." *American Journal of Sociology* 46, no. 4 (January):455–68.

Lasswell, Harold D., and Kaplan, Abraham. 1952. *Power and society: a framework for political inquiry*. London: Routledge & Kegan Paul. Original New Haven: Yale University Press (1950).

Lasswell, Harold D., and Lerner, Daniel, eds. 1966. *World revolutionary elites: studies in coercive ideological movements*. Cambridge, Mass.: MIT Press.

Lasswell, Harold; Lerner, Daniel; and Montgomery, John D. eds. 1976. *Values and development: appraising Asian experience*. Cambridge: MIT Press.

Latouche, Daniel G. 1973. "The process and level of military intervention in the states of tropical Africa, 1960–1971." Ph.D. dissertation, University of British Columbia.

Lawler, Edward J., and Youngs, George A., Jr. 1975. "Coalition formation: an integrative model." *Sociometry* 38, no. 1 (March):1–17.

Lawrence, John. 1970. "Violence." *Social Theory and Practice* 1, no. 2 (Fall):31–49.

Lawson, Reed. 1965. *Frustration: the development of a scientific concept*. New York: Macmillan.

Lazar, Arpad von, and Kaufman, Robert R., eds. 1969. *Reform and revolution: readings in Latin American politics*. Boston: Allyn & Bacon.

Lazarsfeld, P. F., and Rosenberg, M. 1955. "Introduction," in Lazarsfeld/Rosenberg (eds.), *The language of social research*. New York: Free Press, 15–18.

Lazarus, R. S. 1966. *Psychological stress and the coping process*. New York: McGraw-Hill.

LeBon, Gustave. 1913. *The psychology of revolution*. New York: G. P. Putnam's Sons. English ed. London: T. Fisher Unwin (1913).

Lederer, Emil. 1967. *The state of the masses: the threat of the classless society*. New York: Howard Fertig. (Original 1940.)

Lee, Alfred McClung. 1973. "Insurgent and 'peacekeeping' violence in Northern Ireland." *Social Problems* 20, no. 4 (Spring):532–46.

Lee, Hong Young. 1978. *The politics of the Chinese Cultural Revolution.* Berkeley: University of California Press.

Lee, Ta-ling. 1970. *Foundations of the Chinese revolution, 1905–1912.* New York: St. John's University Press.

Lefcourt, Herbert M. 1976. *Locus of control: current trends in theory and research.* Hillsdale. N.J.: Lawrence Erlbaum Associates, Publishers.

Lefebvre, Georges. 1933. "La Révolution française et les paysans." *Annales historiques de la Révolution française* 10:97–128.

Lefebvre, Georges. 1947. *The coming of the French Revolution.* Princeton: Princeton University Press. French ed. *Quatre-vingt-neuf.* Paris: Éditions Sociales (1970). Preface by Albert Soboul. (Original 1939.)

Lefebvre, Georges. 1954. Études sur la Révolution française. Paris: Presses Universitaires de France.

Lefebvre, Georges. 1956. "Le myth de la Révolution française." *Annales historiques de la Révolution française,* no. 145 (October/December): 337–45.

Lefebvre, Georges. 1962, 1964. *The French revolution from its origins to 1799.* 2 vols. New York: Columbia University Press. French ed. George Lefebvre, Raymond Guyot, and Philippe Sagnac. *La Révolution française.* Peuples et Civilisations. Paris: Librairie Félix Alcan (1930).

Lefebvre, Georges. 1963. *La Révolution française.* 3d ed. Paris: Presses Universitaires de France.

Lefebvre, Georges. 1966. "The French Revolution in the context of world history," in Lubasz, 74–86.

Lefebvre, Georges. 1970. *La grande peur de 1789.* Paris: Librairie Armand Colin. (Original 1932.) English ed. *The great fear of 1789: rural panic in revolutionary France.* London: NLB (1973). Introduction by George Rudé.

Lefebvre, Georges. 1972. *Les paysans du nord pendant la Révolution française.* Paris: Armand Colin (Original Lille, 1924.)

Lefever, Ernest W. 1970. *Spear and scepter: army, police, and politics in tropical Africa.* Washington, D.C.: The Brookings Institution.

Lehmbruch, Gerhard. 1975. "Die ambivalenten Funktionen politischer Beteiligung in hochindustrialisierten Demokratien," in Beat Junker, Peter Gilg und Richard Reich (eds.), *Geschichte und Politische Wissenschaft.* Festschrift für E. Gruner. Bern: Francke, 237–64.

Lehtinen, Dexter W. 1974. "Modernization, political development, and stability." *Stanford Journal of International Studies* 9 (Spring):219–45.

Leiden, Carl, and Schmitt, Karl M., eds. 1968. *The politics of violence: revolution in the modern world.* Englewood Cliffs: Prentice-Hall.

Leites, Nathan, and Wolf, Charles, Jr. 1970. *Rebellion and authority: an analytic essay on insurgent conflicts.* Chicago: Markham Publishing Co.

Lemarchand, René. 1974. "Civilian-military relations in former Belgian Africa: the military as a contextual elite," in Schmidt/Dorfman, 69–96.

Lemberg Center for the Study of Violence. 1967. *Six-city study.* Waltham, Mass.: Brandeis University.

Lemberg Center for the Study of Violence. 1968. *Riot data review 1.* Waltham, Mass.: Brandeis University.

Lemert, Edwin. 1967. *Human deviance, social problems, and social control.* Englewood Cliffs: Prentice-Hall.

Lenin, Vladimir I. 1964. "The state and revolution: the Marxist theory of the state and the tasks of the proletariat in the revolution," in *Collected works.* 4th ed. vol. 2. Moscow: Foreign Languages Publishing House, 381–492. (Original 1917.)

Lenin, V. I. 1967. "What is to be done? Burning questions of our movement," in *Selected Works 1.* New York: International Publishers, 97–256. (Original 1902.)

Lenk. Kurt. 1973. *Theorien der Revolution.* Munich: Wilhelm Fink Verlag.

Leonhard, Wolfgang. 1975. *Am Vorabend einer neuen Revolution? Die Zukunft des Sowjetkommunismus.* Gütersloh: C. Bertelsmann Verlag.

Lepsius, M. Rainer. 1968. "The collapse of an intermediary power structure: Germany 1933–1934." *International Journal of Contemporary Sociology* 9:289–301.

Lerner, Daniel. 1957. "Communication systems and social systems: a statistical exploration in history and policy." *Behavioral Science* 2, no. 4 (October):266–75.

Lerner, Daniel. 1958. *The passing of traditional society: modernizing the Middle East.* Glencoe: Free Press.

Lerner, Daniel. 1963. "Toward a communication theory of modernization. A set of considerations," in Pye, 327–50.

Lerner, Daniel. 1969. "Managing communication for modernization: a developmental construct," in Arnold A. Rogow (ed.), *Politics, personality, and social science in the twentieth century: essays in honor of Harold D. Lasswell.* Chicago: University of Chicago Press, 171–96.

Lerner, Daniel, and Robinson, Richard D. 1960. "Swords and ploughshares: the Turkish army as a modernizing force." *World Politics* 13, no. 1 (October):19–44. Also in Bienen (1971), 117–48.

Lerner, Melvin J. 1975. "The justice motive in social behavior: introduction." *Journal of Social Issues* 31, no. 3 (Summer):1–19.

Leventhal, Gerald S. 1976a. "The distribution of rewards and resources in groups and organizations," in Berkowitz/Walster, 91–131.

Leventhal, Gerald S. 1976b. "Fairness in social relationships," in Thibaut et al., 211–39.

Levine, Mark S. 1977. *Canonical analysis and factor comparison.* Sage University Paper Series on Quantitative Applications in the Social Sciences, 12. Beverly Hills: Sage Publications.

LeVine, R.1959. "Anti-European violence in Africa: a comparative analysis." *Journal of Conflict Resolution* 3, no. 4 (December):420–29.

Levitan, Sar A.; Johnston, William B.; and Taggart, Robert. 1975. *Still a dream: the changing status of blacks since 1960.* Cambridge, Mass.: Harvard University Press.

Levy, Burton. 1968. "Cops in the ghetto: a problem of the police system." *American Behavioral Scientist* 11, no. 4 (March/April):31–34.

Levy, Marion J., Jr. 1966. *Modernization and the structure of societies: a setting for international affairs.* 2 vols. Princeton: Princeton University Press.

Lewis, Charlton M. 1976. *Prologue to the Chinese revolution: the transformation of ideas and institutions in Hunan province, 1891–1907.* Cambridge, Mass.: Harvard University Press.

Lewis, Gwynne. 1978. *The second Vendée: the continuity of counter-revolution in the department of the Gard, 1789–1815*. Oxford: Clarendon Press.

Lewis, John Wilson, ed. 1970. *Party leadership and revolutionary power in China*. London: Cambridge University Press.

Lewis, John Wilson, ed. 1974. *Peasant rebellion and communist revolution in Asia*. Stanford: Stanford University Press.

Lewy, Guenter. 1974. *Religion and revolution*. New York: Oxford University Press.

Leyens, Jacques-Philippe, and Parke, Ross D. 1975. "Aggressive slides can induce a weapons effect." *European Journal of Social Psychology* 5, no. 2:229–36.

Leyens, Jacques-Philippe; Camino, Leoncio; Parke, Ross D.; and Berkowitz, L. 1975. "Effects of movie violence on aggression in a field setting as a function of group dominance and cohesion." *Journal of Personality and Social Psychology* 32, no. 2 (August):346–60.

Li, Richard P. Y., and Thompson, William R. 1975. "The 'coup contagion' hypothesis." *Journal of Conflict Resolution* 19, no. 1 (March):63–88.

Liang, Chin Tung. 1962. *The Chinese revolution of 1911*. New York: St. John's University Press.

Liao, Kuang-Sheng. 1976. "Linkage politics in China: internal mobilization and articulated external hostility in the Cultural Revolution, 1967–1969." *World Politics* 28, no. 4 (July):590–610.

Lichbach, Mark Irving, and Gurr, Ted Robert. 1980. "The conflict process: a formal model." Paper presented at the Berlin Conference on Large-Scale Global Modeling, July, Science Center.

Lichtheim, George. 1965. "'All the news that's fit to print.'" *Commentary* 40, no. 3:33–46.

Lieberman, Bernhardt, ed. 1971. *Contemporary problems in statistics*. New York: Oxford University Press.

Lieberson, Stanley, and Silverman, Arnold. 1965. "The precipitants and underlying conditions of race riots." *American Sociological Review* 30, no. 6 (December):887–98.

Liebert, Robert M.; Neale, John M.; and Davidson, Emily S. 1973. *The early window: effects of television on children and youth*. New York: Pergamon Press.

Lief, Harold M. 1969. "Contemporary forms of violence." in Shalom Endleman (ed.), *Violence in the streets*. London: Gerald Duckworth, 49–62.

Lieske, Joel A. 1978. "The conditions of racial violence in American cities: a developmental synthesis." *American Political Science Review* 72, no. 4 (December):1324–40.

Lieuwen, Edwin. 1961. *Arms and politics in Latin America*. New York: Frederick A. Praeger.

Lieuwen, Edwin. 1962. "Militarism and politics in Latin America," in J. J. Johnson, 131–63.

Lieuwen, Edwin. 1964. *Generals vs. presidents: neomilitarism in Latin America*. London: Pall Mall Press.

Lifton, Robert Jay. 1970. *Revolutionary immortality: Mao Tse-tung and the Chinese Cultural Revolution*. Harmondsworth, Middlesex: Penguin. American ed. New York: Random House (1968).

Lijphart, Arend. 1968. *The politics of accommodation: pluralism and democracy in the Netherlands.* Berkeley: University of California Press.

Lijphart, Arend. 1975. "Review article: the Northern Ireland problem: cases, theories, and solutions." *British Journal of Political Science* 5, no. 1 (January):83–106.

Lijphart, Arend. 1977. *Democracy in plural societies: a comparative exploration.* New Haven: Yale University Press.

Lijphart, Arend. 1978. "Majority rule versus democracy in deeply divided societies," in Nic Rhoodie (ed.), *Intergroup accommodation in plural societies.* London: Macmillan, 27–43.

Lindner, Clausjohann. 1972. *Theorie der Revolution.* Munich: Goldmann.

Linehan, William J. 1976. "Models for the measurement of political instability." *Political Methodology* 3, no. 4 (Fall):441–86.

Linz, Juan. 1975. "Totalitarian and authoritarian regimes," in Greenstein/Polsby, vol. 3, 175–411.

Linz, Juan J. 1978. *The breakdown of democratic regimes: crisis, breakdown and reequilibration.* Baltimore: Johns Hopkins University Press.

Linz, Juan J., and Stepan, Alfred, eds. 1978. *The breakdown of democratic regimes.* Baltimore: Johns Hopkins University Press.

Lipset, Seymour Martin. 1959. "Political sociology," in Robert K. Merton, Leonard Broom, and Leonard S. Cottrell, Jr. (eds.), *Sociology today: problems and prospects.* New York: Basic Books, 81–114.

Lipset, Seymour Martin. 1959a. "Some social requisites of democracy: economic development and political legitimacy." *American Political Science Review* 53, no. 1 (March):69–105.

Lipset, Seymour Martin. 1960. *Political man: the social bases of politics.* Garden City, New York: Doubleday. English ed. London: Mercury Books (1963).

Lipset, Seymour Martin. 1967. *The first new nation: the United States in historical and comparative perspective.* New York: Anchor Books. (Original 1964.)

Lipset, Seymour Martin, and Raab, Earl. 1970. *The politics of unreason: right-wing extremism in America, 1790–1970.* New York: Harper & Row.

Lipset, Seymour Martin, and Rokkan, Stein. 1967. "Cleavage structures, party systems and voter alignments," in Seymour Martin Lipset and Stein Rokkan (eds.), *Party systems and voter alignments: cross-national perspectives.* New York: Free Press, 1–64.

Lipsky, Michael. 1968. "Protest as a political resource." *American Political Science Review* 62, no. 4 (December):1144–58. Also in Jackson/Stein (1971), 307–23.

Lipsky, Michael. 1970. *Protest in city politics: rent strikes, housing, and the power of the poor.* Chicago: Rand McNally.

Lipsky, Michael, and Olson, David J. 1977. *Commission politics: the processing of racial crisis in America.* New Brunswick, N.J.: Transaction Books.

Lipsky, William E. 1976. "Comparative approaches to the study of revolution: a historiographic essay." *Review of Politics* 38, no. 4 (October): 494–509.

Liska, Allen E. 1974. "The impact of attitude on behavior: attitude-social support interaction." *Pacific Sociological Review* 17, no. 1 (January): 83–97.

Liska, Allen E., ed. 1975. *The consistency controversy: readings on the impact of attitude on behavior.* Cambridge, Mass.: Schenkman Publishing Co.

Lissak, Moshe. 1964. "Selected literature on revolutions and coups d'état in the developing nations," in Morris Janowitz (ed.), *The new military: changing patterns of organization.* New York: Russell Sage Foundation, 339–62.

Lissak, Moshe. 1967. "Modernization and role-expansion of the military in developing countries: a comparative analysis." *Comparative Studies in Society and History* 9 (April):233–55.

Lissak, Moshe. 1973. "Stages of modernization and patterns of military coups." *International Journal of Contemporary Sociology* 14, nos. 1–2 (March/June):59–75.

Liu, Alan P. L. 1976. *Political culture and group conflict in Communist China.* Santa Barbara, Calif.: Clio Press.

Livingston, Marius H., with Kress, Lee Bruce, and Wanek, Marie G. 1978. *International terrorism in the contemporary world.* Westport, Conn.: Greenview Press.

Llerena, Mario. 1978. *The unsuspected revolution: the birth and rise of Castroism.* Ithaca: Cornell University Press.

Locke, Hubert G. 1969. *The Detroit riot of 1967.* Detroit: Wayne State University Press.

Lodhi, Abdul Qaiyum, and Tilly, Charles. 1973. "Urbanization, crime, and collective violence in 19th-century France." *American Journal of Sociology* 79, no. 2 (September):296–318.

Loehr, William. 1977. "Economic underdevelopment and income distribution," in William Loehr and John P. Powelson (eds.), *Economic development, poverty, and income distribution.* Boulder, Colo.: Westview Press, 3–29.

Lösche, Peter. 1977. *Anarchismus.* Erträge der Forschung, vol. 66. Darmstadt: Wissenschaftliche Buchgesellschaft.

Loewenberg, Gerhard. 1971. "The influence of parliamentary behavior on regime stability: some conceptual clarifications." *Comparative Politics* 3, no. 2 (January):177–200.

Lofchie, Michael F., ed. 1971. *The state of the nations: constraints on development in independent Africa.* Berkeley: University of California Press.

Longworth, Philip. 1975. "Peasant leadership and the Pugachev revolt." *Journal of Peasant Studies* 2, no. 2 (January):183–205.

Lopreato, Sally Cook. 1973. "Toward a formal restatement of Vilfredo Pareto's theory of the circulation of elites." *Social Science Quarterly* 54, no. 3 (December):491–507.

Lorenz, Konrad. 1966. *On aggression.* New York: Harcourt, Brace & World. (Original 1963.)

Lorwin, Val R. 1971. "Segmented pluralism: ideological cleavages and political cohesion in the smaller European democracies." *Comparative Politics* 3, no. 2 (January):141–75.

Louie, Richard. 1964. "The incidence of the terror: a critique of a statistical interpretation." *French Historical Studies* 3:379–89.

Lovell, John P. 1974. "Civil-military relations: traditional and modern concepts reappraised," in Cochran, 11–33.

Lowenstein, Ralph Lynn. 1967. "Measuring word press freedom as a political indicator." Ph.D. dissertation, University of Missouri.

Lowenthal, Abraham F. 1972. *The Dominican intervention.* Cambridge, Mass.: Harvard University Press.

Lowenthal, Abraham F. 1974. "Armies and politics in Latin America." *World Politics* 37, no. 1 (October):107–30.

Lowenthal, Abraham F. 1974a. "Peru's revolutionary government of the armed forces': background and context," in Kelleher (1974), 147–59.

Lowenthal, Abraham F., ed. 1975. *The Peruvian experiment: continuity and change under military rule.* Princeton: Princeton University Press.

Lowenthal, David. 1968. "Review of: Barrington Moore, Jr.: 'Social origins of dictatorship and democracy: lord and peasant in the making of the modern world.'" *History and Theory* 7, no. 2:257–78.

Luard, Evan. 1968. *Conflict and peace in the modern international system.* Boston: Little, Brown.

Lubasz, Heinz, ed. 1966. *Revolution in modern European history.* New York: Macmillan Co.

Lublinskaya, A. D. 1968. *French absolutism: the crucial phase, 1620–1629.* Cambridge: Cambridge University Press.

Lucas, Colin. 1973. "Nobles, bourgeois, and the origins of the French Revolution." *Past and Present* 60 (September):84–126.

Luckham, A. R. 1971. "A comparative typology of civil-military relations." *Government and Opposition* 6, no. 4 (Autumn):5–35.

Ludz, Peter C. 1973. "Alienation as a concept in the social sciences: a trend report and bibliography." *Current Sociology* 21, no. 1.

Lukes, Steven. 1978. "Power and authority," in Tom Bottomore and Robert Nisbet (eds.), *A history of sociological analysis.* New York: Basic Books, 633–76.

Lupsha, Peter. 1969. "On theories of urban violence." *Urban Affairs Quarterly* 4, no. 3 (March):273–96.

Lupsha, Peter A. 1971. "Explanation of political violence: some psychological theories versus indignation." *Politics and Society* 1 (Fall):89–104.

Luttwak, Edward. 1969. *Coup d'état: a practical handbook.* Harmondsworth: Penguin Books. Original London: Allen Lane The Penguin Press (1968). 2d ed.: Cambridge, Mass.: Harvard University Press (1979).

Lutz, William, and Brent, Harry, eds. 1972. *On revolution.* Cambridge: Winthrop Publishers.

Luxemburg, Rosa. 1966–68. *Politische Schriften,* 3 vols., ed. Ossip K. Flechtheim. Frankfort on the Main: Europäische Verlagsanstalt.

Lynch, John. 1973. *The Spanish American Revolution, 1808–1826.* London: Weidenfeld and Nicolson. American ed. New York: W. W. Norton & Co. (1975).

MacCorquodale, Kenneth, and Meehl, Paul E. 1948. "On a distinction between hypothetical constructs and intervening variables." *Psychological Review* 55, no. 2 (March):95–107.

MacDonald, A. P., Jr. 1973. "Internal-external locus of control," in John P. Robinson and Philip R. Shaver. *Measures of psychological attitudes.* Revised ed. Appendix. Ann Arbor: Institute for Social Research, 159–230.

MacEoin, Gary. 1971. *Revolution next door: Latin America in the 1970s*. New York: Holt, Rinehart & Winston.

MacEoin, Gary, ed. 1974. *Chile: under military rule*. New York: IDOC/North America.

MacFarlane, Leslie. 1971. *Political disobedience*. London: Macmillan.

MacFarquhar, Roderick. 1974. *The origins of the Cultural Revolution*, vol. 1: *Contradictions among the people 1956-1957*. London: Oxford University Press.

Mack, Raymond W. 1965. "The components of social conflict." *Social Problems* 12, no. 4 (Spring):388-97.

Mack, R. W., and Snyder, R. C. 1957. "The analysis of social conflict — toward an overview and synthesis." *Journal of Conflict Resolution* 1, no. 2 (June):212-48.

Maier, Pauline. 1970. "Popular uprisings and civil authority in eighteenth-century America." *William and Mary Quarterly*, Third Series 27:3-35.

Maier, Pauline. 1972. *From resistance to revolution: colonial radicals and the development of American opposition to Britain, 1765-1776*. New York: Alfred A. Knopf.

Main, Jackson Turner. 1960. "Charles A. Beard and the constitution: a critical review of Forrest McDonald's 'We the people,' with a rebuttal by Forrest McDonald." *William and Mary Quarterly*, 3d series, 17 (January):86-110.

Main, Jackson Turner. 1965. *The social structure of revolutionary America*. Princeton, N.J.: Princeton Universiy Press.

Majka, Theo. 1980. "Poor people's movements and farm labor insurgency." *Contemporary Crises* 4, no. 3 (July):283-308.

Malaparte, Curzio. 1932. *Coup d'état: the technique of revolution*. New York: E. P. Dutton & Co.

Malefakis, Edward E. 1970. *Agrarian reform and peasant revolution in Spain: origins of the civil war*. New Haven: Yale University Press.

Mallick, Shahbaz K., and McCandless, Boyd R. 1966. "A study of catharsis of aggression." *Journal of Personality and Social Psychology* 4, no. 6: 591-96.

Malloy, James M. 1970. *Bolivia: the uncompleted revolution*. Pittsburgh: University of Pittsburgh Press.

Malloy, James M., and Thorn, Richard S., eds. 1971. *Beyond the revolution: Bolivia since 1952*. Pittsburgh: University of Pittsburgh Press.

Mandrou, Robert. 1959. "Les soulèvements populaires et la société française du XVIIᵉ siècle." *Annales: Économies, Sociétés, Civilisations* 14: 756-65.

Mandrou, Robert. 1969. "Vingt ans àpres, ou une direction de recherches fécondes: Les révoltes populaires en France a XVIIᵉ siècle." *Revue Historique* 242 (July-September):29-40.

Mann, Fritz Karl. 1947. "The fiscal component of revolution: an essay in fiscal sociology." *Review of Politics* 9:331-49.

Mannheim, Karl. n.d. *Ideology and utopia*. New York: Harcourt, Brace & Co. Original published in German: *Ideologie und Utopie*. 2d. ed. Frankfort on the Main: G. Schulte-Bulmke. 3d extended ed. 1952.

Manning, Brian. 1975. "The peasantry and the English Revolution." *Journal of Peasant Studies* 2, no. 2 (January):133-57.

Manning, Brian. 1976. *The English people and the English Revolution 1640–49*. London: Heinemann.

Manning, Sidney A., and Taylor, Dalmas A. 1975. "Effects of viewed violence and aggression: stimulation and catharsis." *Journal of Personality and Social Psychology* 31, no. 1 (January):180–88.

Manuel, Frank E., and Manuel, Fritzie P. 1979. *Utopian thought in the Western world*. Cambridge, Mass.: Harvard University Press.

Mao Tse-tung. 1927. *Report on an Investigation of the Peasant Movement in Hunan*. Peking: Foreign Languages Press, 1953.

(Mao Tse-tung). *Selected works of Mao Tse-tung*. Peking: Foreign Language Press, vol. IV (1961).

Mao Tse-tung. 1961a. *Mao Tse-tung on guerrilla warfare*. Translated and with an introduction by Samuel B. Griffith. New York: Frederick A. Praeger.

Marcuse, Herbert. 1968. "Re-examination of the concept of revolution." *Diogenes* 64 (Winter): 17–26.

Marcuse, Herbert. 1969. "Repressive tolerance," in Robert Paul Wolff, Barrington Moore, and Herbert Marcuse, *A critique of pure tolerance*. London: Jonathan Cape, 93–131. Original published in Boston: Beacon Press (1965).

Marcuse, Herbert. 1972. *Counterrevolution and revolt*. Boston: Beacon Press.

Marine, Gene. 1969. *The black panthers*. New York: New American Library.

Markov, Walter, ed. 1956. *Jakobiner und Sansculotten: Beiträge zur Geschichte der französischen Revolutionsregierung, 1793–1794*. Berlin: Rütten und Loening.

Markov, Walter. 1976. *Volksbewegungen der Französischen Revolution*. Frankfort: Campus Verlag.

Markov, Walter, and Soboul, Albert, eds. 1957. *Die Sansculotten von Paris: Dokumente zur Geschichte der Volksbewegung 1793–1794*. Berlin (East): Akademieverlag.

Markov, Walter and Soboul, Albert. 1973. *1789: Die große Revolution der Franzosen*. Kleine Bibliothek, vol. 100. Berlin (East): Akademieverlag.

Markus, Gregory B. 1970. "Coercion and political instability: cross-national patterns." Senior thesis, San Diego State College.

Markus, Gregory B., and Nesvold, Betty A. 1972. "Governmental coerciveness and political instability: an explanatory study of cross-national patterns." *Comparative Political Studies* 5, no. 2 (July):231–44.

Markus, Gregory B., and Tanter, Raymond. 1972. "A conflict model for strategists and managers." *American Behavioral Scientist* 15, no. 6 (July-August):809–36.

Marquette, Jesse F. 1974. "Social change and political mobilization in the United States: 1870–1960." *American Political Science Review* 68, no. 3 (September):1058–74.

Marquette, Jesse F. 1976. "Social change and political mobilization in the United States: a methodological note." *American Political Science Review* 70, no. 2 (June):545–48.

Marsh, Alan. 1974. "Explorations in unorthodox political behaviour: a scale to measure 'protest potential.'" *European Journal of Political Research* 2, no. 2 (June):107–29.

Marsh, Alan. 1977. *Protest and political consciousness*. Beverly Hills and London: Sage Library of Social Research, 49.

Marshall, Harvey, and Jiobu, Robert. 1975. "Residential segregation in United States cities: a causal analysis." *Social Forces* 53, no. 3 (March):449–60.

Martíc, Milos. 1975. *Insurrection: five schools of revolutionary thought*. New York: Dunellen.

Martines, Lauro, ed. 1972. *Violence and civil disorder in Italian cities 1200–1500*. Berkeley: University of California Press.

Marx, Gary T. 1967. *Protest and prejudice: a study of beliefs in the black community*. New York: Harper & Row.

Marx, G. T. 1970. "Riots," in *Encyclopaedia Britannica*, vol. 19:350–350c.

Marx, Gary T. 1970a. "Issueless riots." *Annals of the American Academy of Political and Social Science*, no. 391 (September):21–33.

Marx, Gary T. 1970b. "Civil disorder and the agents of social control." *Journal of Social Issues* 26, no. 1:19–57.

Marx, Gary T., ed. 1971. *Racial conflict: tension and change in American society*. Boston: Little, Brown & Co.

Marx, Gary T. 1972. "Perspectives on violence." *Contemporary Psychology* 17, no. 3 (March):128–31.

Marx, Gary T. 1974. "Thoughts on a neglected category of social movement participant: the agent provocateur and the informant." *American Journal of Sociology* 80, no. 2 (September):402–42.

Marx, Gary T., and Wood, James L. 1975. "Strands of theory and research in collective behavior." *Annual Review of Sociology* 1:363–428.

Maschke. Günter. 1973. *Kritik des Guerillero: Zur Theorie des Volkskrieges*. Frankfort on the Main: S. Fischer Verlag.

Maslow, Abraham H. 1943. "A theory of human motivation." *Psychological Review* 50:370–96.

Masotti, Lewis. 1967. "Violent protest in urban society." Presented at the Meeting of the American Academy for the Advancement of Science. Mimeographed.

Masotti, Louis H., and Bowen, Don R., eds. 1968. *Riots and rebellion: civil violence in the urban community*. Beverly Hills: Sage Publications.

Masters, Stanley H. 1975. *Black-white income differentials: empirical studies and policy implications*. New York: Academic Press.

Mathiez, Albert. 1922–7. *La Révolution française*. Translated as *The French Revolution* (1928). 2d ed. Paris: Librairie Armand Colin: vol. 1: *La chute de la Royauté* (1925); vol. 2: *La Gironde et la Montagne* (1927); vol. 3: *La terreur* (1928). Also in American ed. *The French Revolution*. New York: Grosset & Dunlap.

Matz, Ulrich. 1970. "Untersuchungen über die Gewalt und ihre Rechtfertigung in der Politik." Habilitation thesis, Munich. Mimeographed.

Matz, Ulrich. 1975. *Politik und Gewalt: Zur Theorie des demokratischen Verfassungsstaates und der Revolution*. Freiburg: Karl Alber.

Maullin, Richard L. 1970. "The private war of a guerrilla." *Transaction* 7, no. 5 (March):45–54.

Maullin, Richard. 1973. *Soldiers, guerrillas, and politics in Columbia*. Lexington, Mass.: D. C. Heath & Co.

Mawdsley, Evan. 1978. *The Russian Revolution and the Baltic fleet: war and politics, February 1917–April 1918*. London: Macmillan.

Mayer, Arno J. 1971. *Dynamics of counterrevolution in Europe: analytic framework, 1870–1956*. New York: Harper & Row.

Mayer, Bernard S., and Mayer, Thomas F. 1976. "Review of Russell (1974)." *American Journal of Sociology* 82, no. 2 (September):452–58.

Mazauric, Claude. 1967. "Réflexions sur une nouvelle conception de la Révolution française." *Annales historiques de la Révolution française* 39:339–68.

Mazauric, Claude. 1970. *Sur la Révolution francaise: contributions à l'histoire de la révolution bourgeoisie.* Paris: Éditions Sociales.

Mazlish, Bruce. 1970. "The French Revolution in comparative perspective." *Political Science Quarterly* 85, no. 2 (June):240–58.

Mazlish, Bruce. 1976. *The revolutionary ascetic: evolution of a political type.* New York: Basic Books.

Mazlish, Bruce; Kaledin, Arthur D.; and Ralston, David B., eds. 1971. *Revolution: a reader.* New York: Macmillan Co.

Mazrui, Ali A. 1976. "Soldiers as traditionalizers: military rule and the re-Africanization of Africa." *World Politics* 28, no. 2 (January):246–72.

Mazrui, Ali A., and Rothchild, Donald. 1967. "The soldier and state in East Africa: some theoretical conclusions on the army mutinies of 1964." *Western Political Quarterly* 20, no. 1 (March):82–96.

McAlister, John T. 1969. *Viet Nam: the origins of revolution.* New York: Alfred A. Knopf.

McAlister, John T., and Mus, Paul. 1970. *The Vietnamese and their revolution.* Harper Torchbooks. New York: Harper and Row.

McAlister, Lyle N. 1961. "Civil-military relations in Latin America." *Journal of Inter-American Studies* 3, no. 3 (July):341–50.

McAlister, Lyle N. 1965. "Changing concepts of the role of the military in Latin America." *The Annals* (July):85–95.

McAlister, Lyle N. 1966. "Recent research and writings on the role of the military in Latin America." *Latin American Research Review* 2, no. 1 (Fall):5–36.

McCagg, William O. 1972. "Jews in revolutions: the Hungarian experience." *Journal of Social History* 6, no. 1 (Fall):78–105.

McCarthy, John, and Zald, Mayer. 1973. *The trend of social movements in America: professionalization and resource mobilization.* Morristown, N.J.: General Learning Press.

McCarthy, John D., and Zald, Mayer N. 1977. "Resource mobilization and social movements: a partial theory." *American Journal of Sociology* 82, no. 6 (May):1212–41.

McColl, Robert W. 1967. "A political geography of revolution: China, Vietnam, and Thailand." *Journal of Conflict Resolution* 11, no. 2 (June): 153–67.

McConaghy, Maureen J. 1975. "Maximum possible error in Guttman scales." *Public Opinion Quarterly* 39, no. 3 (Fall):343–68.

McCord, William, and Howard, John. 1968. "Negro opinions in three riot cities." *American Behavioral Scientist* 11, no. 4:24–27.

McCrone, D. J., and Cnudde, C. F. 1967. "Toward a communication theory of democratic political development: a causal model." *American Political Science Review* 61, no. 1 (March):72–80. Also in Gillespie/Nesvold (1971), 499–512.

McCrone, Donald J., and Hardy, Richard J. 1978. "Civil rights policies and the achievement of racial economic equality, 1948–1975." *American Journal of Political Science* 22, no. 1 (February):1–17.

McCuen, John T. 1966. *The art of counter-revolutionary war: the strategy of counter-insurgency.* London: Faber & Faber.

McDonald, Angus W., Jr. 1978. *The urban origins of rural revolution: elites and the masses in Hunan province, China 1911-1927.* Berkeley: University of California Press.

McDonald, Ronald H. 1975. "The rise of military politics in Uruguay." *Inter-American Economic Affairs* 28, no. 4 (Spring):25–43.

McElroy, Jerome L., and Singell, Larry D. 1973. "Riot and nonriot cities: an examination of structural contours." *Urban Affairs Quarterly* 8, no. 3 (March):281–302.

McEvoy, James, III. 1971. "Political vengeance and political attitudes: a study of Americans' support for political and social violence," in Crotty, 312–42.

McKay, James, and Lewins, Frank. 1978. "Ethnicity and the ethnic group: a conceptual analysis and reformulation." *Ethnic and Racial Studies* 1, no. 4 (October):412–27.

McKinlay, R. D. 1979. "The aid relationship: a foreign policy model and interpretation of the distribution of official bilateral economic aid of the United States, the United Kingdom, France, and Germany, 1960–1970." *Comparative Political Studies* 11, no. 4 (January):411–63.

McKinlay, R. D., and Cohan, A. S. 1974. "Military coups, military regimes, and social change." Paper delivered at the Annual Meeting of the American Political Science Association, 29 August–2 September, in Chicago.

McKinlay, R. D., and Cohan, A. S. 1975. "A comparative analysis of the political and economic performance of military and civilian regimes." *Comparative Politics* 8, no. 1 (October):1–30.

McKinlay, R. D. and Cohan, A. S. 1976a. "The economic performance of military regimes: a cross-national aggregate study." *British Journal of Political Science* 6, no. 3 (July):291–310.

McKinlay, R. D., and Cohan, A. S. 1976b. "Performance and instability in military and nonmilitary regime systems." *American Political Science Review* 70, no. 3 (September):850–64.

McKown, Roberta E. 1975. "Domestic correlates of military intervention in African politics." *Journal of Political and Military Sociology* 3, no. 2 (Fall):191–206.

McKown, Robert E., and Kauffman, Robert E. 1973. "Party system as a comparative analytic concept in African politics." *Comparative Politics* 6, no. 1 (October):47–72.

McLane, John R. 1971. "Archaic movements and revolution in Southern Vietnam," in Miller/Aya, 68–101.

McLellan, Vin, and Avery, Paul. 1977. *The voices of guns.* New York: G. P. Putnam's Sons.

McPhail, Clark. 1971. "Civil disorder participation: a critical examination of recent research." *American Sociological Review* 36, no. 6 (December):1058–73.

McPhail, Clark. 1972. "Theoretical and methodological strategies for the study of individual and collective behavior sequences." University of Illinois at Urbana–Champaign. Mimeographed.

McPhail, Clark. 1978. "Toward a theory of collective behavior." University of Illinois at Urbana–Champaign. Mimeographed.

McPhail, Clark, and Miller, David L. 1973. "The assembling process: a theoretical and empirical examination." *American Sociological Review* 38, no. 6 (December):721–35.

McPhail, Clark, and Pickens, Robert G. 1975. "The explananda of collective behavior: the obvious which eludes us." Paper presented at the Annual Meeting of the American Sociological Association, 26 August, in San Francisco.

McPherson, J. Miller; Welch, Susan; and Clark, Cal. 1977. "The stability and reliability of political efficacy: using path analysis to test alternative models." *American Political Science Review* 71, no. 2 (June):509–21.

McRae, Kenneth D., ed. 1974. *Consociational democracy: political accommodation in segmented societies.* Toronto: Canadian Publishers.

McWilliams, Wilson C., ed. 1967. *Garrisons and government: politics and the military in new states.* San Francisco: Chandler Publishing Co.

McWilliams, Wilson C. 1967a. "Introduction," in McWilliams (1967), 1–41.

Meadows, Paul. 1941. "Sequence in revolution." *American Sociological Review* 6, no. 5 (October):702–709.

Mehden, Fred R. von der. 1964. *Politics of the developing nations.* Englewood Cliffs: Prentice-Hall.

Mehden, Fred R. von der. 1973. *Comparative political violence.* Englewood Cliffs: Prentice-Hall.

Meisel, James H. 1966. *Counterrevolution: how revolutions die.* New York: Atherton Press.

Mercier Vega, Luis. 1969. *Guerillas in Latin America: the technique of the counter-state.* London: Pall Mall Press.

Merelman, Richard M. 1966. "Learning and legitimacy." *American Political Science Review* 60, no. 3 (September):548–61.

Merkl, Peter H. 1969. "Political cleavages and party systems." *World Politics* 21, no. 3 (April):469–85.

Merkx, Gilbert W. 1973. "Recessions and rebellions in Argentina, 1870–1970." *Hispanic American Review* 53, no. 2 (May):285–95.

Merriman, John M., ed. 1975. *1830 in France.* New York: New Viewpoints, a division of Franklin Watts.

Merton, Robert K. 1957. *Social theory and social structure.* Revised and enlarged ed. New York: Free Press.

Merton, Robert K., and Rossi, Alice S. 1957. "Contributions to the theory of reference group behavior," in Merton, 225–80.

Mervielde, Ivan. 1977. "Methodological problems of research about attitude-behavior consistency." *Quality and Quantity* 11, no. 3 (September): 259–81.

Merz, Ferdinand. 1965. "Aggression und Aggressionstrieb," in H. Thomae (ed.), *Handbuch der Psychologie*, vol. 2: *Motivation.* Göttingen: Hogrefe, 569–601.

Meusel, Alfred. 1934. "Revolution and counter-revolution," in *Encyclopaedia of the Social Sciences*, vol. 13. New York: Macmillan Company, 367–76.

Meusel, Alfred. 1952. *Thomas Müntzer und seine Zeit.* Berlin: Aufbau-Verlag.

Meyer, Timothy P. 1972. "Effects of viewing justified and unjustified real film violence on aggressive behavior." *Journal of Personality and Social Psychology* 23, no. 1 (July):21–29.

Michaels, Albert L. 1976. "Background to a coup: civil-military relations in twentieth-century Chile and the overthrow of Salvador Allende," in Welch, 283–311.

Mickolus, Edward. 1978. "Trends in transnational terrorism," in Livingston et al., 44–73.

Mickolus, Edward. 1979. "Transnational terrorism," in Stohl, 147–90.

Mickolus, Edward F. 1980. *Transnational terrorism: a chronology of events, 1968–1979*. London: Aldwych.

Middlebrook, Kevin J., and Palmer, David Scott. 1975. *Military government and political development: lessons from Peru*. Sage Professional Paper in Comparative Politics Series, no. 01–054.

Midlarsky, Manus. 1970. "Mathematical models of instability and a theory of diffusion." *International Studies Quarterly* 14, no. 1 (March):60–84.

Midlarsky, Manus I. 1975. *On war: political violence in the international system*. New York: Free Press.

Midlarsky, Manus I. 1977. "Size effects and the diffusion of violence in American cities." *Papers of the Peace Science Society (International)* 27:39–47.

Midlarsky, Manus I. 1978. "Analyzing diffusion and contagion effects: the urban disorders of the 1960s." *American Political Science Review* 72, no. 3 (September):996–1008.

Midlarsky, Manus, and Tanter, Raymond. 1967. "Toward a theory of political instability in Latin America." *Journal of Peace Research* 3:209–27. Slightly changed also in Feierabend/Feierabend/Gurr (1972), 242–59.

Midlarsky, Manus I.; Crenshaw, Martha; and Yoshida, Fumihiko. 1980. "Why violence spreads: the contagion of international terrorism." *International Studies Quarterly* 24, no. 2 (June):262–98.

Migdal, Joel S. 1974. "Why change? Toward a new theory of change among individuals in the process of modernization." *World Politics* 26, no. 2 (January):189–206.

Migdal, Joel S. 1975. *Peasants, politics, and revolution: pressures toward political and social change in the third world*. Princeton: Princeton University Press.

Miguens, José Enrique. 1975. "The new Latin American military coup," in Fidel, 99–123.

Milbank, David L. 1976. *International and transnational terrorism: diagnosis and prognosis*. Washington, D. C.: CIA Document PR 76–10030.

Milbrath, Lester W., and Goel, M. L. 1977. *Political participation: how and why people get involved in politics*. Chicago: Rand McNally.

Milgram, S., and Shotland, R. L. 1973. *Television and antisocial behavior: field experiments*. New York: Academic Press.

Milgram, Stanley, and Toch, Hans. 1969. "Crowds and social movements," in Gardner Lindzey and Elliot Aronson (eds.), *Handbook of social psychology*. 2d ed. vol. 4. Reading, Mass.: Addison-Wesley, 507–610.

Milgram, Stanley; Bickman, Leonard; and Berkowitz, Lawrence. 1969. "Note on the drawing power of crowds of different size." *Journal of Personality and Social Psychology* 13, no. 2 (October):79–82.

Miller, Abraham H.; Bolce, Louis H.; and Halligan, Mark R. 1976. "The new urban blacks." *Ethnicity* 3 (December) 338–67.

Miller, Abraham H.; Bolce, Louis H.; and Halligan, Mark. 1977. "The J-curve theory and the black urban riots: an empirical test of progressive relative deprivation theory." *American Political Science Review* 71, no. 3 (September):964–82.

Miller, Alden Dykstra. 1971. "Logic of causal analysis: from experimental to nonexperimental designs," in Blalock, 273–94.

Miller, Arthur H. 1974a. "Political issues and trust in government: 1964–1970." *American Political Science Review* 68, no. 3 (September): 951–72.

Miller, Arthur H. 1974b. "Rejoinder to 'Comment' by Jack Citrin: political discontent or ritualism?" *American Political Science Review* 68, no. 3 (September):989–1001.

Miller, Arthur H. 1978. "Partisanship reinstated? A comparison of the 1972 and 1976 U. S. presidential elections." *British Journal of Political Science* 8, no. 2 (April):129–52.

Miller, Arthur H. 1979. "Current trends in political trust." University of Michigan. Mimeographed.

Miller, Arthur H. 1979a. "The institutional focus of political distrust." Paper delivered at Annual Meeting of the American Political Science Association, University of Michigan. Mimeographed.

Miller, Arthur H.; Goldenberg, Edie N.; and Erbring, Lutz. 1979. "Type-set politics: impact of newspapers on public confidence." *American Political Science Review* 73, no. 1 (March):67–84.

Miller, Bowman H., and Russell, Charles A. 1979. "The evolution of revolutionary warfare: from Mao to Marighella and Meinhof," in Kupperman/Trent, 185–99.

Miller, N. E. 1941. "The frustration-aggression hypothesis." *Psychological Review* 48:337–42.

Miller, Norman, and Aya, Roderick, eds. 1971. *National liberation: revolution in the third world.* New York: Free Press.

Miller, S. M. 1973. "On the uses, misuses and abuses of Jencks' inequality." *Sociology of Education* 46, no. 4 (Fall):427–32.

Miller, Warren E., and Levitin, Teresa E. 1976. *Leadership and change: the new politics and the American electorate.* Cambridge, Mass.: Winthrop Publishers.

Mintz, Sidney W. 1973. "A note on the definition of peasantries." *Journal of Peasant Studies* 1, no. 1 (October):91–106.

Mirowsky, John, and Ross, Catherine E. 1979. "Protest group success: the impact of group characteristics, social control, and context." Yale University. Mimeographed.

Mitchell, Edward J. 1968. "Inequality and insurgency: a statistical study of South Vietnam." *World Politics* 28, no. 3 (April):421–38.

Mitchell, Edward J. 1969. "Some econometrics of the HUK rebellion." *American Political Science Review* 63, no. 4 (December):1159–71.

Mitchell, Harvey. 1968a. "The Vendée and counterrevolution: a review essay." *French Historical Studies* 5 (Autumn):405–29.

Mitchell, Harvey. 1974. "Resistance to the revolution in Western France." *Past and Present* 63 (May):94–131.

Modelski, George. 1964. "International relations of internal war," in Rosenau, 14–44.

Modelski, George. 1964a. "International settlement of internal war," in Rosenau (1964), 122–53.

Moinat, Sheryl M.; Raine, Walter J.; Burbeck, Stephen L.; and Davison,

Keith K. 1972. "Black ghetto residents as rioters." *Journal of Social Issues* 28, no. 4:45–62.

Mollat, Michel, and Wolff, Philippe. 1973. *The popular revolutions of the late middle ages.* London: George Allen & Unwin. Original Paris: Calmann-Lévy (1970).

Molnar, Thomas. 1969. *The counter-revolution.* New York: Funk & Wagnalls.

Mols, Manfred, and Tobler, Hans Werner. 1975. "Mexico: Bilanz einer Revolution: Revolution und nachrevolutionäre Entwicklung im Lichte der historischen sozialwissenschaftlichen Forschung." *Jahrbuch für Geschichte von Staat, Wirtschaft und Gesellschaft Lateinamerikas* 12:284–392.

Momboisse, Raymond M. 1967. *Riots, revolts, and insurrections.* Springfield, Ill.: Charles C. Thomas.

Montagu, Ashley. 1973. *Man and aggression.* 2d ed. London: Oxford University Press.

Montanino, Fred. 1977. "Directions in the study of deviance: a bibliographic essay, 1960–1977," in Sagarin, 277–304.

Montesquieu, Charles Louis de Secondat. 1828. "Considerations sur les causes de la grandeur des romains et de leur décadence," in *Oeuvres* vol. I. Paris: Dufour et compagnie.

Montgomery, John D. 1969. "The quest for political development." *Comparative Politics* 1, no. 2 (January):285–95.

Monti, Daniel J. 1979. "Patterns of conflict preceding the 1964 riots: Harlem and Bedford-Stuyvesant." *Journal of Conflict Resolution* 21, no. 1 (March):41–69.

Moore, Barrington, Jr. 1966. *Social origins of dictatorship and democracy: lord and peasant in the making of the modern world.* Boston: Beacon Press.

Moore, Barrington, Jr. 1968. "Thoughts on violence and democracy," in *Proceedings of the Academy of Political Science,* vol. 29, no. 1. New York: The Academy of Political Science, Columbia University, 1–12.

Moore, B., Jr. 1969. "Revolution in America?" *New York Review of Books* (30 January):6–11.

Moore, Barrington, Jr. 1970. "Reply to Rothman." *American Political Science Review* 64, no. 1 (March):83–85.

Moore, Barrington, Jr. 1978. *Injustice: the social bases of obedience and revolt.* New York: M. E. Sharpe.

Moote, Lloyd A. 1972. "The preconditions of revolution in early modern Europe: did they really exist?" *Canadian Journal of History* 7, no. 3 (December):207–34.

Mora y Arauja, M. 1972. "Structural tension, economic development and changes in the level of conflicts," in Heintz, 223–39.

Morales, Waltraud Q. 1973. *Social revolution: theory and historical application.* University of Denver: Graduate School of International Studies, Monograph 11.

Moreno, José A. 1970. "Ché Guevara on guerrilla warfare: doctrine, practice and evaluation." *Comparative Studies in Society and History* 12 (April):114–33.

Moreno, José A. 1970a. *Barrios in arms: revolution in Santo Domingo.* Pittsburgh: University of Pittsburgh Press.

Morgan, Edmund S. 1976. *The challenge of the American Revolution.* New

York: W. W. Norton & Co.

Morgan, William R., and Clark, Terry Nichols. 1973. "The causes of racial disorders: a grievance-level explanation." *American Sociological Review* 38, no. 5 (October):611–24.

Morgan, W. R., and Sawyer, J. 1967. "Bargaining, expectations, and the preference for equality over equity." *Journal of Personality and Social Psychology* 6:139–49.

Morley, Ian, and Stephenson, Geoffrey. 1977. *The social psychology of bargaining.* London: George Allen & Unwin.

Morley, Morris, and Smith, Steven. 1977. "Imperial 'reach': U. S. policy and the CIA in Chile." *Journal of Political and Military Sociology* 5, no. 2 (Fall):203–16.

Morris, Raymond N. 1968. "'Some observations on measurement and statistics': further comment." *Social Forces* 46:541–42.

Morrison, Denton E., and Henkel, Ramon E. 1969. "Significance tests reconsidered." *American Sociologist* 4, no. 2 (May):131–39.

Morrison, Donald G., and Stevenson, Hugh Michael. 1971. "Political instability in independent Black Africa: more dimensions of conflict behavior within nations." *Journal of Conflict Resolution* 15, no. 3 (September):347–68.

Morrison, Donald G., and Stevenson, Hugh M. 1972a. "Integration and instability: patterns of African political development." *American Political Science Review* 66, no. 3 (September):902–27.

Morrison, D. G., and Stevenson, H. M. 1972b. "Cultural pluralism, modernization, and conflict: an empirical analysis of sources of political instability in African nations." *Canadian Journal of Political Science* 5, no. 1 (March):82–103.

Morrison, Donald G., and Stevenson, Hugh Michael. 1974. "Measuring social and political requirements for system stability: empirical validation of an index using Latin American and African data." *Comparative Political Studies* 7, no. 2 (July):252–63.

Morrison, D. G., and Stevenson, H. M. 1974a. "Social complexity, economic development and military coups d'état; convergence and divergence of empirical tests of theory in Latin America, Asia and Africa." *Journal of Peace Research* 11:345–47.

Morrison, Donald George, and Stevenson, Hugh Michael. 1976. "The practice and explanation of coups d'état: measurement or artifact?" *American Journal of Sociology* 82, no. 3 (November):674–83.

Morrison, Donald George; Mitchell, Robert Cameron; Paden, John Naber; and Stevenson, Hugh Michael. 1972. *Black Africa: a comparative handbook.* New York: Free Press.

Moskos, Charles C., Jr. 1976. "The military." *Annual Review of Sociology* 2:55–77.

Moss, Robert. 1970. "Urban guerillas in Latin America." *Conflict Studies* 8 (October):1–15.

Moss, Robert. 1971. "Urban guerilla warfare with an appendix: Minimanual of the urban guerilla by Carlos Marighella." *Adelphi Papers*, no. 79 (August).

Moss, Robert. 1972. *Urban guerillas: the new phase of political violence.* London: Temple Smith.

Moss, Robert. 1975. *The collapse of democracy*. London: Temple Smith.

Mosteller, Frederick, and Moynihan, Daniel P., eds. 1972. *On equality of educational opportunity*. New York: Random House.

Mousnier, Roland. 1958. "Recherches sur les soulèvements populaires en France avant la Fronde." *Revue d'historie moderne et contemporaine* 4:81–113.

Mousnier, Roland. 1970. "The Fronde," in Forster/Greene, 131–59.

Mousnier, Roland. 1971. *Peasant uprisings in the seventeenth century France, Russia and China*. London: George Allen & Unwin. (Original: *Fureurs paysannes: les paysans dans les révoltes du XVIIe siècle [France, Russie, Chine]*, Paris, 1967).

Moy, Roland F. 1971. *A computer simulation of democratic political development: tests of the Lipset and Moore models*. Sage Professional Paper in Comparative Politics Series, no. 01–019.

Moyer, K. E. 1968. "Kinds of aggression and their physiological basis." *Communications in Behavioral Biology*, part A, 2:65–87.

Moyer, K. E. 1969. "Internal impulses to aggression." *Transactions of the New York Academy of Sciences, Series II*, vol. 31:104–14.

Moyer, K. E. 1971. "The physiology of aggression and the implications for aggression control," in Singer, 61–92.

Moyer, Kenneth E. 1971a. *The physiology of hostility*. Chicago: Markham Press.

Moyer, Kenneth E. 1972. "Experimentelle Grundlagen eines physiologischen Modells aggressiven Verhaltens," in Schmidt-Mummendey/Schmidt, 25–57.

Moyer, K. E. 1976. *The psychobiology of aggression*. New York: Harper & Row Publishers.

Mueller, Carol McClurg. 1978. "Riot violence and protest outcomes." *Journal of Political and Military Sociology* 6, no. 1 (Spring):49–63.

Münkler, Herfried. 1980. "Guerillakrieg und Terrorismus." *Neue Politische Literatur* 25, no. 3:299–326.

Mulder, Mauk. 1977. *The daily power game*. The Hague: Martinus Nijhoff Social Sciences Division.

Mulder, Mauk; Veen, Peter; Hijzen, Theo; and Jansen, Peggy. 1973. "On power equalization: a behavioral example of power-distance reduction." *Journal of Personality and Social Psychology* 26, no. 2 (May): 151–58.

Mulkay, M. J. 1971. *Functionalism, exchange and theoretical strategy*. New York: Schocken Books.

Muller, Edward N. 1970. "Cross-national dimensions of political competence." *American Political Science Review* 64, no. 3 (September): 792–809.

Muller, Edward N. 1970a. "The representation of citizens by political authorities: consequences for regime support." *American Political Science Review* 64, no. 4 (December):1149–66.

Muller, Edward N. 1970b. "Correlates and consequences of beliefs in the legitimacy of regime structures." *Midwest Journal of Political Science* 14 (August):392–412.

Muller, Edward N. 1972. "A test of a partial theory of political violence." *American Political Science Review* 66, no. 3 (September):928–59.

Muller, Edward N. 1973. "A nonalienation interaction theory of political protest." Presented at the European Consortium for Political Research Workshop "Political behavior, dissatisfaction, and protest," April in Mannheim. Mimeographed.

Muller, Edward N. 1973a. "Measurement of readiness for unconventional political participation." Mannheim. Mimeographed.

Muller, Edward N. 1975. "Relative deprivation and aggressive political behavior." Presented at the Annual Meeting of the American Political Science Association, in San Francisco. Mimeographed.

Muller, Edward N. 1976. "A model for prediction of participation in collective political aggression." Paper delivered at the World Congress of the International Political Science Association, 16–21 August, in Edinburgh. Mimeographed.

Muller, Edward N. 1977. "Mass politics: focus on participation." *American Behavioral Scientist* 21, no. 1 (September/October):63–86.

Muller, Edward N. 1977a. "Behavioral correlates of political support." *American Political Science Review* 71, no. 2 (June):454–67.

Muller, Edward N. 1978. "Ein Modell zur Vorhersage aggressiver politischer Partizipation." *Politische Vierteljahresschrift* 19, no. 4 (December): 514–58.

Muller, Edward N. 1979. *Aggressive political participation*. Princeton: Princeton University Press.

Muller, Edward N. 1980. "The psychology of political protest and violence," in Gurr, 69–99.

Muller, Edward N., and Jukam, Thomas O. 1977. "On the meaning of political support." *American Political Science Review* 71, no. 4 (December): 1561–95.

Muller, Edward N., and Williams, Carol J. 1980. "Dynamics of political support–alienation." *Comparative Political Studies* 13, no. 1 (April): 33–59.

Munger, Frank W., Jr. 1977. "Popular protest and its suppression in early nineteenth century Lancashire, England: a study of historical models of protest and repression." University of Michigan. Unpublished manuscript.

Murdock, George Peter. (1967). *Ethnographic atlas*. Pittsburgh: University of Pittsburgh Press.

Murphy, Raymond J., and Watson, James M. 1969. "Ghetto social structure and riot support: the role of white contact, social distance, and discrimination," in Grimshaw, 235–49.

Murphy, Raymond J. and Watson, James M. 1970. "The structure of discontent: the relationship between social structure, grievance, and riot support," in Cohen, 140–257.

Murphy, Raymond J., and Watson, James M. 1971. "Level of aspiration, discontent, and support for violence: a test of the expectation hypothesis," in Geschwender, 360–72.

Murray, John O. 1973. "Television and violence. Implications of the surgeon general's research program." *American Psychologist* 28, no. 6 (June): 472–78.

Murray, Paul T. n.d. "War and riots: international conflict as a cause of American racial violence." Jackson, Missouri: Millsaps College.

Naess, Arne. 1958. "A systematization of Gandhian ethics of conflict resolution." *Journal of Conflict Resolution* 2, no. 1 (March):140–55.

Nagel, Jack. 1974. "Inequality and discontent: a nonlinear hypothesis." *World Politics* 26, no. 4 (July):453–72.

Nagel, Jack. 1975. *The descriptive analysis of power*. New Haven and London: Yale University Press.

Nagel, Jack H. 1976. "Erratum." *World Politics* 28, no. 2 (January):315.

Nagin, Daniel. 1978. "General deterrence: a review of the empirical evidence," in Alfred Blumstein, Jacqueline Cohen, and Daniel Nagin (eds.), *Deterrence and incapacitation: estimating the effects of criminal sanctions on crime rates*. Washington, D. C.: National Academy of Sciences, 95–139.

Nagle, John D. 1977. *System and succession: the social bases of political elite recruitment*. Austin: University of Texas Press.

Namboodiri, N. Krishan; Carter, Lewis F.; and Blalock, Hubert M., Jr. 1975. *Applied multivariate analysis and experimental designs*. New York: McGraw-Hill.

Namier, Lewis. 1971. *1848: the revolution of the intellectuals*. Oxford: Oxford University Press. (Original 1946.)

Nardin, Terry. 1971. *Violence and the state: a critique of empirical political theory*. Sage Professional Paper in Comparative Politics Series, no. 01–020.

Nardin, Terry. 1971a. "Theories of conflict management." *Peace Research Reviews* 4 (April):1–98.

Nardin, Terry. 1973. "Conflicting conceptions of political violence," in Cornelius P. Cotter (ed.), *Political Science Annual*, vol. 4. Indianapolis: Bobbs-Merrill, 75–126.

National Advisory Commission on Civil Disorders. 1968. *Report*. (Kerner Report.)

Needler, Martin. 1966. "Political development and military intervention in Latin America." *American Political Science Review* 60, no. 3 (September):616–26.

Needler, Martin C. 1968. "Political development and socioeconomic development: the case of Latin America." *American Political Science Review* 62, no. 3 (September):889–97.

Needler, Martin C. 1968a. *Political development in Latin America: instability, violence, and evolutionary change*. New York: Random House.

Needler, Martin. 1968b. *Latin American politics in perspective, revised printing*. Princeton: D. Van Nostrand Co.

Needler, Martin C. 1970. "Mexico: revolution as a way of life," in Needler (ed.), *Political systems of Latin America*. 2d ed. New York: Van Nostrand Reinhold Co., 1–33.

Needler, Martin C. 1974. "The causality of the Latin American coup d'état: some numbers, some speculations," in Schmidt/Dorfman, 145–59.

Needler, Martin C. 1980. "The military withdrawal from power in South America." *Armed Forces and Society* 6, no. 4 (Summer):615–24.

Nelkin, Dorothy. 1967. "The economic and social setting of military take-overs in Africa." *Journal of Asian and African Studies* 2:230-44.

Nelson, Joan M. 1969. *Migrants, urban poverty, and instability in developing nations*. Occasional Papers in International Affairs, no. 22. Center for International Affairs. Cambridge, Mass.: Harvard University.

Nelson, Joan. 1970. "The urban poor: disruption or political integration in third world cities?" *World Politics* 22, no. 3 (April):393–414.

Nelson, Joan M. 1976. "Sojourners versus new urbanites: causes and consequences of temporary versus permanent cityward migration in developing countries." *Economic Development and Cultural Change* 24, no. 4 (July):721–57.

Nelson, Stephen D. 1971. *The concept of social conflict*. University of Michigan. Institute for Social Research.

Nelson, Stephen D. 1974. "Nature/nurture revisited I: a review of the biological bases of conflict." *Journal of Conflict Resolution* 18, no. 2 (June): 285–335.

Nelson, Stephen D. 1975. "Nature/nurture revisited II: social, political, and technological implications of biological approaches to human conflict." *Journal of Conflict Resolution* 19, no. 4 (December):734–61.

Nelson, William H. 1965. "The revolutionary character of the American Revolution." *American Historical Review* 70, no. 4 (July):998–1014.

Van Ness, Peter. 1970. *Revolution and Chinese foreign policy: Peking's support for wars of national liberation*. Berkeley: University of California Press.

Nesvold, Betty A. 1969. "Scalogram analysis of political violence." *Comparative Political Studies* 2, no. 2 (July):172–94. Also in Gillespie/Nesvold (1971), 167–86.

Nesvold, Betty A. 1971. "Introduction: Studies in domestic conflict," in Gillespie/Nesvold, 31–37.

Nesvold, Betty A. and Martin, Antonia E. 1974. "Analysis of time-lag relationships between coerciveness and conflict." Paper presented to the Annual Meeting of the American Political Science Association, August/September, in Chicago.

Nettl, J. P. 1967. *Political mobilization: a sociological analysis of methods and concepts*. London: Faber & Faber.

Nettl, J. P. 1968. "The state as a conceptual variable." *World Politics* 20, no. 4 (July):559–92.

Nettl, J. P., and Robertson, Roland. 1966. "Industrialization, development, and modernization." *British Journal of Sociology* 17, no. 3 (September):274–91.

Neubauer, Deane E. 1967. "Some conditions of democracy." *American Political Science Review* 61, no. 4 (December):1002–1009.

Neumann, Sigmund. 1965. *Permanent revolution: totalitarianism in the age of international civil war*. 2d ed. New York: Frederick A Praeger.

Newman, Dorothy K. et al. 1978. *Protest, politics, and prosperity: black Americans and white institutions, 1940–75*. New York: Pantheon Books.

Newport, Frank. 1975. "Comment on Burgess and Nielsen." *American Sociological Review* 40, no. 6 (December):838–43.

Newton, George D., Jr., and Zimring, Franklin E. 1970. *Firearms and violence in American life: a staff report submitted to the National Commission on the Causes and Prevention of Violence*. Washington, D. C.: U. S. Government Printing Office.

Ney, Virgil. 1961. *Notes on guerilla war: principles and practices*. Washington, D. C.: Command Publications.

Nickel, Ted W. 1974. "The attribution of intention as a critical factor in the relation between frustration and aggression." *Journal of Personality* 42:482–92.

Nie, Norman H., and Verba, Sidney. 1975. "Political participation," in Greenstein/Polsby, vol. 4, 1–74.

Nieburg, H. L. 1962. "The threat of violence and social change." *American Political Science Review* 56, no. 4 (December):865–73.

Nieburg, H. L. 1963. "Uses of violence." *Journal of Conflict Resolution* 7, no. 1 (March):43–54.

Nieburg, H. L. 1968. "Violence, law, and the social process." *American Behavioral Scientist* 11, no. 4 (March-April):17–19.

Nieburg, H. L. 1969. *Political violence: the behavioral process.* New York: St. Martin's Press.

Nipperdey, Thomas. 1975. *Reformation, Revolution, Utopie: Studien zum 16. Jahrhundert.* Göttingen: Vandenhoeck & Ruprecht.

Nisbet, Robert A. 1969. *Social change and history: aspects of the Western theory of development.* London: Oxford University Press.

Nisbet, Robert. 1977. "Hannah Arendt and the American Revolution." *Social Research* 41, no. 1 (Spring):63–79.

Nixon, Raymond B. 1965. "Freedom in the world's press: a fresh appraisal with new data." *Journalism Quarterly* 42 (Winter):3–14.

Nordlinger, Eric A. 1968. "Political development: time sequences and rates of change." *World Politics* 20, no. 3 (April):494–520.

Nordlinger, Eric A. 1970. "Soldiers in mufti: the impact of military rule upon economic and social change in the non-western states." *American Political Science Review* 64, no. 4 (December):1131–48.

Nordlinger, Eric A. 1972. *Conflict regulation in divided societies.* Occasional Papers in International Affairs, 29. Harvard University: Center for International Affairs.

Nordlinger, Eric A. 1977. *Soldiers in politics: military coups and governments.* Englewood Cliffs: Prentice-Hall.

North, Liisa. 1976. "The military in Chilean politics." *Studies in Comparative International Development* 11, no. 2 (Summer), 73–106.

Nove, Alec. 1974. "On reading André Gunder Frank." *Journal of Developing Studies* 10, nos. 3/4 (April/July):445–55.

Noyes, P. H. 1966. *Organization and revolution: working-class associations in the German revolutions of 1848–1849.* Princeton: Princeton University Press.

Nun, José. 1967. "The middle-class military coup," in Claudio Veliz (ed.), *The politics of conformity in Latin America.* London: Oxford University Press, 66–118.

Nun, José. 1968. "A Latin American phenomenon: the middle-class coup," in Petras/Zeitlin, 145–85.

Nunn, Frederick. 1975. "New thoughts on military intervention in Latin American politics: the Chilean case, 1973." *Journal of Latin American Studies* 7, no. 2:271–304.

Nye, J. S. 1967. "Corruption and political development: a cost-benefit analysis." *American Political Science Review* 61, no. 2 (June):417–27.

Nye, Robert A. 1977. *The anti-democratic sources of elite theory: Pareto, Mosca, Michels.* Sage Professional Paper, Contemporary Political Sociology Series, no. 06–021.

O'Ballance, Edgar. 1967. *The Algerian insurrection, 1954-62*. London: Faber & Faber.

Oberdorfer, D. 1977. "Study says U. S. showed force 215 times since 1945." *Washington Post* (3 January).

Oberschall, A. 1968. "The Los Angeles riot of August 1965." *Social Problems* 15, no. 3 (Winter):322-41. Also in Stuart Palmer and Arnold S. Linsky (eds.), *Rebellion and retreat: readings in the forms and processes of deviance*. Columbus, Ohio: Charles E. Merrill (1972), 248-72.

Oberschall, Anthony R. 1969. "Rising expectations and political turmoil." *Journal of Development Studies* 6, no. 1 (October):5-22.

Oberschall, Anthony. 1973. *Social conflict and social movements*. Englewood Cliffs: Prentice-Hall.

Oberschall, Anthony. 1978a. "Theories of social conflict." *Annual Review of Sociology* 4:291-315.

Oberschall, Anthony. 1978b. "Locker strukturierter kollektiver Konflikt: Eine Theorie und eine Illustration." *Politische Vierteljahresschrift* 19, no. 4 (December):497-513.

Oberschall, Anthony. 1978c. "The decline of the 1960s social movements," in Louis Kriesberg (ed.), *Research in social movements, conflicts and change*. Greenwich, Conn.: JAI Press, 257-89.

Obler, Jeffrey; Steiner, Jürg; and Diericks, Guido. 1977. *Decision-making in smaller democracies: the consociational "burden."* Sage Professional Paper in Comparative Politics, vol. 6, no. 01-064.

O'Brien, Donald Cruise. 1972. "Modernization, order, and the erosion of a democratic ideal: American political science, 1960-1970." *Journal of Development Studies* 8, no. 4 (July):351-78.

O'Brien, Philip J. 1975. "A critique of Latin American theories of dependency," in Ivar Oxaal, Tony Barnett, and David Booth (eds.), *Beyond the sociology of development: economy and society in Latin America and Africa*. London: Routledge & Kegan Paul, 7-27.

O'Brien, Robert M. 1978. "Partial regression coefficients: a 'recomparison' of Kendall's Tau and Pearson's r." *Pacific Sociological Review* 21, no. 4 (October):501-505.

O'Connor, James. 1973. *The fiscal crisis of the state*. New York: St. Martin's Press.

Odom, William E. 1978. "The party-military connection: a critique," in Dale R. Herspring and Ivan Volgyes (eds.), *Civil-military relations in communist systems*. Boulder, Colo.: Westview Press, 27-52.

O'Donnell, Guillermo A. 1973. *Modernization and bureaucratic-authoritarianism: studies in South American politics*. Institute of International Studies. Berkeley: University of California.

Özbudun, Ergun. 1970. "Established revolution versus unfinished revolution: contrasting patterns of democratization in Mexico and Turkey," in Samuel P. Huntington and Clement H. Moore (eds.). *Authoritarian politics in modern society: the dynamics of established one-party systems*. New York: Basic Books, 380-405.

Offe, Claus. 1973. *Strukturprobleme des kapitalistischen Staates*. 2d ed. Frankfort on the Main: Suhrkamp.

O'Kane, R. H. T. 1971. "Coups d'état: an empirical investigation of existing literature; a probabilistic theory proposed and tested; and predictions made." *University of Essex*: Department of Government.

O'Leary, M. R., and Dengerink, H. A. 1973. "Aggression as a function of the intensity and pattern of attack." *Journal of Research in Personality* 7, no. 1 (June):61–70.

Olsen, Marvin E. 1968a. "Perceived legitimacy of social protest actions." *Social Problems* 15 (Winter):297–310.

Olsen, Marvin E. 1968b. "Multivariate analysis of national political development." *American Sociological Review* 33, no. 5 (October):699–712.

Olsen, Marvin E., and Baden, Mary Anna. 1974. "Legitimacy of social protest actions in the United States and Sweden." *Journal of Political and Military Sociology* 2, no. 2 (Fall):173–89.

Olson, Mancur, Jr. 1963. "Rapid growth as a destabilizing force." *Journal of Economic History* 23, no. 4 (December):529–52. Also in Davies (1971), 215–27.

Olson, Mancur. 1965. *The logic of collective action*. Cambridge, Mass.: Harvard University Press.

Olweus, Dan. 1972. "Personality and aggression," in James K. Cole and Donald D. Jensen (eds.), *Nebraska symposium on motivation 1972*. Lincoln: University of Nebraska Press, 261–321.

Onate, Andres D. 1974. "The conflict interactions of the People's Republic of China, 1950–1970." *Journal of Conflict Resolution* 18, no. 4 (December):578–94.

Oppenheimer, Martin. 1969. *The urban guerilla*. Chicago: Quadrangle Book.

Organski, A. F. K. 1967. *The stages of political development*. New York: Alfred A. Knopf.

Orlansky, Jesse. 1970. *The state of research on internal war*. Arlington, Va.: Institute for Defense Analyses.

Orum, Anthony M. 1974. "On participation in political protest movements." *Journal of Applied Behavioral Science* 10, no. 2:181–207.

Osanka, Franklin Mark, ed. 1962. *Modern guerilla warfare: fighting communist guerilla movements, 1941–1961*. New York: Free Press of Glencoe.

Osanka, F. M. 1968. "Internal warfare: guerilla warfare," in *International Encyclopedia of the Social Sciences*, vol. 7. New York: Macmillan Co. and Free Press, 503–507.

Osanka, Franklin Mark. 1971. "Social dynamics of revolutionary guerilla warfare," in Roger W. Little (ed.), *Handbook of military institutions*. Beverly Hills: Sage Publications, 399–416.

Osmond, Russell Lowell. 1979. "Transnational terrorism 1968–1974: a quantitative analysis." Ph.D. dissertation, Syracuse University.

Ostrom, Charles W. 1978. *Time series analysis: regression techniques*. Sage University Paper, Quantitative Applications in the Social Sciences, 9.

Ottaway, David, and Ottaway, Marina. 1970. *Algeria: the politics of a socialist revolution*. Berkeley: University of California Press.

Ottaway, Marina. 1976. "Social classes and corporate interests in the Ethiopian revolution." *Journal of Modern African Studies* 14, no. 3 (September):469–86.

Ottaway, Marina, and Ottaway, David. 1978. *Ethiopia: empire in revolution*. New York: Holmes & Meier.

Otterbein, Keith F. 1968. "Internal war: a cross-cultural study." *American Anthropologist* 70, no. 2 (April):277–89.

Otto, Luther B. and Featherman, David L. 1975. "Social structural and psychological antecedents of self-estrangement and powerlessness." *American Sociological Review* 40, no. 6 (December):701–19.

Overholt, William H. 1977. "Sources of radicalism and revolution: a survey of the literature," in Bialer/Sluzar, 293–335.

Owen, David R. 1972. "The 47, XYY male: a review." *Psychological Bulletin* 78, no. 3 (March):209–33.

Packenham, Robert A. 1964. "Approaches to the study of political development." *World Politics* 17, no. 1 (October):108–20.

Packenham, Robert A. 1970. "Political development research," in Michael Haas and Henry S. Kariel (eds.), *Approaches to the study of political science*. San Francisco: Chandler Publishing Co., 169–93.

Page, Monte M., and Scheidt, Rick J. 1971. "The elusive weapons effect: demand awareness, evaluation apprehension, and slightly sophisticated subjects." *Journal of Personality and Social Psychology* 20, no. 3 (December):304–18.

Page, Stanley W. 1968. *Lenin and world revolution*. Gloucester, Mass.: Peter Smith. (Original 1959.)

Paige, Jeffery M. 1970. "Inequality and insurgency in Vietnam: a re-analysis." *World Politics* 23, no. 1 (October):24–37.

Paige, Jeffery M. 1971. "Political orientation and riot participation." *American Sociological Review* 36, no. 5 (October):810–20.

Paige, Jeffery M. 1975. *Agrarian revolution: social movements and export agriculture in the underdeveloped world*. Riverside, N. J.: Free Press.

Palmer, David Scott. 1974. *Revolution from above: military government and popular participation in Peru, 1968–1972*. Ithaca: Cornell University Press.

Palmer, Monte. 1973. *Dilemmas of political development: an introduction to the politics of the developing areas*. Itasca, Ill.: F. E. Peacock Publishers.

Palmer, Monte, and Thompson, William R. 1978. *The comparative analysis of politics*. Itasca, Ill.: F. E. Peacock Publishers.

Palmer, R. R. 1959. *The age of democratic revolution: a political history of Europe and America, 1760–1800*: vol. 1: *The challenge*. vol. 2: *The struggle* (1964). Princeton: Princeton University Press.

Palmer, R. R. 1959a. "Review of Georges Lefebvre: The peasants and the French Revolution." *Journal of Modern History* 31, no. 4 (December): 329–42.

Palmer, Robert R. 1960. "Popular democracy in the French Revolution: a review article." *French Historical Studies* 1, no. 3 (Fall): 445–69. Also in Kafker/Laux (1968), 279–302.

Palmer, R. R. 1970. *Twelve who ruled: the year of the Terror in the French Revolution*. Princeton: Princeton University Press.

Palmer, R. R. 1971. *The world of the French Revolution*. London: George Allen & Unwin.

Pantaleone, Michele. 1966. *The mafia and politics*. London: Chatto & Windus.

Paranzino, Dennis. 1972. "A note on political coerciveness and turmoil." *Law and Society Review* 6, no. 4 (May):652–55.

Paranzino, Dennis. 1972a. "Inequality and insurgency in Vietnam: a further re-analysis." *World Politics* 24, no. 4 (July):565–78.

Paret, Peter, and Shy, John W. 1962. *Guerillas in the 1960's*. 2d ed. New York: Frederick A. Praeger.

Pareto, Vilfredo. 1901. "Un applicazione di teorie sociologice." *Rivista Italiana di Sociologia*: 402–56. English version: *The rise and fall of the elites: an application of theoretical sociology*. Introduction by Hans L. Zetterberg. Totowa, N.J.: Bedminster Press (1968).

Pareto, Vilfredo. 1916. *Trattato di sociologia generale*. 3 vols. Florence: Barbera. English trans. *Treatise on general sociology*. New York: Dover (1963).

Pareto, Vilfredo. 1965. *Manuale di economia politica*. Rome: Edizioni Bizzari. (Original 1906.)

Parker, Geoffrey, and Smith, Lesley M., eds. 1978. *The general crisis of the seventeenth century*. London: Routledge & Kegan Paul.

Parry, Albert. 1976. *Terrorism: from Robespierre to Arafat*. New York: Vanguard Press.

Parsons, Talcott. 1964. "Some reflections on the place of force in social process," in Eckstein, 33–70.

Parsons, Talcott, and Clark, Kenneth, eds. 1966. *The Negro American*. Boston: Houghton Mifflin Co.

Parvin, Manoucher. 1973. "Economic determinants of political unrest: an econometric approach." *Journal of Conflict Resolution* 17, no. 2 (June):271–96.

Passigli, Stefano. 1973. "On power, its intensity and distribution." *European Journal of Political Research* 1, no. 2 (June):163–77.

Passos, Alaor S. 1968. "Developmental tension and political instability: testing some hypotheses concerning Latin America." *Journal of Peace Research* 5:70–86.

Pastore, N. 1952. "The role of arbitrariness in the frustration-aggression hypothesis." *Journal of Abnormal and Social Psychology* 47:728–31.

Patch, Richard W. 1961. "Bolivia: the restrained revolution." *The Annals*, no. 334 (March):123–32.

Pauker, Guy J. 1959. "Southeast Asia as a problem area in the next decade." *World Politics* 11, no. 3 (April):325–45.

Paukert, Felix. 1973. "Income distribution at different levels of development: a survey of evidence." *International Labor Review* 108, nos. 2–3 (August/September):97–125.

Payne, James L. 1965. *Labor and politics in Peru: the system of political bargaining*. New Haven: Yale University Press.

Payne, James. 1965a. "Peru: the politics of structured violence." *Journal of Politics* 27, no. 2 (May):362–74. Also in Feierabend/Feierabend/Gurr (1972), 359–68.

Payne, James L. 1968. *The patterns of conflict in Columbia*. New Haven: Yale University Press.

Payne, James L. 1969. "Democracy by violence," in Arpad von Lazar and Robert R. Kaufman (eds.), *Reform and revolution: readings in Latin American politics*. Boston: Allyn & Bacon, 90–103.

Payne, Stanley G. 1975. *Basque nationalism*. Reno: University of Nevada Press.

Paynton, Clifford T., and Blackey, Robert, eds. 1971. *Why revolution? Theories and analyses*. Cambridge, Mass.: Schenkman Publishing Co.

Peacock, A. J. 1965. *Bread or blood: the agrarian riots in East Anglia: 1816*. London: Gollancz.

Pearson, Frederic S. 1974a. "Foreign military interventions and domestic disputes." *International Studies Quarterly* 18, no. 3 (September): 259–90.

Pearson, Frederic S. 1974b. "Geographic proximity and foreign military intervention." *Journal of Conflict Resolution* 18, no. 3 (September): 432–60.

Pearson, Frederic S. 1976. "American military intervention abroad: a test of economic and noneconomic explanations," in Satish Raichur and Craig Liske (eds.), *The politics of aid, trade and investment*. New York: Sage Publications, 37–62.

Pearson, Frederic S., and Baumann, Robert. 1974. "Research note: Foreign military intervention by large and small powers." *International Interactions* 1:273–78.

Pearson, Raymond. 1977. *The Russian moderates and the crisis of Tsarism 1914-1917*. London: Macmillan.

Pennock, J. Roland, and Chapman, John W., eds. 1972. *Coercion, Nomos XIV: yearbook of the American Society for Political and Legal Philosophy*. Chicago: Aldine-Atherton.

Pepper, Suzanne. 1978. *Civil war in China: the political struggle 1945-1949*. Berkeley: University of California Press.

Pereira, Nino R., and Salinas, Patricia Wilson. 1978. "A relation between the Gini and Elteto measures of inequality." *Quality and Quantity* 12, no. 2 (June):175–78.

Pérez, Louis A. 1976. *Army politics in Cuba, 1898-1958*. Pittsburgh: University of Pittsburgh Press.

Perinbam, B. Marie. 1973. "Fanon and the revolutionary peasantry–the Algerian case." *Journal of Modern African Studies* 11, no. 3 (September):427–45.

Perlmutter, Amos. 1967. "Egypt and the myth of the new middle class: a comparative analysis." *Comparative Studies in Society and History* 10, no. 1 (October):46–65.

Perlmutter, Amos. 1969. "The praetorian state and the praetorian army: toward a taxonomy of civil military relations in developing societies." *Comparative Politics* 1, no. 3 (April):382–404.

Perlmutter, Amos. 1970. "The Arab military elite." *World Politics* 22, no. 2 (January):269–300.

Perlmutter, Amos. 1974. *Egypt, the praetorian state*. New Brunswick, N.J.: Transaction Books.

Perlmutter, Amos. 1977. *The military and politics in modern times: on professionals, praetorians, and revolutionary soldiers*. New Haven and London: Yale University Press.

Perrie, Maureen. 1972. "The Russian peasant movement of 1905-1907: its social composition and revolutionary significance." *Past and Present* 57 (November):123–55.

Perry, Ronald W.; Gillespie, David F.; and Lotz, Roy E. 1976. "Attitudinal variables as estimates of behavior: a theoretical examination of the attitude-action controversy." *European Journal of Social Psychology* 6, no. 2:227-43.

Peters, Stephen. 1975. "Ingredients of the Communist takeover in Albania," in Hammond (1975a), 273-92.

Peterson, Karen Kay, and Dutton, Jeffrey E. 1975. "Centrality, extremity, intensity: neglected variables in research on attitude-behavior consistency." *Social Forces* 52, no. 2 (December):393-414.

Peterson, Rolf A. 1971. "Aggression as a function of expected retaliation and aggression level of target and aggressor." *Developmental Psychology* 5, no. 1:161-66.

Peterson, Sophia. 1975. "Research on research: events data studies, 1961-1972," in Patrick McGowan (ed.), *Sage International Yearbook of Foreign Policy Studies*, vol. 3. Beverly Hills: Sage Publications, 263-309.

Petras, James, and Zeitlin, Maurice, eds. 1968. *Latin America: reform or revolution?* Greenwich, Conn.: Fawcett.

Pettee, George. 1966. "Revoluton—typology and process," in Friedrich, 10-33.

Pettee, George Sawyer. 1971. *The process of revolution*. New York: Howard Fertig. (Original pub. New York: Harper & Brothers, 1938.)

Pettigrew, T. F. 1964. *A profile of the Negro American*. Princeton: D. Van Nostrand Co.

Pettigrew, T. F. 1967. "Social evaluation theory: convergences and applications," in David Levine (ed.), *Nebraska symposium on motivation 1967*. Lincoln: University of Nebraska Press, 241-311.

Pettigrew, T. F. 1969. "Racially separate or together." *Journal of Social Issues* 25, no. 1:43-69.

Pettigrew, Thomas F. 1971a. "Race relations," in Robert K. Merton and Robert Nisbet (eds.), *Contemporary social problems*. 3d ed. New York: Harcourt, Brace, Jovanovich, 407-65.

Pettigrew, Thomas F. 1971b. *Racially separate or together?* New York: McGraw-Hill.

Pettigrew, Thomas F., ed. 1975. *Racial discrimination in the United States*. New York: Harper & Row.

Pettigrew, Thomas Fraser. 1976. "Race and intergroup relations," in Robert K. Merton and Robert Nisbet (eds.), *Contemporary social problems*. 4th ed. New York: Harcourt Brace Jovanovich, 459-508.

Pfeffer, Richard M. 1971. "Mao Tse-tung and the Cultural Revolution," in Miller/Aya, 249-96.

Phares, E. Jerry. 1976. *Locus of control in personality*. Morristown, N.J.: General Learning Press.

Philip, George D. E. 1978. *The rise and fall of the Peruvian military radicals, 1968-1976*. University of London: Athlone Press.

Phillips, John, and Ba-Yunus, Ilyas. 1976. "Comment on Alan Well's 'The coup d'état in theory and practice: independent Black Africa in the 1960s.'" *American Journal of Sociology* 82, no. 3 (November):684-85.

Phillips, Warren, and Hall, Dennis R. 1970. "The importance of governmental structure as a taxonomic scheme for nations." *Comparative Political Studies* 3, no. 1 (April):63-89.

Pilbeam, Pamela. 1976. "Popular violence in provincial France after the 1830 revolution." *English Historical Review* 91, no. 359 (April):278-97.

Pinard, Maurice. 1967. "Poverty and social movements." *Social Problems* 15, no. 2 (Fall):250–63.

Pinard, Maurice. 1968. "Mass society and political movements: a new formulation." *American Journal of Sociology* 73, no. 6 (May):682–90.

Pinard, Maurice. 1971. *The rise of a third party: a study in crisis politics.* Englewood Cliffs: Prentice-Hall.

Pinard, Maurice. 1976. "The moderation and regulation of communal conflicts: a critical review of current theories." Presented to the European Consortium for Political Research Workshop on "The politics of multicultural societies," 8–14 April, in Louvain (Belgium).

Pinkney, David H. 1964. "The crowd in the French revolution of 1830." *American Historical Review* 70, no. 1 (October):1–17.

Pinkney, David. H. 1972. "The revolutionary crowd in Paris in the 1830s." *Journal of Social History* 5, no. 4 (Summer):512–20.

Pinkney, David H. 1972a. *The French Revolution of 1830.* Princeton: Princeton University Press.

Pipes, Richard, ed. 1968. *Revolutionary Russia.* Cambridge, Mass.: Harvard University Press.

Pitcher, Brian L.; Hamblin, Robert L.; and Miller, Jerry L. L. 1978. "The diffusion of collective violence." *American Sociological Review* 43, no. 1 (February):23–35.

Piven, Frances Fox. 1976. "The social structuring of political protest." *Politics and Society* 6, no. 3:297–326.

Piven, Frances Fox, and Cloward, Richard A. 1971. *Regulating the poor: the functions of public welfare.* New York: Vintage Books.

Piven, Frances Fox, and Cloward, Richard A. 1977. *Poor people's movements: why they succeed, how they fail.* New York: Pantheon.

Piven, Frances Fox, and Cloward, Richard A. 1979. "Electoral instability, civil disorder, and relief rises: a reply to Albritton." *American Political Science Review* 73, no. 4 (December):1012–19.

Pluta, Joseph. 1979. "The performance of South American civilian and military governments from a socio-economic perspective." *Development and Change* 10, no. 3 (July):461–83.

Pollock, David H., and Ritter, Arch R. M., eds. 1973. *Latin American prospects for the 1970s: what kind of revolutions?* New York: Praeger Publishers.

Ponchaud, François. 1977. *Cambodge, année zéro.* Paris: Julliard.

Popper, Frank J. 1971. "Internal war as a stimulant of political development." *Comparative Political Studies* 3, no. 4 (January):413–23.

Popper, Karl Raimund. 1957. *The poverty of historicism.* London: Routledge & Kegan Paul.

Popper, Karl R. 1972. *Conjectures and refutations: the growth of scientific knowledge.* 4th ed. London: Routledge & Kegan Paul.

Porch, Douglas. 1977. *The Portuguese armed forces and the revolution.* London: Croom Helm.

Porchnev, Boris F. 1963. *Les soulèvements populaires en France de 1623 à 1648.* Center de recherches historiques, Oeuvres étrangères, 4. Paris: SEV,PEN; École pratique des hautes études, 6ᵉ section.

Porter, Randall C., and Nagel, Jack H. 1976. "Declining inequality and rising expectations: relative deprivation and the black urban riots." Fels Discussion Paper, no. 96. School of Public and Urban Policy. Philadelphia: University of Pennsylvania.

Portes, Alejandro. 1971. "On the interpretation of class consciousness." *American Journal of Sociology* 77, no. 2 (September):228–44.

Portes, Alejandro. 1973. "Modernity and development: a critique." *Studies in Comparative International Development* 8, no. 3 (Fall), 247–79.

Portes, Alejandro. 1976. "On the sociology of national development: theories and issues." *American Journal of Sociology* 82, no. 1 (July):55–85.

Portes, Alejandro, and Ross, Adreain. 1974. "A model for the prediction of leftist radicalism." *Journal of Political and Military Sociology* 2, no. 1 (Spring):33–56.

Porzecanski, Arturo C. 1973. *Uruguay's Tupamaros: the urban guerilla.* New York: Praeger Publishers.

Potholm, Christian P. 1979. *The theory and practice of African politics.* Englewood Cliffs: Prentice-Hall.

Potter, Jack M.; Diaz, May N.; and Foster, George M., eds. 1967. *Peasant society: a reader.* Boston: Little, Brown & Co.

Powell, John Duncan. 1971. *The political mobilization of the Venezuelan peasant.* Cambridge, Mass.: Harvard University Press.

Powers, Patrick C., and Geen, Russell G. 1972. "Effects of the behavior and the perceived arousal of a model on instrumental aggression." *Journal of Personality and Social Psychology* 23, no. 2 (August):175–83.

Price, H. Edward, Jr. 1977. "The strategy and tactics of revolutionary terrorism." *Comparative Studies in Society and History* 19, no. 1 (January): 52–66.

Price, Robert M. 1971. "A theoretical approach to military rule in new states: reference-group theory and the Ghanaian case." *World Politics* 23, no. 3 (April):399–430.

Price, Roger. 1972. *The French Second Republic: a social history.* London: B. T. Batsford.

Price, Roger, ed. 1975. *Revolution and reaction: 1848 and the Second French Republic.* London: Croom Helm.

Pride, Richard A. 1970. *Origins of democracy: a cross-national study of mobilization, party systems, and democratic stability.* Sage Professional Paper in Comparative Politics Series, no. 01–012.

Pritchard, Robert D. 1969. "Equity theory: a review and critique." *Organizational Behavior and Human Performance* 4, no. 2 (May):176–211.

Prosterman, Roy L. 1976. "'IRI': A simplified predictive index of rural instability." *Comparative Politics* 8, no. 3 (April):339–53.

Przeworski, Adam, and Teune, Henry. 1970. *The logic of comparative social inquiry.* New York: Wiley-Interscience.

Purcell, Susan Kaufman, and Purcell, John F. H. 1980. "State and society in Mexico: must a stable polity be institutionalized?" *World Politics* 32, no. 2 (January):194–227.

Putnam, Robert D. 1967. "Toward explaining military intervention in Latin American politics." *World Politics* 20, no. 1 (October), 83–110. Also in Jason L. Finkle and Richard W. Gable (eds.), *Political development and social change.* 2d ed. New York: John Wiley & Sons (1971), 284–304.

Putnam, Robert D. 1976. *The comparative study of political elites.* Englewood Cliffs: Prentice-Hall.

Pye, Lucian W. 1961. "Armies in the process of political modernization." *Archives Européennes de Sociologie* 2, no. 1:82–92. Also in J. J. Johnson (1962), 69–89.

Pye, Lucian W., ed. 1963. *Communications and political development.* Princeton: Princeton University Press.

Pye, Lucian W. 1964. "The roots of insurgency and the commencement of rebellions," in Eckstein, 157–79.

Pye, Lucian W. 1966. *Aspects of political development.* Boston: Little, Brown & Co.

Pye, Lucian W. 1971. "The legitimacy crisis," in Binder et al., 135–58.

Pye, Lucian W. 1971a. "Foreword," in Binder et al. (1971), vii–x.

Pye, Lucian W. 1972. "Culture and political science: problems in the evaluation of the concept of political culture." *Social Science Quarterly* 53, no. 2 (September):285–96.

Pye, Lucian W. 1976. *Mao Tse-tung: the man in the leader.* New York: Basic Books.

Quandt, Richard E. 1974. "Some statistical characterizations of aircraft hijacking." *Accident Analysis and Prevention* 6 (October):115–23.

Quandt, William B. 1969. *Revolution and political leadership: Algeria, 1954-1968.* Cambridge: MIT Press.

Quanty, Michael B. 1976. "Aggression catharsis: experimental investigations and implications," in Geen/O'Neal, 99–132.

Quarantelli, E. L., and Dynes, Russell R. 1968. "Looting in civil disorders: an index of social change." *American Behavioral Scientist* 11, no. 4 (March/April):7–10.

Quarantelli, E. L., and Dynes, Russell R. 1970. "Property norms and looting: their patterns in community crises." *Phylon: The Atlanta University Review of Race and Culture* 31:168–72. Also in Geschwender (1971), 285–300.

Quinney, Richard. 1970. *The social reality of crime.* Boston: Little, Brown.

Quirk, Robert E. 1960. *The Mexican Revolution 1914-1915: the convention of Aguascalientes.* Bloomington: Indiana University Press.

Qureshi, Saleem. 1976. "Political violence in the South Asian subcontinent," in Alexander, 151–93.

Rabb, Theodore K. 1975. *The struggle for stability in early modern Europe.* New York: Oxford University Press.

Rabinowitch, Alexander. 1968. *Prelude to revolution: the Petrograd Bolsheviks and the July 1917 uprising.* Bloomington: Indiana University Press.

Rabinowitch, Alexander. 1972. "The Petrograd garrison and the Bolshevik seizure of power," in Alexander and Janet Rabinowitch (eds.), *Revolution and politics in Russia: essays in memory of B. I. Nicolaevsky.* Bloomington: University of Indiana Press, 172–91.

Rabinowitch, Alexander. 1976. *The Bolsheviks come to power, the revolution of 1917 in Petrograd.* New York: W. W. Norton & Co.

Rae, Douglas W. 1971. *The political consequences of electoral laws.* New Haven: Yale University Press.

Rae, Douglas W., and Taylor, Michael. 1970. *The analysis of political cleavages.* New Haven and London: Yale University Press.

Raine, Walter J. 1970. "The perception of police brutality in South Central Los Angeles," in Cohen, 380–412.

Raine, Walter J.; Abudu, Margaret J. G.; Burbeck, Stephen; and Davidson, Keith. 1971. "Empirical structure of the urban black subculture as related to riot activity." *Proceedings, 79th Annual Convention, American Psychological Association*, 315–16.

Ramm, Hartmut. 1978. *The marxism of Regis Debray: between Lenin and Guevara*. Lawrence: Regents Press of Kansas.

Rankin, Mary Backus. 1971. *Early Chinese revolutionaries: radical intellectuals in Shanghai and Chekiang, 1902–1911*. Cambridge, Mass.: Harvard University Press.

Ransford, H. Edward. 1968. "Isolation, powerlessness, and violence: a study of attitudes and participation in the Watts riot." *American Journal of Sociology* 73:581–91.

Ransford, H. Edward. 1971. "Comment." *Journal of Social Issues* 27, no. 1: 227–32.

Ransford, H. Edward. 1972. "Blue collar anger: reactions to student and black protest." *American Sociological Review* 37, no. 3 (June):333–46.

Rapoport, Amos. 1975. "Toward a redefinition of density." *Environment and Behavior* 7, no. 2 (June):133–58.

Rapoport, David C. 1962. "A comparative theory of military and political types," in Huntington (1962a), 71–101.

Rapoport, David C. 1966. "Coup d'état: the view of the men firing pistols," in Friedrich, 53–74.

Rau, William C. 1980. "The tacit conventions of the modernity school: an analysis of key assumptions." *American Sociological Review* 45, no. 2 (April):244–60.

Rawls, John. 1971. *A theory of justice*. Cambridge, Mass.: Belknap Press of Harvard University Press.

Ray, James Lee, and Webster Thomas. 1978. "Dependency and economic growth in Latin America." *International Studies Quarterly* 22, no. 3 (September):409–34.

Reichardt, Rolf. 1973. *Reform and Revolution bei Condorcet: Ein Beitrag zur späten Aufklärung in Frankreich*. Bonn: Ludwig Röhrscheid Verlag.

Reiss, Albert, Jr., and Aldrich, Howard. 1971. "Absentee ownership and management in the black ghetto: social and economic consequences." *Social Problems* 18, no. 3 (Winter):319–39.

Rejai, Mostafa. 1973. *The strategy of political revolution*. New York: Doubleday & Co.

Rejai, Mostafa. 1973a. "Survey essay on the study of revolution." *Journal of Political and Military Sociology* 1, no. 2 (Fall): 299–304.

Rejai, Mostafa. 1977. *The comparative study of revolutionary strategy*. New York: David McKay.

Rejai, Mostafa. 1980. "Theory and research in the study of revolutionary personnel," in Gurr, 100–131.

Rejai, Mostafa, with Phillips, Kay. 1979. *Leaders of revolution*. Beverly Hills: Sage Publications.

Renshon, Stanley Allen. 1974. *Psychological needs and political behavior: a theory of personality and political efficacy*. New York: Free Press.

Reynolds, Harry W., Jr. 1968. "Black power, community power, and jobs," in Masotti/Bowen, 237–59.

Rhoads, Edward J. M. 1975. *China's republican revolution: the case of Kwangtung, 1895–1913*. Cambridge, Mass.: Harvard University Press.

Rhoda, Richard. 1978. "Political instability and institutionalization in developing countries: an empirical evaluation of the Huntington model." *Public Data Use* 6 (January):38–44.

Richardson, Lewis F. 1960. *Statistics of deadly quarrels.* Chicago: Boxwood and Quadrangle.

Richardson, R. C. 1977. *The debate on the English Revolution.* London: Methuen & Co.

Richter, Melvin. 1966. "Tocqueville's contributions to the theory of revolution," in Friedrich, 75–121.

Riezler, Kurt. 1943. "On the psychology of the modern revolution." *Social Research* 10, no. 3 (September):320–36.

Rigby, T. H. 1968. *Communist Party membership in the USSR, 1917–1967.* Princeton: Princeton University Press.

Riggs. Fred W. 1963. "Bureaucrats and political development: a paradoxical view," in Joseph LaPalombara (ed.), *Bureaucracy and political development.* Princeton: Princeton University Press, 120–67.

Riggs, Fred W. 1967. "The theory of political development," in James C. Charlesworth (ed.), *Contemporary political analysis.* New York: Free Press, 337–49.

Rights in conflict: the violent confrontation of demonstrators and police in the parks and streets of Chicago during the week of the Democratic National Convention of 1968. A report submitted by Daniel Walker, Director of the Chicago Study Team, to the National Commission on the Causes and Prevention of Violence. (1968). New York: Bantam Books.

Riker, William H. 1962. *The theory of political coalitions.* New Haven: Yale University Press.

Riker, William H., and Ordeshook, Peter C. 1973. *An introduction to positive political theory.* Englewood Cliffs: Prentice-Hall.

Rittberger, Volker. 1971. "Über sozialwissenschaftliche Theorien der Revolution: Kritik und Versuch eines Neuansatzes." *Politische Vierteljahresschrift* 12, no. 4 (December):492–529.

Rittberger, Volker. 1973. "Politische Krisen und Entwicklungsprobleme," in Jänicke, 26–38.

Ritter, Arch R. M., and Pollock, David H. 1973. "Revolution in Latin America: an overview," in Pollock/Ritter, 3–29.

Rivkin, Arnold. 1969. *Nation-building in Africa: problems and prospects.* New Brunswick: Rutgers University Press.

Roach, Janet K., and Roach, Jack L. 1980. "Turmoil in command of politics: organizing the poor." *Sociological Quarterly* 21, no. 2 (Spring): 259–70.

Roberts, Adam, ed. 1967. *The strategy of civilian defense.* London: Faber & Faber.

Roberts, J. M. 1978. *The French Revolution.* Oxford: Oxford University Press.

Robertson, Priscilla. 1952. *Revolutions of 1848: a social history.* Princeton: Princeton University Press.

Robin, Régine. 1970. *La société française en 1789: Semur-en-Auxois.* Paris: Librairie Plon.

Robins, Robert S. 1976. *Political institutionalization and the integration of elites*. Sage Library of Social Research, vol. 21. Beverly Hills: Sage Publications.

Robinson, James A. 1968. "Crisis," in David L. Sills (ed.), *International Encyclopedia of the Social Sciences*, vol. 3. New York: Macmillan Co. and Free Press, 510–14.

Robinson, James A. 1972. "Crisis: an appraisal of concepts and theories," in Herrmann, 20–35.

Robinson, John P., and Shaver, Philip R. 1973. *Measures of social psychological attitudes*. 5th ed. Ann Arbor: Institute for Social Research.

Robinson, Thomas W., ed. 1971. *The cultural revolution in China*. Berkeley: University of California Press.

Rockwell, Richard C. 1975. "Assessment of multicollinearity: the Haitovsky test of the determinant." *Sociological Methods and Research* 3, no. 3 (February):308–20.

Rodrigues, Avelino; Borga, Cesario; and Cardoso, Mario. 1976. *Portugal, despois de Abril*. Lissabon: Bras Monteiro.

Roeder, Philip G. 1979. "Revolting peasants: the role of the peasantry in twentieth-century revolutions." University of New Mexico. Mimeographed.

Röttgers, Kurt, and Saner, Hans, eds. 1978. *Gewalt. Grundlagenprobleme in der Diskussion der Gewaltphänomene*. Basel: Schwabe Verlag.

Rogers, Everett M. 1969. *Modernization among peasants: the impact of communication*. New York: Holt, Rinehart & Winston.

Rogowski, Ronald. 1974. *Rational legitimacy: a theory of political support*. Princeton: Princeton University Press.

Rogowski, Ronald, and Wasserspring, Lois. 1971. *Does political development exist? Corporatism in old and new societies*. Sage Professional Paper in Comparative Politics Series, no. 01–024.

Rokeach, Milton, and Kliejunas, Peter. 1972. "Behavior as a function of attitude-toward-object and attitude-toward-situation." *Journal of Personality and Social Psychology* 22, no. 2 (May):194–201.

Rokkan, Stein. 1969. "Models and methods in the comparative study of nation-building." *Acta Sociologica* 12, no. 2:53–73.

Rokkan, Stein. 1970. "Cross-cultural, cross-societal, and cross-national research," in Unesco (ed.), *Main trends of research in the social and human sciences*, part 1: *social sciences*. Paris: Mouton, 645–89.

Rokkan, Stein. 1970a. *Citizens, elections, parties: approaches to the comparative study of the processes of development*. Oslo: Universitetsforlaget.

Rokkan, Stein. 1973. "Cities, states and nations: a dimensional model for the study of contrasts in development," in S. N. Eisenstadt/Stein Rokkan (eds.), *Building states and nations: models and data resources*, vol. 1. Beverly Hills: Sage Publications, 73–97.

Rokkan, Stein. 1974. "Entries, voices, exits: towards a possible generalization of the Hirschman model." *Social Science Information* 13, no. 1 (February):39–53.

Rokkan, Stein. 1975. "Dimensions of state formation and nation-building: a possible paradigm for research on variations within Europe," in Tilly (1975a), 562–600.

Rokkan, Stein. Forthcoming. "Territories, nations, parties: towards a geo-economic-geopolitical model for the explanation of variations within Western Europe," in Festschrift for Karl Deutsch.

Rokkan, Stein; Sælen, Kirsti; and Warmbrunn, Joan. 1971. "Nation-building: a review of recent comparative research and a select bibliography of analytical studies." *Current Sociology* 13, no. 3.

Ronchey, Alberto. 1979. "Guns and grey matter: terrorism in Italy." *Foreign Affairs* 57, no. 4 (Spring):921–40.

Ronneberger, Franz. 1965. "Militärdiktaturen in den Entwicklungsländern: ein Beitrag zur politischen Formenlehre." *Jahrbuch für Sozialwissenschaft* 16:13–49.

Roots, Ivan. 1966. *The great rebellion, 1642–1660.* London: Batsford.

Rose, Richard. 1969. "Dynamic tendencies in the authority of regimes." *World Politics* 21, no. 4 (July):602–28.

Rose, Richard. 1971. *Governing without consensus: an Irish perspective.* London: Faber & Faber.

Rose, Richard. 1975. "Overloaded government: the problem outlined." *European Studies Newsletter* 5 (December):13–18.

Rose, Richard. 1976. *Northern Ireland: a time of choice.* London: Macmillan.

Rose, Richard. 1977. "Governing and 'ungovernability': a sceptical inquiry." Paper presented at the European Consortium for Political Research Workshop, 28 March–1 April, in Berlin.

Rose, Richard. 1979. "Ungovernability: is there fire behind the smoke?" *Political Studies* 27, no. 3 (September):351–70.

Rose, Thomas, ed. 1969. *Violence in America—a historical and contemporary reader.* New York: Random House.

Rose-Ackerman, Susan. 1978. *Corruption: a study in political economy.* New York: Academic Press.

Rosenau, James, ed. 1964. *International aspects of civil strife.* Princeton: Princeton University Press.

Rosenau, James N. 1973. "Theorizing across systems: linkage politics revisited," in Wilkenfeld, 25–56.

Rosenau, James N., ed. 1974. *Comparing foreign policies: theories, findings, and methods.* New York: Sage Publications.

Rosenbaum, H. Jon, and Sederberg, Peter C., eds. 1976. *Vigilante politics.* Pittsburgh: University of Pennsylvania Press.

Rosenberg, William G. 1974. *Liberals in the Russian Revolution: the Constitutional Democratic Party, 1917–1921.* Princeton: Princeton University Press.

Rosenstock, Eugen. 1931. "Revolution als politischer Begriff in der Neuzeit," in *Festgabe der rechts- und staatswissenschaftlichen Fakultät in Breslau für Paul Heilborn.* Breslau: M. & H. Marcus, 83–124.

Rosenstock-Huessy, Eugen. 1951. *Die europäischen Revolutionen und der Charakter der Nationen.* Stuttgart: W. Kohlhammer Verlag. (Original 1931.)

Ross, Mark Howard and Homer, Elizabeth. 1976. "Galton's problem in cross-national research." *World Politics* 29, no. 1 (October):1–28.

Ross, Steven T., ed. 1971. *The French Revolution: conflict or continuity?* New York: Holt, Rinehart & Winston.

Rossi, Peter H. and Berk, Richard A. 1970. "Local political leadership and popular discontent in the ghetto." *Annals of the American Academy of Political and Social Science*, no. 391 (September):111–27.

Rossi, Peter H.; Berk, Richard A.; and Eidson, Bettye K. 1974. *The roots of urban discontent: public policy, municipal institutions, and the ghetto.* New York: John Wiley & Sons.

Rossi, Peter et al. 1968. "Between white and black—the faces of American institutions in the ghetto," in *Supplemental Studies for The National Advisory Commission on Civil Disorders.* Washington, D. C.: U. S. Government Printing Office, 69–215.

Rostow, W. W. 1960. *The stages of economic growth: a noncommunist manifesto.* Cambridge: Cambridge University Press.

Rotberg, Robert I., and Mazrui, Ali A., eds. 1970. *Protest and power in Black Africa.* New York: Oxford University Press.

Roth, David F., and Wilson, Frank L. 1976. *The comparative study of politics.* Boston: Houghton & Mifflin.

Rothman, Stanley. 1970. "Barrington Moore and the dialectics of revolution: an essay review." *American Political Science Review* 64, no. 1 (March): 61–85.

Rotter, J. B. 1954. *Social learning and clinical psychology.* Englewood Cliffs: Prentice-Hall.

Rotter, Julian. 1966. "Generalized expectancies for internal versus external control of reinforcement." *Psychological Monographs* 609:1–28.

Roucek, Joseph S. 1957. "The sociology of violence." *Journal of Human Relations* 5:9–21.

Rougerie, Jacques. 1964. *Procès des communards.* Paris: René Julliard Collection Archives.

Rougerie, J. 1964a. "Composition d'une population insurgée: L'exemple de la Commune." *Le Mouvement Social*, no. 48 (July/September):31–47.

Rougerie, Jacques. 1971. *Paris libre 1871.* Paris: Edition du Seuil.

Rouquié, Alain. 1973. "Military revolutions and national independence in Latin America: 1968–1971," in Schmitter, 2–56.

Rowe, Edward Thomas. 1974. "Aid and coups d'état: aspects of the impact of American military assistance programs in the less developed countries." *International Studies Quarterly* 18, no. 2 (June):239–55.

Roxborough, J.; O'Brien, Philip; and Roddick, Jackie. 1977. *Chile: the state and revolution.* London: Macmillan.

Rubin, Jeffrey Z. and Brown, Bert R. 1975. *The social psychology of bargaining and negotiation.* New York: Academic Press.

Rubinson, Richard. 1976. "The world-economy and the distribution of income within states: a cross-national study." *American Sociological Review* 41, no. 4 (August):638–59.

Rubinson, Richard. 1977. "Dependence, government revenue, and economic growth, 1955–1970." *Studies in Comparative International Development* 12 (Summer):3–28.

Rubinson, Richard, and Quinlan, Dan. 1977. "Democracy and social inequality: a reanalysis." *American Sociological Review* 42, no. 4 (August): 611–23.

Rudé, George. 1959. *The crowd in the French Revolution.* Oxford: At the Clarendon Press.

Rudé, G. 1961. *Interpretations of the French Revolution.* General Series, Historical Association, no. 47. London: Routledge and Kegan Paul.

Rudé, George. 1962. *Wilkes and liberty: a social study of 1763 to 1774.* London: Oxford University Press.

Rudé, George. 1964. *The crowd in history, 1730-1848.* New York: John Wiley & Sons.

Rudé, George. 1967. "English rural and urban disturbances on the eve of the First Reform Bill, 1830-1831." *Past and Present* 37:87-102.

Rudé, George. 1970. *Paris and London in the 18th century: studies in popular protest.* London: Collins.

Rudé, George. 1971. "Why was there no revolution in England in 1830 or 1848?" in Manfred Kossok (ed.), *Studien über die Revolution.* 2d ed., Berlin (East): Akademie-Verlag, 231-44.

Rudé, George. 1972. *Europe in the eighteenth century: aristocracy and the bourgeois challenge.* London: Weidenfeld and Nicolson.

Rudé, George. 1973. *Revolutionary Europe 1783-1815.* 11th impression. London: Fontana. (Original 1964.)

Rudé, George. 1973a. "The growth of cities and popular revolt, 1750-1850: with particular reference to Paris," in J. F. Bosher (ed.), *French government and society, 1500-1850.* London: Athlone Press, 166-90.

Rudé, George. 1975. *Robespierre: portrait of a revolutionary democrat.* London: Collins.

Rudé, George. 1978. "Popular protest and ideology on the eve of the French Revolution," in Hinrichs et al., 420-35.

Rudé, George. 1980. *Ideology and popular protest.* New York: Pantheon.

Rudolph, Lloyd I. 1959. "The eighteenth century mob in America and Europe." *American Quarterly* 11:447-69.

Ruhl, J. Mark. 1975. "Social mobilization and political instability in Latin America: a test of Huntington's theory." *Inter-American Economic Affairs* 29, no. 2 (Autumn):3-21.

Rule, Brendan Gail, and Nesdale, Andrew R. 1976. "Moral judgment of aggressive behavior," in Geen/O'Neal, 33-60.

Rule, Brendan Gail; Dyck, Ronald; and Nesdale, Andrew R. 1978. "Arbitrariness of frustration: inhibition or instigation effects on aggression." *European Journal of Social Psychology* 8, no. 2 (April-June):237-44.

Rule, James, and Tilly, Charles. 1971. "1830 and the unnatural history of revolution." Ann Arbor: University of Michigan. Mimeographed. Somewhat revised in Merriman (1975), 41-85.

Rule, James, and Tilly, Charles. 1972. "1830 and the unnatural history of revolution." *Journal of Social Issues* 28, no. 1:49-76.

Rummel, Rudolph J. 1963. "Dimensions of conflict behavior within and between nations." *General Systems Yearbook* 8:1-50. Also in Gillespie/Nesvold (1971), 49-84.

Rummel, Rudolph J. 1965. "A field theory of social action with application to conflict within nations." *General Systems* 10:183-211.

Rummel, Rudolph J. 1966. "Dimensions of conflict behavior within nations, 1946-59." *Journal of Conflict Resolution* 10, no. 1 (March):65-73. Also in Gillespie/Nesvold (1971), 39-48.

Rummel, R. J. 1969. "Dimensions of foreign and domestic conflict behavior: a review of empirical findings," in Dean G. Pruitt and Richard C.

Snyder (eds.), *Theory and research on the causes of war*. Englewood Cliffs: Prentice-Hall, 219–28.

Rummel, R. J. 1972. *The dimensions of nations*. Beverly Hills: Sage Publications.

Rummel, R. J. 1976. *Understanding conflict and war*, vol. 2: *The conflict helix*. New York: Sage Publications.

Runciman, W. G. 1961. "Problems of research on relative deprivation." *European Journal of Sociology* 2:315–23. Also in Hyman/Singer (1968), 69–76.

Runciman, W. G. 1966. *Relative deprivation and social justice*. London: Routledge & Kegan Paul.

Runciman, W. G. 1967. "Justice, congruence and Professor Homans." *Archives Européennes de Sociologie* 8, no. 1:115–28.

Rupieper, Hermann-Josef. 1978. "Die Sozialstruktur der Trägerschichten der Revolution von 1848/49 am Beispiel Sachsen," in Hartmut Kaelble, Horst Matzerath, Hermann-Josef Rupieper, Peter Steinbach, and Heinrich Volkmann, *Probleme der Modernisierung in Deutschland: Sozialhistorische Studien zum 19. und 20. Jahrhundert*. Opladen: Westdeutscher Verlag, 80–109.

Russell, Charles A. 1979. "Appendix A. Terrorism—an overview, 1970–78," in Alexander/Kilmarx, 281–296.

Russell, Charles A. 1979–80. "Europe: regional review." *Terrorism* 3:157–71.

Russell, Charles A. 1980. "Latin America: regional review." *Terrorism* 4:277–92.

Russell, Charles A., and Miller, Bowman H. 1977. "Profile of a terrorist." *Terrorism* 1, no. 1:17–34.

Russell, D. E. H. 1974. *Rebellion, revolution, and armed force: a comparative study of fifteen countries with special emphasis on Cuba and South Africa*. New York: Academic Press.

Russett, B. M. 1964. "Inequality and instability: the relation of land tenure to politics." *World Politics* 16, no. 3 (April): 442–54. Also in Davies (1971), 206–13.

Russett, Bruce M. et al. 1964. *World handbook of political and social indicators*. New Haven: Yale University Press.

Rustin, Bayard. 1966. "The Watts manifesto and the McCone Report." *Commentary* 41, no. 3 (March):29–35.

Rustow, Dankwart A. 1963. "The military in Middle Eastern society and politics," in Fisher, 3–20.

Rustow, Dankwart A. 1967. *A world of nations: problems of political modernization*. Washington: The Brookings Institution.

Rustow, Dankwart A. 1969. "The organization triumphs over its function: Huntington on modernization." *Journal of International Affairs* 23, no. 1:119–32.

Rustow, Dankwart A. 1969a. "Change as the theme of political science." Paper delivered at the International Political Science Association Round Table, in Torino.

Rustow, Dankwart A. 1970. "Atatürk as founder of a state" and introduction, in *Philosophers and kings: studies in leadership*. New York: George Braziller, 1–32 and 208–47.

Sabean, David Warren. 1972. *Landbesitz und Gesellschaft am Vorabend des Bauernkriegs: Eine Studie der sozialen Verhältnisse im südlichen Oberschwaben in den Jahren vor 1525*. Stuttgart: Gustav Fischer.

Sagarin, Edward, ed. 1977. *Deviance and social change*. Beverly Hills: Sage Publications.

Salamon, Lester M. 1970. "Comparative history and the theory of modernization." *World Politics* 23, no. 1 (October):83–103.

Salert, Barbara 1976. *Revolutions and revolutionaries: four theories*. New York: Elsevier/North-Holland.

Salmon, J. H. M. 1967. "Venality of office and popular sedition in seventeenth-century France: a review of a controversy." *Past and Present* 37 (July):21–43.

Sampson, Edward E. 1969. "Studies of status congruence" in Leonard Berkowitz (ed.), *Advances in experimental social psychology*, vol. 4. New York: Academic Press, 225–70.

Sampson, Edward E. 1975. "On justice as equality." *Journal of Social Issues* 31, no. 3 (Summer):45–64.

Sanders, David. 1973. "An empirical investigation into Huntington's 'gap hypothesis': five models in search of a theory." M. A. thesis, University of Essex.

Sanders, David. 1978. "Away from a general model of mass political violence: evaluating Hibbs." *Quality and Quantity* 12, no. 2 (June):103–29.

Sanders, David. 1979. "Changes and challenges: patterns of interrelationship among four types of political instability." Paper presented to the European Consortium for Political Research Workshop, April, in Brussels. Mimeographed.

Sanders, David. 1981. *Patterns of political instability*. London: Macmillan.

Sanders, David, and Herman, Valentine. 1976. "Intra- and extra-parliamentary correlates of governmental stability and survival." University of Essex. Mimeographed.

Sanders, David, and Herman, Valentine. 1977. "The stability and survival of governments in Western democracies." *Acta Politica* 12, no. 3 (July): 346–77.

Sandos, James A. 1973. "U. S. military policy toward Latin America." *World Affairs* (Spring):293–308.

Sansom, Robert L. 1970. *The economics of insurgency in the Mekong delta in Vietnam*. Cambridge, Mass.: MIT Press.

Sarkesian, Sam C., ed. 1975. *Revolutionary guerilla warfare*. Chicago: Precedent Publishing.

Sartori, Giovanni. 1976. *Parties and party systems: a framework for analysis*, vol. 1. London: Cambridge University Press.

Saul, Norman E. 1978. *Sailors in revolt: the Russian Baltic fleet in 1917*. Lawrence: Regents Press of Kansas.

Scalapino, Robert A., ed. 1965. *The communist revolution in Asia: tactics, goals, and achievements*. Englewood Cliffs: Prentice-Hall.

Schadee, H. M. A. 1976. "The analysis of event counts." Paper presented to the European Consortium Workshop on "Dissatisfaction and protest," April, in Louvain (Belgium).

Schaefer, David Louis. 1973. "The sense and nonsense of justice: an examination of John Rawl's A theory of justice." *Political Science Reviewer* 3 (Fall):1–41.

Schaefer, James M. 1974. "Studies in cultural diffusion: Galton's problem: a preview." *Behavior Science Research* 9, no. 1:1–26.

Schama, Simon. 1977. *Patriots and liberators: revolution in the Netherlands 1780–1813*. New York: Knopf.

Schapiro, Leonard. 1970. *The communist party of the Soviet Union*. 2d revised and enlarged ed. London: Methuen & Co.

Schapiro, Leonard. (1977). "Two years that shook the world." *New York Review of Books* (31 March):3–4.

Schattschneider, E. E. 1960. *The semi-sovereign people*. New York: Holt, Rinehart & Winston.

Scheff, T. J. 1974. "The labelling theory of mental illness." *American Sociological Review* 39, no. 3 (June):444–52.

Schermerhorn, Richard A. 1961. *Society and power*. New York: Random House.

Schervish, Paul G. 1973. "The labeling perspective: its bias and potential in the study of political deviance." *American Sociologist* 8 (May):47–57.

Scheuch, Erwin K. 1966. "Cross-national comparisons using aggregate data: some substantive and methodological problems," in Richard L. Merritt and Stein Rokkan (eds.), *Comparing nations: the use of quantitative data in cross-national research*. New Haven: Yale University Press, 131–67.

Schieder, Theodor, ed. 1973. *Revolution und Gesellschaft: Theorie und Praxis der Systemveränderung*. Freiburg/Breisgau: Herderbücherei.

Schieder, Wolfgang. 1974. "Die Rolle der deutschen Arbeiter in der Revolution von 1848/49," in Wolfgang Klötzer, Rüdiger Moldenhauer, and Dieter Rebentisch (eds.), *Ideen und Strukturen der deutschen Revolution 1848*. Frankfort on the Main: Verlag Waldemar Kramer, 43–56.

Schieder, Wolfgang. 1978. "Der Rheinpfälzische Liberalismus von 1833 als politische Protestbewegung," in Helmut Berding et al. (eds.), *Vom Staat des Ancien Régime zum modernen Parteienstaat—Festschrift für Theodor Schieder*. Munich: Oldenbourg, 169–95.

Schiffrin, Harold A. 1968. *Sun Yat-sen and the origins of the Chinese revolution*. Berkeley: University of California Press.

Schissler, Jakob. 1976. *Gewalt und gesellschaftliche Entwicklung: Die Kontroverse über die Gewalt zwischen Sozialdemokratie und Bolschewismus*. Meisenheim am Glan: Anton Hain.

Schmidt, Hans Dieter, and Schmidt-Mummendey, Amélie. 1974. "Waffen als aggressionsbahnende Hinweisreize: Eine kritische Betrachtung experimenteller Ergebnisse." *Zeitschrift für Sozialpsychologie* 5, no. 3:201–18.

Schmidt, Peter, and Muller, Edward N. 1978. "The problem of multicollinearity in a multistage causal alienation model: a comparison of ordinary least squares, maximum-likelihood and ridge estimators." *Quality and Quantity* 12, no. 4 (December):267–97.

Schmidt, Steffen W., and Dorfman, Gerald A. eds. 1974. *Soldiers in politics*. Los Altos: Geron-X.

Schmidt, Stuart M., and Kochan, Thomas A. 1972. "Conflict: toward conceptual clarity." *Administrative Science Quarterly* 17, no. 3 (September):359–70.

Schmidt-Mummendey, Amélie, and Schmidt, Hans Dieter, eds. 1972. *Aggressives Verhalten: Neue Ergebnisse der psychologischen Forschung.* 2d ed. Munich: Juventa.

Schmitt, David E. 1974. *Violence in Northern Ireland: ethnic conflict and radicalization in an international setting.* Morristown, N.J.: General Learning Press.

Schmitt, David E. 1976. "Ethnic conflict in Northern Ireland: international aspects of conflict management," in Esman, 228–50.

Schmitt, Eberhard, ed. 1973. *Die Französische Revolution: Anlässe und langfristige Ursachen.* Darmstadt: Wissenschaftliche Buchgesellschaft.

Schmitt, Eberhard. 1976. *Einführung in die Geschichte der Französischen Revolution.* Munich: C. H. Beck.

Schmitter, Philippe C. 1971. "Military intervention, political competitiveness, and public policy in Latin America: 1950–1967," in Janowitz/van Doorn, 425–506.

Schmitter, Philippe C. 1972. "Paths to political development." *Proceedings of The American Academy of Political Science* 30, no. 4:83–105.

Schmitter, Philippe C., ed. 1973. *Military rule in Latin America: function, consequences and perspectives.* Beverly Hills: Sage Publications.

Schmitter, Philippe C. 1973a. "Foreign military assistance, national military spending and military rule in Latin America," in Schmitter (1973), 117–87.

Schmitter, Philippe C. 1975. "Liberation by golpe: retrospective thoughts on the demise of authoritarian rule in Portugal." *Armed Forces and Society* 2, no. 1 (November):5–33.

Schmitter, Philippe C. 1977. "Interest intermediation and regime governability in contemporary Western Europe." University of Chicago. Mimeographed.

Schneider, Peter R., and Schneider, Anne L. 1971. "Social mobilization, political institutions, and political violence, a cross-national analysis." *Comparative Political Studies* 4, no. 1 (April):69–90.

Schneider, Ronald M. 1959. *Communism in Guatemala, 1944–1954.* New York: Frederick A. Praeger.

Schneider, Ronald M. 1975. "Guatemala: an aborted communist takeover," in Hammond (1975a), 563–82.

Schoenberg, Ronald. 1972. "Strategies for meaningful comparison," in Herbert L. Costner (ed.), *Sociological methodology 1972.* San Francisco: Jossey-Bass, 1–35.

Schramm, Wilbur. 1963. "Communication development and the development process," in Lucian W. Pye (ed.), *Communications and political development.* Princeton: Princeton University Press, 30–57.

Schramm, Wilbur. 1964. *Mass media and national development.* Stanford: Stanford University Press.

Schramm, Wilbur, and Lerner, Daniel, eds. 1976. *Communication and change: the last ten years—and the next.* Honolulu: University Press of Hawaii/East-West Center Press.

Schramm, Wilbur, and Ruggels, W. Lee. 1967. "How mass media systems grow," in Daniel Lerner and Wilbur Schramm (eds.), *Communication and change in the developing countries.* Honolulu: East-West Center Press, 57–75.

Schuck, John R. 1976. "Paths to violence: toward a quantitative approach," in Arthur G. Neal (ed.), *Violence in animal and human societies.* Chicago: Nelson Hall, 171–93.

Schuck, John, and Pisor, Kim. 1974. "Evaluating an aggression experiment by the use of simulating subjects." *Journal of Personality and Social Psychology* 29, no. 2 (February):181–86.

Schulman, Irwin J. 1978. "Review of Paige (1975)." *American Political Science Review* 72, no. 2 (June):752–54.

Schulze, Winfried. 1973. "'Reformation oder Frühbürgerliche Revolution?' Überlegungen zum Modellfall einer Forschungskontroverse." *Jahrbuch für die Geschichte Mittel- und Ostdeutschlands* 22:253-69.

Schumaker, Paul D. 1975. "Policy responsiveness to protest-group demands." *Journal of Politics* 33 (May):488–521.

Schumaker, Paul D. 1978. "The scope of political conflict and the effectiveness of constraints in contemporary urban protest." *Sociological Quarterly* 19, no. 2 (Spring):168–84.

Schumaker, Paul D., and Getter, Russell W. 1977. "Responsiveness bias in 51 American communities." *American Journal of Political Science* 21, no. 2 (May):247–81.

Schuman, Howard, and Gruenberg, Barry. 1970. "The impact of city on racial attitudes." *American Journal of Sociology* 76, no. 2 (September): 213–61.

Schuman, Howard, and Hatchett, Shirley. 1974. *Black racial attitudes: trends and complexities.* Ann Arbor: Survey Research Center, Institute for Social Research.

Schuman, Howard, and Johnson, Michael P. 1976. "Attitudes and behavior." *Annual Review of Sociology* 2:161–207.

Schur, Edwin M. 1971. *Labeling deviant behavior: its sociological implications.* New York: Harper & Row.

Schurmann, Franz. 1966; 1971. *Ideology and organization in communist China.* Berkeley: University of California Press.

Schwartz, David C. 1973. *Political alienation and political behavior.* Chicago: Aldine.

Schwarz, Solomon M. 1967. *The Russian Revolution of 1905: the workers' movement and the formation of Bolshevism and Menshevism.* Chicago: University of Chicago Press.

Schweitzer, R. A.; Tilly, Charles; and Boyd, John. 1980. "The texture of contention in Britain, 1828–1829." CRSO Working Paper, no. 211. University of Michigan.

Scolnick, Joseph M., Jr. 1974. "An appraisal of studies of the linkage between domestic and international conflict." *Comparative Political Studies* 6, no. 4 (January):485–509.

Scott, James C. 1969. "Corruption, machine politics, and political change." *American Political Science Review* 63, no. 4 (December):1142-58.

Scott, James C. 1972. *Comparative political corruption.* Englewood Cliffs: Prentice-Hall.

Scott, James C. 1977. "Protest and profanation: agrarian revolt and the little tradition, part II." *Theory and Society* 4, no. 2 (Summer):211-46.

Scott, John Paul. 1975. *Aggression.* 2d and revised ed. Chicago: University of Chicago Press. (Original 1958.)

Scott, Samuel F. 1978. *The response of the royal army to the French Revolution: the role and development of the Line Army, 1787-1793.* Oxford: Oxford University Press.

Scott, Tom. 1979a. "The peasants' war: a historiographical review: part I." *Historical Journal* 22, no. 3 (September):693-720.

Scott, Tom. 1979b. "The peasants' war: a historiographical review: part II." *Historical Journal* 22, no. 4 (December):953-74.

Scribner, Bob, and Benecke, Gerhard, eds. 1979. *The German peasant war of 1515 – new viewpoints.* London: George Allen & Unwin.

Searing, Donald D.; Schwartz, Joel J.; and Lind, Alden E. 1973. "The structuring principle: political socialization and belief systems." *American Political Science Review* 67, no. 2 (June):415-32.

Sears, David O. 1969. "Black attitudes toward the political system in the aftermath of the Watts insurrection." *Midwest Journal of Political Science* 13, no. 4 (November):515-44.

Sears, David O. 1970. "Political attitudes of Los Angeles negroes," in Cohen, 676-705.

Sears, D. O., and McConahay, J. B. 1969. "Participation in the Los Angeles riots." *Social Problems* 17, no. 1 (Summer):3-20.

Sears, David O. and McConahay, John B. 1970a. *"Riot participation,"* in Cohen (1970), 258-87.

Sears, David O., and McConahay, John B. 1970b. "Racial socialization, comparison levels, and the Watts riot." *Journal of Social Issues* 26, no. 1:121-40.

Sears, David O., and McConahay, John B. 1973. *The politics of violence: the new urban blacks and the Watts riot.* Boston: Houghton Mifflin Co.

Sears, David O., and Tomlinson, T. M. 1968. "Riot ideology in Los Angeles: a study of Negro attitudes." *Social Science Quarterly* 49, no. 3 (December):485-503.

Sears, David O.; Tyler, Tom R.; Citrin, Jack; and Kinder, Donald R. 1978. "Political system support and public response to the energy crisis." *American Journal of Political Science* 22, no. 1 (February):56-82.

Seeman, Melvin. 1959. "On the meaning of alienation." *American Sociological Review* 24:783-91.

Seeman, Melvin. 1972. "Alienation and engagement," in Angus Campbell and Philip E. Converse (eds.), *The human meaning of social change.* New York: Russell Sage Foundation, 467-527.

Seeman, Melvin. 1975. "Alienation studies." *Annual Review of Sociology* 1:91-123.

Segre, D. V., and Adler, J. H. 1973. "The ecology of terrorism." *Encounter* 40 (February):17-24.

Seidler, Franz Wilhelm. 1955. "Die Geschichte des Wortes Revolution: Ein Beitrag zur Revolutionsforschung." Ph.D. dissertation, University of Munich.

Seidler, John; Meyer, Katherine; and Mac Gillivray, Lois. 1976. "Collecting data on crowds and rallies: a new method of stationary sampling." *Social Forces* 55, no. 2 (December):507-19.

Selden, Mark. 1971. *The Yenan way in revolutionary China.* Cambridge: Harvard University Press.

Selg, Herbert. 1968. *Diagnostik der Aggressivität*. Göttingen: C. J. Hogrefe.
Selg, Herbert, and Mees, Ulrich. 1974. *Menschliche Aggressivität*. Göttingen: Hogrefe.
Seligson, Mitchell A., and Booth, John A. 1979. "Development, political participation, and the poor in Latin America," in Mitchell A. Seligson and John A. Booth (eds.), *Political participation in Latin America*, vol. II: *Politics and the poor*. New York: Holmes & Meier, 3–8.
Selznick, Philip. 1960. *The organization weapon: a study of Bolshevik strategies and tactics*. Glencoe: Free Press of Glencoe.
Service, Robert. 1979. *The Bolshevik Party in revolution. A study in organisational change 1917–1923*. London: Macmillan.
Seton-Watson, Hugh. 1951. "Twentieth century revolutions." *Political Quarterly* 22, no. 3:251–65. Also in Roy L. Macridis and Bernard E. Brown (eds.), *Comparative politics, notes and readings*. Homewood, Ill.: Dorsey Press, 621–29.
Seton-Watson, Hugh. 1961. *The East European revolution*. New York: Praeger. (Original 1950.) English ed. London: Methuen & Co.
Seton-Watson, Hugh. 1966. *Neither war nor peace*. New York: Praeger.
Seton-Watson, Hugh. 1972. "Revolution in Eastern Europe," in Vatikiotis, 185–97.
Seton-Watson, Hugh. 1977. *Nations and states: an enquiry into the origins of nations and the politics of nationalism*. Boulder, Colo.: Westview Press.
Sewell, William H. 1980. *Work and revolution in France: the language of labor from the old regime to 1848*. New York: Cambridge University Press.
Shamir, Michal. 1979. "Are Western party systems 'frozen'? A comparative dynamic analysis." University of Minnesota. Paper presented to the Annual Meeting of the Midwest Political Science Association, in Chicago.
Shanin, Teodor, ed. 1971. *Peasants and peasant societies: selected readings*. Harmondsworth: Penguin Books.
Shanin, Teodor. 1971a. "The peasantry as a political factor." *Sociological Review* 14, no. 1 (Feburary):5–27. Also in Shanin (1971), 238–63.
Shapiro, Gilbert. 1967. "Review of Moore (1966)." *American Sociological Review* 32:820–21.
Shapiro, Gilbert, and Dawson, Philip. 1972. "Social mobility and political radicalism: the case of the French Revolution of 1789," in William D. Aydelotte, Allan G. Bogue, and Robert William Fogel (eds.), *The dimensions of quantitative research in history*. Princeton: Princeton University Press, 159–91.
Shapiro, Gilbert, and Markoff, John. 1975. "The incidence of the terror: some lessons of quantitative history." *Journal of Social History* 9, no. 2 (Winter):193–218.
Shapiro, Gilbert; Markoff, John; and Weitman, Sasha R. 1973. "Quantitative studies of the French Revolution." *History and Theory* 12, no. 2:163–91.
Sharp, Buchanan. 1980. *In contempt of all authority: rural artisans and riot in the West of England, 1586–1660*. Berkeley: University of California Press.

Sharp, Gene. 1973. *The politics of nonviolent action*. Boston: Porter Sargent Publisher.

Shawcross, William. 1978. "The third Indochina war." *New York Review of Books* 6 April, 15–22.

Shefter, Martin. 1980. "Review of Eisenstadt (1978)." *Journal of Interdisciplinary History* 11, no. 1 (Summer):133–35.

Shelton, Walter J. 1973. *English hunger and industrial disorders: a study of social conflict during the first decade of George III's reign*. London: Macmillan.

Shils, Edward. 1962. "The military in the political development of the new states," in J. J. Johnson, 7–67.

Shingles, Richard D. 1978. "Internal and external control as two separate dimensions of political efficacy: a reformulation and bi-racial comparison." Paper presented to the Midwest Political Science Association Meeting, in Chicago.

Short, James F., Jr., and Wolfgang, Marvin E., eds. 1972. *Collective violence*. Chicago and New York: Aldine-Atherton.

Shorter, Edward, and Tilly, Charles. 1971a. "The shape of strikes in France, 1830–1960." *Comparative Studies in Society and History* 13:60–86.

Shorter, Edward, and Tilly, Charles. 1971b. "Le déclin de la grève violente en France de 1890 à 1935." *Le Mouvement social* 76 (July/September): 95–118.

Shorter, Edward, and Tilly, Charles. 1974. *Strikes in France, 1830–1968*. New York: Cambridge University Press.

Shoup, Paul. 1975. "The Yugoslav revolution: the first of a new type," in Hammond (1975a), 244–72.

Shulim, Joseph I. 1977. "Robespierre and the French Revolution." *American Historical Review* 82, no. 1 (February):20–38.

Siegfried, André. 1956. "Stable instability in France." *Foreign Affairs* 34:394–404.

Sigel, Roberta A., and Hoskin, Marilyn Brookes. 1977. "Affect for government and its relation to policy output among adolescents." *American Journal of Political Science* 21, no. 1 (February):111–34.

Sigelman, Lee. 1971. *Modernization and the political system: a critique and preliminary empirical analysis*. Sage Professional Paper in Comparative Politics Series, no. 01–016.

Sigelman, Lee. 1972. "Do modern bureaucracies dominate underdeveloped polities? A test of the imbalance thesis." *American Political Science Review* 66, no. 2 (June):525–28.

Sigelman, Lee. 1974. "Military intervention: a methodological note." *Journal of Political and Military Sociology* 2, no. 2 (Fall):275–81.

Sigelman, Lee. 1975. "Military size and political intervention." *Journal of Political and Military Sociology* 3, no. 1 (Spring):95–100.

Sigelman, Lee. 1975a. "Rebuttal." *Journal of Political and Military Sociology* 3, no. 1 (Spring): 102–103.

Sigelman, Lee. 1978. "A comment on William Thompson's 'Another look at the Feit-Sigelman dispute over the relative military size-coup propensity hypothesis.'" *Journal of Political and Military Sociology* 6, no. 1 (Spring):101–102.

Sigelman, Lee. 1979. "Understanding political instability: an evaluation of the mobilization-institutionalization approach." *Comparative Political Studies* 12, no. 2 (July):205-28.

Sigelman, Lee, and Simpson, Miles. 1977. "A cross-national test of the linkage between economic inequality and political violence." *Journal of Conflict Resolution* 21, no. 1 (March):105-28.

Sigelman, Lee, and Yough, Syng Nam. 1978. "Some 'trivial' matters that sometimes matter: index construction techniques and research findings." *Political Methodology* 5:369-84.

Silberman, Matthew. 1976. "Toward a theory of criminal deterrence." *American Sociological Review* 41, no. 3 (June):442-61.

Silva, Milton M. da. 1975. "Modernization and ethnic conflict: the case of the Basques." *Comparative Politics* 7, no. 2 (January):227-51.

Silver, Burton B. 1973. "Social mobility and intergroup antagonism: a simulation." *Journal of Conflict Resolution* 17, no. 4 (December):605-23.

Silver, Morris. 1974. "Political revolution and repression: an economic approach." *Public Choice* 17 (Spring):63-71.

Silvert, K. H. 1966. *The conflict society: reaction and revolution in Latin America.* Revised ed. New York: American Universities Field Staff.

Simmel, Georg. 1968. *Soziologie: Untersuchungen über die Formen der Vergesellschaftung.* 5th ed. Berlin: Duncker & Humblot. (Original 1908.)

Simmel, Georg. 1958. "Der Streit," in *Soziologie: Untersuchungen über die Formen der Vergesellschaftung.* 4th ed. Berlin: Duncker & Humblot, 186-255.

Simpson, Dick. 1964. "The congruence of the political, social, and economic aspects of development." *International Development Review* 6, no. 2 (June):21-25.

Sinden, Peter G. 1979. "Inequality and political conflict." *Comparative Social Research* 2:303-20.

Singer, Benjamin D. 1970. "Mass media and communication processes in the Detroit riot of 1967." *Public Opinion Quarterly* 34, no. 2 (Summer): 236-45.

Singer, Benjamin D.; Osborn, Richard W.; and Geschwender, James A. 1970. *Black rioters: a study of social factors and communication in the Detroit riot.* Lexington, Mass.: Heath Lexington Books.

Singer, Daniel. 1970a. *Prelude to revolution: France in May 1968.* New York: Hill & Wang.

Singer, David L. 1972. "Aggression arousal, hostile humor, catharsis." *Journal of Personality and Social Psychology* 8, Monograph Supplement no. 1, part 2 (January).

Singer, J. David, ed. 1968. *Quantitative international politics.* New York: Free Press.

Singer, J. David, and Small, Melvin. 1972. *The wages of war, 1816-1965.* New York: John Wiley & Sons.

Singer, Jerome L., ed. 1971. *The control of aggression and violence: cognitive and physiological factors.* New York: Academic Press.

Skocpol, Theda. 1973. "A critical review of Barrington Moore's Social origins of dictatorship and democracy." *Politics and Society* 4, no. 1 (Fall):1-34.

Skocpol, Theda. 1976. "France, Russia, China: a structural analysis of social revolutions." *Comparative Studies in Society and History* 18, no. 2 (April):175-210.

Skocpol, Theda. 1976a. "Old regime legacies and communist revolutions in Russia and China." *Social Forces* 55, no. 2 (December):284-315.

Skocpol, Theda. 1978. "Review of Keep (1976)." *American Journal of Sociology* 84, no. 1 (July):194-98.

Skocpol, Theda. 1979. *States and social revolutions: a comparative analysis of France, Russia, and China.* Cambridge: Cambridge University Press.

Skocpol, Theda. 1980. "What makes peasants revolutionary?" Paper presented at Symposium on Peasant Rebellions. Johns Hopkins University, January. Mimeographed.

Skocpol, Theda, and Fulbrook, Mary. 1977. "Review of Anderson (1974a; 1974b)." *Journal of Development Studies* 13 (April):290-95.

Skocpol, Theda, and Somers, Margaret. 1978. "Review of Tilly et al. (1975)." *Sociology and Social Research* 62, no. 3 (April):484-87.

Skocpol, Theda, and Trimberger, Ellen Kay. 1978. "Revolutions and the world-historical development of capitalism," in Barbara Hockey Kaplan (ed.), *Social change in the capitalist world economy.* Beverly Hills: Sage Publications, 121-38.

Skolnick, Jerome H. 1969. *The politics of protest: violent aspects of protest and confrontation.* A staff report to the National Commission on the Causes and Prevention of Violence. Washington, D.C.: U. S. Government Printing Office.

Slater, Jerome. 1970. *Intervention and negotiation: the United States and the Dominican revolution.* New York: Harper & Row.

Sloan, Stephen, and Kearney, Richard. 1976. "Non-territorial terrorism: an empirical approach to policy formation." University of Oklahoma: Department of Political Science. Mimeographed.

Smaldone, Joseph P. 1974. "The paradox of military politics in Sub-Saharan Africa," in Cochran, 203-27.

Smaldone, Joseph P. 1976. "Review article: Rebellion, revolution, and war. Perspectives on mass political violence." *Armed Forces and Society* 3, no. 1 (Fall):147-60.

Small, Melvin, and Singer, J. David. 1979. "Conflict in the international system, 1816-1977: historical trends and policy futures," in Charles W. Kegley and Patrick J. McGowan (eds.), *Challenges to America: U. S. foreign policy in the 1980s.* Beverly Hills: Sage Publications, 89-115.

Smelser, Neil J. 1963. *Theory of collective behavior.* New York: Free Press,

Smelser, Neil J. 1968. "Social and psychological dimensions of collective behavior," in Smelser, *Essays in sociological explanation.* Englewood Cliffs: Prentice-Hall, 92-121.

Smelser, Neil J. 1971. "Stability, instability, and the analysis of political corruption," in Bernard Barber and Alex Inkeles (eds.), *Stability and social change.* Boston: Little, Brown & Co., 7-29.

Smelser, Neil J. 1971a. "Alexis de Tocqueville as comparative analyst," in Ivan Vallier (ed.), *Comparative methods in sociology: essays on trends and applications.* Berkeley: University of California Press, 19-47.

Smith, Anthony D. 1973. "Nationalism: a trend report and bibliography." *Current Sociology* 21, no. 3.

Smith, Arthur K., Jr. 1969. "Socio-economic development and political democracy: a causal analysis." *Midwest Journal of Political Science* 13 (February):95-125.

Smith, Robert B. 1974. "Continuities in ordinal path analysis." *Social Forces* 53, no. 2 (December):200–229.

Smith, Robert B. 1978. "Nonparametric path analysis: comments on Kim's 'Multivariate analysis of ordinal variables.'" *American Journal of Sociology* 84, no. 2 (September):437–48.

Smith, Tony. 1979. "The underdevelopment of development literature: the case of dependency myth." *World Politics* 31, no. 2 (January):247–88.

Smock, David R., and Bentsi-Enchill, Kwamena, eds. 1975. *The search for national integration in Africa*. New York: Free Press.

Sniderman, Paul M. 1978. "The politics of faith." *British Journal of Political Science* 8, no. 1 (January):21–44.

Sniderman, Paul; Neuman, W. Russell; Citrin, J.; McClosky, H.; and Shanks, J. Merrill. 1975. "Stability of support for the political system: the initial impact of Watergate." *American Political Quarterly* 3, no. 4 (October):437–57.

Snitch, Thomas H. 1980. "Assassinations and political violence 1968–1978: an events data approach." Washington, D.C.: American University. Mimeographed.

Snow, David A.; Zurcher, Louis A.; and Ekland-Olson, Sheldon. 1980. "Social-networks and social movements: a microstructural approach to differential recruitment." *American Sociological Review* 45, no. 5 (October):787–801.

Snow, Peter G. 1968. "Commentary on: D. P. Bwy: Political instability in Latin America: the cross-cultural test of a causal model." *Latin American Research Review* 3, no. 2 (Spring):74–76.

Snow, Vernon F. 1962. "The concept of revolution in seventeenth-century England." *Historical Journal* 5:167–90.

Snyder, David. 1976. "Theoretical and methodological problems in the analysis of governmental coercion and collective violence." *Journal of Political and Military Sociology* 4, no. 2 (Fall):277–93.

Snyder, David. 1978. "Collective violence: a research agenda and some strategic considerations." *Journal of Conflict Resolution* 22, no. 3 (September):499–534.

Snyder, David, and Kelly, William R. 1976. "Industrial violence in Italy, 1878–1903." *American Journal of Sociology* 82, no. 1 (July):131–62.

Snyder, David, and Kelly, William R. 1977. "Conflict intensity, media sensitivity and the validity of newspaper data." *American Sociological Review* 42, no. 1 (February):105–23.

Snyder, David, and Kelly, William R. 1979. "Strategies for investigating violence and social change: illustrations from analyses of racial disorders and implications for mobilization research," in Zald/McCarthy, 212–37.

Snyder, David, and Kick, Edward L. 1979. "Structural position in the world system and economic growth, 1955–1970: a multiple-network analysis of transnational interactions." *American Journal of Sociology* 84, no. 5 (March):1096–1126.

Snyder, David, and Tilly, Charles. 1972. "Hardship and collective violence in France, 1830 to 1960." *American Sociological Review* 37, no. 5 (October):520–32.

Snyder, David and Tilly, Charles. 1973. "How to get from here to there." *American Sociological Review* 38, no. 4 (September):501–503.

Snyder, David, and Tilly, Charles. 1974. "On debating and falsifying theories of collective violence." *American Sociological Review* 39, no. 4 (August):610–13.

Sobel, Lester A. 1975. *Political terrorism.* New York: Facts on File.

Soboul, Albert. 1956. "Klassen und Klassenkämpfe in der Französischen Revolution," in Markov, 47–76.

Soboul, Albert. 1962. *Les sans-culottes Parisiens en l'an II: mouvement populaire et gouvernement révolutionnaire 2 Juin 1793–9 Thermidor an II.* 2d ed. Paris: Librairie Clavreuil. (Original 1958.) English ed.: *The sans-culottes.* Garden City, N.Y.: Anchor Books (1972).

Soboul, Albert. 1964. *Précis de l'histoire de la Révolution française, 1789–1799.* 2d ed. Paris: Éditions sociales. English ed.: *The French Revolution, 1789–1799: from the storming of the Bastille to Napoleon.* New York: Random House (1975). (Original 1962.)

Soboul, Albert. 1976. *Problèmes paysans de la Révolution (1789–1848): études d'histoire révolutionnaire.* Paris: François Maspero.

Soboul, Albert. 1976a. "Die klassische Geschichtsschreibung der Französischen Revolution: Aktuelle Kontroversen," in Kossok (1976), 48–67. Original in: *Pensée,* no. 177 (September/October 1974):40–58.

Sofranko, Andrew J., and Bealer, Robert C. 1972. *Unbalanced modernization and domestic instability: a comparative analysis.* Sage Professional Paper in Comparative Politics Series, no. 01–036.

Solaún, Mauricio. 1976. "Review of Russell: Rebellion, revolution and armed force—a comparative study of fifteen countries with special emphasis on Cuba and South Africa." *Contemporary Sociology* 5, no. 5 (September):638–39.

Solaún, Mauricio, and Quinn, Michael A. 1973. *Sinners and heretics: the politics of military intervention in Latin America.* Urbana: University of Illinois Press.

Sombart, Werner. 1924. "Die Formen des gewaltsamen sozialen Kampfes." *Kölner Vierteljahreshefte für Soziologie* 5:1–12.

Somers, Margaret R., and Goldfrank, Walter L. 1979. "The limits of agronomic determinism: a critique of Paige's 'Agrarian Revolution.'" *Comparative Studies in Society and History* 21, no. 3 (July):443–58.

Sorel, Georges. 1908. *Réflexions sur la violence.* Paris: Librairie de "Pages libres." American translation *Reflections on violence.* New York: Peter Smith 1915.

Sorokin, Pitirim. 1967. *Sociology of revolution.* New York: Howard Fertig. Original Philadelphia: J. B. Lippincott (1925).

Sorokin, Pitirim. 1937. *Social and cultural dynamics,* vol. 3: *Fluctuations of social relationships, war and revolutions.* New York: American Book Co.

Sorokin, Pitirim. 1957. *Social and cultural dynamics: a study of change in major systems of art, truth, ethics, law and social relationships.* Revised and abridged in one volume by the author. Boston: Porter Sargent Publisher.

Soule, George. 1935. *The coming American revolution.* New York: Macmillan.

Southwood, Ken. 1967. "Riot and revolt: sociological theories of political violence." *Peace Research Reviews* 1, no. 3 (June):1–87.

Spiegel, John P. 1971. "Theories of violence: an integrated approach." *International Journal of Group Tensions* 1, no. 1:77–90.

Spilerman, Seymour. 1970. "The causes of racial disturbances: a comparison of alternative explanations." *American Sociological Review* 35, no. 4 (August):627–49.

Spilerman, Seymour. 1971. "The causes of racial disturbances: tests of an explanation." *American Sociological Review* 36:427–42.

Spilerman, Seymour. 1976. "Structural characteristics of cities and the severity of racial disorders." *American Sociological Review* 41, no. 5 (October):771–93.

Stack, Steven. 1978. "The effect of direct government involvement in the economy on the degree of income inequality: a cross-national study." *American Sociological Review* 43, no. 6 (December):880–88.

Stack, Steven. 1980. "Direct government involvement in the economy: theoretical and empirical extensions." *American Sociological Review* 45, no. 1 (February):146–54.

Stadelmann, Rudolph. 1948. *Soziale und politische Geschichte der deutschen Revolution von 1848*. Munich: Münchner Verlag.

Stadler, Peter. 1964. "Wirtschaftskrise und Revolution bei Marx und Engels: Zur Entwicklung ihres Denkens in den 1850er Jahren." *Historische Zeitschrift* 199, no. 1:113–44.

Staley, Eugene. 1954. *The future of underdeveloped countries*. New York: Harper & Brothers.

Staniland, Martin. 1969. "Frantz Fanon and the African political class." *African Affairs* 58, no. 270 (January):4–25.

Stark, Margaret; Abudu, J.; Raine, Walter J.; Burbeck, Stephen L.; and Davison, Keith K. 1974. "Some empirical patterns in riot process." *American Sociological Review* 39, no. 6 (December):865–76.

Starn, Randolph. 1971. "Historians and 'crisis.'" *Past and Present* 52 (August):3–22.

Starn, Randolph. 1976. "Some uses and abuses of crisis history." Presented at Annual Meeting of the Social Science History Association, University of Pennsylvania. Mimeographed.

Statera, Gianni. 1975. *Death of a utopia: the development and decline of student movements in Europe*. New York: Oxford University Press.

Stavenhagen, Rodolfo, ed. 1970. *Agrarian problems and peasant movements in Latin America*. Garden City: Doubleday & Co.

Stearns, Peter N. 1974. "Measuring the evolution of strike movements." *International Review of Social History* 19, no. 1:1–27.

Stearns, Peter N. 1974a. *The revolutions of 1848*. New York: Norton. English ed. London: Weidenfeld & Nicolson.

Steedly, Homer R., and Foley, John W. 1979. "The success of protest groups: multivariate analyses." *Social Science Research* 8, no. 1 (March):1–15.

Stein, Arthur A. 1976. "Conflict and cohesion: a review of the literature." *Journal of Conflict Resolution* 20, no. 1 (March):143–72.

Stein, Arthur A., and Russett, Bruce M. 1980. "Evaluating war: outcomes and consequences," in Gurr, 399–422.

Steiner, Jürg. 1969. "Nonviolent conflict resolution in democratic systems: Switzerland." *Journal of Conflict Resolution* 13, no. 3 (September): 295–304.

Steiner, Jürg. 1974. *Amicable agreement versus majority rule: conflict resolution in Switzerland*. Revised and enlarged edition. Chapel Hill: University of North Carolina Press.

Steiner, Jürg, and Obler, Jeffrey. 1976. "Does the consociational theory really hold for Switzerland?" in Esman, 324–42.

Steinmetz, Suzanne K., and Straus, Murray A., eds. 1975. *Violence in the family*. New York: Dodd, Mead & Co.

Stepan, Alfred. 1971. *The military in politics: changing patterns in Brazil*. Princeton: Princeton University Press.

Stepan, Alfred, ed. 1973. *Authoritarian Brazil: origins, policies, and future*. New Haven: Yale University Press.

Stepan, Alfred. 1978. *The state and society: Peru in comparative perspective*. Princeton: Princeton University Press.

Stevenson, J. 1974. "Food riots in England, 1792–1818," in R. Quinault and J. Stevenson (eds.), *Popular protest and public order: six studies in British history 1790–1920*. London: George Allen & Unwin, 33–74.

Stevenson, John. 1979. *Popular disturbances in England, 1700–1870*. London: Longman.

Stinchcombe, Arthur L. 1961. "Agricultural enterprise and rural class relations." *American Journal of Sociology* 67, no. 2 (September):165–76.

Stohl, Michael. 1974. "Theory and method in studies of the relationship between foreign and domestic conflict and violence." Paper presented to the Fifth International Peace Research Association Conference, January, in Varanasi, India.

Stohl, Michael. 1975. "War and domestic political violence: the case of the United States 1890–1970." *Journal of Conflict Resolution* 19, no. 3 (September):379–416.

Stohl, Michael. 1976. *War and domestic political violence: the American capacity for repression and reaction*. Sage Library of Social Research, vol. 30. Beverly Hills and London: Sage Publications.

Stohl, Michael, ed. 1979. *The politics of terrorism*. New York: Marcel Dekker.

Stohl, Michael. 1980. "The nexus of civil and international conflict," in Gurr, 297–330.

Stokes, Donald E. 1962. "Popular evaluations of government: an empirical assessment," in Harlan Cleveland and Harold D. Lasswell (eds.), *Ethics and bigness: scientific, academic, religious, political, and military*. New York: Harper & Brothers, 61–72.

Stokes, Eric. 1978. *The peasant and the Raj: studies in agrarian society and peasant rebellion in colonial India*. Cambridge: Cambridge University Press.

Stokes, William S. 1951. "The 'Cuban revolution' and the presidential elections of 1948." *Hispanic American Historical Review* 31, no. 1 (February):37–79.

Stokes, William. 1952. "Violence as a power factor in Latin American politics." *Western Political Quarterly* 5, no. 3 (September):445–68.

Stokols, Daniel. 1976. "The experience of crowding in primary and secondary environments." *Environment and Behavior* 8, no. 1 (March): 49–86.

Stolzenberg, Ross M. 1975. "Education, occupation, and wage differences between white and black men." *American Journal of Sociology* 81, no. 2 (September):299–323.

Stone, L. 1966. "Theories of revolution." *World Politics* 18, no. 2 (January): 159–76.

Stone, Lawrence. 1967. *Social change and revolution in England 1540–1640*. London: Longmans. (Original 1965.)

Stone, Lawrence. 1967a. "News from everywhere." *New York Review of Books* 9, no. 3 (24 August):31–35.

Stone, Lawrence. 1970. "The English Revolution," in Forster/Greene, 55–108.

Stone, Lawrence. 1972. *The causes of the English Revolution 1529–1642*. London: Routledge & Kegan Paul.

Stonner, David M. 1976. "The study of aggression: conclusions and prospects for the future," in Geen/O'Neal, 235–60.

Straka, Gerald M., ed. 1973. *The revolution of 1688 and the birth of the English political nation*. 2d. ed. Problems in European Civilization. Boston: D. C. Heath & Co. (Original 1963.)

Strauss, Harlan J. 1973. "Revolutionary types: Russia in 1905." *Journal of Conflict Resolution* 17, no. 2 (June):297–316.

Strausz-Hupé, Robert; Kintner, William R.; Dougherty, James E.; and Cottrell, Alvin J. 1963. *Protracted conflict: a challenging study of communist strategy*. New York: Harper & Row.

Street, David, and Leggett, John C. 1961. "Economic deprivation and extremism: a study of unemployed negroes." *American Journal of Sociology* 67, no. 1 (July):53–57.

Struwwel, Peter. 1848. *Handbüchlein für Wühler oder kurzgefaßte Anleitung in wenigen Tagen ein Volksmann zu werden*. 2d ed. Leizig: Gustav Mayer.

Sturdivant, Frederick D., ed. 1969. *The ghetto marketplace*. New York: Free Press.

Sturdivant, Frederick D., and Wilhelm, Walter T. 1968. "Poverty, minorities, and consumer exploitation." *Social Science Quarterly* 49, no. 3 (December):643–50.

Suchar, Charles S. 1978. *Social deviance: perspectives and prospects*. New York: Holt, Rinehart & Winston.

Suedfeld, Peter, and Rank, A. Dennis. 1976. "Revolutionary leaders: long-term success as a function of changes in conceptual complexity." *Journal of Personality and Social Psychology* 34, no. 2 (August): 169–78.

Suleiman, Ezra N. 1977. "Self-image, legitimacy and the stability of elites: the case of France." *British Journal of Political Science* 7, no. 2 (April):191–215.

Sullivan, David S., and Sattler, Martin J., eds. 1971. *Revolutionary war: Western response*. New York: Columbia University.

Suls, Jerry M., and Miller, Richard L. 1977. *Social comparison processes: theoretical and empirical perspectives*. New York: Wiley.

Supplemental Studies for the National Advisory Commission on Civil Disorders. Washington, D.C.: U.S. Government Printing Office.

Swart, Christopher, and Berkowitz, Leonard. 1976. "Effects of a stimulus associated with a victim's pain on later aggression." *Journal of Personality and Social Psychology* 33, no. 5 (May):623–31.

Tabb, William K. 1970. *The political economy of the black ghetto*. New York: W. W. Norton & Co.

Tabb, William K. 1971. "Race relations models and social change." *Social Problems* 18, no. 4 (Spring):431–44.

Taeuber, Karl E. 1969. "Negro population and housing: demographic aspects of a social accounting scheme," in Katz/Gurin, 145–93.

Taeuber, Karl E., and Taeuber, Alma F. 1965. *Negroes in cities: residential segregation and neighborhood change.* Chicago: Aldine Publishing Co.

Tai, Chong-Soo; Peterson, Erick J.; and Gurr, Ted Robert. 1973. "Internal versus external sources of anti-Americanism: two comparative studies." *Journal of Conflict Resolution* 17, no. 3 (September):455–88.

Tai, Hung-Chao. 1974. *Land reform and politics: a comparative analysis.* Berkeley: University of California Press.

Taintor, Zebulon C. 1972. "Assessing the revolutionary personality," in Welch/Taintor, 239–49.

Tannahill, R. Neal. 1975. "A methodological note: military intervention in search of a dependent variable." *Journal of Political and Military Sociology* 3, no. 2 (Fall):219–28.

Tannahill, R. Neal. 1976. "The performance of military and civilian governments in South America, 1948–1967." *Journal of Political and Military Sociology* 4, no. 2 (Fall):233–44.

Tannahill, R. Neal. 1978. *The communist parties of Western Europe.* Westport, Conn.: Greenwood Press.

Tanter, R. 1965. "Dimensions of conflict behavior within nations, 1955–1960: turmoil and internal war." *Peace Research Society Papers* 3:159–83.

Tanter, Raymond. 1966. "Dimensions of conflict behavior within and between nations, 1958–60." *Journal of Conflict Resolution* 10, no. 1 (March):41–64. Also in Gillespie/Nesvold (1971), 85–112.

Tanter, Raymond. 1967. "Toward a theory of political development." *Midwest Journal of Political Science* 11, no. 2 (May):145–72.

Tanter, Raymond. 1969. "International war and domestic turmoil: some contemporary evidence," in Graham/Gurr, 550–69.

Tanter, Raymond. 1969a. "Toward a theory of conflict behaviour in Latin America," in Robert W. Cox (ed.), *International organization: world politics.* London: Macmillan, 153–79.

Tanter, Raymond, and Midlarsky, Manus. 1967. "A theory of revolution." *Journal of Conflict Resolution* 11, no. 3 (September):264–80. Also in Welch/Taintor (1972), 154–75.

Taylor, Charles Lewis. 1969. "Communications development and political stability." *Comparative Political Studies* 1, no. 4 (January):557–63.

Taylor, Charles L., and Hudson, Michael C., eds. 1972. *World handbook of political and social indicators.* 2d ed. New Haven: Yale University Press.

Taylor, George V. 1967. "Noncapitalist wealth and the origins of the French Revolution." *American Historical Review* 72, no. 2 (January):469–96.

Taylor, George V. 1972. "Revolutionary and nonrevolutionary content in the *Cahiers* of 1789: an interim report." *French Historical Studies* 7:479–502.

Taylor, Michael, and Herman, V. M. 1971. "Party systems and government stability." *American Political Science Review* 65, no. 1 (March):28–37.

Taylor, Robert L., and Weisz, Alfred E. 1970. "American presidential assassination," in Daniels et al., 291–307.

Television and growing up: the impact of televised violence. 1972. Report to the Surgeon General. Washington, D.C.: United States Public Health Service.

TenHouten, Warren. 1970. "The black family: myth and reality." *Psychiatry* 33, no. 2 (May):145–73.

Terrell, Louis M. 1971. "Societal stress, political instability, and levels of military effort." *Journal of Conflict Resolution* 15, no. 3 (September): 329–46.

Tetsch, Hartmut. 1973. *Die permanente Revolution: Ein Beitrag zur Soziologie der Revolution und der Ideologiekritik.* Opladen: Westdeutscher Verlag.

Thaxton, Ralph. 1977. "On peasant revolution and national resistance: toward a theory of peasant mobilization and revolutionary war with special reference to modern China." *World Politics* 30, no. 1 (October): 25–57.

Thelen, Mark H., and Rennie, David L. 1972. "The effect of vicarious reinforcement on imitation: a review of the literature," in Brendan A. Maher (ed.), *Progress in experimental personality research*, vol. 6. New York: Academic Press, 83–108.

Thibaut, J. W., and Kelley, H. H. (1959). *The social psychology of groups.* New York: Wiley.

Thibaut, John W.; Spence, Janet T.; and Carson, Robert C., eds. 1976. *Contemporary topics in social psychology.* Morristown, N.J.: General Learning Press.

Thomas, Dani B. 1974. "Political development theory and Africa: toward a conceptual clarification and comparative analysis." *Journal of Developing Areas* 8 (April):375–94.

Thomas, Hugh. 1963. "The origins of the Cuban Revolution." *World Today*, October 19:448–60.

Thomas, Hugh. 1967. "Middle-class politics and the Cuban Revolution," in Claudio Veliz (ed.), *The politics of conformity in Latin America.* London: Oxford University Press, 249–77.

Thomas, Hugh. 1971. *Cuba: the pursuit of freedom.* New York: Harper & Row. English ed. London: Eyre & Spottiswoode.

Thomas, Hugh. 1977. "The show of violence." *Times Literary Supplement*, 18 November, 1338–39.

Thomis, Malcolm I. 1970. *The luddites: machine-breaking in regency England.* Newton Abbot: David & Charles Archon Books.

Thomis, Malcolm I., and Holt, Peter. 1977. *Threats of revolution in Britain, 1789–1848.* London: Macmillan.

Thompson, E. P. 1968. *The making of the English working class.* Harmondsworth: Pelican Books. (Original 1963.)

Thompson, E. P. 1971. "The moral economy of the English crowd in the eighteenth century." *Past and Present* 50 (February):76–136.

Thompson, Robert J., Jr., and Kolstoe, Ralph H. 1974. "Physical aggression as a function of strength of frustration and instrumentality of aggression." *Journal of Research in Personality* 7, no. 4 (March):314–23.

Thompson, William Randall. 1972. "Explorations of the military coup." Ph.D. dissertation, University of Washington.

Thompson, William R. 1973. *The grievances of military coup-makers.* Sage Professional Paper in Comparative Politics Series, no. 01–047.

Thompson, William R. 1974. "Toward explaining Arab military coups." *Journal of Political and Military Sociology* 2, no. 2 (Fall):237–50.

Thompson, William R. 1975a. "Systemic change and the Latin American military coup." *Comparative Political Studies* 7, no. 4 (January): 441–59.

Thompson, William R. 1975b. "Regime vulnerability and the military coup." *Comparative Politics* 7, no. 4 (July):459–87.

Thompson, William R. 1976. "Organizational cohesion and military coup outcomes." *Comparative Political Studies* 9, no. 3 (October):255–76.

Thompson, William R. 1978a. "Another look at the Feit-Sigelman dispute over the relative military size-coup propensity hypothesis." *Journal of Political and Military Sociology* 6, no. 1 (Spring):93–99.

Thompson, William R. 1978b. "A reply to Professor Sigelman's comment." *Journal of Political and Military Sociology* 6, no. 1 (Spring):103–104.

Thompson, William R. 1980. "Corporate coup-maker grievances and types of regime targets." *Comparative Political Studies* 12, no. 4 (January): 485–96.

Thompson, William R., and Christopherson, Jon A. 1979. "A multivariate analysis of the correlates of regime vulnerability and proneness to the military coup." *Journal of Political and Military Sociology* 7, no. 2 (Fall):283–89.

Thornton, Thomas Perry. 1964. "Terror as a weapon of political agitation," in Eckstein, 71–99.

Tibi, Bassam. 1973. *Militär und Sozialismus in der Dritten Welt: Allgemeine Theorien und Regionalstudien über arabische Länder.* Frankfort: Edition Suhrkamp.

Tilly, Charles. 1963. "The analysis of a counter-revolution." *History and Theory* 3:30–58.

Tilly, Charles. 1964. *The Vendée.* Cambridge: Harvard University Press. Enlarged paperback ed. 1976.

Tilly, Charles. 1964a. "Reflections on the revolutions of Paris: an essay on recent historical writing." *Social Problems* 12, no. 1 (Summer):99–121.

Tilly, Charles. 1969. "Collective violence in European perspective," in Graham/Gurr, 4–45.

Tilly, Charles. 1969a. "Methods for the study of collective violence," in Ralph W. Conant and Molly Apple Levin (eds.), *Problems in research on community violence.* New York: Praeger, 15–43.

Tilly, Charles. 1970. "The changing place of collective violence," in Melvin Richter (ed.), *Essays in theory and research: an approach to the social sciences.* Cambridge, Mass.: Harvard University Press, 139–64.

Tilly, Charles. 1971. "Review of 'Why men rebel' by Ted Robert Gurr." *Journal of Social History* 4, no. 4 (Summer):416–20.

Tilly, Charles. 1972. "How protest modernized in France, 1845 to 1855," in William O. Aydelotte, Allan G. Bogue, and Robert Fogel (eds.), *The dimensions of quantitative research in history.* Princeton: Princeton University Press, 192–255.

Tilly, Charles. 1972a. "The modernization of political conflict in France," in Edward B. Harvey (ed.), *Perspectives on modernization: essays in memory of Ian Weinberg.* Toronto: University of Toronto Press, 50–95.

Tilly, Charles. 1972b. "Quantification in history, as seen from France," in Val R. Lorwin and Jacob M. Price (eds), *The dimensions of the past:*

materials, problems, and opportunities for quantitative work in history.
New Haven and London: Yale University Press, 93–125.

Tilly, Charles. 1973. "Does modernization breed revolution?" *Comparative Politics* 5, no. 3 (April):425–47.

Tilly, Charles. 1973a. "The chaos of the living city," in Hirsch/Perry (1973), 98–124.

Tilly, Charles. 1974. "Town and country in revolution," in Lewis, 271–302.

Tilly, Charles. 1975. "Revolutions and collective violence," in Greenstein/Polsby, vol. 3, 483–555.

Tilly, Charles, ed. 1975a. *The formation of national states in Western Europe.* Princeton: Princeton University Press.

Tilly, Charles. 1975b. "Food supply and public order in modern Europe," in Tilly (1975a), 380–455.

Tilly, Charles. 1976. "Major forms of collective action in Western Europe 1500–1975." *Theory and Society* 3, no. 3 (Fall):365–75.

Tilly, Charles. 1978. *From mobilization to revolution.* Reading, Mass.: Addison-Wesley.

Tilly, Charles. 1979. "Collective violence in European perspective," in Graham/Gurr, 83–118.

Tilly, Charles. 1979a. "Sociology, meet history." CRSO Working Paper, no. 193. University of Michigan.

Tilly, Charles. 1979b. "Repertoires of contention in America and Britain, 1750–1830," in Zald/McCarthy, 126–55.

Tilly, Charles, and Lees, Lynn. 1974. "Le peuple de Juin 1848." *Annales* 29, no. 5 (September/October):1061–91. (English version: "The people of June, 1848," in Price 1975, 170–209.)

Tilly, Charles, and Rule, James. 1965. *Measuring political upheaval.* Research Monograph, no. 19. Princeton: Princeton Center for International Studies.

Tilly, Charles; Tilly, Louise; and Tilly, Richard. 1975. *The rebellious century 1830–1930.* Cambridge, Mass.: Harvard University Press.

Tilly, Louise A. 1971. "The food riot as a form of political conflict in France." *Journal of Interdisciplinary History* 2, no. 1 (Summer):23–57.

Tilly, Louise A. 1972. "I Fatti di Maggio: the working class of Milan and the rebellion of 1898," in Robert J. Bezucha (ed.), *Modern European social history.* Lexington, Mass.: D. C. Heath & Co., 124–58.

Tilly, Richard. 1970. "Popular disorders in nineteenth-century Germany: a preliminary survey." *Journal of Social History* 4, no. 1 (Fall):1–40.

Tilly, Richard H., ed. 1977. "Sozialer Protest." *Geschichte und Gesellschaft* 3, no. 2. Göttingen: Vandenhoeck & Ruprecht.

Tilly, Richard, and Hohorst, Gerd. 1973. "Sozialer Protest in Deutschland im 19. Jahrhundert: Skizze eines Forschungsansatzes." University of Münster. Mimeographed. Also in Konrad H. Jarausch (ed.), *Quantifizierung in der Geschichtswissenschaft: Probleme und Möglichkeiten.* Düsseldorf: Droste (1976), 232–78.

Tilton, Timothy A. 1974. "The social origins of liberal democracy: the Swedish case." *American Political Science Review* 68, no. 2 (June): 561–71.

Timasheff, Nicholas S. 1965. *War and revolution.* New York: Sheed & Ward.

Tinker, Jerry M.; Molnar, Andrew R.; and LeNoir, John D.; eds. 1969.

Strategies of revolutionary warfare. New Delhi: S. Chand & Co.

Tittle, Charles R. 1969. "Crime rates and legal sanctions." *Social Problems* 16, no. 4 (Spring):409-23.

Tittle, Charles R. 1975. "Deterrents or labeling?" *Social Forces* 53, no. 3 (March):399-410.

Tittle, Charles R. 1977. "Sanction fear and the maintenance of social order." *Social Forces* 55, no. 3 (March):579-96.

Tittle, Charles R., and Logan, Charles H. 1973. "Sanctions and deviance: evidence and remaining questions." *Law and Society Review* 7 (Spring):371-92.

Tittle, Charles R., and Rowe, Alan R. 1974. "Certainty of arrest and crime rates: a further test of the deterrent hypothesis." *Social Forces* 52, no. 4 (June):455-62.

Tocqueville, Alexis de. 1967. *L'ancien régime et la révolution*. Paris: Gallimard. (Original 1856.) English ed.: *The old regime and the French Revolution*. New York: Doubleday & Co. (1955).

To Establish Justice, to insure domestic tranquility. 1969. Final Report of The National Commission on the Causes and Prevention of Violence. Washington, D.C.: U. S. Government Printing Office.

Tökés, Rudolf L. 1967. *Béla Kun and the Hungarian Soviet Republic*. New York: Praeger.

Tønnesson, Kåre D. 1959. *La défaite des sans-culottes: mouvement populaire et réaction bourgeoise en l'an III*. Oslo: Presses Universitaires; Paris: Librairie R. Clavreuil.

Törnblom, Kjell Y. 1977. "Distributive justice: typology and propositions." *Human Relations* 30, no. 1 (January):1-24.

Tolles, Frederick B. 1954. "The American Revolution considered as a social movement: a re-evaluation." *American Historical Review* 60, no. 1 (October):1-12. Abridged in Amann (1963), 49-55.

Tomlinson, T. M. 1968. "The development of riot ideology among urban negroes." *American Behavioral Scientist* 11, no. 4:27-31. Also in Masotti/Bowen (1968), 417-28, and in Grimshaw (1969), 226-35.

Tomlinson, T. M. 1970a. "Ideological foundations for negro action: a comparative analysis of militant and non-militant views of the Los Angeles riot." *Journal of Social Issues* 26, no. 1:93-119.

Tomlinson, T. M. 1970b. "Ideological foundations for Negro action," in Cohen (1970), 326-79.

Tomlinson, T. M., and Sears, David O. 1970. "Negro attitudes toward the riot," in Cohen (1970), 288-325.

Tomlinson, T. M., and TenHouten, Diana L. 1970. "Methodology: negro reaction survey," in Cohen, 127-39.

Tonsor, Stephen J., ed. 1973-74. *America's continuing revolution: an act of conservation*. Washington, D.C.: American Enterprise Institute for Public Policy Research.

Tornow, Walter W. 1971. "The development and application of an input-outcome moderator test on the perception and reduction of inequity." *Organization Behavior and Human Performance* 6, no. 5 (September): 614-38.

Touval, Saadia. 1972. *The boundary politics of independent Africa*. Cambridge, Mass.: Harvard University Press.

Traugott, Mark. 1980. "Determinants of political orientation: class and organization in the Parisian insurrection of June 1848." *American Journal of Sociology* 86, no. 1 (July):32–49.

Traugott, Mark. 1980a. "The mobile guard in the French Revolution of 1848." *Theory and Society* 9, no. 5 (September):683–720.

Trevor-Roper, H. R. 1959. "The general crisis of the seventeenth century." *Past and Present* 16 (November):31–64. Also in Aston (1965), 59–95.

Trimberger, Ellen Kay. 1972. "A theory of elite revolutions." *Studies in Comparative International Development* 7, no. 3 (Fall):191–207.

Trimberger, Ellen Kay. 1976. "Review of Anderson." *Insurgent Sociologist* 6, no. 3 (Spring):55–59.

Trimberger, Ellen Kay. 1978. *Revolution from above: military bureaucrats and development in Japan, Turkey, Egypt, and Peru*. New Brunswick, N.J.: Transaction Books.

Trotsky, Leon. 1965. *Permanent revolution*. New York: Pioneer Publishers.

Trotsky, L. 1965a. *History of the Russian Revolution*. London: Victor Gollancz. American eds. New York: Simon & Schuster, (1932 and Ann Arbor: University of Michigan Press, 1957). Brief excerpt in Joseph Lopreato and Lionel S. Lewis (eds.), *Social stratification: a reader*. New York: Harper & Row, (1974), 288–96.

Tucker, Robert C. 1973. *Stalin as revolutionary, 1879–1929: a study in history and personality*. New York: W. W. Norton & Co.

Tucker, Robert C. 1977. "Stalinism as revolution from above," in Robert C. Tucker (ed.), *Stalinism: essays in historical interpretation*. New York: W. W. Norton & Co., 77–108.

Tucker, Robert C. Forthcoming. *Stalin and the revolution from above, 1929–1939: a study in history and personality*.

Tullis, F. LaMond. 1973. *Politics and social change in third world countries*. New York: John Wiley and Sons.

Tullock, Gordon. 1974. *The social dilemma: the economics of war and revolution*. Blacksburg: University Publications.

Turk, Herman, and Simpson, Richard L., eds. 1971. *Institutions and social exchange: the sociologies of Talcott Parsons and George C. Homans*. Indianapolis and New York: Bobbs-Merrill.

Turner, Charles, and Berkowitz, Leonard. 1972. "Identification with film aggressor (covert role taking) and reactions to film violence." *Journal of Personality and Social Psychology* 21, no. 2 (February):256–64.

Turner, Charles W.; Layton, John; and Simons, Lynn Stanley. 1975. "Naturalistic studies of aggressive behavior: aggressive stimuli, victim visibility, and horn honking." *Journal of Personality and Social Psychology* 31, no. 6 (June):1098–1107.

Turner, Jonathan H. 1974. *The structure of sociological theory*. Homewood, Ill.: Dorsey Press.

Turner, Ralph H. 1964. "Collective behavior," in Robert E. L. Faris (ed.), *Handbook of modern sociology*. Chicago: Rand McNally, 382–425.

Turner, Ralph H. 1969. "The public perception of protest." *American Sociological Review* 34, no. 6 (December):815–31.

Turner, Ralph H., and Killian, Lewis M. 1957. *Collective behavior*. 2d revised ed. Englewood Cliffs: Prentice-Hall (1972).

Tutenberg, Volker, and Pollak, Christl. 1978. *Terrorismus—gestern, heute, morgen: Eine Auswahlbibliographie.* Munich: Bernard Graefe Verlag.

Ulam, Adam B. 1977. *In the name of the people: prophets and conspirators in prerevolutionary Russia.* New York: Viking Press.

Uldricks, Teddy J. 1974. "The 'crowd' in the Russian Revolution: towards reassessing the nature of revolutionary leadership." *Politics and Society* 4:397-413.

Ulrich, R. 1966. "Pain as cause of aggression." *American Zoologist* 6:643-62.

Ulrich, R. E., and Azrin, N. H. 1962. "Reflexive fighting in response to adverse stimulation." *Journal of Experimental Analysis of Behavior* 5:511-20.

Ulrich, R.; Dulaney, S.; Arnett, M.; and Mueller, K. 1973. "An experimental analysis of nonhuman and human aggression," in Knutson, 79-112.

United States Central Intelligence Agency, National Foreign Assessment Center. 1978. *International Terrorism in 1977.* Washington, D.C. August, Doc. no. 5.

United States Congress, House, Committee on Foreign Affairs, Subcommittee on the Near East and South Asia. *International Terrorism.* 93rd Cong., 2d sess., 1974.

United States Congress, House, Committee on Internal Security. *Hearings on Terrorism.* 93rd Cong., 2d sess., 1974.

United States Congress, Senate, Committee on Operations, Subcommittee on Investigations. *Staff Study of Major Riots and Civil Disorders, 1965 through July 31, 1968.* 1968.

United States Department of Commerce, Bureau of the Census. Current Population Reports: The social and economic status of negroes in the United States, 1970. Washington, D.C.: July 1971.

United States Department of Labor, Bureau of Labor Statistics. The Negroes in the United States. Their economic and social situation, Bulletin no. 1511. Washington, D.C.: June 1966.

United States President's Commission on Law Enforcement and Administration of Justice. Task Force Report: Police. 1967.

Urry, John. 1973. *Reference groups and the theory of revolution.* London: Routledge & Kegan Paul.

Useem, Bert. 1977. "Peasant involvement in the Cuban Revolution." *Journal of Peasant Studies* 5, no. 1 (October):99-111.

Useem, Bert. 1980. "Solidarity model, breakdown model, and the Boston anti-busing movement." *American Sociological Review* 45, no. 3 (June):357-69.

Useem, Bert, and Useem, Michael. 1979. "Government legitimacy and political stability." *Social Forces* 57, no. 3 (March):840-52.

Useem, Michael. 1975. *Protest movements in America.* Indianapolis: Bobbs-Merrill.

Valentine, Charles A. 1968. *Culture and poverty: critique and counter-proposals.* Chicago: University of Chicago Press.

Valenzuela, Arturo. 1978. *The breakdown of democratic regimes: Chile.* Baltimore: Johns Hopkins University Press.

Van Valey, Thomas L., and Roof, Wade Clark. 1976. "Measuring residential segregation in American cities: problems of intercity comparison." *Urban Affairs Quarterly* 11, no. 4 (June):453-68.

Van Valey, Thomas L.; Roof, Wade Clark; and Wilcox, Jerome E. 1977. "Trends in residential segregation: 1960-1970." *American Journal of Sociology* 82, no. 4 (January):826-44.

Vatikiotis, P. J., ed. 1972. *Revolution in the Middle East and other case studies.* London: George Allen & Unwin.

Veblen, Thorstein. 1946. *Imperial Germany and the industrial revolution.* New York: Viking Press. (Originally published in 1915 by Macmillan Company.)

Venturi, Franco. 1966. *Roots of revolution: a history of the populist and socialist movements in nineteenth century Russia.* New York: Grosset & Dunlop. (Original 1952.)

Verba, Sidney. 1971. "Sequences and development," in Binder et al., 283-316.

Verba, Sidney, and Nie, Norman H. 1972. *Political participation in America: political democracy and social equality.* New York: Harper & Row.

Verba, Sidney; Nie, Norman H.; and Kim, Jae-On. 1978. *Participation and political equality: a seven-nation comparison.* Cambridge: Cambridge University Press.

Vigderhous, Gideon. 1977. "The level of measurement and 'permissible' statistical analysis in social research." *Pacific Sociological Review* 20, no. 1 (January):61-72.

Villemez, Wayne J., and Rowe, Alan R. 1975. "Black economic gains in the sixties: a methodological critique and reassessment." *Social Forces* 54, no. 1 (September):181-93.

Villemez, Wayne J., and Wiswell, Candace Hinson. 1978. "The impact of diminishing discrimination on the internal size distribution of black income: 1954-74." *Social Forces* 65, no. 4 (June):1019-34.

Völgyes, Iván, ed. 1971. *Hungary in revolution, 1918-19: nine essays.* Lincoln: University of Nebraska Press.

Volkmann, Heinrich. 1975. "Die Krise von 1830: Form, Ursache und Funktion des sozialen Protests im deutschen Vormärz." Habilitation thesis, Free University of Berlin.

Volkmann, Heinrich. 1977. "Soziale Innovation und Systemstabilität am Beispiel der Krise von 1830-1832 in Deutschland," in Otto Neuloh (ed.), *Soziale Innovation und sozialer Konflikt.* Göttingen: Vandenhoeck & Ruprecht, 41-68.

Vroom, Victor H. 1969. "Industrial social psychology," in G. Lindzey and E. Aronson (eds.), *Handbook of social psychology.* 2d ed. vol. 5, 196-268.

Wade, Rex A. 1972. "The Rajonnye Sovety of Petrograd: the role of local political bodies in the Russian Revolution." *Jahrbücher für Geschichte Osteuropas* 20, no. 2 (June):227-40.

Wai, Dunstan M. 1978. "Sources of communal conflicts and secessionist politics in Africa." *Ethnic and Racial Studies* 1, no. 3 (July):286-305.

Waldman, Sidney R. 1972. "Exchange theory and political analysis." *Sociological Inquiry* 42, nos. 3-4:101-28.

Wallace, Michael. 1970–71. "The uses of violence in American history." *American Scholar* 40 (Winter):81–102.

Wallace, Michael D., and Singer, J. David. 1973. "Large scale violence in the global system: definition and some measurement." Paper delivered at the Meetings of the International Political Science Association, August 21, in Montreal.

Walleri, R. Dan. 1978a. "Trade dependence and underdevelopment: a causal-chain analysis." *Comparative Political Studies* 11, no. 1 (April):94–127.

Walleri, R. Dan. 1978b. "The political economy literature on North-South relations: alternative approaches and empirical evidence." *International Studies Quarterly* 22, no. 4 (December):587–624.

Wallerstein, Immanuel. 1974. *The modern world-system: capitalist agriculture and the origins of the European world-economy in the sixteenth century*. New York: Academic Press.

Walsh, Edward J. 1978. "Mobilization theory vis-à-vis a mobilization process: the case of the United Farm Workers' Movement," in Louis Kriesberg (ed.), *Research in social movements, conflicts and change: an annual compilation of research*, vol. 1. Greenwich, Conn.: JAI Press, 155–77.

Walster, Elaine, and Walster, G. William. 1975. "Equity and social justice." *Journal of Social Issues* 31, no. 3 (Summer):21–43.

Walster, Elaine; Berscheid, Ellen; and Walster, G. William. 1973. "New directions in equity research." *Journal of Personality and Social Psychology* 25, no. 2:151–76.

Walster, Elaine; Walster, G. William; and Berscheid, Ellen. 1978. *Equity: theory and research*. Boston: Allyn & Bacon.

Walter, E. V. 1964. "Power and violence." *American Political Science Review* 58, no. 2 (June):350–60.

Walter, E. V. 1964a. "Violence and the process of terror." *American Sociological Review* 29, no. 2 (April):248–57.

Walter, Eugene Victor. 1969. *Terror and resistance: a study of political violence with case studies of some primitive African communities*. New York: Oxford University Press.

Walters, Gary C., and Grusec, Joan E. 1977. *Punishment*. San Francisco: W. H. Freeman & Co.

Walters, Richard H.; Cheyne, J. Allan; and Banks, Robin K., eds. 1972. *Punishment: selected readings*. Harmondsworth, Middlesex: Penguin.

Walton, Jennifer G. 1965. "Correlates of coerciveness and permissiveness of national political systems: a cross-national study." Master's thesis, San Diego State College.

Walzer, Michael. 1963. "Puritanism as a revolutionary ideology." *History and Theory* 3, no. 1:59–90.

Walzer, M. 1965. *The revolution of the saints: a study in the origins of radical politics*. Cambridge, Mass.: Harvard University Press.

Wanderer, Jules J. 1969. "An index of riot severity and some correlates." *American Journal of Sociology* 74, no. 5 (March):500–505.

Ward, Michael Don. 1978. *The political economy of distribution: equality versus inequality*. New York: Elsevier.

Ward, Robert E., and Rustow, Dankwart A., eds. 1964. *Political modernization in Japan and Turkey*. Princeton: Princeton University Press.

Ware, Alan. 1974. "Polyarchy." *European Journal of Political Research* 2, no. 2 (June):179–99.

Warren, D. I. 1969. "Neighborhood structure and riot behavior in Detroit: some exploratory findings." *Social Problems* 16, no. 4 (Spring):464–84.

Warwick, Paul. 1979. "The durability of coalition governments in parliamentary democracies." *Comparative Political Studies* 11, no. 4 (January): 465–98.

Wasserstrom, Robert. 1975. "Revolution in Guatemala: peasants and politics under the Arbenz government." *Comparative Studies in Society and History* 17, no. 4 (October):443–78.

Waterbury, Ronald. 1975. "Non-revolutionary peasants: Oaxaca compared to Morelos in the Mexican Revolution." *Comparative Studies in Society and History* 17, no. 4 (October):410–42.

Watts, Meredith W. 1973. "Efficacy, trust, and commitment to the political process." *Social Science Quarterly* 54, no. 3 (December):623–31.

Wayman, Frank Whelon. 1975. *Military involvement in politics: a causal model.* Sage Papers, International Studies Series, no. 02–035.

Wayman, Frank Whelon. 1981. "Coups or military rule?" *Armed Forces and Society* 7, no. 3 (Spring):487–89.

Weaver, Jerry L. 1973. "Assessing the impact of military rule: alternative approaches," in Schmitter, 58–116.

Weber, Max. 1947. *The Theory of Social and Economic Organization.* New York: Oxford University Press.

Weber, Max. 1964. *Wirtschaft und Gesellschaft: Studienausgabe.* Cologne: Kiepenheuer & Witsch.

Webster, Charles, ed. 1974. *The intellectual revolution of the seventeenth century.* London: Routledge & Kegan Paul.

Weede, Erich. 1970. "Conflict behavior of nation-states." *Journal of Peace Research* 7:229–35.

Weede, Erich. 1975a. "Unzufriedenheit, Protest und Gewalt: Kritik an einem makropolitischen Forschungsprogramm." *Politische Vierteljahresschrift* 16, no. 3 (September):409–28.

Weede, Erich. 1975b. *Weltpolitik und Kriegsursachen im 20. Jahrhundert.* Munich and Vienna: Oldenbourg Verlag.

Weede, Erich. 1977a. "Politische Kultur, Institutionalisierung und Prätorianismus: Überlegungen zur Theorie und empirischen Forschungspraxis, part I." *Kölner Zeitschrift für Soziologie und Sozialpsychologie* 29, no. 3 (September):411–37.

Weede, Erich. 1977b. "Politische Kultur, Institutionalisierung und Prätorianismus: Überlegungen zur Theorie und empirischen Forschungspraxis, part II." *Kölner Zeitschrift für Soziologie und Sozialpsychologie* 29, no. 4 (December): 657–76.

Weede, Erich. 1977c. *Hypothesen, Gleichungen und Daten—Spezifikations- und Meßprobleme bei Kausalmodellen für Daten aus einer und mehreren Beobachtungsperioden.* Kronberg/Ts.: Athenäum Verlag.

Weede, Erich. 1978. "US support for foreign governments or domestic disorder and imperial intervention, 1958–1965." *Comparative Political Studies* 10, no. 4 (January):497–527.

Weede, Erich. 1979. "Der Streik in westlichen Industriegesellschaften: Eine kritische Übersicht der international vergleichenden und quantitativen

Streikforschung." *Zeitschrift für die gesamte Staatswissenschaft* 135, no. 1 (March):1–16.

Weede, Erich. 1979a. "Review of Eisenstadt (1978)." *Kölner Zeitschrift für Soziologie und Sozialpsychologie* 31, no. 4 (December):798–99.

Weede, Erich. 1980. "Beyond misspecification in sociological analyses of income inequality." *American Sociological Review* 45, no. 3 (June): 497–501.

Weede, Erich, and Tiefenbach, Horst. 1981. "Some recent explanations of income inequality: an evaluation and critique." *International Studies Quarterly* 25, no. 2 (June):255–282.

Wehler, Hans-Ulrich, ed. 1973. *Geschichte und Soziologie.* Cologne: Kiepenheuer & Witsch.

Wehler, Hans-Ulrich. 1975. *Modernisierungstheorie und Geschichte.* Göttingen: Vandenhoeck & Ruprecht.

Wehler, Hans-Ulrich, ed. 1975a. "Der deutsche Bauernkrieg, 1524–1526." *Geschichte und Gesellschaft*, Sonderheft 1. Göttingen: Vandenhoeck & Ruprecht.

Wehler, Hans-Ulrich, ed. 1976. "200 Jahre amerikanische Revolution und moderne Revolutionsforschung." *Geschichte und Gesellschaft*, Sonderheft 2. Göttingen: Vandenhoeck & Ruprecht.

Weick, Karl E. 1966. "The concept of equity in the perception of pay." *Administrative Science Quarterly* 11, no. 3:414–39.

Weiher, Gerhard. 1978. *Militär und Entwicklung in der Türkei, 1945–1973.* Opladen: Leske.

Weiner, Myron. 1965. "Political integration and political development." *The Annals* 358 (March):52–64.

Weiner, Myron. 1967. "Urbanization and political protest." *Civilisations* 17:44–50.

Weinert, Richard S. 1966. "Violence in pre-modern societies: rural Columbia." *American Political Science Review* 60, no. 2 (June):340–47.

Weisburd, David. 1979. "Unity, conflict and the necessity of reciprocal causation in conflict theory." Yale University. Mimeographed.

Welch, Claude E., Jr. 1970. "The roots and implications of military intervention," in Welch (1970a), 1–61.

Welch, Claude E., Jr., ed. 1970a. *Soldier and state in Africa: a comparative analysis of military intervention and political change.* Evanston: Northwestern University Press.

Welch, Claude E., Jr., ed. 1971. *Political modernization: a reader in comparative political change.* 2d ed. Belmont, Calif: Wadsworth Publishing Co.

Welch, Claude E., Jr. 1971a. "Cincinnatus in Africa: the possibility of military withdrawal from politics," in Lofchie, 215–37.

Welch, Claude E., Jr. 1974. "Personalism and corporatism in African armies," in Kelleher, 125–45.

Welch, Claude E. 1974a. "The dilemmas of military withdrawal from politics: some considerations from Tropical Africa." *Journal of Modern African Studies* 17 (April):213–27.

Welch, Claude E. 1976. *Civilian control of the military: theory and cases from developing countries.* Albany, N.Y.: State University Press.

Welch, Claude E., Jr., and Smith, Arthur K. 1974. *Military role and rule: perspectives on civil-military relations.* North Scituate, Mass.: Duxbury Press.

Welch, Claude E., Jr., and Taintor, Mavis Bunker, eds. 1972. *Revolution and political change.* North Scituate, Mass.: Duxbury Press.

Welch, Susan. 1975. "The impact of urban riots on urban expenditures." *American Journal of Political Science* 19, no. 4 (November):741-60.

Welch, Susan, and Booth, Alan. 1974. "Crowding as a factor in political aggression: theoretical aspects and an analysis of some cross-national data." *Social Science Information* 13, nos. 4-5:151-62.

Welch, Susan, and Booth, Alan. 1975. "Crowding and civil disorder: an examination of comparative national and city data." *Comparative Political Studies* 8, no. 1 (April):58-74.

Welfling, Mary B. 1973. *Political institutionalization: comparative analyses of African party systems.* Sage Professional Paper in Comparative Politics Series, no. 01-041.

Welfling, Mary B. 1975. "Models, measurement and sources of error: civil conflict in Black Africa." *American Political Science Review* 69, no. 3 (September):871-88.

Welfling, Mary B. 1979. "Terrorism in Sub-Sahara Africa," in Stohl, 259-300.

Weller, J. M., and Quarantelli, E. L. 1973. "Neglected characteristics of collective behavior." *American Journal of Sociology* 79, no. 3 (November):665-85.

Wells, Alan. 1974. "The coup d'état in theory and practice: independent black Africa in the 1960s." *American Journal of Sociology* 79, no. 4 (January):871-87.

Wertheim, W. F. 1974. *Evolution and revolution: the rising waves of emancipation.* Harmondsworth: Penguin.

West, Gerald Thomas. 1973. "The dimensions of political violence in Latin America, 1949-1964: an empirical study." Ph.D. dissertation, University of Pennsylvania.

Weston, Charles H., Jr. 1968. "An ideology of modernization: the case of the Bolivian MNR." *Journal of Inter-American Studies* 10, no. 1 (January):85-101.

Wettig, Gerhard. 1967. "Die Rolle der russischen Armee im revolutionären Machtkampf 1917." *Forschungen zur europäischen Geschichte* 12:46-389.

White, James W. 1973. *Political implications of cityward migration: Japan as an exploratory test case.* Sage Professional Paper in Comparative Politics Series, no. 01-038.

White, James W. 1973a. "State building and modernization: the Meiji restoration," in Almond et al. (1973), 499-599.

White, John G. 1968. "Riots and theory building," in Masotti/Bowen, 157-65.

White, Robert A. 1969. "Mexico: the Zapata movement and the revolution," in Landsberger, 101-69.

Wicker, Allan W. 1969. "Attitudes versus actions: the relationship of verbal and overt behavior responses to attitude objects." *Journal of Social Issues* 25:41-78.

Wicker, Allan W. 1971. "An examination of the 'other variables' explanation of attitude-behavior inconsistency." *Journal of Personality and Social*

Psychology 19, no. 1 (July):18–30.

Widmaier, Ulrich. 1978. *Politische Gewaltanwendung als Problem der Organisation von Interessen: Eine Querschnittsstudie der soziopolitischen Ursachen gewaltsamer Konfliktaustragung innerhalb von Nationalstaaten.* Meisenheim am Glan: Anton Hain.

Wiener, Jonathan M. 1975. "The Barrington Moore thesis and its critics." *Theory and Society* 2, no. 3 (Fall):301–30.

Wildman, Allan. 1970. "The February Revolution in the Russian army." *Soviet Studies* 22, no. 1 (July):3–23.

Wildman, Allan K. 1980. *The end of the Russian imperial army: the old army and the soldiers' revolt (March-April 1917).* Princeton: Princeton University Press.

Wiley, James. 1967. "Political structure, military organization, and revolutionary activity: a comparative analysis." Vanderbilt University. Mimeographed.

Wilkenfeld, Jonathan, ed. 1973. *Conflict behavior and linkage politics.* New York: David McKay Co.

Wilkenfeld, Jonathan. 1973a. "Domestic and foreign conflict," in Wilkenfeld (1973), 107–23.

Wilkenfeld, Jonathan. 1973b. "Domestic conflict in the Middle East: an analysis of international inputs." Paper presented at the 9th World Congress of the International Political Science Association, August, in Montreal.

Wilkenfeld, Jonathan. 1974. "Conflict linkages in the domestic and foreign spheres," in Samuel Kirkpatrick, *Quantitative analysis of political data.* Columbus, Ohio: Charles E. Merrill Publishing Co., 340–58.

Wilkenfeld, Jonathan, and Zinnes, Dina A. 1973. "A linkage model of domestic conflict behavior," in Wilkenfeld, 325–56.

Wilkinson, David. 1975. *Revolutionary civil war: the elements of victory and defeat.* Palo Alto: Page-Ficklin Publications.

Wilkinson, David. 1976. *Cohesion and conflict: lessons from the study of three-party interaction.* London: Frances Pinter.

Wilkinson, Doris Y., ed. 1976. *Social structure and assassination behavior: the sociology of political murder.* Cambridge, Mass.: Schenkman Publishing Co.

Wilkinson, Paul. 1974. *Political terrorism.* London: Macmillan.

Wilkinson, Paul. 1977. *Terrorism and the liberal state.* London: Macmillan.

Willhelm, Sidney M. 1970. *Who needs the negro?* Cambridge, Mass.: Schenkman Publishing Co.

Williams, David. 1955. *The Rebecca riots: a study in agrarian dissent.* Cardiff: University of Wales Press.

Williams, Robin M., Jr. 1975. "Relative deprivation," in Lewis A. Coser (ed.), *The idea of social structure: papers in honor of Robert K. Merton.* New York: Harcourt Brace Jovanovich, 355–78.

Williams, Robin M. 1977. *Mutual accommodation: ethnic conflict and cooperation.* Minneapolis: University of Minnesota Press.

Williams, Roger L. 1969. *The French revolution of 1870–1871.* New York: W. W. Norton.

Williamson, Robert C. 1965. "Toward a theory of political violence: the case of rural Columbia." *Western Political Quarterly* 43 (March):35–44. Also in Lazar/Kaufman (1969), 104–18.

Willner, Ann Ruth. 1968. *Charismatic political leadership: a theory*. Princeton University: Center for International Studies, Monograph 32.

Willner, Ann Ruth. 1970. "Perspectives on military elites as rulers and wielders of power." *Journal of Comparative Administration* 11, no. 3 (November):261–76.

Wilson, James Q. 1960. *Negro politics: the search for leadership*. New York: Free Press of Glencoe.

Wilson, James Q. 1961. "The strategy of protest: problems of Negro civic action." *Journal of Conflict Resolution* 5, no. 3 (September):291–303.

Wilson, John. 1977. "Social protest and social control." *Social Problems* 24, no. 4 (April):469–81.

Wilson, Kenneth, and Orum, Tony. 1976. "Mobilizing people for collective political action." *Journal of Political and Military Sociology* 4, no. 2 (Fall):187–202.

Wilson, Robert A. 1971. "Anomie in the ghetto: a study of neighborhood type, race, and anomie." *American Journal of Sociology* 77, no. 1 (July):66–88.

Wilson, Thomas P. 1971. "Critique of ordinal variables." *Social Forces* 49, no. 3 (March):432–44. Also in Blalock (1971), 415–31.

Wilson, Thomas P. 1974. "On interpreting ordinal analogies to multiple regression and path analysis." *Social Forces* 53, no. 2 (December): 196–99.

Winckelmann, Johannes. 1952. *Legitimität und Legalität in Max Webers Herrschaftssoziologie*. Tübingen: J. C. B. Mohr (Paul Siebeck).

Wingen, John van and Tillema, Herbert K. 1980. "British military intervention after World War II: militance in a second-rank power." *Journal of Peace Research* 17, no. 4:291–303.

Winham, Gilbert R. 1970. "Political development and Lerner's theory: further test of a causal model." *American Political Science Review* 64, no. 3 (September):810–18.

Winkler, Heinrich August. 1974. "Zum Verhältnis von bürgerlicher und proletarischer Revolution bei Marx und Engels," in Hans-Ulrich Wehler (ed.), *Sozialgeschichte heute: Festschrift für Hans Rosenberg zum 70. Geburtstag*. Göttingen: Vandenhoeck & Ruprecht, 326–53.

Winship, Christopher. 1977. "A reevaluation of indexes of residential segregation." *Social Forces* 55, no. 4 (June):1058–66.

Winship, Christopher. 1978. "The desirability of using the index of dissimilarity or any adjustment of it for measuring segregation: reply to Falk, Cortese, and Cohen." *Social Forces* 57, no. 2 (December):717–20.

Wiseman, H. V. 1971. *Political systems: some sociological approaches*. London: Routledge & Kegan Paul.

Wit, Jan de, and Hartup, Willard W., eds. 1974. *Determinants and origins of aggressive behavior*. The Hague and Paris: Mouton.

Wittfogel, Karl A. 1957. *Oriental despotism: a comparative study of total power*. New Haven: Yale University Press.

Wittfogel, Karl A. 1960. "The Marxist view of Russian society and revolution." *World Politics* 12, no. 4 (July):487–508.

Witton, Ronald A. 1971. "Peasants, social conflict, and correlation analysis." *Comparative Political Studies* 4, no. 1 (April):101–106.

Woddis, Jack. 1972. *New theories of revolution: a commentary on the views of Frantz Fanon, Régis Debray, and Herbert Marcuse*. New York:

International Publishers.

Wördemann, Franz. 1977. *Terrorismus: Motive, Täter, Strategien*. Munich: Piper.

Wohlfeil, Rainer, ed. 1972. *Reformation oder frühbürgerliche Revolution*. Munich: Nymphenburger Verlagshandlung.

Wohlfeil, Rainer, ed. 1975. *Der deutsche Bauernkrieg 1524–1526. Bauernkrieg und Reformation*. Munich: Nymphenburger Verlagshandlung.

Wohlfeil, Rainer. 1977. "The 450th anniversary of the German peasants' war of 1524–1526." *Social History* 4 (January):515–20.

Wohlstein, Ronald T., and McPhail, Clark. 1979. "Judging the presence and extent of collective behavior from film records." *Social Psychology Quarterly* 42, no. 1 (March):76–81.

Wolde-Giorgis, Kahsai. 1978. "Aspekte der Revolution in Äthiopien." *Blätter für deutsche und internationale Politik* (April):461–74.

Wolf, Charles, Jr. 1965. "The political effects of military programs: some indicators from Latin America." *Orbis* 8 (Winter):871–93.

Wolf, Charles, Jr. 1966. "Insurgency and counterinsurgency: new myths and old realities." *Yale Review* 56, no. 2 (December):225–41.

Wolf, Charles, Jr. 1969. "The present value of the past." Santa Monica, Calif.: Rand Corporation. Mimeographed.

Wolf, Eric. 1966. *Peasants*. Englewood Cliffs: Prentice-Hall.

Wolf, Eric R. 1969a. "On peasant rebellions." *International Social Science Journal* 21, no. 2:286–93. Also in Shanin (1971), 264–74.

Wolf, Eric. 1971. "Peasant rebellion and revolution," in Miller/Aya, 48–67.

Wolf, Eric R. 1973. *Peasant wars of the twentieth century*. London: Faber & Faber. (Original 1969.)

Wolf, Eric R. 1977. "Review essay: why cultivators rebel." *American Journal of Sociology* 83, no. 3 (November):742–50.

Wolf, Eric R., and Hansen, Edward C. 1966–67. "Caudillo politics: a structural analysis." *Comparative Studies in Society and History* 9:168–79.

Wolfenstein, E. Victor. 1967. *The revolutionary personality: Lenin, Trotsky, Gandhi*. Princeton: Princeton University Press.

Wolfgang, Marvin E. 1970. "Violence and human behavior," in Michael Wertheimer (ed.), *Confrontation: psychology and the problems of today*. Glenview, Ill.: Scott, Foresman & Co., 169–81.

Wolfgang, Marvin E., and Ferracuti, Franco. 1967. *The subculture of violence: towards an integrated theory of criminology*. London: Tavistock Publications.

Wolfinger, Raymond E.; Shapiro, Martin; and Greenstein, Fred I. 1976. *Dynamics of American Politics*. Englewood Cliffs: Prentice-Hall.

Woloch, Isser, ed. 1970. *The peasantry in the old regime: conditions and protests*. New York: Holt, Rinehart & Winston.

Wolpin, Miles D. 1972. *Military aid and counterrevolution in the third world*. Lexington, Mass.: Lexington Books.

Wolpin, Miles D. 1975. "External political socialization as a source of conservative military behavior in the third world," in Fidel, 259–81.

Wolpin, Miles D. n.d. "Egalitarian reformism in the third world vs. the military: a profile of failure." Mimeographed.

Womack, John, Jr. 1972. *Zapata and the Mexican Revolution*. Harmondsworth: Penguin Books.

Woodcock, George, ed. 1977. *The anarchist reader*. Glasgow: Fontana.

Woodside, Alexander B. 1976. *Community and revolution in modern Vietnam*. Boston: Houghton Mifflin.

Worchel, Philip. 1960. "Hostility: theory and experimental investigation," in Dorothy Willner (ed.), *Decision, values, and groups*, vol. 1. New York: Pergamon Press, 254–66.

Worchel, Philip; Hester, Philip G.; and Kopala, Philip S. 1974. "Collective protest and legitimacy of authority." *Journal of Conflict Resolution* 18, no. 1 (March):37–54.

Wright, James D. 1976. *The dissent of the governed: alienation and democracy in America*. New York: Academic Press.

Wright, James D. 1978b. "The political consciousness of post-industrialism." *Contemporary Sociology* 7, no. 3 (May):270–73.

Wright, Mary C., ed. 1968. *China in revolution: the first phase, 1900–1913*. New Haven: Yale University Press.

Wright, Quincy. 1942. *A study of war*. Chicago: University of Chicago Press. Abridged version 1964.

Wright, Sam. 1978a. *Crowds and riots: a study in social organization*. Beverly Hills: Sage Publications.

Wright, Steve. 1978. "The campaign of the British army in Northern Ireland: a case of self-legitimation?" Paper presented to the European Consortium for Political Research, April, in Grenoble. Mimeographed.

Wynn, M. and Smith, M. F. 1973. "The international and domestic event coding system: INDECS." Arlington, Va.: Consolidated Analysis Centers.

Yank, C. K. 1975. "Some preliminary statistical patterns of mass actions in nineteenth-century China," in Frederic Wakeman and Carolyn Grant (eds.), *Conflict and control in late imperial China*. Berkeley: University of California Press, 174–210.

Yankelovich, Daniel. 1974. "A crisis of moral legitimacy?" *Dissent* 21 (Fall): 526–33.

Yates, Aubrey J. 1962. *Frustration and conflict*. New York: John Wiley.

Yoder, Dale. 1926. "Current definitions of revolution." *American Journal of Sociology* 32, no. 3 (November):433–41.

Yough, Syng Nam, and Sigelman, Lee. 1976. "Mobilization, institutionalization, development, and instability: a note of reappraisal." *Comparative Political Studies* 9, no. 2 (July):223–32.

Young, Alfred F., ed. 1976. *The American Revolution*. DeKalb, Ill.: Northern Illinois University Press.

Young, Oran R., ed. 1975. *Bargaining: formal theories of negotiation*. Urbana: University of Illinois Press.

Yu-wen, Jen. 1973. *The Taiping revolutionary movement*. New Haven: Yale University Press.

Zagoria, Donald S. 1974. "Asian tenancy systems and communist mobilization of the peasantry," in Lewis, 29–60.

Zagoria, Donald S. 1976. "Introduction." *Comparative Politics* 8, no. 3 (April):321–26.

Zagorin, Perez. 1959. "The social interpretation of the English Revolution." *Journal of Economic History* 19, no. 3 (September):376–401.

Zagorin, Perez. 1969. *The court and the country: the beginning of the English Revolution.* London: Routledge & Kegan Paul.

Zald, Mayer N., and Ash, Roberta. 1966. "Social movement organizations: growth, decay and change." *Social Forces* 44, no. 3 (March):327–41.

Zald, Mayer N., and McCarthy, John D., eds. 1979. *The dynamics of social movements: resource mobilization, social control, and tactics.* Cambridge, Mass.: Winthrop Publishers.

Zapf, Wolfgang. 1975. "Soziologische Theorie der Modernisierung." *Soziale Welt* 26, no. 2:212–26.

Zapf, W., and Flora, P. 1971. "Some problems of time-series analysis in research on modernization." *Social Science Information* 10, no. 3:53–102.

Zartman, I. William; Paul, James A.; and Entelis, John P. 1971. "An economic indicator of socio-political unrest." *International Journal of Middle East Studies* 2 (October):293–310.

Zashin, Elliot M. 1972. *Civil disobedience and democracy.* New York: Free Press.

Zawodny, J. K. 1962. "Unconventional warfare." *American Scholar* 31, no. 3 (Summer):384–94.

Zeitlin, Irving M. 1971. *Liberty, equality, and revolution in Alexis de Tocqueville.* Boston: Little, Brown & Co.

Zeitlin, Maurice. 1966. "Alienation and revolution." *Social Forces* 45, no. 2 (December):224–36.

Zeitlin, Maurice. 1966a. "Economic insecurity and the attitudes of Cuban workers." *American Sociological Review* 31, no. 1 (February):35–51.

Zeitlin, Maurice. 1970. *Revolutionary politics and the Cuban working class.* New York: Harper & Row. (Original 1967, Princeton University Press.)

Zelditch, Morris. 1978. "Review essay: outsiders' politics." *American Journal of Sociology* 83, no. 6 (May):1514–20.

Zeller, Richard A., and Levine, Zachary H. 1974. "The effects of violating the normality assumption underlying r." *Sociological Methods and Research* 2, no. 4 (May):511–19.

Zillmann, Dolf. 1979. *Hostility and aggression.* Hillsdale: Lawrence Erlbaum Associates.

Zimmermann, Ekkart. 1974. "Zur Soziologie kollektiven Verhaltens: Eine Analyse von Erklärungsversuchen der Negerunruhen der 60er Jahre in den USA." *Soziale Welt* 25, no. 4:479–506.

Zimmermann, Ekkart. 1974a. "Ecological conditions of protest behavior: the case of the American Negro riots in the 1960s." Paper presented at the Annual Meeting of the European Consortium for Political Research. Strasbourg.

Zimmermann, Ekkart. 1975. "Dimensionen von Konflikten innerhalb und zwischen Nationen: eine kritische Bestandsaufnahme des faktoranalytischen Ansatzes in der Makro-Konfliktforschung." *Politische Vierteljahresschrift* 16, no. 3 (September):343–408.

Zimmermann, Ekkart. 1976. "Factor analyses of conflicts within and between nations: a critical evaluation." *Quality and Quantity* 10, no. 4 (December):267–96.

Zimmermann, Ekkart. 1978. "'Bringing common sense back in': some neglected assumptions in status inconsistency theory and research." *European Journal of Sociology* 18, no. 1 (May):53–73.

Zimmermann, Ekkart, guest ed. 1978a. "Makropolitische Konfliktfor-
schung." *Politische Vierteljahresschrift* 19 (December):455–600.
Zimmermann, Ekkart. 1979a. "Crises and crises outcomes: towards a new
synthetic approach." *European Journal of Political Research* 7, no. 1
(March):67–115.
Zimmermann, Ekkart. 1979b. "Toward a causal model of military coups
d'état." *Armed Forces and Society* 5, no. 3 (Spring):387–413.
Zimmermann, Ekkart. 1980. "Macro-comparative research on political pro-
test," in Gurr, 167–237.
Zimmermann, Ekkart. 1981. "Coups or military rule, and when both?"
Armed Forces and Society 7, no. 3 (Spring):491–9.5.
Zimmermann, Ekkart. 1981a. *Krisen, Staatsstreiche und Revolutionen:
Theorien, Daten und neuere Forschungsansätze.* Opladen: West-
deutscher Verlag.
Zimmermann, Ekkart. 1981b. "Legitimität," in Martin Greiffenhagen, Sylvia
Greiffenhagen, and Rainer Prätorius (eds.), *Wörterbuch zur politischen
Kultur der Bundesrepublik Deutschland.* Opladen: Westdeutscher
Verlag, 236–43.
Zimmermann, Ekkart. 1982. "Sozialer Wandel und Konfliktinteraktionen:
Protestgruppen und Systemreaktionen," in Hans.–Joachim. Hoffmann-
Nowotny (ed.), Unbeabsichtigte Folgen sozialen Handelns. Frankfort:
Campus Verlag, 177–91.
Zimring, Franklin E., and Hawkins, Gordon J. 1973. *Deterrence: the legal
threat in civil control.* Chicago: University of Chicago Press.
Zinn, Howard. 1968. *Disobedience and democracy: nine fallacies on law and
order.* New York: Random House.
Zinnes, D., and Wilkenfeld, J. 1971. "An analysis of foreign conflict behavior
of nations," in Wolfram F. Hanrieder (ed.), *Comparative foreign policy:
theoretical essays.* New York: David McKay Co., 167–213.
Zolberg, Aristide R. 1966. *Creating political order: the party-states of West
Africa.* Chicago: Rand McNally.
Zolberg, Aristide R. 1968. "The structure of political conflict in the new
states of tropical Africa." *American Political Science Review* 62, no. 1
(March):70–87.
Zolberg, Aristide R. 1968a. "Military intervention in the new states of
tropical Africa: elements of comparative analysis," in Bienen, 71–98.
Zolberg, Aristide. 1973. "The military decade in Africa." *World Politics* 25,
no. 2 (January):309–31.
Zondag, Cornelius H. 1966. *The Bolivian economy, 1952–65: the revolution
and its aftermath.* New York: Frederick A. Praeger.
Zurcher, Louis A., Jr. 1973. "The arguments of Berkowitz and Davies: two of
the stages in the development of political violence," in Hirsch/Perry,
89–93.
Zurcher, Louis A., and Curtis, Russell L. 1973. "A comparative analysis of
propositions describing social movement organizations." *Sociological
Quarterly* 14, no. 2 (Spring):175–88.
Zurcher, Louis A., and Harries-Jenkins, Gwyn, eds. 1978. *Supplementary
military forces: reserves, militias, and auxiliaries.* Beverly Hills: Sage
Publications.
Zygmunt, Joseph F. 1972. "Movements and motives: some unresolved issues
in the psychology of social movements." *Human Relations* 25, no.
5:449–67.

Index

NAME INDEX

Abeles, R.P. 160
Abell, P. 66
Aberbach, J.D. 158, 482
Aberle, D.F. 33
Abrahamsson, B. 250
Abramson, P.R. 488
Abudu, M.J.G. 154
Acock, A.C. 66
Adams, H.E. 85, 95, 104, 123, 139, 458
Adams, J.S. 28, 29, 31, 160, 441-443
Adas, M. 555
Adelman, I. 102, 137, 252, 263, 264, 269, 520, 538
Adler, J.H. 349
Ahluwalia, M.S. 137
Ahmad, E. 128, 343, 351, 568, 569
Ahn, B.-J. 553
Ajzen, I. 489, 490
Akamatsu, P. 549
Ake, C. 233, 464, 492, 510
Alavi, H. 341
Albright, D.E. 245
Albritton, R.B. 428
Alcock, N. 11
Aldrich, H.E. 183
Alessio, J.C. 29
Alexander, C.N. 441

Alexander, R.J. 323, 561
Alexander, Y. 299, 346, 574
Alioto, J.T. 22
Alker, H.R. 62, 73, 94, 95, 98, 101, 451, 472
Allemann, F.R. 59, 299
Allende, S. 261, 306, 530
Allison, P.D. 472
Allport, F.H. 577
Almond, G.A. 75, 103, 202, 205, 207, 228, 230, 232, 233, 328, 407, 422-424, 451, 494, 496, 497, 508, 511, 528
AlRoy, G.C. 564, 580
Althauser, R.P. 60
Altheide, D.L. 599
Amann, P. 296, 300, 367, 373, 397
Amaro, N. 580
Ames, B. 254, 264, 520
Aminzade, R. 584
Amsel, A. 20, 164, 443, 483
Anderson, Ch.W. 59, 131, 150
Anderson, C.W. 122-125, 127
Anderson, J.L.V. 447
Anderson, N.H. 28
Anderson, P. 328, 562, 563
Anderson, W.A. 490
Andison, F.S. 440
Andrain, C.F. 204, 224, 497

Names appearing in the bibliography have not been listed separately here. However, most of them appear in the text and the footnotes. My thanks go to W. Rossdeutscher for his support.

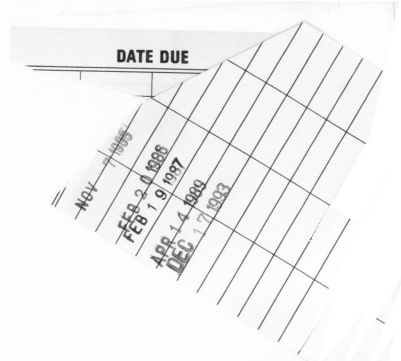